LEGAL ETHICS

FIFTH EDITION

by

DEBORAH L. RHODE
Ernest W. McFarland Professor of Law
Director, Stanford Center on the Legal Profession
Stanford Law School

DAVID LUBAN
University Professor
Professor of Law and Philosophy
Georgetown University Law Center

FOUNDATION PRESS

2009

© 1992, 1995, 2001, 2004 FOUNDATION PRESS

© 2009 By THOMSON REUTERS/FOUNDATION PRESS

      195 Broadway, 9th Floor

      New York, NY 10007

      Phone Toll Free 1–877–888–1330

      Fax (212) 367–6799

      foundation–press.com

Printed in the United States of America

ISBN 978–1–59941–355–6

TEXT IS PRINTED ON 10% POST CONSUMER RECYCLED PAPER

This book is dedicated to the memory of

Helen Luban
1912–1988

Jack Luban
1911–2001

Frederick R. Rhode
1918–1980

Hertha H. Rhode
1920–2007

*

ACKNOWLEDGMENTS

Casebooks are by nature a labor-intensive enterprise and our new edition would have been impossible without the assistance of many individuals over the last four years. However, the final throes of preparation benefited immeasurably from a number of persons who deserve special recognition. Stanford Law Librarians Paul Lomio, Sonia Moss, Erika Wayne, George Wilson, and Kate Wilko were invaluable in tracking down materials. And the exceptional skills, patience, and conscientiousness of Mary Tye at Stanford Law School were essential in preparing the manuscript for publication. At Georgetown, Nicky McMillan and Lindsay Pullen offered indispensable help with the page proofs, as did law librarian Jennifer Locke Davitt and her team of research assistants with the index.

David Luban wishes to express particular gratitude to Jennifer Ang, Georgetown class of 2002, whose research and ideas contributed substantially to several sections of the book. He would also like to thank Jennifer Clark and Nicky McMillan for additional research assistance. In addition, both authors are grateful to their families for their encouragement and forbearance.

We also acknowledge the following authors, journals, and publishers for granting permission to reprint material:

Abel. "Legal Services," Handbook of Applied Sociology. Reprinted by permission of Greenwood Publishing Group, Inc., Westport, CT, from Handbook of Applied Sociology: Frontiers of Contemporary Research, edited by M.E. Olsen and M. Micklin. Copyright by Praeger Publishers and published in 1981 by Greenwood Press, Praeger Publishers.

Allen. A Heaping Serving of Justice: Fifth St. Lawyers Represent the Defenseless and Indefensible in Washington, Dec. 6, 1996.

American Bar Association. American Bar Association Task Force on Minorities in the Legal Profession, Report with Recommendations. (Jan. 1986). Reprinted by permission of the American Bar Association. All rights reserved.

American Bar Association. ABA Committee on Ethics and Professional Responsibility, Formal Opinion 85–352 (1985), Formal Opinion 92–368 (1992), Informal Opinion 1203 (1972) and "... In the Spirit of Public Service." A Blueprint for the Rekindling of Lawyer Professinalism (1986) are copyrighted by the American Bar Association. All rights reserved. Reprinted with permission.

American Bar Association. ABA Standards Relating to the Administration of Criminal Justice, The Prosecution Function, (3d ed. 1992), Reprinted by permission of the American Bar Association. Copyright © 1992 by the American Bar Association. All rights reserved.

American Bar Association. ABA Standards for Imposing Lawyer Sanctions (1986). Reprinted by permission of the American Bar Association. Copyright © 1986 by the American Bar Association. All rights reserved.

American Bar Association. "Report of the Committee on the Code of Professional Ethics," American Bar Association Reports 600–04 (1906). Reprinted by permission of the American Bar Association.

American Bar Association. Institute of Judicial Administration, Juvenile Justice Standards, Standards Relating to Counsel for Private Parties (1979). Reprinted by permission of the American Bar Association.

American Bar Association: Commission on Women in the Profession. "The Unfinished Agenda; Women in the Legal Profession Executive Summary." Reprinted with permission.

American Bar Association. Consortium on Legal Services and the Public, Legal Needs and Civil Justice: Comprehensive Legal Needs Study (1994). Reprinted by permission.

Ames. "Informal Opinion 352: Professional Integrity and the Tax Audit Lottery," 1 Georgetown Journal of Legal Ethics 421 (1987). Reprinted by permission.

Auerbach. Unequal Justice: Lawyers and Social Change in Modern America (1976). Reprinted with permission.

Bankman. "An Academic's View of the Tax Shelter Battle," in The Crisis in Tax Administration, Joel Stemrod and Henry Aaron, eds., (2003). Reprinted with permission.

Barry. "Here's Proof That the Law Has Teeth," Miami Herald Sun, November 21, 1993, p. 5. Reprinted by permission.

Bedford. The Faces of Justice: A Traveller's Report. Copyright © 1961 by Sybille Bedford. Reprinted by permission.

Bok. "A Flawed System of Law Practice and Training," 33 Journal of Legal Education 570 (1983). Reprinted by permission.

Brill. "When a Lawyer Lies," Esquire (Dec. 19, 1975) Steven Brill is President and Editor in Chief, American Lawyer Media, L.P. Reprinted with permission.

Carson. The Lawyer Statistical Report: The U.S. Population in 1995 (1999). Reprinted with permission.

Condlin. "Bargaining in the Dark: The Normative Incoherence of Lawyer Dispute Bargaining Role," 51 Maryland Law Review 1, 4–5, 7–12, (1992). Reprinted by permission.

Corneel. "Guidelines to Tax Practice Second," in 43 Tax Lawyer 297 (1990). Reprinted with permission.

Crenshaw. "Foreword: Toward A Race–Conscious Pedagogy in Legal Education," National Black Law Journal, (Winter 1989). Reprinted by permission of the author.

Darrell. Conscience and Propriety in Tax Practice, New York University Seventeenth Annual Institute on Federal Taxation 1, (Sellin ed. 1959). Reprinted with permission of the author.

Detroit Free Press. (April 5, 1978). Reprinted by permission of the Detroit Free Press.

Falk. "Tax Ethics, Legal Ethics, and Real Ethics: A Critique of ABA Formal Opinion, 85–352," 39 Tax Lawyer, 643 (1986). Reprinted by permission of the author.

Fiss. "Against Settlement," 93 Yale Law Journal 1073 (1984). Reprinted by permission of the author and the Yale Law Journal Company and Fred B. Rothman & Company from The Yale Law Journal, Vol. 93, pp. 1073–1090.

Frankel. Partisan Justice. Excerpt from PARTISAN JUSTICE by Marvin

E.   Frankel. Copyright © 1980 by Marvin E. Frankel. Reprinted by permission of Hill and Wang, a division of Farrar, Straus and Giroux, Inc. Freedman. "The Errant Fax," The Legal Times (Jan. 23, 1995). Reprinted with permission. Freedman. "The Morality of Lawyering," The Legal Times (Sept. 20, 1993). Reprinted with permission.

Friedman. A History of American Law (2nd ed. 1985). Copyright © 1973, 1985 by Lawrence M. Friedman. Reprinted by permission of Simon & Schuster, Inc.

Fuller and Randall. "Professional Responsibility: Report of the Joint Conference of the ABA and AALS," 44 American Bar Association Journal 1159 (1958). Copyright © 1958 the American Bar Association Journal. Reprinted with permission from the ABA Journal. The Lawyer's Magazine, published by the American Bar Association.

Galanter. "The Day After the Litigation Explosion," 46 Maryland Law Review 1 (1986). Reprinted by permission of the Maryland Law Review and the author.

Goldstein. "Ex–Partner in a Major Law Firm Is Spared Disbarment," New York Times, (July 23, 1979). Copyright © 1979 by The New York Times Company Reprinted by permission.

Gordon. "The Ideal and the Actual in the Law: Fantasies and Practices of New York City Lawyers, 1870–1970." Reprinted by permission of Greenwood Publishing Group, Inc. Westport, CT, from The New High Priests: Lawyers in Post–Civil America, edited by Gerard W. Gawalt. Copyright © 1984 by Greenwood Press.

Gordon. "A New Role for Lawyers?: The Corporate Counselor after Enron," 35 Conn. L. Rev. 1185 (2003). Reprinted with permission.

Gordon. "The Independence of Lawyers," 68 Boston University Law Review 1 (1988). Copyright © 1988, Boston University Law Review. Reprinted with permission.

Harvard Program on the Legal Profession. "Philadelphia Legal Aid: Rita's Case," Harvard Program on the Legal Profession, (1982). Copyright ©

1982 by The Foundation Press. A version of this case appeared in P. Haymann and L. Liebman, The Social Responsibility of Lawyers, The Foundation Press. Reprinted with permission.

Heinz and Laumann. Chicago Lawyers: The Social Structure of the Bar. Copyright © 1982, Russell Sage Foundation. Reprinted with permission of the Russell Sage Foundation.

Hurst. The Growth of American Law. Copyright © 1950, Little, Brown and Company. Reprinted with permission of the author and Little, Brown and Company.

Jackall. Moral Mazes: The World of Corporate Managers (1988). Reprinted with permission.

Johnston, Jr. and Schecter. "In the Matter of Kaye, Scholer, Fierman, Hays & Handler: A Symposium of Government Regulation, Lawyers' Ethics, and the Rule of Law," 66 Southern California Law Review 977 (1993). Reprinted with permission of the Southern California Law Review.

Kennedy. Legal Education and the Reproduction of Hierarchy (1983). Reprinted with permission.

Kester. "Correspondence," in Harvard Law School Bulletin 32 (1982). Reprinted with permission.

Koniak. "When the Hurly Burly's Done: The Bar's Struggle With the SEC," 103 Columbia Law Review 1236, 1239–43 (2003). Reprinted by permission of the author and Columbia Bar Review.

Kronman. The Lost Lawyer: Failing Ideals of the Legal Profession (1993). Reprinted with permission.

Kurtz. Discussion on "Questionable Positions," 32 Tax Lawyer 13 (1978). Reprinted with permission.

Kurtz. "Remarks to the American Institute of Certified Public Accountants," 103 Daily Tax Report J–3, (May 26, 1977). Published by The Bureau of National Affairs, Inc. Reprinted with permission from Daily Tax Report.

Langbein. "The German Advantage in Civil Procedure," 52 University of Chicago Law Review 823. Copyright © 1985 University of Chicago Law Review. Reprinted with permission.

Lavelle. "Placing A Price on Human Life: A Legal Puzzle," in National Law Journal, (October 10, 1988). Reprinted with the permission of the National Law Journal. Copyright © 1988, The New York Law Publishing Company.

Lawrence. "The Id, The Ego, and Equal Protection: Reckoning with Unconscious Racism," 39 Stanford Law Review 317. Copyright © 1987 by the Board of Trustees of the Leland Stanford Junior University. Reprinted with permission.

Lee and Lee. "Reflections from the Bottom of the Well: Racial Bias in the Provision of Legal Services to the Poor," Clearinghouse Review 311, 315–316 (1993). Reprinted with permission.

Legal Services Corporation: Documenting the Justice Gap in America (2005). Reprinted by permission of the Legal Services Corporation.

Lempert. "In Settlement Talks, Does Telling the Truth Have Its Limits?" Inside Litigation 1, March 1988, Copyright © 1988 Prentice Hall Law & Business. Reprinted with permission.

Lichtenberg. "Racism in the Head, Racism in the World," in Report from the Institute for Philosophy and Public Policy. Reprinted by permission of the Report from the Institute for Philosophy and Public Policy 12 (1992).

Luban. Lawyers and Justice: An Ethical Study. Copyright © 1988, Princeton University Press. Reprinted with permission.

Luban. "Paternalism and the Legal Profession," 1981 Wisconsin Law Review 454 (1981). Reprinted by permission.

Luban and Millemann. "Good Judgment: Ethics Teaching in Dark Times," 9 Georgetown Journal of Legal Ethics 31, 44–55 (1995). Reprinted with permission.

Luban. "The Ethics of Wrongful Obedience," Ethics in Practice, Deborah L. Rhode, ed. Copyright © 2000. Reprinted with permission.

Luban. "Twenty Theses on Adversarial Ethics," in Beyond the Adversarial System, Helen Stacy and Michael Lavarch, eds. (1999). Copyright © 1999. Reprinted with permission.

Luban. "Taking Out the Adversary: The Assault on Progressive Public-Interest Lawyers," 91 California Law Review (2003). Reprinted with permission.

Macaulay. "Law Schools and the World Outside the Doors: Some Notes on Two Recent Studies of the Chicago Bar," 32 Journal of Legal Education 506 (1982). Reprinted with permission.

MacIntyre. "Utilitarianism and Cost–Benefit Analysis: An Essay on the Relevance of Moral Philosophy to Bureaucratic Theory," in Values in the Electric Power Industry, Kenneth M. Sayre, ed. (1977). Copyright © 1977 by Philosophic Institute of the University of Notre Dame. Reprinted with permission of University of Notre Dame Press.

Mann. Defending White Collar Crime. Pages 103–121, 123 and 166–174. Copyright © 1985 by Yale University Post. Reprinted by permission.

Mitchell. "The Ethics of the Criminal Defense Attorney—New Answers to Old Questions," 32 Stanford Law Review 293. Copyright © 1980 by the Board of Trustees of the Leland Stanford Junior University. Reprinted with permission.

Nasuti. "What Does It Take." Letter to the Editor, California Lawyer (Feb. 1992). Reprinted by permission of Matthew J. Nasuti, Esq.

Neely. "The Primary Caretaker Parent Rule: Child Custody and the Dynamics of Greed," 3 Yale Law Policy Review 168 (1984). Richard Neely is a justice of the West Virginia Supreme Court of Appeals. Reprinted with permission of the author and publisher.

Panel Discussion on Professional Responsibility and the "Model Rules of Professional Conduct." Reprinted from the University of Miami Law

Review, 35 University of Miami Law Review 639 (1981), which holds copyright on this article.

Parsons. "The Professions and Social Structure," in Essays In Sociological Theory. Reprinted with permission of The Free Press, a Division of Macmillan, Inc. from Essays in Sociological Theory by Talcott Parsons. Copyright © 1954 by The Free Press, renewed 1982 by Helen W. Parsons.

Paul. "The Lawyer as Tax Adviser," 25 Rocky Mountain Law Review 412 (1953). Copyright © 1953, Rocky Mountain Law Review. Reprinted with permission of the publisher and author.

Paul. "The Responsibility of the Tax Adviser," 63 Harvard Law Review 377 (1950). Copyright © 1950 by the Harvard Law Review Association. Reprinted with permission.

Posner. "Let Employers Insist If Three Years of Law School Is Necessary," San Francisco Daily Journal, December 15, 1999. Reprinted with permission.

Pound. The Lawyer from Antiquity to Modern Times. Copyright © 1953, West Publishing Company. Reprinted with permission.

Rhode. "Class Conflicts in Class Actions," 34 Stanford Law Review 1183 (1982). Copyright © 1982 by the Board of Trustees of the Leland Stanford Junior University. Reprinted with permission.

Rhode. "The Delivery of Legal Services by Non–Lawyers," 4 Georgetown Journal of Legal Ethics 209 (1990). Reprinted with permission.

Rhode. "Institutionalizing Ethics," 44 Case Western Law Review 665. Copyright © 1994 by Case Western Reserve University School of Law. Reprinted with permission.

Rhode. In the Interests of Justice. Copyright © 2001. Reprinted with permission.

Rhode. "Moral Character as a Professional Credential," 96 Yale Law Journal 481 (1985). Reprinted by permission of the Yale Law Journal Company and Fred B. Rothman & Company from The Yale Law Journal Company, Vol. 94, pp. 491–603.

Rhode. "Perspectives on Professional Women," 40 Stanford Law Review 1163. Copyright © 1988 by the Board of Trustees of the Leland Stanford Junior University. Reprinted with permission.

Rhode. "Foreword: Personal Satisfaction in Professional Practice," 58 Syracuse Law Review 217 (2008). Reprinted by permission of the Syracuse Law Review.

Rhode. "The Rhetoric of Professional Reform," 45 Maryland Law Review 274 (1986). Reprinted by permission of the Maryland Law Review.

Rhode. "Solicitation," 36 Journal of Legal Education 317 (1986). Reprinted by permission.

Ridolfi. Statement on Representing Rape Defendants (July 26, 1989). Reprinted with permission.

Rowen. "When May a Lawyer Advise a Client That He May Take a Position on His Tax Return?," 29 Tax Lawyer 237 (1975). Reprinted with permission of the author.

Schiltz. "On Being a Happy, Healthy, and Ethical Member of an Unhappy, Unhealthy, and Unethical Profession," 52 Vanderbilt Law Review (1999). Reprinted with permission.

Schuck. Agent Orange on Trial: Mass Toxic Disasters in the Courts (1986). Peter Schuck is the Simeon E. Baldwin Professor of Law at Yale Law School. Reprinted by permission of the publishers from Agent Orange on Trial: Mass Toxic Disasters in the Courts by Peter H. Schuck, Cambridge, Mass.: Harvard University Press. Copyright © 1986, 1987, by Marcy Schuck, Trustee.

Shaffer. "The Legal Ethics of Radical Individualism." Published originally in 65 Texas Law Review 963. Copyright © 1987 by the Texas Law Review Association. Reprinted by permission.

Simon. "The Ideology of Advocacy: Procedural Justice and Professional Ethics," 1978 Wisconsin Law Review 29. Copyright © 1978, University of Wisconsin. Reprinted by permission.

Smith. "The Bounds of Zeal in Criminal Defense: Some Thoughts on Lynne Stewart." 44 South Texas L. Review (2002). Reprinted with permission.

Subin "The Criminal Defense Lawyer's 'Different Mission': Reflections on the 'Right' to Present a False Case," 1 Georgetown Journal of Legal Ethics 125. Copyright © 1987, Georgetown Journal of Legal Ethics. Reprinted with permission.

William M. Sullivan et al., Educating Lawyers: Preparation for the Profession of Law (2007). Reprinted by permission of the author and the Carnegie Foundation for the Advancement of Teaching.

Tocqueville. Democracy in America (H. Reeve trans., P. Bradley ed., F. Bowen rev.) (1st ed. 1835). Reprinted with permission.

Uviller. "The Virtuous Prosecutor in Quest of An Ethical Standard: Guidance from the ABA," 71 University of Michigan Law Review 1145 (1978). Reprinted with permission.

Valdez negotiation problem. Adapted from "Dilemmas in Legal Ethics: Negotiation" (videotape), American Bar Association Consortium on Professional Education (1977). Used with permission of the American Bar Association.

vos Savant. "Ask Marilyn," Parade, January 10, 1999. Reprinted with permission of Marilyn vos Savant and Parade Publications, New York, New York. Copyright © 1999.

Wasserstrom. "Lawyers as Professionals: Some Moral Issues," 5 Human Rights 1 (1975). Reprinted by permission.

Wexler. "Practicing Law for Poor People," 79 Yale Law Journal 1049–1059 (1970). Reprinted by permission of the Yale Law Journal Company and Fred B. Rothman & Company from The Yale Law Journal, Vol. 79, pp. 1049–1067.

Williams. "Professionalism and the Corporate Bar," in 36 Business Law 159, 166–167 (1980). Reprinted with permission.

*

SUMMARY OF CONTENTS

ACKNOWLEDGEMENTS v
TABLE OF CASES xxxiii
TABLE OF OTHER AUTHORITIES xli

Introduction 1

CHAPTER I. The Concept of a Profession 35

Introduction 35
A. Historical Frameworks 37
B. Contemporary Controversies 38

CHAPTER II. The American Legal Profession 51

A. Historical Frameworks 51
   Introduction 51
B. Demographic Profiles 64
C. The Conditions of Practice 68
D. Professional Opportunities 81

CHAPTER III. Professional Independence and Professional Codes 106

A. The Historical Backdrop 106
   Introduction 106
B. Self–Regulation: Justifications and Critiques 113
   Introduction 113
C. Professional Regulation and Choice of Law 129

CHAPTER IV. The Advocate's Role in an Adversary System 137

A. The "Neutral Partisanship" Conception of the Lawyer's Role 137
   Introduction 137
B. Neutral Partisanship and Role Morality 148
   Introduction 150
C. The Justification of Neutral Partisanship 154
D. The Adversary System 157
E. Alternatives to Neutral Partisanship 175
F. Judicial Controls on Adversarial Abuses 206

CHAPTER   V.   Confidentiality and the Attorney–Client Privilege 236

A.   The Background of the Attorney–Client Privilege 239
     Introduction 239
B.   The Justification of the Privilege 244
C.   The Crime–Fraud Exception to the Attorney–Client Privilege 250
     1.   Introduction 250
D.   The Attorney–Client Privilege: Organizational Clients 267
E.   The Ethical Duty of Confidentiality 277
F.   Confidentiality and Client Fraud 288
G.   A Final Problem 299

CHAPTER   VI.   Dilemmas of Advocacy: The Criminal Law Paradigm 302

Introduction 302
A.   Defending the Guilty 303
     Introduction 303
B.   The Pursuit of Truth: Honest Witnesses and Lying Clients 323
C.   Smoking Guns and Societal Interests 340
D.   Prosecutorial Ethics 355
     Introduction 355
     Introduction 377

CHAPTER   VII.   Ethics in Organizational Settings 392

A.   Corporate Counseling and Whistleblowing 392
B.   Sarbanes–Oxley: Legislative Requirements 411
C.   In–House Counsel 424
D.   Supervisory and Subordinate Lawyers 438

CHAPTER   VIII.   Negotiation and Mediation 457

Introduction 458
A.   Coercion 465
B.   Truthfulness in Bargaining 467
C.   Cooperative and Competitive Bargaining 484
D.   Mediation 488

CHAPTER   IX.   The Lawyer's Counseling Role 498

Introduction 498
A.   Counseling Frameworks 498
B.   Corporate Practice 505
C.   Family Practice 516
D.   Tax Practice 522
     Introduction 522
E.   Government Lawyers 542

CHAPTER X. Conflicts of Interest ----------------------------------- 563

A. Introduction -- 563
B. Conflicts of Interest in Criminal Defense --------------------------- 570
C. Concurrent Representation of Conflicting Interests in Civil Mat-
    ters --- 589
D. Conflicts Involving Former Clients ---------------------------------- 614
E. Imputed Disqualification -- 625
F. The Former Government Lawyer --------------------------------------- 632
G. Conflicts of Interest in Class Actions ----------------------------- 647
H. Fee–Related Conflicts of Interest ---------------------------------- 671
I. Conflicts of Interest in Context ----------------------------------- 686

CHAPTER XI. Lawyer–Client Decision Making ------------------- 696

A. The Definition of the Problem -------------------------------------- 696
    Introduction --- 696
B. The Justification of Paternalism ----------------------------------- 727
    Introduction --- 727
C. Informed Consent and the Partially Competent Client --------------- 736
    Introduction --- 740

CHAPTER XII. Market Regulation ---------------------------------- 756

Introduction -- 756
A. Advertising -- 757
    Introduction --- 757
B. Solicitation --- 770
    Introduction --- 770
C. Specialization and Group Legal Services Plans --------------------- 794
D. Unauthorized Practice of Law: Nonlawyer Services and Multijuris-
    dictional Practice --- 800
E. Multidisciplinary Practice --- 817
F. Attorneys' Fees -- 821
    Introduction --- 821
    Introduction --- 837
G. Financing Litigation --- 843

CHAPTER XIII. The Distribution of Legal Services ------------ 850

A. Problems of Litigiousness: The Overlawyered Society --------------- 850
B. Problems of Access: The Underlawyered Society -------------------- 866
C. The Right to Legal Services --------------------------------------- 872
D. Public Interest Law --- 877
E. Subsidized Legal Services --- 884
    Introduction --- 884
F. Alternative Dispute Resolution ------------------------------------ 902
G. Pro Bono Representation --- 914
    Introduction --- 914

CHAPTER XIV. Admission to the Bar ------------------------------- 931

A. Introduction--- 931
B. Competence --- 933
    Introduction:Bar Exams-- 933
C. Character and Fitness --- 944
D. Interstate Regulation --- 961

CHAPTER XV. Discipline and Malpractice ----------------------- 967

A. Introduction--- 967
B. Regulatory Structures and Standards ------------------------------ 968
C. Disciplinary Sanctions -- 987
    Introduction-- 987
D. Mental Health and Substance Abuse----------------------------- 1003
    Introduction-- 1003
E. Competence and Malpractice ------------------------------------ 1007
    Introduction-- 1007

CHAPTER XVI. Legal Education--------------------------------- 1021

A. The Structure of Legal Education-------------------------------- 1021
    Introduction-- 1021
B. Diversity--- 1047
C. Professional Responsibility-------------------------------------- 1068
D. Professional Values and Pro Bono Opportunities--------------- 1072

INDEX -- 1075

TABLE OF CONTENTS

ACKNOWLEDGEMENTS v
TABLE OF CASES xxxiii
TABLE OF OTHER AUTHORITIES xli

Introduction 1
Notes: What is the "Ethics" in Legal Ethics? 3
Harvard Program on the Legal Profession, Philadelphia Legal Aid:
    Rita's Case 13
Notes and Questions: Rita's Case 30

CHAPTER I. The Concept of a Profession 35

Introduction 35
A. Historical Frameworks 37
B. Contemporary Controversies 38
    American Bar Association Commission on Professionalism, "...
      In the Spirit of Public Service": A Blueprint for the Rekindling
      of Lawyer Professionalism 38
    Questions 40
    Notes 40
    Deborah L. Rhode, "Professionalism" 42
    Richard A. Posner, Overcoming Law 43
    Questions 46
    Talcott Parsons, "The Professions and Social Structure," in Es-
      says in Sociological Theory 46
    Notes 47
    Questions 50

CHAPTER II. The American Legal Profession 51

A. Historical Frameworks 51
    Introduction 51
    Lawrence Friedman, A History of American Law 52
    Alexis De Tocqueville, Democracy in America 55
    Notes and Questions 58
    Notes: Patterns of Exclusion: Sex, Race, Ethnicity, and Religion 60
B. Demographic Profiles 64
    Notes 66
    Questions 68
C. The Conditions of Practice 68
    Deborah L. Rhode, Foreword: Personal Satisfaction in Profession-
      al Practice 70
    Notes 79
    Questions 80

D. Professional Opportunities 81
   1. Women 81
      Notes 81
      ABA Commission on Women in the Profession, The Unfinished
         Agenda: Women and the Legal Profession, Executive Sum-
         mary 82
      Notes and Questions 89
   2. Racial and Ethnic Minorities 90
      Notes 90
      Charles Lawrence, "The Id, The Ego, and Equal Protection:
         Reckoning with Unconscious Racism" 93
      Judith Lichtenberg, "Racism in the Head, Racism in the
         World" 94
      Notes 97
      Questions 100
   3. Sexual Orientation 100
      Notes 100
   4. Age 103

**CHAPTER III. Professional Independence and Professional
   Codes** 106

A. The Historical Backdrop 106
   Introduction 106
   Roscoe Pound, The Lawyer from Antiquity to Modern Times 106
   James W. Hurst, The Growth of American Law: The Lawmakers .. 107
   Jerold S. Auerbach, Unequal Justice: Lawyers and Social Change
      in Modern America 108
   Problem 1 110
   Notes 111
   Questions 113
B. Self–Regulation: Justifications and Critiques 113
   Introduction 113
   American Bar Association "Report of the Committee on [the]
      Code of Professional Ethics" 114
   Notes 116
   David Luban and Michael Millemann, "Good Judgment: Ethics
      Teaching in Dark Times" 118
   Notes 121
   Judith Lichtenberg, "What's a Code of Ethics For?," In Codes of
      Ethics and the Professions (Margaret Coady & Sidney Bloch
      eds.). 122
   Notes 125
   Deborah L. Rhode, In the Interests of Justice 125
   Questions 127
   Notes 129
C. Professional Regulation and Choice of Law 129
   Problem 2 130
   Problem 3 130
   Questions 131
   Notes: Jurisdiction and Choice of Law 132

CHAPTER IV. The Advocate's Role in an Adversary System 137

A. The "Neutral Partisanship" Conception of the Lawyer's Role 137
   Introduction 137
   Questions 139
   William Simon, "The Ideology of Advocacy: Procedural Justice
      and Professional Ethics" 139
   Notes: The Codes and Neutral Partisanship 140
   Problem 1 141
   ABA Formal Opinion 92–368 Inadvertent Disclosure of Confiden-
      tial Materials 142
   Monroe H. Freedman, "The Errant Fax" 144
   Notes 145
B. Neutral Partisanship and Role Morality 148
   Problem 2 148
   Questions 149
   Introduction 150
C. The Justification of Neutral Partisanship 154
   Notes 154
D. The Adversary System 157
   1. The Historical Background of Adversarial Processes 157
      Notes 157
   2. The "Search for Truth" and the Protection of Rights 158
      Notes 158
      Lon L. Fuller and John D. Randall, "Professional Responsibili-
         ty: Report of the Joint Conference of the ABA and AALS" 159
      David Luban, "Twenty Theses on Adversarial Ethics," in Be-
         yond the Adversarial System (Helen Stacy & Michael La-
         varch Eds.) 161
      Notes and Questions 162
      Deborah L. Rhode, In the Interests of Justice 163
   3. Comparative Perspectives: "Adversarial" Versus "Inquisitori-
      al" Procedures 166
      Notes 166
      John H. Langbein, "The German Advantage in Civil Proce-
         dure" 166
      Notes: An "Inquisitorial" Criminal Trial 170
      Sybille Bedford, The Faces of Justice: A Traveller's Report 171
      Notes and Questions 174
      Problem 3 175
E. Alternatives to Neutral Partisanship 175
   Notes and Questions 175
   1. Alternatives to Neutrality 181
      Problem 4 181
      Notes 182
      Monroe Freedman, "The Morality of Lawyering" 184
      Questions 186
   2. The Limits of Partisanship 187
      Problem 5 187
      United States v. Cueto 189
      Questions 195
      Abbe L. Smith, "The Bounds of Zeal in Criminal Defense:
         Some Thoughts on Lynne Stewart" 199
      Notes and Questions 200

E.   Alternatives to Neutral Partisanship—Continued
   3. Role Morality and Group Identity ----------------------------- 202
     Problem 6 -- 202
     Notes: Role Morality and Group Identity ---------------- 202
     Questions --- 204
F.   Judicial Controls on Adversarial Abuses -------------------- 206
   1. Frivolous Litigation -- 206
     Problem 7 -- 206
     Notes: Sanctions Under Federal Rule 11 --------------- 207
     Questions: Frivolity and Harassment ---------------------- 212
   2. Discovery Abuse --- 213
     Problem 8 -- 213
     Notes: Discovery Abuse ------------------------------------- 215
     Qualcomm Inc. v. Broadcom Corp. ---------------------- 217
     Notes and Questions --- 226
     Notes: Civility and Civility Codes -------------------------- 228
     Lee v. American Eagle Airlines, Inc. ---------------------- 229
     Notes and Questions --- 235

CHAPTER V. Confidentiality and the Attorney–Client Privilege --- 236

Problem 1 -- 236
Notes -- 237
Notes and Questions --- 238
A.   The Background of the Attorney–Client Privilege -------------- 239
   Introduction --- 239
   Problem 2 -- 244
B.   The Justification of the Privilege --------------------------------- 244
   Notes -- 244
   Jeremy Bentham, Rationale of Judicial Evidence, Specially Applied to English Practice ------------------------------------- 246
   Questions --- 247
C.   The Crime–Fraud Exception to the Attorney–Client Privilege ------ 250
   1. Introduction -- 250
   Problem 3 -- 253
   2. Fraud -- 254
     Bersani v. Bersani --- 254
     Notes and Questions --- 256
   3. A Case Study: The Minnesota Tobacco Litigation ------------ 257
     Questions --- 263
   4. The "War on Terror" and the Attorney–Client Privilege --------- 265
     Questions --- 266
D.   The Attorney–Client Privilege: Organizational Clients -------------- 267
   1. The Scope of the Organizational Attorney–Client Privilege ------ 267
     Upjohn Co. v. United States ---------------------------------- 269
     Questions --- 271
   2. The Justifications for the Organizational Privilege --------------- 274
   3. Waiver of the Organizational Privilege ------------------------------ 275

E. The Ethical Duty of Confidentiality ------------------------------- 277
   Notes -- 277
   Spaulding v. Zimmerman --- 279
   Questions -- 282
   Notes: Compliance with Court Orders------------------------------- 285
   Notes: The Exception for Lawyer–Client Disputes ------------------ 287
F. Confidentiality and Client Fraud---------------------------------- 288
   Problem 4 -- 288
   Notes and Questions: The O.P.M. Case ----------------------------- 288
   Notes: Client Fraud and Disclosure Rules-------------------------- 290
   Notes: Bar Responses to Client Fraud ----------------------------- 291
   Questions -- 294
   Notes: Cognitive Bias and Client Fraud---------------------------- 298
G. A Final Problem -- 299
   Problem 5 -- 300

CHAPTER VI. Dilemmas of Advocacy: The Criminal Law Paradigm -- 302

Introduction --- 302
Questions -- 303
A. Defending the Guilty --- 303
   Introduction --- 303
   John B. Mitchell, "The Ethics of the Criminal Defense Attorney—
     New Answers to Old Questions" --------------------------------- 305
   Marilyn Vos Savant, "Ask Marilyn" -------------------------------- 307
   Questions -- 309
   Notes -- 309
   Henry Allen, "A Heaping Serving of Justice; Fifth Street Lawyers
     Represent the Defenseless and the Indefensible of Washington" 314
   Notes -- 316
   Questions -- 322
B. The Pursuit of Truth: Honest Witnesses and Lying Clients---------- 323
   1. Perjury and Disclosure Obligations ---------------------------- 323
      Problem 1 --- 323
      Notes-- 324
      Nix v. Whiteside--- 325
      Notes-- 328
      Questions-- 328
      Notes-- 329
   2. Impeachment--- 332
      Problem 2 -- 332
      Questions-- 334
      Notes-- 335
      Questions-- 337
      Timothy Beneke, Men on Rape-------------------------------- 339
      Cookie Ridolfi, Statement on Representing Rape Defendants --- 339
C. Smoking Guns and Societal Interests------------------------------ 340
   1. Possession of Evidence ------------------------------------- 340
      Problem 3 --- 340
      Notes--- 341
      Questions--- 343

C. Smoking Guns and Societal Interests—Continued
2. Document Retention and Destruction 344
Problem 4 344
Notes 346
Kenneth Mann, Defending White Collar Crime: A Portrait of
Attorneys at Work 348
Questions 350
3. Witness Preparation 351
Problem 5 351
Notes 352
D. Prosecutorial Ethics 355
Introduction 355
1. Prosecutorial Discretion 357
Problem 6 357
Questions 358
Problem 7 359
Problem 8 360
American Bar Association Standards Relating to the Adminis-
tration of Criminal Justice, The Prosecution Function 361
H. Richard Uviller, "The Virtuous Prosecutor in Quest of an
Ethical Standard: Guidance from the ABA" 365
Notes and Questions 368
Questions 370
2. Plea–Bargaining 377
Questions 377
Introduction 377
3. Disclosure Obligations 380
Problem 9 380
Notes 381
Questions 383
4. Press Statements 385
Problem 10 385
Notes and Questions 386
5. Trial Conduct 388
Problem 11 388
Notes 390
Notes: Peremptory Challenges 390

CHAPTER VII. Ethics in Organizational Settings 392

A. Corporate Counseling and Whistleblowing 392
1. Introduction 392
Problem 1 392
David Luban, Lawyers and Justice: An Ethical Study 393
2. Cost/Benefit Frameworks 397
Marianne Lavelle, "Placing a Price on Human Life" 397
Notes: Cost/Benefit Analysis 399
3. Whistleblowing 404
Notes 404
Questions 409
Notes 410

B. Sarbanes–Oxley: Legislative Requirements ------------------- 411
  Susan P. Koniak, "When The Hurlyburly's Done: The Bar's
    Struggle with the SEC" ------------------------------------ 412
  Notes and Questions: Enron ------------------------------------ 413
  Problem 2 --- 415
  Notes: The Sarbanes–Oxley Act ----------------------------- 416
  Part 205—Standards of Professional Conduct for Attorneys Ap-
    pearing and Practicing Before the Commission in the Represen-
    tation of an Issuer --- 416
  Notes and Questions on Sarbanes–Oxley --------------------- 420
C. In–House Counsel --- 424
  Problem 3 --- 424
  Robert Jackall, Moral Mazes: The World of Corporate Managers --- 424
  Questions --- 425
  Robert Jackall, Moral Mazes: The World of Corporate Managers --- 426
  Questions --- 429
  Questions --- 434
  Notes: In–House Counsel ----------------------------------- 434
D. Supervisory and Subordinate Lawyers ----------------------- 438
  Problem 4 --- 438
  Steven Brill, "When a Lawyer Lies" ----------------------- 439
  Notes --- 442
  Questions --- 444
  ABA Comm. on Ethics and Professional Responsibility -------- 445
  Question -- 446
  C.S. Lewis, "The Inner Ring" in They Asked for a Paper: Papers
    and Addresses --- 446
  Patrick J. Schiltz, "On Being a Happy, Healthy, and Ethical
    Member of an Unhappy, Unhealthy, and Unethical Profession" 447
  David Luban, "The Ethics of Wrongful Obedience" in Ethics in
    Practice: Lawyers' Roles, Responsibilities, and Regulation (Deb-
    orah L. Rhode, ed.) --------------------------------------- 448
  Notes and Questions -- 453

CHAPTER VIII. Negotiation and Mediation ----------------- 457

Problem 1: Negotiation Exercise ------------------------------- 457
Introduction --- 458
Problem 2 -- 459
Richard Neely, "The Primary Caretaker Parent Rule: Child Custody
  and the Dynamics of Greed" -------------------------------- 459
Notes -- 460
Questions -- 461
A. Coercion -- 465
  Notes --- 465
B. Truthfulness in Bargaining -------------------------------- 467
  Problem 3 --- 468
  Larry Lempert, "In Settlement Talks, Does Telling the Truth
    Have Its Limits?" --- 470
  Notes and Questions: Candor in Negotiation ---------------- 475
C. Cooperative and Competitive Bargaining ------------------- 484

D. Mediation --- 488

    Problem 4 --- 488

    Notes and Questions: Lawyers and Mediation ----------------- 489

CHAPTER IX. The Lawyer's Counseling Role --------------- 498

Introduction -- 498

A. Counseling Frameworks -- 498

    Lon L. Fuller and John D. Randall, "Professional Responsibility: Report of the Joint Conference" ---------------------------- 498

    Notes on Client–Centered, Collaborative, and Contextual Approaches to Counseling ------------------------------------- 499

B. Corporate Practice --- 505

    Problem 1 --- 505

    Questions --- 506

    Notes --- 507

    Robert W. Gordon, "The Independence of Lawyers" ----------- 507

    Robert W. Gordon: "A New Role for Lawyers?: The Corporate Counselor after Enron" -------------------------------------- 509

    Notes and Questions --- 515

C. Family Practice -- 516

    Problem 2 --- 516

    American Academy of Matrimonial Lawyers, Bounds of Advocacy: Goals For Family Lawyers ------------------------------------ 517

    Notes --- 519

    Questions --- 522

D. Tax Practice --- 522

    Introduction -- 522

    Problem 3 --- 525

    Notes --- 525

    Questions --- 526

    ABA Standing Committee on Ethics and Professional Responsibility Formal Opinion 85–352 ------------------------------- 527

    Report of the Special Task Force on Formal Opinion 85–352 --------- 528

    Matthew C. Ames, "Formal Opinion 352: Professional Integrity and the Tax Audit Lottery" --------------------------------- 531

    Problem 4 --- 531

    Questions --- 532

    Problem 5 --- 533

    Randolph Paul, "The Responsibility of the Tax Adviser" ----------- 533

    Joseph Bankman, "An Academic's View of the Tax Shelter Battle," in The Crisis in Tax Administration --------------------- 534

    Notes and Questions --- 537

    Problem 6 --- 538

    Notes --- 539

    Panel Discussion on Professional Responsibility and the Model Rules of Professional Conduct --------------------------------- 540

    Questions --- 541

E. Government Lawyers -- 542

    Problem 7 --- 542

    Notes: The "Torture Memos" ----------------------------------- 545

    Excerpt from the "Bybee/Yoo Memo" -------------------------- 548

E. Government Lawyers—Continued
    Notes -- 550
    Excerpt from the "Levin Memo" ------------------------------------ 551
    Questions --- 553
    Questions --- 562

CHAPTER X. Conflicts of Interest ------------------------------ 563

A. Introduction --- 563
    United States v. Bronston -- 567
    Notes and Questions -- 569
B. Conflicts of Interest in Criminal Defense ------------------------ 570
    1. Constitutional Standards and Conflicts of Interest -------- 570
        Cuyler v. Sullivan --- 571
        Questions --- 575
        Mickens v. Taylor --- 578
        Notes -- 581
        Questions --- 582
    2. Concurrent Conflicts in Criminal Defense: Strategic Concerns -- 583
        Kenneth Mann, Defending White–Collar Crime ----------- 583
        Notes: Multiple Representation of Criminal Defendants ------ 586
        Questions --- 589
C. Concurrent Representation of Conflicting Interests in Civil Matters --- 589
    Problem 1 --- 589
    Thomas L. Shaffer "The Legal Ethics of Radical Individualism" ---- 589
    Notes and Questions -- 593
    Notes: "The Lawyer for the Situation" ----------------------------- 596
    Questions --- 598
    Notes: Other Common Situations of Concurrent Representation --- 598
    Problem 2 --- 603
    Westinghouse Electric Corporation v. Kerr–Mcgee Corporation ----- 603
    Notes and Questions -- 607
    Problem 3 --- 609
    Notes: Positional Conflicts of Interest ---------------------------- 610
    Questions --- 613
D. Conflicts Involving Former Clients ------------------------------- 614
    Problem 4 --- 614
    1. The Rationale for Disqualification ----------------------------- 615
    2. Confidentiality and the "Substantial Relation" Standard -------- 616
        Westinghouse Electric Corporation v. Gulf Oil Corporation ----- 616
        Notes -- 619
E. Imputed Disqualification --- 625
    Problem 5 --- 625
    Silver Chrysler Plymouth, Inc. v. Chrysler Motors Corporation ----- 627
    Notes -- 630
    Questions --- 631
F. The Former Government Lawyer ---------------------------------- 632
    Problem 6 --- 632
    Armstrong v. McAlpin -- 633
    Notes: The Revolving Door --- 636
    Questions --- 640

G. Conflicts of Interest in Class Actions ----------------------------- 647
 1. Public Interest Class Actions------------------------------------ 649
  Problem 7 --- 649
  Questions --- 650
  Deborah L. Rhode, "Class Conflicts in Class Actions" ------------ 651
  Notes --- 656
  Questions --- 657
  Fiandaca v. Cunningham ------------------------------------- 658
  Notes and Questions -- 663
 2. Mass Torts --- 664
  Problem 8 --- 664
  Notes --- 666
  Problem 9 --- 671
H. Fee–Related Conflicts of Interest------------------------------------ 671
 1. Conflicts in Public Interest Representation ----------------------- 671
  Problem 10-- 671
  Questions --- 672
  Evans v. Jeff D. -- 672
  Notes and Questions -- 678
 2. Attorney Buyouts and Secret Settlements ----------------------- 680
  Problem 11-- 680
  Notes --- 681
  Questions --- 681
 3. Consumer Class Action Abuses --------------------------------- 684
  Questions --- 685
I. Conflicts of Interest in Context ------------------------------------ 686
 Problem 12 -- 686
 Notes: Business Transactions Between Attorneys and Clients ------- 687
 Notes: Media Contracts-- 688
 Notes: The Advocate–Witness Rule----------------------------- 689
 Notes: Conflicts of Interest Involving Prospective Clients ----------- 690
 Notes: Conflicts Based on Personal and Family Relationships ------- 690
 Problem 13 -- 692
 Notes and Questions: Attorney–Client Sexual Relations ------------- 693

CHAPTER XI. Lawyer–Client Decision Making ------------------- 696

A. The Definition of the Problem ------------------------------------- 696
 Introduction-- 696
 Problem 1 --- 698
 Richard Wasserstrom, "Lawyers as Professionals: Some Moral
  Issues" -- 700
 Notes -- 701
 Jones v. Barnes --- 704
 Notes and Questions -- 708
 United States v. Kaczynski ------------------------------------- 715
 Notes and Questions -- 724
B. The Justification of Paternalism ----------------------------------- 727
 Introduction-- 727
 Problem 2 --- 728
 Questions -- 728
 Notes: The Moral Problem of Paternalism ----------------------- 730
 David Luban, "Paternalism and the Legal Profession"------------- 734
 Questions -- 736

C. Informed Consent and the Partially Competent Client 736
Notes and Questions: Informed Consent 736
   1. Defining Competence 740
     Introduction 740
     Questions 743
   2. Representing Clients Under a Disability 743
   3. Representing Juveniles 745
     Problem 3 745
     Notes and Questions 747
     Questions 750
   4. Representing Sophisticated Clients 753
     Problem 4 753
     Notes 754

CHAPTER XII. Market Regulation 756

Introduction 756
A. Advertising 757
   Introduction 757
   Problem 1 761
   Notes 763
   Questions 766
B. Solicitation 770
   Introduction 770
   Jerold S. Auerbach, Unequal Justice: Lawyers and Social Change
     in Modern America 771
   Ohralik v. Ohio State Bar Association 772
   In re Primus 779
   Questions 783
   In re Marshall I. Teichner 784
   Problem 2 786
   Problem 3 787
   Deborah L. Rhode, "Solicitation" 789
   Notes and Questions 791
C. Specialization and Group Legal Services Plans 794
   Problem 4 794
   Notes on Specialization 795
   Questions 796
   Notes on Group Legal Services, Referral Plans, and Legal Insur-
     ance 796
   Questions 799
D. Unauthorized Practice of Law: Nonlawyer Services and Multijuris-
   dictional Practice 800
   Orison S. Marden, "The American Bar and Unauthorized Prac-
     tice" 800
   Florida Bar v. Brumbaugh 801
   Questions 803
   Problem 5 804
   Deborah L. Rhode, Access to Justice 804

D. Unauthorized Practice of Law: Nonlawyer Services and Multijuris-
dictional Practice—Continued
Notes and Questions on Nonlawyer Services 807
Notes and Questions on Multijurisdictional Practice 810
Notes on GATS 814
Notes and Questions on Outsourcing 814
Problem 6 814
E. Multidisciplinary Practice 817
Notes 817
F. Attorneys' Fees 821
Introduction 821
   1. Excessive Fees 824
   In the Matter of Laurence S. Fordham 824
   Questions 828
   Notes 832
   Questions 835
   Problem 6 836
   2. Referral Fees 836
   Notes and Questions 836
   3. Contingent Fees 837
   Introduction 837
   Questions 841
G. Financing Litigation 843
Notes and Questions 843
Peter H. Schuck, Agent Orange on Trial: Mass Toxic Disasters in
the Courts 844
Notes 846
Questions 847

CHAPTER XIII. The Distribution of Legal Services 850

A. Problems of Litigiousness: The Overlawyered Society 850
Charles Dickens, Bleak House 850
Dave Barry, "Here's Proof That the Law Has Teeth" 852
Derek C. Bok, "A Flawed System of Law Practice and Training" ... 855
Notes 857
Questions 866
B. Problems of Access: The Underlawyered Society 866
Legal Services Corporation: Documenting the Justice Gap in
America. 866
Notes 870
C. The Right to Legal Services 872
Notes 872
Richard L. Abel, "Legal Services" 875
David Luban, "Taking Out the Adversary: The Assault on Pro-
gressive Public–Interest Lawyers" 876
Questions 877
D. Public Interest Law 877
Problem 1 877
Shauna Marshall, "Mission Impossible?: Ethical Community Law-
yering" 878
Notes 879

E. Subsidized Legal Services 884
Introduction 884
Omnibus Consolidated Rescissions and Appropriations Act of
1996: Legal Services Corporation 886
Legal Services Corp. v. Velazquez 887
Notes and Questions 889
Questions 894
Problem 2 894
Stephen Wexler, "Practicing Law for Poor People" 896
Problem 3 899
Notes and Questions 900
F. Alternative Dispute Resolution 902
1. The Rationale for Alternative Dispute Resolution 902
Notes 902
2. Forms of Alternative Dispute Resolution 903
Notes 903
3. Alternative Dispute Resolution: Critics and Their Critics 906
Notes 906
4. Ethical Rules 909
Problem 4 909
Owen Fiss, "Against Settlement" 910
Notes and Questions 913
G. Pro Bono Representation 914
1. The Ethical Obligations of Lawyers 914
Introduction 914
Deborah L. Rhode, Access to Justice 915
Questions 925
2. Court–Appointed Pro Bono Representation 927
Notes 927
Questions 929
Questions 930

CHAPTER XIV. Admission to the Bar 931

A. Introduction 931
Notes: Historical Perspectives 931
J. Willard Hurst, The Growth of American Law 932
B. Competence 933
Introduction: Bar Exams 933
Richardson v. McFadden 934
Notes 938
Questions 943
C. Character and Fitness 944
George Sharswood, An Essay on Professional Ethics 944
Schware v. Board of Bar Examiners of the State of New Mexico 944
Notes 946
In re Application of Stewart 948
Problem 1 952
Notes and Questions 956
Problem 2 958
Notes and Questions 961

D. Interstate Regulation -- 961
    Notes --- 961
    Leis v. Flynt -- 962
    Notes --- 964

CHAPTER XV. Discipline and Malpractice ------------------------- 967

A. Introduction --- 967
B. Regulatory Structures and Standards ---------------------------------- 968
    Problem 1 --- 968
    In re Himmel --- 970
    Wieder v. Skala --- 972
    Bohatch v. Butler & Binion, et al. ----------------------------------- 974
    Notes and Questions: Reporting Misconduct ------------------- 976
    The Florida Bar v. Neale -- 979
    Deborah L. Rhode, In the Interests of Justice: Reforming the
       Legal Profession --- 980
    Questions --- 981
    Notes: Disciplinary Structures --- 982
C. Disciplinary Sanctions --- 987
    Introduction -- 987
    Problem 2 --- 987
    Notes --- 991
    Questions --- 993
    American Bar Association, ABA Standards for Imposing Lawyer
       Sanctions -- 995
    Notes and Questions --- 997
D. Mental Health and Substance Abuse ----------------------------------- 1003
    Introduction -- 1003
    In re Kersey --- 1004
    Notes and Questions --- 1005
E. Competence and Malpractice -- 1007
    1. Competence -- 1007
       Introduction --- 1007
       Questions --- 1009
    2. Malpractice -- 1010
       Problem 3 --- 1010
       Notes -- 1011
       Notes and Questions --- 1012
       Questions --- 1014
       Questions --- 1015
       Questions --- 1017
       Questions --- 1019
       Questions: Prevention --- 1020

CHAPTER XVI. Legal Education -- 1021

A. The Structure of Legal Education -------------------------------------- 1021
    Introduction -- 1021
    1. Educational Structure --- 1023
       Richard A. Posner, "Let Employers Insist If Three Years of
          Law School is Necessary" --------------------------------------- 1025
       Notes and Questions --- 1026

A. The Structure of Legal Education—Continued
    2. The Role of Rankings-- 1028
        Questions-- 1029
    3. Educational Content and Methodology -------------------------- 1029
        Duncan Kennedy, Legal Education and the Reproduction of
            Hierarchy-- 1030
        Questions-- 1034
        Notes-- 1035
        Anthony T. Kronman, The Lost Lawyer: Failing Ideals of The
            Legal Profession--- 1036
        Questions-- 1039
        Notes-- 1039
        Questions-- 1041
        William M. Sullivan et al., Educating Lawyers: Preparation for
            the Profession of Law --- 1042
        Notes-- 1044
        Questions-- 1045
B. Diversity-- 1047
    American Bar Association Task Force on Minorities in the Legal
        Profession, Report with Recommendations ----------------------- 1047
    Kimberlé Williams Crenshaw, "Foreword: Toward a Race–Con-
        scious Pedagogy in Legal Education"---------------------------- 1048
    Notes: Perspectives on Race, Ethnicity, and Gender------------------ 1051
    Questions -- 1058
    American Bar Association Commission on Women in the Profes-
        sion, The Unfinished Agenda: Women in the Legal Profession 1061
    Notes -- 1063
    Questions -- 1065
    Questions -- 1067
C. Professional Responsibility-- 1068
    Notes -- 1068
D. Professional Values and Pro Bono Opportunities ---------------------- 1072
    Questions -- 1074

INDEX --- 1075

*

TABLE OF CASES

Principal cases are in bold type. Non-principal cases are in roman type. References are to Pages.

A., In re, 276 Or. 225, 554 P.2d 479 (Or. 1976), 479

Agent Orange Product Liability Litigation, In re, 818 F.2d 216 (2nd Cir.1987), 846

Agent Orange Product Liability Litigation, In re, 800 F.2d 14 (2nd Cir.1986), 658

Agurs, United States v., 427 U.S. 97, 96 S.Ct. 2392, 49 L.Ed.2d 342 (1976), 382

A.H. Robins Co., Inc., In re, 107 F.R.D. 2 (D.Kan.1985), 260

Alabama v. Shelton, 535 U.S. 654, 122 S.Ct. 1764, 152 L.Ed.2d 888 (2002), 873

Alexander v. Cahill, 2007 WL 2120024 (N.D.N.Y.2007), 766, 768

Alexander v. Cahill, 2007 WL 1202402 (N.D.N.Y.2007), 763

Al–Joudi v. Bush, 406 F.Supp.2d 13 (D.D.C. 2005), 730

Aloy v. Mash, 212 Cal.Rptr. 162, 696 P.2d 656 (Cal.1985), 1013

Amchem Products, Inc. v. Windsor, 521 U.S. 591, 117 S.Ct. 2231, 138 L.Ed.2d 689 (1997), 667

American Airlines, Inc., In re, 972 F.2d 605 (5th Cir.1992), 615

Analytica, Inc. v. NPD Research, Inc., 708 F.2d 1263 (7th Cir.1983), 620

Anastaplo, In re, 366 U.S. 82, 81 S.Ct. 978, 6 L.Ed.2d 135 (1961), 955

Anders v. California, 386 U.S. 738, 87 S.Ct. 1396, 18 L.Ed.2d 493 (1967), 711

Ang v. Martin, 154 Wash.2d 477, 114 P.3d 637 (Wash.2005), 1015

Antitrust Grand Jury, In re (Advance Publications, Inc.), 805 F.2d 155 (6th Cir.1986), 252, 253

Applicants v. Texas State Bd. of Law Examiners, 1994 WL 923404 (W.D.Tex.1994), 960

Application of (see name of party)

Argersinger v. Hamlin, 407 U.S. 25, 92 S.Ct. 2006, 32 L.Ed.2d 530 (1972), 873

Armstrong v. McAlpin, 625 F.2d 433 (2nd Cir.1980), **633**

Armstrong, United States v., 517 U.S. 456, 116 S.Ct. 1480, 134 L.Ed.2d 687 (1996), 371

Arthur Andersen LLP v. United States, 544 U.S. 696, 125 S.Ct. 2129, 161 L.Ed.2d 1008 (2005), 346

Attorney U v. Mississippi Bar, 678 So.2d 963 (Miss.1996), 976

Bagley, United States v., 473 U.S. 667, 105 S.Ct. 3375, 87 L.Ed.2d 481 (1985), 382

Bails v. Wheeler, 171 Mont. 524, 559 P.2d 1180 (Mont.1977), 469

Baird v. Koerner, 279 F.2d 623 (9th Cir. 1960), 243

Baldasarre v. Butler, 132 N.J. 278, 625 A.2d 458 (N.J.1993), 600

Balla v. Gambro, Inc., 145 Ill.2d 492, 164 Ill.Dec. 892, 584 N.E.2d 104 (Ill.1991), 408

Banks v. Dretke, 540 U.S. 668, 124 S.Ct. 1256, 157 L.Ed.2d 1166 (2004), 381

Baranyai, Commonwealth v., 296 Pa.Super. 342, 442 A.2d 800 (Pa.Super.1982), 389

Bass, United States v., 536 U.S. 862, 122 S.Ct. 2389, 153 L.Ed.2d 769 (2002), 371

Bates v. State Bar of Arizona, 433 U.S. 350, 51 Ohio Misc. 1, 97 S.Ct. 2691, 53 L.Ed.2d 810 (1977), 759

Batson v. Kentucky, 476 U.S. 79, 106 S.Ct. 1712, 90 L.Ed.2d 69 (1986), 390, 391

Beasley, State ex rel. Oklahoma Bar Ass'n v., 142 P.3d 410 (Okla.2006), 1005

Belge, People v., 50 A.D.2d 1088, 376 N.Y.S.2d 771 (N.Y.A.D. 4 Dept.1975), 237

Belge, People v., 83 Misc.2d 186, 372 N.Y.S.2d 798 (N.Y.Co.Ct.1975), 237

Belli v. State Bar, 112 Cal.Rptr. 527, 519 P.2d 575 (Cal.1974), 758

Benjamin, United States v., 328 F.2d 854 (2nd Cir.1964), 295

Berger v. United States, 295 U.S. 78, 55 S.Ct. 629, 79 L.Ed. 1314 (1935), 355

Berry, State v., 85 Ohio St.3d 1201, 706 N.E.2d 1273 (Ohio 1999), 697

Bersani v. Bersani, 41 Conn.Supp. 252, 565 A.2d 1368 (Conn.Super.1989), **254**

Betts v. Brady, 316 U.S. 455, 62 S.Ct. 1252, 86 L.Ed. 1595 (1942), 873

Bezold v. Kentucky Bar Ass'n, 134 S.W.3d 556 (Ky.2004), 694

Birbrower, Montalbano, Condon & Frank v. Superior Court, 70 Cal.Rptr.2d 304, 949 P.2d 1 (Cal.1998), 812, 964

Blum v. Stenson, 465 U.S. 886, 104 S.Ct. 1541, 79 L.Ed.2d 891 (1984), 679

Boddie v. Connecticut, 401 U.S. 371, 91 S.Ct. 780, 28 L.Ed.2d 113 (1971), 873

Bohatch v. Butler & Binion, 977 S.W.2d 543 (Tex.1998), **974**

Boudreau, In re, 815 So.2d 76 (La.2002), 994

Bradshaw v. Stumpf, 545 U.S. 175, 125 S.Ct. 2398, 162 L.Ed.2d 143 (2005), 373

Bradwell v. State, 83 U.S. 130, 21 L.Ed. 442 (1872), 61

Brady v. Maryland, 373 U.S. 83, 83 S.Ct. 1194, 10 L.Ed.2d 215 (1963), 381

Brickwood Contractors, Inc. v. United States, 2001 WL 793228 (Fed.Cl.2001), 680

Brobeck, Phleger & Harrison v. Telex Corp., 602 F.2d 866 (9th Cir.1979), 831

Bronston, United States v., 658 F.2d 920 (2nd Cir.1981), **567**

Bronston v. United States, 409 U.S. 352, 93 S.Ct. 595, 34 L.Ed.2d 568 (1973), 479

Brotherhood of Railroad Trainmen v. Virginia ex rel. Va. State Bar, 377 U.S. 1, 84 S.Ct. 1113, 12 L.Ed.2d 89 (1964), 798

Brown v. Avvo, Inc., CO7–0920RSL (W.D. Wash., December 18, 2007), 770

Brown v. Legal Foundation of Washington, 538 U.S. 216, 123 S.Ct. 1406, 155 L.Ed.2d 376 (2003), 881, 901

Brown, In re, 912 A.2d 568 (D.C.2006), 1003, 1005

Buckhannon Bd. & Care Home, Inc. v. West Virginia Dept. of Health and Human Resources, 532 U.S. 598, 121 S.Ct. 1835, 149 L.Ed.2d 855 (2001), 679

Burdine v. Johnson, 66 F.Supp.2d 854 (S.D.Tex.1999), 321, 322

Burrow v. Arce, 997 S.W.2d 229 (Tex.1999), 834

Cannon v. United States Acoustics Corp., 532 F.2d 1118 (7th Cir.1976), 598

Cannon v. United States Acoustics Corp., 398 F.Supp. 209 (N.D.Ill.1975), 619

Cargle v. Mullin, 317 F.3d 1196 (10th Cir. 2003), 389

Carolene Products Co., United States v., 304 U.S. 144, 58 S.Ct. 778, 82 L.Ed. 1234 (1938), 882

Central Hudson Gas & Elec. Corp. v. Public Service Commission, 447 U.S. 557, 100 S.Ct. 2343, 65 L.Ed.2d 341 (1980), 792

Chambers v. Baltimore & O.R. Co., 207 U.S. 142, 28 S.Ct. 34, 52 L.Ed. 143 (1907), 874

Chambers v. NASCO, Inc., 501 U.S. 32, 111 S.Ct. 2123, 115 L.Ed.2d 27 (1991), 210

Cintolo, United States v., 818 F.2d 980 (1st Cir.1987), 189

Cipollone v. Liggett Group, Inc., 683 F.Supp. 1487 (D.N.J.1988), 258

City and County of (see name of city)
City of (see name of city)

Clark v. United States, 289 U.S. 1, 53 S.Ct. 465, 77 L.Ed. 993 (1933), 250

Clark v. Virginia Bd. of Bar Examiners, 880 F.Supp. 430 (E.D.Va.1995), 960, 961

Columbia/HCA Healthcare Corp. Billing Practices Litigation, In re, 293 F.3d 289 (6th Cir.2002), 242

Commonwealth v. _____ (see opposing party)

Comden v. Superior Court, 145 Cal.Rptr. 9, 576 P.2d 971 (Cal.1978), 689

Converse, In re, 258 Neb. 159, 602 N.W.2d 500 (Neb.1999), 954

Cooper, In re, 200 A.D.2d 221, 613 N.Y.S.2d 396 (N.Y.A.D. 1 Dept.1994), 988

Cooper, In re, 181 A.D.2d 298, 586 N.Y.S.2d 250 (N.Y.A.D. 1 Dept.1992), 991

Cooperman, In re, 611 N.Y.S.2d 465, 633 N.E.2d 1069 (N.Y.1994), 830

Counsel for Discipline of Nebraska Supreme Court, State ex rel. v. Reilly, 271 Neb. 465, 712 N.W.2d 278 (Neb.2006), 1003

Cronic, United States v., 466 U.S. 648, 104 S.Ct. 2039, 80 L.Ed.2d 657 (1984), 713

Cross & Cross Properties v. Everett Allied Co., 886 F.2d 497 (2nd Cir.1989), 211

Crossman, People v., 850 P.2d 708 (Colo. 1993), 693

C.R.W., In re, 267 Ga. 534, 481 S.E.2d 511 (Ga.1997), 958

Cueto, United States v., 151 F.3d 620 (7th Cir.1998), **189**

Cuyler v. Sullivan, 446 U.S. 335, 100 S.Ct. 1708, 64 L.Ed.2d 333 (1980), **571**

Danville Plywood Corp. v. United States, 899 F.2d 3 (Fed.Cir.1990), 533

Davin v. Daham, 329 N.J.Super. 54, 746 A.2d 1034 (N.J.Super.A.D.2000), 469, 477

Davis, United States v., 285 F.3d 378 (5th Cir.2002), 710

Dawson v. City of Bartlesville, 901 F.Supp. 314 (N.D.Okla.1995), 663

DeSisto College, Inc. v. Line, 888 F.2d 755 (11th Cir.1989), 211

Dillon, United States v., 346 F.2d 633 (9th Cir.1965), 929

Disciplinary Counsel v. Hiltbrand, 110 Ohio St.3d 214, 852 N.E.2d 733 (Ohio 2006), 1005

Disciplinary Proceeding Against Schwimmer, 153 Wash.2d 752, 108 P.3d 761 (Wash. 2005), 1003

Diversified Industries, Inc. v. Meredith, 572 F.2d 596 (8th Cir.1977), 268

Dornay, In re, 160 Wash.2d 671, 161 P.3d 333 (Wash.2007), 989, 993

Douglas v. California, 372 U.S. 353, 83 S.Ct. 814, 9 L.Ed.2d 811 (1963), 874

Dowd & Dowd, Ltd. v. Gleason, 181 Ill.2d 460, 230 Ill.Dec. 229, 693 N.E.2d 358 (Ill. 1998), 794

Duffy, In re, 19 A.D.2d 177, 242 N.Y.S.2d 665 (N.Y.A.D. 2 Dept.1963), 758

Duhaime v. John Hancock Mut. Life Ins. Co., 183 F.3d 1 (1st Cir.1999), 668

Dusky v. United States, 362 U.S. 402, 80 S.Ct. 788, 4 L.Ed.2d 824 (1960), 714, 742

Edenfield v. Fane, 507 U.S. 761, 113 S.Ct. 1792, 123 L.Ed.2d 543 (1993), 791

EEOC v. Sidley Austin Brown & Wood, 406 F.Supp.2d 991 (N.D.Ill.2005), 103

EEOC v. Sidley Austin Brown & Wood, 315 F.3d 696 (7th Cir.2002), 103

Evans v. Jeff D., 475 U.S. 717, 106 S.Ct. 1531, 89 L.Ed.2d 747 (1986), **672**

Family Div. Trial Lawyers v. Moultrie, 725 F.2d 695 (D.C.Cir.1984), 930

Farrar v. Hobby, 506 U.S. 103, 113 S.Ct. 566, 121 L.Ed.2d 494 (1992), 679

Federal Defenders of San Diego, Inc. v. United States Sentencing Com'n, 680 F.Supp. 26 (D.D.C.1988), 610

Feldberg, Matter of, 862 F.2d 622 (7th Cir. 1988), 253

Fiandaca v. Cunningham, 827 F.2d 825 (1st Cir.1987), **658**

Fidelity Federal Sav. and Loan Ass'n v. de la Cuesta, 458 U.S. 141, 102 S.Ct. 3014, 73 L.Ed.2d 664 (1982), 422

Fieger v. Michigan Supreme Court, 2007 WL 2571975 (E.D. Mich. 2007), 229

Fifteenth Judicial Dist. Unified Bar Ass'n v. Glasgow, 1999 WL 1128847 (Tenn.Ct.App. 1999), 804

Finley v. Home Ins. Co., 975 P.2d 1145 (Hawai'i 1998), 600

Firestone Tire & Rubber Co. v. Risjord, 449 U.S. 368, 101 S.Ct. 669, 66 L.Ed.2d 571 (1981), 565

Flanagan v. United States, 465 U.S. 259, 104 S.Ct. 1051, 79 L.Ed.2d 288 (1984), 565

Florida v. Nixon, 543 U.S. 175, 125 S.Ct. 551, 160 L.Ed.2d 565 (2004), 713

Florida Bar v. Brumbaugh, 355 So.2d 1186 (Fla.1978), **801**

Florida Bar v. Went For It, 515 U.S. 618, 115 S.Ct. 2371, 132 L.Ed.2d 541 (1995), 788, 792

Florida Bar, State ex rel. v. Kimball, 96 So.2d 825 (Fla.1957), 101

Florida Bd. of Bar Examiners Re N.R.S., 403 So.2d 1315 (Fla.1981), 101

Fordham, Matter of, 423 Mass. 481, 668 N.E.2d 816 (Mass.1996), **824**

Frazier v. Heebe, 482 U.S. 641, 107 S.Ct. 2607, 96 L.Ed.2d 557 (1987), 965

Fund of Funds, Ltd. v. Arthur Andersen & Co., 567 F.2d 225 (2nd Cir.1977), 566

Gagnon v. Scarpelli, 411 U.S. 778, 93 S.Ct. 1756, 36 L.Ed.2d 656 (1973), 873

Garner v. Wolfinbarger, 430 F.2d 1093 (5th Cir.1970), 249, 274

Gault, In re, 387 U.S. 1, 87 S.Ct. 1428, 18 L.Ed.2d 527 (1967), 748, 873

General Dynamics Corp. v. Superior Court, 32 Cal.Rptr.2d 1, 876 P.2d 487 (Cal.1994), 409

Gentile v. Nevada State Bar, 501 U.S. 1030, 111 S.Ct. 2720, 115 L.Ed.2d 888 (1991), 388

Georgine v. Amchem Products, Inc., 157 F.R.D. 246 (E.D.Pa.1994), 667

Gideon v. Wainwright, 372 U.S. 335, 83 S.Ct. 792, 9 L.Ed.2d 799 (1963), 873

Giglio v. United States, 405 U.S. 150, 92 S.Ct. 763, 31 L.Ed.2d 104 (1972), 381

Ginger, In re, 372 F.2d 620 (6th Cir.1967), 967

Golden Eagle Distributing Corp. v. Burroughs Corp., 801 F.2d 1531 (9th Cir. 1986), 211

Goldfarb v. Virginia State Bar, 421 U.S. 773, 95 S.Ct. 2004, 44 L.Ed.2d 572 (1975), 759, 822

Gonzalez v. State, 117 S.W.3d 831 (Tex.Crim. App.2003), 689

Goodell, Matter of, 39 Wis. 232 (Wis.1875), 61

Goodman v. Kennedy, 134 Cal.Rptr. 375, 556 P.2d 737 (Cal.1976), 1018

Gould v. Harkness, 470 F.Supp.2d 1357 (S.D.Fla.2006), 811

Government of India v. Cook Industries, Inc., 569 F.2d 737 (2nd Cir.1978), 622

Grand Jury Proceedings, In re (FMC Corp.), 604 F.2d 798 (3rd Cir.1979), 252

Grand Jury Proceedings, In re (U.S. v. Doe), 219 F.3d 175 (2nd Cir.2000), 241, 261

Gratz v. Bollinger, 539 U.S. 244, 123 S.Ct. 2411, 156 L.Ed.2d 257 (2003), 1055

Greenberg, In re, 155 N.J. 138, 714 A.2d 243 (N.J.1998), 1006

Greycas v. Proud, 826 F.2d 1560 (7th Cir. 1987), 295, 1019

Grievance Adm'r v. Fieger, 476 Mich. 231, 719 N.W.2d 123 (Mich.2006), 229

Griffin v. Illinois, 351 U.S. 12, 76 S.Ct. 585, 100 L.Ed. 891 (1956), 322, 874

Grimshaw v. Ford Motor Co., 119 Cal.App.3d 757, 174 Cal.Rptr. 348 (Cal.App. 4 Dist. 1981), 402

Grutter v. Bollinger, 539 U.S. 306, 123 S.Ct. 2325, 156 L.Ed.2d 304 (2003), 1055

Grutter v. Bollinger, 16 F.Supp.2d 797 (E.D.Mich.1998), 1055

GTE Products Corp. v. Stewart, 421 Mass. 22, 653 N.E.2d 161 (Mass.1995), 409

Hager, In re, 812 A.2d 904 (D.C.2002), 682

Haines v. Liggett Group, Inc., 814 F.Supp. 414 (D.N.J.1993), 258

Haines v. Liggett Group Inc., 975 F.2d 81 (3rd Cir.1992), 259

Hale v. Committee on Character and Fitness of the Ill. Bar, 530 U.S. 1261, 120 S.Ct. 2716, 147 L.Ed.2d 982 (2000), 954

Hamm, Matter of, 211 Ariz. 458, 123 P.3d 652 (Ariz.2005), 953

Hammad, United States v., 858 F.2d 834 (2nd Cir.1988), 356

Hansen v. Hansen, 43 Colo.App. 525, 608 P.2d 364 (Colo.App.1979), 860

Harper & Row Publishers v. Decker, 423 F.2d 487 (7th Cir.1970), 268

Harrell v. The Florida Bar, 2008 WL 596086 (M.D.Fla.2008), 762, 768

Hatcher, United States v., 323 F.3d 666 (8th Cir.2003), 267

Heelan v. Lockwood, 143 A.D.2d 881, 533 N.Y.S.2d 560 (N.Y.A.D. 2 Dept.1988), 566

Henkel, United States v., 799 F.2d 369 (7th Cir.1986), 329

Hensley v. Eckerhart, 461 U.S. 424, 103 S.Ct. 1933, 76 L.Ed.2d 40 (1983), 679

Herbster v. North American Co. for Life and Health Ins., 150 Ill.App.3d 21, 103 Ill.Dec. 322, 501 N.E.2d 343 (Ill.App. 2 Dist.1986), 408

Hernandez v. New York, 500 U.S. 352, 111 S.Ct. 1859, 114 L.Ed.2d 395 (1991), 389

Hickman v. Taylor, 329 U.S. 495, 67 S.Ct. 385, 91 L.Ed. 451 (1947), 215

Hill v. Norfolk & Western Ry. Co., 814 F.2d 1192 (7th Cir.1987), 211

Himmel, In re, 125 Ill.2d 531, 127 Ill.Dec. 708, 533 N.E.2d 790 (Ill.1988), **970**

Hinson–Lyles, In re, 864 So.2d 108 (La.2003), 956

Hodge & Zweig, United States v., 548 F.2d 1347 (9th Cir.1977), 250

Holloway, In re, 452 N.E.2d 934 (Ind.1983), 988, 991

Hoover v. Ronwin, 466 U.S. 558, 104 S.Ct. 1989, 80 L.Ed.2d 590 (1984), 940

Hopwood v. Texas, 78 F.3d 932 (5th Cir. 1996), 1054

Howard, In re, 912 S.W.2d 61 (Mo.1995), 693

Hull v. Celanese Corp., 513 F.2d 568 (2nd Cir.1975), 565

Hurtado v. United States, 410 U.S. 578, 93 S.Ct. 1157, 35 L.Ed.2d 508 (1973), 928

Imbler v. Pachtman, 424 U.S. 409, 96 S.Ct. 984, 47 L.Ed.2d 128 (1976), 356

Indiana v. Edwards, ___ U.S. ___, 128 S.Ct. 2379, 171 L.Ed.2d 345 (2008), 714

In re (see name of party)

International Shipping Co., S.A. v. Hydra Offshore, Inc., 875 F.2d 388 (2nd Cir. 1989), 211

Iowa Supreme Court Bd. of Professional Ethics and Conduct v. Grotewold, 642 N.W.2d 288 (Iowa 2002), 1003

J.E.B. v. Alabama, 511 U.S. 127, 114 S.Ct. 1419, 128 L.Ed.2d 89 (1994), 390

Jenkens & Gilchrist, P.C., United States v., 2004 WL 870824 (N.D.Ill.2004), 243

Johnson v. State, 453 N.E.2d 365 (Ind.App. 4 Dist.1983), 389

Johnson v. Zerbst, 304 U.S. 458, 58 S.Ct. 1019, 82 L.Ed. 1461 (1938), 873

Johnston, United States v., 690 F.2d 638 (7th Cir.1982), 690

Jones v. Barnes, 463 U.S. 745, 103 S.Ct. 3308, 77 L.Ed.2d 987 (1983), **704**

Jones v. Clinton, 36 F.Supp.2d 1118 (E.D.Ark.1999), 480, 990

Jones, People v., 404 N.Y.S.2d 85, 375 N.E.2d 41 (N.Y.1978), 382

Kaczynski, United States v., 239 F.3d 1108 (9th Cir.2001), **715**

Kamp, In re, 40 N.J. 588, 194 A.2d 236 (N.J.1963), 600

Keller v. State Bar of California, 496 U.S. 1, 110 S.Ct. 2228, 110 L.Ed.2d 1 (1990), 112

Keller, Matter of, 792 N.E.2d 865 (Ind.2003), 762

Kentucky Bar Ass'n v. Gangwish, 630 S.W.2d 66 (Ky.1982), 762

Kersey, In re, 520 A.2d 321 (D.C.1987), **1004**

Kimball, In re, 40 A.D.2d 252, 339 N.Y.S.2d 302 (N.Y.A.D. 2 Dept.1973), 101

Kimball, State ex rel. Florida Bar v., 96 So.2d 825 (Fla.1957), 101

Kinee v. Abraham Lincoln Federal Sav. and Loan Ass'n, 365 F.Supp. 975 (E.D.Pa. 1973), 209

King, Application of, 212 Ariz. 559, 136 P.3d 878 (Ariz.2006), 952

Kling v. Landry, 292 Ill.App.3d 329, 226 Ill. Dec. 684, 686 N.E.2d 33 (Ill.App. 2 Dist. 1997), 1013

Kojayan, United States v., 8 F.3d 1315 (9th Cir.1993), 356

KPMG LLP, United States v., 316 F.Supp.2d 30 (D.D.C.2004), 243

Kras, United States v., 409 U.S. 434, 93 S.Ct. 631, 34 L.Ed.2d 626 (1973), 873

Lamb, In re, 260 Cal.Rptr. 856, 776 P.2d 765 (Cal.1989), 989, 992

Lamplugh, United States v., 334 F.3d 294 (3rd Cir.2003), 344

Lange v. Marshall, 622 S.W.2d 237 (Mo.App. E.D.1981), 489, 493

Laser Industries, Ltd. v. Reliant Technologies, Inc., 167 F.R.D. 417 (N.D.Cal.1996), 252

Lassiter v. Department of Social Services, 452 U.S. 18, 101 S.Ct. 2153, 68 L.Ed.2d 640 (1981), 873, 874, 929

Lathrop v. Donohue, 367 U.S. 820, 81 S.Ct. 1826, 6 L.Ed.2d 1191 (1961), 112

Lawrence v. Texas, 539 U.S. 558, 123 S.Ct. 2472, 156 L.Ed.2d 508 (2003), 692

Lee v. American Eagle Airlines, Inc., 93 F.Supp.2d 1322 (S.D.Fla.2000), **229**

Legal Aid Soc. of Hawaii v. Legal Services Corp., 145 F.3d 1017 (9th Cir.1998), 889

Legal Services Commission v. Mullins, [2006] LPT 012 (2006), 479, 989, 992

Legal Services Corp. v. Velazquez, 531 U.S. 533, 121 S.Ct. 1043, 149 L.Ed.2d 63 (2001), **887**

Leis v. Flynt, 441 U.S. 956, 99 S.Ct. 2185, 60 L.Ed.2d 1060 (1979), 810

Leis v. Flynt, 439 U.S. 438, 99 S.Ct. 698, 58 L.Ed.2d 717 (1979), **962**

Lincoln Sav. & Loan Ass'n v. Wall, 743 F.Supp. 901 (D.D.C.1990), 293, 502

Littleton v. Berbling, 468 F.2d 389 (7th Cir. 1972), 375

Lockwood, In re, 9 Ct.Cl. 346 (Ct.Cl.1873), 61

Louisiana State Bar Ass'n v. Edwins, 329 So.2d 437 (La.1976), 849

Macumber, State v., 112 Ariz. 569, 544 P.2d 1084 (Ariz.1976), 248

Madden v. Township of Delran, 126 N.J. 591, 601 A.2d 211 (N.J.1992), 915

Mallard v. United States Dist. Court for Southern Dist. of Iowa, 490 U.S. 296, 109 S.Ct. 1814, 104 L.Ed.2d 318 (1989), 929

Maltby, In re, 68 Ariz. 153, 202 P.2d 902 (Ariz.1949), 758

Marcus, Matter of, 107 Wis.2d 560, 320 N.W.2d 806 (Wis.1982), 762

Martinez v. Court of Appeal, 528 U.S. 152, 120 S.Ct. 684, 145 L.Ed.2d 597 (2000), 709

Massachusetts School of Law v. American Bar Ass'n, 142 F.3d 26 (1st Cir.1998), 1024

Massachusetts School of Law v. American Bar Ass'n, 107 F.3d 1026 (3rd Cir.1997), 1024

Mathews v. Eldridge, 424 U.S. 319, 96 S.Ct. 893, 47 L.Ed.2d 18 (1976), 873

Matter of (see name of party)

Matzo Food Products Litigation, In re, 156 F.R.D. 600 (D.N.J.1994), 684

Maxwell v. Superior Court, 180 Cal.Rptr. 177, 639 P.2d 248 (Cal.1982), 688

McDaniel v. Gile, 230 Cal.App.3d 363, 281 Cal.Rptr. 242 (Cal.App. 2 Dist.1991), 693

McDonnell Douglas Corp., United States ex rel. O'Keefe v., 132 F.3d 1252 (8th Cir. 1998), 134

McKenzie Const., Inc. v. Maynard, 758 F.2d 97 (3rd Cir.1985), 831

Mendelson, In re, 780 N.Y.S.2d 801 (N.Y.A.D. 3 Dept.2004), 1003

Meredith, People v., 175 Cal.Rptr. 612, 631 P.2d 46 (Cal.1981), 342

Meyerhofer v. Empire Fire & Marine Ins. Co., 497 F.2d 1190 (2nd Cir.1974), 287

Mickens v. Taylor, 535 U.S. 162, 122 S.Ct. 1237, 152 L.Ed.2d 291 (2002), **578**

MIT, United States v., 129 F.3d 681 (1st Cir.1997), 241

Mitchell v. Metropolitan Life Ins. Co., Inc., 2002 WL 441194 (S.D.N.Y.2002), 620

M.L.B. v. S.L.J., 519 U.S. 102, 117 S.Ct. 555, 136 L.Ed.2d 473 (1996), 873

Montanez v. Irizarry–Rodriguez, 273 N.J.Super. 276, 641 A.2d 1079 (N.J.Super.A.D.1994), 603

Moore, In re, 453 N.E.2d 971 (Ind.1983), 988, 991

Morrell v. State, 575 P.2d 1200 (Alaska 1978), 342

Motley v. Marathon Oil Co., 71 F.3d 1547 (10th Cir.1995), 257

Mourad v. Automobile Club Ins. Ass'n, 186 Mich.App. 715, 465 N.W.2d 395 (Mich. App.1991), 409

Mroczko, People v., 197 Cal.Rptr. 52, 672 P.2d 835 (Cal.1983), 577

Musheno v. Gensemer, 897 F.Supp. 833 (M.D.Pa.1995), 598

NAACP v. Button, 371 U.S. 415, 83 S.Ct. 328, 9 L.Ed.2d 405 (1963), 783, 798

Nasik Breeding & Research Farm Ltd. v. Merck & Co., Inc., 165 F.Supp.2d 514 (S.D.N.Y.2001), 477

Nebraska Press Ass'n v. Stuart, 427 U.S. 539, 96 S.Ct. 2791, 49 L.Ed.2d 683 (1976), 387

Nevmerzhitsky v. Ukraine, [2005] ECHR 54825/00 (ECHR 2005), 729

Newby v. Enron, 2007 WL 209923(S.D. Tex. 2007), 414

Newton, Town of v. Rumery, 480 U.S. 386, 107 S.Ct. 1187, 94 L.Ed.2d 405 (1987), 380

New York Cent. & H.R.R. Co. v. United States, 212 U.S. 481, 29 S.Ct. 304, 53 L.Ed. 613 (1909), 1001

Nix v. Whiteside, 475 U.S. 157, 106 S.Ct. 988, 89 L.Ed.2d 123 (1986), 324, **325**

Nolte v. Pearson, 133 F.R.D. 585 (D.Neb. 1990), 689

Non–Punitive Segregation Inmates v. Kelly, 589 F.Supp. 1330 (E.D.Pa.1984), 690, 691

Oakland Cannabis Buyers' Co-op., United States v., 532 U.S. 483, 121 S.Ct. 1711, 149 L.Ed.2d 722 (2001), 554

Ohralik v. Ohio State Bar Ass'n, 436 U.S. 447, 98 S.Ct. 1912, 56 L.Ed.2d 444 (1978), **772**

O'Keefe, United States ex rel. v. McDonnell Douglas Corp., 132 F.3d 1252 (8th Cir. 1998), 134

Oklahoma Bar Ass'n, State ex rel. v. Beasley, 142 P.3d 410 (Okla.2006), 1005

Oklahoma Bar Ass'n, State ex rel. v. Schraeder, 51 P.3d 570 (Okla.2002), 1007

Olwell, State v., 64 Wash.2d 828, 394 P.2d 681 (Wash.1964), 342

Opinion No. 26, In re, 139 N.J. 323, 654 A.2d 1344 (N.J.1995), 809

Oregon State Bar v. Smith, 149 Or.App. 171, 942 P.2d 793 (Or.App.1997), 809

Ortiz v. Fibreboard Corp., 527 U.S. 815, 119 S.Ct. 2295, 144 L.Ed.2d 715 (1999), 668

Ortiz v. State, 265 Ind. 549, 356 N.E.2d 1188 (Ind.1976), 389

Ortwein v. Schwab, 410 U.S. 656, 93 S.Ct. 1172, 35 L.Ed.2d 572 (1973), 873

Oyler v. Boles, 368 U.S. 448, 82 S.Ct. 501, 7 L.Ed.2d 446 (1962), 371

Panel File, In re, 597 N.W.2d 563 (Minn. 1999), 206

Paramount Communications Inc. v. QVC Network Inc., 637 A.2d 34 (Del. Supr.1994), 229

Parents Involved in Community Schools v. Seattle School Dist. No. 1, ___ U.S. ___, 127 S.Ct. 2738, 168 L.Ed.2d 508 (2007), 1059

Passante v. McWilliam, 62 Cal.Rptr.2d 298 (Cal.App. 4 Dist.1997), 687

Peat, Marwick, Mitchell & Co. v. Superior Court, 200 Cal.App.3d 272, 245 Cal.Rptr. 873 (Cal.App. 1 Dist.1988), 607

Peel v. Attorney Registration and Disciplinary Com'n of Illinois, 496 U.S. 91, 110 S.Ct. 2281, 110 L.Ed.2d 83 (1990), 760

Penn Cent. Transp. Co. v. New York City, 438 U.S. 104, 98 S.Ct. 2646, 57 L.Ed.2d 631 (1978), 930

Pennhurst State School & Hosp. v. Halderman, 465 U.S. 89, 104 S.Ct. 900, 79 L.Ed.2d 67 (1984), 650

Pennsylvania v. Delaware Valley Citizens' Council for Clean Air, 483 U.S. 711, 107 S.Ct. 3078, 97 L.Ed.2d 585 (1987), 679

Pennsylvania v. Finley, 481 U.S. 551, 107 S.Ct. 1990, 95 L.Ed.2d 539 (1987), 874

Pennsylvania Coal Co. v. Mahon, 260 U.S. 393, 43 S.Ct. 158, 67 L.Ed. 322 (1922), 930

People v. _____ (see opposing party)

Person v. Association of Bar of City of New York, 554 F.2d 534 (2nd Cir.1977), 842

Petition and Questionnaire for Admission to Rhode Island Bar, In re, 683 A.2d 1333 (R.I.1996), 960

Peyton v. Margiotti, 398 Pa. 86, 156 A.2d 865 (Pa.1959), 841

Philadelphia, City of v. Westinghouse Elec. Corp., 210 F.Supp. 483 (E.D.Pa.1962), 268

Philip Morris, Inc., State v., 1998 WL 154543 (Minn.1998), 263

Picker Intern., Inc. v. Varian Associates, Inc., 670 F.Supp. 1363 (N.D.Ohio 1987), 625

Pirillo v. Takiff, 462 Pa. 511, 341 A.2d 896 (Pa.1975), 587

Plessy v. Ferguson, 163 U.S. 537, 16 S.Ct. 1138, 41 L.Ed. 256 (1896), 212

Powell v. Alabama, 287 U.S. 45, 53 S.Ct. 55, 77 L.Ed. 158 (1932), 872, 929

Primus, In re, 436 U.S. 412, 98 S.Ct. 1893, 56 L.Ed.2d 417 (1978), **779**

Prosecutor v. Barayagwiza, Case No. ICTR 97–19–T (2000), 712

Prosecutor v. Milosevic, Case No. IT–99–37–PT (2000), 712

Qualcomm Inc. v. Broadcom Corp., 2008 WL 66932 (S.D.Cal.2008), **217**

Radiant Burners, Inc. v. American Gas Ass'n, 207 F.Supp. 771 (N.D.Ill.1962), 275

Rancman v. Interim Settlement Funding Corp., 99 Ohio St.3d 121, 789 N.E.2d 217 (Ohio 2003), 848

Ranta v. McCarney, 391 N.W.2d 161 (N.D. 1986), 811

Regents of University of California v. Bakke, 438 U.S. 265, 98 S.Ct. 2733, 57 L.Ed.2d 750 (1978), 1054

Reilly, State ex rel. Counsel for Discipline of Nebraska Supreme Court v., 271 Neb. 465, 712 N.W.2d 278 (Neb.2006), 1003

Reynoso, In re, 477 F.3d 1117 (9th Cir.2007), 804, 809

Rice v. Santa Fe Elevator Corp., 331 U.S. 218, 67 S.Ct. 1146, 91 L.Ed. 1447 (1947), 136, 422

Richardson v. McFadden, 540 F.2d 744 (4th Cir.1976), **934**

Richardson–Merrell, Inc. v. Koller, 472 U.S. 424, 105 S.Ct. 2757, 86 L.Ed.2d 340 (1985), 565

Richmond, United States v., 550 F.Supp. 605 (E.D.N.Y.1982), 379

Rico v. Mitsubishi Motors Corp., 68 Cal. Rptr.3d 758, 171 P.3d 1092 (Cal.2007), 147

Ricoh Co. v. Asustek Computer, Inc., 2007 WL 5462420 (W.D.Wis.2007), 228

Riehlmann, In re, 891 So.2d 1239 (La.2005), 970, 976

Rinella, In re, 175 Ill.2d 504, 222 Ill.Dec. 375, 677 N.E.2d 909 (Ill.1997), 693

R.M. v. Supreme Court, 185 N.J. 208, 883 A.2d 369 (N.J.2005), 984

R.M.J., In re, 455 U.S. 191, 102 S.Ct. 929, 71 L.Ed.2d 64 (1982), 759

Rompilla v. Beard, 545 U.S. 374, 125 S.Ct. 2456, 162 L.Ed.2d 360 (2005), 321

Ronco, In re, 838 F.2d 212 (7th Cir.1988), 211

Ross v. Moffitt, 417 U.S. 600, 94 S.Ct. 2437, 41 L.Ed.2d 341 (1974), 874

Ruffalo, In re, 390 U.S. 544, 88 S.Ct. 1222, 20 L.Ed.2d 117 (1968), 967

Ruiz, United States v., 536 U.S. 622, 122 S.Ct. 2450, 153 L.Ed.2d 586 (2002), 382

Rumsfeld v. Forum for Academic and Institutional Rights, Inc., 547 U.S. 47, 126 S.Ct. 1297, 164 L.Ed.2d 156 (2006), 1066

Russo v. Griffin, 147 Vt. 20, 510 A.2d 436 (Vt.1986), 1012

Rust v. Sullivan, 500 U.S. 173, 111 S.Ct. 1759, 114 L.Ed.2d 233 (1991), 889

Ryder, In re, 263 F.Supp. 360 (E.D.Va.1967), 342

Sakarias, In re, 25 Cal.Rptr.3d 265, 106 P.3d 931 (Cal.2005), 374

San Francisco, City and County of v. Cobra Solutions, Inc., 43 Cal.Rptr.3d 771, 135 P.3d 20 (Cal.2006), 642

Santa Barbara, City of v. Superior Court, 18 Cal.Rptr.3d 403 (Cal.App. 2 Dist.2004), 641, 642

Sattar, United States v., 272 F.Supp.2d 348 (S.D.N.Y.2003), 198

Schatz v. Weinberg & Green, 943 F.2d 485 (4th Cir.1991), 1018

Schaumburg, Village of v. Citizens for a Better Environment, 444 U.S. 620, 100 S.Ct. 826, 63 L.Ed.2d 73 (1980), 793

Scheehle v. Justices of the Arizona Supreme Court, 508 F.3d 887 (9th Cir.2007), 930

Scheehle v. Justices of the Arizona, 211 Ariz. 282, 120 P.3d 1092 (Ariz.2005), 915

Schloetter v. Raiload of Ind., Inc., 546 F.2d 706 (7th Cir.1976), 565

Schraeder, State ex rel. Oklahoma Bar Ass'n v., 51 P.3d 570 (Okla.2002), 1007

Schware v. Board of Bar Exam. of State of N.M., 353 U.S. 232, 77 S.Ct. 752, 1 L.Ed.2d 796 (1957), **944**

Sealed Case, In re, 121 F.3d 729 (D.C.Cir. 1997), 249

Sealed Case, In re, 107 F.3d 46 (D.C.Cir. 1997), 251, 253

Sealed Case, In re, 754 F.2d 395 (D.C.Cir. 1985), 252

Sealed Case, In re, 737 F.2d 94 (D.C.Cir. 1984), 257

Sealed Case, In re, 676 F.2d 793 (D.C.Cir. 1982), 257

SEC v. National Student Marketing Corp., 457 F.Supp. 682 (D.D.C.1978), 291

Serrano v. Priest, 131 Cal.App.3d 188, 182 Cal.Rptr. 387 (Cal.App. 2 Dist.1982), 880

Shapero v. Kentucky Bar Ass'n, 486 U.S. 466, 108 S.Ct. 1916, 100 L.Ed.2d 475 (1988), 760

Silver Chrysler Plymouth, Inc. v. Chrysler Motors Corp., 518 F.2d 751 (2nd Cir.1975), **627**

Singletary v. Costello, 665 So.2d 1099 (Fla. App. 4 Dist.1996), 729

Smith v. Robbins, 528 U.S. 259, 120 S.Ct. 746, 145 L.Ed.2d 756 (2000), 711

Smith v. State, 516 N.E.2d 1055 (Ind.1987), 389

Sparks, ex parte, 368 So.2d 528 (Ala.1979), 928

Spaulding v. Zimmerman, 263 Minn. 346, 116 N.W.2d 704 (Minn.1962), **279**

Spevack v. Klein, 385 U.S. 511, 87 S.Ct. 625, 17 L.Ed.2d 574 (1967), 968

Spivak v. Sachs, 263 N.Y.S.2d 953, 211 N.E.2d 329 (N.Y.1965), 811

Stare v. Tate, 21 Cal.App.3d 432, 98 Cal.Rptr. 264 (Cal.App. 2 Dist.1971), 469, 477

State, By Humphrey v. Philip Morris Inc., 1998 WL 257214 (Minn.Dist.Ct.1998), 260, 262

State ex rel. Humphrey v. Philip Morris, Inc., 1997 WL 33635815 (Minn.Dist.Ct.1997), 261

State v. _____ (see opposing party)

State ex rel. v. _____ (see opposing party and relator)

Steed, In re, 131 P.3d 231 (Utah 2006), 994

Stewart, In re Application of, 112 Ohio St.3d 415, 860 N.E.2d 729 (Ohio 2006), **948**

Strickland v. Washington, 466 U.S. 668, 104 S.Ct. 2052, 80 L.Ed.2d 674 (1984), 320, 929

Stropnicky v. Nathanson, 19 Mass. Discrim. L. Rep. 39 (1997), 206

Suppressed v. Suppressed, 206 Ill.App.3d 918, 151 Ill.Dec. 830, 565 N.E.2d 101 (Ill.App. 1 Dist.1990), 1013

Supreme Court of New Hampshire v. Piper, 470 U.S. 274, 105 S.Ct. 1272, 84 L.Ed.2d 205 (1985), 965

Supreme Court of Virginia v. Friedman, 487 U.S. 59, 108 S.Ct. 2260, 101 L.Ed.2d 56 (1988), 965

Swidler & Berlin v. United States, 524 U.S. 399, 118 S.Ct. 2081, 141 L.Ed.2d 379 (1998), 249

Talton v. Arnall Golden Gregory, LLP, 276 Ga.App. 21, 622 S.E.2d 589 (Ga.App. 2005), 1019

Tante v. Herring, 264 Ga. 694, 453 S.E.2d 686 (Ga.1994), 1013

Taylor, In re, 567 F.2d 1183 (2nd Cir.1977), 588

T.C. Theatre Corp. v. Warner Bros. Pictures, 113 F.Supp. 265 (S.D.N.Y.1953), 619

Teichner, In re, 75 Ill.2d 88, 25 Ill.Dec. 609, 387 N.E.2d 265 (Ill.1979), **784**

The Florida Bar, 425 So.2d 531 (Fla.1982), 101

The Florida Bar v. Heptner, 887 So.2d 1036 (Fla.2004), 1003

The Florida Bar v. Neale, 384 So.2d 1264 (Fla.1980), **979**

The Florida Bar v. Pape, 918 So.2d 240 (Fla. 2005), 768

The Florida Bar re Amendment to Rules Regulating the Florida Bar (Chapter 10)., 510 So.2d 596 (Fla.1987), 807

State ex rel. Humphrey v. Philip Morris, Inc., 1997 WL 33635815 (Minn.Dist.Ct.1997), 261

Thor v. Superior Court, 21 Cal.Rptr.2d 357, 855 P.2d 375 (Cal.1993), 729

Thornton v. Wahl, 787 F.2d 1151 (7th Cir. 1986), 211

Tidwell, In re, D.C. No. 99–B6–1569 (Sep. 11, 2003), 994

Tippins v. Walker, 77 F.3d 682 (2nd Cir. 1996), 321

T.J.S., Application of, 141 N.H. 697, 692 A.2d 498 (N.H.1997), 952

Toledo Bar Assn. v. McGill, 64 Ohio St.3d 669, 597 N.E.2d 1104 (Ohio 1992), 787
Town of (see name of town)

Unauthorized Practice of Law Committee v. Parsons Technology, Inc., 1999 WL 47235 (N.D.Tex.1999), 808
United Mine Workers of America, Dist. 12 v. Illinois State Bar Ass'n, 389 U.S. 217, 88 S.Ct. 353, 19 L.Ed.2d 426 (1967), 798
United States v. _____ (see opposing party)
United States ex rel. v. _____ (see opposing party and relator)
United Transp. Union v. State Bar of Mich., 401 U.S. 576, 91 S.Ct. 1076, 28 L.Ed.2d 339 (1971), 798
Upjohn Co. v. United States, 449 U.S. 383, 101 S.Ct. 677, 66 L.Ed.2d 584 (1981), **269**
UPL Advisory Opinion 2003–2, In re, 277 Ga. 472, 588 S.E.2d 741 (Ga.2003), 809

Village of (see name of village)
Viner v. Sweet, 135 Cal.Rptr.2d 629, 70 P.3d 1046 (Cal.2003), 1014

Wade, United States v., 388 U.S. 218, 87 S.Ct. 1926, 18 L.Ed.2d 1149 (1967), 304
Wamsley, Matter of, 725 N.E.2d 75 (Ind. 2000), 762
Warner, In re, 851 So.2d 1029 (La.2003), 477
Washington v. Harper, 494 U.S. 210, 110 S.Ct. 1028, 108 L.Ed.2d 178 (1990), 729
Washington State Physicians Ins. Exchange & Ass'n v. Fisons Corp., 122 Wash.2d 299, 858 P.2d 1054 (Wash.1993), 216
Westinghouse Elec. Corp. v. Gulf Oil Corp., 588 F.2d 221 (7th Cir.1978), **616**
Westinghouse Elec. Corp. v. Kerr–McGee Corp., 580 F.2d 1311 (7th Cir.1978), **603**
Westinghouse Elec. Corp. v. Rio Algom Ltd., 448 F.Supp. 1284 (N.D.Ill.1978), 607

Wheat v. United States, 486 U.S. 153, 108 S.Ct. 1692, 100 L.Ed.2d 140 (1988), 577
White's Will, In re, 121 N.Y. 406, 31 N.Y.St. Rep. 528, 24 N.E. 935 (N.Y.1890), 742
Wieder v. Skala, 593 N.Y.S.2d 752, 609 N.E.2d 105 (N.Y.1992), **972**
Wiesner v. Nardelli, 2007 WL 211083 (S.D.N.Y.2007), 957
Wiley v. San Diego County, 79 Cal.Rptr.2d 672, 966 P.2d 983 (Cal.1998), 1015
Williams v. General Elec. Capital Auto Lease, 1995 WL 765266 (N.D.Ill.1995), 686
Williams v. State, 805 A.2d 880 (Del. Supr.2002), 610
Williams, United States v., 504 U.S. 36, 112 S.Ct. 1735, 118 L.Ed.2d 352 (1992), 356
Willner v. Committee on Character and Fitness, 373 U.S. 96, 83 S.Ct. 1175, 10 L.Ed.2d 224 (1963), 967
Willy v. Coastal Corp., ARB Case No. 98–060, at 34–36 (U.S. Dept. Of Labor Feb. 27, 2004), 408
Wolters Kluwer Financial Services Inc. v. Scivantage, Adnane Charchour, Sanjeev Doss, Cameron Routh, 525 F.Supp.2d 448 (S.D.N.Y.2007), 227

Yick Wo v. Hopkins, 118 U.S. 356, 6 S.Ct. 1064, 30 L.Ed. 220 (1886), 371
Youngstown Sheet & Tube Co. v. Sawyer, 343 U.S. 579, 72 S.Ct. 863, 96 L.Ed. 1153 (1952), 554

Zant v. Prevatte, 248 Ga. 832, 286 S.E.2d 715 (Ga.1982), 729
Zaruba, Matter of, 177 N.J. 564, 832 A.2d 317 (N.J.2003), 682
Zauderer v. Office of Disciplinary Counsel of Supreme Court of Ohio, 471 U.S. 626, 105 S.Ct. 2265, 85 L.Ed.2d 652 (1985), 760
Zolin, United States v., 491 U.S. 554, 109 S.Ct. 2619, 105 L.Ed.2d 469 (1989), 252
Zubulake v. UBS Warburg LLC, 220 F.R.D. 212 (S.D.N.Y.2003), 351

TABLE OF OTHER AUTHORITIES

ABA Canon of Ethics

Canon	Page
12 (former)	829
27	758, 822
28	822

ABA Model of Judicial Conduct

Canon	Page
3(B)5	978
3(B)6	978

ABA Standards Relating to the Administration of Criminal Justice Defense Function Standards

No.	Page
3–1.2	361
3–1.2 (c)	355
3–1.4	361
3–3.1	362
3–3.1(b)	371
3–3.6	362
3–3.9	362, 369
3–3.9(a)	361
3–3.9(f)	379
3–3.11	363
3–4.1	363, 382
3–5.7	364
3–5.8	364
3–5.9	364
3–5.10	364
3–6.1	364
3–6.2	365
4–7.6	324, 334
4–7.6(b)	336
4–7.7	324

ABA Formal Opinion

No.	Page
85–352	525, 526, 527, 528
87–353	330
88–356	816
92–364	693, 694
92–368	142, 146
93–372	624
93–373	842
93–377	610
93–379	823
94–383	466
94–385	286
96–399	891
00–3	688
00–418	688
06–3	816
06–442	147
07–447	462
07–448	713
08–450	601
284	758
302	822

ABA Formal Opinion

No.	Page
309	758
314	524
340	691
341	290
342	636, 641
352	527
355	798, 799
368	146
371	677, 681
403	603

ABA Informal Opinion

No.	Page
1203	444, 445
1222	758
1457	793
1466	793
1518	478

ABA Model Code of Professional Responsibility—Disciplinary Rules

Rule	Page
1–102(A)(3)	341
1–102(A)(4)	446
1–102(A)(5)	341, 446
1–103(A)	446
2–101(A)	758
2–103	439, 798
2–104(A)	793
2–106	823
2–106(B)	828
2–106(C)	841
2–107(A)(2)	837
2–108	681, 794
2–110(A)(1)	928
2–110(A)(2)	288, 289, 290
2–110(B)	439
2–110(C)	439, 928
2–110(C)(2)	446
3–101(B)	810
4–101	288, 290
4–101(A)	243, 290, 446
4–101(B)	278
4–101(B)(1)	446
4–101(C)	243
4–101(C)(2)	446
4–101(C)(3)	278
4–101(D)	446
5–103(B)	849
5–105	565, 611, 909
5–105(D)	633
6–101(A)(2)	1007
7–101(A)(1)	140
7–101(B)(1)	140, 290
7–102	439
7–102(A)	446

ABA Model Code of Professional Responsibility—Disciplinary Rules

Rule	Page
7–102(A)(1)	210
7–102(A)(2)	210
7–102(B)	446
7–102(B)(1)	290
7–103	369, 381
7–105(A)	466
7–106(C)(7)	341, 439
7–109(A)	341, 439
7–109(C)	842
9–101	633
9–101(B)	566, 637

ABA Model Code of Professional Responsibility—Ethical Considerations

No.	Page
2–20	841
2–25	914
2–27	119, 613
2–28	119
2–29	927
5–9	689
5–20	490
7–7	703, 909
7–8	141, 909
7–9	141
7–12	703
7–13	355
7–14	646
7–17	612
8–1	612
9–3	633
9–4	633

ABA Model Rules of Professional Conduct

Rule	Page
1.0(d)	257
1.0(e)	737
1.1	517, 970, 995, 1007
1.2	31, 141, 178, 236, 288, 324, 393, 507, 517, 650, 672, 708, 728, 747, 889, 900, 909
1.2(a)	33, 141, 478, 670, 699, 754
1.2(c)	896
1.2(d)	130, 297, 728
1.3	141, 995
1.4	130, 478, 507, 517, 666, 754
1.5	215, 686, 687, 688, 730, 823, 829, 831, 836, 970, 995
1.5(d)(1)	841
1.5(d)(2)	841
1.6	33, 236, 243, 279, 285, 286, 288, 291, 301, 324, 408, 411, 415, 424, 483, 603, 621, 622, 666, 728, 747

ABA Model Rules of Professional Conduct

Rule	Page
1.6(a)	278, 286, 483, 737, 747
1.6(b)	284, 280
1.6(b)(1)	8, 282, 410, 411
1.6(b)(2)	278
1.6(b)(3)	278, 287
1.6(b)(5)	409
1.6, Comment	286, 292
1.7	130, 602, 607, 611, 612, 615, 622, 650, 658, 666, 672, 687, 690, 692, 694, 816, 837, 909
1.7(a)(2)	486, 611, 670, 687
1.7(b)	462
1.7(b)(3)	576
1.7(b)(4)	737
1.7, Comment	611, 691, 692
1.8	687, 730, 787, 788
1.8(a)	687, 688
1.8(a)(3)	737
1.8(b)	292, 737
1.8(c)	687
1.8(d)	688
1.8(e)	672, 848
1.8(f)	600, 889
1.8(f)(1)	737
1.8(f)(2)	747
1.8(g)	670, 737
1.8(i)	691
1.8(j)	692, 694
1.8(j), Comment	694
1.8, Comment	669
1.9	615, 621, 622, 626, 690, 633, 816
1.9(a)	619, 737
1.9(b)	621, 630
1.9(b)–(c)	621
1.9(b)(2)	737
1.9(c)	621, 622
1.9, Comment	622
1.10	564, 615, 621, 626, 692, 633, 816
1.10(b)	621, 632
1.11	622, 633, 637
1.11(a)	641
1.11(b)	641
1.11(d)	640
1.13	268, 295, 393, 410, 411, 415, 424, 425, 430, 503, 507, 596, 645
1.13(b)	411
1.13(c)	8
1.13(e)	410
1.13(f)	268
1.14	33, 699, 714, 743, 745, 747
1.14(c)	747
1.16	299, 301, 507, 602, 615, 670, 672
1.16(a)	297
1.16(b)	625
1.16(b)(3)	8
1.16(b)(4)	670

ABA Model Rules of Professional Conduct

Rule	Page
1.16(b)(6)	670, 672
1.16(c)	928
1.16(d)	292
1.18	690
1.18(c)	690
2.1	8, 393, 505, 507, 562, 670
2.1, Comment	499
2.2	490
2.4	491
3.1	210, 215, 295, 296, 324, 970, 995
3.2	215, 683
3.2(b)	683
3.3	33, 236, 301, 324, 330, 331, 439, 666
3.3(a)(1)	135
3.3(a)(2)	211, 554
3.3(a)(4)	332
3.4	215, 236, 324, 341, 439
3.5	633
3.6	386, 388, 901
3.7	689
3.8	369, 381, 383, 385
3.8(g)	385, 386
3.8(h)	385
3.8, Comment	355
3.9	633
4.1	33, 301, 467, 468, 475, 478, 479, 481
4.1(a)	483
4.1(b)	478, 483
4.2	33, 134
4.3	478, 901
4.4	147, 334
4.4(b)	145, 146
5.1	424, 439, 445, 454, 672
5.1(a)	444, 445, 454, 1002
5.1(b)	454
5.1(c)	454
5.2	415, 439, 444, 454, 455, 456, 539
5.2(a)	454
5.2(b)	446, 454
5.4	794
5.4(c)	600, 889
5.5	812, 813, 965
5.5(a)	810
5.6	670, 681, 794
5.6(b)	666, 667, 681, 682
5.7	817
6.1	8, 914, 915
6.2	119, 927
6.3	612
6.4	612
7.1	766
7.2	766, 788, 794
7.3	787, 788, 793, 794
8.1	956
8.3	970
8.4	633
8.4(a)	130, 682
8.4(b)	466

ABA Model Rules of Professional Conduct

Rule	Page
8.4(c)	478, 483, 754, 990
8.4(d)	341, 588, 990
8.5	129, 132, 133, 134, 800
8.5(a)	129, 132, 810
8.5(b)	129, 133
8.5(b)(2)	133

Restatement of Contracts

Sec.	Page
492	465

Restatement (2d) of Contracts

Sec.	Page
161	480
161, Comment (d)	480
174–76	465

Restatement of the Law Governing Lawyers

Sec.	Page
48(2)	849
60, Comment (m)	146
63	286
66(1)	284
66, Comment (c)	284
67	290
68	240
69, Comment (g)	244
78–80	241
79, Comment (f)	242
82(a)	251
82, Comment (d)	257
109	388
122, Comment (d)	623
124(3)	637
132, Comment (b)	616
132, Comment (c)	625
133	603, 637

Restatement (3d) of the Law Governing Lawyers

Sec.	Page
3	813
8	189
34	831
37	1016
46, Comment	829
48	688
49	834
128	610
156	645
201	588

Restatement of Torts

Sec.	Page
551	481
551(b)	481
551(d)	481
551(e)	481

Restatement (2d) of Torts

Sec.	Page
527	481
529	481
552(1)	481

AUTHORS

Abel, Richard L.,
Contradictions of Professionalism, 48
Legal Services, 875

Allen, Henry,
A Heaping Serving of Justice, 314

Ames, Matthew C.,
Formal Opinion 352: Professional Integrity and the Tax Audit Lottery, 531

Auerbach, Jerold S.,
Unequal Justice: Lawyers and Social Change in Modern America, 108, 771

Bankman, Joseph
An Academic's View of the Tax Shelter Battle, in The Crisis in Tax Administration, 534

Barry, Dave,
Here's Proof That the Law Has Teeth, 852

Bedford, Sybille,
Faces of Justice, 171

Beneke, T.,
Men on Rape, 339

Bentham, Jeremy,
Rationale of Judicial Evidence, 246

Bok, Derek,
A Flawed System of Law Practice and Training, 855

Brandeis, Louis D.,
Opportunity in the Law, 38

Brill, Steven,
When a Lawyer Lies, 439

Crenshaw, Kimberle Williams,
Foreword: Toward a Race–Conscious Pedagogy in Legal Education, 1048

De Toqueville, Alexis,
Democracy in America, 55

Dickens, Charles
Bleak House, 850

Fiss, Owen,
Against Settlement, 910

Freedman, Monroe H.,
The Errant Fax, 144
The Morality of Lawyering, 184

Friedman, Lawrence,
A History of American Law, 52

Fuller, Lon L. & Randall, John D.,
Professional Responsibility: ABA–AALS Report, 159, 498

Gordon, Robert W.,
A New Role for Lawyers?: The Corporate Counselor after Enron, 509

Gordon, Robert W.,
The Independence of Lawyers, 507

Hurst, James W.,
The Growth of American Law, 107, 932

Jackall, Robert
Moral Mazes, 424, 426

AUTHORS

Kennedy, Duncan,
Legal Education and the Reproduction of Hierarchy, 1030

Koniak, Susan P.,
When the Hurlyburly's Done: The Bar's Struggle With the SEC, 412

Kronman, Anthony T.,
The Lost Lawyer: Failing Ideals of the Legal Profession, 1036

Langbein, John H.,
The German Advantage in Civil Procedure, 166

Lavelle, Marianne,
Placing a Price on Human Life, 397

Lawrence, Charles,
The Id, the Ego, and Equal Protection: Reckoning With Unconscious Racism, 93

Lempert, Larry
In Settlement Talks, Does Telling the Truth Have its Limits, 470

Lewis, C.S.,
The Inner Ring, 446

Lichtenberg, Judith,
Racism in the Head, Racism in the World, 94
What's a Code of Ethics For?, 122

Luban, David,
The Ethics of Wrongful Obedience, 448
Lawyers and Justice: An Ethical Study, 393
Taking out the Adversary: The Assault on Progressive Public–Interest Lawyers, 876
Paternalism and the Legal Profession, 734
Twenty Theses on Adversarial Ethics, 161

Luban, David, & Milleman, Michael,
Good Judgment: Ethics Teaching in Dark Times, 118

Mann, Kenneth,
Defending White Collar Crime, 348, 583

Marden, Orison S.,
The American Bar and Unauthorized Practice, 800

Marshall, Shauna,
Mission Impossible?: Ethical Community Lawyering

Mitchell, John B.,
The Ethics of the Criminal Defense Attorney, 305

Neely, Richard,
The Primary Caretaker Parent Rule, 459

Parsons, Talcott,
The Professions and Social Structure, 46

Paul, Randolph
The Responsibility of the Tax Adviser, 533

Posner, Richard A.,
Let Employers Insist if Three Years of Law School is Necessary, 1025
Overcoming Law, 43

Pound, Roscoe,
The Lawyer From Antiquity to Modern Times, 35, 40, 106

Rhode, Deborah L.,
Access to Justice, (2004) 804, 915
Class Conflicts in Class Actions, 651

AUTHORS

In the Interests of Justice, 2, 40, 125, 163, 980

Personal Satisfaction in Professional Practice, 70

Professionalism, 42

Solicitation, 789

The Unfinished Agenda: Women and the Legal Profession, 82

Ridolfi, Cookie,
Statement on Representing Rape Defendants, 339

Schlitz, Patrick J.,
On Being a Happy, Healthy, and Ethical Member of an Unhappy, Unhealthy, and Unethical Profession, 41, 69, 447

Schuck, Peter H.,
Agent Orange on Trial: Mass Toxic Disasters in the Courts, 844

Shaffer, Thomas L.,
The Legal Ethics of Radical Individualism, 589

Sharswood, George,
An Essay on Professional Ethics, 944

Simon, William,
The Ideology of Advocacy: Procedural Justice and Professional Ethics, 139

Smith, Abbe L.,
The Bounds of Zeal in Criminal Defense: Some Thoughts on Lynne Stewart, 199

Sullivan, William M., et al.,
Educating Lawyers: Preparation for the Profession of Law, 1042

Uviller, H. Richard,
The Virtuous Prosecutor in Quest of an Ethical Standard, 365

Vos Savant, Marilyn,
Ask Marilyn, 307

Wasserstrom, Richard,
Lawyers as Professionals: Some Moral Issues, 700

AUTHORS

Wexler, Stephen,
Practicing Law for Poor People, 896

AMERICAN BAR ASSOCIATION PROCEEDINGS

Commission on Professionalism,
Rekindling Professionalism: Public Service, 35, 38

Committee on Professional Ethics,
Code of Professional Ethics, Report, 114

Commission on Women in the Profession,
The Unfinished Agenda: Women in the Legal Profession, 82, 1061

Joint Conference,
Professional Responsibility: Report, 498

Standards,
Criminal Justice Standards: Prosecution, 361

Imposing Lawyer Sanctions, 995

Task Force,
Formal Opinion 85–352, p. 527

Minorities in the Legal Profession, Report, 1047

FEDERAL REGULATIONS

Standards of Professional Conduct for Attorneys Appearing and Practicing Before the Commission in the Representation of an Issuer, 17 Code of Federal Regulations Part 205 (2003), p. 416

LAW REVIEWS AND LEGAL PERIODICALS

University of Miami Law Review,
Model Rules of Professional Conduct, 540

MISCELLANEOUS SOURCES

American Academy of Matrimonial Lawyers,
Bounds of Advocacy, 517

Harvard Program on the Legal Profession,
Rita's Case, 13

*

LEGAL ETHICS

*

INTRODUCTION

A course on legal ethics is unique in many ways, but the most prominent is its relevance to all areas of practice. Every lawyer, in every practice specialty, confronts issues of professional responsibility and professional role. The daily life of most attorneys involves often undramatic but important ethical choices about relationships with clients, colleagues, adversaries, judges, governmental officials, and "the law."

This book explores how lawyers forge their professional identities. Its analysis proceeds on two levels. The first concerns issues of personal responsibility; attention centers on the innumerable individual choices that define the kind of lawyers we become, as well as the professional standards that justify or challenge those choices. A second set of issues involves collective responsibilities shared by all members of the bar. These issues often implicate broader questions of social justice. Examples include the distribution of legal services, the regulatory structure of the bar, and the impact of ethical standards on the profession and the public.

The "law of lawyering"—the codes of conduct and the other bodies of law governing legal practice—structures but by no means limits our analysis. Lawyers' professional identities are shaped by a vastly more complex set of values and pressures than those captured in codified rules. For that reason, this textbook takes the law of lawyering as its point of departure but not its only guide. The subject also requires attention to the conditions of practice—to the situational constraints and moral ideals that guide their activities. Our aim is to provide a wide array of materials—drawing not only from law, but also from history, philosophy, psychology, economics, and sociology—that will place questions of professional identity in broader context.

For many years, the subject of legal ethics was unique in most law schools for reasons other than its overarching relevance. The course was the ugly duckling of the curriculum, viewed with distaste by many students and most law professors. Traditionally, the class was short on intellectual content and long on platitudes: students were admonished in the most general terms to be not just good, but very, very good. All too often the result was like a semester-long commencement speech, and its delivery often fell by default to overworked deans or adjuncts.

How could it happen that the course of broadest relevance was also among the most disliked? Part of the difficulty involved the shortage of substantive law; until quite recently, issues of legal ethics seldom reached the courts and received little searching inquiry from scholars. So too, the normative assumptions of the course long remained in an undeveloped state, largely insulated from developments in moral philosophy and social, economic, or political theory. And until the last two decades, little systematic empirical information was available about the legal profession; war stories often expanded to fill the gap. Underlying all of these deficiencies was a sense that the subject was neither very controversial nor very interesting. In some institutions, the field was reduced to a single lecture, and one leading law school's dean was well known for focusing his remarks to the incoming class on a single instruction: never commingle personal and client funds.

One of the most striking changes in the legal world over the past two decades has been the increasing attention to professional responsibility and regulation. Issues concerning the ethics of lawyers and the distribution of their services have become matters of broad concern, both within and outside the profession. Since the 1970s, the law of lawyering has developed at an explosive rate; empirical research has expanded at a corresponding speed; and the philosophical underpinnings of professional roles have attracted more searching examination.

These rapid developments underscore a final sense in which courses in legal ethics are distinctive. Compared with other substantive areas, the subject involves fewer settled principles and more fundamental unanswered questions. Partly for that reason, this book centers on problems, together with discussion notes and questions. Yet the issues raised in these materials are rarely simply hypothetical; they draw on experiences from reported cases, empirical research, personal interviews, and journalistic as well as scholarly publications. They involve real lives and real consequences.

Our reliance on relatively short, distilled versions of actual problems has its limitations. No classroom analysis can replicate the pressures of practice, where job security, professional status, economic rewards, personal friendships, moral principles, and social consequences are often at stake. Yet by the same token, the absence of such pressures in law school settings makes it possible to address fundamental questions of professional role without having vested interests in a particular resolution. Our hope is that this relative freedom from self-interest—coupled with attention to supplemental materials that are not usually accessible under workplace constraints and deadlines—will permit informed reflection. That should, in turn, make it easier to recognize and resolve issues of professional responsibility when they arise later in practice. It is for that reason that surveyed lawyers consistently support more legal ethics coverage in law school.[1]

It is, of course, far easier to take the "moral high road" in class than in life—even when the high road is obvious. This book, however, focuses primarily on contexts where the most appropriate course of conduct is not self-evident. Our attention centers not on issues such as commingling but on areas where there are strong competing values or unresolved doctrinal and policy issues at stake. While many of the problems that follow do not have determinate answers, the materials can suggest better and worse ways of analyzing the right questions. Before addressing these problems, however, it is helpful to focus on certain assumptions about the subject of legal ethics.

1. Deborah L. Rhode, *In The Interests of Justice: Reforming the Legal Profession* 202 (2000); Robert Granfield & Thomas Koenig, " 'It's Hard to be a Human Being and a Lawyer,': Young Attorneys and the Confrontation of Ethical Ambiguity in Legal Practice" 105 *W. Va. L. R.* 495 (2003).

NOTES: WHAT IS THE "ETHICS" IN LEGAL ETHICS?

In one sense, the term "legal ethics" refers narrowly to the system of professional regulations governing the conduct of lawyers. In a broader sense, however, legal ethics is simply a special case of ethics in general, as ethics is understood in the central traditions of philosophy and religion. From this broader perspective, legal ethics cuts more deeply than legal regulation: it concerns the most fundamental moral aspects of our lives as lawyers. As Socrates noted, the subject of ethics "is not about just any question, but about the way one should live."[2]

An organizing premise of this book is that these two aspects of legal ethics cannot be separated. The study of codified ethical rules apart from broader ethical principles makes no sense; a code of professional conduct that ignored the moral commitments of those it governed would be doomed to irrelevance. On the other hand, an abstract study of legal ethics that was unconnected to the institutional and doctrinal basis of law practice would be equally ineffective. Our aim is to integrate both dimensions of ethical analysis.

The study of legal regulations is a familiar part of the law school curriculum; to a certain extent, it *is* the law school curriculum. On the other hand, the study of ethics in the sense Socrates defined it forms the subject matter of moral philosophy, a discipline in which many lawyers, law students, and law teachers lack extended training. However, for our purposes, no such background is necessary: most academic moral philosophy concerns theoretical issues that have little direct bearing on legal ethics, even in the broad, Socratic sense. In this book we will frequently consider philosophical arguments but we need not concern ourselves with their technical dimensions. Our analysis begins with certain recurrent questions that frequently arise in legal ethics classes.

Ethics and Morality

An obvious threshold issue is what exactly is ethics and whether it differs from morality. In everyday conversation, the terms sometimes carry different connotations. When we call lawyers or other professionals "unethical," we usually mean that they have been somehow dishonest—that they have lied, cheated, or become involved in a conflict of interest. By contrast, calling a person "immoral" may conjure up an image of depravity—of cruelty, sexual misconduct, or otherwise illicit behavior. Moral philosophers, however, do not generally use the words "ethics" and "morality" in these restrictive senses, and neither does this casebook.

This is not to imply that the terms have always been interchangeable. Some theorists, including the prominent nineteenth century German philosopher Hegel, have reserved the word "ethics" to refer to the customary norms within a specific society—the society's *ethos*.[3] In Homeric Greece, for

---

2. Plato, *The Republic of Plato* 31 (Allan Bloom trans. 1968), *352D.

3. Georg Wilhelm Friedrich Hegel, *The Phenomenology of Spirit* 266–94 (A. Miller trans. 1977); Bernard Williams, *Ethics and the Limits of Philosophy* 5–7 (1989).

example, concern with personal honor dominated other ethical considerations, while Confucian China emphasized prudence, moderation, and balance. The term "morality," on the other hand, is often used to refer to
philosophical systems involving abstract universal norms of right and
wrong.[4] Immanuel Kant's famous "categorical imperative"—"act so that
you treat humanity ... always as an end, and never as a means only"—is
an example of such a universal moral principle.[5] The categorical imperative,
Kant believed, is valid at all times and in all cultures, and he offered a
purely philosophical demonstration of its truth.

This distinction between theory-based morality and custom-based ethics suggests a sharp separation between everyday judgments and philosophical theories. Yet most contemporary theorists doubt that any clear separation exists. As they note, philosophical theories of morality generally reflect
and reinforce the culture's dominant ethical norms and common sense
understandings. For example, Kant's categorical imperative has two distinctive prescriptions, neither of which are peculiar to his philosophical
system. First, Kant insists that the moral law applies to everyone: it speaks
of "humanity" in general. Second, Kant instructs us to treat others as ends
and not merely as means. The first injunction—to treat everyone, including
those of other races, nationalities, or religions with full moral consideration—is hardly an invention of academic philosophers. Similarly, in everyday life we often criticize people for "using" others merely as means to an
end. What is distinctively philosophical about Kant's approach is not its
core moral insights, but the extended argument on which they are grounded. Because philosophical moral theories such as Kant's overlap with our
customary ethical traditions (secular as well as religious), no general
distinction between ethics and morality seems helpful.

There is, however, an important difference between accepting customary ethical beliefs on faith and subjecting them to critical reflection.
Philosophers capture this difference by distinguishing *positive morality*
from *critical morality*. Positive morality refers to the dominant moral
traditions in a particular society. Critical morality involves a systematic
examination of those traditions to determine whether they should be
obeyed, modified, or abandoned. One of the most important functions of
legal ethics is to offer critical scrutiny of the positive morality of legal
practice. In the chapters that follow, conventional norms such as those
regarding client loyalty, confidentiality, and access to legal services are
subject to such analysis.

Moral Relativism

A related set of questions has to do with the basis of moral judgment.
Values differ significantly within and across particular societies. From this
fact, moral relativists argue that ethics are not universal, but rather
relative to individuals or cultures.[6] In its extreme form, relativism denies

---

4. *Id.*, at 364–74.

5. Immanuel Kant, *Foundations of the Metaphysics of Morals* 46 (Lewis White Beck trans. 1959 2d ed.1990).

6. There is vast literature on relativism. Among the most prominent and useful
treatments are Gilbert Harman & Judith Jar-
vis Thomson, *Moral Relativism and Moral*

the possibility of generalizable moral judgments. This position is often appealing because it reflects healthy instincts of tolerance and humility. "Judge not, lest you be judged" counsels appropriate restraint in contexts of moral complexity.[7]

Yet almost no one—even those who claim to be relativists—accepts relativism in its most extreme form. If someone steals our property or betrays our friendship, it is natural to condemn this behavior. But pursued to its logical extreme, relativism can condemn such practices only if they violate the relativist's own standards; and the relativist will have to concede that the thief or traitor may be justified according to his or her own standards. To find an action repugnant while insisting that others can justifiably pursue it is a feat that few of us are willing or able to perform.

Suppose, for example, that someone you regard as a close friend has taken your work and claimed it as his own, or has blamed you for dishonest acts that he committed. A true relativist would have to acknowledge that "I think it's wrong, but maybe from his point of view what he did was justified. Who am I to say?" If such a response seems morally unsatisfying, that should tip us off that something is wrong with relativism. There is, moreover, an internal contradiction in relativists' claim that because no universal moral standards exist, it is wrong to impose one's own values. If there are no universal principles, by what criteria does the relativist claim that moral condemnation is "wrong"?

There is, however, a more moderate and more defensible form of relativism reflected in much pragmatic and post-modern philosophy. This position denies the possibility of transcendent truths or universally right answers to moral questions independent of context. However, it also acknowledges that some answers are more coherent, consistent, responsive to relevant concerns, and so forth than others. More controversially, the philosopher Richard Rorty has argued that the quest for objectivity in ethics is misplaced. Over time, certain views attract a wide level of consensus and can thus serve as a basis for collective judgment.[8]

Critics of relativism, particularly in its most extreme forms, also note that the fact of moral disagreement does not of itself prove that moral justification is impossible. Scientific claims have been subject to equally widespread dispute. Many societies believed that the earth was flat, but that does not lead us to deny the possibility of making valid claims about geography. Indeed, we sometimes have far more grounds for confidence in our moral than in our factual assessments. We are likely, for example, to be

---

Objectivity (1996); Gilbert Harman, "Moral Relativism Defended," 84 *Phil. Rev.* 3 (1975); Bernard Williams, *Morality: An Introduction to Ethics* 20–26 (1972). For good overviews of the relativism debate as it relates to legal ethics see Paul Tremblay, "Shared Norms: Bad Lawyers and the Virtues of Casuistry," 36 *San Francisco L. Rev.* (2000); W. Bradley Wendel, "Teaching Ethics in an Atmosphere of Skepticism and Relativism," 36 *U. San Francisco L. Rev.* 720 (2002); Katherine R. Kruse, "Lawyers, Justice, and the Challenge of Moral Pluralism," 90 *Minn. L. Rev.* 389 (2005).

7. Matthew 7:1. *See also* John 8:7 ("He who is without sin among you, let him cast out the first stone").

8. See e.g. Richard Rorty, "Human Rights, Rationality, and Sentimentality," in *Truth and Progress* (1998).

more convinced that genocide is wrong than that certain scientific theories about human immune systems are right. Many standards for evaluating ethical claims are no different than standards for evaluating scientific claims: are the claims well-defined, internally consistent, widely shared, and backed up by persuasive evidence and reasoning? For purposes of everyday decision making, as Hilary Putnam has suggested, "that is objectivity enough."[9]

Moreover, moral convictions are often less indeterminate than is commonly supposed. Those who engage in reflective decision-making frequently come to share certain basic moral premises. Given full information and an opportunity for dispassionate and disinterested judgment, individuals appear likely to agree about certain essential values, such as honesty, loyalty, benevolence, and avoidance of unnecessary harm.[10] Some biologists and neuroscientists believe that certain moral convictions have been adaptive for survival and are now hard wired into the brain.[11] All known societies agree on many basic moral judgments, for example that doing a bad thing intentionally is worse than doing it by accident.

Of course, disagreements often arise about how to apply broadly shared values or resolve conflicts between them in particular cases. However, much of the controversy surrounding moral issues involves disputes about facts, not principles. The same is true of most of the hotly contested questions of legal ethics. Lawyers disagree about the duty of confidentiality not because they disagree about what values are important but because they disagree about what rules would best serve those values. Would requiring lawyers to disclose certain confidential information to protect third parties significantly erode client trust and candor? In the long run, would imposing greater disclosure obligations put lawyers in a position to prevent more or less harm?

It also bears emphasis that an argument for tolerance does not depend on a belief in relativism. We can morally disapprove of others' conduct without attempting to dictate their behavior. Indeed, that is what tolerance means. Consider any controversial moral issue, such as that of euthanasia. There is nothing illogical about reasoning: "I believe that euthanasia is morally wrong, but the issue is complicated, and I recognize that my own judgment may be based on limited facts and experience, or biased by self interest. Since it is possible that I am wrong, I am not prepared to condemn those who engage in the practice." This common-sense commitment to tolerance differs from moral relativism in two important respects. First, unlike relativism, this approach does not deny that there *is* a right answer to the moral question. It denies only that one is *sure* enough of the answer

9. Hilary Putnam, *Realism with a Human Face* 178 (James Conant ed. 1990).

10. Alan Wolfe, *Moral Freedom* 168 (2001); Tremblay, *supra* note 6, at 696, 709.

11. See Marc D. Hauser, *Moral Minds* (2006) (suggesting evolution of moral grammar); Rebecca Saxe, "Do the Right Thing: Cognitive Science's Search for a Common Morality," *Boston Rev.*, Sept. Oct., 2005, at 33 (noting high level of consensus across race, sex, wealth, religious affiliation, nationality and educational background on questions such as whether killing one person is justifiable to save five others).

to condemn someone who believes otherwise. Second, the commitment to tolerance is appropriate only for complex moral issues, while relativism in its strong form requires agnosticism about all moral judgments, even the most widely accepted ones such as the evil of genocide.[12]

It is also important not to confuse the assessment of ethical principles with the assessment of those who hold them. One can be a relativist about individual culpability without being a relativist about moral values. For example, we can believe that infanticide is wrong, but make allowances for those who engaged in the practice in a society where it was widely tolerated, because food was scarce, reliable birth control was unavailable, and the practice had not been subjected to critical scrutiny. Moral blameworthiness may be relative, but moral judgment need not be.[13]

In short, a commitment to tolerance does not imply a commitment to relativism. Nor is relativism a position that most of us are prepared to adopt in practice. Rather, we can remain sensitive to the dangers of moral arrogance without abandoning moral convictions. We can also sometimes acknowledge uncertainty about our moral judgments, particularly when the issues are complex or controversial. We can, however, attempt to think the matter through honestly, to consider opposing views, and to make allowances for influences that might distort our judgment. And why ask for more? We must often make decisions in the face of factual uncertainty, yet this does not make us relativists about facts. When we must make a moral decision, we have no choice but to do what seems right to us, even though we recognize that we could be mistaken. After all, the alternative to acting on the judgment that seems best is acting on a judgment that seems worse.

Ethics and Law

To some students, legal ethics seems vague or "squishy," while legal rules seem comparatively clear and determinate. From this perspective, it seems preferable to focus only on the law of lawyering. Yet as every skilled lawyer knows, legal rules are often complex and ambiguous. What constitutes a "reasonable person," an appropriate business judgment, or the right balance between competing constitutional values? The complexity and indeterminacy of moral judgments is no greater than that of corresponding legal judgments. In fact, much legal doctrine incorporates terms and exceptions that will enable decision-makers to take account of ethical norms. The law is at least as "soft" as morality; indeed, in many cases, we will be *more* confident of our moral judgment than we will of our legal or even factual judgments. We may, for example, be certain about the ethical principle that law firms should not represent conflicting interests but have difficulty determining whether such a conflict exists in particular contexts,

---

12. For arguments that the record of Nazi Germany made relativism untenable, *see* Bertrand Russell, *Human Society in Ethics and Politics* 20 (1955); Morris Ginsberg, "On the Diversity of Morals," in *Essays on Sociology and Social Philosophy* (1956).

13. Wendel makes a similar point about slavery. The founders of the Republic who held slaves are not subject to as strong a criticism as someone today who advocated a return to the practice. Wendel, *supra* note 6, at 754–55.

such as those involving large firms with changing members in multiple offices representing large clients with multiple subsidiaries.

This is not to deny that there are "easy cases" in law (as indeed there are in ethics), and that at times the law of lawyering may apparently settle an issue and thereby remove it from the realm of conscience and discretion. Yet even in cases that are clearly covered by formal ethics rules or other law, moral issues inevitably remain.

First, and most fundamentally, there is always the question whether to comply with the law or to engage in conscientious disobedience. *When* disobedience is justified can be controversial, but *that* disobedience is sometimes the right thing to do can hardly be denied. On those (hopefully rare) occasions when settled legal rules clearly demand a course of action that the lawyer finds morally repugnant, serious soul-searching is necessary. To dismiss the issue simply because the law is clear is a rationalization, not a reason, for decision. Second, even in less serious dilemmas, when conscientious disobedience to formal rules is unwarranted, moral deliberation remains necessary to decide whether to comply to the bare minimum degree that the letter of the rules requires, or whether to comply more fully.

In any event, many of the formal ethics rules leave the ultimate decision to the lawyer's discretion. Thus, for example, the ABA's Model Rules of Professional Conduct permit, but do not require, a lawyer to reveal confidential client information "to prevent reasonably certain death or substantial bodily harm."[14] Bar ethical rules permit, but do not require, a corporate lawyer to reveal confidences if the corporation's highest authority insists on violating the law in a way that is likely to injure the corporation.[15] They permit, but do not require, a lawyer to decline or withdraw from representation if the client insists on taking an action that the lawyer finds "repugnant."[16] They permit, but do not require, lawyers to include "moral, economic, social and political factors" in the advice they offer clients.[17] They recommend, but do not require, that lawyers perform fifty hours annually of pro bono service.[18] For these as well as many other issues that arise in legal practice, the law itself invites lawyers to consider their own moral values.

Indeed, as the readings in subsequent chapters make clear, a prominent characteristic of legal practice is the complex, discretionary nature of the judgments that it often requires. Some of those judgments will inevitably implicate ethical principles. As is apparent from the case study that concludes this chapter, lawyers' definition of their professional role and the responsibilities that it entails is necessarily influenced by moral values.

Moral Theories

A basic understanding of the primary frameworks of moral philosophy can sometimes be helpful in addressing the ethical issues that arise in legal

---

14. Model Rule 1.6(b)(1).

15. Model Rule 1.13(c).

16. Model Rule 1.16(b)(3).

17. Model Rule 2.1.

18. Model Rule 6.1.

practice. In essence, moral philosophy is concerned with what makes an action right or wrong. That inquiry has given rise to three basic approaches: those that focus on the consequences of the action; those that emphasize the intrinsic nature of the action itself; and those that center on the character of the actor.

Consequentialism judges the rightness or wrongness of actions based on their consequences. The most familiar consequentialist theory is *utilitarianism*, primarily as developed by Jeremy Bentham, John Stuart Mill, and Henry Sidgwick.[19] In its most familiar form, utilitarianism evaluates actions on the basis of the pleasure they create or the pain they inflict: utilitarians attempt to sum up these consequences, and recommend the action that creates the "greatest good for the greatest number." From this perspective, an individual's moral obligation is to maximize utility.

However, consequentialist theories need not focus on pleasure and pain, which are, after all, hard to measure with any precision. Some economists treat total social wealth as the "good" to be maximized, and judge actions or policies according to their economic effects.[20] They identify utility as the satisfaction of individual preferences. Since it is difficult to make interpersonal comparisons of utility in the absence of some common standard of measure, economists generally rely on money; they assess the strength of preferences by reference to how much individuals would be willing to pay to reach a certain result. Money is thus treated as a stand-in or surrogate for utility (preference-satisfaction). One other prominent consequentialist theory, "ideal utilitarianism," includes less tangible outcomes, such as ideals of fairness, among the goods to be maximized.

Such approaches have two major limitations. One involves indeterminacy; it will often be extremely difficult to predict and weigh all relevant costs and benefits. A second limitation concerns utilitarianism's inability to distinguish legitimate from illegitimate preferences or to protect rights. Individuals' expressed desires are in some measure socially constructed and constrained, and many preference-maximizing approaches provide no basis for challenging those desires, however self-destructive.[21] Moreover, because consequentialists simply add together the gains and losses of society's members, they can justify policies that benefit the many at the expense of the few. For this reason, critics often object that consequentialism cannot

---

19. Jeremy Bentham, "An Introduction to the Principles of Morals and Legislation," in *A Fragment on Government and an Introduction to the Principles of Morals and Legislation* (Wilfrid Harrison ed. 1948); John Stuart Mill, *Utilitarianism* (Mary Warnock ed. 1962); Henry Sidgwick, *Methods of Ethics* (7th ed. 1962). For useful overviews, *see Consequentialism and its Critics* (Samuel Scheffler, ed. 1988); *Utilitarianism and Beyond* (Amartya Sen and Bernard Williams eds. 1985); J.J.C. Smart and Bernard Williams, *Utilitarianism: For and Against* (1973);

H.L.A. Hart, "Between Utility and Rights," 79 *Colum.L.Rev.* 828 (1979).

20. *See* Richard A. Posner, *The Economics of Justice* 48–87 (rev. ed. 1983) for a defense of "wealth maximization" as an ethical principle.

21. Cass R. Sunstein, "Legal Interference With Private Preferences," 53 *U. Chi. L. Rev.* 1129 (1986); Alison Jaggar, *Feminist Politics and Human Nature* 40–42 (1983). *But see* Richard Brandt, *A Theory of the Good and the Right* (1979).

safeguard the rights of minorities against overreaching by a majority, a deficiency that other ethical theories seek to address.

The most prominent of those other theories are *deontological*. The term, derived from the Greek word for duty, refers to approaches that view right action in terms of discharging responsibilities, independent of their consequences. Those responsibilities typically are grounded on universal, generalizable principles.

In a famous passage in *The Brothers Karamazov*, one of Dostoyevsky's characters poses this challenge:

> Imagine that you are creating a fabric of human destiny with the object of making men happy in the end, giving them peace and rest at last. Imagine that you are doing this but that it is essential and inevitable to torture to death only one tiny creature—that child beating its breast with its fist, for instance—in order to found that edifice on its unavenged tears. Would you consent to be the architect on those conditions? Tell me. Tell me the truth.[22]

For a utilitarian, this question is easy: to achieve happiness for millions of individuals one would of course torture a single child. But perhaps there is something suspect about a theory that makes this an easy question. Would we be morally comfortable about enslaving a minority to provide greater wealth and leisure to the majority? Deontologists focus on the intrinsic character of the action—slavery or torture—and argue that some actions are right or wrong quite apart from their consequences. Kant's categorical imperative is a deontological formula: it forbids us from using other individuals as a means, no matter how compelling the end.

Kant is the best-known deontological philosopher. His writings focused heavily on moral duties, which he believed could be deduced from the categorical imperative.[23] These included such obligations as fidelity (keeping promises and avoiding deception); benevolence (helping others and avoiding harm); and cultivating our own abilities. Among contemporary deontologists, however, the focus has shifted from an emphasis on duties to an emphasis on rights, in their moral not legal sense. A modern proponent of deontological approaches would argue that the innocent child in Dostoyevsky's fable has a moral entitlement not to be tortured—an entitlement that overrides the gain in utility to humanity at large. In the words of Ronald Dworkin, whose book title *Taking Rights Seriously* might be seen as a framework for modern deontologists, rights "trump" utility.[24]

Of course, there is plenty of room for debate about what our moral rights are.[25] Moreover, some deontologists believe that in defining rights, it

22. Fyodor Dostoyevsky, *The Brothers Karamazov* 226 (M. Komroff ed., Constance Garnett trans. 1957). For a more general discussion of this issue see John Taurek, "Should the Numbers Count?" 6 *Phil. & Pub. Affairs* 293 (1977).

23. *See* the text accompanying note 5 *supra.*

24. Ronald Dworkin, *Taking Rights Seriously* xi (rev. ed. 1978).

25. For a sophisticated recent treatment, *see* Judith Thomson, *The Realm of Rights* (1990).

is appropriate to take account of consequences. Thus, it is most accurate to think of deontology as a family of theories rather than as a single theory, which all rest on the view that consequences are not determinative.

Critics argue that the strength of deontological approaches is also the source of their limitations. A rule that one is prepared to universalize will often need to be framed at such a level of abstraction that it cannot resolve particular cases. Some formulas, such as the categorical imperative, are devoid of specific content, and cannot easily decide cases where principles are in conflict.[26] Moreover, many critics, including communitarians and feminists, have underscored the inadequacies of frameworks that elevate abstract individual rights over concrete responsibilities and over relationships with family, friends, and communities.[27]

A third group of theories are generally grouped together under the label *virtue ethics*. These theories focus on the character of the actor, rather than on the nature of the act or on its consequences. Aristotle's *Ethics* offered the first systematic expression of this approach. He focused on character and stressed the importance of certain key virtues, such as honesty, courage, temperance, and most importantly, practical wisdom. For Aristotle, virtues enable us to desire good ends, and practical wisdom guides us in actions that will achieve those ends. In the Middle Ages, Christian moralists followed Aristotle's approach, although they also recognized certain virtues, such as mercy, that were quite foreign to Greek thought. A number of contemporary legal ethicists have attempted to revive the Aristotelian tradition, and have insisted that the most important questions of ethics concern our character.[28] In their view, it is important to focus on the development of individual moral judgment, rather than the reduction of morality to abstract impersonal rules.[29]

Alasdair MacIntyre's 1981 book *After Virtue* has played a central role in the revival of virtue ethics. According to MacIntyre, we argue endlessly about moral issues because we no longer share a moral language. Enlightenment and post-Enlightenment developments eroded the Greek and Christian teaching about virtues from which our moral vocabulary evolved. We now face the problem of "ethics after Babel": the language of our disputes—rights and duties, acts and rules, responsibilities and consequences—has become detached from the traditions that gave it force.[30] Individuals who focus on rights talk past those who focus on consequences, and the possibilities for consensus have become increasingly remote. In a

26. See *Consequentialism and its Critics, supra* note 19; James Rachels, *The Elements of Moral Philosophy* 121 (1993); Alisdair McIntyre, *A Short History of Ethics* 197–98 (1966).

27. *See* Carol Gilligan, *In a Different Voice,* (1982); Mark Tushnet, "An Essay on Rights," 62 *Tex.L.Rev.* 1363 (1984).

28. *See* Heidi Li Feldman, "Codes and Virtues: Can Good Lawyers Be Good Ethical Deliberators?" *S.Cal. L. Rev.* 885 (1996);

David Luban, "Epistemology and Moral Education," 33 *J. Legal Ed.* 636 (1983).

29. Rachels, *supra* note 26. See generally Rosalind Hursthouse, *On Virtue Ethics* (1999): Roger Crisp, "Modern Moral Philosophies and the Virtues," in *How Should One Live?: Essays on the Virtues* 1 (Roger Crisp, ed. 1993).

30. Jeffrey Stout, *Ethics After Babel: The Languages of Morals and Their Discontents* (1988).

society where "there is no longer any shared concept of the community's good ... there can be no very substantial concept of what it is that contributes more or less to the achievement of that good."[31]

Moreover, a focus on character seems consistent with how we behave in many situations, and neuroscientific theories emphasize the intuitive nature of much moral decision making. As philosopher Bernard Williams has put it, if a man is consulting ethical theory to decide whether to attempt saving his wife from a burning building, he has having "one thought too many."[32]

To focus on virtue in legal ethics is to shift emphasis from the nature of particular actions and their consequences and to center attention instead on the character of the lawyers who perform these actions. Under this approach, conduct is subject to praise or condemnation primarily on the grounds of what it reflects about the person; acts may be dishonest or forthright, extortionate or generous, disloyal or decent. Yet to critics, this approach yields no more determinate conclusions than other frameworks. As subsequent discussion will note, the central question for legal ethics is often what the good lawyer should do under circumstances of moral complexity or competing values. An approach that focuses on character as a unitary concept may not be helpful in addressing the demands of particular roles under such circumstances. Nor is such a unified concept of character consistent with much contemporary research in psychology and organizational behavior, which documents the situational nature of moral conduct and the extent to which contextual pressures can undermine individuals' ethical commitments.[33]

The Possibility of Pluralism

All of these approaches have something to recommend them; all are subject to significant limitations. To choose among them, it is helpful to reflect on what would make them useful under particular circumstances. The eminent philosopher John Rawls suggested that a moral theory should be tested by our "moral intuitions": the moral judgments we would be inclined to make before we begin to theorize. A useful moral framework offers principles that accommodate our considered moral intuitions. These principles can then help revise our intuitions. Our intuitions thus modified may then assist in further refining our principles, and so on. Eventually, Rawls suggests, we should arrive at a "reflective equilibrium" between principles and intuitions, in which neither requires further adjustment.[34] This approach is consistent with recent work in cognitive psychology, which suggests that individuals generally arrive at moral decisions through intui-

31. Alasdair MacIntyre, *After Virtue* 217 (1981).

32. Bernard Williams, "Persons, Character, and Morality," in *Moral Luck* 1, 18 (1981).

33. *See* research summarized in John Doris, *Lack of Character* 22–47 (2002); Kwame Anthony Appiah, *Experiments in Eth-ics* 39–55 (2007); David Luban, "Integrity: Its Causes and Cures," 72 *Fordham L. Rev.* 279 (2003); Deborah L. Rhode, "If Integrity Is the Answer, What Is the Question?," 72 *Fordham L. Rev.* 333 (2003).

34. John Rawls, *A Theory of Justice* 46–53 (1971).

tive responses, and then consider reasons that support or challenge their initial judgment.[35]

In practice, it may well be that different areas of our moral experience will fall into reflective equilibrium with different moral principles; some judgments may be best systematized by consequentialist theories, some by deontological theories, and some by theories of virtue. Cognitive psychology can also help reconcile our theoretical premises with moral practices. Although the objective of traditional philosophy was to produce unified theoretical frameworks, we have no reason to believe that our individual moral worlds are that tidy. According to many contemporary philosophers, our moral experience is, at its deepest level, *pluralistic;* no single framework is adequate to encompass all aspects of our moral life. As Anthony Appiah puts it, "my philosophy is that everything is more complicated than you thought.... [t]he messiness of ethics goes down deep."[36] n the final analysis, we will often have to rely upon a kind of second-order intuition. While we may look to moral theories for guidance, we still need to make intuitive judgments about which moral theory is most appropriate to the case at hand.

Rita's Case

We begin with an extended case study, one which raises many issues that the book will treat in greater detail. Unlike the bare-bones "P" and "D" in typical hypotheticals, this account provides what anthropologists call "thick description": a narrative sufficiently detailed that the reader may enter into the moral world it describes. In reading the case, it is important to keep several questions in mind:

(1) What ethical issues do the lawyers face?

(2) How much guidance do the ABA's Model Rules of Professional Conduct provide for the lawyers confronting these issues?

(3) What other resources—in terms of background, law, cultural norms, or professional and philosophical traditions—would assist you in addressing the dilemmas of Rita's case?

Harvard Program on the Legal Profession, Philadelphia Legal Aid: Rita's Case*

(1982).

Joan Kiladis sat down in her office to draft a letter to her client, Gladys A., which would close the file dealing with the custody dispute over

35. For useful discussion, see Milton C. Regan, Jr., "Moral Intuitions and Organizational Culture," 51 *St. Louis L.J.* 941 (2007).

36. Appiah, *supra* note 33 at 198, 201. *See,* e.g., Stuart Hampshire, *Morality and Conflict* (1983); Stuart Hampshire, *Innocence and Experience* (1989); Isaiah Berlin, *The Crooked Timber of Humanity* (1991); Wendel,

supra note 6, at 752, 758; Kruse, *supra* note 6.

* This case was prepared by Leila R. Kern under the supervision of Professor Martha Minow and Penny Pitman Merliss for use at the Harvard Law School. Names are disguised.

Gladys's granddaughter Rita. It was April 14, 1982, and the case had been opened over three years ago, in March, 1979. It had been a long and drawn out process, but the closing letter would indicate that Joan Kiladis and Keith Maynard, the two Philadelphia Legal Aid attorneys who had worked on the case, had obtained their objective—Gladys A. had been able to adopt her granddaughter over the initial objection of the Department of Public Welfare. Nonetheless, Kiladis wondered if there was another issue that should be pursued before this case was put to rest. That issue was the allegation of sexual abuse which had precipitated Rita's custody dispute. Although Kiladis was convinced that the alleged sex abuse suffered by the child had been real, she was less sure whether or not the matter should be pursued. She decided to discuss it with Maynard, a poverty lawyer of many years' experience. Kiladis herself, although 40 years old and experienced as a draft counselor and mother of two, was just two years out of law school—more recently than the origin of the case itself—and had never encountered an issue as complex as this one.

At Maynard's office, Kiladis broached the problem with him. It was not the first time. In fact, Kiladis and Maynard had had a running argument for over a year about whether or not to sue the Children's Home, in which Rita had resided for many years, for sexual abuse. Kiladis went in to argue her position one more time. As she had known he would, Maynard refused to turn to the specifics of the allegation until he had reminded both of them of the way the whole system worked when the custody of a child was at stake.

"No one in the system wants to take responsibility for the final decision about the placement of a child, so there is always a shifting of that responsibility, and in the final analysis there is no independent adjudication on any issue," said Maynard. He had learned, over the years, to use that aspect of the system to his clients' advantage. In essence, Maynard believed that attorneys created the history of a case for presentation to a judge by selectively emphasizing and investigating certain events and injuries and letting others fade. They manipulated the other professionals (such as social workers and physicians) involved in the case, and utilized their strengths and weaknesses to the client's advantage. Often, whether knowingly or unknowingly, they steered clients' choices to take advantage of these very efforts. Maynard reminded Kiladis that she had come into the case one and one half years after he did and was therefore reacting in part to the scenario that he had created in the file and in the case. Additionally, he pointed out, Kiladis had become very personally involved with Gladys, the child, and many other members of the family. Although this interest had helped to win the case for Gladys, both of these factors, in Maynard's opinion, affected Kiladis's judgment and objectivity. The two attorneys agreed to look over the files together, one more time, before deciding how to proceed.

Rita's Background

Rita was born in Bellevue Hospital in New York City in December of 1971. Her mother, Carlota, had entered the hospital, in labor, just four hours after taking a shot of heroin. Rita's father, who had been living with Carlota for a number of years and who had fathered her two other children, was not present, nor was his name entered on Rita's birth certificate. Carlota abandoned Rita in the hospital, where the infant remained for three months, being treated for both heroin addiction and syphilis. Her maternal grandmother, Gladys, obtained legal guardianship and took Rita home in March of 1972.

Rita lived with her grandmother for the next two and one half years. First they resided in New York City; then, with the New York court's approval, they moved to West Philadelphia where they lived in a house next door to a low-income public housing project. Although many members of the family—aunts, uncles, cousins—also lived with Gladys at various times during this period, two others were more permanent members of the household, both in New York and in Philadelphia. One was Manuel, Rita's first cousin. Three years older than Rita, Manuel had also been born out-of-wedlock, to Rita's aunt, Maria, and had been raised by Gladys from birth. Maria, like her sister Carlota, was addicted to heroin. The second semi-permanent member of the household, Juan, was to become Rita's step-grandfather. Born in 1950, Juan had been brought up by Gladys since he was 15. He became her third husband in 1977, when he was 27 and Gladys was about 51.

In August 1974 Gladys turned to the Department of Public Welfare (DPW) in Philadelphia for help with Rita. The child, although only two and one half years old, was very difficult to handle; according to Gladys, she had become manipulative, aggressive and generally unmanageable. Gladys was scheduled for gall bladder surgery and needed help caring for Rita. The department suggested that Gladys place Rita in the Catholic Home for Children where the child could be evaluated and receive appropriate therapy, if needed. The Home requested that St. Christophers Hospital evaluate Rita, and then the Home began therapy while Rita resided there.

During the period from August 1974 until June 1976 Rita seemed to thrive in this placement. She visited her family frequently on weekends, and her grandmother was often at the Home during the week as well. Gladys viewed the Catholic Home as a temporary residential facility where children could receive help. The DPW, however, often used the Home as a clearinghouse for children needing foster care. In fact, in June 1976 the Home decided to place Rita with a foster family in Germantown, a lower-middle-class Philadelphia suburb. Gladys continued to visit Rita and take her home on weekends, during the next seven months that Rita lived in Germantown. Relations between Gladys and Rita's foster family quickly became strained. The foster parents complained to the Home that Gladys was not sticking to the visitation schedule, and Gladys complained to DPW that Rita's foster parents were abusing her. Acting on these latter reports, DPW removed Rita from the foster family and returned her to her grand-mother. By this time, February 1977, Juan and Gladys had married.

Four months later Gladys turned once again to DPW. Gladys had been receiving counseling from a social worker, Elizabeth Reilly, who had encouraged her to seek help with Rita. Gladys was depressed, and the child was still aggressive and difficult, biting other children and throwing temper tantrums. Again DPW placed Rita in the Catholic Home for Children. During the following 18 months, Rita again settled into the routine at the Home, and again the Home moved toward a foster placement. Although there were still many home visits, Gladys was having more difficulty maintaining the visiting schedule. She often did not arrive when she had promised to do so, and she often left early. Occasionally, Rita's mother, who had also moved to Philadelphia, visited her at the Home. Home personnel noted that Rita often returned from visits to Gladys appearing distressed.

The move toward placing Rita in a foster home was greatly accelerated in January of 1979. For two months Rita had been in play therapy with a young psychology student who had become increasingly alarmed by the child's apparent sexual sophistication. Rita was then seven years of age. The student believed that Rita was acting out, in therapy, some experience of sexual seduction or observation of sexual behavior. The student, and her supervisor—who was studying sexually abused children—concurred that Rita had had such experiences and that they must have occurred in Gladys's home, or at the least when Rita was in Gladys's care. Suspecting Juan, Rita's step-grandfather, the Home filed a Form CY47 report of possible abuse with DPW. Rita was then moved to a foster placement with a middle-class family in Jenkintown, a well-to-do distant suburb of Philadelphia about 20 miles from Gladys's home in West Philadelphia. Gladys was given neither Rita's address nor her phone number.

Gladys turned for help to her social worker, who contacted Philadelphia Legal Aid (PLA) and asked Maynard to intercede on Gladys's behalf. DPW was about to file a motion for protective custody of Rita and a motion to dispense with Rita's mother's consent to Rita's adoption by the foster family in Jenkintown. It was DPW's position that Gladys, as grandmother, had no standing to intervene.

The legal battle began in the spring of 1979 and resulted, first, in establishing a pattern of visitation between Rita and Gladys, agreed to by the parties; next, in the return of Rita to live with Gladys in March 1981; and finally in the adoption of Rita by Gladys and Juan in April 1982. By then Gladys and Juan were living separately. In the interim both Maynard and Kiladis at PLA had become involved with the case; the court had appointed an attorney, David Slade, an associate at a small downtown law firm, to represent Rita; there had been a complete change in DPW personnel dealing with the case and with the family; and St. Christophers had done two court-ordered psychological evaluations of Rita and her grandparents, to be paid for by the county.

Lawyers' Views

Looking back over their files on Rita, Maynard and Kiladis noted the legal issues that had punctuated the child's short but complex life. There had been prolonged guardianship hearings while Rita was still a patient in the Bellevue nursery in New York, which had continued after Rita went to live with Gladys. Kiladis remarked:

The result was, when Carlota—Rita's mother—realized that she was going to lose all of her children, she actually got herself on methadone. And, although there were lapses, she was eventually given her older two children back, with enormous supervision. She had also come to Pennsylvania. I'm not sure whether legally or not. But she seemed to be doing a reasonably good job with the older children.

It was not clear why Gladys had been named guardian, since grandparents had no special status in guardianship cases, and certain factors in Gladys's home life seemed to argue against court-ordered guardianship. Maynard guessed that some social worker had filed the necessary papers and pushed the guardianship through.

When Gladys contacted DPW in August 1974, her feelings toward Rita seemed to Maynard to indicate ambivalence, "Gladys loves Rita, also can't control her, is somewhat older and not feeling well. There is this, 'I want her away, I want her back.' " As soon as her surgery was scheduled, she sought help in coping with the child. Maynard observed:

> The puzzle here is why, between '74 and '76, Gladys, when she finished her gall bladder operation, did not bring Rita home. I think this is where the ambivalence manifests. That is, once Gladys got home, and a period of time passed as she recovered from major surgery, she found she had a situation that was not so bad. So Gladys left things alone; in the same way, I think, that some parents in other class settings who are ambivalent about their children, have their children in boarding school.

But Gladys couldn't adapt to the "boarding school" regime; she couldn't adapt to the rules. "I think the Home found Gladys to be a pain in the ass," added Maynard. She couldn't do anything on time. She came to visit Rita during the week, she baked birthday cakes for other children's birthdays and came with those. She often brought Rita back late after a weekend home visit. Sometimes after such visits Rita's face and clothes were dirty and her hair uncombed, which shocked Home personnel. The Home staff, accordingly, decided that Rita would be better off in foster care and placed her in Germantown. This decision was reinforced by the fact that they didn't get a clear statement from Gladys that she wanted Rita back before they placed her. Afterwards, however, Glady's interest in Rita's return increased enormously. Maynard mused:

> I believe that Gladys intentionally undermined this placement. She was extremely threatened that she had failed as a mother again, and that she was going to lose Rita permanently. Gladys did not have the ability to directly say to the Home, "I want my child back." So, I think she made it very difficult for the foster family. When she talked to Rita about it, Rita picked up signals about what Gladys wanted to hear. So Rita started saying things about what was being done to her. You couldn't really tell whether they were true or not.

Kiladis, however, was more convinced of the truth of Rita's complaints. She recalled that Rita related to her, almost four years after that first placement, an incident in which the foster father had given her a severe beating for not doing a dance of some kind. Gladys had corroborated this tale with a description of bruises on Rita's buttocks, back and sides. It was at that time that Gladys finally complained to the DPW social worker, and he had Rita returned to Gladys within three days. Kiladis added, "I suspect that that really is the fastest the DPW works."

The PLA lawyers recalled that, at first, everything seemed fine when Rita returned to Gladys. But soon it became clear that Rita was still a very difficult child. Gladys became very depressed. She couldn't handle Rita at all, and something seemed to be wrong with the child. Gladys turned to a social worker therapist, Elizabeth Reilly, and had Rita evaluated at the Learning Disabilities Center where Reilly worked. Reilly not only convinced Gladys to place Rita back at the Home, but she also began a process of convincing Gladys to put Rita up for adoption. According to Maynard:

It was not very long into therapy that Elizabeth Reilly said to herself, "This is a woman with extreme emotional problems, not sick, but with emotional problems; and she has a very complicated relationship with a young man. She is having some trouble raising one child—Manuel; she is having a lot of difficulty with Rita, who seems to be a disturbed child. Gladys can't cope. This is not good for Rita, this is not good for Gladys, so let's move for adoption."

But Reilly was not totally open with Gladys, who seemed to believe that Rita's placement in the Home was again temporary; that the Home would provide treatment for Rita; that she would visit often and bring Rita home on weekends; and, eventually, perhaps when Rita improved, would bring her home again.

Maynard recalled that now Gladys's visits took on a different kind of irregularity. Gladys would say that she was coming on Sunday and then show up on Monday; she would say "I'm coming at noon" and then show up at 6:00 P.M. During Rita's first stay at the Home, Gladys had been late in bringing her back; now she was often late picking her up. The records from the Home's logs indicated that Rita often returned to the Home upset and even had difficulty sleeping on some occasions after a home visit. Kiladis felt that Rita was being torn between her life with Gladys and her life at the Home. Many of the rules were different, and she speculated that Rita must have struggled with Gladys's disapproval of many of the practices at the Home. An example, recalled by Kiladis, was Gladys's anger and concern that Rita was permitted to sleep in a nightgown without panties, and to sleep in the same room as the boys in her cottage. At the same time, a nun at the Home had expressed concern that Rita was allowed to get into bed with Gladys to watch television.

Within a year of Rita's return to the Home, plans were again made to move Rita to a foster family. Maynard remarked:

The planning came from the judgments of the people at the Home that Rita really ought to be permanently placed somewhere, and that Grandma should remain Grandma. There should be visits, but Rita should slowly be weaned away from her Grandmother. This was a judgment that was concurred in by Elizabeth Reilly, Gladys's therapist. And there was something in writing, some document from the Home that indicated consent by Gladys to an adoption. Interestingly enough, when we got discovery that document was missing; but I had seen it.

But the plans to move Rita into a foster placement were greatly accelerated when the young, inexperienced psychology student, after six play-therapy sessions with Rita, concluded that Rita had been sexually abused. Kiladis commented:

The student was being supervised by someone whose "thing" was sexual abuse. What wasn't so clear to us and took us a while to find out was that half of the children in the Home had been placed there as a result of being sexually abused. This student felt that Rita was acting out various sexual behaviors. What was somewhat unfair about it, was that—apparently—this went on all the time. Kids, often, playacted partly as a way of working through some of what they've been through, and obviously it rubbed off on some of the other kids. But this student really freaked out about what was going on.

Although it was quite possible that Rita had been exposed to some sexual behavior, it was not clear exactly what had occurred or where. The Home immediately directed suspicion at Juan and decided to place Rita out of Gladys's reach. Although formally the reason for cutting off visitation was the sexual abuse question, Maynard believed that what was lurking in the background was Gladys's failure to cooperate with the first foster placement. "All of the social workers' notes were loaded with things like that, that Gladys was and had continuously been difficult."

The Home's inappropriate promise to Rita's new foster parents in Jenkintown, the Biancos, that the child was definitely theirs to adopt complicated matters further. Kiladis felt that this promise might have been part of "a deliberate cover-up" of Rita's exposure to either sexual abuse or sexual activity at the Home itself. At first Gladys had reacted passively to Rita's placement in a foster home, as she had when Rita was placed in Germantown the first time. But when the new DPW worker on the case, Mary Nota, who had met Gladys only once before, bluntly told her that Rita was being placed a second time, adding "I'm not going to let you see her," and furthermore made accusations about sexual abuse of Rita by Juan, Gladys's attitude suddenly altered. Maynard recalled: "Gladys went back to Reilly and her staff and drove them crazy, screaming at them, 'You've got to help me!' and they in turn called us." Maynard added:

I got a call from them saying that we had to help this woman. There had been accusations of sexual abuse and her child had been taken away. They didn't say anything to me about the fact that

they had been moving Gladys toward adoption, that they themselves felt that that might be both in Gladys and Rita's best
interests. I learned of these things only after the case came to us.

In a complicated series of moves (see legal strategy below) Maynard
was able to negotiate a visitation schedule while Rita was being evaluated
by a group of specialists at St. Christophers, who dealt with child and sex
abuse victims. After several weeks, however, the "games began again," as
Kiladis put it. She commented that Gladys and the Biancos competed for
Rita like divorcing parents. Gladys was never on time bringing back Rita
and never returned her to the Biancos in the same clothes in which she had
left. The Biancos often dressed her inappropriately—for example, dressing
her in a party dress when they knew that Gladys was taking Rita on a
picnic. The Biancos would then complain when Rita's dress became soiled.
Each family criticized the other's way of life. The Biancos were not
Hispanic, and Jenkintown had essentially no Hispanic population. Rita,
who had been bilingual, could no longer speak much Spanish. In fact, the
Biancos severely reprimanded her for any tendencies to use Spanish. At
school in Jenkintown she was exposed to racial slurs and made to feel very
inferior for being Spanish. Kiladis recalled that Rita had told her that the
Biancos said, "If you go back to West Philadelphia you will become scum
like the rest of them, but we have this wonderful suburban lifestyle." The
attorneys began to believe that the situation in Jenkintown was so bad that
returning Rita to Gladys seemed to be a relatively better course. They were
concerned that Rita was losing her identity as an Hispanic, and that if Rita
were not returned to the Hispanic community, her ethnic roots would be
irreversibly lost.

By the time Kiladis entered the case, Maynard had gotten to know
Gladys well. He didn't believe for one minute that there was sexual abuse
in Gladys's home. He also believed that losing Rita permanently would be a
terrible blow for her. If, during the course of the prolonged legal maneuver-
ings, Gladys's anger and anxiety had dissipated and she had become able
once again to consider adoption as in Rita's best interests, Maynard would
have been amenable. But by the time he had obtained all the information
he needed to represent Gladys, the situation had been reshaped by the
judicial process itself.

He had begun his interviewing of the various professionals involved
knowing that by the time there was a decision about what might be best for
Rita, that decision might not look the same as it would have on the day he
began. Appraising his feelings at the time, Maynard commented:

> Invariably I begin investigating these sorts of cases as if the facts
> are there to be assembled for decision at some future date. But, on
> the ground that then we will make a decision, in my gut, I know
> that the decision is not going to be the same once the investigation
> is completed. Memories, perceptions and positions will all have
> been affected, influenced by the investigation itself. What might
> have looked very bad for a client before a lawyer gets into a case
> can look very different after the lawyer's influence is felt. On the

other hand, what are the choices? This is not an extreme case where I suspected that the child was being abused by my client. I did suspect, and this turned out to be true, that Rita's mother was involved much more than Gladys was telling us. Rita had Carlota's phone number and often spoke with her, and Carlota was often at Gladys's house. In addition, Rita went over to her mother's house more often than any of us had realized, and the exposures over there that would be bad for a child were enormous. But this wasn't enough to alter what I did in the case. I simply chose the right of Gladys to make the decision about her grandchild, over other people. I did not decide that I was the lawyer to the whole situation to decide what was best for Rita. Within certain limits, I really did and do allow my role as an advocate in the situation to take its course.

Kiladis' approach to this was somewhat different. Kiladis had let Maynard know, when she first became involved with the case, that she had to speak with Rita before she made a commitment to represent Gladys. If DPW were correct in its evaluation of the situation and if Rita had developed a strong positive bond with the Biancos, then Kiladis felt she would not have "the emotional energy for the case." But if Rita reported that life with the Biancos was very different from the way both the Home and DPW described it, then "it would be very important to help her." Kiladis recalled:

> Ultimately it put me in a bit of a bind. It wasn't clear whose attorney I was; what I was advocating for, and so on. Knowing Rita's needs as well as Gladys's and eventually even Carlota's created a lot of tension for me. Their needs were different and it was not clear how to bargain them out; whether to try to get the maximum good for everyone or just for our client, Gladys.

Aside from the question of what might or might not be in Rita's best interests, Maynard had first been confronted with the problem of Gladys's best interests. For Maynard, that issue had two distinct parts. First, Gladys wanted Maynard to move immediately to get Rita back for her. Here Maynard had two concerns: first, that he might lose in court if he had to go in at a time when suspicions of sexual abuse were being raised, and, second, that a court battle would take its toll on Gladys herself. At the outset Gladys was not emotionally capable of withstanding the upheaval of a prolonged court procedure. Early in the case Maynard had come to realize that it would be extremely painful for Gladys to confront an outside observer's evaluation of her fitness for parenthood.

Gladys's one emotional peg was her therapist, Reilly. It was Reilly who had called Maynard and implored him to represent Gladys against DPW. Yet it was also Reilly who believed that Rita should be adopted; if DPW called her at trial, she would make a damning expert witness against Gladys. In fact, at the beginning there had been no expert witnesses available who could make a favorable presentation. Maynard believed that Reilly had, as he put it, "screwed Gladys" by not being honest with her about the therapist's concerns, both that Rita was being exposed to a drug-dominated environment through continued contacts with Carlota and that Gladys was too depressed to cope with the situation. He had insisted, after speaking with Reilly, that she become more honest with Gladys and that he was not going to be the one to go back and tell Gladys what the therapist's position actually was.

Maynard felt obligated both to tell his clients everything he discovered and at the same time to protect them. Although he intended to be Gladys's advocate and try to intervene with DPW, his legal instincts told him he could best manage the case by drawing things out for quite a while despite Gladys's desire to act immediately. Maynard therefore decided that it did not make sense to force the issue to a hearing right away:

> One, I couldn't win. Two, I thought this would be bad for Gladys. And three, the expert who had been doing therapy all of this time could not make a good witness for Gladys. So I went back to Gladys and I said: "I don't think that I can win it now. I don't think I can even get you visitation now, although if you tell me that I have to, I will try. I also don't think that Elizabeth Reilly will be as good a witness for you as she needs to be. I have got to do a lot of work with her, and you should start talking to her as well." ... Of course she accepted it, the way she accepts all authorities, in a passive/aggressive manner. But I confronted her with that also. We talked about her anger with me and her inability to challenge me. I think we did so in a healthy way, but long after the initial decision to wait had been made.

Legal Strategy

The first official action taken by Maynard as Gladys's lawyer was a letter which he wrote for her on May 10, 1979, more than two months after she came to him. Essentially the letter was a statement from Gladys that she wished to terminate DPW's custody of Rita, and it included a demand that Rita be returned to her. Maynard knew that this would precipitate action on the part of the department, and it did. But by then Maynard had begun the process he described as "obtaining information from, and trying to neutralize," the professionals involved in the case, and he was ready to proceed. In the March through May period, Maynard had constantly asked for visits at critical times: a confirmation ceremony in the family, illness of a close relative, a whole range of similar events. Each time, the visits were refused. There was constant negotiation with DPW about visits. The Department's hard-line position was later brought up by Maynard in conversations with St. Christophers and with David Slade, whom the court had appointed as Rita's attorney on June 11, 1979. In addition, the staff at PLA had begun to see every person involved in the case. The legal docket in Philadelphia County Probate Court indicates that the DPW moved for temporary custody of Rita on May 25, 1979, and that that motion was allowed by Judge Warren.

On June 8, 1979 Maynard filed two motions: one for visitation and one for the payment of expert assistance for a psychological evaluation. When they went into court on the 11th of June, Maynard did not press the first motion. Instead he again negotiated with DPW about the visitation issue:

> What I said to them was that Gladys should be allowed to visit. I asked them why they felt that she shouldn't. They told me that it was too dangerous, that Gladys, or someone in her household, was going to sexually abuse the child. Then I brought up the notion of having an independent expert decide the issue. I used the two motions to get them to concede to the motion for expert assistance.

In fact, the visitation motion was never acted on in court; Maynard continued to pursue that goal through negotiation. On the other hand, Judge Warren allowed the motion for payment of expert assistance, given that DPW did not oppose it. Had the department opposed it at that time, Maynard believed that he still might have been able to prevail, but he couldn't be sure, given the costs it imposed on the county. Instead, everybody agreed that expert assistance was a good idea; that Gladys really couldn't afford it, that it should be provided and, moreover, that it should be provided by the team of specialists at St. Christophers. Maynard's choice of that team was a deliberate one:

> Before I went on the motion, I went to St. Christophers. I had two meetings with the people there. They had never seen Gladys, but I had two meetings with them. I had a long talk with them about what I saw was going on and about how important it was that they look into it. I also went to see the fellow who runs the clinic, knowing that at that time St. Christophers was involved in an internal struggle over whether to support DPW's approach to child custody issues, an approach which many saw as extreme intervention.

Maynard felt that many of the specialists on the team at St. Christophers had attitudes that were ideal for his client. They were internally involved in a fight about whether they should be supportive of DPW's approach to removing children from their homes; they were sympathetic to poor people; they didn't respect social workers (who generally stood at the bottom of the hierarchy of mental health professionals); and they believed that the social workers' decisions were often ill-advised and unsympathetic to poor people. Maynard recalled, "I knew they would bend over backwards to be non-interventionist in a case with PLA; I knew they would take the general position that these kids belong at home." In this particular case, where a child was being taken from an Hispanic environment and being removed to a distant suburb where she was not being allowed to see her relatives, Maynard thought the team would surely begin with an attitude biased in favor of Gladys. By the time Maynard had met with them twice, he knew that he had a "fairly receptive audience."

Maynard told Judge Warren that he had been to see the people at St. Christophers, and had talked with them. He indicated that they would be willing to accept the appointment from the court. Maynard was relieved that neither Slade nor the DPW counsel objected to the choice of St. Christophers as evaluator. Had he been on the other side, Maynard noted, he would have demanded a different appointment, recognizing that the attorney who got to the expert first established a relationship which invariably sets up the case to some extent in his favor. But, in Maynard's words, "They were so relieved to give up this fight on visitation for a period of time that they went along with the appointment of St. Christophers as an evaluator."

It was not until August of 1980 that Slade voiced some concern about the evaluation being done by St. Christophers. At that time he moved for an additional psychological evaluation and payment of costs. Although this evaluation was also to be conducted by St. Christophers, Slade specified that the report evaluate Gladys's household as a potential home for Rita rather than limiting itself to the question of whether or not abuse had occurred there. Although Maynard knew that Slade might have realized that the St. Christophers team was going over to Gladys's side, Maynard went along with the motion for a new evaluation because "I knew we had St. Christophers; once you've got them that far, you've got them."

The entire evaluation process was very drawn out. But that also, Maynard thought, worked in Gladys's favor in the long run. In the interim, the PLA attorneys were able to build up visitation, bit by bit; they saw Rita's therapist in Jenkintown, the nun at the Home, the DPW social workers, and Gladys's therapist, Reilly. Every interview had a dual purpose: it was an opportunity to get information and an opportunity to in some way "neutralize" the speaker to ensure his or her passive acquiescence in (if not active support for) a result which favored Gladys. Maynard commented that "all of those contacts were negotiations as well as interviews. The whole strategy was to bring the professionals around so that they saw Rita's placement as something that ought to change."

Maynard knew that Gladys's standing to intervene with DPW's attempts to gain custody of Rita might be challenged. Grandparents, unlike parents, had no special status in custody cases, and Maynard was concerned about the legality in Pennsylvania of a guardianship authorized by New York. He had asked students and others at PLA to research the issue, but there seemed to be no law on it. Maynard treated Gladys as if she *were* a substitute mother, but he knew that that status was not clear legally. By the end of the case, the DPW counsel and everyone else involved was referring to Gladys as Rita's legal guardian, and pointing to the New York court's order for authority. In February 1981, PLA filed the New York guardianship records, but Kiladis recalled, "I was reluctant to bring up the issue of Gladys's guardianship from New York because I had researched that and I knew how flimsy it was."

According to Maynard, the DPW social worker on the case when Rita was first placed with the Biancos, Mary Nota, had not only bungled relations with Gladys when the move was made, but also had difficulty managing an adversarial relationship with PLA. He recalled he was able to take advantage of Nota's mistakes: "We worked on Mary Nota to the point where she was so angry with us that she made a terrible witness at St. Christophers. All she did was rant and rave about us and not talk about

Rita.'' Maynard deliberately did nothing to decrease Nota's vindictiveness nor to improve her relationship with Gladys. Kiladis had also seriously questioned Nota's choice of Betty Bianco as a foster mother. Betty was known as someone who became very attached to the children placed with her, and then was very upset when any one of them left. This bonding, in Kiladis's opinion, was certain to exacerbate the relationship between Betty and Gladys. Both women were fighting to be Rita's mother.

During this period, there were many personnel shifts at DPW; among them, the replacement of Mary Nota by Margaret Kamin. Kiladis and Maynard both perceived this change to be a very beneficial one for their client. People from PLA were in Kamin's office within a week after she started, talking to her about the situation from their point of view. Maynard recalled that Kamin wasn't completely taken in by this strategy, but she was willing to give the case a fresh look.

A great deal had changed under the influence of PLA. A schedule of day visits had been established. The St. Christophers team was evaluating the situation, and though Gladys was cooperating fully with them, Betty Bianco was not. Because Betty refused to bring Rita in to Philadelphia to go to St. Christophers, Joan Kiladis and then Margaret Kamin, were driving out to Jenkintown to pick up Rita and bring her downtown. Gladys was still in therapy with Elizabeth Reilly, whom Maynard felt he had "turned around."

The team at St. Christophers was aware that Rita was feeling a great deal of tension because of the racism in the Jenkintown school she was attending. By March 1980 a talk between Gladys's attorneys and the staff at St. Christophers indicated that they were coming to three conclusions, summarized in a memo in the PLA file:

> (1) While the St. Christophers team cannot state categorically that there has been no sexual abuse, nothing in Rita's language or behavior indicates any basis for the CY47. If she was abused, she is no longer cognizant of the fact. The team believes that the filing of the CY47 was ill-advised; that a lot of the behavior cited is characteristic of institutional living. (2) Rita wants to go home to her grandmother, cannot understand why she is moved from place to place and is apprehensive that her therapists will be taken away from her. (3) Because of the above, the team would recommend that Rita be returned to Gladys's home and continue in therapy at St. Christophers.

Kiladis remembered that St. Christophers was unwilling officially to exonerate Juan of sexual abuse; nor would the evaluators address the possibility that Rita was being beaten by the Biancos. Rita had written a letter to her therapist at St. Christophers, saying that she was being beaten and generally mistreated by the Biancos and that she wanted to go home to her grandmother and "pappy," her name for Juan. Although Kiladis had not actually handed Rita the pencil and paper to write it, she felt somewhat implicated in the letter-writing process because she frequently urged Rita to be frank with the people at St. Christophers, reassuring her that what she told her therapist there would not get back to the Biancos.

Kiladis had also told Rita to be frank with David Slade, but as it had turned out, Rita never got to talk with Slade. Although he was the child's attorney, and according to Maynard had left "no legal stone unturned," he never went out to see the child or asked to have her brought to his office. Maynard recalled, "We did not sit down with Slade and say, 'you should see the kid.' If we had, I think that he would have gone. But we didn't do that."

Assessing Slade's representation, Maynard observed there were two dimensions to cases like Rita's. First, there was the purely legal obligation to pursue certain issues and employ certain procedural tactics. Maynard thought that Slade clearly understood his legal obligations and met them by moving for, and then supporting, evaluation of Rita's situation by an independent source. He did have a conversation with the team at St. Christophers. He did talk with the social worker. But he never met Rita: he never dealt with the second dimension, never became involved with his client as a person, never tried to make the legal objective fit the person's needs. Kiladis said that both Rita and Gladys had called Slade's office on numerous occasions and left messages on his answering machine, but their calls were never returned. Maynard added:

> Slade lived in another world. He lived in the downtown world of big firms; those attorneys don't go to Jenkintown, and they don't go out to people's houses, and the last thing he was going to do was to go to Gladys's house in West Philadelphia. I think that that is part of the class structure of the bar, and I think it's a shame. Those attorneys miss the chance for the type of practice that a doctor who is a general practitioner has. I have a life as full of people as of law, law as a human service. It's not for everybody, but it's for more people than you'd think if they'd give it a chance.

It was not clear to Maynard what Slade was advocating. At first he had gone along with DPW, but later he opposed them as well and asked for continuances. Slade seemed to feel that Rita had already lost her identification as an Hispanic, and that therefore ethnicity was no longer at issue. Slade was not even present at the final two hearings in the case.

Further, the PLA attorneys were able to turn Kiladis's coincidental friendship with two of the women at DPW who were involved with Rita's case to Gladys's advantage. Memos in the PLA file indicate that Kiladis had long telephone conversations with Susan Goldman, the supervisory social worker. Goldman had often called Kiladis at her home to discuss her worry over Margaret Kamin's extreme emotional involvement in Rita's case. They also discussed the CY47, which at that point was two years old and had never been substantiated or officially pursued. Goldman felt that the psychology student who had made the first report of sexual abuse had been under considerable pressure, pressure to find instances of such abuse for her supervisor's book. She and Kiladis discussed the question of why the Home had chosen to move Rita into foster placement at a time when many of the professionals involved were warning against any change. Kiladis told Goldman of her own belief that Juan was a stabilizing influence on the family, and that his youth counted in the family's favor if any concerns about Gladys's failing health might arise. Kiladis reassured Goldman that DPW need not rely upon Kamin's judgment that Gladys and Juan were "okay as parents," since St. Christophers was certainly very competent and would be making a favorable report.

Similarly, Kiladis was continually in contact with Grace Myers, the counsel for DPW. Before Grace Myers became the attorney of record on the case, Kiladis had met her at the Philadelphia County Courthouse. Kiladis explained:

> I had several long conversations with Grace. I knew her from law school. When I talked with her at the courthouse, I knew that some of what I was saying would get back to the department. I told her that we had a lot of cases with the department in which we concurred with the moves that the department was making, but that we had a few where we felt that the department's behavior was off-the-wall. The department occasionally overreacted, and Rita's case was an example of that; they were much more upset than was warranted.

Kiladis knew that her relationship with Myers "cut through a lot of red tape." Kiladis did not tell Myers that she thought Gladys would fall apart if she had to take care of Rita without the necessary support services from DPW, but rather that there were support mechanisms in place, that Gladys was doing well with them, that Gladys was being very cooperative; when the department told Gladys to do something differently with Rita she did. Myers, according to Kiladis, "knew that I believed in what I was saying, that Rita wanted to go to Gladys; that Gladys wanted her, and that there were support mechanisms at work that I had no objection to."

According to Maynard, "it was Joan's involvement in the case that finally won it for Gladys." Kiladis not only spent many hours talking with Margaret Kamin, Susan Goldman and Grace Myers, she also spent a great deal of time with Gladys and Rita. From Jenkintown she drove Rita to and from St. Christophers and to and from Gladys's for visits. She met Carlota and recognized the extensive contact that Rita still had with her mother. Indeed, Kiladis felt that the entire custody issue might never have arisen if Carlota had been legally represented from the start. Kiladis in many ways became an advisor and counselor to Gladys, talking with her about the best school placement for Manuel, and eventually, Rita, as well as answering Gladys's questions about various presents for Rita while the child was still living with the Biancos. Kiladis recalled, "I had to set limits or I would have been making up grocery lists for her."

On January 29, 1981, Kiladis filed a petition for Gladys and Juan to adopt Rita. By then Kiladis herself had been with the case since the fall of 1980 and had gotten to know (or knew previously) all of the professionals involved, as well as the "principals": Rita, Gladys, Betty Bianco, and even Carlota and Juan. Since Juan spoke very little English, Kiladis's acquaintance with him was very limited. She had participated in a conference at St. Christophers and knew that the hospital team's second report, which would come out on February 1, 1981, would contain a recommendation that Rita be returned to Gladys after a period of gradually increasing visitation. The adoption petition, although filed, was not immediately acted upon.

DPW agreed to St. Christophers' recommendations, and Rita returned to live with Gladys, Juan and Manuel in March 1981. She was, however, still under the legal custody of DPW. Rita and Gladys attended therapy sessions each week at St. Christophers. Manuel went along at first, but since the sessions interfered with his first love, baseball, he soon asked to be allowed not to attend. This was agreed to by the therapist at St. Christophers. Juan refused to go from the very beginning. Kiladis believed that his resistance arose from a combination of his remaining distress about having been accused of sexually abusing Rita and the traditional "macho" notion that men did not talk about their feelings. For whatever reasons, Juan said that if he had to attend therapy sessions, he was moving out. And shortly thereafter he did so, moving in with a woman his own age.

Gladys, Manuel and Rita were now living together at Gladys's home in West Philadelphia. Gladys was in therapy with Elizabeth Reilly, and Rita and Gladys continued to go to therapists at St. Christophers. Margaret Kamin of DPW remained involved. Finally, in February of 1982, Kiladis convinced Susan Goldman that it was time for DPW to release Rita from its custody by moving to dismiss the original DPW motions for custody and to dispense with Carlota's consent to Rita's adoption. A hearing was set before Judge Yates on February 2. Because Rita was ill that day, she and Gladys did not attend. Kiladis was there, along with Grace Myers and Margaret Kamin for DPW; David Slade was not present. Since there was no opposition to the dismissal of the two motions filed by DPW, the judge was willing to dismiss them. But, he asked, who would then be Rita's guardian? Myers mentioned that Gladys was legally Rita's guardian because of the New York court order. Kiladis, not convinced of the validity of that order in Pennsylvania, told the judge that she had filed an adoption petition for Gladys and Juan. Kamin voiced some concern about allowing Rita to be adopted by Gladys and Juan. All three women were concerned about the possibility that if adopted, Rita might become the object of a custody dispute between Gladys and Juan in the event that their separation ended in divorce. Judge Yates ordered a continuance.

In April, when Rita's case appeared before Judge Yates again, the cast of characters had changed slightly. Rita and Gladys were present with Kiladis, and DPW was represented by Grace Myers and Susan Goldman. David Slade again did not appear. Judge Yates allowed DPW to dismiss its two motions, entered into the record an agreement between Gladys and DPW for after-care services, and allowed the petition for Gladys and Juan to adopt Rita, even though Juan was not present and the judge knew that Juan and Gladys were living separately. Rita ran up to the bench and hugged the judge.

Loose Ends

When they had finished reviewing the case, Maynard stepped out of his office to get some coffee and mused about Kiladis's involvement with the case.

> She came as a new student and gradually became more experienced. As she began to grow and I had more confidence in her, I gave her more and more of the case. She developed an excellent relationship with Gladys. I was anxious for that to happen because I needed to separate myself from it psychologically. But, what I also saw develop was the classic problem of over-commitment. It seemed to me that Joan took every little piece of anything that was there and blew it up. At the same time she was driving Rita around town and making Gladys's domestic arrangements. She made the case because of the amount of energy and effort that she put into it. But I never really believed that there was a staff person at the Children's Home who had sexually abused Rita. I don't really know, but I didn't believe it.

Kiladis meanwhile had rediscovered in the files a number of memos that she had written to Maynard describing conversations that she had had with Rita and with Susan Goldman from DPW. In one memo, dated December 13, 1980, Kiladis had recounted Rita's response to her direct question as to whether or not any of the males she knew ever "got fresh with her."

> She didn't know what I meant, except for hitting, and when I explained she said, "like Steve at the Home?" (only it took her a little while to remember his name). Gladys explained that Steve was a social worker who came to the Home about once a month. She often saw him fondling several of the girls, including Rita. He was around in 1978 and is, from what Rita indicated, almost certainly the cause of the CY47.

This conversation had taken place in Kiladis's automobile, as did the next one, described in a memo from Kiladis to Maynard dated December 27, 1980.

> Rita then asked me if I would forgive her for not having told me the truth. "That man at the home who kept bothering me was not named Steve, his real name was Joe or Joey." He had told her that she would get into a lot of trouble if ever she told. She said that she felt badly about telling me his wrong name, and that she had known his name all along.

Kiladis remembered checking with Susan Goldman from DPW to see if the social worker knew of any "Joe" or "Joey" at the Home. In a memo dated January 18, 1981, she put into the file a synopsis of a lengthy telephone conversation that she had had with Goldman:

> Joe/Joey is the groundskeeper at the Home and is still there. He had little contact with the kids, Susan thinks, but says that since Rita was often sick with ear infections and officially confined to bed in her cottage, what the child says is possible. Susan promises to check into it, if just because

she is under pressure to get greater accountability from people and places that DPW uses for placement.

While Kiladis and Maynard were both convinced that Juan had never abused Rita sexually or in any other way, Maynard had reminded Kiladis of the many other opportunities in Rita's environment for sexual exposure or stimulation: with other children at each of the two foster homes; with other children at the Catholic Home; with children in the neighborhood around Gladys's home; when Rita stayed at Carlota's house or even at the home of her Aunt Maria.

Yet Kiladis had always been puzzled by the timing of the Home's placement of Rita with the Biancos. Even the Home's psychologist, who filed the CY47, had put into his report at that time that he did not "think this is an appropriate time to attempt to place this child in a foster home. Her power and control struggles, her volatile emotional state mean that she will be a considerable handful for any foster parents." Perhaps, as Kiladis believed, someone at the Home knew that the "father figure" referred to in the report, who was exposing the child to "sexual overstimulation," was actually a member of their own staff. Rita then had been whisked out to Jenkintown for protection, not from Juan but from Joe.

Although convinced by this evidence that there had been sexual abuse at the Home, Kiladis was not committed to the idea of suing the Home on behalf of Gladys and Rita. She knew that type of trial was a very difficult one. Rita, who was not an easy child to deal with, would be placed in a very vulnerable position. Old wounds would be reopened. Gladys's anger and feelings of betrayal by the Home, an institution which was supposed to have helped Rita, would be rekindled.

As Maynard returned to his office, Kiladis thought about how many other loose ends remained in this case, as in most others like it. PLA knew many things about the family that DPW did not know. She thought of Carlota's continuing involvement with Gladys and Rita and the potential dangers in Rita's exposure to a drug-dominated environment. Moreover, there was the fact that Gladys received a full monthly allowance from the federal AFDC (Aid to Families with Dependent Children) program, even though (unbeknownst to the government) Gladys and Juan who owned the building that Gladys and the children were living in, had not reported the rent they were receiving from the two apartments in the building, the fact that they owned a building in Puerto Rico (which not being occupied by either of them would have disqualified Gladys from welfare), nor that Gladys was working one job under a false Social Security number given to her employer by Margaret Kamin. Where did Maynard's and Kiladis's duty to their client begin and end? What did it require them to overlook, and what did it require them to pursue? Should they leave Rita's case, and close the file?

NOTES AND QUESTIONS: RITA'S CASE

Rita's case reflects many of the central themes of this book. Perhaps the most crucial is the definition of the lawyer's role—or, more accurately, the need for self-definition, which lawyers confront throughout their legal careers. Of the three lawyers who figure in the case, one remains in the background. David Slade, Rita's court-appointed attorney, plays at best a walk-on part, largely, it seems, by his own choice. As seen through Maynard's eyes, Slade has chosen to offer technical expertise but little sensitivity to the personal and relational aspects of his cases. This downtown lawyer leaves "no legal stone unturned" but finds it unnecessary actually to meet with Rita. Maynard's judgment of Slade's performance is unsympathetic. How might Slade himself assess his representation? What might account for his conduct?

The other two lawyers in the case, Maynard and Kiladis, define their roles quite differently. Maynard sees his function primarily as representing Gladys, the Legal Aid Society's client:

I did not decide that I was the lawyer to the whole situation to decide what was best for Rita. Within certain limits, I really did and do allow my role as an advocate in the situation to take its course.

Kiladis, by contrast, admits that:

It wasn't clear whose attorney I was; what I was advocating for, and so on. Knowing Rita's needs as well as Gladys's and eventually even Carlota's created a lot of tension for me. Their needs were different and it was not clear how to bargain them out; whether to try to get the maximum good for everyone or just for our client, Gladys.

1. In the end, is it clear how Kiladis resolves this tension? Is it appropriate for her even to consider trying "to get the maximum good for everyone" rather than only for Gladys? Does this approach breach any obligations to the client? On the other hand, Maynard is convinced that "it was Joan's involvement in the case that finally won it for Gladys"—an involvement that included spending many hours with Rita. Would attorneys who define their roles purely as "advocates" for their client be likely to invest this amount of time to help another party?

Suppose that you were one of the Legal Aid attorneys in this case. If you believed that the best outcome for Gladys would be inconsistent with the best outcome for Rita, would that affect your choice of roles? Would your answer turn on the inadequacy of Rita's representation by David Slade? If so, what about other individuals whose interests were unrepresented—Juan, Carlota, the children in the Catholic home? How should such concerns of third parties affect attorneys' ethical obligations?

What factors should guide lawyers in choosing between the role of advocate and what Maynard calls "lawyer to the whole situation"? Consider the following issues.

The Law of Lawyering

To what extent does Model Rule 1.2 dictate a particular role? Should a lawyer be subject to discipline for choosing the "wrong" role? Did either

Maynard's or Kiladis's approach violate any of the bar's codified requirements?

The Traditions and Practices of the Bar

To what extent do the conventional practices and traditions of the bar help lawyers define their obligations in circumstances like Rita's case? What if there are competing norms and traditions? Obviously, the zealous advocate is a well-established role, but so is the nonpartisan counselor who attempts to reconcile competing interests. Maynard's term "lawyer to the whole situation" paraphrases Louis Brandeis's description of his own practice of mediating between clients and other parties.[37] As Chapter X makes clear, Brandeis' approach has been highly influential.

The role of "lawyer for the situation" implies greater independence from the client than the advocate's role. Thus Brandeis once wrote in a memorandum to himself: "Advise client what he should have—not what he wants."[38] How desirable is this role definition? Is it the one Kiladis adopted? Should it matter whether the client can afford to hire another attorney who might see the issues differently?

Ethical Principles

To what extent should lawyers' choice of roles depend on their ethical principles? What arguments might be made on behalf of Maynard's and Kiladis's different visions of professional responsibility?

Personal Style

How much discretion should lawyers have to select or adapt a role to fit their personalities and priorities? Should so important an issue be left to the preferences of individual attorneys? Is there any practical alternative?

Confidentiality, Advocacy, and Contextual Decision Making

How easily can or should lawyers shift from one role to another depending upon the particular context? Maynard acknowledges that if he had believed that Rita was being abused in Gladys's home, he might not have adopted the advocate's stance. So too, Kiladis's choice of role apparently depended in large measure on the inadequacy of representation of a vulnerable child. In a different context, she might not have experienced the same tensions in the advocate's role.

If such contextual factors affect a lawyer's definition of role, do they also impose any obligations to third parties? If Maynard had known of child abuse, should he have disclosed it? Should Kiladis have informed the Biancos and Carlota that they were entitled to court-appointed attorneys?

At the end of the case, Maynard and Kiladis are deliberating about whether to sue the Catholic Home for Children. Kiladis has become convinced that a child abuser works as one of the Home's groundskeepers, but fears that such a suit might have devastating effects on Rita and

---

37. *See* John P. Frank, "The Legal Ethics of Louis D. Brandeis," 17 *Stan.L.Rev.* 683 (1965).

38. Philippa Strum, *Louis D. Brandeis: Justice for the People* 40 (1984) (quoting Brandeis).

Gladys. Yet failing to bring formal charges could expose other children to severe risks. How should the lawyers resolve this dilemma? Should the considerations be different for "an advocate" than for a "lawyer for the situation"? Are there any alternatives besides litigation that might avoid the dilemma?

2. Are any of Maynard's and Kiladis's legal tactics problematic? For example, is it appropriate for them to "neutralize" other professionals in the case: the psychiatrists at St. Christophers, Mary Nota, Margaret Kamin, Susan Goldman, and Grace Myers? Kiladis withholds from Grace Myers, a law school acquaintance, the belief that Gladys is unable to care for Rita without outside support services, as well as the knowledge that the legal basis for Gladys's guardianship is dubious. Kiladis and Maynard also keep this information from the court. Is that proper? Does it matter whether nondisclosure involves a matter of fact or a matter of law? What about the knowledge that Gladys is collecting AFDC payments based on false representations of her income? Under what, if any, circumstances should a lawyer reveal such facts? Consult Model Rules 1.6, 3.3, and 4.1.

Maynard and Kiladis have several private conversations with DPW personnel, including Mary Nota and Margaret Kamin. From one perspective, these conversations appear perfectly appropriate: Gladys's lawyers should be able to discuss her case with the relevant officials. However, Maynard and Kiladis structure these encounters for adversarial purposes; the objective is to "neutralize" the officials. DPW has its own legal counsel, and the Model Rules forbid lawyers to engage in ex parte contacts with other represented parties unless authorized by law. (Model Rule 4.2). Did Maynard and Kiladis violate these rules? Or were the conversations the kind of communications with government officials that are "authorized" by law? Did Kiladis's extensive personal involvement with Rita without her lawyer's consent violate bar ethical codes?[39]

3. Another important issue in Rita's case involves the allocation of power between lawers and clients. In theory, attorneys are agents of those they represent. In practice, the Legal Aid lawyers in this case "whether knowingly or unknowingly, [often] steered clients' choices." For example, at one point Maynard talks Gladys out of seeking immediate visitation rights, because "his legal instincts told him he could best manage the case by drawing things out for quite awhile despite Gladys's desire to act immediately." When Maynard advises Gladys that they should not immediately seek visitation because they could not win, is he giving her any real choice? Such opposition to the client's wishes for the client's own good is an example of paternalism, discussed more fully in Chapter XII. Under what circumstances is it justified? Is paternalism ever consistent with the advocate's role? Consult Model Rules 1.2(a) and 1.14.

In the end, Gladys adopts Rita. Is this an outcome that Gladys genuinely desires, or is it an instance of lawyers' shaping client choices to

---

39. For further discussion of the advocate's role and alternatives, *see* Chapter IV. On the "lawyer for the situation," *see* Chapter X.

fit the legal alternatives readily available? From the outset of the case, Gladys expresses ambivalence. She wants to keep Rita, but she also wants public agencies to provide care in those intervals when she is unable to cope. Should Kiladis and Maynard have tried to formalize such an arrangement rather than pursuing adoption? What would the likely response have been by the court, by welfare officials, or by Rita's attorney? Does the adoption raise other ethical concerns? Should Juan have been a party, given that he is likely to separate from Gladys? What about the rights of Carlota? How should their interests have been handled?

4. Does the fact that this is a legal aid case present special problems of legal ethics and legal process? Most of the parties whose interests are at stake have no representation or inadequate representation. To what extent are the difficulties in Rita's case attributable to the distribution (or maldistribution) of legal assistance? To what extent do they reflect inadequacies in legal and social welfare alternatives? Would more or better lawyers have led to a better process? A better result? Are you satisfied with the outcome of Rita's case? If not, what reforms would you propose?

CHAPTER I

THE CONCEPT OF A PROFESSION

INTRODUCTION

American lawyers have long prided themselves on being part of a profession. Their status as professionals has been critical to attorneys' self-esteem, social standing, and regulatory independence. Since the concept of professionalism carries so much significance for lawyers both individually and collectively, this book begins by trying to get a better sense of what exactly the concept means.

The term "profession" is both elastic and elusive. Its meaning has varied considerably over time and cultures, and has inspired continued debate among contemporary social theorists. The most common definition, reflected in a report by the American Bar Association's Commission on Professionalism, has stressed professionals' special expertise and ethical responsibilities. Borrowing from an influential work by Roscoe Pound, former Dean of Harvard Law School, the Commission defined professionalism as the practice of a "learned art in the spirit of a public service."[1]

This approach builds on various intellectual traditions, particularly "functionalist" sociological theory. Functionalism's central premise is that professional structures emerge in response to social needs, rather than to the profession's own interests and efforts. From this perspective, lawyers' privileged position derives from their performance of tasks that are critical in developed societies. The failure of various nations' efforts to abolish the bar is often taken as evidence that its role is indispensable.[2]

In defining that role, sociologists generally have stressed the importance of specialized knowledge and ethical obligations. Drawing on works such as Max Weber's *Economy and Society*, some theorists view professional specialization as one of the foundations of a complex economic order.[3] Other theorists, including Emile Durkheim, have emphasized the need for vocational groups with distinctive ethical ideals. In *Professional Ethics and Civil Morals*, Durkheim argued that the erosion of religious and community controls had contributed to an "amoral" economic order. To prevent a decline in public morality and to insure loyalty to client and societal

---

1. *See In the Spirit of Public Service: A Blueprint for the Rekindling of Lawyer Professionalism*, Commission on Professionalism, American Bar Association (1986) *infra*, quoting Roscoe Pound, *The Lawyer from Antiquity to Modern Times* 5 (1953).

2. France, Russia, and China are the most celebrated examples. *See* A.A. Berle,

"Legal Profession and Legal Education," 9 *Encyclopedia of the Social Sciences* 340 (1933). Some American colonies also attempted to abolish or restrict attorneys' role. *See infra*. For discussion of Japan, *see* Chapter XIV.

3. Max Weber, *On Law*, in *Economy and Society* (Max Rheinstein ed. 1922).

interests, occupations like law must instill a sense of collective ethics in their members.[4]

This need for occupational groups with special knowledge and moral commitments has, in turn, been thought to account for other distinguishing features of professions, such as ethical codes, regulatory autonomy, prescribed forms of training, and a monopoly over certain services. According to sociologist Eliot Freidson, whose definition is quoted with approval by the ABA Commission, a profession is:

> An occupation whose members have special privileges, such as exclusive licensing, that are justified by the following assumptions:
>
> 1.   That its practice requires substantial intellectual training and the use of complex judgments.
>
> 2.   That since clients cannot adequately evaluate the quality of the service, they must trust those they consult.
>
> 3.   That the client's trust presupposes that the practitioner's self-interest is overbalanced by devotion to serving both the client's interest and the public good, and
>
> 4.   That the occupation is self-regulating—that is, organized in such a way as to assure the public and the courts that its members are competent, do not violate their client's trust, and transcend their own self-interest.[5]

Such assumptions, as well as their underlying functionalist framework, have attracted criticism from all points on the ideological spectrum. Many commentators have challenged the tendency of prevailing frameworks to ignore variations within and across professional groups in particular cultural settings. Other theorists have questioned the evidentiary basis for conventional accounts. In the view of these critics, the profession's claims to specialized competence are no different in kind from the claims of other groups that have not attained professional status (information services experts, investment bankers, and so forth). Many commentators have also challenged the profession's assertion of a distinctive "public service" orientation or commitment to the "public good." As critics note, bar rhetoric on this issue is often vague or circular. For example, the report of the ABA Commission on Professionalism defines professionalism as practice "in the spirit of public service" and then defines "public service" as "representing individual clients and advocating their interests in a professional manner."[6] Yet however public service commitments are defined, it is by no means clear that they are more widely shared by those with recognized professional status, such as accountants or architects, when compared with non-professionals such as community organizers or health care workers.

---

4.   Emile Durkheim, *Professional Ethics and Civil Morals* (1957).

5.   Eliot Freidson, quoted in Commission on Professionalism, *supra* note 1. See also Herbert Kritzer, "The Professions Are Dead: Long Live the Professions," 22 *Law & Social Inq.* 713 (2001); Section B *infra*.

6.   ABA Commission on Professionalism, *supra* note 1, at 6 n. 22.

From critics' perspective, the primary reasons for professionals' distinctive roles and influence lie elsewhere. Inspired by work ranging from neoclassical economics to Marxist analysis, many of these commentators view the concept of professionalism as an assertion of occupational power, although they often disagree on its origins and consequences.

The following excerpts offer a sample of these views. In evaluating their arguments, consider how well they account for both the pervasiveness of lawyers in the industrialized world and the diversity in their social status and tasks. Although virtually no developed country has found it possible to do without a legal profession, many nations have granted attorneys far less power, prestige, and economic rewards than has the United States. What might explain American attorneys' distinctive position in what de Tocqueville labeled the nation's "highest public class?"

A. HISTORICAL FRAMEWORKS

At the turn of the twentieth century, in a famous address before the Harvard Law School, Supreme Court Justice Louis Brandeis identified a central and continuing challenge to the American bar. As he noted, the American legal profession has "unusual opportunities for usefulness."

> The great achievement of the English-speaking people is the attainment of liberty through law. It is natural, therefore, that those who have been trained in the law should have borne an important part in that struggle for liberty and in the government which resulted. Accordingly, we find that in America the lawyer was in the earlier period almost omnipresent in the State. Nearly every great lawyer was then a statesman; and nearly every statesman, great or small, was a lawyer.

But, Brandeis maintained, this distinguished tradition had eroded.

> Instead of holding a position of independence, between the wealthy and the people, prepared to curb the excesses of either, able lawyers have, to a large extent, allowed themselves to become adjuncts of great corporations and have neglected the obligation to use their powers for the protection of the people. We hear much of the "corporation lawyer," and far too little of the "people's lawyer...."

> For nearly a generation the leaders of the Bar have, with few exceptions, not only failed to take part in constructive legislation designed to solve in the public interest our great social, economic and industrial problems; but they have failed likewise to oppose legislation prompted by selfish interests. They have often gone further in disregard of common weal. They have often advocated, as lawyers, legislative measures which as citizens they could not approve, and have endeavored to justify themselves by a false analogy. They have erroneously assumed that the rule of ethics to be applied to a lawyer's advocacy is the same

where he acts for private interests against the public, [whose interest is not represented] as it is in litigation between private individuals.[7]

Brandeis, like other leaders of the American progressive reform movement, held beliefs that were similar to functionalist theories of the professions. Both the functionalists and the progressive lawyers opposed the commercialization of the profession, and insisted that lawyers had an ethical responsibility to counsel clients and to modify laws in ways that would serve the common good. Both groups also believed that the bar could advance the public interest by reducing class conflict. Brandeis' well known progressive call was for members of the legal profession to become "people's lawyers" as well as corporate lawyers.[8] Attorneys, in Brandeis' view, had distinctive qualities of mind that suited them for public service: "logical thinking, a nose for facts, good judgment of people, [and] toleration [of opposing views]...."[9]

Concerns about the decline in lawyers' reputation and moral stature remain a common theme in contemporary debates on the profession. The following excerpt from the Report by the ABA's Commission on Professionalism offers a prominent example.

B. CONTEMPORARY CONTROVERSIES

American Bar Association Commission on Professionalism, "... In the Spirit of Public Service": A Blueprint for the Rekindling of Lawyer Professionalism

1, 3, 10, 17, 55–56, 95, 96 (1986).

"Professionalism" is an elastic concept, the meaning and application of which are hard to pin down. That is perhaps as it should be. The term has a rich, long-standing heritage, and any single definition runs the risk of being too confining.

Yet the term is so important to lawyers that at least a working definition seems essential. Lawyers are proud of being part of one of the "historic" or "learned" professions, along with medicine and the clergy, which have been seen as professions through many centuries.

When he was asked to define a profession, Dean Roscoe Pound of Harvard Law School said:

> The term refers to a group ... pursuing a learned art as a common calling in the spirit of public service—no less a public service

---

7. Louis P. Brandeis, "The Opportunity in the Law," (1905) reprinted in *Business: A Profession* (1913).

8. David Luban, "The Noblesse Oblige Tradition in the Practice of Law," 41 *Vand. L.Rev.* 717, 723–24 (1988). See also William H. Simon, "Babbitt v. Brandeis: The Decline of the Professional Ideal," 37 *Stan.L.Rev.* 565 (1985).

9. Luban, *supra* note 8, at 725.

because it may incidentally be a means of livelihood. Pursuit of the learned art in the spirit of a public service is the primary purpose.

The rhetoric may be dated, but the Commission believes the spirit of Dean Pound's definition stands the test of time. The practice of law "in the spirit of a public service" can and ought to be the hallmark of the legal profession.

[A central question facing today's bar is]: Has our profession abandoned principle for profit, professionalism for commercialism?

The answer cannot be a simple yes or no. The legal profession is more diverse and provides more legal services to more people today than ever before. These are not inconsiderable achievements. Further, most lawyers, the Commission believes, are conscientious, fair, and able. They serve their clients well and are a credit to the profession. Yet the practices of some lawyers cry out for correction. Without denigrating the Bar generally, this report proposes some needed changes in the practices of law schools, practicing lawyers and judges. We believe the future of the legal profession will be bright if all elements of the profession resolve to confront their problems and deal with them forthrightly. . . .

The public views lawyers, at best, as being of uneven character and quality. In a survey conducted by this Commission, under the thoughtful direction of Commission member Gustave H. Shubert, only 6% of corporate users of legal services rated "all or most" lawyers as deserving to be called "professionals." Only 7% saw professionalism increasing among lawyers; 68% said it had decreased over time. Similarly, 55% of the state and federal judges questioned in a separate poll said lawyer professionalism was declining. The primary question for this Commission thus becomes what, if anything, can be done to improve both the reality and the perception of lawyer professionalism.

Perhaps the golden age of professionalism has always been a few years before the time that the living can remember. Legend tends to seem clearer than reality. Still, it is proper—indeed it is essential—for a profession periodically to pause to assess where it is going and out of what traditions it has come.

Clearly, the legal profession is in a process of evolution. This is inevitable. The challenge for individual lawyers and the organized Bar is to understand these changes and to preserve those principles of professionalism which endure despite the changing legal landscape.

Even with our shortcomings, all is far from bleak on the legal horizon. Examples abound—even in this anti-heroic age—of lawyers who have given of themselves unselfishly and at considerable personal sacrifice to provide their services to the public at large. . . .

Similarly, it behooves the legal profession to work voluntarily toward the implementation of these and other reforms that will make us more a profession "in the spirit of a public service." If such action is not taken, far more extensive and perhaps less-considered proposals may arise from governmental and quasi-governmental entities attempting to regulate the profession. The challenge remains. It is up to us to seize the opportunity while it is ours.

QUESTIONS

1.   What should we make of this consistent harkening back to an assumed golden age of professionalism?

2.   To what extent does the commercialization of legal practice erode its commitment to professionalism? Are there inherent distinctions between professions and other highly regarded occupations? Does it matter?

3.   What accounts for American lawyers' relatively high status but poor public image?

4.   How does the ABA Commission define the problems facing the profession and how realistic are its prescriptions?

NOTES

Is it realistic to expect most lawyers not "to put profits first?" According to Dean Pound, whom the Commission earlier quotes, members of professions, unlike other vocations, make the pursuit of profit "incidental" rather than primary to the provision of service.[10] How plausible is that account as a description or aspiration for the American bar?

As the preceding materials suggested, concerns about the increase in commercialization and the decline of professionalism have recurred throughout the last century. However, the current sense of disquiet does have certain distinctive features. It is accompanied by widespread public criticism of the profession, and responsibility is placed on the bar as a whole, not on some single subgroup of offending practitioners. Less than a fifth of Americans have confidence in the honesty and integrity of lawyers.[11] Moreover, concerns are widely shared among lawyers themselves. Following the release of the ABA Report, most state and local bar associations convened their own committees on professionalism, which generally expressed concerns similar to that of the national commission. So too, prominent leaders of the bar and legal ethics experts have become increasingly outspoken critics. Mary Ann Glendon's *A Nation Under Lawyers* (1994), Anthony Kronman's *The Lost Lawyer* (1994), William Simon's *The Practice of Justice* (1998), and Deborah Rhode's *In the Interests of Justice* (2000) all reflect a widespread sense that traditional ideals, although honored in bar rhetoric, have been increasingly devalued in legal practice. The lawyer-statesman is losing ground to the lawyer-entrepreneur. In

---

10. Roscoe Pound, *The Lawyer from Antiquity to Modern Times* 5 (1953).

11. Deborah L. Rhode, *In the Interests of Justice* 4, 215 n.4 (2000); Mary P. Gallagher, "Lawyers Still Struggling With Image Problem," *Boston Law Tribune*, May 31, 2002, at 6. See also Roper Center for Public Opinion Research, 2002 Gallup Survey (finding that only 18 percent of Americans rated the honesty and ethical standards of lawyers as very high or high; 35 percent rated them as low or very low), and 2002 Harris Survey (finding that only 65 percent of Americans would trust lawyers to tell the truth).

many professional contexts, rewards are based less on character and craft than on business development and billable hours.

For the contemporary American bar, these are the "best of times and the worst of times."[12] In no country do lawyers enjoy greater power, wealth, and status. The number of lawyers has doubled over the past quarter century. Law is the highest paying profession and a common path to leadership in both the public and private sector. Demand for corporate legal services has continued strong, corporate lawyers' income has remained high, and the profession continues to expand. Yet that overall economic prosperity has also been accompanied by increasing insecurity, acrimony, and pressure. Escalating costs and competition has resulted in greater focus on the bottom line, and higher billable hour requirements. Partnership means less and is harder to obtain. Recent law graduates face a tougher job market with higher debt burdens than their predecessors. Moreover, among practitioners who represent primarily individual rather than corporate clients, the demand for services has been relatively weak, lay competition has increased, and average earnings have been modest. The consequence has been to widen income disparities within the profession. Dissatisfaction with certain key aspects of professional life is reflected in lawyers' exceptionally high rates of stress, depression, and substance abuse.[13]

The result, as Robert Nelson and David Trubek observe, is a sense that:

> lawyers, both individually and collectively, have lost control over forces that are reshaping the markets in which they compete, the law firms to which they traditionally devoted their careers, the pace and quality of their worklives, and their status in society.
>
> To be sure, many within the legal profession might have preferred to operate in more stable markets and to abide by more stable relationships guided by "professional" as opposed to market place values. But this option was not available in the last twenty years—and has never really been available in recent history. The bar is too split easily to agree on what relationships and values should be fostered. It has been too tolerant of entrepreneurship and too leery of effective professional association or governmental control to develop truly powerful regulatory mechanisms. The concerns of both the losers and at least some of the winners in the recent growth and restructuring of the industry made it important for bar leaders to say something comforting about professionalism and its value as an integrating element for

---

12.   Robert L. Nelson & David M. Trubek, "New Problems and New Paradigms in Studies of the Legal Profession," in *Lawyers' Ideals/Lawyers' Practices: Transformation in the American Legal Profession* (Robert L. Nelson, David M. Trubek, & Rayman L. Solomon, eds. 1992) at 14. *See also* Rhode, *supra* note 11, at 23–38. Robert W. Gordon, "The American Legal Profession, 1870–2000," in *The Cambridge History of Law in America* (Christopher Tomlins & Michael Grossberg, eds. 2008).

13.   *See* Rhode, *supra* note 11, at 25; Patrick J. Schiltz, "On Being a Happy, Healthy, and Ethical Member of an Unhappy, Unhealthy, and Unethical Profession," 52 *Vand. L. Rev.* 871 (1999).

the profession. The general sense that lawyers had lost control of their markets, workplaces, and careers created a climate in which such rhetoric found a ready response. But a long tradition of entrepreneurship, segmentation, and weak control made it impossible for the leaders of the bar to say anything very concrete or do anything significant about the trends they decried. The result was a vague and general invocation of "shared" values that really aren't shared, a symbolic and nostalgic crusade in the name of an ideology almost no one really believes in fully and which has little to do with the everyday working visions of American lawyers.[14]

Other commentators have come to similar conclusions. Some fifteen years after the release of the ABA Commission report, the introductory address at a conference on professionalism offered the following assessment.

Deborah L. Rhode, "Professionalism"

52 South Carolina Law Review 458, 459–61, 463 (2001).

A threshold question is whether we are all on the same page, or even in the same book, with respect to what we are trying to fix. I have long argued that a central part of the "professionalism problem" is a lack of consensus about what exactly the problem is, let alone how best to address it. "Professionalism" has become an all-purpose prescription for a broad range of complaints, including everything from tasteless courtroom apparel to felonies like document destruction. For some lawyers, the term evokes some hypothesized happier era, "just over the horizon of personal experience, when law was less competitive and commercial, and more collegial and civil." For other lawyers, the concept carries less appealing symbolic freight. These nostalgic appeals seem like an opportunities for pompous platitudes and selective recollection. After all, the good old days were never all that good for many lawyers who didn't fit within well-off white male circles, or for many clients who bore the costs of anticompetitive bar practices.

Moreover, whatever consensus exists at the symbolic level often fades when concrete practices or sanctions are at issue. It is no accident that the bar's strategies of choice for addressing professionalism have been education and voluntary civility codes, which run the risk of papering over much that is problematic in bar regulatory structures. Educational programs can focus on uncontroversial topics or raise, without resolving, disputed ones. And bar civility codes [which over a hundred jurisdiction have adopted] are adept at fudging contentious choices. For example:

> [A lawyer should] be a vigorous and zealous advocate on behalf of [a] client while recognizing that, as an officer of a court, that excessive zeal may be detrimental to many clients' interests as well as to the proper functioning of our system of justice;

14. Nelson & Trubek, *supra* note 12.

[A lawyer should], within the framework of vigorous representation, advocacy, and duty to the client, be firm, yet tolerant and non-abusive of ineptness or the inexperience of opposing counsel . . .

[A lawyer should] attempt to avoid bullying, intimidating, or sarcastic questioning of witness except as reasonably proper under circumstances reasonably related to trial tactics.

Such standards command widespread support because they dodge the difficult issues. Who can disagree with rules that aren't really rules but only aspirations, and that tell lawyers not to be bullies unless "necessary" or "proper"? The issue really worth discussion is how to determine when zeal is unnecessary or "excessive." When does "vigorous" representation demand taking advantage of opposing counsel's ineptness? On questions involving hard tradeoffs between individual clients' interests and societal values, most civility codes are diplomatically vague. [And] . . . [i]t is scarcely self-evident that those most in need of instruction in civility will pay attention to anything provided in aspirational form. . . .

The same is true of educational programs on professionalism. . . . Although most states now require attorneys to take several hours a year of continuing legal education courses in ethics, no jurisdictions have attempted to determine whether these episodic, largely exhortatory experiences have any affect on practice. Yet research in other professions such as medicine and engineering has found no relationship between performance and participation in continuing education.

In short, the popularity of recent professionalism initiatives rests not on evidence that they are effective, but rather on evidence that they are innocuous. Educational programs and voluntary codes are a relatively inexpensive and uncontested form of symbolic politics. They affirm our professional aspirations without the inconvenience of actual adherence.

———

One prominent observer who does not criticize the greater competitiveness and commercialism of law practice is Judge Richard Posner. Posner analogizes the closed, cartelized legal profession of the "good old days" to medieval craft guilds, which restricted membership, valued skilled workmanship, and produced custom-made goods for the elites who could afford them. The end of the guilds and the rise of competitive markets and mass production made goods cheaper in both senses of the word: lower in quality but also in cost. The great transformation from a guild system to a market economy improved the lot of consumers but made the condition of producers harder by increasing competitive pressure. In the following excerpt, Posner examines similar dynamics in the American legal profession.

Richard A. Posner, Overcoming Law
63–68, 92–93 (1995).

Today, all is changed [with the legal profession], changed utterly. Although the profession has not been thrown open to free entry, an accelerating accumulation of legal and especially economic changes over the past three decades has transformed the profession in the direction of competitive enterprise. It is not so profound a transformation as the change from medieval weavers' guilds to the modern mass-production textile industry—it does not signify the deprofessionalization, let alone the proletarianization, of the legal profession. But there are sufficient parallels to make the analogy an illuminating one.

Although part of a larger movement aptly described as the industrialization of service, the transformation of the profession is the proximate consequence of a surge in demand for legal services. The causes of this surge are not well understood, though some causal factors, such as the creation of new rights, much higher crime rates, greatly relaxed rules of standing, more generous remedies (including relaxed standards for class actions) as part of a general tilt in favor of civil plaintiffs and against civil defendants, and the increased subsidization of lawyers for indigent criminal defendants and indigent civil plaintiffs, can be identified. The most conspicuous manifestations of the surge in demand for legal services are the litigation explosion and concomitant rapid growth in the number of lawyers. . . .

The accommodation of the increased demand for legal services has taken a variety of forms, all of which involve expanding the supply of those services . . . [T]he supply of legal services was expanded through increases in the number of suppliers, increased competition among suppliers, and technical and organizational innovations that enhanced the productivity of legal services. The first response is illustrated by the creation of new law schools, the expansion of existing ones, and the reduction in the rate of flunking out students. . . . The motor for this expansion in supply was competition among law firms to add lawyers in order to cope with the higher demand for legal services. . . .

The second response to the rising demand for legal services—increased competition within the profession—is the result in part of a series of decisions by the Supreme Court that invalidated on one ground or another a number of traditional restrictions on competition among lawyers. The judge-made exemption of the learned professions from antitrust law has gone, and with it price-fixing by bar associations. Most limitations on lawyers' advertising, not only media advertising but also the personal solicitation of legal business from persons having potential legal claims, have been invalidated, as have many barriers to lawyers' relocating to states other than the ones in which they were originally licensed.

Technical and organizational innovations have increased the vigor of competition in the legal-services market, but they have also an independent significance for the transformation of the profession. The rise of the paralegal has demonstrated that much of the traditional work of lawyers can be done by nonlawyers. . . .

As the legal problems of business firms grow, more firms find it profitable to create large in-house legal staffs. These staffs not only provide greater competition for law firms but also enable corporate clients to engage in shrewder negotiations with them—to play off one against the other, to solicit competitive bids, and so forth—thus further stimulating competition among law firms. We should not be surprised that the price of legal services fell (in real, that is, inflation-adjusted, terms), rather than, as popular and professional opinion alike supposes, rose, between 1970 and 1985. The growing ratio of associate to partner income is consistent with the hypothesis of growing competition: reduction in monopsony power has increased law firms' labor costs.

As law firms grow, opportunities for professional specialization—for a more complete division of labor—grow apace. I mentioned the paralegal. Large law firms also hire professional managers, English professors, accountants, economists, computer experts, and other nonlawyer specialists to perform services formerly performed by lawyers. Lawyers become proficient in narrow fields of law or in particular techniques, learn to work in large teams, and engage in activities characteristic of competition—such as marketing—or of large enterprises—such as supervision. Competition makes them work harder, too, and reduces their security of tenure. There are more cases of firms dissolving, restructuring, regrouping; of firms firing associates and even partners; and of wide fluctuations in earnings within firms.

These changes have psychological consequences. Harder work, even when well remunerated, greater uncertainty of tenure, and the inevitably bureaucratic "feel" of practicing law in a huge organization all reduce job satisfaction. Many lawyers claim with evident sincerity not to enjoy the practice of law as much as they once did. Many say they wouldn't have gone to law school had they known what the practice of law would become. The increasingly competitive character of the legal-services market makes lawyers feel like hucksters rather than the proud professionals they once were, and brings forward to positions of leadership in the profession persons whose talents, for example for marketing ("rainmaking"), are those of competitive business rather than of professionalism. Gone are the days of artisanality and the security of the guild. . . .

The practice of law has become more competitive. . . . Naturally it is less fun. Competitive markets are no fun at all for most sellers; the effect of competition is to transform most producer surplus into consumer surplus and in more or less time to drive the less efficient producers out of business.

The implications for legal ethics are complex. It is necessary to distinguish between two types of ethical obligation. One is to the client and is illustrated by the rule that the lawyer is the fiduciary of his client, whom he must therefore treat as he would himself rather than as he would treat the other party to a normal arms'-length contract. The other type of ethical obligation is to the court or the community and is illustrated by rules against suborning perjury and abusing pretrial discovery. Competition will not greatly erode the first kind of ethical obligation; competitive markets are not notable for disserving their customers. . . . It may, however, erode the second type of ethical obligation significantly. The lawyer's performance of his ethical obligations to people and institutions that are not his clients disserves his clients, his customers; and competition implies the subordination of other interests to those of the consumer.

QUESTIONS

1.   In what respects do Posner and the authors of the ABA's professionalism report agree? What are their disagreements?

2.   If Posner is correct, how should we view the demise of professionalism? Consider Posner's distinction between ethics rules protecting clients from those protecting the courts and the community. He argues that increased competition may erode the second sort of rule, but not the first. Is this an acceptable trade-off?

3.   If Rhode is correct about the limited usefulness of the professionalism campaign to date, should the effort be abandoned? Or could it be more profitably redirected? If you were asked to chair a bar professionalism task force, how would you respond?

Talcott Parsons, a leader of functionalist sociology, is known among legal theorists partly for his distinction between businesses and professions. The following excerpt sets forth Parson's claim that the distinction lies not in individual motivations but in institutional structures.

Talcott Parsons, "The Professions and Social Structure," in Essays in Sociological Theory

34, 43–46 (Talcott Parsons rev. ed. 1958).

[S]tudy of the relation of social structure to individual action in [the professions can] throw light on certain other theoretically crucial aspects of the problem of the role of self-interest itself. . . . [T]he difference between business and the professions in this respect has strongly tended to be interpreted as mainly a difference in the typical motives of persons acting in the respective occupations. The dominance of a business economy has seemed to justify the view that ours was an "acquisitive society" in which every one was an "economic man" who cared little for the interests of others. Professional men, on the other hand, have been thought of as standing above these sordid considerations, devoting their lives to "service" of their fellow men. . . .

Perhaps the best single approach to the distinction of these two elements is in the question, in what do the goals of ambition consist? There is a sense in which, in both cases, the dominant goal may be said to be the same, "success." To this there would appear to be two main aspects. One is a satisfactory modicum of attainment of the technical goals of the respective activities, such as increasing the size and improving the portion of the business firm for which the individual is in whole or in part responsible, or attaining a good proportion of cures or substantial improvement in the condition of patients [or clients]. The other aspect is the attainment of high standing in one's occupational group, "recognition" in Thomas' term. In business this will involve official position in the firm, income, and that rather intangible but none the less important thing, "reputation," as well as perhaps particular "honors" such as election to clubs and the like. In medicine it will similarly involve size and character of practice, income, hospital and possibly medical school appointments, honors, and again reputation. The essential goals in the two cases [business and the professions] would appear to be substantially the same, objective achievement and recognition: the difference lies in the different paths to the similar goals, which are in turn determined by the differences in the respective occupational situations.

There are two particularly important empirical qualifications to what has been said. In the first place certain things are important not only as symbols of recognition, but in other contexts as well. This is notably true of money. Money is significant for what it can buy, as well as in the role of a direct symbol of recognition. [In some instances, actual achievement may fail to bring appropriate recognition. Such circumstances place great strains on the individual and may result in inappropriate "commercialism" in the professions and "shady" practices in business. Where achievement does not bring recognition, individuals have conflicting needs.] . . . Commercialism and dishonesty are to a large extent the reactions of normal people to this kind of conflict situation. The conflict is not generally a simple one between the actor's self-interest and his altruistic regard for others or for ideals, but between different components of the normally unified goal of "success". . . .

If this general analysis of the relation of motivation to institutional patterns is correct two important correlative conclusions follow. On the one hand the typical motivation of professional men is not in the usual sense "altruistic," nor is that of business men typically "egoistic." Indeed there is little basis for maintaining that there is any important broad difference of typical motivation in the two cases, or at least any of sufficient importance to account for the broad differences of socially expected behavior. On the other hand there is a clear-cut and definite difference on the institutional level [in terms of what behavior is rewarded].

NOTES

Other sociologists, following approaches similar to Parsons, have suggested that a key function of professional identity and regulatory structures is to subordinate practitioners' self-interested concerns to higher social values. As Robert Merton put it in *Some Thoughts on the Professions in American Society* (1960), the organization of professions does not require members to "feel altruistic (though that might do no harm); it only requires them to act altruistically" in the service of societal interests. Is this notion of mandatory altruism a contradiction in terms? Is it a fair description of the legal profession's actual practices?

Critics of professional practices span a broad ideological spectrum. Unlike functionalists, who have viewed professional structures primarily as a response to social needs, these theorists have stressed practitioners' role in creating and molding such needs to their own ends. Critics from the anti-regulation right have objected to restrictive practices that unduly limit entry, discourage competition, and stifle innovation.[15] Critics from the left often echo these concerns, and add the objection that professional organizations often privilege their own and clients' interests to those of society and underserved groups. In a series of works beginning in 1970, Eliot Freidson has argued that the privileges of professionals are more attributable to their power and self-interest than to their societal functions.[16] In *Disabling Professions*, Ivan Illich makes related arguments about professional authority, and submits that:

> the new dominant professions claim control over human needs.... All trade associations are attempts by those who sell their labour to determine how work shall be done, and by whom. Professions also do this, but they go further: they decide what shall be made, for whom and how their decrees shall be enforced. They claim special, incommunicable authority to determine not just the way things are to be made, but also the reason why their services are mandatory. Many professions are now so highly developed that they not only exercise tutelage over the citizen-become-client, but also determine the shape of his world-become-ward....
>
> Professionals tell you what you need and claim the power to prescribe. They not only recommend what is good, but actually ordain what is right. Neither income, long training, delicate tasks nor social standing is the mark of the professional. Rather, it is his authority to define a person as client, to determine that person's need and to hand the person a prescription.[17]

Other critics, such as law professor Richard Abel, make similar claims. In his view, the bar's claims to distinctive forms of knowledge and ethical conduct serve more to legitimate than to explain its prerogatives. Abel's work describes efforts by the profession to create and control its market position. Major strategies have included efforts to upgrade educational standards, restrain competition within the profession, prevent competition from outside, and maintain regulatory autonomy.[18] However, as Abel also notes, these efforts confront both economic and political obstacles. In a market economy, efforts to restrict supply increase incentives for other

---

15. Milton Friedman, *Capitalism and Freedom* (1962); Sylvia Ostry, "Competition Policy and the Self–Regulating Professions," in *The Professions and Public Policy* 17, 19–22 (Philip Slayton & Michael J. Trebilcock eds. 1978).

16. Eliot Freidson, *Profession of Medicine* (1970); Eliot Freidson *Professional Powers: A Study of the Institutionalization of Formal Knowledge* (1986).

17. Ivan Illich, "Disabling Professions," in Ivan Illich *et al.*, *Disabling Professions* 16, 17 (1977).

18. Richard L. Abel, "United States: The Contradiction of Professionalism," in 1 *Lawyers in Society: The Common Law World* 186–243 (Richard Abel and Philip Lewis eds. 1989).

producers to enter the market, and provoke resistance by underserved groups who want access to the profession or to the assistance that it provides. Moreover,

> Although self-governance is the principal impetus behind the professional project, it is theoretically contradictory and hopelessly flawed in practice. Justified in terms of "independence," it ultimately depends on state power to enforce its rules and often to compel membership. Claiming to promote the public interest, it inevitably pursues parochial advantages.... External observers—consumers and the general public—are even less contented with the performance of professional associations. Expressing this dissatisfaction, courts strike down restrictive practices, legislatures create independent regulatory bodies, and clients sue for malpractice. Professional associations will survive, but with impaired legitimacy and diminished authority.[19]

Analyses such as Abel's have been challenged along several lines. One criticism involves reductionism, that is, the tendency of structural market-control theories to undervalue noneconomic motives and professional ideologies. A related criticism concerns the conclusory tendencies of such theories and their reliance on the same general explanation for inconsistent behaviors. For example, if lawyers under these approaches do not provide pro bono legal assistance, they are assumed to be acting out of narrow economic self-interest. Conversely, if they do offer such assistance, they are said to be legitimating the profession's claim to special status, which also serves economic self-interests. A final criticism involves the extent to which some market-control theories homogenize professions and obscure divisions within and across their memberships.

Several recent works have proposed alternative models of professionalism. Some theorists, after noting the decline in "cohesion, consensus, and community" within the bar, question the usefulness of talking about *a* profession. In their view, lawyers constitute less a unified group than an "amalgamation ... [of members] pursuing different objectives in different manners and more or less delicately held together under a common name ..."[20] From this perspective, attorneys now practice in an era of "postmodern professionalism," with increasing diversity along lines of personal background, substantive specialty, and practice setting. Although commissions on professionalism have long insisted that more unites than separates attorneys, such claims seem closer to aspirations than descriptions. The concerns of a small-town divorce lawyer in a solo practice bear little resemblance to those of an urban federal prosecutor or a Wall Street associate specializing in "corporate mergers."[21] This diversity raises questions about the bar's reliance on a unified regulatory structure and uniform standards of education and admission.

19. *Id.*

20. Sharyn L. Roach Anleu, "The Legal Profession in the United States and Australia: Deprofessionalization or Reorganiza-

tion?," 19 *Work and Occupations* 184, 188 (May, 1992).

21. Rhode, *supra* note 11, at 20. See also Kritzer, *supra* note 5, at 720–21.

A final group of theorists propose frameworks that integrate ideological as well as structural features. So, for example, Robert Nelson and David Trubek stress the importance of lawyers' "agency," and the ideological "norms, traditions, and practices" which make up professionalism.

> They generate the claims that allow lawyers to maintain jurisdiction over work. They become part of each lawyers' professional identity, to some extent providing coherence and meaning in everyday life and allowing lawyers to respond to new situations in "appropriate ways".... [Professionalism] provides a set of dispositions which lawyers use to interpret their situations and orient their choices. It constitutes a world view which delimits but does not necessarily determine action ... [Such a framework sees] professional ideals as partially formed within the workplace and consciously or unconsciously designed for the promotion of the economic, power, and status goals of lawyers. Thus lawyers' "ideals" carry within themselves heavy traces of what we have called "structure." But they also can be seen as sets of dispositions that have a logic partially independent of the structures that produced them.[22]

QUESTIONS

1.   How would you assess these competing theories? What is at stake in the bar's claim to be a profession rather than a business?

2.   What accounts for the legal profession's relative success in creating a market for its services, restricting non-lawyer competition, and maintaining professional independence?

3.   To what extent do any of these theorists adequately describe your own sense of what being a professional means?

4.   One state bar director active in the professionalism campaign put its fundamental objective this way: "Bottom line—better people make better lawyers. Better lawyers make for a better profession."[23] If that is the mission, how can it be achieved? Are there strategies for the bench, bar, and law schools that you would recommend?

---

22.   Nelson & Trubek, *supra* note 12, at 22–23.

23.   John T. Berry, "A Check–Up on the Health of the Legal Profession," 17 Professional Lawyer 2, 9 (2006).

CHAPTER II

THE AMERICAN LEGAL PROFESSION

A. HISTORICAL FRAMEWORKS

INTRODUCTION

Although the term "profession" did not come into use until around the sixteenth century, individuals have been performing services that we would now associate with the legal profession for at least 2,000 years. By the fourth century B.C., advocates were assisting parties in Greek tribunals, and were involved in counseling and legislative work. However, these individuals did not form a cohesive "profession" in the sense we now use the term. Training was informal, ethical standards were lax, and discipline was lacking.[1]

A somewhat more professionalized culture developed in early Rome. Between the first and third centuries A.D., legal advisors and advocates began to form communities around the courts in major cities. These groups attempted to standardize training and provide some disciplinary oversight, as well as to assist the development of a systematic jurisprudence.[2]

With the fall of the Holy Roman Empire, this professional tradition also declined. As Chapter IV indicates, early Anglo–Saxon methods of dispute resolution, particularly trials by ordeal, presented less need for trained advocates. However, in England, after the Norman conquerors imported certain innovations, including trial by jury, the usefulness of partisan assistance increased.[3] During the twelfth and thirteenth centuries, the foundations for a professional community began to emerge. It was, however, highly stratified, with different specialities having monopolies over certain functions and certain courts. Ultimately the English bar divided into two groups. The most elite were the barristers, who provided trial representation. They prepared for their role by attending one of several Inns of Court and then by serving as apprentices to practicing barristers. The educational requirements of the Inns varied over time, but

---

1. Thomas Holton, *Preface to Law: The Professional Milieu* 2–4 (1980); George Calhoun, *Introduction to Greek Legal Science* 44–48 (1944); Robert J. Bonner, *Lawyers and Litigants in Ancient Athens* 200–43 (1927).

2. J.A. Crook, *Legal Advocacy in the Roman World* (1995); Hans Julius Wolff, *Roman Law* 95–117 (1951); Wolfgang Kunkel, *An Introduction to Roman Legal and Constitutional History* 105–116 (J. Kelly trans. 1973).

3. *See* Stroud Frances Milsom, *Historical Foundations of the Common Law* 28 (1969); Marion Neef & Stuart Nagel, "The Adversary Nature of the American Legal System: A Historical Perspective," in *Lawyers' Ethics: Contemporary Dilemmas* 73, 76, 80 (Allan Gerson ed. 1980); Henry S. Drinker, *Legal Ethics* 12–14 (1953).

during the American bar's formative era, they were anything but rigorous. The remaining legal work was performed by solicitors, who were governed by rules of court and professional associations, supplemented by legislation. That division remains in contemporary Great Britain, although the boundaries have blurred over the last quarter century, and areas of overlapping jurisdiction have increased.

By contrast, the American bar began without such formal stratification and gradually developed into more specialized groups. The following excerpts from Friedman and de Tocqueville indicate the course of that evolution.

Lawrence Friedman, A History of American Law

94–98, 633–635, 638–639 (2d ed. 1985).

THE LEGAL PROFESSION

The early colonial years were not friendly years for lawyers. There were few lawyers among the settlers. In some colonies, lawyers were distinctly unwelcome. In Massachusetts Bay, the *Body of Liberties* (1641) prohibited pleading for hire. The "attorneys" of early Virginia records were not trained lawyers, but attorneys-in-fact, laymen helping out their friends in court. In 1645, Virginia excluded lawyers from the courts; there had been a ban in Connecticut too. The Fundamental Constitutions of the Carolinas (1669) was also hostile; it was considered "a base and vile thing to plead for money or reward." Apparently, no lawyers practiced law in South Carolina until Nicholas Trott arrived in 1699. The Quaker colony at Burlington, West New Jersey, made do with a single lawyer until the end of the seventeenth century. In Pennsylvania, it was said, "They have no lawyers. Everyone is to tell his own case, or some friend for him ... 'Tis a happy country."

There is some evidence, then, to back Daniel Boorstin's comment that "ancient English prejudice against lawyers secured new strength in America ... [D]istrust of lawyers became an institution." Distrust of lawyers arose from various sources. The Puritan leaders of Massachusetts Bay had an image of the ideal state. Revolutionary or Utopian regimes tend to be hostile to lawyers, at least at first. Lawyers of the old regime have to be controlled or removed; a new, revolutionary commonwealth must start with new law and new habits. Some colonists, oppressed in England, carried with them a strong dislike for all servants of government. Merchants and planters wished to run their affairs, without intermediaries. The theocratic colonies believed in a certain kind of social order, closely directed from the top. The legal profession, with its special privileges and principles, its private, esoteric language, seemed an obstacle to efficient or godly government. The Quakers of the Middle Atlantic were opposed to the adversary system in principle. They wanted harmony and peace. Their ideal was the "Common Peacemaker," and simple, nontechnical justice. They looked on lawyers as sharp, contentious—and unnecessary—people. For all these reasons, the lawyer was unloved in the 17th century.

In the 18th century, too, there was sentiment against lawyers. The lower classes came to identify lawyers with the upper class. Governors and their royal parties, on the other hand, were not sure of the loyalty of lawyers, and were sometimes afraid of their influence and power. In 1765, Cadwallader Colden, lieutenant governor of New York, told the Board of Trade in England that the "Gentlemen of the Law" had grown overmighty. They ranked just below the large landowners, and just above the merchants in society. Lawyers and judges, said Colden, had such power that "every Man is afraid of offending them"; their "domination" was "carried on by the same wicked artifices that the Domination of Priests formerly was in the times of ignorance." Lay judges, too, may have resented the lawyers' threats to their competence and prestige. And as law became more "rational" and "professional," it became more confusing and remote to merchants and businessmen.

How strong the resentment against lawyers was, how deep it went, is hard to say. The evidence is partly literary; pamphlets and speeches are notoriously unreliable as measures of actual feeling among a diverse population. Some hatred was surely there; there is hard evidence of riots and disorders against lawyers and judges. Lawyers, like shopkeepers, moneylenders, and lower bureaucrats, are social middlemen; they are lightning rods that draw rage during storms in the polity. In 18th-century New Jersey, the "table of the Assembly groaned beneath the weight of petitions . . . invoking vengeance on the heads of the attorneys." The "Regulators," in late colonial North Carolina—a kind of vigilante group—rose up to smash corrupt and incompetent government. Lawyers were in the camp of the enemy. They perverted justice; they were "cursed hungry Caterpillars," whose fees "eat out the very Bowels of our Common-wealth." In Monmouth and Essex counties (New Jersey), in 1769 and 1770, mobs rioted against the lawyers.

But the lawyers were, in the end, a necessary evil. In the end, no colony could even try to make do without lawyers. In the very beginning, to be sure, there were makeshift alternatives. Lay judges knew enough English law to run their local courts; and a few practical books of English law circulated in the colonies. . . .

As soon as a settled society posed problems for which lawyers had an answer or at least a skill, lawyers began to thrive, despite the hostility. Courts were in session; merchants were drawn into litigation; land documents had to be written, and the more skill the better. Men trained in law who came from England found a market for their services; so did laymen with a smattering of law; there were semiprofessionals, too, with experience for sale. In the late 17th century, justices of the peace, sheriffs, and clerks, acted as attorneys in New Jersey. In the literature, there are constant complaints against unauthorized lawyers, pettifoggers, shysters, and lowlifes—unprincipled men stirring up unprincipled litigation. These complaints, like the outcry against ambulance chasers more than a century later, sometimes had a curiously inconsistent quality. Lawyers were criticized both for incompetence and for wrongful competence. And an unauthorized or underground bar has been common in many societies; it crops up when the need for legal services outstrips the supply of legitimate lawyers. At any rate, there was a competent, professional bar, dominated by brilliant and successful lawyers ... in all major communities by 1750, despite all bias and opposition.

No law schools in the colonies trained these men. Particularly in the South, where there were no colleges, some young men went to England for training, and attended the Inns of Court, in London. The Inns were not law schools as such; they had "ceased to perform educational functions of a serious nature," and were little more than living and eating clubs. Theoretically, a man could become a counselor-at-law in England without reading "a single page of any law book." But the Inns were part of English legal culture; Americans could absorb the atmosphere of English law there; they read law on their own, and observed English practice.

The road to the bar, for all lawyers, was through some form of clerkship or apprenticeship. The aspiring lawyer usually entered into a contract with an established lawyer. The student paid a fee; in exchange, the lawyer promised to train him in the law; sometimes, too, the lawyer would provide food and lodging. Apprenticeship was a control device as well as a way of learning the trade. It kept the bar small; and older lawyers were in firm command. How much the apprentice learned depended greatly on his master.... [The first law schools] grew out of law offices which became so good at teaching that they gave up practice entirely....

THE NIMBLE PROFESSION

In 1850 there were, according to one estimate, 21,979 lawyers in the country. As we have seen, the number of lawyers grew very rapidly after the Revolution. In the last half of the century, there was even greater increase. The transformation of the American economy after the Civil War profoundly affected the demand for lawyers, and hence the supply. By 1880, there were perhaps 60,000 lawyers; by 1900, about 114,000.

The functions of the profession changed along with its numbers. The New York Code of Civil Procedure, of 1848, symbolized one kind of change.... The codes in turn dethroned the ancient pleading arts. The slow estrangement of the lawyer from his old and natural haunt, the court, was an outstanding fact of the practice in the second half of the century. Most lawyers still went to court; but the Wall Street lawyer, who perhaps never spoke to a judge except socially, made more money and had more prestige than any courtroom lawyer could.

The change of function reflected changes in the law itself. Life and the economy were more complicated; there was more, then, to be done, in the business world especially; and the lawyers proved able to do it. There was nothing inevitable in the process. It did not happen, for example, in Japan. The legal profession might have become smaller and narrower, restricted like the English barrister, or the brain surgeon, to a few rare, complex, and lucrative tasks. Automation and technological change posed dangers to lawyers, just as they posed dangers to other occupations. Social invention constantly threatened to displace them. It was adapt or die. For example, lawyers in the first half of the century had a good thing going in title searches and related work. After the Civil War, title companies and trust companies proved to be efficient competitors. By 1900, well-organized, efficient companies nibbled away at other staples of the practice, too: debt collection and estate work, for example.

Nevertheless the lawyers prospered. The truth was that the profession was exceedingly nimble at finding new kinds of work and new ways to do it. Its nimbleness was no doubt due to the character of the bar: open-ended, unrestricted, uninhibited, attractive to sharp, ambitious men. In so amorphous a profession, lawyers drifted in and out; many went into business or politics because they could not earn a living at their trade. Others reached out for new sorts of practice. At any rate, the profession did not shrink to (or rise to) the status of a small, exclusive elite. Even in 1860, the profession was bigger, wider, more diverse than it had been in years gone by. In 1800, lawyers in Philadelphia came "predominantly from families of wealth, status, and importance." In 1860, a much higher percentage came from the middle class—sons of shopkeepers, clerks, small businessmen. In Massachusetts, too, in the period 1870–1900, there was an increase in the percentage of lawyers who were recruited from business and white-collar backgrounds, rather than professional or elite backgrounds, compared to the prewar period.

The external relations of the bar were always vitally important. After 1870, there was another line of defense against competition: the lawyers' unions (never called by that name), which fought vigorously to protect the boundaries of the calling. The organized profession raised (or tried to raise) its "standards"; tried to limit entry into the field, and (above all) tried to resist conversion of the profession into a "mere" business or trade. In fact, lawyers did not incorporate and did not become fully bureaucratized. The bar was able to prevent the corporate practice of law. Large private law firms were able to compete with captive legal departments and house counsel staffs of large corporations. For the time being, at least, the private lawyer kept his independent status as a middle-class craftsman and entrepreneur. The lawyer's role in American life had never been too clearly defined. The practice of law was what lawyers did. This was a truth as well as a tautology. The upper echelons of the profession never quite succeeded in closing the doors against newcomers and outsiders. They dreamt of a close-knit, guildlike bar. They longed for the honor and security of the barrister. But because it was easy to pass in and out of the profession, their dream could never be fulfilled.

Alexis De Tocqueville, Democracy in America

Vol. I, 283–90 (H. Reeve trans., P. Bradley ed., F. Bowen rev., 1973) (1st ed. 1835).

In visiting the Americans and studying their laws, we perceive that the authority they have entrusted to members of the legal profession, and the influence that these individuals exercise in the government, are the most powerful existing security against the excesses of democracy. This effect seems to me to result from a general cause, which it is useful to investigate, as it may be reproduced elsewhere. . . .

Men who have made a special study of the laws derive from this occupation certain habits of order, a taste for formalities, and a kind of instinctive regard for the regular connection of ideas, which naturally render them very hostile to the revolutionary spirit and the unreflecting passions of the multitude. . . .

Some of the tastes and the habits of the aristocracy may consequently be discovered in the characters of lawyers. They participate in the same instinctive love of order and formalities; and they entertain the same repugnance to the actions of the multitude, and the same secret contempt of the government of the people. I do not mean to say that the natural propensities of lawyers are sufficiently strong to sway them irresistibly; for they, like most other men, are governed by their private interests, and especially by the interests of the moment.

In a state of society in which the members of the legal profession cannot hold that rank in the political world which they enjoy in private life, we may rest assured that they will be the foremost agents of revolution. . . .

I am in like manner inclined to believe that a monarch will always be able to convert legal practitioners into the most serviceable instruments of his authority. There is a far greater affinity between this class of persons and the executive power than there is between them and the people, though they have often aided to overturn the former; just as there is a greater natural affinity between the nobles and the monarch than between the nobles and the people, although the higher orders of society have often, in concert with the lower classes, resisted the prerogative of the crown.

Lawyers are attached to public order beyond every other consideration, and the best security of public order is authority. It must not be forgotten, also, that if they prize freedom much, they generally value legality still more: they are less afraid of tyranny than of arbitrary power; and, provided the legislature undertakes of itself to deprive men of their independence, they are not dissatisfied. . . .

The government of democracy is favorable to the political power of lawyers; for when the wealthy, the noble, and the prince are excluded from the government, the lawyers take possession of it, in their own right, as it were, since they are the only men of information and sagacity, beyond the sphere of the people, who can be the object of the popular choice. If, then, they are led by their tastes towards the aristocracy and the prince, they are brought in contact with the people by their interests. They like the government of democracy without participating in its propensities and without imitating its weaknesses; whence they derive a two-fold authority from it and over it. The people in democratic states do not mistrust the members of the legal profession, because it is known that they are interested to serve the popular cause; and the people listen to them without irritation, because they do not attribute to them any sinister designs. The lawyers do not, indeed, wish to overthrow the institutions of democracy, but they constantly endeavor to turn it away from its real direction by means that are foreign to its nature. Lawyers belong to the people by birth and interest, and to the aristocracy by habit and taste; they may be looked upon as the connecting link between the two great classes of society.

The profession of the law is the only aristocratic element that can be amalgamated without violence with the natural elements of democracy and be advantageously and permanently combined with them. I am not ignorant of the defects inherent in the character of this body of men; but without this admixture of lawyer-like sobriety with the democratic principle, I question whether democratic institutions could long be maintained; and I cannot believe that a republic could hope to exist at the present time if the influence of lawyers in public business did not increase in proportion to the power of the people.

This aristocratic character, which I hold to be common to the legal profession, is much more distinctly marked in the United States and in England than in any other country. This proceeds not only from the legal studies of the English and American lawyers, but from the nature of the law and the position which these interpreters of it occupy in the two countries. The English and the Americans have retained the law of precedents; that is to say, they continue to found their legal opinions and the decisions of their courts upon the opinions and decisions of their predecessors. In the mind of an English or American lawyer a taste and a reverence for what is old is almost always united with a love of regular and lawful proceedings. . . .

In America there are no nobles or literary men, and the people are apt to mistrust the wealthy; lawyers consequently form the highest political class and the most cultivated portion of society. They have therefore nothing to gain by innovation, which adds a conservative interest to their natural taste for public order. If I were asked where I place the American aristocracy, I should reply without hesitation that it is not among the rich, who are united by no common tie, but that it occupies the judicial bench and the bar.

The more we reflect upon all that occurs in the United States, the more we shall be persuaded that the lawyers, as a body, form the most powerful, if not the only, counterpoise to the democratic element. In that country we easily perceive how the legal profession is qualified by its attributes, and even by its faults, to neutralize the vices inherent in popular government. When the American people are intoxicated by passion or carried away by the impetuosity of their ideas, they are checked and stopped by the almost invisible influence of their legal counselors. These secretly oppose their aristocratic propensities to the nation's democratic instincts, their superstitious attachment to what is old to its love of novelty, their narrow views to its immense designs, and their habitual procrastination to its ardent impatience. . . .

The influence of legal habits extends beyond the precise limits I have pointed out. Scarcely any political question arises in the United States that is not resolved, sooner or later, into a judicial question. Hence all parties are obliged to borrow, in their daily controversies, the ideas, and even the language, peculiar to judicial proceedings. As most public men are or have been legal practitioners, they introduce the customs and technicalities of their profession into the management of public affairs. The jury extends this habit to all classes. The language of the law thus becomes, in some measure, a vulgar tongue; the spirit of the law, which is produced in the schools and courts of justice, gradually penetrates beyond their walls into the bosom of society, where it descends to the lowest classes, so that at last the whole people contract the habits and the tastes of the judicial magistrate. The lawyers of the United States form a party which is but little feared and scarcely perceived, which has no badge peculiar to itself, which adapts itself with great flexibility to the exigencies of the time and accommodates itself without resistance to all the movements of the social body. But this party extends over the whole community and penetrates into all the classes which compose it; it acts upon the country imperceptibly, but finally fashions it to suit its own purposes.

NOTES AND QUESTIONS

1. Legal historian Robert Gordon summarizes the American bar's more recent evolution as follows.

> The period from 1870 to 1930 sees the rise of the corporate law firm, plaintiff's personal-injury practice and public-interest lawyering. The second period, 1930–1970 [witnesses] the new specialities emerging from the statutory and administrative innovations of the New Deal and the postwar political-economic order; and from the "rights revolution" of the 1960s and 1970s. [The third period, from 1970 to 2000, reflects major shifts in the size, composition, and structure of the bar]. In these years, the profession tripled in size and admitted women and minorities in significant numbers. Corporate law firms multiplied, grew to enormous size, and began to claim the largest share of total legal business. Personal injury practice entered the age of the mass-tort class action. Public interest "cause" lawyers added new constituencies and began to play a regular role in governance. . . . The ideal of a single unified profession receded as social distance and income differentials widened between its upper and lower tiers.[4]

Compare Friedman's and de Tocqueville's accounts of the early American legal profession with the contemporary bar described by Gordon and by the materials excerpted in Chapter I and Part B below. What have been the most significant changes in the practice of law during the last century?

4. Robert W. Gordon, "The American Legal Profession, 1870–2000," in *The Cambridge History of Law in America* (Christo- pher Tomlins & Michael Grossberg, eds., 2008).

What social, economic, and technological forces appear most significant in accounting for these changes?

2.   To what extent is the organized bar's experience distinctive? As historian Burton Bledstein notes in *The Culture of Professions,* the mid-nineteenth century witnessed the rise of various professions, all with their own "intellectual pretensions and social aspirations," and their desire for spheres of "cultural authority and autonomy." However, some occupational groups were more successful than others in that effort. Indeed, according to de Tocqueville's analysis, lawyers were at the pinnacle of the social pecking order. Is that view reconcilable with Friedman's description of public attitudes toward lawyers? How does the status of the contemporary bar compare with that of the nineteenth-century legal profession?

3.   Historical research suggests that not all attorneys experienced being part of a natural aristocracy in the sense de Tocqueville implied. Accounts by frontier lawyers during the mid-nineteenth century indicate that many practitioners were barely able to piece together a livelihood, and that much of their difficulty stemmed from the absence of public respect. Young attorneys often reported considerable difficulty in receiving payment for services they provided. As one struggling Texan wrote home to relatives, "I wish the fees came in half as fast as the cases."[5]

Similarly, Joseph Baldwin, in his wry caricature, *The Flush Times of Alabama and Mississippi* 37–38 (1957), offered the following description of his legal community:

> thirty or forty young men armed with a plentiful stock of brass ... standing ready to supply any distressed citizen who wanted law, with their wares counterfeiting the article. I must confess it looked to me something like a swindle.... There was one consolation: the clients were generally as sham as the counsellors. For the most part, they were either broke or in a rapid decline. They usually paid us the compliment of retaining us, but they usually retained the fee too, a double retainer we did not much fancy. However, we got as much as we were entitled to and something over.... The most that we made was experience. We learned before long, how every possible sort of case could be successfully lost; there was no way of getting out of court that we had not tested.... The way was infested and ambushed, with all imaginable points of practice, quirks and quibbles, that had strayed off from the litigation of every sort of foreign judicature,—that had been successfully tried in, or been driven out of, regularly organized forums, besides a smart sprinkling of indigenous growth. Nothing was settled. Chaos had come again, or rather, had never gone away.

Does this portrait cast doubt on the profession's current lament about the recent decline of law from a profession to a business?

---

5.   Maxwell Bloomfield, "The Texas Bar in the Nineteenth Century," 32 *Vand.L.Rev.* 261, 269–71 (1979).

Experts dispute the extent to which lawyers in the nineteenth and early twentieth century had a more civic-minded conception of their professional role than contemporary practitioners. Some scholars argue that the American bar once embraced a more ethically robust view of the lawyer as statesman.[6] Other experts believe that moral activism by nineteenth century attorneys is vastly overstated, and that the notion of ethically neutral, client-centered advocacy was widely accepted then as now.[7] What turns on this dispute? How does the bar's history inform contemporary debates?

NOTES: PATTERNS OF EXCLUSION: SEX, RACE, ETHNICITY, AND RELIGION

For much of its history, the Anglo–American bar was unreceptive to women and minorities. In eighteenth and early nineteenth-century England, efforts to establish law as a "gentlemen's" profession led to restrictive admission practices. For a substantial period, barristers excluded certain presumptively unfit groups, including Catholics, tradesmen, journalists, and women. Wealth was also a significant filtering device; the cost of education and establishing a practice limited access to those of considerable means. Although solicitors were more democratic in their entrance practices, lengthy apprenticeship requirements and class-based selection networks discouraged membership from socially and economically disadvantaged groups.

In America, until the late nineteenth century, formal admission requirements were fairly lax, but informal screening also occurred through apprenticeship practices and clients' unwillingness to retain members of certain subordinate groups. Chapter XV explores the history of the bar's general efforts to upgrade admission requirements. What is of principal relevance here is the way that legal doctrine, social practices, and economic barriers influenced the composition of the profession.

Discrimination on the Basis of Sex

During much of the eighteenth and nineteenth centuries, gender defined the geography of the workplace, and woman's primary place was in domestic rather than professional spheres. There were, however, exceptions to this general pattern. Particularly in the Colonial era, when labor was scarce and relatively few occupations required formal licenses, some white women managed to participate in legal transactions either by acting as their husband's representative or successor, or by obtaining special authorization to proceed as independent agents. Few women, however, managed to

6. Anthony T. Kronman, *The Lost Lawyer: Failing Ideals of the Legal Profession* 1, 11–23, 165–314 (1993); Robert W. Gordon "Legal Thought and Legal Practice in the Age of American Enterprise: 1870–1920," in *Professions and Professional Ideologies in America* 70 (Gerald L. Geison ed. 1983); Russell Pearce, "Lawyers as America's Governing Class: The Formation and Dissolution of the Original Understanding of the American Lawyer's Role," 8 *U. Chi. L. Sch. Roundtable* 381 (2001).

7. Norman Spaulding, "The Myth of Civic Republicanism: Interrogating the Ideology of Antebellum Legal Ethics," 71 *Ford. L. Rev.* 1397 (2003).

attain positions of significant public power or recognition, and those who did generally acquired an anomalous status. The first American female attorney was an "honorary male" in a literal as well as figurative sense; she was frequently addressed in person and in seventeenth-century court records as Gentleman Margaret Brent.[8]

During the late eighteenth century, the gradual formalization of bar admission criteria made it increasingly difficult for women to act as lawyers. And, of course, African–American women under slavery had no capacity to assert legal rights. However, after the Civil War, the expansion of women's educational opportunities and political activism contributed to a growing stream of female applicants to the bar. In 1867, Iowa became the first state to license a woman attorney, and the following decades witnessed a gradual increase in female candidates from largely white middle and upper middle class backgrounds.

Women's initial reception in most jurisdictions was less than enthusiastic. In a celebrated 1873 decision denying Myra Bradwell admission to the Illinois bar, three concurring Supreme Court Justices invested the sexes' "separate spheres" with both spiritual and constitutional significance:

> The family organization, which is founded in the divine ordinance, as well as in the nature of things, indicates the domestic sphere as that which properly belongs to the domain and functions of womanhood. The harmony, not to say identity, of interests and views which belong[s], or should belong, to the family institution is repugnant to the idea of a woman adopting a distinct and independent career from that of her husband.[9]

Although the precise method of divine communication was never elaborated, it remained accessible to other decision makers as well. Judges in Wisconsin, Pennsylvania, and the District of Columbia similarly concluded that women's nature was to nurture, and that any professional pursuits constituted a departure from the natural order and "when voluntary, treason against it."[10] As one late nineteenth-century judge explained, the "peculiar qualities of womanhood, its gentle graces, its quick sensibility, [and] its tender susceptibility" were surely not qualifications for "forensic strife."[11]

Many female applicants, however, remained unconvinced. By the turn of the century, various political, legal, and social forces had coalesced to secure women's rights to admission in about half the states, and by 1920, formal barriers were largely removed. Informal obstacles, however, remained. "Bring on as many women lawyers as you choose," predicted one

---

8. Deborah L. Rhode, *Justice and Gender: Sex Discrimination and the Law* 20–21 (1989); Deborah L. Rhode, "Perspectives on Professional Women," 40 *Stan.L.Rev.* 1163 (1988); Karen Morello, *The Invisible Bar: The Woman Lawyer in America 1638 to the Present* (1986).

9. Bradwell v. State, 83 U.S. 130, 141 (1872).

10. In the Matter of Goodell, 39 Wis. 232, 245 (1875); Rhode, *Justice and Gender*, *supra* note 8, at 21–23.

11. In the Matter of Goodell, 39 Wis. 232, 245 (1875). *See also* In re Lockwood, 9 Ct.Cl. 346, 348, 355 (1873).

District of Columbia judge, "I do not believe they will be a success."[12] Clarence Darrow agreed. As he explained in an early twentieth century address to a group of Chicago women attorneys: "You can't be shining lights at the bar because you are too kind. You can never be corporation lawyers because you are not cold-blooded. You have not a high grade of intellect." Although conceding that female practitioners might be acceptable as counsel for divorce and nonpaying criminal cases, he doubted that women would "ever make a living" in the law.[13]

Such attitudes became self-fulfilling prophesies. Female professionals who rejected their maternal mission were typically treated as social deviants, but women who restricted work to raise families were denounced for squandering educational opportunities that should be reserved for full-time male breadwinners. Many bar associations and law schools denied female applicants or limited their admission; Harvard remained all-male until 1950 and not until 1972 did all accredited law schools eliminate explicit sex-based restrictions.[14] Substantial disparities also prevailed in hiring, salaries, and promotion. Private firms frequently declined to employ women, and almost no rationalization was too trivial. As one Wall Street partner explained to a female applicant, much as his firm would like to hire a woman, the logistical difficulties were simply too great: she couldn't use the attorney's bathroom; she couldn't be relegated to the secretaries' bathroom; and the firm couldn't afford to build another facility.[15] In 1960, women constituted less than 3% of the American bar, and were largely excluded from fields of practice with the greatest status, influence, and financial rewards.[16]

Major changes came with the rise of the contemporary women's movement, and the broader social, economic, and demographic changes that it reflected. By 1983, women constituted over a third of new entrants to the profession, and by the turn of the century, about half.[17]

Discrimination on the Basis of Race, Religion, and Ethnicity

Prejudice against racial, ethnic, and religious minorities was also pervasive, as is clear from Jerold Auerbach's account in Chapter III and the materials on admission and legal education in Chapters XV and XVII. In the late nineteenth and early twentieth centuries, many employers, edu-

---

12. Belva Lockwood, "My Efforts to Become a Lawyer," in *Women and the American Economy: A Documentary History*, 1675–1929, 297–301 (W. Elliot Brownlee & Mary M. Brownlee eds. 1976).

13. Clarence Darrow, quoted in Michael Grossberg, "Institutionalizing Masculinity: The Law as a Masculine Profession," in *Meanings for Manhood: Constructions of Masculinity in Victorian America* 133, 149 (Mark Carnes and Clyde Griffen eds. 1990).

14. Donna Fossum, "Women in the Legal Profession: A Progress Report," 67 *Women's L.J.* 1 (1981).

15. Cynthia Epstein, *Women in Law* 85 (1981).

16. *Id.*, at 61, 66–67; James White, "Women in the Law," 65 *Mich.L.Rev.* 1051 (1967); Rosabeth Kanter, "Reflections on Women and the Legal Profession: A Sociological Perspective," 1 *Harv. Women's L.J.* 1 (1978); Rhode, Perspectives on Professional Women, *supra* note 8.

17. Gordon, *supra*, note 4.

cators, and bar associations openly discriminated against immigrants from Eastern Europe and Asia, as well as Jews from all ethnic backgrounds.[18] A 1939 report found that Jewish lawyers accounted for half the practitioners in New York city, but few were working in corporate firms; the exceptions were mainly in firms with predominantly Jewish clients.[19]

Racial discrimination was more pervasive and persistent. Although the first black lawyer was admitted to the bar in 1844 (Macon Allen, Maine), few blacks had any realistic possibility of membership until after the Civil War. The family of the first black to graduate from a law school (George Ruffin, Harvard, 1869) moved from Virginia, where it had been a crime to teach any black to read.[20] Discriminatory admission policies, inadequate educational backgrounds, and lack of financial resources restricted access to law school, and the small number of lawyers of color restricted opportunities for apprenticeships. At the turn of the twentieth century, there were only about 730 black lawyers in the entire country.[21] Once admitted to the bar, minority lawyers faced continued resistance from potential employers and clients. Few firms were willing to hire lawyers of color, and blacks who could afford the services of an attorney often hired whites, who were assumed to function more effectively in a racist legal system.

Barriers to women of color were especially great. Access to higher educational and professional programs was extremely limited, and the few institutions that did not discriminate on the basis of race often did so on the basis of sex. Charlotte Ray, one of the first black women to graduate from law school (Howard, 1873), gained admittance by using her initials rather than first name on application papers. After an unsuccessful struggle to obtain legal work, she returned to her earlier career of teaching in public schools. Between 1875 and 1925, no more than 25 black women were reportedly practicing law. By 1940, the number had only doubled.[22]

In 1890, when the census first began classifying lawyers by race, blacks constituted under .5% of the profession; in 1960 they were slightly over 1%. Not until the late 1940's was an African–American appointed to the federal bench or to the full-time faculty of a non-minority law school.[23] Although the Supreme Court held racially segregated legal education unconstitutional in 1950, informal policies of racial discrimination persisted at some accredited law schools. It took the Civil Rights movement of the 1960s to bring major changes. Between 1969 and 1985, the number of black attorneys roughly tripled, increasing from about 2000 to 6000.[24]

---

18. Jerold Auerbach, *Unequal Justice: Lawyers and Social Change in Modern America* (1976).

19. Gordon, *supra* note 4.

20. Geraldine Segal, *Blacks in the Law* 240 (1983).

21. Gordon, *supra* note 4.

22. *Id.*, at 1, 4, 215.

23. Edward Littlejohn & Leonard Rubinowitz, "Black Enrollment in Law Schools: Forward to the Past," 12 *Thurgood Marshall L.Rev.* 415 (1987); Kellis Parkes & Betty Stebeman, "Legal Education for Blacks," 407 *Annals of the American Academy of Political Social Science* 144 (1973). *See* Chapter XVII *infra.*

24. Gordon, *supra* note 4.

Other minority groups have also been subject to discrimination. Class as well as racial and ethnic barriers has had a major impact. Poor educational preparation and the absence of financial assistance placed law school out of reach for the vast majority of minorities. As late as 1968, only about 3% of the nation's law students were black, Hispanic, or Native American compared with about 20% today.[25]

B.   DEMOGRAPHIC PROFILES

American Bar Association, Lawyer Demographics (2007)

NUMBER OF LICENSED LAWYERS—2006

1,116,967

Source: ABA Market Research Department, 6/2006

GENDER

	2000
Male	73%
Female	27%

Source: *The Lawyer Statistical Report*, American Bar Foundation, 2004 edition

AGE

	2000
29 yrs. or less	7%
30–34	12%
35–39	14%
40–44	15%
45–54	28%
55–64	13%
65 +	12%
Median age	45

Source: *The Lawyer Statistical Report*, American Bar Foundation, 2004 edition

RACE/ETHNICITY

	2000*
White, not Hispanic	88.8%
Black, not Hispanic	4.2%
Hispanic	3.4%
Asian Pacific, American, not Hispanic	2.2%

25. American Bar Association Task Force on Minorities in the Legal Profession, *Report with Recommendations* (Jan. 1986), excerpted in Chapter XVII.

American Indian, not Hispanic	0.2%
Native Hawaiian or Pacific Islander, not Hispanic	.04%
2 + races	1.2%

* Source: 2000 U.S. Census, Bureau of the Census
NOTE: U.S. Census considers Hispanic an ethnicity, not a race. Persons of Hispanic origin can be of any race.

LAW STUDENTS

Academic Year	**2003–2004**
Total JD enrollment	**137,676**
Gender	
Male	51%
Female	49%
Minority enrollment	20.6%

Source: ABA Section of Legal Education & Admissions to the Bar
http://www.abanet.org/legaled/statistics/stats.html

PRACTICE SETTING

% of lawyers in	**2000**
Private Practice	74%
Government	8%
Private Industry	8%
Retired/Inactive	5%
Judiciary	3%
Education	1%
Legal Aid/Public Defender	1%
Private Association	1%

Source: *The Lawyer–Statistical Report*, American Bar Foundation, 2004 edition

PRIVATE PRACTITIONERS

% of private practitioners ...	**2000**
Solo	48%
2–5 lawyers	15%
6–10 lawyers	7%
11–20 lawyers	6%
21–50 lawyers	6%
51–100 lawyers	4%
101+ lawyers	14%

Source: *The Lawyer–Statistical Report*, American Bar Foundation, 2004 edition

LAW FIRM SIZE

% of law firms with ...	2000
2–5 lawyers	76%
6–10 lawyers	13%
11–20 lawyers	6%
21–50 lawyers	3%
51–100 lawyers	1%
101+ lawyers	1%
Total # firms	47,563

Source: *The Lawyer–Statistical Report*, American Bar Foundation, 2004 edition
Note: Numbers may not add to 100 due to rounding. Compiled by the ABA Market Research Department.
© 2006 American Bar Association

NOTES

Over the last century, the American bar has become increasingly specialized, and the work lives of lawyers in various fields are often quite different. In a landmark study of the Chicago bar, first published in 1980 and updated in 1998, sociologists John Heinz and Edward Laumann portrayed a profession sharply divided into two hemispheres. Most lawyers represented either individuals and small businesses or large organizations such as corporations, unions, and the government. Few ever "crossed the equator" and there were marked distinctions in their practices and backgrounds, including the kind of law schools they attended, their professional development, and their social networks and political values. Although there were distinctions within the groups,

> this fundamental difference in the nature of the client served appears to be the principal factor that structures the social differentiation of the profession.... Fields that serve corporate, wealthier, more "establishment" clients are accorded more deference within the profession than are those that serve individual, poorer clients. This suggests the thesis that prestige within law is acquired by association, that it is "reflected glory" derived from the power possessed by the lawyers' clients....[26]

Heinz and Laumann also noted that the traditional view of the bar as a single, unified profession no longer fits the facts.

> First of all, lawyers, of course, are not merely lawyers. They are advisors to businessmen and are businessmen themselves; they are politicians, lobbyists, and judges or potential judges; they are real estate and insurance salesmen, claims adjustors, facilitators of zoning variances, scholars, and rich lie-abouts. But even those roles that are usually thought of as lawyers' work, more narrowly defined, display considerable variety.... [The lawyer who commutes to Brussels or Tokyo to negotiate international franchise agreements] will have little in common with the lawyer who haunts the corridors of the criminal courts hoping that a bailiff will, in return for a consideration, commend his services to some poor wretch charged with a barroom assault.

26. John P. Heinz and Edward O. Laumann, *Chicago Lawyers: The Social Structure of the Bar* 319 (1982).

Both of those private practitioners will differ from the government-employed lawyers who prosecute criminal cases or who practice public international law in the employ of the State Department, as the two sorts of government-employed lawyers differ from one another.[27]

In the 1998 update of their study, Heinz and Laumann found that some distinctions between the two hemispheres had grown less pronounced. In general, lawyers were more highly specialized, and their fields were less sharply separated by the corporate and individual representation boundary. Attorneys practicing in the two sectors also had fewer differences in personal characteristics than in earlier decades because of the broader diversity recruitment efforts by firms. However, some important distinctions between the hemispheres persisted, and the income gap between corporate and non-corporate practitioners had widened. Demand for services had grown more rapidly in the business sector and by the late 1990s, about 60% of lawyers' time was devoted to corporate clients compared with half in the 1970s. A third of attorneys worked in only one field, up from a quarter two decades earlier, and it appeared doubtful that the profession's current organizational structures "provided enough interchange to produce a bar that functioned as a community of common pursuit."[28]

A pathbreaking study of new lawyers by the American Bar Foundation and the National Association of Law Placement also provides a window into how the bar is evolving, The study, *After the JD*, is following 5000 lawyers after their law school graduation and the study's first report describes their careers two to three years into practice.[29] The new lawyers are significantly more diverse than their predecessors: 46% are women, up from 5% in 1970, and 17% are nonwhite, compared to 5% in 1970. In terms of sexual orientation, 2.5% report being gay, lesbian, bisexual or transgendered, a figure in line with reports by college graduates (3.5%). In terms of religious affiliation, 30% are Protestant, 27% Roman Catholic, 7% Jewish, and 23% report no religious affiliation. Most come from relatively privileged backgrounds. About two thirds had fathers who graduated from college, and half had college-graduate mothers, a figure three times the national average.

Almost all surveyed lawyers, 94%, work full time, 90% in legal practice. Most are in private practice: two thirds of women and three quarters of men work for firms. Over a quarter are in small firms (2–20 lawyers), a fifth are in midsized firms (21 to 100 lawyers) and close to another fifth are in firms over 100 lawyers. Government employs 16%, business, 9% and legal services, public defenders, and public interest organizations, 3%.

---

27. *Id.*

28. John P. Heinz, Edward O. Laumann, Robert L. Nelson, Ethan Michelson, "The Changing Character of Lawyers' Work: Chicago in 1975 and 1995," 32 *Law & Soc. Rev.* 751 (1998). For the full study, see John P. Heinz, Robert L. Nelson, Rebecca L. Sandefur, & Edward O. Laumann, *Urban Lawyers* (2005).

29. Ronit Dinovitzer et al., NALP Foundation and American Bar Foundation, *After the JD: First Results of a National Study of Legal Careers* (2004), available at http://abfn.org/ajd.pdf.

Another 5% are in solo practice and 2% are in nonprofit or educational settings. The median work week is 50 hours compared with 40 for fulltime American workers. However, a fifth (most in large firms) report working 60 hours a week or more. More than two thirds report that at least half of their work is in a single substantive field.

There are wide income gaps within this group. About 35% of the lawyers have salaries over $110,000, while 25% have salaries under $50,000. About a third have changed jobs once, and almost a fifth, twice or more during their first three years in practice.

QUESTIONS

1. How does the structure of legal practice affect legal ethics? Will the increasing diversity and specialization of the bar work against consensus on issues such as self-regulation, competition, and the delivery of legal service? To what extent do lawyers feel a sense of common professional identity and interests? Does it still make sense to talk of *the* legal profession?

2. What are the causes and consequences of the trend toward larger law firms and greater specialization?

C. The Conditions of Practice

Lawyers' different practice settings all present distinctive rewards and difficulties. Solo practice offers the greatest opportunities for control, flexibility, independence, and direct client contact. Some solo practitioners work out of home offices, which can reduce expenses and work/family conflicts. The price for these advantages is generally paid in greater isolation, lower status and income, and more economic uncertainty and instability than other types of private practice. The absence of mentors and back up support from colleagues and staff pose additional problems. Some attorneys also lack the time and contacts for adequate business development. However, many solo practitioners have found ways to mitigate these difficulties through sharing office space, advice, and client referrals with other attorneys or professional service providers.[30]

Partnerships in small firms present many of the same obstacles and opportunities as solo practice. Attorneys in these firms generally have substantial control and flexibility in schedules but equally substantial economic pressures and insecurities. Some small firms have attempted to obtain greater economies of scale and managerial efficiencies through national franchise arrangements, but at the cost of losing some of their

---

30. See Carol Seron, *The Business of Practicing Law: The Work Lives of Solo and Small Firm Attorneys* (1996); Leslie C. Levin, "The Ethical World of Solo and Small Firm Practitioners," 41 *Houston L. Rev.* 309 (2004); Jay Eisman, "The Ups and Downs of Practicing Alone," *N.Y. L. J.* November 12, 1999, at 24; Boston Bar Association Task Force on Professional Fulfillment, *Expectations, Realities, and Recommendations for Change* 12 (1997).

independence and flexibility.[31] Other attorneys from small firms, together with many in solo practice, have obtained support from bar association networks and consortia sponsored by law schools.[32]

Practice in larger firms typically offers a different range of advantages, such as relatively high status and income, significant intellectual challenges, and opportunities to work in cutting edge and high-stakes matters. But with these practice settings also come long hours and competitive working environments. The size and geographic dispersion of large firms makes it hard to sustain collegiality, cooperation, and firm wide norms. And the increasing competitiveness of the market has reinforced a profit orientation that threatens other values.[33] For those at the bottom of the hierarchy, much of the work can be tedious, with little chance for client contact, trial experience, or development of professional skills. Many of these junior attorneys are in the kind of practice settings that are most likely to lead to depression, stress, and poor physical health: i.e., environments that impose high job demands but offer little control over the terms of work.[34] It is not surprising to researchers on quality of life that associates at large firms report the highest levels of dissatisfaction within the legal profession, despite their generous pay.[35]

For lawyers dissatisfied with law firms, in-house counsel positions have become an increasingly attractive option. Opportunities for such positions have expanded substantially over the last two decades, and their status and intellectual challenge have also grown. Since the 1980s, in-house counsel have assumed greater responsibility for providing corporate clients with an array of basic legal services, as well as selecting and monitoring outside attorneys, implementing legal compliance programs, and preventing legal difficulties. Departments range in size from one to hundreds of attorneys and perform a wide variety of tasks that reflect the organization's nature and scope. In-house counsel positions are attractive to many lawyers because they typically offer somewhat more regular hours and greater job security than law firms, along with an escape from the up-or-out promotion structures and client development obligations.[36] In recent national surveys,

31. Levin, *supra* note 30; Jerry Van Hoy, *Franchise Law Firms and the Transformation of Personal Legal Services* (1997).

32. The resources provided have included mentoring, assistance with information technology and client development, access to law libraries, training in office management and substantive law areas, case referrals, anda forum to share advice. Deborah Howard, "The Law School Consortium Project: Law Schools Supporting Graduates to Increase Access to Justice for Low and Moderate–Income Individuals and Communities," 29 *Fordham Urban L. J.* 1245, 1246–47 n.7, 1249, 1254 (2002). *See also* Levin, *supra* note 30.

33. Marc Galanter & William Henderson, "The Elastic Tournament: A Second Transformation of the Big Law Firm," *Stanford L. Rev.* (2008).

34. Martin P. Seligman, Paul R. Verkuil, and Terry H. Kang, "Why Lawyers Are Unhappy," 23 *Cardozo L. Rev.* 33, 42 (2001).

35. Ronit Dinovitzer & Bryant Garth, "Lawyer Satisfaction in the Process of Structuring a Legal Career," 41 *Law & Soc'y Rev.* 1 (2007); Dinovitzer, *After the JD, supra* note 29; Deborah L. Rhode, *In the Interests of Justice: Reforming the Legal Profession* 33 (2000); Marc Galanter, "Old and in the Way," *Wis. L. Rev.* 1081, 1108 (1999); Patrick J. Schiltz, "On Being a Happy, Healthy, and Ethical Member of an Unhappy, Unhealthy, and Unethical Profession," 52 *Vand. L. Rev.* 871 (1999).

36. Boston Bar Association Task Force, *supra* note 30, at 14. *See generally*, Carl D. Liggio, "A Look at the Role of Corporate Counsel–Back to the Future—or Is it the Past?," 44 *Ariz. L. Rev.* 621 (2002).

about two-thirds to three-quarters of corporate counsel indicated that gaining a better balance between their professional and personal life was a major reason for their current job choice.[37] Many attorneys also like the opportunities for proactive problem solving and management positions that are available in corporate settings. Yet not all organizations have provided the advantages that lead attorneys to move in-house. In some companies, downsizing and cost-containment strategies have created economic pressures that compromise the quality of life for all employees, including lawyers. Despite the reputation of shorter hours in corporate counsel offices, the most comprehensive recent research finds that in-house lawyers do not report significantly less difficulty balancing their professional and personal lives than lawyers in firms.[38]

Government service promises some of the same advantages commonly associated with corporate counsel positions, such as manageable schedules and freedom from business development and up-or-out promotion pressures. Many public sector positions, including those in legal aid, public defender, and public interest organizations, also offer a degree of independence and connection with social justice issues that hold substantial appeal. The downside is generally lower salaries, fewer support services, and more limited opportunities for advancement than in private practice. As Chapters VI and XIII note, severe underfunding for most public defender and civil legal aid services can lead to crushing caseloads and corresponding problems of stress and attrition.

The following excerpt from a symposium on lawyers' happiness explores the extent and causes of lawyers' dissatisfaction with some aspects of contemporary legal practice. Although the primary focus is on private practice, many of the problems are not unique to that setting.

Deborah L. Rhode, "Foreword: Personal Satisfaction in Professional Practice"

58 Syracuse Law Review 217 (2008)

> One is happy as the result of one's own efforts, once one knows the necessary ingredients of happiness—simple tastes, a certain degree of courage, self-denial to a point, love of work, and above all, a clear conscience.
>
> George Sand

Ethics, said Socrates, is "not just about any question, but about the way one should live." [Given its relatively high rates of dissatisfaction, the legal profession needs to pay more attention to that question, and to research that addresses it]. A wide range of benefits follow from increased life satisfaction, including greater productivity and career success, better

---

37. Catherine Amon, "Despite the Mergers and Fast Pace, In–House Lawyers Are Basically Happy," *Conn. L. Trib.*, Oct. 9, 2000 (77%); Catalyst, *Women in Law: Making the Case* 11 (2001).

38. Catalyst, *supra* note 37, at 46.

interpersonal relationships, fewer disciplinary problems, more charitable contributions, enhanced physical and mental health, and longer life expectancy. Employers, clients, and society generally also have a stake in strategies that increase attorneys' well being and performance. Given the centrality of law and lawyers in American life, these issues deserve more serious attention. . . .

I.   The Profession and its Discontents

How happy are lawyers? That, of course, depends on how we define and assess happiness. Most experts distinguish between positive emotions (or pleasure), engagement, and meaning, and find that the most satisfied people orient their activities toward engagement and meaning. . . . Unlike momentary pleasure, which may not be a frequently recurring state, full engagement of one's talents in some valued activity produces a more lasting sense of fulfillment.

To gauge this more sustained form of happiness in professional life, researchers typically ask people how satisfied they are and whether they would choose the same career again or recommend it to someone else. . . . Surveys by the American Bar Association and National Opinion Research Center find that only about half of lawyers are satisfied or very satisfied with their work. That percentage is substantially lower than for Americans in general; 86% are satisfied with their work and law does not rank among the top twelve professions for satisfaction. Lawyers rate their jobs about the same as accountants, civil engineers and car salesman, and significantly below dentists, engineers, physicians, police officers, and real estate agents. Although four fifths of legal practitioners are proud to be a lawyer, only about half that number would recommend their career to a young person.

Lawyers' discontent is reflected in other measures, such as high rates of attrition and psychological difficulties. Almost half of associates leave law firms within three years; three quarters leave within five. An estimated one-third of lawyers suffer from depression or alcohol or drug addiction; attorneys have about three times the rate of depression and almost twice the rate of substance abuse of other Americans. . . .

Satisfaction rates vary somewhat across different practice settings and demographic groups, and highlight the range of factors contributing to disaffection. Attorneys in large firms are the least satisfied (44%) and attorneys in the public sector are the most (66%). Graduates of the highest ranked law schools who work in the most prestigious large law firm settings are the least likely to be extremely satisfied with their decision to become a lawyer and the most likely to plan on leaving their position within two years. . . . Such variations reflect differences both in working conditions and expectations for attorneys with different backgrounds, values, and credentials.

Race, gender and ethnicity also play a role. In the American Foundation study of recent graduates, Blacks were most satisfied with their decision to become lawyers and with the substance of their work but the least satisfied with the social conditions and opportunities for professional development and influence. Women were more satisfied than men with the substance of what they did and less satisfied with its context and opportunities; they were also more likely to leave their position, particularly if it was is in a large firm. Other studies ... find that women of color are the least satisfied of all groups with almost all aspects of their workplaces. Such variations underscore the progress that remains to be made in valuing equal opportunity in practice as well as principle.

II.   Sources of Dissatisfaction

What would make lawyers happier? [Research findings] suggest that professional satisfaction reflects a combination of genetic predispositions, working conditions, and personal efforts. Experts generally believe that people have a genetically determined set point for happiness, and that at least 50 percent of the variation in satisfaction reflects this physiological baseline. Changes in circumstances, such as health, finances, and personal relationships, move people up or down in happiness levels, but over time, most individuals return to their set points.... However, even researchers who stress the importance of genetic predispositions also note the potential for individual improvement. People need not let their "genetic steersman have his way.... [W]ithin wide latitude, they can control their destination...."

The nature and conditions of work are also important. Job satisfaction depends on how well a position meets basic psychological needs for self-esteem, control, competence, security, and relationships with others. People are happiest when they feel they are being effective, exercising strengths and virtues, meeting life's challenges, and contributing to socially valued ends that bring meaning and purpose. Individuals also benefit from benefiting others. Volunteer work is correlated not only with greater satisfaction but also with greater physical and mental health, and self-esteem. For lawyers, pro bono activities enhance career development; they are a way to build skills, reputation, and contacts, while advancing causes to which individuals are committed. By these standards, the opportunities available in many legal workplaces fall short.

One cluster of problems involves the substance of legal practice and the gap between expectations and realities. Individuals often choose law as a career with little knowledge of what lawyers actually do. Law in prime time media offers some combination of wealth, power, drama, or heroic opportunities. Law in real time is something else, particularly for those at the bottom of the pecking order. The sheer drudgery of many legal matters, particularly in large firms, exacts a heavy price.... [and the] adversarial, zero-sum and uncivil aspects of practice [can make lawyers] scapegoats for acrimony not of their own making.... [In the ABA's studies of young lawyers] the greatest source of disappointment ... was the "lack of contribution to the social good." Individuals who chose legal careers partly out of concerns for social justice have often shared Archibald's MacLeish's inability to care very much "whether $900,000 belongs this way or that."

. . .

Other sources of dissatisfaction involve the increasing pace, pressure, and competitiveness of modern practice. Technological innovations have intensified pressures for instant responsiveness, and predictably unpredictable demands can amplify the problem. Legal life lurches from deadline to deadline, as lawyers remain tethered to their offices with email, blackberries, cell phones, and faxes. Although these developments have made it easier for attorneys to work from home, they have also made it harder not to.

The pressure for constant accessibility is compounded by growing competition. Over the last three decades, the number of American lawyers has more than doubled and they face increasing challenges from nonlawyers and international providers of legal services. Corporate clients, who are experiencing greater pressures in their own markets, have responded by curtailing costs, refusing to subsidize associate training, and parceling out work on the basis of short-term competitive considerations, rather than long-term relationships. That, in turn, has increased the time lawyers have to spend on marketing their services and reduced the time and opportunities available for mentoring junior colleagues. Those most likely to fall through the cracks are women and minorities, who remain out of the loop of informal support. In the ABA's most recent survey, 62 percent of women of color, 60 percent of white women, but only 4 percent of white men feel excluded from formal and informal networking opportunities.

Competition within as well as across law firms has also intensified, leading to more internal rivalries and less collegial relationships. Partnership has become less accessible and less attractive. Fewer lawyers gain full equity status and it no longer promises life time security or saner schedules. In effect, private practice has become "leaner and meaner." To many attorneys, the struggle looks increasingly like a "pie eating contest where the prize is more pie." These problems have been exacerbated by the priority of profits and its affect on pro bono work and billable hours. In *The Paradox of Success*, John O'Neil notes that monetary success brings many rewards, but not necessarily the ability to enjoy them. For lawyers, escalating incomes come with escalating demands and have squeezed out time for family, friends, public service, and personal interests that would ultimately prove more satisfying. Only a quarter of surveyed lawyers are in workplaces that fully count pro bono work toward billable hours and almost two thirds feel that such work is a negative or unimportant factor in promotion and compensation decisions.

What is, however, highly rewarded is a willingness to work extended hours and inflexible schedules. A New Yorker cartoon captures the prevailing ethic: it features a well-heeled professional advising a younger colleague that "all work and no play makes you a valued employee." Yet these norms are a major cause of dissatisfaction and attrition, particularly among women lawyers, who bear a disproportionate share of family responsibilities. . . . Most surveyed lawyers report that they do not have sufficient time for themselves and their families. Only a third to a half believe that their employers support balanced lives and flexible workplace arrangements.

Recent surveys find that most men as well as women indicate a willingness to take lower salaries in exchange for more time with their families. Four fifths of associates responding to an *ABA Journal* Poll would make that tradeoff.

Excessive hours carry a substantial cost. Overwork is a leading cause of disproportionately high rates of stress, substance abuse, reproductive dysfunction, and mental health difficulties. In a profession in which half the talent pool is now female and most men as well as women want a balanced life, employers can ill afford policies that prevent it. Today's generation of lawyers grew up expecting fulfillment in both work and family, and are increasingly unhappy about settling for less.

III.   Misplaced Priorities

Why do so many lawyers put up with unfulfilling practice, and why do so many legal employers fail to make adjustments that would improve not only satisfaction, but also recruitment, retention, and performance? The explanations are, of course interrelated. If too few disaffected lawyers vote with their feet, employers have too little incentive to respond. By the same token, if too few workplaces are implementing effective reforms, too few attorneys will see somewhere else to go.

Part of the problem is that people are surprisingly inaccurate judges of what will make them happy, and lawyers are no exception. Psychologists identify a number of factors that interfere with rational choices. One is that focusing on a highly salient event or other extrinsic rewards inflates their importance. So, for example, lawyers may overestimate the well-being that will flow from making partner or scoring a large bonus because they overlook contextual factors and adaptive mechanisms that moderate the effect. Desires, expectations, and standards of comparison tend to increase as rapidly as they are satisfied. People become trapped on a "hedonic treadmill:" the more they have the more they need to have. . . .

In particular, money plays a much smaller role in promoting personal satisfaction than most people, including lawyers, commonly assume. Americans' income, controlled for inflation, is twice what it was in the late 1950s, but fewer report being very happy and more objective evidence concerning mental health difficulties also suggests a decline in well-being. Researchers consistently find that for individuals at lawyers' income levels, differences in compensation bear little relationship to differences in satisfaction. Individuals earning $200,000 are not significantly happier than those earning half that much. There is also no relationship between compensation and fulfillment across different fields of practice. Discontent is greatest among well-paid large firm associates and least pronounced among relatively low-earning academics and public sector employees.

One reason for this disconnect between wealth and satisfaction is that most of what high incomes can buy does not yield enduring happiness. The novelty of new purchases or circumstances quickly wears thin, and the transitory pleasure that they bring is less critical in promoting well-being than other factors, such as individuals' relationship with families, friends, and communities, and their sense of contributing to larger societal ends. A second reason for the limited effect of money is that satisfaction is most affected by relative not absolute income, and increases in wealth are generally offset by changes in reference groups. To large extent, pay is a "positional good;" individuals' satisfaction with their economic status depends on its position relative to others. Yet the increasingly public nature of lawyers' salaries has made the competition for relative status easier to play and harder to win. This kind of arms race has few winners and many losers. There is, in fact, no room at the top. Attorneys who look hard enough can always find someone getting something more.

Other dynamics help trap lawyers into overvaluing income. One is the difficulty of downward economic mobility. Attorneys who initially chose well-paying jobs in order to gain training and prestige, or to pay off student loans, often become accustomed to the lifestyle that such positions make possible. So too, the work required to generate high income creates needs that fuel financial demands. Attorneys working sweatshop hours feel entitled to goods and services that will make their lives easier and more pleasurable. This pattern of compensatory consumption can become self-perpetuating. As one refugee from large firm practice observes, lawyers frequently use the "substantial income from their jobs in an attempt to fill the voids created by their jobs." Professionals who accept grueling schedules to afford comfort for themselves or their families often find that they have little time to enjoy it. Yet luxuries can readily become necessities, and many attorneys feel unable to afford a more satisfying balance of personal, professional, and public service pursuits.

The desire for status and the equation of money with merit pushes in equally counterproductive directions. For many individuals, including lawyers, income is a key measure of achievement and self-esteem, and a marker of social status. The desire to impress and display is deeply rooted in human nature, and in America's increasingly materialist culture, self-worth is linked to net worth.

These dynamics skew the priorities not only of individual lawyers but also of the firms that employ them. Because money is at the top of almost everyone's scale, it is easier to reach consensus on maximizing compensation than on other values such as reducing hours or subsidizing substantial pro bono commitments. Firms that sacrifice profits for other workplace satisfactions risk losing talented rainmakers and recruits who prefer greater earnings. Once high pay scales are established, they are difficult to dislodge. Downward mobility is painful, and the working conditions necessary to sustain such incomes then encourage the sense of deprivation and entitlement that fuel desires for more compensation. It is also easier for employers to offer money or perks than to address deeper problems in workplace culture. The result is bigger bonuses and widening arrays of glitzy amenities, everything from massages and pet insurance to take-out dinners delivered on silver trays.

Yet as experts note, these extrinsic rewards are less likely to be effective than strategies that heighten the intrinsic satisfaction of work and that ensure sufficient time for life outside it. That message has been slow to catch on.... Part of the problem is that billable hours have assumed symbolic significance. A willingness to work extended schedules has become a proxy for harder to measure qualities such as commitment, ambition, and reliability under pressure. Attorneys who have made the sacrifices that such schedules require are often resentful of colleagues who want "special" accommodation. Backlash is particularly likely if those working "normal" hours have to assume a disproportionate share of inconvenient weekend, holiday, and late-night work.

Yet a growing body of evidence suggests that humane schedules, alternative work arrangements, and other family-friendly policies are cost-effective strategies. Such initiatives improve recruitment and retention, and help reduce stress and other health-related disorders. Some recent estimates suggest that every dollar invested in these policies concerning quality of life results in two dollars saved in other costs. Other surveys find that part-time employees are generally more efficient than full-time counterparts, particularly bleary, burned out professionals clocking sweatshop hours; any additional overhead expenses are more than offset by reduced attrition. In short, balanced lives boost bottom lines.

The same is true of pro bono opportunities. They enable lawyers to develop new skills, areas of expertise, and potential client contacts, as well as enhance their reputations and self-esteem. As one attorney notes, such activity can be "an enormous morale booster for the entire firm. Everyone feels that they touched a life ... no office picnics or parties can give you that." ...

Strategies for Reform

A profession that has built its reputation on solving problems for others has been curiously passive in the face of its own discontent. Recent changes in the conditions of practice have left many lawyers in a state of wistful resignation. They see workplace demands increasing, and civility and collegiality heading in the opposite direction. Yet many seem to lack a sense of control over their collective future. What most needs to change is a belief about what change is possible. In an influential essay, "The Importance of What We Care About," philosopher Harry Frankfurt emphasized a point that also emerges from the psychological research summarized [above]. Individuals are most fulfilled when they engage in work that they find meaningful and reflect at the deepest level about what meets this definition. It is, in short, important to remind ourselves what we care most about, and to refuse to settle, at least in the long term, for workplaces that fall short. Although not all the downsides of legal practice are easily avoided, lawyers could do much more, both individually and collectively, to reduce the gap between expectations and experience in their professional lives.

At the individual level, lawyers need to be more proactive in identifying and developing their strengths, and finding work that will engage their capacities and aspirations. That, in turn, will require individuals to become more informed and self-reflective in their career choices. One step to that end is the emergence of rankings and data bases, like building a Better Legal Profession, and the *American Lawyer* A List, which grade selected law firms on factors such as diversity, work/life programs, associate satisfaction and pro bono activities. Students should demand, and insist that their placement offices demand, more such information, including how workplace policies function in practice. How does part time status or substantial pro bono involvement affect promotion and compensation decisions? How much control do lawyers exercise over their schedules and over the kinds of assignments and public service opportunities available?

Once employed, practitioners also need to press for such control. That is particularly important for women, who are socialized not to appear pushy or aggressive. As the title of pathbreaking book on negotiating behavior noted, *Women Don't Ask*. But when it comes to professional development and work/family tradeoffs, lawyers of both sexes need to ask; they must actively pursue what is necessary for fulfillment. In one study on career advancement, the most effective strategy was impatience; individuals benefited from seizing every opportunity and leaving a position when a more challenging opportunity became available. So too, professionals committed to improving their current situation often find strength in numbers. Organizing colleagues both within and across workplaces can significantly improve diversity and work/family policies.

At the institutional level, legal employers must do more to address sources of discontent and to evaluate the adequacy of their responses. A commitment to quality of life needs to be reflected in workplace priorities, policies, and reward structures. That, in turn, will require systematic evaluation of lawyers' satisfaction, and of practices that affect it, such as mentoring, diversity, and work/family initiatives. Decision makers must track whether underrepresented groups such as women and minorities are advancing in numbers equal to white male counterparts, whether all groups feel equally well supported in their professional development, and whether they find part-time and mentoring policies effective. So, for example, do lawyers working reduced hours find that their schedules are respected, that their pay and benefits are proportionate to their performance, and that they retain opportunities for advancement and desirable assignments? Do participants in formal mentoring programs feel that their assigned mentor has sufficient time, interest, incentives, and knowledge to provide the necessary support? Are supervising attorneys adequately trained and evaluated in mentoring, performance appraisals, and treatment of subordinates? Do junior attorneys have an opportunity to rate supervisors in forms that matter in the organization's reward structure? Too many employers now lack adequate evaluation structures, and invest substantial time and money in initiatives that fail to meet the needs of their ostensible beneficiaries.

[Reforms] are also necessary in the treatment of pro bono work and the structure of practice.... Employers must make a visible commitment to public service that is reflected in resource allocation and rewards. [Another] promising initiative involves law firm tracks that allow different hours and compensation tradeoffs without second-class status ... [or] that match attorneys with projects that fit their substantive and scheduling preferences. Fee arrangements that reduce reliance on hourly billing can also be helpful in reducing pressures for overwork.

Clients should also pressure legal employers to address sources of chronic dissatisfaction. On some issues, clients have an obvious financial interest. They seldom get cost-effective service from bleary, burned out practitioners, and high rates of attrition involve disruption, inconvenience, and additional training expenses. So too, a growing number of corporate counsel see diversity as an economic as well as moral imperative. They want firms that make full use of available talent, and that offer lawyers with a range of backgrounds and perspectives. To that end, many large corporations have pledged to consider diversity in allocating legal work. More clients need to follow suit, to put teeth in their commitments, and to add concerns like pro bono activities.

Bar associations, for their part, could also do more to support diversity, public service, and quality of life reforms. For example, some local bar groups have enlisted law firms to support goals and timetables for racial and gender equity. Others have developed initiatives to increase pro bono involvement, and a few states have required lawyers to report pro bono work.... By raising the visibility of pro bono involvement, bar associations can pressure employers to support work that would be rewarding to all concerned.

V.   The Role of Legal Education

Law schools have an obvious role to play in addressing issues of professional satisfaction, but it is not one that most have been inclined to assume ... Issues concerning [pro bono work], the conditions of practice and lawyer satisfaction are ... noticeable for their absence. And with reason. Law schools have strong interests in maximizing student applications, retention, and job placement; an institution's financial well being depends on a steady stream of tuition, and its status depends partly on selectivity in admissions and employment of its graduates. None of those interests are served by delivering unwelcome messages about the downsides of practice.

Yet legal academics are also the branch of the profession best situated to address its problems, and with that opportunity comes a corresponding obligation. In his celebrated 1934 address on the "Public Influence of the Bar," United States Supreme Court Justice Harlan Stone noted that legal academics were the members of the profession "most detached from those pressures of the new economic order which have so profoundly affected their practicing brethren." That independence gave them a unique capacity for disinterested analysis of the "[b]ar as an institution" and for "an informed understanding of its problems...."

Legal education also can do more to prepare future generations to address, individually and collectively, the sources of professional discontent. For example, law schools can expose students to different practice settings and the literature on satisfaction; help them identify and exercise their own core strengths; and require employers conducting campus interviews to disclose relevant information. More law faculty should also pursue research that would promote professional fulfillment. We need to know much more about what works in the world. For example, what law school and employer initiatives are most effective in improving health and satisfaction over the long term? What incentives and pressures are most likely to secure practices that we know are effective?

Legal academics take pride in working at the forefront of social change. We like to believe that our teaching and research contribute to more just and efficient governance institutions. We need now to turn more of our efforts toward our own profession, and to promote forms of practice that fulfill lawyers' deepest needs and aspirations.

NOTES

The dissatisfactions chronicled above have surfaced in a variety of forms: blogs, legal commentary, and bar association studies and surveys.[39] Such dissatisfaction also emerged in an internal law firm memo by associates in one prominent law firm that was leaked to the press and widely circulated on the web and in media publications. In an *American Lawyer's* survey of 132 firms, the firm in question rated lowest in associate satisfaction, and the memo offered a scathing analysis of the reasons why. Major problems included: a 2200 billable hour target (2420 for the maximum bonus); insufficient training, mentoring, and pro bono opportunities; inequitable work assignment systems; and partner indifference to such problems.[40]

Other more trivial complaints and proposed reforms earned some equally scathing responses by legal commentators. For example:

- Allegedly, partners have a monthly budget for socializing with associates. We call on all partners to spend it. If you choose to do one thing to improve partner-associate relations, at least say "hello" in the hallways. It sounds like a small thing, but simply talk to us. Get to know the associates: you might even like a few.

- Get an online food delivery system ... so that people working late can order food easily.

- Set up a recreation room with a TV.

- Get concierge service for things like dry cleaning.

- Free shoeshines.

Dahlia Lithwick, a former lawyer who writes for *Slate*, observes: "Associates in law firms knowingly sign away their health, leisure time, and

---

39. See Symposium on Lawyer Happiness, 58 *Syracuse L. Rev.* 217 et seq (2008); Jean Stefanic & Richard Delgado, *How Lawyers Lose Their Way: A Profession Fails Its Creative Minds* (2005); Douglas Litowitz, *The Destruction of Young Lawyers* (2006); Ashby Jones, "Law Firm Life Doesn't Suit Some Associates," *Wall St. J.*, May 2, 2006, at B6.

40. Http://www.internalmemos.com

relationships for a monstrous salary and hefty bonuses. This is not news. What is news is that the associates . . . ask for both too much and too little. They want law firm life to be about more than just the commodification of their time, even when it is. And yet faced with an opportunity to reclaim their lives, they are willing to settle for a 'hi' in the hallways and a better appointed cage. . . . The absurdity of the . . . memo isn't that these associates regret their Faustian bargain. It is that they just want shiny shoes for their troubles."[41]

As the preceding excerpt notes, however, such criticisms have done little to stem the arms race in perks, despite evidence suggesting that neither such amenities nor increased compensation are a major influence on attrition.[42] Another approach is the student-run Building a Better Legal Profession, a coalition from a number of schools which rates firms on diversity, billable hours, and pro bono work.[43] Recent evidence suggests that many associates might welcome changes along those dimensions. In a 2007 ABA Journal on-line survey, 84% of associates indicated that they would be willing to earn less money in exchange for lower billable-hour requirements. Almost a third of respondents favored a 20% reduction in hours, although only a small minority were willing to take a proportionate reduction in pay.[44]

QUESTIONS

1. What conclusions do you draw from this research on satisfaction? In considering your own job choice, what factors are most important?

2. As the preceding excerpt notes, the factors most critical to individual satisfaction include self-esteem, autonomy, competence, and relations with others. How can change along these dimensions be realized? Is Lithwick's characterization fair, or were associates simply being realistic about what they thought they could achieve? If you had been an associate at the firm, what strategies would you have recommended for reforming firm policies and practices? If you were planning to join a large firm, would you join Building a Better Legal Profession? What are the barriers to organizing associates or students, and what strategies might address them?[45]

---

41. Dahlia Lithwick, "Free the Baby Lawyers," October 29, 2002. Http://slate.msn.com/toolbar.aspx?action=print&id=2073302.

42. Lynnley Browning, "For Lawyers, Perqs to Fit a Lifestyle," *N.Y. Times*, Nov. 22, 2007, at C1. See NALP, *Toward Effective Management of Associate Mobility: A Status Report on Attrition* (2005); Peter H. Huang & Rick Swedloff, "Authentic Happiness and Meaning at Law Firms," 58 *Syr. L. Rev.* 341 (2008).

43. Peter Lattman, "The Nerve! Students Tell Big Firms They Want a Life," *Wall St. J.*, April 4, 2007, at 82; Andrew Bruck and Andrew Cantor, "Why the Center Will Not Hold: How Supply–Side and Demand Side Market Forces Are Changing the Economics of Large Law Firms," *Stan. L. Rev.* (2008).

44. Stephanie Ward, "The Ultimate Time–Money Trade–Off," *ABA J.,* February 2007, at 24.

45. *See* Marion Crain, "The Transformation of the Professional Workplace," 79 *Chicago–Kent L. Rev.* 543 (2004) (discussing barriers to collective organization among professionals, particularly lawyers); Bruck & Cantor, *supra* note 43.

3.   What accounts for the mismatch between workplace conditions likely to yield greatest professional fulfillment and the conditions prevailing in many legal workplaces? To what extent does the pursuit of profits explain the disjuncture?[46] An increasing body of research suggests that opportunities for mentoring, skills development, participation in workplace decision-making, and manageable schedules can lead to higher profitability. Such opportunities generally increase morale and retention, lower recruitment and training costs, and reduce health problems related to stress and overwork.Why have so many legal employers failed to respond accordingly?

D.   Professional Opportunities

1.   Women

NOTES

As the preceding historical overview noted, the gender composition of most traditionally male professions, including law, has changed dramatically over the last four decades. Women's representation has grown from about three to thirty percent, and they now constitute almost half of law school classes.

Women's equal access has not, however, ensured their equal acceptance, a fact that has gained increasing attention. As late as 1980, only one article on the entire subject of gender bias in the courts had appeared in mainstream legal literature. A decade later, thirty states had gender bias commissions and the National Judicial Education Association had an active program to promote equality for women and men in the courts. Increasing attention has also focused on the intersection of gender bias with other forms of prejudice such as those based on race, ethnicity, and sexual orientation, and on women's underrepresentation in positions of greatest legal influence. They constitute less than a fifth of law firm partners, federal judges, law school deans, U.S. Attorneys, state attorney generals, and Fortune 500 general counsels. The gap widens for women of color, who account for only about 1–2 percent of corporate officers, top earners, law firm partners, and general counsels[47]

---

46. Deborah L. Rhode, "Profits and Professionalism," 33 *Ford. Urban L. J.* 44 (2006). See Galanter & Henderson, *supra* note 33 (arguing that competition and the mobility of rain-making partners makes it difficult for firms to give priority to non-economic objectives); Ben W. Heineman & David B. Wilkins, "The Lost Generation," *American Lawyer*, March, 2008, at 85 (noting the adverse effects of the focus on profits per partner; as well as the need for mentoring, professional development and pro bono opportunities to address associate attrition).

47. Deborah L. Rhode & Barbara Kellerman, "Women and Leadership," in *Women and Leadership: The State of Play and Strategies for Change* (Barbara Kellerman & Deborah L. Rhode, eds., 2007); Lynne Marek, "Large Firms Have Trouble Retaining Women," *Nat'l L. J.*, June 18, 2007, 1; Theresa M. Beiner, "Not All Lawyers are Created Equal: Difficulties that Plague Women and Women of Color," 58 *Syr. L. Rev.* (2008); ABA Commission on Women in the Profession, *Current Glance at Women in the Law* (2006); Janet E. Gans Epner, *Visible Invisibility: Women of Color in Law Firms* (ABA Commission on

Researchers have documented gender bias in multiple areas: (1) opportunities for professional advancement, mentoring, compensation, and recognition; (2) work family policies; (3) the treatment of female lawyers, litigants, and witnesses; and (4) the structures and resources for dealing with these issues. The following reading describes some of the barriers still confronting women in the bar. How would you explain and address the gender inequalities described below?

ABA Commission on Women in the Profession, The Unfinished Agenda: Women and the Legal Profession, Executive Summary

(Prepared by Deborah L. Rhode) (2001).

[In recent decades,] the status of women has dramatically improved ... At the turn of this century, women accounted for almost a third of the nation's lawyers and for the first time constituted a majority of entering law students.

Yet despite substantial progress, substantial challenges remain. Women in the legal profession remain underrepresented in positions of greatest status, influence, and economic reward.... On average, female lawyers earn about $20,000 less than male lawyers, and significant disparities persist even for those with similar qualifications, experience, and positions. Studies involving thousands of lawyers find that men are at least twice as likely as similarly qualified women to obtain partnerships. The underrepresentation of women of color is still greater. What limited data are available also find significant inequalities in pay and promotion for minority, lesbian, and disabled attorneys.

The problems are compounded by the lack of consensus that there are in fact serious problems. In the ABA's 2000 poll, only about a quarter of female lawyers and three percent of male lawyers believed that prospects for advancement were greater for men than for women. Most attorneys equate gender bias with intentional discrimination, and the contexts in which they practice produce few overt examples. Yet a wide array of research finds that women's opportunities are limited by factors other than conscious prejudice. Major barriers include unconscious stereotypes, inadequate access to support networks, inflexible workplace structures, sexual harassment, and bias in the justice system.

I. Barriers for Women in the Legal Profession

A. Gender Stereotypes

A longstanding obstacle to equal opportunity involves the mismatch between characteristics associated with women and those associated with

Women in the Profession, 2006); National Association of Law Placement, [NALP], "Women and Attorneys of Color at Law Firms" (NALP, 2004); Association of American Law Schools, Statistical Report on Law School Faculty and Candidates for Law Faculty Positions, http://www.aals.org/statistics/0405/html/0405_T4B_tit.html. *See* generally, Elizabeth Chambliss, *Miles to Go: Progress of Minorities in the Legal Profession* (ABA Commission on Racial and Ethnic Diversity in the Legal Profession, 2004).

professional success, such as assertiveness and competitiveness. Women still face a longstanding double standard and a double bind. They risk criticism for being too "soft" or too "strident," too "aggressive" or "not aggressive enough." And what is assertive in a man is often abrasive in a woman. A related obstacle is that female attorneys often do not receive the same presumption of competence or commitment as their male colleagues. In large national surveys, between half and three quarters of women believe that they are held to higher standards than men. The problem is compounded for women of color or other identifiable minorities including lesbians and disabled women. The performance of these groups is subject to special criticism, and their achievements often are attributed to special treatment rather than professional qualifications.

The force of traditional stereotypes is reinforced by other biases in decision making. People are more likely to notice and remember information that confirms prior assumptions than information that contradicts them. For example, attorneys who assume that working mothers are less committed tend to remember the times they left early, not the nights that they stayed late. People also want to believe that their own evaluations and workplaces are meritocratic. If women are underrepresented, the most psychologically convenient explanation is that they lack the necessary qualifications and commitment.

B. Support Networks

An equally persistent problem is inadequate access to informal networks of mentoring, contacts, and client development. Despite recent progress, many attorneys are most comfortable supporting others who seem most similar in backgrounds, experiences, and values. The small number of women, particularly women of color, in senior positions prevents adequate mentoring for all the junior colleagues who need assistance. Female attorneys who have substantial family commitments also have difficulty making time for mentoring relationships and for the informal social activities that generate collegial support and client contacts.

The result is that many female lawyers remain out of the loop of career development. They aren't given enough challenging high visibility assignments. They aren't included in social events that yield professional opportunities. And they aren't helped to acquire the legal and marketing skills that are central to advancement.

These barriers can become self-perpetuating. Senior attorneys are reluctant to support and mentor women who have difficulty advancing. Women who are not supported are in fact less likely to advance. Their inability to reach senior positions then reduces the pool of women mentors and perpetuates the assumptions that perpetuate the problem. Again, the problem is particularly pronounced for women of color; in recent national surveys, fewer than a third were satisfied with the availability of mentors and fewer than one percent remain at firms where they are initially hired.

C. Workplace Structures

A further obstacle involves workplace structures that fail to accommodate substantial family responsibilities and pro bono commitments. About two-thirds of surveyed lawyers report experiencing work/family conflict and most believe that it is the greatest barrier to women's advancement. Only a fifth of surveyed lawyers are very satisfied with the allocation of time between work and personal needs, or with their connection to issues of social justice.

The most obvious failures in workplace structures are excessive hours and resistance to reduced or flexible schedules. Client expectations of instant responsiveness and total availability, coupled with lawyers' expectations of spiraling salaries, have pushed working hours to new and often excessive levels. Hourly requirements have increased dramatically over the last two decades, and what has not changed is the number of hours in the day. Unpredictable deadlines, uneven workloads, or frequent travel pose further difficulties for those with substantial family obligations.

Unsurprisingly, most female attorneys feel that they do not have sufficient time for themselves or their families, and half report high levels of stress in juggling their responsibilities. Moreover, women who do not have families often have difficulty finding time for relationships that might lead to them. Unmarried associates frequently report ending up with disproportionate work because they have no acceptable reason for refusing it. Yet many lawyers who would like to adjust or reduce their hours bump up against considerable resistance. A wide gap persists between formal policies and accepted practices. Although over 90 percent of surveyed law firms allow part time schedules, only about three to four percent of lawyers actually use them. Most women surveyed believe that any reduction in hours or availability would jeopardize their prospects for advancement.

The result is yet another double standard and another double bind. Working mothers are held to higher standards than working fathers and are often criticized for being insufficiently committed, either as parents or professionals. Those who seem willing to sacrifice family needs to workplace demands appear lacking as mothers. Those who want extended leaves or reduced schedules appear lacking as lawyers. These mixed messages leave many women with the uncomfortable sense that whatever they are doing, they should be doing something else. Assumptions about the inadequate commitment of working mothers can influence performance evaluations, promotion decisions, and opportunities for the mentoring relationships and challenging assignments that are crucial for advancement.

Yet contrary to conventional wisdom, there is little basis for assuming that working mothers are less committed to their careers than other lawyers. Women are not significantly more likely to leave legal practice than men. Rather, they typically move to positions with greater flexibility. Also contrary to popular assumptions, taking a reduced schedule does not necessarily signal reduced professional commitment. In fact, it generally takes exceptional dedication for women to juggle competing work and family responsibilities in unsupportive working environments.

Although the inadequacy of family-friendly policies is not just a "women's issue," the price is paid disproportionately by women. Despite a significant increase in men's assumption of domestic work over the last two decades, women in two-career couples continue to shoulder the major burden. Part of the reason involves longstanding socialization patterns and workplace practices that deter men from taking part-time schedules or family leaves for more than a few weeks. Only about 10–15 percent of surveyed law firms and Fortune 1000 companies offer the same paid parental leave to men and women.

Yet these norms make little sense, even from the most narrow economic calculus. A wide array of research indicates that part time employees are more productive than their full time counterparts, particularly those working extended hours. Bleary, burned-out lawyers seldom provide cost-effective services, and they are disproportionately prone to stress, substance abuse, and other health-related disorders. Moreover, full-time employees are not necessarily more accessible than those on reduced or flexible schedules. Lawyers at a deposition for another client are less available than the woman at home with cell phones, e-mails, and fax machines. The limited research available finds no negative impact on client relations from reduced or flexible schedules.

Considerable data also indicate that such arrangements save money in the long run by reducing absenteeism, attrition, and corresponding recruitment and training costs. Adequate opportunities for alternative schedules and reasonable working hours are becoming increasingly important in attracting as well as retaining talented lawyers. Almost half of surveyed women and a third of men placed work/life balance among their top reasons for selecting their current legal employer.

Similar points could be made about other workplace policies that affect lawyers' quality of life. Organizations that fail to provide benefits for domestic partners, and to welcome them at social events, are overlooking cost-effective ways of making lesbian attorneys feel valued and comfortable in their workplaces. And organizations that fail to offer reasonable accommodations for lawyers with disabilities are paying a similar price. Greater efforts to insure the inclusiveness of legal workplaces would serve the interests of both lawyers and their employers....

D.   Sexual Harassment

Another context in which inadequate policies assume particular significance for women involves sexual harassment. Of course, considerable progress has been made since the Commission was founded in 1987, when only about a third of surveyed law firms had sexual harassment policies. Almost all firms now have such policies. Yet here again, the gap between formal policies and actual practices remains substantial. In the most recent surveys, about half to two-thirds of female lawyers, and a quarter to half of female court personnel, reported experiencing or observing sexual harassment. Almost three-quarters of female lawyers thought harassment was a problem in their workplaces.

It is a problem for which women pay a substantial and disproportionate price. They account for about 90% of reported complaints, and many experience both economic and psychological injuries, such as loss of employment opportunities, unwanted transfers, anxiety, depression, and other stress-related conditions. Organizations pay another price in decreased productivity, increased turnover, and risks of legal liability.

The problem is often magnified by the costs of identifying it. Many women justifiably fear ridicule or retaliation. Those who complain are often dismissed as humorless and hypersensitive, and are subject to informal blacklisting. As a result, surveys from a wide variety of occupational contexts find that few women, typically well under 10 percent, make any formal complaint; fewer still can afford the financial and psychological costs of litigation. Yet while the likelihood of complaints is small except for the most serious behavior, concerns about unjust accusations often deter men from mentoring or socializing informally with younger women. . . .

II. Gender Issues in Context

Although many of the opportunities and obstacles for women in the legal profession and legal system are widely shared, there are also some important differences across practice contexts. This report reviews key variations in women's experience. About a third of female attorneys now work in law firms or in solo practice. About 10 percent are in government or corporate counsel offices. About three percent are in the judiciary or in public interest, public defender, or legal aid organizations. And about one percent are in legal education. Compared with men, women are less likely to work in law firms, and more likely to work in public interest and public sector offices.

Part of the reason for such gender disparities may reflect perceptions about the different opportunities for women and men in these practice settings. Most studies find that men's chances of becoming partners in law firms are two to three times higher than women's. Gender disparities are especially pronounced for managing and equity partners, and for women of color. Minority women hold fewer than 1 percent of equity partnerships and their attrition rate after 8 years is virtually 100 percent. By contrast, women, particularly women of color, have traditionally perceived more hospitable environments in public interest and public sector positions. When relieved of the obligation to reward business development and maximize profits, many governmental and public interest organizations find it easier to advance women and to establish flexible work structures.

So too, many in-house counsel offices have attracted women by offering reasonable hours and freedom from client development obligations. However, the most recent national survey data indicate that only a quarter of women in corporate law departments are satisfied with opportunities for advancement, and that they experience no less difficulty in balancing personal and professional lives than women in law firms.

III.   The Difference Gender Difference Makes

In assessing the consequences of gender inequality, a crucial question is what difference it makes, not simply for individual women but also for the profession and public. Do women bring demonstrably different qualities than men to their work? The evidence is mixed, but the best answer appears to be some women, some of the time. And the differences are smaller than often thought. In general, psychological research finds few respects in which men and women consistently vary, and even for those characteristics, gender typically accounts for only a small part of the variation among individuals. Contextual forces and other factors like race and ethnicity can be equally or more significant.

Systematic evidence concerning women in the legal profession is limited and not entirely conclusive. The most extensive research involves judicial behavior. Some, but not all studies, find gender differences, although not necessarily on issues of gender equality. Unsurprisingly, however, there is ample evidence that women as a group attach particular importance to such issues. Professional organizations like the National Association of Women Judges, the ABA Commission on Women and the Profession, women's bar associations, and women's networks all have helped transform the legal landscape on women's issues. Yet it also bears emphasis that many of these initiatives have been actively supported by men.

It is equally critical to emphasize that gender differences are experienced differently by different groups of women in different practice contexts. There is no "generic woman." Race, class, ethnicity, disability, age, and sexual orientation can be as important as gender in defining professional opportunities and concerns. In order to ensure equality for all women, it is crucial to build alliances across these groups. A candid acknowledgment of differences encourages a better understanding of commonalities and a stronger collective effort to address shared concerns.

IV.   An Agenda for Change

A.   Guiding Principles: Commitment and Accountability

The most important factor in ensuring equal opportunity for women in the legal profession is a commitment to this objective, a commitment that is reflected in both institutional and individual priorities. Legal employers and bar associations must be prepared to translate principles into practice, and to hold their leadership accountable for the results. Lawyers in positions of influence need to build a moral and a pragmatic case for diversity, and to incorporate diversity goals into their organization's policies and reward structures. Progress toward those goals should be a factor in evaluating supervisors, law firms, and other legal employers. Bar associations, women's organizations, and corporate and governmental clients can assist this effort by monitoring the performance of employers, and by steering business or providing special recognition to those with successful records. What strategies are most effective will depend on the particular workplace, but the information available suggests certain best practices that are most likely to be successful.

B. Strategies for Legal Employers and Bar Associations

1. Assessment of Problems and Responses: Policy Evaluation, Benchmarks, and Training

- Organizations should collect systematic information concerning women's experience in areas such as promotion, leadership opportunities, compensation, alternative work schedules, sexual harassment, and satisfaction levels.

- Organizations should review formal policies, procedures, and educational materials to ensure that they reflect adequate commitments to equal opportunity and inclusiveness. Model policies from the ABA Commission on Women and other bar organizations can provide useful guidance. At a minimum, employers need to specify diversity-related objectives, prohibited conduct, and remedial processes.

- Organizations should establish formal benchmarks for monitoring progress on diversity-related goals, and should consider progress toward these goals in evaluating lawyers' performance.

- Organizations should consider providing management training and employee education on diversity issues and enlisting assistance from expert consultants. Such initiatives should be seen as a catalyst, not substitute for, broader changes

2. Evaluation Structures, Leadership Opportunities, and Professional Development

- Organizations should review their evaluation, work assignment, and compensation procedures to ensure equal opportunity.

- Legal employers and bar organizations should provide adequate opportunities for formal and informal training in areas that affect professional development, such as marketing leadership, communication, and related skills.

- Organizations should reexamine leadership selection criteria and structures to ensure adequate opportunities and diversity.

3. Quality of Life and Work—Family Initiatives

- Employers need to develop adequate policies and practices concerning flexible and reduced schedules, family leaves, telecommuting, child care assistance, domestic partners, disability accommodations, and related quality of life initiatives.

- Organizations need to monitor implementation to ensure that options that are available in principle are acceptable in practice and that standard billable hour expectations are not excessive.

4. Mentoring Programs and Women's Networks

- Legal employers and bar organizations should establish formal mentoring programs and support voluntary women's networks that provide informal mentoring and career assistance. Well-designed programs should assess and reward mentoring efforts.

- Women's networks should receive adequate assistance for activities such as workshops, seminars, speaker series, and informal events, and for outreach to particular groups of women who may encounter special obstacles, such as women of color, lesbians, women with disabilities, and women on part-time schedules. Where appropriate, support staff should be included in network initiatives.

5.   Sexual Harassment

- Organizations should develop or review sexual harassment policies to ensure adequate procedures for receiving complaints, providing effective sanctions, and preventing retaliation. These procedures should also establish adequate safeguards against unwarranted accusations, and overly punitive responses to genuine misunderstandings or inadvertent offenses.

- Bar ethical authorities should treat sexual harassment as a form of professional misconduct. . . .

This is not a modest agenda. But it is critical to maintaining a legal system that is committed to equal justice in practice as well as principle.

NOTES AND QUESTIONS

Many lawyers attribute women's underrepresentation in positions of greatest influence to women's different choices and commitments; they are more likely to drop out of the paid labor force or to reduce their hours than similarly credentialed men.[48] The differences are not, however, as pronounced as many believe. One recent study by the MIT Workplace Center found that for every female lawyer who left a law firm to have more time for family or unpaid pursuits, three took non-firm jobs and one took a non-law position.[49] To the extent that more women are dropping out, some observers find it unproblematic—a function of priorities that society should respect. Others, like Linda Hirshman, believe that women are "cutting their ambitions off at the knees." In her view, those who put family first have "fewer opportunities for full human flourishing" in public life. Assigning this role to women "is unjust. Women assigning it themselves is equally unjust."[50] Other commentators fault the workplace for its failure to provide flexible, reduced hour and leave policies that do not penalize those who take advantage of them.[51]

Researchers also believe that women's "choices" are socially constrained and at least partly a function of the unequal pay, advancement opportunities, and quality of work available to them. In addition to the

48. Galanter & Henderson, supra note 33; Sylvia Ann Hewlett & Carolyn Buck Luce, "Off Ramps and On Ramps: Keeping Talented Women on the Road to Success," *Harvard Business Review,* 43–45 (March 2005).

49. Marek, *supra* note 47; "Large Firms Have Trouble Retaining Women," *Nat'L L. J.,* June 18, 2007.

50. Linda R. Hirshman, *Get to Work* 23, 24–25 (2006).

51. Hewlett & Luce, *supra* note 48; Rhode & Kellerman, *Women and Leadership, supra* note 47; National Association of Women Lawyers, *Retention and Promotion of Women in Law Firms* (2006).

studies cited in the Commission report, subsequent research has confirmed significant gender disparities.[52] For example, the *After the J.D.* survey found that recent female law graduates received lower salaries than recent male graduates, even when both were in the same practice context.[53] A survey of the average pay of equity partners at large law firms found a similar gap.[54] The first national study of the experiences of women of color in law firms reported further disparities in mentoring and work assignments. About 62 percent of women of color and 60 percent of white women, but only 4 percent of white men, felt excluded from formal and informal networking opportunities. Similarly, 44 percent of women of color, compared with 39 percent of white women and only 2 percent of white men, reported being passed over for desirable work assignments.[55] Other research similarly documents inequalities in mentoring and career development opportunities, as well as persistent gender stereotypes and inadequate implementation of work/family policies.[56]

How should lawyers and law firms respond to these disparities? Some bar associations have initiatives in which firms pledge to have a certain representation of women in partnership and management positions by a given date.[57] Would you support such an approach? What other strategies would you recommend?

2. RACIAL AND ETHNIC MINORITIES

NOTES

Beginning in the late 1960s, the representation of lawyers of color in the legal profession began to increase substantially, but progress has

52. Lauren Stiller Rikleen, *Ending the Gauntlet: Removing Barriers to Women's Success in Law* (2006); Elena Kagan, "Women and the Legal Profession—A Status Report," 61 *The Record* 37 (2006); Timothy L. O'Brien, "Up the Down Staircase," *N.Y. Times*, March 19, 2006, at Section 3,1; Lindsay Blohm & Ashley Riveira, *Presumed Equal: What America's Top Women Lawyers Really Think About Their Firms* (2006); Nancy J. Reichman & Joyce S. Sterling, "Sticky Floors, Broken Steps, and Concrete Ceilings in Legal Careers," 14 *Tex. J. Women & L.* 27 (2004); Dinovitzer, *supra* note 29; National Association of Women Lawyers, *supra* note 51.

53. Dinovitzer, *supra* note 29 (noting gap of $66,000 for women and $80,000 for men, and $15,000 gap for lawyers at largest firms).

54. "Pay for Women Partners Is Lagging Behind Men," 6 *Nat'l L. J.*, (Oct. 23, 2006) (noting average salary for women was $429,169 and men was $510,375).

55. Epner, *supra* note 47.

56. For mentoring and work assignments see Rikleen, *supra* note 52 at 105–110, 139–43; Rhode & Kellerman, *supra* note 47. For stereotypes, *see id.*, and Catalyst, *The Double–Bind Dilemma for Women in Leadership* (2007). For work family policies, *see* Rhode & Kellerman, *supra* note 47; Symposium, Work/Life Conflict in the Legal Profession, 27 *Women's Rights Law Reporter* 1 (2006). For "schedule creep," in which part time lawyers end up working more than their status and compensation reflects, *see* Rikleen, *supra* note 52, at 131–36; and Joan Williams & Cynthia Calvert, "Balanced Hours Effective Part-time Policies for Washington Law Firms: The Project for Attorney Retention," 8 *Will. & Mary J. of Women & Law*, 376 (2002). *See* generally, Beiner, *supra* note 47; Lynne Marek, "Exit Women," *Nat'l. L J.*, June 18, 2007, at 1.

57. *See* the San Francisco Bar No Glass Ceiling Initiative, and the Chicago Bar Alliance for Women, Call to Action discussed in Rikleen, *supra* note 52, at 372–74. *See also* Rhode & Kellerman, *supra* note 47.

remained limited. At a time when African Americans, Hispanics, Native Americans and Asian Americans account for almost 30% of the American population, they constitute only about 20% of the nation's law students, 10% of its lawyers, and 4% of law firm partners and general counsel of Fortune 1000 companies. Forty percent of firms have no partners of color. Attorneys of color are also more likely to be unemployed and underpaid, to experience lower promotion rates to partnership, and to express dissatisfaction with their current job.[58]

Explanations for the underrepresentation vary. Leaders of large firms tend to blame the inadequate pool from which they must recruit in order to maintain their "standards," typically lawyers from the top of their class and from the top law schools. Leaders of mid size firms blame the limited pool and their inability to compete in terms of salary, resources, and status, with other employers. Small firm lawyers stress the close relationships that are necessary in such settings, which lead to employment of those with similar backgrounds.[59]

Experts, however, attribute at least part of the problem to implicit, largely unconscious, racial bias. Such bias diminishes minorities' aspirations and opportunities to enter law school, and constrain their performance and advancement once they graduate.[60] Some of the problems are comparable to those confronting women: the devaluation of competence; the special scrutiny that accompanies token status; the exclusion from informal networks of advice and assistance; the lack of quality assignments; and the absence of mentors and role models. In addition, barriers of race and ethnicity intersect with barriers of class. As the materials in Chapter XVI reflect, minorities' underrepresentation in the law school applicant pool is partly attributable to inadequate financial resources and educational preparation. These factors, together with pressures resulting from isolation and unconscious bias, contribute to minorities' disproportionate attrition rate during law school.[61]

Theories of racial prejudice proceed on several levels. Some research, based on psychoanalytic approaches, suggests that groups with highly visible differences become targets for rejection and displaced hostility. Individuals who experience frustration in their interpersonal relationships, or who cannot live up to their own aspirations, often subconsciously project their conflicts into racial stereotypes. In the process, they attribute undesir-

---

58. Chambliss, *supra* note 47, at 2, 5, 9; Dinovitzer, *supra* note 29; Emily Barker, "Trickle–Up Theory," *Minority Law Journal*, Summer 2007, at 1. *See* J. Cunyon Gordon, "Painting by Numbers: 'And, Um, Let's Have a Black Lawyer Sit at Our Table,'" 71 *Fordham L. Rev.* 1257 (2003).

59. John M. Conley, "Tales of Diversity: Lawyers' Narratives of Racial Equity in Private Firms," 31 *Law & Soc. Inquiry* 831, 838–41.

60. Chambliss, supra note 47; Epner, supra note 47; Richard H. Sander, "The Ra-

cial Paradox of the Corporate Law Firm," 84 *N.C. L. Rev.* 1225 (2006); David B. Wilkins & G. Mitu Gulati, "Why Are There So Few Black Lawyers in Corporate Law Firms: An Institutional Analysis," 84 *Cal. L. Rev.* 493 (1996).

61. As Chapter XIV notes, applicants of color also have somewhat lower pass rates on bar exams, which may be partly attributable to their lower representation among repeat test takers.

able characteristics, such as lower intelligence, laziness, or aggression, to other groups.[62]

A second framework stresses the historical, socioeconomic and political forces that help determine when and which groups become targets of subordination. According to some theorists, social and economic dislocation that generates widespread anxiety often triggers a search for scapegoats. So too, groups that have achieved dominance generally seek to legitimize their position by magnifying group differences.[63] Early socialization processes leave individuals with images, assumptions, and expectations that inhibit later efforts to build cross-racial relationships of comfort and equality.[64]

A final approach, informed by cognitive psychology, stresses the role of social categories in perpetrating racial stereotypes. Individuals' needs to simplify experience, to maintain group affiliations, and to believe in a "just world" often result in assigning characteristics to subordinate groups that explain their subordination. Most people want to assume that life follows orderly, predictable, and equitable patterns in which everyone gets what he deserves and deserves what he gets. To sustain this view, people will often adjust their evaluations of merit to justify existing inequalities.[65] Because individuals are largely unaware of their biases, researchers have developed tests of implicit attitudes, some of which are available on-line. Such tests find, for example, that both white and black subjects more readily associate positive words and images with whites than blacks; the association is strong for white survey participants, and weak for blacks. This pattern is consistent with other laboratory studies finding that black students show explicit attitudes that are strongly favorable to their own racial group, but implicit associations that are not. Such findings reflect the strength of racial stereotypes even among individuals whose conscious beliefs are to the contrary.[66] In the excerpts that follow, Charles Lawrence and Judith Lichtenberg explore such unconscious underpinnings of racial bias and the cultural practices that sustain them.

---

62. See Gordon Allport, *The Nature of Prejudice* (25th ed. 1979); David A. Thomas & Karen L. Proudford, "Making Sense of Race Relations in Organizations," in *Addressing Cultural Issues in Organizations* 51, 61 (Robert T. Carter, ed., 2000).

63. Joel Kovel, *White Racism: A Psychohistory* 44 (1984).

64. Thomas and Proudford, *supra* note 62, at 59.

65. Irwin Katz, *Stigma—A Social Psychological Analysis* 121 (1981); Michael Lerner, *The Belief in a Just World: A Fundamental Delusion* vii-viii (1980). Thomas and Proudford cite an example in which consultants interviewed midlevel professionals in an investment organization concerning issues related to the quality of life. In their initial interviews, white professional employees de-

scribed the organization as highly political, and the promotion process as not based on merit. Yet when consultants later introduced data indicating that employees of color were most disadvantaged by the process, the white professionals shifted ground and maintained that race-based differentials were the product of a system in which the "best" employees got the greatest opportunities. When the inconsistency was pointed out, the interviewees became defensive and some felt tricked because the data on race had not been conveyed before the initial interview. Thomas & Proudford, *supra* note 62, at 57–58.

66. *See* Brian A. Nosek, Mahzarin Banaji, and Anthony G. Greenwald, "Harvesting Implicit Group Attitudes and Beliefs From a Demonstration Web Site," 6 *Group Dynamics: Research and Practice*, 101, 105–06 (2002).

Charles Lawrence, "The Id, The Ego, and Equal Protection: Reckoning with Unconscious Racism"

39 Stanford Law Review, 317, 335–339 (1987).

How is the unconscious involved when racial prejudice is less apparent—when racial bias is hidden from the prejudiced individual as well as from others? Increasingly, as our culture has rejected racism as immoral and unproductive, this hidden prejudice has become the more prevalent form of racism. The individual's Ego must adapt to a cultural order that views overtly racist attitudes and behavior as unsophisticated, uninformed, and immoral. It must repress or disguise racist ideas when they seek expression.

Joel Kovel refers to the resulting personality type as the "aversive racist" and contrasts this type with the "dominative racist," the true bigot who openly seeks to keep blacks in a subordinate position and will resort to force to do so. The aversive racist believes in white superiority, but her conscience seeks to repudiate this belief or, at least, to prevent her from acting on it. She often resolves this inner conflict by not acting at all. She tries to avoid the issue by ignoring the existence of blacks, avoiding contact with them, or at most being polite, correct, and cold whenever she must deal with them. Aversive racists range from individuals who lapse into demonstrative racism when threatened—as when blacks get "too close"—to those who consider themselves liberals and, despite their sense of aversion to blacks (of which they are often unaware), do their best within the confines of the existing societal structure to ameliorate blacks' condition. . . .

Cognitivists see the process of "categorization" as one common source of racial and other stereotypes. All humans tend to categorize in order to make sense of experience. Too many events occur daily for us to deal successfully with each one on an individual basis; we must categorize in order to cope. When a category—for example, the category of black person or white person—correlates with a continuous dimension—for example, the range of human intelligence or the propensity to violence—there is a tendency to exaggerate the differences between categories on that dimension and to minimize the differences within each category.

The more important a particular classification of people into groups is to an individual, the more likely she is to distinguish sharply the characteristics of people who belong to the different groups. Here, cognitivists integrate the observations of personality theorists and social psychologists with their own. If an individual is hostile toward a group of people, she has an emotional investment in preserving the differentiations between her own group and the "others." Thus, the preservation of inaccurate judgments about the out-group is self-rewarding. This is particularly so when prejudiced judgments are made in a social context that accepts and encourages negative attitudes toward the out-group. In these cases, the group judgment reinforces and helps maintain the individual judgment about the out-group's lack of worth.

The content of the social categories to which people are assigned is generated over a long period of time within a culture and transmitted to individual members of society by a process cognitivists call "assimilation." Assimilation entails learning and internalizing preferences and evaluations. Individuals learn cultural attitudes and beliefs about race very early in life, at a time when it is difficult to separate the perceptions of one's teacher (usually a parent) from one's own. In other words, one learns about race at a time when one is highly sensitive to the social contexts in which one lives.... Lessons learned at this early developmental stage are not questioned: They are learned as facts rather than as points of view.

Furthermore, because children learn lessons about race at this early stage, most of the lessons are tacit rather than explicit.... If we do learn lessons about race in this way, we are not likely to be aware that the lessons have even taken place. If we are unaware that we have been taught to be afraid of blacks or to think of them as lazy or stupid, then we may not be conscious of our internalization of those feelings and beliefs.

All of these processes, most of which occur outside the actor's consciousness, are mutually reinforcing.... In ambiguous social situations, it will always be easier to find evidence supporting an individual's assumed group characteristics than to find contradictory evidence.... Case studies have demonstrated that an individual who holds stereotyped beliefs about a "target" will remember and interpret past events in the target's life history in ways that bolster and support his stereotyped beliefs and will perceive the target's actual behavior as reconfirming and validating the stereotyped beliefs. While the individual may be aware of the selectively perceived facts that support his categorization or simplified understanding, he will not be aware of the process that has caused him to deselect the facts that do not conform with his rationalization. Thus, racially prejudiced behavior that is actually the product of learned cultural preferences is experienced as a reflection of rational deduction from objective observation, which is non-prejudicial behavior. The decisionmaker who is unaware of the selective perception that has produced her stereotype will not view it as a stereotype. She will believe that her actions are motivated not by racial prejudice but by ... the attributes she has "observed" in the groups she has favored or disfavored.

Judith Lichtenberg, "Racism in the Head, Racism in the World"

12 Report from the Institute for Philosophy and Public Policy, 3–5 (Spring/Summer 1992).

Different perceptions among blacks and whites in our society about what racism is, and where it is, constitute an important source of racial tension. For many white Americans today, the word "racism" is a red flag. They don't see themselves as harboring animosity toward black people as such; they believe they hold to an ideal of equality, and of equal opportunity. So they feel insulted to be called racists, baffled by charges that we live in a racist society. A white supremacist would not be so wounded.

On the other hand, those who say our society is racist are not speaking rhetorically or hyperbolically. The claim that racism is dead or insignificant, in the face of overwhelming asymmetries between blacks and whites, . . . must produce anger or humiliation or incomprehension.

In general, white people today use the word "racism" to refer to the explicit conscious belief in racial superiority (typically white over black, but also sometimes black over white). For the most part, black people mean something different by racism: they mean a set of practices and institutions that result in the oppression of black people. Racism, in this view, is not a matter of what's in people's heads but of what happens in the world.

The white picture of the racist is the old-time Southern white supremacist, who proclaimed his beliefs proudly. Your typical late twentieth-century American is, at some important level, an egalitarian who rejects the supremacist creed. In her mind, then, she is not a racist.

That a person is not a racist in this sense makes a difference. . . . [T]hings are worse when people explicitly believe and proclaim supremacist doctrines, and a special moral culpability attaches to holding such beliefs. But not to be a racist "in the head" is insufficient to prevent injustice and suffering that divides along racial lines.

The alternative view is that the evil we call racism is not fundamentally a matter of what's in people's heads, not a matter of their private, individual intentions, but rather a function of public institutions and practices that create or perpetuate racial division and inequality. Who cares if your intentions are good if they reinforce or permit racial discrimination and deprivation?

Racism as overt or out-and-out racism reflects a powerful strain in our attitudes toward moral responsibility. On this view, you are responsible only for what you intend; thus, if consciously you harbor no ill-will toward people of another race or background you are in that respect innocent. For those who would be deemed the oppressors, such a view is abetted by what psychologists call "cognitive dissonance"—essentially, the desire to reduce psychological discomfort. It is comfortable for white people to believe racism is dead just as long as they harbor no conscious feelings of antipathy or superiority to blacks. And, conversely, it is less painful for blacks, seeing what they see, to think otherwise.

Less–Than–Conscious Racism

Over the last thirty or forty years it has become publicly unacceptable, in most circles, to express racist views openly. . . . It doesn't follow, however, that such beliefs vanish altogether.

How do they manifest themselves? It's common for people to find— even without any awareness on their part—the behavior of a person of another race more threatening or obnoxious or stupid (or whatever) than they would the behavior of a member of their own group. And just as their threshold of intolerance may be lower for negative behavior, they may have higher standards for members of other groups than for their own when it comes to positive traits: thus the claim that women and minorities have to be "twice as good" as white males to get the same credit. A related phenomenon is what psychologists call "aversive racism." In an experiment by Samuel Gaertner, subjects received a phone call, seemingly a wrong number, from a person who said that his car had broken down, that he had just used his last dime and that he needed someone to call a tow truck for him. Young white liberals who presumably saw themselves as racially well-intentioned, were almost six times more likely to hang up on callers when the voice on the phone sounded black than when the person sounded white.... There's considerable evidence that murderers who kill white people are more likely to get the death penalty than those who kill black people, a disparity that implies the belief on the part of juries that white life is more valuable than black life....

People sometimes justify discrimination not in terms of their own beliefs but in terms of other people's.... So too, borrowing a term from Mary Anne Warren, we can define "secondary racism" as discrimination based not on race itself but according to race-correlated factors that unfairly affect racial minorities.... [For example] [e]ntrance examinations and other tests may contain biases against some groups that are unintended by and opaque to their creators....

The Disadvantages of Being Disadvantaged

This last category has no common name, although it is perhaps the broadest and most intractable form by which racial inequalities are perpetuated. Whereas secondary racism involves discriminating (however inadvertently) on the basis of factors irrelevant to merit, this form employs criteria that are appropriate and relevant.

Most people would agree that we ought to admit people to jobs or schools on the basis of ability and talent, past or potential performance. Yet even if we could purge our screening devices of irrelevant biases, fewer blacks would gain entry than their numbers in the general population would suggest. They will on the whole be less competitive, given past deprivation, than their more privileged white counterparts....

Even if "racism-in-the-head" disappeared, then, "racism-in-the-world" would not. One reason is the continued existence of facially race-neutral practices, like seniority systems and the old-boy network, that discriminate unfairly against minorities and women. The other reason is that people who as a historical consequence of overt racism have had substandard prenatal care, nutrition, housing, health services, and education, people who live in drug-and crime-infested neighborhoods, will on the whole fare less well than those more privileged.

Conclusion

[A]n individual whose attitudes and beliefs are not overtly racist, are not even covertly racist, can inhabit a racist society or participate in racist *institutions*. A society or an institution is racist if it discriminates on grounds of race, either "primarily" or "secondarily," or if it perpetuates inequalities produced by primary or secondary racism. Sometimes, the society or the institution is so corrupt that a morally decent person arguably ought not have anything to do with it. More often, however, we hold individuals to less stringent standards. We want to know whether they simply go along with the objectionable practices, or if in the course of their involvement they do something to make the system less discriminatory. What can they do? How much ought they to do? That's another story.

NOTES

The American Bar Association's Commission on Racial and Ethnic Diversity in the Legal Profession, together with other experts in the field, has issued a broad set of recommendations to promote diversity within the profession. These efforts focus on increasing accountability and racial comfort, and challenging racial bias.[67] For example, employers should intensify their efforts in hiring, retaining, and promoting lawyers of color. In particular, employers should reassess evaluation procedures and criteria that have a disproportional racial impact. Recruiters should make greater contact with law schools that have substantial minority enrollments, either through on site interviews or letters to minority student associations and visits to regional minority placement conferences. Hiring standards should avoid excessive reliance on first year grades, LSAT scores, and law review experience, which disproportionately exclude students of color and do not measure the full range of skills that are necessary for successful practice. Promotion criteria such as collegiality and ability to attract client business need to take into account the special obstacles facing minorities. Employers should also ensure a favorable working environment for underrepresented groups. Providing adequate mentoring and opportunities for challenging assignments, supervisory experiences, and client contact should be key priorities.[68]

National, state, and local bar organizations have also attempted to expand access to the bar by underrepresented groups. Strategies have included increased recruitment of talented minority high school and college students, greater financial assistance for disadvantaged students, more support for outreach and educational preparation programs by groups like the Council on Legal Educational Opportunities, and additional initiatives that assist minority graduates to pass the bar.

Other diversity efforts have focused on encouraging government and in-house legal departments to channel business to lawyers of color and demand that their counsel demonstrate adequate commitment to diversity. For example, since 1999 about five hundred corporate counsel signed a

67. Devon Carbado & Mitu Gulati, "Race to the Top of the Corporate Ladder: What Minorities Do When They Get There," 61 *Wash. & Lee L. Rev.* 1645, 1662–1663 (2004).

68. Chambliss, *supra* note 47, at 97–98; Sam Reeves, "The Carrot Didn't Work So Let's Apply the Stick," S6, S8, *National L. J.*, (Oct. 23, 2006); Edgardo Ramos & Lynn Anne Baronas, "What Works: Ways to Increase Diversity at Law Firms," *Nat'l L. J.*, Jan 16, 2006, at 13. Wilkins & Gulati, *supra* note 60.

statement indicating that they valued diversity when choosing outside counsel. Beginning in 2004, in an effort to intensify client pressure, a growing number of corporate counsel agreed to "end or limit relationships with firms whose performance consistently indicated a lack of meaningful interest in being diverse."[69] Similarly, the California Minority Counsel Program, sponsored by the Bar Association of San Francisco, enlists corporations who agree to hire and promote more lawyers of color, to use more minority-owned firms for outside legal work, and to encourage other firms that it employs to assign lawyers of color to its work. The Bar also asks firms to accept specified affirmative action goals.[70]

Paul Barrett's profile, *The Good Black*, provides a case history of the profession's difficulties in addressing diversity-related issues. It chronicles the efforts of Lawrence Mungen, an African–American graduate of Harvard College and Harvard Law School, to fit the model that Barrett's title invokes. As a senior associate, Mungen joined the Washington, D.C. branch office of a Chicago law firm, Katten, Muchen and Zavis, and attempted to "play by the rules." After being hired to do complex bankruptcy work in an office that generated too little of it, he fell through the cracks, and landed off the partnership track. But until late in the process, Mungen failed to complain or to raise race-related concerns. He didn't want to be typecast as the "angry black," and he declined to support or mentor any of the small number of other minority lawyers at the firm. When his difficulty in obtaining work became clear, some partners made a few well meaning but ineffectual responses. They slashed his billing rate, which enabled him to take over some routine matters, but also undermined his reputation as someone capable of demanding, partnership-caliber work. Although the senior partners eventually offered to relocate him in another office, they did not provide assurances of opportunities that would lead to promotion. He sued for race discrimination and alleged multiple examples, such as the firm's failure to provide formal evaluations, informal mentoring, invitations to client meetings, or help with business development. A largely black District of Columbia jury found in his favor, but a divided appellate panel reversed. Unable to find another comparable position, Mungen made do with temporary, low-level assignments at other firms and, by the end of the book, was contemplating an alternative career.

As many commentators have noted, the case was a kind of "racial Rorschach test" in which observers saw what they expected to see. To lawyers in the firm and sympathizers outside it, including the appellate court, this was a morality play in which no good deed went unpunished. From their perspective, Mungen was treated no worse than white associates, and in some respects considerably better. The slights and oversights that he alleged at trial were "business as usual mismanagement." And the

---

69. Karen Donovan, "Pushed by Clients, Law Firms Step Up Diversity Efforts," *N.Y. Times*, July 21, 2006, at C6. For the Call To Action initiative, see www.clocalltoaction.com

70. *See* Bruck and Cantor, *supra* note 43; "Diversity Counts," *Cal. Lawyer*, Nov. 2005, at 12; David Wilkins, "Do Clients Have Ethical Obligations to Lawyers? Some Lessons From the Diversity Wars," 11 *Georgetown J. Leg. Ethics* 855, 964–65 (1998).

extra efforts that the firm made to keep Mungen were evidence of a commitment to equal opportunity. By contrast, critics, including Barrett, saw this as a textbook case of "a reckless indifferent affirmative action." From their vantage, the firm's efforts were too little too late. Unsurprisingly, these competing perceptions usually divided along racial lines and typified attitudes within the profession generally. In an ABA survey around the time, only 8 percent of black lawyers, but 41 percent of whites, believed that firms had a genuine commitment to diversity.[71]

Much, of course, depends on what counts as commitment. Katten's management, like that at many firms, undoubtedly did want minority lawyers to succeed. Even from a purely pragmatic standpoint, it helps in recruitment and business development if a firm includes more than the single black lawyer that Katten's Washington office had during Mungen's employment. But while many attorneys want to achieve greater diversity, they do not necessarily want to rethink the structures that get in the way. Nor do they support preferential treatment. The ABA's survey found that only 42 percent of white lawyers, compared with 92 percent of blacks, favored affirmative action. To opponents, reliance on race, ethnicity, or gender perpetuates a kind of preferential treatment that society should be seeking to eradicate. In critics' view, such treatment implies that women and men of color require special advantages, which reinforces the very assumptions of inferiority that society should be trying to counteract.

By contrast, supporters of affirmative action generally acknowledge that stigma can present substantial problems, but argue that critics mistake its most fundamental causes and plausible solutions. Assumptions of inferiority predated affirmative action and would persist without it. The absence of women and men of color in key legal roles is also stigmatizing. Moreover, in proponents' view, the profession is unlikely to reduce racial or gender prejudices if it ignores their continuing effects, or treat all forms of preferential treatment as equally objectionable. Disfavoring attorneys of color stigmatizes and subordinates in a way that disfavoring white males does not. In some contexts, "special" treatment may be essential to counteract the special obstacles facing underrepresented groups.

However, as even supporters of affirmative action note, it is by no means adequate to deal with the diversity-related challenges facing the legal profession. An undue reliance on preferences at the hiring stage may deflect attention from the obstacles that lawyers of color face in subsequently trying to forge the relationships that will enable them to succeed within primarily white organizations.[72] The stigma associated with affirmative action can compound those obstacles. Significant progress will require legal employers to implement a broad range of strategies that can address the problems of unconscious bias in mentoring, work assignments, and evaluation practices, as well as mitigate any backlash that results from diversity initiatives.

---

71. Walter La Grande, "Getting There, Staying There," *ABA Journal*, 54 (Feb. 1999).

72. Wilkins & Gulati, *supra* note 60, at 501.

QUESTIONS

1. What is your view on affirmative action in legal workplaces? In a letter to the editor of the *National Law Journal,* a self-described "young, white, straight male attorney who happens to be politically progressive," wrote to protest employment termination decisions attributable to "meeting an important client's newly asserted diversity demands." In his view, "surely firing people even partially on the basis of an immutable characteristic is as unjust when done in the name of increasing diversity as it is when done to maintain homogeneity."[73] Do you agree?

2. If you had been managing partner at Katten, what would you have done when Mungen's problems surfaced? What would you have done after the litigation ended?

3. Can even "positive" race-based characterizations work against the stereotyped group? What barriers might confront Asian–Americans who are cast as the "Model Minority" based on their intelligence and hard work?[74] Consider the description Senator Joseph Biden offered of lawyer and presidential candidate Barack Obama, as the "first mainstream African–American who is articulate and bright and clean and a nice-looking guy."[75] If this statement had been made in the context of a candidate for legal employment, would it be evidence of unconscious racism? How should lawyers respond?

4. How would you evaluate the bar's progress in reducing barriers for lawyers of color? What strategies strike you as most promising.

3. SEXUAL ORIENTATION

NOTES

"Don't have any. Don't want any." That was one employer's response to a Los Angeles bar survey about gay and lesbian attorneys in the mid–1990's.[76] Until relatively recently, those attitudes were all too typical. The experience of gays and lesbians in the legal profession has paralleled their experience in society generally. Until the late 1960s, criminal prohibitions on homosexual conduct and cultural assumptions about sexual "deviance" inhibited public expression of gay and lesbian identity. Individuals whose non-heterosexual practices became known suffered substantial sanctions, including pervasive discrimination in employment. Law was no exception, although the closeted nature of most homosexual practices presented few

73. Ben Martin, Letter to the Editor, *National L. J.* Nov., 6, 2006, at 23.

74. Mirand O. McGowne & James Lindgren, "The First Century: Celebrating 100 Years of Legal Scholarship Essay: Testing the Model Minority Myth," 100 *Nw. U. L. Rev.* 331 (2006): Pat Chew, "Asian Americans: The 'Reticent' Minority and Their Paradoxes," 36 *Wm. & Mary* l. Rev. 1, 24, 1994.

75. Lynette Clemetson, "The Racial Politics of Speaking Well," *N. Y. Times,* Feb. 4, 2007, Sec. 4, at 1.

76. "Los Angeles County Bar Association Report on Sexual Orientation Bias," 45 *S. Cal. Rev. of Law & Women's Studies* 295, 305 (1995).

occasions for bar pronouncements. During the 1950s and 1960s, there were only three reported judicial cases concerning denial of professional licenses to gays and lesbians, and only one involved an attorney. In 1955, Harris Kimball, a Florida civil rights attorney, was disbarred after being convicted of having sexual relations with another man on an Orlando beach.[77]

Beginning in the 1970s, the growth of a gay rights movement contributed to substantial changes. Partly in response to such activism, as well as to new research and new interpretations of prior research, the American Psychiatric Association in 1973 removed homosexuality from its list of mental illnesses. Legal challenges to discrimination based on sexual orientation also began to meet with limited success, and the next several decades witnessed the increasing passage of bans on such discrimination. However, openly gay and lesbian individuals faced widespread discrimination in areas such as employment, family law, immigration policy, benefit programs and criminal codes.[78]

Experience within the legal profession has mirrored this partial progress. In 1973, on petition from Harris Kimball, the New York Court of Appeals became the first state to hold that homosexuality was not a ground for exclusion from the bar.[79] A series of bar admission cases in Florida subsequently prompted its supreme court to limit moral character scrutiny to inquiries bearing a "rational relationship to fitness for legal practice," and to determine that private noncommercial sexual acts between consenting adults bore no such relationship.[80] Beginning in the late 1970s, a number of organizations, including the National Lesbian and Gay Lawyers Association, formed to provide support networks and press for changes on issues involving sexual orientation. In 1989, the American Bar Association passed a resolution condemning discrimination on the basis of sexual orientation. In 1996, the Association adopted a resolution aimed at protecting the civil rights of gay and lesbian attorneys in the justice system. It urged state and local bar associations to study the issue and to make appropriate recommendations. By the late 1990s, about 30 states had prohibitions on judicial bias based on sexual orientation. So too, the Association of American Law Schools and American Bar Association forbid discrimination by law schools on grounds of sexual orientation as well as race, color, religion, national origin, sex, age, handicap, or disability.

Yet despite this progress, bias against gay and lesbian attorneys remains a problem. In surveys by the National Law Placement Association, about 1.4% of lawyers identify as gay, lesbian, or bisexual, and in large firms the number is 1.9%. These percentages are significantly lower than

77. State *ex rel.* Florida Bar v. Kimball, 96 So.2d 825 (Fla.1957).

78. For overview of problems and progress, *see* William N. Eskridge, Jr. and Nan D. Hunter, *Sexuality, Gender, and the Law* (2d ed. 2004).

79. In re Kimball, 40 A.D.2d 252, 339 N.Y.S.2d 302 (1973), *rev'd per curiam,* 33 N.Y.2d 586, 347 N.Y.S.2d 453, 301 N.E.2d 436 (1973). Florida courts subsequently affirmed a recommendation that Kimball be readmitted to the bar if he passed the state bar examination. Florida Bar In re Kimball, 425 So.2d 531 (Fla.1982) (assessing costs of the proceeding against Kimball).

80. Florida Board of Bar Examiners Re N.R.S., 403 So.2d 1315 (Fla.1981).

the 3%–7% estimated to be in the population generally.[81] The reasons may have much to do with sexual orientation bias that lawyers have frequently reported in professional settings.[82] Openly gay and lesbian attorneys often experienced adverse career impacts as well as a lack of benefits for domestic partners.[83] Although the situation has recently improved, particularly in terms of formal policy, the philosophy in some workplaces continues to be "Don't ask, don't tell."[84]

Rarely does discrimination based on sexual orientation result in complaints, and seldom do complaints result in effective responses. Only 7 percent of some 1100 Legal Aid attorneys in a New York survey were aware of a complaint involving sexual orientation bias although six times that number were aware of bias-related incidents. A related New York bar survey of some 220 gay and lesbian attorneys found that disciplinary action occurred in less than 4 percent of reported incidents of discrimination.[85]

Inadequate remedies both mask and perpetuate the problem. Most victims of discrimination see little point in raising concerns that might harm their own reputations more than those of their offenders. Risks of blacklisting make litigation involving employment discrimination particularly unlikely. As a Los Angeles bar report notes, gay and lesbian practitioners generally would "rather have a career than a lawsuit."[86] Remedial approaches available for other forms of discrimination have been unavailable for discrimination based on sexual orientation. Although an increasing number of gay and lesbian attorneys have become open about their sexual orientation, others are deterred by fears of workplace bias and social ostracism, and the lack of legal and policy protection from bias.[87]

The lack of prohibitions against bias based on sexual orientation has often been justified on the ground that such discrimination is different from that directed at other underrepresented groups. Yet the reasons most

81. Vivan Chen, "Rainbow Revolution," *American Lawyer*, March 2007, at 15; Leigh Jones, "Gay, Lesbian Lawyers Gain at Larger Firms," *National Law J.*, March 26, 2007, at 1.

82. *See* studies cited in ABA Section of Individual Rights and Responsibilities, Report to the House of Delegates (2007) available at www.ABA.net.org/yld/midyear07/docs.115.pdf; New Jersey Final Report of the Task Force on Gay and Lesbian Issues (2001); Judicial Council Advisory Commission on Access and Fairness, Sexual Orientation Fairness in the California Courts (2001); Greta Schnetzler and Laurie K. Simonson, "Sexual Orientation Bias," *California Lawyer*, 37, 38 (December 2001); Report of the Special Committee on Lesbians and Gay Men in the Legal Profession, Association of the Bar of the City of New York, 48 *The Record* 843, 860 (1993); Los Angeles County Bar Report, *supra* note 76, at 197. For less systematic evidence suggesting progress, *see* "Gay Friendlier," *American Lawyer*, at 26, 27 (January 2003).

83. California Bar Association, *Report and Recommendations Regarding Sexual Orientation Discrimination in the California Legal Profession* (1996); Los Angeles County Bar Report, *supra* note 76.

84. Chen, *supra* note 76, at 16.

85. New York Committee Report, *supra* note 82, at 854.

86. Los Angeles County Bar Report, *supra* note 76, at 355. For a recent suit against Sullivan and Cromwell that has attracted widespread adverse publicity for the gay attorney claiming discrimination, *see* Chen, *supra* note 81.

87. Only sixteen states and the District of Columbia prohibited employment discrimination on the basis of sexual orientation. ABA Section of Individual Rights and Responsibilities, *supra* note 82. For general discussion of workplace barriers, *see* Catalyst, *Making Change: LGBT Inclusion: Understanding the Challenges* (2007).

often given for sexual orientation bias are comparable to justifications once offered for discrimination on the basis of race, ethnicity, or gender: i.e., lawyers who are "different" along these lines would not fit in, or would be unacceptable to clients.

Efforts to respond to these patterns are increasing. Bar associations have sponsored surveys and recommendations concerning sexual orientation bias. In February 2007, the ABA added "persons of differing sexual orientation and gender identity" to its Goal IX, which calls on the bar to promote "full and equal participation in the legal profession" of targeted groups including minorities, women, and persons with disabilities. The ABA also created a Commission on Sexual Orientation and Gender Identity to address bias.[88] Recommended strategies have included: lobbying for antidiscrimination initiatives by judicial bodies, governmental decision makers, professional associations, and employing institutions; recognition of openly gay and lesbian attorneys as a positive contribution to diversity programs; inclusion of domestic partners in employment-related benefits and activities; limitation of bar admission and disciplinary oversight to exclude noncommercial sexual practices among consenting adults; bans on law school recruiting by employers who discriminate on the basis of sexual orientation; greater coverage of issues concerning sexual orientation in law school curricula and journals; pro bono assistance to gay and lesbian organizations; and educational activities designed to promote tolerance concerning sexual orientation.

What is your view? What should be the role of lawyers in responding to bias based on sexual orientation?

4.   Age

Discrimination based on age is likely to become an increasingly important concern over the next two decades as the number of senior lawyers grows dramatically. Lawyers over fifty now constitute about 30 percent of the profession. This group is expected to double over the next twenty years and reach about 560,000 or 45% of the profession.[89] A full quarter of the American bar is expected to start retiring by 2011.[90]

A central and unsettled issue of similarly increasing importance is whether partners in law firms are covered by the federal Age Discrimination in Employment Act (ADEA) 28 U.S.C. §§ 623(a), 630(f). That act protects employees, not employers, and the EEOC, in a recent widely publicized case, has claimed that partners who lack sufficient management prerogatives may qualify for protection. The case, *EEOC v. Sidley Austin Brown & Wood*, 406 F.Supp.2d 991 (N.D. Ill. 2005), and 315 F.3d 696 (7th Cir. 2002), arose after Sidley's executive committee demoted 32 partners to

---

88. Siobhan Morrissey, "Overlooked No Longer," *ABA J.*, Dec. 2007, at 62.

89. Marc Galanter, "Second Chances," *American Lawyer*, June, 2000, at 116.

90. Leigh Jones, "Dealing with the R Word," *Nat'l Law J.* April 16, 2007, at 1, 10; Leigh Jones, "Firms Face New Rules for Retirement," *Nat'l Law J.*, November 19, 2007, at A1.

nonequity counsel or senior counsel status and altered retirement rules for other partners. Almost all of these partners were in their fifties or sixties, and the EEOC opened an investigation to determine if they had a valid claim under the ADEA. According to the EEOC, these partners were employees because they had no meaningful opportunity to vote on issues of most importance to them or their firm, which were all decided by a self-perpetuating executive committee (36 of 500 partners). The district court denied Sidley's motion to dismiss, and the court of appeals, in an opinion by Judge Posner affirmed. His opinion signaled considerable support for the EEOC's position, and noted that decisions about ADEA coverage should not be determined by the "tyranny of labels." 315 F.3d, at 705. Sidley subsequently settled the suit under a consent decree awarding the demoted partners $27.5 million, and barring the firm from using age as a basis for requiring retirement, terminating partners, or altering their partnership status.

That case, together with the shifting demographics of the profession, is causing many employers to reconsider their policies. About half of all firms have mandatory retirement rules, which vary widely and are enforced inconsistently.[91] Many allow retirees to stay on with some "of counsel" or "senior counsel" status, but with diminished earnings and influence over firm policy. About 40 percent of surveyed lawyers favor mandatory retirement, largely on the grounds that it makes room in the ranks for younger lawyers, encourages an orderly transition in client relationships, and avoids awkward conversations with non-productive partners.[92] Most lawyers, however, believe that such age-based rules are too inflexible. In 2007, following recommendations of an influential New York Bar Association report, the ABA passed a resolution calling on firms to end mandatory retirement. The preferable approach, according to supporters of the resolution, is individualized evaluation and planning, with incentives for senior lawyers to transition into a status that meets employers' needs as well as their own.

How should the profession deal with these demographic challenges? Are there ways of more effectively involving retired lawyers in pro bono or other public service?

The result in *Sidley,* and the partnership structure that it reflects, are likely to have broader consequences. In order to protect themselves from liability in discrimination suits based not just on age but on race and sex, law firms are likely to move toward increasingly objective evaluation criteria. As David Wilkins notes, this trend could be a mixed blessing. It may help reduce bias against disadvantaged groups, but at the expense of enshrining criteria that "will be all about money. . . . To be sure, firms will continue to pay lip service to factors such as institutional citizenship and public service. At the end of the day, however, rigorously holding partners to rigid standards on billing and revenue generation is likely to seem the

---

91. Jones, "Dealing with the R Word," *supra* note 90, at 10.

92. Jones, "Firms Face New Rules," *supra* note 90, at A10; Elizabeth Goldberg,

"Gray Matters," *American Lawyer*, December, 2007, at 119.

best way both to protect the firm from discrimination claims and to ensure its continued survival in today's cutthroat global marketplace."[93] If Wilkins is right, are there ways that the profession could respond to these trends?

93. David   B.   Wilkins,   "Partner,   Wood," 120 *Harv. L. Rev.* 1264, 1272 (2007). Shmartner: EEOC v. Sidley Austin Brown &

CHAPTER III

PROFESSIONAL INDEPENDENCE AND PROFESSIONAL CODES

A. THE HISTORICAL BACKDROP

INTRODUCTION

American lawyers formed bar associations during the Colonial period, but these organizations declined after the Revolution. The decline was partly due to the exodus of Tory leaders and partly to broader social, economic, and political forces working against professional cohesion. In the late nineteenth century, bar associations re-emerged to meet a variety of needs described in the excerpts that follow.

Roscoe Pound, The Lawyer from Antiquity to Modern Times

10–15 (1953).

The bar association as an organization of those practicing the profession is an essential element of professional life. It is only through organization that the spirit of public service can be developed and maintained and crucial types of public service can be rendered effectively. It is the bar association, not the individual lawyer, that can maintain high educational standards insuring a learned profession, that can maintain high standards of character as a prerequisite of admission to practice, that can formulate and maintain high standards of ethical conduct in relations both with clients and with courts. The public has a deep interest in having a well organized bar part of the machinery of administering justice in a complex social and economic order. . . .

By a bar association, then, we mean an organization of lawyers to promote and maintain the practice of law as a profession, that is, as a learned art pursued in the spirit of a public service—in the spirit of a service of furthering the administration of justice through and according to law. This is brought out in the declared purposes of bar associations. . . . (1) To advance the science of jurisprudence, (2) to promote the administration of justice in the jurisdiction in which the association exists, (3) to uphold the honor of the profession of the law, and (4) to establish cordial intercourse among the members of the bar of the jurisdiction. These are set forth in the Constitution of the American Bar Association (1878) adding to the second a further purpose "to promote uniformity of legislation throughout the Union." This formula has been followed by most of the state associations since 1878.

James W. Hurst, The Growth of American Law: The Lawmakers

285–289, 290–292 (1950).

During most of the years after the American Revolution, in the local communities, in the states, and in the nation, there was no bar in any but a courtesy use of the title. A "bar" implies internal organization and cohesion, and on the whole lawyers in the United States were among the most unthinkingly and stubbornly individualistic members of the loosely organized American society. In the late eighteenth century the more populous places had local bar associations, which the lawyers formed for social, library, or disciplinary purposes, or for a combination of these ends. In the Northern states some local bar associations—for example, the Suffolk County bar in Massachusetts—attained a high degree of guild organization, and for a generation firmly controlled admissions and professional conduct. In the first two generations after independence the popular temper demanded relaxation of bar standards, and most of these local associations disappeared, or became wholly social. . . .

Planned bar organization revived first in the great cities. It marked a reaction against the corruption in local government. In 1870 a number of leading lawyers organized the Association of the Bar of the City of New York, primarily to fight the Tweed ring. The activities of a notorious fringe of unlicensed practitioners gave impetus to the formation of the Chicago Bar Association, in 1874. Between 1870 and 1878 eight city and eight state bar associations, in twelve states, were formed largely under the motive of reform of municipal government and of conditions within the bar. . . .

By 1925 all the states and territories could claim some sort of association. It was hard to get reliable counts of city or county bar organizations . . . Estimates put the total at . . . above 1100 by 1930. The great growth in numbers in both cases came after the turn of the century. However, like the American Bar Association, most state and local associations originated primarily for social reasons; and, like the national organization, most of them held to this character until the 1920s. . . . Structurally, the organized bar was weak because of the ill-considered adoption of the practice of a select instead of an all-inclusive membership . . . The new associations did not fix reasonably objective, uniform, and defensible criteria for the selection of their members. Hence they weakened their authority to speak either to laymen or to lawyers, as representatives of the profession. . . . After 1910 state and local associations . . . sought broader membership. Some of them went from the extreme of restriction to an extreme in which they emphasized merely quantitative growth. By 1935 it was estimated that 60 percent of lawyers in the United States belonged to some professional association. . . .

At Saratoga, [a fashionable summer resort in] New York, in August, 1878, seventy-five lawyers from twenty-one jurisdictions organized the American Bar Association.... For many years election was a highly selective, personalized matter [and the organization was mainly social]. Though the Association early began discussion of reforms in legal education, its outstanding field of action during its first generation was in the preparation and recommendation of uniform laws for adoption by the states.

Jerold S. Auerbach, Unequal Justice: Lawyers and Social Change in Modern America

62–67 (1976).

The bar association movement was a characteristic feature of the decades surrounding 1900. Lawyers, in common with doctors, social workers, teachers, and engineers, flocked into professional associations, whose growth—the number of bar associations jumped from 16 in 1880 to more than 600 by 1916—expressed the impulse for professional cohesion in a fragmented society undergoing rapid change. Their local revival after the Civil War was attributable to unease over urban corruption. Nationally, the American Bar Association, organized in 1878, had more diffuse purposes: to promote the administration of justice, to advance jurisprudence, to uphold professional honor, and to encourage social intercourse among lawyers. But the ABA exuded the genial tone of a social club, set by its predominantly Southern members who came to Saratoga Springs each year to escape the summer heat. The "benefit of the waters," one member declared, rivaled in importance the professional business of the association. Simeon Baldwin, the moving spirit behind the association, labored to confine membership "to leading men or those of high promise...." Local associations often were similarly exclusive. The Chicago Bar Association, founded (in the words of one of its presidents) to bring "the better and the best elements of the profession together," charged high admission fees and annual dues to achieve its purpose. The strongest pillars of the Association of the Bar of the City of New York were Yale, Harvard, and Protestantism.

Bar associations were not the exclusive preserve of corporate lawyers, but lawyers whose practices provided them with a sufficient margin of wealth and leisure to pay fees, attend conventions, and participate in committee work were bound to predominate.... State associations were more diversified [than the ABA]; even in the most heavily urbanized and industrialized states general practitioners [as well as corporate lawyers] retained a strong voice. In fact, in states like New York, Massachusetts, and Illinois, metropolitan and state associations, representing respectively the urban and rural wings of the profession, engaged in constant internecine sniping. Whether corporate or country lawyers predominated, however, the "best men" used bar associations as a lever of control over professional ethics, educational qualifications, and bar admission. Claiming the right to represent and to police the entire profession, they discriminated against an increasingly substantial number of urban practitioners from ethnic minority groups.

Understandably, bar associations defended stability, order, and control.... Bar associations did venture timidly into the shallower waters of law reform, but they usually skirted the dangerous shoals of substantive change. In 1912 ABA president Stephen Gregory declared that professional associations were "the chief instrumentality of constructive legal reform." Rarely, however, did their concern extend to such problems as the provision of legal services. At best, they preoccupied themselves with the most technical, professional aspects of legal issues—for example, the ethical proprieties of contingent fees rather than the social and individual costs of lives broken in industrial accidents.... Law was supposed to be socially relevant; but the areas chosen for reform were not the areas of law most socially relevant.

During the second decade of the twentieth century the American Bar Association began to assert itself aggressively as a professional protective organization. Its purpose was twofold: to preserve its own exclusiveness (and the status that accompanied its preservation) and to exert professional leverage upon the political process. Two prewar episodes provided a test of its strength and scope: the admission of black lawyers and the nomination of Louis D. Brandeis to the Supreme Court.

In 1912 the executive committee of the American Bar Association unknowingly admitted three black lawyers to membership. Informed of its carelessness, it quickly passed a resolution rescinding the admission and— "since the settled practice of the Association has been to elect only white men as members"—referring the matter for determination by the entire association. Attorney General George W. Wickersham protested (one of the contested members, a Harvard Law School graduate, was his assistant in the Department of Justice)—not from any commitment to racial equality but from disgust with procedural irregularities that violated association by-laws. He was assured by the association's secretary that the recission resolution had been adopted only with "a sincere purpose to do what seemed ... to be right and just...." And he was sternly chastised for his "discourteous and dogmatic" criticism, a display of pique unbecoming an association member. But Moorfield Storey, a past president of the bar association and the first president of the National Association for the Advancement of Colored People, was incensed. "It is a monstrous thing," he complained, "that we should undertake to draw a color line in the Bar Association." Storey repudiated the notion that blacks were excluded by association policy, although he conceded that none had ever been admitted. The association was in a quandary. Claiming to be a national organization, it functioned as a restricted social club. The admission of blacks, in the words of its membership chairman, posed "a question of keeping pure the Anglo–Saxon race." A compromise resolution precluded future associational miscegenation. Prodded by Storey, members permitted the three duly elected black lawyers to remain but provided that all future applicants must identify themselves by race. The association thereby committed itself to lily-white membership for the next half-century. It had elevated racism above professionalism.

Professionalism converged with politics in the Brandeis donnybrook. The first of several dramatic twentieth-century Court nomination controversies, it brought into sharp focus the public implications of professional parochialism. More was at stake than a judicial seat, although a place on the Supreme Court was hardly inconsequential at a time when the judiciary was praised or blamed as the most reliable defender of vested property interests against public regulation. On the surface the division seemed clear. Brandeis' opponents, drawn largely from State Street law firms and from the American Bar Association, could plausibly view the Boston people's attorney as a threat to their restricted professional world. They spoke of law as a bulwark of private property; Brandeis, who would not have disagreed, had often used it as an instrument of social change to make property owners more responsible to the public. They devoted their careers to counseling private interests; Brandeis committed much of his to public service. . . .

The challenge to Brandeis would cut across every major professional concern of the day: ethnicity; the social function of law; the role of lawyers; and standards of professional character, conduct, and ethics. As "an outsider, successful, and a Jew," Brandeis was suspect. His confirmation fight was a symbolic crusade, pitting the newest defenders of the established professional order against the outsider who was especially dangerous because he shared so many of their attributes yet put them to such different use. It was precisely because Brandeis' credentials were so impeccable—a brilliant record at Harvard Law School and a lucrative corporate practice—that the opposition to his appointment was so revealing. Even the most qualified of outsiders—qualified according to professional terms set by the insiders—encountered a wall of antipathy from the elite. Their resistance, and their defeat, exposed both the sources of their professional power and its limits. [Despite opposition by the ABA and six of its former presidents, Brandeis was confirmed in 1916 by a vote of 47–22.]

PROBLEM 1

You are the president of your state bar association and an influential member of the ABA's governing body, the House of Delegates. Your state requires all lawyers who practice within its jurisdiction to belong to your bar association. However, proposals are now under discussion to convert the association to a voluntary organization, like the one in a neighboring state. What is your view? Why?

As long as your association is mandatory, do you believe that it should take a position or actively lobby on legal issues such as abortion, physician-assisted suicide, or the death penalty? What about issues more directly connected with lawyers' activities, such as the licensing of trained legal technicians to provide routine form-processing services? Should the ABA take positions on such issues?

NOTES

Although the terminology is confusing, there is an important difference between membership in the bar and membership in a bar association. Membership in a state's bar means simply that one is licensed to practice in that state. The term "state bar" does not refer to an organization; it refers to lawyers who are admitted to practice in the state. A bar association, on the other hand, is a membership organization—a trade association of lawyers. In addition to the ABA, which is a national bar association, there are bar organizations on the city, county, and state level. Many lawyers belong to several bar associations.

By its own account, the American Bar Association is the world's largest voluntary professional organization. By the first part of the 21st century, it had over 400,000 members, about 40 percent of the country's practicing attorneys. Its constitution, originally adopted in 1936 and revised in 1971, provides for governance through a House of Delegates, subject to referenda by the entire membership of participating state and local bar associations. Representatives to the House of Delegates include past and present officers of the Association, members elected by state and local bar associations, and representatives of certain professional groups. According to a 1981 resolution by that House, the organization's objectives are to:

1) promote improvements in the system of justice;

2) improve the delivery of legal services;

3) provide leadership in the improvement of the law;

4) increase understanding of the legal system;

5) assure the highest standards of professional competence and ethics;

6) serve as the national representative of the legal profession;

7) enhance the professional growth of its members.

Critics of the organized bar have suggested that its unstated agenda looks somewhat different. In their view, bar organizations generally have pursued only those "improvements" that serve to enhance their members' economic and social status. As evidence, critics cite the organized bar's opposition to reforms that might reduce the need for lawyers and the size of legal fees. In addition, opponents note that much of the bar's work occurs through committee, where attorneys with strong personal or client interests may wield disproportionate influence. Because large-firm lawyers are disproportionately represented among the ABA's membership and leadership, critics also question whether it should attempt to speak for the entire legal profession on controversial issues.

Disputes have also centered on the Association's role concerning issues that do not directly concern the profession. An ABA resolution in February 1990 supporting women's constitutional right to abortion prompted about 1500 resignations. Six months later, by a closely divided vote, the House of Delegates rescinded the resolution in favor of a statement taking no position on the issue, and then later passed another pro-choice resolution.

Proponents noted that one of the Association's stated purposes was to promote the administration of justice and uniformity of legislation, and that the House of Delegates had previously supported the Uniform Abortion Act (a fact noted by the Supreme Court in *Roe v. Wade*). Opponents claimed that the broader mission of the ABA would be compromised by taking a position on an extremely divisive issue that would run counter to the moral and religious convictions of many members. In response, the ABA's then-president, Talbot D'Alemberte, spoke in favor of the measure:

> In the 1950s, I'm ashamed to say we were neutral when issues of racial justice were before the courts. The ABA may not, without grave risk to our credibility, withdraw from the debate over this vital issue today.

D'Alemberte further argued that the ABA had grown in size and stature after it finally decided to become involved with civil rights and that it should address the "one issue that women care most about."[1]

What is your view on whether the ABA should take positions on politically controversial issues? Aren't all issues that are important enough to warrant an ABA position likely to be politically controversial? Should the ABA take positions that have primarily symbolic effect?

Similar issues arise at the state and local level. About two thirds of the states have "integrated bars," which require lawyers to belong to the state bar association as a condition of practice. (The term refers to the integration of the state bar with the state's bar association, not to integration in any other sense of the word.) The formation of such mandatory associations began during the 1920s as an effort to promote greater control over admissions and discipline. Since then their role has been a matter of continuing controversy. Some critics complain that the merger of a "regulatory agency and trade association" ill serves the public interest. Others object that mandatory bar organizations' involvement on issues beyond self-regulation violates members' First Amendment rights.[2] In *Keller v. State Bar of California*, 496 U.S. 1 (1990), the Supreme Court held that compulsory bar dues may not be used over a member's objection to finance lobbying on issues unrelated to the regulation of the profession or the improvement of legal services. This decision, coupled with similar rulings by lower courts, has influenced some mandatory state bar organizations to curtail their lobbying activities. Other bars permit members to withhold the small portion of their dues that would be used for lobbying.

These challenges to the bar's lobbying activities raise broader issues about lawyers' collective interests and social responsibilities. Consider the following observation by Bayles Manning, former dean of the Stanford Law School:

1. Mark Curriden, "ABA Leadership Votes to Back Abortion Rights: Bush May Stop Seeking Group's Advice on Judges," *The Atlanta Constitution*, Aug. 12, 1992, at A2; Jennifer Warren, "Bar Association Renews Fight on Abortion," *L.A. Times*, Aug. 11, 1992, at A3.

2. Compulsory bar membership was sustained against First Amendment challenge in Lathrop v. Donohue, 367 U.S. 820 (1961).

I have no quarrel whatever with the concept of a trade association for lawyers. Lawyers are a distinctive, self-identified group of citizens; they have their own interests and concerns; they are and should be free to organize to express those proprietary interests through the political process.... But when an organization of lawyers is acting as a trade association for its own interests, it is no longer entitled to fly the colors of the licensed preserver of the public interest.

Today the organized profession acts through the same organizations, uses the same names, uses the same speaking platforms, draws on the same rhetoric, and uses the same public relations machinery whether acting as a trade association or for the broader improvement of the law. The inevitable consequence is a fearful cynicism and loss of credibility when the duality is perceived by the public—as it inevitably will be.[3]

Some commentators have similarly maintained that professionals should be expected to avoid self-deception, if not always self-interest, on issues of regulatory policy. Given the risks of bias, it is often argued that lawyers should not control the regulation of lawyers. The readings below address such arguments as they relate to ethical codes.

QUESTIONS

1.   What are bar associations' most important functions?

2.   To what extent can these associations represent the public's interest in regulating lawyers?

3.   How should bar organizations deal with conflicts in their objectives? For example, what role should these organizations play on proposals that are likely to increase the public's access to law by reducing the need for lawyers or curtailing their monopoly over legal services?

B.   SELF-REGULATION: JUSTIFICATIONS AND CRITIQUES

INTRODUCTION

The first formulations of professional ethics date back 2500 years to principles established by medical practitioners. Some groups of Roman legal advisors and advocates also developed ethical standards, as did certain medieval guilds. The first British barristers were subject to rules of their Inns of Court, and in the mid-eighteenth century, Parliament passed a comprehensive statute regulating solicitors. However, it was not until the

---

3. Bayles Manning, "If Lawyers Were Angels: A Sermon in One Canon," 60 *A.B.A.J.* 821, 825 (July 1974). For a similar, more recent argument that bar associations should rely more heavily on other regulators to restrain lawyer misconduct and concentrate on functions that professional organizations are uniquely able to fulfill, see Fred Zacharias, Reform or Professional Responsibility as Usual: Whither the Institutions of Regulation and Discipline?, 2003 U. Ill. L. Rev. 1505.

early twentieth century that American lawyers formalized a similar body of standards in an official code.

During the bar's early years, its ethical norms arose largely through professional traditions and informal community oversight. Judicial sanctions were relatively rare, and usually occurred in response to violations of criminal or civil law.[4] In 1836, David Hoffman, a University of Maryland professor, attempted to summarize the bar's most important ethical traditions in his *Fifty Resolutions in Regard to Professional Deportment*. As the title implies, Hoffman was concerned with etiquette as well as ethics. His standards accordingly discouraged any conduct that might reflect adversely on lawyers' public image, including all forms of advertising, solicitation, involvement in unjust causes, or disingenuous tactics.

The other important nineteenth-century work on legal ethics was by George Sharswood, a Pennsylvania judge. His 1854 *Essay on Professional Ethics* was a major influence on the first state bar association's Code of Professional Ethics (Alabama, 1887) and the American Bar Association's first Canons of Ethics (1908). Although he shared Hoffman's disapproval of commercialism and competition, Sharswood set forth a more complex understanding of lawyers' obligations to clients and the system of justice. In effect, Sharswood asserted differences between personal and professional morality that remain central to contemporary debates over legal ethics.

In 1906, the ABA issued an influential report recommending a formal ethical code. The immediate impetus for the Committee's formation was a Harvard University address by then President Theodore Roosevelt that, like Justice Louis Brandeis' celebrated 1913 speech (excerpted in Chapter 1), rebuked corporation lawyers for helping powerful clients to evade regulatory legislation. The ABA's president authorized a Committee to consider whether the "ethics of our profession rise to the high standards which its position of influence in the country demands."[5] As the following Report reflects, the Committee's concerns were rather different than Roosevelt's.

American Bar Association "Report of the Committee on [the] Code of Professional Ethics"

600, 600–04 (1906 American Bar Association Reports).

To the American Bar Association:

Your instructions direct us to report upon the "advisability and practicability" of the adoption of such a code [of ethics].

---

4. *Professionalization* 129 (Howard M. Vollmer & Donald L. Mills eds. 1966); Deborah L. Rhode, "Moral Character as a Professional Credential," 94 *Yale L.J.* 491 (1985).

5. Jerold S. Auerbach, *Unequal Justice, Lawyers and Social Change in Modern America* 40 (1976).

First, *as to advisability.*

We are of opinion that the adoption of such a code is not only advisable, but under existing conditions of very great importance. There are several considerations moving us to this conclusion:

1. With Wilson, Webster and others, we believe that "justice is the great interest of man on earth." And here in America, where justice reigns only by and through the people under forms of law, the lawyer is and must ever be the high priest at the shrine of justice. Under our form of government, unless the system for establishing and dispensing justice is so developed and maintained that there shall be continued confidence on the part of the public in the fairness, integrity and impartiality of its administration, there can be no lasting permanence to our republican institutions. Our profession is necessarily the keystone of the republican arch of government. Weaken this keystone by allowing it to be increasingly subject to the corroding and demoralizing influence of those who are controlled by graft, greed and gain, or other unworthy motive, and sooner or later the arch must fall. It follows that the future of the republic depends upon our maintenance of the shrine of justice pure and unsullied. We know it cannot be so maintained unless the conduct and motives of the members of our profession, of those who are the high priests of justice, are what they ought to be. It therefore becomes our plain and simple duty, our patriotic duty, to use our influence in every legitimate way to help make the American Bar what it ought to be. A code of ethics, adopted after due deliberation and promulgated by the American Bar Association, is one method in furtherance of this end.

2. With the marvelous growth and development of our country and its resources, with the ranks of our profession ever extending, its fields of activities ever widening, the lawyer's opportunities for good and evil are correspondingly enlarged, and the limits have not been reached. We cannot be blind to the fact that, however high may be the motives of some, the trend of many is away from the ideals of the past and the tendency more and more to reduce our high calling to the level of a trade, to a mere means of livelihood or of personal aggrandizement. With the influx of increasing numbers, who seek admission to the profession mainly for its emoluments, have come new and changed conditions. Once possible ostracism by professional brethren was sufficient to keep from serious error the practitioner with no fixed ideals of ethical conduct; but now the shyster, the barratrously inclined, the ambulance chaser, the member of the Bar with a system of runners, pursue their nefarious methods with no check save the rope of sand of moral suasion so long as they stop short of actual fraud and violate no criminal law. These men believe themselves immune, the good or bad esteem of their co-laborers is nothing to them provided their itching fingers are not thereby stayed in their eager quest for lucre. Much as we regret to acknowledge it, we know such men are in our midst. Never having realized or grasped that indefinable ethical something which is the soul and spirit of law and justice, they not only lower the *morale* within the profession, but they debase our high calling in the eyes of the public. They hamper the administration and even at times subvert the ends of justice. Such men are enemies of the republic; not true ministers of her courts of justice robed in

the priestly garments of truth, honor and integrity. All such are unworthy of a place upon the rolls of the great and noble profession of the law.

3. Members of the Bar, like judges, are officers of the courts, and like judges should hold office only during good behavior. "Good behavior" should not be a vague, meaningless or shadowy term devoid of practical application save in flagrant cases. It should be defined and measured by such ethical standards, however high, as are necessary to keep the administration of justice pure and unsullied. Such standards may be crystallized into a written code of professional ethics, and a lawyer failing to conform thereto should not be permitted to practice or retain membership in professional organizations, local or national, formed, as is the American Bar Association, to promote the administration of justice and uphold the honor of the profession. Such a code in time will doubtless become of very great practical value by leading to action through the judiciary, for the courts may, as conditions warrant, require all candidates for the Bar to subscribe to suitable and reasonable canons of ethics as a condition precedent to admission. If this be done, the courts will be in an indisputable position to enforce, through suspension or disbarment, the observance of proper ethical conduct on the part of members of the Bar so admitted. Action by the national Association will also tend to develop uniformity between the various states, not only in form and method of statement, but also in application, and this we deem of practical importance. . . .

4. A further reason why we report the advisability of canons of ethics being authoritatively promulgated arises from the fact that many men depart from honorable and accepted standards of practice early in their careers as the result of actual ignorance of the ethical requirements of the situation. Habits acquired when professional character is forming are lasting in their effects. The "thus it is written" of an American Bar Association code of ethics should prove a beacon light on the mountain of high resolve to lead the young practitioner safely through the snares and pitfalls of his early practice up to and along the straight and narrow path of high and honorable professional achievement.

NOTES

The Evolution of Bar Ethical Rules

Following this Report, an ABA Committee drafted 32 proposed Canons of Ethics, which the Association approved in 1908 with little controversy or debate. By 1920, courts or legislatures in all but 13 states and the District of Columbia had adopted the Canons, in some instances with local modifications. In most other states, the Canons were treated as a source of guidance to practitioners, courts, and disciplinary tribunals. However, substantial problems in enforcement persisted, in part because of the standards' brevity, generality, and attempt to combine moral exhortation with disciplinary mandates. The situation worsened as the number of Canons multiplied. By the late 1960s, there were 47 Canons, and some 1400 formal and informal opinions interpreting them by the ABA Standing Committee on

Ethics and Professional Responsibility. These opinions lacked the force of law but were designed to guide practitioners and courts. The result was a proliferation of precedents lacking in coherence and consistency. Despite the unwieldy multiplication of texts, many significant ethical problems remained unacknowledged and unaddressed.[6]

The obvious inadequacies of this structure prompted the formation of an ABA Committee on Evaluation of Ethical Standards. In 1969, that Committee recommended a new Code of Professional Responsibility. Again, the proposed standards generated relatively little controversy. After approval by the ABA House of Delegates, the Code was ultimately adopted by every state except California, which enacted a similar body of rules.

In an effort to avoid the confusion that had surrounded the Canons, drafters of the Code divided the text into three parts: Canons, Ethical Considerations, and Disciplinary Rules. As the Code's Preliminary Statement explains:

> The Canons are statements of axiomatic norms, expressing in general terms the standards of professional conduct expected of lawyers in their relationships with the public, with the legal system, and with the legal profession.... The Ethical Considerations are aspirational in character and represent the objectives toward which every member of the profession should strive.... The Disciplinary Rules, unlike the Ethical Considerations, are mandatory in character. The Disciplinary Rules state the minimum level of conduct below which no lawyer can fall without being subject to disciplinary action.

The inspiration for this approach came from Lon Fuller, whose book *The Morality of Law* (1964) argued for a distinction between moralities of duty and moralities of aspiration.[7] Other commentators similarly supported including ethical considerations in addition to disciplinary rules not simply because such considerations could "aim higher" than minimally decent conduct, but also because they could "deal with questions less easily codified."[8] As these commentators emphasized, many ethical issues confronting lawyers called "not for simple 'do's' and 'don't's', but for an enlarged and more sensitive consciousness of the variety of values at stake."[9] Such values could not be adequately explored in a text consisting only of minimum rules.

Soon after the Code's adoption, its content and structure began to provoke increasing criticisms. According to some observers, the disparity

---

6. For a general history of the Canons, see James M. Altman, "Considering the A.B.A.'s 1908 Canons of Ethics," 71 *Fordham L. Rev.* 2395 (2003); *see also* Susan D. Carle, "Lawyers' Duty to Do Justice: A New Look at the History of the 1908 Canons," 24 *Law & Soc. Inquiry* 1 (1999). On the Canons' predecessor, the 1887 Alabama Code, see Allison Marston, "Guiding the Profession: The 1887 Code of Ethics of the Alabama State Bar Association," 49 *Ala. L. Rev.* 471 (1998).

7. See David Luban, "Rediscovering Fuller's Legal Ethics," 11 *Geo. J. Legal Ethics* 801 (1998); John M. A. DiPippa, "Lon Fuller, The Model Code, and The Model Rules," 37 *S. Tex. L. Rev.* 303 (1996).

8. Charles Frankel, "Review of *Code of Professional Responsibility*," 43 *U. Chi. L. Rev.*, 874, 880 (1976).

9. *Id.*, at 880.

between what the Ethical Considerations exhorted and what the Disciplinary Rules required was fostering cynicism about the bar's aspirational norms and creating confusion in enforcement efforts. Other critics identified further problems with the Code, including its failure to distinguish among various functions that lawyers performed (*e.g.*, advocate, counselor, intermediary) and the inconsistency of its rules on competition with newly emerging Supreme Court decisions. Within a decade after the Code's adoption, a special ABA Commission was already recommending an alternative set of standards, the Model Rules of Professional Conduct.

Unlike their predecessors, these Rules inspired considerable dispute within the profession. After heated debates over a series of preliminary drafts, the ABA in 1983 approved a final version. Controversy then shifted to the states. By the beginning of the twenty-first century, all but six states had adopted the Model Rules in large part, although with changes in certain substantive provisions, particularly the rules governing confidentiality.[10] Federal courts generally have adopted the ethical provisions in force in the jurisdiction in which they sit.

The Regulatory Framework

The format of the Model Rules marks a significant departure from earlier codes. It provides black-letter rules with interpretative comments and little of the moral exhortation characteristic of its predecessors. A note on the Rules' scope states that "the comments are intended as guides to interpretation, but the text of each rule is authoritative." Although the Model Rules, like the Code, disclaim any role in setting standards for civil liability, courts have often invoked their provisions in malpractice actions.

David Luban and Michael Millemann, "Good Judgment: Ethics Teaching in Dark Times"
9 Georgetown Journal of Legal Ethics 31, 44–55 (1995).

The move from the [ABA] Canons [of Ethics] to the Model Code of Professional Responsibility was a watershed event, because the DRs marked the first time that legal ethics was regulated by hard law. Because of the anomaly of the Model Code's Canons and Ethical Considerations, however, the legal force of which was unclear, the ABA's transition to hard law was not complete until it adopted the Model Rules of Professional Conduct in 1983. The Model Rules adopted a rule-and-comment format wholly familiar from the Uniform Commercial Code, the Model Penal Code, and the various Restatements. . . .

The very titles of the documents indicate the change:

> *Canons* of *Professional Ethics*;
>
> *Code* of *Professional Responsibility*;
>
> *Rules* of *Professional Conduct*.

10. State Ethics Rules, ABA/BNA Lawyers' Manual on Professional Conduct, April 20, 2006, 273.

The term "canon" derives initially from biblical studies, where "the canon" referred to those sacred texts officially included in the Bible (the antonym was "apocrypha"). Canons of Professional Ethics were those sacred principles officially endorsed by the ABA. As the 1906 ABA report put it, the idea was to replace the "rope of sand of moral suasion" with a

> "thus it is written" of an American Bar Association code of ethics [that] should prove a beacon light on the mountain of high resolve to lead the young practitioner safely through the snares and pitfalls of his early practice up to and along the straight and narrow path of high and honorable professional achievement.

"Thus it is written"! Evidently the word "canons" was not lightly chosen. However, by 1969, the ABA had decided to descend from Sinai and create a code. The term "ethics" dropped out of the title, to be replaced by the more technical-sounding "professional responsibility." Finally, the Model Rules announced itself as nothing more than an effort to regulate conduct. The de-moralization of the ethics rules was complete.

Geoffrey Hazard's views of the transformation are particularly significant, because as the Kutak Commission's reporter who drafted the Model Rules he occupies the dual role of chronicler and prime mover of the final stage of the transition. The guiding vision of Hazard's effort to legalize and de-moralize the ethics codes is this: "It is time that lawyers and the organized bar came to understand that they are governed by law, bound by law, and answerable before the law, like other people." To Hazard, this ideal seems to have meant several things: First, the ethics . . . rules should be drafted with meticulous craftsmanship in a lawyerly manner, and should be readily interpretable by anyone with legal training. Hence, no more anomalies like Canons and Ethical Considerations. Second, the rules should "track" obligations imposed on lawyers through other laws. This the Model Rules did by modeling its own provisions on decisional or other law, to avoid a conflict of legal obligations. Third, in cases of conflict the rules should defer to other sources of legal obligation. A continuing theme of Hazard's writing has been that professional self-regulation does not permit lawyers to exempt themselves from other law, and that it is a persistent professional self-delusion to believe otherwise.

[He also argued that ethical aspirations are matters of personal values, and have no place in a legal code. Other lawyers continue to favor aspirational rules, however.] An example will illustrate what is lost in a de-moralized code of conduct. Consider EC 2–27's proposition that "a lawyer should not decline representation because a client or a cause is unpopular or community reaction is adverse," together with EC 2–28's reminder that "[t]he personal preference of a lawyer to avoid adversary alignment against judges, other lawyers, public officials, or influential members of the community does not justify his rejection of tendered employment." These aspirations simply vanish from the Model Rules, which replaces them with a rule stating that a lawyer "shall not seek to avoid appointment by a tribunal to represent a person except for good cause . . ." (Model Rules 6.2).

Not only is the latter rule narrower than the ECs, it omits any tincture of the Model Code's suggestion that professional honor takes guts, that lawyers may sometimes have to stand up against the community and the establishment. These are properly aspirations rather than duties, since it is too much to require every lawyer to have the courage and steadfastness of Atticus Finch; but it is one property of an aspiration that we properly feel ashamed of ourselves for not living up to it. The Model Rules, by contrast, don't offer the slightest suggestion that a lawyer should feel ashamed of turning away a client out of a lack of nerve. . . .

[The argument in defense of ECs] is that rules such as EC 2–27 and EC 2–28 can fortify a lawyer's conscience. If a lawyer has "other lawyers, public officials, or influential members of the community" telling her that if she knows what's good for her, she will stop fighting so hard for her client, it is not only her courage but her confidence in her own judgment that is likely to need fortification. Can she really be sure that she is right when the mandarins of the local bar, the bureaucrats of city hall, and business leaders who have sent clients her way in the past are all telling her that she's upsetting the apple-cart on behalf of a client who isn't good enough for her in the first place? It is in a crisis like this that it might help to have an official statement of the profession's commitments. . . .

Whatever the ultimate merits of the argument . . . Hazard's impetus toward legalizing and de-moralizing the codes has triumphed in the field of professional regulation. Indeed, the next giant step—the Restatement of the Law Governing Lawyers that now exists in draft—brings professional rules into full parity with the other departments of the law. What seems to have been overlooked, however, is that this triumph has gone a long way toward undermining the whole enterprise of lawyer self-regulation.

. . . Hazard's stern dictum that lawyers must be made to understand that they are answerable before the law, like other people, suggests that lawyers habitually misunderstand this point, and seems like an effort to break through the profession's carapace of self-proclaimed and self-serving superiority. But then why should lawyers be allowed to regulate themselves? Isn't that a case of the fox guarding the henhouse? If it is true that "public law ha[s] come to define the profession's duties and responsibilities," then why shouldn't the public take that part of the lawmaking process out of the profession's hands? . . .

And, as a matter of fact, that is precisely what has been happening. Within the past two decades, it has become abundantly clear that the ethics codes are just one piece of the law governing lawyers, and not necessarily the most important. To take a few examples:

> Item: The domain of professional regulation of lawyer advertising and solicitation has eroded steadily in the face of constitutional decisions over the twenty years since *Bates* [Bates v. State Bar of Arizona, 433 U.S. 350 (1977), struck down many restrictions on lawyer advertising on free-speech grounds].
>
> Item: Rule 11 sanctions have been orders of magnitude more important for regulating frivolous or harassing litigation than the code counterparts whose language rule 11 more or less replicates.

Item: The enormous explosion in legal malpractice has become the most prominent feature of the contemporary landscape of lawyer behavior. In the 1960s, malpractice liability insurance was largely unavailable on the domestic market, because the claims were so few. By contrast, some contemporary estimates suggest that as many as ten percent of lawyers face malpractice charges. Multi-million dollar malpractice settlements arising from the savings and loan collapses have sent a massive shudder through the large-firm bar, and may well change the way such firms structure themselves and practice law.

Item: Over the vigorous protests of the criminal defense bar, lawyers' fees were brought under the fee-forfeiture provisions of RICO and the Continuing Criminal Enterprises Act.

. . .

Item: The legal profession is subject to antitrust legislation. Law firms are subject to Title VII strictures in promotion decisions. Constitutional principles governing labor unions apply to mandatory bar associations as well. IRS disclosure provisions for large cash transactions apply to lawyers' fees, and IRS rules include lawyers among the tax-preparers who are subject to civil fines for taking hyper-aggressive positions without flagging them.

The list could go on. In fifty years, we may come to regard the by-then-defunct Model Rules as merely an unstable halfway-point between robust self-regulation and fully external regulation of lawyers. . . .

NOTES

Other commentators have also noted the costs of substituting minimum rules for ethical aspirations. Consider the following observation:

The danger [with an ethics code reflecting rules not ethics] is that it will pass for ethics. In that respect, the bar's insistence on minimal, enforceable standards may have missed the mark. No such code, however well-drafted, can definitively respond to the complexities of professional practice. Where a threat of formal sanctions is remote, as is generally the case in professional contexts, the most significant function of official codes will be symbolic and pedagogic. To the limited extent that codified precepts can affect behavior, an exclusively minimalist approach could prove misguided. The consequence may be socialization to the lowest common denominator of conduct that a highly self-interested constituency will publicly brand as deviant. . . .

To be sure, a codified catechism that aspires too far beyond the capacity of "ordinary men on ordinary occasions" may seem irrelevant to the resolution of practical problems. The ABA is not a plausible source for a Sermon on the Mount. Undoubtedly, the infusions of cant in the prior code have undermined its credibility in professional socialization. But it by no means follows that a less platitudinous document, expressing certain core notions of honest and equitable conduct, would generate comparable cynicism simply because many practitioners would occasionally stray from the prescribed path.

At the least, a more ethically rigorous code might perform a salutary function by sensitizing professionals to the full normative dimensions of their choices. Whatever the likelihood of enforcement, a collective affirmation of professional values may have some effect simply by supplying, or removing, one source of a rationalization for dubious conduct.[11]

Do you agree? How might Hazard respond?

Critics of the Model Rules approach have often argued that a reliance on minimum prohibitions to govern an increasingly diverse bar will inevitably lead to a higher level of abstraction and lower common denominator in regulatory standards than is desirable for ethical codes. An alternative strategy would be to expand the use of specialized standards that are more specific and more demanding than the ABA Code and Model Rules. The potential of this approach is reflected in the Standards of Conduct of the American Academy of Matrimonial Lawyers and the Guidelines of Tax Practice by the ABA Tax Section Committee on Standards of Tax Practice.[12] District Judge Stanley Sporkin, former director of enforcement for the Securities and Exchange Commission, has similarly advocated an ethical code for corporate and securities lawyers that would impose greater public responsibilities than current norms.[13]

Such codes, if reinforced by courts, bar ethics committees, and law firms, could encourage more ethically reflective decision making. And lawyers who agreed to abide by these heightened standards would be sending an important reputational signal to clients, judges, other lawyers, and job applicants. However, the proliferation of multiple potentially inconsistent standards also carries a price. And if compliance was difficult to monitor, that price might not be worth paying.

How would you assess that tradeoff? Consider the general purposes of ethical rules described below. How well do lawyers' codes serve these objectives? What, if any, changes would you support?

Judith Lichtenberg, "What's a Code of Ethics For?," In Codes of Ethics and the Professions (Margaret Coady & Sidney Bloch eds.).

13–28 (1996).

Who needs a code of ethics? Something in the very idea arouses suspicion or even ridicule. On the one side, we may suspect that codes of

---

11. Deborah L. Rhode, "Ethical Perspectives on Legal Practice," 37 *Stan. L. Rev.* 589, 647–48 (1985).

12. See the discussion of the matrimonial standards and the tax guidelines in Chapter IX.

13. Stanley Sporkin, "The Case for Specialty Codes of Conduct," *Legal Times*, Feb. 17, 1992, at 24.

ethics are merely platitudinous—that they state obvious truths or prescriptions that everybody knows. Codes of ethics are from this perspective pointless: decent people follow their prescriptions as a matter of course, and thus have no need of codes; while less savory types ignore their dictates, snickering all the while, we suspect, at the naivete of supposing that a code of ethics could make a difference. On the other side, a detailed and specific code raises concerns that its pronouncements are too controversial, requiring behavior about which reasonable people can disagree and so infringing the autonomy of those who come within its purview. Since such people are typically what we call professionals—people who jealously guard their independence and who generally do not lack in the conviction of their intellectual and moral worth—a specific and demanding code may seem to threaten individual autonomy.

Why would anyone want a code of ethics? What purposes can a code serve? What good can it do? Is its point simply to get people to act in certain ways, or does it have other goals as well? In what follows I want to suggest some answers to these questions....

John Ladd has argued that the imposition of principles on other people "in the guise of ethics contradicts the notion of ethics itself, which presumes that persons are autonomous moral agents." A code of "ethics," Ladd believes, by its nature converts ethical issues into something else: matters of legal or other authoritative rules, perhaps, but certainly not ethics. Ethics cannot be imposed from without.

Whatever appeal Ladd's view has derives from an undue emphasis on the word "ethics." Of course, if we insist that insofar as we act ethically we act autonomously, and that we therefore do not obey rules externally imposed, then a code of ethics is an oxymoron, ruled out from the start. We may also admit that for some purposes the identification of the ethical with autonomous, freely chosen action is appropriate. But if we take at least one purpose of a code of ethics to be the simple and straightforward one of increasing the probability that people will behave in some ways rather than others, then a code of ethics may be both possible and effective, just as a system of law is possible and effective. A code of ethics can give a person a reason, sometimes a decisive reason, to act in one way rather than another.... For contrary to the slogan, you can legislate morality. The civil rights movement and the progress of desegregation demonstrate that over time, changes in the law can significantly change people's attitudes, so that what is perfectly acceptable, the conventional wisdom, in one era can become an embarrassment to the next. So even if our ultimate aim is to change people's characters and their reasons for acting, we could do a lot worse than to begin by manipulating their incentives to act by requiring certain behavior and attaching penalties to noncompliance.... [For this purpose] a useful code will be detailed and specific. For, from this point of view, we need a code precisely for those situations that are not clear....

A different objection to codes of ethics is that a virtuous person would not need one. For such a person knows what to do, and doesn't need a code for instructional purposes; nor does she need an external incentive, such as a code would provide, to motivate her.

The obvious response is that even if this is true of the virtuous person, such virtue is scarcer than it suggests. One does not have to believe that immorality is rampant or that human nature is nasty and brutish to admit that many people who qualify as perfectly normal and typical easily stray from the virtuous path where one or more of the following conditions are met: the temptations are significant, the price of adherence (in terms, for example, of the sacrifice involved to our interests) is high, the costs of violation are low. These costs are certainly lower when no explicit rule (let alone sanctions) exists to remind us of what we ought to do. With or without sanctions, a code of ethics can persuade a person to do what she might not be sufficiently moved to do on her own. . . .

Often, a person is not adequately motivated to do the right thing because he has not brought to consciousness the character of what he is doing (or not doing). It would be a mistake to say he doesn't *know* that what he is doing is wrong, for the problem is not simple ignorance. It is rather that he has not thought about just what it is he is doing; he has not described it to himself properly, if at all. . . . [A] code of ethics can force to people's consciousness descriptions of what they are doing that will render at least those of typical sensibilities uncomfortable. . . . Like a legal system, a code of ethics can [also] resolve coordination problems. A code requiring certain behavior can not only give people a reason to do what they might not be sufficiently moved to do on their own—thus overcoming the problem of inadequate virtue mentioned earlier—it can also change the nature, implications, or consequences of the behavior required. In part, this can be a matter of reducing the amount of sacrifice required of any given individual: a code that prohibits certain advertising practices, for example, disadvantages everybody equally—and therefore disadvantages no one—whereas a person who adopts the rule in isolation may suffer disproportionately. (Of course, compliance is never complete; but compliance above a certain threshold probably suffices in most cases. And in cases like advertising, where noncompliance is fully public, those who defy the code may suffer disapproval by the profession and incur other losses as a result.)

In addition, whereas the contribution of an isolated individual's adherence to the rule would be minimal, when everybody acts in the same way we see significant results. This can affect a person's motive to act, because it now seems that one's adherence to the rule, when conjoined with the adherence of others, really makes a difference and is thus worth doing. But it's not simply a matter of changing a person's dispositions. The dispositions are changed precisely because the act, or at least the consequences of the act, is changed. . . . Codes of ethics, then, by encouraging or even requiring standards of behavior among a group of people with some similarity of needs and interests, can affect both their motivation to act and the nature of their acts. When the encouragement provided by codes is reinforced by sanctions for noncompliance, their effect on these principles will be even greater.

The arguments I have been making so far suggest material reasons for thinking that a code of ethics can get people to comport themselves differently than they might in the absence of the code. But there are other reasons one might want a code of ethics. If we call those reasons discussed so far "material," we would call these by contrast "symbolic" or "expressive": they concern the value of the public expression of ideals, values, or rules, apart from their material effects. . . .

[Codes of ethics, like legal rules, publicly announce a group's] commitment to a certain moral standard. It not only prohibits certain conduct but also publicly avows our rejection of it—which is a different and stronger commitment.

NOTES

A related issue involves the process for formulating bar ethical rules. Once a profession's regulatory focus shifts from expressing shared values to specifying minimum disciplinary standards, how much control should it exercise over the drafting and enforcement process? A recurrent critique of the legal profession's regulatory codes is that they have been established by the group to be regulated.

The following excerpt challenges the traditional justifications for the bar's control over its own ethical codes and enforcement structures. How would bar leaders respond to this critique? How would you?

Deborah L. Rhode, In the Interests of Justice

(2000).

In an influential history of the legal profession sponsored by the American Bar Association, former Harvard Law School Dean Roscoe Pound assured ABA leaders that their organization was not the "same sort of thing as a retail grocers' association." If he was right, it was for the wrong reason. Lawyers, no less than grocers, are motivated by their own occupational interests. What distinguishes the American bar is its ability to present self regulation as a societal value. Lawyers retain far more control over their own oversight than any other group. Such freedom from external accountability too often serves the profession at the expense of the public. . . . The problem is not that bar policies are baldly self-serving. Lawyers and judges who control regulatory decisions generally want to advance the public's as well as the profession's interests. Rather, the difficulty is one of tunnel vision, compounded by inadequate accountability. No matter how well intentioned, lawyers and former lawyers who regulate other lawyers cannot escape the economic, psychological, and political constraints of their position. Without external checks, these decision makers too often lose perspective about the points at which occupational and societal interests conflict. . . .

Historically, the profession itself has controlled the regulatory process. For centuries, courts have asserted "inherent power" to regulate the practice of law. One rationale for this authority is that judges need to control the conduct and qualifications of lawyers in order to assure the proper administration of justice. A second justification is that self regulation preserves the separation of powers and protects the independence of the legal profession from government domination. As a practical matter, American courts have delegated much of their regulatory authority to the organized bar, which defends its autonomy on similar grounds. According to the Preamble of the ABA's Model Rules of Professional Conduct, "An independent legal profession is an important force in preserving government under law, for abuse of legal authority is more readily challenged by a profession whose members are not dependent on government for the right to practice."

These arguments have considerable force, but they cannot justify the current regulatory structure. Protecting the bar from state control clearly serves important values, and nations that lack an independent profession have had difficulty safeguarding individual rights and checking official misconduct. But professional autonomy and government domination are not the only alternatives. Many countries with an independent bar impose far more checks on its self-regulatory powers. Such governmental efforts to increase lawyers' accountability do not necessarily pose significant risks of retaliation or threats to the proper administration of justice. Indeed, American courts often recognize as much, and increasingly permit some regulation of attorneys by legislatures and administrative agencies.

Yet on the whole, lawyers retain considerable control over their own regulation. Bar codes of conduct claim to protect the public, but the public has had almost no voice in their formulation or enforcement. Only one nonlawyer served on the commissions that drafted the American Bar Association's Model Code of Professional Responsibility and the Model Rules of Professional Conduct. Only one was represented on the thirteen member Ethics 2000 Commission that recommended revisions. The ABA House of Delegates, which has power to accept or amend model ethical codes, is composed exclusively of lawyers. And the state supreme courts that ultimately adopt, reject, or modify ABA standards, rely heavily on recommendations from their local bars. Although nonlawyers often have token representation on other regulatory bodies such as discipline committees, these lay members typically are selected by the profession. Almost never do they have the information, resources, leverage or accountability to consumer groups that would be necessary to check bar control.

The limitations of such a structure are obvious. Political and economic theorists have long recognized the self-regarding tendencies of self-regulating occupations. As former Stanford Law School Dean Bayless Manning has noted, American lawyers normally are "splendidly scrupulous" about creating safeguards against conflicts of interests. But that sensitivity vanishes when the profession's own governance structure is at issue. The vast majority of surveyed lawyers favor bar control over regulatory processes despite the obvious potential for bias.

In justifying this control, lawyers often claim that ultimate governance authority rests with state judges, who do not face the same conflicts of interests as practitioners. Yet the history of self-regulation suggests the limitations of such oversight. Most judges are by training and temperament sympathetic to bar interests. Moreover, their reputation, effectiveness, and, sometimes, reelection, depend partly on cooperative relations with the profession. Seldom has the judiciary attempted to impose regulation that might seriously compromise lawyers' status, income, or power. As a result, bar standards of conduct have been insufficiently demanding and inadequately enforced.

QUESTIONS

1.   What follows from this critique of self-regulation? What would be the advantages and risks of reducing professional control over regulatory processes?[14]

2.   Other countries, including those with comparable legal traditions, such as Great Britain, New Zealand and Australia, have moved to replace the profession's self-regulatory powers with oversight by more independent bodies.[15] Would such changes be desirable in this country? If so, how could they be achieved?[16]

3.   What changes would you expect in the American bar's codes of conduct if groups other than lawyers played a central role in the codification process?

4.   How would you evaluate the trend from ethical principles to legal rules? Would you support specialized codes of conduct for particular groups of lawyers? How should such codes be designed and enforced?

Other sources of law and interpretation

Lawyers also have forms of ethical guidance apart from codes. Prominent among them is the American Law Institute's *Restatement (Third) of*

---

14.   For critiques of the current structure, see Jonathan Macey, "Occupation Code 541110: Lawyers, Self–Regulation, and the Idea of a Profession," 74 *Fordham L. Rev.* 1079 (2005); Benjamin Barton, "Do Judges Systematically Favor the Interests of the Legal Profession, 59, *Ala. L. Rev.* (2007); Benjamin Barton, An Institutional Analysis of Lawyer Regulation: Who Should Control Lawyer Regulation, Courts, Legislatures, or the Market," 37 *Ga. L. Rev.* 1167 (2003). See also Gillian Hadfield, Legal Barriers to Innovation: The Growing Economic Costs of Professional Control Over Corporate Legal Markets, *Stan. L. Rev.* (2008) (arguing that decreased professional control would increase innovative, cost-effective ways of delivering services).

15.   Richard Parnham, "The Clementi Reforms in a European Context—Are the Proposals Really That Radical?," 8 *Legal Ethics* 195 (2007).

16.   For recent reform efforts, which in some states would increase bar control over admission and discipline, and in other states would decrease that authority, see Vesna Jaksic, "Some States Seek Change in How Lawyers Regulated," *Nat'l Law Journal*, Jan. 21, 2008, at A6. For discussion of other countries' approach to lawyer discipline, see Chapter XVI.

the Law Governing Lawyers (2000). Like other ALI Restatements, the *Law Governing Lawyers* aims not merely to restate the existing law but also to suggest improvements.

In addition, bar organizations provide formal and informal opinions interpreting ethical rules. The ABA has issued hundreds of Formal Opinions, which are frequently quoted in judicial decisions. Less cited, but often more important, are state bar ethics opinions, typically issued to respond to lawyers' queries. In most jurisdictions, these—like the ABA's opinions—are advisory and non-binding. However, in fourteen states, accounting for about a quarter of all practitioners, ethics opinions are legally binding. Not only are lawyers required to conform to ethics opinions in these jurisdictions, compliance sometimes provides a safe harbor against discipline.[17] Given their importance, the process by which most states generate these opinions is often troublingly haphazard. They are typically issued by committees of volunteer lawyers who are unrepresentative of the bar and unaccountable to the public. The process often poses potential conflicts of interest, because lawyers may wish to interpret ethics rules in ways that favor their own practices. In many states, opinions are uneven in quality, unreviewable in substance, and slow to respond to significant issues.[18]

International Regulation

Increasing globalization in the market for legal services has correspondingly increased the importance of international standards that affect American lawyers. Since 1994, some 160 countries have signed GATS, the General Agreement on Trades in Services, which requires states to engage in efforts to liberalize rules affecting services including law that are imported or exported. Under GATS, member World Trade Organization governments, including the United States, have agreed to consider regulations that would affect domestic governance structures, potentially including lawyers' ethical codes.[19]

Other codes of conduct may affect lawyers practicing abroad. The United Nations in 1990 adopted Basic Principles on the Role of Lawyers as part of an effort to implement international standards in criminal justice. The Council of Bars and Law Societies of the European Union (CCBE), as the representative of bar associations in European Union countries, adopted a Code of Conduct in 1988, which was revised in 1998 and 2006.[20] When adopted by member countries, the code is binding, and it now covers most European lawyers. It includes topics such as confidentiality, conflicts

---

17. Peter A. Joy, "Making Ethics Opinions Meaningful: Toward More Effective Regulation of Lawyers' Conduct," 15 *Geo. J. Legal Ethics* 313, 337 (2002). Joy's overview is based on a detailed empirical study of different states' approaches to the legal force of ethics opinions.

18. *Id.*, at 349–63.

19. Laurel S. Terry, "But Who Will the WTO Disciplines Apply To?, Distinguishing Among Market Access, National Treatment, and Article VI 4 Measures When Applying the GATS to Legal Services," 2003 *Prof. Lawyer* 83 (2003).

20. The Code is available at http://www.ccbe.org/en/documents/code_deonto.htm. For general discussion, see Laurel Ter-of interest, and fees, in a black letter format analogous to the Model Rules of Professional Conduct. The International Bar Association also has a non-binding Code of Ethics, adopted in 1958 and revised in 1988, which states broad ethical standards. Article I of the Code includes a brief statement about conflicting ethical norms. It provides that "A lawyer who undertakes professional work in a jurisdiction where he is not a full member of the profession shall adhere to the standards of professional ethics in the jurisdiction in which he has been admitted. He shall also observe all ethical standards which apply to lawyers of the country where he is working." What happens when the standards of the two countries directly conflict is left unspecified, and such conflicts are bound to increase as legal practice becomes more international.[21]

NOTES

In the chapters that follow, it is important to analyze bar standards not as fixed mandates but as evolving norms and starting points for discussion about appropriate policy. As Charles Frankel noted after the ABA's adoption of the Code of Professional Responsibility:

> In the legal profession, as in most other domains of life, the elevation of standards comes in the main from neither exhortation nor codification. It comes from renewed attention to first principles, from a freshened awareness of the changed problems people confront, and from a sustained debate about the best ways to deal with them.[22]

That debate is the subject of much of this book.

C. PROFESSIONAL REGULATION AND CHOICE OF LAW

Much of lawyers' practice crosses state lines. Where state ethics rules conflict, Model Rule 8.5 offers guidance. Rule 8.5(a) provides that lawyers are subject to disciplinary authority in a state where they are licensed and where they offer or provide services. As to the choice of law, Rule 8.5(b) provides:

> (1) for conduct in connection with a matter pending before a tribunal, the rules of the jurisdiction in which the tribunal sits, unless the rules of the tribunal provide otherwise; and (2) for any other conduct, the rules of the jurisdiction in which the lawyer's conduct occurred, or, if the predominant effect of the conduct is in a different jurisdiction, the rules of that jurisdiction shall be applied to the conduct. A lawyer shall not be subject to discipline if the lawyers conduct conforms to the rules of a jurisdiction in which the lawyer

ry, "An Introduction to the European Community's Legal Ethics Code Part I: An Analysis of the CCBE Code of Conduct," 7 *Geo. J. Legal Ethics* 1 (1993).

21. See James S. Moliterno & George Harris, *Global Issues in Legal Ethics* (2007); Laurel S. Terry, "U.S. Legal Ethics: The Coming Age of Global and Comparative Perspectives," 4 *Wash. U. Global Studies L. Rev.* 463 (2005).

22. Charles Frankel, "Review of Code of Professional Responsibility," 43 *U. Chi. L. Rev.* 874, 886 (1976).

reasonably believes the predominant effect of the lawyer's conduct will occur.

PROBLEM 2

a) You are bar counsel in State X. You have successfully prosecuted a discipline case against James Mark, a lawyer licensed in X. Mark had filed a consumer class action against Ajax Pharmaceuticals, the manufacturer of a widely-used shampoo for head lice. The action alleged that the shampoo is ineffective. Ajax's lead defense counsel, Shannon Ross, had negotiated a settlement agreement with Mark in which Mark obtained a large fee while his clients obtained minimal damages. The agreement also required Mark not to tell his clients the details of the negotiation, or their likelihood of obtaining a higher recovery if they declined the settlement offer. The representative clients learned of the agreement through a whistleblower on Ajax's defense team. Mark was suspended for violating Rules 1.4 (on communicating with clients) and 1.7 (on conflicts of interest).

You are now considering disciplinary action against Ross, Ajax's counsel, for violating Rule 8.4(a), which states that "It is unprofessional misconduct for a lawyer to violate or attempt to violate the Rules of Professional Conduct, *knowingly assist or induce another to do so*, or do so through the acts of another" (emphasis added). You believe that Ross has assisted or induced Mark to commit disciplinary violations. However, Ross is licensed in State Y (the state where Ajax is located) but not in State X. None of the members of Mark's client class live in State Y.

If Ross and Mark negotiated the settlement agreement at Ajax's offices in State Y, do you have jurisdiction to seek discipline against Ross in State X? What if they had negotiated the settlement agreement in Mark's office in State X?

b) Alternatively, you are bar counsel in State Z. On Ross's advice, employees of Ajax have made fraudulent misrepresentations about the shampoo and the progress of the lawsuit to consumer protection officials in State Z. Ross is not licensed in State Z, and none of Mark's clients live in Z. Do you have jurisdiction to pursue disciplinary charges against Ross in Z for violating Rule 1.2(d), "A lawyer shall not counsel a client to engage . . . in conduct that the lawyer knows is criminal or fraudulent"?

PROBLEM 3

You work for the St. Louis, Missouri office of a large national law firm. Currently you are representing Hypertronics, a closely-held technology company that is negotiating its own sale to ALS, a high-tech company whose headquarters and principal facilities are located in Princeton, New Jersey. You have done a variety of paperwork for the pending sale.

Together with Hypertronics executives and the company's general counsel, you have flown to New York City, where the deal will be closed at a meeting with ALS executives. Their offices are in Princeton; the meeting will take place at your firm's New York offices. In New York, Hypertronics's general counsel mentions in your presence that, due to unanticipated technical problems in some of its new designs, the company may default on several major contracts. These contracts had figured prominently in setting the purchase price for Hypertronics. Without them, it is highly unlikely that ALS would have agreed to buy Hypertronics for the agreed-upon price. If, as seems likely, Hypertronics defaults on the contracts after being purchased, ALS could lose a substantial amount of money.

Hypertronics' general counsel maintains that the risk of default is not sufficiently high, and its materiality is not sufficiently clear, to require disclosure. Over your protests, counsel insists that the closing proceed at the agreed-upon price. You believe that this would constitute a civil fraud under both Missouri and New Jersey law.

You are a member of the Missouri and New Jersey bars, having previously practiced for several years in your firm's New Jersey office. The relevant confidentiality rules in the two states are as follows.

> Missouri Rules of Professional Conduct 4–1.6: "(a) A lawyer shall not reveal information relating to representation of a client unless the client consents after consultation, except for disclosures that are impliedly authorized in order to carry out the representation, and except as stated in paragraph (b)."

The two exceptions provided in paragraph (b) do not include revealing confidences in cases of client fraud.

> New Jersey Rules of Professional Conduct 1.6(b)(1): "A lawyer shall reveal [information relating to representation of a client] to the proper authorities, as soon as, and to the extent the lawyer reasonably believes necessary, to prevent the client from committing a criminal, illegal or fraudulent act that the lawyer reasonably believes is likely to result in . . . substantial injury to the financial interest of property of another."

> New Jersey Rule 1.6(d): "Reasonable belief for purposes of [Rule] 1.6 is the belief or conclusion of a reasonable lawyer that is based upon information that has some foundation in fact and constitutes prima facie evidence of the matters referred to in subsection . . . (b)."

Finally, New York's confidentiality rules permit you to reveal "[t]he intention of a client to commit a crime and the information necessary to prevent the crime," and "[c]onfidences or secrets to the extent implicit in withdrawing a written or oral opinion or representation previously given by the lawyer and believed by the lawyer still to be relied upon by a third person where the lawyer has discovered that the opinion or representation was based on materially inaccurate information or is being used to further a crime or fraud."

QUESTIONS

1. Under the current version of ABA Model Rule 8.5, what should you do?

2. Is the "predominant effect" of your conduct in Missouri, New Jersey, or New York? Or is there no predominant effect in one state rather than another? If not, which state's ethics rules apply?

3. Which state's confidentiality rule applies?

    Statutory reference: Model Rule 8.5.

NOTES: JURISDICTION AND CHOICE OF LAW

The steady growth of interstate legal practice, coupled with the numerous variations in state ethics rules, have raised concerns that lawyers may find themselves under inconsistent ethical obligations. States have always reserved the right to discipline lawyers they license regardless of where the lawyer's misconduct occurred, and Model Rule 8.5(a) restates this "long-arm jurisdiction" principle. Until recently, however, the Model Rules were silent on the extent of states' disciplinary authority over lawyers not licensed in the state. In August 2002, the ABA amended Model Rule 8.5(a), adding the sentence "A lawyer not admitted in this jurisdiction is also subject to the disciplinary authority of this jurisdiction if the lawyer provides or offers to provide any legal services in this jurisdiction." Problem 2 raises the question of whether this standard includes only lawyers who are representing or offering to represent clients in the "foreign" jurisdiction, or whether it extends to all the lawyer's professional activities in the jurisdiction that affect its citizens. The amended rule also does not include language to cover situations like that illustrated in Problem 2(b), where a lawyer is *not* providing or offering legal services in a jurisdiction, but is engaged in conduct that has consequences for citizens of the jurisdiction.

It may at first seem puzzling that a state can exercise any disciplinary authority over a lawyer not licensed to practice in that state. After all, suspension and disbarment—the ultimate sanctions in lawyer discipline—by definition apply only when the lawyer has a state license that can be suspended or revoked. However, courts and bar agencies have other sanctions available that can extend to lawyers from other states. A state can issue a private or public reprimand and it can refuse ever to admit the lawyer to its own bar, even on a *pro hac vice* basis. Perhaps most importantly, many states have reciprocal discipline relationships with other states. Under these reciprocity agreements, another state's discipline of a lawyer may trigger discipline in the lawyer's home state as well.

According to Model Rule 8.5(a), a disciplinary action against a lawyer can be brought in any state in which the lawyer is licensed. In that case, the disciplinary body must decide whether to apply its own ethical rules ("forum law") or another state's ethical rules ("foreign law"). Choice of law is a different issue than that of disciplinary authority. One is a question of jurisdiction, the other a question of which rules apply in a court or disciplinary body that has jurisdiction.

In 1993 the American Bar Association amended Model Rule 8.5 to resolve such choice-of-law problems. However, many lawyers found the solution inadequate, and in 2002, following the recommendation of an ABA Commission on Multijurisdictional Practice, the ABA revised the choice-of-law provision and adopted a very different approach from the 1993 version. Because not all states have adopted the Model Rule as amended, choice of law doctrine can vary.[23]

Both the older and newer versions of Rule 8.5 provide that in litigation settings, the ethical rules of the forum tribunal apply. In non-litigation settings, the 1993 version made the governing rules those of the jurisdiction where the lawyer principally practices. Under the 2002 approach, the ethics rules that apply are those of the state where the conduct occurred

The 2002 approach reflects the traditional "territorial" focus, embodied in the First Restatement of Conflict of Laws (1934). Under this approach, a forum should apply the law of the state in which the disputed conduct occurred. The primary exception to this rule arises when the choice-of-law question concerns procedural issues, in which case the forum should apply its own law. About one-third of the states continue to use this traditional approach to choice-of-law issues.

The Second Restatement of Conflict of Laws (1971) adopted an alternative approach; in the absence of a statute, the applicable law is that of the state with "the most significant relationship" to the issue. In determining significance, courts balance the expectations of the parties, the interests of government, and the ease of administration.[24] About half the states currently employ the "most significant relationship" test. This approach, too, finds its way into Model Rule 8.5(b). Both the 1993 and 2002 versions of the Model Rule contain exceptions to the general choice-of-law rule for non-litigation settings when the "predominant effect" of the lawyer's conduct occurs in a different jurisdiction. In that circumstance, the ethics rules of the predominant-effect jurisdiction will apply.

While the territorial approach arguably errs on the side of rigidity, the "most significant relationship" test has been criticized for indeterminacy. Judges employing this test engage in a case-by-case balancing of factors to determine which jurisdiction has the most significant relationship to the case. It is often difficult for a lawyer to predict the outcome of such a balancing approach, so the lawyer will face considerable uncertainty about which ethics rule to obey.[25] It may be impossible to determine in advance whether Missouri or New Jersey has the most significant relationship to the situation in Problem 3. Interest analysis also may yield no clear answer.

These drawbacks demonstrate why a clear rule such as Model Rule 8.5 is useful. However, both versions of Model Rule 8.5(b)(2) can lead to choosing the law of a state with little or no interest in the matter at hand.

---

23. *See* Geoffrey J. Ritts, "Professional Responsibility and the Conflict of Laws," 18 *J.Leg.Prof.* 17 (1993).

24. *Restatement (Second) of Conflict of Laws* § 6.

25. Ritts, *supra* note 23, at 75–76.

Problem 3 illustrates the problem. It is at least arguable that New York's rules should apply in this case because the conduct took place at a meeting in New York, and neither Missouri nor New Jersey can claim that the "predominant effect" of the conduct took place in that state alone. Yet isn't it likely that New York has less interest in the conduct than either Missouri or New Jersey?[26]

Federal–State Choice–of–Law

Determining applicable standards of professional conduct by lawyers in federal courts has turned out to raise additional vexing problems. Current practice varies widely among the 94 federal districts, and lack of uniformity of each district's rules of professional conduct makes it difficult for lawyers even to find out what the local rules are. Some districts adopt the ethics rules of the state in which the court sits; others modify those rules slightly; still others have rules of their own, usually the ABA Model Rules. Furthermore, federal districts vary in their answers to the *"Erie* question" of whether to adopt state-court interpretations of state rules or to develop a federal common law of professional responsibility.

For all these reasons, many commentators have advocated some uniform approach. Debate has evolved along two parallel tracks, one concerning ethics rules for federal government lawyers, especially federal prosecutors, and one concerning ethics rules for private practitioners in federal courts.

Federal Government Lawyers

The first major issue developed in the late 1980s, over whether federal prosecutors must abide by Model Rule 4.2's "no contact" provision, which forbids lawyers from directly contacting parties represented by their own counsel. Federal prosecutors strongly believe that they must be able to speak directly with lower-level members of organized crime outside the presence of defense counsel—who are often paid by the organization's leaders and whose presence may deter cooperation with an ongoing investigation. Attorney General Richard Thornburgh circulated a memo asserting that the Supremacy Clause of the U.S. Constitution exempts federal prosecutors from discipline by state bar associations for violating state ethics rules such as the no-contact rule. Five years later, Attorney General Janet Reno expressly adopted this policy as a formal Department of Justice rule. However, in 1998 the Reno rule was invalidated in *U.S. ex rel. O'Keefe v. McDonnell Douglas Corp.,* 132 F.3d 1252 (8th Cir.1998) on the ground that the DOJ lacks statutory authority for promulgating such a regulation. Later in 1998, Congress passed an amendment that ended all debate over the rule, stating in pertinent part: "An attorney for the government shall be subject to State laws and rules, and local Federal court rules, governing attorneys in each State where such attorney engages in that attorney's duties, to the same extent and in the same manner as other attorneys in that State." Citizens Protection Act of 1998, 28 U.S.C. § 530B.

---

26. For further reading on Model Rule 8.5, see the Final Report of the ABA Commission on Multijurisdictional Practice, at *www. abanet.org/cpr.*

The amendment was informally known as the "McDade Amendment," after sponsor Rep. John McDade (R–Pa.), who was acquitted in 1996 after an eight-year investigation and trial for federal conspiracy and racketeering charges involving allegations that he accepted gifts from defense contractors in return for support in granting federal contracts. The amendment's co-sponsor, Rep. John P. Murtha (D–Pa.) had also been targeted in a criminal inquiry involving allegations of bribery, but was never indicted. Rep. McDade sponsored the legislation, he said, to curb "rampant" abuse by "overaggressive prosecutors." "These guys play rough," McDade warned. "Their mantra used to be, 'Let justice be done.' Now it's, 'Winning is everything.' "[27]

Disciplinary Authority of Government Agencies and Entities

In addition to state ethics codes and opinions, some state and federal agencies have adopted their own rules governing the conduct of lawyers practicing before them. Violation of these rules can result in loss of the right to practice before the agency. For example, lawyers practicing before federal immigration courts are forbidden from engaging in "contumelious or otherwise obnoxious conduct . . ."—an unusually-worded rule that may well send immigration practitioners scurrying to their dictionaries. 8 CFR 1003.102(g). So too, immigration lawyers are forbidden from "knowingly or with reckless disregard" making a false statement of fact or law—arguably a more stringent rule than Model Rule 3.3(a)(1), which forbids knowingly false, but not reckless, statements. See 8 CFR 1003.102(c). As Chapter IX indicates, the Treasury Department also has promulgated a detailed set of regulations to govern all professionals, nonlawyers as well as lawyers, who practice before the Internal Revenue Service. Courts have generally upheld the agencies' inherent power to discipline lawyers by limiting or disbarring them from practicing before the agency. However, federal agencies cannot impose other disciplinary sanctions, and no consensus exists about how to reconcile conflicts between state rules of conduct and agency rules.

To take a far more prominent example, in the wake of the Enron disaster and other corporate scandals in 2001, Congress passed the Sarbanes–Oxley Act, which authorizes the Security and Exchange Commission to adopt rules of conduct for lawyers practicing in a wide range of corporate settings. The resulting regulations—which will receive detailed treatment in other chapters of this book—include requirements for reporting potential securities frauds "up the corporate ladder," sometimes going to higher corporate authority over the head of the lawyer's superiors. These highly-publicized regulations proved tremendously controversial within the bar. Nevertheless, within months of their adoption, the ABA amended the Model Rules to bring them into conformity with the SEC's new requirements.

---

27. Richard Willging, "Federal Prosecutors Have New Hurdle," *USA Today*, April 19, 1999, at 12A.

In 2003, the Washington State Bar Association issued Interim Formal Opinion 197, which found that Washington state lawyers must continue to abide by confidentiality obligations regardless of Sarbanes–Oxley's disclosure authorizations. The Washington Bar Association argued that case law about whether SEC regulations could pre-empt state ethics rules is undeveloped, and therefore that until the courts authoritatively resolve this issue, the state rules continue to bind lawyers. A few months later, a committee of the California State Bar wrote a letter to the SEC informing the agency that it was taking a similar anti-disclosure possession.[28] The SEC's rule clearly states, "Where the standards of a state or other United States jurisdiction where an attorney is admitted or practices conflict with this part, this part shall govern." 17 C.F.R. 205.1 However, questions of when federal law pre-empts state law are notoriously thorny. One traditional doctrine holds that in a subject where states traditionally regulate, Congress's intention to pre-empt must be "clear and manifest." *Rice v. Santa Fe Elevator Corp.*, 331 U.S. 218, 230 (1947). Under this standard, it is unclear whether an SEC regulation has pre-emptive force. To date, no court has resolved this question.

One other example of a section of the bar governed by its own rules of professional responsibility is the JAG Corps—military lawyers, known as judge-advocates. Although these are government lawyers, they are not covered by the McDade Amendment. The Army, Navy, and Air Force each have their own rules of professional conduct, based on the ABA's Model Rules but with significant differences. Judge-advocates must along be licensed in a state, and the JAG rules of conduct state that they must abide by both their state rules and the service-specific rules. In case of a conflict, the service-specific rules state that they govern.

28.   The letter is available at http://cal   tions/2003–10–08_SEC.pdf.
bar.ca.gov/calbar/pdfs/sections/buslaw/corpora

CHAPTER IV

THE ADVOCATE'S ROLE IN AN ADVERSARY SYSTEM

The preamble to the ABA's Model Rules of Professional Conduct begins with the observation that "[a] lawyer is a representative of clients, an officer of the legal system and a public citizen having special responsibility for the quality of justice." In addition, of course, lawyers have obligations to the organization that employs them, and public sector lawyers serve societal interests. These multiple responsibilities can impose significant ethical, financial and other career pressures.

The Model Rules recognize as much. According to their Preamble, lawyers' obligations "are usually harmonious.... In the nature of law practice, however, conflicting responsibilities are encountered. Virtually all difficult ethical problems arise from conflict between a lawyer's responsibilities to clients, to the legal system and to the lawyer's own interest in remaining an upright person while earning a satisfactory living." Perhaps the most important question that lawyers must answer for themselves is how to rank these responsibilities. What should a lawyer do when representing a client effectively conflicts with the lawyer's own sense of "remaining an upright person," either because the lawyer disapproves of the client's ends or has qualms about the means necessary to pursue them effectively? Law students and practicing attorneys are sometimes discomfited to discover that there is no settled answer to this question, either in the bar's traditions or in the rules governing the profession. Yet this ambiguity is not altogether surprising, nor should it be disturbing. If the question "How shall I lead my professional life?" had a pat answer set forth in some hypothesized *Restatement of Virtue*, that would surely signify an overly rigid and implausibly homogenized character to the practice of law. The fact that American lawyers have approached their role in different ways through different traditions is in some respects a positive reflection of the diversity and creativity of the bar.

A. THE "NEUTRAL PARTISANSHIP" CONCEPTION OF THE LAWYER'S ROLE

INTRODUCTION

Many issues in legal ethics that raise the most perplexing questions— zealous advocacy, confidentiality at the expense of innocent third parties, and the demand that lawyers divorce their own sense of right and wrong from their pursuit of client objectives—all seem to flow from a small group of principles. In the excerpt that follows, William Simon explores these principles. The most important are:

> • the requirement of pursuing the client's ends diligently (Simon's "principle of partisanship"); and

> • the requirement that lawyers should not judge the justness of the client's lawful ends, and may not be held morally accountable for those ends (Simon's "principle of neutrality").

Other writers have also focused on these requirements. In fact, some have argued that these principles constitute the "standard conception of the lawyer's role."[1] In a famous 1820 speech, Lord Henry Brougham declared:

> An advocate, in the discharge of his duty, knows but one person in all the world, and that person is his client. To save that client by all means and expedients, and at all hazards and costs to other persons, and amongst them, to himself, is his first and only duty; and in performing this duty he must not regard the alarm, the torments, the destruction which he may bring upon others.[2]

Lord Brougham's speech prompted vigorous opposition at the time, and its premise continues to provoke controversy. Contemporary critics have objected that there is nothing "standard" about conceiving the lawyer's role in terms of these two principles; many lawyers would energetically reject both principles.[3] For this reason we identify these principles as the "Neutral Partisanship" framework without suggesting that it is the sole "standard" view of legal ethics.

In addition to the principles of partisanship and neutrality, Simon includes a third element in Neutral Partisanship:

> the justification of these two principles by reference to the adversary system or, more generally, to procedural norms. The idea is that because we have an adversary system lawyers must adhere to the principles of partisanship and neutrality.

Simon calls this third element the "principle of procedural justice." He adds one final element as well: "professionalism," the idea that issues of legal ethics can only be resolved by lawyers in their occupational capacity,

---

1. The term "standard conception of the lawyer's role" originated in Gerald J. Postema, "Moral Responsibility in Professional Ethics," 55 *N.Y.U.L.Rev.* 63, 73 (1980), and also appears in David Luban, *Lawyers and Justice: An Ethical Study* 7, 11, 52 (1988).

2. *Trial of Queen Caroline* 8 (J. Nightingale ed. 1820–21).

3. Ted Schneyer, "Moral Philosophy's Standard Misconception of Legal Ethics," 1984 *Wisc.L.Rev.* 1529; Stephen Ellmann,

"Lawyering for Justice in a Flawed Democracy," 90 *Colum.L.Rev.* 116, 120–29 (1990). For a discussion of Brougham's view in historical and contemporary contexts, see Deborah L. Rhode, "An Adversarial Exchange on Adversarial Ethics," 41 *J. Legal Ed.* 29 (1991); Fred C. Zacharias & Bruce A. Green, "Reconceptualizing Advocacy Ethics," 74 *Geo. Wash. L. Rev.* 1 (2005); and Monroe H. Freedman, "Henry Lord Brougham, Written By Himself," 19 *Geo. J. Legal Ethics* 1213 (2006).

not by individual attorneys in light of personal convictions or by nonlawyers.

QUESTIONS

1. To what extent do the Model Rules reflect principles of partisanship, neutrality, and professionalism?

2. Are ethical rules any more difficult for nonlawyers to understand and evaluate than the legal requirements that they are expected to interpret in other contexts, such as filing tax returns or serving on juries? Consider those questions in light of the materials that follow.

William Simon, "The Ideology of Advocacy: Procedural Justice and Professional Ethics"

1978 Wisconsin Law Review 29, 36–38 (1978).

The first principle of conduct is the principle of neutrality. This principle prescribes that the lawyer remain detached from his client's ends. The lawyer is expected to represent people who seek his help regardless of his opinion of the justice of their ends. In some cases, he may have a duty to do so; in others, he may have the personal privilege to refuse. But whenever he takes a case, he is not considered responsible for his client's purposes. Even if the lawyer happens to share these purposes, he must maintain his distance. In a judicial proceeding, for instance, he may not express his personal belief in the justice of his client's cause.

The second principle of conduct is partisanship. This principle prescribes that the lawyer work aggressively to advance his client's ends. The lawyer will employ means on behalf of his client which he would not consider proper in a non-professional context even to advance his own ends. These means may involve deception, obfuscation, or delay. Unlike the principle of neutrality, the principle of partisanship is qualified. A line separates the methods which a lawyer should be willing to use on behalf of a client from those he should not use. Before the lawyer crosses the line, he calls himself a representative; after he crosses it, he calls himself an officer of the court. Most debates within the Ideology of Advocacy concern the location of this line. . . .

The principles of neutrality and partisanship describe the basic conduct and attitudes of professional advocacy. The two principles are often combined in the terms "adversary advocacy" or "partisan advocacy". . . . However, it should be noted that the two principles are distinct in important respects. Many occupational roles, for instance the bureaucrat and the doctor, are expected to serve the general public without regard to the ends of those who seek their help. Yet, they are not expected to engage in the partisan pursuit of individual ends. On the other hand, political representatives are expected to be partisan, but they are not expected to serve all comers without regard to their ends. Only the lawyer seems to insist on making a virtue of both neutrality and partisanship.

Two further principles, though less obvious, are also assumed.... The first is the principle of procedural justice.... In this essay, the term "procedural justice" is used ... to refer to the notion that there is an inherent value or legitimacy to the judicial proceeding (and to a more qualified extent, the entire legal system) which makes it possible for a lawyer to justify specific actions without reference to the consequences they are likely to promote....

The second foundation principle of the Ideology of Advocacy is professionalism.... [Professionalism means that ethical questions about the limits of advocacy] are to be resolved in terms of legal doctrine and that they should be resolved by lawyers collectively in their occupational capacities and not by lawyers individually in terms of personal or social norms or by broad-based political institutions.

NOTES: THE CODES AND NEUTRAL PARTISANSHIP

The extent to which lawyers ethical codes embody the Neutral Partisanship conception of the lawyer's role is a surprisingly contested issue, one that is important enough to justify a careful review of the rules. Although the ABA's 1969 Code of Professional Responsibility has long been superseded by the Model Rules, its provisions offer a still influential conception of the lawyer's role, and its terminology is significant for understanding current rules.

The Code's principal text of partisanship is Canon 7: "A lawyer should represent a client zealously within the bounds of the law."[4] Several ECs and DRs spell out the notion of zeal within the bounds of the law. For example, DR 7–101(A)(1) provides that: "A lawyer shall not intentionally fail to seek the lawful objectives of his client through reasonably available means permitted by law and the Disciplinary Rules...." This implies that lawyers cannot allow their own moral scruples about a client's ends or the means used to pursue them to interfere with zealous representation, as long as the ends and means are lawful. The lawyer's only alternative is to withdraw from the representation. However, DR 7–101(A)(1) also adds that a "lawyer does not violate this Disciplinary Rule, however, by acceding to reasonable requests of opposing counsel which do not prejudice the rights of his client, by being punctual in fulfilling all professional commitments, by avoiding offensive tactics, or by treating with courtesy and consideration all persons involved in the legal process." DR 7–101(B)(1) further permits lawyers to refuse to aid conduct they believe to be unlawful even though there is "some support for the argument that the conduct is lawful." EC 7–

---

4. The "zeal" terminology comes from Canon 15 of the Code's predecessor, the ABA Canons of Professional Ethics: "The lawyer owes 'entire devotion to the interest of the client, warm zeal in the maintenance and defense of his rights and the exertion of his utmost learning and ability,' to the end that nothing be taken or be withheld from him, save by the rules of law, legally applied."

8 and 7–9, which emphasize that a lawyer should raise issues of justice and morality with their clients. These amount to a kind of "counter-text" stressing that zeal has limits and that a lawyer is not merely a "hired gun."

The Model Rules includes no requirement of zeal as such—the closest it comes is the requirement in Rule 1.3 of "reasonable diligence" in pursuit of the client's interest. Moreover, the Comments to Rules 1.2 and 1.3 explicitly counsel that a lawyer is *not* obligated to do anything a client asks. Model Rule 1.2(a) requires the lawyer to "abide by" client decisions about the objectives of representation, but only to "consult" with the client about means.

On its face, then, the Model Rules weakens the ethic of zealous representation. However, a Comment to Rule 1.3 specifies that a lawyer "must . . . act with commitment and dedication to the interests of the client and with zeal in advocacy upon the client's behalf"; the word "must" was deliberately added to this Comment in 2002, replacing the less forceful word "should" in prior versions. About 40 jurisdictions include "zeal" in this Comment and one rule, that of the District of Columbia, includes it in the text. Rule 1.3, which is titled "Diligence *and Zeal*" (emphasis added), begins: "A lawyer shall represent a client zealously and diligently within the bounds of the law." About ten jurisdictions have no reference to zeal in their code.[5] In practice, many lawyers believe that "zeal" continues to be the ethical standard that the Model Rules embody, and that lawyers have no right to refrain from effective tactics even if they find them morally offensive.

Perhaps the question of whether or not to use the word "zeal" in a rule seems like a trivial semantic issue. But precisely because rule-drafters have consciously used or refrained from using the word, it has taken on a larger significance. To include "zeal" or "zealous" in a rule signifies a commitment to Neutral Partisanship; to omit these words signifies, at the very least, greater openness to alternative visions of the lawyer's role.

PROBLEM 1

You are a litigator in a large law firm. During the discovery phase of a complicated commercial proceeding, involving tens of millions of dollars, you are reviewing several boxes of documents that the adversary has turned over. In one box you find a file of documents marked "CONFIDENTIAL: CONTENTS PROTECTED BY ATTORNEY–CLIENT PRIVILEGE. UNAUTHORIZED PARTIES ARE PROHIBITED FROM READING THIS DOCUMENT." On the assumption that this may be standard "boilerplate," you begin to read one of the documents, and quickly realize that it concerns the pending litigation and undoubtedly is protected by the attorney-client privilege. Apparently the file of documents was sent to you by

---

5. Panel Discussion, "Zealous Representation: How Low Can You Go?," discussed in 21 ABA/BNA Lawyers' Man. Prof. Conduct 312 (2006).

mistake. You suspect that it contains information that would be quite valuable to your side in the litigation.

May you read the documents? *Should* you read the documents? May you use the information contained in the documents? Must you notify the adversary law firm that you have received the documents by mistake? Must you return the documents?

ABA Formal Opinion 92–368
Inadvertent Disclosure of Confidential Materials
(November 10, 1992).

The Committee has been asked to opine on the obligations under the Model Rules of Professional Conduct of a lawyer who comes into possession of materials that appear on their face to be subject to the attorney-client privilege or otherwise confidential, under circumstances where it is clear that the materials were not intended for the receiving lawyer.... This opinion is intended to answer a question which has become increasingly important as the burgeoning of multi-party cases, the availability of xerography and the proliferation of facsimile machines and electronic mail make it technologically ever more likely that through inadvertence, privileged or confidential materials will be produced to opposing counsel by no more than the pushing of the wrong speed dial number on a facsimile machine.

A satisfactory answer to the question posed cannot be drawn from a narrow, literalistic reading of the black letter of the Model Rules. But it is useful, and necessary, to bear in mind the thoughts in the Preamble to the Model Rules that "many difficult issues of professional discretion ... must be resolved through the exercise of sensitive professional and moral judgment guided by the basic principles underlying the Rules," and that "the Rules do not exhaust the moral and ethical considerations that should inform a lawyer, for no worthwhile human activity can be completely defined by legal rules." In that larger, and more fundamental, framework, the Committee's views, expressed in this opinion, have been informed by the importance the Model Rules give to maintaining client confidentiality, ... the similarity between the circumstances here addressed and other conduct the profession universally condemns, and the receiving lawyer's obligations to his client.

Giving due weight to each of the foregoing considerations, it is the view of the Committee that the receiving lawyer, as a matter of ethical conduct contemplated by the precepts underlying the Model Rules, (a) should not examine the materials once the inadvertence is discovered, (b) should notify the sending lawyer of their receipt and (c) should abide by the sending lawyer's instructions as to their disposition....

The concept of confidentiality is a fundamental aspect of the right to the effective assistance of counsel. As reflected in each iteration of the rules of professional responsibility, the obligation of the lawyer to maintain and to refuse to divulge client confidences is virtually absolute....

If the Committee were to countenance, or indeed encourage, conduct on the part of the receiving lawyer which was in derogation of this strong policy in favor of confidentiality, the Committee would have to identify a more important principle which supports an alternative result. As the Committee examines the potentially competing principles, we conclude that their importance pales in comparison to the importance of maintaining confidentiality. . . .

[I]t might be urged that a receiving lawyer has an obligation to maximize the advantage his client will gain from careful scrutiny of the missent materials. While the "zealous" representation of Canon 7 of the Model Code of Professional Responsibility does not appear in haec verba [in these exact words] in the Model Rules, it could be argued that a lawyer's "commitment and dedication to the interests of the client," referred to in the Comment to Model Rule 1.3 (calling on a lawyer to act with "reasonable promptness and diligence"), includes an obligation to capitalize on an error of this sort on the part of opposing counsel.

However, there are many limitations on the extent to which a lawyer may go "all out" for the client. . . . For example, if during a lunch break in a deposition, lawyer B left notes or other materials in a conference room, either in an unlocked briefcase or on the conference room table, there is no respectable argument that competent and diligent representation requires or even permits lawyer A, arriving back from lunch early, to review the materials to which he now has easy access. Nor if, after a closing at lawyer A's office, lawyer B accidentally leaves a file or a briefcase behind would it be proper to assert that lawyer A could take advantage of this inadvertence and rifle the file or inspect the briefcase before returning it. Indeed, in the view of the Committee that lawyer would have an obligation to notify the lawyer who left her briefcase that it had been found. Finally, if in positioning an overhead projector on a shared counsel table in a courtroom during a recess, court personnel inadvertently move the prosecutor's notes into a position in front of the defense counsel's place at the table, it seems clear to the Committee that defense counsel would have an absolute obligation to return the materials without any examination or copying.

The analysis of this issue as an ethical matter should not obscure some more practical considerations that suggest the correct course for the receiving lawyer is to inform sending lawyer and return the documents. The immediate reaction of receiving counsel might be that the use of the missent materials can only serve to advantage his client. Nonetheless, it is clear there are advantages to doing just the opposite. First, instances of inadvertent production of documents tend not to occur only on one side. While a lawyer today may be the beneficiary of the opposing lawyer's misstep, tomorrow the shoe could be on the other foot. . . . [Furthermore], the credibility and professionalism inherent in doing the right thing can, in some significant ways, enhance the strength of one's case, one's standing with the other party and opposing counsel, and one's stature before the Court.

Monroe H. Freedman, "The Errant Fax"

Legal Times (Jan. 23, 1995).

From her fax machine to yours comes the smoking-gun document that could win your client's case. But it's addressed to her co-counsel, labeled "LAWYER–CLIENT PRIVILEGE" and "WORK PRODUCT," and a cover sheet demands that it be returned by any unintended recipient. What should you do?

Don't read it, says the American Bar Association's ethics committee in Opinion 92–368. Inform the lawyer who sent it, and obey her instructions about what to do with the document.

But two state ethics committees have read the ABA opinion and have found it unpersuasive. The Ohio committee, in its Opinion 93–11, concluded that the unintended recipient is free to use the document, but that he should inform opposing counsel about it. And just last month, the Maine ethics committee, in Opinion 146 (Dec. 9, 1994), reached a similar conclusion. A California court, in *Aerojet–General Corp. v. Transport Indemnity Insurance*, 22 Cal.Rptr.2d 862 (1993), went further, holding that the lawyer may keep the document and need not inform opposing counsel.

My vote is with the authorities recommending using the document, and I agree with the California court that opposing counsel need not be informed. Here's why....

[The ABA committee's] analysis begins with the admission that a "satisfactory answer cannot be drawn from a narrow, literalistic reading of the black letter of the Model Rules." A translation from the doublespeak is that there is no rule that supports the "satisfactory answer" that the committee wanted to reach.

So the committee went to the preamble of the Model Rules for some of the most Delphic guidance this side of Delphi.... Having cut loose from the rules themselves, the ABA committee was free to analogize at will—to the importance of client confidences, ... similar conduct that the profession "universally condemns," and even "the receiving lawyer's obligations to his client." The committee also relied on "professionalism" and on the lawyer's "personal conscience and the approbation of professional peers."
. . .

The committee's best argument for its result is the ethic of confidentiality.... I find the committee's contention [that returning the errant fax is required by confidentiality] misplaced. The obligation of confidentiality runs, after all, between the lawyer and her client—not between the lawyer and your client. And that's what we're talking about here.

Your adversary has been careless in protecting her client's confidences. Therefore, says the committee, you should protect her client's confidences. As fabled Harvard Law Professor Austin Scott used to say, "I understand everything but the 'therefore.'"

At the same time, the committee overrides the search for truth. Surely, there are values, including the lawyer-client privilege, that take precedence over truth-seeking. But you—the adversary of the party who holds the privilege—are not bound by that privilege.

Also devalued is the ethic of zealous representation. The Model Rules have replaced the Model Code's "zeal" with "commitment and dedication." But University of Pennsylvania Law Professor Geoffrey Hazard Jr., Reporter for the Model Rules, in his (and co-author W. Hodes') *The Law of Lawyering*, has noted that zealousness continues to be "the fundamental principle of the law of lawyering." . . .

As the ABA committee says, zealousness has always been subject to express limitations. But that is hardly an excuse for adding unexpressed limitations, as the committee does. You have received the document that could win your client's case, yet the committee holds that you should give more weight to your adversary's obligation of confidentiality than to your own obligation of zealous representation. . . .

With regard to the secondary issue—informing opposing counsel of her blunder—that is an issue that is covered by a black-letter rule. Model Rule 1.6 says that a lawyer "shall not reveal information relating to representation of a client unless the client consents. . . ." (The exceptions are inapplicable here.) The most efficacious use of the document might be to impeach the adverse party at trial—a tactic that could be defeated by premature disclosure.

Of course, if the client consents, the lawyer can send back the document—although I would hope that the lawyer would first make his own determination of whether the document is in fact privileged. Even a faxed invitation to lunch is likely to have a cover sheet with the standard language about lawyer-client privilege and threats of cruel and unusual punishment for any unauthorized use. How do you know that a document is privileged unless you read it?

And where is the committee's stopping point? What if opposing counsel's blunder is not a misdirected document but a failure to assert the lawyer-client privilege in court, or a failure to plead the statute of limitations, or an initial offer of settlement far in excess of what your client is willing to take? How far is the current vogue for "professionalism" to take us in sacrificing our clients' interests to protect opposing counsel from embarrassment or a malpractice action?

NOTES

In its 2002 amendments to the Model Rules, the ABA addressed the "errant fax" issue by requiring that a lawyer "who receives a document relating to the representation of the lawyer's client and knows or reasonably should know that the document was inadvertently sent shall promptly notify the sender." Model Rule 4.4(b). A Comment to this Rule adds that whether the lawyer chooses to return the document unread "is a matter of professional judgment ordinarily reserved to the lawyer."

As both the ABA Formal Opinion and Professor Freedman's response indicate, Problem 2 presents a straightforward conflict between the ethics of neutral partisanship and what we might consider the ethics of fair play. No Model Rule explicitly prohibits a lawyer from reading the opponent's missent document, or, for that matter, from any of the forms of snooping that the Opinion cites, such as peeking at the adversary's notes. Yet the Opinion is probably correct in assuming that most lawyers disapprove of such tactics, and it may well be correct that such widely condemned tactics violate the spirit of the Model Rules as expressed in its preamble.

However, Professor Freedman—an outspoken proponent of zealous advocacy—is on strong ground when he reads this argument as an admission that no rule prohibits a lawyer from reading and using the "errant fax." Does the new Rule 4.4(b) change this situation? Freedman is also on strong ground when he asks rhetorically whether a client should lose the case because his or her lawyer doesn't wish to be unsportsmanlike. The Comment to Rule 4.4(b) leaves this question to the lawyer, not the client. Is this a proper resolution of the issue?

Numerous state and municipal bar associations have published ethics opinions on this subject. Most opinions require a lawyer who has inadvertently received privileged material *and is aware of its confidential nature before reading it* to refrain from examining the material—the position taken in ABA Formal Opinion 368. Of course, it is very likely that the receiving lawyer will not know that a document is privileged without first reading it, so perhaps the more significant questions are whether lawyers can use the information and whether they must return the documents. Most opinions advise that lawyers *may* take advantage of confidential information that they have inadvertently received in order to further client interests.[6] A few hold that lawyers *must not* use such information, and should return all inadvertently disclosed materials to opposing counsel.[7] The *Restatement of the Law Governing Lawyers*, on the other hand, holds that "[t]he receiving lawyer may be required to consult with that lawyer's client about whether to take advantage of the lapse." *Restatement*, § 60 Comment *m*.

Significantly, only the Massachusetts bar has declared that the receiving lawyer *must* use the information if doing so would help the client—and yet this result seems to follow from an unqualified ethic of neutral partisanship. Does this mean that the profession is *not* committed to such an ethic? Do you agree with Formal Opinion 92–368 that "there are many limitations on the extent to which a lawyer may go 'all out' for the client"? How much say should the client have in the matter? If lawyers misuse a

---

6. This position is taken by the bars of the District of Columbia, the City of New York, Illinois, Kentucky, Maine, Maryland, Michigan, New Hampshire, Ohio, Oregon, and Pennsylvania.

7. Louisiana, North Carolina, Utah, and Virginia. The sixteenth state, Florida, requires the receiving lawyer to notify the sending lawyer, but otherwise declines to address the ethical questions.

document in violation of their state's ethics rule, should they be disqualified?[8]

Similar questions have arisen in recent years about "metadata." Metadata is information embedded in electronic documents about the creation or modification of the document. It is usually invisible on the screen, but it can often be retrieved through word-processing or spread sheet software. Much metadata is innocuous, but sometimes it reveals important confidences through tracked changes, comments, and deleted material. An opinion by the D.C. Bar explains:

> A lawyer who is preparing a document may electronically circulate the document in draft form among other lawyers in the firm for their review and comment. The other lawyers may insert their suggested revisions and other comments, some of which might address the strengths and weaknesses of the client's position. If the final version of the document is electronically transmitted to opposing counsel, it may be possible for opposing counsel to discover the comments. The sender of the document may not be aware of the metadata embedded within the document, or that it remains in the electronic document despite the sender's good-faith belief that it was "deleted."[9]

The results can be highly damaging. "Examples of unintended releases . . . include one firm that posted a Word document online and, with two knowledgeable 'clicks,' a savvy viewer was able to discover that the client initially intended to sue someone other than the named defendant. In another case, a motion in a national security lawsuit was posted with what the lawyers thought had been redacted sensitive information."[10] Should lawyers be subject to sanctions for mining metadata, such as earlier versions of a file, that are not readily visible? Or is looking for metadata that opposing counsel could have scrubbed part of effective representation?

Bar committees and commentators have come to different conclusions on that question. The American Bar Association's Committee on Professional Ethics in Formal Opinion 06–442 interpreted Model Rule 4.4 as requiring only notification of opposing counsel of any discovered material. Maryland's Ethics Committee in Opinion 2007–09 comes to a similar conclusion. In effect, these committees place responsibility on the transmitting attorney to scrub their documents. By contrast, New York and Florida

---

8. A New York City Bar Opinion takes the position that the lawyer should not be disqualified because otherwise opposing counsel might deliberately send a privileged document in an effort to force replacement of an effective adversary. N.Y. City Ethics Op. 2003–4 (2003). By contrast, the California Supreme Court requires disqualification of a litigator who receives opposing counsel's work product and exploits the knowledge in impeaching two experts rather than notifying opposing counsel. In the court's view, it does not matter whether use of the confidential material reveals false testimony; exceptions to attorneys' ethical obligations cannot depend on the content of the privileged document. Rico v. Mitsubishi Motors Corp., 42 Cal.4th 807, 171 P.3d 1092 (2007). For fuller discussion see Andrew M. Perlman, "Untangling Ethics Theory From Attorney Conduct Rules: The Case of Indadvertent Disclosures," 13 *Ge. Mason L. Rev.* 767 (2005).

9. "Review and Use of Metadata in Electronic Documents," D.C. Bar Opinion 341 (2007).

10. Marcia Coyle, " 'Metadata' Mining Vexes Lawyers, Bars," *Nat'l. L. J. Online*, Feb. 18, 2008.

have held that lawyers should refrain from proactively mining metatdata but also should take reasonable care to avoid sending it. New York State Bar Association Committee on Professional Ethics, Opinions 749 (2004) and 782 (2007); Professional Ethics Committee of the Florida Bar, Opinion 06–2 (2006). Which position makes most sense? Does your answer depend on the adequacy of technology to perfectly scrub a document?[11]

If lawyers are prohibited from peeking at metadata, what would stop a sophisticated client from demanding that the lawyer forward the documents so that the client can examine them? Must the lawyer refuse to send such documents to the client? Whose documents are they? Alternatively, what if the client obtains confidential documents surreptitiously and gives them to the attorney? Must the attorney disclose that fact to the other side? See Professional Ethics Committee of the Florida Bar, Opinion 07–1 (2007).

B.   NEUTRAL PARTISANSHIP AND ROLE MORALITY

PROBLEM 2

Consider four examples of defense by intimidation:

a) A law firm defended pharmaceuticals manufacturer A. H. Robins Corporation in thousands of law suits over the Dalkon Shield, an intrauterine contraceptive device that Robins marketed during the 1970s to over three million women. Because of a design flaw, the Dalkon Shield caused an estimated 66,000 miscarriages and sterilized thousands of women by infecting them with pelvic inflammatory disease (PID).

One tactic of Robins's counsel soon acquired the nickname "the dirty questions list." Defense lawyers taking depositions asked plaintiffs very specific, graphic questions about intimate details of their personal hygiene and sexual practices—questions that one plaintiff described as "more like an obscene phone call" than a pretrial inquiry. Firm lawyers argued that the answers were relevant to the law suits because they might reveal alternative sources of PID infection. The questions also served, however, to intimidate plaintiffs into dropping their law suits or settling them for inadequate amounts. The message was clear that they might have to reveal the same information in open court. Among other things, defense lawyers asked plaintiffs for the names of all their past and present sexual partners ("besides your husband"), raising the possibility that the partners' names might be revealed and that they might be called as witnesses for purposes of impeaching plaintiffs' testimony. Potential litigants filed affidavits indi-

---

11. See David Hricik, "Mining for Embedded Data: Is it Ethical to Take Intentional Advantage of Other People's Failures?," 8 *N.C. J. L. & Tech.* 231, 232–34 (2007) (noting that the best tools for removing metadata become obsolete and incapable of perfect scrubbing in a short space of time); Toby Brown, Electronic Discovery Basics, 52 *R.I. Bar J.* 7 (2003); David Hricik, I Can Tell When You're Telling Lies: Ethics and Embedded Confidential Information, 30 *J. Legal Prof.* 79 (2006).

cating that they had dropped their own lawsuits because of the questions that other women had been asked.[12]

b) A law firm defended a major petroleum corporation against a hostile takeover by another large corporation. The acquiring corporation's board chairman is a well-known pro-Israel Jewish activist. Takeover defense lawyers recommended notifying the governments of Islamic oil-producing states about the impending acquisition, in the hope that they would threaten to cut off oil supplies if the takeover went forward. By provoking religious antagonisms and raising international tension, the law firm hoped to block the takeover.[13]

c) Lawyers representing corporations and government entities have sometimes pursued SLAPP suits—*Strategic Lawsuits Against Public Participation*. In a typical case, citizens protesting corporate policies or actions face claims for defamation or tortious interference with business. Some of the alleged defamation has been based on speech as innocuous as testifying against a real estate developer at a zoning hearing, complaining to a school board about incompetent teachers, or collecting signatures on a petition. Although the vast majority of SLAPP suits are dismissed before trial, the aim of the suits is not legal victory but intimidation. Defendants faced with the prospect of ruinous legal bills and the risk of substantial personal liability often agree to cease protest activities in return for withdrawal of the SLAPP suits.[14]

d) A seasoned trial litigator repeatedly makes unsustained evidentiary objections in order to disrupt the flow of her adversary's presentation and distract the jury from damaging evidence.[15] She also refuses to consent to a rescheduling request by an opposing lawyer whose wife is undergoing major surgery on the grounds that it would seriously inconvenience her expert witnesses. Her firm has hired investigators to look into the private lives of adversaries and their counsel.

QUESTIONS

1. Are such tactics proper?

2. Who should decide whether to use tactics that may well affect the outcome of litigation?

3. Would a lawyer who declined to use these tactics at a client's request be in violation of the Model Rules?

4. Do lawyers bear moral responsibility for using such tactics? For proposing them to clients who never thought of them?

---

12. Ronald J. Bacigal, *The Limits of Litigation: The Dalkon Shield Controversy* 19–20 (1990).

13. Philip B. Heymann & Lance Liebman, *The Social Responsibilities of Lawyers* 117–18 (1988).

14. George W. Pring & Penelope Canan, *SLAPPs: Getting Sued for Speaking Out* (1996).

15. David D. Blinka, "Ethics, Evidence, and the Modern Adversary Trial," 19 *Geo. J. Legal Ethics* 1 (2006).

INTRODUCTION

A central moral problem in legal ethics—and professional ethics more generally—arises from the Neutral Partisanship vision. Advocates, it is sometimes said, must do things for the client that they would never do for themselves. They must represent causes that they personally find repugnant, and employ methods that harm the innocent, such as intimidating injured plaintiffs through intrusive questions, stirring up international incidents, filing SLAPP suits, and intimidating opposing counsel. Thus, lawyers acting in their professional role seem to be governed by a distinctive set of moral rules. Parallel problems arise for other professions. Journalists publish the truth even if doing so injures innocent parties; military leaders cause thousands of enemy casualties in order to save small numbers of their own troops; physicians treating AIDS patients keep the knowledge of infection secret even from the patient's unprotected sexual partners. In the case of lawyers, the Neutral Partisanship vision insists on narrowing the range of the advocate's moral concern to focus solely on the client.

Is this concept of *role morality* different from ordinary morality justifiable? The puzzle may be illustrated by a celebrated anecdote in which a parishioner approaches a priest and says, "Father, I don't understand how, if God is good and loves us, He can permit so much pain in the world." The priest hesitates, then replies: "God has to do a lot of things in his professional capacity that He would never do if it were up to Him personally."

One critic of role morality is the lawyer-philosopher Richard Wasserstrom. In a well-known essay, Wasserstrom considers the "accusation . . . that the lawyer-client relationship renders the lawyer at best systematically amoral and at worst more than occasionally immoral in his or her dealings with the rest of mankind."[16] According to Wasserstrom,

> Once a lawyer represents a client, the lawyer has a duty to make his or her expertise fully available in the realization of the end sought by the client, irrespective, for the most part, of the moral worth to which the end will be put or the character of the client who seeks to utilize it. Provided that the end sought is not illegal, the lawyer is, in essence, an amoral technician whose peculiar skills and knowledge in respect to the law are available to those with whom the relationship of client is established.[17]

Wasserstrom observes that being an "amoral technician" requires some sort of justification—one cannot simply opt out of moral obligations at will. He believes that this problem is especially acute for lawyers:

> The lawyer—and especially the lawyer as advocate—directly says and affirms things. The lawyer makes the case for the client. He or she tries to explain, persuade and convince others that the client's cause

---

16. Richard Wasserstrom, "Lawyers as Professionals: Some Moral Issues," 5 *Human Rights* 1, 1 (1975).

17. *Id.* at 5–6.

should prevail. The lawyer lives with and within a dilemma that is not shared by other professionals. If the lawyer actually believes everything that he or she asserts on behalf of the client, then it appears to be proper to regard the lawyer as in fact embracing and endorsing the points of view that he or she articulates. If the lawyer does not in fact believe what is urged by way of argument, if the lawyer is only playing a role, then it appears to be proper to tax the lawyer with hypocrisy and insincerity. To be sure, actors in a play take on roles and say things that the characters, not the actors, believe. But we know it is a play and that they are actors. The law courts are not, however, theaters, and the lawyers both talk about justice and they genuinely seek to persuade. The fact that the lawyer's words, thoughts, and convictions are, apparently, for sale and at the service of the client helps us, I think, to understand the peculiar hostility which is more than occasionally uniquely directed by lay persons toward lawyers. The verbal, role-differentiated behavior of the lawyer *qua* advocate puts the lawyer's integrity into question in a way that distinguishes the lawyer from the other professionals.[18]

If lawyers seldom take such worries seriously, Wasserstrom suggests, that may be because a role morality like Neutral Partisanship, which permits lawyers to set moral deliberation to one side, creates a "simplified intellectual world ... that ... is often a very comfortable one to inhabit."[19]

In another essay, Wasserstrom insists on "a comprehensiveness, a universalistic dimension of morality, that is at odds with the more particularistic focus ... that occurs within and through the perspective of roles."[20] Morality is "universalistic," on this view, because to be moral is to transcend one's own particular desires and loyalties, to recognize that all people have equal and intrinsic moral worth, and therefore to treat all those one encounters with equal respect and concern.

However, other philosophers have objected that this universalistic approach misses an important dimension of moral life: the significance of our attachments to particular people and groups-our friends, our family, our community, and our clients. In the words of one philosopher, "[l]oyalty is neither egoism nor impersonal morality.... There is the morality of rules ... and thou-shalt-nots. There is enlightened, rational egoism that fancies it can see that being a nice guy pays. And, different from these, but sharing features with each, are loyalties. Loyalties are part of what make our societal worlds go around...."[21] The author concludes that in the end "all morality is tribal morality."[22]

---

18. *Id.* at 14.

19. *Id.* at 9.

20. Richard Wasserstrom, "Roles and Morality," in *The Good Lawyer: Lawyers' Roles and Lawyers' Ethics* 28 (David Luban ed. 1983).

21. Andrew Oldenquist, "Loyalties," 79 *J. Phil.* 173, 176 (1982). *See also* George P. Fletcher, *Loyalty: An Essay on the Morality of Relationships* (1992); Michael K. McChrystal, "Lawyers and Loyalty," 33 *Wm. & Mary L.Rev.* 367 (1992).

22. *Id.* at 179.

Here we see the decisive contrast. When does morality *prevent* us from playing favorites (notably, on behalf of clients)? When does it *require* us to play favorites? Does everyone share the same moral obligations, or does each "station" in life have its own unique "duties," each tribe its own loyalties, each role its own script?

The view that morality imposes universal responsibilities appears across a wide range of cultures. It finds expression in the Golden Rule ("Do to men what you would wish men to do to you," Matt. vii. 12), its cousins in the Hebrew Bible ("Love the stranger as thyself," Levit. xix. 34), and the teachings of Confucius ("Never do to others what you would not like them to do to you," Analects xv. 23).[23] Each of these mandates implies that, from the moral point of view, our common humanity demands that we should treat each other alike regardless of differences in social roles.

This idea was central to the work of the eighteenth century philosopher Immanuel Kant, who claimed that the defining feature of the moral law is its *universality*—that it applies with equal force to everyone. Kant proposed that the test of whether a rule of action, or "maxim," is morally acceptable is found in this formula: "Act only according to that maxim by which you can at the same time will that it should become a universal law."[24] In other words, one tests whether an act is morally permissible by asking "what if everyone were permitted to do that?" Kant argued that his formula is equivalent to another rule: "Act so that you treat humanity, whether in your own person or in that of another, always as an end and never as a means only."[25] He stressed the *dignity* that all humans share and argued that morality requires us to honor that dignity in everyone with whom we have dealings.

There are really two distinct propositions here: first, that everyone is bound by the same moral rules or obligations, and second, that everyone should be treated alike (as an end rather than a means). Though they are distinct, both propositions arise from the same source: the belief that we all possess human dignity and thus that, from a moral point of view, we are all each other's equals. It is the second idea, that everyone should be treated with equal respect, that is of primary importance to legal ethics, for Neutral Partisanship requires systematically favoring clients over others.

Wasserstrom appears to be arguing from a Kantian understanding of ethics. It is a powerful position. In response, however, critics have argued this understanding should be modified to make room for special loyalties. Even if the moral point of view demands that we ask whether our maxims could be accepted as universal laws, perhaps some of those laws extend only over our own occupational community, not over all human beings.

---

23. C.S. Lewis finds similar precepts in the Egyptian Book of the Dead, the Old Norse *Volospa,* the Babylonian *Hymn to Samas,* and miscellaneous other Egyptian, Hindu, Roman, and Biblical sources. C.S. Lewis, *The Abolition of Man* 97–100 (1947).

24. Immanuel Kant, *Foundations of the Metaphysics of Morals* 39 (Lewis White Beck trans. 1959). For further discussion, see the material on moral reasoning in the Introduction.

25. *Id.* at 47.

A similar view of morality was articulated by the German philosopher G.W.F. Hegel and, in 1876, by F.H. Bradley, a British follower of Hegel. Bradley's famous essay "My Station and Its Duties" argued that the Kantian formulas are too abstract to be useful: it is hard to say what "treating people as ends, not means" requires without fleshing out the formula by looking at the customs of a particular community.[26] According to Hegel and Bradley, it is only in a concrete community, which has moral traditions already in place, that we will be able to apply Kantian principles.Such a community will include roles, or stations, and duties that apply to all individuals who occupy those stations. Thus, Neutral Partisanship can perhaps be universalized over all lawyers.

In his overview of professional ethics, philosopher Arthur Applbaum summarizes other common defenses of role morality—for example, the claim that it is morally permitted, or even required, for a litigator to use intimidating tactics such as those in Problem 2.[27] The arguments come in pairs:

Expectation: Adversaries expect hardball tactics. *Consent*: Adversaries consent to hardball tactics.

Rules of the Game: The rules of the litigation game permit hardball tactics. *Fair Play*: Fair play in the litigation game morally permits hardball tactics.

Increased Net Benefit: More social benefit than burden is caused by zealous advocacy in litigation. *Pareto Superiority*: No one on balance is burdened, and some benefit, from zealous advocacy in litigation.

No Difference: If I don't use hardball tactics against my adversary, some other lawyer will. *Self–Defeat*: If I don't use hardball tactics against my adversary, some other lawyer will use them even more ruthlessly.

Role Obligation: The rules of the lawyer's role require engaging in any lawful tactics that help my client, including "dirty questions" and SLAPP suits. *Moral Obligation*: Morality requires that lawyers obey the rules of the lawyer's role.

Selflessness: A lawyer representing a client should filter out his or her own self-interest. *Person Neutrality*: A lawyer representing a client should filter out his or her own moral judgments.

Applbaum points out that it is easy to confuse the arguments in each pair with each other, but this is a mistake: "in each pair, the first claim might hold, but does not justify much. The second claim would justify much, but does not hold. In no pair does the second proposition follow from the first."[28] Is he right?

Two legal commentators famously defined a lawyer as "a person who on behalf of some people treats other people the way bureaucracies treat all

---

26. In F.H. Bradley, *Ethical Studies* (1876).

27. Arthur Isak Applbaum, *Ethics for Adversaries: The Morality of Roles in Public and Professional Life* 4 (1999). Applbaum illustrates his arguments with the example of political consultants who engage in slander and deception; we substitute legal examples instead.

28. *Id.*

people—as nonpeople."[29] Is this unfair or does it contain a grain of truth? Can the lawyer's role be justified in Kantian terms?

C.   THE JUSTIFICATION OF NEUTRAL PARTISANSHIP

NOTES

Any defense of role morality must include a defense of the role itself. Neutral Partisanship (or any other understanding of legal ethics, for that matter) cannot establish ethical obligations unless the role it creates is morally justifiable. Defenders of Neutral Partisanship generally have relied upon three arguments to justify the lawyer's "amoral" role: (a) the rights of the *client*, (b) the moral interests of the *lawyer,* and (c) the needs of the *legal system.*

a) *The client's autonomy.* American society traditionally has placed significant value on individual autonomy, on the liberty to order our own affairs, within wide limits defined by law. Many writers on legal ethics defend Neutral Partisanship in these terms. For example, Stephen Pepper writes:

> Our first premise is that law is intended to be a public good which increases autonomy. The second premise is that increasing individual autonomy is morally good. The third step is that in a highly legalized society such as ours, autonomy is often dependent upon access to the law.... For most people most of the time, meaningful access to the law requires the assistance of a lawyer. Thus the resulting conclusion:.... If the conduct which the lawyer facilitates ... is not unlawful—then this line of thought suggests that what the lawyer does is a social good.[30]

Wasserstrom similarly notes that if lawyers decline on moral grounds to pursue their clients' legal rights, the legal profession may exercise undue power as it determines who gets to exercise their legal rights and who does not. Pepper echoes this fear that moral "screening submits each ... to rule by an oligarchy of lawyers."[31]

Other commentators also have argued that clients' rights should be lawyers' paramount concern and have criticized lawyers who follow their own consciences and by doing so diminish client autonomy. The legal system is designed to accommodate many people's different conceptions of how to live; for lawyers to interfere with clients' exercise of their legal rights undermines the authority of law.[32]

---

29. Edward A. Dauer & Arthur A. Leff, "Correspondence: The Lawyer as Friend," 86 *Yale L.J.* 573, 581 (1977).

30. Stephen L. Pepper, "The Lawyer's Amoral Ethical Role: A Defense, A Problem, and Some Possibilities," 1986 *Am.B.Found. Res.J.* 613, 617.

31. *Id.*

32. W. Bradley Wendel, "Civil Obedience," 104 *Colum. L. Rev.* 363 (2004); Stephen Ellmann, "Lawyers and Clients," 34

To critics of Neutral Partisanship, these are strong arguments, but they are by no means decisive. First, clients' rights are not the only moral values, and when enhancing a client's liberty or autonomy injures other individuals, it must be shown that the gain excuses the wrong. Second, the "oligarchy" argument relies on an imperfect analogy. As Alan Goldman has remarked,

> [t]he major fallacy in this argument . . . is the implicit assumption that lawyers act as a corporate body to determine collectively how clients may act. In fact they do not form such a body. They do not vote on how cases should be pursued, but rather act as individuals whose moral opinions may differ among themselves. . . . If an individual lawyer refuses to do for a client that which he feels the client has no right to do, the client can always seek another lawyer.[33]

Only in the exceptional case in which the lawyer is the "last in town" are the client's rights necessarily at risk.

Finally, proponents of client autonomy generally contrast their preferred model with paternalistic models, in which lawyers decide what is in the client's best interests, even when the client does not agree. (See Chapter XI). In proponents' view, it is objectionable for advocates to substitute their own judgments for those of clients who will have to live with the results. But for the purpose of justifying Neutral Partisanship, the question is not who should determine the client's interests, but whether lawyers should pursue interests they find repugnant. Even from the standpoint of protecting rights, there are rights of third parties to be considered as well.

b) *The moral interests of the lawyer.* In a well-known article, Charles Fried argued that a lawyer is a "special-purpose friend" of the client.

> A lawyer is a friend in regard to the legal system. He is someone who enters into a personal relation with you—not an abstract relation as under the concept of justice. That means that like a friend he acts in your interests, not in his own; or rather he adopts your interests as his own. I would call that the classic definition of friendship. To be sure, the lawyer's range of concern is sharply limited. But within that limited domain the intensity of identification with the client's interests is the same.[34]

Fried then presses two points. First, each of us has a right to privilege the interests of our own friends, even if we could benefit more people by

---

U.C.L.A.L.Rev. 717 (1987). As one litigator put it, "I personally would have a problem even conveying my own view of the morality of the situation to a client. I think morality is a very slippery concept, primarily in the eye of the beholder." Robert L. Nelson, "The Discovery Process as a Circle of Blame: Institutional, Professional, and Socioeconomic Factors That Contribute to Inefficient and Amoral Behavior in Corporate Litigation," 67 *Fordham L. Rev.* 773, 778–80 (1998).

33. Alan Goldman, *The Moral Foundations of Professional Ethics* 129–30 (1980); *see* Deborah L. Rhode, *In the Interests of Justice* 57 (2000).

34. Charles Fried, "The Lawyer as Friend: The Moral Foundations of the Lawyer–Client Relation," 85 *Yale L.J.* 1060, 1071–72 (1976).

distributing our concern more broadly. We are not morally obligated to treat everyone in the world equally. An essential component of the good life is to be able to pay special attention to one's family and friends. To deny us that right would be to infringe on our moral personality.

Fried's second point is that favoring our friends is justifiable because friendship is itself a source of moral value. Reasoning by analogy, Fried concludes that since clients are special-purpose friends, an advocate cannot be criticized for favoring their interests. Neutral Partisanship follows from this conception of "the lawyer as friend."

Fried's argument has attracted numerous comments and criticisms. Edward Dauer and Arthur Leff object that the friendship analogy is weak, because lawyers and friends share no common bond apart from their professional relationship, which Fried has arbitrarily analogized to friendship. In effect, "a lawyer is like a friend ... because, for Professor Fried, a friend is like a lawyer."[35] William Simon goes further. Focusing on the fact that typically a lawyer becomes the client's "friend" only for pay, Simon maintains that Fried has formulated the classical definition not of friendship but of prostitution.[36]

By contrast, Susan Wolf agrees with much of Fried's argument; however, she objects that by using it to defend Neutral Partisanship, Fried has drawn the wrong conclusion: "If one adopts some interests as one's own, it would seem one becomes to that extent personally accountable for them. Thus, if the interests are immoral, one can be personally blamed for having them. If, on the other hand, the lawyer is not to be blamed for the immorality of the client's goals, this would have to be because these goals are *not* identified with the lawyer's goals."[37]

Despite these objections, many lawyers will recognize a large grain of truth in Fried's insistence on the personal and intimate character of legal services, which implies a large measure of trust on the part of the client. This "special-purpose" trust and loyalty may be very hard for the client to distinguish from personal trust and loyalty. As an empirical matter, "the lawyer as friend" can at times be quite an apt metaphor.[38]

c) *The interests of the system.* Some commentators seek to justify Neutral Partisanship by reference not only to the interests of clients, or of lawyers, but also to the nature of the American legal system. The prior excerpt from William Simon suggested that the most frequent argument for such partisanship rests on principles of procedural justice and thus, implicitly, on the adversary system.

---

35. Dauer & Leff, *supra* note 29, at 578.

36. William Simon, "The Ideology of Advocacy: Procedural Justice and Professional Ethics," 1978 *Wisc.L.Rev.* 29, 108–09.

37. Susan Wolf, "Ethics, Legal Ethics, and the Ethics of Law," in *The Good Lawyer:*

Lawyers' Roles and Lawyers' Ethics 59 n. 4 (David Luban ed. 1983).

38. See Robert J. Condlin, " 'What's Love got To Do With It?—Its Not Like They're Your Friends for Christ's Sake': The Complicated Relationship between Lawyer and Client," 82 *Neb. L. Rev.* 211 (2003).

At its core, the adversary system consists of three features: adjudication by an impartial tribunal, formal procedural rules, and party responsibility for the presentation of their own cases.[39] This third feature inspires the principles of partisanship and neutrality: lawyers' role is to advance their clients' cases (partisanship), without regard to their own view of its moral implications (neutrality).

The following discussion focuses on the adversary system and the justifications it provides for this Neutral Partisan role.

D. The Adversary System

1. The Historical Background of Adversarial Processes

NOTES

The Anglo–American adversary system has its roots in various rituals of dispute resolution. Among the oldest and most widespread were trials by ordeal. Disputes that could not be settled informally or that presented conflicting evidence often resulted in an ordeal procedure that placed the accused at considerable disadvantage. Under this system, defendants were put in a situation of severe physical danger, such as drowning or burning, and appeals were made for divine intervention. Depending on the ritual, the accused party's survival unharmed served as proof of guilt or innocence.

An alternative procedure, trial by compurgation, was designed to test the credibility of the accused. Under this system, a defendant established innocence by denying the offense and presenting a specified number of witnesses who swore to his or her honesty. For their oaths to be valid, the witnesses had to make a perfect recitation. According to some historical accounts, the precursors of our modern legal profession were witnesses hired for their ability to complete an oath without sneezes or stumbles.

In eleventh century England, William the Conqueror introduced trial by combat. To resolve criminal charges, the accuser and accused fought each other personally. In disputes over land, the plaintiff could hire a professional combatant to represent him. The purpose of the battle was not to kill one's opponents but to force them to "cry craven," and admit their perjury. In civil cases, the losers typically paid a fine. In criminal cases, hanging or mutilation was common.

The Normans also imported a system of jury trials, which gradually came to supplant these more primitive predecessors. Unlike their modern counterparts, however, jurors under this early procedure were not impartial peers who lacked prior knowledge of the case before them. Rather, they

---

39. Lon L. Fuller, "The Adversary System," in *Talks on American Law* 30–32 (Harold J. Berman ed. 1961).

were male landowners from the community (a small minority of the adult population) and lack of personal information about the matter in dispute was a ground for disqualification rather than qualification. During its early stages, this system had few of the safeguards that form the mainstay of contemporary adversarial processes. The defendant had no right to counsel, and confessions obtained under torture were freely admissible. Until the sixteenth century, when witnesses began to be part of established procedures, jurors did their own fact-finding outside the courtroom.

By the seventeenth century, when colonists began to transplant English legal practices into American soil, more formal procedural safeguards had developed. Initially, however, some settlers viewed this formalism as too expensive and cumbersome for American needs. A general distaste for lawyers—who were thought to be fomenters of strife—also inspired efforts to develop simple dispute resolution procedures. Yet as American society became more complex, and its commercial activity more extensive, the need for procedural regularity and professional intermediaries became apparent.

Other forces were also at work. Many members of the emerging middle and upper classes in America were intent on restricting the power of the state as well as preventing the development of an aristocracy comparable to that in England. An adversarial legal process appeared consistent with these objectives. It limited the role of the judge, and placed considerable responsibility in the hands of parties and their chosen representatives. As long as those representatives were members of an independent professional class, they could provide an important check on central governmental authority.

This complex set of historical, political, and socioeconomic forces played an influential role in American constitutional development. The framers of the Bill of Rights included provisions that fortified an adversarial structure, such as rights to counsel, due process, and trial by jury. Those provisions were, in turn, interpreted by a legal profession interested in maintaining its own autonomy and influence. Over the course of the next two centuries, the American bar developed a deep commitment to an adversarial system and to the values underlying it, which are reviewed in the readings that follow.

2.   THE "SEARCH FOR TRUTH" AND THE PROTECTION OF RIGHTS

NOTES

Justifications for the adversary system generally rest on two premises: first, adversary procedures offer the best means of discovering truth; and second, zealous advocacy protects fundamental individual rights from public and private infringement.

Problems with the adversary system reflect the flip side of these two justifications. Obligations of zeal and confidentiality encourage attorneys to avoid disclosing truth and may infringe upon adversaries' legal rights. The tension between the general justifications and the particular consequences that the system occasionally entails has inspired a longstanding debate.

The following excerpt provides perhaps the best-known defense of the adversary system. Co-authored in the 1950s by Lon Fuller, one of the nation's most prominent philosophers of law, it represents a semi-official statement by a joint committee of the American Bar Association and the Association of American Law Schools. This Report offered a reasoned argument for the superiority of the adversary system to other procedural systems such as those in Continental Europe, where the judge exercises primary control over the fact-finding process.

Lon L. Fuller and John D. Randall, "Professional Responsibility: Report of the Joint Conference of the ABA and AALS"

44 American Bar Association Journal 1159, 1160–61 (1958).

The lawyer appearing as an advocate before a tribunal presents, as persuasively as he can, the facts and the law of the case as seen from the standpoint of his client's interest. It is essential that both the lawyer and the public understand clearly the nature of the role thus discharged. Such an understanding is required not only to appreciate the need for an adversary presentation of issues, but also in order to perceive truly the limits partisan advocacy must impose on itself if it is to remain wholesome and useful.

In a very real sense it may be said that the integrity of the adjudicative process itself depends upon the participation of the advocate. This becomes apparent when we contemplate the nature of the task assumed by any arbiter who attempts to decide a dispute without the aid of partisan advocacy.

Such an arbiter must undertake, not only the role of judge, but that of representative for both of the litigants. Each of these roles must be played to the full without being muted by qualifications derived from the others. When he is developing for each side the most effective statement of its case, the arbiter must put aside his neutrality and permit himself to be moved by a sympathetic identification sufficiently intense to draw from his mind all that it is capable of giving—in analysis, patience and creative power. When he resumes his neutral position, he must be able to view with distrust the fruits of this identification and be ready to reject the products of his own best mental efforts. The difficulties of this undertaking are obvious. If it is true that a man in his time must play many parts, it is scarcely given to him to play them all at once.

It is small wonder, then, that failure generally attends the attempt to dispense with the distinct roles traditionally implied in adjudication. What generally occurs in practice is that at some early point a familiar pattern will seem to emerge from the evidence; an accustomed label is waiting for the case and, without awaiting further proofs, this label is promptly assigned to it. It is a mistake to suppose that this premature cataloguing must necessarily result from impatience, prejudice or mental sloth. Often it proceeds from a very understandable desire to bring the hearing into some order and coherence, for without some tentative theory of the case there is no standard of relevance by which testimony may be measured. But what starts as a preliminary diagnosis designed to direct the inquiry tends quickly and imperceptibly to become a fixed conclusion, as all that confirms the diagnosis makes a strong imprint on the mind, while all that runs counter to it is received with diverted attention.

An adversary presentation seems the only effective means for combating this natural human tendency to judge too swiftly in terms of the familiar that which is not yet fully known. The arguments of counsel hold the case, as it were, in suspension between two opposing interpretations of it. While the proper classification of the case is thus kept unresolved, there is time to explore all of its peculiarities and nuances. . . .

It is only through the advocate's participation that the hearing may remain in fact what it purports to be in theory: a public trial of the facts and issues. Each advocate comes to the hearing prepared to present his proofs and arguments, knowing at the same time that his arguments may fail to persuade and that his proofs may be rejected as inadequate. It is a part of his role to absorb these possible disappointments. The deciding tribunal, on the other hand, comes to the hearing uncommitted. It has not represented to the public that any fact can be proved, that any argument is sound, or that any particular way of stating a litigant's case is the most effective expression of its merits.

The matter assumes a very different aspect when the deciding tribunal is compelled to take into its own hands the preparations that must precede the public hearing. In such a case the tribunal cannot truly be said to come to the hearing uncommitted, for it has itself appointed the channels along which the public inquiry is to run. . . . The result may be that the hearing loses its character as an open trial of the facts and issues, and becomes instead a ritual designed to provide public confirmation for what the tribunal considers it has already established in private. When this occurs adjudication acquires the taint affecting all institutions that become subject to manipulation, presenting one aspect to the public, another to knowing participants.

These, then, are the reasons for believing that partisan advocacy plays a vital and essential role in one of the most fundamental procedures of a democratic society. But if we were to put all of these detailed considerations to one side, we should still be confronted by the fact that, in whatever form adjudication may appear, the experienced judge or arbitrator desires and actively seeks to obtain an adversary presentation of the issues. Only when he has had the benefit of intelligent and vigorous advocacy on both sides can he feel fully confident of his decision.

Viewed in this light, the role of the lawyer as a partisan advocate appears not as a regrettable necessity, but as an indispensable part of a larger ordering of affairs. The institution of advocacy is not a concession to the frailties of human nature but an expression of human insight in the design of a social framework within which man's capacity for impartial judgment can attain its fullest realization.

When advocacy is thus viewed, it becomes clear by what principle limits must be set to partisanship. The advocate plays his role well when zeal for his client's cause promotes a wise and informed decision of the case. He plays his role badly, and trespasses against the obligations of professional responsibility, when his desire to win leads him to muddy the headwaters of decision, when, instead of lending a needed perspective to the controversy, he distorts and obscures its true nature.

————

The following excerpt is a contemporary summary of objections to the argument that the adversary system is the best way to establish truth. The excerpt labels this the "argument from truth."

David Luban, "Twenty Theses on Adversarial Ethics," in Beyond the Adversarial System (Helen Stacy & Michael Lavarch Eds.)

143–45 (1999).

The argument from truth is implausible, misleading, unrealistically abstract, empirically unconfirmed, and contrary to common sense.

Implausible: If the argument were right, then legal cultures with non-adversarial, or less adversarial, systems (for example, those of Germany and France) would be systematically less efficient at finding facts and arriving at accurate interpretations of the law. There is no evidence, even anecdotal, that this is true. . . .

Misleading: The argument from truth often invokes an analogy between adversarial adjudication and an idealized image of scientific inquiry, in which every thesis is subjected to raking criticism aiming to probe for weaknesses, unearth contrary evidence, and ensure that no proposition enters the corpus of scientific doctrine based on wishful thinking.

However, the adversary system bears scant resemblance to this idealized, critical-rationalist, picture of scientific inquiry. Science doesn't, or at least shouldn't, try to exclude probative evidence, discredit opposing testimony known to be truthful, fight efforts at discovery, use procedural devices to delay trial in hopes that opponents will run out of money or witnesses die or disappear, exploit the incompetence of opposing counsel, shield material facts from a tribunal based on privilege, or indulge in sophistry and rhetorical manipulation—all, arguably, tactics required by the principle of partisanship.

Unrealistically abstract: Conspicuously absent from the critical-rationalist fantasy-portrait of the adversary system is any mention whatever of money (specifically, of the costs of litigation and the inequality of resources among parties). Nor does it take account of inequalities of skill among advocates; the compressed time-frame of a trial; the prejudices and frailties of all-too-human judges; [and] tactical manipulation by lawyers.

Empirically unconfirmed: Even the most sophisticated experimental efforts to model adversarial and non-adversarial procedures have failed to find a comparative advantage in either.

Contrary to common sense: Suppose that you faced a crucial life-decision, for example a choice between two attractive but very different job possibilities. If the adversary system really is the best method of finding the truth, you would ask friends, or hire lawyers, to investigate the possibilities and then use every trick in the litigator's bag to try to persuade you of one or the other—tricks that might include efforts to hide or exclude material facts. It is obvious that no sane person would make a life-decision in such a perverse way. This shows how contrary to common sense the argument from truth is.

NOTES AND QUESTIONS

1.   Fuller and Randall believe that the adversary system works properly only if lawyers do not "muddy the headwaters of decision." What does that mean? Does it muddy the waters to use skillful cross-examination to discredit the testimony of a truthful opposing witness? To exclude probative evidence from trial? To resist discovery requests? These are all accepted tactics of adversarial advocacy. Are Fuller and Randall defending Neutral Partisanship or attacking it?

2.   Is the adversary system as good as Fuller and Randall suggest or as irrational as Luban suggests? How could their opposing views be tested?

3.   Elsewhere, Luban discusses Fuller and Randall's argument that a single, neutral decision-maker cannot take one side of an argument, then the other, then resume the neutral role.

> One problem is that [the argument] begs the question. When Fuller writes, "Each of these [representative] roles must be played to the full without being muted by qualifications derived from the others," he is presupposing that inquiry proceeds best by unmuted adversary presentation—in which case, of course, an inquisitorial investigation becomes by definition a mere copy of the real thing.... But is it not equally possible that a decision-maker can form a more reliable picture if the opposed positions *are* muted by qualifications derived from each other? After all, the strongest form of each side's case may be strongest because it is exaggerated and misleading.... Sometimes the opponent may be able to smoke out the exaggeration, but there will inevitably be cases in which the decision-maker simply cannot sort through the exaggerations, strategic omissions, and false implications, and as a result decides wrongly.[40]

40.   David Luban, "Rediscovering Fuller's Legal Ethics," 11 *Geo. J. Legal Eth.* 801, 822 (1998).

How might Fuller and Randall reply?

Other writers argue that the purpose of the adversary system is not simply to establish the truth, but also to protect individual rights even at the expense of truth. As Monroe Freedman points out, "a trial is far more than a search for truth, and the constitutional rights that are provided by our system of justice may well outweigh the truth-seeking value—a fact which is manifest when we consider that those rights and others guaranteed by the Constitution may well impede the search for truth rather than further it. What more effective way is there, for example, to expose a defendant's guilt than to require self-incrimination, at least to the extent of compelling the defendant to take the stand and respond to interrogation before a jury? [However,] even the guilty accused has an 'absolute constitutional right' to remain silent...."[41] Good criminal defense lawyers often counsel a client to keep silent during interrogation and trial. They also attempt to suppress persuasive inculpatory evidence, even though doing so will obstruct the search for truth. Criminal procedure allows the defense attorney to take these and similar actions in order to safeguard legal rights. Similarly, in civil trials, counsel frequently invoke the attorney-client privilege or challenging discovery requests, even though such actions interfere with the search for truth.

What can justify ranking the preservation of the legal rights, even of guilty clients, ahead of accurate fact-finding? The most plausible answer seems to be that rights are values of a different, more fundamental, order than the pursuit of factual accuracy. In the words of Ronald Dworkin, "[i]ndividual rights are political trumps held by individuals. Individuals have rights when, for some reason, a collective goal is not a sufficient justification ... for imposing some loss or injury upon them."[42] Individual rights trump collective goals, even a goal as important as legal fact-finding.

Under this reasoning, the adversary system exists in order to provide litigants with the best opportunity to promote their legal rights, and the advocate's job is to serve as a champion of those rights. The following selection criticizes this familiar argument on behalf of the adversary system.

Deborah L. Rhode, In the Interests of Justice

53–58 (2001).

[In addition to truth-related justifications, another] defense of neutral partisanship involves the protection of rights and the relationships necessary to safeguard those rights. Here again, the priority we place on personal liberties is rooted in more general cultural commitments....

If ... advocates were held morally accountable for their clients' conduct, less legal representation would be available for those most vulnerable

---

41. Monroe H. Freedman, *Lawyers' Ethics in an Adversary System* 2 (1975).

42. Ronald Dworkin, *Taking Rights Seriously* 11 (1978 ed.).

to popular prejudice and governmental repression. Our history provides ample illustrations of the social and economic penalties directed at attorneys with unpopular clients. It was difficult enough to find lawyers for accused communists in the McCarthy era, and for political activists in the early southern civil rights campaign. Those difficulties would have been far greater without the principle that legal representation is not an endorsement of client conduct.

These justifications of neutral partisanship assume special force in criminal cases. Individuals whose lives, liberty, and reputation are at risk deserve an advocate without competing loyalties to the state. Guilt or innocence should be determined in open court with due process of law, not in the privacy of an attorney's office. The consequences of an alternative model are readily apparent in many totalitarian countries. Where defense lawyers' role is to "serve justice," rather than their clients, what passes for "justice" does not commend itself for export. Often the roles of counsel for the defendant and the state are functionally identical and the price is paid in innocent lives. This country has had similar experiences when the crime has been especially heinous or the accused has been a member of a particularly unpopular group.... Without the prospect of defense counsel willing to challenge law enforcement conduct, government officials have inadequate incentives to respect constitutional rights or to investigate facts thoroughly. Providing uncompromised advocacy for defendants who are guilty is the best way of protecting those who are not.

Although these rationales for zealous advocacy are not without force, they fall short of justifying current partisanship principles. A threshold weakness is the bar's overreliance on criminal defense as an all-purpose paradigm for the lawyer's role. A relatively small amount of legal work involves either criminal proceedings or civil matters that raise similar concerns of individual freedom and governmental power. An advocacy role designed to insure the presumption of innocence and deter prosecutorial abuse is not necessarily transferable to other legal landscapes. Bar rhetoric that casts the lawyer as a "champion against a hostile world" seems out of touch with most civil practice. The vast majority of legal representation assists corporate and wealthy individual clients in a system that is scarcely hostile to their interests. When a Wall Street firm representing a Fortune 500 corporation squares off against understaffed regulators or a victim of unsafe products, the balance of power is not what bar metaphors imply. . . .

[T]he bar's traditional rights-based justifications offer inadequate support for prevailing adversarial practices. Such justifications implicitly assume that clients are entitled to assistance in whatever the law permits. This assumption confuses legal and moral rights. Some conduct that is socially indefensible may remain lawful because adequate prohibitions appear unenforceable, or because decision making bodies are too uninformed or compromised by special interests to impose effective regulation. An ethic of undivided client loyalty in these contexts has encouraged lawyers' assistance in some of the most socially costly enterprises in recent memory: the distribution of asbestos and Dalkon Shields; the suppression of health information about cigarettes; and the financially irresponsible ventures of savings and loan associations.

Defenders of neutral partisanship typically respond that protection of client rights is ethically justifiable despite such consequences because individual liberty and autonomy are of paramount value in a free society. Moral philosophers generally make no such mistake. As David Luban notes, this standard justification for zealous advocacy blurs an important distinction between the "desirability of people acting autonomously and the desirability of their autonomous acts." It is, for example, morally desirable for clients to make their own decisions about whether to attempt to defeat a needy opponent's valid claim through a legal technicality; it is not morally desirable for them actually to make the effort. Autonomy does not have intrinsic value; its importance derives from the values it fosters, such as personal creativity, initiative, and responsibility. If a particular client objective does not, in fact, promote those values, or does so only at much greater cost to third parties, then neither that objective, nor an advocate's assistance, is ethically justifiable.

Lawyers manage to avoid this conclusion only by selectively suspending the moral principle they claim to respect. Under the bar's ethical codes and prevailing practices, the legal rights and personal autonomy of clients assume paramount concern; the rights and autonomy of third parties barely figure. As a practical matter, this difference in treatment makes perfect sense. Clients are, after all, the ones footing the bill for advocates' services. But from a moral standpoint, such selective concern is impossible to justify. Particularly when the client is an organization, values of autonomy often cut against the bar's traditional priorities. A corporation's "right" to maximize profits through unsafe but imperfectly regulated methods can hardly take ethical precedence over a consumer's or employee's right to be free from reasonably avoidable risks. And contrary to bar leaders' claims, an attorney's refusal to assist legal but morally dubious conduct does not necessarily compromise individual autonomy or impose a professional oligarchy. Unless the lawyer is the last in town, his or her refusal to provide representation will not foreclose client choices. It may simply prompt reevaluation of their ethical consequences or impose the financial and psychological costs of finding alternative counsel. It is, of course, true that lawyers have no special expertise in evaluating those consequences. But attorneys at least will have a more disinterested perspective than clients on the moral dimensions of client activities. Moreover, the bar's willingness to suspend moral judgement is highly selective. When clients' conduct is at issue, advocates readily become agnostics. Lawyers insist that they are not "presumptuous enough to pass judgment" on what constitutes the "public interest," or to cast themselves as "unique guardians of the public good." Yet when a regulation involving attorneys' own conduct is at issue, they generally have no similar difficulty in determining where the public interest lies. Indeed, the organized bar has sought exclusive authority to pass judgment on many ethical questions, such as whether protecting client confidences should trump other societal values, or whether lawyers should have obligations to prevent foreseeable injuries to third parties.

The real question is not "by what right" do lawyers "impose" their moral views, but by what right should they evade a fundamental moral responsibility of all individuals: to accept accountability for the consequences of their actions. Of course, reasonable people often disagree about whether particular conduct is ethically justifiable. They also disagree about whether it is possible to reach any "right" answer in moral disputes. But even if a lawyer believes that objectively valid moral decisions are impossible, it does not follow that all views are equally valid. Some positions are more coherent, free of bias or self interest, and supported by reliable evidence. Lawyers can, and should, act on the basis of their own principled convictions, even when they recognize that others could in good faith hold different views.

3.   COMPARATIVE PERSPECTIVES: "ADVERSARIAL" VERSUS "INQUISITORIAL" PROCEDURES

NOTES

Attorneys in Great Britain and the United States generally believe that the adversary system is superior to the "inquisitorial" system of civil law countries such as France and Germany. In fact, few Anglo–American lawyers are familiar with that alternative.

To many, the term "inquisitorial" procedure evokes images of the Spanish Inquisition. This implication is wildly misleading. In fact, the principal difference between contemporary inquisitorial systems and adversary systems lies in the role of lawyers. Many of the functions assumed by advocates in adversary settings—such as the primary responsibility for questioning witnesses, selecting experts, and shaping the case—are performed by judges or magistrates under inquisitorial procedures. Although in both systems attorneys present arguments to the court, the model of an inquisitorial proceeding is that of an official inquiry into an event, rather than a contest between opposing camps.

Any fair assessment of the adversary system should rest on an informed understanding of the leading alternative. The readings that follow provide a starting-point for that understanding. They focus on one example of an inquisitorial system, the Federal Republic of Germany (pre-unification West Germany).

John H. Langbein, "The German Advantage in Civil Procedure"

52 University of Chicago Law Review 823, 826–31 (1985).

I.   Overview of German Civil Procedure

There are two fundamental differences between German and Anglo–American civil procedure, and these differences lead in turn to many others. First, the court rather than the parties' lawyers takes the main responsibility for gathering and sifting evidence, although the lawyers exercise a watchful eye over the court's work. Second, there is no distinction between pretrial and trial, between discovering evidence and presenting it. Trial is not a single continuous event. Rather, the court gathers and evaluates evidence over a series of hearings, as many as the circumstances require.

Initiation. The plaintiff's lawyer commences a lawsuit in Germany with a complaint. Like its American counterpart, the German complaint narrates the key facts, sets forth a legal theory, and asks for a remedy in damages or specific relief. Unlike an American complaint, however, the German document proposes means of proof for its main factual contentions. The major documents in the plaintiff's possession that support his claim are scheduled and often appended; other documents (for example, hospital files or government records such as police accident reports or agency files) are indicated; witnesses who are thought to know something helpful to the plaintiff's position are identified. The defendant's answer follows the same pattern. It should be emphasized, however, that neither plaintiff's nor defendant's lawyer will have conducted any significant search for witnesses or for other evidence unknown to his client. Digging for facts is primarily the work of the judge.

Judicial preparation. The judge to whom the case is entrusted examines these pleadings and appended documents. He routinely sends for relevant public records. These materials form the beginnings of the official dossier, the court file. All subsequent submissions of counsel, and all subsequent evidence-gathering, will be entered in the dossier, which is open to counsel's inspection continuously.

When the judge develops a first sense of the dispute from these materials, he will schedule a hearing and notify the lawyers. He will often invite and sometimes summon the parties as well as their lawyers to this or subsequent hearings. If the pleadings have identified witnesses whose testimony seems central, the judge may summon them to the initial hearing as well.

Hearing. The circumstances of the case dictate the course of the hearing. Sometimes the court will be able to resolve the case by discussing it with the lawyers and parties and suggesting avenues of compromise. If the case remains contentious and witness testimony needs to be taken, the court will have learned enough about the case to determine a sequence for examining witnesses.

Examining and recording. The judge serves as the examiner-in-chief. At the conclusion of his interrogation of each witness, counsel for either party may pose additional questions, but counsel are not prominent as examiners. Witness testimony is seldom recorded verbatim; rather, the judge pauses from time to time to dictate a summary of the testimony into the dossier. The lawyers sometimes suggest improvements in the wording of these summaries, in order to preserve or to emphasize nuances important to one side or the other.

Since the proceedings in a difficult case may require several hearings extending across many months, these summaries of concluded testimony—by encapsulating succinctly the results of previous hearings—allow the court to refresh itself rapidly for subsequent hearings. The summaries also serve as building blocks from which the court will ultimately fashion the findings of fact for its written judgment. If the case is appealed, these concise summaries constitute the record for the reviewing court. (We shall see that the first appellate instance in German procedure involves review de novo, in which the appellate court can form its own view of the facts, both from the record and, if appropriate, by recalling witnesses or summoning new ones.)

Anyone who has had to wade through the longwinded narrative of American pretrial depositions and trial transcripts (which preserve every inconsequential utterance, every false start, every stammer) will see at once the economy of the German approach to taking and preserving evidence. Our incentives run the other way; we pay court reporters by the page and lawyers mostly by the hour.

A related source of dispatch in German procedure is the virtual absence of any counterpart to the Anglo–American law of evidence. German law exhibits expansive notions of testimonial privilege, especially for potential witnesses drawn from the family. But German procedure functions without the main chapters of our law of evidence, those rules (such as hearsay) that exclude probative evidence for fear of the inability of the trier of fact to evaluate the evidence purposively. In civil litigation German judges sit without juries (a point to which this essay recurs); evidentiary shortcomings that would affect admissibility in our law affect weight or credit in German law.

Expertise. If an issue of technical difficulty arises on which the court or counsel wishes to obtain the views of an expert, the court—in consultation with counsel—will select the expert and define his role. . . .

Further contributions of counsel. After the court takes witness testimony or receives some other infusion of evidence, counsel have the opportunity to comment orally or in writing. Counsel use these submissions in order to suggest further proofs or to advance legal theories. Thus, nonadversarial proof-taking alternates with adversarial dialogue across as many hearings as are necessary. The process merges the investigatory function of our pretrial discovery and the evidence-presenting function of our trial. Another manifestation of the comparative efficiency of German procedure is that a witness is ordinarily examined only once. Contrast the American practice of partisan interview and preparation, pretrial deposition, preparation for trial, and examination and cross-examination at trial. These many steps take their toll in expense and irritation.

Judgment. After developing the facts and hearing the adversaries' views, the court decides the case in a written judgment that must contain full findings of fact and make reasoned application of the law.

II.   Judicial Control of Sequence

From the standpoint of comparative civil procedure, the most important consequence of having judges direct fact-gathering in this episodic
fashion is that German procedure functions without the sequence rules to
which we are accustomed in the Anglo–American procedural world. The
implications for procedural economy are large. The very concepts of "plaintiff's case" and "defendant's case" are unknown. In our system those
concepts function as traffic rules for the partisan presentation of evidence
to a passive and ignorant trier. By contrast, in German procedure the court
ranges over the entire case, constantly looking for the jugular—for the
issue of law or fact that might dispose of the case. Free of constraints that
arise from party presentation of evidence, the court investigates the dispute
in the fashion most likely to narrow the inquiry. A major job of counsel is
to guide the search by directing the court's attention to particularly cogent
lines of inquiry.

Suppose that the court has before it a contract case that involves
complicated factual or legal issues about whether the contract was formed,
and if so, what its precise terms were. But suppose further that the court
quickly recognizes (or is led by submission of counsel to recognize) that
some factual investigation might establish an affirmative defense—illegality, let us say—that would vitiate the contract. Because the court functions
without sequence rules, it can postpone any consideration of issues that we
would think of as the plaintiff's case—here the questions concerning the
formation and the terms of the contract. Instead, the court can concentrate
the entire initial inquiry on what we would regard as a defense. If, in my
example, the court were to unearth enough evidence to allow it to conclude
that the contract was illegal, no investigation would ever be done on the
issues of formation and terms. A defensive issue that could only surface in
Anglo–American procedure following full pretrial and trial ventilation of
the whole of the plaintiff's case can be brought to the fore in German
procedure.

Part of what makes our discovery system so complex is that, on
account of our division into pretrial and trial, we have to discover for the
entire case. We investigate everything that could possibly come up at trial,
because once we enter the trial phase we can seldom go back and search for
further evidence. By contrast, the episodic character of German fact-
gathering largely eliminates the danger of surprise; if the case takes an
unexpected turn, the disadvantaged litigant can count on developing his
response in another hearing at a later time. Because there is no pretrial
discovery phase, fact-gathering occurs only once; and because the court
establishes the sequence of fact-gathering according to criteria of relevance,
unnecessary investigation is minimized. In the Anglo–American procedural
world we value the early-disposition mechanism, especially summary judgment, for issues of law. But for fact-laden issues, our fixed-sequence rule
(plaintiff's case before defendant's case) and our single-continuous-trial
rule largely foreclose it.

The episodic character of German civil procedure—Benjamin Kaplan called it the "conference method" of adjudication—has other virtues: It lessens tension and theatrics, and it encourages settlement. Countless novels, movies, plays, and broadcast serials attest to the dramatic potential of the Anglo–American trial. The contest between opposing counsel; the potential for surprise witnesses who cannot be rebutted in time; the tricks of adversary examination and cross-examination; the concentration of proof-taking and verdict into a single, continuous proceeding; the unpredictability of juries and the mysterious opacity of their conclusory verdicts—these attributes of the Anglo–American trial make for good theatre. German civil proceedings have the tone not of the theatre, but of a routine business meeting—serious rather than tense. When the court inquires and directs, it sets no stage for advocates to perform. The forensic skills of counsel can wrest no material advantage, and the appearance of a surprise witness would simply lead to the scheduling of a further hearing. In a system that cannot distinguish between dress rehearsal and opening night, there is scant occasion for stage fright.

NOTES: AN "INQUISITORIAL" CRIMINAL TRIAL

In her book *The Faces of Justice: A Traveller's Report* (1961), journalist Sybille Bedford reports on trials in five European countries. In Germany she witnessed a remarkable criminal trial. Dr. Brach, an army physician, home for a visit, shot to death a man who had exposed himself to the doctor's twelve-year-old daughter. The daughter had reported to her parents on several occasions that the same man had exposed himself as she walked to and from school through a park. On the final occasion, the doctor was home; he took his revolver, found the man in the park, placed him under arrest and, with the help of a passer-by, began to take him to the police station. The man attempted to climb over a wall out of the park; the passer-by grabbed his legs, and Dr. Brach began shooting, trying to hit the escapee's foot. The man was killed by one of the doctor's three shots.

The German criminal court is presided over by a chief judge and two assistant judges. This court also included six lay jurors, who deliberate together with the judges. There are few exclusionary rules, on the theory that the judges can provide expert assistance to the jurors in assessing the credibility of the evidence. The state is represented by a state's attorney or Staatsanwalt, a career civil servant who may not engage in the private practice of law. The defendant is represented by an attorney. However, the bulk of the examination of witnesses is performed by the judges. After they finish, the state's attorney and defense attorney can ask additional questions, but usually have little or nothing to add. The defendant himself also may directly question witnesses. The defendant has no privilege against self-incrimination, but is not put under oath and therefore cannot be guilty of perjury.

The judges are well-prepared for the trial, as Bedford explains:

Continental judges have it all in front of them. They have had weeks to go through it at home. They sit by no means every day, and the best of their working time is spent on paperwork. The accused may have been questioned—by another judge, the Untersuchungsrichter [investigating judge] in the German-speaking countries, the Juge d'instruction in France—for a number of weeks or months. Everything he said has been taken down in writing, and this evidence, in a fat dossier, lies open now at the relevant page before the presiding judge.

All the same, here too the evidence must be heard again at the trial, must be, as in English courts, oral and direct. . . . It all has to be said again for the last and final time that counts and, as in England, it will often turn out to be rather different from the original deposition.[43]

The result of the trial may be appealed as of right by either side, and the appellate court will engage in *de novo* review of the evidence.

The following brief excerpts from the trial of Dr. Brach will give some sense of the feel of an "inquisitorial" criminal trial. The first excerpt is from the extensive examination of the doctor, the second from the examination of his daughter.

Sybille Bedford, The Faces of Justice: A Traveller's Report

124–125 (1961).

It was a strange experience to hear this presentation of a case by both sides, as it were, in one; not a prosecution case followed by a defence case, but an attempt to build the whole case, the case as it might be presented in a summing-up, as it went. A strange experience to hear the (attenuated) inquisitorial procedure at work, to hear all questions, probing questions and soothing questions, accusatory and absolving questions, questions throwing a favourable light and questions having the opposite effect, flow from one and the same source, the bench, and only from the bench, while public prosecutor and counsel for the defence sat mute, taking notes.

"Dr. Brach, were you accustomed to handling a revolver?"

"No. It was a new weapon. I had never used it before."

"You must have had some instruction or practice in the Army?"

"None at all. As a medical officer I had nothing to do with such things."

"You told us earlier today that you were called up and served during the war—before you were even a medical student—you must have had small-arms instruction then? Didn't you know that a revolver is a most unreliable weapon—?"

"Yes, but—"

43. Sybille Bedford, *The Faces of Justice: A Traveller's Report* 110–11 (1961).

"Well, in heaven's name, man, didn't you know that it is about *the* most *uncertain, unsafe* weapon there is?" This was said with considerable severity, although not so much in the manner of a judge addressing an exhortation to the dock, as in the tone of man to man.

"When it comes to one's child being indecently molested twice a week—"

"Twice a week? This is the first time you told this court anything of the kind!"

"It happened all the time."

"You did not give that figure, or anything like it, to the examining judge?"

[It had already come out that the doctor had said very little during the preliminary investigation; instead he had given a detailed interview to an illustrated weekly. "Why did you do that?" "I don't know." "Don't you know the motives for your actions, Dr. Brach?" "Well, the editor had asked me to."]

"My wife went to the police," said Dr. Brach.

"How often? Twice a week?"

"Again and again. It didn't do any good."

"Herr Oberstaatsanwalt, have you any information about complaints to the police?" The prosecutor answered that his department knew only of the one that had been lodged in the spring of 1958.

"My wife went at least a dozen times," said Dr. Brach, "and she didn't go every time it happened."

"And these alleged visitations always took place in the park?"

"Yes, on the girl's way to school."

"Couldn't she have taken another way?" asked the younger judge.

"She could have gone through the town," said the judge president, "by making a slight detour she need not have gone through the park at all."

"Yes, she could have."

"Did you not tell her?"

"I think I did. I know my wife told her."

The younger judge, the one who spoke with the Baden accent, said, "You *think* you told her? Didn't you say, Look here, you mustn't go to school through the park, I forbid you to go to school through the park?"

"I did speak to her," Dr. Brach said, deadpan and helpless.

"One or two more points. Can you tell us something more about your state of mind on that Saturday noon, Doctor? You hadn't slept, luncheon was late, you were pretty irritable? When your girl came in with the news, did you feel annoyed at your weekend being spoilt?"

"That didn't occur to me," said Dr. Brach. [This question of the judge was later harshly criticized in the press.]

At that point a jolly blare drowned all other sound. A troop of Bundeswehr with brass band was marching by in the street below. "Are they serenading you, Dr. Brach?" asked the judge, whereupon court and public broke into a common gust of good-natured laughter. Dr. Brach cracked an uneasy smile.

"To wind up, we should like to know something about your general attitude.... How do you personally feel about the phenomenon of exhibitionism? Do you think exhibitionists are people who act under a pathological compulsion? Do you think they are sick people? Or perverts? Are they particularly repulsive to you?"

"I think an adult who exposes himself indecently to a child is a criminal." . . .

After the adjournment came the children's evidence, always a disagreeable experience, here remarkable chiefly for the way in which the judges handled it.

The doctor's girl was sent in. Girls of twelve can look almost anything, this one was just a nice child. "Come up, my dear," said the judge president; "up here, come to me." Up on the dais she went, round the judges' table, to his chair. He turned sideways to face her, and asked her name. The child sketched a curtsy. He asked her some questions about school; he nearly made her laugh; then, friendly and matter of fact, he told her that now they must speak about those disagreeable things. He and the younger judge asked all that had to be made known or clear. Where they could, they were offhand; they minced no words where words could not be minced. The jury heard the precise evidence. His voice, though distinct enough, stayed private, and by keeping the girl turned to him, he never allowed her to become quite aware of her surroundings. Once the prosecutor rose to submit exclusion of the public on grounds of decency, but the judge president turned it down. Once the public guffawed and he silenced it with a rebuke as sharp as the guillotine. The girl, throughout, sounded cheerful and detached.

It was well done. Almost anyone else in the judges' position would have attempted to do the same—although perhaps not with quite that degree of informality—but it might not have come off. Those two men had the touch that cannot be learnt. Perhaps the secret of it was the lack of sentimentality and condescension; there was nothing false about their manner, it seemed informed by moderation, good sense and a respect for other people's feelings. I should perhaps say that it was a performance of high human quality and that a German court of law was the last place where I should have dreamt to encounter it. (Perhaps I should also say that I had not put a foot inside Germany for nearly thirty years and that I had decided never to enter it again as long as I lived; unless it were to do a job.)

The substance of the girl's evidence was that there had been indecent exposure, but no attempt at assault, by the same man.

NOTES AND QUESTIONS

The trial of Dr. Brach received wide comment in the German press, which noted that a lengthy sentence would cost him his commission in the army due to official regulations. The case carried political overtones, largely because in post-World War II Germany the army had become a controversial institution, and Dr. Brach's case became a vehicle for wider controversy over military values. In the end Dr. Brach was convicted, but at the prosecutor's recommendation received a sentence short enough to permit him to retain his commission. This in turn led to criticisms that the judges were overly deferential to the prosecutor's viewpoint—a recurring charge among critics of the German system.

1.   What are the relative advantages and disadvantages of the German "inquisitorial" and American "adversarial" processes?

2.   The judiciary constitutes over one-fourth of the German legal profession. By contrast, in the United States, judges comprise about 4% of the legal profession. The German judiciary is part of the civil service: a law graduate enters the judiciary at the bottom through an examination and works his or her way up. Judges almost never change careers to become practicing lawyers, and lawyers almost never change careers to become judges.

One observer writes, "In civil law, judges are active front-line workers. The civil law, with its judicial workforce, requires a vastly larger judicial plant and relatively fewer lawyers.... Comprehensive figures on the number of judges and lawyers are hard to come by, but civil law countries tend to have one judge for every three to four lawyers, whereas the ratio in common law countries is typically one judge for every 25 to 50 attorneys. Judicial capacity in common law countries is presently stretched thin. In an era of distrust of government, downsizing and privatization, it is difficult to imagine a major enlargement of judicial facilities and authority."[44]

Does it follow that moving away from the adversarial system is not an option in the United States?

3.   Fuller and Randall, in the preceding excerpt from "Professional Responsibility: Report of the Joint Conference of the ABA–AALS," raise several objections to non-adversary adjudication. Do these objections seem well-taken when applied to the German procedures described by Langbein and Bedford?

4.   If the United States were to adopt a system resembling Germany's, what else in our law would have to change?

5.   Consider two contrasts between American and German procedure:

a) In Germany, courts will appoint an expert witness if they believe one is necessary; however, litigants rarely are able to rebut the adverse testimony of such an expert with an expert of their own. In America, the

---

44.   Marc Galanter, "Dining at the Ritz: Visions of Justice for the Individual In the Changing Adversarial System," in *Beyond the* *Adversarial System* 126 (Helen Stacy & Michael Lavarch eds. 1999).

parties engage their own experts, whose testimony is more malleable but, as a consequence, less credible. Paid expert witnesses are sometimes nicknamed "saxophones": the derisive implication is that they play the music their employer wants to hear.

b) In Germany, lawyers are ethically forbidden from attempting to coach or otherwise influence the testimony of witnesses; in America, norms of competence and zeal imply that a lawyer who does not "prepare" a witness may violate their ethical obligations.[45]

What are the relative advantages of these contrasting practices?

PROBLEM 3

Consider Rita's Case from the Introduction. How well did the adversary system work there? Would the process or outcome have been improved by more vigorous adversarial advocacy? By less vigorous adversarial advocacy? By a system modeled on inquisitorial procedures?

Were both Maynard and Kiladis (Gladys's attorneys) equally committed to Neutral Partisanship? How would you describe the differences in their ways of approaching the lawyer's role? Which do you prefer?

E. Alternatives to Neutral Partisanship

NOTES AND QUESTIONS

A natural question at this juncture is what alternatives are available in the United States to the Neutral Partisanship conception of the lawyer's role. Some experts believe that alternative conceptions of professional ethics were prevalent in the eighteenth and nineteenth centuries[46] Clearly the historical record reveals considerable disagreement on the proper relationship between the lawyer's and the client's conscience. A well-known example involved a debate between the two leading antebellum writers on legal ethics concerning the justifiability of pleading the statute of limitations to enable a client to evade a legitimate debt.

In 1836, David Hoffman, dean of the University of Maryland's law school, published the first systematic analysis of American legal ethics.

---

45. For additional material on witness preparation *see* Chapter VI. For further comparative readings on procedural norms, legal professions, and legal ethics in civil law systems *see* Geoffrey C. Hazard, Jr. & Angelo Dondi, *Legal Ethics: A Comparative Study* (2004); Mirjan Damaska, *The Faces of Justice and State Authority: A Comparative Approach to the Legal Process* (1986); Richard L. Abel & Philip S.C. Lewis, *Lawyers in Society* (3 volumes) (1989): Vol. 1: *The Common Law World;* Vol. 2: *The Civil Law World;* Vol. 3: *Comparative Theories;* John Leubsdorf, *Man in His Original Dignity* (2000) (France);

David Luban, "The Sources of Legal Ethics: A German–American Comparison of Lawyers' Professional Duties," 48 *Rabels Zeitschrift* 245 (1984).

46. L. Ray Patterson, "Legal Ethics and the Lawyer's Duty of Loyalty," 29 *Emory L.J.* 909, 912–13 (1980). *See also* Russell Pearce, "Lawyers as America's Governing Class: The Formation and Dissolution of the Original Understanding of the American Lawyer's Role," 8 *U. Chi. L. Sch. Roundtable* 381 (2001).

That analysis took the form of "Fifty Resolutions in Regard to Professional Deportment." They included the following:

> XII.   I will never plead the Statute of Limitations, when based on the *mere efflux of time*; for if my client is conscious he owes the debt; and has no other defence than the *legal bar*, he shall never make me a partner in his knavery.

> XIV.   My client's conscience, and my own, are distinct entities: and though my vocation may sometimes justify my maintaining as facts, or principles, in doubtful cases, what may be neither one nor the other, I shall ever claim the privilege of solely judging to what extent to go. In *civil* cases, if I am satisfied from the evidence that the *fact* is against my client, he must excuse me if I do not see as he does, and do not press it: and should the *principle* also be wholly at variance with sound law, it would be dishonourable folly in me to endeavour to incorporate it into the jurisprudence of our country, when, if successful, it would be a gangrene that might bring death to my cause of the succeeding day.

Eighteen years later, Pennsylvania Judge George Sharswood published the first American treatise on legal ethics. As Chapter III indicated, Sharswood's 1854 *Legal Ethics* provided the foundation for Alabama's code of ethics, which, in turn, became the model for the 1908 ABA Canons of Professional Ethics. Sharswood approached the statute of limitations situation differently from Hoffman:

> ... a defendant who knows that he honestly owes the debt sued for, and that the delay has been caused by indulgence or confidence on the part of his creditor, ought not to plead the statute. . . . [Nevertheless,] the lawyer, who refuses his professional assistance because in his judgment the case is unjust and indefensible, usurps the functions of both judge and jury.

Who is right?

Even in the late nineteenth century, the legal profession remained divided over the commitment to Neutral Partisanship. Elihu Root, a founder of the firm that later became Cravath, Swaine & Moore, is remembered for the adage "[t]he client never wants to be told he can't do what he wants to do; he wants to be told how to do it, and it is the lawyer's business to tell him how"—a view that comes quite close to Neutral Partisanship.[47] Yet Root's contemporary, Louis Brandeis—also a major corporate lawyer before ascending to the Supreme Court—once wrote a memorandum to himself (entitled "The Practice of Law") which directed, "[a]dvise client what he should have—not what he wants"[48]—an uncanny counterpoint to Root's adage. Legal historian Robert Gordon has argued that in practice as well as theory, the nineteenth century corporate bar found itself divided: on the one hand, offering its clients zealous represen-

---

47. *Quoted in* 1 Robert T. Swaine, *The Cravath Firm and Its Predecessors, 1819–1947* 667 (1946).

48. *Quoted in* Philippa Strum, *Louis D. Brandeis: Justice for the People* 40 (1984).

tation, while, on the other hand, engaging in progressive reforms sometimes antithetical to client interests.[49]

There is no uniform commitment to Neutral Partisanship among
contemporary lawyers—not surprisingly, given the diversity of the bar.
Many attorneys hesitate to act as full-fledged neutral partisans if doing so
requires them to act unfairly, for example, by taking advantage of another
lawyer in a negotiation because a client wants the lawyer to. Consider an
example drawn from a study of lawyers in a New England town in the
1980s. At the time of the study, an out-of-town developer had recently
evicted an artist's colony from the building that the artists had occupied for
years, so that the developer could raise the rent beyond what the artists
could pay. The artists brought suit, and were defeated by a local lawyer
representing the developer. The result was that the artists' colony dis-
persed and disappeared, much to the dismay of town residents for whom
the colony was a point of local pride. The developer's lawyer came in for
intense criticism, and other local attorneys differed dramatically over
whether he had done the right thing. Some said yes:

> It wasn't fair that [the developer's lawyer] took all that flak.... [F]or
> my money he's the best, a real pro, you know, top of the line lawyer.
> And it's not as if it was his idea to put the arts people out onto the
> street.... People who criticize him don't know what they are talking
> about.... Lawyers, we can't make decisions for our clients. It ain't for
> us to dictate to them and it isn't as if [the developer] needs advice.

> Far as I can tell he did exactly what every good lawyer does.... He
> knew the law and there was nothing complicated, really quite rou-
> tine.... So see, this client comes to you and asks you to do what you
> and he both know the law allows him to do.... Maybe I remember too
> much all that law school talk about how everybody should have a
> lawyer.... You know it all comes down to how we aren't priests, [and
> how] we take our clients as they come.

Others disagreed:

> [The developer's lawyer] sold out ... yeah, the community's suffered
> because of it. I mean, what's the good of making a few extra dollars if
> you can't walk down the street with your head up.

> What do they care about this town; they'd bulldoze Main Street and
> City Hall to help the bottom line and ... [the developer's lawyer's
> would] be right beside them.

> Clients can have lots of rights that they don't and shouldn't exer-
> cise.... Look, when I deal with clients I want them, I expect, to think
> about things other than what they want or what some law says they
> can have. If I don't do that I'm just a plumber and it kills me, but I

---

49. Robert Gordon, *Lawyers as the
American Aristocracy* (unpublished lectures).
For further discussion of this history, *see*
Susan D. Carle, "Lawyers' Duty to Do Jus-
tice: A New Look at the History of the 1908
Canons," 24 *Law and Soc. Inquiry* 1 (1999);
David Luban, "The *Noblesse Oblige* Tradition
in the Practice of Law," 41 *Vand.L.Rev.* 717
(1988).

don't think [the developer's lawyer] did that. He should have talked to them about how, down the road, they'd be better off, everybody been better off, if they'd been more generous with the artists and with the town. You might wonder whether [the developer's lawyer] forgot he was a lawyer. . . . Might just as well have been the developer himself.[50]

1. Which of these positions is closest to your own view of what professionalism requires? Why?

2. Are the positions of any of the lawyers quoted above inconsistent with the provisions of Model Rule 1.2?

Several contemporary writers have proposed alternatives to Neutral Partisanship. Kenney Hegland has argued that

[i]n civil matters, it [should] be unprofessional conduct for a lawyer to assert any legal doctrine or rule on behalf of a client unless the lawyer has a good faith belief that the assertion of the doctrine or rule in the particular case will further a policy behind the doctrine or rule.[51]

Under Hegland's framework, lawyers should not, for example, assert the statute of limitations unless doing so would serve statutory purposes. Such a framework would not, in Hegland's view, require lawyers to play moral guardians. Rather it would simply deny clients the "quibbles, nit-picks and afterthoughts [that] are the product of the legal imagination. If the profession creates them, it can prohibit them."[52] In response to objections that the purposes of rules may be indeterminate or that it would be too costly to make exceptions to general rules, Hegland writes:

To deny the possibility of determining situations in which a doctrine should not apply (that is, [to] deny the possibility of agreeing when something is a quibble), [is also to deny] the possibility of determining situations in which a doctrine should apply. If this is right, God help us. . . .

The efficiency argument is that we should apply rules without reference to underlying policies because it is simply too costly to figure out when to make exceptions. . . . "Even though our goal is to protect defendants from stale claims, it is too costly to determine staleness as a matter of fact; we must simply assume, pursuant to our rule, that claims are stale after four years." I have always had problems with this cavalier approach to the pressing problem of citizens. "Yes, you should probably win this case but, quite frankly, it would take us too much time to figure out why, so best of luck in life."[53]

In a similar vein, William Simon argues that lawyers should pursue legal justice, which he carefully distinguishes from the lawyer's own moral values. What legal justice requires depends upon the context.[54] When a

---

50. All quotations from Austin Sarat, "Ideologies of Professionalism: Conflict and Change Among Small Town Lawyers," 11–13 (unpublished manuscript 1988).

51. Kenney Hegland, "Quibbles," 67 *Tex.L.Rev.* 1491, 1494 (1989).

52. *Id.* at 1500.

53. *Id.* at 1502, 1506–07.

54. William H. Simon, *The Practice of Justice: A Theory of Lawyers' Ethics* (1998), ch. 6.

statute or rule is itself consistent with the basic values of a legal system, "pursuing justice" might lead to the same approach that Hegland recommends. But if the statute itself violates more fundamental legal values (such as fairness), pursuing justice might lead a lawyer to find loopholes around the statute, treating it narrowly and formalistically even if that frustrates its purpose. In situations where an advocate can count on opposing counsel to uphold his or her client's rights, legal justice may be served if both sides act as neutral partisans. But in a context such as Rita's Case, where opposing counsel is effectively out of the loop, an approach that considers the child's interests as well as the client's may be necessary to achieve the kind of legal justice that the adversary system contemplates.

By contrast to Simon's and Hegland's emphasis on legal justice, David Luban has argued that the adversary system is too weakly justified to support a role morality that diverges widely from non-professional morality. As a result, lawyers in their professional roles should be just as accountable for their actions as they would be in ordinary, non-legal circumstances. Thus, if intimidating injured women into dropping legitimate lawsuits by forcing them to answer humiliating "dirty questions" (see Problem 2, *supra*) is wrong for a non-lawyer to do, it is wrong for a lawyer to do as well.[55] The primary exception is in criminal defense, where adversarial advocacy is strongly justified by the (liberal and constitutional) values of protecting people from the abuse of state power.

Deborah Rhode has similarly argued for:

an alternative framework for the advocate's role that needs to be ethically justifiable in principle and consistently reinforced in practice. At its most basic level, such a framework would require lawyers to accept personal moral responsibility for the consequences of their professional actions. Attorneys should make decisions as advocates in the same way that morally reflective individuals make any ethical decision. Lawyers' conduct should be justifiable under consistent, disinterested, and generalizable principles.

These moral principles can, of course, recognize the distinctive needs of lawyers' occupational role. Ethically responsible decision making always takes into account the context and capacity in which a person acts. The extent of attorneys' responsibilities for client conduct will depend on their knowledge, involvement, and influence, as well as on the significance of values at stake.

However, unlike the bar's prevailing approach, this alternative framework would require lawyers to assess their obligations in light of all the societal interests at issue in particular practice contexts. An advocate could not simply retreat into some fixed conception of role that denies personal accountability for public consequences or that unduly privileges clients' and lawyers' own interests. Client trust and confidentiality are entitled to weight, but they must be balanced against other equally important concerns. Lawyers also have responsi-

---

55. David Luban, *Lawyers and Justice: An Ethical Study (1988), ch. 8.*

bilities to prevent unnecessary harm to third parties, to promote a just and effective legal system, and to respect core values such as honesty, fairness, and good faith on which that system depends. In accommodating those responsibilities, lawyers should, of course, be guided by relevant legal authority and bar regulatory codes. Respect for law also is a fundamental value, particularly among those sworn to uphold it. Adherence to generally accepted rules also serves as a check against the decision maker's own bias or self-interest. But ... attorneys may at times confront exceptional cases in which the applicable rules are so inadequate that reference to broader moral principles is necessary.[56]

All these authors argue that Neutral Partisanship is defective because it generates a defective system of justice. In addition to this "systemic" approach, other writers criticize Neutral Partisanship on the grounds that it creates a morally indefensible relationship between lawyer and client. Noteworthy among these "relational" alternatives to Neutral Partisanship is the work of Thomas L. Shaffer; he develops a complex argument, based partly on secular notions of civic virtue and partly on Judeo–Christian religious traditions, to forge an ethic close in spirit to David Hoffman's resolutions.[57]

None of these alternatives is as easy to apply as Neutral Partisanship: each of them calls on attorneys to engage in situation-specific judgment to determine what course of action fulfills legal justice or moral principle. No doubt, this greater complexity is a drawback of the alternatives; different lawyers will arrive at different judgments. This is inevitable, however, once personal accountability gets back into the picture. As Wasserstrom remarks in the passage cited earlier, the world of Neutral Partisanship is a "simplified moral world." That is both its strength and its weakness.

Under the Neutral Partisanship conception, lawyers are not morally accountable for their clients' ends, provided these are lawful. Nor can lawyers cannot be held morally responsible for their choice of clients or for lawful means in pursuing client's ends.

Alternatives to Neutral Partisanship insist on some measure of accountability. In the first group of readings that follows, Monroe Freedman argues that lawyers *should* be held morally responsible for their choice of clients, though Freedman argues elsewhere that once a lawyer has agreed to represent a client that lawyer must carry out the representation with undiluted zeal. Problem 4, and its accompanying Notes, address Freedman's point through a specific case.

---

56. Rhode, *supra* note 33, at 67. See also Deborah L. Rhode, "Legal Ethics in an Adversary System: The Persistent Questions," 34 *Hofstra L. Rev.* 641 (2006).

57. *See* Thomas L. Shaffer, "The Unique, Novel, and Unsound Adversary Ethic," 41 *Vand.L.Rev.* 697 (1988); Thomas L. Shaffer, *On Being a Christian and a Lawyer: Law for the Innocent* (1981); *American Legal Ethics: Text, Readings, and Discussion Topics* (1985). *See also* Jack Sammons, *Lawyer Professionalism* (1988); and Jack Sammons, "Meaningful Client Participation: An Essay Toward a Moral Understanding of the Practice of Law," 6 *J.L. & Religion* 61 (1988), from which the distinction between "systemic" and "relational" conceptions of legal ethics is drawn.

The second section centers on cases, such as those involving terrorists or members of organized crime, in which lawyers have faced felony charges for actions taken on behalf of widely despised clients. These examples suggest the legal limits of neutral partisanship.

Finally, we consider an alternative offered by David Wilkins, who argues that lawyers' professional responsibilities should sometimes be influenced by their other roles and identities. Wilkins offers this conclusion as part of an argument that black corporate lawyers may have special obligations to avoid forms of practice that are injurious to the interests of other African Americans.

1.   ALTERNATIVES TO NEUTRALITY

PROBLEM 4

You are an associate with a large international law firm, working mostly on banking cases. The firm has just taken on a new case, representing several banks in the Cayman Islands in a highly volatile matter. The national press has seized on the story, and the firm has come under heavy criticism. Here is the background.

Under current U.S. law, victims of torture and other human rights violations can bring claims for damages in U.S. courts under the Alien Tort Statute, 28 U.S.C. § 1350, even though neither the plaintiff nor defendant is an American citizen. Although successful plaintiffs, such as victims of atrocities in the Bosnian War, may be unable to collect monetary judgments, human rights advocates generally regard Alien Tort claims as a crucial symbolic means of condemning abuses and vindicating victims' need for legal justice.

The case your firm has taken grows out of the 1994 genocide in Rwanda. During a few terrible weeks, an estimated 800,000 members of the Tutsi minority group were murdered by racist militias of the majority Hutu ethnic group. Many of these murders were grisly atrocities in which the victims (of all ages) were hacked to death with machetes. Members of the Hutu-controlled Rwandan government organized and instigated the genocide. Subsequently, many were brought to trial, either in Rwandan national courts or before an international tribunal.

Mr. M. held ministerial rank in the Rwandan government, and was deeply implicated in the genocide. He had negotiated large-scale purchases of machetes and small arms to distribute to the death squads; he made inflammatory anti-Tutsi speeches on the radio, referring to Tutsi as "cockroaches" and calling for their extermination; and he participated in the government throughout the genocide. It is also widely known that Mr. M. corruptly siphoned off millions of dollars and placed it in secret bank accounts in the Cayman Islands. Mr. M. was tried before the International Criminal Tribunal for Rwanda, and sentenced to life imprisonment for genocide and crimes against humanity.

A group of female Rwandan survivors, all of whom had been raped, tortured, and severely injured during the genocide, filed an Alien Tort Claim action against Mr. M. A New York jury has awarded them one billion dollars. Currently, their attorneys have launched a vigorous effort to pierce the veil of bank secrecy and seize the money in Mr. M.'s accounts in the Cayman Island banks.

The banks have retained your firm to fight this effort. Bank secrecy is big business in the Caymans, where, because of the extremely protective banking laws, many possessors of illicit fortunes have accounts. Furthermore, whichever banks hold Mr. M.'s money have a good chance of keeping it after his death—provided that they can fend off legal claims such as this one.

a) Some of the associates in your firm are shocked and repelled by the firm's willingness to take the case. Should they be? The firm's management committee has issued a statement reaffirming the right of all clients to representation by the lawyer of their choice.

b) Several associates have begun drafting a letter asking the firm to drop the client. You have agreed to help. What should the letter say?

c) Alternatively, suppose that you are one of the lawyers representing the banks. How do you respond to the associates?

d) Would it make a difference if Mr. M. had been acquitted of the criminal charges, due to insufficient legal evidence, and is now living in luxury in Paris?

NOTES

In February 1997, the prestigious new York law firm of Cravath, Swaine & Moore agreed to represent Crédit Suisse, one of three big Swiss banks to come under international scrutiny for laundering stolen Nazi gold. The banks were under investigation by the New York State Attorney General and the New York City Council. Official U.S. documents from the 1940s detail how Crédit Suisse dealt with Nazi gold, most of which was looted from countries overrun by German forces and some of which was taken from Jewish victims of the Holocaust. These documents, based on extensive electronic surveillance by U.S. and British intelligence, show that the bank accepted gold bars from Germans and made millions of Swiss francs available to Germany. A 1945 report by the U.S. Foreign Economic Administration names Crédit Suisse Zurich as the most frequent violator of the Allied Code of Conduct concerning Swiss banks.[58]

Before deciding to represent the bank, the firm heard objections from several partners during an unusual "all hands" meeting at which the issue was extensively discussed. After the meeting, presiding partner Samuel C. Butler wrote a firm-wide memorandum explaining that the decision to represent the bank was "a matter of great moral consequence," but

---

58. Blaine Harden & Saundra Torry, "N.Y. Law Firm to Advise Swiss Bank Accused of Laundering Nazi Loot," *Wash. Post*, Feb. 28, 1997, at A3.

arguing that Cravath could "make a terrible situation better" by helping the bank reach a "fair and just" solution that would bring "a satisfactory closure to a very dark chapter in history."[59]

A dozen of the firm's associates wrote a memorandum protesting the decision. Several threatened to resign.

> It is our conviction that one cannot represent Crédit Suisse in its role as bankers to those who committed genocide and do the justice we are all obliged to do the victims and survivors of the slaughter. The two are simply incompatible. It seems implausible that Cravath could both serve Crédit Suisse and bring about the fair and honorable resolution for those who suffered at the hands of the Nazis and their collaborators. We suspect, even with the best intentions, Crédit Suisse's interest may be too closely connected with containing the financial consequences of scandal for justice to be served by our representation of them.[60]

The associates argued that the firm's decision to represent Crédit Suisse would lend the "imprimatur" of Cravath's sterling reputation. "Whatever settlement is 'cut,' " they wrote,

> Crédit Suisse earns through the Firm's involvement a legitimacy worth more to it than the wealth it has hoarded. In other words, the fee they pay the Firm buys them that which one is most obligated not to give those implicated in Nazi crimes. . . . The continuing problem of the Holocaust is that all reactions are inadequate, and this is why one must be very aware of the messages now sent to the survivors and perpetrators and collaborators. How can we take on the role of counsel to Crédit Suisse and send the right message about the catastrophe of the Holocaust and the actions that led to it, let alone the actions that profited from it.[61]

On the other hand, several "senior statesmen" of the New York City bar and leaders in New York's Jewish community supported Cravath's representation. Arthur Liman argued that Cravath would provide "effective lawyers who will try to find a fair solution."[62] If responsible firms turn away such a controversial case, Liman argued, it might end up in the hands of lawyers who see "dollar bills," and "that would be a disaster. . . . I would not like to see this becoming a lawyer's feast."[63] Ezra Levin, a Jewish community leader and name partner at New York's Kramer, Levin, Naftalis & Frankel, similarly viewed this case as "an opportunity [for Cravath] to perform a service to its client which is also likely to coincide with the interest" of Jews seeking to recover their assets.[64] Levin hoped that

59. *Id.*; Edward A. Adams & Daniel Wise, "Controversy Ruffles Cravath Over Representing Swiss Bank," *N.Y.L.J.*, March 3, 1997, at col. 4.

60. *Quoted in* Blaine Harden, "When Client, Justice Are 'Incompatible'; Lawyers Protest Firm's Representation of Bank That Laundered Nazi Loot," *Wash. Post*, March 13, 1997, at A15.

61. *Id.*

62. *Id.*

63. *Id.*

64. Saundra Torry, "When the Sins of the Client are Visited on the Firm," *Wash. Post*, March 3, 1997, at F7.

Cravath would persuade the banks "that cooperation, rather than stonewalling, will best help them maintain their valued franchise and recapture their goodwill."[65]

Harvard law professor Laurence Tribe reacted skeptically to the suggestion that Crédit Suisse's interest would coincide with those of the Jewish community. "If push comes to shove and something seems fairer to the American Jewish Congress but really means Crédit Suisse is taking quite a soaking," Tribe wrote, "it's hard for me to imagine how a firm would go about not putting the client's interest first."[66] Tribe suggested that Cravath donate its fees to "appropriate causes in light of the evil the client [has] done."[67]

An analogous case arose when former federal judge Abraham Sofaer agreed to represent Libya after the Libyan-sponsored bombing of Pan Am Flight 103 over Lockerbie, Scotland. He, too, said he was seeking to negotiate a settlement that would satisfy everyone, including the families of the 259 people killed in the bombing. Lawyers denounced the representation as a conflict of interest because of Sofaer's previous role as the top lawyer for the State Department. Within days, Sofaer's firm dropped Libya as a client.

Harvey L. Pitt, at the time a lawyer at Fried, Frank, Harris, Shriver & Jacobson, said he saw "a huge difference between [representing] Crédit Suisse and Moammar Gadhafi," and that Cravath should not be criticized. "The essential difference is that [Crédit Suisse] is an upstanding financial institution whose general policy is to comply with all the rules and laws applicable. If it makes a mistake, it is entitled to a defense. But if someone is deliberately assassinating people and is an affront to the world of nations they don't earn the same entitlement to legal representation."

Paul Wolff, a partner at Williams & Connolly, thought this analysis makes the question sound too easy. "I totally agree with the distinction Harvey made between Gadhafi and Crédit Suisse, if in fact he properly depicts Crédit Suisse," Wolff said. "The tough one is if this is not a bank that simply went astray ... but in fact acted beyond the law, that provided assistance to the Third Reich and is hiding behind a polished image over the years.... What does a firm do?"[68]

Monroe Freedman, "The Morality of Lawyering"

Legal Times, September 20, 1993.

My views are "worse than absurd." They are "dangerous" and "pernicious." "Joe McCarthy," I am told, "would be proud of you." I am, it appears, the devil personified, and all because I asked a simple question: Why you? ... [Why should you represent a client you find immoral].

65. *Id.*

66. *Id.*

67. *Id.*

68. *Id.*

My question ... relates to one of the most fundamental issues of lawyers' ethics and the nature of the lawyer's role. That issue is frequently posed by asking whether one can be a good person and a good lawyer at the same time. Or whether the lawyer forfeits her conscience when she represents a client. Or whether the lawyer is nothing more than a hired gun. Essentially, these questions ask whether the lawyer, in her role as a lawyer, is a moral being. There are three answers to that question:

- *The amoral lawyer.* One answer has been dubbed "the standard conception." It holds that the lawyer has no moral responsibility whatsoever for representing a particular client or for the lawful means used or the ends achieved for the client. Critics have accurately pointed out that under the standard conception, the lawyer's role is at best an amoral one and is sometimes flat-out immoral.

- *Moral control of the client.* A second answer insists that the lawyer's role is indeed a moral one. It begins by agreeing with the standard conception that the lawyer's choice of client is not subject to moral scrutiny. But it holds that the lawyer can impose his moral views on the client by controlling both the goals pursued and the means used during the representation.

According to this view, the lawyer can properly stop the client from using lawful means to achieve lawful goals. For example, the lawyer, having taken the case and having induced the client to rely upon her, can later threaten to withdraw from the representation—even where this would cause material harm to the client—if the client does not submit to what the lawyer deems to be the moral or prudent course. I recently criticized this view....

- *Choice of client as a moral decision.* The third answer also insists that the lawyer's role is a moral one. It begins by agreeing with the standard conception that the client is entitled to make the important decisions about the client's goals and the lawful means used to pursue those goals. But this answer recognizes that the lawyer has the broadest power—ethically and in practice—to decide which clients to represent. And it insists that the lawyer's decision to accept or to reject a particular client is a moral decision. Moreover, that decision is one for which the lawyer can properly be held morally accountable.

Although critics have erroneously, and repeatedly, identified me with the standard conception, I have consistently advocated the third answer for 17 years. It is refreshing, therefore, to be criticized at last for what I believe, rather than for what I don't believe....

One letter in response to my column said that the question [Why you?] was "impertinent." No lawyer, the writer said, should be under a burden of public moral accountability. That, indeed, is the standard conception. As I have indicated, one reason I reject that view is that I believe that the lawyer's role is neither an immoral nor an amoral one.

Moreover, we are a profession that exists for the purpose of serving the public, and we hold a government-granted monopoly to do so. As the U.S.

Supreme Court has repeatedly held, lawyers are an essential part—a constitutionally required part—of the administration of justice. It is therefore contrary to democratic principles for lawyers to contend that we owe the public no explanation of what we do and why we do it. . . .

QUESTIONS

1.   In other common-law jurisdictions, solicitors (office lawyers) have the same freedom to reject clients as American lawyers, but barristers (trial lawyers) are subject to the "cab rank rule," which requires them as a matter of professional ethics to accept any brief that is offered.[69] Does this rule make the barrister's role, in Freedman's words, either an amoral or immoral one? Should American trial lawyers operate under a similar ethical requirement?

2.   It may seem at first that Freedman's argument would prevent lawyers from ever representing morally repugnant clients. However, Freedman makes it clear that lawyers can justify representing such clients if the representation serves constitutional, procedural, or other public values. For example, in Freedman's view, lawyers are justified in representing guilty criminal defendants because doing so furthers Fifth and Sixth Amendment values and helps safeguard civil liberties against potential government abuses. Civil cases can likewise serve important public values, even when one's clients are morally odious.[70]

Deborah Rhode makes a similar claim in arguing for a framework that would "make the merits matter" and would require the lawyer

to assess them from a moral as well as legal vantage. . . . Of course, in a profession as large and diverse as the American bar, different lawyers will reach different judgments about what is in fact equitable. Although such judgments should be defensible under accepted ethical principles, their application will necessarily reflect individuals' own experiences and commitments. As William Kunstler once put it in explaining why he would defend the World Trade Center bombers but not the Ku Klux Klan, "everyone has a right to a lawyer, that's true. But they don't have a right to me." [T]he framework proposed here does not demand that lawyers reach the same results in hard cases. It demands rather that lawyers recognize that such cases *are* hard, and that they call for contextual moral judgments.[71]

Bearing these points in mind, how should a lawyer decide which cases to take and which to avoid? What happens if moral problems with the client's position do not become clear until after an attorney has begun representation?

---

69.   The rule creates exceptions when the barrister has too much pending work or the case would create a financial hardship. In practice, many observers believe that the exceptions come close to swallowing the rule.

70.   See Monroe H. Freedman and Abbe Smith, *Understanding Lawyers' Ethics* 24–31 (2nd ed. 2002).

71.   Rhode, *supra* note 33, at 79.

2.   The Limits of Partisanship

PROBLEM 5

You are a federal prosecutor, considering whether to convene a grand jury to seek an unusual indictment. The targets would be law firms and lawyers who, over a period of decades, coordinated the legal defense of the tobacco industry. During the 1990s, through a combination of whistle-blowers, litigation, and the tobacco settlement, millions of pages of previously-secret documents have fallen into the hands of the government. In your opinion, these documents show that the tobacco industry's in-house "Committee of Counsels," as well as some lawyers from outside law firms, were the architects of a vast strategy of deception. That strategy sought to mask the health hazards posed by cigarettes, as well as to disguise nicotine's addictive powers; and, above all, to ensure defeat of products-liability suits. For almost fifty years, the tobacco industry had an unblemished record of litigation victories, invariably triumphing with the twin arguments that smoking is chosen behavior (plaintiffs had assumed the risk) and that the harmful effects of cigarette smoke were scientifically controversial.

Early in the 1950s, on the advice of a public relations firm, tobacco companies set up the Tobacco Industry Research Council, later renamed the Council on Tobacco Research (CTR). Its original stated purpose was to fund independent scientific research on the connection between smoking and health. However, beginning in 1966, in response to a report by the Surgeon General on the connection between smoking and disease, tobacco company lawyers formed a "special projects" unit within CTR. Decisions about special projects grants would be made by lawyers rather than scientists. This enabled the lawyers to protect the results of the research by asserting the attorney-client privilege, based on the claim that the research was litigation-connected.[72] Other research received funding directly by the tobacco companies under the supervision of lawyers.

A review of the available evidence has persuaded you that the lawyers consciously engineered a decades-long coverup. For example, in a 1978 memo, one tobacco company CEO wrote, "We have again 'abdicated' the scientific research directional management of the Industry to the 'Lawyers' with virtually *no* involvement on the part of scientific or business management side of the business."[73]

You have learned that attorneys advised their tobacco company clients to steer clear of research into the health effects of cigarette smoke, in order to enable management and scientists to deny knowledge of smoking-related risks. Ironically, this advice eventually became the basis for a claim of fraud, because of the tobacco industry's repeated assurances over the years that "it would make an honest attempt to learn whether the smoking of

72. For discussion of this claim of attorney-client privilege, see Chapter V.

73. *Quoted in* Minnesota v. Philip Morris et al., Report of Special Master: Findings of Fact, Conclusions of Law and Recommendations Regarding Non–Liggett Privilege Claims (Feb. 10, 1998), <<http://stic.neu.edu/MN/specialmaster2–10–98.html>>.

cigarettes created health hazards.''[74] Lawyers also carefully edited scientific reports to ensure consistency with their legal theories. Philip Morris conducted potentially controversial research in Germany, and produced reports written in German, with the aim of making discovery as difficult as possible. CTR-funded scientists provided a stable of expert witnesses to testify, again and again, that the connection between cigarettes and illness was unproven; as one lawyer wrote to the chairman and CEO of a tobacco company in 1978: "Finally the industry research effort has included special projects designed to find scientists and medical doctors who might serve as industry witnesses in lawsuits or in a legislative forum."[75]

In effect, the lawyers created a scientific institution whose primary function was to create favorable evidence for litigation and conceal unfavorable evidence. For years, on the advice of counsel, litigation strategy drove scientific as well as business strategy. In the words of former Food and Drug Administration Commissioner David Kessler:

> The old lawyers wrote the script; the new lawyers perpetuated it. Certainly the members of the Committee of Counsels were more than agents of their clients. Those lawyers helped create the positions of their clients. They interpreted the science for the industry scientists and then told the scientists what they could say. They also told the CEOs what to say. These lawyers were the producers and enforcers of the script.[76]

In 1999, the federal government filed a civil racketeering claim against eleven tobacco companies, based on their "fraudulent and tortious activities."[77] But you have become convinced that the tobacco industry's legal counsel were equally responsible for the decades of deception—and thus, that if the industry had committed frauds, so had its lawyers. Federal law states that accomplices in criminal acts are charged as principals (18 U.S.C. § 2); and organizations (including law firms) are liable for crimes committed by their employees in the course of their duties. You are considering seeking indictments for mail fraud, wire fraud, and conspiracy against the individual lawyers and law firms most centrally involved in "producing and enforcing the script."

The federal mail fraud statute (18 U.S.C. § 1341) requires proof of two elements: a "scheme or artifice" to defraud, and the use of the mails in that scheme. (The second element establishes the federal nexus.) The wire fraud statute (18 U.S.C. § 1343) is parallel, except that instead of the use of the mails, it requires that the telephone, radio, or television were employed in the scheme. Finally, the conspiracy statute (18 U.S.C. § 371)

74. Minnesota v. Philip Morris et al., Order Regarding Privilege and the Crime–Fraud Exception and Setting Forth Procedures to Determine the Privilege Beginning With the Liggett Documents (redacted), May 8, 1997, <<http://stic.neu.edu/MN/MNOrder regardingprivilege–Liggett.htm>>

75. Memorandum from Ernest Pepples to J. E. Edens, April 4, 1978, *quoted in* Stanton A. Glantz et al., *The Cigarette Papers* (1996), at 44.

76. David Kessler, *A Question of Intent* (2001), at 372.

77. The case is currently under litigation; relevant documents may be found in the DOJ website, <<http://www.usdoj.gov/civil/cases/tobacco2/index.htm>>.

requires that two or more persons conspired to commit a federal offense or to defraud the United States "or any agency thereof." Your theory would be that the entire strategy employed by the Committee of Counsels amounted to a vast "scheme or artifice to defraud" potential tobacco plaintiffs of legitimate compensation for their tobacco-induced injuries, as well as to defraud state governments, which paid billions for medical treatment of smokers. Planning the strategy would be conspiracy to commit the federal offenses of wire fraud and mail fraud.

Some attorneys in your office disagree strongly with your plan— indeed, they are appalled. They remind you that former FDA Commissioner Kessler, who battled the tobacco industry for years, is hardly a disinterested party. They believe that the tobacco industry's lawyers were doing nothing other than what any good lawyer does for a business client: they devised ways to safeguard the client's legal interests, and told the clients how to create a favorable record by legitimate means. These were respectable, honest lawyers, who crossed no ethical boundaries. It would be morally and legally wrong, under those circumstances, to prosecute them.

These attorneys in your office direct you to the *Restatement (Third) of the Law Governing Lawyers*, which cautions in § 8: "The traditional and appropriate activities of a lawyer in representing a client in accordance with the requirements of the applicable lawyer code are relevant factors for the tribunal in assessing the propriety of the lawyer's conduct under the criminal law." They believe that nothing done by tobacco industry counsel falls outside of "traditional and appropriate activities of a lawyer."

Should you proceed? There are a number of cases in which lawyers have faced criminal charges for their zealous representation of clients. Usually, this occurs when the client is a notorious criminal figure—for example, an organized crime boss—and the prosecutor concludes that the lawyer has crossed the line between a "criminal lawyer" and a "lawyer-criminal."[78] Such cases raise, in the starkest terms, the question of when zealous advocacy makes a lawyer accountable for pursuing the client's ends. The following case provides a striking example.

United States v. Cueto

United States Court of Appeals, Seventh Circuit, 1998.
151 F.3d 620.

■ BAUER, CIRCUIT JUDGE.

After a jury trial, Amiel Cueto was convicted of one count of conspiracy to defraud the United States, in violation of 18 U.S.C. § 371, and three counts of obstruction of justice, in violation of the omnibus clause of 18 U.S.C. § 1503. The district court sentenced Cueto to 87 months imprison-

78. U.S. v. Cintolo, 818 F.2d 980, 990   license to act as a lawyer-criminal").
(1st Cir.1987) ("a criminal lawyer has no

ment and imposed monetary penalties. Cueto now appeals his convictions and sentence. . . . For the following reasons, we affirm.

BACKGROUND

[Venezia owned B & H, a vending machine and video-game business through which he operated an illegal gambling operation in East St. Louis, Illinois. The business placed video-games in taverns, where they were used for gambling. Cueto, a lawyer, represented Venezia and several tavern owners, all of whom were targeted in an investigation by the Illinois Liquor Control Commission (ILCC), the police, and the FBI. Robinson was an ILCC agent who worked undercover for the FBI and posed as a corrupt liquor agent. When the state police raided a tavern that was participating in Venezia's gambling business, Robinson solicited a bribe from Venezia in return for promises to call off the investigation. Venezia asked Cueto for advice. Cueto told Venezia not to pay the bribe, and began a litigation campaign against Robinson and his investigation. Cueto had one of his partners file a complaint with the State's Attorney depicting Robinson as a corrupt agent engaged in extortion. Next, Cueto obtained an injunction forbidding Robinson from interfering with Venezia's businesses. When Robinson persisted in the investigation, Cueto filed additional complaints against him, including a "show cause" hearing asking that Robinson be held in contempt for violating the injunction. When Robinson prevailed by proving that he was an undercover FBI agent, Cueto appealed, first to the Seventh Circuit and then to the United States Supreme Court. Both appeals were unsuccessful.

Subsequently, Robinson testified in a gambling prosecution against one of B & H's customers, and Cueto cross-examined him. Cueto sent transcripts of this cross-examination to the State's Attorney, charging that Robinson had committed perjury and should be investigated. Cueto lobbied a congressman (who was a partner with Cueto and Venezia in a gambling establishment) to exert influence to get Cueto appointed State's Attorney; he also published a newspaper and wrote articles in it in which he attacked the prosecutors in the racketeering investigation, and announced that he would run for State's Attorney and, if elected, would prosecute Robinson. When a grand jury was impaneled to investigate Venezia, Cueto worked on his defense, and filed numerous motions to hinder the investigation and to get the grand jury dissolved. Although Cueto succeeded in delaying the investigation, Venezia was eventually convicted on various gambling and racketeering charges.

Throughout this period, Cueto was involved in real estate deals and other business ventures with Venezia, including an asbestos removal business and a topless bar at which Venezia's illegal gambling devices were used. The financial viability of these businesses depended on the revenues from Venezia's gambling business, which secured loans and covered debts.

Cueto was indicted for "conspiracy to defraud the United States," in violation of 18 U.S.C. § 371, alleging that he misused his office as an attorney and unlawfully and intentionally conspired with Venezia ... to impede, impair, obstruct, and defeat the lawful function of the FBI, the grand jury, and the federal district court in connection with the investigation, indictment, and prosecution of Venezia, B & H, and the illegal gambling operation and racketeering enterprise. The indictment alleged that Cueto and Venezia's business relationship created Cueto's financial motive for his participation in the conspiracy, in which he endeavored to protect the illegal gambling enterprise and to maintain its continued operation in order to safeguard his personal financial interests. In addition to the conspiracy charges, the government "charged obstruction of justice . . ., alleging that Cueto endeavored to use his office as an attorney to influence, obstruct, and impair the due administration of justice in various court proceedings. . . .")

ANALYSIS

Before we begin our analysis, we discuss the appropriate standard of review, our particular role in this review, and the limited scope of this decision. Our ruling today does not interfere with legitimate avenues of advocacy of even the most zealous of attorneys; we do nothing more than consider the constitutionality of certain criminal statutes aimed at protecting the sanctity and integrity of our justice system from corrupt influences and apply them in a sober and impartial fashion. . . .

I.   Obstruction of Justice

Cueto asserts several arguments with respect to his convictions on Counts 2, 6, and 7 for obstruction of justice, contending that the omnibus clause of § 1503 is unconstitutionally vague as applied to the conduct charged in the indictment. . . . Cueto argues that "much of what lawyers do—are attempts to influence the justice system," and that the omnibus clause of § 1503 was not intended to apply to the type of conduct charged in the indictment. Questions regarding the constitutionality or scope of a statute are reviewed de novo.

. . . The omnibus clause of § 1503 is a catch-all provision that states:

> Whoever . . . corruptly or by threats or force, or by any threatening letter or communication, influences, obstructs, or impedes or endeavors to influence, obstruct or impede, the due administration of law, shall be imprisoned. . . .

18 U.S.C. § 1503. This clause was intended to ensure that criminals could not circumvent the statute's purpose "by devising novel and creative schemes that would interfere with the administration of justice but would nonetheless fall outside the scope of § 1503's specific prohibitions" [citation omitted]. "The obstruction of justice statute was drafted with an eye to 'the variety of corrupt methods by which the proper administration of justice may be impeded or thwarted, a variety limited only by the imagination of the criminally inclined.' "[citation omitted].

Cueto also contends that the vagueness problems are exacerbated by this court's broad construction of the term "corruptly," arguing that it fails to provide meaningful and adequate notice as to what conduct is proscribed by the statute. The Seventh Circuit has approved a jury instruction which articulates a definition for the term "corruptly," and the district court judge included this definition in its instructions to the jury:

> Corruptly means to act with the purpose of obstructing justice. The United States is not required to prove that the defendant's only or even main purpose was to obstruct the due administration of justice. The government only has to establish that the defendant should have reasonably seen that the natural and probable consequences of his acts was the obstruction of justice. Intent may be inferred from all of the surrounding facts and circumstances. Any act, by any party, whether lawful or unlawful on its face, may violate Section 1503, if performed with a corrupt motive.

The mere fact that a term "covers a broad spectrum of conduct" does not render it vague, and the requirement that a statute must give fair notice as to what conduct is proscribed "cannot be used as a shield by one who is already bent on serious wrongdoing."

There is little case authority directly on point to consider whether an attorney acting in his professional capacity could be criminally liable under the omnibus clause of § 1503 for traditional litigation-related conduct that results in an obstruction of justice. "Correct application of Section 1503 thus requires, in a very real sense, that the factfinder discern—by direct evidence or from inference—the motive which led an individual to perform particular actions.... 'Intent may make any otherwise innocent act criminal, if it is a step in a plot.'" Therefore, it is not the means employed by the defendant that are specifically prohibited by the statute; instead, it is the defendant's corrupt endeavor which motivated the action. Otherwise lawful conduct, even acts undertaken by an attorney in the course of representing a client, can transgress § 1503 if employed with the corrupt intent to accomplish that which the statute forbids....

We are not persuaded by Cueto's constitutional challenges, and his focus is misplaced. The government's theory of prosecution is predicated on the fact that Cueto held a personal financial interest in protecting the illegal gambling enterprise, which formed the requisite corrupt intent for his conduct to qualify as violations of the statute.[10] Cueto focuses entirely on the legality of his conduct, and not the requisite criminal intent proscribed by § 1503. It is undisputed that an attorney may use any lawful means to defend his client, and there is no risk of criminal liability if those means employed by the attorney in his endeavors to represent his client remain within the scope of lawful conduct. However, it is the corrupt endeavor to protect the illegal gambling operation and to safeguard his own

---

10. This theory of prosecution brings us some pause. With the government's emphasis on Cueto's involvement in Venezia's illegal gambling operation and the racketeering enterprise, we are puzzled why the government did not indict and prosecute Cueto in the underlying racketeering case for his participation in the illegal gambling operation. Although the government's decision not to prosecute Cueto in the previous case is fundamentally inconsequential to the instant appeal, we are concerned about the relationship between the instant appeal and the underlying prosecution of the gambling operation and the racketeering enterprise.

financial interest, which motivated Cueto's otherwise legal conduct, that separates his conduct from that which is legal.

Even though courts may be hesitant, with good reason and caution, to include traditional litigation-related conduct within the scope of § 1503, the omnibus clause has been interpreted broadly in accordance with congressional intent to promote the due administration of justice and to prevent the miscarriage of justice, and an individual's status as an attorney engaged in litigation-related conduct does not provide protection from prosecution for criminal conduct.... Cueto's arguments have no merit. As a lawyer, he possessed a heightened awareness of the law and its scope, and he cannot claim lack of fair notice as to what conduct is proscribed by § 1503 to shield himself from criminal liability, particularly when he was already "bent on serious wrongdoing." More so than an ordinary individual, an attorney, in particular a criminal defense attorney, has a sophisticated understanding of the type of conduct that constitutes criminal violations of the law. There is a discernable difference between an honest lawyer who unintentionally submits a false statement to the court and an attorney with specific corrupt intentions who files papers in bad faith knowing that they contain false representations and/or inaccurate facts in an attempt to hinder judicial proceedings. It is true that, to a certain extent, a lawyer's conduct influences judicial proceedings, or at least attempts to affect the outcome of the proceedings. However, that influence stems from a lawyer's attempt to advocate his client's interests within the scope of the law. It is the "corrupt endeavor" to influence the due administration of justice that is the heart of the offense, and Cueto's personal financial interest is the heart of his corrupt motive.

An amicus brief submitted by the National Association of Criminal Defense Lawyers ("Association") also questions the proper scope of the omnibus clause of § 1503, and the Association articulates its fears that if we affirm Cueto's convictions, criminal defense attorneys will be subject to future prosecutions not only for actual misconduct, but also for apparent and inadvertent wrongdoing, notwithstanding a lawyer's good faith advocacy. The Association believes that this type of sweeping prosecution will sufficiently chill vigorous advocacy and eventually destroy the delicate balance between prosecution and defense which is necessary to maintain the effective operation of the criminal justice system. Although the Association discusses valid policy concerns and asserts legitimate arguments, some of which we generally agree with, we are also concerned with the flipside of its argument. If lawyers are not punished for their criminal conduct and corrupt endeavors to manipulate the administration of justice, the result would be the same: the weakening of an ethical adversarial system and the undermining of just administration of the law. We have the responsibility to ensure that the integrity of the criminal justice system is maintained and that protection includes granting to both the prosecution and the defense flexibility and "discretion in the conduct of the trial and the presentation of evidence," in addition to enforcing mechanisms of punishment, which necessarily include criminal prosecution, to prevent abuses of the system.

We have carefully examined the fears articulated by the National Association of Criminal Defense Lawyers, in addition to the arguments put forth by the defendant, that a decision upholding the application of the omnibus clause of § 1503 to litigation-related conduct may deter or somehow chill the criminal defense lawyers in zealous advocacy, and we find those concerns to be exaggerated, at least as considered in light of the facts in the present case. Although we appreciate that it is of significant importance to avoid chilling vigorous advocacy and to maintain the balance of effective representation, we also recognize that a lawyer's misconduct and criminal acts are not absolutely immune from prosecution. We cannot ignore Cueto's corrupt endeavors to manipulate the administration of justice and his clear criminal violations of the law. As the First Circuit recognized in *Cintolo*:

> Nothing in the caselaw, fairly read, suggests that lawyers should be plucked gently from the maddening crowd and sheltered from the rigors of 18 U.S.C. § 1503 in the manner urged by appellant and by the amici. Nor is there sufficient public policy justification favoring such a result. To the contrary, the overriding public policy interest is that "the attorney-client relationship cannot ... be used to shield or promote illegitimate acts...." "Attorneys, just like all other persons, ... are not above the law and are subject to its full application under appropriate circumstances."

Accordingly, we conclude that the omnibus clause of § 1503 may be used to prosecute a lawyer's litigation-related criminality and that neither the omnibus clause of § 1503 nor this court's construction of the term "corruptly" is unconstitutionally vague as applied to the conduct charged in the indictment for which Cueto was convicted.... [T]he record adequately supports the conclusion that Cueto's conduct, though nominally litigation related conduct on behalf of his client, was undertaken with the corrupt intent to protect Venezia, Venezia's associates, and his business from criminal prosecution and to safeguard his personal financial interest in the illegal gambling operation, whatever the costs and consequences to the due administration of justice.

The charges in Count 2 of the indictment included allegations of a corrupt endeavor to obstruct the due administration of justice in *Venezia v. Robinson* by filing pleadings in federal district court and a continued attempt to hinder the proceedings by filing an appeal in this court and a petition for certiorari in the United States Supreme Court. The evidence demonstrates that Cueto successfully exposed the FBI's investigation, uncovered the evidence it had gathered, obtained the injunction against Robinson, and continued to file frivolous appeals after the district court dismissed the injunction and the complaint. Government agents, in fact, testified that the investigation was disrupted and that Cueto "blew the lid off the ongoing investigation." The jury was amply justified in concluding that Cueto's repeated filings were motivated by his attempt to protect his client from prosecution and to safeguard his financial interest. Cueto's actions may qualify as traditional litigation-related conduct in form, but not in substance, and the evidence presented at trial demonstrates that Cueto clearly intended and corruptly endeavored to obstruct the due administration of justice in *Venezia v. Robinson....*

For the reasons discussed above, keeping in mind the limited scope of our holding, we AFFIRM the defendant's convictions and the sentence imposed by the district court.

QUESTIONS

1.   Cueto published articles that criticized federal prosecutors, and lobbied a Congressman to help him get an appointment as State's Attorney. Apart from these activities, presumably protected by the First Amendment, he engaged in the typical activities of a litigator: he filed motions, he sought and obtained an injunction, he appealed decisions that he lost, he complained to the authorities that a witness had perjured himself, he prepared a criminal defense for a client, he conducted a cross-examination, and, when a federal agent, pretending to be corrupt, solicited a bribe from his client, he advised the client not to pay it and complained to the proper authorities that the agent had attempted extortion. Has Cueto been sentenced to seven years in the penitentiary for activities that criminal defense lawyers perform for clients every day?

2.   What is the difference between zealous advocacy on behalf of a suspected racketeer and obstruction of justice? Is it only the lawyer's "corrupt" motive? What made Cueto's motive corrupt? Is it only his business dealings with his client? Many lawyers have business dealings with clients. Is it his financial dependence on his client? If so, how is Cueto different from corporate in-house counsel, many of whom are paid in shares of the company? Is it that the client is engaged in criminal activity? Isn't that often true of criminal defenders' clients? What if a corporation is convicted of criminal activity? Could their general counsel also be criminally liable?

3.   How, if at all, can *Cueto* be reconciled with the proposition that lawyers are not accountable for pursuing their clients' ends through use of the legal system? At what point did Cueto's representation of Venezia cross the line to criminal liability?

One possible answer is that Cueto's business dealings with Venezia made him a partner in Venezia's racketeering, rather than simply a lawyer representing a racketeer. However, as the court notes with some concern in footnote 10, the government did not prosecute Cueto as a racketeer or as an accomplice in racketeering. The government prosecuted him only for his lawyering activities, which obstructed justice by disrupting the government's investigation of Venezia. (The conspiracy charge is basically conspiracy to obstruct justice.) Was that prosecution appropriate?

The Cali Cartel's Lawyers

One of the most highly-publicized prosecutions of lawyers for their conduct as advocates concerned half-a-dozen attorneys representing members of the Cali cocaine cartel. After raiding their offices in October, 1994, the government indicted three lawyers for money laundering, soliciting false statements from drug defendants, and conspiring with their clients to import cocaine. The latter charge was the most controversial. The government's theory was that the lawyers were so deeply involved in advising their clients how to continue their activities with impunity that they had become co-conspirators. According to federal prosecutors, some of the lawyers conveyed death threats from Cali, or paid hush money, to captured suspects in Florida. Some allegedly sought to protect the Rodriguez brothers (the reputed heads of the Cali cartel) by obtaining false affidavits. The lawyers were also accused of arranging bail with the knowledge that their clients would leave the country.

Three of the lawyers were former federal prosecutors, and another, Michael Abbell, was a Harvard Law School graduate who had served nearly twenty years at the Department of Justice, rising to head the Office of International Affairs. An expert in extradition, he went into private practice in 1984 and was hired to help Miguel Rodriguez–Orejuela, a reputed Cali cartel kingpin, fight extradition from Spain to the United States. He later helped Rodriguez in other matters.

The Miami defense bar believed that the indictments were an attempt to intimidate defense lawyers representing drug clients (the so-called "white powder defense bar"). "They're charging [the lawyers] with the crimes of their clients," commented Miami attorney Roy Black, who represented Abbell. "The worst part of this," he added, "is the prosecutors who obtained the indictment were the same prosecutors who opposed these lawyers in a drug case."[79] Other defense counsel believed that the indictments broke new ground by criminalizing client-representation activities that had not previously been regarded as illegal.

After several trials, Abbell and attorney William Moran were convicted on a number of charges, but Senior U.S. Judge William M. Hoeveler threw out all their convictions except those for money-laundering conspiracy. "The lawyers did some things that were highly unprofessional and, indeed, unethical," Judge Hoeveler explained. "I don't think they should practice law again. That doesn't make them part of a racketeering conspiracy."[80] Abbell was sentenced to seven years, Moran to five years, and former federal prosecutor Donald Ferguson to two years.

Perhaps the most startling of the convictions was that of another former federal prosecutor, Joel Rosenthal. When a Cali member was arrested in Texas in 1991, Rosenthal retained a lawyer there to represent him. He did so with $65,000 in cash from Miguel Rodriguez, which he deposited in his trust account before paying the fees. Rosenthal did not disclose the source of the fees to the Texas lawyer. The government claimed that this activity constituted money laundering and concealment. The

---

79. David Lyons, "Feds Snare Lawyers in Cali Cartel Net: The Defense Bar Sees, In Raids, Taps and Novel Theories, an Unprecedented Attack," *Nat'l. Law J.*, June 19, 1995, at A1.

80. Mary Hladky, "Two Lawyers' Convictions Junked: Federal Judge Reverses Jury on Some Florida Drug Counts, Though Others Stand," *Nat'l. Law J.*, June 21, 1999, at A5.

money-laundering statute, 18 U.S.C. § 1957, penalizes anyone who "knowingly engages or attempts to engage in a monetary transaction in criminally derived property that is of a value greater than $10,000...." Rosenthal pled guilty. Norman Muscowitz, a former federal prosecutor who represented Rosenthal, calls the outcome "tragic." He explains: "Except for this crime, Joel has had a long and honorable career as an attorney."[81]

Did Rosenthal's act cross the line from criminal lawyer to lawyer-criminal? Do such prosecutions deter lawyers from vigorously defending those accused of notorious criminal activity? Or does the government have a legitimate interest in discouraging attorneys from being "on retainer to the Mafia"?[82]

Lawyers for Terrorists: The Lynne Stewart Case

The War on Terror raises parallel questions. How far can a lawyer go in representing a terrorist? In pursuit of terrorism suspects, the government has frequently relied on two criminal statutes prohibiting "material support" for terrorism. Material support receives a broad definition, which includes providing "expert advice or assistance"—meaning "advice or assistance derived from ... specialized knowledge"—and "personnel (1 or more individuals who may be or include oneself)." 18 U.S.C. § 2339A(b)(1) and (3). The crucial question for lawyers is whether, by representing an alleged terrorist, a lawyer has provided expert advice or assistance, or personnel. If so, the lawyer runs the risk of prosecution and lengthy imprisonment.

The answer may depend on which of the two material support statutes is involved. 18 U.S.C. § 2339A prohibits providing material support items "knowing or intending that they are to be used in preparation for, or in carrying out" terrorist crimes, while 18 U.S.C. § 2339B prohibits knowingly providing material support to a foreign terrorist organization (abbreviated 'FTO'), knowing that they have been so designated by the U.S. government. The statutes also criminalize attempts and conspiracies to provide material support to terrorists. Notice the difference in mens rea between the two statutes. Section 2339A requires that the accused not only provided material support to terrorism, but did so knowing or intending that the support items would be used to facilitate terrorist crimes. Section 2339B requires no such knowledge or intention. All it requires is that the accused has knowingly provided material support to an organization that he or she knows has been designated as an FTO. Thus, for example, someone who donates money to a known FTO has violated section 2339B even if he or she believes that the money would not be used to commit crimes.

The leading case on lawyers and material support concerns lawyer Lynne Stewart, who represented Sheik Abdul Rahman, the "blind sheik." He was the leader of the Islamic Group ("IG"), a militant organization

---

81. Lyons, *supra* note 71, at A1.

82. Rhode, *supra* note 33, at 74 (quoting Geoffrey Hazard). For a detailed account of the case of the Cali cartel's lawyers, see James L. Kelley, *Lawyers Crossing Lines: Nine Stories of Greed, Disloyalty, and Betrayal of Trust* (2001).

engaged in jihad against the United States, which planned bombings of several sites around New York City. Sheik Rahman was convicted of several crimes and sentenced to life plus 65 years. Fearing that Sheik Rahman would continue to direct the IG from prison, the Attorney General ordered the imposition of Special Administrative Measures (SAMs) that limit the Sheik's communications with the outside world. Before visiting the Sheik in prison, Stewart was required to sign an affirmation that she would abide by the SAMs. She was accused of violating the SAMs in at least two ways. First, she disguised the Sheik's IG-related conversations with the interpreter, "by making extraneous comments in English to mask the conversation in Arabic between [the interpreter] and Sheikh Abdel Rahman." Second, "Stewart then released her client's statement to the press . . . 'withdrawing his support for the cease-fire [in Egypt] that currently exists.' " As a result, Stewart was indicted for material support under § 2339B, as well as for making false statements to the government by signing the statement that she would abide by the SAMs.

In a first round of litigation, the judge dismissed the indictment on the ground that the material support statute was unconstitutionally vague. He wrote, "the Government fails to explain how a lawyer, acting as an agent of her client, an alleged leader of an FTO, could avoid being subject to criminal prosecution as a 'quasi-employee' allegedly covered by the statute. At the argument on the motions, the Government expressed some uncertainty as to whether a lawyer for an FTO would be providing personnel to the FTO before the Government suggested that the answer may depend on whether the lawyer was 'house counsel' or an independent counsel—distinctions not found in the statute." *U.S. v. Sattar*, 272 F. Supp. 2d 348, 359 (S.D.N.Y. 2003).

The government re-indicted Stewart under § 2339A, with its more demanding *mens rea* requirement. Here, the judge declined to find the statute void for vagueness, and a jury convicted Stewart; the jurors were persuaded by wiretap evidence that Stewart actually knew that her assistance was furthering crimes. Some objected that the prosecution attempted to inflame the jury by trying Stewart together with the interpreter, and by playing a tape of Osama bin Laden. Stewart was sentenced to 28 months in prison; the case is currently under appeal.

Stewart's case received widespread attention, in part because Stewart herself was an appealing 62–year–old grandmother who had no ideological sympathy with Islamic terrorism. In an interview, Stewart said, "There are a hundred lawyers who would do exactly what I did. There are a million lawyers who would do almost exactly what I did. Because this is the way you have to represent clients."[83] Some have suggested that Stewart seemed to "revel" in violations of the SAMs.[84] A sympathetic commentator wrote that "Stewart crossed the line between zealous advocacy and wrongful

---

83. Susie Day Interview with Lynn Stewart, http://www.frontpagemag.com/Articles/ReadArticle.asp?ID=4764.

84. William Glaberson, "Defenders of the Unpopular Feel a Little Less Popular," *N.Y. Times*, Feb. 11, 2005, at A21.

conduct. But she is no terrorist."[85] Criminal defender and legal theorist Abbe Smith expands on this point.

Abbe L. Smith, "The Bounds of Zeal in Criminal Defense: Some Thoughts on Lynne Stewart"
44 S. Tex. L. Rev. 31 (2002).

. . . [H]ow did Stewart go from being an exemplary client-centered lawyer, doing what she could do to legitimately advance her client's case and cause, to allegedly aiding him directly in his criminal activities? Although the line may be easy to discern after the fact, it may not have looked so clear to Stewart at the time. Defense lawyers often become intensely identified with clients, perhaps especially so when the client is a social or political pariah. When everyone else is against the client the lawyer "pumps up the volume" a bit. Add to this the criminal defender's tendency to flaunt authority, and you get defenders who are willing to break a rule here or there, especially when it comes to autocratic places like jails and prisons. Stewart may not have meant to further violence when she communicated her client's message; she may have seen herself as resisting overly harsh prison rules and asserting what she deemed to be her client's fundamental right of self-expression.

You have to get close to clients—no matter who the client is or what he or she is alleged to have done—in order to work with that client and fashion a defense. The longer a case goes on and the higher the stakes, the closer the lawyer sometimes gets. This is especially so if the lawyer likes the client, if he or she has any real feeling for the client. Stewart clearly got close to the sheik. She liked him. She may have gotten too close.

. . . I have often thought that excessive devotion is a greater peril than excessive zeal on behalf of a client. When lawyers get too close to clients— when they become their client's "best friend," their client's "family," or worse, succumb to the "eros [that] finds its way into most lawyer-client relationships"—things can go off-course. There need not be a clear breach of professional norms, like sleeping with a client, for lawyers to get too close.

Excessive devotion to, interest in, and identification with clients can happen to lawyers who have perfectly good boundaries the rest of the time. There is this one client, this one case that gets under the lawyer's skin. Maybe the lawyer perceives the client to be a victim of a horrible injustice. Maybe the lawyer feels a real affinity for the client, something approaching love. Maybe the client or case is filling some sort of need in the lawyer that the lawyer isn't even aware of—a need for connection, for love, for meaning.

The problem is this line is especially hard to draw. Lawyers are bound to become attached to clients out of a sense of shared humanity, and

85. David Cole, "The Lynne Stewart Trial," *The Nation*, March 7, 2005.

because the lawyer-client relationship is a relationship after all. Attachment is not a bad thing. The best defenders are often the most attached, the most connected to clients. From the outside, it may seem obvious where natural and appropriate attachment ends and boundary violations begin. From the inside, it is not always so easy. . . .

The truth is zealous lawyers contemplate getting in a little trouble from time to time, though they do not expect to be criminally prosecuted. What defender has not on occasion violated a prison rule, passed on a communication they probably should not have passed on, attempted to soften an otherwise harsh criminal justice system? More importantly, what zealous, devoted defender refrains from speaking for clients simply because they are told not to?

I find it hard to believe that Stewart acted as she did to promote or carry out terrorism in the name of the suffering people of Egypt. Prior to agreeing to represent the sheik—about which Stewart initially had misgivings—there is no indication that Stewart knew anything about, much less passionately believed in the sheik's cause. There is no indication she had especially strong views about politics in the Middle East. . . .

If Stewart—after weighing the risks of her conduct and deciding it was worth it in this particular context—simply misjudged the government's reaction, there is an explanation for this that may be "political" without involving any intent to "provide material assistance to a terrorist organization." Stewart's client was incarcerated under the harshest of circumstances—he was basically being held incommunicado—and Stewart no doubt felt this was both unjust and cruel. The only thing that mattered to the sheik was his voice. And yet it was unlikely at best that petitioning the court to change the conditions of his confinement would be productive. This coupled with the belief that the sheik had been wrongly convicted may have made Stewart want to stretch the bounds of advocacy on her client's behalf.

NOTES AND QUESTIONS

1. Assume that Abbe Smith is correct that Stewart's conduct arose out of excessive identification with her client's plight: old, blind, sentenced to life in prison, barred from human contact with anyone but Stewart. Should that exonerate her from the charge of providing material support to terrorism? Smith suggests that every good defender stretches rules and expects to get in trouble sometimes, especially when the rules are part of a draconian prison regimen. "Everyone does it" is, of course, not a morally acceptable excuse. But Smith's argument is subtler than this. She argues that an anti-authoritarian, emotionally involved, client-centered personality, suspicious of red tape and feisty in opposing the government, may be a prerequisite for an effective criminal defender. Nevertheless, Smith draws the line differently from Stewart. "I take a pragmatic approach to professional boundaries. I may feel a lot for some clients—I may want to move mountains on their behalf, and weep when I cannot do it—but I will not do anything to jeopardize my ability to practice law. I may offer a prisoner a

piece of gum or candy in clear violation of prison rules, but I will not help him escape. I may arouse a prosecutor's or judge's ire because of impassioned advocacy—even going so far as to risk being cited for contempt—but I won't risk my law license."

Did Lynne Stewart cross an ethical as a well as a pragmatic line?

2.   Stewart signed an agreement to abide by the SAMs before she was permitted to visit her client in prison. In the sheik's case, the SAMs—authorized by a federal regulation—specified that he would "not be permitted to talk with, meet with, correspond with, or otherwise communicate with any member, or representative, of the news media, in person, by telephone, by furnishing a recorded message, through the mails, through his attorney(s), or otherwise." Stewart denied that at the time she signed the agreement, she intended to violate the SAMs; she formed that intention only after meeting with the sheik and perceiving how harsh his regime of forced isolation is. The jury did not believe her.

Should a defender be compelled to sign an agreement not to violate SAMs? At least one federal judge thinks the answer is no. William Young, the trial judge in the case of Richard Reid—the Al Qaeda "shoe bomber" who attempted to detonate explosives packed into his sneakers on board an air liner—declined to require Reid's counsel to sign an affirmation that they would abide by SAMs.

> The affirmation here unilaterally imposed by the Marshals Service as a condition of the free exercise of Reid's Sixth Amendment right to consult with his attorneys fundamentally and impermissibly intrudes on the proper role of defense counsel. They are zealously to defend Reid to the best of their professional skill without the necessity of affirming their bona fides to the government....

> Nor is this all. The Court takes judicial notice, pursuant to Federal Rule of Evidence 201, that the government has indicted attorney Lynne Stewart, Esq., inter alia, for violating 28 U.S.C. § 1001 [the false statements statute], in that having signed the required affirmation, she violated the SAMs applicable to one Sheikh Abdel Rahman, and therefore knowingly made a false statement. Evidently, the government theorizes that the affirmation was knowingly false when made. Whatever the merits of this indictment, its chilling effect on those courageous attorneys who represent society's most despised outcasts cannot be gainsaid. U.S. v. Reid, 214 F.Supp.2d 84, 94–95 (D. Mass. 2002).

Although Judge Young's opinion makes extensive reference to the Sixth Amendment right to counsel, and suggests that he might have found unconstitutional the requirement that Reid's counsel sign an agreement to abide by the SAMs, he did not reach the constitutional issue because the government agreed not to require Reid's counsel to sign. Should the Sixth Amendment prevent the government from using SAMs to stop terrorists from running their operations from a prison cell and using their lawyers as conduits?

3.   In a letter to Judge Koeltl after the verdict before her sentencing, Stewart reiterated that she did not support Rahman's objectives, and that in retrospect, wished that she had challenged the SAMS or conditions of his confinement. Instead, "I tested the limits of what the courts and law would allow for my clients because I believe I was, as criminal defense lawyers often say, 'liberty's last champion.' ... [I]t did not for a moment occur to me that I was venturing anywhere near breaking the law ... I believed that the worst case scenario was that I would be barred from visiting my client."[86] The government requested a sentence of thirty years. If you had been the trial court, how would you have exercised your sentencing discretion?

4.   Much of the evidence against Stewart comes from secret tapings of her prison conversations with Sheik Rahman and the interpreter. The government's taping of confidential attorney-client conversations in prison itself raises controversial issues. These are discussed in Chapter V.

3.   ROLE MORALITY AND GROUP IDENTITY

PROBLEM 6

Your firm represents a real estate developer who, through high pressure but legally permissible tactics, is able to take advantage of the lack of resources and sophistication among a recent immigrant group. As a result, he manages to sell them homes at prices substantially above market value. Over the last several years, this client's work has generated over a million dollars in legal fees for your firm.

1.   Do lawyers at the firm who are part of the same ethnic group as the immigrants have any special moral obligations to challenge the client's practices? If so, how far do those obligations extend? Do they require more from the lawyers than refusing to work on the matter?

2.   Do members of the firm who are *not* members of the ethnic group have any similar ethical obligations regarding this matter? Must they protect lawyers with the same ethnicity as the immigrant group from adverse financial or career consequences if they challenge the developer's practices or refuse to do his work? Should the firm drop the client out of loyalty to its minority attorneys?

3.   Do any of your answers change if the client is also a member of the ethnic group?

4.   Is this a problem of role morality?

NOTES: ROLE MORALITY AND GROUP IDENTITY

Problem 6 is modeled on a case that David Wilkins explores in an article on the responsibilities of black corporate lawyers.[87] He begins by raising one fundamental question:

---

86. Lynne Stewart, Letter to Hon. Judge John Koeltl, September 16, 2006.

87. This problem is based on a case discussed by David B. Wilkins in "Two Paths

What is the moral justification for focusing on the obligations blacks in corporate law firms allegedly owe to other blacks? For example, if it would be morally wrong (or at least morally troubling) for a black lawyer to assist a real estate developer to sell houses at double their market value by exploiting the ignorance of moderate income buyers, wouldn't it be equally wrong for a white lawyer to do so? Would the moral calculus be any different if the prospective homebuyers were all poor whites? Indeed, to the extent that race is relevant at all, shouldn't whites, as the perpetrators (or the descendants of the perpetrators) of racist oppression, have the greatest obligation to rectify the results of past injustices to blacks? Why should those few blacks who have finally managed to squeak past the unjust barricades of a hostile and racist world be required to carry the additional burden of worrying about whether their actions will "uplift the race?"[88]

Wilkins offers several reasons why blacks should have that burden. Like other critics of role morality, he rejects the Neutral Partisanship conception that denies lawyers' ethical "accountability for either the means employed or the ends achieved."[89] Wilkins believes that all lawyers have to accept moral responsibility for the consequences of their representation, and that part of this responsibility for black lawyers is to consider how their actions will affect the black community.

In defending this position, Wilkins starts from the premise that "[c]ertain relationships create special moral obligations."[90] The bonds between parent and child, citizen and state, and lawyer and client are obvious examples. For racial and ethnic minorities, membership in an "identifiable common culture" constitutes such a relationship.

> For those blacks whose membership in the black community is central to their identity, recognizing the existence of such an obligation promotes both a healthy self-love and a firm foundation for helping other blacks who are truly in need.... But the interdependency between individual blacks and blacks as a group gives black professionals a moral reason for valuing the interests of other blacks even in circumstances where they do not see group membership as central to their own identity. Given the link between individual opportunity and group advancement, even those blacks who ultimately care only about their own moral right to be free from racist constraints ought to recognize a moral responsibility to participate in collective projects to end racist oppression....
>
> Finally, morality requires that individual blacks take account [of] the unintended but nevertheless predictable consequences of their actions. Consider, for example, a black corporate lawyer who is asked to defend a company accused of discriminating against blacks in employment. No matter how much that lawyer protests that his race is irrelevant to the performance of his professional role, his very presence

---

to the Mountaintop? The Role of Legal Education in Shaping the Values of Black Corporate Lawyers," 45 *Stan.L.Rev.* 1981, 1989 (1993).

88. *Id.* at 1995.

89. *Id.* at 2018.

90. *Id.* at 1996.

at the counsel table sends a message to the jurors (both black and white) about the merits of the discrimination claim. To the extent that this implicit message (i.e., a company that discriminated would not hire a black lawyer) helps the company defeat a valid claim of discrimination, the black lawyer has helped inflict a moral wrong on the black plaintiffs.[91]

In Wilkins's view, attorneys of color can fulfill their obligations in many different ways, in every practice setting, including corporate law. Although he acknowledges that such practice may help solidify inequalities in the distribution of wealth and power, he finds countervailing benefits from having a minority presence within the corporate bar.

First, if nothing else, the presence of blacks within these elite ranks undermines the stereotype of black intellectual inferiority. Second, as a corollary to the first point, the achievements of black corporate lawyers might inspire other young black women and men to strive harder to become successful in their own right. Indeed, in addition to being passive role models, black corporate lawyers might work actively to open up additional opportunities for blacks, in law or elsewhere. Third, corporate law practice gives black lawyers access to money and other resources that can be directed toward projects to benefit the black community. Fourth, in addition to offering material rewards, corporate law practice traditionally has been a stepping stone to politics and political influence. As a result, black corporate lawyers may be able to translate their private power into public power in ways that benefit the black community. Finally, the very fact that corporations have such power to impose costs on the black community underscores the benefits that could accrue if black lawyers are able to persuade corporations to act in ways that are less harmful (and perhaps even beneficial) to the black community.[92]

Wilkins does not speak explicitly to what lawyers of color should have done on the facts of Problem 6. Nor is his purpose to prescribe appropriate conduct in more complicated cases where the minority community is itself divided about its own interests or the consequences of particular client actions. Rather, Wilkins's aim is to establish that lawyers of color have an obligation to consider those issues and to make some contribution to advancing the interests of their racial or ethnic community.

QUESTIONS

1. Do you agree with Wilkins's position? How would you assess the conduct of Anthony Griffin, a black lawyer working as NAACP general counsel in Texas who, while acting as cooperating counsel for the American Civil Liberties Union, represented the Ku Klux Klan in a free speech case? The case involved the government's attempt to compel disclosure of Klan membership lists in order to identify individuals who had been tyrannizing black residents of a local housing project. In resisting disclosure, Griffin

---

91. *Id.* at 2001–02.   **92.** *Id.* at 1991.

relied on Supreme Court precedents protecting the confidentiality of NAACP membership lists. The current NAACP management felt the cases were distinguishable because Klan members were allegedly engaged in illegal activity. It fired Griffin. Was that response appropriate?[93]

2.   A study of Harvard Law School graduates several years into their legal careers revealed that many had confronted dilemmas similar to the one presented in Problem 6. These attorneys often fell back on traditional justifications for the advocacy role that left them morally uncomfortable.

In the words of one young African–American attorney who was experiencing the pressures of an associate seeking to be promoted to partner:

> We represented a client in a plant closing case that was opposed by the community. That one made me think a lot because I grew up in (a poor community) which used to have a heavy manufacturing base and everyone worked in the mills. I watched the plants close and watched the parents of friends get laid off and watched the community go down the hill from there. I recognize that was very possible in this case. While I'm representing the company, I recognize the community's interests also. Intellectually, though, it's easy to see that the basis for the community's lawsuit has no merit. . . . I guess what I ended up doing was concentrating on the legal issues because that was really all that I had control over. . . .

Another attorney recalled:

> We had a case where a company wanted to develop a hazardous waste incinerator in a poor area. What we did was perfectly legal. We bought the land from the owners. We told them we were developing an industrial park, which was semi-true. But, this case went against my general convictions about environmental issues, particularly putting something like this in a poor area where people can't or won't resist. But I convinced myself that there's always another side. By the time I was done, I thought our client was closer to the right side of things than the townspeople. The stuff has to go somewhere. I tended to accept what the client was saying about all the precautions they would take.

However, the most effective technique is sometimes to simply ignore ethical implications altogether. In the words of one typical respondent, "I used to care about how the things I did as a lawyer affected people, but I don't find myself asking these questions anymore."[94]

How would you assess the decision making framework of these attorneys? How would you approach such issues?

3.   Do members of nonracial identity groups have similar obligations? For example, should a woman lawyer decline to represent clients who she

---

93. For extensive discussion, see David B. Wilkins, "Race, Ethics, and the First Amendment: Should a Black Lawyer Represent the Ku Klux Klan?" 63 *G.W. L. Rev.* 1030 and reprinted in *Legal Ethics: Law Stories* 17 (Deborah L. Rhode & David. Luban, eds. 2006).

94. Robert Granfield and Thomas Koenig, " 'It's Hard to be a Human Being and a Lawyer': Young Attorneys and the Confrontations with Ethical Ambiguity in Legal Practice," 105 *West Virginia L. Rev.* 495 (2003).

believes are guilty of sex discrimination or sexual harassment? Does she have the right to decline to represent male clients because her practice is devoted to the well-being of women? In *Stropnicky v. Nathanson*, 19 Mass. Discrim. L. Rep. 39 (1997), a female lawyer specializing in divorce problems facing women refused to review the divorce settlement of a man because she had a "wives only" matrimonial practice. He filed a gender discrimination claim against her, and the Massachusetts Commission Against Discrimination (MDAC) found that she had violated public accommodations law and fined her $5,000. Many Massachusetts lawyers objected to MDAC's finding that a law practice is a public accommodation; others suggested that it violates a lawyer's First Amendment rights to force her to accept male clients if doing so runs contrary to her beliefs. Many individuals, however, including some feminists, sided with the Commission on the grounds that lawyers were free to reject clients based on the justness of their causes, but not on the basis of their sex or the color of their skin.[95]

4. Is it unlawful discrimination for a legal employer to assign, or refuse to assign, a lawyer to a particular case on the basis of race, sex, or ethnicity? Consider the decision of prosecutors in the O. J. Simpson case to ensure that at least one prominent member of the team was an African American, and the assignment of a woman prosecutor in the Martha Stewart case to avoid the image of a "man beating up on a woman."[96] What if a client requests a lawyer of a particular race because she believes that will help with a jury, or requests a woman because she is more comfortable talking about the details of domestic abuse or sexual harassment with someone of her own sex?[97]

F. JUDICIAL CONTROLS ON ADVERSARIAL ABUSES

1. FRIVOLOUS LITIGATION

PROBLEM 7

a) You are a partner in a small firm that handles real estate cases, including landlord-tenant cases, some on a pro bono basis. In one eviction

---

95. For discussion of this case, see Deborah L. Rhode, "Can A Lawyer Insist on Clients of One Gender?," *Nat'l L. J.* (Dec. 1, 1997); "Symposium: A Duty to Represent? Critical Reflections on Stropnicky v. Nathanson," 20 *W. New Eng. L. Rev.* 5 (1998); Steve Berenson, "Politics and Plurality in a Lawyer's Choice of Clients: The Case of Stropnicky v. Nathanson," 35 *San Diego L. Rev.* 1 (1998).

96. Laurie P. Cohen, "U.S. Wants 'Gender Card' Out of Stewart Case," *Wall St. J.* 2003, at C1 (quoting jury consultant JoEllen Dimitrius). For the Simpson case, see Christopher A. Darden, *In Contempt* (1996); Margaret M. Russell, "Representing Race: Beyond Sellouts and Race Cards: Black Attor-

neys and the Straightjacket of Legal Practice," 95 *Mich. L. Rev.* 766 (February 1997). See In re Panel File, 597 N.W.2d 563 (Minn. 1999) (prosecutor admonished for moving to prohibit public defender from assigning an African American to try a case based on a memo from his predecessor suggesting that the public defender believed race to be an issue in the case and was planning to recruit an African–American assistant for the trial).

97. Ernest F. Lidge III, "Law Firm Employment Discrimination in Case Assignments at the Client's Insistence: A Bona Fide Occupational Qualification?," 38 *Conn. L. Rev.* 159 (2005).

matter that your firm is handling pro bono, an associate presents pleadings for your signature. Your client is without funds and is two months delinquent in his rent. Unless the court is prepared to overlook a well-established line of cases holding that building code violations are not a defense in suits for non-payment of rent, your client has no chance of success. The associate has prepared a general denial to the complaint and requested a jury trial. This defense strategy, a common practice by local Legal Aid offices, will delay the proceeding for sixty days, during which time the client can save up enough for a security deposit and the first month's rent on another apartment. Your state code of civil procedure contains a rule identical in wording to federal Rule 11. See *infra*. Do you sign the pleading? Would it matter why your client had not paid the rent?

Assume that the trial court finds that building code violations are not a defense in your non-payment of rent case. You believe that the chances that an appellate court will overrule that determination are minimal, but the appointment of two new judges leaves some slight hope. However, your client would like to pursue the appeal, because he will have use of the money pending final judgment. He also hopes that the strategy will impose some appropriate costs on a landlord who is unwilling to repair major defects in his apartment. Do you file the appeal?

b) In another paying case, your client has vacated an expensive apartment in a luxury building. The landlord has withheld the security deposit after a quarrel with your client, and the client wishes to sue for recovery. The security deposit is over the limit for small claims court. Before vacating the apartment the client photographed it, since she suspected that the landlord would withhold her deposit; the pictures show the apartment in good condition. You explain to your client that even though she is likely to win if the case goes to trial, your fee and litigation expenses will together cost her considerably more than she can recover. She insists that she wishes to proceed even if the matter costs her money, since, in her words, "I'm right and he's wrong and I'm going to prove it in public. It's worth it to see him squirm in court."

Your associate drafts the complaint, but appends a memo raising concerns that because the case is clearly a financial loser for the client, the judge will view it either as harassment or as a nuisance suit designed to extract an unjustified settlement. The associate warns that in either eventuality the firm may be sanctioned under the state's version of Rule 11 for undertaking an action merely to harass the landlord. Do you file the complaint?

NOTES: SANCTIONS UNDER FEDERAL RULE 11

Some of the most hotly litigated issues in professional responsibility in the last two decades have arisen from rules in the Federal Rules of Civil Procedure that permit courts to impose sanctions, including financial sanctions, on lawyers and parties who abuse the adversary system. Prominent among these are Rule 26(g), directed at discovery abuse, and Rule 11, directed at meritless claims, defenses and motions.

For decades, Rule 11 was close to a dead letter: between 1950 and 1983, fewer than sixty reported cases involved Rule 11 sanction motions. In 1983, however, the rule was amended to give it longer reach and sharper teeth, and in the ensuing five years almost one thousand Rule 11 cases were reported.[98] The 1983 rule permitted financial sanctions against offending lawyers payable to their adversaries. To aggressive litigators, this was an invitation to move for sanctions as an intimidation tactic. Ironically, a rule designed to curb adversarial excesses quickly morphed into a new source of them. Furthermore, some, although not all, studies suggested that in practice Rule 11 was biased in application: it was invoked three times as often by defendants as by plaintiffs, and some judges seemed more predisposed to think of plaintiffs' filings as meritless and sanctionable than defendants' responses and counter-claims.

In response to these and other difficulties, in 1994 the Rule was again amended. One new feature was a "safe harbor" provision that allowed lawyers or parties to avoid sanction by withdrawing the offending document. This, too, proved to be a handy tool for aggressive litigators, who used the threat of sanctions to intimidate adversaries into withdrawing their pleadings. In December 2007, the Rules Committee again amended Rule 11 by removing the safe harbor provision. The core of the amended Rule reads:

> By presenting to the court a pleading, written motion, or other paper—whether by signing, filing, submitting, or later advocating it—an attorney or unrepresented party certifies that to the best of the person's knowledge, information, and belief, formed after an inquiry reasonable under the circumstances—
>
>> 1) it is not being presented for any improper purpose, such as to harass, cause unnecessary delay, or needlessly increase the cost of litigation;
>>
>> 2) the claims, defenses, and other legal contentions are warranted by existing law or by a nonfrivolous argument for extending, modifying, or reversing existing law or for establishing new law;
>>
>> 3) the factual contentions have evidentiary support or, if specifically so identified, will likely have evidentiary support after a reasonable opportunity for further investigation or discovery; and
>>
>> 4) the denials of factual contentions are warranted on the evidence or, if specifically so identified, are reasonably based on belief or a lack of information.[99]

The rule is directed at three abuses of the litigation process:

---

98. As reported in 4 *ABA/BNA Lawyers' Manual of Professional Conduct* 217 (July 20, 1988). *See also* Herbert M. Kritzer et al., "The Use and Impact of Rule 11," 86 *N.W.U.L.Rev.* 943 (1992).

99. Fed.R.Civ.P. 11(b) (1994).

- presenting a pleading *for an improper purpose* (subsection 1);

- presenting a pleading that is *unwarranted by law* (subsection 2); and

- presenting a pleading that makes or denies *factual claims* without appropriate support (subsections 3 and 4). By signing, filing, submitting, or later advocating the claim, an attorney or party certifies that he has made a reasonable inquiry into the factual and legal basis of the claim.

Moreover, the Committee Notes to the rule explain that an attorney may be sanctioned for "insisting on a position after it is no longer tenable." Thus, if subsequent research or factual investigation reveals that the claim is insufficiently supported by law or fact, even though reasonable inquiry at the time of filing did not reveal the insufficiency, the attorney must withdraw the claim or face sanctions. Typically, an adversary will move for Rule 11 sanctions, but a court can order sanctions on its own initiative. Several other features of the rule are worth noting:

First, sanctions are discretionary—courts need not sanction lawyers who violate the rule.

Second, "A sanction imposed under this rule must be limited to what suffices to deter repetition of the conduct or comparable conduct by others similarly situated. The sanction may include nonmonetary directives; an order to pay a penalty into court; or, if imposed on motion and warranted for effective deterrence, an order directing payment to the movant of part or all of the reasonable attorney's fees and other expenses directly resulting from the violation." Fed.R.Civ.P. 11(c)(4) (2007).

Third, Rule 11(c)(1)(A) provides that "[a]bsent special circumstances, a law firm shall be held jointly responsible for violations committed by its partners, associates, and employees."

Fourth, clause (2) (quoted *supra*) requires that pleadings be warranted by law or by "a nonfrivolous argument for extending, modifying, or reversing existing law or for establishing new law." The word *nonfrivolous*, the Committee Notes explain, makes it clear that the standard is objective, so attorneys' sincere but unreasonable beliefs in the plausibility of their claims will not satisfy the rule. This eliminates the so-called "empty head, pure heart" defense to sanctions.

Fifth, the rule permits so-called "fishing expeditions," where a plaintiff alleges wrongdoing without much evidence, but hopes to develop the evidence through the discovery process. Clearly, there is some point to forbidding such expeditions. A striking example of abuse is *Kinee v. Abraham Lincoln Fed. Sav. and Loan Ass'n.*, 365 F.Supp. 975, 982–83 (E.D.Pa.1973), in which a group of homeowners sued mortgage lenders over an allegedly improper method of mortgage collection. To learn which lenders employed this method, plaintiffs' lawyers named as defendants all 177 mortgage brokers listed in the Philadelphia telephone book, provoking a sanction under the older version of Rule 11.

To most commentators and courts, however, a categorical prohibition on fishing expeditions seemed excessively harsh, particularly in actions where a plaintiff is required to show that the defendant knew or was aware of certain facts, or that the defendant had engaged in a conspiracy. These include securities fraud, antitrust, RICO, and employment discrimination cases. Often, the plaintiff will need some kind of "smoking gun" from the defendant's own files. In such cases, the crucial evidence can be found only through discovery after the complaint has been filed. The current version of Rule 11 recognizes these difficulties, and requires only that filings "have evidentiary support or, if specifically so identified, are likely to have evidentiary support after a reasonable opportunity for further investigation or discovery."

Some observers believe that the current version of Rule 11 does to little to curb abuse. In both 2004 and 2005, the House of Representatives approved the Lawsuit Reduction Act, which would require courts to impose sanctions against attorneys found to have filed a frivolous lawsuit or legal pleading. No similar bill reached the Senate, and surveyed federal judges dispute the need for the measure. Eighty-five percent report that groundless litigation is "no more than a small problem in their courtrooms."[100]

The language of Rule 11 parallels and to an extent replicates the language of the bar ethical codes. Model Rule 3.1 explicitly enjoins a lawyer from "frivolous" actions, and defines frivolity in language nearly identical to Rule 11: "A lawyer shall not bring or defend a proceeding, or assert or controvert an issue therein, unless there is a basis for doing so that is not frivolous, which includes a good faith argument for an extension, modification or reversal of existing law."[101]

In addition to Rule 11, courts have other statutory and procedural provisions to deter abuse. For example, under 28 U.S.C. § 1927, an attorney who multiplies proceedings unreasonably and vexatiously may be required to pay the costs and attorneys' fees that result from such conduct. Federal Rule of Civil Procedure 37 provides for sanctions against unjustified resistance of discovery, and Rules 16 and 26 seek to deter abuse through judicial management of pretrial proceedings. Under its inherent power, a court may also award reasonable attorneys' fees for bad faith litigation conduct. *Chambers v. NASCO, Inc.*, 501 U.S. 32 (1991).

A crucial issue in the interpretation of Rule 11 concerns its underlying policy. Is it intended primarily to keep frivolous cases out of court? Or is it intended primarily to prevent lawyers from employing frivolous claims in

---

100. "Federal Judges See No Need for Legislation to Address Frivolous Lawsuits, Survey Finds," 21 *ABA/BNA Lawyers Manual of Professional Conduct* 214 (2005).

101. Similarly, DR 7–102(A)(1) states: "[I]n his representation of a client, a lawyer shall not file a suit, assert a position, conduct a defense, delay a trial, or take other action on behalf of his client when he knows or when it is obvious that such action would serve merely to harass or maliciously injure another." DR 7–102(A)(2) continues: "[I]n his representation of a client, a lawyer shall not knowingly advance a claim or defense that is unwarranted under existing law, except that he may advance such claim or defense if it can be supported by good faith argument for an extension, modification, or reversal of existing law."

cases that might not themselves be frivolous? How much of courts' concern involves their own caseloads; how much involves expense, delay and unfairness for parties; and how much involves the ethics of the bar? These policy questions bear on how to interpret Rule 11's requirement that legal positions must be backed by nonfrivolous legal arguments. Does this requirement mean that the lawyers must actually make the good faith arguments, or does it mean only that such arguments exist (whether or not the lawyers made them)? Courts have divided on that issue.[102] If the rule is meant as an ethics regulation, the arguments the lawyers actually made are the ones that matter. If, on the other hand, the purpose of Rule 11 is to keep frivolous cases out of court, then sanctions should not apply if nonfrivolous arguments exist for the legal position, regardless of whether the lawyers actually made those arguments.

Frequently courts address the related issue of whether a party that offers both frivolous and nonfrivolous arguments for a position should be sanctioned. Some judges believe that withholding sanctions "would allow a party with one or more patently meritorious claims to pepper his complaint with one or more highly advantageous, yet wholly frivolous, claims." *Cross & Cross Properties v. Everett Allied Co.*, 886 F.2d 497, 505 (2d Cir.1989). Other courts hold that as long as a party can make some nonfrivolous claim, no Rule 11 or ethical violation has occurred. What is your view?

Is a Rule 11 violation automatically a violation of professional ethics as well? Should every Rule 11 sanction be accompanied by a disciplinary referral?

Does a lawyer's failure to disclose adverse legal authority in a legal paper violate Rule 11? A well-known Ninth Circuit opinion answers in the negative: "neither Rule 11 nor any other rule imposes a requirement that the lawyer, in addition to advocating the cause of his client, step first into the shoes of opposing counsel to find all potentially contrary authority, and finally into the robes of the judge to decide whether the authority is indeed contrary or whether it is distinguishable. It is not in the nature of our adversary system to require lawyers to demonstrate to the court that they have exhausted every theory, both for and against their client."[103]

In fact, however, Model Rule 3.3(a)(2) states, "A lawyer shall not knowingly fail to disclose to the tribunal legal authority in the controlling jurisdiction known to the lawyer to be directly adverse to the position of the client and not disclosed by opposing counsel." What policy would justify this rule?

---

102. International Shipping Co., S.A. v. Hydra Offshore, Inc., 875 F.2d 388 (2d Cir. 1989), In re Ronco, 838 F.2d 212, 218 (7th Cir.1988), Thornton v. Wahl, 787 F.2d 1151, 1154 (7th Cir.1986) (sanctions imposed for not identifying argument as one for the extension or modification of existing law), and Hill v. Norfolk & W. Ry. Co., 814 F.2d 1192, 1198 (7th Cir.1987) (upholding sanctions for neglecting contrary authority), DeSisto College, Inc. v. Line, 888 F.2d 755, 766 (11th Cir.1989). *See* Ellen P. Quackenbos, "Rule 11 and Papers not Warranted By Law," 58 *Fordham L.Rev.* 1085 (1990).

103. Golden Eagle Distributing Corp. v. Burroughs Corp., 801 F.2d 1531, 1541–42 (9th Cir. 1986).

QUESTIONS: FRIVOLITY AND HARASSMENT

It is not at all obvious what constitutes a frivolous legal argument. As many commentators note, "[t]oday's frivolity may be tomorrow's law, and the law often grows by an organic process in which a concept is conceived, then derided as absurd (and clearly not the law), then accepted as theoretically tenable (though not the law), then accepted as the law."[104] Imposing sanctions for frivolity may interrupt this organic process of growth by discouraging lawyers from venturing theories that will one day work their way into the law. Monroe Freedman notes that: "Depending on how one counts the cases, the Supreme Court has overruled its own decisions 200 to more than 300 times. On at least sixteen occasions, this has happened within three years. At other times, the most venerable of precedents have fallen, including at least ten cases that were overruled after as many as 94 to 126 years."[105]

1.   In *Plessy v. Ferguson,* 163 U.S. 537 (1896), the Supreme Court upheld racial segregation. Could a lawyer have made a nonfrivolous argument that *Plessy* should be reversed one year after it was decided? Clearly such an argument would be wasting the Court's time, at least in the sense that the outcome would be a foregone conclusion. Would such an argument therefore be frivolous? What if the lawyer sincerely believed that *Plessy* was wrongly decided and that his case had a stronger factual record concerning the harms of "separate but equal"?

2.   Suppose the lawyer had waited three years, during which time new Justices were appointed. If Rule 11 had been in effect, should sanctions have been imposed? If not, does that suggest that a legal argument can be sanctioned as frivolous if it is presented before an unsympathetic judge but not before a sympathetic judge? Does this hypothetical case differ from *Brown v. Board of Education,* which overturned *Plessy* in 1954, in any respect other than the passage of time?

If, on the other hand, you believe that an argument to reverse *Plessy* would not have been frivolous even in 1897, do you also believe that an argument to reverse *any* case immediately after its decision can be offered in good faith? What would then become of the principles of *res judicata* and *stare decisis*? Consider the implications for overburdened courts and underfinanced opponents.

3.   Federal Judge Frank Easterbrook has suggested that "something is frivolous only when (a) we've decided the very point, and recently, against the person reasserting it, or (b) 99 of 100 practicing lawyers would be 99% sure that the position is untenable, and the other 1% would be 60% sure it's untenable."[106] How would you assess this suggestion?

---

104.   D. Michael Risinger, "Honesty in Pleading and Its Enforcement: Some 'Striking' Problems with Federal Rule of Civil Procedure 11," 61 *Minn.L.Rev.* 1, 57 (1976).

105.   Monroe H. Freedman, "The Professional Obligation to Raise Frivolous Issues In Death Penalty Cases," 31 *Hofstra L. Rev.* 1167 (2006).

106.   *Quoted in* Sanford Levinson, "Frivolous Cases: Do Lawyers Really Know Anything at All?" 24 *Osgoode Hall L.Rev.* 353, 375 (1987).

4.   Rule 11 forbids lawyers and parties from filing paper for such improper purposes as delay, harassment, or unnecessarily raising the costs of litigation. Arguably, however, *every* paper filed in a lawsuit imposes some delay and harassment on the adversary: a response costs time, money, and annoyance. Moreover, every skilled trial lawyer considers the tactical effects as well as the legal merits of papers filed in a lawsuit. For this reason, the "improper purpose" prong of Rule 11 has universally been understood to forbid only filings that have no colorable justification other than delay, harassment, or imposition of costs. Sanctionable conduct may include pleadings frivolous on either the law or the facts, but these filings are independently forbidden by the other prongs of Rule 11(b). If frivolous claims were the only filings forbidden by the "improper purpose" prong, it would be unnecessary.

One possible kind of filing that is nonfrivolous on the law and facts but nevertheless has no colorably proper purpose is a paper that asserts a genuine legal claim, but that confers no tangible advantage on the party that files it. For example, a complaint requesting damages that are less than the minimum costs of going to trial would, on this interpretation, be interposed for an improper purpose. The justification for reading the rule this way would be that the plaintiff is using the court, a scarce public resource, merely to work off a grudge. A response might be that parties should be entitled to go to court to establish a principle, not just to secure financial gain. But what if the party's overriding motive is to punish the adversary, not vindicate some important right?

Should courts ever interpret Rule 11(b)(1) as a prohibition on filings whose economic costs outweigh their anticipated benefits? Under what circumstances, if any, should courts sanction parties that are willing to sacrifice money in order to make a legal point? What constitutes an "improper purpose" under Rule 11? Will the difference between vindictiveness and vindication often lie in the eye of the beholder?[107] If so, what follows from that fact?

2.   Discovery Abuse

PROBLEM 8

You are an associate in a firm representing the defendant Fisons, a drug manufacturer, in a products liability case. The defendant marketed a drug, Somophyllin Oral Liquid, used to treat viral infections. An excess of its active ingredient, theophylline, caused seizures and brain damage to the infant daughter of the plaintiffs. They sued the doctor and Fisons, and the doctor cross-claimed against Fisons. His insurance company, which is prosecuting the claim, initially sought discovery of all documents related to Somophyllin as well as theophylline. Your firm objected on the ground that the request was "overly broad, unduly burdensome, harassing, and not

---

107.   For examples of the difficulty, see Deborah L. Rhode, "Frivolous Cases and Civil Justice Reform: Misconceiving the Prob- lem, Recasting the Solution," 54 *Duke L. J.* 447 (2004).

reasonably calculated to lead to the discovery of admissible evidence." You agreed instead to turn over documents related only to Somophyllin. After discovery has proceeded for a considerable period, you discover documents relating to theophyllline toxicity in a file for another drug, Intal, which Fisons also markets. The supervising partner does not believe that the documents need to be disclosed, because the plaintiff did not move to compel production of documents other than those concerning Somophyllin. How should you proceed?

b.   You are a managing partner in a firm representing a plaintiff construction company in a products liability case. Your client alleges defects in the defendant's steel manufacturing process which, if proven, could expose the corporation to extensive liability in subsequent suits by other customers. Accordingly, the defendant is waging a war of attrition in the hopes of convincing your client and any other potential plaintiffs that their costs in trying the case would exceed any likely recovery. To that end, the defendants have:

1) made repeated requests to extend the date for compliance with subpoenas, refused your good faith requests to reschedule depositions, and produced an ostensibly "misfiled" document only when confronted by a reference to the document in an inadvertently disclosed attachment;

2) responded to discovery requests by bombarding you with every remotely relevant document and, in one instance, referring you to thousands of pages of material that contained only one reference of even tangential relevance.

3) referred to one of your female associates as "babycakes."

Lawyers for your firm have determined that the court is unlikely to impose meaningful sanctions for such conduct, and have decided instead to respond in kind. The trial team has:

4) deposed opposing witnesses on the most peripheral possible matters in the most inconvenient possible locations;

5) reminded witnesses that "I don't recall" is a response that generally avoids the risks of disclosure or prosecution for perjury;

6) filed answers to interrogatories that are technically accurate but not responsive to the stated question.

The client has now objected to the escalating costs of discovery and accused your firm of meter-running. They insist that you reduce your own fees substantially. How should the firm proceed? Should it have handled the discovery phases differently?

If the firm now moves for sanctions and opponents respond with a cross-motion for sanctions, how should the court rule? What further facts would be relevant to the court's decision? In determining whether you or your opponents have engaged in sanctionable practices, should it matter who "started it"? Should any of the attorneys be personally subject to liability? Should the ethics of your firms discovery tactics be relevant in any subsequent disputes with the client over fees?

References: Model Rules 1.5, 3.1, 3.2. See also Model Rule 3.4.[108]

NOTES: DISCOVERY ABUSE

One of the primary purposes of discovery, according to the United States Supreme Court, is to assure "[m]utual knowledge of all the relevant facts gathered by both parties [that] is essential to proper litigation."[109] It is instructive to compare this characterization with a Chicago litigator's candid description of the aims of discovery: "The purpose of discovery . . . is to give as little as possible so [your opponents] will have to come back and back and maybe will go away or give up."[110] Civil discovery is intended to enhance the search for truth in adversary litigation and to eliminate surprise tactics by allowing lawyers access to facts in the possession of their adversaries. But, as the litigator's cynical description indicates, the discovery process is often abused for tactical reasons, and many litigators agree with then federal judge Marvin E. Frankel that discovery has become an occasion for "beating plowshares into swords"—turning a rule intended to control adversarial excess into an adversarial weapon in its own right.[111]

One common abuse includes overdiscovery and its complement, overproduction of information in response to discovery. As one lawyer put it: "Discovery is trial by avalanche of documents. . . . I bombard opponents with mounds of information and see if they will wade through it."[112] Both of these tactics serve multiple purposes: they distract opponents by mixing useful information with irrelevancies, they burden the adversaries—attorneys and clients—with exhausting and annoying work, and they impose economic pressures as well.

Many lawyers and judges believe that discovery abuse is a problem, at least in high-stakes litigation, and incivility is too common in all areas of practice. They complain of "antics with semantics," such as "hypertechnical" definitions of words used in discovery requests as a method for withholding obviously discoverable information, refusing to come to any agreements with opposing counsel concerning discovery . . . and scheduling depositions and hearings at times he knows are terribly inconvenient for opposing counsel and his client.[113]

It is important to notice, however, that much of the evidence for widespread discovery abuse is less than rigorous: it comes from anecdotes, war stories, the personal impressions of lawyers and judges, and opinion

---

108. For the "babycakes," reference, see Amy Gardner, "What Were They Thinking?," *Litigation,* Winter–Spring, 2005, 1.

109. Hickman v. Taylor, 329 U.S. 495, 507 (1947).

110. Quoted in Wayne D. Brazil, "Civil Discovery: Lawyers' Views of Its Effectiveness, Its Principal Problems and Abuses," 1980 *Am.B.Found.Res.J.* 789, 829.

111. Marvin E. Frankel, *Partisan Justice* 18 (1980).

112. Brazil, supra note 102, at 854.

113. Alex W. Albright, "Waging Unconditional Warfare: An Exasperated Court Speaks its Mind," *Tex.Law.,* Sept. 5, 1988, at 18, col. 1. *See* sources summarized in Rhode, *supra* note 33, at 83–84; Allen K. Harris, "Increasing Ethics, Professionalism, and Civility: Key to Preserving the American Common Law and Adversarial Systems," *2005 Professional Lawyer* 92.

polls of professionals. Professor Linda S. Mullenix has argued that discovery abuse is largely a myth, unsupported by any rigorous quantitative study, and spread by civil justice "reformers" who have an anti-litigation political agenda.[114] The most systematic studies find that serious discovery abuse is largely confined to a minority of cases, particularly high-stakes matters in large legal communities that lack informal sanctions and significant judicial oversight. The amount of time lawyers spend on discovery is low in the majority of cases, and in most cases discovery is not a major contributor to litigation cost.[115] However, in many other cases, adversaries engage in more modest forms of incivility and distortion that obstruct the dispute resolution process.[116]

Problem 8a is based on *Washington State Physicians Insurance Exchange & Association v. Fisons Corp.*, 858 P.2d 1054 (Wash. 1993). There, a smoking gun document on toxicity came to light when a whistleblower within the company sent it to one of the plaintiffs. The Washington Supreme Court concluded that, given the way defense counsel Bogle & Gates had chosen to narrow and then interpret the discovery requests, "It appears clear that no conceivable discovery request could have been made by the doctor that would have uncovered the relevant documents." In the court's view, Bogle and Gates failure to produce documents should be sanctioned because it was "misleading" and "contrary to the purposes of discovery and the fairness of the litigation process." After that decision, the firm settled the sanctions case for $325,000, one of the highest penalties ever reported at the time. The litigation was settled for 6.9 million. The case prompted a cover story in *The American Lawyer* (April 1994) titled "Sleazy in Seattle."

Is discovery manipulation the occupational disease of litigators, or is it their occupation? Bogle & Gates had fourteen prominent litigation experts testify on its behalf in the sanctions hearing, including Professor Geoffrey Hazard, Jr., the nation's most well-known legal ethics commentator. These experts testified that interpreting discovery requests narrowly and technically to avoid turning over inculpating documents was "typical" and "proper;" indeed, several claimed that it was required by lawyers "ethical obligation to zealously represent their client."

In commenting on the *Fisons* case, Monroe Freedman asked a key question:

114. Linda S. Mullenix, "Discovery in Disarray: The Pervasive Myth of Pervasive Discovery Abuse and the Consequences for Unfounded Rulemaking," 46 *Stan.L.Rev.* 1393 (1994); Mullenix, "The Pervasive Myth of Pervasive Discovery Abuse: The Sequel," 39 *B.C. L. Rev.* 683 (1998).

115. Mullenix, "Pervasive Myth," *supra* note 106, at 684, discussing James S. Kakalik et al., "Discovery Management: Further Analysis of the Civil Justice Reform Act Evaluation Data," 39 *B.C. L. Rev.* 613 (1998)—a study by the RAND Corporation.

116. These problems vary according to the legal and judicial culture that prevails. For example, a quarter of Boston litigators surveyed felt that the discovery process worked well, compared with three quarters of those in Kansas City. James S. Kakalik, et al., *Discovery Management: Further Analysis of the Civil Justice Reform Act Evaluation Data* 55 (1998); Susan Keilitz, et al., "Attorneys' Views of Civil Discovery," *Judges J.*, Winter, 1993, 2–6, 34–35. On incivilities and minor problems, see Rhode, *supra* note 33, at 82–96, and Harris, *supra* note 105.

What does this [consensus among experts] tell us? It tells us that lawyers throughout the bar (including those who later became judges) had known for decades that discovery rules were being systematically frustrated by disingenuous responses to discovery demands. It tells us that the Washington Supreme Court was itself being disingenuous in pronouncing itself shocked that such things were going on.[117]

If the legal ethics experts were correct about normal practice, how should this figure in litigators' decisions and in courts' interpretation of discovery rules. Were the legal ethics experts suggesting that if everybody engages in misleading conduct, that is acceptable practice? Consider the observation of Robert Aronson, a Seattle law professor who supported sanctions: "there were kids out there dying because [Fisons's lawyers and managers] were hiding information so they could win a lawsuit."[118]

Two years after the *Fisons* case, a federal judge sanctioned Bogle & Gates for a similar discovery violation. Representing Subaru of America, Bogle & Gates responded to a discovery request by claiming that certain records did not exist. When later depositions showed that they did in fact exist, Bogle & Gates was ordered to pay the other side's legal fees.[119] In 1998, Bogle & Gates dissolved, although the reasons were not directly connected with the sanctions cases.

A recent widely publicized case represents a judicial effort to discourage the kind of conduct reflected in *Fisons*.

Qualcomm Inc. v. Broadcom Corp.

U.S. District Court, S.D. Cal., 2008.
2008 WL 66932.

■ Barbara L. Major, United States Magistrate Judge.

ORDER GRANTING IN PART AND DENYING IN PART DEFENDANT'S MOTION FOR SANCTIONS AND SANCTIONING QUALCOMM, INCORPORATED AND INDIVIDUAL LAWYERS

At the conclusion of trial, counsel for Broadcom Corporation ("Broadcom") made an oral motion for sanctions after Qualcomm Incorporated ("Qualcomm") witness Viji Raveendran testified about emails that were not produced to Broadcom during discovery. The trial judge, United States District Court Judge Rudi M. Brewster, referred the motion to this Court. . . .

Having considered all of the written and oral arguments presented and supporting documents submitted, and for the reasons set forth more fully below, the Court GRANTS IN PART and DENIES IN PART Broadcom's

117. Monroe H. Freedman, "Masking the Truth to Resolve Competing Duties," *Legal Times*, Sept. 11, 1996, at 22.

118. Robert Aronson, quoted in Ralph Nader & Wesley J. Smith, *No Contest* 126 (1996).

119. Alex Fryer, "Clout of State's Big Law Firms Wards Off Misconduct Cases," *Seattle Times*, May 3, 1998, at F1.

motion for sanctions against Qualcomm, REFERS TO THE STATE BAR OF CALIFORNIA six attorneys, and SANCTIONS Qualcomm and six of its retained lawyers.

BACKGROUND

[Qualcomm is a telecommunications company, while Broadcom is a manufacturer of integrated circuits for broadband communications. In 2005, Qualcomm sued Broadcom for patent infringement "based on its manufacture, sale, and offers to sell H.264—compliant products." H. 264 is an industry standard for video coding. The two patents in question are called the 104 and 767 patents. Broadcom responded that Qualcomm had waived its right to enforce the patents by participating in the Joint Video Team (JVT), the standards-setting body that created the H.264 standard. As the court explains, "if Qualcomm had participated in the creation of the H.264 standard, it would have been required to identify its patents that reasonably may be essential to the practice of the H.264 standard, including the 104 and 767 patents, and to license them royalty-free or under non-discriminatory, reasonable terms. Thus, participation in the JVT in 2002 or early 2003 during the creation of the H.264 standard would have prohibited Qualcomm from suing companies, including Broadcom, that utilized the H.264 standard."]

B.   Evidence of Qualcomm's Participation in the JVT

Over the course of discovery, Broadcom sought information concerning Qualcomm's participation in and communications with the JVT through a variety of discovery devices. For example, as early as January 23, 2006, Broadcom served its First Set of Requests for the Production of Documents and Things, in which it requested:

> [a]ll documents given to or received from a standards setting body or group that concern any standard relating to the processing of digital video signals that pertains in any way to any Qualcomm Patent, including without limitation communications, proposals, presentations, agreements, commitments, or contracts to or from such bodies? [and]

> [a]ll documents concerning any Qualcomm membership, participation, interaction, and/or involvement in setting any standard relating to the processing of digital video signals that pertains in any way to any Qualcomm Patent. This request also covers all proposed or potential standards, whether or not actually adopted.

>   . . .

Broadcom also requested similar information via interrogatories and multiple . . . deposition notices. . . . On their face, Qualcomm's written discovery responses did not appear unusual. In response to Broadcom's request for JVT documents, Qualcomm, in a discovery response signed by attorney Kevin Leung, stated "Qualcomm will produce non-privileged relevant and responsive documents describing QUALCOMM's participation in the JVT, if any, which can be located after a reasonable search." Similarly, Qualcomm committed to producing "responsive non-privileged documents that were given to or received from standards-setting body responsible for the ... standard, and which concern any Qualcomm participation in setting the ... standard." ...

[Broadcom's counsel had obtained a December 2002 email list of JVT participants (entitled avc_ce) on which was the email address of a Qualcomm employee, Raveendran.]

As the case progressed, Qualcomm became increasingly aggressive in its argument that it did not participate in the JVT during the time the JVT was creating the H.264 standard. . . .

C.   Trial and Decision Not to Produce avc_ce Emails

Trial commenced on January 9, 2007, and throughout trial, Qualcomm argued that it had not participated in the JVT in 2002 and early 2003 when the H.264 standard was being created. . . .

While preparing Qualcomm witness Viji Raveendran to testify at trial, attorney Adam Bier discovered an August 6, 2002 email to viji@qualcomm. com welcoming her to the avc_ce mailing list [a list of JVT participants]. Several days later, on January 14, 2007, Bier and Raveendran searched her laptop computer using the search term "avc_ce" and discovered 21 separate emails, none of which Qualcomm had produced in discovery. The email chains bore several dates in November 2002 and the authors discussed various issues relating to the H.264 standard. . . . The Qualcomm trial team decided not to produce these newly discovered emails to Broadcom, claiming they were not responsive to Broadcom's discovery requests. The attorneys ignored the fact that the presence of the emails on Raveendran's computer undercut Qualcomm's premier argument that it had not participated in the JVT in 2002. The Qualcomm trial team failed to conduct any investigation to determine whether there were more emails that also had not been produced.

Four days later, during a sidebar discussion, Stanley Young argued against the admission of the December 2002 avc_ce email reflector list, declaring: "Actually, there are no emails—there are no emails ... there's no evidence that any email was actually sent to this list. This is just a list of email ... addresses. There's no evidence of anything being sent." None of the Qualcomm attorneys who were present during the sidebar mentioned the 21 avc_ce emails found on Raveendran's computer a few days earlier. During Raveendran's direct testimony on January 24th, attorney Lee Patch pointedly did not ask her any questions that would reveal the fact that she had received the 21 emails from the avc_ce mailing list; instead, he asked whether she had "any knowledge of having read" any emails from the avc_ce mailing list. But on cross-examination, Broadcom asked the right question and Raveendran was forced to admit that she had received emails from the avc_ce mailing list. . . .

... On January 26, 2007, the jury returned unanimous verdicts in favor of Broadcom regarding the non-infringement of the 104 and 767 patents. . . .

... After a thorough overview of the JVT, the JVT's policies and guidelines, and Qualcomm's knowledge of the JVT and evidence of Qualcomm's involvement therein, Judge Brewster found:

> by clear and convincing evidence that Qualcomm, its employees, and its witnesses actively organized and/or participated in a plan to profit heavily by (1) wrongfully concealing the patents-in-suit while participating in the JVT and then (2) actively hiding this concealment from the Court, the jury, and opposing counsel during the present litigation.

Judge Brewster further found that Qualcomm's "counsel participated in an organized program of litigation misconduct and concealment throughout discovery, trial, and post-trial before new counsel took over lead role in the case on April 27, 2007." Based on "the totality of the evidence produced both before and after the jury verdict," and in light of these findings, Judge Brewster concluded that "Qualcomm has waived its rights to enforce the 104 and 767 patents and their continuations, continuations-in-part, divisions, reissues, or any other derivatives of either patent."

Also on August 6, 2007, Judge Brewster granted Broadcom's Motion for an Award of Attorneys' Fees pursuant to 35 U.S.C. § 285. Judge Brewster found clear and convincing evidence that Qualcomm's litigation misconduct ... justified Qualcomm's payment of all "attorneys' fees, court costs, expert witness fees, travel expenses, and any other litigation costs reasonably incurred by Broadcom" in the defense of this case. On December 11, 2007, Judge Brewster adopted this court's recommendation and ordered Qualcomm to pay Broadcom $9,259,985.09 in attorneys' fees and related costs, as well as post-judgment interest on the final fee award of $8,568,633.24 at 4.91 percent accruing from August 6, 2007.

D. Qualcomm's Post–Trial Misconduct

Following trial, Qualcomm continued to dispute the relevancy and responsiveness of the 21 Raveendran emails. Qualcomm also resisted Broadcom's efforts to determine the scope of Qualcomm's discovery violation. . . .

But, on April 9, 2007, James Batchelder and Louis Lupin, Qualcomm's General Counsel, submitted correspondence to Judge Brewster in which they admitted Qualcomm had thousands of relevant unproduced documents and that their review of these documents "revealed facts that appear to be inconsistent with certain arguments that [counsel] made on Qualcomm's behalf at trial and in the equitable hearing following trial." Batchelder further apologized "for not having discovered these documents sooner and for asserting positions that [they] would not have taken had [they] known of the existence of these documents."

As of June 29, 2007, Qualcomm had searched the email archives of twenty-one employees and located more than forty-six thousand documents (totaling more than three hundred thousand pages), which had been requested but not produced in discovery. Qualcomm continued to produce additional responsive documents throughout the summer.

DISCUSSION

. . .

A.   Legal Standard

The Federal Civil Rules authorize federal courts to impose sanctions on parties and their attorneys who fail to comply with discovery obligations and court orders. Rule 37 authorizes a party to file a motion to compel an opponent to comply with a discovery request or obligation when the opponent fails to do so initially. If such a motion is filed, the rule requires the court to award reasonable attorney's fees to the prevailing party unless the court finds the losing party's position was "substantially justified" or other circumstances make such an award unjust. Depending upon the circumstances, the court may require the attorney, the client, or both to pay the awarded fees. If the court grants a discovery motion and the losing party fails to comply with the order, the court may impose additional sanctions against the party. Fed. R. Civ. P. 37 (b). There is no requirement under this rule that the failure be willful or reckless; "sanctions may be imposed even for negligent failures to provide discovery."

The Federal Rules also provide for sanctions against individual attorneys who are remiss in complying with their discovery obligations:

> [e]very discovery request, response or objection made by a party . . . shall be signed by at least one attorney [and] [t]he signature of the attorney . . . constitutes a certification that to the best of the signer's knowledge, information, and belief, formed after a reasonable inquiry, the request, response, or objection is: consistent with the rules and law, not interposed for an improper purpose, and not unreasonable or unduly burdensome or expensive.

Fed. R. Civ. P. 26 (g)(2). . . .

If an attorney makes an incorrect certification without substantial justification, the court must sanction the attorney, party, or both and the sanction may include an award of reasonable attorney's fees. . . .

In addition to this rule-based authority, federal courts have the inherent power to sanction litigants to prevent abuse of the judicial process. . . .

B.   Broadcom Did Not File a Motion to Compel Discovery

As summarized above, Broadcom served interrogatories and requested documents relating to Qualcomm's participation in the JVT. Qualcomm responded that "Qualcomm will produce non-privileged relevant and responsive documents describing QUALCOMM's participation in the JVT, if any, which can be located after a reasonable search." Qualcomm also committed to producing "responsive non-privileged documents that were given to or received from standards-setting body responsible for the [H.264] standard, and which concern any Qualcomm participation in setting the [H.264] standard."

Despite these responses, Qualcomm did not produce over 46,000 responsive documents, many of which directly contradict the non-participation argument that Qualcomm repeatedly made to the court and jury. Because Qualcomm agreed to produce the documents and answered the interrogatories (even though falsely), Broadcom had no reason to file a motion to compel.[4] And, because Broadcom did not file a motion to compel, Broadcom's possible remedies are restricted. If Broadcom had filed a motion to compel, it could have obtained sanctions against Qualcomm and its attorneys. Because Broadcom did not file a motion to compel, it may only seek Rule 37 sanctions against Qualcomm. Fed. R. Civ. P. 37(c). Thus, Qualcomm's suppression of documents placed its retained attorneys in a better legal position than they would have been in if Qualcomm had refused to produce the documents and Broadcom had filed a motion to compel.

. . .

C. Sanctions

The Court's review of Qualcomm's declarations, the attorneys' declarations, and Judge Brewster's orders lead this Court to the inevitable conclusion that Qualcomm intentionally withheld tens of thousands of decisive documents from its opponent in an effort to win this case and gain a strategic business advantage over Broadcom. Qualcomm could not have achieved this goal without some type of assistance or deliberate ignorance from its retained attorneys. Accordingly, the Court concludes it must sanction both Qualcomm and some of its retained attorneys.

. . .

2. Attorneys' Misconduct

The next question is what, if any, role did Qualcomm's retained lawyers play in withholding the documents? The Court envisions four scenarios. First, Qualcomm intentionally hid the documents from its retained lawyers and did so so effectively that the lawyers did not know or suspect that the suppressed documents existed. Second, the retained lawyers failed to discover the intentionally hidden documents or suspect their existence due to their complete ineptitude and disorganization. Third, Qualcomm shared the damaging documents with its retained lawyers (or at least some of them) and the knowledgeable lawyers worked with Qualcomm to hide the documents and all evidence of Qualcomm's early involvement in the JVT. Or, fourth, while Qualcomm did not tell the retained lawyers about the damaging documents and evidence, the lawyers suspected there was additional evidence or information but chose to ignore the evidence

---

4. Qualcomm attempts to capitalize on this failure, arguing "Broadcom never raised any concern regarding the scope of documents Qualcomm agreed to produce in response to Request No. 50, and never filed a motion to compel concerning this request. Accordingly, there is no order compelling Qualcomm to respond more fully to it." Qualcomm made the same argument with regard to its other discovery responses. This argument is indicative of the gamesmanship Qualcomm engaged in throughout this litigation. Why should Broadcom file a motion to compel when Qualcomm agreed to produce the documents? What would the court have compelled: Qualcomm to do what it already said it would do? Should all parties file motions to compel to preserve their rights in case the other side hides documents?

and warning signs and accept Qualcomm's incredible assertions regarding the adequacy of the document search and witness investigation.

Given the impressive education and extensive experience of Qualcomm's retained lawyers, the Court rejects the first and second possibilities. It is inconceivable that these talented, well-educated, and experienced lawyers failed to discover through their interactions with Qualcomm any facts or issues that caused (or should have caused) them to question the sufficiency of Qualcomm's document search and production. Qualcomm did not fail to produce a document or two; it withheld over 46,000 critical documents that extinguished Qualcomm's primary argument of non-participation in the JVT. In addition, the suppressed documents did not belong to one employee, or a couple of employees who had since left the company; they belonged to (or were shared with) numerous, current Qualcomm employees, several of whom testified (falsely) at trial and in depositions. Given the volume and importance of the withheld documents, the number of involved Qualcomm employees, and the numerous warning flags, the Court finds it unbelievable that the retained attorneys did not know or suspect that Qualcomm had not conducted an adequate search for documents.

The Court finds no direct evidence establishing option three. Neither party nor the attorneys have presented evidence that Qualcomm told one or more of its retained attorneys about the damaging emails or that an attorney learned about the emails and that the knowledgeable attorney(s) then helped Qualcomm hide the emails. While knowledge may be inferred from the attorneys' conduct, evidence on this issue is limited due to Qualcomm's assertion of the attorney-client privilege.[8]

Thus, the Court finds it likely that some variation of option four occurred; that is, one or more of the retained lawyers chose not to look in the correct locations for the correct documents, to accept the unsubstantiated assurances of an important client that its search was sufficient, to ignore the warning signs that the document search and production were inadequate, not to press Qualcomm employees for the truth, and/or to encourage employees to provide the information (or lack of information) that Qualcomm needed to assert its non-participation argument and to succeed in this lawsuit. These choices enabled Qualcomm to withhold hundreds of thousands of pages of relevant discovery and to assert numer-

---

8. Qualcomm asserted the attorney-client privilege and decreed that its retained attorneys could not reveal any communications protected by the privilege. Several attorneys complained that the assertion of the privilege prevented them from providing additional information regarding their conduct. This concern was heightened when Qualcomm submitted its self-serving declarations describing the failings of its retained lawyers. Recognizing that a client has a right to maintain this privilege and that no adverse inference should be made based upon the assertion, the Court accepted Qualcomm's assertion of the privilege and has not drawn any adverse inferences from it. However, the fact remains that the Court does not have access to all of the information necessary to reach an informed decision regarding the actual knowledge of the attorneys. As a result, the Court concludes for purposes of this Order that there is insufficient evidence establishing option three.

ous false and misleading arguments to the court and jury. This conduct warrants the imposition of sanctions.[9]

a.   Identity of Sanctioned Attorneys

The Court finds that each of the following attorneys contributed to Qualcomm's monumental discovery violation and is personally responsible: James Batchelder, Adam Bier, Kevin Leung, Christopher Mammen, Lee Patch, and Stanley Young ("Sanctioned Attorneys").

Attorneys Leung, Mammen and Batchelder are responsible for the initial discovery failure because they handled or supervised Qualcomm's discovery responses and production of documents. The Federal Rules impose an affirmative duty upon lawyers to engage in discovery in a responsible manner and to conduct a "reasonable inquiry" to determine whether discovery responses are sufficient and proper. In the instant case, a reasonable inquiry should have included searches using fundamental terms such as JVT, avc_ce or H.264, on the computers belonging to knowledgeable people such as Raveendran, Irvine and Ludwin. As the post-trial investigation confirmed, such a reasonable search would have revealed the suppressed documents. Had Leung, Mammen, Batchelder, or any of the other attorneys insisted on reviewing Qualcomm's records regarding the locations searched and terms utilized, they would have discovered the inadequacy of the search and the suppressed documents.[10] . . . .

Attorneys Bier, Mammen and Patch are responsible for the discovery violation because they also did not perform a reasonable inquiry to determine whether Qualcomm had complied with its discovery obligations. When Bier reviewed the August 6, 2002 email welcoming Raveendran to the avc_ce email group, he knew or should have known that it contradicted Qualcomm's trial arguments and he had an obligation to verify that it had been produced in discovery or to immediately produce it. If Bier, as a junior lawyer, lacked the experience to recognize the significance of the document,

9.   The applicable discovery rules do not adequately address the attorneys' misconduct in this case. Rule 26(g) only imposes liability upon the attorney who signed the discovery request or response. Similarly, Rule 37(a) authorizes sanctions against a party or attorney only if a motion to compel is filed; Rule 37(b) authorizes sanctions against a party or an attorney if the party fails to comply with a discovery order; and, Rule 37(c) only imposes liability upon a party for the party's failure to comply with various discovery obligations. Under a strict interpretation of these rules, the only attorney who would be responsible for the discovery failure is Kevin Leung because he signed the false discovery responses. However, the Court believes the federal rules impose a duty of good faith and reasonable inquiry on all attorneys involved in litigation who rely on discovery responses executed by another attorney. . . . The facts of this case also justify the imposition of sanctions against these attorneys pursuant to the Court's inherent power.

10.   Leung's attorney represented during the OSC hearing that Leung requested a more thorough document search but that Qualcomm refused to do so. If Leung was unable to get Qualcomm to conduct the type of search he deemed necessary to verify the adequacy of the document search and production, then he should have obtained the assistance of supervising or senior attorneys. If Mammen and Batchelder were unable to get Qualcomm to conduct a competent and thorough document search, they should have withdrawn from the case or taken other action to ensure production of the evidence. Attorneys' ethical obligations do not permit them to participate in an inadequate document search and then provide misleading and incomplete information to their opponents and false arguments to the court.

then a more senior or knowledgeable attorney should have assisted him. . . .

Similarly, when Bier found the 21 emails on Raveendran's computer that had not been produced in discovery, he took the appropriate action and informed his supervisors, Mammen and Patch. Patch discussed the discovery and production issue with Young and Batchelder. While all of these attorneys assert that there was a plausible argument that Broadcom did not request these documents, only Bier and Mammen actually read the emails. Moreover, all of the attorneys missed the critical inquiry: was Qualcomm's document search adequate? If these 21 emails were not discovered during Qualcomm's document search, how many more might exist? The answer, obviously, was tens of thousands. If Bier, Mammen, Patch, Young or Batchelder had conducted a reasonable inquiry after the discovery of the 21 Raveendran emails, they would have discovered the inadequacy of Qualcomm's search and the suppressed documents. . . . Finally, attorneys Young, Patch, and Batchelder bear responsibility for the discovery failure because they did not conduct a reasonable inquiry into Qualcomm's discovery production before making specific factual and legal arguments to the court. . . .

Patch was an integral part of the trial team—familiar with Qualcomm's arguments, theories and strategies. He knew on January 14th that 21 avc_ce emails had been discovered on Raveendran's computer. Without reading or reviewing the emails, Patch participated in the decision not to produce them. Several days later, Patch carefully tailored his questions to ensure that Raveendran did not testify about the unproduced emails. And, after Broadcom stumbled into the email testimony, Patch affirmatively misled the Court by claiming that he did not know whether the emails were responsive to Broadcom's discovery requests. . . . Batchelder also is responsible because he was the lead trial attorney and, as such, he was most familiar with Qualcomm's important arguments and witnesses. Batchelder stated in his opening statement that Qualcomm had not participated in the JVT before late 2003. Despite this statement and his complete knowledge of Qualcomm's legal theories, Batchelder did not take any action when he was informed that JVT documents that Qualcomm had not produced in discovery were found on Raveendran's computer. He did not read the emails, ask about their substance, nor inquire as to why they were not located during discovery. And, he stood mute when four days later, Young falsely stated that no emails had been sent to Raveendran from the avc_ce email group. . . .

For all of these reasons, the Court finds that these attorneys did not conduct a reasonable inquiry into the adequacy of Qualcomm's document search and production and, accordingly, they are responsible, along with Qualcomm, for the monumental discovery violation.

. . .

3. Imposed Sanctions

. . .

b. Referral to the California State Bar

As set forth above, the Sanctioned Attorneys assisted Qualcomm in committing this incredible discovery violation by intentionally hiding or recklessly ignoring relevant documents, ignoring or rejecting numerous warning signs that Qualcomm's document search was inadequate, and blindly accepting Qualcomm's unsupported assurances that its document search was adequate. The Sanctioned Attorneys then used the lack of evidence to repeatedly and forcefully make false statements and arguments to the court and jury. As such, the Sanctioned Attorneys violated their discovery obligations and also may have violated their ethical duties. To address the potential ethical violations, the Court refers the Sanctioned Attorneys to The State Bar of California for an appropriate investigation and possible imposition of sanctions.[18] . . .

c. Case Review and Enforcement of Discovery Obligations

The Court also orders Qualcomm and the Sanctioned Attorneys to participate in a comprehensive Case Review and Enforcement of Discovery Obligations ("CREDO") program. This is a collaborative process to identify the failures in the case management and discovery protocol utilized by Qualcomm and its in-house and retained attorneys in this case, to craft alternatives that will prevent such failures in the future, to evaluate and test the alternatives, and ultimately, to create a case management protocol which will serve as a model for the future.

. . .

While no one can undo the misconduct in this case, this process, hopefully, will establish a baseline for other cases. Perhaps it also will establish a turning point in what the Court perceives as a decline in and deterioration of civility, professionalism and ethical conduct in the litigation arena. To the extent it does so, everyone benefits—Broadcom, Qualcomm, and all attorneys who engage in, and judges who preside over, complex litigation. If nothing else, it will provide a road map to assist counsel and corporate clients in complying with their ethical and discovery obligations and conducting the requisite "reasonable inquiry."

NOTES AND QUESTIONS

1. In a subsequent March 5, 2008 order, district court Rudi Brewster vacated Judge Major's sanction judgment so that Qualcomm attorneys could assert a self-defense exception to the attorney-client privilege and justify their conduct. However, while the matter was pending, the decision

---

18. Monetary sanctions would be appropriate to address the discovery violations. However, the Court declines to impose monetary sanctions against the Sanctioned Attorneys for several reasons. First, if the imposed sanctions do not convince the attorneys to behave in a more ethical and professional manner in the future, monetary sanctions are unlikely to do so. Second, it is possible that Qualcomm will seek contribution from its retained attorneys after it pays Broadcom's attorneys' fees and costs and, in light of that significant monetary sanction, an additional fine is unlikely to affect counsel's future behavior. . . .

caused widespread concern in the bar and the legal blogosphere. It seemingly imposes a stringent obligation on litigators: in the words of the judge, the three lawyers supervising discovery and document production should have "insisted on reviewing Qualcomm's records regarding the locations searched and terms utilized." Does this require litigators to adopt a mistrustful or even adversarial stance toward their own client? Under what circumstances does the court's "reasonable inquiry" standard require attorneys to do their own electronic searches of the computers of knowledgeable clients?

Consider one expert's advice about "Qualcom Lessons:

• 'If labor [for discovery is divided with the client or its in house counsel), demand an advance privilege waiver for communications relevant to any discovery disputes;

• Don't trust standard procedures or formal systems. Don't trust; verify.

• Err in favor of production.

• The more you don't want to produce a document, the more important it is to produce it.' "[120]

2. The six sanctioned lawyers belong to a "boutique" forty-lawyer Silicon Valley intellectual property firm. They include two named partners, two other partners, and two associates, including a junior associate. How blameworthy were the lawyers after discovering the August 6, 2002 email to Raveendran welcoming her to avc_ce? Were the associates more or less culpable than the partners? Under what, if any, circumstances is it appropriate to sanction lawyers involved in the discovery process who do not sign pleadings or appear in court?

3. What is Judge Major's factual basis for finding that Qualcomm's lawyers were "intentionally hiding or recklessly ignoring relevant documents"? She states that they are highly educated and experienced, and in an appendix not included in this excerpt she summarizes their credentials. Is it proper to infer from a lawyer's resume that he or she is too smart to have been fooled by a client? Are you persuaded by the court's conclusion that the lawyers were at least reckless? If so, should they have received monetary sanctions?

4. In 2007, federal district court Harold Baer issued a widely reported discovery sanction against Dorsey and Whitney, in which he faulted "naked competition and singular economic focus of the marketplace" as eroding professionalism and respect for court orders. Wolters Kluwer Financial Services, Inc. v. Scivantage, Adnane Charchour, Sanjeev Doss, Cameron Routh, and Gregory Alves, 525 F.Supp.2d 448, 450 (S.D.N.Y. 2007). If that is correct, how should the profession respond? Some litigators believe that monetary sanctions are too often simply "chump change," and unlikely to be a significant deterrent given the stakes involved. In response to such criticisms, some judges have imposed alternative sanctions. One district

120. David McGowan, "11 Qualcomm Lessons," *Cal. Bar Journal,* February, 2008, at 6.

court in Wisconsin initially revoked permission to appear pro hac vice to two associates guilty of discovery abuse. They protested that such penalties would follow them for the rest of their careers whenever they applied for temporary admission in other courts. In response, the court agreed to vacate the revocation on condition that they provide pro bono representation for prisoners pursuing a constitutional claim. Ricoh Company v. Asustek Computer Inc., 2007 WL 5462420 (W.D. Wis. 2007). Is that an appropriate remedy? What other strategies might be most effective in curing abuse?

NOTES: CIVILITY AND CIVILITY CODES

Since the American Bar Association issued a widely-publicized report in 1986 decrying the loss of "professionalism" among attorneys, over a hundred bar organizations have proposed or adopted "codes of civility."[121] Almost all of these address litigation abuses. Thus, the Kentucky Bar Association's Code of Professional Courtesy states: "A lawyer should not seek sanctions against or disqualification of another attorney unless necessary for the protection of a client and fully justified by the circumstances, not for the mere purpose of obtaining a tactical advantage." California's civility standards advise lawyers to agree to "reasonable extension requests" and avoid filing continuances or using document requests as "harassing tactics." The Virginia Bar's Principles of Professional Courtesy include the following:

> A lawyer should, whenever possible, attempt and cooperate in any reasonable effort to limit discovery by forbearance in number and detail of interrogatories propounded. A lawyer should seek voluntary and informal production of exhibits and documents and cooperate in the release thereof when the client's interest will not be prejudiced thereby. A lawyer should make fair disclosures to discovery without needless qualifications.[122]

In 1988, The ABA House of Delegates adopted a recommendation that state and local bar associations "encourage their members to accept as a guide for their individual conduct, and to comply with, a lawyers' creed of professionalism." The ABA Torts and Insurance Practice Section issued an example of such a "Lawyer's Creed of Professionalism." It reads in part:

> 4. I will endeavor to consult with opposing counsel before scheduling depositions and meetings and before re-scheduling hearings, and I will cooperate with opposing counsel when scheduling changes are requested;

> 5. I will refrain from utilizing litigation or any other course of conduct to harass the opposing party;

> 6. I will refrain from engaging in excessive and abusive discovery, and I will comply with all reasonable discovery requests;

> 7. I will refrain from utilizing delaying tactics....

121. *Report of the Commission on Professionalism to the Board of Governors and the House of Delegates of the American Bar Association,* 112 F.R.D. 243 (1986); Rhode, *supra* note 33, at 82.

122. "Principles of Professional Courtesy," *Va.Law.,* July 1989, at 30.

The ABA House of Delegates made clear that "nothing in such a creed shall be deemed to supersede or in any way amend the Model Rules of Professional Conduct or other disciplinary codes, alter existing standards of conduct against which lawyer negligence might be judged or become a basis for the imposition of civil liability of any kind."

Appended to this creed is a "Lawyer's Pledge of Professionalism," including a provision stating: "I will honor the spirit and intent, as well as the requirements, of the applicable rules or code of professional conduct for my jurisdiction, and I will encourage others to do the same." Are these codes "uneasy bedfellows" with ethical rules requiring pursuit of a client's interest?[123] How useful are such codes of civility likely to be in curbing the conduct reflected in Problem 8 and accompanying notes? Should a court rely on such codes in assessing lawyer conduct?

Could the bar's binding rules do more to discourage uncivil conduct? In Fieger v. Michigan Supreme Court, 2007 WL 2571975 (E.D. Mich. 2007), the trial judge struck down as vague and overbroad two Michigan's Rules of Professional Conduct. Rule 3.5(c) provided that a lawyer shall not "engage in undignified or discourteous conduct toward the tribunal," and Rule 6.5(a) provided that a lawyer "shall treat with courtesy and respect all persons involved in the legal process...." One plaintiff challenging the rules was an attorney who had been disciplined by a divided Michigan Supreme Court for making profane public comments about appellate judges who had overturned a verdict he had won. See Grievance Administrator v. Fieger, 719 N.W.2d 123 (Mich.2006) (finding that references to the judges as jackasses and Nazis, who deserved to be anally violated were not protected speech). Fieger did not contest his discipline, but challenged the rules as overbroad on their face. Do you agree with the district court's ruling? Should attorneys be subject to discipline for characterizations of judges or opposing counsel?

Perhaps the leading case on lawyer incivility is *Paramount Communications v. QVC Network*, 637 A.2d 34, 58 (Del.Supr.1994), where the Delaware Supreme Court attached a blistering "Addendum" to an opinion concerning other issues, criticizing the well-known litigator Joseph Jamail for "rude, uncivil, and vulgar" behavior during depositions. The court elected not to sanction Jamail. In the following case, a trial judge similarly attempts to give civility teeth.

Lee v. American Eagle Airlines, Inc.

Southern District of Florida, 2000.
93 F.Supp.2d 1322.

■ MIDDLEBROOKS, J.:

ORDER ON ATTORNEY'S FEES AND COSTS

This Cause came before the Court upon Plaintiff's Amended Verified Motion for Attorney's Fees and Costs, filed November 4, 1999 (DE #310).

---

123. Robert S. Huie, "Uneasy Bedfellows?," *Nat'l L. J.* March 6, 2006, at 23.

The Court has reviewed the pertinent portions of the file and is otherwise fully informed in the premises.

I.   Introduction

"Let's kick some ass," Marvin Kurzban said loudly to his client, Anthony Lee, and his co-counsel, Ira Kurzban. I had taken the bench, and Court was in session. Opposing counsel and their client representatives were seated across the aisle. The jury was waiting to be called into the courtroom. Mr. Kurzban's comment was suited more to a locker room than a courtroom of the United States, and the conduct of Plaintiff's counsel that followed disrupted the adversary system and interfered with the resolution of a civil dispute.

The trial of this case lasted approximately fourteen days. The jury found that American Eagle Airlines had subjected Mr. Lee to a racially hostile work environment in violation of Title VII of the Civil Rights Act of 1964, 42 U.S.C. § 2000e, et seq., and 42 U.S.C. § 1981. As compensation, the jury awarded Mr. Lee $300,000. In addition, the jury awarded Mr. Lee $650,000 in punitive damages. The jury denied Mr. Lee's other claim, also premised on Title VII and § 1981, finding that Mr. Lee had not been terminated because of his race. This motion seeking attorney's fees and costs pursuant to 42 U.S.C. § 1988 followed.

As the prevailing party in a Title VII action, the Plaintiff now seeks $1,611,910.50 in attorney's fees. This request presents the question of whether unprofessional and disruptive conduct of counsel which prolongs the proceedings and creates animosity which interferes with the resolution of a cause can be considered in determining an award of attorney's fees.

In their post-trial motions, counsel for the parties filed opposing affidavits concerning additional misconduct that was not directly observed by the Court. Since these affidavits presented vastly different versions of events, an evidentiary hearing was held; counsel and other witnesses testified.

These issues have been distasteful and time consuming. There is a great temptation to simply move on and ignore the issue. It is unpleasant to hear lawyers accusing each other of lies and misrepresentations. Unprofessionalism on the part of lawyers is a distraction and takes time away from other pending cases; it also embroils the Court in charges and counter charges. However, the functioning of our adversary system depends upon being able to rely upon what a lawyer says. So, confronted by affidavits of counsel that were directly contradictory, I decided to hear testimony and make credibility findings. These findings are based upon direct observations by the Court, the transcript of the trial, and the evidentiary hearing.

In addition, we contacted the Florida Bar to determine whether counsel had been the subject of complaints regarding unprofessional conduct.

The Florida Bar forwarded a record of a previous complaint by a state court judge concerning the conduct of Marvin Kurzban. In response to that complaint, and immediately before the trial in this cause, the Florida Bar had directed Mr. Kurzban to attend an ethics class and pay a fine.

II.   Findings of Fact Pertaining to Misconduct by Counsel

Discovery in this case was rancorous from the beginning. As is often the case, counsel for both sides contributed to the lack of civility. The tone of depositions was harsh, witnesses were treated with discourtesy, and discovery disputes were abundant. The transcripts of the depositions in this case are weighted down with bitter exchanges between the lawyers.…

Testimony at the evidentiary hearing reflected that this uncivil conduct also continued during conversations between counsel. The testimony of a young lawyer formerly with the Defendant's counsel's law firm was particularly poignant. This lawyer testified that during telephone conversations with Ira Kurzban, she was hung up on, told that she had only been assigned to work on the case because she was African–American, and wrongly accused of misrepresentations. She testified that her experience with opposing counsel in this case was a factor in her decision to leave her litigation practice.

This testimony was not only powerful and credible, but it also reflects the corrosive impact this type of unprofessional behavior can have upon the bar itself. A litigation practice is stressful and often exhausting. Unprofessional litigation tactics affect everyone exposed to such behavior and the ripple effect of incivility is spread throughout the bar.

The trial began. Testimony at the evidentiary hearing reveals that Mr. Kurzban's "Let's kick some ass" comment was not an aberration. A client representative of the Defendant, a lawyer for American Airlines, testified that she and others were subjected to a barrage of comments out of the hearing of the Court and jury which she likened to trash talk at a sporting event. Local counsel for the Defendant was called a "Second Rate Loser" by Marvin Kurzban. She testified that each day as court began, Marvin Kurzban would say, "Let the pounding begin." In front of defense counsel's client, Mr. Kurzban would ask, "How are you going to feel when I take all of your client's money?" When walking out of the courtroom, Marvin Kurzban would exclaim, "Yuppies out of the way." …

[The judge details several examples of alleged misbehavior by Marvin and Ira Kurzban, including speaking with a witness during a break after being warned not to, looking upward at the ceiling when their objections were overruled, making belligerent comments directly to opposing counsel, and insulting the court reporter—then complaining to the judge about the reporter's bias when the reporter responded to the insult with an epithet.]

I required the Court Reporter to apologize for his behavior. Because of the accusation of bias, I arranged for other Court Reporters to cover the remainder of the trial.

I learned that accusations of bias followed any disagreement with positions espoused by Plaintiff's counsel: "There's no question that he's entitled to it, so it's no—if I understand what Your Honor's saying, you don't want it to go in front of the jury for whatever reason." "Your Honor, I know you're angry at me, but I hope you're not taking it out on my client." "In fact, I think that the Court has exhibited extreme bias in this case and your rulings on objections." "Well, Your Honor, I respectfully disagree with you, that's for a court of appeals ultimately to decide, but to put a motive on it I think it exhibits a substantial amount of bias on behalf of Your Honor." "And I concur with what my brother has said. There's been clear animus by this Court to this side." "I've practiced 26 years and I've tried over 50 cases, and I've won multimillion dollar verdicts on more than a dozen cases. I don't need for this Court to allow a witness to have his wife introduced. I can't think of any reason or purpose, other than prejudice, that this Court would allow such an act to occur."

[The judge details other instances of alleged misbehavior by the Kurzban brothers, including "the rolling of eyes; exasperated looks at the ceiling; and flailing of arms" whenever the judge made an adverse ruling. When the judge admonished him for laughing at one adverse ruling, "Ira Kurzban then listed a litany of complaints about rulings which he stated should result in a mistrial." The judge added: "When offered a mistrial, the Plaintiff declined." During another disagreement, the judge admonished Ira Kurzban as follows: "If I can't rely on lawyers being able to respect each other and be respected and accept what other people say in the courtroom, this system can't work. It's as important to me as whether or not you have a law degree. . . . "] . . .

During a cross-examination concerning how much time the witness spent on various shifts, Marvin Kurzban held a file towards the witness and asked:

Marvin Kurzban: I have your personnel file (indicating). How many times did you have to work between 1992 and 1994, sir? Do you think it was more than a handful of times?

After an objection, and out of the presence of the jury, I asked Mr. Kurzban for the witness's personnel file. He responded:

Marvin Kurzban: Actually, we do have Mr. Blades's personnel file, when it was produced among all the other personnel files in Miami of the people. I don't know if that box is here or I left it in the office. I think the personnel files that we were given by counsel is in the office.

The Court: So it wasn't in the folder that you picked up and carried to the stand?

Marvin Kurzban: No it wasn't, Your Honor.

The Court: You said, "Mr. Blades, we have your personnel file here!"

* * *

The Court: You believe it is permissible to pick up a file from your desk, carry it to the witness stand and tell the witness "Mr. Blades, we have your personnel file," and then begin questioning him? You believe that's appropriate court examination?

Marvin Kurzban: I do, on hostile witnesses; on cross-examination, I believe that I'm entitled to have that witness believe I'm going to question him on something whether or not I have that in my hand or not. Yes, I do.

* * *

The Court: I believe, frankly, that it is inappropriate to make a deliberate misrepresentation to a witness or to ask, implying in your questioning something that is not true.

Marvin Kurzban: Neither was I implying something that wasn't true, nor was I making a misrepresentation. The question was about how many times he worked, Your Honor. The question wasn't: In your personnel file it says something. I didn't make any such misrepresentation.

Mr. Kurzban insisted that he had the personnel file back at his office. He was asked to produce it and he responded that he would the following day. The file was never produced.

At the end of the trial, defense counsel Connor approached Ira Kurzban and offered his hand in congratulations. Mr. Kurzban refused to shake his hand. The trial ended much like it had begun.

At the evidentiary hearing, Plaintiff's counsel were unrepentant, attacking opposing counsel and accepting no responsibility for their own actions. They argued that the perceived misconduct was only a matter of style and the exercise of first amendment rights. In keeping with that "style," Marvin Kurzban ended the hearing with the proclamation that he had called his opponent a loser, but not a second-rate loser because, "I don't rate losers." Mr. Kurzban's testimony reflects that he has no clue about what it means to be a lawyer.

III. Analysis

Courts presiding over civil rights actions may, in their discretion, award the prevailing party a "reasonable attorney's fee (including expert fees)" as part of its costs. See 42 U.S.C. § 1988; 42 U.S.C. § 2000e–5(k). Although the presiding court has discretion, a prevailing plaintiff is to be awarded attorney's fees "in all but special circumstances." This presumption in favor of awarding attorney's fees is a reflection of Congress' clear intent to "cast the Title VII plaintiff in the role of 'a private attorney general,' vindicating a policy of the highest priority." By awarding prevailing plaintiffs their attorney's fees, the section "makes it easier for a plaintiff of limited means to bring a meritorious suit."

Courts determining attorney's fee awards begin by determining the "lodestar": the product of the number of hours reasonably expended on the litigation and a reasonable hourly rate for the attorney's services. This lodestar may then be adjusted for the results obtained.

1. The reasonable hourly rate

"A reasonable hourly rate is the prevailing market rate in the relevant legal community for similar service by lawyers of reasonably comparable skills, experience, and reputation." The party seeking attorney's fees, in this case Mr. Lee, bears the burden of producing "satisfactory evidence that the requested rate is in line with prevailing market rates." To be satisfactory, evidence must consist of "more than the affidavit of the attorney performing the work."

Prior to adoption of the lodestar formula, the so-called "Johnson factors" governed fee awards. See *Johnson v. Georgia Highway Express, Inc.*, 488 F.2d 714, 717–19 (5th Cir.1974). Although the lodestar formula has since displaced the "Johnson factors," the Eleventh Circuit has permitted district courts to consider the factors in establishing a reasonable hourly rate. See *Loranger*, 10 F.3d at 781 n. 6. Among those factors is the experience, reputation, and ability of the attorneys and the skill requisite to perform the legal service properly. See *Johnson*, 488 F.2d at 717–19. As explained more fully in the findings of misconduct, contained in Section II, supra, the conduct of Ira Kurzban and Marvin Kurzban both during and prior to trial was very troubling. In my estimation, the manner in which a lawyer interacts with opposing counsel and conducts himself before the Court is as indicative of the lawyer's ability and skill as is mastery of the rules of evidence. Upon review of the trial transcripts and the evidence presented during the evidentiary hearing on attorney conduct and based on observations at trial, I find that the conduct of Ira Kurzban and Marvin Kurzban in the litigation of this case fell far below acceptable standards, especially in light of the $300 hourly rate the attorneys claim. Accordingly, I find "special circumstances" justifying a departure from counsels' requested rates: Ira Kurzban shall be awarded $150 per hour for his pretrial work and $0 for his trial work; Marvin Kurzban's rate for this action is $0. . . .

V. Conclusion

As I considered this issue, I reflected upon a letter recently received from a trial lawyer following a discussion on civility and professionalism with the Miami Chapter of the American Board of Trial Advocates. This lawyer stated:

> It seems to me that the courts are basically facing this issue as one of education. Hence we have seminars, guidelines and articles from both the state and federal bench explaining what lawyers should do to be civil and professional to each other. However, I do not think the problem is that lawyers do not know how to act in a civil manner. Rather, I think some lawyers will simply do that with which they can get away.
>
> Special masters, grievance committees and educational seminars are not as effective as a sanction for uncivil behavior.
>
> I know our federal court is quite busy and that the time it takes to consider uncivil behavior may have to be taken from some other pending case. However, I would submit that eliminating uncivil behavior not only helps that case, but every other case in which that lawyer

is involved. Moreover, as the word spreads as to the price to be paid for unprofessionalism, other lawyers and other cases will be implicated.

I believe that this reduction in attorney fees is an appropriate response to the conduct by Plaintiff's counsel in this case, but I am not convinced it will deter future misconduct. I frankly considered denying fees altogether but while I have reviewed many of the depositions, I did not observe everything that happened during the pretrial phase of the case. The reduction in attorneys' fees based upon misconduct of counsel is therefore approximately $358,423.20.

For the foregoing reasons, it is hereby ORDERED AND ADJUDGED that Plaintiff's Amended Verified Motion for Attorney's Fees and Costs (DE #310) is GRANTED. Based on the foregoing we award Plaintiff $312,324.63 in fees and costs.

Furthermore, because of the misconduct of counsel which occurred in this case, a copy of this order shall be sent to the Florida Bar and the Peer Review Committee for the Southern District of Florida for any action deemed appropriate.

DONE and ORDERED in Chambers at Miami, Florida this 13th day of March 2000.

NOTES AND QUESTIONS

1.   Notice that the judge awards the Kurzbans $312,324.63 in fees and costs, and "fines" them (in the form of fee-reduction) $358,423.20. The Kurzbans had requested $1.6 million in attorneys' fees. Was the fee reduction excessive? Was the judge abusing his discretion when he held that "the manner in which a lawyer interacts with opposing counsel and conducts himself before the Court is . . . indicative of the lawyer's ability and skill," and therefore cut back the Kurzbans' hourly rate because of their uncivil behavior?

2.   Among the instances of "incivility" on the part of the Kurzbans that the judge details are several remarks they made during trial about the judge's bias against them. The opinion notes that the Kurzbans did not request a mistrial on account of judicial bias. If attorneys believe that a judge is behaving in a biased manner, but do not wish to ask for a mistrial—perhaps because they believe that they are persuading the jury—how should they respond? Are the Kurzbans being punished for standing up for their client? Does civility require lawyers to act as though they agree with a judge's unfavorable rulings? If so, could civility harm their client's case in the eyes of the jury?

3.   Was it misconduct for Marvin Kurzban to pretend that papers in his hand were a witness's personnel file when in fact they were not? If so, what sanction would be appropriate?

4.   The Kurzbans claimed that their "perceived misconduct was only a matter of style and the exercise of first amendment rights." Is this correct? Is it a violation of free speech to sanction them for insulting opposing counsel out of earshot of the court?

CHAPTER V

CONFIDENTIALITY AND THE ATTORNEY–CLIENT PRIVILEGE

PROBLEM 1

Francis Belge and Frank Armani, New York attorneys, were appointed to defend Robert Garrow on charges of murder. During the course of representation, Garrow revealed to them the commission of several rapes, two other unsolved murders, and the location of the victims' bodies. Belge and Armani confirmed the location and photographed the bodies. Belge and Armani kept this information to themselves, despite the pleas of the frantic parents of the missing murder victims, who correctly surmised that Garrow may have killed their daughters and that Garrow's attorneys knew one way or the other. The information finally came out 10 months later at Garrow's trial, when Belge and Armani attempted to use Garrow's public confession to help establish an insanity defense. Earlier, during secret plea negotiations with the District Attorney, Belge and Armani had suggested that they could provide information concerning two unsolved murders in return for a favorable plea bargain.

Belge and Armani were subsequently indicted for violating two sections of a New York public health law which require, respectively, that a decent burial be accorded to the dead and that anyone knowing of the death of a person without medical attendance report the fact to the proper authorities. After that indictment was dismissed, the New York Bar Association Committee on Professional Ethics was asked to consider whether the lawyers had violated relevant ethics rules.

References:

Model Rules 1.16, 1.2, 1.6, 3.3, 3.4

1. You are a member of the committee. What is your recommended disposition? (For purposes of considering this question, use the Model Rules rather than New York's Code of Professional Responsibility.)

2. Suppose Belge and Armani had learned the information from a source other than their client. Would their obligations have been different?

3. Alternatively, assume that Belge and Armani knew that another person had been charged with the kidnaping of one of the victims. If Garrow had not wanted his guilt revealed in plea negotiations, what would their responsibilities have been?

4. What if there had been no plea negotiations and the attorneys had anonymously informed the authorities of the location of the bodies? Would

the appropriateness of their conduct have depended on whether investigators were able, or might have been able, to link Garrow to the murders?

5. What should Belge and Armani have done if they had strongly suspected that Garrow would attempt other assaults or dispose of the victims' bodies while on bail? See the discussion in Part B below concerning disclosures to prevent death or substantial bodily harm.

NOTES

In dismissing the indictment against Belge, the New York trial court concluded that the information was privileged and applauded counsel for acting with "all the zeal at [his] command to protect the constitutional rights of his client." In so holding, the court acknowledged that its task would have been "much more difficult" had Belge been indicted for obstructing justice rather than circumventing the "trivia of a pseudo-criminal statute." *People v. Belge,* 372 N.Y.S.2d 798, 803 (1975). The appellate court, while affirming dismissal of the indictment, expressly declined to reach the "ethical questions" underlying the case. It did, however, voice "serious concern" as to invocation of the attorney-client privilege in a context where counsel had obligations dictated not only by the Code but by "basic human standards of decency." *People v. Belge,* 376 N.Y.S.2d 771, 772 (1975).

Although a jury convicted Garrow, public sentiment against Belge and Armani ran high. They received death threats and their practices encountered severe difficulties. Armani had to dismiss two associates and three secretaries; Belge left for St. Croix.[1] Several years after the Garrow case, a television documentary, "Ethics on Trial," profiled Armani and others involved in the proceedings. The District Attorney who prosecuted Garrow acknowledged that disclosure of the bodies could have led to incriminating information, and defended the decision of Garrow's counsel to maintain confidentiality. What was "reprehensible," he believed, was Armani's and Belge's attempt to use the information about Garrow's past crimes to bargain for an insanity plea that would have put the defendant back on the street. This, he maintained, was inconsistent with a lawyer's role as officer of the court.

In a television interview, Armani reflected on his dilemma, which he understood in rather different terms than did the District Attorney:

Armani: This was something that was really momentous for us because of the conflict within us. Your mind screaming one way "Relieve these parents [of the murder victims]!" You know—what is your responsibility? Should you report this? Shouldn't you report it? One sense of morality wants you to relieve the grief.

Interviewer: And the other?

Armani: The other is your sworn duty. . . .

---

1. *See* "Lawyer Privilege Gets Severe Test," 64 *A.B.A.J.* 664 (1978).

Interviewer: Didn't you think that there was a factor of just common decency here?

Armani: I can't explain it—but to me it was a question of which was the higher moral good.

Interviewer: Between what?

Armani: The question of the Constitution, the question of even a bastard like him having a proper defense, having adequate representation, being able to trust his lawyer as to what he says.

Interviewer: As against what?

Armani: As against the fact that I have a dead girl, the fact that her body's there. As against the breaking hearts of her parents. But they are—[pause]. It's a terrible thing to play God at that moment, but in my judgment—and I still feel that way—that their suffering is not worth jeopardizing my sworn duty or my oath of office or the Constitution.[2]

NOTES AND QUESTIONS

1.   Do you agree with Armani's way of posing the issue? If so, did he resolve the issue correctly? In the same interview, Armani added that if constitutional protections don't "belong to the worst of us, they won't apply to the best of us. Where do you make exceptions?" Do you agree?

After his conviction on the initial murder charge, Garrow pled guilty to the other offenses in exchange for concurrent sentences. He then sued Belge and Armani for several million dollars based on allegedly ineffective assistance of counsel, and sued the state for $10 million based on allegedly improper medical treatment of wounds he sustained while being captured by police. In exchange for dropping the claims against the state, he received a transfer to a medium security correctional facility for elderly and handicapped prisoners. The security proved inadequate to his talents and he escaped shortly after his transfer.

The police then asked Armani for any information that might help recapture his former client. According to Armani's subsequent account of the case, he attempted to

> recall some of the tactics Garrow had told him about using to elude the police. "He once told me that he would hole up in the underbrush until the cops gave up the search in that area and pulled out.... That's how he broke out of [an earlier police dragnet]."[3]

Based in part on that information, police concentrated search efforts on the underbrush near the prison. As they approached his cover, Garrow fired on the patrol. They fired back and he was killed instantly.

2.   Did Armani breach any ethical rules in disclosing confidential information about Garrow's past tactics for eluding police? Was Armani obligated—

---

2. *Ethics on Trial* (WETA–TV video 1987).

3. Tom Alibrandi with Frank H. Armani, *Privileged Information* 199 (1984).

morally or legally—to volunteer what he knew? What would you have done?

3.   As it turns out, Armani had his own reasons for wanting to make sure that Garrow was recaptured. Garrow's escape terrified him, because of a chilling moment that had occurred during Garrow's trial. Armani's wife and daughter Dorina came to court to watch the trial, and Garrow greeted Dorina by name. Surprised, Armani had asked Dorina how she knew Garrow, and she replied that she didn't. At that moment, Armani realized that at some point, Garrow had been stalking Dorina as he had stalked his other rape and murder victims.[4] Now, Garrow was loose. Should the risks to Dorina affect Armani's disclosure responsibilities?

4.   The New York trial court stated that it might have had difficulty dismissing obstruction of justice charges against the two lawyers. How can keeping a client's confidences be obstruction of justice? Compare the *Cueto* case in Chapter IV. Were Belge's and Armani's motives comparable to Cueto's?

A.   THE BACKGROUND OF THE ATTORNEY-CLIENT PRIVILEGE

INTRODUCTION

Recall Lord Brougham's definition of the lawyer's role in a criminal defense context:

> An advocate, in the discharge of his duty, knows but one person in all the world, and that person is his client. To save that client by all means and expedients, and at all hazards and costs to other persons, and, amongst them, to himself, is his first and only duty; and in performing this duty he must not regard the alarm, the torments, the destruction which he may bring upon others.[5]

One of the central requirements of this intensely focused loyalty to clients is the duty of confidentiality. Although Belge and Armani found the decision an agonizing one, they felt themselves bound by the duty of confidentiality, and they revealed the location of the bodies only when they believed that doing so would be to their client's advantage. The result was to compound the "alarm" of the community and the "torments" of the victims' families, but at great "hazards and costs" to the lawyers themselves; their reputations were shattered and lives were threatened.

Few attorneys will ever face confidentiality issues quite so wrenching as these, but many will at some point confront troubling dilemmas, in civil as well as criminal practice. For example, a criminal defense lawyer may believe that her client committed a crime for which someone else is about to be sentenced. A client may ask a lawyer to negotiate without revealing to opposing parties that they are bargaining under a material misapprehen-

---

4. *Id.* at 157.

5. 2 *Trial of Queen Caroline* 8 (J. Nightingale ed. 1820–21).

sion.[6] A litigator may know of the existence of a "smoking gun" that the other side has not requested in discovery. A lawyer representing a family member may learn a secret that she is keeping from other family members, who also trust the lawyer.[7] A corporate lawyer may learn that her client is marketing a product that could cause life-threatening injuries.[8]

Confidentiality rules that speak to these dilemmas arise from two main sources: laws of evidence concerning the attorney-client privilege and bar ethical codes.

Evidence Law

The Elements of the Attorney–Client Privilege

The laws of evidence establishing an attorney-client privilege date back to the sixteenth century. In the classic formulation by John Wigmore, these laws provide:

> (1) Where legal advice of any kind is sought (2) from a professional legal adviser in his capacity as such, (3) the communications relating to that purpose, (4) made in confidence (5) by the client, (6) are at his instance permanently protected (7) from disclosure by himself or by the legal adviser, (8) except the protection be waived.[9]

The *Restatement of the Law Governing Lawyers* preserves the kernel of Wigmore's analysis:

> [T]he attorney-client privilege may be invoked ... with respect to: (1) a communication (2) made by privileged persons (3) in confidence (4) for the purpose of obtaining or providing legal assistance for the client.[10]

Each clause of Wigmore's formula gives rise to important questions. What kind of advice is "legal"? Can only a lawyer be a "professional legal adviser"? What about an accountant working with a lawyer on a white-collar criminal case? What is a "communication"? Is it only verbal, or can it include a tangible object that the client would like to give to the lawyer for safekeeping? What determines whether the client has disclosed information in confidence? What counts as "disclosure"? Does it encompass disclosures of otherwise unprivileged information from which privileged communications could be inferred? When is the privilege inadvertently waived? An extended body of law has evolved around these and other questions. A similar body of law has evolved around the related work-product privilege, which protects material prepared for litigation except on a showing of necessity by a third party. See Federal Rules of Civil Procedure Rule 26.

Waiver

One of the most significant areas of development involves waivers. The privilege will presumptively be waived if: the communication takes place in

---

6. *See* Chapter VIII, *infra.*

7. *See* Chapter X, Problem 1, *infra.*

8. *See* Chapter IX, *infra.*

9. John H. Wigmore, 8 *Wigmore on Evidence* § 2292, at 554 (John T. McNaughton rev. ed. 1961).

10. *Restatement of the Law Governing Lawyers,* § 68 (2000).

the presence of a third party; the client and lawyer fail to assert the privilege; the client discloses the communication to an unprivileged third party (e.g., a close friend); or the client or his agent implicitly or explicitly consents to disclosure.[11] Related principles deny any confidentiality protection between co-clients of the same lawyer in the same matter: thus, no privilege applies in subsequent litigation between co-clients. On the other hand, a co-client generally cannot waive the privilege unilaterally, without first securing the consent of the other co-clients.

One court has observed that waiver is a "loose and misleading label for what is in fact a collection of different problems," and explains:

> Cases under this "waiver" heading include situations as divergent as an express and voluntary surrender of the privilege, partial disclosure of a privileged document, selective disclosure to some outsiders but not all, and inadvertent overhearings or disclosures.[12]

Particularly important in many cases of corporate misconduct is the issue of selective waiver: a company may wish to reveal privileged information to the government in order to persuade officials to take no action, without waiving the privilege against a host of potential civil plaintiffs waiting in the wings. The problem of selective waiver arises when a client wishes to make partial revelation of privileged material—presumably, those portions whose content is favorable to the client—without waiving the privilege on the rest of the material. Courts are divided on the issue but most do not permit such selective waivers. Part of the concern is fairness to an adversary if partial revelation is allowed:

> a party cannot partially disclose privileged communications or affirmatively rely on privileged communications to support its claim or defense and then shield the underlying communications from scrutiny by the opposing party. "The quintessential example is the defendant who asserts an advice-of-counsel defense and is thereby deemed to have waived his privilege with respect to the advice that he received."[13]

As courts often put it, once a party decides to waive the privilege on some communications in order to use them as a "sword," the party cannot use the privilege as a "shield" to protect similar information. As is clear from the materials in section C, *infra*, this was an issue in tobacco litigation, where the tobacco industry released favorable scientific studies while shielding unfavorable ones under the attorney-client privilege.

However, some government agencies, including the SEC, have taken the position that in order to encourage full disclosure to regulators, organizations should be able to retain a privilege in subsequent suits by third parties. Many judges have been unconvinced. In the view of the Sixth Circuit Court of Appeals, "the investigatory agencies of the government

---

11. *See also Restatement of the Law Governing Lawyers*, §§ 78–80 (2000).

12. United States v. MIT, 129 F.3d 681, 684 (1st Cir. 1997). For a discussion of representative cases on many of these issues, see In re Grand Jury Proceedings (United States v. Doe), 219 F.3d 175 (2d Cir.2000).

13. *In re* Grand Jury Proceedings (United States v. Doe), 219 F.3d 175, 182 (2d Cir.2000).

should act to bring to light illegal activities," not support "wrongdoers in concealing the information from the public domain."[14] Subsequent discussion of the organizational privilege explores this issue of third party rights in contexts where the government insists that corporations waive the privilege and work-product protection as a condition of favorable treatment in prosecutorial and sentencing decisions.

What if a lawyer inadvertently discloses a privileged communication to an adversary, for example by mistakenly turning over a privileged document during discovery? As Chapter 4, Problem 1 indicated, lawyers differ about the ethical obligations of the lawyer who receives the "errant fax"; courts similarly differ over whether inadvertent disclosure waives the privilege. Most but not all recent decisions preserve the privilege in the face of accidental disclosure, and the *Restatement of the Law Governing Lawyers* agrees (see § 79, Illustration to Comment f). The Advisory Committee on Evidence Rules to the Judicial Conference of the United States has proposed a Federal Rule of Evidence, Rule 502, providing that privileged materials inadvertently shared during discovery in federal litigation or federal administrative proceedings are not waived "if the holder of the privilege or work product protection took reasonable precautions to prevent disclosure and took reasonably prompt measures, once the holder knew or should have known of the disclosure, to rectify the error." Congressional approval is required for the rule to become effective.

The Distinction Between the Duty of Confidentiality and the Attorney–Client Privilege

Though they are related, the ethical duty of confidentiality and the attorney-client privilege are not the same. The ethical duty of confidentiality under the Model Rules covers a much broader range of communication than the attorney-client privilege. The attorney-client privilege is a rule of evidence, which protects only attorney-client communications from disclosure in a proceeding before a tribunal. By contrast, the ethical duty of confidentiality forbids lawyers from divulging confidential information to anyone, not just to a tribunal. The rules governing the attorney-client privilege have been developed by courts and legislatures; the duty of confidentiality, though nominally promulgated by the jurisdiction's highest court, is in fact part of the bar's self-regulatory structure. The attorney-client privilege is riddled with exceptions that are generally not exceptions to the duty of confidentiality. Of all the exceptions identified above, only explicit or implied consent by the client can waive the lawyer's ethical obligations of secrecy.

To take a conspicuous example, discussed further in section C, *infra*, conversations concerning future client crimes or frauds do not fall under the attorney-client privilege, but in some states they are nevertheless protected by the ethical duty of confidentiality. When courts determine that information is not covered by the attorney-client privilege, they may order

---

14. *In re* Columbia/HCA Healthcare Corp. Billing Practices Litigation, 293 F.3d 289 (2002). See also *In re* Quest Commissions Int. Inc., Securities Litigation, 22 *Lawyers Manual of Professional Conduct* 300 (19th Cir. 2006).

the lawyer to divulge the information or respond to a subpoena, even though the information remains confidential under bar ethical rules. Lawyers who refuse to testify when directed to do so may be guilty of contempt of court.

The distinction between the ethical duty of confidentiality and the evidentiary privilege is underscored in the ABA Model Rules of Professional Conduct. Model Rule 1.6 protects all "information relating to representation of a client."[15] By contrast, the attorney-client privilege protects only confidential communications from a client, and only from disclosure to a tribunal.

Information About Client Identity and Lawyers' Fees

One category of information that has traditionally fallen outside the privilege involves basic information about the attorney-client relationship itself: the identity of the client, the size of the lawyer's fee, the name of the person paying the fee if it is someone other than the client, and the fact that the attorney-client relationship exists.

In recent years, federal prosecutors have attempted with increasing frequency to subpoena attorneys in order to obtain such information. Lawyers representing low-level participants in organized crime can be asked to reveal who is paying their fees and how much they are receiving. Such information can be useful in building a "net worth" case against organized crime bosses. (In a net worth case, the prosecution proves that the defendant has spent more money than his lawful sources of income can explain.) Defense counsel complain that prosecutors are using subpoenas for harassment, in an effort to drive a wedge between them and their clients. Despite such complaints, however, courts have declined to view information about client identity or attorney's fees as privileged communications. Courts have also rejected claims of privilege to shield clients who allegedly purchased illegal tax shelters.[16]

One exception occurs when identifying the client would be tantamount to revealing otherwise-privileged information as well. In the leading case, *Baird v. Koerner*, 279 F.2d 623 (9th Cir.1960), a group of taxpayers instructed their attorney to make an anonymous payment of back taxes, presumably to improve their position in any subsequent criminal investigation. The Ninth Circuit Court of Appeals held that the clients' identities were privileged, because to reveal their identities would be tantamount to revealing the privileged information that they owed back taxes. As the *Restatement* summarizes the doctrine, "The privilege applies if the testimo-

---

15. The ABA's 1969 Code of Professional Responsibility also protects a broader category of material than the privilege. It encompasses all "information gained in the professional relationship that the client has requested be held inviolate or the disclosure of which would be embarrassing or would be likely to be detrimental to the client." DR 4–101(A). Several important jurisdictions, such

as the District of Columbia and New York state, follow this older rule. The Code protects such categories of information from disclosure to anyone in any setting, apart from the few exceptions noted in DR 4–101(C).

16. United States v. KPMG LLP, 316 F.Supp.2d 30 (D.D.C.2004); United States v. Jenkins & Gilchrist, P.C., 2004 WL 870824 (N.D. Ill. 2004).

ny [about the client] directly or by reasonable inference would reveal the content of a confidential communication." § 69, Comment *g*.

PROBLEM 2

A pedestrian is killed in a hit-and-run automobile accident in which the identity of the driver is unknown. A few days later, an attorney representing the driver approaches the district attorney and states that his client will turn himself in provided that a favorable plea agreement can be worked out in advance. The victim's parents subsequently file a wrongful death action against "Doe I," the driver of the car. They subpoena the attorney for purposes of obtaining information as to the client's identity, and the attorney claims an attorney-client privilege. What results?

B. THE JUSTIFICATION OF THE PRIVILEGE

NOTES

The theory behind the attorney-client privilege is explicitly instrumental in character: sealing the lawyer's lips is a means of serving wider societal goals, not an end in itself. The underlying assumption, as McCormick summarizes it, is that:

> the law is complex and in order for members of the society to comply with it in the management of their affairs and the settlement of their disputes they require the assistance of expert lawyers. Second, lawyers are unable to discharge this function without the fullest possible knowledge of the facts of the client's situation. And last, the client cannot be expected to place the lawyer in full possession of the facts without the assurance that the lawyer cannot be compelled, over the client's objection, to reveal the confidences in court. The consequent loss to justice of the power to bring all pertinent facts before the court is, according to the theory, outweighed by the benefits to justice (not to the individual client) of a franker disclosure in the lawyer's office.[17]

This line of argument presumes that without the privilege, candid disclosure from client to lawyer will be chilled; the adversary system will function less effectively, and societal interests in justice will be ill-served.

This justification for the privilege rests on certain assumptions about both the effectiveness of the adversary system and the impact of the privilege on clients' willingness to disclose compromising information to their lawyers. Chapter IV raised questions about the efficacy of the adversary system, and current research casts doubt on the significance of the privilege in insuring candid communication. Public defenders report that many clients commonly lie and withhold information despite the privilege; indigent defendants often are unpersuaded that an appointed lawyer works

---

17. *McCormick on Evidence* § 87, at 120–21 (John W. Strong, ed., 4th ed. 1992).

for them and not for the state. White collar defenders similarly report that clients are often unwilling to supply damaging facts even though they have no reason to question their counsel's loyalty. On the other hand, some defendants will tell their story to anyone with a seemingly sympathetic ear, even someone that will not be shielded by the privilege—police, cell mates, prison guards or reporters.

The most systematic studies available reveal only a tenuous connection between confidentiality rules and the willingness of clients to reveal sensitive information to their lawyers. An early *Yale Law Journal* study found that "more people would talk to a lawyer without a privilege, than to a marriage counselor. . . . In fact, . . . most people were either unaware of the attorney-client privilege or believed that it extended to other professional relationships as well."[18] A *Journal of Corporation Law* survey of confidentiality in corporate practice found "no statistically significant association . . . between how often the attorney raises the issue of confidentiality and whether the employee shows concern over the issue."[19]

Professor Fred Zacharias's research on New York lawyers and clients produced a number of significant findings:

- Many of the lawyers he studied almost never informed their clients about the duty of confidentiality (and fewer than one in five informed their clients of confidentiality in the majority of cases);

- many of the clients misunderstood the nature and scope of confidentiality;

- only 30% of former clients said that they gave information to their lawyers that they would not have given without a guarantee of confidentiality; and

- only about half of the lay respondents predicted that they would withhold information without a guarantee of confidentiality.[20]

What accounts for these finding is not entirely clear. Perhaps confidentiality mattered to only 30% of the former clients because only 30% had sensitive information. Nevertheless, Zacharias's survey raises questions about how often confidentiality is necessary and sufficient to avoid chilling client disclosures.

A study of New Jersey lawyers found that the vast majority tell at least some of their clients about confidentiality. However, almost none inform their clients about the exceptions to confidentiality. Apparently, most lawyers fear that doing so will undermine the very trust they are trying to create.[21]

---

18. Note, "Functional Overlap Between the Lawyer and Other Professionals: Its Implications for the Privileged Communications Doctrine," 71 *Yale L.J.* 1226, 1232 (1962).

19. Eric Slater & Anita Sorenson "Corporate Legal Ethics—An Empirical Study: The Model Rules, the Code of Professional Responsibility, and Counsel's Continuing Struggle Between Theory and Practice," 8 *J.Corp.L.* 601, 622 (1983).

20. Fred C. Zacharias, "Rethinking Confidentiality," 74 *Iowa L. Rev.* 351, 380–83 (1989).

21. Leslie C. Levin, "Testing the Radical Experiment: A Study of Lawyer Responses to Clients Who Intend to Harm Others,"

Even granting the background assumptions about client candor, however, the instrumental argument for the privilege is not self-evidently correct. Jeremy Bentham's famous and forceful critique suggests why. (Bentham, one of the founders of utilitarianism, was also a celebrated jurist.)

Jeremy Bentham, Rationale of Judicial Evidence, Specially Applied to English Practice

302–04, 309–11 (Garland Publishing, Inc. 1978; reprint, 1827).

SECT. II.—*Lawyer and Client.*

English judges have taken care to exempt the professional members of the partnership from so unpleasant an obligation as that of rendering service to justice. . . .

When, in consulting with a law adviser, attorney or advocate, a man has confessed his delinquency, or disclosed some fact which, if stated in court, might tend to operate in proof of it, such law adviser is not to be suffered to be examined as to any such point. The law adviser is neither to be compelled, nor so much as suffered, to betray the trust thus reposed in him. Not suffered? Why not? Oh, because to betray a trust is treachery; and an act of treachery is an immoral act.

An immoral sort of act, is that sort of act, the tendency of which is, in some way or other, to lessen the quantity of happiness in society. In what way does the supposed cause in question tend to the production of any such effect? The conviction and punishment of the defendant, he being guilty, is by the supposition an act the tendency of which, upon the whole, is beneficial to society. Such is the proposition which for this purpose must be assumed. . . .

But if such confidence, when reposed, is permitted to be violated, and if this be known, (which, if such be the law, it will be), the consequence will be, that no such confidence will be reposed. Not reposed?—Well: and if it be not, wherein will consist the mischief? The man by the supposition is guilty; if not, by the supposition there is nothing to betray; let the law adviser say every thing he has heard, every thing he can have heard from his client, the client cannot have any thing to fear from it. That it will often happen that in the case supposed no such confidence will be reposed, is natural enough: the first thing the advocate or attorney will say to his client, will be,—Remember that, whatever you say to me, I shall be obliged to tell, if asked about it. What, then, will be the consequence? That a guilty person will not in general be able to derive quite so much assistance from his law adviser, in the way of concerting a false defence, as he may do at present. . . .

47 *Rutgers L. Rev.* 81, 122–23 (1994). For overviews of the critiques of broad confidentiality rules, see Deborah L. Rhode, *In the Interests of Justice* 106–14 (2001); William H. Simon, *The Practice of Justice: A Theory of Lawyers' Ethics* 54–62 (1998).

Thus much as to the case where the effect of the disclosure may be to subject the client to suffer as for an offence. Where the effect of it does not go beyond the subjecting him to some non-penal obligation to which he otherwise might not be subjected, or to debar him from some right of which he otherwise might have come into possession, or remained possessed,—the objection is no more reconcilable with the main object of the law than in the other case. In every such case, though by a process grievously and unnecessarily dilatory and expensive, what the law does, or to be consistent ought to do, is to compel each party, out of his own mouth, (or, to speak literally, by his own hand), to make disclosure of such facts as, lying within his own knowledge, are of a nature to contribute towards substantiating the claim of the adversary. Can there be any reason why that information, which he is compelled to give by his own hand, should not be obtained with equal facility from another hand, from which, if there be any difference, it may be extracted with less reluctance? . . .

QUESTIONS

1.   Wigmore summarizes Bentham's argument thus: "It always comes back to this, that the deterring of a guilty man from seeking legal advice is no harm to justice, while the innocent man has nothing to fear and therefore will not be deterred."[22] How would you respond to this argument?

One response is to question whether deterring a guilty man from seeking legal advice in fact poses no harm to justice. Bentham seems to define justice as convicting the guilty. This definition focuses on outcomes but ignores fair process—or rather, it assumes that fair procedures are whatever result in correct outcomes. Do you agree? Is such a view consistent with the due process clause of our Constitution or with the Fourth and Fifth Amendments, both of which may impede the search for truth and allow the guilty to escape? Some writers have argued that to restrict or remove the attorney-client privilege would have the effect of forcing criminal defendants to choose between constitutional rights. Either they would hide facts from their own attorneys, in effect nullifying the constitutional right to effective assistance of counsel, or else tell the attorneys facts that could later be revealed, in effect nullifying the right against self-incrimination (which Bentham also believed should be abolished).[23] Quite apart from these constitutional concerns, are there moral objections to convicting the guilty by deterring them from candid legal consultations?

2.   Moreover, is it always true that "the innocent man has nothing to fear and therefore will not be deterred" from speaking openly to his attorney? What about cases in which individuals falsely believe that they are guilty, perhaps because they are unaware of the availability of legal defenses (duress, necessity, self-defense, diminished capacity)? What about civil cases where an available defense (such as contributory negligence) is contingent on initially admitting fault, which defendants may be unwilling

---

22. Wigmore, *supra* note 9, at 552, § 2291.

23. David Luban, *Lawyers and Justice: An Ethical Study* 192–95 (1988).

to do because they do not understand the defense?[24] Bentham might respond that such cases are infrequent, so that the gains to law enforcement of abolishing the attorney-client privilege outweigh the wrongful convictions. What is your view? How much weight should we give to the prospect of wrongfully convicting the innocent?

3. Bentham's argument chiefly concerns criminal matters, in which a defendant will be found either guilty or not. But in civil disputes, as Wigmore notes, both sides may have disadvantageous facts that they wish to keep secret.[25] However, Bentham was convinced that his argument was even stronger in civil lawsuits than in criminal cases, for in the civil case, the effect of abolishing the privilege is less harsh than in criminal cases: the penalty for losing does not include punishment. Is this persuasive?

4. Wigmore also suggests that Bentham's proposal would have an adverse effect on the legal profession.

> The consideration of "treachery," so inviting an argument for Bentham's sarcasms, is after all not to be dismissed with a sneer.... Certainly the position of the legal adviser would be a difficult and disagreeable one, for it must be repugnant to any honorable man to feel that the confidences which his relation naturally invites are liable at the opponent's behest to be laid open through his own testimony. He cannot but feel the disagreeable inconsistency of being at the same time the solicitor and the revealer of the secrets of the cause. This double-minded attitude would create an unhealthy moral state in the practitioner.[26]

Consider this argument in the context of the Garrow case in Problem 1. Would the attorneys have been in a more "difficult and disagreeable" position if they had been required to reveal the location of victims' bodies rather than to keep the information confidential? Surely when lawyers wish for humanitarian reasons to blow the whistle on clients who have trusted them, the lawyers' position is "difficult and disagreeable" whatever they do. What is Wigmore's basis for suggesting that abolishing the privilege would induce a more "unhealthy moral state" in practitioners than does obligating them to stay silent against their will?

5. In *State v. Macumber*, 544 P.2d 1084 (Ariz.1976), a client on his deathbed confessed to his lawyers that he had committed murders for which another man, Macumber, was being tried. When the lawyers later attempted to testify for Macumber about this confession, the prosecutor invoked the attorney-client privilege on behalf of the deceased client. The prosecutor argued that traditionally the attorney-client privilege remains intact after the client's death. The trial judge agreed, and rejected the lawyers' proposed testimony. Macumber was convicted. On appeal, the Arizona Supreme Court upheld the invocation of the attorney-client privi-

---

24. See Ronald J. Allen, et al., "A Positive Theory of the Attorney–Client Privilege and the Work Product Doctrine," 19 *J. Legal Stud.* 359, 371 (1990).

25. Wigmore, *supra* note 9, at 552, § 2291.

26. *Id.* at 553.

lege, arguing that the legislature must have anticipated such cases when it codified a privilege that does not end at the client's death. Fortunately for Macumber, the court found other, unrelated errors in his conviction. If such errors had not been present, how should the case have been decided, and on what grounds? Consider that issue in light of cases discussed in Chapter VI, in which defense lawyers knew that their clients were guilty of crimes for which innocent men had been convicted.

The issue raised in *Macumber* re-emerged dramatically during the 1994 Whitewater investigation of President Bill Clinton and Hillary Rodham Clinton. (Whitewater was a dubious Arkansas real estate venture in which the Clintons had invested years earlier.) During that investigation, the Independent Counsel attempted to compel testimony from a law firm that had represented Vincent Foster. Foster, a White House aide, had committed suicide, and the special prosecutor wished to learn what he had told attorneys that may have been relevant to Whitewater inquiries. The D. C. Circuit held that the importance of the ongoing federal criminal investigation outweighed the importance of maintaining the privilege after the client's death. *In re Sealed Case*, 121 F.3d 729 (D.C.Cir.1997). However, the Supreme Court reversed. On the majority's view, "knowing that communications will remain confidential even after death encourages the client to communicate fully and frankly with counsel." The Court reaffirmed the traditional contours of the common-law attorney-client privilege, and rejected attempts to limit the privilege by balancing it against other concerns. *Swidler & Berlin v. United States*, 524 U.S. 399 (1998). Justice O'Connor's dissenting opinion argued that the privilege should yield in the face of compelling law enforcement needs, such as when information may be necessary to exonerate an innocent defendant.

The only well-established line of cases that permits balancing the privilege against other interests involves the so-called "corporate fiduciary exception" to the privilege in stockholder derivative suits. The leading precedent is *Garner v. Wolfinbarger*, 430 F.2d 1093 (5th Cir.1970), *cert. denied*, 401 U.S. 974 (1971), which considered whether shareholders in a derivative action should have access to otherwise-privileged communications between management and corporate attorneys. Rather than declaring the privilege absolute, *Garner* held that courts must balance the benefits of disclosure against the costs. Courts that follow *Garner* generally note that the parties seeking privileged information are stockholders of the corporation, who thus have some claim to being the "real" clients of corporate attorneys. Since management-defendants owe fiduciary obligations to these shareholders, the latter have a specially protected interest in obtaining sufficient information to ensure that such obligations are met. Thus, these cases do not represent genuine exceptions to the no-balancing approach affirmed by the Supreme Court in *Swidler & Berlin*.

The issue of whether the privilege should be balanced against other societal concerns is fundamental to its justification. If the justification of the privilege is basically utilitarian, it seems appropriate to weigh its objectives against other utilitarian ends. If, on the other hand, the justification rests on non-utilitarian values, such as respecting the rights and dignity of the client, the Supreme Court's no-balancing framework of *Swidler & Berlin* seems appropriate. Which approach seems to you to make the most sense? Where should the rights and dignity of non-clients figure in this analysis? Does the Court's ruling in *Swidler* imply that *Macumber* correctly decided the privilege issue?

6.   Ultimately, Bentham's argument against the attorney-client privilege is that it defeats justice by allowing wrongdoers to hide guilty facts with the assistance of a lawyer. When all else is said, does Bentham have a point?

C. THE CRIME–FRAUD EXCEPTION TO THE ATTORNEY–CLIENT PRIVILEGE

1. INTRODUCTION

The most significant exception to the attorney-client privilege arises when a client attempts to use an attorney's services to further a crime or fraud. Thus, for example, in *United States v. Hodge & Zweig*, 548 F.2d 1347 (9th Cir.1977), a drug dealer offered a lawyer a retainer to provide legal services for himself and his associates if any of them were arrested while importing drugs. Since the dealer approached the lawyer in furtherance of crimes, his conversations with the lawyer were outside the privilege.

Why the crime-fraud exception? Historically, many courts explained that when clients have misconduct in mind, they are not consulting attorneys in their professional capacity—as officers of the court—and thus no attorney-client relationship has formed.[27] Yet this argument seems artificial: it implies that the attorney-client relationship switches on and off as the conversation shifts from honest to dishonest topics. There are other, more straightforward, rationales for the crime-fraud exception. The purpose of the attorney-client privilege is to encourage clients to obtain legal advice that will facilitate their compliance with legal obligations or their vindication of legal rights. Such objectives do not encompass client efforts to violate the law. In Justice Cardozo's words, "the privilege takes flight if the relation is abused. A client who consults an attorney for advice that will serve him in the commission of a fraud will have no help from the law. He must let the truth be told." *Clark v. United States*, 289 U.S. 1, 15 (1933).

The crime-fraud exception has four primary conditions. First, a client's *intent* to commit a crime or fraud is enough to create the exception, regardless of whether the client believes the act to be a crime or fraud, and even if the client forms the wrongful intent after the lawyer-client conversation. Although most courts hold that wrongful intent without action is sufficient to trigger the crime-fraud exception, a minority position, en-

---

27. Geoffrey C. Hazard, Jr., "An Historical Perspective on the Attorney–Client Privilege," 66 *Calif. L. Rev.* 1061 (1978).

dorsed by the *Restatement*, maintains that the crime-fraud exception should apply only if the client later accomplishes the wrongful purpose. A contrary view, the *Restatement* argues, would penalize clients for consulting lawyers and being talked out of wrongful plans.[28] However, Paul Rice, the author of the principal treatise on the attorney-client privilege, rejects the *Restatement* argument:

> The client's communications should not retroactively be afforded the protection of the privilege simply because . . ., as a result of some fortuity, [he] did not have an opportunity or was unable to accomplish his illegal end. The wrong is the seeking of legal advice with the improper motive. If that is established, the client is not innocent. . . .[29]

Most courts agree with this traditional view, and view wrongful intent as sufficient to negate the privilege.[30]

Second, it is the *client's* intent to commit crime or fraud that is relevant, not the lawyer's. The crime-fraud exception applies even if lawyers have no knowledge of the client's illicit motive. Conversely, if the client has no criminal or fraudulent intent, the attorney-client privilege remains applicable even if the attorney's intentions are wrongful. For example, if an attorney knowingly assists one client in a crooked deal, communications between the attorney and innocent co-clients participating in the same transaction remain privileged.

Third, the exception applies only to conversations that are in furtherance of the crime or fraud. Thus, discussion of ongoing or future crimes and frauds typically falls outside the privilege, but professional conversations about a client's past misconduct usually remains protected.

Typically, a conversation about a past crime or fraud is not "in furtherance" of it, and that is why, in most cases, the crime-fraud exception is inapplicable. However, if a criminal tells a lawyer about a past crime in order to solicit the lawyer's help in fleeing the jurisdiction, the conversation *is* in furtherance of the crime, and therefore not privileged. Similarly, professional consultations between attorneys and clients about ongoing or future crimes and frauds typically are in furtherance of the misconduct, which is why the crime-fraud exception applies. However, if the client has come to the lawyer to ask for advice about the safest way to quit a criminal conspiracy before a crime is committed, the conversation is not in furtherance of the future crime, and the privilege remains intact.[31] Thus, although many lawyers and courts continue to declare that past frauds are privileged but future frauds are not, the most accurate way of stating the crime-fraud exception makes reference only to the "in furtherance of" test: was the conversation in furtherance of a crime or fraud? Whether the client-lawyer

---

28.   *Restatement of the Law Governing Lawyers*, § 82(a); *see* Comment c., at 615.

29.   1 Paul R. Rice, *Attorney–Client Privilege in the United States*, § 8.2 at 26 (1999).

30.   The influential District of Columbia Court of Appeals is the most prominent court

to follow the *Restatement*. *See In re* Sealed Case, 107 F.3d 46 (D.C.Cir.1997).

31.   Harry I. Subin, "The Lawyer as Superego: Disclosure of Client Confidences to Prevent Harm," 70 *Iowa L. Rev.* 1091, 1117 n. 51 (1985).

conversation concerns past, ongoing, or future conduct is simply a useful rule of thumb.

In distinguishing between "past," "ongoing," and "future" events, the baseline is the time that clients communicate with a lawyer, not the time at which they assert the privilege. If clients consult attorneys in furtherance of a crime or fraud before or during its commission, the conversation is unprivileged, and remains so after the unlawful act is complete.[32] Although this seems like a simple point, confusion often arises in practice. Suppose a client consults an attorney on Monday, uses what the attorney tells him to commit a crime on Tuesday, is arrested on Wednesday, and the attorney is subpoenaed to testify about the prior conversation on Thursday. The attorney may instinctively think "past crime," because the crime was committed two days before. But the crime wasn't past at the time of the attorney-client conversation, and so the crime-fraud exception applies and the conversation is not privileged.

Fourth, the party attempting to pierce the privilege bears the burden of proving that the crime-fraud exception applies. The Supreme Court held in *United States v. Zolin*, 491 U.S. 554 (1989), that when a party attempts to defeat the attorney-client privilege by invoking the crime-fraud exception, part of its evidentiary case that the crime-fraud exception applies may include the contested document itself, reviewed in camera by the judge. To obtain in camera review, the party moving the crime-fraud exception "must present evidence sufficient to support a reasonable belief that in camera review may yield evidence that establishes the exception's applicability." *Id.* at 574–75. This, the Court states, is "a lesser evidentiary showing ... than is required ultimately to overcome the privilege." *Id.* at 572.

But how much evidence is required to overcome the privilege? Under the standard test, to overcome the privilege through the crime-fraud exception "[t]here must be a showing of a prima facie case sufficient to satisfy the judge that the light should be let in."[33] Courts disagree, however, about what makes a prima facie case. Here are a few examples:

1.   An influential California opinion requires a preponderance of evidence: "if a judge in the pretrial period concludes that the evidence and argument are essentially in equipoise, i.e., that the evidence commands exculpatory and inculpatory inferences equally, the judge must deny the motion to penetrate the privilege under the crime-fraud exception." *Laser Industries, Ltd. v. Reliant Technologies, Inc.*, 167 F.R.D. 417 (N.D.Cal. 1996).

2.   D.C. Circuit: "The government satisfies its burden of proof if it offers evidence that if believed by the trier of fact would establish the elements of an ongoing or imminent crime or fraud." In re *Sealed Case*, 754 F.2d 395 (D.C. Cir. 1985)

---

32.   *In re* Grand Jury Proceedings (FMC Corp.), 604 F.2d 798, 803 (3d Cir.1979), provides a lucid explanation of this point.

33.   Clark v. United States, 289 U.S. at 14. For a more detailed exegesis of this prima facie case test, see *In re* Antitrust Grand Jury (Advance Publications, Inc.), 805 F.2d 155, 165–66 (6th Cir.1986).

3.   Sixth Circuit: "The evidence produced ... must raise more than a strong suspicion that a crime was committed to establish a *prima facie* violation, but it need not be as strong as that needed to effect an arrest or secure an indictment." In re *Antitrust Grand Jury (Advance Publications, Inc.)*, 805 F.2d 155, 166 (6th Cir.1986).

4.   Seventh Circuit: Noting that the D.C. Circuit's test requires "enough [evidence] to support a verdict in favor of the person making the claim," the Seventh Circuit disagrees, writing, "The question here is not whether the evidence supports a verdict but whether it calls for inquiry. Courts often use 'prima facie evidence' to refer to enough to require explanation rather than evidence that by itself satisfies a more-likely-than-not standard.... [A] prima facie case must be defined by regard to its function: to require the adverse party, the one with superior access to the evidence and in the best position to explain things, to come forward with that explanation." *In the Matter of Feldberg*, 862 F.2d 622, 625–26 (7th Cir.1988).

The California and D.C. Circuit's tests are the most demanding. The Sixth Circuit's standard is less rigorous, and the Seventh Circuit's appears to be the easiest of all for a party seeking to pierce the attorney-client privilege. The differences between the tests can make a large practical difference. For example, a D.C. Circuit decision upheld the privilege when the case for the crime-fraud exception rested on evidence that the attorney and client had discussed the subject-matter of an alleged crime shortly before the crime was committed. According to the court,

> That is not enough. One cannot reasonably infer from the meeting that the Company was consulting its general counsel with the intention of committing a crime.... True enough, within weeks of the meeting about campaign finance law, the vice president violated that law. But the government had to demonstrate that the Company sought the legal advice with the intent to further its illegal conduct. Showing temporal proximity between the communication and the crime is not enough.[34]

It seems clear that on the Seventh Circuit's less demanding test, a court should find the crime-fraud exception: surely the evidence of temporal proximity "calls for inquiry," which is all the Seventh Circuit requires.

PROBLEM 3

You are representing a client for violation of anti-spamming laws. On April 10, your client asks you whether, if he lists last year's profits from his computer activities on his current federal income tax return, the information might be used as evidence against him in the anti-spamming case. You answer that it might indeed, although you are certainly not recommending that he fail to report income. He changes the subject and does not mention his taxes again.

---

34.   *In re* Sealed Case, 107 F.3d 46, 50 (D.C. Cir. 1997).

A few months after the April 15 income tax filing date, the government convenes a grand jury to investigate possible income tax evasion by your client, based on the fact that his federal tax return lists no income from his computer activities. The federal prosecutor subpoenas you to testify about any conversations you had with your client about his federal income tax prior to April 15. You assert the attorney-client privilege, based on the fact that your conversations with your client concerned his defense against the anti-spamming charges. In response, the prosecutor argues that the crime-fraud exception applies.

Is the conversation privileged? What evidence might the prosecutor offer to establish the crime-fraud exception? What evidence might you offer in response?

2.   FRAUD

Conversations in furtherance of a crime or fraud are unprivileged; but what constitutes a fraud? Many frauds are crimes, specified as such by statute. Thus, for example, frauds are defined in ninety-two federal criminal statutes.[35] But the phrase "crime *or* fraud" makes it clear that the exception applies to civil conduct as well, and the boundaries of civil fraud are less well defined.

Bersani v. Bersani

Connecticut Superior Court, 1989.
565 A.2d 1368.

■ OPINION BY FREEDMAN, J.:

[The plaintiff wife filed for divorce, and received temporary custody of the two minor children. Without permission from the court, she took the children to Spain. The court found her in contempt, granted the divorce in a hearing that she did not attend but in which she was represented by counsel, and awarded custody of the children to the defendant husband. The plaintiff's attorney acknowledged that she knew her client's location, and the husband moved to compel the attorney to divulge this information.]

The defendant acknowledges in his memorandum in support of his motion to compel that Rule 1.6 of the Rules of Professional Conduct precludes, except as specifically authorized, disclosures by an attorney of confidential information imparted to the attorney by a client in the course of the attorney's representation. He argues, however, that sustaining the privilege in the present circumstances would "tend to immunize a flagrant violation of this court's orders and to inflict an unjustifiable harm to the interests of the defendant and of the children."

The plaintiff argues in her memorandum of law in opposition to the defendant's motion to compel that, while the court has an obligation to apply the best interests of the child standard in custody disputes, "the issue

---

35. Ellen S. Podgor, "Criminal Fraud,"
48 *Am. U. L. Rev.* 729, 740 (1999).

presently before this court does not involve custody, it involves disclosure of privileged information." The plaintiff further argues that the "best interests of the child" does not provide an exception to the confidentiality rule, and that providing too many exceptions would erode the rule and thereby impede the attorney's ability competently and earnestly to represent her client.

[The court notes that Wigmore's standard formulation of the attorney-client privilege, set out in Section A, *supra*, has been adopted by Connecticut courts.].

Subsection (c) (2) of Rule 1.6 of the Rules of Professional Conduct provides that a lawyer may reveal information relating to the representation of a client to the extent that the lawyer believes that it is necessary to "[r]ectify the consequence of a client's criminal or fraudulent act in the commission of which the lawyer's services had been used." Rule 3.3(a)(2) of the Rules of Professional Conduct states that "[a] lawyer shall not knowingly ... fail to disclose a material fact to a tribunal when disclosure is necessary to avoid assisting a criminal or fraudulent act by the client...."

It is the opinion of this court that the plaintiff's wilful contempt in leaving the country in violation of the court's order constitutes a fraud on the court, a fraudulent act under Rule 1.6 (c) (2). While it is clear to this court that the plaintiff's attorney did not assist or advise the plaintiff to violate the court's order, the attorney's present refusal to disclose her client's whereabouts does serve to assist the plaintiff in her ongoing violation of the court's order.

The New Jersey Supreme Court in *Fellerman v. Bradley*, 493 A.2d 1239 (1985), stated that in the context of the "crime or fraud" exception to the attorney-client privilege ..., "our courts have generally given the term 'fraud' an expansive reading." In *Fellerman*, the failure of the defendant's attorney to disclose the whereabouts of his client prevented the court from enforcing a provision of the final judgment in a dissolution action, to which the defendant had previously agreed, requiring the defendant to pay an expert's fee. The court stated that "the client, through his attorney, attempted to perpetrate a fraud on the court—to 'mock' justice—by consenting to and subsequently flouting a judgment that obligated him to bear the costs of an accountant."

The situation in the present case presents more compelling facts than those in *Fellerman* to justify the expansion of the meaning of fraud in Rule 1.6 (c) (2) beyond traditional tort or criminal law definitions to include those which constitute "a fraud on the court." The court in *Fellerman* concluded that the defendant's attempt to escape payment of a court ordered expense constituted a fraud on the court. The plaintiff's deliberate violation of the court's order in the present case has extended ramifications because it impedes the court's ability to implement its subsequent orders regarding custody, orders made in the best interests of the two minor children, not in the interests of either the plaintiff or the defendant.

The New York Court of Appeals in *Matter of Jacqueline F.*, 391 N.E.2d 967 (1979), required an attorney representing the guardian of a minor to disclose his client's address notwithstanding the attorney's claim that the information was protected under the attorney-client privilege.... The court ... noted that the attorney's client appeared to keep her address secret for the sole purpose of thwarting the mandate of the court's judgment awarding custody of the minor to her parents. The court held that "[u]nder these circumstances the attorney-client privilege, which exists to foster 'lawful and honest purposes' ... must yield to the best interests of the child."

[The court next reviews similar decisions from Missouri and Washington.]

This court, mindful of the importance of the attorney-client privilege and the function it serves in our adversary system, must nevertheless weigh the benefits of that privilege against the state's vital interest as parens patriae in determining the best interests of the minor children. While the plaintiff would have this court hold that the issue before it does not involve custody, the issue of custody here is inextricably intertwined with the issue of attorney-client privilege. The facts reveal: (1) that the plaintiff has left the country with the children in direct violation of a court order; (2) that the plaintiff's attorney knows the precise whereabouts of her client and declines to disclose that information; (3) that the failure to disclose that information assists the plaintiff in her ongoing contempt of the court's order; and (4) that the court's ability to effectuate subsequent orders issued in the best interests of the children has been thwarted.

It is this court's opinion, that, under the circumstances, the attorney-client privilege does not apply to information imparted to an attorney by a client in the course of perpetrating a fraud on the court. Moreover, any claim of privilege must yield in these circumstances to the best interests of the children. Accordingly, the defendant's motion to compel counsel to reveal the whereabouts of the plaintiff and the children is granted.

NOTES AND QUESTIONS

1. What is the court's rationale for denying the plaintiff's claim of privilege? Is it that the "privilege must yield ... to the best interests of the children," or that "the plaintiff's wilful contempt in leaving the country in violation of the court's order constitutes a fraud on the court" and thus creates the crime-fraud exception? The first theory seems too broad: it virtually eliminates the attorney-client privilege in cases involving minor children. The second theory is also very broad: it seems to imply that any violation of a court order constitutes a fraud on the court. A third possibility is that violating a court order contrary to the best interests of minor children constitutes a fraud on the court. What might be the rationale for this more limited theory?

2. a) *Black's Law Dictionary* offers several definitions of "fraud." All of them include two central elements: (1) knowing or reckless misrepresentation of the truth or concealment of a material fact, and (2) a purpose to

induce someone else to act to his or her detriment.[36] The absent parents in *Bersani* and in the cases it discusses are all concealing a material fact—their location and that of their children. But where is the second element, inducement to act?

b) The "Terminology" section of the Model Rules states that " 'Fraud' or 'Fraudulent' denotes conduct that is fraudulent under the substantive or procedural law of the applicable jurisdiction and has a purpose to deceive." Model Rule 1.0(d). Under this characterization, is Ms. Bersani engaged in fraud by refusing to reveal her location?

c) The *Restatement* states that "[f]raud, for the purpose of the [crime-fraud] exception, requires a knowing or reckless misrepresentation (or nondisclosure when applicable law requires disclosure) likely to injure another," a concept of fraud that it draws from the law of torts. *Restatement*, § 82, cmt. *d*.

d) In his hornbook on legal ethics, Charles Wolfram writes:

> More likely, *fraud* in the catchword phrase used to describe the [crime-fraud] doctrine stands as synecdoche for all intentional wrongs involving a client acting with bad faith and intending, or purposefully oblivious to, serious harm to another.[37]

In line with this formulation, some courts have extended the crime-fraud exception to encompass abuse of the attorney-client relationship to commit torts as well as crimes or frauds.[38] Does Wolfram's formulation, or the "crime-fraud-tort" exception, apply in *Bersani*?

e) In an influential opinion, the District of Columbia Circuit held that the crime-fraud doctrine applies in the context of a "crime, fraud, or other type of misconduct fundamentally inconsistent with the basic premises of the adversary system." *In re Sealed Case*, 676 F.2d 793, 812 (D.C.Cir.1982). Is this broader or narrower than Wolfram's formulation? Does it apply in *Bersani*?

3.   Is any concealment in breach of a legal duty a fraud for purposes of the crime-fraud exception? What arguments would justify a broad or narrow interpretation of the exception?

3.   A Case Study: The Minnesota Tobacco Litigation

One of the nation's most dramatic examples of the crime-fraud exception involves the multitude of state lawsuits against the tobacco industry in the 1990s. The example is not only highly controversial, it is also highly illuminating about the practicalities of proving a prima facie case for the exception. To understand the context of the confidentiality issues, it is

---

36.   *Black's Law Dictionary* 670–71 (7th ed. 1999).

37.   Charles Wolfram, *Modern Legal Ethics* 280 (1986).

38.   *See, e.g., In re* Sealed Case, 737 F.2d 94, 98–99 (D.C.Cir.1984); *but cf.* Motley v. Marathon Oil Co., 71 F.3d 1547, 1551 (10th Cir.1995) (declining to extend crime-fraud exception to torts).

helpful to review the material on the tobacco litigation included in Chapter IV, Problem 5. Other relevant information is summarized below.

Background to Minnesota Tobacco Litigation: The Three "Waves"

It has become customary to distinguish three "waves" of litigation over smoking-related injuries. From the 1950s until the 1990s—the "first wave" of litigation—the tobacco industry never lost a personal injury lawsuit. In part, this was because juries regularly regarded smoking as chosen, voluntary behavior, and for much of this period the industry also succeeded in casting doubt on the causal connection between cigarettes and illness. However, the industry's spectacular litigation success-record depended as well on what observers termed "General Patton"-style discovery tactics. As one tobacco defense lawyer explained:

> [T]he aggressive posture we have taken regarding depositions and discovery in general continues to make these cases extremely burdensome and expensive for plaintiffs' lawyers, particularly sole practitioners. To paraphrase General Patton, the way we won these cases was not by spending all of [R. J. Reynolds]'s money, but by making that other son of a bitch spend all his.[39]

The first meaningful disclosure of tobacco industry documents came during the second wave of cigarette litigation in the 1980s. In *Cipollone v. Liggett Group, Inc.*, 683 F.Supp. 1487 (D.N.J.1988), the most notable second wave case, the court ordered the tobacco industry to release thousands of pages of confidential documents. A companion case to *Cipollone* provided the first indications of the extent of the role of tobacco company lawyers in shielding documents from discovery on debatable claims of privilege. In *Haines v. Liggett Group Inc.*, U.S. District Judge H. Lee Sarokin reviewed documents in camera, and concluded as follows:

> Despite the industry's promise to engage independent researchers to explore the dangers of cigarette smoking and to publicize their findings, the evidence clearly suggests that the research was not independent; that potentially adverse results were shielded under the caption of "special projects;" that the attorney-client privilege was intentionally employed to guard against such unwanted disclosure; and that the promise of full disclosure was never meant to be honored and never was. 140 F.R.D. 681, 684 (D.N.J.1992).

According to Sarokin, industry lawyers invoked the privilege to shield documents that were sent to lawyers not to obtain legal advice, but merely to obtain the attorney-client privilege. On this basis, Judge Sarokin found a prima facie showing of crime-fraud against the industry, and rejected the industry's claims of privilege. However, Judge Sarokin's decision was vacated and remanded on other grounds; furthermore, the court of appeals

---

39. Haines v. Liggett Group, Inc., 814 F.Supp. 414, 421 (D.N.J.1993) (quoting Apr. 29, 1998, Memorandum from J. Michael Jordan, counsel for RJR.)

removed Judge Sarokin—who the industry believed was biased against them—from the case.[40]

The Minnesota Tobacco Case

On August 17, 1994, Minnesota Attorney General Hubert H. "Skip" Humphrey III filed suit in Ramsey County District Court against seven tobacco companies and two tobacco research institutes for alleged violations of state consumer protection and antitrust laws. Several days later, Blue Cross and Blue Shield of Minnesota joined the litigation, becoming the first corporate insurers of health services to sue the tobacco industry on issues related to smoking.

Minnesota set out on a "determined discovery quest," according to plaintiffs' lawyer Michael Ciresi.[41] The state refused the tobacco industry's initial offer to comply with its discovery obligations by producing only those documents that it had previously disclosed in litigation elsewhere. In challenging the industry's claim of privilege, the state argued that certain categories of documents were not protected in the first instance, and that others fell under the crime-fraud exception.

One important precedent that may have reassured the Minnesota plaintiffs was the prior application of the crime-fraud exception by a Kansas district court to compel discovery of industry scientific research. An almost identical situation involving the misuse of the privilege by industry lawyers to conceal health hazards arose in the Dalkon Shield litigation. As noted in Problem 2 in Chapter IV, the Shield was an intrauterine contraceptive device manufactured by the A. H. Robins Corporation. It sometimes caused infections in its users that resulted in injuries, miscarriages, and sterility. Several thousand women became infertile as a result of Dalkon Shields. When reports of medical problems began to emerge, Robins directed its research scientists to report their findings on safety to the company's lawyers, rather than executives or doctors, in order to shield them behind the attorney-client privilege. During subsequent litigation, a court found a prima facie case that Robins

> failed to adequately test the Dalkon Shield before marketing it; attempted to develop hard evidence which misrepresented the nature, quality, safety and efficacy of the Dalkon Shield; ignored the mounting evidence against the Dalkon Shield, with knowledge of the potential harm caused by the product; relied upon invalid studies in an effort to refute or ignore the dangers potentially caused by the Dalkon Shield; and attempted, with the assistance of counsel, to devise strategies to

40. *See* Haines v. Liggett Group Inc., 975 F.2d 81, 91–94 (3d Cir.1992), vacating 140 F.R.D. 681 (D.N.J.1992) (finding the district court's characterization of the Federal Magistrate's Act erroneous); *id.* at 98 (removing Judge Sarokin). On remand, the plaintiffs' law firm sought permission to withdraw (citing financial hardship) before the claims of privilege were ever resolved.

41. Michael Ciresi et al., "Decades of Deceit: Document Discovery in the Minnesota Tobacco Litigation," 25 *Wm. Mitchell L. Rev.* 477, 489 (1999).

cover up Robins' responsibilities and lessen its liability with respect to the Dalkon Shield . . .[42]

The court regarded counsel's efforts to prevent evidence against the Shield from coming to light as fraudulent. On this basis, the court required disclosure of a number of otherwise-privileged documents.

Minnesota's strategy in the tobacco litigation succeeded brilliantly. In total, Minnesota would eventually compel the production of approximately thirty-five million pages of documents from all defendants.

The plaintiffs won a key, early battle by obtaining document indices that tobacco industry lawyers had created over many years to manage the millions of documents relating to smoking and health. Judge Fitzpatrick held that certain portions of the indices were discoverable, notwithstanding the fact that they were work products prepared in anticipation of litigation.[43] At bottom, the court's argument rested on the sheer impossibility of the plaintiffs carrying out meaningful discovery without the indices:

> If five attorneys were to devote twelve hours each per day, five days per week, to the task of reviewing those nine million pages—and limit their review to one minute per page—it would take nine years to review those documents alone.[44]

The indices gave the plaintiffs' lawyers a detailed "roadmap" to documents the tobacco industry lawyers had spent decades classifying and protecting.

In the spring of 1997, another major turning-point occurred in the tobacco litigation. Liggett Company, the smallest of the cigarette manufacturers, decided to make a "separate peace," breaking ranks with the rest of the industry to settle its cases on its own. In its settlement agreement, Liggett waived all of its claims of privilege and gave crucial documents to the Minnesota depository. The non-Liggett industry defendants, however, objected to the production of approximately 2,400 of the Liggett privileged documents, claiming that they were subject to a joint-defense privilege that could not be unilaterally waived by Liggett. They had a point. The Liggett documents included notes from off-the-record meetings of industry lawyers, and other secrets that would otherwise have remained privileged. The court directed the parties to file memoranda of law on the claims of privilege and joint defense.

Using documents produced in discovery and the privilege logs, Minnesota presented evidence that the industry had "engaged in a decades-long campaign to suppress scientific knowledge about the dangers of smoking, manipulated evidence of its knowledge of those dangers to conceal it from the public and the courts, and intentionally breached its duties to the public to truthfully research and report those dangers."[45] This evidence,

---

42. *In re* A.H. Robins Co., 107 F.R.D. 2, 14–15 (D.Kan.1985).

43. State *ex rel.* Humphrey v. Philip Morris, Inc., No. C1–94–8565, slip op. at 12 (Minn.Dist.Ct. Nov.1, 1995).

44. *Id.* at 13.

45. Ciresi, *supra* note 41, at 519.

Minnesota argued, established a prima facie case of crime-fraud that defeated the privilege.

The trial court agreed.[46] In support of its conclusion, the court cited to extensive documentary evidence, including:

- The defendants' assurances that they "would not knowingly distribute a dangerous product" and "that the tobacco industry was committed to providing safe products";

- defendants' "intentionally den[ying] or minimiz[ing] known health risks ..." and attempting "to create doubt as to a connection between smoking and illness" and "to create doubt that cigarette smoking causes illness"; and

- defendants' use of attorneys and claims of privilege to suppress information and documents "which appear to be scientific in nature and specifically related to health issues."[47]

The court further criticized the tobacco industry for using the attorney-client privilege as both a "shield" and a "sword," by disclosing only favorable scientific findings while hiding unfavorable ones. In its view, the defendants should not "be permitted to use in its advertising and public relations campaigns, health-related research which support their economic interests, and to claim privilege for research which may lead to the opposite conclusion."[48] This holding is consistent with the view of partial waiver quoted earlier from In re *Grand Jury Proceedings (United States v. Doe)*, 219 F.3d 175, 182 (2d Cir.2000). The court added:

> In considering whether the crime-fraud exception may be applied to the facts of this case, this Court ... concludes that the Defendants had an independent obligation to conduct research into the safety of its product, and to warn the product's consumers if the research results supported negative conclusions. A manufacturer has a special duty, apart from litigation, to keep abreast of the hazards posed by its products.... The cigarette industry itself has recognized this duty. Plaintiffs have presented evidence, and this Court has found, however, that the Defendants have claimed safety-related scientific research conducted by the Defendants has been the subject of claims of attorney-client privilege.[49]

The trial court's order provided the industry with an additional opportunity to rebut the prima facie findings of crime-fraud in proceedings before a court-appointed special master. The trial court also set up a novel procedure for determination of the industry's privilege claims for the Liggett documents. For all practical purposes, it was physically impossible for the special master to conduct an in camera review of all the docu-

---

46. Order Regarding Privilege and the Crime Fraud Exception and Setting Forth Procedures to Determine Privilege Beginning with the Liggett Documents, State *ex rel.* Humphrey v. Philip Morris, Inc., 1997 WL 33635815 (Minn.Dist.Ct.1997).

47. *Id.* at 3–11.

48. *Id.* at 28.

49. *Id.*

ments—the judge calculated that doing so would take the special master more than six years, doing nothing but reading documents 2,000 hours a year. Instead, the judge ruled that the special master could "sample" documents from each category and on this basis make a determination of privilege for the entire category.[50]

Unsurprisingly, the tobacco companies objected strongly to the "sampling" method. Their appeal to the Minnesota Supreme Court was, however, unsuccessful. Eventually, Special Master Mark Gehan would examine just 3% of the papers to determine which of the remaining 97% ought to be made public. The tobacco companies had argued that the category method would erroneously expose certain privileged documents filed in several different categories (some privileged, some not). This fear turned out to be well-founded. A 1985 Jones, Day, Reavis & Pogue memo that traces the involvement of R. J. Reynolds lawyers in directing and occasionally suppressing research into the effects of tobacco, for example, was eventually classified in four non-privileged categories and one privileged category. Judge Fitzpatrick ordered reluctant tobacco lawyers to produce the memo, which found its way onto the Internet later in the year.[51]

In 1997, the special master issued a report regarding the Liggett documents; three months later, the trial court adopted the special master's recommendation and held that almost half of approximately 2,000 Liggett documents were not within the scope of the privilege or, if privileged, were discoverable under the crime-fraud exception.[52] According to the special master, some documents were not within the privilege because they "reflect attorneys selecting and directing research projects" rather than giving legal advice.[53] Similarly, scientific research documents and public statements "do not demonstrate a process of a client seeking advice or an attorney providing advice."[54] Other documents were subject to disclosure under the crime-fraud exception, because "they demonstrate the actual involvement of the attorneys for the defendant companies in the selection, funding, and funding continuation for [Council on Tobacco Research] special projects and because these documents provide relevant evidence of the response by the defendants to allegations from external sources to the effect that the defendants' products were unsafe."[55]

Almost simultaneously with the trial court's December order, the tobacco companies submitted the Liggett documents to Rep. Thomas Bliley in response to a congressional subpoena. Rep. Bliley then published most of the documents on the Internet for the public to view.

50. *Id*. at 11.

51. Alison Frankel, "Stubbing Out the Privilege," *American Lawyer*, June 1998.

52. Report of the Special Master: Findings of Fact, Conclusions of Law and Recommendations, State *ex rel*. Humphrey v. Philip Morris Inc., No. C1–94–8565 (Minn.Dist.Ct. Sept.10, 1997); Order With Respect to Non–Liggett Defendants' Objections to the Special Master's Report Dated September 10, 1997, State *ex rel*. Humphrey v. Philip Morris Inc., No. C1–94–8565 (Minn.Dist.Ct. Sept.12, 1997).

53. Report of the Special Master, at 43.

54. *Id*. at 45, 48–49.

55. *Id*. at 43.

Next, the special master turned his attention to the 200,000 non-Liggett documents; again, he relied on the controversial "sampling" method. On grounds similar to those given in the decision about the Liggett documents, he concluded that approximately 39,000 non-Liggett documents fell outside the attorney-client privilege. Tobacco industry appeals proved unavailing, and the Minnesota Supreme Court found that the "extraordinary relief" the industry sought—document-by-document review—was "an impossibility."[56]

On May 8, 1998 the industry agreed to a settlement which was "unprecedented in terms of monetary relief, injunctive requirements, and disclosure of internal tobacco company documents."[57] The Minnesota settlement called for the tobacco industry to pay the state $6.1 billion over the next 25 years and another $466 million (or about 7.1%) to the state's lawyers. In a separate agreement announced on the same day, industry defendants agreed to pay Blue Cross and Blue Shield of Minnesota $469 million over five years. Lawyers were awarded an additional $126 million from defendants for their representation of Blue Cross.[58] The tobacco companies agreed to further measures that included maintaining a warehouse document depository for the next ten years, open to the public, and dissolving the Center for Tobacco Research.[59]

QUESTIONS

1. According to the Minnesota court, the industry's "special duty" to conduct research on the safety of cigarettes and to warn the public of hazards implied that the industry's efforts to hide the hazards amounted to a fraud. Through deceit, the state and public had been deprived of something to which they were legally entitled. Does this mean that any attempt by a manufacturer to withhold information about product hazards (for example, by quietly settling products liability cases and signing secrecy agreements with the plaintiffs) amounts to fraud that negates the attorney-client privilege? Is that too broad a theory?

2. During the third wave of tobacco litigation, virtually every court that reviewed the industry's allegedly privileged documents in camera found that some documents were not within the privilege or were subject to disclosure under the crime-fraud exception. Industry lawyers objected to these findings. An R.J. Reynolds attorney told reporters that what happened to tobacco company documents could happen in other industries that have similar committees of counsel meeting about common concerns. "Don't think it can only apply to a politically unpopular industry."[60] In the

---

56. State *ex rel.* Humphrey v. Philip Morris Inc., Nos. CX–98–414, CX–98–431, 1998 WL 154543, at 1 (Minn.1998).

57. Ciresi, *supra* note 41, at 478.

58. "Tobacco Companies to Pay Minnesota, Blue Cross $6.6 Billion Plus Fees," *Mealey's Litigation Reports: Tobacco*, May 21, 1998.

59. *Id.*

60. Rex Bossert, "A Splintered Privilege: Two Judges Have Taken Exception to Tobacco's Confidentiality Claims," *Nat'l. L. J.*, April 7, 1997, at A1.

same vein, lawyers for Philip Morris argued that the "radical incursions on privilege law" in the Minnesota litigation could threaten traditional protections of privilege in suits against other companies.[61]

How radical are these incursions? The Minnesota court's method of determining privilege by categorizing documents and sampling a small number from each category was novel, and provoked intense controversy. "This is completely and utterly without precedent," claimed counsel to Brown & Williamson. "You can't even find sweepings in the corners of law libraries to suggest that this is appropriate."[62] Jones, Day litigation chairman John Strauch agreed: "I can't think of a worse system for something as important as attorney-client privilege."[63] One of the plaintiffs' lawyers countered that defense counsel had only themselves to blame. First they stonewalled, and then they made a "calculated decision" not to handpick documents within each category to show the special master before he made his recommendations.[64]

Given the practical impossibility of reviewing thirty-five million documents in camera, how else could the court have determined the issue of privilege? On the other hand, given the inevitable errors that led to disclosure of privileged documents, how can the sampling technique satisfy the requirements of justice?

3. Professors Edward J. Imwinkelried and James R. McCall applaud the Minnesota special master's report for sending a strong legal ethics message to the bar and for ordering disclosure of tobacco research, but contend that the report erred in evaluating the discoverability of the research solely in terms of the traditional attorney-client and work product privileges. They argue that such an application of the crime-fraud exception might, in the future, discourage product safety research in other industries.[65] Is this a valid concern? How should courts respond?

4. The Minnesota court removed the privilege from tobacco industry documents using two different theories. First, the court held that some of the documents should not have been protected in the first place, because they were not communicated to attorneys for purposes of helping them in legal representation. Rather, they were communicated to attorneys only to allow the attorneys to shield them under a claim of privilege. Second, the court held that attempting to conceal health information about cigarettes was fraudulent, and thus the exception to the privilege applies. Why did the court use both theories?

5. After the U.S. Supreme Court declined to halt the release of tobacco industry documents, an unidentified spokesman for the industry stated:

> This decision eviscerates effective legal representation that lies at the core of our system of civil justice. Unless our nation has openly decided

---

61. John J. Mulderig et al., "Tobacco Cases May be Only the Tip of the Iceberg for Assaults on Privilege," 67 *Def. Counsel J.* 16 (January 2000).

62. Frankel, *supra* note 51.

63. *Id.*

64. *Id.*

65. Edward J. Imwinkelried and James R. McCall, "Minnesota v. Philip Morris, Inc.: An Important Legal Ethics Message Which Neglects the Public Interest in Product Safety Research," 87 *Ky. L.J.* 1127 (1999).

that the normal standards of law apply to everyone except tobacco companies, this decision continues to tilt what should be the fair and level playing field that has been a hallmark of the American judicial process for more than 200 years.[66]

Is this fair? Did the tobacco industry's own conduct justify the treatment it received?

4. The "War on Terror" and the Attorney-Client Privilege

Less than two months after the September 11, 2001 terrorist attacks, the Department of Justice published an amendment to federal regulations pertaining to prison inmates who may be terrorists. The amended regulation states:

> In any case where the Attorney General specifically so orders, based on information from the head of a federal law enforcement or intelligence agency that reasonable suspicion exists to believe that a particular inmate may use communications with attorneys or their agents to further or facilitate acts of terrorism, the Director, Bureau of Prisons, shall ... provide appropriate procedures for the monitoring or review of communications between that inmate and attorneys or attorneys' agents who are traditionally covered by the attorney-client privilege, for the purpose of deterring future acts that could result in death or serious bodily injury to persons, or substantial damage to property that would entail the risk of death or serious bodily injury to persons.
>
> . . .
>
> (2) Except in the case of prior court authorization, the Director, Bureau of Prisons, shall provide written notice to the inmate and to the attorneys involved, prior to the initiation of any monitoring or review under this paragraph (d). The notice shall explain:
>
> > (i) That ... all communications between the inmate and attorneys may be monitored, to the extent determined to be reasonably necessary for the purpose of deterring future acts of violence or terrorism;
> >
> > (ii) That communications between the inmate and attorneys or their agents are not protected by the attorney-client privilege if they would facilitate criminal acts or a conspiracy to commit criminal acts, or if those communications are not related to the seeking or providing of legal advice.
>
> (3) The Director, Bureau of Prisons, with the approval of the Assistant Attorney General for the Criminal Division, shall employ appropriate procedures to ensure that all attorney-client communications are reviewed for privilege claims and that any properly privileged materials (including, but not limited to, recordings of privileged communications)

---

66. "Commerce Committee Puts Documents on Web After Supreme Court Rejects Stay Sought by Industry," *Mealey's Litigation Reports: Tobacco*, April 24, 1998.

are not retained during the course of the monitoring. To protect the attorney-client privilege and to ensure that the investigation is not compromised by exposure to privileged material relating to the investigation or to defense strategy, a privilege team shall be designated, consisting of individuals not involved in the underlying investigation. The monitoring shall be conducted pursuant to procedures designed to minimize the intrusion into privileged material or conversations. Except in cases where the person in charge of the privilege team determines that acts of violence or terrorism are imminent, the privilege team shall not disclose any information unless and until such disclosure has been approved by a federal judge.[67]

An ABA task force strongly opposed the taping of prison conversations between lawyers and clients, on several grounds. The most basic is, quite simply, that monitoring will unduly chill essential conversations between attorneys and their clients. The task force argues that the new regulation violates a federal statute requiring that federal detainees "be afforded reasonable opportunity for private consultation with counsel." 18 USC § 3142(e). In the task force's view, the privilege team (which the task force refers to as the "taint team") will in reality provide no protection of privileged conversations.

> Existing case law ... clearly establishes that when an inmate makes telephone calls over a telephone line that he or she knows is monitored, the necessary expectation of confidentiality is lacking and the calls therefore do not qualify as privileged *ab initio*.... Thus, under established case law, the taint team would have legal support for finding that *none* of the recorded attorney-client consultations they are called upon to review fall within the scope of the privilege, because the requisite expectation of confidentiality is lacking. And even if the government is willing to foreswear taking such an approach, there is nothing to prevent co-defendants, defendants in related cases, or private plaintiffs, for example from maintaining that these conversations were unprivileged and should be discoverable, either by subpoenaing the tapes or by subpoenaing the attorney involved. Indeed, where a taint team learns information in the course of monitoring an interview that may exculpate another individual, the government will be required—under *Brady v. Maryland*, 373 U.S. 83 (1963)—either to disclose that exculpatory information to the interested party or to dismiss the relevant criminal charges against that individual.[68]

The ABA task force accordingly concluded that the new regulation interferes with vital Fifth and Sixth Amendment rights.

QUESTIONS

1. How useful is the regulation likely to be in deterring terrorists? How much is it likely to interfere with candid attorney-client conversations?

---

67.   28 C.F.R. § 501.3(d).

68.   ABA Criminal Justice Section and Task Force on Terrorism and the Law, letter from Robert E. Hirshon to General Counsel, Rule Unit, Bureau of Prisons, Dec. 28, 2001.

2. The regulation states "[t]hat communications between the inmate and attorneys or their agents are not protected by the attorney-client privilege if they would facilitate criminal acts or a conspiracy to commit criminal acts." Is this a correct statement of the crime-fraud exception? Can a communication facilitate criminal acts without the client intending the conversation to further those acts?

3. The regulation permits secret taping of attorney-client conversations in prison, without notification, if a federal judge approves it. Such secret taping occurred in Lynne Stewart's conversations with Sheik Abdul Rahman. The regulation also permits the privilege team to reveal privileged information if a judge so orders. Are these provisions justified?

4. The ABA fears that review of tapes by a privilege team will not protect any attorney-client conversations because no conversations that occur while the parties know they are being taped will be protected in the first place. Is this realistic? In *United States v. Hatcher,* 323 F.3d 666, 674 (8th Cir. 2003), the Eighth Circuit Court of Appeals held that taped prison conversations between inmates and their attorneys are not privileged, because the knowledge that the conversations were being taped waives the privilege; to date, no courts have disagreed.

5. In a related issue, lawyers representing clients in terrorism cases have complained that their conversations with their clients are being wiretapped by the government's terrorist surveillance program.[69] Should the government be allowed to do so?

D. The Attorney-Client Privilege: Organizational Clients

In one sense, the issues surrounding the attorney-client privilege are no different when the client is an organization than when the client is a natural person. In both situations, the objective is to promote full and frank communication between lawyers and clients, which is necessary to insure loyalty, trust, and competence in professional practice. In another sense, however, the differences between an individual, natural person as client and an artificial person composed of many individuals raise unique questions that affect both the scope and the rationale of the privilege.

1. The Scope of the Organizational Attorney-Client Privilege

A fundamental principle of representing an organization is that professional obligations run to the entity itself, not to any of its officers,

---

69. Philip Shenon, "Lawyers Fear Monitoring in Cases on Terrorism," *N.Y. Times,* Apr. 28, 2008 at A14.

directors, or employees. Model Rule 1.13. Obviously, the organization speaks through management, but no member of management is "the client" of the organization's lawyer. This raises questions about which communications between a lawyer and the organization's officers and employees lie within the attorney-client privilege. Whose confidences must be kept? And from whom?

If, for example, a corporation's CEO tells the lawyer in confidence that he has committed acts constituting embezzlement, the lawyer's fiduciary duties clearly run to the corporation. Counsel must therefore inform the board of directors of the embezzlement. Yet the situation remains one of some delicacy, because the CEO may have been relying on the lawyer's duty of confidentiality. For this reason, Model Rule 1.13(f) states:

> In dealing with an organization's directors, officers, employees, members, shareholders or other constituents, a lawyer shall explain the identity of the client when it is apparent that the organization's interests are adverse to those of the constituents with whom the lawyer is dealing.

In effect, the lawyer must issue "Miranda warnings" to corporate officers and employees if it is clear that they are communicating information that cannot be held in confidence.

Another thorny issue involves which employees and agents of the organization personify the client for purposes of the privilege. For many years, courts employed two different approaches in identifying the client for purposes of the attorney-client privilege. One approach restricted the privilege to conversations between the corporation's lawyer and members of its "control group," that is, senior management.[70] The alternative "subject matter" test originated in *Harper & Row Publishers, Inc. v. Decker,* and was elaborated as a five-part test in *Diversified Industries, Inc. v. Meredith.*

> [T]he attorney-client privilege is applicable to an employee's communication if (1) the communication was made for the purpose of securing legal advice; (2) the employee making the communication did so at the direction of his corporate superior; (3) the superior made the request so that the corporation could secure legal advice; (4) the subject matter of the communication is within the scope of the employee's corporate duties; and (5) the communication is not disseminated beyond those persons who, because of the corporate structure, need to know its contents. We note, moreover, that the corporation has the burden of showing that the communication in issue meets all of the above requirements.[71]

---

70. The control group test originated in City of Philadelphia v. Westinghouse Electric Corp., 210 F.Supp. 483 (E.D.Pa.1962), *mandamus denied sub nom.* General Elec. Co. v. Kirkpatrick, 312 F.2d 742 (3d Cir.1962), *cert. denied* 372 U.S. 943 (1963).

71. 572 F.2d 596, 609 (8th Cir.1977) (citing Harper & Row Publishers v. Decker, 423 F.2d 487, 491–92 (7th Cir.1970), aff'd by an equally divided Court, 400 U.S. 348 (1971)).

In the following decision, the Supreme Court addressed the question of which employees' conversations with lawyers are covered by the organizational privilege.

Upjohn Co. v. United States

Supreme Court of the United States, 1981.
449 U.S. 383, 386–92, 394–96.

[Auditors working for Upjohn, a pharmaceutical manufacturer, discovered that one of the company's subsidiaries had made illegal payments to foreign officials in return for government business. Gerard Thomas, Upjohn's general counsel, began an internal investigation that included employee interviews and questionnaires. In 1976, Upjohn voluntarily reported on the illegal payments to the Securities and Exchange Commission and the Internal Revenue Service (IRS). The IRS began its own investigation, and demanded that Upjohn produce the questionnaires and Thomas's interview notes. Upjohn refused the discovery request on the grounds of attorney-client privilege. The District Court rejected the claim of privilege. The Sixth Circuit supported the District Court and remanded for determination of who was in Upjohn's control group. Upjohn appealed to the Supreme Court.]

■ JUSTICE REHNQUIST delivered the opinion of the Court.

We granted certiorari in this case to address important questions concerning the scope of the attorney-client privilege in the corporate context.... With respect to the privilege question the parties and various *amici* have described our task as one of choosing between two "tests" which have gained adherents in the courts of appeals. We are acutely aware, however, that we sit to decide concrete cases and not abstract propositions of law. We decline to lay down a broad rule or series of rules to govern all conceivable future questions in this area, even were we able to do so. We can and do, however, conclude that the attorney-client privilege protects the communications involved in this case from compelled disclosure....

II

Federal Rule of Evidence 501 provides that "the privilege of a witness ... shall be governed by the principles of the common law as they may be interpreted by the courts of the United States in light of reason and experience." The attorney-client privilege is the oldest of the privileges for confidential communications known to the common law. Its purpose is to encourage full and frank communication between attorneys and their clients and thereby promote broader public interests in the observance of law and administration of justice. The privilege recognizes that sound legal advice or advocacy serves public ends and that such advice or advocacy depends upon the lawyer's being fully informed by the client....

The Court of Appeals, however, considered the application of the privilege in the corporate context to present a "different problem," since the client was an inanimate entity and "only the senior management, guiding and integrating the several operations, . . . can be said to possess an identity analogous to the corporation as a whole." . . . Such a view, we think, overlooks the fact that the privilege exists to protect not only the giving of professional advice to those who can act on it but also the giving of information to the lawyer to enable him to give sound and informed advice. . . .

In the case of the individual client the provider of information and the person who acts on the lawyer's advice are one and the same. In the corporate context, however, it will frequently be employees beyond the control group as defined by the court below—"officers and agents . . . responsible for directing [the company's] actions in response to legal advice"—who will possess the information needed by the corporation's lawyers. Middle-level—and indeed lower-level—employees can, by actions within the scope of their employment, embroil the corporation in serious legal difficulties, and it is only natural that these employees would have the relevant information needed by corporate counsel if he is adequately to advise the client with respect to such actual or potential difficulties. This fact was noted in *Diversified Industries, Inc. v. Meredith,* 572 F.2d 596 (C.A.8 1978) (en banc):

> In a corporation, it may be necessary to glean information relevant to a legal problem from middle management or non-management personnel as well as from top executives. The attorney dealing with a complex legal problem is thus faced with a "Hobson's choice". If he interviews employees not having "the very highest authority," their communications to him will not be privileged. If, on the other hand, he interviews *only* those employees with "the very highest authority," he may find it extremely difficult, if not impossible, to determine what happened.

The control group test adopted by the court below thus frustrates the very purpose of the privilege by discouraging the communication of relevant information by employees of the client to attorneys seeking to render legal advice to the client corporation. The attorney's advice will also frequently be more significant to noncontrol group members than to those who officially sanction the advice, and the control group test makes it more difficult to convey full and frank legal advice to the employees who will put into effect the client corporation's policy. . . .

The narrow scope given the attorney-client privilege by the court below not only makes it difficult for corporate attorneys to formulate sound advice when their client is faced with a specific legal problem but also threatens to limit the valuable efforts of corporate counsel to ensure their client's compliance with the law. In light of the vast and complicated array of regulatory legislation confronting the modern corporation, corporations, unlike most individuals, "constantly go to lawyers to find out how to obey the law," particularly since compliance with the law in this area is hardly an instinctive matter. . . .[2]

---

2. The Government argues that the risk of civil or criminal liability suffices to ensure that corporations will seek legal advice in the absence of the protection of the

The communications at issue were made by Upjohn employees to counsel for Upjohn acting as such, at the direction of corporate superiors in order to secure legal advice from counsel. . . . Consistent with the underlying purposes of the attorney-client privilege, these communications must be protected against compelled disclosure.

The Court of Appeals declined to extend the attorney-client privilege beyond the limits of the control group test for fear that doing so would entail severe burdens on discovery and create a broad "zone of silence" over corporate affairs. Application of the attorney-client privilege to communications such as those involved here, however, puts the adversary in no worse position than if the communications had never taken place. The privilege only protects disclosure of communications; it does not protect disclosure of the underlying facts by those who communicated with the attorney. . . .

Here the Government was free to question the employees who communicated with Thomas and outside counsel. Upjohn has provided the IRS with a list of such employees, and the IRS has already interviewed some 25 of them. While it would probably be more convenient for the Government to secure the results of petitioner's internal investigation by simply subpoenaing the questionnaires and notes taken by petitioner's attorneys, such considerations of convenience do not overcome the policies served by the attorney-client privilege. As Justice Jackson noted in his concurring opinion in *Hickman v. Taylor,* 329 U.S., at 516: "Discovery was hardly intended to enable a learned profession to perform its functions . . . on wits borrowed from the adversary."

QUESTIONS

1.   Though the Court repudiates the control group test, it "decline[s] to lay down a broad rule," and proposes a case-by-case determination of the scope of the privilege. Does the decision offer sufficiently concrete guidance to corporate attorneys or employees as to whether their conversations are protected?

The *Upjohn* majority stresses that the disclosures at issue came from employees who were acting like clients in a crucial respect: informing attorneys about the case. The Court concludes that the attorney-client privilege must therefore protect communications with any corporate employees from whom the attorney must obtain information for purposes of the representation. How, if at all, does this differ from the subject matter test? Note that in the *Meredith* formulation, the privilege attaches to a communication only if "the subject matter of the communication is within

privilege. This response ignores the fact that the depth and quality of any investigations to ensure compliance with the law would suffer, even were they undertaken. The response also proves too much, since it applies to all communications covered by the privilege: an individual trying to comply with the law or faced with a legal problem also has strong incentive to disclose information to his lawyer, yet the common law has recognized the value of the privilege in further facilitating communications.

the scope of the employee's corporate duties." Does *Upjohn* impose this requirement? How does the Court's framework compare with the *Restatement of the Law Governing Lawyers*, § 79, which protects communications between any agent of the organization and the organization's lawyer "concern[ing] a legal matter of interest to the organization" if "disclosed only to: (a) privileged persons . . . . .; and (b) other agents of the organization who reasonably need to know of the communication in order to act for the organization"?

2.   The most common argument for the attorney-client privilege is that it encourages frank disclosures. The assumption is that with the privilege in place, the client has little to fear in disclosing sensitive information to the attorney. How realistic is this assumption when the attorney is investigating possible wrongdoing by a corporate employee? Management, after all, is very likely to sanction, fire, or sue an employee who has landed the company in legal difficulties. And if the lawyer provides "Miranda warnings" that the corporation has sole discretion to waive or assert the privilege, how comfortable will employees feel in discussing possible misconduct? Does this imply that the usual argument for the attorney-client privilege is inapplicable in cases such as *Upjohn?* How else might the corporate attorney-client privilege be justified?

One possible justification, somewhat different from *Upjohn*'s, proceeds in four steps. (1) Without extensive protection for lawyer-client communication, corporate counsel will be cut "out of the loop"—employees and management will withhold sensitive information from legal advisers. (2) In that case, attorneys will be unable to counsel their clients in order to prevent illegal behavior. (3) A significant part of a corporate attorney's role includes attempting to prevent misconduct. (4) Clients are often willing to be dissuaded from improper activities by their attorneys, for if they were not, they would not seek costly legal advice in the first place.[74] The conclusion is that a broad attorney-client privilege enhances corporate compliance with legal standards.

Do you find this argument persuasive? Are any steps of the argument questionable?[75]

3.   The *Upjohn* Court argues that restricting the privilege "threatens to limit the valuable efforts of corporate counsel to ensure their client's compliance with the law," and that the adversary is placed at no disadvantage by the privilege because the underlying facts remain discoverable. If these arguments are correct, why did Upjohn assert the privilege, particularly since it had voluntarily disclosed the questionable payments to the SEC and IRS?

74. This last proposition has been forcefully defended in Steven Shavell, "Legal Advice About Contemplated Acts: The Decision to Obtain Advice, Its Social Desirability, and Protection of Confidentiality," 17 *J. Legal Stud.* 123 (1988).

75. For further discussion of *Upjohn,* see David Luban, note 23, at 222–28 (1988); John E. Sexton, "A Post–*Upjohn* Consideration of the Corporate Attorney–Client Privilege," 57 *N.Y.U.L. Rev.* 443 (1982).

One answer is that asserting the privilege would allow Upjohn to control the flow of information: Upjohn had "forbidden its employees to answer questions it considers irrelevant." More fundamentally, Upjohn and the government were in an adversarial posture despite Upjohn's voluntary disclosure of questionable payments. Asserting the privilege can be a useful litigation tactic, because it forces the adversary to obtain its information "the hard way" by seeking facts through an expensive and time-consuming discovery process.

These arguments explain why the privilege serves the corporation's advantage. Do they undercut any of the Court's explanations of how the privilege serves societal interests?

4. Justice Rehnquist's opinion in *Upjohn* quotes the words of Justice Jackson: "Discovery was hardly intended to enable a learned profession to perform its functions ... on wits borrowed from the adversary." John Stuart Mill once criticized jurists who look on legal procedure through "fox-hunting eyes":

> [H]ow little, as yet, even instructed Englishmen are accustomed to look upon judicature as a means to an end, and that end the execution of the law. They speak and act, every now and then, as if they regarded a ... trial as a sort of game, partly of chance, partly of skill, in which the proper end to be aimed at is, not that the truth may be discovered, but that both parties may have fair play.[76]

Are Justice Jackson and Justice Rehnquist looking at the corporate attorney-client privilege through fox-hunting eyes? How might they respond to Mill's criticism?

5. The *Upjohn* Court expressly reserved the question of whether the corporate attorney-client privilege applies to communications with former employees. How would you resolve this question?

6. Critics of *Upjohn* have claimed that giving a broad scope to the corporate attorney-client privilege will turn corporate attorneys into "black holes" of information. Attorneys investigating corporate internal affairs on behalf of management may well be the only corporate officers with a full and clear picture of the matter being investigated. All the attorneys' conversations on the subject are privileged, including conversations in which they report to management the findings of their internal investigation, and thus the total picture drops into a black hole. Information goes in, but it never comes out.

Consider the Dalkon Shield and tobacco cases, discussed in Section C.3, *supra*. Research scientists working for the Shield's manufacturer were directed to report their findings on safety to the company's lawyers, rather than executives or doctors, in order to shield them behind the attorney-client privilege. Tobacco research was similarly channeled through industry lawyers, who then claimed that it was protected by the privilege—a black

---

76. 5 Jeremy Bentham, *Rationale of Judicial Evidence, Specially Applied to English Practice 318 (1827).*

hole that lasted for decades. To critics, *Upjohn's* broad protection for corporate communications assists such coverups of corporate wrongdoing and impedes regulatory oversight. Do the Supreme Court's arguments persuade you otherwise?

2. THE JUSTIFICATIONS FOR THE ORGANIZATIONAL PRIVILEGE

As the discussion in Section B suggests, the privilege rests on two central arguments. The first is utilitarian and instrumental: society benefits from encouraging clients to disclose the information necessary for effective legal representation and legal compliance. The second cluster of arguments rests on the need to protect individual rights such as privacy and freedom from self-incrimination.

Some commentators and courts have suggested that neither the utilitarian nor the rights-based justifications for the attorney-client privilege are persuasive when the client is an organization rather than a natural person. From a utilitarian standpoint, the benefit of encouraging disclosure may be less when the client is an entity rather than an individual for the reason explored above: corporate attorneys are unable to promise a full measure of confidentiality because they must tell management what they learn from corporate employees. Thus, even with the privilege, frank disclosure from employees to corporate counsel is often unlikely if employees have options about cooperation. In at least some cases, however, employees or officers will have to consult with counsel irrespective of the privilege because their jobs depend on it or because such consultation can later shield them from liability through the "advice of counsel" defense.[77] On the other side of the ledger, the social costs of extending the privilege to corporations are greater. As one of the earliest commentators on the corporate attorney-client privilege argued: "where corporations are involved, with their large number of agents, masses of documents and frequent dealings with lawyers, the zone of silence grows large. Few judges—or legislators either, for that matter—would long tolerate any common law privilege that allowed corporations to insulate all their activities by discussing them with legal advisors."[78] It is not at all obvious that a utilitarian, balancing approach to the privilege argues for honoring it fully.

Unsurprisingly, then, courts in some contexts have rejected the *per se* corporate privilege in favor of case-by-case balancing of utilities. As discussed in section B, *supra*, stockholder derivative suits against corporations have provided the major "corporate fiduciary" exception to the privilege. Because corporate managers and counsel owe fiduciary obligations to shareholders, when the shareholders file suit alleging managerial misconduct, courts may compel disclosure of communications between management and counsel. Under the leading precedent, *Garner v. Wolfinbarger,* 430 F.2d 1093 (5th Cir.1970), *cert. denied,* 401 U.S. 974 (1971), courts must

77. William Simon, "After Confidentiality: Rethinking the Professional Responsibilities of the Business Lawyer," 75 *Fordham L. Rev.* 1453, 1468 (2006).

78. David Simon, "The Attorney–Client Privilege As Applied to Corporations," 65 *Yale L.J.* 953, 955–56 (1956).

balance the benefits of disclosure against the costs. Subsequent decisions have extended the *Garner* doctrine to other fiduciary relationships. For example, beneficiaries of an employee benefit plan may pierce the attorney-client privilege between the trust management and the trust's lawyer, and union members have pierced the privilege between union officers and the union's lawyer.

Like the utilitarian rationale, non-utilitarian arguments for the attorney-client privilege carry considerably less weight when the client is an organization instead of an individual. As Charles Wolfram writes, "arguments [for the corporate privilege] based on human dignity are irrelevant. The corporation as an entity has no legal or moral claims to dignity. The humans who act as the agents of the corporation are entitled to such dignity, but individually they are not the client...."[79]

Yet the weakness of the corporate privilege in theory has not been reflected in doctrine. The leading modern case that viewed the privilege as a personal rather than corporate right was reversed on appeal.[80]

3. WAIVER OF THE ORGANIZATIONAL PRIVILEGE

In the wake of corporate scandals around the turn of the twenty first century, federal officials began pressuring organizations under investigation to waive the attorney-client privilege and work product doctrine. In 2001, the Securities and Exchange Commission issued what is commonly called the Seaboard Report (Exchange Act Release No. 44969), which outlines the criteria the Commission considers when determining whether to bring an enforcement action. These include whether a company has "cooperated completely with appropriate regulatory and law enforcement bodies," conducted a thorough internal review and made the results available to SEC staff, and voluntarily disclosed information that was not directly requested and might not have been otherwise discovered. Waiver of the privilege and work product doctrine is commonly considered to be part of the necessary disclosure.[81] Other regulatory and prosecutorial agencies have begun adopting similar policies.[82]

Most significantly, in 2003 the Justice Department issued the so-called "Thompson Memorandum" addressing "Principles of Federal Prosecution of Business Organizations." The Thompson Memorandum identified factors that federal prosecutors should consider in deciding whether to charge organizations with an offense. These factors include the organization's timely and voluntary disclosure of wrongdoing, and its willingness to cooperate in investigation of its agents, even if that involves waiver of the

---

79. Wolfram, *supra* note 37, at 283–84; *see also* Luban, *supra* note 23, at 228–33.

80. Radiant Burners, Inc. v. American Gas Ass'n, 207 F.Supp. 771, 773, 775 (N.D. Ill.1962), *reversed,* 320 F.2d 314 (7th Cir. 1963).

81. Bruce A Green & David C. Clifton, "Feeling a Chill," *ABA J.,* Dec. 2005, at 61, 63–64.

82. Id., at 64, discussing the New York Attorney General's office and the New York Stock Exchange.

attorney client privilege and work product doctrine.[83] The rationale for the policy was that it will conserve government resources, and produce more candid information than that available if prosecutors conducted their own investigation.

The Thompson Memo ignited a firestorm of criticism from the bar, including from such unusual partners as the ACLU and the Association of Corporate Counsel. Facing Congressional legislation to overturn its policy, the Department withdrew the Thompson Memorandum and replaced it with the 2006 "McNulty Memorandum," containing new guidelines on Principles of Federal Prosecution of Business Organizations. The McNulty Memorandum provides that prosecutors may not penalize a company in charging decisions for refusing to waive the privilege. Furthermore, it allows prosecutors to request privilege waivers only after approval from the Deputy Attorney General based on demonstration of a "legitimate need" for privileged material. The Department would also give favorable considerable to companies that voluntarily waived the privilege.[84]

Whether the revised policy will adequately address concerns remains unclear. Some critics doubt that the revised Justice Department policy will reduce pressure on corporations to waive the privilege, because "more often than not requests for waivers are not . . . [made] outright but are coercively inferred."[85] The ABA's President protested that the McNulty Memo's guidelines "fall far short of what is needed to prevent further erosion of . . . fundamental attorney-client privilege, work product, and employee protections during government investigations."[86] Some commentators have argued that the prospect of coerced waivers encourages counsel not to make written notes of their investigations. It also poses ethical problems in their interviews with employees. Corporate lawyers routinely disclose that they are representing the corporation, but practices differ over giving more explicit warnings about what that might imply for individual employees.[87] Employees may not appreciate the risks that waiver poses to them, but clarifying their exposure is likely to diminish their willingness to provide internal investigators with full information. Other commentators, however, dispute that the Justice Department policies will chill the zeal or quality of internal corporate investigations, because corporations cannot afford *not* to know everything that a government investigation might unearth.[88]

83. See http://www.usdoj.gov/dag/cftf/corporate_guidelines.htm.

84. See Memorandum from Paul J. McNulty, U.S. Deputy Att'y Gen., to Heads of Dep't Components & U.S. Att'ys (Dec. 12, 2006), at http://www.usdoj.gov/dag/speeches/2006/mcnulty_memo.pdf.

85. Ralph Lindeman & Robert Wilhelm, "Justice Department Limits Consideration of Privilege Waivers in Criminal Matters," 22 *Lawyer's Manual on Professional Conduct* 634, 635 (2006) (quoting Frederick J. Krebs).

86. Statement of Karen J. Mathis, President, ABA, March 8, 2007, available at http://www.abanet.org/poladv/letters/attycli ent/2007mar08_privwaivh_t.pdf.

87. Thomas Brom, "Read My Lips," *California Lawyer*, April 2006, at 12; Susan L. Merrill, "Internal Investigations," in *Securities Litigation: Planning and Strategies* 91, 100, 101 (2002).

88. Julie R. O'Sullivan, "The Last Straw: The Department of Justice's Privilege Waiver Policy and the Death of Adversarial Justice in Criminal Investigations of Corporations," 57 *DePaul L. Rev.* 329, 332–34 (2008); Daniel Richman, "Decisions About Coercion: The Corporate Attorney–Client Privilege

Controversy also erupted over a 2004 amendment to the federal sentencing guidelines. That amendment initially included commentary providing that waiver of the attorney-client privilege would not be a prerequisite to a more lenient sentence, "unless such waiver is necessary in order to provide timely and thorough disclosure" of relevant information. In 2006, the U.S. Sentencing Commission removed the quoted language in response to concerns that it unduly pressured organizations to waive the privilege.[89]

One commentator argues that the privilege waiver has become a symbolic issue to the bar. Because corporations lack the Fifth Amendment privilege against self-incrimination, defense counsel regard the attorney-client privilege as their only weapon. In the eyes of defense counsel, the government seems to believe "that the proper role of corporations confronted with allegations of wrongdoing is, quite simply, to roll over. Individual defendants can fight like hell, but corporations should self-report, remediate harm, cooperate fully, and take whatever prosecutors and regulators believe they have coming. Zealous defense counsel find this assumption beyond galling."[90] What might be the Justice Department's rejoinder to this sentiment?

A converse problem arises when an organization's interest lies in not waiving the privilege, but it is in individual directors' interest for it to do so. For example, when directors are sued for corporate misconduct, they may wish to raise the defense that they relied on advice of counsel. In order for them to establish the defense, and for opponents to challenge their assertions, disclosure of privileged materials will be necessary. How should this dilemma be resolved?[91]

E.   THE ETHICAL DUTY OF CONFIDENTIALITY

NOTES

Lawyers' duties of confidentiality are defined not only by the attorney-client privilege, but also by the Code and Model Rules. Curiously, however, the view that lawyers have an ethical obligation to keep client confidences is a relative newcomer compared with the privilege. The earliest treatments of legal ethics in the United States, David Hoffman's 1836 "Resolutions" and George Sharswood's 1854 *Essay on Professional Ethics,* identify no such obligation. The duty of confidentiality appears to have been the

---

Waiver Problem," 57 *DePaul L. Rev.* 295, 305 (2008).

89.   U.S. Sentencing Comm'n, Amendments to the Sentencing Guidelines 45 (May 18, 2006), available at http://www.ussc.gov/2006guid/FinalUserFrdly.pdf.

90.   O'Sullivan, *supra* note 88, at 335.

91.   Mark A. Kressel, Note, "Contractual Waiver of Corporate Attorney–Client Privilege," 116 *Yale L. J.* 412 (2006) (arguing that directors and corporations should contract to allow waiver before the situation arises and in the absence of such an agreement, directors should not be allowed to assert the defense).

invention of the eminent late-nineteenth-century corporate lawyer David Dudley Field.[92]

As noted earlier, the attorney-client privilege prevents lawyers only from offering evidence in legal proceedings about confidential communications with clients. Bar ethical mandates, by contrast, enjoin lawyers from revealing confidential information received from anyone to anyone, in or out of courtrooms. As previous discussion indicates, moreover, the attorney-client privilege is riddled with waivers and exceptions that significantly narrow its scope. By contrast, bar ethical rules offer sweeping protections from disclosure. DR 4–101(B) protects secrets as well as confidences, and thus forbids a lawyer from disclosing any information related to the representation that would be detrimental to the client. This includes information obtained from sources other than the client. Model Rule 1.6(a) states simply that "[a] lawyer shall not reveal information relating to representation of a client . . . ."

These ethical mandates include some exceptions. Both the Code and the Model Rules permit lawyers to reveal confidences if the client consents. Both permit lawyers to reveal confidences to defend themselves from accusations of wrongful conduct or to collect a fee. Both permit lawyers to reveal confidences if required by law or court order.

Finally, both the Code and Model Rules grant lawyers a limited freedom to violate confidentiality in order to safeguard the interests of others. Disciplinary Rule 4–101(C)(3) allows a lawyer to reveal "the intention of his client to commit a crime and the information necessary to prevent the crime." For many years, the Model Rules were much more protective than this, permitting lawyers to reveal confidences only if doing so was necessary to prevent their clients from committing crimes "likely to result in imminent death or substantial bodily harm." In 2002, the ABA broadened the exception very slightly, permitting lawyers to reveal confidences "to prevent reasonably certain death or substantial bodily harm" even if the cause was not a criminal act by the client.

However, in 2003, in the aftermath of the Enron scandals and the Sarbanes–Oxley Act, the ABA House of Delegates once again expanded the circumstances under which lawyers could reveal confidential information. The vote was very narrow: 218–201. Model Rule 1.6(b)(2) now permits a lawyer to disclose confidential information "to the extent the lawyer reasonably believes necessary to prevent the client from committing a crime or fraud that is reasonably certain to result in substantial injury to the financial interests or property of another and in furtherance of which the client has used or is using the lawyer's services." In addition, Rule 1.6(b)(3) now allows lawyers to reveal confidences when the client has used the lawyer's services to commit a crime or fraud that is reasonably certain to result (or has resulted) in substantial injury to someone's financial interests or property. Some commentators—most notably Geoffrey Hazard,

92. L. Ray Patterson, "Legal Ethics and the Lawyer's Duty of Loyalty," 29 *Emory L.J.* 909, 941–42 (1980).

the original reporter of the Model Rules, and a noted authority on legal ethics—had argued for years that without these rules, lawyers would be unable to take steps necessary to disentangle themselves from illegal conduct and might therefore be civilly or criminally liable as accomplices to their clients' misdeeds.[93] See Section F, *infra*. Prior to the scandals that erupted in Enron et al., such arguments had always been unavailing in the ABA, where efforts to broaden the exceptions to confidentiality invariably ignited political firestorms.

Similar battles have recurred in states that have adopted the Model Rules. Most jurisdictions enacted versions of Rule 1.6 that are much closer to the current ABA version than to its more protective predecessors. Indeed, states have adopted a broad variety of confidentiality exceptions: discretion or obligation to reveal confidences to prevent client crimes against life or bodily injury; obligation to reveal confidences to save human life, regardless of whether a crime is involved; permission to reveal any criminal conduct; permission or obligation to reveal crimes or non-criminal frauds against property; permission or obligation to reveal crimes or frauds in which the lawyer's services were unwittingly used; and various combinations of these provisions.

The following case illustrates the potential problems created by restrictive disclosure obligations, which continue to exist in many state codes.

Spaulding v. Zimmerman

Supreme Court of Minnesota, 1962.
116 N.W.2d 704, 706–10.

■ THOMAS GALLAGHER, JUSTICE.

Appeal from an order of the District Court of Douglas County vacating and setting aside a prior order of such court dated May 8, 1957, approving a settlement made on behalf of David Spaulding on March 5, 1957, at which time he was a minor of the age of 20 years; and in connection therewith, vacating and setting aside releases executed by him and his parents, a stipulation of dismissal, an order for dismissal with prejudice, and a judgment entered pursuant thereto.

The prior action was brought against defendants by Theodore Spaulding, as father and natural guardian of David Spaulding, for injuries sustained by David in an automobile accident, arising out of a collision which occurred August 24, 1956, between an automobile driven by John Zimmerman, in which David was a passenger, and one owned by John Ledermann and driven by Florian Ledermann.

On appeal defendants contend that the court was without jurisdiction to vacate the settlement solely because ... their counsel then possessed information, unknown to plaintiff herein, that at the time he was suffering

93. Geoffrey C. Hazard, Jr., "Lawyers and Client Fraud: They Still Don't Get It," 6 Geo.J.Legal Ethics *701 (1993).*

from an aorta aneurysm which may have resulted from the accident, because no duty rested upon them to disclose information to plaintiff which they could assume had been disclosed to him by his own physicians....

After the accident, David's injuries were diagnosed by his family physician, Dr. James H. Cain, as a severe crushing injury of the chest with multiple rib fractures; a severe cerebral concussion, probably with petechial hemorrhages of the brain; and bilateral fractures of the clavicles. At Dr. Cain's suggestion, on January 3, 1957, David was examined by Dr. John F. Pohl, an orthopedic specialist, who made X–ray studies of his chest. Dr. Pohl's detailed report of this examination included the following:

"... The lung fields are clear. The heart and aorta are normal."

Nothing in such report indicated the aorta aneurysm with which David was then suffering. On March 1, 1957, at the suggestion of Dr. Pohl, David was examined from a neurological viewpoint by Dr. Paul S. Blake, and in the report of this examination there was no finding of the aorta aneurysm.

In the meantime, on February 22, 1957, at defendants' request, David was examined by Dr. Hewitt Hannah, a neurologist. On February 26, 1957, the latter reported to Messrs. Field, Arveson, & Donoho, attorneys for defendant John Zimmerman, as follows:

"The one feature of the case which bothers me more than any other part of the case is the fact that this boy of 20 years of age has an aneurysm, which means a dilatation of the aorta and the arch of the aorta. Whether this came out of this accident I cannot say with any degree of certainty and I have discussed it with the Roentgenologist and a couple of Internists.... Of course an aneurysm or dilatation of the aorta in a boy of this age is a serious matter as far as his life. This aneurysm may dilate further and it might rupture with further dilatation and this would cause his death.

"It would be interesting also to know whether the X-ray of his lungs, taken immediately following the accident, shows this dilatation or not. If it was not present immediately following the accident and is now present, then we could be sure that it came out of the accident."

Prior to the negotiations for settlement, the contents of the above report were made known to counsel for defendants Florian and John Ledermann.

The case was called for trial on March 4, 1957, at which time the respective parties and their counsel possessed such information as to David's physical condition as was revealed to them by their respective medical examiners as above described. It is thus apparent that neither David nor his father, the nominal plaintiff in the prior action, was then aware that David was suffering the aorta aneurysm but on the contrary believed that he was recovering from the injuries sustained in the accident.

On the following day an agreement for settlement was reached wherein, in consideration of the payment of $6,500, David and his father agreed to settle in full for all claims arising out of the accident.

. . .

Early in 1959, David was required by the army reserve, of which he was a member, to have a physical checkup. For this, he again engaged the services of Dr. Cain. In this checkup, the latter discovered the aorta aneurysm. He then reexamined the X-rays which had been taken shortly after the accident and at this time discovered that they disclosed the beginning of the process which produced the aneurysm. He promptly sent David to Dr. Jerome Grismer for an examination and opinion. The latter confirmed the finding of the aorta aneurysm and recommended immediate surgery therefor. This was performed by him at Mount Sinai Hospital in Minneapolis on March 10, 1959.

Shortly thereafter, David, having attained his majority, instituted the present action for additional damages due to the more serious injuries including the aorta aneurysm which he alleges proximately resulted from the accident. As indicated above, the prior order for settlement was vacated. In a memorandum made a part of the order vacating the settlement, the court stated: . . .

"The mistake concerning the existence of the aneurysm was not mutual. For reasons which do not appear, plaintiff's doctor failed to ascertain its existence. By reason of the failure of plaintiff's counsel to use available rules of discovery, plaintiff's doctor and all his representatives did not learn that defendants and their agents knew of its existence and possible serious consequences. Except for the character of the concealment in the light of plaintiff's minority, the Court would, I believe, be justified in denying plaintiff's motion to vacate, leaving him to whatever questionable remedy he may have against his doctor and against his lawyer.

"That defendants' counsel concealed the knowledge they had is not disputed. The essence of the application of the above rule is the character of the concealment. Was it done under circumstances that defendants must be charged with knowledge that plaintiff did not know of the injury? If so, an enriching advantage was gained for defendants at plaintiff's expense. There is no doubt of the good faith of both defendants' counsel. There is no doubt that during the course of the negotiations, when the parties were in an adversary relationship, no rule required or duty rested upon defendants or their representatives to disclose this knowledge. However, once the agreement to settle was reached, it is difficult to characterize the parties' relationship as adverse. At this point all parties were interested in securing Court approval. . . .

"But it is not possible to escape the inference that defendants' representatives knew, or must be here charged with knowing, that plaintiff under all the circumstances would not accept the sum of $6500.00 if he or his representatives knew of the aneurysm and its possible serious consequences. Moreover, there is no showing by defendants that would support an inference that plaintiff and his representatives knew of the existence of the aneurysm but concluded that it was not causally related to the accident.

"When the adversary nature of the negotiations concluded in a settlement, the procedure took on the posture of a joint application to the Court, at least so far as the facts upon which the Court could and must approve settlement is concerned. It is here that the true nature of the concealment appears, and defendants' failure to act affirmatively, after having been given a copy of the application for approval, can only be defendants' decision to take a calculated risk that the settlement would be final. . . .

"To hold that the concealment was not of such character as to result in an unconscionable advantage over plaintiff's ignorance or mistake, would be to penalize innocence and incompetence and reward less than full performance of an officer of the Court's duty to make full disclosure to the Court when applying for approval in minor settlement proceedings." . . .

[I]n the instant case the court did not abuse its discretion in setting aside the settlement which it had approved on plaintiff's behalf while he was still a minor. It is undisputed that neither he nor his counsel nor his medical attendants were aware that at the time settlement was made he was suffering from an aorta aneurysm which may have resulted from the accident. The seriousness of this disability is indicated by Dr. Hannah's report indicating the imminent danger of death therefrom. This was known by counsel for both defendants but was not disclosed to the court at the time it was petitioned to approve the settlement. While no canon of ethics or legal obligation may have required them to inform plaintiff or his counsel with respect thereto, or to advise the court therein, it did become obvious to them at the time, that the settlement then made did not contemplate or take into consideration the disability described. This fact opened the way for the court to later exercise its discretion in vacating the settlement and under the circumstances described we cannot say that there was any abuse of discretion on the part of the court in so doing. . . .

QUESTIONS

1. The district court opinion in *Spaulding v. Zimmerman* insisted (and the Minnesota Supreme Court agreed) that during adversary settlement negotiations "no rule required or duty rested upon defendants or their representatives" to disclose that David Spaulding suffered from an aortic aneurysm. What is your view? Did defense counsel have a moral duty to provide that information? Would the Code, which was in force at the time, or the Model Rules in their current formulation, permit the defendants' lawyers to tell Spaulding of his condition?

Consider Model Rule 1.6(b)(1), which permits a lawyer to disclose client confidences "to the extent the lawyer reasonably believes necessary to prevent reasonably certain death or substantial bodily harm." Was David Spaulding's impending death or substantial bodily harm "reasonably certain"? Would defense counsel be permitted to tell David about his medical condition under this rule? Would they be permitted not to?

2. The district judge overturned the settlement on the theory that once the parties were before the court they were no longer in an adversary posture and "[i]t is here that the true nature of the concealment appears." Is the implication that although defendants' counsel had no duty to save Spaulding's life, they did have a duty not to mislead the trial judge?

Was the district judge grasping for ways to reach the equitable result? Once he had conceded that defense counsel acted properly in keeping their knowledge of Spaulding's aneurysm confidential, the judge was unable to vacate the settlement by offering the most natural argument—that defense counsel should have warned the plaintiff of his peril. Was the judge straining to find any argument, however unnatural, to vacate it? If so, was the court's decision justified? Was there a better alternative?

3. a) According to the district judge: "[T]here is no doubt of the good faith of both defendants' counsel." Do you agree? What does good faith mean in this context? Is it relevant (or disturbing) that, according to a later interview with the judge, he was a friend of a senior partner in the defendant's law firm and didn't want to expose it to criticism?[94]

b) The court reserves its criticism for Spaulding's lawyer, who failed "to use available rules of discovery" to obtain the medical reports of defendants' physician. Only the fact that Spaulding was a minor prevented the judge from "denying plaintiff's motion to vacate, leaving him to whatever questionable remedy he may have against his doctor and against his lawyer." In your view, does the fault lie more with plaintiff's counsel than with defendants'? Should the result of the case have depended on the plaintiff's age?

4. Did Dr. Hewitt Hannah, the physician retained by the defense, violate any ethical obligation in failing to warn Spaulding of his aneurysm? If so, did Hannah's unethical behavior relieve the defense lawyers of responsibility or mitigate their conduct?

5. Within the criminal defense context, the most vivid analogy to *Spaulding v. Zimmerman* involves a lawyer who lets an innocent person go to prison or even to execution for a crime that his client has privately acknowledged committing. In an 1847 English case, the "Mirfield Murders," two itinerant peddlers, Reid and M'Cabe, were arrested on suspicion of a grisly triple murder.[95] Barrister William Seymour, representing Reid, argued that M'Cabe was the murderer; however, both men were convicted and sentenced to die. Reid then confessed that he alone had committed the murders.

In response to rumors that Reid had previously confessed his guilt and acknowledged M'Cabe's innocence to his lawyer Seymour, the latter conceded that "I had reason strongly to presume Reid's guilt" but denied that he knew of M'Cabe's innocence. In a letter to the London *Times,* Seymour went further:

> And now, Sir, assuming that to be true which I deny, and admitting for a moment that a "full confession" was made to me "previous to the trial which wholly exculpated M'Cabe," I am yet to learn that I would

94. Roger C. Cramton & Lori P. Knowles, "Professional Secrecy and Its Exceptions: *Spaulding v. Zimmerman* Revisited," 83 *Minn. L. Rev.* 63, 126 (1998). See also Roger Cramton, "*Spaulding v. Zimmerman*: Confidentiality and its Exceptions," in *Legal Ethics: Law Stories* 175 (Deborah L. Rhode & David Luban, eds, 2006).

95. The account of the Mirfield Murders comes from David Mellinkoff, *The Conscience of a Lawyer* 194–98 (1973).

be deserving of blame for endeavouring to throw the whole guilt upon M'Cabe if the evidence warranted such a course. I am yet to learn that this would be either morally or professionally wrong. . . . I esteem it in the first place to be [counsel's] strict and solemn duty to keep faithful to his client during the trial, and to hold his secrets as a religious trust. . . .

And in the next place, it is equally his bounden duty to frame the best defence in his power from the evidence at trial. . . . When a veto is put upon this exercise of a counsel's discretion . . . the independence of the bar will be violated, and the principle of advocacy will be abolished altogether.[96]

In an editorial, *The Times* (of London) offered an outraged reply:

We have . . . not one shadow of doubt that to save a client by the sacrifice of an innocent man, whom counsel know to be innocent, is a direct violation of honour, of morality, and of the laws of God and man.[97]

Do you agree with Seymour or with *The Times* editorialist? Consider that question again in the context of similar American cases described in the Introduction to Chapter VI, Section A. Is *The Times* editorial comment as applicable to *Spaulding v. Zimmerman* as to Seymour's defense of Reid? Is it more or less persuasive?

The *Restatement of the Law Governing Lawyers* parallels Model Rule 1.6(b) and provides in § 66(1) that "[a] lawyer may use or disclose confidential client information when the lawyer reasonably believes that its use or disclosure is necessary to prevent reasonably certain death or serious bodily harm to a person." In the comments to this section, the *Restatement* explains that the risk "need not be the product of a client act; an act of a nonclient threatening life or personal safety is also included, as is a threat created through accident or natural causes." "Serious bodily harm" within the meaning of the Section includes . . . the consequences of events such as imprisonment for a substantial period. . . . *Restatement*, § 66 cmt. c.

Under the *Restatement* doctrine, would Seymour be permitted to reveal Reid's guilt? Does the doctrine mean that criminal defense lawyers whose clients admit that they are guilty of a crime for which someone else is likely to be imprisoned may always reveal this information to the authorities? Should lawyers have an obligation to disclose facts that might exculpate an innocent defendant?

6. In their case history of *Spaulding v. Zimmerman*, Roger C. Cramton and Lori P. Knowles interviewed the surviving participants of the litigation as well as reviewed court records. Among their findings were that the two defense lawyers never informed their clients about Spaulding's aneurism; indeed, they appear to have made the decision not to disclose entirely on

---

96. *Id.* at 196–97 (*quoting The Times* (London), Dec. 30, 1847, at 6).

97. *Id.* at 198 (*quoting* The Times (London), Dec. 30, 1847, at 4). *See generally* "Symposium: Executing the Wrong Person: The Professionals' Ethical Dilemmas," 29 *Loyola of Los Angeles Law Review* 1547 (1996).

their own, without consulting either their clients or the insurers who were paying them.[98] What might account for such conduct? If their decision had become a matter of public knowledge, how might it have affected their practice? Should they have considered this consequence?

Cramton and Knowles also shed light on one of the puzzling features of the case, the failure on the part of Spaulding's lawyer to request Dr. Hannah's report. In part, this lapse may be attributable to the lawyer's youth and inexperience, but he also had a legitimate worry about demanding the report. He feared that it might lead defense counsel to request reports by Spaulding's physicians, one of which recommended waiting a year to settle the case in order to make sure of the extent of Spaulding's injuries. Spaulding's lawyer feared that if this report came to light, the court might not approve the immediate settlement that all parties desired.[99] Does this affect your appraisal of responsibility in the case?

As Cramton and Knowles report, the story does not have a happy ending. Although David Spaulding's aortic aneurism was discovered in time for corrective surgery, a side-effect of the surgery was that David lost the power of speech. Not all the lawyers lived happily ever after. Richard Pemberton, a young lawyer who argued the case for Zimmerman in the Supreme Court, believed that he received the assignment because a senior partner found it distasteful. Pemberton did as well and subsequently had this to say about his assignment.

> After 20 years of practice, I would like to think that I would have disclosed the aneurysm of the aorta as an act of humanity and without regard to the legalities involved, just as I surely would now. You might suggest to your students in the course on professional responsibility that a pretty good rule for them to practice respecting professional conduct is to do the right thing.[100]

Is it that simple? If the bar's ethical rules at the time had prevented disclosure, is the "right" course of conduct self-evident?

NOTES: COMPLIANCE WITH COURT ORDERS

What should a lawyer do when a court rules against an assertion of attorney-client privilege, for example in a case involving client identity or tainted fees, and orders the attorney to reveal confidential information? It may seem obvious that the attorney must comply with the court order—the alternative is to face jail or fines for contempt—but the bar has resisted this conclusion. An early draft of the Model Rules included an exception to Model Rule 1.6 (the confidentiality rule) to permit lawyers to reveal confidences in order to comply with a court order. But the ABA House of Delegates deleted the exception, which was not restored until the 2002 revisions of the Model Rules, nearly twenty years after the deletion. In the meantime, lawyers and commentators searching for a way to allow lawyers

98. Cramton & Knowles, *supra* note 94, at 69.

99. *Id.* at 74.

100. *Id.*, at 201.

to comply with court orders without violating Model Rule 1.6 argued that complying with court orders comes under the rubric of "disclosure . . . impliedly authorized in order to carry out the representation" (Model Rule 1.6(a)). Thus, the deletion's significance was more symbolic than practical—but the symbolism is important. It shows how profoundly reluctant lawyers are to disclose confidential information, even when a court declares that it is not privileged.

The *Restatement of the Law Governing Lawyers*, § 63, explicitly provides that "[a] lawyer may use or disclose confidential client information when required by law, after the lawyer takes reasonably appropriate steps to assert that the information is privileged or otherwise protected against disclosure." Similarly, the current version of Model Rule 1.6 explicitly permits lawyers to reveal confidences "to comply with other law or court orders," but the Comment adds that without informed consent of the client to do otherwise, the lawyer "should assert on behalf of the client all nonfrivolous claims that the order is not authorized by other law or that the information sought is protected against disclosure by the attorney-client privilege or other applicable law." Model Rule 1.6, Comment [13]. The Comment adds that "the lawyer must consult with the client about the possibility of appeal. . . ."

State bar ethics committee opinions have exhibited similar reluctance about disclosing confidences even in the face of a court order. Most of these opinions conclude that lawyers are permitted but not required to reveal confidential information. A New Mexico opinion goes further, urging lawyers to challenge statutes requiring lawyers to disclose client identity or large cash transactions. "[T]he Committee is of the opinion that an attorney who chooses not to decline the representation and who rather chooses to represent the client while challenging the law would uphold the highest ideals and traditions of our profession."[101] So too, a 1994 ABA ethics committee formal opinion declares that a lawyer must resist subpoenas for confidential information on any legitimate available grounds, and cannot reveal confidential information until confronted by the final order of a court.[102]

If the bar's foot-dragging in the face of court orders seems puzzling, and inconsistent with the time-honored conception of lawyers as "officers of the court," it bears note that journalists sometimes prefer going to jail to revealing the identity of their news sources. Although bar opinions do not go so far as to instruct lawyers to resist court orders, the opinions imply some sympathy with the journalists' tenacious defense of confidentiality. One flamboyant lawyer—Oscar Goodman, a Las Vegas lawyer so well-known that the press referred to him simply as "the Big O"—preferred paying a $2,500 a day fine (which, accompanied by reporters, he hand-carried each day to the clerk of court) rather than turn over records of how

---

101. State Bar of N.M. Advisory Opinions Comm., Advisory Op. 1989–2 (1989). For discussion of bar resistance to court-ordered disclosure of confidences, see Susan P. Koniak, "The Law Between the Bar and the State," 70 *N.C. L. Rev.* 1389 (1992).

102. ABA Formal Opinion 94–385 (July 5, 1994).

much he had been paid by a client who was an alleged mobster. His client finally permitted Goodman to turn over the records. Goodman commented, "Money can't coerce me.... Jail time can't coerce me. But my ticket to practice law was of great importance. And my client told me that I was throwing away money for no purpose."[103] His resistance did Goodman no harm: within five years of the incident, "the Big O" was elected to the first of three terms as mayor of Las Vegas.

Are lawyers who resist valid court orders to reveal confidential information professional heroes, or obstructors of justice? Does it matter why the court is seeking the information?

NOTES: THE EXCEPTION FOR LAWYER–CLIENT DISPUTES

One conspicuous exception to the bar's passionate defense of confidentiality arises when a client sues a lawyer for malpractice or files a grievance against a lawyer, or when a lawyer must sue a client to collect unpaid fees. The Model Rules, like its predecessor, allows disclosure "to establish a claim or defense on behalf of the lawyer in a controversy between the lawyer and the client, to establish a defense to a criminal charge or civil claim against the lawyer based upon conduct in which the client was involved, or to respond to allegations in any proceeding concerning the lawyer's representation of the client." Rule 1.6(b)(3). On the basis of such rules, one well-known court decision permitted a lawyer to reveal confidential information to parties suing his client for fraud, in order to persuade the plaintiffs that the lawyer should not be joined as an additional defendant.[104]

The discrepancy between the bar's otherwise-wholehearted embrace of confidentiality and the self-defense exception has prompted unfavorable comment from some commentators:

> The same lawyer who is prohibited from disclosing information learned while representing a client to exonerate someone falsely accused of a capital crime, in other words, is perfectly free to disclose confidential information when he or she is the one accused, falsely or not. Nor is there any requirement that the lawyer's liberty be at stake, or even that the lawyer be accused of anything criminal. A simple fee dispute with a client is sufficient grounds to disclose confidential information. The lawyer's interest in collecting a fee is apparently a higher priority than exonerating an innocent defendant about to be convicted of a capital crime or helping a distraught family locate an abducted child. Confidentiality means everything in legal ethics unless lawyers lose money, in which case it means nothing.[105]

Is this unfair? Are the bar's priorities justifiable?

103. Richard Bernstein, "Lawyer Risks Jail to Protect Client Information," *N.Y. Times*, Dec. 23, 1994, at A28.

104. Meyerhofer v. Empire Fire & Marine Insurance Co., 497 F.2d 1190 (2d Cir. 1974).

105. Daniel R. Fischel, "Lawyers and Confidentiality," 65 *U. Chi. L. Rev.* 1, 10 (1998).

F.   CONFIDENTIALITY AND CLIENT FRAUD

PROBLEM 4

Assume that you were a senior partner with Singer, Hutner, Levine & Seeman under the circumstances described below. What would you have done? Note that the lawyers practiced in New York while it was governed by the Code of Professional Responsibility. Consider whether your answers would be different under the Model Rules.

References:

DR 2–110(A)(2), DR 4–101; Model Rules 1.2, 1.6, 1.16

NOTES AND QUESTIONS: THE O.P.M. CASE

In a well-known client fraud case from the 1970s, O.P.M., a computer leasing firm, obtained more than $210 million in fraudulent loans. The two partners who owned O.P.M. bought computers that they then leased to other companies. They used their existing leases as collateral for loans to buy additional computers that were necessary for future leases. O.P.M. won a sizable market share by slashing its prices, but as a result, its lease revenues were too small to provide collateral for the loans needed. So the partners forged leases for much higher amounts—leases that their lawyers unknowingly presented to lenders as documentation for new loans. Every increase in their business required new computers, new loans, and new forgeries; incoming revenues went to service past loans. In essence, O.P.M. (the initials stood for *Other People's Money*) was a pyramid scheme. The partners' methods were hardly subtle. They committed their forgeries by what they called the "glass table method": one partner would crouch beneath a glass table in their private office at night, with the lights off, and shine a flashlight upward through a genuine lease to enable his partner to trace the signatures on to a fraudulent lease.

Most of these loans were negotiated and the paperwork processed by O.P.M.'s outside counsel, the law firm of Singer, Hutner, Levine & Seeman. A year before the two partners who ran O.P.M. were finally caught, their accountant warned Singer, Hutner of the frauds. At this point, O.P.M. was generating sixty per cent of the firm's billings.

1.   What should the firm have done at this point?

Singer, Hutner engaged two legal ethics experts as consultants. On the basis of their advice, Singer, Hutner continued to close new loans for O.P.M. A few months later, it became clear to Singer, Hutner, partly as a result of one O.P.M. partner's admissions, that $60 million of the new loans it had closed were fraudulent.

2.   What should the firm have done now?

On advice of the legal ethics experts, Singer, Hutner gradually terminated its representation without informing O.P.M.'s new counsel that anything was amiss. Before the fraud finally unraveled, the new attorneys had unwittingly closed another $15 million in fraudulent loans for O.P.M. After the O.P.M. partners were convicted of criminal violations and sentenced to ten and twelve years in prison, Singer, Hutner paid $10 million to settle a suit brought by defrauded lenders.[106]

What accounts for the firm's behavior? When Singer, Hutner lawyers first learned of the frauds, they told their ethics consultants that the firm wanted to do what was proper but also wished, if possible, to continue representing O.P.M., its bread-and-butter client. In response, the consultants gave three crucial pieces of advice. First, because the frauds were past, Singer, Hutner could not disclose them. Second, Singer, Hutner had no obligation to "police" its client in order to make certain that the new loans it was closing were honest. Third, because Singer, Hutner had no information positively suggesting that O.P.M.'s partners would continue the frauds, the firm did not have to withdraw. Considerable evidence suggests that Singer, Hutner took great pains to "know" as little as possible about O.P.M.'s frauds, so that the law firm could maintain that it was not intentionally involved in illegal activity. Although Singer, Hutner eventually insisted that the O.P.M. partners arrange to have customers send the law firm independent verifications of deals, the O.P.M. partners had little difficulty intercepting the verification forms and substituting forgeries.

When, several months later, Singer, Hutner partners discovered that they had closed an additional $60 million in fraudulent new loans, the ethics consultants advised that these too had now become past frauds, and were therefore protected by the bar's confidentiality rules. When Singer, Hutner decided to withdraw, the consultants warned that a sudden resignation could violate the firm's ethical responsibilities under DR 2–110(A)(2): "[a] lawyer shall not withdraw from employment until he has taken reasonable steps to avoid foreseeable prejudice to the rights of his client." It followed from the consultants' opinion that Singer, Hutner should not reveal O.P.M.'s past frauds to successor counsel, even though the new counsel asked whether anything was amiss. Thus, Singer, Hutner's lawyers found themselves in the painful position of deceiving their successor counsel, who then closed additional fraudulent transactions.

3.   Singer Hutner lawyers claimed that at no point in the O.P.M. history did they clearly "know" that the loans it was closing were fraudulent. Do you find this excuse adequate? If the only way that Singer, Hutner could have known about the loans it was closing was to police its own client, what should the firm have done?

---

106.   This account is drawn from Stuart Taylor, Jr., "Ethics and the Law: A Case History," *N.Y. Times*, Jan. 9, 1983, § 6 Magazine, at 31 and from "OPM Leasing Services, Inc.," *in The Social Responsibilities of Lawyers* 184 (Philip B. Heymann & Lance Liebman eds., 1988).

4.   Was the advice given by the ethics consultants sound? Consider DR 7–102(B)(1), DR 4–101, and DR 2–110(A)(2). Notice that DR 7–102(B)(1) protects "privileged communications." ABA Formal Opinion 341 interprets "privileged communications" to refer to confidences and secrets as defined in DR 4–101(A).

5.   At what step, if any, did Singer, Hutner go wrong? Why? Would Model Rules giving lawyers the discretion but not the obligation to reveal frauds have made a difference? If not, what else might have been more effective?

NOTES: CLIENT FRAUD AND DISCLOSURE RULES

Some of the most common, and therefore troubling, confidentiality dilemmas are those arising out of client fraud. As Geoffrey Hazard puts it, "[r]esponsible law-giving require[s] recognition . . . that honest lawyers can suffer the misfortune of having dishonest clients."[107] Hazard cautions that lawyers representing such clients risk criminal sanctions for aiding and abetting fraud if the lawyers protect client confidences too zealously.[108] Some lawyers seem to believe that the attorney-client relationship insulates them from criminal or civil liability for crimes and frauds involving their professional assistance. This is simply not so.

As noted earlier, it was not until 2003 that the ABA's Model Rules incorporated exceptions to confidentiality permitting lawyers to divulge client confidences (a) to prevent client fraud; or (b) to rectify client fraud in which lawyers had unwittingly participated. Remarkably, however, all but eight states and the District of Columbia had already abandoned the Model Rules' across-the-board protection of confidences concerning client fraud. The remaining states adopted one or both of the proposed permissions to divulge confidences; some even strengthened them to *require* disclosure.

Required disclosure. Florida, New Jersey, Virginia, and Wisconsin require lawyers to disclose confidential information if that is the only way to prevent a client's criminal fraud; New Jersey and Wisconsin also require the lawyer to disclose such information to prevent a non-criminal fraud; and Hawaii and Ohio require lawyers to disclose confidences to rectify a client's crime or fraud in which the lawyer's services were used.

Permitted disclosure. Only Alabama, California, the District of Columbia, Kentucky, Missouri, Montana, Nebraska, Rhode Island, and South Dakota forbid the disclosure of confidences to prevent criminal conduct (unless it threatens life or limb). Other states have a variety of rules permitting the disclosure of confidences to prevent criminal or non-criminal frauds or to rectify frauds in which the lawyer's services were used.

Similarly, the *Restatement of the Law Governing Lawyers*, § 67 permits lawyers to disclose confidences to prevent or rectify client crime or fraud threatening "substantial financial loss," if the lawyer's services are being used in the same matter.

---

107.   Hazard, *supra* note 93, at 720.   **108.**   *Id.* at 706–07.

These state responses recognize that, as Hazard puts it, "an honest lawyer with a dishonest client is at risk of being drawn into a transaction which is tainted with fraud or other illegality; that in such an eventuality the lawyer can be charged with being an accessory to the client's wrongdoing; that honest lawyers should be able effectively to disengage themselves from client fraud; and that being able to effect such a disengagement requires clear legal authority to disclose client confidences if necessary to that purpose. [Responsible law-giving] also requires having no tears for clients who draw their lawyers into fraudulent schemes."[109]

NOTES: BAR RESPONSES TO CLIENT FRAUD

The O.P.M. debacle is only one of a series of hotly-debated cases involving lawyers who, by honoring the duty of confidentiality, permitted clients to engage in fraud. Perhaps coincidentally, in each decade since the 1970s, one notorious case of lawyers implicated in client frauds has grabbed headlines; the names of these cases have become shorthand for the entire problem and the debates surrounding them. In the 1970s, the case involved "National Student Marketing"; in the 1980s, "O.P.M" What some called "*the* ethics case of the '90s" involved the Wall Street law firm of Kaye, Scholer, Fierman, Hays & Handler, and for some time "Kaye, Scholer" displaced O.P.M. as the quintessential client fraud case. After 2001, the case is "Enron." (As of late 2008, it seems entirely possible that the subprime mortgage crash will eventually produce its own client fraud scandals.) The notes that follow briefly relate the history of these episodes.

The modern debate over lawyer responses to client fraud began with the 1972 complaint filed in *SEC v. National Student Marketing Corp.,* 457 F.Supp. 682 (D.D.C.1978). In that case, the SEC accused several lawyers and their firms of aiding their clients' violations of securities law. The court held that the lawyers were obligated to prevent their clients from closing a merger after the lawyers discovered that it had been approved on the basis of materially misleading documents. However, the decision failed to specify what steps the lawyers should have taken to prevent the merger from going forward. Was it withdrawal? Disclosure? Although the district court opinion was silent in the face of these questions, the SEC took the position that the lawyers should have disclosed the fraud. The securities bar objected strenuously, arguing that the SEC proposal would compel securities lawyers to violate their duties of confidentiality. The ABA responded by strengthening the protections for confidences in the Model Code of Professional Responsibility.

Most states did not adopt the ABA's strengthened protection of confidentiality in the Code, just as most states rejected the ABA's highly protective pre–2002 version of Rule 1.6. Yet the organized bar has continued to resist disclosure mandates: as we saw earlier in the Chapter, several state ethics committees have issued opinions declaring that lawyers should

109.   Hazard, *supra* note 93, at 720.

not comply with court orders to reveal confidential information without first appealing them.

The O.P.M. case broke in 1981, while an ABA Commission headed by Robert Kutak was in the process of drafting the Model Rules of Professional Conduct. Several influential members of the Kutak Commission favored broader exceptions to confidentiality, and O.P.M. became a poster child for the perils of rules that prevent lawyers from disclosing client fraud. Early drafts of the Model Rules included exceptions to confidentiality if disclosure was the only way for lawyers to prevent such fraud or rectify frauds that they had unwittingly assisted. Again the bar objected and the ABA rejected those exceptions.[110] The one concession in the Model Rules to the pro-disclosure side of the argument was a so-called "noisy withdrawal" suggestion in a Comment to MR 1.6: "Neither this Rule nor Rule 1.8(b) nor Rule 1.16(d) prevents the lawyer from giving notice of the fact of withdrawal, and the lawyer may also withdraw or disaffirm any opinion, document, affirmation, or the like." Noisy withdrawal would clearly tip off other parties to a transaction that something is amiss without actually revealing client confidences. Because the most recent version of MR 1.6 permits lawyers to reveal confidences in the face of client fraud, noisy withdrawal is no longer necessary, and the Comment about noisy withdrawal has been deleted from the current Model Rules.

The Kaye, Scholer case arose out of the massive and enormously costly collapse of the savings and loan industry (the so-called "thrift industry") in the late 1980s. Deregulation of the industry in the early '80s had led to a rash of risky investments by thrift owners, who were able to attract depositors because of taxpayer-funded deposit insurance. When the industry crashed, the taxpayers were left with losses estimated to total nearly half a trillion dollars. One of the most notorious of the thrift owners was Charles Keating (whose large political contributions tainted a number of U.S. senators). Keating retained Kaye, Scholer to help fight off bank examiners whose job was to make sure that thrifts were run prudently. Kaye, Scholer's lawyers informed the bank examiners—who were entitled by law to full access to a thrift's records—that all requests for information were to be channeled through the law firm. Then the firm allegedly stonewalled the examiners; one described Kaye, Scholer's tactics as "a stiff-arm day in and day out." At the same time that the firm was asserting that Keating's Lincoln Savings and Loan was making sound, prudent investments, the thrift was involved in fraudulent and high risk transactions that put it in a deep financial hole. By 1989 it was insolvent and owed $2.6 billion.[111]

The Office of Thrift Supervision (OTS)—a government agency charged with recovering as much money as possible from the savings and loan

---

110. *See* Ted Schneyer, "Professionalism as Bar Politics: The Making of the Model Rules of Professional Conduct," 14 *Law & Soc. Inquiry* 677 (1989).

111. For a chronology of the Kaye, Scholer case, *see* "In The Matter of Kaye,

Scholer, Fierman, Hays & Handler: A Symposium on Government Regulation, Lawyers' Ethics, and the Rule of Law: Introduction," 66 *S. Cal. L. Rev.* 977, 979–83 (1993).

mess—took Lincoln over as its receiver. Suddenly, Kaye, Scholer's adversary had become the client, and the attorney-client privilege no longer shielded Lincoln's records of dealings with Kaye, Scholer lawyers. Based on Lincoln's own files, OTS filed charges against the law firm, alleging that Kaye, Scholer had knowingly misrepresented or failed to disclose information to the bank examiners that would have indicated Lincoln's pattern of unsafe, unsound, and unlawful practices, as well as Lincoln's efforts to conceal these practices. In a widely-denounced tactic, OTS froze Kaye, Scholer's assets in order to force a quick settlement, and the firm paid OTS $41 million without any adjudication of the charges. The organized bar was furious at the government's hardball methods, but the case also provoked debate over whether Kaye, Scholer's lawyers had behaved improperly. In a widely-quoted judicial opinion, federal judge Stanley Sporkin blasted the lawyers and accountants who worked for Keating:

> The questions that must be asked are: Where were these professionals . . . when these clearly improper transactions were being consummated? Why didn't any of them speak up or disassociate themselves from these transactions? Where also were the outside accountants and attorneys when these transactions were effectuated? What is difficult to understand is that with all the professional talent involved (both accounting and legal), why at least one professional would not have blown the whistle to stop the overreaching that took place in this case.[112]

A final, ironic, note is that the successor counsel in O.P.M. who Singer, Hutner deceived was none other than Peter Fishbein of Kaye, Scholer—the same attorney whose aggressive representation of Charles Keating had precipitated the firm's difficulties.

The wave of accounting scandals that began with the collapse of energy giant Enron in 2001 did not originate in a change in law, in the way that the savings and loan crisis can be traced back to a deregulation of the industry that invited risky speculation. Rather, the cause appears to be the stock market bubble of the late 1990s, which created tremendous incentives for unsound businesses to manipulate their financial statements in order to look more profitable than they were. The hope was that this would keep stock prices afloat while the company grew out of its financial woes. But the desire of business managers to cover up losses, roll the dice once more, and hope that later success would redeem earlier losses is entirely parallel to similar desires of thrift operators. Enron's manipulation consisted of extremely intricate transactions designed to move losses off Enron's books and onto the books of "special purpose entities" (SPEs) that were nominally independent from Enron but actually were created by Enron for no purpose other than parking losses. All of these transactions involved many professionals: executives, accountants, and lawyers. Enron's in-house legal department consisted of 250 attorneys, and at least two outside law firms (Vinson & Elkins and Andrews & Kurth) played a substantial role in papering Enron's deals. To date, no single set of events as dramatic as the

---

112.   Lincoln Sav. & Loan Ass'n v. Wall,
743 F.Supp. 901, 920 (D.D.C.1990).

O.P.M. or Kaye, Scholer cases has emerged from lawyers' behavior.[113] A lengthy report by a court-appointed bankruptcy examiner suggests that the failure of the lawyers to blow the whistle (internally as well as externally) on Enron's many dubious transactions came in part because they did not always understand the transactions, in part because they relied on the accountants, and in part because they chose to remain wilfully blind. The examiner nevertheless concludes that substantial grounds exist for malpractice actions against some lawyers.[114] The basis for liability is that these lawyers took no remedial measures in the course of papering deals that they often recognized to be improper.[115] So too, a Report of the Bar of the City of New York concluded that lawyers were in a position to question possible misconduct, but only some did so and none raised their concerns with the Board of Directors.[116] Vinson & Elkins settled lawsuits for $30 million.

These are not isolated cases. A survey by the New York City Bar of nine recent scandals found that in at least seven, lawyers were well positioned to ask questions about the conduct leading to the litigation, and in one of the two exceptions, lawyers knew of other violations of fiduciary obligations.[117] Litigation over lawyers' responsibilities in such cases of client fraud are likely to remain a prominent feature of the contemporary legal landscape. Underlying all of these cases are fundamental problems of adversarial ethics. What, if any, obligations do lawyers have to protect innocent third parties from unscrupulous clients? What obligations do lawyers owe to a client's shareholders, whose interests might be jeopardized by managerial misconduct? How are those responsibilities to be balanced against the duty of confidentiality?

QUESTIONS

1. If you suspect that your client is involved in fraudulent or hazardous conduct, can you keep your hands clean by keeping your eyes closed? Under what circumstances might you have an obligation to investigate your client's activities? Under what circumstances might you have an obligation to report managerial misconduct to a board of directors? See the discussion

---

113. Robert W. Gordon, "A New Role for Lawyers?: The Corporate Counselor After Enron," 35 *Conn. L. Rev.* 1185 (2003) (excerpted in Chapter IX *infra*).

114. In re Enron Corp., Final Report of Neal Batson, Court–Appointed Examiner, Appendix C (Role of Enron's Attorneys).

115. Discussion of the Enron lawyers is voluminous. For examples, see Simon, *supra* note 77; Gordon, *supra* note 113; Deborah L. Rhode & Paul D. Paton, "Lawyers, Ethics, and Enron," 8 *Stan. J.L. Bus. & Fin.* 9 (2002); Colloquium: Ethics in Corporate Representation, 74 *Fordham L. Rev.* 947–1352 (2005); "Symposium–Enron and the Future

of U.S. Corporate Law and Policy," 89 *Cornell L. Rev.* 269 (2004); John R. Kroger, "Enron, Fraud and Securities Reform: An Enron Prosecutor's Perspective," 76 *Colo. L. Rev.* 57 (2003). For an overview of lawyers involvement in nine scandals including Enron, World Com, and HealthSouth, see Association of the Bar of the City of New York, Report of the Lawyer's Role in Corporate Governance 21–30 (2006).

116. Association of the Bar of the City of New York, *supra* note 115, at 26, 102.

117. *Id.*, at 26–29.

of organizational clients, Model Rule 1.13, and the Sarbanes–Oxley statute in Chapter VII.

Most business lawyers deny that they have any responsibilities to investigate potential client misconduct, but there is distinguished judicial authority to the contrary. Consider Judge Friendly's opinion in *United States v. Benjamin*, 328 F.2d 854 (2d Cir. 1964) and Judge Posner's in *Greycas v. Proud*, 826 F.2d 1560 (7th Cir.1987). *Benjamin* sustained the criminal conviction of a lawyer who had "shut [his] eyes to what was plainly to be seen," namely that his services were being used by his client in financial frauds.[118] In *Greycas*, the lawyer Proud wrote a letter assuring a would-be lender that no prior liens existed on the collateral that Proud's client was putting up for a loan. Proud relied on his client's statement that no liens existed under circumstances plainly suggesting a need for further inquiry. The client was lying, and after he had defaulted on the loan, the court imposed substantial civil liability on Proud for "negligent misrepresentations that induce detrimental reliance."[119] Both *Benjamin* and *Greycas* are considered leading cases on lawyers' liability for client frauds.

An individual's conscious avoidance of guilty knowledge satisfies the *mens rea* requirement for criminal liability, under the doctrine of "wilful ignorance" (sometimes referred to as "wilful blindness" or "connivance"). The paradigm case is the drug courier who deliberately refrains from looking in the satchel he is transporting, in order to be able to say truthfully that he didn't know he was carrying drugs. There is little settled law defining when this doctrine or its civil counterparts apply to lawyers. To avoid liability, is it enough for a lawyer simply to accept at face value a client's assurances about the propriety of a transaction or the soundness of the client's business? If you are writing an opinion letter to a regulator based on these assurances, can you present yourself as a mere scrivener, reporting whatever your client says? If you suspect that your client is concealing material facts, may you adopt a "don't ask, don't tell" approach to client interviewing? Under what circumstances would you be putting your own word on the line?[120]

2.   When a regulatory agency requires corporations to disclose information, how adversarial may lawyers be in presenting it or fending off regulators? This issue played a prominent role in the Kaye, Scholer matter. Geoffrey Hazard, a nationally-renowned ethics expert, gave an expert opinion on behalf of Kaye, Scholer maintaining that the firm was acting in the traditional role of litigation counsel in administrative or judicial proceedings that Lincoln reasonably anticipated. That role, he suggested, is one in which the lawyer's obligations to third parties are at a minimum, and obligations of confidentiality and zealous advocacy are at a maximum. According to Hazard, the standard governing what litigation counsel can say on behalf of their clients is set forth in Model Rule 3.1. This rule requires only that lawyers have a non-frivolous basis for any position that

---

118.   328 F.2d at 854, 863.
119.   826 F.2d at 1565.

120.   *See* David Luban, "Contrived Ignorance," 87 *Geo. L. J.* 957 (1999).

they assert. Under this standard, Hazard argued, Kaye, Scholer had behaved properly.[121]

William H. Simon takes issue with Hazard's position. In particular, Simon rejects the view that the ethical obligations of "litigation counsel" are only to refrain from taking frivolous positions:

> Professional responsibility doctrine provides no support for this position whether or not we call the lawyers "litigation counsel." The argument's spurious force depends entirely on its disregard for the distinction between factual assertion and argument. Rule 3.1 and its "not frivolous" standard applies to the latter; it governs *positions* that counsel takes, not assertions containing *information*. In a pleading, brief, or argument in court, the lawyer refers to evidence that has been or will be presented to the tribunal. Argument involves assertions as to how this evidence should be interpreted or characterized.... The dangers of deception are limited, and counsel can be given wide latitude....
>
> The situation is different if the lawyer provides information, especially under a disclosure duty.... In these situations, counsel's task does not consist of suggesting characterizations for evidence of record but rather of providing information within their control in response to the other party's requests. When counsel represent expressly or implicitly that they have provided all the information responsive to the request, they put their credibility in issue in ways that they do not in argument.[122]

In response to Simon, Donald Langevoort objects that

> [e]mbedded in both the law of fraud and conventional legal ethics is a "tit for tat" norm of fair play that sometimes allows for Machiavellian behavior.... [W]hen a relationship is adversary, law and ethics default to something closer to *caveat emptor*.... In other words, advocacy talk, of the sort commonly found in highly contested negotiations, is the accepted norm when a relationship is adversary....
>
> I certainly don't know enough about the relationship between the Bank Board and Kaye Scholer to be totally confident in drawing inferences. But I strongly suspect that it was recognized by both sides as highly adversarial, thus triggering a sense that Kaye Scholer had fairly free rein to make overstatements of opinion and inference, such as describing the client's "prudent underwriting" or "managerial skill." ... I strongly disagree with Simon's inference that Kaye Scholer was offering anything like a due diligence opinion on which the regulators could reasonably rely in substitution for their own investiga-

121. "Summary of the Expert Opinion of Geoffrey C. Hazard, Jr." (Feb. 25, 1992), *reprinted in The Attorney–Client Relationship After Kaye, Scholer* 381, 394–402 (PLI Corp. Law & Practice Course Handbook Series No. B4–7009, 1992).

122. William H. Simon, "The Kaye Scholer Affair: The Lawyer's Duty of Candor and the Bar's Temptations of Evasion and Apology," 23 *Law & Soc. Inquiry* 243, 271 (1998).

tion. I doubt that anyone mistook the firm's advocacy for anything else.[123]

What is your view? Is a lawyer reporting client information to a regulatory agency like litigation counsel, and thus subject to the norms of the adversary system, or do regulatory contexts call for less spin and more candor?

3.   Some commentators draw a distinction between *gatekeeping* and *whistleblowing* rules. A gatekeeping rule, such as Model Rule 1.2(d), prohibits lawyers from assisting in fraudulent conduct. Coupled with Rule 1.16(a), this gatekeeping rule requires lawyers to withdraw from representations whenever their involvement would further client frauds. If lawyers are essential to the transaction, their refusal to provide assistance "shuts the gate" before it can be completed. An example of a gatekeeping rule is the 1989 Financial Institutions Reform, Recovery & Enforcement Act (FIR-REA), which makes banking attorneys liable for large civil penalties and restitution payments if they knowingly or recklessly participate in violations of law, fiduciary duty, or unsafe and unsound banking practice.[124] A whistleblowing rule goes further. Not only must lawyers refuse to assist fraud, they must (or may) inform others of the misconduct, or divulge weaknesses in the client's financial position.[125]

In arguing against gatekeeping and whistleblowing requirements, lawyers strongly object to being forced to police their clients. They often claim that it is unfair to mandate a standard of behavior that will be impossible to enforce and that less scrupulous members of the bar will not honor. The result will be to place honest lawyers at a competitive disadvantage among clients looking for undivided loyalty.

Do you find this argument persuasive? How do you respond to the concern that taking this argument seriously will drive ethical standards to the lowest common denominator? This is not an unrealistic concern. In his account of the thrift catastrophe, Martin Mayer quotes a banker—a former lawyer—who said that before the industry collapsed, "for half a million dollars you could buy any legal opinion you wanted from any law firm in New York."[126] According to Mayer,

> [t]he failure of the Bank Board to control the egregious crookedness of so many S & Ls must be laid in large part at the doorsteps of the great Washington, New York, Chicago, Dallas, and Los Angeles law firms. More than eighty firms, for example, represented Charles Keating and American Continental Corporation (the parent of Lincoln Savings) in his five years of tussles with the Bank Board. . . . [Many of] these firms

123.   Donald C. Langevoort, "What Was Kaye Scholer Thinking?," 23 *Law & Soc. Inquiry* 297, 298–99 (1998).

124.   Pub.L. No. 101–73, § 907, 103 Stat. 183, 473 (1989).

125.   Reinier H. Kraakman, "Gatekeepers: The Anatomy of a Third–Party Enforcement Strategy," 2 *J.L. Econ. & Organization* 53 (1986).

126.   Martin Mayer, *The Greatest–Ever Bank Robbery: The Collapse of the Savings and Loan Industry* 20 (1990).

have more than two hundred lawyers to feed; and Keating has estimated his legal fees as high as $70 million.[127]

Similar points have been made about the lawyers implicated in more recent financial scandals including Enron.

4.   Reinier Kraakman cautions that attempting to regulate an industry by increasing the gatekeeping and whistleblowing obligations of lawyers or accountants will prove ineffective if members of the industry can easily switch to less scrupulous providers.[128] How significant is that concern? Could Keating have dispensed with lawyers in dealing with banking regulations, or could Enron have structured its special purpose entities without legal assistance?

A related argument, developed by the New York City bar, is that lawyers who have gatekeeping or whistleblowing obligations will be excluded from information channels, and may let their own concerns about avoiding liability skew their advice to clients.[129] How should this risk be balanced against the benefits of increasing lawyer's responsibilities to investigate and prevent possible misconduct?

To what extent should lawyers be asked to play gatekeeping and whistleblowing roles?[130]

NOTES: COGNITIVE BIAS AND CLIENT FRAUD

Investigators of business frauds sometimes report that the lawyers they interview are stunned to discover that the deals they worked on were fraudulent. Enron lawyers told investigators that they were proud of the cutting-edge deals they put together; somehow, they failed to recognize that the deals were illegal. Social psychology research suggests common patterns that may work against lawyers' recognition of client fraud. One such tendency is "cognitive conservatism." Individuals are more likely to register and retain information when it is compatible with established beliefs or earlier decisions. A related phenomenon is reduction of "cognitive dissonance." After making a decision, individuals tend to suppress or reconstrue information that casts doubt on that decision. Accordingly, once lawyers have determined to represent a particular client, they may become less sensitive to ethical problems arising from that choice.

---

127. *Id.* at 122–23.

128. Kraakman, *supra* note 125, at 72–74.

129. Association of the Bar of the City of New York, *supra* note 115, at 5, 57–64.

130. For further discussion *see* Fred C. Zacharias, "Coercing Clients: Can Lawyer Gatekeeping Rules Work?," 47 *Boston Coll. L. Rev.* 455 (2006); John Coffee, "The Attorney as Gatekeeper: An Agenda for the SEC," 103 *Colum. L. Rev.* 1293 (2003); Sung Hui Kim, "The Banality of Fraud: Re-Situating

the Inside Counsel as Gatekeeper," 74 *Fordham L. Rev.* 983 (2005); David B. Wilkins, "Making Context Count: Regulating Lawyers After Kaye, Scholer," 66 *S.Cal.L. Rev.* 1145, 1164 (1993); Howell E. Jackson, "Reflections on Kaye, Scholer: Enlisting Lawyers to Improve the Regulation of Financial Institutions," 66 *S.Cal.L. Rev.* 1019, 1053–54 (1993); George H. Brown, "Financial Institution Lawyers as Quasi–Public Enforcers," 7 *Geo. J. Legal Ethics* 637 (1994).

Other problems involve overconfidence and overcommitment. Those who obtain decision making positions often have high confidence in their own capacities and judgment. That can readily lead to arrogance, over-optimism, and an escalation of commitment to choices that turn out to be wrong, either factually or morally. As a result, individuals may ignore or suppress dissent, overestimate their ability to rectify adverse consequences, and cover up mistakes by denying, withholding, or sometimes destroying information. An incremental slide into ever more dubious conduct can readily produce "the boiled frog" problem. As legend would have it, a frog thrown into boiling water will jump out of the pot. A frog placed in tepid water that gradually becomes hotter and hotter will calmly boil to death.

Other cognitive processes push in similar directions. Individuals are more likely to retain information that reflects favorably on themselves and to form positive impressions of someone on whom their own success partly depends. So too, the very act of advocating a particular position increases the likelihood that proponents will themselves come to adopt that position. In many practice settings, these cognitive biases, together with financial self-interest, collegial pressure, and diffusion of responsibility skew ethical judgment.[131]

How should ethical codes and civil liability rules respond to these psychological tendencies? Are they reasons to give the benefit of the doubt to lawyers who overlook client fraud? Or should regulatory structures seek to provide greater incentives for lawyers to identify and prevent client misconduct?

G.   A FINAL PROBLEM

The client-fraud cases we have examined present a context—the representation of clients in a heavily regulated industry—in which lawyers' duties of confidentiality were complicated by federal law mandating disclosure of sensitive client information. This is not by any means unusual: the law often creates special disclosure obligations that may affect the lawyer's professional responsibilities. What this means in practice is that lawyer's decisions about when to preserve client confidences may involve the interaction of several different bodies of law. For analytical purposes, we have found it useful to distinguish between the ethical requirement of confidentiality and the law of attorney-client privilege, but in real life, lawyers will have to consider them in tandem, alongside any other bodies of law that bear on disclosure obligations. We conclude this chapter with a problem requiring analysis along all these dimensions.

---

131. *See*, e.g., Deborah L. Rhode, "Moral Counseling," 75 *Fordham L. Rev.* 1317 and sources cited in notes 23–25; Douglas C. Langevoort, "The Organizational Psychology of Hyper–Competition: Corporate Irresponsi- bility and the Lessons of Enron," 70 *George Wash. L. Rev.* 968 (2002); Langevoort, "The Epistemology of Corporate–Securities Law- yering: Beliefs, Biases and Organizational Be- havior," 63 *Brook. L. Rev.* 629 (1997).

PROBLEM 5

You are representing an executive in her divorce. She and her husband have two children, ages 4 and 10. Currently, your client is romantically involved with another man, Shane. You have negotiated a temporary joint custody arrangement pending the final divorce settlement. For the past few weeks, your client has had sole custody of the children while her husband is out of town making new living arrangements for his elderly mother.

Ten days ago, you telephoned your client at home to discuss the ongoing divorce negotiations. Her ten-year-old daughter answered the phone and said that her mother was not home. To your dismay, you learned from her that her mother had left her and her younger sister alone for more than 24 hours, while the mother stayed with Shane. You reached your client on her cell phone, and explained to her that leaving small children alone as she had done may constitute neglect. Not only could it harm her custody request, neglect is a criminal violation—to say nothing of the danger of leaving the children unaccompanied. Your client explained that the ten-year-old is exceptionally mature and capable, and that she had left meals for the children.

This week, however, you telephoned your client's home at 7 a.m., hoping to reach her before she left for the day, because she needed to sign some documents. Once again the ten-year-old answered the telephone and told you that her mother was not there. When you eventually spoke with your client, she explained that she had spent the night caring for Shane, who had flu. She did not bring the children with her because she did not want to expose them to the virus. You warned her that leaving the children unattended is neglect even if her motives were commendable.

Today, you received a call from your client, who informed you that the four-year-old had been treated for minor burns she received while being bathed by her sister. Running the bath, the ten-year-old had turned on the hot water tap before the cold and scalded the younger child. You asked your client bluntly whether she was home at the time. Instead of answering, however, she became angry, and told you to mind your own business. She had called, she said, only to alert you to an incident her husband might raise in the ongoing divorce negotiations—not to get a lecture from her own lawyer about how to live her life.

In your state, child neglect is a misdemeanor punishable by fine or up to a year in jail. The statute defines criminal neglect as "knowing failure to provide ordinary and proper care and attention" to a child. Furthermore, the state has enacted a Child Abuse and Neglect Reporting Act. The Act requires any person other than a health practitioner "who has reason to believe that a child has been subjected to abuse or neglect" to report the evidence to the Department of Child Welfare. However, the Act specifically exempts from this obligation anyone who "would be (a) disclosing matter communicated in confidence by a client to the client's attorney or other information relating to the representation of the client; or (b) violating the attorney-client privilege." One more legal rule seems relevant: Your state permits, but does not require, lawyers to reveal otherwise-confidential information necessary to prevent a client from committing any crime (and not, as in the Model Rules, only those crimes "likely to result in imminent death or substantial bodily harm"). Furthermore, the rule permits disclosure of confidences when necessary to rectify a client crime or fraud in which the lawyer's services were used.

What are your obligations the child abuse reporting statute? In upcoming settlement negotiations with the wife's attorney? In future dealings with the court?

References:

Model Rules 1.6, 3.3, 4.1, 1.16.

CHAPTER VI

DILEMMAS OF ADVOCACY: THE CRIMINAL LAW PARADIGM

INTRODUCTION

Among the most familiar roles lawyers play is that of advocate in a courtroom. The advocate's role raises familiar and sometimes dramatic ethical quandaries. How zealous should lawyers be on behalf of disagreeable causes or clients? What should they do if a client commits perjury? How far can they go in discrediting truthful opposing witnesses? How forthcoming must they be about the truth? Should their goal be victory or justice? Such issues can arise in any litigation, civil or criminal; but in the public imagination criminal cases are the most central and most controversial. This chapter therefore treats criminal law as a paradigm for examining the ethics of advocacy. It pursues two goals: understanding the role lawyers play in the criminal justice system, and examining the dilemmas of advocacy more generally.

The general public is often ambivalent about the role of defense counsel. As a matter of abstract principle, most people agree that those accused of a crime should be presumed innocent until proven guilty and that they should have the right to legal assistance in defending their case. But when the presumption becomes concrete, opinion often shifts. Lawyers' role in freeing guilty, sometimes dangerous, offenders often provokes considerable outrage. At the same time, however, lawyers' assistance in protecting individuals unjustly accused accounts for some of the most heroic and widely respected moments in the bar's history. Criminal cases thus require attorneys to withstand competing pressures and to serve multiple interests. These cases have traditionally served as the paradigm of the advocate's role because crucial values are at stake on both sides. Interests of life, liberty, and reputation are at issue not only for defendants but also for victims, potential victims, and other individuals who might be charged with criminal offenses.

Such issues were starkly presented in a celebrated 1943 autobiography by a prominent Atlanta attorney, Arthur Powell. There, Powell disclosed that a former client had acknowledged committing the murder for which another man had been convicted. In that case, a Jewish factory-owner, Leo Frank, was found guilty of murdering his 14–year–old employee, Mary Phagan. Antisemitic prejudice ran high and the local papers demanded the death penalty. Powell's client, after a promise of complete confidentiality, revealed his guilt. He would not, however, surrender to authorities or allow

Powell to disclose his confession. Powell then contacted the governor and asserted Frank's innocence, but refused to identify the source of his information. After the governor commuted Frank's sentence, a lynch mob gathered under the banner "Knights of Mary Phagan." They hanged Leo Frank and formed a group that subsequently folded into the Ku Klux Klan.[1]

Powell later defended his actions on the ground that the constitution guaranteed the privilege of counsel, and that "we lawyers, no matter what we think of it, have no duty but to protect and obey it. Such is our duty; such is our oath." However Powell also added, "I would be strongly tempted to break my oath before I would let an innocent man hang, but would know that I was violating the law and my oath if I did so."[2]

QUESTIONS

1. How would you assess Powell's conduct? What would you have done in his place? Would your response change after your client died?

2. How broadly should the privilege of confidentiality and assistance of counsel extend when the lawyer is sure of his client's guilt? Should the answer depend in part on whether the attorney believes that his client will commit further offenses or that another individual might be wrongfully convicted for the client's crime? Consider that issue in light of the sentencing oversight that freed a convicted rapist, described in Problem 1(b), *infra*.

A. DEFENDING THE GUILTY

INTRODUCTION

David Hoffman, in the first American treatise on legal ethics, proposed the following resolution:

> xv. When employed to defend those charged with crimes of the deepest dye, and the evidence against them, whether legal, or moral, be such as to leave no just doubt of their guilt, I shall not hold myself privileged, much less obliged, to use my endeavours to arrest, or to impede the course of justice, by special resorts to ingenuity—to the

---

1. *See* Leonard Dinnerstein, *The Leo Frank Case* 125 (1987 ed.); Robert Frey & Nancy Thompson–Frey, *The Silent and the Damned: The Murder of Mary Phagan and the Lynching of Leo Frank* (1988).

2. Arthur Powell, "Privilege of Counsel and Confidential Communications," 6 *Ga. B.J.* 334, 335 (1944) (discussing *I Can Go Home Again* (1943)). For recent examples, see Adam Liptak, "When Law Prevents Righting a Wrong," *N.Y. Times*, May 4, 2008, at E3; (discussing a North Carolina lawyer who revealed, after his client's death, that the client had acted alone in committing a murder for which another man was serving a life sentence); Adam Liptak, "Lawyer Reveals Secret Toppling Death Sentence," *N.Y. Times*, Jan. 19, 2008, at A1, A13 (discussing case in which a defense lawyer disclosed, after his client's death, that prosecutors had inappropriately coached his client to implicate a man still serving a life sentence).

artifices of eloquence—to appeals to the morbid and fleeting sympathies of weak juries, or of temporizing courts. . . . Persons of atrocious character, who have violated the law of God and man, are entitled to no such special exertions from any member of our pure and honourable profession; and indeed, to no intervention beyond securing to them a fair and dispassionate investigation of the *facts* of their cause, and the due application of the law: all that goes beyond that, either in manner or substance, is unprofessional, and proceeds, either from a mistaken view of the relation of client and counsel, or from some unworthy and selfish motive, which sets a higher value on professional display and success, than on truth and justice, and the substantial interests of the community.[3]

A century later, Supreme Court Justice Byron White defined the obligation of defense counsel very differently:

Law enforcement officers have the obligation to convict the guilty and to make sure they do not convict the innocent. They must be dedicated to making the criminal trial a procedure for the ascertainment of the true facts surrounding the commission of the crime . . . [Unlike prosecuting attorneys,] defense counsel has no comparable obligation to ascertain or present the truth. Our system assigns him a different mission. He must be and is interested in preventing the conviction of the innocent, but . . . we also insist that he defend his client whether he is innocent or guilty. The State has the obligation to present evidence. Defense counsel need present nothing, even if he knows what the truth is. He need not furnish any witnesses to the police, or reveal any confidences of his client, or furnish any other information to help the prosecution's case. If he can confuse a witness, even a truthful one, or make him appear at a disadvantage, unsure or indecisive, that will be his normal course. Our interest in not convicting the innocent permits counsel to put the State to its proof, to put the State's case in the worst possible light, regardless of what he thinks or knows to be the truth. Undoubtedly, there are some limits which defense counsel must observe but more often than not, defense counsel will cross-examine a prosecution witness, and impeach him if he can, even if he thinks the witness is telling the truth, just as he will attempt to destroy a witness who he thinks is lying. In this respect, as part of our modified adversary system and as part of the duty imposed on the most honorable defense counsel, we countenance or require conduct which in many instances has little, if any, relation to the search for truth.[4]

Consider those contrasting descriptions in light of the materials that follow. What are lawyers' obligations to criminal defendants, to the justice system, and to society generally when they believe their client is guilty?

---

3. David Hoffman, *Fifty Resolutions in Regard to Professional Deportment* xv in *A Course of Legal Studies* (1836).

4. United States v. Wade, 388 U.S. 218, 256–258 (1967) (White, J., dissenting in part and concurring in part).

John B. Mitchell, "The Ethics of the Criminal Defense Attorney—New Answers to Old Questions"

32 Stanford Law Review 293, 320–321 (1980).

II. Why I Defend the Guilty

By defending the guilty at trial, the defense attorney assures that those who are supposed to operate the screens [that protect the innocent] do so properly. By defending the guilty at trial, the defense attorney dispels at least some of the coercive effects of the plea-bargaining system. In short, by defending the guilty, the defense attorney protects the freedom of the innocent. But I defend the guilty not simply to protect all of us but also to protect the guilty from the corrupting influences of the criminal justice system. . . .

Many judges in large urban court systems, interested only in clearing their dockets, and often given to a martinet's temperament, shuttle the 20 or so new faces represented by the same public defender each day from arraignment through guilty plea. Police often lie, while prosecutors suppress evidence favorable to the defense. This governmental lawbreaking passes without the slightest notice. Under the umbrella of almost limitless discretion, judges are often guided only by their inclinations. . . .

Most people in our society do not respect the mandate of the law just because it is the law. Most refrain from beating or mugging others because of some internal sense that it is wrong to treat people that way rather than from a fear of the law. The values that our criminal law teaches to those poor, minority defendants who confront it, however, lead to different conclusions. If human beings are worthy of so little respect, if having money is everything, if power itself is the justification for fulfilling one's desire at the expense of the powerless, and if law is merely one tool of such power, then the only reason not to commit any type of crime is fear of the law's power. . . .

Our criminal courts must teach better lessons. It is to this end that I defend the guilty, for they, above all, must be taught the right lesson. It is not that I naively believe that most convicted defendants would thank a judge for being "fair" while sending them to prison. From my experience, however, the prevalent injustice in the current process does do harm by further lessening respect for the law, not just in the criminal defendants, but also in friends, family, witnesses, and spectators. The lessons are communicated to all of those who are touched by the process. . . .

B. The Ravages of Conviction

1. The prisons.

A lengthy exposition on the nightmarish conditions in our jails and prisons would cover little new ground. Literature and reports documenting the horrors are extensive. . . .

I will not dwell on this. Those guilty of serious crimes merit the wrath of our society. But almost no one deserves the hell holes that we call jails and prisons. There is almost no case I would not defend if that meant keeping a human being, as condemnable as he or she may be, from suffering the total, brutal inhumanity of our jails and prisons. . . .

When people ask how I can defend someone who is "dangerous," they are referring to a person who is more than just factually guilty of a crime; they mean someone who poses immediate physical danger to them in a very special sense. Statistically, drunk or negligent drivers are responsible for more deaths annually than murderers. But this kind of immediate physical danger does not frighten us. We do not like it, but we understand it. It does not involve some stranger totally disregarding our personal integrity by violently entering our world and using us as an object of his wishes. When people say "dangerous," they mean the violent offender.

I do not consider every person who commits a violent offense to be dangerous. When I speak of "dangerous" I refer to a quality of the person, not of the crime. While the nature of the crime may reflect this quality, it will not necessarily do so. Murderers rarely endanger lives a second time, and even those who assault their victim in the course of a robbery generally do so only when surprised by the victim's resistance. . . .

In my view a dangerous person is one for whom violence is a customary response, who is willing to attack a stranger without reason, and who is likely to do so in the future. The type of person I consider dangerous in a way that poses ethical problems greater than the basic problem of defending the factually guilty is a person likely to commit another act of violence the very same day. The question that arises, then, is how certain must I be that a person is "dangerous" before I will consider that factor in my ethical calculus?

Scientific studies attempting to predict future dangerous behavior have been unable to do so to a standard of "more likely than not," let alone "beyond a reasonable doubt." Nevertheless, there are defendants who, after interviews and review of their present charge and past criminal history, I have reasonably believed to be dangerous. The fact that I cannot validate this belief by some scientifically devised scale of deviance does not mean that this belief has no importance in my own calculation of the morality of my actions. A reasonable belief is a sufficient level of certainty to define a defendant as dangerous for my purposes.

Even if the defendant is guilty and dangerous, I can, yet, posit several reasons to justify his or her defense. First, it is through the defense of just such cases that an attorney can most influence the functioning of the screens. Government can best be educated in a serious case, especially one in which the police and prosecutor perceive the defendant as dangerous. The agents of the government really want to win convictions in such cases and it is in just such cases that all of the abuses the system generates are most likely to appear. Acquittals or even difficulties at trial due to inadequate investigation or the use of poor evidence will be remembered. In addition, making the screens operate effectively when serious charges are involved is especially important because the consequences of convicting an innocent person of a serious offense are so severe.

Second, it is important to ensure that the dangerous are treated fairly in the process. Such persons are the last ones in whom to reinforce values that disregard the worth of other human beings. Finally, aside from the general aversion I have to seeing anyone go to prison, incarceration presents some special problems for me when dealing with the dangerous offender. Almost all of the defendants I have met who I believed were dangerous had committed assaults, not murders. Their prison sentences would therefore be short—especially since over half of all violent crimes are committed by persons under 18 years of age. Even if we lock them up for quite a while, when they get out they will still be young and strong and probably more dangerous to the society than they were before they entered prison.

* * *

Marilyn vos Savant's weekly question-and-answer column, "Ask Marilyn," appears in *Parade Magazine*, a nationally-distributed Sunday magazine. In a column that preceded the next selection, Marilyn asked her readers whether private attorneys should accept or decline criminal cases in which the attorney knows that the client is guilty.

Marilyn Vos Savant, "Ask Marilyn"

Parade Magazine, Jan. 10, 1999.

You asked, "Should a private attorney defend a criminal case in which he or she knows that the defendant is guilty? Or should that attorney say, 'No, thank you'?" You also noted that if a client couldn't obtain representation, the court would appoint an attorney or assign a public defender (in the case of an indigent client), as required by law.

I believe that the private attorney should not take the case—so strongly that I fear having missed some novel argument to the contrary. No system is perfect, but I can't understand why a process for finding objective truth and holding citizens accountable should permit a legal representative to knowingly work against discovery of such truth.

—Frank A. Hansen, Chicago, Ill.

Our system works best when parties are represented by zealous advocates. As Dr. Samuel Johnson (1709–84) said, "The lawyer has no business with the justice or injustice of the cause. The justice or injustice of the cause is to be decided by the judge."

—Larry S. Pozner, National Association of Criminal Defense Lawyers, Denver, Colo.

Among those in agreement with the last reader, the most common sentiment was that if criminal defense attorneys turned down the cases of guilty defendants, they would be "assuming the role of the prosecutor, judge and jury." I believe this is not true. No one is suggesting that the attorney should gather evidence like a prosecutor, be allowed to make a legal decision about guilt like a jury or actually sentence the defendant like a judge. The suggestion is merely that the attorney turn down the case.

I pride myself on being open. To me, this means always searching for more truth, refining my opinion accordingly and moving to a better position if and when I find one. But when I asked readers to tell me if they think (A) the attorney should take a case in which he or she knows the defendant is guilty, or (B) the attorney should *not* take the case, I was unprepared for the results. For one thing, I was surprised by the visceral antipathy toward attorneys in general . . .

Here are the results: Of the readers who are not attorneys, 72% believe (B) that an attorney should *not* defend a guilty client in a criminal case and 25% believe (A) that an attorney *should* defend a guilty client. However, most of the latter included serious restrictions, such as an insistence that the attorney advise the client to plead guilty, thus considerably softening their support of position A. The remaining 3% had mixed feelings.

Among attorneys who responded, 92% (A) *would* defend a client they knew to be guilty. Just 7% chose B: They would *not* defend a guilty client. The remaining 1% had mixed emotions.

The principles stated by the attorneys who chose A include:

● A vigorous defense, even of the guilty, will force the prosecution to maintain high standards of proof for all cases.

● Even a guilty client should have an appropriate charge.

● Even a guilty client should have a fair sentence.

● A guilty client might not be legally responsible, as in cases of self-defense or insanity.

● An innocent person might give a false confession.

. . .

Before I conducted the poll, I had chosen A. Upon reading the arguments of those who also chose A, however, I felt my position was weak. I now choose B—the attorney should *not* take the case—except for the following cases:

1) When the attorney believes that the guilty client is still morally, ethically or spiritually in the right.

2) When the attorney believes that the broken law is morally, ethically or spiritually wrong.

3) *When the attorney knows in his or her heart that he or she is doing the right thing, regardless of what anyone else thinks.* This covers cases in which the attorney thinks the State has behaved badly, cases in which he or she thinks the client may be charged inappropriately or sentenced unfairly, cases in which the attorney thinks the client may not be legally responsible and cases in which the attorney suspects a false confession.

NOTES AND QUESTIONS

1. Savant's survey of her readers is not a scientific study, not only because her readership may not be representative of the public as a whole, but also because the responses came only from readers who felt strongly enough about the issue to write to her. The results may be skewed toward non-lawyers who dislike the legal profession and lawyers who feel they must defend it. However, even granting these potential distortions, there remains a sizable gap between public and professional views about defending the guilty. Other more systematic evidence finds similar gaps: over two-thirds of the public believes that "lawyers spend too much time finding technicalities to get criminals released."[5]

2. Vos Savant claims that the arguments on behalf of defending the guilty generally are weak, but also seems to believe that some arguments are appropriate, such as those seeking a fair charge or sentence, an insanity defense, or an acquittal based on false confession. Do you agree with that distinction?

3. Are there clients that you would not defend even if no other lawyers were willing to accept the case? In a survey shortly after the 9/11 attack on the World Trade Center, a majority of surveyed attorneys indicated that they would not defend accused terrorists.[6] Would you? Why or why not?

NOTES

Truth

The first justification for zealous representation of clients whom an attorney believes to be factually guilty is that it is necessary to protect those who are factually or legally innocent.[7] Defendants seldom have reason to confess their culpability to counsel, and circumstantial evidence may be misleading or incomplete. As Barbara Babcock notes,

> Facts are indeterminate, contingent, and in criminal cases, often evanescent. A finding of guilt is not necessarily the truth, but a legal conclusion arrived at after the role of the defense lawyer has been fully played.... [T]here is [often] a difference between legal and moral guilt.[8]

Accordingly, our system proceeds on the assumption that guilt is generally best determined not in the privacy of one lawyer's office but in open court under due process. As Lord Erskine observed in the trial of Thomas Paine for publishing *The Rights of Man* (1792), "If the advocate

5. ABA, *Perceptions of the U.S. Justice System* 59 (1999).

6. Amanda Bronstad, "Lawyer Poll—Most Lawyers Would Not Defend Terrorists," *Los Angeles Business Journal*, November 5, 2001, at 1. 1

7. The commentary on criminal defense lawyers' ethical obligations to guilty clients is extensive. For representative selections, *see*

Deborah L. Rhode, *In the Interests of Justice* 53–64 (2000); Cynthia Siemen, *Emotional Trials: The Moral Dilemma of Women Defense Attorneys* (2004); Barbara A. Babcock, "Defending the Guilty," 32 *Clev.St.L.Rev.* 175 (1983); and sources cited below.

8. Babcock, *supra* note 7, at 177–78.

refuses to defend from what he may think of the charge or the defense, [the lawyer] assumes the character of the judge ... before the hour of judgment."[9]

The risks of allowing lawyers to curtail their efforts in accordance with their own perceptions of guilt are particularly great under a system in which some 90 percent of all defendants never go to trial, acquittal is extremely rare, and resources for pretrial preparation are usually far from adequate.[10] One large survey of indigent criminal cases found that 99 percent included no motion for expenses for experts or investigation.[11] In a quarter of the cases in which innocent defendants have recently been exonerated by DNA evidence, their trial attorneys were demonstrably ineffective.[12] The reasons for their inadequacy are often rooted in the economic structure of the indigent defense system. As a federal oversight Commission candidly noted, most lawyers who take these cases face an "inherent conflict between remaining financially solvent and providing vigorous advocacy."[13]

About three-quarters of felony defendants are poor enough to qualify for court-appointed counsel. Systems for indigent defense take several forms but they generally share one defining feature: they are grossly underfunded. Of the $100 billion that America spends annually on criminal justice, only 2–3% goes to indigent defense, and the funds for defense counsel average about an eighth of the resources available to prosecutors.[14]

The risks of underfunding are generally greatest in indigent defense systems that rely on contracts with private practitioners awarded through competitive bids. Under this system, lawyers agree to provide representation for a specified percentage of the courts' total criminal caseload for a fixed annual amount, irrespective of the number or complexity of cases. Such systems discourage zealous advocacy by selecting attorneys who are able to turn over high volumes of clients at low cost. Where, as is typically the case, these systems lack adequate quality controls, a race to the bottom is difficult to avoid.[15]

Similar disincentives for effective representation occur in jurisdictions that rely on an assignment system for indigent defense in which courts appoint counsel on a case-by-case basis. These lawyers receive minimal flat fees or hourly rates, coupled with a ceiling on total compensation. Low

9. Lloyd P. Stryker, *For the Defense* 217 (1947) (quoting Erskine).

10. Felony acquittal rates in the state courts average about 1 percent and in the federal district courts about 3 percent. *See* David Luban, "Are Criminal Defenders Different?," 91 *Mich.L.Rev.* 1729 (1993). For resources, see sources cited in Deborah L. Rhode, *Access to Justice* 12, 126–28 (2004) and notes 14–17 *infra*.

11. ABA Standing Committee on Legal Aid and Indigent Defense, *Gideon's Broken Promise: America's Continuing Quest for Equal Justice* 19 (2005).

12. Barry Scheck, Peter Neufeld, & Jim Dwyer, *Actual Innocence* 187 (2000).

13. Report of the Commission to Review the Criminal Justice Act, reprinted in 52 *Crim. L. Reporter* 2265, 2284–85 (March 10, 1993).

14. Rhode, *supra* note 10, at 123; David Cole, *No Equal Justice* 64, 84 (1999).

15. Rhode, *supra* note 10, at 127–28; Cole, *supra* note 14, at 83–85; Amy Bach, "Justice on the Cheap," *The Nation*, May 21, 2001, at 21.

ceilings apply even for defendants facing the death penalty, and attorneys subject to such compensation caps have ended up with hourly rates below $100 and sometimes even below $10. For most court-appointed lawyers, "thorough preparation is a quick route to financial ruin."[16]

Analogous problems often arise under the third system for indigent defense, which relies on public defender offices. Where funding is adequate, the quality of representation in these offices is generally quite high. But many operate with crushing caseloads and grossly inadequate resources.[17]

Defendants who hire their own counsel do not necessarily fare better. Most of these individuals are just over the line of indigency and cannot afford substantial legal expenses. Their lawyers typically charge a flat fee, payable in advance. This practice creates obvious incentives to cut corners on factual investigation and to negotiate a quick plea bargain. Only defendants who can pay steep fees, usually in white-collar or organized crime cases, have ready access to the highly skilled advocacy that the public sees in publicized trials. Where defendants lack such resources, counsel face further temptations to curtail their advocacy. A plea bargain spares lawyers the strain and potential humiliation of an unsuccessful trial. Such settlements also preserve good working relationships with judges and prosecutors, who face their own, often overwhelming caseload demands. In this system, "zealous advocacy is the exception not the rule, and it is generally better to be rich and guilty than poor and innocent."[18]

Given all the structural pressures working against effective representation, arguments like vos Savant's, which encourage attorneys to judge, not defend, their clients, carry obvious risks. Court-appointed lawyers who adopt a "meet 'em, greet 'em, plead 'em" approach to their high volume practice often rationalize their conduct on the grounds that extensive preparation is wasted on the guilty. As one of these practitioners put it, if defendants "want Clarence Darrow, they should hire Clarence Darrow."[19] A striking example involves a lawyer who acknowledged that he had deliberately missed a deadline for filing a post-conviction appeal because he "did not like" his client and thought that the man "deserved to die."[20]

Disincentives for adequate representation are particularly strong where the crime is heinous or the accused is a member of an especially unpopular group. To take only the most obvious example, for most of this

---

16. *See* sources cited in Rhode, *supra* note 10, at 123; Vesna Jaksic, "Capital Case Crisis," *National L. J.*, July 2, 2007, at A1.

17. Tresca Baldas, "As Caseloads Swell, Public Defenders Feel the Heat," *National L. J.*, Sept. 24, 2007, at A7; Vesna Jaksic, "A Crisis in Funding," *National L. J.*, March 26, 2007, at 1, 10; ABA Standing Committee, *supra* note 11, at 16–19; David S. Udell & Rebekah Diller, Access to the Courts: An Essay for the Georgetown University Law Center Conference on the Independence of the Courts, 95 *Geo. L. J.* 1127, 1138 (2007).

18. Rhode, *supra* note 7, at 52; Stephen Bright, "Keep the Dream Alive," *Yale Law Report*, Fall, 1999, 27.

19. Adam Liptak, "County Says Its Too Poor to Defend the Poor," *N.Y. Times*, April 15, 2003 (Quoting Thomas Pearson).

20. Sara Rimer, "Lawyer Sabotaged Case of a Client on Death Row," *N.Y. Times*, Nov. 24, 2000, at A27. When the lawyer received formal notification of an execution date, he came to regret his conduct and filed a motion seeking an extension of the deadline and his removal from the case. *Id.*

nation's history, southern blacks accused of an offense against a white victim stood little chance of anything approximating a fair trial.[21] Despite substantial progress, discrimination against racial and ethnic minorities remains common.[22] Defendants charged with particularly heinous crimes also face enormous obstacles securing effective assistance of counsel.

So too, in many dictatorships and totalitarian countries, where defense counsel's role is ostensibly to "serve justice," what passes for "justice" does not commend itself for export. Often the roles of counsel for the defendant and the state are functionally identical and the price is paid in innocent lives. For example, in the celebrated Chinese trial of the Gang of Four, the lawyer for the widow of Mao Tse Tung refused to assert her plea of innocence. He and the other defense lawyers conducted no independent investigation, cross-examined no prosecution witnesses, and called no defense witnesses. There was no need to do so, the lawyer explained, because the "police and the prosecutors worked on the case a very long time and the evidence they found that wasn't true they threw away."[23]

So too, in this country, trial records even in capital cases reveal similar examples of counsel who functioned more as spectators than advocates— who failed to conduct any investigation, introduce any evidence, cross-examine any witnesses, or even remain awake and sober during the proceedings.[24] Whether or not their clients are guilty—legally as well as factually—this level of representation is cause for concern. Particularly in a system that relies heavily on plea-bargaining, the government's case needs to receive vigorous challenge in the small percentage of proceedings that do reach a jury. As John Mitchell argues in the preceding excerpt, without the prospect of a zealous defense in some cases, prosecutors and police have far fewer incentives to investigate the facts thoroughly, to corroborate a complainant's story, and to ensure, in short, that they are not trying the wrong person.

Critics of this rationale for unqualified partisanship make several responses. Former law professor and federal judge Richard Posner puts a common view with uncommon candor:

> I can confirm from my own experience as a judge that criminal defendants are generally poorly represented, but if we are to be hardheaded we must recognize that this may not be an entirely bad thing. The lawyers who represent indigent criminal defendants seem to be good enough to reduce the probability of convicting an innocent

21. For representative examples, *see* Dan T. Carter, *Scottsboro: A Tragedy of the American South* (1969); Daniel H. Pollitt, "Counsel for the Unpopular Cause: The Hazard of Being Undone," 43 *N.C.L. Rev.* 9 (1964).

22. *See* Cole, *supra* note 14; Leadership Conference on Civil Rights, *Justice on Trial: Racial Disparities in the American Criminal Justice System* (2000); Amnesty International, *Death by Discrimination—The Continuing Role of Race in Capital Cases* (2002).

23. Monroe Freedman, "Our Constitutionalized Adversary System," 1 *Chapman L. Rev.* 57, 59–60 (1998). For other examples, *see* James E. Moliterno & George C. Harris, Global Issues in Legal Ethics 90, 145, Rhode, *supra* note 7, at 54, 72–73.

24. *See* Rhode, *supra* note 10, at 137–38; Cole, *supra* note 14, at 86–87, Texas Defender Service, *Lethal Indifference* (December 2002); Anthony Lewis, "The Silencing of Gideon's Trumpet," *New York Times Magazine*, April 20, 2003, at 50, 51.

person to a very low level. If they were much better, either many guilty people would be acquitted or society would have to devote much greater resources to the prosecution of criminal cases. A bare-bones system for defense of indigent criminal defendants may be optimal.[25]

William Simon challenges the zealous advocate role on different grounds. In his view, arguments that guilt should be considered only by judges or jurors, not by lawyers, are convincing only to the extent that those triers of fact have all crucial information. The difficult ethical issue, however, arises where that is not the case—where, for example, only the defense attorney knows that the defendant has destroyed inculpating information or offered four other noncredible alibis before settling on the current version. We need not attribute "cosmic certainty" to lawyers to believe that they are sometimes better able to make a judgment about guilt than a judge or juror.[26]

On similar reasoning, Harry Subin argues that lawyers can provide appropriate checks on law enforcement abuses without resorting to the kind of "special ... ingenuity" that the nineteenth century ethics expert David Hoffman condemned. In Subin's view:

> it is one thing to attack a weak government case by pointing out its weakness. It is another ... to attack a strong government case by confusing the jury with falsehoods.... [Accordingly] I would limit my representation at that stage to putting forth the strongest argument I could that the facts presented by the state did not sustain its burden. In these ways, the defendant would receive the services of an attorney in subjecting the state's case to the final stage of the screening process provided by the system to insure against unjust convictions. That, however, would be all that the defense attorney could do.[27]

Where defense counsel lack the willingness or capacity to provide effective representation, many commentators argue that the appropriate response is to address those problems directly, not to inculcate an ideology oblivious to truth. Thus, greater resources could be made available for appointed counsel to undertake adequate trial preparation, and more effective oversight of lawyers' performance could be institutionalized through civil malpractice or disciplinary liability as well as through preventive monitoring and reversals. For example, many bar associations have established guidelines for effective representation in individual cases and effective administration of indigent defense systems. These guidelines could be adopted by states as a condition of funding public defender offices or reimbursing private practitioners. Courts could then apply such standards in establishing qualifications and monitoring conduct of appointed counsel. Such guidelines typically include limits on caseloads, support for litigation-related expenses, and requirements concerning factual investigation and

25. Richard Posner, *The Problematics of Moral and Legal Theory* 163–64 (1999).

26. William Simon, "The Ethics of Criminal Defense," 91 *Mich.L.Rev.* 1703 (1993).

27. Harry I. Subin, "The Criminal Lawyer's 'Different Mission': Reflections on the 'Right' to Present a False Case," 1 *Geo.J. Legal Ethics* 125, 148, 151 (1987).

communication with clients, all of which could significantly improve the quality of legal representation. Even without adoption of such explicit standards, courts could find constitutional violations in indigent defense systems that set statutory fees too low or demand caseloads too high to permit effective representation.[28] More defense lawyers could follow the guidelines set forth by the ABA Standing Committee on Ethics and Professional Responsibility in Formal Opinion 06–441 (2006). It requires attorneys for indigent defendants to refuse cases, or withdraw from representation, if an excessive workload prevents competent representation. The opinion also requires supervising attorneys to monitor workloads and take appropriate remedial action if they become excessive, including support for a refusal to accept new matters. Some attorneys have even risked contempt charges rather than go to trial when overwhelming caseloads prevented inadequate preparation.[29]

Consider the following reading in light of these concerns and proposals. The article vividly portrays the world of Washington, D.C.'s "Fifth Street lawyers"—lawyers with offices on the street across from the courthouse, who make their living from fees authorized for court-appointed counsel under the District's Criminal Justice Act (CJA).

Henry Allen, "A Heaping Serving of Justice; Fifth Street Lawyers Represent the Defenseless and the Indefensible of Washington"

Wash. Post, Dec. 6, 1996, B1.

Some of these lawyers are like guys who will never be contenders but hang around the boxing gym because they like to hit, no matter how many punches they have to take to do it. Some talk to themselves and comb their hair with their fingers. Some are too mouthy and egotistical to work anywhere else. They are loners, mavericks, freelance gladiators, anarchists, spitball artists, true believers, class warriors.

Some are very good criminal lawyers, a few are very bad criminal lawyers. You see them sitting in the cafeteria with eyes half-closed or half-open and skin the color of mythical New York sewer alligators; with their derelict night-school dreams of enthralled juries and fame, of Darrow and the Revolution, of starting at the bottom and building a paid and retained practice while they fight for the rights of the always poor and almost-always guilty who look so much the same after a while that the lawyers write down what they're wearing when they meet them in the cellblock down the hall so they can identify them an hour later at their arraignment.

---

28. *See* ABA Standing Committee, *supra* note 11, at 31–34; Udell & Diller, *supra* note 17, at 1139; Baldas, supra note 17, at A7; Institute for Law and Justice, Bureau of Justice Assistance, United States Department of Justice, *Compendium of Standards for Indigent Defense Systems*; ABA, *Guidelines for the Appointment and Performance of Defense Counsel in Death Penalty Cases*, 18–19 (Revised ed. 2003); Rhode, *supra* note 7.

29. For a similar proposal, see Monroe Freedman, "An Ethical Manifesto for Public Defenders," 39 *Valparaiso L. Rev.* 911 (2005).

You may have an office at home or someplace like the Bob Hope Building on D Street, but you can run your whole practice down here. . . . You meet with your clients in the hallways, the cellblock. You face them across the fake butcher block tables of the cafeteria—the same meeting over and over, the lawyer saying, "I want you to understand . . ." and the defendant . . . talking to you in a collection of phrases that become a generic conversation after you spend enough time hanging around down here. Like:

"Prosecutor just wants me to plead out, is what it is," the defendant says. He has eyes that look like they've just come to a slow but very final decision, and a mouth that looks like it's got a toothpick in it whether it does or not. "Wants me to plead out because there ain't no case, is what it is."

"That's not what it is," you say. You're not sure what he's driving at, you know he doesn't know what you're driving at, and you're not sure yet either. You've got your professional face on, a face that doesn't listen as much as it simply waits. You see him checking out your rumpled collar that still smells scorched from where you ironed it this morning. He doesn't understand how somebody can look and live like you, so gray and broke-down.

"Make no sense," the defendant says. "I'm looking at 10 years anyway you look at it."

"You take it to trial, they've got four witnesses—you must've made somebody mad."

"They lie. They say they saw me with those Ziplocs, I didn't have no Ziplocs, I don't do nothing with cocaine. Man dump them by my feet and bucked on me, he's gone."

"Man dumped them," you say. "You find Man, I'll put him on the stand. One of these days we're going to catch Man and the crime rate in this city is going to drop like a stone."

"I should get me a paid lawyer. Get me a Jew. Jew get me out of this."

"You got a paid lawyer last time. He sent his runner out to your mother's house and talked her into taking the case away from the CJA attorney. She paid all that money and you still went down. You can't find any better lawyers than you find right here."

"Can't find any worse ones neither," the young man says.

"You make up your mind which one I am and call me."

It's a hard dollar, being nobody for $50 an hour—a fee that's a quarter, a fifth, a tenth of what you might get in the uptown firms. Uptown, the lawyers are somebody. They can tell from the Martha's Vineyard tans on their faces when they look in the mirror every morning, from the . . . Neiman Marcus suspenders, . . . Princeton stickers on their car windows. When uptown lawyers go to lunch at the Palm, Tommy the manager knows their names. Tommy is the uptown lawyers' pet tough guy. He makes them feel real. Here in the Superior Court cafeteria you feel very real but you're nobody.

. . . Here's how it works: You phone in with your CJA number when your name comes up alphabetically on a rotation of hundreds of lawyers. If the supervising judge approves, your name goes up on a cratered old bulletin board down the hall from the cafeteria—it's known as the Wailing Wall. Lawyers, family, investigators—they swarm when they see those lists go up, looking for names. They squat, they bob, like some kind of oompah-band routine.

If the cases get papered and the prosecution is going forward, you interview them back in the cellblock, get an address and phone number, see if they're who they say they are, don't bother talking about guilt and innocence, just start working on getting your client out at arraignment.

When you're new, you get misdemeanors—fugitives, shoplifting. When the judges think you're good enough, you get felonies, which are more hours, more money, more fun: burglary, unauthorized use of a vehicle, moving up to possession of drugs with intent to distribute, then distribution, armed robbery, and then the real prize, the top of the line: murders.

NOTES

Rights

The second principal justification for zealous representation of the guilty involves the protection of rights. Where individuals' lives, liberty, and reputation are so directly at risk, they deserve one advocate without competing loyalties to the state. That is particularly the case when those who commit crimes are themselves the victims of procedural injustice or misconduct by law enforcement officials.

Rights-based concerns also arise from the conditions of confinement in most of this nation's prisons, the inadequacy of alternatives to incarceration, the severe penalties for many offenses, and the disabling consequences of a criminal record, especially for low income, low-skilled, defendants of color. These distinctive features of penal sanctions, coupled with the potential for governmental repression, justify many of the special protections of the criminal process, including the Sixth Amendment right to effective assistance of counsel and the Fifth Amendment privilege against self-incrimination. For many commentators, these protections also entail a commitment of unqualified partisanship beyond that justifiable in civil proceedings.[30] Enforcement of constitutional guarantees are critical not only because they promote more accurate outcomes, but also because, as Laurence Tribe notes, they are "affirmations of respect for the accused as a human being—affirmations that remind him and the public about the sort of society we want to become. . . ."[31]

---

30. *See* David Luban, *Lawyers and Justice* 58–63 (1988); Richard Wasserstrom, "Lawyers as Professionals: Some Moral Issues," 5 *Human Rights* 1, 12 (1975).

31. Laurence H. Tribe, "Trial by Mathematics: Precision and Ritual in the Legal Process," 84 *Harv. L. Rev.* 1329, 1391–92 (1971).

Challenges to Partisanship

These justifications for partisanship have been subject to several lines of challenge. While acknowledging the unique features of criminal punishment, some commentators argue that it would be preferable to address these concerns directly. Misleading the judge and jury in the few cases that go to trial does nothing to address the problems in the vast number of cases that do not. More attention should focus directly on disproportionate sentences, inhumane prison conditions, and inadequate opportunities for ex-offenders.

Others notice that the rights of defendants may victimize other defendants: thus, the right against self-incrimination of one person may prevent another person from obtaining the only witness who could exonerate him.[32] In the Leo Frank case, Arthur Powell's duty to his client prevented him from saving Frank by revealing the identity of Mary Phagan's actual killer.

To the extent that our concern is with protecting individual rights, many commentators argue that the rights of victims also deserve some consideration in defense counsel's moral universe. "Private" conduct by criminal offenders can constitute no less a threat to personal liberty than misuse of "public" authority by the state. Thus, William Simon maintains that lawyers should make case-by-case judgments about whether to engage in aggressive defense tactics that are legal but that are likely to distort the fact-finding process. In making those judgments, attorneys should consider the extent to which values justifying zealous partisanship are in fact implicated in particular prosecutions. For example, does the case involve abuses of state power, racial bias, or disproportionate sentences?[33]

In a *New York Times* article, "How to Defend Someone You Know is Guilty," Bronx Public Defender David Feige describes the defender's mindset in a way that suggests that Simon's proposal for sensitive, case-by-case weighing of values unrealistic:

> It's as simple as this: I care about the person I know. In most cases, the complainant is an abstraction to me. His victimization is an abstraction. My client, on the other hand is very human and very real. It is his tears I see, his hand I hold and his mother I console.... I empathize with my clients the way everyone else in the system empathizes with the complainants. And ultimately, I do to the complainants what the rest of the system does to my clients. I dehumanize them. I learn their facts and statistics from police reports, but I don't linger over their faces.... "UC #4225 [threatened] with a screwdriver." That's the victim. Somewhere behind that language is the person that prosecutors and cops and judges and politicians and friends and family all rally round....

32. Akhil Reed Amar & Renee B. Lettow, "Fifth Amendment First Principles," 93 *Mich. L. Rev.* 857, 861 (1995).

33. Simon, *supra* note 26.

So defending the reviled, even those who are guilty, is not some mental trick, nor even a moral struggle for me. I don't lack imagination or willfully close my eyes to another's suffering. Rather, the reality of my clients—their suffering, their fear—is more vivid to me than that of the victims. My clients are the ones left exposed. They are the ones who are hated. They are the ones who desperately need my protection. Everyone else can look out for the victims.[34]

If Feige has accurately described what it takes to defend the guilty day in and day out, asking defenders also to take victims into account might make their job impossible. Is that an argument against Simon's proposal, or for it?

Other accounts of criminal defense lawyers reflect similar strategies of selective empathy, and note that they may come at a personal cost for defenders. As one describes the psychic numbing, "You don't get worn out from all the pain and sadness. You get worn out from not feeling the pain and sadness. You get tired of not feeling."[35]

Structural Constraints and Lawyer–Client Relationships

Part of the difficulty in establishing effective lawyer-client relationships in the criminal context stems from certain structural features: the inability of most defendants to afford and choose their own attorney; and the absence of sufficient resources to enable most court-appointed counsel to spend sufficient time on the vast majority of cases. Roy Fleming summarizes these concerns:

Skepticism about the accountability of criminal defense attorneys is not a new concern. [Several decades ago] Abraham Blumberg described the private practice of criminal law as a "confidence game." The intangible quality of the attorney's work, the concern over fees, and the need to prepare clients for guilty pleas or trial convictions while satisfying the interests of the court system all came together as ingredients in this game. A few years later, however, it became clear that clients distrust their public defenders and court-appointed attorneys and hold them in low esteem. Jonathan Casper neatly captured their views and caught the tone of subsequent studies with the title of his seminal article, "Did You Have a Lawyer When You Went to Court? No, I Had a Public Defender." A rather substantial body of research agrees that in contrast with their attitudes toward privately retained attorneys, criminal defendants see publicly paid and assigned counsel as part of the "system"—overly eager to plead them guilty, disinclined to give them much time, and little concerned about their welfare. . . .

---

34. David Feige, "How to Defend Someone You Know Is Guilty," *New York Times Magazine*, April 8, 2001, at 59–60.

35. James S. Kunen, *"How Can You Defend These People?": The Making of a* *Criminal Lawyer* 143(1983). See also Siemen, *supra* note 7; Susan Bandes, "Repression and Denial in Criminal Lawyering," 9 *Buffalo Crim. L. Rev.* 339, 364–83 (2006).

[However ...] when viewed in light of systematic, comparative analyses of the impact of defense attorneys on other measures of case outcomes ... public clients are not treated in significantly different ways than are private clients. In this sense, attorney-client relations may be best viewed as part of procedural justice, in which style, approach, rapport, attitudes, and perception define "fairness." Thus, in games between attorneys and clients, clients perceive fairness if they trust their attorneys and believe they have a say or voice in the handling of their cases. . . .

In the eyes of criminal clients, professional accountability hinges on a market conception and fee-for-service definition of lawyer responsibility. They place little faith in the notion that ethical concerns and feelings of professional obligation by themselves are sufficient guarantees that a lawyer picked seemingly "out of the hat" will adequately represent their interests. . . . Stuck with their attorneys, and their attorneys stuck with them, they are caught up in a confidence game in which competing interests and the need for accommodation are resolved in ways that are not as self-evidently effective as choosing and paying a lawyer to represent them.

From this perspective, it can be asked whether indigent defense systems might be designed to allow criminal defendants to select their own attorneys. If organized along the lines of a voucher system, attorney fees and costs would still be paid publicly, but defendants could, if they wished, select an attorney from among those who wanted to represent indigent criminal clients. Indigent defendants with the freedom to choose might express fewer apprehensions about their attorneys.[36]

Other, more recent research reinforces these concerns. One of the few systematic studies of lawyer-client decision making in criminal cases concludes:

Many public defenders are able to overcome their client's initial resentment and are able to forge good working relationships with most clients. For other defendants, however, client hostility and lack of trust make it difficult to forge effective attorney-client relationships. Rather than take the time to allay client suspicion and foster a good relationship, some public defenders opt simply to minimize client consultation and participation in decisionmaking. . . . [T]he client's general low intelligence and a concern that the client would make a poor, hurtful decision were identified by the highest percent of respondents as the two factors that almost always or most of the time limit the client's participation in decision making.[37]

---

36. Roy B. Fleming, "Client Games: Defense Attorney Perspectives on Their Relations with Criminal Clients," 1986 *A.B.F. Res.J.*, at 253–54, 257–58, 261, 268, 276.

37. Rodney J. Uphoff & Peter B. Wood, "The Allocation of Decisionmaking Between Defense Counsel and Criminal Defendant: An Empirical Study of Attorney–Client Decisionmaking," 47 *Kan. L. Rev.* 1, 54 (1998).

Some contexts pose a special challenge for lawyer-client relations. For example, it is estimated that a third of Guantanamo detainees are refusing to cooperate with appointed counsel. Many believe that their lawyers are at best useless and at worst government agents in disguise. That suspicion is reportedly encouraged by interrogators' disparaging comments about the lawyers, and by their singular lack of success not only in securing releases, but even in accommodating detainees' minor requests such as access to reading material or toothpaste.[38]

The inability of many court-appointed lawyers to forge effective client relationships comes through clearly in other recent research. Common findings are that most criminal defendants are not satisfied with their lawyer's representation; the most dissatisfied defendants are those with court-appointed counsel; client-relation skills, such as keeping defendants informed, spending time with them, and listening to their concerns, are just as important as legal abilities in promoting client satisfaction; and court-appointed lawyers lack adequate incentives to improve client relations.[39]

One recent study of some 5000 felonies also found that clients of public defenders received on average prison sentences that were three years longer than those of privately represented defendants. Researchers speculated that the reason was that "marginally indigent" defendants chose to tap resources of family and friends to hire private counsel when they had a good chance of avoiding conviction—particularly when they were innocent. Public defenders ended up with a disproportionate share of matters in which the government's case was overwhelming.[40]

What follows from these findings? How should those who oversee indigent defense systems respond to such findings?

Ineffective Assistance of Counsel

One obvious way to address the inadequate representation of indigent defendants is to provide more judicial oversight of lawyers' performance. In *Strickland v. Washington,* 466 U.S. 668 (1984), the Court set forth the relevant Sixth Amendment standard: defendants have a right to reasonably effective representation under prevailing professional norms. However, counsel should be "strongly presumed to have rendered adequate assistance." Courts should overturn convictions only if there is a "reasonable probability that, absent [counsel's] errors, the fact finder would have a reasonable doubt respecting guilt." 466 U.S. at 695.

This burden traditionally has been extremely difficult to meet. Courts have declined to find inadequate representation where attorneys were

38. David Luban, "Lawfare and Legal Ethics in Guantánamo," 60 *Stanford L. Rev.* 1981 (2008).

39. Marcus T. Boccaccini & Stanley L. Brodsky, "Characteristics of the Ideal Criminal Defense Attorney from the Client's Perspective: Empirical Findings and Implications for Legal Practice," 25 *Law & Psychol Rev.* 81, 101–105 (2001).

40. Morris B. Hoffman, Paul H. Rubin, & Joanna M. Shepherd, "An Empirical Study of Public Defender Effectiveness: Self–Selection By the 'Marginally Indigent,' " 3 *Ohio State J. Crim. L.* 223 (2005). See Morris B. Hoffman, "Free Market Justice," *N.Y. Times,* Jan. 8, 2007, at A23.

drunk, on drugs, or parking their car during key parts of the prosecution's case. And defendants have been executed despite their lawyers' lack of any prior trial experience, ignorance of all relevant death penalty precedents, or failure to offer any witnesses, closing argument or mitigating evidence.[41] One systematic survey found that over 99 percent of ineffective assistance claims were unsuccessful.[42]

The ineffective enforcement of the constitution's "effective" representation requirement has recently prompted further Supreme Court intervention. In *Wiggins v. Smith,* U.S. (2003), a majority of Justices voted to overturn the conviction of a death row defendant whose attorneys failed to conduct a reasonable investigation of mitigating circumstances. Even the most cursory review would have revealed facts about the defendant's experience of abuse that could well have affected the jury's sentencing deliberations. However, as in *Strickland,* the Court emphasized the limits of its ruling. The majority opinion made clear that defense counsel would not always be required to present mitigating evidence or even to do a full investigation. As long as "reasonable professional judgments" supported an attorney's limited inquiry or failure to raise mitigation claims, the constitutional standard would be met. Although legal experts generally viewed *Wiggins* as a step in the right direction, many questioned its limited scope. Virtually all commentary and bar guidelines on capital cases underscore the critical importance of mitigating evidence.[43] Given this consensus, it is by no means clear how counsel could ever reasonably conclude that investigation of potentially mitigating circumstances was unnecessary.

The Court took a step further in *Rompilla v. Beard,* 545 U.S. 374 (2005). There, the majority set aside a death sentence after finding that the defendants' trial lawyers failed to examine a prior conviction file that they knew the prosecution intended to use as evidence of aggravation in the sentencing phase of the proceedings.

How much impact these decisions will have on the conduct of defense lawyers or courts that review their performances remains unclear. But certainly they signal less tolerance for defective lawyering than many prior decisions over the last decade, including ones that have applied a three step analysis to determine how much dozing by trial counsel is constitutionally permissible: "(1) did counsel sleep for repeated and/or prolonged lapses; (2) was counsel actually unconscious; and (3) were the defendant's interests at stake while counsel was asleep?"[44] Some trial judges have allowed cases to

---

41. Cole, *supra* note 14, at 87; Rhode, *supra* note 10, at 115; Bright, *supra* note 18; Robert Sherrill, "Death Trip: The American Way of Execution," *The Nation*, January 8/15, 2001, 20.

42. Victor E. Flango and Patricia McKenna, "Federal Habeas Corpus Review of State Court Convictions," 31 *Cal. West. L. Rev.* 237, 259–60 (1995).

43. *See,* e.g. ABA, *Guidelines, supra* note 28.

44. Tippins v. Walker, 77 F.3d 682, 687 (2d Cir.1996); Burdine v. Johnson, 66 F.Supp.2d 854, 863–66 (S.D. Tex.1999), aff'd., sub. nom. Burdine v. Johnson, 262 F.3d 336 (5th Cir.2001), cert. den. sub. nom. Cockrell v. Burdine, 535 U.S. 1120 (2002).

proceed when defense lawyers were in a deep slumber on numerous occasions for substantial periods.[45]

Such tolerance has come at a substantial cost. The refusal to provide adequate resources or oversight for criminal defense increases the likelihood of serious errors at trial, the risks of inaccurate verdicts, and the costs of appellate review. The challenge remaining is to convince a greater number of courts and policy makers that in the long run, it would be less expensive, as well as more equitable, to invest in better representation at trial.

QUESTIONS

1. Richard Uviller claims that "[i]n all but the rare case of an innocent client, the defendant's lawyer must strive to make the true appear false and the false appear true."[46] Is that how you would describe the attorney's role? What would you do if you were assigned to represent a defendant whom you believed to be guilty of a serious crime? Is that what you would want all defense lawyers to do? Is it a standard of representation that you would want for yourself or a close family member?

2. In *Griffin v. Illinois*, Justice Black wrote "There can be no equal justice where the kind of trial a man gets depends on the amount of money he has." 351 U.S. 12, 18 (1956). Do you agree? Do the courts? Does the public? If Americans truly accepted that principle, could it be institutionalized? What obstacles stand in the way?

3. Under current resource constraints, how should indigent defense attorneys allocate their efforts? Drawing on analogous approaches from medical ethics, John Mitchell suggests the need for a triage system, in which counsel systematize their allocation decisions and give priority based first on the likelihood of innocence; second on severity of consequences; third, on the need to make the system work; and fourth, on "concrete justice . . .—cases that touch the attorneys' hearts."[47] Are these the priorities that you would choose?

4. An increasing number of public defenders believe that truly effective representation calls for "holistic" "problem-solving" approaches that focus not just on the criminal charges at issue but on services that may help keep their clients out the criminal justice system in the future. By addressing needs involving employment, housing, substance abuse, mental health, and education, defense counsel may be able to obtain a better disposition or reduce the chances of recidivism.[48] Many lawyers also define their role to include working for systemic reforms that will help prevent crime and

---

45. Burdine v. Johnson, 66 F.Supp.2d 854 (S.D. Tex.1999).

46. Richard Uviller, *The Tilted Playing Field* 298 (1999).

47. John B. Mitchell, "Redefining the Sixth Amendment," 67 *S. Cal. L. Rev.* 1215 (1994).

48. Cait Clarke, "Problem–Solving Defenders in the Community: Expanding the Conceptual and Institutional Boundaries of Providing Counsel to the Poor," 14 *Geo. J. Legal Ethics* 401 (2001).

increase the fairness of the criminal justice system. Community outreach, lobbying, and collaboration with other service providers are a critical part of some defenders' daily activities. Such efforts do, however, take time away from trial preparation of individual cases. In a world of limited resources, what priority would you place on problem-solving activities?

B.   The Pursuit of Truth: Honest Witnesses and Lying Clients

References to the "criminal defense paradigm" reflect the special place that criminal defense occupies in American legal ethics. One reason for that influence is that, as noted earlier, many moral dilemmas that arise in criminal cases occur in civil contexts as well. These include problems of client perjury, document destruction, witness preparation, and impeachment in cross-examination. The materials that follow explore these chronic dilemmas of litigation practice. The focus, however, is on criminal proceedings, where the stakes are often highest, and the issues most sharply drawn.

1.   Perjury and Disclosure Obligations

PROBLEM 1

a) You represent a defendant on charges of robbery. Your client claims that he was elsewhere on the evening in question. First, he indicates that he was at a shopping mall with two friends; investigation reveals that the two friends were at a sports event on that night. Then your client remembers that he was at a party, which the alleged host does not recall giving. Finally, your client recalls that he was at the movies with his sister. His sister confirms the story, but is unable to provide further corroboration.

The case goes to trial. May you, or must you, call the sister as a witness? Assume that the prosecution establishes that the robbery could have taken place after the movie. On cross-examination, your client states that after the movie he went to the party that your previous investigation failed to confirm. He explains his failure to disclose this information during direct examination on the ground that the party involved drugs and he did not want to implicate his friends in possible criminal activities. What are your responsibilities?

b) Assume that another of your clients is convicted for sexual assault and then released on bond pending completion of a pre-sentence report. Due to an administrative oversight, however, no date for sentencing is ever set. What are your obligations? What considerations would be relevant to your decision?

c) Suppose that you are the partner of the lawyer in the sentencing case described above. Your partner defends his refusal to disclose the mistake on the ground that his client might not in fact have committed the crime and did not seem like "the kind of guy [who] would [rape] on a regular basis."[49] Given the inability of trained experts accurately to predict future dangerousness, are an attorney's subjective impressions relevant? What would you advise your partner about the consequences of disclosing, or not disclosing, the error?

d) You are a member of your state bar disciplinary authority. Local judges have filed complaints against several defense lawyers who knowingly failed to inform them of legislation that imposed new presumptive mandatory minimum sentences for child sex offenses absent exceptional circumstances. Neither the judges nor the prosecutors were aware of the legislation for a period following its enactment and the lawyers' clients were sentenced under the old law. How do you proceed?[50]

e) You are a law student in a criminal justice clinic, representing a homeless client on a shoplifting charge. At the initial hearing, a few minutes after you meet your client for the first time, the judge states that he will release the client with no bail if he has somewhere to stay; otherwise, the client will remain in jail. The client tells you that he will stay with his brother, and after you tell this to the judge, the judge releases him. As you leave the courtroom, the client tells you he has no brother. What are your responsibilities?

References:

Model Rules 1.2, 1.6, 3.1, 3.3, 3.4; ABA Crim. Defense Standards 4–7.6 and 4–7.7.

NOTES

No issue in legal ethics has attracted greater attention than the problem of perjury by criminal defendants. The issue is critical *not* because it arises frequently in practice. Indeed, many advocates insist that they rarely have actual knowledge that their client is lying, and those cases (like 90 percent of all criminal matters) are likely to be resolved through plea bargains. Rather, the question remains crucial because it establishes the boundaries of clients' trust and lawyers' obligations of confidentiality. Those issues affect an attorney-client relationship in every case. Duties of confidentiality influence what lawyers tell criminal defendants in their first meetings, what defendants believe they can tell lawyers, how investigations are conducted, and how trial strategies are formulated.

In *Nix v. Whiteside,* 475 U.S. 157 (1986), the Supreme Court cast light on the issue by holding that a lawyer did not provide ineffective assistance of counsel by discouraging his client from giving what the lawyer believed would be false testimony.

49. Tom Coakley, "N.M. Rapist Free 10 Years in Court Foul–Up," *Denver Post,* March 23, 1983, at 12A.

50. Cary Spivak & Dan Bice, "Ignorance of DAs, Judges, Benefits Child Sex Felons," *Milwaukee Journal Sentinel,* Feb. 10, 2007.

Nix v. Whiteside

Supreme Court of the United States, 1986.
475 U.S. 157.

[Editors' Note: The case involved a defendant convicted of the second degree murder of Calvin Love. The crime took place in Iowa when Whiteside and two companions visited Love's apartment seeking marijuana. An argument began over the ownership of a certain amount of marijuana, and at one point Love directed his girlfriend to get his "piece." According to Whiteside's testimony, Love then started to reach under his pillow and move toward Whiteside. Whiteside stabbed Love in the chest, inflicting a fatal wound. After Whiteside was charged with murder, he gave a statement to Gary Robinson, his court-appointed attorney. In that statement, Whiteside indicated that he had stabbed Love as the latter "was pulling a pistol from underneath the pillow on the bed." Upon questioning by Robinson, however, Whiteside indicated that he had not actually seen a gun, but that he was convinced that Love had a gun. A police search revealed no weapon, and none of Whiteside's companions reported seeing a gun. Robinson advised Whiteside that the existence of a gun was not necessary to establish the claim of self-defense, and that only a reasonable belief that the victim had a gun nearby was necessary even though no gun was actually present.

Chief Justice Burger wrote the majority opinion in which Justices White, Powell, Rehnquist and O'Connor joined.]

Until shortly before trial, Whiteside consistently stated to Robinson that he had not actually seen a gun, but that he was convinced that Love had a gun in his hand. About a week before trial, during preparation for direct examination, Whiteside for the first time told Robinson and his associate Donna Paulsen that he had seen something "metallic" in Love's hand. When asked about this, Whiteside responded: "[I]n Howard Cook's case there was a gun. If I don't say I saw a gun, I'm dead."

Robinson told Whiteside that such testimony would be perjury and repeated that it was not necessary to prove that a gun was available but only that Whiteside reasonably believed that he was in danger. On Whiteside's insisting that he would testify that he saw "something metallic" Robinson told him, according to Robinson's testimony:

"[W]e could not allow him to [testify falsely] because that would be perjury, and as officers of the court we would be suborning perjury if we allowed him to do it; . . . I advised him that if he did do that it would be my duty to advise the Court of what he was doing and that I felt he was committing perjury; also, that I probably would be allowed to attempt to impeach that particular testimony."

Robinson also indicated he would seek to withdraw from the representation if Whiteside insisted on committing perjury.[51]

---

51. Whiteside's version of the events at this pretrial meeting is considerably more cryptic:

"Q: And as you went over the questions, did the two of you come into conflict with regard to whether or not there was a weapon?"

Whiteside testified in his own defense at trial and stated that he "knew" that Love had a gun and that he believed Love was reaching for a gun and he had acted swiftly in self-defense. On cross-examination, he admitted that he had not actually seen a gun in Love's hand. Robinson presented evidence that Love had been seen with a sawed-off shotgun on other occasions, that the police search of the apartment may have been careless, and that the victim's family had removed everything from the apartment shortly after the crime. Robinson presented this evidence to show a basis for Whiteside's asserted fear that Love had a gun.

The jury returned a verdict of second-degree murder, and Whiteside moved for a new trial, claiming that he had been deprived of effective assistance of counsel. The Supreme Court of Iowa affirmed respondent's conviction. That court held that the right to have counsel present all appropriate defenses does not extend to using perjury, and that an attorney's duty to a client does not extend to assisting a client in committing perjury. . . . The court commended "both Mr. Robinson and Ms. Paulsen for the high ethical manner in which this matter was handled."

[Editors' Note: Whiteside then petitioned for a writ of habeas corpus, claiming that he had been denied effective assistance of counsel. The district court denied the writ and the Court of Appeals for the Eighth Circuit reversed. In the appellate panel's view, Robinson's warning to Whiteside that he would inform the court of the perjury constituted a threat to violate the attorney's obligation to preserve client confidences.

The United States Supreme Court unanimously disagreed. Justice Burger's majority opinion noted that the right of an accused to testify in his own behalf is of relatively recent origin. Until the end of the nineteenth century, criminal defendants were disqualified as witnesses on grounds of bias; under current due process standards, the right to testify is generally assumed. However, in the Court's view, that right does not extend to false testimony. *Nix* was decided three years after the ABA adopted the Model Rules of Professional Conduct, at a time when many states still used rules based on the previous Model Code of Professional Responsibility. The Court therefore discusses both sets of standards. According to Justice Burger's opinion:]

. . . Both the Model Code of Professional Responsibility and the Model Rules of Professional Conduct also adopt the specific exception from the attorney-client privilege for disclosure of perjury that his client intends to commit or has committed. DR 4–101(C)(3) (intention of client to commit a crime); Rule 3.3 (lawyer has duty to disclose falsity of evidence even if disclosure compromises client confidences). Indeed, both the Model Code and the Model Rules do not merely *authorize* disclosure by counsel of client

"A: I couldn't—I couldn't say a conflict. But I got the impression at one time that maybe if I didn't go along with—with what was happening, that it was no gun being involved, maybe that he will pull out of my trial."

perjury they *require* such disclosure. See Rule 3.3(a)(4); DR 7–102(B)(1)....

These standards confirm that the legal profession has accepted that an attorney's ethical duty to advance the interests of his client is limited by an equally solemn duty to comply with the law and standards of professional conduct; it specifically ensures that the client may not use false evidence. This special duty of an attorney to prevent and disclose frauds upon the court derives from the recognition that perjury is as much a crime as tampering with witnesses or jurors by way of promises and threats, and undermines the administration of justice.

The commentary [to Model Rule 3.3] ... also suggests that an attorney's revelation of his client's perjury to the court is a professionally responsible and acceptable response to the conduct of a client who has actually given perjured testimony. Similarly, the Model Rules and the commentary, as well as the Code of Professional Responsibility adopted in Iowa, expressly permit withdrawal from representation as an appropriate response of an attorney when the client threatens to commit perjury. Model Rules of Professional Conduct, Rule 1.16(a)(1), Rule 1.6, Comment (1983); Code of Professional Responsibility, DR 2–110(B), (C) (1980). Withdrawal of counsel when this situation arises at trial gives rise to many difficult questions including possible mistrial and claims of double jeopardy.... Whether Robinson's conduct is seen as a successful attempt to dissuade his client from committing the crime of perjury, or whether seen as a "threat" to withdraw from representation and disclose the illegal scheme, Robinson's representation of Whiteside falls well within accepted standards of professional conduct and the range of reasonable professional conduct acceptable under *Strickland*....

The Court of Appeals' holding that Robinson's "action deprived Whiteside of due process and effective assistance of counsel" is not supported by the record since Robinson's action, at most, deprived Whiteside of his contemplated perjury. Nothing counsel did in any way undermined Whiteside's claim that he believed the victim was reaching for a gun. Similarly, the record gives no support for holding that Robinson's action "also impermissibly compromised Whiteside's right to testify in his own defense by conditioning continued representation ... and confidentiality upon Whiteside's *restricted* testimony." The record in fact shows the contrary: (a) that Whiteside did testify, and (b) he was "restricted" or restrained only from testifying falsely and was aided by Robinson in developing the basis for the fear that Love was reaching for a gun. Robinson divulged no client communications until he was compelled to do so in response to Whiteside's post-trial challenge to the quality of his performance. We see this as a case in which the attorney successfully dissuaded the client from committing the crime of perjury....

On this record, the accused enjoyed continued representation within the bounds of reasonable professional conduct and did in fact exercise his right to testify; at most he was denied the right to have the assistance of counsel in the presentation of false testimony. Similarly, we can discern no breach of professional duty in Robinson's admonition to respondent that he would disclose respondent's perjury to the court. The crime of perjury in this setting is indistinguishable in substance from the crime of threatening or tampering with a witness or a juror. A defendant who informed his counsel that he was arranging to bribe or threaten witnesses or members of the jury would have no "right" to insist on counsel's assistance or silence. Counsel would not be limited to advising against that conduct. An attorney's duty of confidentiality, which totally covers the client's admission of guilt, does not extend to a client's announced plans to engage in future criminal conduct. . . .

In short, the responsibility of an ethical lawyer, as an officer of the court and a key component of a system of justice, dedicated to a search for truth, is essentially the same whether the client announces an intention to bribe or threaten witnesses or jurors or to commit or procure perjury. No system of justice worthy of the name can tolerate a lesser standard.

NOTES

Justice Brennan concurred separately, emphasizing that the Court has no constitutional or statutory authority to establish rules of ethics for lawyers practicing in state courts. He also joined a concurrence by Justice Blackmun, in which Justices Marshall and Stevens similarly joined. These concurring Justices emphasized that the only issue before the Court was whether Whiteside's Sixth Amendment right to a fair trial had been violated. In their view it had not. The only effect that Robinson's threat had on the trial was that Whiteside did not testify falsely. And, "[t]o the extent that Whiteside's claim rests on the assertion that he would have been acquitted had he been able to testify falsely, he claims a right that the law does not recognize." 475 U.S. at 186. Moreover, if Whiteside had lied on the stand, he would have faced a potential perjury prosecution and could have been subject to impeachment by other witnesses. Accordingly, he could not claim prejudice from his counsel's decision.

However these concurring Justices also emphasized that

[t]his Court . . . *cannot* tell the States or the lawyers in the States how to behave in their courts, unless and until federal rights are violated.

Unfortunately, the Court seems unable to resist the temptation of sharing with the legal community its vision of ethical conduct. But let there be no mistake: the Court's essay regarding what constitutes the correct response to a criminal client's suggestion that he will perjure himself is pure discourse without force of law. As Justice Blackmun observes, *that* issue is a thorny one . . . but it is not an issue presented by this case. Lawyers, judges, bar associations, students, and others should understand that the problem has not now been "decided."

QUESTIONS

1. What problem has *Nix v. Whiteside* decided? What ethical issues has it left unresolved?

2. Notice that the Model Rules' duty to remedy client perjury lasts only until the end of the proceeding. Why? What should lawyers do if, while a case is on appeal, they learn facts suggesting that a witness may have testified falsely?[52]

3. How certain do lawyers need to be that their client is lying before they take some remedial measures? For example, suppose that Whiteside had stated from the beginning that he had seen "something metallic" in Love's hand, and never remarked to his lawyers "If I don't say I saw a gun, I'm dead."

4. The Court states, "An attorney's duty of confidentiality, which totally covers the client's admission of guilt, does not extend to a client's announced plans to engage in future criminal conduct. See *Clark v. United States*, 289 U.S. 1, 15 (1933)." The case cited, however, discusses the attorney-client privilege rather than the ethical duty of confidentiality. Based on the quoted language, a 1986 case asserts that *Nix v. Whiteside* "approved an explicit statement to the court of the fact that perjury is about to be committed."[53] Is this a correct reading of current ethical standards? If Whiteside had said to Robinson, "I'm going to tell the court that I saw something metallic, and you're not going to stop me," could Robinson inform the court of this conversation before Robinson testified?

NOTES

Nix v. Whiteside raises two key questions: what standard of knowledge is required before the lawyer concludes that a defendant's testimony is (or would be) false; and what the lawyer and court should do if the defendant nonetheless insists on exercising his constitutional right to testify.

Standards of Knowledge

How certain should courts and counsel be that proposed testimony is false before denying defendants the right to make such statements? If a client were on trial for perjury, the standard would be proof beyond a reasonable doubt. Is a lesser requirement permissible in denying defendants the right to give certain testimony on their own behalf?

That issue is critical, since many criminal trial attorneys insist that they virtually never "know" that their client intends to lie. Defendants who plan to commit perjury seldom have a reason to announce it to their lawyer. In many cases, lawyers facing severe constraints of time and resources have similarly little incentive to pursue investigations that would establish beyond a reasonable doubt that a client's final story is false. But it is by no means self-evident that certainty beyond a reasonable doubt should be the standard; that is not our common-sense understanding of what knowledge requires.

---

52. Maryland State Bar Committee on Ethics, Op. 2005–15 (2005) (holding that a lawyer must investigate the possible perjury and inform the court if false testimony has been given).

53. U.S. v. Henkel, 799 F.2d 369, 370 (7th Cir. 1986).

Courts and commentators have divided on the level of certainty that is appropriate in this context. After *Nix v. Whiteside*, the American Bar Association Standing Committee on Ethics issued Formal Opinion 87–353, which advised lawyers to disclose to the court testimony that they "know" is false, but failed to define "know."[54] Under the Model Rules' somewhat circular standard, "knowingly" means "actual knowledge of the facts in question ... which may be inferred from circumstances." This definition rules out the criminal law's "willful blindness" standard, which makes intentionally avoiding knowledge legally equivalent to knowledge. (Thus, for example, drug couriers who deliberately refrain from looking in the suitcase they are hired to transport across the border can be convicted on a willful blindness theory of knowingly transporting drugs.) The Model Rules' standard, by insisting on actual knowledge, protects lawyers from disciplinary charges in cases where they carefully refrained from asking their clients questions that would have revealed that the clients' subsequent testimony was perjurious. Some criminal defenders report that they never ask their clients "Did you do it?" or even "Tell me what happened." Instead, they ask narrowly-focused questions like "What did you tell your friends about where you were going?"

Courts have proceeded with varying definitions of knowledge. Common formulations include "beyond a reasonable doubt," "firm factual basis," and "good faith determination."[55] However, trial judges frequently have failed to make any factual inquiry into the basis of the lawyer's conclusions about client perjury, or have implied that a client's inconsistent representations would be sufficient to justify an attorney's judgment of perjury. In 2002, after considering recommendations of the Ethics 2000 Commission, the ABA House of Delegates added the following language to the comment to Rule 3.3:

> [8]   The prohibition against offering false evidence only applies if the lawyer knows that the evidence is false. A lawyer's reasonable belief that the evidence is false does not preclude its presentation to the trier of fact. A lawyer's knowledge that the evidence is false, however, can be inferred from the circumstances. See Rule 1.0(f). Thus, although a lawyer should resolve doubts about the veracity of testimony or other evidence in favor of the client, the lawyer cannot ignore an obvious falsehood.

How much guidance does this language provide? Does it resolve the issue posed by the uncorroborated alibi in Problem 1(a)?

54.   ABA Comm. on Legal Ethics Formal Opinion 87–353 (1987). The Opinion states that in the "unusual case, where the lawyer does know, on the basis of the client's clearly stated intention, that the client will testify falsely at trial, and the lawyer is unable to effectively withdraw from the representation, the lawyer cannot examine the client in the usual manner." *Id.* at 8. However, since the Opinion endorses the conduct of the attorney in *Nix v. Whiteside*, it seems clear that clients need not admit that their testimony will be untrue; they need only communicate clearly their intent to make statements that lawyers "know" to be untrue.

55.   Developments, "Client Perjury and the Duty of Candor," 6 *Geo.J.Leg.Ethics* 1005, 1008–09 (1993).

Should questions by clients concerning the likelihood of perjury prosecutions be convincing evidence of an intent to lie if their testimony is implausible but not conclusively established as false? Consider the case of a defendant who expressed concerns on email about "telling a complete lie" about how much she had been drinking prior to being stopped for driving while intoxicated. She asked her attorney if the prosecution would be able to "obtain some witness that can testify how much I have been drinking". The attorney responded by email that "You won't be charged with perjury. I've never seen them charge anyone with perjury, and everybody lies in criminal cases, including the cops. If you want to go tell the truth, then we'll just plead guilty and you can get your jail time over with." The client later disclosed the emails to the trial judge. How should the court respond?[56]

Remedial Measures

A related question involves the procedure that courts should use if a client insists on giving testimony that the lawyer expects will be false, or if a client offers such testimony while on the witness stand. In most other settings, the prescribed response to client misconduct is withdrawal. However, courts and commentators have generally found this an unsatisfactory way of coping with the perjury dilemma in criminal cases, because it would simply transfer the problem to the next attorney and would give a defendant the opportunity to trigger mistrials by insisting on the right to testify.

What should be done if a client insists on testifying over counsel's objections is subject to dispute. One unresolved question is whether the trial court must conduct an inquiry or make findings on whether the proposed testimony would constitute perjury. If the perjury cannot be definitely established, a related question is whether defendants should have the option of testifying in narrative form—that is, without the attorney asking questions. Model Rule 3.3's commentary rejects that approach on the ground that it "compromises both contending principles; it exempts the lawyer from the duty to disclose false evidence, but subjects the client to an implicit disclosure of information imparted to counsel." However, many courts and commentators have disagreed. In their view, the narrative approach is the best accommodation of the competing principles; it avoids implicating lawyers in perjury, but avoids penalizing confidential disclosures and gives clients whose life and liberty are at risk an opportunity to plead their cases. The trial judge's ability to take a defendant's apparent perjury into account in sentencing provides some check on obvious fabrication. What is your view?

An alternative approach that has commanded support among many defense lawyers is to give priority to one of the contending principles—that of confidentiality. Under this approach, lawyers should attempt to dissuade their clients from perjury and should conduct direct examination in a way that minimizes risks of false testimony. However, if they are unable to

56. Nate Morabito, "Tri–Cities Attor-
ney Arrested for Contempt of Court," News   Channel 11, Nov. 30, 2005.

prevent perjury, they should not disclose it either directly to the court or implicitly to the jury through an unguided narrative. What limited survey data are available suggests that many practicing attorneys have preferred this approach although it is contrary to Model Rule 3.3(a)(4).[57] Other nations have also had problems resolving this issue. The European CCEB Code of Conduct Rule 4.1 prohibits lawyers from knowingly giving false or misleading information to the court but neither the rule nor the accompanying commentary explains how they should respond when they believe a client or witness has testified falsely.

Monroe Freedman is a leading defender of this position. It arises from what Freedman characterizes as the "perjury trilemma"—a trio of jointly inconsistent obligations. In order to fulfill one obligation, that of zealous advocacy, the attorney must learn all the significant facts of the client's case. At the same time, the attorney labors under a second duty of confidentiality, as well as a third obligation of candor to the court. Freedman argues that attorneys whose clients commit perjury can fulfill at most two of these three obligations. If they have learned all significant facts, they will know that the testimony is perjurious, and then must either violate confidentiality or be less than candid to the court. Thus, they can reconcile the duties of confidentiality and candor only if they do not know that their clients' testimony is perjurious, but this implies that they have neglected their duties of zealous advocacy by failing to learn significant facts. Freedman argues that candor to the court is the principle that should give way. In his view, the duties of confidentiality and zealous advocacy are of paramount constitutional and moral significance; they are essential to effective assistance to counsel, which is "one of the most significant manifestations of our regard for the dignity of the individual," and a critical protection against governmental abuses.[58]

Do you agree? Is respect for the rule of law and the integrity of the justice system an equally critical value in a free society? Another way of accommodating these competing principles would be to follow the approach of some European countries and allow the defendant to make an unsworn statement. Would such an approach be preferable to either the full disclosure or narrative strategies that now prevail?

2.   IMPEACHMENT

PROBLEM 2

a) You represent a lawyer on criminal charges growing out of his representation of an 85–year–old widow with no family who lived alone.

---

57. See Monroe Freedman, "Getting Honest About Client Perjury," 21 *Georgetown J. Legal Ethics* 133, 148 (2008); Lauren Reskin, "How Lawyers Vote in Tough Ethical Dilemma," *ABA J.* Feb. 1, 1986 (41 percent of polled attorneys believed that informing the court of perjury would violate client's rights to effective assistance of counsel). Since such a strategy avoids a potentially acrimonious conflict with the client and an almost certain defeat at trial, lawyers' preferences are scarcely surprising.

58. Monroe H. Freedman, *Lawyers' Ethics in an Adversary System* 4 (1975). *See* his more recent treatment, Freedman, *supra* note 57; Monroe H. Freedman & Abbe Smith, *Understanding Lawyers' Ethics.* 153–90 (rev. ed. 2002).

She had retained the lawyer to take care of a few monthly expenses such as rent and utility bills, and had given him her bankbooks to withdraw the necessary funds. He did so but also withdrew over $100,000, which he used for purchase of a Cadillac and investments listed in his own and his wife's names. A neighbor's discovery of these withdrawals led to a criminal indictment.

Your client's defense is that the woman had lent him some of the money and had asked him to invest the remainder. However, he neglected to keep copies of the promissory notes. The woman recalls no such agreement and prosecutors have located no such notes. After your client refused to plea bargain or to make any restitution, the case proceeded to trial. You cross-examined the woman about details unrelated to the incident in an effort to establish her faulty memory. She became quite confused about the date of her birth and her husband's death, but was clear about the recent events surrounding the lawyer's conduct. After lengthy deliberations, the jury deadlocked 11 to 1 in favor of conviction and the judge declared a mistrial.

While waiting for a new trial you learn that the woman is in ill health and lacks sufficient funds to pay for housing and medical expenses. Although the bar has filed disciplinary charges against your client, its backlog of cases is so extensive that the woman will probably not survive long enough to establish a case. The client is pleased with your representation and again refuses any plea bargains. He asks if there is anything you can do to further delay the proceeding. Your partners ask if there is anything you can do to withdraw from representation. How do you respond?[59]

b) The facts are the same as above except that the case involves civil fraud charges brought by the woman rather than a criminal prosecution.

c) You represent one co-defendant in a campus rape case. The incident took place after the complainant, a sophomore, accepted a ride home with your client following rifle club practice. According to the complainant, on the evening in question your client said he needed to stop off at his fraternity house and invited her in. A number of his friends were drinking. They pressured her into joining them. One guided a cup to her lips. When she indicated that she felt sick, she was taken to a couch in an upstairs room. When the defendant began undressing her, she protested. She later told the police she was too sick and scared to resist physically. She passed out and, when she awoke, another fraternity member was having sex with her. Your client insists that he believed the woman consented. His fraternity has a history of initiating "little sisters" through drinking and group sex, and he thought this woman was aware of the tradition. He also tells you that he had heard from "other people" that she was "hot-blooded" and "highly sexed," and that she "led him on" by her conduct and clothing. You have learned that this is the second time in his college career that he has been accused of sexual assault.

59. This problem is modeled on cases discussed in E.R. Shipp, "Fear and Confusion in Court Plague Elderly Crime Victims," *N.Y. Times*, Mar. 13, 1983, at A1.

Investigators hired by the defendant's well-to-do family have discovered a disaffected former boyfriend of the victim. He is willing to testify that she enjoyed "rough sex" with him. According to the investigators' reports, the woman is from a conservative and deeply religious family. You suspect that vigorous pretrial disclosures about her provocative dress and her prior sexual relationship might discourage her from testifying for fear of embarrassing her family. Under your state's rape shield statute, a victim's prior sexual history is only admissible if the judge makes an in camera determination that it is "material . . . to negating force or coercion," and that its probative value outweighs its prejudicial effects. You are convinced that some judges might view this woman's sexual history as more probative than prejudicial, and might resolve doubts in favor of admitting evidence in order to avoid reversal on appeal. It is also likely that humiliating facts could be brought out in pretrial disclosures.

You are equally convinced that a prior allegation of date rape against your client will be deemed too prejudicial and too dissimilar from this incident to be admissible at trial. In that earlier case, the victim decided not to press charges after her complaint to campus authorities resulted in harassment by the defendant's friends. You are concerned that a similar outcome in this case would discourage other women from coming forward and would add to the well-documented problems of campus sexual assault. You also worry that as defense counsel, that is not what you should be worrying about.

How do you proceed?[60]

References:

Model Rule 4.4; ABA Crim. Defense Standard 4–7.6.

QUESTIONS

Problem 2 raises a number of fundamental questions of legal ethics:

1.   How persuasive are lawyers' justifications for defending a claim that they believe is false or a client whom they believe is guilty? (See the discussion in Section A of this chapter.)

2.   Are clients entitled to a defense that includes impeaching a witness whom the lawyer believes is telling the truth? Does it matter if one purpose of impeachment is to induce a witness to drop charges?

3.   Do the answers to those questions vary depending on whether that case is civil or criminal? Should lawyers' obligations take into account the costs to potential witnesses and the impact on society generally? If so, does rape stand on a different footing from other civil or criminal proceedings? Alternatively, do other matters involving intimate conduct or particularly vulnerable victims also present special considerations?

4.   Should the lawyer's gender affect resolution of these issues? Does a defendant gain an extra and unwarranted advantage from representation

60.   This problem is a composite based on several reported cases.

by a female attorney in a case where the sexual conduct of a female witness is relevant? Might jurors assume that no woman would zealously attack another woman's credibility without a belief that she was testifying untruthfully?

NOTES

Few skills are more prized by trial lawyers and despised by the public than the art of impeaching a truthful witness. Jerome Frank's *Courts on Trial* describes the process:

> As you may learn by reading any one of a dozen or more handbooks on how to try a law-suit, an experienced lawyer uses all sorts of stratagems to minimize the effect on the judge or jury of testimony disadvantageous to his client, even when the lawyer has no doubt of the accuracy and honesty of that testimony. The lawyer considers it his duty to create a false impression, if he can, of any witness who gives such testimony. If such a witness happens to be timid, frightened by the unfamiliarity of court-room ways, the lawyer, in his cross-examination, plays on that weakness, in order to confuse the witness and make it appear that he is concealing significant facts. Longenecker, in his book *Hints On The Trial of a Law Suit* (a book endorsed by the great Wigmore), in writing of the "truthful, honest, overcautious" witness, tells how a "skillful advocate by a rapid cross-examination may ruin the testimony of such a witness." The author does not even hint any disapproval of that accomplishment. Longenecker's and other similar books recommend that a lawyer try to prod an irritable but honest "adverse" witness into displaying his undesirable characteristics in their most unpleasant form, in order to discredit him with the judge or jury. "You may," writes Harris, "sometimes destroy the effect of an adverse witness by making him appear more hostile than he really is. You may make him exaggerate or unsay something and say it again." Taft says that a clever cross-examiner, dealing with an honest but egotistic witness, will "deftly tempt the witness to indulge in his propensity for exaggeration, so as to make him 'hang himself.' And thus," adds Taft, "it may happen that not only is the value of his testimony lost, but the side which produces him suffers for seeking aid from such a source"—although, I would add, that may be the only source of evidence of a fact on which the decision will turn....[61]

The American Bar Association Standards on the Criminal Defense Function (3rd ed. 1993) provide that "defense counsel's belief or knowledge that the witness is telling the truth does not preclude cross-examination." An earlier edition of that standard included the qualification that the lawyer's belief "should, if possible, be taken into consideration by counsel in conducting the cross-examination."[62] What follows from this omission? Are there considerations that should be taken into account in Problem 2?

---

61. Jerome Frank, *Courts on Trial* 82 (1949).

62. ABA Standards Relating to the Administration of Criminal Justice, The Defense

To some commentators, impeachment of a truthful witness is especially problematic when the witness is the complainant in a rape case. Zealous advocacy in that context may carry special costs because of the particularly grave potential for humiliation, the deterrent that such conduct creates for other victims, and the societal impact of sanctioning rape myths—of fostering the impression that women who claim rape often provoked, permitted, or deserved what they got. Lawyers' appeals to such myths are often effective. Jurors are less likely to convict a defendant if evidence suggests that the complainant engaged in non-marital sex, drank, used drugs, dressed "provocatively," or knew the defendant, however brief their acquaintance.[63] The same information affects judicial decision-making, and racial bias has been found to amplify these effects when the complainant is a woman of color.[64] In addition, rape victims often suffer from rape trauma syndrome, which may lead them to suppress details of an assault.[65] Zealous cross-examination can exploit confusion that may discredit a complainant's basically accurate account. The risk is particularly great in cases involving child sex abuse.[66]

Exploitation of rape complainants' special vulnerability can have a corrosive impact on the entire law enforcement system. Rape is the most under-reported felony, in part because of a victimization of victims that rape shield statutes have only partially addressed. Some states bar admission of sexual history evidence except for relations with the accused and explanation of physical evidence (such as the presence of semen). Other states permit the admission of sexual history evidence if the judge makes an in camera determination of relevance, and the remaining jurisdictions allow such evidence under specified conditions.[67] David Luban draws the following conclusion:

> Matters would be different if rape were rare and false accusations of rape occurred regularly. Then the advocate's role would properly focus on the vulnerability of men, not of women. Suffice it to say that the world is not this way. [Susan] Estrich speculates that the law of rape has been shaped by "[t]he male rape fantasy . . . a nightmare" in

Function, 4–7.6(b) (1979).

63. Henry F. Fadell & Kagan Brown, "The Effects of Using Social Science Rape Typologies on Juror Decisions to Convict," 31 *Law & Psych. Rev.* 1, 1–16 (2007); Deborah L. Rhode, *Speaking of Sex* 121–127 (1998).

64. Jeffrey J. Pokorak, "Rape as A Badge of Slavery: The Legal History and Remedies for Prosecutorial Race of Victim Charging Disparities," 7 *Nevada L. J.* 1, 39 (2006). Deborah L. Rhode, *The Unfinished Agenda: Women and the Legal Profession* 21–22 (ABA Commission on Women in the Profession, 2001).

65. *See* Patricia Frazier & Eugene Borgida, "Juror Common Understanding and the Admissibility of Rape Trauma Syndrome Evidence in Court," 12 *Law and Hum. Behavior* 101 (1988).

66. Livia L. Gilstrap, Kristina Fritz, Amanda Torres, & Annika Melinder, "Child Witnesses: Common Ground and Controversies in the Scientific Community," 32 *Wm. Mitchell L. Rev.* 59, 69 (2005); Maggie Bruck & Stephen J. Ceci, "The Suggestibility of Children's Memory," 50 *Ann. Rev. Psychol.* 419, 436 (1999).

67. Katharine T. Bartlett & Deborah L. Rhode, *Gender and Law:Theory, Doctrine, Commentary* 797 (4th Ed. 2006). For examples of the way that information about victims is exploited in sex crime cases, see id., at 798–99; Aviva Orenstein, "Special Issues Raised by Rape Trials," 76 *Forham L. Rev.* 1585, 15941605 (2007).

which the man is accused of rape after having sex with a woman who said no but did not resist.... In my view, then, the advocate's role should stop well short of an all-out assault on the [truthful] prosecutrix.... The lawyer can ask the victim whether she consented. The lawyer can also argue reasonable doubt to the jury. What she cannot do is cross-examine her to make her look like a whore.[68]

QUESTIONS

1.   Do you agree? Consider various objections that might be raised against Luban's argument that lawyers should be less zealous in defending rape than other crimes. (a) It does not sufficiently consider the costs to male defendants who may misjudge consent. Given the brutal conditions of this nation's prisons and the permanent stigma that may attach to rape convictions, defendants are entitled to have the jury see the case from their perspective. (b) The defense attorney's role is to protect those accused of crimes from the state—it is not to protect rape victims from rapists. It simply is not a defender's job to pull punches out of solicitude for rape victims. (c) Victims sometimes lie or are mistaken and the costs to defendants can be substantial, as illustrated by the highly publicized accusations against Duke lacrosse players discussed in Part B. (d) Rape is not the only context in which complainants are vulnerable and particularly wary about reporting abuse, nor is it the only context in which the only effective defense is to "taint the victim."[69]

2.   Do rape complainants face a unique combination of intrusiveness, stigma, and credibility problems that pose unique ethical concerns for opposing lawyers? Alternatively, is rape just one example of why a contextual "do justice" approach like William Simon's makes sense? Simon believes that lawyers should tailor their tactics to achieve the just result. But is there consensus within society generally, or the criminal defense bar in particular, about what "justice" requires in matters like acquaintance rape? What about cases involving child witnesses, where aggressive cross examination may unjustly confuse or discredit truthful testimony, but gentle examination may fail to reveal suggestive pretrial preparation tactics?[70] What would be the risks and benefits of a discretionary approach to "hard cases?"[71]

3.   Should women defense attorneys feel special ethical responsibilities in cases involving women victims of sexual assault, particularly given the

68. David Luban, "Partisanship, Betrayal and Autonomy in the Lawyer–Client Relationship: A Reply to Stephen Ellmann," 90 *Colum.L.Rev.* 1004, 1028–1031 (1990).

69. David Margolick, "At the Bar," *N.Y. Times*, Jan. 22, 1988 at A4 (quoting defense attorney Jack Litman's justification for claiming that the victim liked "rough sex.")

70. See Bruck and Ceci, supra note 66.

71. For discussion of hard cases in the criminal context, *see* Rhode, *supra* note 7, at 71–74. For an example of such a case in a context other than rape, *see* "Avila's Old Lawyer Says He's Rethinking Career," CMM/cp,//lawcenter, July 26, 2002 (describing lawyer's response to the news that a former client whom he had successfully defended on child molestation charges was arrested for the kidnaping and murder of a five-year-old child).

influence that their involvement may have with juries? Or should the advocate's role not be affected by gender-related considerations? In *Emotional Trials: The Moral Dilemma of Women Criminal Defense Attorneys* (2004), Cynthia Siemsen draws on interviews with women defense attorneys who have grappled with ethical issues in cases involving sexual abuse: rape, domestic violence, and child molestation. These women had encountered endless variations on the same question: "How can you defend him?" Some responded with procedural justifications along the lines noted earlier: "everyone is entitled to representation;" "it's not our role to judge them;," "I'm not defending the act ... I'm defending the right to a fair proceeding." Others worked hard to empathize with their client, regardless of the heinousness of the act. Often factors in defendants' own life histories helped to explain or mitigate the offense; they were victims of child sexual abuse or domestic violence; they had drug or mental health disabilities that called for institutionalized treatment not extended incarceration. In many cases, harsh penalty structures, particularly California's three strikes law, created incentives to provide the best possible defense. Many of these lawyers found special satisfaction in the "social work" aspect of their work: they looked for opportunities to help "turn someone's life around."

Although some female attorneys made efforts to minimize the costs to women victims, others acknowledged the difficulties this created when their objective was in essence to make the witness "look like a liar." Typically, the strategy for defense counsel was to fall back on role: "I can't be concerned about [them].... It's not my job." Such experiences sometimes left the lawyer with emotional scars or an unwillingness to accept certain kinds of cases, especially child molestation.

But for the vast majority of defenders in the vast majority of cases, their practice was not in tension with their principles. Rather, they saw defending the "poorest of the poor" as an extension of feminist values. It reflected a commitment to individual rights, a respect for human dignity, and a compassion for those who had been victims as well as victimizers.

Do you find these responses adequate? Would Luban? What about Ridolfi, given her account reprinted below?

4. One of the only public opinion surveys of legal ethics presented a hypothetical in which defense counsel believed that an opposing witness's testimony was accurate and truthful but that skillful cross-examination could discredit the witness's memory or motives. Three-quarters of surveyed lawyers, but fewer than half of non-lawyers, believed that an attack on memory was appropriate. Two-thirds of lawyers, but only 40 percent of non-lawyers, believed that an attack on motives was proper.[72] What follows from this difference in views? Does it argue for, or against, giving the public a greater voice in the formulation of professional rules?

72. Wes Hansen, "Lawyers, Lawyers, Lawyers," *Ethics: Easier Said than Done* 38 (1993).

5.   How would you weigh the competing values in Problem 2? Consider the following statements by criminal defense attorneys. Do any describe your own position?

Timothy Beneke, Men on Rape

104–105 (1982).

... The bottom line is in getting my client off. If I saw myself appealing to the jury's sexism I would probably wonder about it and, it's true, I don't look at it as harshly as appealing to the jury's racism. The effect of the women's movement on me has been as strong as on anyone else, but I'm no one special; I try to win my cases. If I could get my client off by appealing to the jury's sexism I probably would, because I'd be more concerned with this one guy and his freedom than the ethical issue of sexism. If I didn't appeal to their sexism and I thought I could've to get my client off, and he went to prison, I probably would feel pretty bad about it. In the heat of the battle I probably pull out a lot of stops and I may have appealed to the jury's sexism without even realizing it.

Cookie Ridolfi, Statement on Representing Rape Defendants

(July 26, 1989) (unpublished manuscript, Santa Clara Law School).

I have never felt conflicted about what side I stand on in a criminal trial. My political sensibilities keep me firmly planted on the side of the defendant. As a public defender for nearly seven years, I have seen that my clients are victims of poverty, racism, and a criminal justice system that, despite its lofty ideals, presumes guilt, not innocence. My experience has shown me that the system is stacked against an accused and doubly stacked against those who are not white or are poor....

However, my role as a defender in sexual assault cases is not clear or simple. These cases frequently require that I, a feminist who rejects harmful stereotypes of women, exploit those same stereotypes in defense of my client. In the majority of sexual assault cases, the complainant and defendant know one another and fabrication or consent is raised as a defense.... As a consequence, in most sex cases, my role is to charge the complainant with having agreed to the sexual encounter, or having asked for it, or of being a woman scorned whose feeling of rejection caused her to cry rape as an act of revenge.

Some defense attorneys believe that effective cross-examination can be done in a way that does not demean the complainant. I disagree. No matter what tone of voice is used or how politely the questions are put, a good cross-examination must still ultimately demonstrate that the complaining witness is a liar.

Moreover, if the defense attorney is respectful of the complainant's feelings, she lends credibility to the prosecution's case. The more successful the defense counsel is at cutting away at the complainant's credibility, the more effective the defense and necessarily, more damaged the complainant is. An attorney who is concerned about a complainant's feelings necessarily compromises her client's right to an advocate with exclusive loyalty.

In the conflict between my commitment to defender work and my increasing distress over what is required of me in a sex case, the fact that my own gender is also an issue at trial weighs heavily. Last year I defended a man charged with assault and rape. He and the complainant were dance partners in a club featuring provocative "live dancing." She testified that the defendant appeared at her door late one night, forced his way inside, then dragged her into the basement where he viciously raped and beat her. The client said that he had been invited into the house for sex which was interrupted when the complainant's husband came home; it was her husband who beat her, not him.

After more than a week of trial where emotions ran high for everyone, the jury acquitted him. Afterwards, I met with jurors. One woman juror told me that she believed in his innocence because she was certain that I could not have fought for him in the way that I did had he committed that crime. . . . I later learned that he was arrested and convicted in two new rape/assault cases similar to the one I had tried. . . . [T]hat trial and that complainant still haunt me. I think of the horror described from the witness stand and I believe now that it is true. I think about the fact that the defendant left the courthouse a free man and returned to a community that pitied him as a victim and despised her as the victimizer. I think about the two women that were beaten and raped by him just a few months later. Finally, I think about my role in that.

Despite this experience and my growing discomfort with my own participation in the defense of rape cases, I remain firm in my belief that every person, no matter what the charge or circumstances of the case, deserves dedicated and competent counsel. I also know that some men are victims of a woman's false charges of rape and agree strongly that this defense must be pursued when a defendant makes this claim. I am not critical of any other woman who chooses to defend a man charged with rape. But for all of the reasons I have given, I would find it difficult to again be in the position where I would have to challenge a woman's claim of rape knowing that what she claims may be true.

C. SMOKING GUNS AND SOCIETAL INTERESTS

1. POSSESSION OF EVIDENCE

PROBLEM 3

How should a lawyer respond in the following situations? Does it matter whether a legal proceeding is pending or imminent? Should it?

a) A client leaves in the lawyer's possession the fruits or instrumentalities of a crime such as stolen property or a weapon.

b) A third party turns over such evidence to the lawyer or reveals its location.

c) The lawyer receives from a client documents implicating him in criminal activity.

d) A client describes to the lawyer the location of incriminating evidence. After finding that evidence, the lawyer realizes that it will be irretrievably lost or destroyed if she takes no action.

e) The client, a prominent African American athlete, is incarcerated during trial for the murder of his white ex-wife. Before the predominantly black female jury visits the defendant's home, his lawyer removes photographs of white celebrities and nude white girl friends. The lawyer replaces them with photographs of the defendant's family that defense staff has enlarged and made suitable for display, along with a civil rights poster that the lawyer supplies from his own office picturing an African American school-girl being accompanied to a segregated school by a federal marshal.[73]

f) A client under investigation by a U.S. Attorney asks the lawyer whether certain documents could establish criminal liability and what the consequences would be if the documents were lost or inadvertently destroyed. After that conversation, the lawyer discovers that incriminating documents have vanished. The client denies any responsibility for their removal.

NOTES

Lawyers' ethical obligations concerning evidence are essentially those defined by statute and procedural rules. Model Rule 3.4 provides that a lawyer shall not falsify evidence or "unlawfully obstruct another party's access to evidence or unlawfully alter, destroy, or conceal a document or other material having potential evidentiary value." Nor may a lawyer "counsel or assist another person to do any such act," *id.*, or engage in conduct "prejudicial to the administration of justice." Rule 8.4(d). The Code of Professional Responsibility includes similar prohibitions.[74]

Laws concerning the retention of evidence vary in scope. Some statutes prohibit intentional destruction or concealment if the material is relevant to a pending criminal proceeding; other prohibitions also cover material relevant to an ongoing investigation. Model Penal Code § 241.7 and its state analogues criminalize destruction or concealment if the actor believes that an official proceeding or investigation is pending or about to be instituted. A few states impose liability for actions intended to prevent

73. The description is of defense lawyer Johnnie Cochran's strategy in the trial of football great O. J. Simpson for murdering his wife and a friend. Jeffrey Rosen, "The Bloods and the Crits," *The New Republic*, Dec. 9, 1996, at 27.

74. Disciplinary Rule 7–109(A) provides that "[a] lawyer shall not suppress any evidence that he or his client has a legal ob-ligation to reveal or produce." Other provisions direct that a lawyer shall not "[i]ntentionally or habitually violate any established rule of procedure or of evidence" (DR 7–106(C)(7)), nor engage in "illegal conduct involving moral turpitude" (DR 1–102(A)(3)), nor engage "in conduct that is prejudicial to the administration of justice." DR 1–102(A)(5).

production of evidence in a legal proceeding regardless of when the actions take place. In the aftermath of massive document shredding in the Enron case, the federal Sarbanes–Oxley Act of 2002 enacted a new prohibition on destruction of documents "in relation to or contemplation of any ... matter" "within federal jurisdiction." 18 U.S.C. § 1519. A proceeding "need not be pending or about to be instituted" to trigger liability. 18 U.S.C. § 1512(f). Thus, attorneys' ethical responsibilities regarding potential evidence will vary depending upon when destruction or concealment is contemplated, what statutes are controlling, and whether the material is subject to any court order.

Interpretation of attorneys' ethical and statutory obligations has produced several clear rules and certain murky norms. Prevailing case law generally holds that attorneys may not actively participate in concealing the "fruits or instrumentalities" of a crime. Lawyers who come into possession of such material must turn it over to the prosecution.

The leading cases are *State v. Olwell*, 394 P.2d 681 (Wash.1964); *In re Ryder*, 263 F.Supp. 360 (E.D.Va.), *aff'd,* 381 F.2d 713 (4th Cir.1967); and *Morrell v. State*, 575 P.2d 1200 (Alaska 1978). In *Olwell,* the court held that an attorney must turn over an incriminating weapon when requested by subpoena and should do so on his own initiative without revealing the source or manner in which it was obtained. *Ryder* reached a similar result, and suspended a lawyer who moved a sawed-off shotgun and apparently stolen money from his client's safety deposit box to his own. In *Morrell,* a friend of the defendant cleaned out his car at his attorney's request. On discovering a kidnap plan, he turned it over to the attorney. The attorney consulted the Alaska bar ethics committee, which advised him to return the plan to the friend, to counsel the friend on laws governing concealment of evidence, and to withdraw from the case if it became obvious that an ethical violation would result. The attorney then withdrew and attempted to return the evidence. When the friend proved reluctant to accept it, the attorney helped arrange its transfer to the police. The defendant was convicted and appealed on grounds of ineffective assistance of counsel. In rejecting that claim, the court reasoned that the attorney would have been obligated to see that the evidence reached the prosecutor even if he had received it from the defendant, and that his obligation was even stronger because he had acquired it from a third party. 575 P.2d at 1211.

Although attorneys are required to turn over evidence in their possession, they cannot be compelled to disclose its origin or how they learned of its location. A leading case is *People v. Meredith*, 631 P.2d 46 (Cal.1981). There, a murder suspect told his lawyer that he had taken a wallet from the victim and had left it in a trash can near his home. The lawyer retrieved it, turned it over to the prosecution, and subsequently withdrew as defense counsel. At trial, the location of the evidence became crucial as a means of linking the defendant to the crime. Accordingly, the court required the lawyer to testify about where he had found the wallet, but not to disclose his representation of the defendant or his reasons for searching the trash can. The court also suggested that attorneys in future cases could avoid any harmful effects of its ruling by leaving evidence in its original location.

The *Meredith* holding attempted to accommodate competing concerns: the court wanted probative evidence to reach the jury but not through disclosure of privileged communications. Other courts have taken different approaches. Some judges have required the defendant to stipulate where evidence originated. Others have excluded material when the prosecutor had no way except through defense counsel to establish its link with the defendant (such as through fingerprints, bank serial numbers, or the like).[75]

Each of these approaches has attracted significant criticism. Excluding the evidence entirely allows defendants to dispose of incriminating material by leaving it with their lawyers. Requiring defendants to stipulate facts linking themselves to such material penalizes confidential disclosures and accomplishes indirectly what the privilege was meant to prevent. *Meredith*'s compromise has the same effect unless counsel responds by informing clients of attorneys' obligations to turn over incriminating material. If that occurs with some frequency, then the compromise position takes on an "air of unreality"; as Geoffrey Hazard and William Hodes note, it would be a "very dim client indeed who did not think to move the evidence to a safer location or do a better job of destroying it." But, they conclude, "at least the legal system is not much worse off than if the client had never consulted a lawyer."[76]

By contrast, other commentators object that this entire line of cases unduly penalizes certain defendants. If citizens generally have no affirmative obligation to produce evidence, why should attorneys be treated differently, particularly given the values underlying the attorney-client privilege? Moreover, as a practical matter, the *Olwell* rule is almost never invoked in white-collar cases; attorneys are not penalized for failure to volunteer incriminating records in their possession.[77] However, one might equally ask whether citizens should be affirmatively required to produce non-self-incriminating evidence if they know it will assist in a criminal investigation, and whether lawyers, as officers of the court, should have some special responsibility to disclose such evidence.

QUESTIONS

1. What results does this line of cases suggest on the facts of Problem 3?

2. Do these results make sense? Are they consistent with the *Garrow* "buried bodies" case discussed in Chapter V? Is photographing physical evidence qualitatively different from receiving it?

---

75. Geoffrey Hazard Jr. & William Hodes, *The Law of Lawyering* § 1.6:401, at 194; § 3.4:204, at 631 (2d ed. 1990).

76. *Id.*, § 1.6:402, at 196.

77. Kevin R. Reitz, "Clients, Lawyers and the Fifth Amendment: The Need for a Projected Privilege," 41 *Duke L.J.* 572, 597–602, 627 (1991).

3.   Is redecorating a defendant's home before a jury visit consistent with lawyers' ethical obligations? Is it different than suggesting changes in a defendant's wardrobe or physical appearance? How should the trial judge or bar disciplinary committee have responded to the facts of Problem 3(e)?

4.   Consider the case of *United States v. Lamplugh*, 334 F.3d 294 (3d Cir. 2003), in which a gun show promoter was convicted along with her late husband of not filing federal income tax returns for 1991 and 1992. The couple's defense at trial was that they had filed their returns, but that the Internal Revenue Service had either lost or misplaced them. Just prior to the start of their trial, the couple gave their lawyer a box of what they claimed were newly discovered financial records, including what appeared to be copies of their 1991 and 1992 tax returns. Midway through the trial, the lawyer turned the documents over to prosecutors, who waited until their closing argument to show the jury that the purported returns for tax years 1991 and 1992 were dated for those respective years. Taxes for those years would not be due until the following spring and appropriately filed returns would be dated for those later years. The Lamplughs were both convicted. On appeal, the wife contended that her attorney had rendered ineffective assistance of counsel for not having recognized that the returns were fakes and for not having warned her that the government could use the false returns to bolster its case. The trial judge upheld that claim and granted a new trial. The Third Circuit Court of Appeals reversed. According to the appellate panel, the defendant should not be allowed to "manipulate the justice system by knowingly presenting fabricated written documents...." 334 F.3d, at 301.

Do you agree? Should the attorney be liable for malpractice or be subject to bar disciplinary sanctions?

2.   DOCUMENT RETENTION AND DESTRUCTION

PROBLEM 4

a) In *The Superlawyers,* Joseph Goulden describes one of his interviews with a Washington criminal defense lawyer over a candid three-martini lunch. Partway through the interview, the lawyer pointed across the room to a former client. Several years ago, he had represented the client in an FTC investigation. The client had been doing some "odd-ball accounting" which discriminated against certain customers. One of them had complained to the FTC. In the lawyer's view, the practice constituted a "clear cut violation" of the Robinson–Patman Act. "Trouble was coming," the lawyer recalled. "It was just a matter of time."

> Now, in a situation like this, the documents should tell the whole story and I don't see any reason why a man should help the federal government build a gallows for himself. At the same time, the bar rules are pretty simple: If I advise him to go burn everything, I can be disbarred for interfering with the processes of justice.

> So I take another route. I tell him just what I told you. I tell him ... without all his sales records the FTC will have a hell of a time

making a case. Oh, they could, but only by backtracking to customers. But I know the FTC is so short-handed they won't do that except in a major case. "Do you still have any documents around that could hurt you?" I asked him. "Some of this stuff must be getting pretty old, and most people turn over their records fairly fast."[78]

As the lawyer had predicted, the FTC subpoenaed enough records to make a case which "cost the poor bastard one hell of a lot of time and trouble." The client was furious. "But why didn't you tell me I should have cleaned out the files?" he kept asking me. I finally unloaded on him and gave him an informative little talk. The client remained mad, haggled over the bill, and complained all over Washington. But, as the lawyer concluded, "I don't give a damn, though; I still have my law license."[79]

Should he?

b) You are a state bar counsel who is considering whether to file disciplinary charges against Nancy Temple. Temple served as an in-house lawyer for the Arthur Andersen accounting firm prior to its dissolution in connection with the Enron scandal. The conduct at issue involves Temple's instructions to Andersen staff concerning documents related both to the audit of questionable investment vehicles for Enron, and to the certification of the company's potentially misleading financial statements. Andersen had a detailed document retention policy calling for the destruction of all nonessential draft documents or conflicting documentation relating to an audit.[80] The policy itself is not unusual. Your concerns arise from the timing and context of a memo that Temple sent on October 12, 2002, calling for compliance with that policy.

Temple's conduct was the subject of a 2002 Congressional hearing in which she characterized her actions as customary housekeeping duties. In that hearing, she admitted awareness, prior to October 8, of allegations by an Enron employee of inappropriate accounting procedures, as well as an investigation of those allegations by outside counsel. The SEC placed Enron under investigation in early October, and it confirmed that fact publicly in an October 22 press release. Temple's notes from a conference call on October 8 anticipated that outcome: "Highly probable some SEC investigation."[81] Temple also knew that outside counsel had been retained on October 9 to assist Andersen with legal difficulties arising out of its financial reporting for Enron.

78. Joseph Goulden, *The Superlawyers,* 287–89 (1972).

79. *Id.*

80. A complete copy of the Andersen policy, Client Engagement Information–Organization, Retention and Destruction, Feb. 1, 2000, is reprinted in Destruction of Enron-Related Documents by Andersen Personnel: Hearing Before the House of Representatives Committee on Energy, 107th Cong. 1 (Jan.

24, 2002), at 79–103. For discussion, *see* Deborah L. Rhode & Paul Paton, "Lawyers, Ethics and Enron," 8 *Stanford J. Law, Bus. & Fin.* 9 (2002), reprinted in Enron: Corporate Fiascos and Their Implications (ed. Nancy B. Rapoport & Bala G. Dahran, eds. 2004).

81. April Witt & Peter Behr, "Losses, Conflicts Threaten Survival," *Washington Post,* July 31, 2002, at A1.

Despite her knowledge, Temple sent an e-mail on October 12 to Andersen's Houston practice director stating: "It might be useful to consider reminding the engagement team of our documentation and retention policy. It will be helpful to make sure that we have complied with that policy."[82] On October 23, the lead engagement partner on the Enron audit ordered his team to comply with Andersen's policy. The result was an extraordinary volume of document destruction over the next several weeks. Media reports chronicled the shredding of more than 18 trunks and 30 boxes of material on only one of the days at one of the offices, compared with an average of one trunk per week in the preceding period.[83] Not until November 10, after the SEC had subpoenaed documents from Andersen concerning its Enron investigation and after Andersen had received a second subpoena in a related lawsuit, did Temple instruct the Enron engagement team "to preserve documents, computer files and other information relating to Enron."[84]

In subsequent criminal proceedings against Andersen for obstructing the SEC investigation, prosecutors argued that Temple's "reminder" about the audit firm's document shredding policies encouraged destruction of materials relevant to that investigation. Andersen was convicted under 18 U.S.C. § 1512, which made it a crime to "knowingly ... corruptly persuad[e]" another person to withhold documents. The U.S. Supreme Court overturned that conviction because jury instructions did not require findings of the required degree of knowledge.[85] The influence of that holding is limited because, as noted earlier, Congress subsequently enacted a new prohibition on document destruction with somewhat different language. Section 1519 criminalizes destruction "in relation to or in contemplation of any matter," and is not limited to proceedings about to be instituted. Could Anderson have been prosecuted under that new prohibition?[86]

How would you evaluate Temple's conduct? Was it ethical? Was it prudent? Arthur Anderson, a $9 billion partnership in 2002, imploded after Enron and its parent company settled with Enron investors for $40 million.[87]

NOTES

Businesses are generating an increasing number of documents and government decision-makers are generating an increasing number of regulations concerning document retention. By 1980, the federal government

---

82. Andersen internal e-mail message from Nancy Temple to Michael C. Odom, Oct. 12, 2001, reprinted in Andersen Hearing, *supra* note 80, at 45.

83. Witt & Behr, *supra* note 81, at A1; Robert E. Hinerfeld, "A Broader View of Discovery Ethics: The Societal Context," *Professional Lawyer*, 35, 55 (2002).

84. Andersen internal e-mail memorandum from Nancy Temple to David Duncan, Nov. 10, 2001, reprinted in Andersen Hearing, *supra* note 80, at 63.

85. Arthur Andersen v. United States, 544 U.S. 696 (2005).

86. See Daniel K. Joseph, "Stop the Shredding: Document Retention after U.S. v. Anderson," *Professional Lawyer* 13 (2006).

87. Id., at 14, n. 4.

had over 1,300 statutes or regulations requiring retention of certain records for certain periods, and every state and most municipalities had comparable rules.[88] In order to ensure compliance with such requirements while minimizing costs, corporations and their counsel have focused greater attention on information retention policies.

Establishing a general retention program has multiple advantages. It can minimize the expense of storage and retrieval of documents, as well as reduce the legal risks from records that are erroneous, misleading, or inculpating. As one Washington, D.C. corporate litigator put it: "Paper kills and more paper kills more."[89] Document control programs speak to this problem by targeting entire categories of material for elimination once they reach a certain age to avoid the suggestion that any selective destruction occurred. Employees also receive counseling about the need to "think about how [something] would sound in court." If they "wouldn't care to explain it from the witness stand," they shouldn't write it.[90]

Yet such programs also have costs, including the administrative expenses of ensuring compliance; the difficulties of establishing facts once certain documents are destroyed; and the adverse inferences observers may draw from selective compliance with the program or destruction outside its boundaries. The situation has grown more complicated as organizations increasingly rely on electronic documents that are easily stored and hard to eliminate. The average computer can retain millions of pages of documents, and deletion is not necessarily final. Documents can continue to exist in other locations such as backup tapes, hard drives, other terminals in an organization's network, and attachments of emails saved by other users. The ease of creating and deleting documents has given individuals a false sense of security. They often "hit the trash button to delete things that they shouldn't have written" and that are retrievable in later legal proceedings.[91] Such human tendencies have led organizations to attempt to design systems that will more effectively delete inessential and potentially compromising documents, as well keep their information storage within manageable boundaries. Courts have recognized the legitimacy of those storage concerns, and in 2006, the Supreme Court approved an amendment to the Federal Rules of Civil Procedure. Rule 37(f) provides: "Absent exceptional circumstances, a court may not impose sanctions under these rules on a party for failing to provide electronically stored information lost as the result of the routine, good-faith operation of an electronic information system."

Attorneys often play a pivotal role in designing and administering such good faith information systems. Part of that role, as lawyers have increasingly recognized, is to provide counseling once litigation is pending or

88. John M. Fedders & Lauryn H. Guttenplan, "Document Retention and Destruction: Practical, Legal, and Ethical Considerations," 56 *Notre Dame Law.* 5, 8–9 (1980).

89. Michael Allen, "Cleaning House: U.S. Companies Pay Increasing Attention to Destroying Files," *Wall Street J.*, Sept. 2, 1987, at 1 (quoting Judah P. Best).

90. Goulden, *supra* note 78, at 292.

91. Jason Krause, "A Tangled Tale of Discovery," *ABA J.*, March 2007, at 37, 41 (quoting attorney Ted Meyer).

imminent about the retention of all the material clients wish hadn't been written. If particular employees may have motives to destroy particular documents, counsel should take immediate steps to ensure that those records are secure and that reliable individuals are in charge of storage and file searches. In many cases, pragmatic and ethical considerations point in similar directions; destruction that can be proven can also be disastrous. Compromising statements can often be explained; destruction removes that possibility. Moreover, as experienced litigators note, in an age of widespread photocopying and electronic transmission, it is usually "impossible to destroy all copies of documents. They inevitably show up."[92] Judges and juries are entitled to draw adverse inferences from destruction, and they sometimes impose stiff sanctions on clients and counsel who engage in such conduct.

Yet as the preceding discussion suggests, statutory prohibitions leave significant gaps. In some jurisdictions, destruction is legal if a proceeding is foreseeable but not pending. And lawyers who suspect but do not "know" that their client has engaged in illegal destruction may not reveal that fact. As the next excerpt explains, lawyers sometimes go to considerable lengths to avoid knowing whether their client has unlawfully destroyed incriminating evidence.

Kenneth Mann, Defending White Collar Crime: A Portrait of Attorneys at Work

103–07, 109–13, 117–18, 120–23 (1985).

Two possible goals related to information control motivate the attorney in his meetings with clients. The first goal is to obtain adequate information about the situation being investigated. . . . The second goal, which can exist only in conjunction with the first, is to keep the client from communicating too much information to the attorney, information that would interfere with his building a strong defense. . . . But many attorneys pursue the two goals simultaneously, encouraging disclosure of certain facts, discouraging disclosure of other facts. They want to extract all the information from the client that will facilitate good defense decisions: details about the potential charge, what the government might use to prove it, and what the "worst case" picture for the client looks like. But they also want clients to conceal from them information that is not essential to these ends and that either limits the attorney's ability to argue certain defenses or puts him in a difficult ethical position.

Some attorneys, for instance, discourage the disclosure of facts that would negate a defense of lack of knowledge. They would not want to find out that a client actually had knowledge of a fact that would prove criminal intent—knowledge of a report or the action of another person—if the government was also not going to find this out. The attorney can then more

---

92. Michael Orey, "Document Shredding Shows Importance Of Having a Policy on What Is Preserved," *Wall Street J.*, Jan. 14, 2002, at A6 (quoting Judith Best).

forcefully argue that the client did not know of the report or action. In other cases, attorneys prefer not to know that the client is continuing to commit the very crime that the government is investigating. In still other cases, clients commit new crimes aimed at obstructing the advancement of an investigation. Knowledge of these acts could raise the problem of deciding how to respond to an ethical precept that allows the attorney either to report the client to authorities or to cease representation in midcourse, both of which would undermine the client's chances of avoiding prosecution.

Defense attorneys know that they walk a narrow line between helping and hurting their case when they facilitate or allow a client to hide facts from the attorney himself. Not having knowledge of an inculpatory fact that the government discovers can completely destroy a defense attorney's argument, which is why some attorneys reject this approach. But of the attorneys I studied, most either said that they sometimes preferred not to get certain facts from a client or showed by their actions that they felt this way. . . .

Here is an archetype scenario of the attorney in the inquiry avoidance role: a subpoena is issued by a court calling for the client to produce all documents related to a certain transaction. Upon receipt, the client takes the subpoena to an attorney and asks, "How do I proceed?" In the characteristic case of avoidance, the attorney begins by explaining to the client what is called for by the subpoena and what significance certain types of documents would have for the course of the investigation. He will not blandly ask the client what documents currently exist but will explain to the client what the subpoena indicates about the subject and scope of the investigation. Some attorneys go one step further and explain to the client what kinds of documents could be used against the client "*if* they exist." . . .

An attorney who is avoiding inquiry will not ask, "Did such documents ever exist?" or "Was document X or document Y found?" His interaction with the client is likely to be limited to a narrower question: "Do you have anything to present in response to the subpoena?" . . . Another attorney was asked directly about the attorney-client relationship in IRS summons compliance procedures. He stated:

> There are many cases in which one would surmise that documents summoned from the client existed at the time the summons was issued. My function in this procedure is a very limited one. I, of course, do not want the client convicted of an obstruction of justice charge, and I do warn him of the dire consequences of such a happening. But in the end it is the client's choice. I have no doubt that clients destroy documents. Have I ever "known" of such an occurrence? No. But you put two and two together. You couldn't convict anyone on such circumstantial evidence, but you can draw your own conclusion.

Facilitation of Concealment

. . . A large number of respondents indicated that some clients make open proposals to destroy or manipulate evidence. One attorney stated the following:

When you have a client who's in a very bad bind and he's going to have to essentially convict himself by turning over bank records, or accountant records, or what have you, the client has a very strong impulse to do something about it, to save his own neck. From the client's point of view, there is not much to lose at that stage—he knows he's stuck if he doesn't do something. Occasionally, a client will say something like, "If I get rid of the records now, isn't it true that no one will know the difference?" . . . I don't say, "Look, I can't allow you to do that." That puts me in a one-up moral position and is most embarrassing for the client. I usually say something like, "The penalties are very severe, and it is true that it may turn up later and cause you more trouble, so I advise you not to do it." That makes it seem more like I'm helping him protect himself rather than demonstrating some kind of moral superiority. . . .

Justifications

. . . [M]any attorneys would not see effective—as opposed to intentional—facilitation of evidence destruction as a malfunction in the system of adversarial representation, even if it were in fact partially the consequence of the way attorneys handled their clients. Rather, it would be seen as the inevitable by-product of an adversarial system whose higher value requires that the attorney be able to maximize his zeal for his client's cause while minimizing, if not eliminating altogether, any law *enforcement* role on his part. Attorneys believed this strongly and were prepared to defend it vigorously. As one stated,

> It's my mission and obligation to defend the client, not to sit in moral, ethical, or legal judgment of him. I cannot join him in transgressing the law, but whatever he does of his own impetus, whatever way he conducts himself in attempting to protect himself, is a decision he has to make independent of what I do. I must inform him of the consequences and significance of his action but not punish him or sanction him or in other ways initiate law enforcement actions against him. My role in the adversary system is to protect him.

. . .

The underlying notion of an adversary system helps the attorney to cope with uneasiness he may have about specific actions he takes. The adversary system as a whole is assumed to serve the greater social good, even if some of its details do not appear so. Thus, if a rule mandates or permits a specific behavior—such as an attorney's answering questions posed by the clients as hypotheticals—that behavior is legitimate because it is part of a system that works. It is a deductive logic: if the system works, then the specific rules are right.

QUESTIONS

1. As Chapter V indicates, the standard justification for the attorney-client privilege and the duty of confidentiality stresses the obligation of

advocates to learn all the details of their clients' cases. To fulfill this obligation, attorneys must be able to reassure their clients that everything they reveal will remain confidential. But most of the lawyers that Mann interviewed do not want to learn all the details of their clients' cases. Is their "don't ask, don't tell" policy consistent with the justification for sweeping confidentiality protections?

2. Consider Mann's final observation concerning the world-view of white-collar defense lawyers. They justify a selective ignorance that undermines the effectiveness of the adversary system by arguing that such practices are "part of a system that works. It is a deductive logic: if the system works, then the specific rules are right." But don't those practices make the system work less well?

3. The federal obstruction of justice statute authorizes criminal penalties for: "whoever corruptly . . . endeavors to . . . impede any . . . officer in or of any court of the United states . . . in the discharge of his duty. . . ." 18 U.S.C. § 1503(a). It is well-settled that shredding incriminating documents in an ongoing investigation violates section 1503. Would it be permissible for an attorney to avoid knowledge of incriminating documents, but inform a client that if such documents exist, they would be very damaging? Could an attorney be liable as an accomplice of a client who then shreds the documents? Note that federal law punishes accomplices as principals. 18 U.S.C. § 2. Suppose that the client testifies that he shredded the documents only because his lawyer gave advice along the lines set forth in Problem 4(a)?

4. Are current ethical rules adequate to cope with these circumstances? Are there situations where civil and disciplinary sanctions are appropriate for attorneys who keep their "sharp eye[s] . . . demurely averted."[93] Should lawyers and clients face tort liability for "spoliation" of evidence: the intentional or negligent destruction of material "[known] to be essential to a civil action"?

5. Should bar disciplinary authorities automatically initiate investigations of attorneys who have been subject to discovery sanctions for document destruction? If the facts are as stated in Problem 4(b), should Nancy Temple be subject to sanctions?

6. Should lawyers be accountable for failing to make efforts to prevent document destruction? A growing number of courts and commentators have maintained that lawyers have such an affirmative responsibility.[94]

3. Witness Preparation

PROBLEM 5

You are representing defendants in a case involving a crucial witness from the West African country of Guinea. He has never participated in a

---

93. Marvin Frankel, "The Search for Truth: An Umpireal View," 123 *U. Penn. L. Rev.* 1031, 1035 (1975).

94. See Zubulake v. UBS Warburg LLC, 220 F.R.D. 212, 218 (S.D.N.Y. 2003); Joseph, *supra* note 86, at 17–197; Rhode & Paton, *supra* note 80.

legal proceeding before and is quite nervous. His English, although perfectly adequate, is heavily accented and unpleasant to listen to, a fact that worries you if the case goes to trial. When you prepare him for testifying, he gives cautious, heavily qualified, "two-handed" answers ("on the one hand . . .; on the other hand"). He frequently uses technical jargon which he cannot explain clearly, or even correctly (as you know from your own preparations for the case, which included carefully studying textbooks on the scientific issues). When you repeat questions, he occasionally gives different answers the second time around.

a) Can you tell him not to use technical terminology? Alternatively, can you tell him the correct definitions of technical concepts and rehearse him until he is able to explain them clearly?

b) Can you tell him that his cautious answers are no good? Can you tell him which of his ". . . on the other hands" to leave out because they are damaging? Can you explain the legal theory of the case to him so that he better understands why certain ways that he put things might be damaging? Can you propose alternative phrasings to him?

c) Can you insist that he testify through an interpreter?

d) After two hours of the trial preparation, the witness says in frustration and panic, "Just tell me what to say." How do you respond?

NOTES

One of the most common problems in criminal as well as civil trials, involves witness preparation, a practice forbidden in most countries. Marvin Frankel summarizes the process as follows:

> [t]he [adversary] contest by its very nature is not one in which the objective of either side, or of both together, is to expose "the truth, the whole truth, and nothing but the truth."
>
> That the quoted words, from the witness's oath, are not meant quite literally may be seen from more than one perspective. Consider the lawyer's major work of interviewing and "preparing" witnesses, including the client who plans to take the stand. . . . [E]very lawyer knows that the "preparing" of witnesses may embrace a multitude of other measures, including some ethical lapses believed to be more common than we would wish. . . . Whatever word is used to describe it, the process often extends beyond helping organize what the witness knows, and moves in the direction of helping the witness to know new things. At its starkest, the effort is called subornation of perjury, which is a crime, and which we are permitted to hope is rare. Somewhat less stark, short of criminality but still to be condemned, is the device of telling the client "the law" before eliciting the facts—i.e., telling the client what facts would constitute a successful claim or defense, and only then asking the client what the facts happen perchance to be. . . . [A famous] instance is fictional but apt: *Anatomy of a Murder,* a 1958 novel by Robert Traver, was an account by a pseudonymous state

supreme court justice of a murder defendant educated by his lawyer about a defense of impaired mental capacity and then, conveniently, but obviously not truthfully, recounting "facts" that fit the defense and won an acquittal. It is not unduly cynical to suspect that this, if not in such egregious forms, happens with some frequency.

Moving away from palpably unsavory manifestations, we all know that the preparation of our witnesses is calculated, one way and another, to mock the solemn promise of the whole truth and nothing but. To be sure, reputable lawyers admonish their clients and witnesses to be truthful. At the same time, they often take infinite pains to prepare questions designed to make certain that the controlled flow of truth does not swell to an embarrassing flood. "Don't volunteer anything," the witnesses are cautioned. The concern is not that the volunteered contribution may be false. The concern is to avoid an excess of truth, where the spillover may prove hurtful to the case....

The simple point to be stressed, here and throughout, is that many of us trained in the learned profession of the law spend much of our time subverting the law by blocking the way to the truth. The subversion is not for the most part viewed as a pathology; rather, if somewhat paradoxically, it follows from the assigned roles of counsel in the very system of law which thus finds its purposes thwarted.[95]

A longstanding dispute has centered on the technique, summarized by Mann and Frankel, of counseling the client about the law or about other witnesses' testimony before inquiring about the facts. Some commentators have defended the practice on the ground that:

it is not the lawyer's function to prejudge his client as a perjurer. He cannot presume that his client will make unlawful use of his advice ... [t]here is a natural predisposition in most people to recollect facts, entirely honestly, in a way most favorable to their own interest.... Before he begins to remember essential facts, the client is entitled to know what his own interests are ... [t]o decide otherwise would ... penalize the less well-educated defendant....[96]

Other commentators work from similar factual assumptions, but arrive at different conclusions. In their view, it is asking too much of human nature to provide a reason for lying and then ask for the truth. Advising the client about the law under circumstances that will tempt them to conceal documents or misrepresent facts is imprudent as well as unethical. It is "hard enough to get essential facts without supplying a motive to distort them."[97]

---

95. Marvin Frankel, *Partisan Justice* 16–17 (1980).

96. Monroe Freedman, "Professional Responsibility of the Criminal Defense Lawyer: The Three Hardest Questions," 64 *Mich. L. Rev.* 1469, 1479 (1966). Freedman subsequently changed his view and came to regard the practice as improper. Monroe H. Freed-

man, *Lawyers' Ethics in an Adversary System* 59–77 (1975). *See* also Jerold S. Solovy & Robert Byman, "What's Wrong With Witness Coaching?," *Nat'l L. J.*, August 2, 1999, at B19.

97. Anthony Amsterdam, "Lectures on Trial Practice," Stanford Law School, 1981.

Where should lawyers draw the line between helping individuals recollect and helping them revise reality? Preparing witnesses can assist as well as distort truth-finding processes; it can aid nervous, unsophisticated, or reticent individuals in making effective presentations and can facilitate careful choice of language. Skillful coaching can also bring about dramatic improvements. Witnesses can learn to avoid annoying mannerisms, suspicious hesitations, unduly technical language, and prejudicial phrasing. Such assistance will often make a material difference in the way fact-finders perceive a case. For example, in one study of perceptual biases, individuals who watched the same collision gave differing estimates of the speed of the vehicles depending on how the question described the impact: "smashed" (41 mph); "hit" (34 mph); "contacted" (32 mph).[98]

An interesting historical case study in the rationale and risks of witness preparation emerged in a 1986 *New York Law Journal* exchange on the seventy-fifth anniversary of the famous Triangle Shirtwaist factory fire. That disaster, in which 146 young, mostly immigrant women burned to death, became a turning point in the struggle for protective labor legislation. It also resulted in a celebrated criminal prosecution of the factory owners for violation of safety statutes. After poignant testimony from one of the victims, defense counsel requested her to repeat her narrative. When she provided an almost verbatim repetition, the lawyer asked about one word she had used in her first but not second account. After repeating the testimony silently to herself, moving her lips slightly in the process, the witness confirmed that she had erroneously omitted the word. After briefly changing the subject, counsel then repeated the strategy with similar results. The obviously rehearsed nature of the victim's testimony helped to undermine the credibility of the prosecution's case and to secure an acquittal. A *New York Law Journal* article commending the defense counsel's performance provoked an angry letter to the editor in response. Its authors noted that many women who testified in the case needed rehearsing; they spoke little or no English and were traumatized by the fire and court proceedings.[99]

Compare that case with the *Anatomy of a Murder* script. Should a lawyer ever start an inquiry by saying: "Before I ask about your recollection, let me tell you what another key witness recalls."? How would you distinguish appropriate and inappropriate counseling? What should the attorney have said in response to the client email quoted earlier about the likelihood of perjury prosecutions?[100] A preliminary draft of the Model Rules of Professional Conduct included a standard that would have prohibited lawyers from giving advice that they could "reasonably foresee will aid a client in giving false testimony." Would you favor adoption of such a rule?

98. Monroe Freedman, "Counseling the Client: Refreshing Recollection or Prompting Perjury?," 2 *Litigation* 35, 46 (1976).

99. Daniel J. Kornstein, "A Tragic Fire—A Great Cross–Exam," *N.Y.L.J.*, March 28, 1986, at 2; Ann Ruben & Emily Ruben, Letter to the Editor, reprinted in Stephen Gillers & Norman Dorsen, *Regulation of Lawyers: Problems of Law and Ethics* 492–496 (2d ed. 1989).

100. See text accompanying note 56 *supra.*

D. PROSECUTORIAL ETHICS

INTRODUCTION

Codes and commentary on prosecutorial ethics generally build on a shared premise. Prosecutors have a dual role as advocates and officers of justice; their obligation is to "seek justice, not merely to convict."[101] Yet what that mandate means and whether it can be given useful content are subject to considerable dispute. To some commentators, "seek justice" is an unhelpful cliché. It establishes no identifiable standards, and what prosecutor would admit to any other objective? As Justice Robert Jackson once put it, "the qualities of a good prosecutor are as elusive and as impossible to define as those which [mark] a gentleman. And those who need to be told would not understand it anyway."[102]

Yet many commentators also believe that the prosecutor's unique role imposes unique ethical responsibilities that can and should be enforced. These lawyers have exceptional power: they have full access to the coercive and investigatory resources of the government, but none of the accountability demanded by an identifiable client.[103] Because abuses that occur under color of law erode public confidence in the legal system, prosecutors' compliance with ethical standards is especially critical.

Such compliance is all the more important in light of the ineffectiveness of other review mechanisms. Formal oversight of prosecutorial conduct has often been minimal. Concerns about separation of powers, together with the absence of legal standards for assessing discretionary decisions have made courts reluctant to second guess many prosecutorial actions. Except in extreme cases, most judges have been equally unwilling to overturn convictions of guilty defendants in response to violations of ethical rules, typically on the ground that the violations are harmless errors.[104]

In theory, misconduct that does not rise to the level of constitutional violations should be addressed through professional disciplinary proceedings. In practice, such proceedings are rare. Surveys of cases reversed for prosecutorial misconduct find that none result in disciplinary sanctions.[105]

---

101. *See* Berger v. United States, 295 U.S. 78 (1935); ABA Standards Relating to the Administration of Criminal Justice 3–1.2(c) (3d ed. 1992). *See also* Model Rules, Rule 3.8 comment ("A prosecutor has the responsibility of a minister of justice and not simply that of an advocate."); Code of Professional Responsibility, EC 7–13 (1981).

102. Robert Jackson, "The Federal Prosecutor," 24 *J. Judicature Soc.* 18 (1940).

103. Angela J. Davis, *Arbitrary Justice: The Power of the American Prosecutor* (2007); Professional Responsibility, Report of the Joint Conference of the ABA and AALS, 41

ABA Journal, 1159 (1958). By contrast, some commentators argue that the distinctiveness of the prosecutor's role has been overstated. In their view, all lawyers occupy a dual role, but the standards to which they are subject sometimes strike a different balance. See Kevin McMunigal, "Are Prosecutorial Ethics Standards Different?," 88 *Fordham L. Rev.* 1453, 1472 (2000).

104. *See* Barry Scheck, Peter Neufeld, and John Dwyer, *supra* note 12, at 173.

105. Davis, *supra* note 103, at 128–29. In one study of 1,283 New York cases alleging prosecutorial misconduct, and 277 finding

Studies of bar disciplinary proceedings similarly find almost no cases involving prosecutors.[106] Defendants, defense counsel, or judges generally have few incentives to file complaints and bar enforcement agencies have few incentives to proceed on their own initiative. Lawyers and judges have little to gain from arousing a district attorney's ire, and prosecutorial immunity from civil liability discourages citizens' grievances. (Prosecutorial immunity from civil suits was established in *Imbler v. Pachtman*, 424 U.S. 409 (1976)). Clients who plead guilty are sometimes reluctant to reopen their cases after discovery of misconduct out of fear that they will be subject to additional charges and more severe sanctions on retrial. And bar disciplinary authorities facing substantial resource constraints have little reason to initiate disciplinary charges that are likely to be contentious, controversial, and costly to litigate.

Other remedies for prosecutorial misconduct are available, but seldom imposed. These include suppression of unethically-obtained evidence, dismissal of cases, or disqualification for conflicts of interest.[107] Political accountability is equally limited. Although state DAs are generally elected and U.S. attorneys are high-level political appointees, their subordinates are not. The vast majority of enforcement decisions are neither publicized nor memorable. Nor are most voters and politicians who control appointments adequately informed about the complex considerations underlying many enforcement practices. That is not to deny the influence of public opinion on some prosecutorial decisions. But where political considerations play a role, they often reinforce pressures to win cases at the expense of other values.[108]

reversible error, none resulted in discipline. "APR Panelists Examine Why Prosecutors Are Largely Ignored by Disciplinary Offices," 22 *ABA/BNA Lawyers' Manual on Professional Conduct* 90 (2006) (citing study by the Center for Public Integrity). In another survey of 381 homicide convictions that were reversed because of prosecutors' misconduct between 1963 and 1999, not one prosecutor was convicted or publicly sanctioned by bar disciplinary authorities. Only two were disciplined by their District Attorney's office and many were later promoted or appointed to the bench. Ken Armstrong and Maurice Possley, "The Verdict: Dishonor," *Chicago Tribune*, Jan. 10, 1999, at A1; Ken Armstrong and Maurice Possley, "Break Rules Be Promoted," *Chicago Tribune*, Jan. 14, 1999 at 1. See generally Adam Liptak, "Prosecutor Becomes Prosecuted," *N.Y. Times*, June 24, 2007, at E4.

106. Bruce Gordon and the Center for Public Integrity, Misconduct and Punishment: State Disciplinary Authorities Investigate Prosecutors Accused of Misconduct (2003), available at www.publicintegrity.org (finding only 44 cases of prosecutorial discipline since 1970); Fred Zacharias, "The Professional Discipline of Prosecutors," 79 *North*

Car. L. Rev. 721 (2001) (finding only about one hundred reported cases of disciplinary action against prosecutors in the last century); Mike Zapler, "State Bar Ignores Errant Lawyers," *San Jose Mercury News*, Feb. 12, 2006, at A1 (finding only one out of 1500 California bar disciplinary actions over 5 years involving prosecutorial misconduct); Ellen Yaroshefsky, "Wrongful Conviction: It Is Time to Take Prosecutorial Discipline Seriously," 8 *U.D.C. L. Rev.* 275 (2004) (describing failures of Department of Justice and judicial oversight structures).

107. *See* e.g., U.S. v. Hammad, 858 F.2d 834 (2d Cir.1988) (suppression); U.S. v. Kojayan, 8 F.3d 1315 (9th Cir.1993) (dismissed); Turbin v. Arizona Superior Court, 797 P.2d 734 (Ariz. App.1990) (conflict). But *see* U.S. v. Williams, 504 U.S. 36 (1992) (dismissal inappropriate remedy when prosecutor does not disclose exculpatory material to grand jury).

108. Stanley J. Fisher, "In Search of the Virtuous Prosecutor: A Conceptual Framework," 15 *Am. J. Criminal Law* 197, 205 (1988); Robert L. Gershman, "The Prosecutor's Duty to Truth," 14 *Geo. J. Legal Ethics* 309, 350 (2001).

These pressures arise from multiple sources. For most prosecutors, conviction records are the most tangible measure of status and success; acquittals are often taken as evidence of incompetence or overzealousness. Law enforcement agents and victims of crime often serve as surrogate clients—their concerns are more immediately felt than those of defendants and their families. Many prosecutors are relatively young, inexperienced, and ambitious, which makes them particularly vulnerable to competitive pressures. All too often, winning—or at least not losing—can become the preeminent value.[109] Particularly in well-publicized cases, a desire to secure convictions can lead to unconscious bias; even well-intentioned prosecutors may suppress doubts or undervalue exculpatory evidence.[110]

When serving as Attorney General, Richard Thornburgh described a common view among attorneys holding law enforcement positions:

> You're putting bad guys in jail. You're trying to get every edge you can on those people who are devising increasingly more intricate schemes to rip off the public, hiring the best lawyers, providing the best defenses.
>
> So you're constantly pushing the edge of the envelope out to see if you can get an edge for the prosecution . . . not to abolish constitutional rights, but to give the law enforcement officer an even break.[111]

Is that an appropriate description of the prosecutorial role? Consider that issue in light of the problems that follow.

1.   PROSECUTORIAL DISCRETION

PROBLEM 6

You are the elected district attorney in a Southwestern state capital. A disgruntled former employee of your city comptroller comes to you with allegations that his employer has overlooked certain irregularities in financial dealings with major campaign contributors. The employee also claims to have attended several small gatherings at which the comptroller used

---

109. Uviller, *supra* note 46, at 57; Robert L. Misner, "Recasting Prosecutorial Discretion," 86 Crim. L. and Crim. 717, 720 (1996); Kenneth Bresler, "I Never Lost a Trial," 9 *Geo. J. Legal Ethics* 537 (1996).

110. Susan Bandes, "Loyalty to One's Convictions: The Prosecutor and Tunnel Vision," 49 *Howard L. Rev.* 475 (2006); Alafair Burke, "Improving Prosecutorial Decision Making: Some Lessons of Cognitive Science," 47 *Wm & Mary L. Rev.* 1587 (2006). For an egregious example of a prosecutor's suppression of evidence to secure a desired conviction in the heavily publicized rape case involving Duke lacrosse players, see the text accompanying notes 116 and 162 *infra*. For discussion of the general problem, see Evan P. Gold-

stein, "The Power of the Prosecutor," *Chron. Higher Ed.*, May 11, 2007, and Liptak, *supra* note 105.

111. Jim McGee, "War on Crime Expands U.S. Prosecutor's Powers: Aggressive Tactics Put Fairness at Issue," *Wash. Post*, Jan. 10, 1993, at A1, 36. In the mid 1990s, in an effort to counteract abuses that may accompany such objectives, the Justice Department launched a major new ethics policy board and training program for federal prosecutors. For evaluations, *see* Fred C. Zacharias & Bruce A. Green, "The Uniqueness of Federal Prosecutors," 88 *Geo. L.J.* 207, 238–39 (2000) and "Regulating Federal Prosecutors' Ethics," 55 *Vand. L. Rev.* 381 (2002).

cocaine. A disagreement over the employee's promotion motivated him to come forward with public charges.

After some investigation, you believe that the comptroller has knowingly ignored financial improprieties but you have no direct evidence that he did so in exchange for campaign support. You also learn, as a result of unlawful (and, therefore, inadmissible) wiretap recordings, that the comptroller has had frequent contact with suspected drug dealers, and that he is aware of more serious financial misconduct by other public officials.

QUESTIONS

1.   Can you file charges of financial mismanagement against the comptroller and threaten to bring charges of drug use if he does not plead guilty? Could you also demand that he resign from office in return for your dropping charges? Alternatively, may you call the comptroller to testify before the grand jury in the hope that if he does not provide useful information, he will commit perjury and enable you to use the threat of a perjury prosecution to compel his cooperation in a broader investigation?

2.   Assume that before you take action concerning the comptroller, several of your assistant prosecutors advise you not to file charges. As they note, the comptroller is the first African–American to hold that office and is one of your city's only high-ranking non-white politicians. Filing a case without proof beyond a reasonable doubt may deprive the black community of an important role model, invite charges of racism, and compromise the office's efforts to recruit more attorneys of color. Needless to say, claims of racial bias would scarcely further your own political career.

In making your decision to prosecute, can you consider—or avoid considering—such factors? Are your personal attitudes toward occasional drug use relevant? Would it matter that your understaffed office has an informal policy of not prosecuting occasional drug users who have no prior criminal record?

3.   Assume that you have filed charges for financial misconduct. While plea negotiations are in progress, you learn that the disgruntled employee, your leading witness, has a history of psychiatric treatment for depression. That history is unknown to the defendant, but could be relevant to a jury if the case proceeds to trial. Are you obligated to disclose the employee's treatment to the defendant? Must you reveal evidence that the employee has used a racial epithet to describe the comptroller? Does it matter whether your own confidence in the witness's credibility remains unshaken? Should you advise the witness that he need not speak with the defendant's investigators, and that any statement he makes could be used for impeachment at trial?

4.   Suppose that the defendant refuses to consider a plea and that his lawyer releases a statement denouncing the charges as politically and racially motivated. May you respond by detailing the facts that led to your decision, including the allegations of drug use? Can you assert that the

evidence demonstrates a "slam dunk" case of improprieties? Suppose that you do not disclose the drug use but the press reports it and attributes the information to an unnamed source in your office. How should you respond?

5. If you decide to proceed against the comptroller, should racial considerations affect any of your decisions, such as where to file charges, who should try the case, how to select the jury, and what to advise your lead witness? If, in your experience, young non-white males are least likely to convict defendants for drug offenses, may that fact influence any of your strategic decisions?

PROBLEM 7

Consider the following conduct. Which actions are impermissible under existing standards? Which actions should be impermissible? What should be the appropriate sanctions?

a) A local district attorney's office has a policy of not filing rape charges where the victim and accused are acquainted unless there is substantial corroborating evidence. Although the state's recent rape reform legislation eliminated corroboration requirements as a precondition of conviction, many prosecutors' offices have declined to proceed without such evidence because of juror skepticism.

b) Where unable to obtain sufficient evidence to convict certain labor leaders for suspected corruption, the Department of Justice has successfully prosecuted them for income tax violations. Some of those leaders had previously been critical of administration policy in general and the Attorney General in particular. Other federal prosecutors have reviewed tax records and international adoption proceedings of witnesses and their families in an effort to discover legal offenses, which might then pressure targeted individuals to cooperate with government investigations.[112]

c) A prosecutor receives a sexual assault complaint by a young African–American woman. She claims that she was raped by several white members of a university lacrosse team that had asked her to perform as a stripper. Several of the university's athletic teams have a record of alcohol-related offenses, and town-gown relations have been complicated by class and racial tensions. The woman has a history of drug, alcohol, and mental health difficulties, and gives inconsistent accounts of the number of assailants. Although she is unable to identify assailants from two lineups, she does make a positive identification of three players from pictures of those present at the party. However that photo spread did not conform to accepted practice because it included no other pictures that might have produced a false identification. One of the players whom the woman identifies has photographic and telephone records that place him elsewhere. DNA tests on the woman's underwear show traces of semen and other

---

112. Deborah L. Rhode, "Conflicts of Commitment: Legal Ethics in the Impeachment Context," 52 *Stan. L. Rev.* 269, 335–38 (2000) (describing pressure that the Independent Counsel placed on women who had ex-perienced sexual advances from then President William Clinton); Monroe Freedman, "Professional Responsibility of the Criminal Defense Lawyer: The Three Hardest Questions," 64 *Mich. L Rev.* 146 (1966).

material that fail to match any of the lacrosse players. The prosecutor is facing a difficult election campaign, in which support from the African–American community will be critical. He maintains that as long as the woman says " 'yes, it's them,' I have an obligation to put that to the jury."[113]

PROBLEM 8

You are a prosecutor in a large city. You must currently decide which (if either) of two suspects to charge in the brutal killing of a police officer. The facts are as follows.

Shortly after midnight on the night of the killing, police officers Robert Wood and Teresa Turko pulled over an automobile to tell the driver that his lights were off. Wood and Turko were unaware that the car had been stolen a few days earlier by 16–year–old David Harris. When Wood reached the car, its driver shot him dead and sped off. Officer Turko was unable to get its license number or to describe the driver.

Harris was arrested a month later after boasting to friends that he had been involved in the highly-publicized murder. He acknowledged having stolen the car, and directed the police to the murder weapon—a .22 caliber pistol that he had stolen from his father and concealed in a bayou that washed off any fingerprints.

However, Harris denied having committed the murder. He accused a 28–year–old drifter named Randall Adams. According to Harris, he had picked up Adams hitchhiking and they had spent the day together. They had gotten a bite to eat, drunk a few beers, smoked some marijuana, and watched some pornographic movies. Harris said that Adams was driving the car when the police officers pulled them over; Harris, who knew that the car was stolen, slumped down in the seat to avoid being seen. Next, he said, Adams reached under the seat to where he had seen a pistol, grabbed it, and killed Officer Wood. On Harris's account, they parted at Adams's motel, with Adams telling Harris to forget all about what had happened.

Adams's story corroborates Harris's up to a point, but only up to a point. According to Adams, after the food, marijuana, and movies, he returned to his motel at 10 P.M. and watched television for the rest of the night with his brother. The brother corroborates this, but the two have different recollections of what they watched that night. Adams's brother has stated that he does not wish to testify. Adams has no criminal record, while Harris has a lengthy juvenile record. Both seem sincere, and Harris is

---

113. Bennett L. Gershman & Joel Cohen, "No Gatekeeper of Justice," *National L. J.*, Feb. 19, 2007, at A22 (quoting Michael Nifong, the prosecutor in the rape case involving Duke lacrosse players). See also Duff Wilson, "More Ethics Charges Brought Against Official in Duke Case," *N.Y. Times*, Jan. 25, 2007, at A14 (discussing Nifong's claim that the DNA evidence that showed no matches with the accused defendants was not important to disclose because he was not pursuing the case on the basis of DNA evidence). For critical accounts of the prosecutors conduct, see Stuart Taylor, Jr., and KC Johnson, *Until Proven Innocent* (2007); Robert P. Mosteller, "The Duke Lacrosse Case, Innocence, and False Identifications: A Fundamental Failure to "Do Justice," 76 *Fordham L. Rev.* 1337 (2007).

an appealing youth whom you believe will make a sympathetic impression on a jury.

The case has attracted considerable public attention, in part because the murder was unsolved for a month and in part because of its sheer cold-bloodedness. The public reaction strongly favors the death penalty for the killer; however, your state does not permit the death penalty for 16–year–olds.

How do you proceed? According to ABA Standard 3–3.9(a), (below), do you have sufficient evidence to charge Harris? Adams? If you believe that the evidence is sufficient to charge either one, whom do you charge for Wood's killing? If you do not believe the evidence is sufficient, how do you explain to the media and the public that you have released both men despite the fact that one of them almost certainly killed Officer Wood?

How convinced of guilt do you have to be to charge one of the two? Can considerations of whom you think a jury would be more willing to convict enter into your decision? If you charge Adams, how certain must you be of his guilt to seek the death penalty?[114]

American Bar Association Standards Relating to the Administration of Criminal Justice, The Prosecution Function

(1992).

Standard 3–1.2 The Function of the Prosecutor

(a) The office of prosecutor is charged with responsibility for prosecutions in its jurisdiction.

(b) The prosecutor is an administrator of justice, an advocate, and an officer of the court; the prosecutor must exercise sound discretion in the performance of his or her functions.

(c) The duty of the prosecutor is to seek justice, not merely to convict. . . .

(e) It is the duty of the prosecutor to know and be guided by the standards of professional conduct as defined by applicable professional traditions, ethical codes, and law in the prosecutor's jurisdiction. . . .

Standard 3–1.4 Public Statements

(a) A prosecutor should not make or authorize the making of an extrajudicial statement that a reasonable person would expect to be disseminated by means of public communication if the prosecutor knows or reasonably should know that it will have a substantial likelihood of prejudicing a criminal proceeding.

---

114. This problem is adapted from Errol Morris's 1988 documentary film *The Thin Blue Line*.

(b) A prosecutor should exercise reasonable care to prevent investigators, law enforcement personnel, employees or other persons assisting or associated with the prosecutor from making an extrajudicial statement that the prosecutor would be prohibited from making under this standard.

Standard 3–3.1 Investigative Function of Prosecutor

(b) A prosecutor should not invidiously discriminate against or in favor of any person on the basis of race, religion, sex, sexual preference, or ethnicity in exercising discretion to investigate or to prosecute. A prosecutor should not use other improper considerations in exercising such discretion.

Standard 3–3.6 Quality and Scope of Evidence Before Grand Jury

(a) A prosecutor should only make statements or arguments to the grand jury and only present evidence to the grand jury which the prosecutor believes is appropriate or authorized under law for presentation to the grand jury. In appropriate cases, the prosecutor may present witnesses to summarize admissible evidence available to the prosecutor which the prosecutor believes he or she will be able to present at trial. The prosecutor should also inform the grand jurors that they have the right to hear any available witnesses, including eyewitnesses.

(b) No prosecutor should knowingly fail to disclose to the grand jury evidence which tends to negate guilt or mitigate the offense.

(c) A prosecutor should recommend that the grand jury not indict if he or she believes the evidence presented does not warrant an indictment under governing law.

(d) If the prosecutor believes that a witness is a potential defendant, the prosecutor should not seek to compel the witness's testimony before the grand jury without informing the witness that he or she may be charged and that the witness should seek independent legal advice concerning his or her rights.

(e) The prosecutor should not compel the appearance of a witness before the grand jury whose activities are the subject of the inquiry if the witness states in advance that if called he or she will exercise the constitutional privilege not to testify, unless the prosecutor intends to judicially challenge the exercise of the privilege or to seek a grant of immunity according to the law.

Standard 3–3.9 Discretion in the Charging Decision

(a) A prosecutor should not institute, or cause to be instituted, or permit the continued pendency of criminal charges when the prosecutor knows that the charges are not supported by probable cause. A prosecutor should not institute, cause to be instituted, or permit the continued pendency of criminal charges in the absence of sufficient admissible evidence to support a conviction.

(b) The prosecutor is not obliged to present all charges which the evidence might support. The prosecutor may in some circumstances and for good cause consistent with the public interest decline to prosecute, notwithstanding that sufficient evidence may exist which would support a conviction. Illustrative of the factors which the prosecutor may properly consider in exercising his or her discretion are:

(i) the prosecutor's reasonable doubt that the accused is in fact guilty;

(ii) the extent of the harm caused by the offense;

(iii) the disproportion of the authorized punishment in relation to the particular offense or the offender;

(iv) possible improper motives of a complainant;

(v) reluctance of the victim to testify;

(vi) cooperation of the accused in the apprehension or conviction of others; and

(vii) availability and likelihood of prosecution by another jurisdiction....

(d) In making the decision to prosecute, the prosecutor should give no weight to the personal or political advantages or disadvantages which might be involved or to a desire to enhance his or her record of convictions....

(f) The prosecutor should not bring or seek charges greater in number or degree than can reasonably be supported with evidence at trial or than are necessary to fairly reflect the gravity of the offense.

Standard 3–3.11 Disclosure of Evidence by the Prosecutor

(a) A prosecutor should not intentionally fail to make timely disclosure to the defense, at the earliest feasible opportunity, of the existence of all evidence or information which tends to negate the guilt of the accused or mitigate the offense charged or which would tend to reduce the punishment of the accused.

(b) A prosecutor should not fail to make a reasonably diligent effort to comply with a legally proper discovery request.

(c) A prosecutor should not intentionally avoid pursuit of evidence because he or she believes it will damage the prosecution's case or aid the accused.

PART IV. PLEA DISCUSSIONS

Standard 3–4.1 Availability for Plea Discussions

(c) A prosecutor should not knowingly make false statements or representations as to fact or law in the course of plea discussions with defense counsel or the accused.

Standard 3–5.7 Examination of Witnesses

(a) The interrogation of all witnesses should be conducted fairly, objectively, and with due regard for the dignity and legitimate privacy of the witness, and without seeking to intimidate or humiliate the witness unnecessarily.

(b) The prosecutor's belief that the witness is telling the truth does not preclude cross-examination, but may affect the method and scope of cross-examination. A prosecutor should not use the power of cross-examination to discredit or undermine a witness if the prosecutor knows the witness is testifying truthfully.

(c) A prosecutor should not call a witness in the presence of the jury who the prosecutor knows will claim a valid privilege not to testify.

(d) A prosecutor should not ask a question which implies the existence of a factual predicate for which a good faith belief is lacking.

Standard 3–5.8 Argument to the Jury

(a) In closing argument to the jury, the prosecutor may argue all reasonable inferences from evidence in the record. The prosecutor should not intentionally misstate the evidence or mislead the jury as to the inferences it may draw.

(b) The prosecutor should not express his or her personal belief or opinion as to the truth or falsity of any testimony or evidence or the guilt of the defendant.

(c) The prosecutor should not make arguments calculated to appeal to the prejudices of the jury.

(d) The prosecutor should refrain from argument which would divert the jury from its duty to decide the case on the evidence.

Standard 3–5.9 Facts Outside the Record

The prosecutor should not intentionally refer to or argue on the basis of facts outside the record whether at trial or on appeal, unless such facts are matters of common public knowledge based on ordinary human experience or matters of which the court may take judicial notice.

Standard 3–5.10 Comments by Prosecutor After Verdict

The prosecutor should not make public comments critical of a verdict, whether rendered by judge or jury.

PART VI. SENTENCING

Standard 3–6.1 Role in Sentencing

(a) The prosecutor should not make the severity of sentences the index of his or her effectiveness. To the extent that the prosecutor becomes involved in the sentencing process, he or she should seek to assure that a fair and informed judgment is made on the sentence and to avoid unfair sentence disparities.

Standard 3–6.2 Information Relevant to Sentencing

(b) The prosecutor should disclose to the defense and to the court at or prior to the sentencing proceeding all unprivileged mitigating information known to the prosecutor, except when the prosecutor is relieved of this responsibility by a protective order of the tribunal.

H. Richard Uviller, "The Virtuous Prosecutor in Quest of an Ethical Standard: Guidance from the ABA"

71 University of Michigan Law Review 1145, 1145–1156 (1973).

I.   Selective Prosecution and Differential Justice

At first encounter, the widely supported brief for uniformity in the enforcement of the criminal laws appears to need little argumentation. To most, the proposition "Equal justice under law," chiselled on the courthouse pediment, is both elegant and self-evident. Indeed, this slogan expresses for many the quintessence of the American system of justice. Yet, the phrase is fundamentally deceptive. While wide or irrational disparities in treatment are deplorable, equality in the sense of uniformity in result is neither the fact nor the ideal in the system of justice. A given piece of human behaviour, described grossly by statute as a crime, does not and should not generate an automatic and standardized response from police, juries, or judges. Nor should we expect an undiscriminated prosecutorial reflex.... Professor Monroe H. Freedman ... uses a blunter instrument to probe prosecutorial ethics. He attacks ... the prosecutor who singles out a target for determined prosecution. Citing Al Capone and James Hoffa as the victims of overzealous prosecution, he decries "prosecutions that are directed at individuals rather than at crimes."

The ethical standard so casually suggested by Professor Freedman is somewhat baffling. What does he mean by a prosecution directed against an individual? Does he mean that in deciding where to investigate or how vigorously to prosecute, the district attorney should have no regard for the personal characteristics of the actual or potential defendant? Surely, he does not argue that in deciding on the acceptability of a lesser plea, the prosecutor should pay no heed to whether the offender is a novice or a seasoned professional, treating all cases alike according to the deed that was done. But if the prosecutor may ethically take the background or reputation of the defendant into consideration in electing an appropriate disposition, why not in fixing his investigative sights? ...

I recognize the significance of my disparagement of objective consequences. Unequal results are unequal regardless of the motivation of the official who achieved them. But if Robert Kennedy, as Attorney General, was convinced that the Teamsters Union, and Hoffa in particular, was destructive to trade unionism and a powerful, dangerous, and gangster-ridden force in the economy of the nation, would not his pursuit of Hoffa seem more ethical than if (as Freedman hypothesizes) Kennedy resolved to imprison Hoffa in revenge for a trivial personal insult and brought the armies of the Justice Department against him on that account?[115] The prosecutor who senses the outrage of his constituency against the aggressive and unsightly hordes of prostitutes infesting the streets may ethically respond by stricter application of valid laws against prostitution. More questionable, it seems to me, is the same campaign waged by the prosecutor as self-appointed custodian of community morality, impelled by personal distaste generated by his own values. I do not suggest that the honorable prosecutor be the slave of his electorate. Indeed, in many matters his duty clearly lies in the defiance of community pressures. But, within the confines of law, I would rather see his discretion guided by an honest effort to discern public needs and community concerns than by personal pique or moralistic impertinence. . . .

While [the current] ABA standard 3.9(a) condemns in its strongest terms the prosecutor who institutes or causes to be instituted criminal charges when he knows them to be unsupported by "probable cause," paragraph (b)(i) of the same standard suggests that the prosecutor may decline to prosecute a case when he himself entertains a "reasonable doubt that the accused is in fact guilty." . . . Read together, then, the trio of provisions sounds like this: The prosecutor *must* abjure prosecution without probable cause, *should* refuse to charge without a durable prima facie case, and *may* decline to proceed if the evidence fails to satisfy him beyond a reasonable doubt.

The interesting part of the standard is the suggestion that if the prosecutor, imagining himself in the seat of a juror, would not vote for a verdict of guilty, he may decline to present the matter to the system's designated fact finder. I have heard prosecutors, as a matter of personal conscience, take this notion as an ethical imperative. "I never try a defendant," so runs the credo, "unless I am personally convinced of his guilt beyond a reasonable doubt." Or, for some: "beyond any doubt." Realistically, the prosecutor figures that, inflamed by the brutal facts of the crime or for some other reason, the jury may overlook the basis for the doubt which nags his own judgment. And he could not sleep at night having contributed to the conviction of a man who might just possibly be innocent. Of course, in reaching this extra-judicial judgment, the prosecutor will allow himself to consider relevant items which might be excluded from trial evidence. Nor would his refusal to prosecute the case necessarily mean he would decline to recommend the acceptance of a guilty plea, for the confession which normally accompanies the plea may remove the prosecutor's doubt.

Yet withal, the prosecutor's conscientious stand represents a notable modification of our system of determining truth and adjudicating guilt. At

---

115. [Editors' note: The author is referring to Jimmy Hoffa, who headed the union in the 1960s and was widely reported to have ties with organized crime, not to one of his successors as Teamster President, James Hoffa, Jr.]

the least it creates a new subtrial, informal and often ex parte, interposed between the determinations of the accusing and judging authorities.

Can there be any objection to the prosecutor's transformation of the standard's "may" into a personal "must"? A defendant, of course, can only benefit from this additional safety procedure, and its adoption may move the prosecutor to more diligent and painstaking pretrial investigation, including an open-minded search for persuasive defense evidence. This latter effort comports nicely with the familiar injunction duly intoned by standard 1.1(c): "The duty of the prosecutor is to seek justice, not merely to convict." From these features it may appear that the standards should have placed this burden of internal persuasion on the prosecutor in every case. I think not.

A concrete, commonplace example may illustrate the operation of the precept and flesh out our appraisal of its wisdom. Practitioners know too well a sticky item: the one-eye-witness-identification case. For instance, an elderly white person is suddenly grabbed from behind in a dimly lit vestibule by a black youth who shows a knife and takes the victim's wallet. The entire incident occupies thirty seconds. Some days later, the victim spots the defendant in the neighborhood and has him arrested by the nearest policeman. Although the prosecutor presses him hard, the victim swears he has picked the right man. There is nothing unusual about the defendant's appearance, the victim never saw him before the crime, and he admits he does not know many blacks personally, but his certainty cannot be shaken. He insists that in those few moments of terror his attacker's face was "indelibly engraved on his memory." The defendant may have an alibi: his mother will testify that at the time of the crime he was at home watching television with her (not evidence readily credited). And that is the entire case.

Many prosecutors, I think, would concede that as jurors they would hesitate to vote "guilty" on this evidence. His sincerity unmistakable, the victim might well be correct in his identification of the defendant; perhaps it is more likely than not that the defendant is the perpetrator. And juries regularly convict in such cases. But since he knows the fallibility of identification under such circumstances, the basis for reasonable doubt is clear to the prosecutor.

Should the ethical prosecutor refuse to put this sort of evidence before the jury, withhold from the regular fact-finding process the opportunity to decide the issue? Indeed, should the conscientious prosecutor set himself the arduous task of deciding whether in this instance the complainant is right? If it is his duty to do so, how does he rationally reach a conclusion? For this purpose, are his mental processes superior to the jurors' or the judge's? Or may he—should he—abstain from prejudging the case and simply pass the responsibility to those who cannot escape it?

[Let us consider how this standard would apply to a common problem]. The defendant, let us assume, is charged with the illegal possession of a quantity of narcotics. There is little doubt of his guilt; indeed, he is ready to plead guilty. However, he claims that the drug was obtained by an illegal search of his automobile and should therefore be suppressed. The police officer insists that he retrieved the bag of drugs after the defendant abandoned it by throwing it from the window of the vehicle at the officer's approach. Now, the prosecutor knows that some drug carriers do try to divest themselves of the contraband when approached by police, but he also knows that many police seek to escape the strictures of the exclusionary rule by reciting an abandonment to cover an illegal search and seizure. Despite his general suspicion, however, the prosecutor has no reason to believe that the case in question is based on false testimony. Moreover, he has every reason to believe that on the ultimate issue of the defendant's guilt, justice will be done. What is his ethical course?

I confess I have no clear release from the prosecutor's predicament. I recognize as laudable the taking of one more precaution to avert the horror of convicting an innocent person. Yet, on balance, I do not believe the prosecutor must—or should—decide to proceed only in those cases where he, as a fact finder, would resolve the issue for the prosecution.

Where the prosecutor, from all he knows of the case, believes that there is a substantial likelihood that the defendant is innocent of the charge, he should, of course, not prosecute. Similarly, if he has good reason to believe that a witness is lying about a material fact, he should not put the witness on the stand, and if his case falls without the witness' testimony he should dismiss it regardless of whether inadmissible evidence persuades him of the culpability of the defendant. Short of these grounds for declining prosecution on the merits, I deem the ethical obligations of the prosecutor satisfied if he makes known to the court, or the defense, discovered adverse evidence and defects of credibility in witnesses.

Thus, when the issue stands in equipoise in his own mind, when he is honestly unable to judge where the truth of the matter lies, I see no flaw in the conduct of the prosecutor who fairly lays the matter before the judge or jury. . . . Although the prosecutor's discretionary powers may be important, and his detached and honorable presence vital, he is not, after all, the sole repository of justice. Thus, I do not believe that the system is served by canons which overplay the prosecutor's "quasi-judicial" role. He is, let us remember, an advocate as well as a minister of public justice.

NOTES AND QUESTIONS

Two areas of greatest prosecutorial power involve the choice of targets for investigation and offenses to charge. Unlike other countries, in which the state is expected to file indictments for every felony supported by sufficient evidence, American prosecutors have substantial discretion in selecting cases to pursue and do not bring charges in a majority of potential felony proceedings. Principal reasons for non-prosecution include insufficient admissible evidence, the unavailability of parties, the appropriateness of alternative remedies, the characteristics of defendants, the insignificance of the offense, and resource constraints.

The Decision to Charge

Consider Problems 6 through 8, and Uviller's hypotheticals, in light of the standards set forth in Model Rule 3.8, DR 7–103, ABA Standard 3–3.9 and the following principles for federal prosecution adopted by the Justice Department.

Section 9–27–230 Initiating and Declining Charges–Substantial Federal Interest

1.   In determining whether prosecution should be declined because no substantial federal interest would be served by prosecution, the attorney for the government should weigh all relevant considerations, including:

(1) Federal law enforcement priorities;

(2) The nature and seriousness of the offense;

(3) The deterrent effect of prosecution;

(4) The person's culpability in connection with the offense;

(5) The person's history with respect to criminal activity;

(6) The person's willingness to cooperate in the investigation or prosecution of others; and

(7) The probable sentence or other consequences if the person is convicted.[116]

In 2003, then Attorney General John Ashcroft issued a memorandum with revised guidelines on charging.

Section 9–27 300 Selecting Charges–Charging Most Serious Offense

1.   ... Once the decision to prosecute has been made, the attorney for the government should charge, or should recommend that the grand jury charge, the most serious offense that is consistent with the nature of the defendant's conduct, and that is likely to result in a sustainable conviction....

2.   However, a faithful and honest application of the Sentencing Guidelines is not incompatible with selecting charges or entering into plea agreements on the basis of an individualized assessment of the extent to which particular charges fit the specific circumstances of the case, are consistent with the purposes of the Federal criminal code, and maximize the impact of Federal resources on crime.... [i]t is appropriate that the attorney for the government consider.... whether the penalty yielded.... is proportional to the seriousness of the defendant's conduct and whether the charge achieves such purposes of the criminal law as punishment, protection of the public, specific and general deterrence, and rehabilitation.[117]

116. United States Department of Justice, Section 9–27.230, Principles of Federal Prosecution (Sept. 1997).

117. Memorandum from Attorney General John Ashcroft, to all Federal Prosecutors 2 (September 22, 2003, available at http://

The commentary to this principle adds that charges "should not be filed simply to exert leverage to induce a plea, nor should charges be abandoned in an effort to arrive a bargain that fails to reflect the seriousness of the defendant's conduct." Rather, the principle "provides the framework for ensuring equal justice in the prosecution of Federal criminal offenders. It guarantees that every defendant will start from the same position, charged with the most serious criminal act he/she commits...."

QUESTIONS

1.   On the facts in Problems 6–8, how much evidence of guilt should the district attorney demand before filing charges? Notice that bar ethical rules and the ABA Standards require, at a minimum, probable cause. Should prosecutors require more? Some commentators agree with Uviller that prosecutors who insist on proof beyond a reasonable doubt usurp the functions of the judge and jury. In response, critics point out that in 90 percent of all cases, such functions are already displaced through plea bargaining; anything short of a beyond-a-reasonable-doubt standard for cases that do not go to trial thus creates the risk that an innocent person will suffer criminal penalties. Even in cases that do go to trial, it is doubtful that juries will be more accurate than prosecutors in assessing reasonable doubt. Empirical research suggests that jurors can readily be influenced by a range of non-evidentiary, prejudicial factors, and often lack access to inadmissible but highly probative information that is available to the government.[118]

The costs of pursuing questionable cases are substantial. In two-thirds of the death penalty cases in which defendants have recently been exonerated by DNA evidence, misconduct by the police or prosecutors played a role.[119] In most of these cases, prosecutors had actual knowledge of undisclosed exculpatory evidence or reason to suspect the information provided by law enforcement officials. So too, other investigations of misconduct have found substantial evidence of convictions based on perjury, fabricated evidence, suggestive identification procedures, dishonest jailhouse informants, biased experts, and misuse of scientific data.[120] Would ethical standards that required prosecutors to be convinced beyond a reasonable doubt help prevent such wrongful convictions? Or would other strategies be more productive, such as ethical code provisions or formal policies requiring

www.usdoj.gov/usao/eousa/foia_reading_room/usam/title9/27mcrm.htm)

118. Gershman, *supra* note 108, at 340–341.

119. Scheck, Neufeld, & Dwyer *supra* note 12, at 175.

120. Erwin Chemerinsky, "The Role of Prosecutors in Dealing with Police Abuse: The Lessons of Los Angeles," 8 *Virg. J. Social Pol'y & L.* 305, 308–09 (2001) (citing studies such as one in Los Angeles that re-sulted in over 100 overturned convictions); Myrna S. Raeder, "See No Evil: Wrongful Convictions and the Prosecutorial Ethics of Offering Testimony by Jailhouse Informants and Dishonest Experts," 76 *Fordham L. Rev.* 1413 (2007) (advocating Model Rule requiring prosecutors to have a factual basis for belief in the reliability of evidence); Mosteller, *supra* note 113 (arguing for rules governing identification procedures); Kevin C. McMunigal "Prosecutors and Corrupt Science," 36 *Hofstra L. Rev.* 437 (2007).

prosecutors to have a factual basis for believing evidence is reliable, or specific rules governing practices such as identification procedures?

2. How would you evaluate the principle embraced by the Ashcroft memorandum? If you were a federal prosecutor, how would it affect your decision making?

The Role of Race

3. Would it be appropriate for the prosecutors in Problem 6 and 7 to allow race to play any role in their deliberations? Consult ABA Standard 3–3.1(b). As noted earlier, courts have been extremely reluctant to second-guess prosecutors' charging decisions, but they have made clear that such decisions should not be adversely affected by defendants' race or religion, or by their exercise of constitutionally protected interests such as freedom of speech.[121] To establish an equal protection violation based on racially selective prosecution, a defendant must prove that the conduct at issue had a discriminatory purpose as well as effect.[122] Although a wide array of evidence finds racially disparate impacts in charging decisions involving homicides, drugs, and political corruption, discriminatory purpose has generally been impossible to demonstrate.[123] There is no settled precedent on whether prosecutors may consider race when it would influence the decision in the defendant's favor. Nor is it clear that anyone would have standing to complain. Does that suggest that "benign" discrimination is permissible? What about resolving doubts in favor of minority victims, as happened in the Duke lacrosse case on which Problem 7 (c) is based?

Some commentators claim that black politicians have been subject to particular prosecutorial scrutiny.[124] A case similar to Problem 6 involved former Washington D.C. mayor Marion Barry. A lengthy federal investigation regarding possible corruption in his administration revealed information concerning Barry's own drug use. A sting operation then resulted in evidence that led to his conviction on cocaine charges. In other instances, African–American officials later cleared of wrongdoing have suffered irreparable political damage. In light of this history, is it reasonable for a prosecutor to give black politicians the benefit of the doubt in charging decisions?

To what extent should public attitudes affect those decisions? A recent movement toward "community prosecution" has stressed the importance of prosecutorial efforts to reach out to local citizens, and to partner with other organizations on issues involving crime prevention and law enforcement

---

121. Yick Wo v. Hopkins, 118 U.S. 356 (1886); Oyler v. Boles, 368 U.S. 448 (1962). Vindictive or retaliatory prosecution is also forbidden, and is grounds for dismissing a case.

122. United States v. Armstrong, 517 U.S. 456 (1996); United States v. Bass, 536 U.S. 862 (2002).

123. See cases cited in note 121; Yoav Sapir, "Neither Intent Nor Impact: A Cri-

tique of the Racially Based Selective Prosecution Jurisprudence and a Reform Proposal," 19 *Harv. Blackletter L. J.* 127, 130–133 (2003).

124. Sapir, *supra* note 123, at 132; Mark Curridan, "Selective Prosecution: Are Black Officials Investigatory Targets?" *ABA J.*, Feb. 1992, at 54, 57.

priorities.[125] One ongoing challenge within that movement is how to reconcile the need for both prosecutorial independence and accountability. That challenge has often been greatest where law enforcement practices have a strong racially disparate impact. To what extent should community views matter on issues such as how to treat crack cocaine offenses, as opposed to other forms of illegal drug activities? What if the community's views are divided?[126] How should the prosecutor have handled race and class concerns among the local and national black community in the case involving Duke lacrosse players?

4. What, if any, role should race, ethnicity, and gender play in the assignment of cases? How should attorneys of color respond if they are selected to prosecute cases carrying special racial significance? Do these attorneys have any special responsibilities in a system in which defendants of color are disproportionately likely to be prosecuted, convicted, and sentenced to death or extended prison terms? How can prosecutors respond effectively to racial bias within their own offices and police departments without jeopardizing the support necessary to handle other cases?[127]

Are the concerns different in cases involving gender? The choice of a female United States attorney to head the prosecution of Martha Stewart was widely perceived as an effort to "neutralize" the "gender card."[128] According to one jury consultant, the government was " 'clearly trying to make [the case] appear as two strong women doing battle with one another,' rather than [as] a man beating up on a woman."[129] If that analysis is correct, was the government's decision appropriate? Would a male trial attorney who was passed over for the lead counsel position have a valid claim of gender discrimination?

The Role of Politics

5. In 2007, Congress launched an investigation of allegations that the Bush administration had dismissed eight U.S. Attorneys for political reasons. Attorney General Alberto Gonzales denied the allegations. He and President Bush repeatedly stressed that U.S. Attorneys serve at the "plea-

125. Anthony Alfieri, "Community Prosecutors," 90 *Cal. L. Rev.* 1465 (2002); Anthony C. Thompson, "It Takes a Community to Prosecute," 77 *Notre Dame L. Rev.* 321 (2002).

126. See Sapir, *supra* note 123, at 164; Thompson, *supra* note 125. For community opposition to the Barry prosecution, which was estimated to cost between 2 and 50 million dollars, see Davis, supra note 105, at 168. For arguments that the law-abiding minority community benefits from targeting disproportionate enforcement resources on minority offenders, see Randall Kennedy, "The State, Criminal Law, and Racial Discrimination: A Comment," 107 *Harv. L. Rev.* 1255 (1994). William J. Stuntz, "Race, Class, and Drugs," 98 *Colum. L. Rev.* 1795 (1998).

127. See Roscoe C. Howard, Jr., "Changing the System From Within: An Essay Calling on More African Americans To Consider Being Prosecutors," 6 *Wid. L. Symp. J.* 139 (2000); Anthony V. Alfieri, "Prosecuting Race," 48 *Duke L. J.* 1157 (1999). For discussion of the problems and proposed responses see Leadership Conference on Civil Rights, *Justice on Trial: Racial Disparities in the American Criminal Justice System*, 9–19, 52–54 (recommending greater training, oversight, and publication of data concerning racial disparities).

128. Laurie P. Cohen, "U.S. Wants 'Gender Card' Out of Stewart Case," *Wall Street J.*, July 7, 2003, C1 (quoting Deborah Rhode).

129. *Id.*, (quoting JoEllan Dimitrius).

sure of the president" and may be dismissed for any performance reason. Congressional testimony and government documents provided little evidence of performance concerns for most of those fired, and seven of the eight U.S. Attorneys had received excellent job evaluations. Three were dismissed while pursuing cases involving current or former Republican members of Congress. A fourth had failed to pursue voting fraud charges against Democrats, which he claims were not adequately supported by the evidence.[130]

It is customary for U.S. Attorneys to resign when an administration changes, and for the president to take political considerations into account when selecting replacements. It is not customary for presidents to fire U.S. attorneys for political reasons.[131] Does that distinction make sense? If political considerations can play a legitimate role in the appointment of U.S. Attorneys, do they also a role in their retention? How should concerns about the accountability of prosecutors be balanced against concerns about the fairness and impartiality of the justice system?

Other nations attempt to provide prosecutors with greater insulation from political pressures by placing them in the civil service or other semi autonomous agency. Would you support such an approach for this country? What about requiring that U.S. attorneys be dismissed only for cause, as is the case with independent prosecutors?

Inconsistent Theories

6. How should prosecutors deal with cases involving more than one defendant who may be responsible for the offense, as in Problem 8? The United States Supreme Court cast light on that question in *Bradshaw v. Stumpf*, 545 U.S. 175 (2005). There, the government brought charges against Stumpf and Wesley for armed robbery and murder. Stumpf pleaded guilty to aggravated murder. However, in a contested penalty hearing before a three-judge panel, he claimed in mitigation that he had acted at Wesley's urging and that Wesley had killed the victim. The state argued that Stumpf had fired the fatal shot. The panel agreed and sentenced him to death. At Wesley's subsequent jury trial, the state presented evidence that Wesley admitted shooting the victim. Wesley responded that the state had taken a different position at Stumpf's hearing. Wesley was convicted but sentenced not to death, but to life imprisonment with the possibility of parole. Stumpf then moved to withdraw his plea or vacate his sentence on the basis of the prosecutor's reliance on inconsistent theories to convict both defendants of the same offense.

---

130. 28 U.S.C. § 541 provides simply that "each U.S. Attorney is subject to removal by the President." For Gonzales' claims and contrary evidence indicating that political considerations played a role, *see* Alberto Gonzales, "They Lost My Confidence: Attorneys' Dismissals were Related to Performance, Not to Politics," *USA* Today, March 7,

2007, at A10; 1; David C. Iglesias, "Why I was Fired," *N.Y. Times*, March 21, 2001, at A21; Dan Eggen, "6 of 7 Dismissed U.S. Attorneys Had Positive Job Evaluations," *Washington Post*, Feb. 18, 2007, at A1.

131. David Fontana, "Make It Less Political," *National L. J.* April 30, 2007, at 27.

The Sixth Circuit Federal Court of Appeals found for Stumpf, and the Supreme Court reversed in part and remanded. In the majority's view, which defendant pulled the trigger was immaterial to Stumpf's conviction because state law made aiders and abettors liable for murder. However, because Stumpf's role may have been material to sentencing, the Court remanded for findings on that point.

The California Supreme Court took a stronger position against inconsistent theories in *In re Sakarias*, 106 P.3d 931 (Cal. Sup. Ct.), cert. denied sub nom. *Waidla v. California*, 546 U.S. 939 (2005). There, the Court vacated a death sentence for one defendant where a prosecutor had manipulated evidence without a "good faith justification" to advance inconsistent theories about which defendant had delivered the fatal blow. However, the Court found that the other defendant had suffered no "constitutionally significant prejudice" because the evidence clearly established that he was responsible for the victim's death.

Do these cases help resolve what the prosecutor should do on the facts of Problem 8?

Internal Policies

7.   In Problem 6, what, if any, significance should attach to the office's informal policy of not prosecuting occasional drug use by individuals without a prior criminal record? When the district attorney makes an exception, should offenders have any standing to complain? Some commentators have urged prosecutors to establish internal guidelines or presumptive policies to ensure greater consistency in responses to similar offenses. However, as advocates of such standards acknowledge, if they become public and enforceable by defendants, some of the deterrent power of criminal sanctions might be lost, incentives to cooperate would be reduced, and courts could become enmeshed in difficult evidentiary issues. Commentators have also worried that offices would respond by withdrawing guidelines or framing them at a level of generality that would eliminate their usefulness.[132] Are such risks worth accepting?

Public Involvement and Professional Accountability

8.   Should internal policies of prosecutors' offices be subject to external review? Consider the concern raised by former prosecutor and law professor, now judge Gerald Lynch:

> In effect, as the overbreadth of the formal substantive criminal law drives an increase in prosecutorial power [the pressure will increase] . . . on prosecutors to develop internal administrative practices and standards for the exercise of discretion that will become a separate de

---

132.   For example, the federal principles quoted above not only are framed in extremely general terms, they also add that an attorney may depart from their mandates "as necessary in the interests of fair and effective law enforcement." United States Department of Justice Principles of Federal Prosecution, *supra* note 116, at 3278. Moreover, the guidelines are intended for internal use and may not be relied upon "to create a right or benefit, substantive or procedural, enforceable at law by a party at litigation with the United States." *Id.*

facto substantive criminal law. The problem is that this body of law is largely unwritten and may vary from district attorney to district attorney, or even from individual prosecutor to individual prosecutor.[133]

What might be appropriate responses to this concern? Did the Ashcroft memo reflect a constructive step toward greater consistency or does it compound problems in the nation's reliance on incarceration as an approach to crime?

9. Should victims have any right to complain about nonenforcement of certain offenses, such as those falling under the rape corroboration policy described in Problem 7? Some have argued that victims and complaining witnesses be granted standing to challenge a decision not to prosecute and that courts be permitted to order prosecution in cases involving an abuse of discretion.[134] Would you favor such a policy? Do the facts of Problem 7 suggest such an abuse? Would bringing acquaintance-rape cases despite fact finders' reluctance to convict be one way of increasing deterrence, educating the community about the seriousness of the offense, and enhancing the likelihood of conviction in later cases? What about victims' claims of overly aggressive enforcement? For example, some prosecutors' offices operate with "no drop" policies for domestic violence cases, which means that the government will proceed even when a survivor requests that her complaint be dismissed. How would you assess the merits of such a policy, which often tradeoff additional risks to one victim in order to achieve greater deterrence and protect other victims from pressure to withdraw their complaints?[135]

10. If prosecutors should be free to ignore public opinion concerning acquaintance-rape cases, does it follow that they should feel similarly unconstrained in other contexts where local views run against enforcement? If public opinion should play a role, how should it be assessed? Could courts develop manageable standards for reviewing prosecutors' allocation of enforcement resources? On relatively rare occasions, judges have held prosecutorial policies of nonenforcement to be outside constitutional or statutory limits and have issued writs of mandamus to compel action.[136] Should courts be more willing to review prosecutorial conduct under principles analogous to those developed for monitoring abuses of discretion by federal administrative agencies? Or should courts simply demand that individual prosecutors adhere to their own offices' policies?[137]

---

133. Gerald E. Lynch, "The Role of Criminal Law in Policing Corporate Misconduct," 60 *Law & Contemp. Problems* 23, 61 (1997).

134. National Advisory Commission on Criminal Justice Standards and Goals, Standard 1.2 at 24 (1973).

135. For a review of the competing evidence concerning these claims, see Deborah L. Rhode, "Social Research and Social Change: Meeting the Challenge of Gender Inequality and Sexual Abuse," 30 *Harv. J. Law & Gender* 11, 19–20 (2007).

136. Littleton v. Berbling, 468 F.2d 389, 416 (7th Cir.1972), *rev'd on other grounds sub nom.*, O'Shea v. Littleton, 414 U.S. 488 (1974) (holding that alleged failure to prosecute white citizens for assaults on blacks was subject to review and reversal for abuse of discretion).

137. *See* Leslie C. Griffin, "The Prudent Prosecutor," 14 *Geo. J. Legal Ethics* 259, 305–07 (2001) (arguing for precise inter-

Pursuit of Offenses or Offenders

11.   Is it ethically permissible or appropriate under current standards for prosecutors to target labor leaders or star witnesses as described in Problem 7? Should the government pursue offenses rather than offenders, or should it allocate enforcement resources in light of the character and prior conduct of particular individuals? In the article that Uviller discusses, Monroe Freedman takes issue with the contention that "if the individual is in fact guilty of the crime with which he is charged, the motive of the prosecutor is immaterial. This contention overlooks the fact that there are few of us who have led such unblemished lives as to prevent a determined prosecutor from finding some basis for an indictment...."[138] Do you agree? Is there anything unjust about a prosecutor drawing up an "enemies list" if its membership is based on suspected but unprovable criminal activity and not on prosecutor's personal or political considerations? How would you assess the decision by Independent Counsel Kenneth Starr to expand his investigation of possible financial misconduct by then President Bill Clinton arising from a failed real estate development and related matters? The expanded investigation encompassed possible perjury in a civil sexual harassment proceeding and a consensual extramarital relationship on the theory that a broader inquiry might reveal a pattern of inducing false testimony.[139] What about the decision of the U.S. Attorney to bring perjury charges against White House Aid Scooter Libby for lying before a grand jury about who leaked confidential information to a reporter about the identity of a CIA agent? The prosecutor already knew the source of the leak when he questioned Libby.[140]

12.   If the current ethical standards that prohibit prosecutors from considering political gain are unenforced and unenforceable, would other measures be appropriate? Consider the proposal by Bruce Fein, former associate deputy attorney general:

> Prosecutors should be barred from non-prosecutorial electoral office for five years following a resignation. They should be prohibited from commercial exploitation of particular criminal investigations or prosecutions ... [and from] broadcast appearances to discuss ongoing investigations or pending indictments.[141]

---

nal ethical directives or rebuttable presumptions, and internal review procedures).

138.   Monroe H. Freedman, "The Professional Responsibility of the Prosecuting Attorney," 55 *Geo.L.J.*, 1030, 1034–35 (1967).

139.   See Rhode, *supra* note 30.

140.   Diane Rabinowitz, "A Tale of Two Prosecutors," *Wall St. J*, June 22, 2007, at A11.

141.   Bruce Fein, "Time to Rein in the Prosecution: New Rules are Necessary to Limit Potential Abuse of Power," *ABA J.*, July, 1994, at 96.

2.   PLEA-BARGAINING

QUESTIONS

1.   In the political corruption case discussed in Problem 6, would it be proper for the prosecutor to offer an advantageous plea bargain on condition that the comptroller resign from office?

2.   In the multiple defendant case described in Problem 8, how convinced of guilt should the prosecutor be before accepting a plea that a defendant accepts to avoid prosecution on a capital offense?

INTRODUCTION

In a criminal justice system where few cases go to trial, prosecutors' ethical responsibilities in plea bargaining assume considerable significance. And those responsibilities, like the bargaining process itself, provoke substantial dispute.

To some commentators, plea-bargaining is an invitation to injustice—a violation of individuals' most fundamental rights and society's most fundamental values. From this perspective, our elaborate constitutional protections serve largely as window dressing for a system that in fact imposes sanctions under a process resembling a street bazaar. John Langbein suggests that contemporary plea-bargaining functions in much the same fashion as medieval torture. Extorting confessions became an apparent necessity in order to bypass the continental criminal system's idealistic but impractical prohibition against the use of circumstantial evidence. In Langbein's view, the level of complexity and safeguards in our current criminal procedures has produced similar reliance on coercive methods. "Like the medieval Europeans," he argues, "we have preserved an unworkable trial procedure in form, we have devised a substitute nontrial procedure to subvert the formal procedure, and we have arranged to place defendants under fierce pressure to 'choose' the substitute."[142] What is particularly objectionable about this system is that it leads to "innocent defendants being offered (and taking) the same deals as guilty ones."[143]

The system also encourages sloppy lawyering, because any inadequacy in prosecutor's or defense counsel's preparation remains largely invisible when cases quickly settle. Since prosecutors are particularly disposed to plead their weakest cases, the incentives to forgo trial are strongest for those at greatest risk of an unjust conviction. The problem is compounded by severe minimum penalties for certain offenses and by the horrendous conditions in many jails, which sometimes encourage defendants to take whatever bargain offers the quickest release. Limitations on pre-trial

---

142.   John H. Langbein, "Torture and Plea Bargaining," 46 *U.Chi.L.Rev.* 3, 20 (1978).

143.   Robert E. Scott & William J. Stuntz, "Plea Bargaining as Contract," 101 *Yale L.J.* 1909, 1911 (1992). For disputes about the frequency of pleas by innocent defendants, see John G. Douglass, "Fatal Attraction: The Uneasy Courtship of Brady and Plea Bargaining," 50 *Emory L. J.* 439, 489 (2001).

discovery, and inequalities in resources can inappropriately distort outcomes.[144] Moreover, the high volume of cases and lack of pre-sentence reports at the plea bargaining stage leaves many prosecutors ill informed about the offenders' background and other relevant circumstances.[145]

Critics of plea bargaining have proposed a variety of alternatives, including: less coercive sentencing structures; extension of pre-trial disclosure obligations; centralized screening and review of bargains; and nonnegotiable concessions for those who forego trials.[146] Such a system could be imposed by legislation or adopted by policy and would exert less pressure on innocent defendants who fear arbitrary or unduly harsh penalties if they risk trial.

By contrast, defenders of plea bargaining see it as an acceptable, indeed essential, way of conserving scarce resources. Although the plea-bargaining process may not always separate the innocent from the guilty, the same is true of trials, given evidentiary restrictions and juror biases. Defense lawyers are free to present exculpating evidence during negotiations and if they lack the resources or incentive to do so, the problem is not inherent in plea-bargaining. Nor would these problems of inadequate representation be eliminated by eliminating plea negotiation, since they are also likely to emerge at trial if resource constraints remain unchanged. From this perspective, reform efforts should focus on reducing caseloads and increasing resources and regulatory oversight of both prosecutors and defense counsel.[147]

However, even defenders of plea bargaining generally acknowledge that it is subject to abuse and that prosecutors operate with multiple objectives apart from pursuing justice:

> their goal may be to enhance their personal batting average, to avoid a potentially embarrassing loss in a particular case ... to cultivate good relationships with influential private attorneys, or simply to avoid staying too late at the office.[148]

How do these general assessments of the plea bargaining structure affect your view of the conduct in the preceding problems? What, if any, reforms would you advocate for the bargaining process?

Overcharging

1. Is it acceptable for a prosecutor to file charges, or threaten to file charges, that he has no intention of trying in the hopes of forcing a guilty plea or encouraging cooperation with government investigations? For ex-

---

144. Stephanos Bibas, "Plea Bargaining Outside the Shadow of Trial," 117 *Harv. L. Rev.* 2463, 2528–31 (2004); Douglass, *supra* note 143.

145. David Lynch, "The Impropriety of Plea Agreements: A Tale of Two Counties," 19 *Law & Soc. Inquiry* 115 (1994).

146. Douglass, *supra* note 143; Ronald Wright & Marc Miller, "The Screening/Bar-gaining Tradeoff," 55 *Stan. L. Rev.* 29, 35 (2002).

147. Scott & Stuntz, *supra* note 143, at 1910; Frank Easterbrook, "Plea Bargaining as Compromise," 101 *Yale L.J.* 1969 (1992).

148. Stephen J. Schulhofer, "A Wake–Up Call from the Plea–Bargaining Trenches," 19 *Law & Soc. Inquiry* 135, 137 (1994).

ample, in Problem 6, suppose the district attorney believes beyond a reasonable doubt that the comptroller is guilty of drug use but doubts a jury's willingness to convict, given the inadmissibility of the wiretap evidence and the credibility problems with the employee. May he include drug offenses in the indictment?

How would you evaluate the conduct of a prosecutor who charged an eighteen year old boy with rape, statutory rape, sexual battery, and aggravated child molestation for a single act of intercourse with a fifteen year old girl? She claimed the act was forcible; he claimed it was consensual. The jury acquitted on the offenses requiring proof of force, but convicted the defendant for statutory rape and aggravated child molestation. The latter offense carried a ten year minimum, and when community opinion ran against the verdict, the prosecutor acknowledged that he had used the molestation charge as a "backstop" in case the defendant was acquitted of rape.[149]

Can you envision circumstances apart from those in Problem 6 that would make the practice of overcharging more or less acceptable? What about Problem 8? Consult ABA Standard 3–3.9(f) the Principles of Federal Prosecution, Commentary to 9–27–300, excerpted above.

Conditional Agreements: Public Officials and Public Liability

2. In contexts involving public officials, may prosecutors insist on resignation as a condition of accepting a guilty plea? In the Marion Barry case, news media reported that the prosecutor offered to let Barry plead to misdemeanors if he would resign his office. Is such a bargain appropriate?

Federal District Judge Jack Weinstein found such a practice unconstitutional in *United States v. Richmond,* 550 F.Supp. 605 (E.D.N.Y.1982). There, the defendant Congressman agreed to plead guilty to income tax evasion, possession of marijuana, and unlawful salary supplements, as well as to resign from Congress and to terminate his reelection campaign. In return, the prosecutor agreed to forego prosecution for various other crimes. Judge Weinstein concluded:

> This portion of the agreement [concerning resignation and reelection] was invalid for three reasons. First, it conflicted with the fundamental right of the people to elect their representatives. Second, it interfered with the principle of separation of powers. Third, it contravened public policy by utilizing a technique latent with the possibility of Executive domination of members of Congress through the threat of forced resignations....
>
> Power to strip a member of Congress of elective office was committed to neither the executive nor the judiciary. It was explicitly reserved to Congress itself.... The possibility of the executive utilizing the threat of prosecution to force the resignation of a congressional representative involves potentially dangerous political consequences. It represents an opportunity for an assault on the composition and integrity

---

149. Davis, *supra* note 105, at 54–55   that was ultimately reversed).
(discussing the conviction of Marcus Dixon

of a coordinate branch of government.... The enormous spectrum of criminal laws that can be violated, the powerful investigative and prosecutorial machine available to the executive, and forced resignations through plea bargaining would provide an intolerable threat to a free and independent Congress.... *Id.* at 606–609.

Would you come to a similar conclusion?

3. In response to the *Richmond* decision, the Justice Department promulgated guidelines that encourage U.S. attorneys to consider voluntary offers of resignation from office as a desirable objective in plea negotiations. *Richmond*'s reasoning has not been followed elsewhere in the nation, and prosecutors divide about the appropriateness of including resignation as part of a formal plea agreement.[150] What factors should be relevant to their decision? Do similar considerations apply to decisions by an Independent Counsel appointed to investigate wrongdoing by federal officials?

4. Is it appropriate for a prosecutor to condition dismissal of criminal charges on an accused's agreement to release public officials from civil liability? Yaser Hamdi, an American citizen by birth, was captured in Afghanistan and held in U.S. military confinement for nearly three years without access to a lawyer or an opportunity to challenge his detention. After the Supreme Court held that he was entitled to such an opportunity, the government instead agreed to release him from custody. However, the agreement included several conditions, including Hamdi's renunciation of American citizenship and release of all liability claims against the United States for violation of his civil rights. Are these conditions ethical?

In *Town of Newton v. Rumery*, 480 U.S. 386 (1987), a divided Supreme Court held that release-dismissal agreements are enforceable if they reflect some legitimate law enforcement objective, not just a desire to save taxpayer dollars. Many prosecutors consider such agreements unethical, and they are relatively uncommon. However, in the small number of cases challenging their validity, over four-fifths of these agreements have been upheld, generally without mention of any specific law enforcement objective.[151] The relinquished civil claims typically involve excessive force, false imprisonment, and related abuses. What, if any, law enforcement objectives might justify requiring defendants to give up potentially valid civil claims in exchange for favorable treatment in a criminal matter?

3. DISCLOSURE OBLIGATIONS

PROBLEM 9

a) You are the prosecutor in a robbery case with strong evidence of guilt. The victim had an excellent opportunity to observe the robber and

150. Elsa Walsh, "U.S. Plea Guidelines Encourage Resignations," *Wash. Post*, June 2, 1990, at A8, 1.

151. One survey found only 26 agreements in a decade of reported cases, 85 percent of which were upheld. Only 7 percent of surveyed prosecutors had executed such agreements in the last 5 years, and almost half considered them either never ethical (27 percent) or rarely ethical (20 percent). Andrew B. Coan, "The Legal Ethics of Release–Dismissal Agreements: Theory and Practice," 1 *Stan. J. C.R. & C.L.* 371 (2005).

readily identified him at a lineup shortly after the incident. Defense counsel is a private practitioner who accepts a high volume of cases at flat fees and generally pleads his clients guilty with little or no pretrial investigation. Several days before trial, you learn that the complaining witness has fled the jurisdiction and cannot be located. Must you disclose that fact in plea negotiations? Should you?

b) Suppose the complaining witness is available, but the defense has an eyewitness to the assault who claims that the assailant was not the defendant. That eyewitness does not know the parties and has no obvious motives to lie. However, he also has a prior criminal conviction for lying on a credit report that would be admissible as impeachment material. In plea negotiations, can you threaten to call in the witness to discuss his testimony and question him about the conviction? You suspect that the threat of public disclosure of this information might cause him to refuse to testify or change his story to avoid testifying.[152]

c) In another case, you have charged the defendant with aggravated assault. The victim is the defendant's former girlfriend and shortly before trial you learn that she is unwilling to testify. Part of her reluctance stems from fear that the defendant will retaliate. She is also concerned that if the prosecutor discloses facts about her history of psychiatric treatment for depression, the defendant will make them public.

How do you proceed? What factors would be most relevant to your judgment?

NOTES

Under the ABA's Model Rule 3.8 and Model Code DR 7–103, the prosecutor is obligated to make timely disclosure of evidence that tends to negate guilt or mitigate the offense. This rule has constitutional underpinnings. Under standards first set forth in *Brady v. Maryland,* 373 U.S. 83 (1963) and clarified more recently in *United States v. Bagley,* 473 U.S. 667 (1985), "the suppression by the prosecution of evidence favorable to an accused upon request violates due process where the evidence is material either to guilt or to punishment irrespective of the good or bad faith of the prosecution." *Brady*, 373 U.S. at 87. This includes evidence useful in impeaching prosecution witnesses as well as evidence that is directly exculpatory.[153]

Unlike Model Rule 3.8 and DR 7–103, the *Brady* rule conditions a prosecutor's disclosure obligations on a defense request, and requires disclosure of exculpatory material only if it is "material either to guilt or to punishment." In *Bagley*, the Supreme Court explained that "evidence is material only if there is a reasonable probability that, had the evidence been disclosed to the defense, the result of the proceeding would have been

---

152. This fact pattern is modeled on a case in Adventures in Legal Ethics, produced by Stephen Gillers for New York Law School.

153. Banks v. Dretke, 540 U.S. 668 (2004); Giglio v. U.S., 405 U.S. 150, 154 (1972).

different. A 'reasonable probability' is a probability sufficient to undermine confidence in the outcome."[154]

The application of these requirements in plea bargaining remains unsettled. Some prosecutors disclose their entire case file, either as a result of legislative mandate, office policy, or personal principle. Others are reluctant to expose witnesses to potential harassment and intimidation, or to give defendants an advance opportunity to revise their recollections in light of the state's evidence.[155]

Controversy continues about whether all information involving the availability or credibility of witnesses is "exculpatory" and therefore subject to disclosure.[156] In *People v. Jones,* 375 N.E.2d 41 (N.Y.1978), *cert. denied,* 439 U.S. 846 (1978), the New York Court of Appeals found no denial of due process where the prosecutor failed to disclose that the complaining witness in a robbery prosecution had died four days before the entry of the plea. In the court's view, although such information would have been a significant factor influencing the defendant's determination to plead guilty, it was not relevant to the legal issue of guilt. Nor was it significant that the prosecutor, before learning of the witness' death, had made representations about the witness' availability for trial; the silence later did not constitute misrepresentation when there was no affirmative duty to disclose. The prosecutor was not "obliged to share his appraisal of the weaknesses of his own case (as opposed to specific exculpatory evidence)" and the witness's unavailability was not "evidence." However, somewhat inconsistently, the court left open the possibility that a prosecutor might have disclosure obligations if a defendant "staunchly and plausibly maintains his innocence" but explicitly states he will accept a plea to avoid the risk of a stiffer sentence. 375 N.E.2d at 44.

In *United States v. Ruiz,* 536 U.S. 622 (2002), the Supreme Court settled the constitutional issue for a broad category of *Brady* information: evidence that the defense could use to impeach prosecution witnesses. The Court argued that *Brady* is fundamentally a trial right, and requiring the prosecution to reveal impeachment evidence before plea bargaining could undermine the government's "interest in securing those guilty pleas that are factually justified, desired by defendants, and help to secure the efficient administration of justice." *Id.* at 631. It concluded that "the Constitution does not require the Government to disclose material impeachment evidence prior to entering a plea agreement with a criminal defendant." *Id.* at 633.

154. U.S. v. Bagley, 473 U.S. 667 (1985). An earlier case described the constitutional standard of materiality as requiring a determination of whether "the omitted evidence creates a reasonable doubt that did not otherwise exist." U.S. v. Agurs, 427 U.S. 97, 112 (1976).

155. Uviller, *supra* note 46, at 93–97, 108; Ellen S. Podgor, "The Ethics and Professionalism of Prosecutors in Discretionary Decisions," 68 *Fordham L. R.* 1511 (2000).

156. Code provisions do not discuss disclosure obligations in plea contexts. ABA Standard 3–4.1 prohibits prosecutors from making false representations in plea negotiations but does not require disclosure of exculpatory evidence.

That decision leaves open whether prosecutors ever have an ethical, if not constitutional, obligation to make such disclosures.

QUESTIONS

1. Is the *Jones* court's reasoning persuasive? In Problem 9, is the leading witness's treatment for depression exculpatory? Should prosecutors disclose any evidence that discredits a witness or can they decide that some material is more prejudicial than probative? If evidence is subject to disclosure requirements, does the defendant have a right to receive it before entering a plea?[157]

2. How far does the prosecution need to go in facilitating discovery of exculpatory material? Is it permissible for a district attorney to counsel government witnesses that it may be imprudent to speak to defense investigators? Should a prosecutor be subject to discipline for failure to disclose the location of exculpatory witnesses or a lab test revealing exculpatory DNA evidence?

Courts have begun to take more seriously misrepresentations concerning such evidence.[158] In the case involving Duke lacrosse players, the prosecutor, Michael Nifong, was disbarred, in part for his false representation to the court concerning DNA. Nifong claimed that the "state is not aware of any additional material or information which may be exculpatory in nature...."[159] In fact, the director of a private laboratory had found DNA traces of other men on the rape complainant's underwear, and after consultation with the prosecutor, did not include that finding in a summary of lab data that the prosecutor gave to the defense. One of the defendant's lawyers stumbled on the information in reviewing the 1844 pages of laboratory data.

Suppose that Nifong had made no affirmative misstatement but simply failed to disclose the exculpatory material before accepting a plea from one of the defendants? Could he have been disciplined for failure to make timely disclosure of the evidence under Model Rule 3.8?[160] If not, does that suggest a need to amend the Rule?

3. May a prosecutor decide not to pursue certain leads for fear of discovering exculpatory material? Do the government's obligations increase where defense counsel has inadequate resources for trial preparation or where the police department has been lax in turning over exculpatory evidence to the

157. Courts and bar ethics committees have divided over whether the death of witnesses must be disclosed in negotiation of civil and criminal cases. Richard Zitrin & Carol Langford, *Legal Ethics in the Practice of Law* 371 (1995).

158. Tom Perotta, "Ex–Prosecutor Suspended for Misleading Trial Court," *New York L. J.*, Oct. 4, 2005 (discussing case of Claude Stuart, who was suspended for falsely informing the court that he did not know the whereabouts of a key murder witness when he had in fact interviewed the witness the day before).

159. David Barstow & Duff Wilson, "DNA Witness Jolted Dynamic of Duke Case," *N.Y. Times*, December 24, 2006, at A1, A10.

160. Davis, *supra* note 105, at 149 (suggesting the difficulties of reading Model Rule 3.8 to require discipline).

district attorney? Should more jurisdictions follow the lead of some European nations in which all police evidence is available to the defense?[161]

4. Some commentators have been highly critical of prosecutors' limited discovery obligations. As David Luban notes:

> [A]n unscrupulous prosecutor needs to get caught before *Brady* does any good and it is a matter of conjecture how often the prosecutor gets away with undisclosed *Brady* material. . . .
>
> *Brady*, moreover, holds only that the prosecution must turn over exculpatory material to the defense. The defense still has no right to depose prosecution witnesses or even to interview an unwilling witness, and in some jurisdictions the prosecution lies under no obligation even to divulge the names of its witnesses to the defense. Nor need the prosecution divulge the results of scientific tests or expert evaluations unless the prosecutor believes these to be exculpatory. Though some prosecutors maintain an "open file" policy, granting defenders access to the prosecution's case files, this is purely a policy choice on the prosecutor's part, not a legal right of defendants. . . .
>
> Although the principal rationale for this no-discovery procedural regime is the protection of prosecution witnesses, it appears to be justified as well by the ideal of adversary balance. After all, because of the defendant's right against self-incrimination, the prosecution has no discovery rights. Fair is fair. But fair is not fair. In fact, the prosecution retains significant discovery rights. By obtaining a warrant, prosecutors and police can search the defendant's possessions. . . . Prosecutors can [also] plant informants in the defendant's cell . . . [and] the harmless error rule embodied [in *Bagley*] effectively insulates prosecutorial misconduct.[162]

5. What follows from this critique? For example, should courts require prosecutors to have an "open file" policy, and impose more severe penalties for non-disclosure? Should any materials that are arguably exculpatory be submitted to an internal ethics officer or to the trial judge for *in camera* review?[163] Should defendants who plead guilty and acknowledge commission of the crime in open court be able to withdraw the plea if they can prove that the prosecutor knowingly failed to disclose exculpatory evidence?

As these questions suggest, the enforcement of disclosure requirements in plea bargaining raises a host of practical difficulties. "Open file" policies have not entirely solved the problem because different prosecutors have different ideas of what that means and often lack the time or incentives to ensure that their files include all exculpatory material in government

---

161. *See* Stanley Z. Fisher, "The Prosecutor's Ethical Duty to Seek Exculpatory Evidence in Police Hands: Lessons from England," 68 *Fordham L. Rev.* 1379 (2000) (arguing for regulation of police record keeping); Beatrix Elsner & Julia Peters, "The Prosecution Service Function Within the German Judicial System," in *Coping With Overloaded Criminal Justice Systems: The Rise of Prosecutorial Power Across Europe* 207 (Jorg–Martin Hehle & Marianne Wade, eds. 2006).

162. Luban, *supra* note 10, at 1737.

163. See Uviller, *supra* note 46, at 46.

hands.[164] Because judges generally are reluctant either to condone *Brady* violations or to overturn guilty pleas, most courts have settled on an awkward compromise. Defendants may withdraw their plea if they can prove that undisclosed exculpatory material would have materially affected a reasonable person's decision to plead guilty. However, the absence of a record indicating what considerations most influenced a decision has made it easy for courts to find that the undisclosed information was not material.[165] Moreover, this compromise offers least to those who need it most. As noted earlier, prosecutors offer greatest inducements in their weakest cases, which are the ones where innocence is most likely. Yet because defendants in those cases receive the most generous offers, they will also have the most difficulty showing that the *Brady* material would have altered their plea decision.

How to address these enforcement difficulties is subject to dispute. Some commentators have argued that courts should allow defendants to waive *Brady* claims but should require a record insuring that the defendants knew what material they were giving up.[166] Other commentators have argued for modification of the materiality standard. In the absence of active oversight by courts and disciplinary agencies, some experts have also recommended creation of prosecutorial conduct commissions.[167] Would you support any of these strategies? Are there other reforms that strike you as more promising?

6.   *Ruiz* settles the constitutional question of whether prosecutors must disclose impeachment evidence before plea bargaining. Should the ethical question be settled the same way?

7.   What if a prosecutor receives evidence after a case is over that the wrong individual was convicted? In 2008, the ABA House of Delegates amended the Model Rules to include two new sections of Model Rule 3.8 to deal with this question. Rule 3.8(g) requires a prosecutor who learns of "new, credible, and material evidence creating a reasonable likelihood that a convicted defendant did not commit an offense of which the defendant was convicted," the prosecutor must disclose the evidence to the proper authorities as well as the defendant, and initiate an investigation. And Rule 3.8(h) requires a prosecutor who receives clear and convincing evidence that a defendant was convicted of a crime he did not commit to "seek to remedy the conviction."

4.   PRESS STATEMENTS

PROBLEM 10

a) On the facts of Problems 6 and 7, what statements may the prosecutor make to the press? Should they all be on the record?

---

164. Douglass, *supra* note 143, at 461.

165. *Id.* at 4, 44.

166. Douglass, *supra* note 143, at 515–17.

167. Lyn M. Morton, "Seeking the Elusive Remedy for Prosecutorial Misconduct: Suppression, Dismissal, or Discipline?," 7 *Geo.J.Legal Ethics* 1083, 1114–15 (1994).

b) In the Duke lacrosse case, the prosecutor described the defendants as "a bunch of hooligans" who were "stonewalling" his investigation, who "don't want to admit the enormity of what they have done," and whose "daddies" would "buy big time lawyers." Should any of these statements subject the prosecutor to discipline or to a judicial order barring further statements?[168]

c) Various pretrial publicity issues arose in the widely reported acquaintance rape prosecution of William Kennedy Smith, a member of the Kennedy family. The alleged rape occurred after a woman he had picked up in a bar drove him back to the Kennedy beachfront estate from the club where he, Senator Edward Kennedy, and another family member had been drinking. Although the media traditionally has not disclosed the names of rape victims, a number of newspapers and broadcast networks identified the complainant and revealed a wide array of unfavorable details about her life, including her single motherhood, prior abortions, cocaine use, and family's reputation for social climbing. It was widely rumored that reporters obtained much of this information from investigators for the defense. Unfavorable information concerning the defendant subsequently emerged when the prosecutor filed, and released to the press, a pretrial motion. That motion indicated her intent to call three witnesses who claimed that Smith had raped or attempted to rape them while on dates. Their testimony would be admissible at trial only if the court found that these prior acts were so similar to the Palm Beach charges as to indicate a common pattern and that their probative value outweighed their prejudicial impact. Critics of the prosecutor's action claimed that publicly releasing the document (rather than filing it under seal) was unethical and prejudicial, particularly since the defense counsel was under a no-comment order to refrain from further public discussion of the case. Supporters of the prosecutor's conduct argued that public disclosures were appropriate to corroborate the charges and to counteract earlier negative images of acquaintance rape victims in general and the Palm Beach complainant in particular.

What is your view? How would you have handled press disclosures if you had been the lead prosecutor? Suppose that you had filed the motion under seal and then someone from your office had anonymously leaked it to the press? If you had cautioned all individuals working on the case not to make unauthorized disclosures, but leaks had continued to occur, how should you respond? Should courts and bar disciplinary agencies impose sanctions in such circumstances?

References: Model Rules 3.6, 3.8(g).

NOTES AND QUESTIONS

Ethical rules on lawyers' press statements attempt to accommodate competing values. On one hand, litigants have rights to adjudication

---

168. Gershman & Cohen, *supra* note 113, at A22 (quoting Nifong); Barstow and Wilson, *supra* note 159, at A10 (quoting Nifong).

untainted by pretrial publicity.[169] Participants in certain categories of cases such as rape and sexual abuse also have interests in keeping their identities or prior intimate relationships confidential. On the other hand, individuals subject to false and prejudicial accusations have an interest in clearing their names, and the public in general has a right to "guard against the miscarriage of justice by subjecting [the process] ... to extensive public scrutiny and criticism."[170]

1. How would you evaluate the issue facing the prosecutor in Problem 10(b)? Did release of the motions pose a substantial likelihood of material prejudice or was it consistent with government counsel's general obligation to "do justice"? Alan Dershowitz, in commenting on the prosecutor's conduct, argued that even if the judge excluded testimony about the prior charges, public release of the motion would irrevocably prejudice the defendant's interests:

> [I]f jurors in the Smith case learn of the three previous alleged crimes, they will no longer think he is a nice boy. They will think that maybe one woman or even two could be overreacting, mistaken or on a vendetta. But all four? No way! This guy is a rapist, the jurors will think, even if the evidence is less than entirely convincing. They will see the Florida woman as someone who finally had the courage to blow the whistle on Mr. Smith.
>
> Even if Judge Lupo eventually rules the evidence inadmissible ... it is likely to have a pervasive influence on the jury as well as on Mr. Smith's ongoing trial in the court of public opinion. This kind of evidence is called "skunk evidence" by criminal lawyers because even if you get rid of the skunk, the smell remains.[171]

By contrast, defenders of the prosecutor's conduct claimed that her actions ensured a more accurate public understanding of the acquaintance rape charges. Observers also noted that some social science evidence indicates that even when jurors have been exposed to extensive pretrial publicity, they are generally able to disregard it and base their verdict on evidence presented in court.[172]

How would you have resolved the issue? Is your opinion affected by the ultimate outcome in the case? The judge excluded evidence of Smith's prior sexual conduct, and the jury acquitted despite the prosecutor's media disclosures.

169. For an overview of the adverse affects of pretrial publicity and the inability of voir dire selection processes to prevent selection of biased jurors, see Solomon M. Fulero, "Afterward: The Past, Present, and Future of Applied Pretrial Publicity Research," 26 *L. & Human Behavior* 127, 127–28 (2002).

170. Nebraska Press Assn. v. Stuart, 427 U.S. 539, 560 (1976).

171. Alan Dershowitz, "Two Rape Cases—Against Smith," *N.Y. Times*, July 26, 1991, at A27.

172. Robert E. Drechsel, "An Alternative View of Media–Judiciary Relations: What the Non-Legal Evidence Suggests About the Fair Trial–Free Press Issue," 18 *Hofstra L.Rev.* 1 (1989).

In *Gentile v. Nevada State Bar*, 501 U.S. 1030 (1991), the Supreme Court held that states may prohibit lawyers' speech if it creates a "substantial likelihood of material prejudice" by influencing potential jurors. Following *Gentile*, the ABA amended Model Rule 3.6 to reflect the same standard and added Rule 3.8(f). It requires prosecutors to take "reasonable care" to prevent affiliated law enforcement personnel from making statements that violated Rule 3.6. How would these Rules and the *Gentile* standard apply to conduct in Problem 6? If defense counsel has challenged the prosecutor's integrity, should the prosecutor be expected to turn the other cheek in order to protect the defendant's sixth amendment interests?

2.   Should prosecutors follow any special principles concerning press disclosures for certain kinds of cases? Consider the arguments surrounding the appropriate policy for the media regarding rape victims' identity and personal history. Should prosecutors or journalists take special pains to avoid disclosing information that would exacerbate victims' sense of shame and fear, or would such a policy violate the public's right to know and compound the special stigma that attaches to sexual assault cases? Do cases involving conduct of public figures present a strong need for accurate press coverage, including anonymous off the record confirmations or denials? Or are these cases in which prosecutors should be accountable for every statement, including anonymous leaks, that come from their office?[173]

3.   The *Restatement of Law Governing Lawyers*, § 109, acknowledges prosecutors' need to issue statements that inform the public of their actions and that serve other legitimate law enforcement purposes. However, the *Restatement* also cautions prosecutors to avoid extrajudicial remarks "that have a substantial likelihood of heightening public condemnation of the accused." Should such a standard be enforced by courts and disciplinary agencies? How would it apply to any of the statements in Problems 6 or 10? Would it ever be proper for a district attorney to state that a defendant's grand jury testimony "is full of such blatant lies [that] it's clear she is just making things up"?[174]

5.   Trial Conduct

PROBLEM 11

Consider the following trial tactics. Which are impermissible or ethically objectionable?

173.   In the widely publicized rape case involving Los Angeles Laker Star Kobe Bryant, lawyers and court clerks disclosed the complainant's identity in violation of court order. Her name address, telephone number, and humiliating personal information quickly became available and was posted on the web. In the wake of death threats, harassment, and humiliating media coverage, she refused to testify and the prosecutor dropped charges. See Kirk Johnson, "As Accuser Balks, Prosecutor Dumps Bryant Rape Case," *N. Y. Times*, Sept. 2, 2004.

174.   Ana Gorman, "Lawyer in Dog–Attack Case May Be Cited," *Los Angeles Times*, March 8, 2002 at B1 (quoting San Francisco Terence Hallinan in a widely publicized dog mauling prosecution).

1) The prosecutor characterizes the defendant police officer as a "punk behind a badge" who used "Gestapo tactics," and refers to defense counsel as "tricky."[175]

2) In response to defense counsel's claim that the guilty parties were still at large, the prosecutor claims that the killers were not at large but were in the courtroom.[176]

3) The prosecutor states that defense counsel's function is to "get his client off" by bringing out "insignificant facts" and "legal technicalities."[177]

4) The prosecutor refers to testimony of a black defense witness as "shucking and jiving" on the stand.[178]

5) "The prosecutor quotes from Biblical passages about the taking of life in order to justify capital punishment as a deterrent."[179]

6) The prosecutor states:

"Ladies and gentlemen, all we want is justice.... What in the world have I or [the assistant attorney general] or the DA's office or the police department got to gain by even trying to convict an innocent person? It would destroy our credibility.... This defendant ... committed a crime so vile, so vicious, so despicable, so unnecessary that the death penalty is the only answer. Sure, your job is hard, but you can do it. Only you can do it. The police department has done all that it can do.... [We] have done all that we can do. Only the 12 of you can finish the job by going up in that jury room and bringing back a verdict of death. Unless you do that, the efforts of the police department and my office have all been in vain."[180]

7) The prosecutor uses peremptory challenges to exclude:

• three black men, wearing blue jeans on the ground that their choice of clothing showed disrespect for the court trying a black defendant;[181]

• two Hispanics who had family members with criminal records, and two other Hispanics who were proficient in Spanish and allegedly might be reluctant to "accept the interpreter as the final arbiter of what was said by ... [a Spanish-speaking] witness" in a prosecution of a Hispanic defendant.[182]

---

175. Commonwealth v. Baranyai, 442 A.2d 800, 801 (Pa.Super.1982).

176. Ortiz v. State, 356 N.E.2d 1188 (Ind.1976).

177. Johnson v. State, 453 N.E.2d 365, 368 (Ind.App.1983).

178. Smith v. State, 516 N.E.2d 1055, 1064 (Ind.1987), cert. denied, 488 U.S. 934 (1988).

179. "The Use of Scriptures ...," *Nat'l. Law J.*, March 20, 2000, at A6.

180. Cargle v. Mullin, 317 F.3d 1196 (10th Cir.2003).

181. Carey Goldberg, "Simpson Again, Race Again," *N.Y. Times*, Sept. 29, 1996, at E4.

182. Hernandez v. New York, 500 U.S. 352, 356 (1991).

NOTES

The boundary between zealous advocacy and prosecutorial abuse during trial has been a matter of continuing dispute. Some of that controversy may be inevitable, given adversarial dynamics and professional standards that are clear in principle but arguable in application. In general, codified rules and existing case law prohibit a prosecutor from: expressing a personal opinion; making arguments calculated to inflame the jury; arguing facts not in evidence; engaging in unduly harsh characterizations of the defense; commenting on a defendant's failure to testify; or excluding a prospective juror based solely on the belief that the juror would be partial to a defendant on grounds of race or gender. Under these standards, how would you evaluate the specific comments in Problem 11? Which of the following sanctions might be appropriate: bar disciplinary actions, reversal of the conviction, judicial contempt citations, or instructions to the jury?

NOTES: PEREMPTORY CHALLENGES

In *Batson v. Kentucky*, 476 U.S. 79 (1986), the Supreme Court held that prosecutors may not exercise peremptory challenges to exclude potential jurors based on race. In *J.E.B. v. Alabama,* 511 U.S. 127 (1994), the Court extended that ruling to ban discrimination based on gender. In the majority's view, such discrimination injures litigants, potential jurors, and the community; the state's "perpetuation of invidious stereotypes" inevitably erodes confidence in the fairness of the judicial system. Under the Court's holdings in *Batson* and *J.E.B.,* a party alleging unlawful bias must make a *prima facie* showing of intentional discrimination; the opposing party must then provide an explanation that is not pretextual and that is based on juror characteristics other than race or gender. What sort of explanation would be sufficient on the facts of Problem 11(7)? Can prosecutors legitimately invoke "neutral" criteria that correlate with race or gender as screening devices? Would other strategies, such as the use of confidential questionnaires, be as effective in identifying biased jurors as group-based characteristics?

How realistic is it to expect lawyers to suspend their assumptions about race, gender, and ethnicity in selecting jurors whose own assumptions are likely to matter? Surveyed practitioners and case files suggest that *Batson* is difficult to enforce. One study of 500 trials and 23,000 jurors over an eight year period found that black jurors were three times more likely to be struck by a prosecutor than whites.[183]

The O.J. Simpson case provided a widely publicized case history of *Batson* violations. There, jury consultants for both sides found that black women were the group most likely to vote for acquittal and least likely to credit the domestic violence evidence, or to respond favorably to Marcia

---

183. "Jeff Juries Formed Unfairly," *Times–Picayune,* Sept 23, 2003. *See also* Leonard Post, "A Loaded Box of Stereotypes: Despite Batson, Race, Gender Play Big Role in Jury Selection," *National L. J.* April 25, 2005 (describing stereotypes such as African Americans distrust of police).

Clark, the white woman lead prosecutor.[184] Although the judge submitted a detailed 79 page questionnaire to prospective jurors, this information did not prevent defense counsel from using peremptory challenges to increase black women's representation on the jury.[185] If you had been one of the lawyers in the *Simpson* case, what would you have done? In his concurring opinion in *Batson v. Kentucky*, 476 U.S. 79, 106–07 (1986), Justice Marshall predicted that "even if all parties approach the court's mandate with the best of conscious intentions, that mandate requires them to confront and overcome their own racism on all levels—a challenge I doubt all of them can meet." If Marshall was right, what follows from his conclusion?

184.   Albert W. Alshuler, "How to Win the Trial of the Century: The Ethics Lord Brougham and the O.J. Simpson Defense Team," 29 *McGeorge L. Rev.* 311–312 (1998).

185.   For acknowledgments by defense lawyers, see sources cited in *id*.

CHAPTER VII

ETHICS IN ORGANIZATIONAL SETTINGS

A. CORPORATE COUNSELING AND WHISTLEBLOWING

1. INTRODUCTION

Most lawyers today work in organizational settings and most of their clients are also organizations. This structure of practice complicates ethical decision-making because lawyers are subject to institutional pressures, incentives, and customs that may sometimes conflict with their personal values or bar codes of conduct.

The materials that follow focus on common organizational contexts such as corporate counsels' office or corporate law firms. The opening case study poses questions about how lawyers in those settings balance competing values such as cost and safety of clients' products. To what extent do these tradeoffs involve ethical as well as business decisions? Is cost/benefit analysis an adequate strategy for resolving such issues?

A related set of issues that arise in many organizational settings involves decision making authority. Where reasonable people disagree on what the appropriate tradeoff should be or what ethical rules require, whose view should prevail? How much deference should an attorney give to judgments by clients' management or by their supervising attorneys?

A final cluster of questions involve lawyers' responsibilities when they disagree on ethical grounds with a client's or a supervisor's decision? Is there a point at which lawyers have a responsibility to blow the whistle on an organizational decision? Should such disclosures about unethical or unlawful activities by clients or colleagues be encouraged? If so, what protections should be available for lawyer-whistleblowers?

PROBLEM 1

You are a senior lawyer in Ford Motor Company's in-house counsel office. One of the company's most respected engineers seeks your advice. He is concerned that Ford, in its rush to market a model competitive with small foreign cars, has been unwilling to make certain safety improvements in the fuel tank placement of Pinto automobiles. Based on your preliminary investigation, management undertakes a full review of safety test results and alternative design plans for the Pinto fuel system. After extensive consultation with the engineering and legal staff, Ford's top executive officers determine that the system, although susceptible to explosion if punctured from the rear, nonetheless meets federal safety standards and that the cost of improving the system would exceed the costs of liability in foreseeable tort litigation. Accordingly, the officers determine not to redesign or recall the model. There is no reason to believe that the Board of Directors would arrive at a different conclusion.

Assume that you disagree with the chief executive officer's decision, but are unable to alter his views. What should you do? What alternatives would you consider? What factors would be relevant to your judgment?

References:

Model Rules 1.2, 1.13, 2.1.

David Luban, Lawyers and Justice: An Ethical Study

206–13 (1988).

The shockers came on three successive days, October 13, 14 and 15, 1979, in three successive front-page *Chicago Tribune* headlines:

OCTOBER 13 FORD IGNORED PINTO FIRE PERIL, SECRET MEMOS SHOW

OCTOBER 14 HOW FORD PUT A PRICE TAG ON AUTOS' SAFETY

OCTOBER 15 U.S. OFFICIAL SEES COVER–UP IN FORD SAFETY TEST POLICY

Of course, everyone knew about the celebrated exploding Pinto long before that time. In February 1978, a California jury had awarded $125 million—later reduced to $6.6 million by a judge—to a teenager who had suffered horrendous burns in a Pinto accident. By the summer of 1978, the macabre gagline "Shut up or I'll back my Pinto into you" was circulating. And the *Tribune*'s research was initiated because a grand jury in Indiana had indicted Ford for reckless homicide in the burning deaths of three teenage women whose 1973 Pinto had exploded after being struck from behind by a van on August 10, 1978.

The secret internal Ford memos revealed in the first two *Tribune* articles made it all worse. They seemed to show a level of foreknowledge and coldblooded calculatedness on Ford's part that appalled many readers.

The first day's memos showed that Ford engineers knew that Pinto gas tanks would be pierced by bolts when struck from behind at speeds as low as 21 m.p.h. This would allow gasoline to leak out, so that any spark, caused, for example, by metal scraping over pavement, would explode the fuel supply. Other memos discussed several modifications in the Pinto design that would make it safer. These were rejected on the grounds that they cost too much money (various figures were cited, ranging from $5.08 to $11 per car), and because some would decrease trunk space.

According to the first *Tribune* article, a Ford memo of November 10, 1970 commented that government-proposed fuel tank safety standards "are too strict and come too soon. Ford executives list lesser standards that the

Department of Transportation 'can be expected to buy' as alternatives.'' A "confidential" memo dated April 22, 1971 recommended that one of the safety devices not be installed until 1976, to save Ford $20.9 million. Another "confidential" memo of October 26, 1971 stated that no additional "fuel system integrity" changes would be made until "required by law." As a result of lobbying by the auto industry, the more stringent legal requirements did not go into effect until 1977; the 1977 Pinto was designed to meet the new requirements. Ford, faced with a government investigation, voluntarily recalled 1.5 million 1971–76 Pintos and Bobcats; as it happened, however, the recall notice was not sent out until twelve days after the Indiana accident.

These memos, in short, indicated that Ford engineers and executives were aware of Pinto's design problem, and that instead of repairing it, they acted deliberately to avoid regulatory and financial consequences to the company.... [Another document contained a cost/benefit analysis in which, according to media accounts, Ford concluded that "[s]aving 180 people from burning to death and another 180 from suffering serious burns in car fires each year would not be worth the cost of adding $11 per car in safety improvements."] The document was prepared by Ford as an argument to the federal government against a higher safety standard. According to a Ford spokesman, "who uttered a profanity when a *Tribune* reporter mentioned the study to him," the government itself had established the dollar value assigned to death and injury by the study. The government, however, claimed that these numbers had been prepared for an entirely different purpose, a federal study of the loss to the national economy brought about by traffic accident injuries.

TABLE 2.

BENEFITS AND COSTS RELATING TO
FUEL LEAKAGE ASSOCIATED WITH THE
STATIC ROLLOVER TEST PORTION OF FMVSS 208

Benefits: *Savings*—180 burn deaths, 180 serious burn injuries, 2100 burned vehicles.
Unit Cost—$200,000 per death, $67,000 per injury, $700 per vehicle.
Total Benefit—180 × ($200,000) + 180 × ($67,000) + 2100 × ($700) = $49.5 million.

Costs: *Sales*—11 million cars, 1.5 million light trucks.
Unit Cost—$11 per car, $11 per truck.
Total Cost—11,000,000 × ($11) + 1,500,000 × ($11) = $137 million.

Source: Strobel, Lee, "How Ford put a price tag on auto's safety," *Chicago Tribune,* October 14, 1979, p. 18. [Table taken from Ford's study]

The final day's stories focused on statements by federal officials that Ford's way of handling the crash-test data on Pinto might amount to a cover-up. . . .

Ford was acquitted of reckless homicide in the Indiana trial. The defense was able to prevent 280 of the 300 Ford documents from being introduced as evidence. It argued that after the recall was initiated, federal regulations actually prevented Ford from notifying Pinto owners of the dangerous gas tank, and thus Ford was not legally reckless. But the key to the defense lay in the facts of the Indiana case. The young women's car was struck by a van moving fifty m.p.h., enough to rupture the fuel tank on any comparable car. The prosecution argued that the Pinto was moving between fifteen and thirty-five m.p.h. when struck (so that the relative speed of the crash was between fifteen and thirty-five m.p.h.). The defense, interviewing possible witnesses as far away as Costa Rica, turned up two hospital employees who reported a deathbed conversation with one of the victims, who said she had stopped the car. Prosecutor Michael Cosentino's grisly attempt to impugn this testimony—by arguing that since the victim's lips were totally burned off, she could not possibly have articulated the word "stopped"—failed, and Ford was acquitted of murder.

According to the *Tribune*, Ford engineers had known since 1968 that fuel tanks in the position of the Pinto's were liable to rupture "at very low speed," and discussions of how to deal with the problem in Pintos had been going on since at least 1970. Yet until the lawsuits began, the public had no inkling of the matter. And the consequences were severe: the company itself could estimate how many people would be immolated in their Pintos. During 1976 and 1977 alone "thirteen Pintos—more than double the number that might be expected in proportion to their numbers—were involved in fiery rear-end crashes resulting in deaths" while the VW Rabbit and Toyota Corolla suffered none. Some might say that it is a mistake to dwell on the particulars: it makes our reactions too emotional. On the contrary, I think that in problems such as these we cannot afford to forget the three teenagers who perished in a one-thousand-degree fire. And, if the *Tribune* stories are accurate, Ford knew precisely what it was doing. . . .

[In particular,] [a]ccording to former Ford executive Harley Copp, the lawyers [in Ford's legal department] "definitely knew" what was in those documents. . . .

. . .

Before turning to our principal question, however, the question of whether Ford's attorney should have blown the whistle, we must address a prior one: assuming that the facts of the case are as the newspapers stated them, did Ford do anything immoral?

This question sounds absurd. If allowing innocent people to be immolated for no other reason than cold, cold cash isn't immoral, what is? Only one thing, we might answer: doing a study on it first and then covering up the whole horrible process.

Despite this understandable reaction, there is another way to look at the matter. What was it that Ford did? It traded off cost for safety. But that is what car manufacturers must always do. Safety costs money, and people may not be willing to pay the price. Hence, the cheaper, in both senses, car. ([Ford executive Lee] Iacocca introduced the Pinto to break into the under-two-thousand-pounds-and-two-thousand-dollars market.) Government regulations set minimum safety standards, but after these were met, the marketplace sets the level of safety.

. . . Pinto's gastank was punctured at twenty-one m.p.h. collisions. For $6.65 extra, it would have withstood thirty m.p.h. But it still would have gone at forty. For more money, it would have stood up to fifty-five (Pinto would then have resembled an armored half-track). But no car is totally safe, and thus they will all generate their grotesque cost-benefit analyses. Indeed, a standard test of negligent design in tort law is simply that the risk of the design outweighs the benefits; even in strict liability, where the only issue is whether the product is defective and not whether the manufacturer was negligent, one well-known definition of "defective design" is just "design that is not optimally risk-beneficial." Thus, not only does the law contemplate the trade-off of safety against price, compliance with it will require cost-benefit studies such as Ford's.

This brings us to the second part of the response. To a sophisticated reader, Ford's cost-benefit study is nothing to get excited about. First of all, that number of deaths is simply an actuarial statistic and does not by any means show a callous attitude toward human life, any more than does a similar study by your insurance company or by the manufacturer of the safest car money can buy. Every car has a small but calculable probability of burning you to death. Multiply a tiny probability by millions of cars and you will get a body count like Ford's. One hundred and eighty deaths out of 12.5 million vehicles translates into the statistic that the gastank Ford was using increased your chance of death by one in seventy thousand over the safer alternative. That doesn't sound as bad as actually writing down the number of deaths; nevertheless, mathematically the numbers are equivalent. (Many people would bet their lives against eleven dollars at seventy thousand to one odds: you take a worse bet by far every time you ride without a seatbelt.)

Nor is that two hundred thousand dollars per death figure beyond the pale of humanity. Personal injury lawyers use formulas for computing the value of a wrongful death: it's just one of the things that must be done to compensate, as far as possible, for irreversible losses. The fact that we normally do not put a price tag on human life does not mean that its economic meaning is incalculable, and indeed we "calculate" it every time we choose not to invest in a piece of safety equipment.

So, at any rate, goes the argument. It says that Ford was not doing anything improper or out of the ordinary: it just got caught with a lot of embarrassing memos that made for good copy but really signified nothing.

2. Cost/Benefit Frameworks

Marianne Lavelle, "Placing a Price on Human Life"

National Law Journal, Oct. 10, 1988, at 1, 28–29.

What is the worth of a human life?

The question, unthinkable to some, is a key consideration for the people balancing the cost of government regulation against the benefit of saving lives. . . .

Putting a price tag on life seems "harsh or cold-blooded" to some critics, say . . . Boston University Law Prof. Clayton P. Gillette and Thomas D. Hopkins, an economist at Rochester Institute of Technology. The two scholars themselves view the valuing of human life as a common and necessary practice.

If the government wants to force a change in the design of automobiles that costs car-makers $10 million and will save 10 lives a year, the professors say life valuation inevitably comes into play. The regulation obviously would be worth the cost if a human life is valued at $1 million or more. But what if a human life is worth less? Strict cost-benefit analysis adherents might call that proposal too expensive to implement—and perhaps would urge weighing other alternatives.

The problem, according to Messrs. Gillette and Hopkins, is that Uncle Sam has decided, on different days and in different ways, that the dollar value of a life is as little as $70,000, as much as $132 million, anywhere in between and impossible to measure.

Separate numbers and philosophies have been adopted by many of the 90–some agencies charged with assuring Americans have clean air and safe food and products, according to the report. . . .

To Ralph A. Luken, a chief economist with the Environmental Protection Agency, using dollars to represent lives saved by regulation is a straightforward process that helps the agency compare oranges with oranges. "We try to the extent possible to monetize things, because otherwise it's relatively difficult to make comparisons," he says. "How do you compare crop loss to sick days? You need to integrate information."

At the opposite end of the spectrum, Barry Felrice, an administrator at the National Highway Traffic Safety Authority, says his agency eschews quantification of life as a matter of principle. Although the agency estimates how many lives could be saved by air bags, child restraints or the like, NHTSA refuses to translate that benefit into dollars. "Our statute tells us explicitly that safety shall be given an overriding concern," he says.

That doesn't mean regulation at all costs; the proposals are analyzed for their "practicability," says Mr. Felrice. "We interpret that to mean we don't put the car companies out of business." . . .

Different philosophies have bred differing values of life, according to the Gillette–Hopkins report, prepared for the Administrative Conference of the United States, a government think tank that looks for ways to improve efficiency in the federal bureaucracy.

At the extremes, the Consumer Product Safety Commission judged a life to be worth $70,000 in a 1980 proposal for regulation of space heaters, while the Food and Drug Administration's 1979 ban of the pesticide DES in cattle feed judged each life saved to be worth $132 million.

The Nuclear Regulatory Commission, meanwhile, has a unique system that takes into account the number of people affected multiplied by possible amounts of radiation released. By one calculation, the professors found the NRC's so called person-rem standard translates to $7.4 million per life saved.

Juries, on average, award $950,000 as the value of a man in his 30s, according to Jury Verdict Research Co. of Solon, Ohio. The approach used in most courtrooms can be summed up in the phrase, "You are what you earn," a theory articulated as long ago as 1776, by Adam Smith in "Wealth of Nations." . . .

But what is standard operating procedure in the courtroom is considered passé in most of the regulatory world. If human value is equivalent only to potential earnings, then women, children, minorities and the elderly lose their worth. As Jury Verdict Research Co. documents, the average jury settlement for the death of a woman over 65 years old is $85,000.

Most agencies, therefore, have moved to a life valuation method called "willingness-to-pay," which has gained wide acceptance among economists.

How much is a person willing to pay to avoid death? Economists derive this seemingly unknowable number by looking at workers in high-risk jobs such as mining and construction. How much of a pay premium do employers have to offer to lure employees into these dangerous occupations? Using those premium figures and a complex formula, economists have determined value-of-life figures that, for the most part, put jury verdicts to shame.

The value of life appears to be about $1.95 million, give or take $500,000, according to about 25 studies judged credible by economist Ted R. Miller of the liberal Washington think tank, the Urban Institute. . . . Despite high praise, willingness-to-pay has its drawbacks. For example, it assumes workers fully know and understand the risks involved in jobs, and freely accept the wages fairly offered.

That particular set of assumptions proves the economists are "not in commuting distance with this galaxy," says lawyer David Vladeck of Ralph Nader's Public Citizen Litigation Group. Because the real world rarely achieves the free-market ideal, economists have not quite perfected the willingness-to-pay process.

Although the figures do hover around $2 million, Mr. Miller has seen studies come up with life values ranging from $500,000 to more than $10 million. At the EPA, which has studied the process more than any other federal agency, willingness-to-pay has produced values ranging from $400,000 to $7 million. . . .

Mr. Gillette admits, "Everyone is a little uneasy about charging government with the responsibility of deciding how much a life's worth." But he argues that more serious thought about the worth of human life in regulation could lead to greater care for safety, not less. The highly publicized case of Jessica McClure, the baby saved after two days trapped in an open well in 1987, serves as an example of how money might have been better spent on prevention.

"We were willing to spend all sorts of money to save her," says Mr. Gillette, "even though no one thought for a minute about whether it was worth spending any money at all to plug up the wells."

NOTES: COST/BENEFIT ANALYSIS

In his study of decisionmaking by corporate management, Robert Jackall writes that:

> scientific theories of decision making . . . provide managers with a whole range of conceptual tools—cost/benefit analysis, risk/benefit analysis, . . . and so on—that purport to "take the black magic out of management" and routinize administration. It is worth noting that even managers who are skeptical about the efficacy of such measures are among the principal consumers of such techniques and of analytical devices of every sort. In trying to come to grips with what seem at times to be incalculable, irrational forces, one must be willing to use whatever tools are at hand. Moreover, in an increasingly professional-ized managerial environment, to eschew a vocabulary of rationality or the opportunity to routinize decisions when possible, can only make one vulnerable to the charge of "managing by the seat of the pants."[1]

Jackall illustrates with an incident involving White, a hearing safety expert working for a textile manufacturer. When White proposed potential-ly costly safeguards to protect the hearing of workers in a noisy mill, he found himself increasingly isolated and ignored. Jackall comments that

> White's moral squint on the hearing issue, manifested by his obvious emotional commitment to the problem and his insistence on the company's obligation to workers, made other managers uncomfortable. The only publicly acceptable way to discuss such an issue, of course, is in rational/technical, emotionally neutral terms like "liability conse-quences," the "trade-off between noise reduction and efficiency," or the "linkage of compliance with regulation to productivity improve-ment. . . ."[2]

White's experience can be viewed as a cautionary tale. Lawyers are often most effective when they couch their advice in the pragmatic terms

---

1. Robert Jackall, *Moral Mazes: The World of Corporate Managers* 76 (1988).

2. *Id.* at 104.

that make clients and colleagues comfortable. This strategy allows attorneys to raise ethical concerns without sounding preachy or judgmental: objectionable conduct can be characterized as "unduly risky, as something that will not play well with jurors, governmental regulators, the media, or the general public."[3] By contrast, approaches that implicitly impugn clients or colleagues' moral sensibilities may often arouse anger and resistance.[4]

However, the issue is one of substance as well as style. Underlying the rhetoric of cost-benefit analysis are several key assumptions: that, in some sense, everything, including human life, has a price; that the price can be ascertained objectively; that all issues should be seen as economic issues; and that ethical appeals reflect personal, subjective, and often emotional concerns that cloud rational decision making. A central question is whether these assumptions are themselves defensible.

Economists use the term "cost-benefit analysis" to refer to a set of formal techniques for evaluating the economic value of projects. Conceptually, it is closely aligned with utilitarian analysis, and it plays an important role in guiding policy, particularly when the economics of a project is the only issue on the table. But as the Luban and Lavalle excerpts indicate, the technique becomes more controversial when it requires assigning dollar values to goods, such as human life and safety, or the natural environment, that people value for moral, religious, aesthetic, or emotional reasons over and above their economic worth. Economists have developed sophisticated techniques to study how people implicitly place price-tags on these "fragile values," but the efforts strike some critics as a crass category-mistake: judging the value of someone's religious convictions by asking how much they are worth in dollars misses the point, in just the way that judging economic theories by asking how much economists would be willing to pay to have them be true misses the point.[5] To these critics, the assumption that all values have a price overlooks what Justice Oliver Wendell Holmes, Jr. called "the importance of the uneconomic to man...."[6] To defenders of cost-benefit analysis, no better method is available for evaluating public investment decisions and regulations.[7]

One important question is how objective cost-benefit analysis actually is. Put another way, would all of its practitioners arrive at the same conclusion? The answer appears to be no, because the outcome depends on

---

3. Deborah L. Rhode, "Moral Counseling," 75 *Fordham L. Rev.* 1317, 1319 (2006).

4. Ian Ayers & John Braithwaithe, *Responsible Regulation: Transcending the Deregulation Debate* 92 (1992); Sally S. Simpson, "Corporate–Crime Deterrence and Corporate–Control Policies: Views from the Inside," in *White Collar Crime Reconsidered* 289–291 (Kip Schlegel & David Weisburd, eds. 1992) (noting management's tendency to marginalize moral concerns that appear to clash with business considerations).

5. Mark Sagoff, "At the Monument to General Meade, or On the Difference Between Beliefs and Benefits," 42 *Ariz. L. Rev.* 433, 452 (2000).

6. Oliver Wendell Holmes, Jr., "Address of Chief Justice Holmes," in *Collected Legal Papers* 272, 273–74 (Mark de Wolfe Howe, ed. 1920).

7. Matthew D. Adler & Eric A. Posner, "Rethinking Cost–Benefit Analysis," 109 *Yale L.J.* 165 (1999). *See generally* Matthew D. Adler & Eric A. Posner, *Cost–Benefit Analysis: Legal, Ethical, and Philosophical Perspectives* (2001).

which method analysts employ for assigning prices to fragile values. Yet in everyday life we seldom think in purely monetary terms about the value of human life, so analysts must resort to indirect methods of pricing life, such as those summarized by philosopher Alasdair MacIntyre:

> Writers on cost-benefit analysis techniques have devised four alternative methods for computing the cost of a person's life. One is that of discounting to the present the person's expected future earnings; a second is that of computing the losses to others from the person's death so as to calculate their present discounted value; a third is that of examining the value placed on an individual life by presently established social policies and practices, e.g., the benefits in increased motor traffic which society at the present moment is prepared to exchange for a higher fatal accident rate; and a fourth is to ask what value a person placed on his or her own life, by looking at the risks which that person is or was prepared to take and the insurance premiums which he or she was prepared to pay.

MacIntyre, like other contemporary economists, observes that these criteria sometimes yield different answers, so that however rigorous the analysis, the result may be arbitrarily determined by the initial choice of method for pricing human life.[8]

Furthermore, decision-makers must find a way to limit the alternative courses of action under consideration. The decision about which options to consider can often determine the outcomes reached. So, for example, in the Ford Pinto case, it matters which safety improvement the decision-maker subjects to cost-benefit calculation. Should it be the $11 it would cost per car to fix the problem, or the much more modest cost involved in reducing the hazard through partial adjustments or in averting the risk through better design in the first instance? Similar questions have arisen in cases following the Ford Pinto litigation that presented analogous facts.[9]

Another contentious point about cost-benefit analysis concerns the technique of "discounting"—assigning lower dollar values to human lives lost later than to those lost earlier (for the same reason that a dollar lost ten years from now is worth less than a dollar lost now). Proponents of discounting argue that it not only represents sound economics, but also mirrors the way we ordinarily think: most of us are more concerned with the near future than the further future. Critics reply that discounting the

---

8. Alasdair MacIntyre, "Utilitarianism and Cost–Benefit Analysis: An Essay on the Relevance of Moral Philosophy to Bureaucratic Theory," *in Values in the Electric Power Industry* 221 227–28 (Kenneth M. Sayre ed. 1977); W.Kip Vicusi, "The Value of Life in Legal Contexts: Survey and Critique," 2 *Am. L. & Econ. Rev.* 195 (2000) (noting disparity between the "valuation of life," which reflects how individuals respond to risk and the "cost of death," which reflects quantifiable losses when individuals die); Bill Marsh, "Putting a Price on the Priceless: One Life,"

N.Y. Times, Sept. 9, 2007, at E 4 (noting differences between average jury values of $4 million, 9/11 benefit fund values, which averaged 2 million, and individuals' valuation based on price they pay to reduce various risks, which ranges from about $500,000 to $6 million).

9. For example, in the Pinto case, installation of a $5 safety device would have resulted in a considerably lower rate of risk. *See* Mark Dowie, "Pinto Madness," *Mother Jones*, Sept./Oct. 1977, at 28–29.

value of death and illness for future generations wrongly treats them as beings of lesser worth than ourselves.[10]

It is important to distinguish formal cost-benefit analysis—a mathematical methodology—from what might more loosely be described as thinking in terms of costs and benefits. Business lawyers and their clients often discuss choices in terms of costs and benefits even without a formal cost-benefit analysis prepared by economic experts. Informal cost-benefit thinking will seldom employ controversial techniques such as discounting, but it may still backfire if it assigns dollar figures to values like human life that many people think should not be assessed in the same way that we price potatoes. The jurors in one Pinto case were so outraged at Ford's cost-benefit analysis that they awarded the injured plaintiffs punitive damages exactly equal to the money that the cost-benefit analysis said Ford was saving by not repairing the Pinto.[11]

Cost-benefit analysis is most defensible when it considers the consequences to all concerned; in these cases, its affinity to utilitarian moral frameworks is strongest. But lawyers typically examine the consequences only to their clients, and their clients frequently consider consequences only to themselves. As one expert on corporate misconduct and social responsibility notes, the reality is that it is sometimes economically rational for companies to ignore health and safety laws, given the low risks of detection and of serious penalties. As a result, "any compliance policy that relies totally on cost benefit calculations is 'doomed to fail.' You cannot take the moral content out of social control and expect social control to work."[12]

Critics of cost benefit analysis often suggest that a rights-based approach is preferable in many health and safety contexts. This approach might call for recognition of a right not to be subject to unreasonable risks. Or, under the approach of the highway traffic administrators described by Lavelle, the standard might be the maximum level of safety that is economically practical.

Formulating a right in these terms would, of course, require consideration of most of the same factors that would be relevant under a cost-benefit utilitarian analysis. To decide what is reasonable or practical, decisionmakers would need to limit the range of alternatives under review, assess their costs, predict their consequences, and so forth; these evaluations would involve the same indeterminacies noted earlier. However, a rights-based framework could nevertheless yield somewhat different questions and outcomes than a pure utilitarian approach because it can presuppose certain priorities, such as safety, or establish certain minimum standards and benchmarks.

---

10. The point is debated in Lisa Heinzerling, "Regulatory Costs of Mythic Proportions," 107 *Yale L.J.* 1981 (1998), John J. Donohue III, "Why We Should Discount the Views of Those Who Discount Discounting," 108 *Yale L. J.* 1901 (1999), Lisa Heinzerling, "Discounting Life," 108 *Yale L.J.* 1911 (1999).

11. Grimshaw v. Ford Motor Co., 119 Cal.App.3d 757, 790 (Cal. 1981).

12. John Braithwaite, *Crime, Shame, and Reintegration* 141 (1989).

Thus, in the Pinto case, a rights-based approach would not focus directly on Ford's costs and benefits of remedying the design defect but rather on the degree of risk that an informed buyer should reasonably expect in light of prevailing industry standards. This is, in effect, the California tort standard. Consumer expectations would, of course, be affected by the costs and benefits of safety features for the industry as a whole. However, the final outcome would not be skewed by Ford's initial mistake or its restricted choice of alternatives in comparing price and risk.

To be sure, this approach is subject to many of the same ambiguities as utilitarian analysis. For example, should we assess consumer expectations in light of an automobile's overall safety record or on the basis of rear-end fire fatalities? Is the latter issue one on which most consumers have expectations? Which framework we select is highly relevant in cases like the Ford Pinto. According to tort expert Gary Schwartz's research, the Pinto's overall safety record during the relevant period was quite "respectable," in part because only 1 percent of all traffic crashes result in fires and only 4 percent of accident fatalities occur in fire crashes. However, because of its gas tank placement the Pinto did perform much worse regarding rear-end fire fatalities than most subcompacts.[13]

Decision-makers in a situation like the Pinto case could thus arrive at much the same outcome through either a utilitarian or rights-based approach. A utilitarian who began with a less limited set of alternatives than Ford might end up protecting a reasonable expectation of safety. But there are recurrent situations in which the two ethical frameworks can yield quite different outcomes, particularly where the values at stake are fragile and significant. To take an example involving the valuation of life, suppose that a worker is trapped in a mine explosion. Rescue is possible but extremely expensive. For about the same cost, it would be possible to institute safety investments that would, on the average, save three lives over the next decade. Alternatively, suppose that it would be possible to save the life of a child involved in a Pinto crash but only through quite costly intensive care and rehabilitative therapy. If she is allowed to die, the same resources could be used for prenatal programs that would save the lives of several other children. A strict utilitarian might prefer to maximize the lives saved; an alternative approach, grounded in respect for each individual life, would decline to sacrifice one innocent person for the good of several anonymous others.

Which of these ethical frameworks makes most sense on the facts in Problem 1? How would you judge Ford's decision under each standard? Consider Gary Schwartz's claim that cases like the Pinto reflect a "two cultures problem." On the one hand, we expect both governmental and corporate decision-makers to consider cost-benefit trade-offs when setting safety standards or evaluating design alternatives. Indeed, product liability

---

13. During the period in question, the Pinto accounted for about 2 percent of automobiles and about 2 percent of fatal accidents accompanied by fire, but about 4 percent of all rear-end fire-related fatalities. Gary T. Schwartz, "The Myth of the Ford Pinto Case," 43 *Rutgers L.Rev.* 966, 1032 (1992).

law requires such an evaluation. On the other hand, when we are dealing not with statistics and probabilities but with identifiable victims such as the trapped miner or Pinto passenger, the prospect of trading cash for lives offends deeply felt moral values.

How the tort system should respond to this ambivalence has been a subject of considerable debate. However one resolves that question in general, and however one assesses Ford's conduct in particular, the point that bears emphasis here is that lawyers counseling corporations need to consider the ethical limitations of cost-benefit analysis. Such considerations are crucial for attorneys not only in their own comfort level with a decision, but in predicting their clients' potential legal liabilities and public relations consequences.

Given such considerations, was the conduct of Ford Motor Company in the Pinto case wrong? Do the Luban, Lavelle, and MacIntyre excerpts suggest problems in the figures Ford used to make its cost-benefit calculations or in the method itself? Did Ford managers' seemingly utilitarian analysis rest on any implicit non-utilitarian assumptions about what consequences mattered and how they should be measured? If so, were those assumptions reasonable?

3.   Whistleblowing

NOTES

Studies of hazardous or illegal conduct in organizational settings suggest a common pattern. A bad decision is often made under circumstances of inadequate time and information. Reversing that decision later would impose serious financial costs and delays. Individuals would lose credibility. Organizations would lose profits. The likely harms are abstract, remote, and frequently uncertain in dimensions. Victims are anonymous probabilities; information and accountability for consequences are fragmented. Under these circumstances, individuals face substantial temptation to avoid knowledge and dodge responsibility. And when someone else challenges their conduct, the tendency is often to rally around the original decision.[14] As one summary of the problem concludes:

> A wide array of research evidence documents the role of cognitive biases in distorting individual judgment on health, safety, and financial matters that may pose ethical concerns. Two related problems involve overconfidence and overcommitment. Those who obtain decision making positions often have high confidence in their own capacities and judgment. That can readily lead to arrogance, over-optimism, and an escalation of commitment to choices that turn out to be wrong, either factually or morally As a result, individuals may ignore or suppress dissent, overestimate their ability to rectify adverse consequences, and

14. John M. Darley, "How Organizations Socialize Individuals Into Evildoing," in *Codes of Conduct: Behavior Research Into* *Business Ethics* 31–35 (David M. Messick & Ann E. Tenbrunsel eds. 1996).

cover up mistakes by denying, withholding, or sometimes destroying information. An incremental slide into ever more dubious conduct can readily produce "the boiled frog" problem. A frog thrown into boiling water will jump out of the pot. A frog placed in tepid water that gradually becomes hotter and hotter will calmly boil to death.[15]

How should law and lawyers respond to this pattern?

In the Pinto case, suppose that Ford's lawyers tried but failed to obtain internal review of management's safety decisions. Should those attorneys be permitted or encouraged to disclose the relevant facts to a government agency or consumer organization? Should disclosure of confidential information be mandatory rather than permissive in circumstances posing clear threats to life and safety? Under Nuclear Regulatory Commission mandates, an employee who becomes aware of certain nuclear safety risks must inform governmental officials. Engineering codes of conduct similarly require disclosure of conditions posing a risk to public health or welfare.[16] Should comparable requirements be applicable for lawyers in other contexts likely to involve serious health hazards?

As Chapter V and discussion in Part B below indicate, earlier drafts of the Model Rules would have obligated disclosure to prevent a client from committing an act that would result in death or substantial bodily harm to a third party. The ABA House of Delegates chose rather to approve a discretionary provision in response to concerns that lawyers would face undue risk of liability for nondisclosure, and that clients would withhold information necessary for effective representation. Consider those arguments in light of the materials in Chapter V regarding confidentiality, including Fred Zacharias' study of New York lawyer and client attitudes. Under one of the hypothetical situations in Zacharias' survey:

> The general counsel to a firm that produces a metal alloy used in the manufacture of airplanes learns of a company study that suggests that in some high-altitude flight patterns the alloy might weaken and cause a plane to explode. The alloy does, however, meet the minimum safety standards set by the government. The lawyer urges the Board of Directors to recall the alloy or at a minimum to inform users of its potential danger. The Board decides that the study is too inconclusive to warrant action in light of the dire financial consequences of disclosure to the company.[17]

Over three quarters of surveyed lawyers indicated that they would not disclose the information, a decision consistent with New York code provisions. Approximately half of the surveyed clients believed (incorrectly) that

---

15. Rhode, *supra* note 3, at 1321.

16. Nat'l. Society of Professional Engineers, "Code of Ethics for Engineers," Rule II.1(a), in *Codes of Professional Responsibility* 102 (Rena A. Gurlin ed., 4th ed. 1999). See Michael C. McFarland, "The Public Health, Safety, and Welfare: An Analysis of the Social Responsibilities of Engineers," in *Social, Ethical and Policy Implications of Engineering:* *Selected Readings* 121 (Joseph R. Herkert ed., 2000).

17. Fred Zacharias, "Rethinking Confidentiality," 74 *Iowa L. Rev.* 351 (1989). The hypothetical comes from John Ferren, "The Corporate Lawyer's Obligation to the Public Interest," 33 *Bus.Lawyer* 1253 (1978).

attorneys had discretion to disclose under current rules, 85% believed that attorneys should disclose, and only 15% indicated that disclosure would affect their willingness to use an attorney's services.[18]

If you were on a bar commission charged with recommending rules on confidentiality, what formulation would you propose? What effect do you think a different rule might have on attorney conduct under circumstances described in Problem 1? In his discussion of the Pinto problem, Luban concludes that if Ford's lawyers could not convince the company to redesign or recall the car, they should have alerted the public to the danger. Do you agree? Are there persuasive reasons why lawyers should defer to other decision-makers on cost and safety decisions? Consider the following arguments.

Government Regulation

A common claim by corporate clients and their lawyers is that responsibility for protecting public welfare rests with government. It is for politically accountable officials, not self-appointed attorney moralists, to make difficult trade-offs. As long as clients comply with existing regulations, their duties are satisfied. This argument surfaces in a wide array of organizational settings. So, for example, defenders of Enron's lawyers claimed that the techniques the company used to mislead investors about its financial condition were not clearly unlawful. And, as noted in the materials on the Hewlett Packard pretexting scandal discussed below, both in-house and outside lawyers advised the company that using fraudulent representations to obtain private phone records of board members and reporters was not illegal and therefore was acceptable.

An obvious problem with this view is that it fails to acknowledge the limits of regulation. In contexts like the Ford Pinto case, industry organizations typically exercise far more influence over regulatory structures and enforcement than unorganized and uninformed consumers. Inadequate information among regulators may allow distribution of a product without adequate review of risks, as was the case with asbestos, Dalkon shield contraceptive devices, and many automobile safety features.[19] In some contexts, corporate or industry organizations are reluctant even to conduct adequate research on safety risks for fear of creating adverse evidence that may cause future legal or regulatory problems.[20]

---

18. Zacharias, *supra* note 17, at 392–395.

19. See, e.g., Paul Brodeur, *Outrageous Misconduct: The Asbestos Industry on Trial* (1985); Susan Perry & Jim Dawson, *Nightmare: Women and the Dalkon Shield* 208 (1985); Bob Egelko, "Court Upholds Big Award Against Ford," *San Francisco Chronicle*, October 24, 2002, at A7 (discussing $290 million punitive damage award against Ford for defects in Ford Bronco design that company's safety engineers concluded would make deaths in a rollover particularly likely even though the vehicle met federal safety standards); Laurie J. Flynn, "Love in the Time of Benzene," *N.Y. Times*, November 17, 2003, at C1.

20. See the discussion in Chapter V of judicial findings that the Dalkon Shield manufacturer and the tobacco industry refrained from safety research because of liability concerns.

The Market

A related issue of decision-making authority involves the rights of consumers, workers, or other affected parties to make their own trade-offs between dollars and risks. Corporate clients and their counsel often claim that it is not their role to impose personal preferences on others about what level of safety to demand.

How plausible is this alternative in circumstances such as the Pinto case? How much information about how many features of how many comparable models would consumers need in order to make a truly rational choice? Studies of informed consent in medical contexts indicate that most individuals do not adequately understand or recall disclosures concerning risky or experimental procedures. When faced with hard treatment choices, most surveyed patients do not want decision-making control and responsibility.[21] When making car purchases, how many prospective buyers are likely to focus on rear-end collision fatalities? Even when the issue was brought to their attention, about half of Pinto purchasers did not respond to Ford's recall notice and obtain free safety improvements.[22] Indeed Dennis Gioia, the company's former recall coordinator, now notes with some chagrin that he not only owned a Pinto at the time of the fires, but also that he sold it to his sister.[23]

Was he right, however, in the priorities that the company drew from that fact? Does it follow that consumers are unconcerned with safety simply because they do not make it central to their final decisions? Might they simply assume that government standards establish adequate protection? And if such standards in fact fall short, is there a role for disclosures that would enable consumers and regulators to make informed choices?

Studies of whistleblowers who make such disclosures in various public and private sectors find that disclosure can result in substantial personal costs, but also substantial societal benefits. Some individuals experience harassment, isolation, and economic retaliation as well as the pain that comes from exposing colleagues' misjudgments. As Sissela Bok notes: "the message of the whistleblower is seen as a *breach of loyalty* because it comes from within. . . . The conflict is strongest for those who take their responsibilities to the public seriously, yet have close bonds of collegiality and duty to clients as well."[24] One lawyer who became unemployable after bearing

---

21. See e.g., Jon F. Merz & Baruch Fischoff, "Informed Consent Does Not Mean Rational Consent," 11 *J. Legal Med.* 321, 343–344 (1990); Barry Schwartz, *The Paradox of Choice: Why More is Less* (2004).

22. Schwartz, *supra* note 13, at 1041–1043.

23. Dennis Gioia, "Pinto Fires and Personal Ethics: A Script Analysis of Missed Opportunities," 11 *J. Bus. Ethics* 380, 384 (1992).

24. Sissela Bok, *Secrets* 214–15 (1982). *See* Roberta Ann Johnson, *Whistleblowing: When It Works—and Why* (2003); Fred C. Zacharias, "Coercing Clients: Can Lawyer Gatekeeper Rules Work?," 47 *Boston C. L. Rev.* 455 (2006); Sung Hui Kim, "The Banality of Fraud: Resituating the Inside Counsel as Gatekeeper," 74 *Fordham L. Rev.* 983, 1064–65 (2005).

an unwelcome message noted, "People think whistleblowers are great but they don't necessarily want one in their organizations."[25]

Yet leaks of confidential information have been critical in exposing major government scandals, and in preventing or remedying hazardous products and environmental disasters. And lawyers have been subject to substantial criticism and sometimes financial liability for failing to protect innocent third parties. The most widely publicized cases include those involving tobacco, asbestos, automobiles, contraceptives, and savings & loan associations.[26]

Should any steps be taken, apart from changes in bar ethical codes, to permit or encourage whistleblowing? Beginning in the 1970s, the federal government began passing legislation that protects government employees who disclose abuses, and private employees who report violations of certain federal safety and environmental standards. A few states have laws protecting all employees, not only those in regulated industries, who report violations to a government body. About half of all jurisdictions also have established public policy exceptions to employers' rights to fire at will in response to ethical resistance. Yet although most courts have allowed employees to sue for wrongful discharge if they are fired for refusing to do something illegal, similar protection has not been available where employees lose their jobs after aggressively reporting illegalities to management.

In the few cases that have arisen involving lawyers who blew the whistle on clients, courts have reached varying results. Several well-publicized decisions have not permitted attorneys' claims to proceed to trial. In *Herbster v. North American Co. for Life and Health Ins.*, 501 N.E.2d 343 (Ill.App.1986), *cert. denied*, 484 U.S. 850 (1987), an attorney sought $250,000 compensatory damages and $10 million punitive damages after he was fired for allegedly disobeying management's request to destroy certain files. The district court granted the insurance company's motion to dismiss on the ground that the communications alleged in the complaint were confidences protected by the attorney-client relationship. In *Balla v. Gambro, Inc.*, 584 N.E.2d 104 (Ill.1991), an in-house lawyer was fired after he told his superior that he would do anything in his power to stop the company from selling kidney dialysis machines known to be ineffective. Denying his cause of action, the Illinois Supreme Court reasoned that wrongful discharge suits were not necessary to encourage lawyer whistleblowing because professional ethics already compel attorneys to promote the public interest. Illinois's version of Model Rule 1.6 requires lawyers to disclose confidential information to the extent necessary "to prevent the client from committing an act that would result in death or serious bodily injury." In *Willy v. Coastal Corp.*, ARB Case No. 98–060, at 34–36 (U.S.

---

25. John Gibeaut, "Telling Secrets," *ABA J.* Nov. 2004, at 73 (quoting Susan W. Ausman).

26. *See* Deborah L. Rhode, *In the Interests of Justice* 106–109 (2001); Martin Mayer, *The Greatest–Ever Bank Robbery* (1990);

Richard Zitrin & Carol M. Langford, *The Moral Compass of the American Lawyers* 94–11 (1999); Morton Mintz, *At any Cost: Corporate Greed, Women, and the Dalkon Shield* (1985); and sources cited in notes 19 and 24 *supra*.

Dept. Of Labor Feb. 27, 2004), the U.S. Department of Labor's Administrative Review Board held that federal common law prevented a discharged lawyer from using privileged or confidential information of his former lawyer to prove his claim.

Other courts have been more receptive to the plight of fired whistle-blowers. These decisions have relied on three major theories. Discharges of whistle-blowers have been held to violate public policy; to breach an implied covenant of good faith and fair dealing; or to violate an implicit term of attorneys' employment contract. For example, in *Mourad v. Automobile Club Ins. Assn.,* 465 N.W.2d 395 (Mich.App.1991), the Michigan Court of Appeals upheld a $1.25 million jury award to an in-house lawyer who sued for retaliatory discharge and demotion. He claimed that the defendant insurance company had punished his resistance to cutting corners and costs in defending policyholders. In the appellate court's view, the company should have known in hiring the attorney that he would be bound by the Code of Professional Responsibility and should have "incorporated this fact in creating a just cause employment contract."

So too, in *General Dynamics Corporation v. Superior Court,* 876 P.2d 487 (Cal.Sup.Ct.1994), and GTE Products Corp. v. Stewart, 653 N.E.2d 161 (Mass.1995), both the California and Massachusetts Supreme Courts upheld corporate counsel's right to sue for retaliatory discharges under certain circumstances. Those circumstances included discharges exposing criminal conduct or violations of clear public policy that could be proved without violating the attorney's obligations of confidentiality.

Parallel issues arise when lawyers report misconduct by fellow lawyers. Although both the Model Rules and the Code mandate such reports, courts have divided over whether lawyers who are fired in retaliation for blowing the whistle have a valid claim of wrongful discharge. For discussion and cases, see Chapter XV.

QUESTIONS

1.   Does it make sense, as in *Herbster,* that an attorney can disclose confidences to collect a fee or to establish a defense in claims initiated by a client, but cannot make similar disclosures to establish a retaliatory discharge action? Notice that the result would be different under Model Rule 1.6(b)(5), which permits lawyers to reveal client confidences to establish claims against the client, not merely to collect fees or establish defenses. See the discussion of the "self-defense" exception to confidentiality in Chapter V, *supra.*

2.   In the aftermath of the *Herbster* case, Illinois enacted legislation that would explicitly allow in-house lawyers to sue for retaliatory discharge if they were fired for refusing to obey corporate orders to violate a law or rule of ethics. The legislation also permits lawyers bringing such actions to reveal confidences obtained in the course of employment.[27] However, the

27.   Ill. Public Act 86–1029, Private Sector Advisory Group (1990).

Illinois legislation creates no cause of action for outside counsel or for in-house attorneys fired for attempting to have their employers comply with law. What might be the basis for these distinctions? Are they appropriate?

3. What other structures might be helpful in encouraging ethical resistance in contexts such as those described below? Could more be done through internal corporate and law firm policies or through external support from professional associations? Consider for example:

> • creation of internal hotlines, inspector general/ ombudsperson positions, or ethics committees to receive reports of misconduct and prevent retaliation.

> • state or federal legislation making it an unfair labor practice to discharge an employee who reports to management or governmental agencies conduct reasonably believed to be illegal, against public policy, or inconsistent with employer policies;

> • whistleblowing exceptions to employment-at-will doctrine;

> • support for whistleblowers by professional organizations, such as legal funds to pursue wrongful discharge claims or awards for ethical resistance;

> • including ethical conduct in training programs, performance evaluations, and compensation decisions.[28]

Which of these suggestions seem most promising? What other measures would you propose?

4. In 2003, the ABA amended Model Rule 1.13, adding a new clause requiring lawyers who reasonably believe that they have been fired in retaliation for reporting misconduct under circumstances specified in the rule to "assure that the organization's highest authority is informed of the lawyer's discharge or withdrawal." Model Rule 1.13(e). How much is this provision likely to help?

NOTES

Under Model Rule 1.6(b)(1), a lawyer may reveal information "to the extent the lawyer reasonably believes necessary to prevent reasonably certain death or substantial bodily harm," a standard that appears in the *Restatement* as well. Given the numbers in Ford's cost-benefit analysis— 180 anticipated deaths and 180 serious burns out of a total of 12.5 million vehicles—should a lawyer conclude that marketing the Pinto will lead to reasonably certain death or substantial bodily harm? Statistically speaking, there is an overwhelming likelihood that someone will die because of Pinto's gas tank but a minuscule likelihood that any particular individual will be one of the anticipated victims; the chances for a given driver or passenger are less than three-one-thousandths of a percent. Given these

---

28. See Terance D. Miethe, Whistleblowing at Work; Kim, *supra* note 24, at 1067. For an overview of proposed legislation and related materials, see the website of the National Whistleblower Center, http://www.whistleblower.org.

odds, does Rule 1.6(b)(1) permit or forbid whistleblowing? What kind of "reasonable certainty" is it talking about? Is the rule designed for mass-tort situations like this? According to the Ethics 2000 Commission, Rule 1.6(b)(1) allows disclosure where, for example, a toxic discharge in drinking water may not produce injury for many years.

Does Model Rule 1.13, concerning the organization as client, change the analysis? In response to the SEC's implementation of the Sarbanes–Oxley bill (discussed below), the ABA amended the rule in 2003. The new Rule 1.13(b) considers situations in which misconduct by an organizational officer or employee is unlawful and likely to result in substantial injury to the organization. The previous version of the rule had instructed the lawyer to take steps in the best interest of the organization, which might include referring the matter to higher authority, and if necessary, to the organization's highest authority (so-called "reporting up the ladder" or, more simply "reporting up"). If the highest authority failed to remedy the situation, the lawyer was permitted to resign.

The new version of the Rule dramatically alters its predecessor. Now, rather than merely permitting the lawyer to report up the ladder, the rule states that the lawyer must report up the ladder "unless the lawyer reasonably believes that it is not necessary in the best interest of the organization." Model Rule 1.13(b). Furthermore, if the highest authority insists upon unlawful conduct or fails to address it in a timely and appropriate manner, the lawyer may reveal confidential information "whether or not Rule 1.6 permits such disclosure" in order to prevent substantial injury to the organization. In the now-prevalent terminology, the lawyer not only must "report up," but if that proves inadequate, the lawyer may "report out"—blow the whistle.

Other countries have no comparable requirements. The Code of the Council of the Bars and Law Societies of Europe (CCBE) has no provision analogous to Rule 1.13 and no provisions that speak directly to the bar's obligations in representing organizational clients. Japan has a requirement comparable to Rule 1.13(b), which obligates in-house lawyers to report wrongdoing up the chain of the command, to the board of directors if necessary, but does not authorize reporting out if the organization fails to act.[29]

B.   SARBANES–OXLEY: LEGISLATIVE REQUIREMENTS

As noted above, these revisions of Model Rule 1.13 came in response to the SEC's regulations implementing the Sarbanes–Oxley Act, which Congress enacted in the wake of high-profile corporate scandals including Enron, WorldCom, Global Crossings, and Tyco. The materials that follow begin with a discussion of lawyers' responsibility in the Enron debacle.

---

29. Japanese Federation of Bar Associations, Basic Rules on the Duties of Practicing Attorneys, art. 51, discussed in James E. Moliterno & George C. Harris, *Global Issues in Legal Ethics* 131–32 (2007).

Discussion then turns to the Sarbanes–Oxley response and an analysis of the SEC's implementing regulations.

Susan P. Koniak, "When The Hurlyburly's Done: The Bar's Struggle with the SEC"

103 Columbia Law Review 1236, 1239–43 (2003).

We lawyers are guilty. To commit most complex corporate frauds, companies need legal help. The trick is to make everything look legitimate, and lawyers are critical to that task. The allegations against lawyers in the Enron case demonstrate what I mean.

[Professor Koniak describes the creation of so-called "special purpose entities" (SPEs) by Enron. The SPEs (two of which were named JEDI and Chewco) were designed so that under the relevant accounting rules their profits would appear on Enron's books but their debts would not. To avoid SEC disclosure obligations, a non-Enron employee named Michael Kopper was placed in charge of the Chewco; in reality, Kopper worked for Enron's CFO.]

What did the lawyers do? First, it should be apparent from what has been said thus far that the involvement of lawyers was necessary to implement these machinations. The point of the scheme was to create the impression of compliance with rules of law and accounting that would justify keeping JEDI's profits on Enron's books and its debts off those books. Yes, accountants can be helpful for these tasks, but all in all, creating the impression of compliance with rules is work lawyers are especially "qualified" to do. And the complaint in the Enron securities litigation alleges that lawyers did just that in this case.

According to the complaint, two large and prestigious law firms, Vinson & Elkins (Vinson) and Kirkland & Ellis (Kirkland), were involved in this scheme and in many of Enron's later, similarly fraudulent, transactions. Vinson represented Enron, and Kirkland represented both Chewco and JEDI, and later other Enron-related partnerships or entities.. . .

The above cursory description just begins to scratch the surface of Enron's scandalous conduct. Thus far, it might appear that only two law firms were involved in this mess, but that is not true. To provide even a hint of how many lawyers and law firms were part of these schemes, another aspect of Enron's conduct must be described. Here, Enron made money and other assets go round in circles to inflate its profits. For example, J.P. Morgan (which was by no means the only bank to engage in this kind of behavior with Enron) set up an SPE of its own, Mahonia. Mahonia was controlled by J.P. Morgan (as was, for example, Delta, Citigroup's version of Mahonia), and its purpose was to engage in money-go-round deals. J.P. Morgan would arrange to "pre-pay" Mahonia for oil or gas; Mahonia would arrange to "pre-pay" Enron for the designated commodity; and finally, Enron would arrange to "buy" the commodity from J.P. Morgan in the future for a price that appeared to be the amount J.P.

Morgan originally laid out (to Mahonia that ended up at Enron via the Mahonia–Enron leg of the deal) plus interest. In other words, J.P. Morgan was lending Enron money through Mahonia and calling it something else, so that Enron would not have to disclose this debt on its balance sheets. Instead, Enron would book as trading profit the money transferred to it from Mahonia and list as a trading liability the money it was due to pay back to J.P. Morgan.

.   .   .

These money-go-round deals are especially important to my claim that lawyers were central, even more central than accountants, to the corporate fraud at Enron. Accountants cannot book such circles as "sales" instead of "loans" without two legal opinions, a "true sale" opinion and a "nonconsolidation" opinion. The accountants, in other words, could not act without the lawyers vouching for these deals—not the other way around, as many lawyers would have people believe. Vinson apparently issued "true sales" opinions in a number of these transactions, although it was surely not the only firm to do so. More importantly, each of the banks had lawyers who helped the banks with their part of the sham. The banks' lawyers set up puppet SPEs to allow the banks to funnel loans to Enron disguised as trades or sales. The lawyers also helped the banks to protect themselves from the prospect that Enron would go belly-up from the weight of all this undisclosed debt by helping the banks to sell off or insure against their exposure to Enron "defaulting" on its promise to "buy" its own oil or gas back from the bank—that is, to repay the loan.

How many major law firms were helping banks in what appear to be fraudulent transactions? The Texas court denied motions to dismiss charges of securities fraud in connection with Enron's shady deals against Citigroup, J.P. Morgan, Credit Suisse First Boston, and Merrill Lynch. I have no doubt that those banks were represented by the "best" legal talent in this country—law firms considered to be of the highest caliber. And none of those lawyers noticed anything amiss? We are not just to believe that the banks are all innocent, something I personally do not believe, having watched every single minute of the testimony given by Citigroup's and J.P. Morgan's managers before the Senate Permanent Subcommittee on Investigations. Are we also to believe that all the lawyers who worked on these deals were incapable of grasping just what it was they were doing? I rest my case.

NOTES AND QUESTIONS: ENRON

1.   Review the discussion of the Enron case in Chapter V. That discussion presupposed honest lawyers representing dishonest clients. Koniak challenges that assumption. If she is right about the facts, does that suggest that dozens of lawyers, perhaps more, were unethical? Not necessarily. She argues that the bar regards its ethos of loyalty to clients as a kind of higher law governing its behavior.

I am often asked whether I am accusing lawyers of getting up in the morning intent on breaking the law, and helping their clients to do so, too. I am not. I think that lawyers believe what they are doing is lawful, that advising their clients in a manner that I believe ends up undermining state law is their job. I think that they believe at the end of the day that they have done the right thing, acted not just as law permits, but as it commands them to act. In other words, the bar's legal vision functions as law; it operates not just plausibly, but also convincingly, to coat lawyer behavior, at least in the minds of those acting (lawyers), with a veneer that changes the nature of the activity itself, making it "right."[30]

How plausible is this explanation? Consider the defense that Vinson and Elkins offered of its conduct in Enron: "When clients ask us [if they can do something] our job is to . . . figure out if there is a legally appropriate way to do it. That's what we do. And so does every other law firm in America."[31] How might Koniak respond? How would you?

2.   What other factors might account for lawyers' involvement in ethically problematic transactions? In 2000, Enron was Vinson and Elkin's largest client and a frequent source of lateral employment for its attorneys. The firm billed the company between $27 and $30 million in services, and almost two dozen lawyers had obtained jobs in Enron since 1991. Both the general counsel and deputy general counsel were former V & E partners.[32] In many cases like Enron, problems are exacerbated by eat what-you-kill compensation structures that tie individual partners' financial and professional status to their client billings. And when lawyers believe that a client will readily find some other firm to push the envelope, they may see little point in withholding assistance.[33] Are there measures that firms, bar associations, or legislators could take?

3.   Although Enron's top management were convicted of frauds and conspiracies, many would disagree with Koniak that their lawyers were complicit. The lengthy report by Neal Batson, Enron's bankruptcy examiner, details possible grounds of liability for Enron's lawyers, but also possible defenses of fact and law. *In re Enron*, Appendix C, Case No. 01–16034 (AJG). The issue was never resolved. In 2006, Vinson & Elkins agreed to pay $30 million to Enron's bankruptcy estate in exchange for relinquishment of any claims that it had aided and abetted fraud that contributed to the company's collapse. The firm was subsequently dismissed from a

30.   Susan P. Koniak, "When the Hurlyburly's Done: The Bar's Struggle With the SEC," 103 *Colum. L. Rev.* 1236, 1245 (2003). For another analysis of the responsibility of Enron's lawyers, see Deborah L. Rhode & Paul D. Paton, "Lawyers, Ethics, and Enron," 8 *Stan. J.L. Bus. & Fin.* 9 (2002).

31.   Patty Waldmeir, "Inside Track: Don't Blame the Lawyers for Enron," *Financial Times*, Feb. 21, 2002, at 14.

32.   Rhode & Paton, *supra* note 30; Dan Ackman, "Enron's Lawyers: Eyes Wide Shut," *Forbes.com*, Jan. 28, 2002.

33.   Geoffrey Miller, "From Club to Market: The Evolving Role of Business Lawyers," 74 *Fordham L. Rev.* 1105, 1124 (2006).

shareholder suit against Enron participants. Newby v. Enron, 2007 WL 209923 (S.D. Tex. 2007).

PROBLEM 2

You are an associate in a large corporate law firm representing Planetary Telecom (PT), an innovative telecommunications firm that has become highly successful in the past five years. You are asked to assist in drafting opinion letters required by securities law in connection with some complex transactions that PT's chief financial officer wishes to undertake. These transactions involve selling unprofitable assets to a company created solely for the purpose of holding those assets (the company is a "special purpose entity" or SPE). The SPE is held in the name of the CFO's grandmother. By getting the assets off the books, the sale will help PT show a year-end profit and boost its stock prices. Securities law requires that the sale be genuine, which means that the assets must be effectively insulated from PT's control. The SEC requires an opinion letter attesting that the sale is a "true sale" complying with the effective-insulation requirement. In fact, however, the CFO has structured the deal so that the liabilities will be transferred back to PT in a month. As a consequence, no true sale letter can appropriately be issued. Instead, PT's accounting firm has stated that a different kind of opinion letter will suffice. This kind of opinion letter, called a "true issuance" opinion, does not assert that the SPE's assets are insulated from PT's control. It merely offers an opinion about who owns the assets if the SPE goes bankrupt. Based on your knowledge of securities law, you believe that the true issuance letters you have been asked to draft do not comply with securities law: only a true sale letter will suffice. You are also concerned because securities law requires that such deals have a legitimate business purpose, and you know that the SPEs exist only for the purpose of moving liabilities off the books for accounting purposes—a violation of the law. The accounting firm, however, insists that a true issuance letter is good enough.

You raise your concerns at a meeting with other lawyers working on the project, including the supervising partner. He informs you that PT has done many deals structured this way in the past, and that in his view, there is nothing wrong with it. The other lawyers working on the project seem discomfited by your analysis of the securities law, but they do not participate in the discussion. In your view, it is not even a close call that the transactions are illegal.

a) What are your obligations under the Sarbanes–Oxley regulations? Under Model Rule 1.13? Under Model Rule 5.2?

b) Suppose that you decide to bring the matter to the attention of the general counsel—the chief legal officer—of the client company. He indicates that the matter will be reviewed. After two weeks, you remind the general counsel and he expresses confidence in the supervising partner's judgment. What should you do?

c) Your state ethics code has a version of Rule 1.6 that does not allow revealing client confidences to prevent financial frauds. Its version of Rule 1.13 also does not permit disclosure of confidences outside the corporation. However, Section 205.3(d)(2) of the Sarbanes–Oxley Act authorizes lawyers to reveal client confidences to prevent material violations of securities law and to rectify frauds that utilized their services. May you disclose your client's confidences to the SEC? Must you disclose?

NOTES: THE SARBANES–OXLEY ACT

Section 307 of the Sarbanes–Oxley Act of 2002 provides that the Securities and Exchange Commission:

> shall issue rules, in the public interest and for the protection of investors, setting forth minimum standards of professional conduct for attorneys appearing and practicing before the Commission in any way in the representation of issuers, including a rule—
>
> > (1) requiring an attorney to report evidence of a material violation of securities law or breach of fiduciary duty or similar violation by the company or any agent thereof, to the chief legal counsel or the chief executive officer of the company (or the equivalent thereof); and
> >
> > (2) if the counsel or officer does not appropriately respond to the evidence (adopting, as necessary, appropriate remedial measures or sanctions with respect to the violation), requiring the attorney to report the evidence to the audit committee of the board of directors of the issuer or to another committee of the board of directors comprised solely of directors not employed directly or indirectly by the issuer, or to the board of directors.

In spring 2003, after substantial back-and-forth in the period for commenting on proposed regulations, the SEC issued the following regulations to implement Section 307. Following selected text of the regulation, we summarize their principal features.

Part 205—Standards of Professional Conduct for Attorneys Appearing and Practicing Before the Commission in the Representation of an Issuer

17 C.F.R. Part 205 (2003).

§ 205.1　Purpose and scope.

This part sets forth minimum standards of professional conduct for attorneys appearing and practicing before the Commission in the representation of an issuer. These standards supplement applicable standards of any jurisdiction where an attorney is admitted or practices and are not intended to limit the ability of any jurisdiction to impose additional obligations on an attorney not inconsistent with the application of this part. Where the standards of a state or other United States jurisdiction where an attorney is admitted or practices conflict with this part, this part shall govern.

§ 205.2 Definitions.

For purposes of this part, the following definitions apply:

(e) *Evidence of a material violation* means credible evidence, based upon which it would be unreasonable, under the circumstances, for a prudent and competent attorney not to conclude that it is reasonably likely that a material violation has occurred, is ongoing, or is about to occur. . . .

(g) *In the representation of an issuer* means providing legal services as an attorney for an issuer, regardless of whether the attorney is employed or retained by the issuer. . . .

(i) *Material violation* means a material violation of an applicable United States federal or state securities law, a material breach of fiduciary duty arising under United States federal or state law, or a similar material violation of any United States federal or state law. . . .

(n) *Report* means to make known to directly, either in person, by telephone, by e-mail, electronically, or in writing.

§ 205.3 Issuer as client.

(b) *Duty to report evidence of a material violation.* (1) If an attorney, appearing and practicing before the Commission in the representation of an issuer, becomes aware of evidence of a material violation by the issuer or by any officer, director, employee, or agent of the issuer, the attorney shall report such evidence to the issuer's chief legal officer (or the equivalent thereof) or to both the issuer's chief legal officer and its chief executive officer (or the equivalents thereof) forthwith. By communicating such information to the issuer's officers or directors, an attorney does not reveal client confidences or secrets or privileged or otherwise protected information related to the attorney's representation of an issuer.

(2) The chief legal officer (or the equivalent thereof) shall cause such inquiry into the evidence of a material violation as he or she reasonably believes is appropriate to determine whether the material violation described in the report has occurred, is ongoing, or is about to occur. If the chief legal officer (or the equivalent thereof) determines no material violation has occurred, is ongoing, or is about to occur, he or she shall notify the reporting attorney and advise the reporting attorney of the basis for such determination. Unless the chief legal officer (or the equivalent thereof) reasonably believes that no material violation has occurred, is ongoing, or is about to occur, he or she shall take all reasonable steps to cause the issuer to adopt an appropriate response, and shall advise the reporting attorney thereof. In lieu of causing an inquiry under this paragraph (b), a chief legal officer (or the equivalent thereof) may refer a report of evidence of a material violation to a qualified legal compliance committee under paragraph (c)(2) of this section if the issuer has duly established a qualified legal compliance committee prior to the report of evidence of a material violation.

(3) Unless an attorney who has made a report under paragraph (b)(1) of this section reasonably believes that the chief legal officer or the chief executive officer of the issuer (or the equivalent thereof) has provided an appropriate response within a reasonable time, the attorney shall report the evidence of a material violation to:

(i) The audit committee of the issuer's board of directors;

(ii) Another committee of the issuer's board of directors consisting solely of directors who are not employed, directly or indirectly, by the issuer and are not, in the case of a registered investment company, "interested persons" . . .; or

(iii) The issuer's board of directors. . . .

(4) If an attorney reasonably believes that it would be futile to report evidence of a material violation to the issuer's chief legal officer and chief executive officer (or the equivalents thereof) under paragraph (b)(1) of this section, the attorney may report such evidence as provided under paragraph (b)(3) of this section.

. . .

(8) An attorney who receives what he or she reasonably believes is an appropriate and timely response to a report he or she has made pursuant to paragraph (b)(1), (b)(3), or (b)(4) of this section need do nothing more under this section with respect to his or her report.

(9) An attorney who does not reasonably believe that the issuer has made an appropriate response within a reasonable time to the report or reports made pursuant to paragraph (b)(1), (b)(3), or (b)(4) of this section shall explain his or her reasons therefor to the chief legal officer (or the equivalent thereof), the chief executive officer (or the equivalent thereof), and directors to whom the attorney reported the evidence of a material violation pursuant to paragraph (b)(1), (b)(3), or (b)(4) of this section.

(10) An attorney formerly employed or retained by an issuer who has reported evidence of a material violation under this part and reasonably believes that he or she has been discharged for so doing may notify the issuer's board of directors or any committee thereof that he or she believes that he or she has been discharged for reporting evidence of a material violation under this section.

. . .

(d) *Issuer confidences.* (1) Any report under this section (or the contemporaneous record thereof) or any response thereto (or the contemporaneous record thereof) may be used by an attorney in connection with any investigation, proceeding, or litigation in which the attorney's compliance with this part is in issue.

(2) An attorney appearing and practicing before the Commission in the representation of an issuer may reveal to the Commission, without the issuer's consent, confidential information related to the representation to the extent the attorney reasonably believes necessary:

(i) To prevent the issuer from committing a material violation that is likely to cause substantial injury to the financial interest or property of the issuer or investors;

(ii) To prevent the issuer, in a Commission investigation or administrative proceeding from committing perjury . . .; suborning perjury . . .; or committing any act proscribed in 18 U.S.C. 1001 that is likely to perpetrate a fraud upon the Commission; or

(iii) To rectify the consequences of a material violation by the issuer that caused, or may cause, substantial injury to the financial interest or property of the issuer or investors in the furtherance of which the attorney's services were used.

§ 205.4   Responsibilities of supervisory attorneys.

(a) An attorney supervising or directing another attorney who is appearing and practicing before the Commission in the representation of an issuer is a supervisory attorney. An issuer's chief legal officer (or the equivalent thereof) is a supervisory attorney under this section.

(b) A supervisory attorney shall make reasonable efforts to ensure that a subordinate attorney, as defined in § 205.5(a), that he or she supervises or directs conforms to this part. To the extent a subordinate attorney appears and practices before the Commission in the representation of an issuer, that subordinate attorney's supervisory attorneys also appear and practice before the Commission.

(c) A supervisory attorney is responsible for complying with the reporting requirements in § 205.3 when a subordinate attorney has reported to the supervisory attorney evidence of a material violation.

(d) A supervisory attorney who has received a report of evidence of a material violation from a subordinate attorney under § 205.3 may report such evidence to the issuer's qualified legal compliance committee if the issuer has duly formed such a committee.

§ 205.5   Responsibilities of a subordinate attorney.

(a) An attorney who appears and practices before the Commission in the representation of an issuer on a matter under the supervision or direction of another attorney (other than under the direct supervision or direction of the issuer's chief legal officer (or the equivalent thereof)) is a subordinate attorney.

(b) A subordinate attorney shall comply with this part notwithstanding that the subordinate attorney acted at the direction of or under the supervision of another person.

(c) A subordinate attorney complies with § 205.3 if the subordinate attorney reports to his or her supervising attorney under § 205.3(b) evidence of a material violation of which the subordinate attorney has become aware in appearing and practicing before the Commission.

(d) A subordinate attorney may take the steps permitted or required by § 205.3(b) or (c) if the subordinate attorney reasonably believes that a supervisory attorney to whom he or she has reported evidence of a material violation under § 205.3(b) has failed to comply with § 205.3.

§ 205.6 Sanctions and discipline.

(a) A violation of this part by any attorney appearing and practicing before the Commission in the representation of an issuer shall subject such attorney to the civil penalties and remedies for a violation of the federal securities laws available to the Commission in an action brought by the Commission thereunder.

(b) An attorney appearing and practicing before the Commission who violates any provision of this part is subject to the disciplinary authority of the Commission, regardless of whether the attorney may also be subject to discipline for the same conduct in a jurisdiction where the attorney is admitted or practices. An administrative disciplinary proceeding initiated by the Commission for violation of this part may result in an attorney being censured, or being temporarily or permanently denied the privilege of appearing or practicing before the Commission.

(c) An attorney who complies in good faith with the provisions of this part shall not be subject to discipline or otherwise liable under inconsistent standards imposed by any state or other United States jurisdiction where the attorney is admitted or practices.

(d) An attorney practicing outside the United States shall not be required to comply with the requirements of this part to the extent that such compliance is prohibited by applicable foreign law.

§ 205.7 No private right of action.

(a) Nothing in this part is intended to, or does, create a private right of action against any attorney, law firm, or issuer based upon compliance or noncompliance with its provisions.

(b) Authority to enforce compliance with this part is vested exclusively in the Commission.

NOTES AND QUESTIONS ON SARBANES–OXLEY

1. Who is governed by Part 205? The regulation governs any lawyers who advise clients in the preparation of documents that foreseeably may become part of submissions to the SEC. § 205.2(a) (omitted in the excerpt reprinted above). This includes a wide range of corporate documents. The regulation also governs lawyers who advise that certain information does not need to be included in a filing. Foreign attorneys who do not appear before the SEC are exempt from coverage.

2. What is an "appropriate response" by a chief legal officer to an attorney's report of evidence of misconduct? It is a response that would lead a reasonable attorney to believe that the problem is being addressed in accordance with applicable laws. This includes a determination that the

client has a colorable argument that its conduct is legal. § 205.2(b) (omitted in the excerpt reprinted above).

3. What standard triggers a lawyer's reporting obligations? Part 205.2(e) provides:

> (e) *Evidence of a material violation* means credible evidence, based upon which it would be unreasonable, under the circumstances, for a prudent and competent attorney not to conclude that it is reasonably likely that a material violation has occurred, is ongoing, or is about to occur.

Many practitioners and commentators have found this standard confusing, with its convoluted syntax, multiple probabilistic terms ("material," "credible," "unreasonable," "reasonably likely"), and double-negative construction.[34] The double-negative "unreasonable not to conclude" standard appears to be higher than a "reasonable lawyer" standard. If the rule required only that a reasonable lawyer would conclude that it is reasonably likely that a material violation had occurred, then the "reporting up" obligation might be triggered even if another reasonable lawyer concluded the opposite. The double-negative construction rules out that possibility; it requires that no reasonable lawyer could avoid the conclusion that a material violation is reasonably likely. "Reasonably likely" means more than "merely possible," but something short of "more likely than not."

Apparently, this convoluted standard emerged as a compromise between two positions. Initially, the SEC wanted an objective standard triggering lawyers' reporting obligations, which would have defined "evidence of a material violation" as "evidence that would cause a lawyer to reasonably believe that a violation is occurring." Nearly all practicing lawyers who commented on the proposed standard maintained that it was too demanding. They preferred a subjective standard that would have required reporting only if the attorney knew that a violation was occurring. How different is the compromise standard from a subjective knowledge requirement?

4. Section 205.3(b) provides the basic "reporting up the ladder" framework: An attorney who becomes aware of evidence of a material violation of securities law must report it to the chief legal officer of the issuing company, who must in turn investigate, take steps to make sure that the issuer responds appropriately, and report back to the attorney who initially made the report. If that attorney does not receive a satisfactory response, he or she must go up the ladder once again, and report the evidence to members of the company's board of directors. Alternatively, the issuing company can set up a "Qualified Legal Compliance Committee" (QLCC) consisting of independent members of the board of directors. (In the excerpt reproduced above, we have omitted regulations concerning QLCCs.) Both the attorney and the chief legal officer can discharge their reporting requirements by reporting to the QLCC. Section 205.3(b)(4) provides that if

---

34. *See* George M. Williams III, "The SEC's New 'Not Unreasonable Man' Standard," 229 *N.Y.L.J.*, Feb. 27, 2003, at 1 (a linguist dissects the standard).

an attorney "believes that it would be futile to report evidence of a material violation to the issuer's chief legal officer and chief executive officer (or the equivalents thereof)," the attorney may bring the evidence of a material violation directly to the board of directors.

5.   The most controversial aspect of the regulation is section 205.3(d)(2). It permits lawyers representing issuers before the SEC to reveal client confidences in order to prevent fraud or rectify fraud in which the lawyer's services have been used. In July 2003, the Washington State Bar issued an ethics opinion asserting that it would continue to enforce the states' own confidentiality rule against lawyers who violate it, even if the violation is authorized by the Sarbanes–Oxley regulations. In August 2003, the Corporations Committee of the Business Law Section of the California State Bar sent a letter to the SEC general counsel agreeing with the Washington Bar and arguing that the SEC lacks authority to preempt state ethics rules. The General Counsel's response was that the agency had such authority, and one of its Commissioners characterized the Washington bar ethics opinion as an "essentially lawless act."[35] The preemption issue is likely to be the subject of ongoing controversy between state and national authorities. It is a technically intricate issue. *Rice v. Santa Fe Elevator Corp.*, 331 U.S. 218, 230 (1947), states that courts should "start with the assumption that the historic police powers of the States [are] not to be superseded by the Federal Act unless that was the clear and manifest purpose of Congress." Because the regulation of lawyers has historically rested with the states, the *Rice* presumption favors the California and Washington bar positions. However, the Supreme Court has often failed to follow *Rice* on preemption issues.

The North Carolina Bar has concluded that under prevailing Supreme Court precedent, *Fidelity Federal v. de la Cuesta*, 458 U.S. 141 (1982), federal regulation preempts conflicting law if the agency clearly intended preemption and its action was within the scope of its delegated authority. Unless and until a court ruled that the SEC had exceeded its authority, its regulations should preempt contrary state bar standards. North Carolina State Bar Ethics Comm. Formal Op. 2005–9 (Jan. 20, 2006). Which side do you believe should prevail?

What if the reporting attorney is fired? Under § 205.3(b)(10), the attorney may report the discharge to the board of directors. Does this provision rule out a cause of action for retaliatory discharge? Should it?

6.   The regulations state that attorneys violating the rule will be subject to civil sanctions and penalties by the SEC; that they are immunized against penalties under inconsistent state standards by good faith efforts to comply; that the SEC will not seek criminal penalties; and that the regulations create no private right of action. The net result is to create a "safe harbor" for attorneys from civil lawsuits based on violation of the regulations. Does

---

35. Letter from Giovanni Prezioso, SEC General Counsel, to J. Richard Manning & David W. Savage, President and President Elect, Washington State Bar Association, July 23, 2002; Harvey J. Goldschmid, Speech before Association of the Bar of the City of New York, Nov. 17, 2003.

that categorical exemption serve the public interest? Are regulatory violations likely to be relevant in malpractice litigation despite the disclaimer in Section 205? See Chapter XVI.

7.   The SEC has also considered a "noisy withdrawal" rule. Under its provisions, if a reporting lawyer does not get an appropriate response in a reasonable time, the lawyer must withdraw, disaffirm relevant documents, and notify the SEC and successor counsel that he or she has withdrawn for professional reasons. The proposal met with considerable support from academic experts, but overwhelming opposition from the organized bar.[36] What is your view of its merits?

8.   The Sarbanes–Oxley regulations have not been well received by the practicing bar. The "up the ladder" reporting structure creates the unpleasant possibility that lawyers may be required to go over the heads of their superiors—those who hired them, evaluate them, pay them, and often work side by side with them—and inform the board of directors that those same individuals may be engaged in illegal conduct. Furthermore, attorneys must do this based on evidence that is not conclusive. If the attorney is fired, the only recourse specified is informing the board of directors. An additional complication arises for in-house counsel in multinational corporations operating in countries where whistleblowing is not permitted.[37] It is not hard to see why these regulations are unpopular within the profession. As one lawyer puts it:

> An attorney has many roles in society—client representative, officer of the legal system, and public citizen responsible for justice, to name a few. Now, thanks to a group of forty law professors, a former plaintiffs' attorney, and a Congress faced with a disillusioned public in an important election year, an attorney representing clients before the Securities and Exchange Commission also has another title: corporate snitch.[38]

Do you agree? Would most members of the public? Millions of innocent investors and employees lost life savings as a result of recent corporate misconduct in which lawyers' services were implicated. Is the SEC's response unreasonable in light of widespread demands for greater professional accountability? Why or why not?

9.   In light of Koniak's description of the role of lawyers in the Enron scandal, how likely is it that the Sarbanes–Oxley regulations will successfully address the problem?

---

36.   For arguments in support, see John C. Coffee, Jr., "The Attorney as Gatekeeper: An Agenda for the SEC," 103 *Colum. L. Rev.* 1293, 1307–10 (2003); Miller, *supra* note 33, at 1129–35; Rhode *supra* note 3, at 1336. For opposition, see "Federal Lawmakers Get Earful at Hearing on SEC's Proposed 'Noisy Withdrawal' Rules," 20 *ABA/BNA Lawyer's Man. On Prof. Conduct* 69 (Feb. 11, 2004).

37.   In some countries, including France and Germany, whistleblowers are regarded as informants, a legacy from Nazi practices in the World War II era. For discussion of the difficulties of reconciling Sarbanes–Oxley protections for whistleblowers under some European countries' laws, see John Gibeaut, "Culture Clash," *ABA J.*, May 2006, at 10.

38.   Jennifer Wheeler, "Section 307 of the Sarbanes–Oxley Act: Irreconcilable Conflict with the ABA's Model Rules and the Oklahoma Rules of Professional Conduct?" 56 *Okla. L. Rev.* 461 (2003).

C.   In-House Counsel

PROBLEM 3

Assume that you are a lawyer for Covenant Corporation, the pseudonym for one of the companies that sociologist Robert Jackall studied in *Moral Mazes: The World of Corporate Managers,* excerpted below. How would you respond to the situations facing Black and Reed? Do the responsibilities of inside and outside counsel differ in such circumstances? How helpful are Model Rules 1.13, 1.6, and 5.1?

Robert Jackall, Moral Mazes: The World of Corporate Managers

Oxford University Press 122–123 (1988).

. . . Drawing lines when information is scarce becomes doubly ambiguous, a problem that often emerges in shaping relationships with one's colleagues. For instance, Black, a lawyer at Covenant Corporation, received a call from a chemical plant manager who had just been served with an order from the local fire department to build retaining dikes around several storage tanks for toxic chemicals so that firemen would not be in danger of being drenched with the substance should the tanks burst if there were a fire at the plant. The plant manager indicated that meeting the order would cause him to miss his numbers badly that year and he wondered aloud if the fire chief might, for a consideration, be persuaded to forget the whole thing. Black pointed out that he could not countenance even a discussion of bribery; the plant manager laughed and said that he was only joking and would think things over and get back to Black in a few weeks. Black never heard from the plant manager about this issue again; when they met on different occasions after that, the conversation was always framed around other subjects. Black did inquire discreetly and found out that no dikes had been built; the plant manager had apparently gone shopping for a more flexible legal opinion. Should he, Black wondered, pursue the matter or in the absence of any firm evidence just let things drop, particularly since others, for their own purposes, could misconstrue the fact that he had not acted on his earlier marginal knowledge? Feeling that one is in the dark can be somewhat unnerving.

More unnerving, however, is the feeling that one is being kept in the dark. Reed, another lawyer at Covenant, was working on the legal issues of a chemical dumpsite that Alchemy Inc. [a subsidiary of Covenant] had sold. He suddenly received a call from a former employee who had been having trouble with the company on his pension payments; this man told Reed that unless things were straightened out in a hurry, he planned to talk to federal officials about all the pesticides buried in the site. This was alarming news. Reed had no documentation about pesticides in the site; if Alchemy had buried pesticides there, a whole new set of regulations might apply to the situation and to Covenant as the former owner. Reed went to the chemical company's director of personnel to get the former employee's file but was unable to obtain it. Reed's boss agreed to help, but still the director of personnel refused to release the file. After repeated calls, Reed was told that the file had been lost. Reed went back to his boss and inquired whether it might be prudent for Covenant to repurchase the site to keep it under control. This was deemed a good idea. However, the asking price for the site was now three times what Covenant had sold it for. Everyone, of course, got hesitant; another lawyer became involved and began working closely with Reed's boss on the issue. Gradually, Reed found himself excluded from discussions about the problem and unable to obtain information that he felt was important to his work. His anxiety was heightened because he felt he was involved in a matter of some legal gravity. But, like much else in the corporation, this problem disappeared in the night. Eventually, Reed was assigned to other cases and he knew that the doors to the issue were closed, locked, and bolted.

QUESTIONS

1.   Black and Reed find themselves cut "out of the loop" of information when they raise questions concerning possible violations by other company officials. Yet both of them sense that the problems they noted—the possibility of bribery by the chemical plant manager (Black) and the possibility that the company was doing nothing about dangerous pesticides (Reed)— have not gone away. How should they respond? Are there any affirmative steps they may take to find out what has happened? If so, *must* they follow up on the matter?

2.   William Simon writes: "Every corporate lawyer knows that the manager is not the client. . . . [F]ew corporate lawyers have a coherent idea of what a corporate client could be other than the manager."[39] How much help do the Model Rules provide in figuring out what a corporate client could be other than the manager? Rule 1.13 states that an organization's lawyer represents the organization, and has special duties to safeguard the organization from employees' illegal action that might harm the organization. Does that Rule tell Black and Reed how to proceed? Does it adequately take account of the public's interest? Does it provide lawyers with adequate leverage in conversations with corporate officers? That is, does the rule permit them to say truthfully something like "I could be subject to discipline if I didn't follow through on this matter!" If not, how would you draft an ethical rule or statutory provision that would help Black and Reed?

3.   Jackall notes that "drawing lines when information is scarce becomes doubly ambiguous"—"doubly," because there is no clear answer either to the question "what happened?" or to the question "is what happened acceptable?" Does the scarcity of information absolve a lawyer from responsibility for drawing lines? It may seem that the answer is clearly "yes": one

---

39.   William H. Simon, "After Confidentiality: Rethinking the Professional Responsibilities of the Business Lawyer," 75 *Fordham L. Rev.* 1453, 1464 (2006).

cannot be held responsible for what goes on behind one's back. But in that case, an organization could absolve all but a handful of its employees from responsibility simply by dividing and controlling information within the organization. If an organization should not be able to restrict responsibility so easily, how would you prevent it?

Robert Jackall, Moral Mazes: The World of Corporate Managers

17–22, 101, 118–19, 106–12 (1988).

... The hierarchical authority structure that is the linchpin of bureaucracy dominates the way managers think about their world and about themselves. Managers do not see or experience authority in any abstract way; instead, authority is embodied in their personal relationships with their immediate bosses and in their perceptions of similar links between other managers up and down the hierarchy. . . . [The role of the subordinate is to keep his boss from making mistakes, particularly public ones; he must keep his boss informed, lest his boss get "blindsided." . . . A subordinate must also not circumvent his boss nor ever give the appearance of doing so. He must never contradict his boss's judgment in public. To violate the last admonition is thought to constitute a kind of death wish in business. . . .

In return, [the subordinate] can hope for those perquisites that are in his boss's gift. . . . He can hope to be elevated when and if the boss is elevated, though other important criteria intervene here. He can also expect protection for mistakes made, up to a point. . . . It is characteristic of this authority system that details are pushed down and credit is pulled up. Superiors do not like to give detailed instructions to subordinates. The official reason for this is to maximize subordinates' autonomy. The underlying reason is, first, to get rid of tedious details. . . .

Moreover, pushing down details relieves superiors of the burden of too much knowledge, particularly guilty knowledge. A superior will say to a subordinate, for instance: "Give me your best thinking on the problem with [X]." When the subordinate makes his report, he is often told: "I think you can do better than that," until the subordinate has worked out all the details of the boss's predetermined solution, without the boss being specifically aware of "all the eggs that have to be broken." It is also not at all uncommon for very bald and extremely general edicts to emerge from on high. For example, "Sell the plant in [St. Louis]; let me know when you've struck a deal," or "We need to get higher prices for [fabric X]; see what you can work out," or "Tom, I want you to go down there and meet with those guys and make a deal and I don't want you to come back until you've got one." This pushing down of details has important consequences.

First, because they are unfamiliar with—indeed deliberately distance themselves from—entangling details, corporate higher echelons tend to expect successful results without messy complications. This is central to top executives' well-known aversion to bad news and to the resulting tendency to kill the messenger who bears the news.... Managers have a myriad of aphorisms that refer to how the power of CEOs, magnified through the zealous efforts of subordinates, affects them.... "When he sneezes, we all catch colds." ...

The moral ethos of managerial circles emerges directly out of the social context that I have described. It is an ethos most notable for its lack of fixedness. In the welter of practical affairs in the corporate world, morality does not emerge from some set of internally held convictions or principles, but rather from ongoing albeit changing relationships with some person, some coterie, some social network, some clique that matters to a person. Since these relationships are always multiple, contingent, and in flux, managerial moralities are always situational, always relative. Business bureaucracies thus place a great premium on the virtue of "flexibility," as it is called.... [P]rinciples and those who raise them do not generally fare well in back rooms. ....

Brady [an accountant] came across ... serious and potentially damaging information. Key people in the corporation—at this stage, Brady was not sure just who was involved—were using about $18 million from the employee pension fund as a profit slush fund. Essentially, there was too much money in the pension fund. Explicit rules govern such a contingency but these were being ignored. The money was not declared as an asset but concealed and moved in and out of the corporation's earning statements each year so that the corporation always came in exactly on target.

This knowledge deeply upset Brady. He feels that there are rules in accounting that one can break and rules that one cannot break ..... In his view, the point of being an accountant is precisely to account, that is to find out the facts—Brady uses the word "truth"—and report them accurately. When one deals with other people's money, one has to be especially careful and forthright. Brady saw the pension fund manipulation as a direct violation of fiduciary trust, as depriving stockholders not only of their rightful knowledge but also of material benefits and as a misuse of other people's money for personal gain. It was, he felt, a practice that could in hard times jeopardize the employees' pension fund. He now had no way of reporting the matter through normal channels. His boss, the corporate vice-president for finance, had been hostile to him ever since Brady came under his control.... While his boss, the corporate vice-president, was in Europe, Brady went to the chief lawyer in the whole corporation and laid out the case for him. The lawyer "did not want to touch the issue with a barge pole." He sent a friend of Brady's, yet another corporate vice-president, to Brady to cool things down. According to Brady, the vice-president argued: "Look, why don't you just forget the whole thing. Everyone does it. That's just part of the game in business today." When Brady persisted, the vice-president asked if Brady could not just go along with things even if he did not agree. Brady said that he could not. Brady mentioned the managerial bonus program and acknowledged that that too could be adversely affected by his action. The vice-president blanched and became quite upset. Right after Brady's boss returned from Europe, Brady was summarily fired and he and his belongings were literally thrown out of the company building.

It is important to note the sharp contrast between Brady's reasons for acting as he did and other corporate managers' analyses of his actions. For Brady, the kinds of issues he confronted at work were distinctly moral issues, seen through the prism of his professional code. He says:

> I was in jeopardy of violating my professional code. And I feel you have to stick up for that If your profession has standing, it has that standing because someone stood up for it. If the SEC had come in and did an analysis and then went into the details of the cases and put me up on the stand and asked me—What is your profession? Was this action right or wrong? Why did you do it then? I would really be in trouble ... with myself most of all. I was frightened of losing respect, my self-respect in particular.... I was just too honest for that company. What is right in the corporation is not what is right in a man's home or in his church. *What is right in the corporation is what the guy above you wants from you.* That's what morality is in the corporation.

The corporate managers to whom I presented this case see Brady's dilemma as devoid of moral or ethical content. In their view, the issues that Brady raises are, first of all, simply practical matters. His basic failing was, first, that he violated the fundamental rules of bureaucratic life. These are usually stated briefly as a series of admonitions. (1) You never go around your boss. (2) You tell your boss what he wants to hear, even when your boss claims that he wants dissenting views. (3) If your boss wants something dropped, you drop it....

Second, the managers that I interviewed feel that Brady had plenty of available legitimations to excuse or justify his not acting. Clearly, they feel, a great many other executives knew about the pension fund scam and did nothing; everybody, especially the top bosses, was playing the game. The problem fell into other people's areas, was their responsibility, and therefore their problem. Why, then, worry about it? Besides, Brady had a number of ways out of the situation if he found it intolerable, including resigning. Moreover, whatever action he took would be insignificant anyway so why bother to act at all and jeopardize himself? Even a fool should have known that the CEO was not likely to take whatever blame resulted from the whole affair.

Third, these managers see the violations that disturbed Brady—irregular payments, doctored invoices, shuffling numbers in accounts—as small potatoes indeed, commonplaces of corporate life ..... Moreover, as managers see it, playing sleight of hand with the monetary value of inventories, post-or predating memoranda or invoices, tucking or squirreling large sums of money away to pull them out of one's hat at an opportune moment are all part and parcel of managing in a large corporation where interpretations of performance, not necessarily performance itself, decide one's fate. Furthermore, the whole point of the corporation is precisely to put other people's money, rather than one's own resources, at risk.

Finally, the managers I interviewed feel that Brady's biggest error was in insisting on acting according to a moral code, his professional ethos, that had simply no relevance to his organizational situation. "When the rubber hits the road," they say, abstract ethical and moral principles are not of much use.... Even more to the point, Brady called others' organizational morality, their acceptance of the moral ethos of bureaucracy, into question, made them uncomfortable, and eroded the fundamental trust and understanding that make cooperative managerial work possible. One executive elaborates a general sentiment:

> What it comes down to is that his moral code made other people uncomfortable. He threatened their position. He made them uncomfortable with their moral standards and their ethics. If he pursued it, the exposé would threaten their livelihood and their way of life. So they fired him. I personally believe that people in high places in big companies at some stage lose sight of the objectives of their companies and begin to focus on their positions. That's the only way you can really rationalize the pension fund issue.... Eventually, if the thing hits the newspapers, the big guys will lose. But, in the meantime, within the organization that guy is going to lose. And he will go through life feeling that he was honest and wasn't as crooked as the guys above him....

Karl Mannheim points out that bureaucracy turns all political issues into matters of administration. One can see a parallel alchemy in managers' responses to Brady's dilemma. Bureaucracy transforms all moral issues into immediately practical concerns. A moral judgment based on a professional ethic makes little sense in a world where the etiquette of authority relationships and the necessity for protecting and covering for one's boss, one's network, and oneself supercede all other considerations and where nonaccountability for action is the norm. As a matter of survival, not to mention advancement, corporate managers have to keep their eye fixed not on abstract principles but on the social framework of their world and its requirements. Thus, they simply do not see most issues that confront them as moral concerns even when problems might be posed in moral terms by others.

QUESTIONS

1.   Jackall describes a conflict between the ethical worlds of Brady, the accountant, and the corporate managers with whom Jackall discussed the case. Brady saw the CEO's pension fund manipulation as an issue of ethics, while the corporate managers saw the problem as practical. From their perspective, to get along you have to go along, and Brady simply ignored this truth of corporate life. What is your view?

2.   Is the professional responsibility of a lawyer different from that of an accountant in the circumstance that Brady describes? According to Brady, "the point of being an accountant is precisely to account, that is, to find out the facts (Brady uses the word 'truth') and report them accurately." Is the

role of an attorney different? Lawyers are often deeply suspicious of the very notion that there is a single, objective "truth"; much of legal argument consists in casting facts in the light most favorable to a client. That world view is hard to reconcile with Brady's notion of truth that is "just out there" independent of the interpretations of parties to the transaction. Which view do you find most compelling. Is it *true* that the corporation's pension fund manipulation violated its fiduciary obligations? Is that as *true* for a lawyer as for an accountant? And is a lawyer, just like an accountant, ethically required to react in the same way Brady reacted? What do Model Rule 1.13 and Sarbanes–Oxley require? After Sarbanes–Oxley, the particular pension-fund manipulation Jackall reports is unlikely; but few observers will claim that the Act means the end of business and accounting scams.

3. Brady was concerned with the spirit as well as the letter of his code of professional ethics. When he encountered the problem of the pension fund manipulation, his reaction was to ask the question: "Does this violate my code of ethics?" A more cynical response, in line with the Holmesian "bad man" theory of the law, would be to ask: "How can I construe my code of ethics to allow me to do what the client wants?" The German code of legal ethics includes a rule instructing lawyers to follow the spirit rather than merely the letter of the rules; no similar provision appears in the ABA Code or Model Rules. Would addition of such a provision be useful?

Brady's defense of his approach is simple: "If your profession has standing, it has that standing because *someone stood up for it*." Is it that simple?

4. In a recent account of the barriers to whistleblowing, Jackall notes:

> The fantastically complicated division of authority that marks all large organizations separates most actors from the consequences of their actions. In particular.... Plausible deniability is part and parcel of these fragmented authority structures. If actors have networked well— a prerequisite for survival, let alone success, in the bureaucratic wilderness—they can count on loyal allies and subordinates to circle the wagons and protect them when arrows begin to fly . . . . . When one choses to point out the wrongdoing of colleagues or especially that of superiors, one inevitably jars these intricate affiliations.... [Such an assertion of principle] threatens established social order and makes everyone wonder whose actions will next come under unwanted scrutiny with unforeseeable results . . . . . Even those who welcome the consequences of betrayal mistrust the betrayer.
>
> In the end, blowing the whistle is a lonely business....[40]

Consider the parallels between the world Jackall describes and the world of Enron described above, and of Hewlett Packard, described below. How are these cases similar. How well do current code and legislative requirements deal with their fundamental dynamics?

40. Robert Jackall, "Whistleblowing & Its Quandries," 20 *Geo. J. Legal Ethics* 1133, 1135–36 (2007).

HEWLETT PACKARD: A CASE STUDY[41]

In 2006, the Silicon Valley computer company Hewlett Packard became embroiled in a highly publicized scandal. The problems arose from "pre-texting," the use of investigators to obtain confidential information through false pretenses. The case provides a highly illuminating portrait of "how the good go bad"—how well intentioned lawyers and managers can become complicit in conduct widely viewed as unethical if not unlawful.

In 2005, leaks of confidential information accompanied the widely publicized firing of HP C.E.O. Carly Fiorina. Patricia Dunn, a member of the board of directors became its new chair and Mark Hurd became C.E.O. Neither had legal background; Dunn came from investment services and Hurd had headed a technology company. Among Dunn's first challenges was to address leaks that could only have come from board members or top executives. Dunn launched an investigation headed by a Boston-based private investigator, Ron DeLia, who had done work for HP in the past. In the late spring of 2005, DeLia sent a report to Dunn, which she forwarded to General Counsel Ann Baskins. DeLia explained that investigators had obtained phone records through pretexting. Baskins expressed concerns about the legality of the process, and DeLia responded that he was aware of no laws that made it illegal and no criminal prosecutions for such activities. Although the investigation failed to identify the leakers, HP leadership hoped that the process would deter future disclosures.

However, in January 2006, reporter Dawn Kawamoto ran a story on HP's long term strategies. Board member George Keyworth, a board member, later acknowledged having been the anonymous source. He did not believe he had disclosed any proprietary information and considered the story to be good press. Hewlett Packard's leadership, by contrast, viewed the story with alarm, particularly because it addressed potential acquisitions. Baskins asked an HP employment lawyer, Ken Hunsaker, to head an investigation. Through pretexting, the investigation team obtained phone records of two HP employees, seven directors and nine reporters. It also created a fictional disgruntled HP employee who contacted Kawamoto by e-mail, and attached a file with tracking capability. Investigators hoped that she would forward the e-mail to her source for confirmation. Hurd, the C.E.O., authorized the process but later denied knowledge of the tracking aspect.

Around the same time, Baskins asked Hunsaker to explore the legality of pretexting. He put the question to Anthony Gentilucci, an HP security manager. Gentilucci responded that pretexting was common. In his view, although phone operators shouldn't give the information out and were in

41. This case study is based on extensive journalist coverage and Congressional testimony. Among the best treatments of the lawyers' role and their interaction with HP leaders are James B. Stewart, "The Kona Files: Hewlett–Packard's Surveillance Scandal," *The New Yorker,* Feb. 19 & 26, 2007, at 152; and Sue Reisinger, "Did Ann Baskins See No Evil at HP?," *Corporate Counsel,* Jan. 2007, at 68; Peter Waldman & Don Clark, "Probing the Pretexter," *Wall St. Journal,* September 25, 2006, at B1; and Lawrence Hurley, "Congress Asks HP Where Were the Lawyers?," *San Francisco D. J.,* Sept. 29, 2006, at 1, 9.

some sense "liable," the practice was "on the edge, but above board." Hunsaker's now infamous e-mail answer was "I should not have asked." Hunsaker also spent about an hour researching the issue on line. It is not clear what sources he consulted, but had he looked at the websites of the Federal Trade Commission or the Federal Communications Commission, he would have discovered that both considered the practice illegal.

In February, the issue arose again. Two HP security employees sent an e-mail to Hunsaker stating that pretexting "is very unethical at the least and probably illegal." So too, Baskins again asked Hunsaker about the legality of pretexting and he again put the question to DeLia. This time DeLia consulted his outside counsel. That lawyer offered a quick judgment that pretexting was not illegal, based on research done by a summer associate the preceding year; the lawyer later claimed that he had not been hired to research the issue. DeLia then sent an e-mail to Hunsaker indicating that no state or federal laws prohibited pretexting but that there was "a risk of litigation."

In March, Hunsaker circulated a report connecting Keyworth to the leaks. In preparation for a meeting with Hurd, Baskins asked Hunsaker to talk to outside counsel about pretexting. Hunsaker asked Gentilucci to consult DeLia's lawyer. This time, the lawyer had a paralegal prepare a response. She told Gentilucci that she was unable to find any criminal charges to indicate that pretexting was illegal. In April, at Baskin's request, Hunsaker prepared a memo on the issues raised by pretexting. He noted his online research and his contacts with DeLia and his outside counsel. According to the memo, counsel's firm had conducted "extensive research" and found the practice "not unlawful." Mark Hurd then met with Keyworth privately and gave him an opportunity to acknowledge his leaks. Keyworth did not do so. As he later recalled the meeting, Hurd did not ask him about the reporter and Keyworth was not aware that her story was the focus of the investigation.

In May, a divided board asked Keyworth to resign. One of its most influential members, Tom Perkins, objected to the decision and resigned in protest. He also recalled objecting to the legality of pretexting. Dunn and other board members recalled no such objection and Dunn denied making any promise to keep the leaker's identity confidential. Larry Sonsini, HP's outside counsel, then contacted Perkins about how to handle the resignation. Post–Enron reforms require that a company report board resignations to the SEC, and if the resignation stems from any disagreement with the company or the board, the reasons must also be disclosed. Perkin's said his disagreement was with Dunn not the company, and the SEC report included no reasons.

Perkins subsequently consulted law professor Viet Dinh, who served with him on another board. Dinh raised concerns about pretexting that Perkins then conveyed to Sonsini. Sonsini responded that pretext calls were a "common investigatory method" and that "It appears, therefore, that the process was well done and within legal limits." Perkins relayed this to Dinh who then expressed doubts that the records could have been lawfully obtained. Perkins's dissatisfaction continued to escalate after receiving a notice from the phone company suggesting that his phone records were "hacked." He was also angry that the minutes of his final board meeting did not reflect the objections to pretexting that he recalled making. Perkins demanded that the minutes be amended, and that the company file a notice with the S.E.C. since he now considered his dispute to be with the company. Baskins subsequently wrote to Perkins denying his requests, because the minutes had been approved and were accurate as drafted, and because he had earlier characterized the reasons for his resignation as personal. Perkins, represented by Dinh, then contacted the SEC, the California Attorney General, and the U.S. Attorney for the Northern District of California, which all launched investigations.

A national scandal erupted, fueled by Congressional hearings at which Dunn and Hurd testified and Baskins and Hunsaker invoked their 5th amendment privilege. Dunn, Baskins Hunsaker, and Gentilucci were all forced to resign. The California Attorney General charged Dunn, Hunsaker, DeLia, and two private investigators with four felony counts: fraudulent wire communications, wrongful use of computer data, identity theft, and conspiracy. The counts were later reduced to misdemeanors. A state court dismissed the charges against Dunn, and then later against all other defendants based on evidence that they had performed community service. One investigator pleaded guilty to federal charges.

In his Congressional testimony, Hurd apologized for the "rogue" investigation and for authorizing the fake email. While denying knowledge of certain other pretexting activity that others had permitted, he acknowledged that failing to read a report that described it was not "my finest hour." Patricia Dunn stated: "I do not accept personal responsibility for what happened." She added: "I relied on the expertise of others in whom I had full confidence. I deeply regret that so many people, including me, were let down." Larry Sonsini maintained that his response to Perkins about the legality of pretexting was not a "legal opinion. It was conveying the truth of what I was told." Ann Baskin made no public statement. Her lawyer told New Yorker reporter James Stewart: "A general counsel has to be able to rely on her senior counsel's research and advice, particularly when she has hundreds of lawyers working for her worldwide." Hunsaker's lawyer assured Stewart that "There cannot be a violation without intent to violate the law and Kevin absolutely believed that the investigation was being done in a legal and proper way."

The financial and personal affects of the scandal varied considerably. HP reimbursed both Perkins for $1.5 million in legal expenses and agreed to pay Keyworth's as well. Ann Baskin, in exchange for cooperating with HP's investigation and releasing the company from liability, received the right to exercise stock options worth over $3.7 million, with another million in options to vest immediately. Mark Hurd, who according to Dunn, had received the same legal advice that she had received, got a bonus of $8.6 million in 2007, along with options on over 500,000 shares of stock. HP stock rose to its highest value in over six years.

Both Congress and the California legislature subsequently passed legislation making pretexting a criminal defense.

QUESTIONS

1.   How would you evaluate the conduct of the lawyers in the HP case? What accounts for their conduct? Could, or should, any of the attorneys be subject to discipline or malpractice liability? Did any fail to exercise appropriate supervisory responsibility?[42] What would you have done in their place?

2.   In the aftermath of the scandal, HP hired Bart M. Schwartz, a former federal prosecutor, to evaluate the company's ethical policies and its conduct of investigations. He told a *New York Times* reporter that he was struck by the lack of consideration of ethical issues in the company's efforts to trace press leaks. "Doing it legally should not be the test; that is given. You have to ask what is appropriate and what is ethical."[43] What might explain the absence of ethical considerations for HP lawyers and managers? What lessons does their experience hold for general counsel? Is one message that whatever else is outsourced, ethics shouldn't be among them?

NOTES: IN–HOUSE COUNSEL

The evolution of in-house counsel positions has placed certain issues of ethical responsibility in new contexts. Although the percentage of lawyers working for private industry has remained fairly stable over the last quarter-century, the absolute size and status of corporate legal departments has grown substantially. In-house counsel have increasingly assumed central functions in providing basic legal services, selecting and monitoring outside attorneys, and attempting to prevent legal problems.

A number of factors account for this increase. Corporations can often achieve substantial savings by relying on inside counsel who are familiar with their structure, employees, records, and objectives; who do not have to accommodate other clients' demands; and who have no incentive to bill unnecessary hours. However, outside counsel remain useful for needs that are episodic and non-repetitive, that require special staffing or expertise, or that call for independent judgment. Whether inside or outside counsel is more cost-effective for particular matters depends on a complicated set of factors involving the nature of the legal work and the particular fee arrangements that outside firms are willing to negotiate.

How the allocation of work to in-house counsel affects the exercise of ethical responsibility is a matter of longstanding debate. The traditional view has been that inside counsel would have less ability to check corporate

---

42.   See the discussion in Section d below, and "Analysis and Perspective: Scandals Involving Investigators Ensnare Lawyers," 21 *ABA/BNA Lawyers' Man. Prof. Conduct* 507 (2006).

43.   Damon Darlin, "Advisor Urges H.P. to Focus on Ethics Over Legalities," *N.Y. Times*, Oct. 4, 2005, at C3.

misconduct because of their greater economic and psychological dependency on the company and their socialization into organizational culture. (In Germany, where ethical rules place special emphasis on lawyers' independence from their clients, house counsel are a separate profession whose members do not belong to the bar.) Where a significant part of in-house attorneys' compensation involves stock options, there may be economic incentives to overvalue the company's short-term profit objectives at the expense of long-term values. To the extent that in-house counsel participate in shaping policies and transactions, these lawyers may have difficulty later exercising independent judgment concerning the legal issues involved.[44] As the Jackall and HP case studies make clear, lawyers, like other managerial employees, face considerable pressure to remain team players. The same has been true of general counsel in other corporate scandals, such as Enron and Tyco. According to Steve Gillers, the job of in-house attorney is the most "ethically challenged position in the legal profession," because "the client is the corporation but the directions come from management."[45] That difficulty is reflected in the growing number of criminal prosecutions of in-house counsel for aiding and abetting fraud.[46] In recognition of these compromising influences, audit companies composed of independent directors increasingly rely on outside counsel for advice on ethics and compliance issues.[47]

Yet comparable pressures can exist for outside counsel as well. Many firm lawyers bill a substantial percentage of their time to a single client and find that it is "sometimes easier to say 'no' to a captive client than to a client who may take its business elsewhere."[48] Moreover, outside lawyers often may be less able to exercise their independence because they have less access to information and fewer informal channels of influence. Eve Spangler's study of lawyers working for organizations comments on this debate:

> In any comparison of in-house and outside legal services, law firms maintain that their independence is their single most significant asset. One law firm partner explains:
>
>> It is not uncommon for us to tell the president that he's a turkey. You know, "You're a goddamn fool, and you've got an environmental problem right now and you've got to spend a million dollars to fix it even though it will lose you money this year, or you're going to go to jail. That's the magnitude of your problem." I'd like to

44. Deborah A. DeMott, "The Discrete Roles of General Counsel," 74 *Fordham L. Rev.* 955 (2005).

45. Michael Orey, "In-House Attorneys, Watch Your Step," *Business Week,* Aug. 6, 2007, at 36 (quoting Gillers).

46. *Id;* DeMott, *supra* note 44, at 974–75, and 978–79; Stephanie Francis Ward, "The Hammer Goes In-House," ABA J., January, 2008, at 14. (describing prosecutions and the failure of Enron's general counsel to address ethical concerns raised by the company's accounting practices and its CFO's con-

flicts of interest); Kim, *supra* note 24, at 1019 and 1054–56 (describing the case against Tyco's general counsel).

47. DeMott, *supra* note 44, at at 980; Geoffrey C. Hazard and Edward B. Rock, "A New Player in the Boardroom: The Emergence of Independent Directors' Counsel," 59 *Bus. Law.* 1389, 1395–96 (2004).

48. David S. Machlowitz, "Lawyers Move In-House," *ABA J.* May 1989, at 69 (quoting counsel for Chase Manhattan Corp).

hear an in-house lawyer say that to a president who just had a stockholders meeting where he's promised them the world. I'd like to see an in-house lawyer tell his board of directors that his president is violating the Foreign Corporate Practices Act. The fact is, there's just no room for willful blindness at that level. If you have both loyalties and accountability to the superior, you can't be independent.

This stance is in sharp contrast to that of the in-house lawyers who say, "I am first a corporate officer and second I happen to be a lawyer," or, again, "I'm pretty much [a company man] through and through."

Nevertheless, the staff attorneys Spangler interviewed insisted that they rarely face situations where job pressures would force them to compromise their judgment. They meet their ethical obligations by counseling executives to look to the long-term interests of the company rather than short-term advantage. And, when executives reject their advice, they report up the ladder when they have to even though it creates difficulties relating to people " 'after you've brought the world down on their heads.' "[49]

In a practical sense, much of the debate over inside and outside lawyers' ethical autonomy may have missed the mark. As Elliot Freidson observes, "surely the more critical matter is the relationship one has to the market" and to one's superiors, whether they are corporate managers or senior attorneys in a firm.[50] Lawyers' economic and psychological sense of vulnerability and the support available for ethical resistance is likely to be more significant than whether they practice in a corporate or law firm setting.

The American Bar Association Task Force on Corporate Responsibility recommended that a public company's board of directors, not management, have responsibility for the selection, retention, and compensation of general counsel, and that the attorneys in that position have regular meetings with the board's independent directors to discuss legal compliance matters. Other commentators have made similar recommendations.[51] To what extent would this practice assist in-house counsel facing difficult ethical issues?

Under what circumstances should either in-house or outside counsel withdraw from representation because a client declines to accept their advice? Geoffrey Hazard observes that representation of clients on an ongoing basis imposes moral responsibility for their conduct in a sense that representation of clients for past acts does not. To defend an individual charged with murder is not the same as being "on retainer to the Mafia."

What follows from that distinction? Hazard goes on to argue:

49. Eve Spangler, *Lawyers for Hire* (1986).

50. Elliot Freidson, *Professional Powers: A Study of the Institutionalization of Formal Knowledge* 124–25 (1986).

51. American Bar Association, Report of the Bar Association Task Force on Corporate Responsibility, 59 *Bus. Law.* 145 (2003); Kim, *supra* note 24, at 1054–63.

The obvious answer for the advisor whose advice is ignored is that he can resign. In some circumstances that is the only honorable course to be followed, but it is impractical as a response to all except fundamental disagreements. More important, though not often recognized by the critics of legal and other advisors to corporations, the sanction of resignation involves some ethical problems of its own. If taken seriously, it should be applicable only when any right-thinking advisor would resign. But this is to say that such a client ought to have no right-thinking advisor at all, at least until the client redirects his conduct so that it would no longer be objectionable to a right-thinking advisor. There are situations in which it seems proper that the client should suffer that kind of penalty, for example if he insists on fabricating evidence or carrying out a swindle. But if the case is less extreme than this, the sanction of resignation is too severe. It implies that the client should have to function without proper guidance, or perhaps cease functioning at all, because its managers do not see fit to follow the advice of its advisors. . . .

If this were the consequence that should ensue from a client's refusal to follow advice, it would mean that the advice was in effect peremptory—not an informed suggestion but a command. When an advisor's advice is in effect peremptory, however, the result is a reversal of the underlying structure of responsibility for the organization's conduct. The advisor becomes the ultimate arbiter and the client a subordinate. . . .

It seems unlikely that such a transfer of responsibility is contemplated by those who say that an advisor has some kind of responsibility for what his principal does. Probably it is assumed that the organization will not be left helpless for want of essential assistance, but rather that some other advisor will come along to take the place of the right-thinking advisor who resigns. This assumption, however, has some curious implications. It may mean that an equally high-minded advisor can step in as successor because he was not involved before. As a result, that which is reprehensible when done by one advisor in continuous service becomes acceptable when done by multiple advisors acting in a relay. A lot of moral knots are cut this way but it surely is an Alexandrine technique. On the other hand, the assumption may be that a less high-minded successor can be expected to take over. If so, it reduces the significance of resignation to a merely personal matter and perhaps a case of narcissism. (It may also have the result of simply insulating the client from conscientious advisors in the future.) Still another possibility is that the client will figure out how to retain high-minded advisors without creating situations in which they will feel impelled to resign; the client will learn not to ask for advice in the cases that might put his counsel under that kind of pressure.[52]

Do you agree? Would you accept such rationales for continued employment in less respectable contexts (for example, by accused war criminals

52. Geoffrey Hazard, Jr., *Ethics in the Practice of Law 144 (1978).*

who argued that their replacements would have been worse)? Is it possible that lawyers' threats of resignation could up the moral ante and encourage clients to rethink their conduct as well as encourage other attorneys to do the same? Is advice really peremptory as long as the advisor is not the proverbial "last lawyer in town," a presumably rare circumstance for corporate counsel?

D.   Supervisory and Subordinate Lawyers

PROBLEM 4

1.   Suppose the facts had been as follows in the Berkey–Kodak case described below.

a) You are an associate with Donovan Leisure. For the past two years you have worked principally for one senior partner on a large antitrust suit brought by Berkey Photo against your client, Eastman Kodak. One of the major issues in the suit concerns whether Kodak's acquisitions of early competitors or its superior product innovations were the primary cause of its dominant market position. In connection with that issue, Kodak has retained a highly regarded Yale economics professor to study the photography industry in the hope that he will develop an expert opinion that Kodak's innovations, rather than its acquisitions, enabled it to attain dominance. Ultimately, the professor does develop such a theory. However, in one early letter to the senior partner, the expert indicates he is unable to explain how Kodak's early acquisitions could be irrelevant to its present market position.

This letter and certain documents reviewed by the economist have not been produced in response to Berkey's discovery demand for all such documents and for "interim reports" prepared by the economist. The partner in charge of the case has executed an affidavit under oath stating that he inadvertently destroyed the documents, believing them to be duplicates of material still available. The partner also privately maintains that he does not consider the economist's correspondence to be a "report" within the meaning of the discovery demand.

You find that interpretation contrived, and try unsuccessfully to convince the partner that the expert's preliminary expression of doubt is precisely the sort of interim statement that Berkey is seeking for cross-examination purposes. At the very least, you believe the trial court should be asked to rule on the question. You also know that the documents have not been destroyed, although they reveal nothing of critical substantive value to Berkey. You greatly respect the senior partner and are at a loss to explain his behavior. What is your response?

b) Assume that you describe the situation to another senior partner whose opinion you value. He expresses doubt that the facts could be as you described them. He points out that if it were the case that the partner had suppressed evidence and lied under oath, and if the deception became public, that man's life would be ruined and the firm's reputation would be tainted. In addition, the partnership could lose a major client and be subject to a multi-million dollar malpractice suit. What do you do?

c) Assume that before you take any action, Berkey makes a settlement offer that Kodak is willing to accept. Does that alter your plans?

2. Suppose that Steven Brill's account of the Berkey–Kodak litigation excerpted below is essentially correct.

a) Assume you are a member of the New York Bar Disciplinary committee, to whom the matter has been referred. What, if any, disciplinary action do you recommend for the attorneys involved?

b) Assume you are a member of the firm's management committee. You have worked with the attorneys whose conduct is now open to question and, prior to this incident, you had respect and affection for all of those involved. What action do you believe the firm should take with respect to those individuals? If Kodak had not lost the trial and left the firm, would that affect your decision?

References:

DRs 7–102, 7–106(C)(7), 7–109(A), 2–103, 2–110(B) & (C); Model Rules 3.3, 3.4, 5.1, 5.2.

Bibliographic References: Walter Kiechel III, "The Strange Case of Kodak's Lawyers," *Fortune,* May 8, 1978, at 188; James B. Stewart, Jr., "Kodak and Donovan Leisure: The Untold Story," *The American Lawyer,* Jan. 1983, at 24.

Steven Brill, "When a Lawyer Lies"

Esquire 23–24 (Dec. 19, 1979).

Eighteen months ago, Joseph Fortenberry, Harvard College '66 and Yale Law '69, was on the perfect big-time lawyer's career path. At thirty-three, he had a federal court of appeals clerkship under his belt and was a senior associate at the New York law firm of Donovan Leisure Newton & Irvine working on the all-important antitrust case that Kodak was defending against Berkey Photo.

His prospects for being made a partner at the prestige firm the following year were excellent: He was regarded not only as brilliant but also as engaging and enjoyable to work with; Kodak was the firm's biggest case (occupying twenty lawyers full time, with gross billings of some $4 million a year); and he was working hand in hand with Mahlon Perkins Jr., one of the firm's most respected partners.

Then came April 20, 1977. That morning, in the middle of one of hundreds of depositions (on-the-record question-and-answer sessions with a witness prior to the trial) that he had sat through for months, Joe Fortenberry's career unraveled.

Alvin Stein, the lawyer for Berkey Photo, was questioning a Kodak "expert witness," Yale economics professor Merton Peck, about files and other materials the professor had received from Kodak in order to prepare his testimony. In such suits, each side is allowed to obtain—or "discover"—almost any documents that the other side has used to prepare and bolster its case. Such materials can often be used to attack the credibility of witnesses.

Peck told Berkey lawyer Stein that he had shipped all the materials back to Perkins of Donovan Leisure earlier that year. What happened, then, to the documents, Stein asked Perkins. I threw them out as soon as I got them, the Donovan Leisure partner replied.

Perkins was lying. He'd saved all the documents in a suitcase, frequently taking them back and forth between his office at the firm and a special office he'd leased near the federal courthouse for the trial. And Joe Fortenberry, sitting at Perkins's side during this deposition, knew his boss was lying. He'd worked with the suitcase full of documents, and at least once he'd carried it between Perkins's two offices. Two weeks later, Perkins submitted a sworn statement to the court confirming he'd destroyed the documents.

In January of 1978, Perkins's perjury came to light when Stein, at the end of the Kodak–Berkey trial, asked Peck about any reports he had submitted prior to the trial to Kodak's lawyers. This led back to more probing questions about the materials Peck had used to prepare his testimony. Then—in what has since become a much-reported, pinstriped soap opera—on the Sunday night before the last week of the trial, a frightened Perkins broke down and confessed to Kodak lead lawyer John Doar that he'd never destroyed the documents but had actually hid them in a cupboard in his office. Perkins told the judge the next day, then resigned from the firm; Stein used Donovan Leisure's withholding of documents to help convince the jury of Kodak's bad faith and guilt; Kodak lost the case in a spectacular $113 million verdict (since reduced to $87 million); Kodak dropped Donovan Leisure; and Perkins was convicted of contempt of court for his perjury and sentenced to a month in prison.

But what about Joe Fortenberry?

The rules by which the bar disciplines lawyers—the Code of Professional Responsibility—require that "a lawyer who receives information clearly establishing that . . . a person other than his client has perpetrated a fraud upon a tribunal shall promptly reveal the fraud to the tribunal." Moreover, the code requires that a lawyer who knows that another lawyer has engaged in dishonesty, deceit, or misrepresentation must report the offending lawyer to proper prosecutorial authorities.

In short, Fortenberry was obligated to speak up when Perkins lied. Instead, he said nothing to anyone. To be sure, Perkins, perhaps thinking he was helping Fortenberry, told the federal prosecutors who later investigated the case that Fortenberry had whispered in his ear and reminded him of the existence of the documents when Perkins told Stein he'd destroyed them. Fortenberry denies this. What's undisputed, and more relevant, is that Fortenberry never said a word about Perkins's lie to the judge, as he was obligated to, or even to any other Donovan Leisure partner.

Throw the book at him, right? Wrong. Law firms teach young associates that they are apprentices to the partners, not whistle blowers. The partners, after all, are supposed to be the ones with the experience and standing to make decisions about right and wrong. Fortenberry had worked for Perkins for more than six months. In an environment like Donovan Leisure, this means that he respected the fifty-nine year-old "Perk," as his admiring partners called him, for the well-liked senior litigator that he was. It also means that he was intimidated by Perkins and, of course, that he knew Perkins was his ticket to a partnership when the firm partners would decide in the following year which of the associates at Fortenberry's level would be offered that golden prize. "What happened to Joe" says a close associate "was that he saw Perk lie and really couldn't believe it. And he just had no idea what to do. I mean, he knew Perkins was lying, but he kept thinking that there must be a reason. Besides, what do you do? The guy was his boss and a great guy!"

As stung as Donovan Leisure is by the Perkins affair, the firm's partners have treated Fortenberry with the compassion that suggests that they understand his dilemma. They've paid for him to retain his own lawyer for the investigation that resulted in Perkins's guilty plea and for possible bar association disciplinary action. (Federal prosecutors say there's no evidence of criminal misconduct on Fortenberry's part, but the Association of the Bar of the City of New York never comments on its own investigations regarding possible violations of the Lawyers Code of Professional Responsibility, even to the point of acknowledging whether there is one going on.) And they've kept him on at the firm and gone out of their way with signs ranging from work assignments to lunch invitations to show that they hold him blameless. In many ways, it hasn't helped. Friends say that Fortenberry—"a well-liked, personable genius," as one puts it—has been severely hurt emotionally by the Perkins episode. "He just looks and acts like a beaten man," as another associate explained.

There's one thing that Donovan Leisure could do to revive Fortenberry. They could make him a partner this June, when the decision on partners of his seniority is normally made. The odds are he'd have been made a partner had the Perkins affair never happened; so if, as Samuel Murphy of the firm's management committee told me recently, "in judging Joe for partnership, we're not going to hold the tragedy with Perk against him in any way," it stands to reason that he will get the offer. Then again, how does Donovan Leisure look, its reputation already hurt by the Perkins affair, offering a partnership to the man who apparently violated the Code of Professional Responsibility and kept quiet while Perkins perpetrated his fraud on the court?

With Donovan Leisure beginning to recover from the Perkins affair . . . the upcoming decision on what to do with Fortenberry may be the one last hurdle they have to pass. (A once-feared malpractice suit by Kodak is now unlikely, a source at the camera maker says.)

But there are larger questions, too, that Fortenberry's sad situation should raise. Donovan Leisure senior partner Murphy says that "the firm is trying to create an atmosphere in which associates in positions like Fortenberry's will feel free to take the story of one partner acting improperly to another partner." But Perkins's impropriety—a clear, deliberate lie—is an easy call. What about an associate who thinks his partner is filing a frivolous motion or is bilking a client? "You know, when you come to work at a big firm you do give up independence," Murphy concedes. "And a young lawyer's ideas about what is frivolous, for example, can't always be accepted, though we do encourage them to tell the partners they're working for what they think."

And what about firms other than Donovan Leisure that haven't been clubbed by a Perkins disaster into thinking about "open doors" and the like? I asked eight different associates, ages twenty-seven to thirty-two, at major firms around the country what they'd do in Fortenberry's situation. None said that they'd speak up to the judge in the case as their Code of Professional Responsibility requires; only four suggested that there was another partner at the firm they'd feel free to go to if their boss did something like that; and one told a story of watching a partner bill a client (a major utility) for three times the hours worked and, not knowing what to do, doing nothing.

Judge Marvin E. Frankel, the trial judge in the Kodak–Berkey case, was highly critical of Donovan Leisure's conduct during the trial and so outraged by Perkins's lie that he personally called it to the attention of the federal prosecutors. Frankel has since left the bench and become a partner at the midtown firm of Proskauer Rose Goetz & Mendelsohn. An associate there told me last week he'd "have no idea" what to do in a Perkins situation. "There isn't any way for an associate to handle that problem," Frankel concedes. Yet, unexplainably, the once-outraged judge shifts the direct responsibility from the individual law firms, where it belongs, to the organized bar generally: "All firms, including this one, should push the bar association to evolve procedures so that an associate doesn't have to be a hero to do what's ethical."

Every year more and more of the best brains in our society go from law school to firms like Donovan Leisure. And every year these firms get larger—and more competitive. Without some real effort from those at the top, this is an environment that is destined to make automatons out of those who get by and tragedies out of those, like Fortenberry, who have the bad luck to get tripped up.

NOTES

According to case histories of the Berkey–Kodak litigation, the perjury in Perkins's affidavit became public as a result of his own disclosure, first to fellow partner John Doar and then to the court. The existence of the expert's early correspondence emerged after cross-examination when Berkey's counsel asked him whether there were any documents "on this matter" prepared prior to a given date. When the expert responded by seeking a definition of "on this matter," counsel for Berkey pursued the issue and district Judge Frankel required disclosure of the letter.[53]

In his summary to the jury, counsel made the most of the incident:

> That sordid spectacle of dissembling, evasiveness, deception, and con-cealment disgraces the dignity of this court, this proceeding, and you jurors. And there is no doubt, I believe, based upon the evidence presented to you, and the conclusions to be drawn from that evidence, that the witness deliberately and purposefully concealed material evi-dence, and—I think it has got to be said—lied to you under oath. Not once, repeatedly. [The expert] has proven himself utterly unworthy of belief.[54]

Judge Frankel also made clear his own dissatisfaction with Donovan Leisure's performance. He began by noting that Perkins had executed his false affidavit in response to his partner's request for something stronger that would "satisfy" the court as to why documents could not be produced. Frankel then questioned whether it was sufficient "for Mr. Perkins' partners to demand more positiveness or whether it wasn't incumbent on everyone concerned to press Mr. Perkins more vigorously than he appears to have been pressed for the truthful account we received so many months later." As for the failure to disclose the expert's early letter, Frankel questioned why lead counsel John Doar "did not see fit to let me look at the document," and added:

> All of those things it seems to me reflect—and I have said it in just words of one or two syllables—a kind of single-minded interest in winning, winning, winning, without the limited qualification of that attitude that the Court, I think, is entitled to expect and which I feel must have infected Perkins and has infected certain aspects of this case from time to time in ways that I find upsetting.[55]

A week after the jury awarded Berkey a total of $113 million in damages, Kodak announced that Sullivan and Cromwell was taking over the litigation. On appeal, the Second Circuit reversed and remanded the lower court judgment. Kodak eventually settled the case for $6.75 million. Donovan Leisure paid $675,000 to Kodak to prevent a malpractice claim for failure to turn over documents.[56] John Doar, who was widely criticized by Donovan Leisure colleagues for his "cold, distant, and morally arrogant manner" and his ineffective supervision of the Kodak litigation, resigned from the firm. According to James Stewart's case history:

> Fortenberry's role in the scandal had nothing to do with his failure to be made a partner. The firm had actually passed him over two months before the Perkins matter ever came to light, partners there say. It

---

53. Walter Kiechel III, "The Strange Case of Kodak's Lawyers," *Fortune*, May 8, 1978, at 188.

54. Trial Transcript at 16,739 (Jan. 21, 1978).

55. *Id.* at 16,742.

56. Stephen Wermiel, "Lawyers' Public Image Is Dreadful, Spurring Concern by At-torneys," *Wall St. J.*, Oct. 11, 1983, at 1.

later concealed its decision so as to enhance Fortenberry's chances of getting another job, keeping him working so that prospective employers would not see his immediate dismissal from the firm and conclude that Fortenberry was indeed implicated in Perkins's wrong-doing. Even so, Fortenberry was not hired by any private law firm to which he applied for a job.

Perkins emerged relatively well. Although he served 27 days in jail for contempt of court, he was never disbarred. Subsequently he traveled extensively, taught English in Japan, and served as president of his local orchestra. One of his former partners described him as "happier, I believe, than he had been as a practicing lawyer."[57]

In the mid–1980s, the then–65–year–old Perkins began working as a volunteer at the Center for Constitutional Rights, a prominent public interest law firm. "Intellectually, the work here is every bit as satisfying as what I did before," he told a *New York Times* reporter. "And politically, I derive a lot more satisfaction than I did at Donovan, Leisure. I'm helping in causes I believe in very deeply. This wasn't a very good way to have gotten out, but at this point, I'm very happy not to be there, and very happy to be here."[58]

QUESTIONS

1.   What implications can be drawn from the Berkey–Kodak case for the structure of law firms and content of ethical rules? Do the ABA's Informal Opinion 1203 excerpted below and Model Rule 5.2 provide adequate guidance for associates?

2.   Can firms create better formal or informal channels of communications regarding ethical issues? What might have encouraged Fortenberry to disclose Perkins's conduct to other partners in the firm at a point when the affidavit could have been withdrawn without major scandal?[59]

3.   Should associates be subject to formal or informal sanctions for failure to make such disclosures?

4.   Does Perkins's subsequent career affect your view about whether he should have been disbarred?

5.   Rule 5.1(a) makes partners in a law firm responsible for ensuring that the firm's policies give "reasonable assurance that all lawyers in the firm conform to the rules of professional conduct." How stringently should it be applied? Consider the following situation. Law firm B is well-known for its extremely aggressive litigation tactics, which sometimes have led to sanctions under Rule 11 and Rule 26 of the Federal Rules of Civil Procedure. In

57. James B. Stewart, Jr., "Kodak and Donovan Leisure: The Untold Story," *The American Lawyer,* Jan. 1983, at 24, 62.

58. David Margolick, "The Long Road Back for a Disgraced Patrician," *N.Y. Times,* Jan. 19, 1990, at B6.

59. *See* Lawrence K. Hellman, "The Effects of Law Office Work on the Formation of Law Students' Professional Values: Observation, Explanation, Optimization," 4 *Geo. J. Legal Ethics* 537 (1991).

one recent high-stakes case, after repeated complaints by opposing attorneys that the firm's lawyers resisted legitimate discovery requests, the trial judge rebuked the supervising partner. Afterwards the abusive tactics become more subtle but do not stop. As the partner privately explains, "delay is worth a great deal to the firm." Should any other lawyers in the firm be subject to discipline under Model Rule 5.1(a)? Should firms as entities be subject to discipline? Could courts and lawmakers take more effective measures to address these circumstances? Should Donovan Leisure have been subject to sanctions if Rule 5.1 had been in effect?

6. At the turn of this century, New York and New Jersey are the only states with an ethical rule that permits firms as well as individual lawyers to be disciplined for ethical and legal violations. New York Code of Professional Responsibility DR 1–102(2); N.J. Rules of Professional Conduct 5.1(a). Under what circumstances should a law firm be disciplined for misconduct of lawyers in the firm? What sanctions are appropriate for firms? See Ted Schneyer, "Professional Discipline for Law Firms?," 77 *Cornell L. Rev.* 1 (1991); Julie Rose O'Sullivan, "Professional Discipline for Law Firms? A Response to Professor Schneyer's Proposal," 16 *Geo. J. Legal Ethics* 1 (2002). See Chapter XV.

Under federal law, organizations can be charged with crimes committed by their employees in the actual or apparent scope of their duties. In 2006, the prominent plaintiffs' firm of Milberg Weiss (currently Milberg LLP) was indicted because of illegal kickbacks partners paid to clients who would become named plaintiffs in class action suits.[60] Several partners pled guilty to fraud and conspiracy charges. As of summer 2008, charges remain pending against the law firm.

ABA Comm. on Ethics and Professional Responsibility

Informal Op. 1203 (1972).

You have asked the Committee for an Opinion based on the following factual situation.

"In a law office a junior attorney forms a firm conviction that it is necessary in connection with a client matter pending before a tribunal to call some information to the attention of the tribunal—that it would be a fraud on the tribunal to maintain some part of the client's claim without revealing the information. In accordance with the customary practice of the office the junior operates under the general supervision of a senior attorney. The senior directs the junior not to reveal the information. The senior states that the withholding is not fraud or misrepresentation under then prevailing state of law and that the information is privileged. The junior, after thoughtful consideration and weighing the greater experience and

---

60. Julie Creswell, "Milberg Weiss Is Charged With Bribery and Fraud," *New York*   *Times*, May 18, 2006 at A1.

learning of his elder colleague, disagrees. What is required of the junior under the Code of Professional Responsibility?"

You have correctly identified the relevant provisions of the Code of Professional Responsibility as DR 1–102(A)(4), (5), 1–103(A), 4–101(A), (B)(1), (C)(2), (D), 7–102(A), (B). However, we believe that the procedure to be followed under the circumstances given is governed by DR 2–110(C)(2). Whether or not the continued employment of the particular junior attorney will result in the violation of a Disciplinary Rule may be a matter of judgment, and great weight should be given to the senior attorney's judgment that it will not. But if the views of the two are irreconcilable, then the junior attorney should withdraw. To do more at this stage of the proceedings would be premature. Of course, if a violation of a disciplinary rule occurs of which the junior attorney has unprivileged knowledge, then the provisions of DR 1–103(A) should be followed.

QUESTION

How does this opinion differ from Rule 5.2(b)? Which is superior?

C.S. Lewis, "The Inner Ring" in They Asked for a Paper: Papers and Addresses

146–47(1962).

. . .

It would be polite and charitable, and in view of your age reasonable too, to suppose that none of you is yet a scoundrel. On the other hand, by the mere law of averages (I am saying nothing against free will) it is almost certain that at least two or three of you before you die will have become something very like scoundrels. There must be in this room the makings of at least that number of unscrupulous, treacherous, ruthless egotists. The choice is still before you: and I hope you will not take my hard words about your possible future characters as a token of disrespect to your present characters. And the prophecy I make is this. To nine out of ten of you the choice which could lead to scoundrelism will come, when it does come, in no very dramatic colours. Obviously bad men, obviously threatening and bribing, will almost certainly not appear. Over a drink or a cup of coffee, disguised as a triviality and sandwiched between two jokes, from the lips of a man, or woman, whom you have recently been getting to know rather better and whom you hope to know better still—just at the moment when you are most anxious not to appear crude, or naif or a prig—the hint will come. It will be the hint of something which is not quite in accordance with the technical rules of fair play: something which the public, the ignorant romantic public, would never understand: something which even the outsiders in your own profession are apt to make a fuss about: but something, says your new friend, which "we"—and at the word "we" you try not to blush for mere pleasure—something "we always do". And you will be drawn in, if you are drawn in, not by desire for gain or ease, but simply because at that moment, when the cup was so near your lips, you cannot bear to be thrust back again into the cold outer world. It would be so terrible to see the other man's face—that genial, confidential, delightfully sophisticated face—turn suddenly cold and contemptuous, to know that you had been tried for the Inner Ring and rejected. And then, if you are drawn in, next week it will be something a little further from the rules, and next year something further still, but all in the jolliest, friendliest spirit. It may end in a crash, a scandal, and penal servitude: it may end in millions, a peerage and giving the prizes at your old school. But you will be a scoundrel.

Patrick J. Schiltz, "On Being a Happy, Healthy, and Ethical Member of an Unhappy, Unhealthy, and Unethical Profession"

52 Vand. L. Rev. 871, 917–18 (1999).

Let me tell you how you will start acting unethically: It will start with your time sheets. One day, not too long after you start practicing law, you will sit down at the end of a long, tiring day, and you just won't have much to show for your efforts in terms of billable hours. It will be near the end of the month. You will know that all of the partners will be looking at your monthly time report in a few days, so what you'll do is pad your time sheet just a bit. Maybe you will bill a client for ninety minutes for a task that really took you only sixty minutes to perform. However, you will promise yourself that you will repay the client at the first opportunity by doing thirty minutes of work for the client for "free." In this way, you will be "borrowing," not "stealing."

And then what will happen is that it will become easier and easier to take these little loans against future work. And then, after a while, you will stop paying back these little loans. You will convince yourself that, although you billed for ninety minutes and spent only sixty minutes on the project, you did such good work that your client should pay a bit more for it. After all, your billing rate is awfully low, and your client is awfully rich.

And then you will pad more and more—every two minute telephone conversation will go down on the sheet as ten minutes, every three hour research project will go down with an extra quarter hour or so. You will continue to rationalize your dishonesty to yourself in various ways until one day you stop doing even that. And, before long—it won't take you much more than three or four years—you will be stealing from your clients almost every day, and you won't even notice it.

You know what? You will also likely become a liar. A deadline will come up one day, and, for reasons that are entirely your fault, you will not be able to meet it. So you will call your senior partner or your client and make up a white lie for why you missed the deadline. And then you will get busy and a partner will ask whether you proofread a lengthy prospectus and you will say yes, even though you didn't. And then you will be drafting a brief and you will quote language from a Supreme Court opinion even though you will know that, when read in context, the language does not remotely suggest what you are implying it suggests. And then, in preparing a client for a deposition, you will help the client to formulate an answer to a difficult question that will likely be asked—an answer that will be "legally accurate" but that will mislead your opponent. And then you will be reading through a big box of your client's documents—a box that has not been opened in twenty years—and you will find a document that would hurt your client's case, but that no one except you knows exists, and you will simply "forget" to produce it in response to your opponent's discovery requests.

Do you see what will happen? After a couple of years of this, you won't even notice that you are lying and cheating and stealing every day that you practice law. None of these things will seem like a big deal in itself—an extra fifteen minutes added to a time sheet here, a little white lie to cover a missed deadline there. But, after a while, your entire frame of reference will change. You will still be making dozens of quick, instinctive decisions every day, but those decisions, instead of reflecting the notions of right and wrong by which you conduct your personal life, will instead reflect the set of values by which you will conduct your professional life—a set of values that embodies not what is right or wrong, but what is profitable, and what you can get away with.

David Luban, "The Ethics of Wrongful Obedience" in Ethics in Practice: Lawyers' Roles, Responsibilities, and Regulation (Deborah L. Rhode, ed.)

95–97, 102–03, 105 (2001).

One of the best-known and most painful examples of [wrongful obedience by lawyers] was the Berkey–Kodak antitrust litigation in 1977, a bitterly contested private antitrust action brought by Berkey Photo against the giant of the industry. In the heat of adversarial combat, Mahlon Perkins, an admired senior litigator for the large New York law firm representing Kodak, snapped. For no apparent reason, he lied to his opponent to conceal documents from discovery, then perjured himself before a federal judge to cover up the lie. Eventually he owned up, resigned from his firm, and served a month in prison. Perhaps this sounds like an instance of chickens coming home to roost for a Rambo litigator. But by all accounts, Perkins was an upright and courtly man, the diametrical opposite of a Rambo litigator.

Joseph Fortenberry, the associate working for him, knew that Perkins had perjured himself but kept silent. "What happened . . ." recalls another associate, "was that he saw [the partner] lie and really couldn't believe it. And he just had no idea what to do. I mean, he . . . kept thinking there must be a reason. Besides, what to you do? The guy was his boss and a great guy!"

Notice the range of explanations here. First, the appeal to hierarchy: the guy was his boss. Second, to personal loyalty: the guy was a great guy. Third, to helplessness: Fortenberry had no idea what to do. Fourth, Fortenberry couldn't believe it. He kept thinking there must be a reason. The last is an explanation of a different sort, suggesting that Fortenberry's own ethical judgment was undermined by the situation he found himself in.

As a matter of fact, the same may be said of Perkins. He wasn't the lead partner in the litigation; he belonged to a team headed by a newcomer to the firm, an intense, driven, focused, and controlling lawyer. In a situation of supreme stress, Perkins's judgment simply failed him.

In Berkey–Kodak, neither Perkins nor Fortenberry received an explicit order to break the rules, but sometimes lawyers do. What guidance do the ethics rules give when this happens? ABA Model Rule 5.2(a) denies the defense of superior orders to a subordinate lawyer ordered to behave unethically, but Rule 5.2(b)states that a subordinate may defer to "a supervisory lawyer's reasonable resolution of an arguable question of professional duty." The problem is that the pressures on subordinate lawyers may lead them to misjudge when a question of professional duty is arguable and when the supervisor's resolution of it is reasonable. Remember Fortenberry, who "kept thinking there must be a reason" when he heard Perkins perjure himself before a federal judge. This was not even close to an arguable question, and there's nothing reasonable about perjury—but the very fact that it was Fortenberry's respected supervisor who committed it undermined his own confidence that he understood what was reasonable and what was not. When that happens, Rule 5.2(b) will seem more salient to an associate than the bright-line prohibition on wrongful obedience that the first half of the rule articulates.

I want to see what we can learn about wrongful obedience from the most celebrated effort to study it empirically, Stanley Milgram's experiments conducted at Yale thirty-five years ago. Even though these experiments are very well-known, I will begin by reviewing what Milgram did and what he discovered.

Imagine, then, that you answer Milgram's newspaper advertisement, offering twenty dollars if you volunteer for a one-hour psychology experiment.[61] When you enter the room, you meet the experimenter, dressed in a grey lab coat, and a second volunteer, a pleasant, bespectacled middle-aged man. Unbeknownst to you, the second volunteer is in reality a confederate of the experimenter.

The experimenter explains that the two volunteers will be participating in a study of the effect of punishment on memory and learning. One of you, the learner, will memorize word-pairs; the other, the teacher, will punish the learner with steadily-increasing electrical shocks each time he makes a mistake. A volunteer, rather than the experimenter, must administer the shocks because one aim of the experiment is to investigate punishments administered by very different kinds of people. The experimenter leads you

61. [Ed. Milgram actually offered $4, but this was in 1960 dollars.]

to the shock-generator, a formidable-looking machine with thirty switches, marked from 15 volts to 450. Above the voltages labels are printed. These range from "Slight Shock" (15–60 volts) through "Danger: Severe Shock" (375–420 volts); they culminate in an ominous-looking red label reading "XXX" above 435 and 450 volts. Both volunteers experience a 45–volt shock. Then they draw lots to determine their role. The drawing is rigged so that you become the teacher. The learner mentions that he has a mild heart problem, and the experimenter replies rather non-responsively that the shocks will cause no permanent tissue damage. The learner is strapped into the hot seat, and the experiment gets underway.

The learner begins making mistakes, and as the shocks escalate he grunts in pain. Eventually he complains about the pain, and at 150 volts announces in some agitation that he wishes to stop the experiment. You look inquiringly at the man in the grey coat, but he says only, "The experiment requires that you continue." As you turn up the juice, the learner begins screaming. Finally, he shouts out that he will answer no more questions. Unflapped, the experimenter instructs you to treat silences as wrong answers. You ask him who will take responsibility if the learner is injured, and he states that he will. You continue.

As the experiment proceeds, the agitated learner announces that his heart is starting to bother him. Again, you protest, and again the man in the lab coat replies, "The experiment requires that you continue." At 330 volts, the screams stop. The learner falls ominously silent, and remains silent until the bitter end.

But it never actually gets to the bitter end, does it? You may be excused for thinking so. In a follow-up study, groups of people heard the Milgram setup described. They were asked to guess how many people would comply all the way to 450 volts, and to predict whether they themselves would. People typically guessed that at most one teacher out of a thousand would comply—and no-one believed that they themselves would.

In reality, sixty-three percent of subjects complied all the way to 450 volts. Moreover, this is a robust result: it holds in groups of women as well as men, and experimenters obtained comparable results in Holland, Spain, Italy, Australia, South Africa, Germany, and Jordan; indeed, the Jordanian experimenters replicated the 65% result not only among adults but among seven-year-olds. Originally, Milgram had intended to run his experiments in Germany, to try to understand how so many Germans could participate in the Holocaust; his American experiments were merely for the purpose of perfecting his procedures. After the American dry run, however, Milgram remarked: "I found so much obedience, I hardly saw the need of taking the experiment to Germany."

In my view, we should regard the underestimates of subjects' willingness to inflict excruciating shocks on an innocent person as a finding just as important and interesting as the 65% compliance rate itself. The Milgram experiments demonstrate not only that in the right circumstances we are quite prone to destructive obedience, but also that we don't believe this about ourselves, or about our neighbors—nor do we condone it.

Milgram demonstrates that each of us ought to believe three things about ourselves: that we disapprove of destructive obedience, that we think we would never engage in it, and, more likely than not, that we are wrong to think we would never engage in it. . . .

The Milgram experiments place moral norms in conflict. One is what I will call the performance principle: the norm of obeying authority, coupled with the norm of doing your job. The other is the no-harm principle: the prohibition on torturing, harming, and killing innocent people. In the abstract, we might think, only a sadist or a fascist would subordinate the no-harm principle to the performance principle. But the Milgram experiments seem to show that what we think in the abstract is dead wrong. Two out of three people you pass in the street would electrocute you if a laboratory technician ordered them to.

The question is why. . . .

The feature I wish to focus on is the slippery-slope character of the electrical shocks. The teacher moves up the scale of shocks by 15–volt increments, and reaches the 450 volt level only at the thirtieth shock. Among other things, this means that the subjects never confront the question "Should I administer a 330 volt shock to the learner?" The question is "Should I administer a 330 volt shock to the learner given that I've just administered a 315 volt shock?" It seems clear that the latter question is much harder to answer. As Milgram himself points out, to conclude that administering the 330 volt shock would be wrong is to admit that the 315 volt shock was probably wrong, and perhaps all the shocks were wrong.

Cognitive dissonance theory teaches that when our actions conflict with our self-concept, our beliefs and attitudes change until the conflict is removed. We are all pro se defense lawyers in the court of conscience. Cognitive dissonance theory suggests that when I have given the learner a series of electrical shocks, I simply won't view giving the next shock as a wrongful act, because I won't admit to myself that the previous shocks were wrong.

Let me examine this line of thought in more detail. Moral decision-making requires more than adhering to sound principles, such as the no-harm principle. It also requires good judgment, by which I mean knowing which actions violates a moral principle and which do not. Every lawyer understands the difference between good principles and good judgment—it is the difference between knowing a rule of law and being able to apply it to particular cases. As Kant first pointed out, you can't teach good judgment through general rules, because we already need judgment to know how rules apply. Judgment is therefore always and irredeemably particular.

Let's assume that most of Milgram's subjects do accept the no-harm principle, and agree in the abstract that it outweighs the performance principle. *They still need good judgment to know at what point the electrical shocks violate the no-harm principle.* Virtually no-one thinks that the slight tingle of a 15 volt shock violates the no-harm principle: if it did, medical researchers would violate the no-harm principle every time they take blood samples from volunteers. Unsurprisingly, only two of Milgram's thousand subjects refused to give any shocks at all.

But how can 30 volts violate the no-harm principle if 15 volts didn't? And if a 30–volt shock doesn't violate the no-harm principle, neither does a shock of 45 volts.

Of course we know that slippery slope arguments like this are bad logic. At some point, the single grains of sand really do add up to a heap, and at some point shocking the learner really should shock the conscience as well. But it takes good judgment to know where that point lies. Unfortunately, cognitive dissonance generates enormous psychic pressure to deny that our previous obedience may have violated a fundamental moral principle. That denial requires us to gerrymander the boundaries of the no-harm principle so that the shocks we've already delivered don't violate it. However, once we've kneaded and pummelled the no-harm principle, it becomes virtually impossible to judge that the next shock, only imperceptibly more intense, crosses the border from the permissible to the forbidden. By luring us into higher and higher level shocks, one micro-step at a time, the Milgram experiments gradually and subtly disarm our ability to distinguish right from wrong. Milgram's subjects never need to lose, even for a second, their faith in the no-harm principle. Instead, they lose their capacity to recognize that administering an agonizing electrical shock violates it.

What I am offering here is a corruption of judgment explanation of the Milgram experiments. The road to Hell turns out to be a slippery slope, and the travellers on it really do have good intentions—they "merely" suffer from bad judgment. . . .

Let me return to the Berkey–Kodak case and see what light the corruption-of-judgment theory may shed on it. The theory suggests that we should find the partner's and associate's misdeeds at the end of a slippery slope, beginning with lawful adversarial deception and culminating with lies, perjury, and wrongful obedience. Following this lead, one fact leaps out at us: the misdeeds occurred during a high-stakes discovery process.

Every litigator knows that discovery is one of the most contentious parts of civil litigation. Civil discovery is like a game of Battleship. One side calls out its shots—it files discovery requests—and the other side must announce when a shot scores a hit. It makes that announcement by turning over a document. There are two big differences. First, unlike Battleship, it isn't always clear when a shot has scored a hit. Lawyers get to argue about whether their document really falls within the scope of the request. They can argue that the request was too broad, or too narrow, or that the document is privileged, or is attorney work-product. Second, unlike Battleship, lawyers don't always get to peek at the opponent's card after the game. When the opponent concludes that a shot missed her battleship, she makes the decision ex parte—she doesn't have to announce it to her adversary, who may never learn that a smoking-gun document (the battleship) was withheld based on an eminently debatable legal judgment.

Every litigation associate goes through a rite of passage: She finds a document that seemingly lies squarely within the scope of a legitimate discovery request, but her supervisor tells her to devise an argument for excluding it. As long as the argument isn't frivolous there is nothing improper about this, but it marks the first step onto the slippery slope. For better or for worse, a certain kind of innocence is lost. It is the moment when withholding information despite an adversary's legitimate request starts to feel like zealous advocacy rather than deception. It is the moment when the no-deception principle encoded in Model Rule 8.4(c)[62] gets gerrymandered away from its plain meaning. But, like any other piece of elastic, the no-deception principle loses its grip if it is stretched too often. Soon, if the lawyer isn't very careful, every damaging request seems too broad or too narrow; every smoking-gun document is either work-product or privileged; no adversary ever has a right to "my" documents. At that point the fatal question is not far away: Is lying really so bad when it is the only way to protect "my" documents from an adversary who has no right to them? If legitimate advocacy marks the beginning of this particular slippery slope, Berkey–Kodak lies at its end.

NOTES AND QUESTIONS

The Independence of Associates

1.   In a widely discussed article in the *Harvard Law School Bulletin*, Professor Duncan Kennedy notes that

> There are many variations on law firm hierarchy. There are firms in which senior partners test associates to see if they are such sell-outs that they'll do anything, no matter how ethically questionable, and firms in which someone will put a black mark in a mental book if you show the slightest hesitation about putting your arm to the elbow in muck. There are firms where you can get out of doing bad things with the equivalent of "please, not tonight, dear, I have a headache," and firms where you can engage your coworkers in a serious dialogue about the ethics of particular cases.[63]

In Kennedy's view, associates have a responsibility to try and ensure that their firm falls into the final category.

> If you fight now, if you come to stand for something now you'll be able to make things different when you own the place. If you've done nothing during the long interval but cave in, and cave in, and cave in, you won't even know it when you own the place, or if you know it you won't care. . . .

In correspondence responding to Kennedy's article, Harvard Law School alumnus John Kester wrote:

---

62. [Eds. The rule reads: "It is professional misconduct for a lawyer to engage in conduct involving dishonesty, fraud, deceit or misrepresentation"].

63. Duncan Kennedy, "Rebels From Principle: Changing the Corporate Law Firm From Within," *Harv. L. Sch. Bull.* 36 (Fall, 1981).

One should not barter one's soul to practice law, and one does not have to. It is inconceivable to me that any attorney in my firm would be forced to work on a case if he found it morally offensive. But you can't expect to be a habitual conscientious objector and still plan to be a general. No law graduates were ever conscripted to join my firm (or to go to law school, for that matter). If they do so, it's because they seek challenging work, development of skills, able co-workers, an opportunity to help people, and wealth for themselves. If you are far to the left and only support causes you like, then you ought not be offering yourself for general hire as a lawyer. The problem is not with the clients or the cases, it's with you—you are in the wrong line of work.[64]

How would you respond? What do the reading by Lewis, Schiltz, and Luban suggest about the pressures and responsibilities of subordinate lawyers?

Legal Responsibility in Organizational Settings

2. An extensive body of law addresses how to control organizational misconduct and how to assign individual responsibility in organizational settings. Issues of enterprise liability, corporate crime, aiding and abetting, wilful ignorance, conspiracy, and liability of managers and directors all have well-developed doctrine. Such topics are also the subject of an immense theoretical literature in economics, law, psychology and organization theory.[65] These doctrinal and theoretical frameworks have some direct application to law firms, corporate counsel offices, and other legal employers.

The Model Rules of Professional Conduct summarize the allocation of responsibility between supervisors and subordinates in Rule 5.1, "Responsibilities of a Partner or Supervisory Lawyer," and Rule 5.2, "Responsibilities of a Subordinate Lawyer." The Code of Professional Responsibility includes no comparable provisions. Model Rule 5.1(c) holds supervisory lawyers accountable for subordinates' disciplinary violations *either* when the supervisory lawyer orders or ratifies the conduct *or* when the supervisory lawyer knows of the conduct but fails to take "reasonable remedial action." In addition, Rule 5.1(b) instructs supervisory lawyers to make reasonable efforts to ensure that their subordinates conform to the rules of professional conduct, while Rule 5.1(a) makes partners in a law firm responsible for ensuring that the firm's policies give "reasonable assurance that all lawyers in the firm conform to the rules of professional conduct."

As for the individual accountability of subordinate lawyers, Rule 5.2(a) states, "A lawyer is bound by the rules of professional conduct notwithstanding that the lawyer acted at the direction of another person." However, Rule 5.2(b) also states, "A subordinate lawyer does not violate the rules of professional conduct if that lawyer acts in accordance with a supervisory

---

64. John G. Kester, "Correspondence" *Harv. L. Sch. Bull* 32 (Spring 1982).

65. For a sophisticated survey of the literature, *see* Brent Fisse & John Braithwaite, *Corporations, Crime and Accountabil-* *ity* (1993). For a review of the social psychology literature, *see* Philip Zimbardo, *The Lucifer Effect: Understanding How Good People Turn Evil* (2007).

lawyer's reasonable resolution of an arguable question of professional duty." Thus, subordinate lawyers could be excused from disciplinary liability if a supervisor made a reasonable but incorrect judgment about their ethical responsibilities.

Other professions do not provide a comparable "superior orders" defense. Rather, most other ethical codes explicitly underscore individuals' obligations to use independent judgment and to comply with relevant standards. For example, Rule 102 of the American Institute of Certified Public Accountants' Code of Professional Conduct provides that ". . . in the performance of any professional service, a member . . . shall not subordinate his judgment to others." Similarly Section 9.055 of the American Medical Association's Code of Ethics advises medical students, resident physicians, and other staff to "refuse to participate in patient care ordered by their supervisors in those cases in which they believe the orders reflect serious errors in clinical judgment or physician impairment that could result in a threat of imminent harm." Subordinates should also "communicate their concerns to the physicians issuing the orders and, if necessary, to the appropriate person for mediating such disputes." So too, Rule 9(a) of the National Society of Professional Engineers' Code of Ethics for Engineers provides that engineers must "accept responsibility for all professional acts," and Rule 1(a) requires that if their judgment is overruled under circumstances where the "safety, health, property, or welfare of the public are endangered, they shall notify their employer or client and such other authority as may be appropriate."[66] Are any of these formulations preferable to the Model Rules? What might account for their different approaches?

Defenders of the Model Rules approach generally claim that it provides appropriate recognition of the reality of legal practice in organizational contexts: namely that the situation of the junior attorney is "more precarious and more pressured" than that of senior attorneys.[67] Studies of ethical decisions in law firms find considerable incentives for lawyers to adopt, or leave unchallenged, the norms of dominant partners.[68]

By contrast, critics of the Model Rules approach believe that special protection for subordinates is neither necessary nor appropriate. Given the political and financial constraints under which bar disciplinary agencies operate, they pursue clear cases, not those involving "reasonable resolutions of an arguable question of professional duty," whatever the status of the attorney. In fact, the most comprehensive review of Model Rule 5.2 found no reported case in which a junior attorney has been absolved of sanctions for following a superior's order.[69]

66. Bureau of National Affairs, *Codes of Professional Responsibility, supra* note 16, at 15, 102, 409; Carol M. Rice, "The Superior Orders Defense in Legal Ethics: Sending the Wrong Message to Young Lawyers," 30 *Wake Forest L. Rev.* 887, 908–09 (1997).

67. Marc Galanter & Thomas Palay, "The Transformation of the Big Law Firm," in *Lawyers' Ideals/Lawyers' Practices* 31, 60 (Robert L. Nelson, et al., eds. 1992).

68. See Kimberly Kirkland, "Ethics in Large Firms: The Principles of Pragmatism," 35 *U. Memphis L. Rev.* 631 (2005); Milton C. Regan, Jr., "Moral Intuitions and Organizational Culture," 51 *St.Louis L. Rev.* 941, 965–66 (2007).

69. Rice, *supra* note 66, at 902.

Yet to the extent that the Rule serves primarily to provide ethical guidance for lawyers rather than to affect disciplinary proceedings, critics believe that it provides the wrong message. In their view, subordinate attorneys should be encouraged to raise ethical concerns with their supervisors or with others in a position to review a supervisor's questionable decisions. Such decisions may in some instances be the product of hasty, self-interested, or ill-informed judgments. And in some of those cases, associates who are under less direct pressure than their supervisors to achieve a final result, may be in a better position to evaluate ethical concerns. As Chapter III noted, one function of ethical codes is to provide justifications and support for lawyers who might otherwise have difficulty raising moral concerns. According to critics, Model Rule 5.2 fails to provide that support.

Do you agree? What other steps could law firms or other legal employers take to encourage junior attorneys to raise their concerns?

CHAPTER VIII

NEGOTIATION AND MEDIATION

PROBLEM 1: NEGOTIATION EXERCISE[1]

Rules for Both Sides

You should be assigned as counsel for either the plaintiffs or defendants in the negotiation exercise and follow the instructions for your side that are included in the Teacher's Manual.

1. You should read the materials on negotiation in this chapter.

2. You should develop a strategy for resolving the matter and then meet with the student representing the other side.

You should make yourself available for one to two hours of negotiation and discussion with your partner, which need not be continuous. It may be spread across more than one day or interrupted for caucusing. You should make every effort to reach a settlement, but you are not required to do so.

3. Do not discuss the problem with other students who have the opposite side of your case until after you have completed negotiations. You may discuss the problem with other students representing the *same* party as you are, so long as neither of you has begun negotiations or both of you have completed negotiations. Do not talk to anyone else on the same side while either of you is in the process of negotiating.

4. If you reach a settlement, you should record the terms and both negotiators should sign it. If you cannot reach a settlement, that too should be recorded, together with the last offer on either side, signed again by each side. The sheets recording this information should be turned in prior to classroom discussion.

5. After completing the negotiation, you and opposing counsel should discuss your approaches and strategies. You should exchange confidential instructions and explore any concerns regarding unethical or inappropriate conduct.

6. You should also complete a short summary of the exercise to be turned in prior to class discussion. That summary should address the following questions:

a) What bargaining position did you expect from your opponent? How did it differ from what he or she presented?

---

1. This problem, developed by Henry Hecht, is based on a hypothetical originally published by the American Bar Association Consortium for Professional Education and the American Bar Association Center for Professional Responsibility in *Dilemmas in Legal Ethics* (1977).

b) How would you evaluate your own conduct? Were you honest? Competent? Effective? Would an informed client's evaluation differ from your own?

c) What could or should you have done differently?

d) How would you evaluate your opponent's conduct? How did it affect your own? If this had been a real case involving significant legal fees or an important client, would your conduct have been substantially different? Would it have changed the outcome?

INTRODUCTION

About ninety percent of both criminal and civil cases conclude without trial. Some are dropped by a party, or are dismissed by a court, but the overwhelming majority are settled. As Marc Galanter points out, "negotiation is not ... some unusual alternative to litigation. It is only a slight exaggeration to say that it *is* litigation. There are not two distinct processes, negotiation and litigation; there is a single process of disputing in the vicinity of official tribunals that might fancifully be called LITIGOTIATION."[2]

Lawyers also bargain in a broad variety of other non-litigation settings on matters such as contracts, incorporations, adoptions, mergers, wills, and divorces. Theorists often distinguish "dispute negotiation"—negotiation to settle disputes about past events—from "transactional negotiation"—negotiation to structure future arrangements. Both forms of bargaining take place "in the shadow of the law."[3] In dispute resolution contexts, if the negotiators fail to reach agreement, the case may result in litigation; accordingly, the parties can evaluate each others' offers by estimating the likelihood and dollar value of a favorable outcome at trial. In transactional contexts, parties' choices and bargaining leverage are often shaped by background legal rights and remedies.

The dynamics of negotiation are also affected by the ethical values of participants. Because so much bargaining takes place in settings where formal oversight is absent, a lawyer's own internal sense of honesty and fair dealing play a critical role. Consider the relationship of law and ethics in the negotiations described below. In evaluating the appropriateness of bargaining conduct and the professional rules that regulate it, consider the following principles.

Universality: "Could I recommend that everyone in my situation act this way?"

Reciprocity: "Would I want others to treat me this way?"

---

2. Marc Galanter, " '. . . A Settlement Judge, not a Trial Judge:' Judicial Mediation in the United States," 12 *J.L. & Soc'y* 1 (1985); Marc Galanter & Mia Cahill, "Most Cases Settle: Judicial Promotion and Regulation of Settlements," 46 *Stan.L.Rev.* 1339 (1994).

3. The phrase comes from Robert H. Mnookin & Lewis Kornhausert, "Bargaining in the Shadow of the Law: The Case of Divorce," 88 *Yale L.J.* 950 (1979).

Publicity: "Would I be comfortable if I read about what I had just done on the front page of the Wall Street Journal?"[4]

Legality: "Do substantive laws of tort, contract, fraud, or extortion permit this negotiating tactic? What about the rules of professional conduct?"

PROBLEM 2

If you were the lawyer in the circumstances Judge Neely describes below, what would you do?

Richard Neely, "The Primary Caretaker Parent Rule: Child Custody and the Dynamics of Greed"

3 Yale Law & Policy Review 168, 177–79 (1984).

A [divorcing] parent concerned with paying as little child support as possible can use the threat of a custody fight, with its never-certain outcome, as a lever during settlement negotiations. The result is that one parent—typically the father—winds up paying less in child support than the needs of the child or children warrant, while the other parent—typically the mother—is forced to scrape by on inadequate support, a problem exacerbated by the generally lower earning power of women....

B.   Unequal Bargaining Power Out-of-Court

Divorce decrees are typically drafted for the parties after compromises reached through private negotiation. These compromises are then approved by a judge, who generally gives them only the most perfunctory sort of review. The result is that parties (usually husbands) are free to use whatever leverage is available to obtain a favorable settlement. In practice this tends to mean that husbands will threaten custody fights, with all of the accompanying traumas and uncertainties discussed above, as a means of intimidating wives into accepting less child support and alimony than is sufficient to allow the mother to live and raise the children appropriately as a single parent. Because women are usually unwilling to accept even a minor risk of losing custody, such techniques are generally successful.

To make these abstract statements more concrete, I would like to use an example from my own experience. My first encounter with the manner in which the unpredictability of divorce proceedings can be used to terrorize women came early in my career as a small-town lawyer.[15] My client was

4. "More Tips for When Mediation Impasse Strikes Also: Ethical Dilemmas at the Negotiating Table," 23 *Alternatives to the High Cost of Litigation* 179, 181 (2005) (paraphrasing Carrie Menkel–Meadow).

15. I realize that some readers, particularly those who are unfamiliar with the realities of the practice of law, may find this anecdote unattractive. Lawyers, however, respond keenly to incentives, and the current custody system in states following "best interests" or similar standards provides a strong incentive to behave like Simon Legree. Lawyers who do not do so are sacrificing their clients' interests in order to feel good about themselves; to the extent that clients figure this out, such lawyers are also likely to go broke. Those interested in ending such

a railroad brakeman who had fallen out of love with his wife and in love with motorcycles. Along the way, he had met a woman who was as taken with motorcycles as he. After about a year, my client's wife filed for divorce. My client had two children at home—one about nine and the other about twelve. Unfortunately for him, the judge in the county where his wife had filed her suit was notorious for giving high alimony and child support awards. The last thing that I wanted to do was go to trial. The wife had a strong case of adultery against my client, and the best my client could come up with was a lame countersuit for "cruel and inhuman treatment"—not exactly a showstopper in a rural domestic court.

During the initial interview, I asked my client about his children, and he told me that he got along well with them. He also indicated, however, that two children were the last thing he wanted from his divorce. Nonetheless, it occurred to me in my role as zealous advocate that if my client developed a passionate attachment to his children and told his wife that he would fight for custody all the way to the state supreme court, we might settle the whole divorce fairly cheaply. My client was a quick study: That night he went home and began a campaign for his children. His chance of actually getting custody from the judge was virtually nonexistent, but that did not discourage our blustering threats.

My client's wife was unwilling to take any chance, no matter how slight, on losing her children. Consequently, the divorce was settled exactly as we wanted. The wife got the children by agreement, along with rather modest alimony and child support. All we had needed to defeat her legitimate claims in the settlement process was the halfway credible threat of a protracted custody battle. As Solomon showed us, the better a mother is as a parent, the less likely she is to allow a destructive fight over her children.

The above story is more than just a homey example, for it is repeated across the nation every day. Under our purportedly sex-neutral system, women on statistical average come out of divorce settlements with the worst of all possible results: They get the children, but insufficient money with which to support them. They are forced to scrape along to support their families at inadequate standards of living, and the children are forced to grow up poor, or at least poorer than they should be. Yet the dynamic demonstrated above is seldom discussed, despite its importance in promoting the growth of a rapidly-expanding class of poor people, the female-headed household.

NOTES

In Justice Neely's example, the mother gives up some child support to which she is entitled. She makes this financial sacrifice because she is highly *risk-averse:* she will not gamble on custody, even if the odds are

behavior should look to changes in the law that will put an end to such incentives, rather than pinning their hopes on any sudden change in the realities of legal practice in a world well supplied with Simon Legrees and economically disadvantaged women.

excellent that she will prevail. A parent who is less risk averse will be less susceptible to what is often called "custody blackmail". However, there are other reasons besides risk-aversion for yielding to such coercion. One is to spare children from the trauma of litigation. A second reason arises from the "friendly parent" provisions applicable in many states that give preference to the parent who has demonstrated willingness to share custody or to grant more extensive visitation rights. These provisions create a bargaining opportunity for parties interested in minimizing spousal and child support payments. By demanding joint custody over their former spouse's opposition, they can qualify as the friendly parent. That gives them leverage to trade uncontested custody in return for reduced financial obligations.

The frequency of "custody blackmail" is hard to gauge. The limited evidence available suggests that it is sufficiently common to cause concern and that women are almost always the vulnerable party.[4] Their vulnerability is compounded by other disadvantages, such as greater risk aversion, lower wage earning capacity, less self-esteem, and higher likelihood of dependence and deference in marital relationships.[5]

QUESTIONS

1. The term "custody blackmail" was obviously coined by opponents of the practice, and suggests that the strategy is always improper. Is it?

2. Is it unethical for a lawyer to propose this tactic to a client who has not indicated a desire for custody but who has indicated a desire to minimize his support obligations? Does the appropriateness of the strategy depend on whether the lawyer or the client initially suggests it? Does it depend on whether the financial demands by the other spouse seem excessive? If a client claims to want sole or joint physical custody, but the lawyer believes the client does not really mean it or should not obtain it, must the lawyer withdraw? See ABA Section on Litigation, Ethical Guidelines for Settlement Negotiations, 3.3.3 (Aug. 2002) (providing that lawyers who find a client's goal or strategy repugnant may withdraw or continue representation on the condition that they will not assist that goal or strategy). Suppose the client wants to negotiate directly with the former spouse? See *id.*, Rule 4.3.3, Committee Notes (indicating that lawyers need not discourage a client's contact with an opposing party but citing division in authority over whether a lawyer may encourage or advise a client in that contact).

3. Raol Felder, one of the nation's leading divorce lawyers, describes his role as a "technician, a how-to man," not a "moralist." "It is not my intention to stand in judgment.... [W]hen I take a case, I am not

4. Scott Altman, "Lurking in the Shadow," 68 *S. Cal. L. Rev.* 493, 497–504 (1995).

5. Penelope Eileen Bryan, "Legions of Women in Divorce Settlement Negotiations," *Denver U. L. Rev* 931 (1997); Scott H. Hughes, "Elizabeth's Story: Exploring Power Imbalances on Divorce Mediation," 8 *Geo. J. Leg. Ethics* 553 (1995). For an overview of women's difficulties negotiating for themselves, see Linda Babcock & Sara Laschever, *Women Don't Ask: Negotiation and the Gender Divide* (2003).

concerned with whether my client is right or wrong. As far as I am concerned, my client is always right."[6]

What is your view? Few would argue that clients in the middle of acrimonious divorces are always "right" about what is in their long-term interest.[7] Particularly where parties will have continuing contact after the divorce, do hardball bargaining strategies make sense? Is part of a family lawyer's role to help clients live up to their best rather than worst instincts? Or are such efforts an inappropriate exercise in paternalism by lawyers who will not have to cope with the consequences?

4. A growing number of family practitioners are addressing these issues through what they term "collaborative lawyering." Their aim is to offer a more cooperative form of dispute resolution than traditional adversarial processes.[8] Under this approach, parties commit to collaborate with each other as well as with their lawyers in an attempt at mutual problem solving. Each client is represented by counsel, and signs a retainer agreement providing that the lawyer is to assist them in reaching a fair, out-of-court agreement. If the parties fail to reach such a settlement, the lawyers may not represent them in further proceedings. The clients also commit to act in good faith and to disclose all relevant information. This dispute resolution process involves joint settlement meetings with parties and their lawyers, all of whom have a substantial stake in preserving cooperative relationships and engaging in creative, mutually beneficial problem solving.

A Colorado Bar Ethics Opinion, Op. 115 (2007) held that agreements requiring termination of representation if the parties do not reach settlement violate Model Rule 1.7(b). That Rule bars attorneys from representing a client where their responsibilities to that client may be "materially limited by responsibilities to . . . a third person" unless the lawyer reasonably believes that the representation will not be "adversely affected" and the client gives informed consent. According to the Colorado Bar Ethics Committee, client consent could not cure the potential conflict because whenever the collaborative process is unsuccessful, the lawyers' obligation to the opponent to withdraw would trump the lawyer's obligation to pursue the client's best interest, which might be litigation.

Do you agree? Other bar ethics opinions, including ABA Formal Op. 07–447, have permitted lawyers to enter into termination agreements as part of the collaborative process. Kentucky Ethics Op. E–425 (2005), and New Jersey Bar Ethics Op. 699 (2005).[9] How would you advise a client about the appropriateness of entering into a collaborative process?

6. Raol Lional Felder, *Divorce* 7 (1971). For similar views, see Michael Gross, "Trouble in Splitsville," *New York Magazine*, Dec. 13, 1999, at 39 (discussing New York's "matrimonial mafia").

7. Many divorces trigger severe anger, anxiety, stress, depression and guilt. See sources cited in Rhode, *Professional Responsibility: Ethics by the Pervasive Method* 694 (1998); Pauline H. Tesler, "Collaborative Law A New Paradigm for Divorce Lawyers," 5 *Psychol. Pub. Pol'y & L.* 967 (1999).

8. *See* Shiela M. Gutterman, *Collaborative Law: A New Model For Dispute Resolution* (2004); Pauline H. Tesler, *Collaborative Law: Achieving Effective Resolution in Divorce Without Litigation* (2001).

9. For an overview of the ethical issues, see Christopher Fairman, "A Proposed Model Rule for Collaborative Law," 21 *Ohio State J.*

Clearly, this approach is not practical for all dispute resolution settings. Nor does it resolve the most troubling negotiation issues that arise in family practice. By definition, parties who are most likely to engage in morally problematic conduct are among those least likely to commit to fair and cooperative problem solving. A collaborative process also cannot compensate for inequities in substantive law, gross inequalities in power, or the absence of representation for vulnerable third parties like children whose welfare is directly implicated.[10] But for parties willing to engage in the collaborative process, it at least creates incentives to come to fair agreements.

If you practiced in the area of family law, where on the spectrum between technician and collaborator would you feel most comfortable? Why? In one of the few available empirical studies on lawyers' negotiation ethics, family law had the highest percentage of lawyers considered by practitioners to be adversarial and unethical (15%), and one of the lowest percentages of lawyers considered to be problem solvers (38%).[11] Should courts, bar associations, and ethical rules do more to encourage cooperative approaches?

5. Ethical issues often arise in family law because the interests of children are materially affected but seldom formally represented. To what extent should this fact influence a lawyer's negotiating strategies? Do existing ethical rules adequately provide for the interests of unrepresented third parties? Consider as an alternative, *The Bounds of Advocacy: Goals for Family Lawyers*, of the American Academy of Matrimonial Lawyers, a voluntary association of qualified specialists in family law. Goal 6.1 provides that "[a]n attorney representing a parent should consider the welfare of, and seek to minimize the adverse impact of the divorce on, the minor children." The Comment adds:

> One of the most troubling issues in family law is determining a lawyer's obligations to children. The lawyer must competently represent the interest of the client but not at the expense of children. The parents' fiduciary obligations for the well-being of a child provide a basis for the attorney's consideration of the child's best interests consistent with traditional advocacy and client loyalty principles. It is accepted doctrine that the attorney for a trustee or other fiduciary has

Dispute Res. 73 (2005); Larry R. Spain, "Collaborative Law: A Critical Reflection on Whether a Collaborative Orientation Can Be Ethically Incorporated into the Practice of Law," 56 *Baylor L. Rev.* 141 (2004). The disagreement between the Colorado and ABA opinions is analyzed in Scott R. Peppet, "The (New) Ethics of Collaborative Law," 14 *Disp. Resol. Mag.* 23–27 Winter (2008) and Peppet, "The Ethics of Collaborative Law," 2008 *J. Disp. Resol.* (forthcoming 2008).

10. Penelope Eileen Bryan, "Collaborative Divorce: Meaningful Reform or Another Quick Fix?," 5 *Psychology, Public Policy, & Law* 1001 (1999); Pauline H. Tesler, "The Believing Game, the Doubting Game, and Collaborative Law: A Reply to Penelope Bryan," 5 *Psychology, Public Policy & Law* 1008 (1999).

11. Andrea Kupfer Schneider, "Shattering Negotiation Myths: Empirical Evidence on the Effectiveness of Negotiation Style," 7 *Harvard Negotiation L. Rev.* 143 (2002).

an ethical obligation to the beneficiaries to whom the fiduciary's obligations run.

In particular, Goal 6.2 provides: "An attorney should not permit a client to contest child custody, contact, or access for either financial leverage or vindictiveness." Its Comment states:

> Tactics oriented toward asserting custody rights as leverage toward attaining some other, usually financial, goal are destructive. The matrimonial lawyer should counsel against, and refuse to assist, such conduct. Proper consideration for the welfare of the children requires that they not be used as pawns in the divorce process. Thus, for example, in states where child support is determined partly on the basis of the amount of time a parent spends with the child, the lawyers should negotiate parenting issues based solely on considerations related to the child, then negotiate child support based on financial considerations. If despite the attorney's advice, the client persists, the attorney should seek to withdraw.

The Preliminary Statement to these goals makes clear that they "aspire" to a level of practice above the minimum required by the Model Rules, but should not be used to determine malpractice liability. Should they? Or should bar ethical rules and court decisions impose some obligations to highly vulnerable third parties like children? Alternatively, should bar regulatory authorities or voluntary associations develop certification systems to identify lawyers willing to abide by heightened ethical standards?

6. Commentators have proposed a variety of ways of determining "fairness" in negotiation. One is to assess substantive results by criteria such as:

> Equality: participants share equally in benefits and burdens;

> Need: participants receive resources adequate to their needs; or

> Equity: participants benefit in relation to their contributions.[12]

Another possibility is to evaluate the process. Consider three possible approaches. The first is the *free market theory*: a fair settlement is whatever the parties agree to, provided that the agreement has not resulted from coercion or fraud. The second is the *shadow verdict theory*: a fair settlement is whatever approximates the result the court would have reached if the case had gone to adjudication—the so-called "shadow verdict." A final approach is the *perceptions of fairness*: a fair settlement is what emerges from a process that participants consider just. Major factors that influence those perceptions include whether the parties had an adequate opportunity for their concerns to be heard and whether they were treated with dignity and respect.[13]

---

12. Nancy A. Welsh, "Perceptions of Fairness," in *The Negotiator's Fieldbook* (Andrea Kupfer Schneider & Christopher Honeyman, eds.) ABA Section on Dispute Resolution 165, 166–67 (2006).

13. Welsh, *supra* note 12, at 168–70.

Which of these approaches should legal rules and legal ethics seek to promote? How would they help in assessing the fairness of Judge Neely's negotiation?

A.   Coercion

NOTES

Consider the "ultimatum bargaining game": Rich and Poor are offered $1000 to divide as they choose, provided that they agree on a division. If they don't agree, neither of them gets any money at all. Rich offers Poor $100, threatening to walk unless Poor accepts. Since Rich can afford to make good on the threat, and Poor needs the money, Poor accepts. Is this a coercive or otherwise unfair use of bargaining power?

If, under conventionally accepted free market principles, a fair bargain is whatever agreement results from a process untainted by coercion or fraud, a key question is how to define those terms. The *Restatement of Contracts* defines "duress" as either:

a) a wrongful act that compels agreement without a party's volition (such as when a person is drunk); or

b) a wrongful threat that precludes a party's exercise of free will and judgment and was intended or should reasonably have been expected to do so.[14]

Part (b) adopts what Alan Wertheimer labels a "two-pronged" theory of duress. Wertheimer, who has developed the most thorough contemporary account of the legal and ethical status of coercion, argues that two conditions must be met for an offer or a threat to qualify as duress. First, the statement must leave the victim no reasonable choice but to acquiesce; and second, it must be independently wrongful.[15] For example, under the approach of Wertheimer and the *Restatement*, exploiting a party's vulnerability may be coercive without constituting duress if the offer was not fraudulent or otherwise illegal. Versions of this theory inform not only the law of contracts, but also the law governing crime, torts, marriage, and wills. If, however, the parties stand in a fiduciary relationship, the law of undue influence may give additional protection to a vulnerable party.

For purposes of establishing duress, a threat or offer is wrongful if it proposes something that is illegal. A threat to exercise a legal right is generally not considered wrongful, although some bar ethical codes include

14. *Restatement of Contracts* § 492 (1932). The *Restatement of Contracts (Second)* does not define duress, but its discussion of duress in §§ 174–76 is consistent with the definition quoted here.

15. Alan Wertheimer, *Coercion* 29–45 (1987). *Accord*, Russell Korobkin, Michael L. Moffitt, & Nancy A. Welsh, "The Law of Bargaining," in *The Negotiator's Fieldbook*, *supra* note 12, at 183, 186. For a classic legal realist argument that exploiting another party's vulnerability can be coercive and therefore unethical, *see* Robert L. Hale, "Coercion and Distribution in a Supposedly Non–Coercive State," 38 *Pol. Sci. Q.* 470 (1923).

an important exception. Under DR 7–105(A) of the Model Code of Professional Responsibility, a lawyer may not threaten to file criminal charges to obtain an advantage in a civil matter, even though individuals have the right under most circumstances to inform prosecutors of criminal violations. California Rule of Professional Conduct 5–100 also bans threats to invoke administrative and disciplinary processes. Clients can themselves make such threats, although attorneys may not advise them to do so. Cal State Bar Formal Op. 1983–73. The basis for these prohibitions is a desire to prevent parties from manipulating the criminal justice and other regulatory processes for personal gain because those processes are designed to protect society as a whole. Ethical Consideration 7–21, Cal State Bar Formal Op. No 1989–106. No corresponding provision exists in the Model Rules because drafters considered it unrealistic to expect lawyers to refrain from discussing potential criminal liability in negotiations over related civil claims.[16] Some jurisdictions nevertheless include the prohibition in their versions of the Rules—thus, the D.C. Rules of Professional Conduct contain rule 8.4(g), "It is professional misconduct for a lawyer to seek or threaten to seek criminal charges or disciplinary charges solely to obtain an advantage in a civil matter."

However, Model Rule 8.4(b) forbids criminal conduct adversely reflecting on a lawyer's fitness. And some jurisdictions define extortion to include threats to expose criminal conduct or secrets that could impair reputation or livelihood in order to gain financial advantages.[17] Other jurisdictions' extortion statutes follow the Model Penal Code, § 223.4, cmt.f, which specifically exempts threats to bring criminal charges made during negotiation of a civil claim relating to those same charges. For example, if a customer defrauds a merchant, and the merchant's attorney writes a letter giving the customer one last chance to make restitution before the merchant seeks criminal charges, the Model Penal Code would not consider the letter to be extortionate, and Model Rule 8.4(b) would not apply to the attorney's conduct. If, on the other hand, the letter demanded more money than the customer owed, it could constitute extortion.

Similarly, ABA Ethics Committee Opinion 92–363 (1992) concludes that a lawyer may use the possibility of pressing criminal charges against an opposing party in a private civil matter to gain relief for the client, provided that the criminal matter is related to the civil claim, that both the civil claim and the possible criminal charge are legally and factually justifiable, and that the lawyer does not attempt to exert improper influence over the criminal process. A lawyer may also agree as part of a settlement to refrain from presenting criminal charges against an opposing party so long as the settlement agreement does not violate existing law.

In a related opinion, Formal Op. 94–383 (1994), the ABA Ethics Committee concluded that a lawyer's threat to report opposing counsel to

---

16. Geoffrey C. Hazard, Jr. & W. William Hodes, *The Law of Lawyering, A Handbook on the Model Rules of Professional Conduct* 4.4:103 (2001, 3d ed.).

17. "Threatening Criminal Prosecution," 71 *ABA/BNA Manual on Professional Conduct,* 601 (2003).

disciplinary authorities in order to obtain advantage in a civil case may violate the Model Rules of Professional Conduct even though they do not expressly prohibit such threats. Under the ABA Committee's analysis, filing disciplinary charges may not be used as a bargaining chip if the misconduct raises a substantial question as to opposing counsel's honesty, trustworthiness, or fitness as a lawyer because reporting is already mandatory under such circumstances. See Chapter XV, *infra*. A threat to file charges would also be improper if the misconduct is unrelated to the civil claim, if the charges would not be well founded in fact and law, or if the threat has no substantial purpose or effect other than to embarrass or burden opposing counsel or his client, or to prejudice the administration of justice. See also Ethical Guidelines 4.3.2 (lawyers may not attempt to obtain a settlement through extortionate or wrongful threats); 4.2.3 Committee Notes (lawyers should avoid negotiating, "in a threatening or extortionate manner," terms relating to the reporting of criminal or disciplinary misconduct)

Whether or not hardball bargaining strategies meet the legal definition of coercion, the research available suggests that they often seem unfair to most people. In one study, subjects played a version of the ultimatum bargaining game. In this version, players received a sum of money to divide; the first player gets one chance to make an offer, and the second player has one opportunity to take it or leave it (in which case both players get nothing). Although most people are unwilling to forego all advantages of superior bargaining power, most are also unwilling to exploit it fully or to acquiesce in such tactics by adversaries. A quarter of first players proposed a 50–50 split, and the average first player offer was a 67–33 split. Only 10 percent of first players demanded more than 90 percent of the money—and in almost all of those six cases, second players refused the offer, despite the fact that doing so cost them money. In a similar study, where subjects observed other players in action before playing ultimatum with them, three-fourths of the subjects preferred splitting a small amount of money with a "fair" player than a slightly higher amount with a "hardball" player.[18] Such research suggests that exploitative bargaining can be ethically offensive and tactically unwise, even if it is legally permissible. Consider whether any of the tactics that you or your opponent used in the Problem 1 simulation were inappropriately coercive under legal or bar ethical principles.

B.   Truthfulness in Bargaining

Model Rule 4.1 prohibits a lawyer from making a false statement of material fact or law to an adversary, as well as from failing to disclose a material fact when disclosure is necessary to avoid assisting a criminal or fraudulent act by a client. On its face, this rule apparently forbids lying to

---

18.   Robert A. Frank, *Passions Within Reason: The Strategic Role of Emotions* 170–71 (1988).

an adversary in a negotiation. However, according to the comment to Rule 4.1, as amended in 2001:

> Whether a particular statement should be regarded as one of fact can depend on the circumstances. Under generally accepted conventions in negotiation, certain types of statements ordinarily are not taken as statements of material fact. Estimates of price or value placed on the subject of a transaction and a party's intentions as to an acceptable settlement of a claim are ordinarily in this category, and so is the existence of an undisclosed principal except where nondisclosure of the principal would constitute fraud. Lawyers should be mindful of their obligations under applicable law to avoid criminal and tortious misrepresentation.

What statements fall under this qualification is not entirely clear. Gross exaggerations? Half-truths? Intentional misstatements? When is a lie not a lie for purposes of bar ethical rules? See ABA Bar Ethics Committee Formal Op. 06–439 (2006) (distinguishing between impermissible misstatements of fact and acceptable puffing such as exaggerated claims about the strength and weakness of factual and legal positions).

Under conventional definitions, lying involves an attempt to create a belief at odds with one's own. Lies in negotiation may involve the nature and value of property; the consequences of certain decisions; and the parties' interests, priorities, minimum settlement point, alternatives to agreement, readiness for trial, and so forth.[19] Consider the examples in Problem 3. When do such lies violate "generally accepted conventions" in negotiation? What does the Lempert reading below suggest about the extent to which there are any such generally accepted norms?

PROBLEM 3

a) In negotiations over a hotel's breach of contract to host an organization's conference, the attorney for the defendant hotel makes an initial settlement offer of $15,000. The lawyer for the plaintiff organization maintains that his client's officers would never accept such an offer, that damages from the breach are likely to be much higher, and that any jury award would be more substantial. The lawyer actually believes that if the case went to trial, his client would receive a substantially smaller sum. Based on that advice, the plaintiff's president has authorized the lawyer to settle for any amount over $10,000.

In responding to the initial offer, the plaintiff's lawyer also represents that it would be impossible for his client to find another suitable hotel under such short notice. When the lawyer later contacts his client to report the settlement offer, he learns that another hotel has orally agreed to host

---

19. Gerald B. Wetlaufer "The Ethics of Lying in Negotiations," 77 *Iowa L.Rev.* 1219, 1223–1226 (1990).

the conference. When he then calls the defendant's attorney to accept the settlement, the attorney opens the conversation by asking, "How are efforts to mitigate the damages coming along?" The plaintiff's lawyer responds, "nothing definite yet." The settlement is then finalized at $15,000.

b) In negotiating the sale of a ranch, the seller's lawyer states that the property is an outstanding business opportunity and that its acreage and crop yield should produce an income of at least $160,000 per year. The out-of-state buyer, who is unfamiliar with the layout of the ranch, relies on that representation, which significantly overstates the ranch's profitability.

c) In lease negotiations, the lawyer representing the owner of a shopping center did not inform the lessee that the center was about to go into foreclosure. The lessee incurred significant expenses in getting the space ready for use, only to be evicted by the company that bought the property at the foreclosure sale.

d) In negotiations over the property settlement in an uncontested divorce, the husband and wife disagree about the value of certain assets, including real estate and stock in a family corporation. When reviewing the wife's proposed settlement, the husband's lawyer notices a $50,000 calculation error by opposing counsel that understates her alleged interest in jointly owned real estate. The lawyer brings the matter to the attention of his client, who believes that the understated figure is a more accurate reflection of the property's true worth. Accordingly, the lawyer prepares a counteroffer replicating the error in a way that minimizes the likelihood of its discovery. On the mistaken belief that the husband has surrendered his challenge to the value of the real estate, the wife abandons her challenge to the value and ownership of the stock. Both parties ultimately accept a version of the husband's counteroffer and sign a final agreement that recites the disposition of assets without specifying their value.

e) In negotiations over an eviction action, the tenant has no lawyer and is unaware that conditions she has complained about would establish housing code violations entitling her to a setoff against the rent. The attorney for the landlord advises her to accept his client's final offer, which is a "generous" stipulated settlement that includes no setoff. The attorney further suggests that she should avoid looking doubtful in front of the judge, who must approve the agreement.[20]

f) If you were a lawyer in the four situations described by Lempert in the next excerpt, how would you respond?

20. Problem 3(a) is based on a case described in Monroe Freedman, "Lying: Is it Ethical?" *Legal Times* Dec. 12, 1994, at 20; *see* Monroe Freedman, "Acceptable Lies," *Legal Times,* Feb. 20, 1995. Problem 3(b) is modeled on Bails v. Wheeler, 559 P.2d 1180 (Mont.1977). Problem 3(c) describes the facts in Davin v. Daham, 746 A.2d 1034 (N.J. Super. A.D. 2000). Problem 3(d) is modeled on Stare v. Tate, 21 Cal.App.3d 432, 98 Cal. Rptr. 264 (1971). Problem 3(e) draws on Russell Engler, "Out of Sight and Out of Line; The Need for Regulation of Lawyers' Negotiations With Unrepresented Poor Persons," 85 *Cal. L. Rev.* 79 (1997).

Larry Lempert, "In Settlement Talks, Does Telling the Truth Have Its Limits?"

2 Inside Litigation 1 (1988).

> *"For truth itself does not have the privilege to be employed at any time and in every way; its use, noble as it is, has its circumscriptions and limits."*

—Montaigne

Law professor Charles Craver, who teaches courses and workshops on legal negotiation and settlement, likes to begin by saying, "I've never been involved in legal negotiations where both sides didn't lie." It tends to get some "shocked responses," he admits.

Craver, a former litigator and labor law practitioner, does not stop there. He goes on to defend some lies in the course of settlement talks as perfectly proper.

To U.S. Magistrate Wayne Brazil, on the other hand, lying is anathema, and nothing about the settlement setting excuses it. "My opinion is, no lying," he says, adding, somewhat wryly, "Strike one blow for naiveté."

Whether naive or not, Brazil does seem to be in a minority. Not all lawyers are as unapologetic as Craver, but interviews with experts who have focused on negotiation and ethics, plus several litigators and judicial officers, indicate that most believe lying in settlement talks is not always prohibited (and that volunteering the truth is not always required).

In the 15 interviews, *Inside Litigation* asked what a lawyer ought to do in each of four hypothetical settlement situations.

Participants included nine law professors who have written on ethics, negotiation, or both; five experienced litigators, a federal circuit court judge, and a U.S. magistrate ... Most specified what they believed prevailing ethics rules would allow. A few answered in terms of what they would do but did not venture opinions on the formal ethics rules. In several instances, some noted that ethics rules might permit lying but that, personally, they would not do it. The lawyers also volunteered suggestions on tactics....

Situation No. 1: Lying About Authorized Limits

> *Your clients, the defendants, have told you that you are authorized to pay $750,000 to settle the case. In settlement negotiations, after your offer of $650,000, the plaintiffs' attorney asks, "Are you authorized to settle for $750,000?" Can you say, "No, I'm not?"*

(Two of the litigators well-known for representing plaintiffs were asked essentially the same question with the roles reversed, so that the plaintiffs' attorney is asked whether he or she is authorized to settle for a specific amount.)

Of those willing to give a straight yes or no answer, six say no, you cannot say that. Seven say yes, you can—but all but one of these add that as a matter either of personal ethics or strategy, they would not give such an answer.

"Outright lying always is out of bounds," according to David Luban.... It's not that one can never be misleading in the admittedly adversarial game of negotiation, he explains. But the way the process works, when one side makes an evasive statement, the other side can ask a question to clarify that position. A flat, declarative statement sends no signal that clarification is needed. "People have to be able to rely on flat-out declarations," Luban says, or the process breaks down or, at best, becomes "incredibly time-consuming."

Geoffrey Hazard Jr., the author of the ABA Model Rules, agrees that "you're allowed to make an evasive statement." He too says that an outright lie in Situation No. 1 would violate Rule 4.1....

Litigator Jacob Stein, however, argues that this is one of those statements, referred to in the comment to Rule 4.1, that "ordinarily are not taken as statements of material fact." If the opponent says he or she is not authorized to pay more, "I don't rely on that," says Stein. "In the realm of negotiation, the issue is whether there's reliance."

Several participants contend that the ethics rules would permit the lie but their personal standards would not. Stein is in this camp. So is James White of the University of Michigan. "A flat denial of that sort"—although permissible—"makes me uncomfortable. It's questionable morally," White says. In the view of Judge Alvin Rubin, a representation about settlement authority should not be considered a representation of fact under the ethics rules. But he, too, says, "Personally, I would avoid the question rather than answer untruthfully."

Craver, on the other hand, not only believes that lying is permissible in Situation No. 1 but says, "I don't have any hesitancy in lying about my authorized limits"; he has done it before and would do it again, he says. Lying is an acceptable response to the inquiry, in his view, because "the other side has no right to that information." ...

Most of those interviewed point out that a negotiator who is asked about authorized settlement limits can dodge the question or deflect it in a variety of ways. "The way to avoid [the problem] is to think ahead and have answers ready," says White. He recalls, for example, negotiators who would simply laugh and say, "You don't think I'm going to tell you answers to questions like that." Or the negotiator can answer the question with a question, White adds: When the plaintiff's lawyer asks, "Are you authorized to settle for $750,000," the defendant's lawyer asks, "Are you willing to come below $750,000?" According to Craver, treating the question as an offer sometimes can be an effective strategy: "I appreciate your movement; it's in the right direction, but $750,000 is still too much." Ronald Rotunda of the University of Illinois suggests responding, "I'll bring back to my client the best offer I can get."

The interviewees agree that whatever response the lawyer chooses, consistency is important. If you refuse to answer questions about authorized limits in the course of the settlement talks, you must always refuse, or the exception will be obvious to the opponent.

A no-lying rule, Craver complains, means that the negotiator would always have to swear off the "limited authority" technique—a Mutt-and-Jeff kind of approach that casts the negotiator as a nice guy whose flexibility is limited by a tough-minded client. "The negotiator could never say, 'I'm sorry, I'm just not authorized . . .,' even when the statement is true, because he or she would be forced to tell the truth—and cut off a possible better deal for the client—when the opponent probes further and hits on the actual authorized figure. Yet, 'limited authority' is a very, very common technique," Craver says. And saying, "No, I'm not authorized," he notes, is much more forceful than saying, "You know you can't ask me that."

Some experienced practitioners, however, eschew that technique anyway. For one thing, they say, it would imply a lack of influence with the client that the opponent would not find credible. Says plaintiffs' lawyer Leonard Ring, "I don't use the word authorize. I have a lot of persuasion with my client."

(Invoking limited authority—at the $750,000 level, for example—can pose a slight practical problem if $750,000 turns out to be the best figure you can get, and you want to settle. You then have to discover, in a phone call, perhaps, that your client has been "persuaded after all." Whether you actually phone the client or call your spouse to discuss grocery shopping, as far as Craver is concerned, does not raise an ethical issue. "I would have no qualms lying about the phone call," he says.)

Situation No. 2: Lying About an Injury

You represent a plaintiff who claims to have suffered a serious knee injury. In settlement negotiations, can you say your client is "disabled" when you know she is out skiing?

The score: no, fourteen; yes, one. This question was the only one of the four that yielded a solid consensus. . . .

Situation No. 3: Exaggerating an Injury

You are trying to negotiate a settlement on behalf of a couple who charge that the bank pulled their loan, ruining their business. Your clients are quite upbeat and deny suffering particularly severe emotional distress. Can you tell your opponent, nonetheless, that they did?

The score: no, eight; yes, five (with two not answering directly).

Brazil says no. "Lawyers should try to get for clients what they need, and not more," he argues. "Measuring our value as lawyers by how much we get for the client," he adds, is an "insidious trend" and a "source of great ethical strain on the system."

Some see No. 3 as a closer question but believe that pushing the emotional distress element in settlement talks would be an unacceptable misrepresentation of fact. Says Rubin, "It moves closer to the permissible [than No. 2] but does not yet reach it."

But several lawyers who find the assertion of disability in No. 2 to be unethical do not object to the assertion of emotional distress in No. 3. Obviously, some distress has occurred—"if they didn't care at all, there wouldn't be a legal matter," says Craver. "I'm embellishing the concern." White agrees that exaggeration of the degree of pain experienced by a client is "well within the range of puffing." The fundamental question, says White, is "what are your and my legitimate expectations [as opposing negotiators]?" The opponent expects exaggeration of pain, White believes.

Explaining further, White draws an analogy to sales law, which distinguishes between puffing and making a warranty by asking whether reliance on the statement would be reasonable. In this analogy, lawyers are sophisticated buyers and sellers: the defense lawyer is a buyer, the plaintiff's lawyer, a seller. "Because they're sophisticated, a fair amount of puffing is permitted without it being a warranty," White says. "It's like two car dealers" negotiating the sale and purchase of a car. (Independently, Rotunda arrives at a similar analogy but draws a different conclusion. Contending that the exaggeration in Situation No. 3 is improper, Rotunda observes, "If lawyers want to be like used car salesmen, this is a good place to start.") . . .

Rex Perschbacher of the University of California agrees that reasonableness of reliance is one criterion—working in combination, he believes, with the degree of specificity. That is, as questions become more specific, the negotiator has less freedom to lie because the opponent's reliance on the answer becomes more reasonable. Thus, Perschbacher says no to No. 1 and no to No. 2, but would allow the claim for emotional distress in No. 3.

Several who say the lawyer in No. 3 cannot make an outright assertion about emotional distress do acknowledge that the issue can be raised in a more oblique way. Hazard, for example, would let the negotiator say that cutting off a loan is the *kind of act* that can produce serious distress. "You can suggest that the other party ought to think about it, with a carefully chosen phrase," says Hazard. Or you can ask a rhetorical question, says Luban: "Wouldn't *you* feel as though the world has caved in on you?"

Stein, who says no to No. 3, adds that the assertion of emotional distress in that situation would be unwise. "A good negotiator would ask for medical reports, and you wouldn't have any," he says. McNamara, too, questions the effectiveness of exaggeration. "Stick to the facts," he advises. "Somewhere or other there are pieces of paper that make it clear what the facts are." Surely, he says, you can point out that "one of the items the jury can consider is not just the plaintiffs' loss but the effect on these people." And that, he says, "is exactly how far I'd take it.... You don't want to hurt the client's case ... by losing credibility as an advocate."

Situation No. 4: A Mistaken Impression

   In settlement talks over the couple's lender liability case, your opponent's comments make it clear that he thinks the plaintiffs have gone out of business, although you didn't say that. In fact, the business is continuing, and several important contracts are in the offing. You are on the verge of settlement; can you go ahead and settle without correcting your opponent's misimpression?

The score: no, four; yes, nine (with two not answering directly).

The participants agree that you cannot say anything to further or ratify the misimpression. But beyond that point, disagreement sets in.

Hazard says no on the ground that the ethics rules incorporate the law of fraud—"and the law of fraud," adds Hazard, "is more exacting than most lawyers think." The opponent's belief that the client is out of business is "a manifest misapprehension that goes to the bargain itself," Hazard says. McNamara, too, says, "It does not pass the smell test with me. . . . [In this situation], failure to speak up is fraud." But White disagrees with this conclusion, referring again to the bargaining between two car dealers—there is no obligation under the common law of fraud to correct the savvy dealer's error, White says.

Interestingly, Craver, outspoken in his support for lying in Situation No. 1, finds No. 4 so difficult a situation that he cannot give a definite answer. If he thought that correcting the misimpression would not hurt the client, he says, he would do it. But if it looked like the settlement would fall apart on that issue alone, he's not so sure. By contrast, Luban—who flatly says no to the outright lie in No. 1—generally approves keeping quiet in No. 4.

The difference for Luban lies in his rule that flat-out declarations have to be true—No. 4, obviously, involves no such declaration. "It's not my job to do their job for them," Luban says of the opponent in No. 4, "as long as my word isn't on the line." Similarly, says plaintiffs' lawyer David Shrager, "I'm not in litigation to educate the opponent." . . .

Several interviewees who say the misimpression need not be corrected add that there are factors that could tip the answer [the] other way. Perschbacher would want to consider whether circumstances beyond those stated in the hypothetical, give rise to a claim that the opponent is placing particular reliance on the negotiator who keeps quiet. For example, Perschbacher says, if the misimpression relates to a fact that the opponent cannot determine on his own, then failure to correct his misimpression might be improper. Luban agrees, and adds that the consequences for the opponent probably should be weighed in as well.

Luban cites a Minnesota Supreme Court case from 1962 to show what he means about consequences. In *Spaulding v. Zimmerman* (116 N.W.2d 704), a car crash had led to a personal injury suit. The defense doctor examined the plaintiff and discovered a potentially fatal medical problem that neither the plaintiff, the plaintiff's lawyer, nor the plaintiff's doctor knew about. The defense doctor revealed his finding to the defendant's lawyer, who settled the case without mentioning that the plaintiff could drop dead any second (presumably, that fact would have affected the settlement value adversely from the defense point of view). The defendant's lawyer was not responsible for the plaintiff's misimpression about the value of the case. "But it's perfectly clear that any lawyer with a grain of conscience would tell the plaintiff he had to see a doctor. You don't let somebody drop dead to save your client some money," Luban says. . . .

In *Spaulding v. Zimmerman,* the Minnesota court did not say the defendant's lawyer had acted unethically, but it did void the settlement, as the plaintiff had asked it to do. As a practical matter, that points to a problem with keeping quiet in Situation No. 4, as several interviewees emphasize—if an attack on the settlement ensues once the opponent learns the facts, your client might not have the peace he thought he was buying. "That's one practical reason for taking the ethical high road," says Brazil. But Stein, who says that correction of the misimpression is not required, believes that a well-crafted release would probably foreclose an attack on the settlement. . . . Not surprisingly, given the range of reactions to the hypotheticals, experts approach the issue of truth in the settlement process from a variety of perspectives. "I don't see why the law should allow attorneys to tell a bald-faced lie," says Rotunda. As he sees it, the comments to Rule 4.1, which forgive certain lies because of "generally accepted conventions in negotiation," are an attempt to "slice the baloney [too] thin."

Others attach more weight to the dynamics of the negotiation process. "I can't expect the opponent to reveal all his information to me," says White. "It's appropriate for him to try to get me to believe some things that are not true." Negotiation, according to McNamara, becomes "orderly capitulation" unless the negotiator misrepresents to some degree.

Hazard describes negotiation as a process of "communicating without giving away the store." The communication occurs through the exchange of incomplete signals; it "necessarily entails an exploratory process" and "a certain amount of acting," Hazard says.

At the same time, countervailing forces exist—and not just moral or religious ones—in favor of candor. One such force is reputation. Legal practice would be cumbersome indeed if other lawyers were never willing to take you at your word, Craver notes. "There has to be a level of candor if one is going to practice law," he says. Moreover, he observes, candor can be a good tactic. In this regard, he says a possible approach to Situation No. 4 would be to correct the misimpression and build on the boost in credibility with the opponent that such a step would bring.

McNamara has another reason to tell the truth—he knows he would not be a good liar. "I can't be my most convincing when I'm lying," he says.

NOTES AND QUESTIONS: CANDOR IN NEGOTIATION

1.   How would you respond to the cases in Problem 3 and the hypothetical situations in Lempert's article? Do any of these examples involve misrepresentations of fact within the meaning of Model Rule 4.1? If, under this

Rule, statements about settlement authority are "ordinarily" not viewed as statements of fact, what is meant by "ordinarily"? Consider the Ethical Guidelines 4.1.1, Committee Notes (identifying factors relevant to whether a statement should be considered one of fact, such as the parties' past relationship, the opponent's apparent sophistication, the phrasing of the statement, and the negotiating practices of the community). Are misrepresentations about settlement authority or related matters justifiable when there are other alternatives available? Experienced practitioners often sidestep direct inquiries on these issues with responses such as "I'm not free to disclose that" or "I would advise my client that the case justifies $20,000." Would it be preferable to require that lawyers avoid direct misstatements of their clients' willingness to accept certain settlements?

What about other forms of bluffing, such as false claims by a buyer that he has seen a better price in a discount catalogue, or by a seller that she has another buyer at the asking price?[21] Those who argue that such misrepresentations are harmless generally assume that the opposing party will recognize bluffing or "puffing" for what it is. But if that were always true, the practice would also be ineffective. Bluffing and puffing continue because sometimes they work and some opponents are deceived. To commentators such as Judge Alvin Rubin, parties dealing with a lawyer should not need to exercise the same degree of caution as they would if trading at a Far Eastern bazaar.[22] What is your view? How much prudence is it reasonable to expect concerning such statements?

Game theorist Thomas Schelling writes:

A bargain is struck when somebody makes a final, sufficient concession. Why does he concede? Because he thinks the other will not. "I must concede because he won't. He won't because he thinks I will. He thinks I will because he thinks I think he thinks so...." There is some range of alternative outcomes in which any point is better for both sides than no agreement at all. To insist on any such point is pure bargaining, since one always *would* take less rather than reach no agreement at all, and since one always *can* recede if retreat proves necessary to agreement. Yet if both parties are aware of the limits to this range, *any* outcome is a point from which at least one party would have been willing to retreat and the other knows it! There is no resting place.[23]

If Schelling is correct, it will be difficult for negotiators to reach agreement unless they have managed to keep their bottom lines hidden from each other. Total candor becomes an obstacle to agreement, even when both sides want to agree. From this perspective, negotiation is like the game of chicken. It ends when one side has successfully bluffed the other, and

---

21. For arguments that the claims about price may be legally permissible if not honorable, but that the claims about another buyer may be fraudulent, *see* G. Richard Shell, *Bargaining for Advantage: Negotiation Strategies for Reasonable People* 201–11 (1999).

22. Alvin B. Rubin, "A Causerie on Lawyers' Ethics in Negotiations," 35 *La. L. Rev.* 577 (1975).

23. Thomas Schelling, *The Strategy of Conflict* 21–22 (rev. ed. 1980).

bluffing is impossible if either party knows his opponent's settlement point. What does this analysis suggest about obligations of candor and disclosure on the part of negotiators? Under what circumstances would full disclosure of relevant facts assist or impede the negotiation process? What interpretation of existing rules would best serve societal interests?

2.   Are the claims in Problem 3(b) about the ranch's profitability statements of fact? Should a buyer be entitled to rely on such statements? Should it matter whether information about the property's recent financial performance was accessible to the buyer? What about claims that poultry breeding stock had "very high productive traits"? *Nasik Breeding and Research Farm Ltd. v. Merck & Co.*, 165 F.Supp.2d 514, 530 (S.D.N.Y. 2001).

3.   On the facts of 3(c), the New Jersey court held that the lessee's lawyer may have committed malpractice, but that the lessor's lawyer may be liable as well. Under the court's analysis, an attorney has a duty not only to represent a client "effectively and vigorously" but also to "act fairly and in good faith." At a minimum, the lawyer had an obligation to counsel his client to disclose the impending foreclosure and if the client refused to withdraw from representation. In the court's view, the lawyer was in a "difficult position," but "the practice of law is not easy." *Davin v. Daham*, 746 A.2d 1034 (N.J.Super. A.D. 2000). Is that your view? Compare Ethical Guideline 2.3 (providing that lawyers' negotiating conduct "should be characterized by honor and fair dealing"); 4.1.2 Committee Note (indicating that lawyers generally have no obligation to make disclosures unless silence would constitute fraud). Would it be unethical for a personal injury lawyer to settle a claim without disclosing that his client had died? See *In re Warner*, 851 So.2d 1029 (La. 2003).

4.   Problem 3(d) is based on *Stare v. Tate*, 21 Cal.App.3d 432, 98 Cal.Rptr. 264 (1971). There, the court noted,

> the mistake might never have come to light had not the husband desired to have the exquisite last word. A few days after [the wife] had obtained the divorce he mailed her a copy of the offer which contained the errant computation. On top of the page he wrote with evident satisfaction: "PLEASE NOTE ... MISTAKE IN YOUR FIGURES." A month later the wife filed suit action to reform the agreement.

98 Cal.Rptr., at 266.

The court reformed the agreement under § 3399 of the California Code to conform to the wife's understanding. The Code provides: "When through fraud or mutual mistake of the parties, or a mistake of one party, which the other at the time knew or suspected, a written contract does not truly express the intention of the parties, it may be revised on the application of a party aggrieved, so as to express that intention, so far as it can be done without prejudice to rights acquired by third persons, in good faith and for value."

What would you have done as counsel for the husband? If you had consulted your client and he had refused to authorize disclosures of the mistake, how would you have responded? What factors would have been most relevant in guiding your conduct? Would it have been appropriate to consider the likely effect of nondisclosure on your reputation or the fairness of the underlying divorce settlement? Note that Model Rule 4.1 requires disclosure to avoid tortious or criminal misrepresentation. See Comment [2].

Should lawyers have an obligation to seek their clients' approval before correcting a scrivener's error? In Informal Opinion 86–1518 (Feb. 9, 1986), the ABA's Standing Committee on Ethics reviewed a situation in which a lawyer discovered that the final draft of a contract prepared by opposing counsel's office did not contain a material, previously disputed, provision. In the Committee's view, the lawyer should contact opposing counsel to correct the error and had no obligation under either the Model Rules or the Code to obtain the client's permission. Rule 1.2(a) provides that lawyers "shall abide by a client's decisions concerning the objectives of representation and shall consult with the client as to the means by which they are to be served." However, the Comment to the Rule acknowledges the lawyer's responsibility for technical and strategic issues. Rule 1.4 requires lawyers to explain matters "reasonably necessary to permit the client to make informed decisions regarding the representation." Under the Committee's analysis, once the client had accepted the disputed provision, no informed decision remained to be made. In addition, the Committee relied on general prohibitions on conduct involving dishonesty, fraud, deceit, or misrepresentation, in Model Rule 8.4(c) and DR 1–102(A)(4), and the provision in Rule 4.1(b) that lawyers shall not fail to disclose a material fact to a third person when disclosure is necessary to avoid assisting a fraudulent act by a client unless the information is privileged. Accord, Ethical Guidelines 4.3.5 (providing that is unprofessional for a lawyer to knowingly exploit a drafting error). Does it follow that knowing failure to disclose an error would constitute fraud and grounds for discipline?

Suppose that in Problem 3(d) the attorney had not noticed the scrivener's error until the husband showed him the letter about to be sent to the wife. How should the attorney have responded? If the attorney had persuaded the husband not to mail the letter or disclose the error, and that fact later came to light, could the attorney be subject to civil liability or disciplinary sanctions?

5. How should lawyers deal with unrepresented, unsophisticated adversaries? Is it enough for lawyers in cases like 3(e) to comply with Model Rule 4.3, which requires them to avoid implying that they are disinterested; to correct misunderstandings concerning their role; and to refrain from giving legal advice when the lawyer "knows or reasonably should know that the interests of such a person are or have a reasonable possibility of being in conflict with the interests of the client"? Accord, Ethical Guidelines, 4.3.4?

An early draft of the Model Rules would have required lawyers to avoid "exploiting unrepresented parties' ignorance of the law or the practices of the tribunal." Discussion Draft Rule 8.6 (1980). Would you support such a rule? How could it be enforced? Did the lawyer in Problem 3(e) behave ethically? If not, how could such behavior be prevented or remedied?

6. Is it unethical for a negotiator to make representations that are highly misleading even though they are not literally false? How would you assess the conduct of the plaintiff's lawyer in Problem 3(a)?

The case on which the problem is based arose during the 1960s, when the Washington, D.C., Mattachine Society planned what it billed as the first national conference to focus on gay and lesbian rights. The Manger Hotel agreed to host the conference with knowledge of its subject. Then, two weeks before the event, after publicity and invitations had been mailed, management in the hotel chain's home office ordered cancellation of the agreement. Monroe Freedman, the Society's lawyer, later defended his conduct:

> Was anything definite about mitigation at that point? Is anything ever definite in this life? After all, the Mattachine Society had thought that the deal with the Manger was definite, and it turned out that it wasn't.... The statement about mitigation wasn't a flat-out denial: it was equivocal—an evasion that a careful listener could have picked up on. "What do you mean 'nothing definite'?" he might have said....[24]

According to Freedman, the new offer of a hotel site was confidential information and as long as he did not make a false statement of material fact, he did not need to disclose it under Model Rule 4.1. Do you find his reasoning persuasive? What would you have done in his circumstances?

7. Are half-truths equivalent to lies? Consider *In re A.*, 554 P.2d 479 (Ore.1976), in which a client testified at a deposition that his mother was "in Salem." He neglected to mention that she was dead and buried in Salem, in order to suggest that she was still alive and potentially in need of his financial support. The Oregon court believed that the client's attorney should have withdrawn, because in the court's view, the half-truth was fraudulent. In a recent Australian case, the Legal Services Commissioner for Queensland, a non-lawyer, disciplined a barrister who did not reveal, when settling a personal injury case, that he had recently learned that his client was seriously ill with cancer, and unlikely to have the 27 year life expectancy which he had previously claimed.[25]

By contrast, in a landmark Supreme Court case on perjury, *Bronston v. United States,* 409 U.S. 352, 354 (1973), the following colloquy occurred:

"Q. Do you have any bank accounts in Swiss banks, Mr. Bronston?

A. No, sir.

Q. Have you ever?

A. The company had an account there for about six months in Zurich."

---

24. Freedman, *supra* note 20, at 20.

25. Legal Services Commission v. Mullins [2006]LPT 012. The barrister, a promi- nent member of the bar, received a reprimand and a $20,000 fine.

Although Bronston's answers were literally true, he failed to disclose that he himself had used a personal account in a Geneva bank for five years between 1959 and 1964. The Supreme Court overturned his conviction for perjury on the ground that in an adversary proceeding, his questioner had responsibility to smoke out Bronston's deception.[26] Should the same standard apply in a negotiation? What are the similarities and differences between negotiation and adversary proceedings?

Should negotiators who are acting as agents for others have some duty to protect themselves from deceptive non disclosures? Research on negotiation ethics suggests that a range of factors influence the likelihood of deception, including personal characteristics, situational incentives, and the relationship between the parties. In general, parties are more willing to deceive by omission than commission, so prudent negotiators will ask as many specific questions as possible, particularly in circumstances in which they have no ongoing relationship.[27]

The Duty of Disclosure

Suppose that in the course of negotiations it becomes apparent that your opposing counsel lacks certain crucial information. Your obligations depend partly on doctrines of fraud and mistake, which are summarized in section 161 of the *Restatement (Second) of Contracts*. Section 161 provides that non-disclosure of a fact will be treated as a lie in several situations. Two are particularly relevant in negotiation contexts. Disclosure is required when necessary to correct a previous assertion that is erroneous, or when the fact in question concerns a basic assumption of the negotiation and non-disclosure would violate "good faith and . . . reasonable standards of fair dealing." And when is that? The accompanying comment explains merely that "reasonable standards of fair dealing" refers to prevailing business practices.[28] But as the Lempert excerpt suggests, among lawyer-negotiators it is not always clear what the prevailing business practices are.

A growing body of contract and tort caselaw provides some guidance. Under prevailing doctrine, the more a negotiator's statement invokes or implies actual knowledge, the more likely courts will be to find the buyer's reliance justifiable. Liability is also increasingly common for negotiators who: deliberately attempt to deceive; deal with an unusually gullible party; make partial disclosures that are literally true but misleading; have material information not available to the other side; or reasonably appear to have special skill and judgment related to the matter in question.[29]

---

26. Lawyers for then-President Clinton invoked *Bronston* as precedent during impeachment proceedings in claiming that some of their client's deposition statements concerning Monica Lewinsky were misleading but not perjurious. The trial court rejected those claims and in post-impeachment proceedings found Clinton in contempt "notwithstanding tortured definitions and interpretations of the term 'sexual relations' " to exclude oral sex. Jones v. Clinton, 36 F.Supp.2d 1118, 1130 (E.D. Ark. 1999).

27. Maurice E. Schweitzer & Rachel Croson, "Curtailing Deception: The Impact of Direct Questions on Lies and Omissions," in *What's Fair Ethics for Negotiators* 175, 195–96 (Carrie Menkel–Meadow & Michael Wheeler, eds. 2004).

28. *Restatement (Second) of Contracts* § 161 cmt. (d) (1981).

29. Shell, *supra* note 21, at 208–10; Robert Mnookin, Scott R. Peppet, & Andrew Tulumello, *Beyond Warning: Negotiating to*

Caselaw summarized in the *Restatement of Torts* takes a less permissive view of puffing than Model Rule 4.1. Under prevailing doctrine, an injured party can recover damages caused by materially misleading misrepresentations, including ambiguous statements with a false meaning made without regard for how they will be understood. Partially true statements can be materially misleading if they fail to state qualifying information.[30]

Most importantly, Section 551 of the Restatement specifies several situations in which nondisclosure will result in liability. They include circumstances where the undisclosed fact is basic to the transaction and one party, "because of the relationship [with the other party], the customs of the trade or other objective circumstances, would reasonably expect a disclosure.... "§ 551(e). Section 551(d) requires a party to disclose "the falsity of a representation not made with the expectation that it would be acted upon, if he subsequently learns that the other is about to act in reliance upon it in a transaction with him." Thus, a negotiator may engage in puffing only so long as those on the other side don't indicate that they take it seriously. A negotiator must also disclose "matters known to him that he knows to be necessary to prevent his partial or ambiguous statement of the facts from being misleading." § 551(b). In short, Section 551 does not distinguish between lies, "generally accepted" puffery, half-truths, and truthful-but-misleading statements. All are tortious frauds if other parties rely on them to their detriment.

Law professor Donald Langevoort offers an economic justification for treating "half-truths" as deceptive:

> Why do we have law barring affirmative misrepresentations in the first place? Why don't we say that reasonable people should always do their own "due diligence" investigation rather than rely on information provided by someone with an obviously conflicting interest? ... [T]he orthodox answer is that the law of fraud is efficient. It allows the less informed party to forego the costly and duplicative process of factual investigation and information discovery, thereby reducing transaction costs. The law offers a credibility bond for the reliability of factual representations by the informed party.
>
> It is not at all hard to extend this same logic to the half-truth. That is, it facilitates efficient transacting to say that the law will offer a credibility bond when a person speaks not only for the technical accuracy of the statement but also its natural and normal implication as a matter of ordinary communication (putting aside any expectations

Create Value in Deals and Disputes 281–82 (2000); Gary Tobias Lowenthal, "The Bar's Failure to Require Truthful Bargaining by Lawyers," 2 *Geo. J. Legal Ethics* 383, 421 (1988); *Restatement (Second) of Contracts* §§ 159, 168 (1981).

30. *Restatement (Second) of Torts* § 527, § 529 (1977). See also *id.*, § 552 (1), on negligent misrepresentation, which has sometimes served as a basis for liability claims against lawyers. It provides: "One

who, in the course of his business, profession or employment, or in any transaction in which he has a pecuniary interest, supplies false information for the guidance of others in their business transactions, is subject to liability for pecuniary loss caused to them by their justifiable reliance upon the information, if he fails to exercise reasonable care or competence in obtaining or communicating the information."

created by law). Language is inherently imprecise; it is not functional to force people to stop and analyze statements to see if there is some subtle limit or ambiguity that must be clarified. . . . A certain level of protection for reasonable inferences is thus appropriate. . . .

This strikes me as a helpful approach, but I want to consider a significant refinement. . . . [T]here are some contexts [such as the hearing in *Bronston v. U.S.*, supra] in which the half-truth doctrine has little necessary place. If there is in fact little or no trust between two parties—a truly adversarial setting—it is difficult to justify the doctrine at all. At least ex ante, I suspect that in these settings parties will often prefer a default rule of mere technical accuracy, with its reduced risk of ex post litigation. While I have seen no explicit statement in the case law that the half-truth doctrine adjusts downward to reflect a lack of trust between the parties, it should.

Conversely, we should expect that negotiations characterized by a high degree of trust should lead to an upward adjustment: a broad half-truth doctrine, one with little privilege to conceal once a matter is addressed at all.[31]

By contrast, Professor Alan Strudler argues that even in some less adversarial business negotiations, half-truths should be permissible. In his view, negotiators who have invested time and effort in acquiring useful information should be able to capitalize on their efforts. Strudler proposes a "deserved advantage principle: other things being equal, the more value one brings to the bargaining table, the more one may fairly insist upon as return. . . . According to the deserved advantage principle account, a buyer's acquisition of information that increases the value of the object being sold in a negotiation warrants some additional measure of bargaining strength, and a privilege of buyer nondisclosure . . . protects the buyer in getting a fair return on the valuable information that she brings to the table."[32] If, for example, the buyer's hard work has unearthed information indicating that the seller's property is worth more than the seller thinks it is, the buyer should not have to disclose the information. As Strudler notes,

The commercial world teems with . . . intermediaries or middlemen, from jobbers and distributors to stockbrokers and real estate agents. A financial intermediary is a bargain hunter; whether searching garage sales for impressionist works of art or inexpensive farm land for mineral deposits, she seeks to buy low and sell high. A bargain hunter's job involves exploiting a seller's lack of knowledge.[33]

Are Langevoort's and Strudler's proposals consistent? If not, which seems more convincing? Consider negotiating experts' concern that reinforcing an ethic of non-disclosure will lead too many negotiators to lose credibility and miss opportunities for mutually advantageous agreements.

---

31. Donald C. Langevoort, "Half–Truths: Protecting Mistaken Inferences by Investors and Others," 52 *Stan. L. Rev.* 87, 94, 98 (1999).

32. Alan Strudler, "Moral Complexity in the Law of Nondisclosure," 45 *UCLA L. Rev.* 337, 374–75 (1997).

33. *Id.*, at 345.

Richard Shell argues instead for "information-based bargaining" in which negotiators try to get as much reliable knowledge about the situation and other party as possible. That will enable participants to "think outside the box" and to devise agreements that fall within a "zone of overlap" of parties' settlement points. Howard Raiffa similarly argues that maximum value creation for the parties occurs under conditions of full, open, truthful exchange.[34]

How should bar ethical rules deal with disclosure? An early draft of the Model Rules included a separate section on the lawyer as negotiator that closely paralleled the Restatement position. However, as noted above, Rule 4.1(a) in the version ultimately adopted bars only false statements of material fact. Model Rule 4.1(b) requires disclosure of material fact "when disclosure is necessary to avoid assisting a criminal or fraudulent act by a client, unless disclosure is prohibited by Rule 1.6." The "unless" clause imposes a major limitation because Rule 1.6(a) forbids a lawyer from revealing confidential information without client consent "except for disclosures that are impliedly authorized in order to carry out the representation. . . ." The Comment to this rule indicates that a lawyer is impliedly authorized to make a disclosure in negotiation "that facilitates a satisfactory conclusion," but only if the client's instructions do not limit that authority. If a client instructs the lawyer to keep certain information secret, Rules 1.6 and 4.1(b) together seem to require confidentiality.

However, as the Comment to Rule 1.6 also makes clear, lawyers must withdraw from representation rather than allow their services to be used to further a fraud. Model Rule 8.4(c) similarly provides that: "[i]t is professional misconduct for a lawyer to engage in conduct involving dishonesty, fraud, deceit or misrepresentation." If their choice is to have a lawyer withdraw midway through negotiations or to disclose material information, many clients will prefer disclosure, particularly if failure to do so could later void the transaction. Given these ethical obligations, a lawyer's role in negotiation may sometimes requires bargaining with clients as well as opposing parties.

The bargaining process needs also to take account of ethical as well as legal considerations. In this, as in other contexts, the law and morality of lawyering are not necessarily coextensive. Legal doctrine and bar disciplinary rules often establish only minimal requirements due to the costs of enforcement, the problems of proof, the need for stability in transactions, and the consequences of widespread noncompliance. Accordingly, legal requirements do not exhaust the ethical considerations that are relevant in shaping negotiation behavior. Lawyers also have an individual interest in maintaining their own reputations and a shared interest in supporting standards of good faith and fair dealing on which any efficient bargaining process depends. The world of legal practice, like society more generally, relies on a "background of trust that makes sharp practices conspicuous

---

34. Shell, *supra* note 21, at iv, 218 (1999); Howard Raiffa, *Lectures on Negotiation Analysis* 6 (1996).

and jarring,'' as well as counterproductive in any context involving ongoing relationships.[35]

The late federal Judge Alvin Rubin puts the point directly:

It is inherent in the concept of professionalism that the profession will regulate itself, adhering to an ethos that imposes standards higher than mere law observance. Client avarice and hostility neither control the lawyer's conscience nor measure his ethics. Surely if its practitioners are principled, a profession that dominates the legal process in our law-oriented society would not expect too much if it required its members to adhere to two simple principles when they negotiate as professionals: Negotiate honestly and in good faith; and do not take unfair advantage of another, regardless of his relative expertise or sophistication.[36]

Do you agree?

C.   COOPERATIVE AND COMPETITIVE BARGAINING

Clearly, many of the ethical problems arising in negotiation result from the view that successful bargaining requires an adversarial stance toward other parties. Many experts, however, believe that a cooperative approach to bargaining is not only more ethical but also more widespread and generally more effective.[37] The few empirical studies available on lawyer-negotiators are consistent with these claims. One found that about two-thirds of surveyed lawyers were consistently cooperative and a quarter were consistently competitive; the remainder used mixed styles. Of those rated effective by their peers, three-quarters were cooperative.[38] In another large scale study involving Chicago and Milwaukee practitioners, three quarters of lawyers evaluated as "true problem solvers" were described by peers as effective. By contrast, only 14 percent of those classified as ethical and adversarial, and only 1 percent of those classified as unethical and adversarial were rated effective.[39]

Advocates of cooperative negotiation claim that high ethical standards and collaborative approaches enhance opportunities for creative, mutually advantageous solutions. Hardball negotiators often "walk away leaving money on the table": that is, they reach an agreement without noticing that a better agreement for both sides was available, such as a structured settlement or nonmonetary provisions equivalent to financial payments. Some feminists also argue that cooperative negotiation is more consistent

---

35. Kevin Gibson, "Ethics and Morality in Negotiation," in *The Negotiator's Fieldbook, supra* note 12, at 175, 176.

36. Rubin, *supra* note 22, at 592.

37. *See* Shell, *supra* note 21; Mnookin, Pepper, and Tulmelo, *supra* note 29; Roger Fisher & William Ury, *Getting To Yes* (1981); Howard Raiffa, *The Art and Science of Negotiation* (1982); Tesler, *supra* note 7.

38. Gerald Williams, *Legal Negotiations and Settlement* 19 (1983).

39. Catherine H. Tinsley, Jack J. Cambria, & Andrea Kupfer Schneider, "Reputations in Negotiation," in The Negotiator's Fieldbook, *supra* note 12, at 203.

with values traditionally associated with women and that further societal interests in facilitating equitable agreements.[40]

In essence, the key technique of cooperative negotiation is to avoid getting overly invested in a client's bargaining position, and to look instead at the underlying needs and interests that led the client to assert the position in the first place. In that way, negotiators can achieve their clients' ends without getting trapped in competitive game-playing. Major principles of cooperative bargaining include:

- Appeal to objective criteria, such as principles and standards that the other party views as legitimate, rather than merely trading offers in a test of will and skill.

- Make the goal of the negotiation the highest realistic expectation of what can be achieved; do not allow your client's bottom line to become the main reference point.

- Stay focused on the client's real needs, not winning the competition or getting the most money. It is often possible to satisfy those needs without getting the best financial settlement, and thus without turning negotiation into a zero-sum game.

- Instead of reaching a stalemate over one central issue, try to place another concern on the table, one that matters more to the other side than to your own client, so that concessions can be traded. Ask open ended questions to identify potential interests. The key to cooperative negotiation is reciprocity and logrolling among issues.

- Remember that issues other than money may be less obvious but more divisive. Avoid letting questions of control, turf, ego, and reputation sabotage an otherwise acceptable bargain.[41]

A key concern among those who prefer cooperative approaches is whether they will work when the other negotiator is non-cooperative. The answer is a qualified "yes." Successful negotiators adopt four basic strategies for these situations:

---

40. Whether women negotiate differently or do better in cooperative contexts has generated a large body of research with conflicting results. The most accurate generalization appears to be that gender sometimes matters, but its importance depends heavily on context, such as the power relations between the parties, the sex of the opponent, and whether women are bargaining for themselves or others. See Babcock & Laschever, *supra* note 5; Deborah M. Kolb & Linda L. Putnam, Negotiation Through a Gender Lens, in *The Handbook of Dispute Resolution* 135 (Michael L. Moffitt & Robert C. Bordone eds. 2005); Carrie Menkel–Meadow, "Teaching about Gender and Negotiation: Sex, Truths, & Videotape," *Negotiation Journal*, Oct. 2000, at 357.

41. Shell, *supra* note 21, at 28–43.See also sources cited in Robert C. Bordone, "Fit-ting the Ethics to the Forum: A Proposal for Process–Enabling Ethical Codes," 21 *Ohio State J. Dispute Res.* 1,19 (2005). A notorious example involves a multi-billion dollar bid from one of Henry Kravis's rivals for RJR Nabisco. The deal collapsed when two major investment banking firms, Drexel Burnham Lambert and Salomon Brothers, could not agree on which firm's name would appear on the left hand side of the *Wall Street Journal* ad announcing the financing of the transaction. The position of the firms' name would signal to the financial community which of the two was the "lead" bank, and neither would accept second place status. *Id.*, at 30; Bryan Burrough & John Helyar, *Barbarians at the Gate: The Fall of RJR Nabisco* 30–31 (1990).

- They never initiate the use of "dirty tricks" or hard ball strategies; *but*

- they don't let the other side use such tactics without retaliating in some form; *but*

- after retaliating, they don't hold grudges—they return to a "no-first-use" policy on exploitative strategies; *and*

- they make it plain to the other side that their strategy follows the first three rules.

In short, successful approaches are *nice, provokable, forgiving,* and *transparent.*[42] A bargainer who follows these rules will occasionally risk being exploited by a non-cooperative adversary. However, research has shown that if negotiators encounter each other in repeat transactions, or have knowledge of their adversary's reputation, non-cooperative negotiators will be "punished" for excessively competitive past behavior. Across a wide range of settings, cooperation works better over the long run.[43]

Yet as experts also note, there are also limits to the effectiveness of cooperation. For example, Robert Condlin argues that some degree of competition is inherent in the negotiation process. A common "bargainer's dilemma" involves whether to seek the long-term gains of cooperative bargaining, or the one-time advantage that successful competitive bargaining can sometimes confer. In Condlin's view, the duty of zealous advocacy for a current client may require lawyers to seek the one-time advantage. Otherwise, they are trading off the client's interests for their own long-term bargaining effectiveness, which benefits only themselves, their future clients, and the present client's adversary. Such a strategy appears to violate Model Rule 1.7(a)(2), "A lawyer shall not represent a client if . . . the representation of one or more clients will be materially limited by the lawyer's responsibilities to another client or . . . a third person or by a personal interest of the lawyer. . . ."[44] How would you respond to this argument?

Building on such insights, some experts agree with Condlin that it is self-deceiving to think that ethical conduct in negotiation can always be viewed as enlightened self-interest. Lies that are unlikely to be revealed may be highly effective and, as Gerald Wetlaufer notes, the world in which

42. Robert Axelrod, *The Evolution of Cooperation* 20, 54 (1984). For a more technical presentation, see Michael Taylor, *The Possibility of Cooperation* (1987). For a critique of this account of cooperative bargaining, see Ken Binmore, Review of *Complexity and Cooperation*, 1 JASSS (1998), at http://jasss.soc.surrey.ac.uk/1/1/review1.html. *See also* David A. Lax & James K. Sebenius, *The Manager as Negotiator: Bargaining for Cooperation and Competitive Gain* 38–41 (1986).

43. Axelrod, *supra* note 42, at 35–36, 53. See also Lynn Mather, "What Do Clients Want? What Do Lawyers Do?," 52 *Emory L.*

J. 1076, 1065–86 (2003) (noting the importance to divorce lawyers of not appearing unreasonable); Catherine Dupree, "Integrity Has its Price," *Harv. Mag*, July–Aug. 2003, available at http://ww2w.harvardmag.com/online/070378.html. (finding that a good reputation for a seller on e bay led to a 12 percent increase in profits).

44. Robert J. Condlin, "Bargaining in the Dark: The Normative Incoherence of Lawyer Dispute Bargaining Role," 51 *Maryland L. Rev.* 1, 11–12 (1992).

we live "honors instrumental effectiveness above all else."[45] However, Wetlaufer also argues that many of our common excuses for lying are equally self-deceptive. To rely on excuses such as "everyone does it" or "the other side is doing it" presupposes an impoverished view of morality and one that we would reject in other contexts. Moreover, as other experts note, it is important for negotiators to maintain their own standards of fairness, self respect, and credibility. Those who stoop to their opponents' level forfeit both their moral and legal advantage, which may be especially relevant if the bargain is ever challenged. In the long run, unethical practices impair reputations and weaken fundamental values of trust and integrity on which effective lawyering depends.[46] As social psychologists note, because people tend to remember information that confirms preexisting impressions, reputations are "sticky" attributes; one developed, they are relatively easy to maintain, but once tarnished, are hard to build back again.[47]

At the same time, it is also important to minimize clients' risk of suffering exploitation when bargaining with parties who appear willing to cut ethical corners. The risks are greatest in one shot bargaining contexts where the stakes matter and reputations or relationships do not. Commonly recommended strategies of self-protection include:

- Verify information.

- Put representations in writing.

- Do not tolerate shady tactics such as "low balling" or "nibbling," in which a manipulative negotiator gets the other a party committed to an attractive deal and then reveals that the true price is higher or adds demands for minor concessions at the last minute.

- Give an opponent who has engaged in unethical tactics a face-saving way to forfeit any undeserved advantage and agree to a reasonable resolution.

Although such strategies may not always be fully effective, both moral and legal experts note that sometimes

ethics and integrity are things for which a price may have to be paid.... [To that end] we might clearly define winning in a way that leaves room for ethics. It might, for instance, be understood not as "getting as much as we can" but "winning as much as possible without engaging in unacceptable behavior," and "unacceptable behavior" might then be understood to exclude not just those things that are stupid or illegal but also those other things that are unethical. And finally we might give up our claim that ... [we have no choice between] the harsh individualist reality of instrumental effectiveness

---

45. Gerald Wetlaufer, "The Ethics of Lying in Negotiations," 75 *Iowa L.Rev.* 1219, 1223–26, 1272–73 (1990).

46. Shell, *supra* note 21, at 227; Sissela Bok, *Lying: Moral Choice in Public and Professional Life* (1978); Reed Elizabeth Loder,

"Moral Truthseeking and the Virtuous Negotiator," 8 *Geo.J.Leg. Ethics* 45 (1994).

47. Tinsley, Camria, & Schneider, *supra* note 39, at 204. See also Roy J. Lewicki, "Trust and Distrust" in *The Negotiator's Fieldbook, supra* note 12, at 191.

and the elusive possibilities of ethics, integrity, reciprocity and community.[48]

D. Mediation
PROBLEM 4

With some reservations, you agreed to serve as a mediator in a divorce action involving the son of an old friend. The couple insisted that they had no substantial disagreements and wished to avoid the costs of separate representation. Each spouse willingly signed an informed consent form acknowledging that you were serving as a mediator rather than an advocate, and that you had advised them to obtain independent counsel.

The couple was married for 12 years. The wife worked to put the husband through law school and then deferred paid employment for several years in order to care for their two children. She recently returned to her job as a nutrition consultant for medical facilities. The couple plans to share legal custody of the young children; the wife will have physical custody.

After several sessions, the parties have reached an agreement. Although the terms clearly favor the husband, the settlement is still within the range of what you believe a court will approve. The agreement does, however, have several disturbing aspects. First, you have reason to believe that neither party may have been entirely candid in disclosing financial assets. You suspect that the wife receives consulting income that does not appear on the couple's tax returns. You also believe that the husband has understated the potential value of separate property investments in technology companies that are soon likely to go public.

A second difficulty is that the wife has waived spousal maintenance and all interest in certain community property purchased by the husband with his salary income during the marriage. You do not believe that her income will be sufficient to adequately support herself and the children. You are uncertain whether the waiver is attributable to a sense of guilt, principles of fairness, or an unwillingness to take a strong bargaining stance that would provoke conflict. You also have observed patterns of verbal and psychological abuse in the way that the husband relates to his wife. However, she denies that he has ever engaged in physical violence.

A final problem is that, in exchange for the wife's financial concessions, the husband has agreed to reduce his claims for time with the children. He plans to see them only once a month, which you believe is inadequate for their needs. He will also cease taking them for visits to their paternal grandparents, whom the wife dislikes but the children adore.

What is your role if you believe that the financial agreement is unreasonably lopsided? How should you handle the financial disclosure

48. Wetlaufer, *supra* note 45, at 1272–73.

issue? Suppose that you discuss the matters with each party separately and that both affirm their original financial statements without responding fully to your concerns? Are you obligated or permitted to raise your suspicions with the ignorant party or to conduct any independent investigation? How should you handle the husband's concessions concerning visitation if you believe that they are not in the children's best interests?

Assume that you do not further discuss your suspicions about financial disclosures with either party and that the couple disregards the concerns that you note about fairness and visitation. The court grants the divorce and incorporates the mediated settlement in the final decree. Subsequently, the wife decides to return to graduate school and seeks to reopen the decree. Among other things, she claims that her husband fraudulently concealed the true value of his investments and that you failed to inform her of that possibility or to provide adequate financial counseling. She also threatens to sue you for malpractice and seeks damages based on the cost of relitigating the original agreement. What is your likely liability?[49]

NOTES AND QUESTIONS: LAWYERS AND MEDIATION

The Functions of Mediation

A form of dispute resolution that has become increasingly popular over the last two decades is mediation. As defined by the Standard I of the ABA's Model Standards of Practice for Family and Divorce Mediation (2001), this is a process that "relies upon the ability of participants to make their own voluntary and informed decisions." In this process, the primary role of a mediator is "to assist the participants to gain a better understanding of their own needs and the needs and interests of others and to facilitate agreement among the participants." Mediation serves a different function than arbitration, in which a neutral third party imposes a resolution. Rather, in the words of Lon Fuller, the "central quality of mediation [is] its capacity to reorient the parties toward each other, not by imposing rules on them, but by helping them to achieve a new and shared perception of their relationship...."[50] The strengths and limitations of mediation as a form of alternative dispute resolution are explored in Chapter XIII. Discussion here focuses on the ethical issues that arise for lawyer-mediators.

Mediation generally takes two forms: evaluative and facilitative. In evaluative mediation, a neutral third party attempts to help parties resolve their disputes by performing tasks such as providing legal information and assessing the relative strengths and weaknesses of each side's positions. In facilitative mediation, a neutral third party attempts to promote dispute

---

49. See Robert A. Baruch–Bush, "The Dilemmas of Mediation Practice: A Study of Ethical Dilemmas and Policy Implications," *A Report on a Study for the National Institute for Dispute Resolution* 8, 19 (1992); Lange v. Marshall, 622 S.W.2d 237 (Mo.App. 1981).

50. Lon L. Fuller, "Mediation—Its Forms and Functions," *in* Lon L. Fuller, *The Principles of Social Order* 144 (Kenneth I. Winston ed. 1981).

resolution by assisting parties to identify and communicate their interests, and to reach mutually acceptable agreements.[51]

Mediation can occur in disputes of any sort, but has come to special prominence in labor, employment, and family contexts. Family courts often recommend and sometimes require divorcing parties to participate in mediation to work out the details of property and custody settlements. Most professional mediators are not lawyers; their backgrounds are often in psychology, social work, or industrial relations. Yet an increasing number of lawyers have become involved in mediation and some have begun to specialize in the practice.

In disputes involving legal issues, lawyer-mediators can promote agreement by helping the parties minimize conflict, understand their rights, explore underlying problems, and draft a legally enforceable agreement. Lawyers can also be of assistance in representing one of the parties during mediation sessions or in reviewing an agreement afterward. Standard VI of the ABA's Standards of Practice advises consultation with an attorney before concluding an agreement. But engaging separate attorneys imposes some of the financial costs that mediation is often intended to avoid. Moreover, the participation of counsel may compromise parties' control and autonomy, and push them into excessively adversarial bargaining positions. Having a lawyer later review a mediated agreement can be equally problematic. An attorney who has not participated in the negotiations, who does not know what facts came out or what logs were rolled, often cannot judge the fairness of the resulting agreement. In determining whether to obtain independent legal advice, parties need to consider whether they are willing to accept the additional expense and risk of unraveling part of a mediated settlement.

The Lawyer's Role in Mediation

When can a lawyer serve as mediator? The ABA Code treats the issue only briefly in EC 5–20, which notes that lawyers are often asked to assume that role and that when they do, they should not subsequently represent in the dispute any of the parties involved. In the absence of explicit code provisions, some state bar ethics committees initially prohibited lawyers from mediating divorce disputes. Underlying these decisions were concerns about conflicts of interest and inadequate protection for confidentiality. Other bar committees authorized divorce mediation on the theory that the lawyer represents neither party. A third view, put forth by many experts, was that a lawyer-mediator represents both parties.[52] That view inspired a now withdrawn Model Rule (Rule 2.2) on intermediaries. That Rule specified requirements for lawyers serving mediation roles, and included provi-

51. Carrie Menkel–Meadow, "Ethics and Professionalism in Non–Adversarial Lawyering," 27 *Fla. St. U. L. Rev.* 153, 170 (1999).

52. See generally Jonathan A. Beyer, "Practicing Law at the Margins: Surveying Ethics Rules for Legal Associates and Lawyers Who Mediate," 11 *Geo. J. Legal Ethics* 411 (1998); Linda Galler, " 'Practice of Law' in the New Millennium: New Roles, New Rules, But No Definitions," 72 *Temple L. Rev.* 1001 (2000).

sions on conflicts of interest, informed consent, confidentiality, and related issues.

However, many commentators believed that these minimum requirements fell short of establishing an adequate framework for mediation. Accordingly, on recommendation of the Ethics 2000 Commission, the ABA in 2002 deleted the rule. In its place appears Rule 2.4, which merely defines the term "third-party neutral" and requires a lawyer to "explain the difference between the lawyer's role as a third-party neutral and a lawyer's role as one who represents a client."

In comparing the different bar approaches, most experts view the flat ban on lawyer-mediators in divorce cases as unduly restrictive. Recent surveys suggest that in most uncontested divorces, at least one party goes without legal representation. Where parties' resources are limited, joint access to a single attorney-mediator may be preferable to leaving one spouse unrepresented. Whether mediators are nominally "representing" both or neither party seems less critical than the concrete obligations that the relationship entails, such as requirements of impartiality and informed consent.

Standards Governing Mediation

About three quarters of states have adopted some standards to govern the mediation process. Roughly half the states have adopted their own rules governing court-connected mediation programs and a quarter have adopted standards promulgated by some professional associations. The ABA, the American Arbitration Association, and the Society for Professionals in Dispute Resolution (SPIDR) have jointly prepared Model Standards of Conduct for Mediators, revised in 2005. The ABA and National Conference of Commissioners on Uniform State Laws has promulgated a Uniform Mediation Act, which about eight states had adopted by 2007.[53] Other organizations have also developed standards for mediation or alternative dispute resolution generally, or standards for particular areas of practice.[54]

Although these standards differ in some respects, most set forth similar provisions concerning impartiality, conflicts of interest, and confidentiality. For example, the ABA's Model Family Mediation Standards, Standard III and IV require mediators to:

- explain their role and the process;

- discuss obligations concerning confidentiality and ground rules for any separate sessions with one of the parties;

---

53. Susan Nauss Exon, "How Can a Mediator Be Both Impartial and Fair: Why Ethical Standards of Conduct Create Chaos for Mediators," 2006 *J. Dispute Res.* 387, 394–95 (compiling state standards).

54. See the Commission on Ethics and Standards in ADR, cosponsored by the Insti-

tute for Conflict Prevention and Resolution and Georgetown University Law School, which produces standards found at www.cpradr.org, and the ABA Family Mediation Standards noted above.

• inform the parties that they may seek independent advice from attorneys, accountants, therapists, religious advisors, or other professionals during the process;

• disclose any potential grounds of bias or conflict of interest upon which a mediator's impartiality may reasonably be questioned;

• advise the parties of their right to suspend or terminate mediation and the circumstances under which the mediator may suspend or terminate the process;

• obtain parties' written consent (unless they are legally required to enter mediation).

A lawyer may mediate disputes involving past or present clients, provided that all parties give their informed consent and the lawyer has appropriate qualifications and is able to be impartial. In contexts involving family issues, mediators should have knowledge not only concerning the relevant law and the mediation process, but also domestic violence and child development, abuse, and neglect. Standard II. The parties' written agreement to mediate a dispute should include provisions regarding fees, and mediators should not make charges contingent on the resolution of the matter. Standard V.

Under all of these standards, a mediated negotiation is still a negotiation. Accordingly, it presents many of the same ethical problems such as confidentiality and unequal bargaining power that arise in other bargaining contexts.

Confidentiality in Mediation

In contexts of joint representation, the attorney-client privilege generally protects the confidentiality of statements only from disclosure to third parties; the privilege does not apply between the joint clients. The privilege also does not protect disclosures to lay practitioners or to lawyers who do not "represent" either party unless the jurisdiction has specifically extended protection to mediation. The Uniform Mediation Act, Sections 4 and 5, and many analogous state codes, allow mediators and/or parties to assert a privilege against disclosure except under specified conditions, such as where a person has used mediation to plan, commit, or conceal a crime.[55] Rule 408 of the Federal Rules of Evidence and its state analogues hold that statements made in settlement negotiations including mediation are not admissible in subsequent proceedings.[56] Most codes of conduct for mediators advise them to discuss confidentiality requirements at the outset of the process and to maintain parties' reasonable expectations of confidentiality.

55. For an overview of state provisions, see Alan Kirtley,"The Mediation Privilege's Transition from Theory to Implementation: Designing a Mediation Privilege Standard to Protect Mediation Participants, the Process, and the Public Interest," in *Mediation Theory and Practice* 220 (James J. Alfini, Sharon B. Press, Jean R. Sternlight, & Joseph B. Stulberg, eds. 2006).

56. Charles W. Ehrhardt, "Confidentiality, Privilege and Rule 408: The Protection of Mediation Proceedings in Federal Court," in *Mediation Theory and Practice*, *supra* note 54, at 213.

Many mediators also have parties sign confidentiality agreements, although these may not always be enforceable in subsequent disputes.

During the mediation process itself, practitioners differ in the arrangements they make with parties concerning the sharing of information. In some litigation and labor contexts, shuttle diplomacy between opposing camps is the norm; disclosures from these sessions will not be revealed without a party's authorization. By contrast, in divorce cases, separate meetings are less common and information is generally shared.

How should the mediator have handled the disclosure issue in Problem 4? In a case with similar facts, a Missouri appellate court assumed *arguendo* that the attorney had breached his duties by failing to inquire fully into the husband's financial affairs or to advise the wife to litigate the issue. However, the court dismissed the malpractice complaint because the plaintiff had failed to establish that if the attorney had acted differently, she would have obtained a better mediated settlement without the expense of litigation.[57]

How can lawyer-mediators minimize the risks of such complaints? For example, should mediators confront a party whom they suspect is lying in a private caucus and threaten to terminate the mediation unless full disclosure is made? Alternatively would it be enough to require a sworn affidavit with financial disclosures?[58]

Fairness and Impartiality

A fundamental question for mediators is how to balance concerns of fairness and impartiality, particularly in light of inequalities in bargaining power. State codes have adopted differing, sometimes internally inconsistent standards, and practitioners are divided.[59] On one end of the spectrum are mediators who insist on remaining neutral, however skewed the process or outcome. For example, mediators in labor and commercial contexts "regularly deal with parties who are of unequal power, and most have no problem with this inequality. For [these] mediators, the primary function is to have the parties come to an agreement."[60] Such neutrality has the advantage of preserving mediators' credibility and maximizing the chances that participants with superior bargaining leverage will agree to mediated solutions. As Christopher Honeyman notes, there are practical constraints on mediators' abilities to reduce power disparities or to protect unrepresented interests: "If mediators ignored the 'real world' and attempted to base all settlements on reason and brotherly love, stronger parties would obtain little benefit from mediation and would soon avoid it."[61]

57. Lange v. Marshall, 622 S.W.2d 237 (Mo. App.1981).

58. Mark D. Bennett & Michelle S. G. Hermann, *The Art of Mediation* 120–121 (1996).

59. For an overview, see Exon, *supra* note 53, at 401–07.

60. Pamela S. Engram & James R. Markowitz, "Ethical Issues in Mediation: Divorce and Labor Compared," *Mediation Q.*, June 1985, at 19, 23.

61. Christopher Honeyman, "Patterns of Bias in Mediation," 1985 *J. Disp. Resolution* 141, 146.

On the other end of the spectrum are mediators who intervene in order to balance power and to ensure a process as well as a result that meet some minimum standards of fairness. For example, mediators may interrupt intimidating negotiation patterns; meet with the parties separately; structure the bargaining session to equalize participation; provide premediation training to improve participants' negotiating skills; discuss strategies for addressing power disparities with each party; or propose that the disadvantaged party seek therapy or separate legal representation.[62] Many commentators and some ethical codes recommend that mediators withdraw rather than facilitate an unjust settlement.[63] Under Standard XI of the ABA's Model Family Mediation Standards, mediators may consider suspending or terminating the process if:

4. the participants are about to enter into an agreement that the mediator reasonably believes to be unconscionable;

5. a participant is using the mediation to further illegal conduct;

6. a participant is using the mediation process to gain an unfair advantage.

What constitutes unfairness or unconscionability in a particular case is, however, often open to dispute.

Underlying these issues are more fundamental questions about the meaning of neutrality in mediation. To some commentators, neutrality requires mediators to prevent their own values from biasing the process. By contrast, others believe that neutrality requires structuring a process that will ensure meaningful participation, informed decision making and a reasonable balance of power.[64] Model Rule 4.5.6 proposed by the Commission on Ethics and Standards in ADR attempts to strike a balance. It provides that:

c) The third party neutral should use all reasonable efforts to conduct the process with fairness to all parties....

d) The third party neutral should make reasonable efforts to prevent misconduct that would invalidate any settlement. The third party neutral should also make reasonable efforts to determine that the parties have reached agreement of their own volition and knowingly consent to any settlement.

The comment to the proposed Rule adds:

62. Bennett & Hermann, *supra* note 58, at 120–21; Hughes, *supra* note 5; Albie M. Davis & Richard A. Salem, "Dealing with Power Imbalances in the Mediation of Interpersonal Disputes," *Mediation Q.*, Dec. 1984, at 17, 20–21, 25.

63. See "More Tips for When Mediation Impasse Strikes Also: Ethical Dilemmas at the Negotiating Table," *supra* note 4, at 181 (quoting Carrie Menkel–Meadow regarding withdrawal to avert a settlement that is substantively unfair or has resulted from false information) Hughes, *supra* note 5, at 594–95 (advising mediators not to accept an agreement outside the range that a court would approve unless the weaker party is making an informed and voluntary decision and is not subject to a disability).

64. Exon, *supra* note 53, at 402–06.

[2] This section requires third party neutrals to make reasonable efforts to determine that the parties have reached an agreement of their own volition, one that is not coerced. While some have suggested that third party neutrals should bear some moral accountability or legal responsibility for the agreements they help facilitate, these Rules do not make the third party neutral the guarantor of a fair or just result.

So too, as noted above, the ABA Model Family Mediation Standards permit, but do not require, mediators to withdraw rather than facilitate an unfair agreement. Standard XI. In commenting on this approach, Andrew Schepard, reporter for the Standards, notes that while they impose some requirements of procedural fairness, no dispute resolution process, including mediation, can "remedy fundamental preexisting inequities in power or legal entitlements between participants. That job is for legislatures or courts."[65] Do you agree? How would you proceed in Problem 4?

A related issue is the extent to which mediators should consider fairness to unrepresented parties such as children. Standard VIII of the ABA Model Family Mediation Standards states that "a family mediator shall assist participants in determining how to promote the best interests of the children." Is that version preferable to other codes which impose a duty on mediators to promote the best interest of the children? What would such standards require on the facts of problem 4?

Cases Inappropriate for Mediation

Given the difficulties for mediators in simultaneously addressing power disparities and maintaining impartiality, many experts believe that certain cases involving such disparities are inappropriate for mediation. Domestic violence cases are a commonly cited example. Court-sponsored diversion programs that provide for mediation of minor abuse charges have been subject to considerable criticism. According to critics, mediation places the parties on equal footing and invites compromise. As a result, it may lead to inappropriate concessions and fail to deter abusive conduct or coercive bargaining. By implying that parties share responsibility for past problems and future solutions, the process may pressure victims to modify their own behavior in exchange for a batterers' promises not to commit further crimes. Moreover, successful mediation generally requires that both parties desire to settle the conflict, that weaker parties be able to assert their interests, and that stronger parties be willing to abide by concessions reflected in a final agreement. Such characteristics are often missing in domestic violence cases. Critics also claim that allowing mediation "undermines the criminal justice system's message to batterers that their conduct is illegal and wrong."[66]

---

65. Andrew Schepard, "An Introduction to the Model Standards of Practice for Family and Divorce Mediation," 35 *Fam. L. Q.* 1, 16 (2001).

66. Joanne Fuller and Rose Mary Lyons, "Mediation Guidelines" 33 *Willamette L. Rev.* 905, 911 (1997). See sources cited in René L. Rimelspach, "Mediating Family Disputes in a World With Domestic Violence:

However, critics of mediation often are equally critical of conventional law enforcement and adjudicatory strategies, because penalties are often minor and leave fundamental problems unacknowledged. In divorce and custody contexts where abuse is present, adversarial approaches can escalate conflict and encourage patterns of blame, denial, and intimidation that perpetuate the problem. By contrast, a properly structured mediation process can encourage parties to acknowledge abusive patterns and devise workable responses. Some evidence suggests that such a process can lessen incidents of abuse and that women who have experienced violence generally want the right to choose whether mediation is in their best interest.[67]

Many supporters of mediation accordingly conclude that a carefully designed mediation process may be preferable to the alternatives for some parties. Such a process should include safeguards such as:

- providing adequate training for the mediator;
- screening to exclude cases where concerns about safety, intimidation, and control cannot be adequately addressed;
- encouraging parties to obtain assistance from an attorney or lay advocate;
- referring parties to appropriate therapeutic and community resources;
- permitting either party to opt out of the process at any time;
- suspending or terminating the process if concerns such as safety and intimidation arise.[68]

Is such an approach consistent with a mediator's impartiality? Should it be extended to other contexts of power imbalance?

Some commentators also have been critical of mediation in divorce contexts, particularly the mandatory mediation programs that many states have established for contested child custody cases. From critics' perspective, the empowering potential of mediation is undermined when the process is imposed rather than chosen. Subordinate groups may be particularly vulnerable to a process that lacks checks on racial, ethnic, or gender bias and that excludes advocates who can assert weaker parties' rights. The risks are particularly great for women who are unequally situated in income and power, and in mediation programs that do not make appropriate provision for cases involving allegations of abuse.[69] Supporters of mediation respond that the evidence does not show that women fare worse in mediation than in litigation or in other negotiation or dispute resolution processes.

How to Devise a Safe and Effective Court–Connected Mediation Program," 17 *Ohio St. J. Dispute Resolution* 95, 96–98 (2001).

67. Rimelspach, *supra* note 66; Peter Salem & Ann L. Milne, "Making Mediation Work in a Domestic Violence Case," *Fam. Advoc.* Winter 1995, at 34.

68. ABA Model Family Mediation Standards, Standard X; Rimelspach, *supra* note 66.

69. Penelope Eileen Bryan, "Collaborative Divorce: Meaningful Reform or Another Quick Fix?" 5 *Psych. Pub. Pol. & L.* 1001 (1999); Rita Henley Jensen, "Divorce–Mediation Style," *ABA J.* Feb. 1997, at 57.

Indeed, in most studies, men and women express approximately equal satisfaction with mediation as a dispute resolution process. Furthermore, women report that mediation is helpful to them in "standing up" to their spouses, and rated themselves more capable and knowledgeable as a result of participation in mediation.[70]

What is your view? How would you handle the fairness issues in Problems 4 and 5?[71]

---

70. Schepard, *supra* note 65, at 17.

71. For further reading, *see Mediation: Theory, Policy and Practice* (Carrie Menkel–Meadow ed. 2001).

CHAPTER IX

THE LAWYER'S COUNSELING ROLE

INTRODUCTION

In an influential joint report on professional responsibility, the American Bar Association and the Association of American Law Schools emphasized that lawyers' opportunities for ethical influence are generally greatest in their counseling and advising role. This chapter explores that role in four representative contexts: corporate, tax, family, and government practice.

Each of these areas raises distinctive challenges. Ethical dilemmas in corporate counseling often involve the competing interests of various groups: management, shareholders, employees, customers, and the broader community. Tax practice presents special ethical pressures partly because the temptations for clients to cut corners are particularly great. Their risk of suffering significant penalties is generally small and their sense of moral responsibility to government tax collectors is generally limited. Family practice poses other difficulties because the issues involved often carry considerable emotional as well as ethical freight. Parties have more personally at stake and have greater difficulties making rational decisions than in most other contexts. Moreover, the interests of vulnerable third parties—typically children—may be directly implicated but not formally represented. And government lawyers offering opinions on the meaning of legal constraints can have immense effect on the formulation of public policy. In our chief example—the role of executive branch lawyers in the formulation of interrogation policy in the "war on terror"—many people believe that highly permissive legal opinions paved the way to torture and abuse. Consider how these concerns should affect the lawyer's counseling role in the circumstances described below.

A. COUNSELING FRAMEWORKS

Lon L. Fuller and John D. Randall, "Professional Responsibility: Report of the Joint Conference"

44 A.B.A.J. 1159, 1161 (1958).

The Lawyer's Role as Counselor

Vital as is the lawyer's role in adjudication, it should not be thought that it is only as an advocate pleading in open court that he contributes to the administration of the law. The most effective realization of the law's aims often takes place in the attorney's office, where litigation is forestalled by anticipating its outcome, where the lawyer's quiet counsel takes place of public force. Contrary to popular belief, the compliance with the law thus brought about is not generally lip-serving and narrow, for by reminding him of its long-run costs the lawyer often deters his client from a course of conduct technically permissible under existing law, though inconsistent with its underlying spirit and purpose.

Although the lawyer serves the administration of justice indispensably both as advocate and as office counselor, the demands imposed on him by these two roles must be sharply distinguished. The man who has been called into court to answer for his own actions is entitled to a fair hearing. Partisan advocacy plays its essential part in such a hearing, and the lawyer pleading his client's case may properly present it in the most favorable light. A similar resolution of doubts in one direction becomes inappropriate when the lawyer acts as counselor. The reasons that justify and even require partisan advocacy in the trial of a cause do not grant any license to the lawyer to participate as legal adviser in a line of conduct that is immoral, unfair, or of doubtful legality. In saving himself from this unworthy involvement, the lawyer cannot be guided solely by an unreflective inner sense of good faith; he must be at pains to preserve a sufficient detachment from his client's interests so that he remains capable of a sound and objective appraisal of the propriety of what his client proposes to do.

NOTES ON CLIENT–CENTERED, COLLABORATIVE, AND CONTEXTUAL APPROACHES TO COUNSELING

Model Rule 2.1 requires lawyers in an advisory role to "exercise independent professional judgment and render candid advice." The rule continues, "In rendering advice, a lawyer may refer not only to law but to other considerations such as moral, economic, social and political factors, that may be relevant to the client's situation." Although there is no caselaw interpreting this rule, the Comments explain the meaning of the twin requirements of independence and candor:

> Legal advice often involves unpleasant facts and alternatives that a client may be disinclined to confront. In presenting advice, a lawyer endeavors to sustain the client's morale and may put advice in as acceptable a form as honesty permits. However, a lawyer should not be deterred from giving candid advice by the prospect that the advice will be unpalatable to the client.[1]

The rule also gives lawyers substantial leeway to base their advice on non-legal factors. Here too, the Comment on the rule explains the point:

> Advice couched in narrow legal terms may be of little value to a client, especially where practical considerations, such as cost or effects on

---

1. Model Rules of Professional Conduct, Rule 2.1, cmt 1.

other people, are predominant. Purely technical legal advice, therefore, can sometimes be inadequate. It is proper for a lawyer to refer to relevant moral and ethical considerations in giving advice. Although a lawyer is not a moral advisor as such, moral and ethical considerations impinge upon most legal questions and may decisively influence how the law will be applied.[2]

These standards raise important questions about how lawyers should bring moral and ethical standards into their counseling role. Most contemporary approaches to ethics in counseling have taken three basic forms: client-centered, collaborative, and contextual.[3] Although the boundaries among these approaches often blur, they do help identify different understandings of lawyers' moral responsibilities in advising clients.

What distinguishes client-centered counseling, as the term suggests, is the priority that it places on client autonomy.[4] Underlying this approach is a belief that clients have the right and capacity to determine their own objectives. In the often-quoted words of Elihu Root, "The client never wants to be told he can't do what he wants to do; he wants to be told how to do it, and it is the lawyer's business to tell him how."[5] As proponents note, the lawyer-client relationship is one of agency, which presupposes that attorneys will defer to the party who has retained them, and who will have to live with the results of the representation. This emphasis on autonomy has distinguished philosophical ancestry: Immanuel Kant argued that individual autonomy is the supreme value, the only thing that is good in itself. That is because the exercise of free will is what distinguishes rational beings from the rest of nature.[6] Many philosophers follow Kant in the special value they place on autonomy.[7] Because autonomy counts as a pre-eminent moral value, enhancing the client's autonomy is a morally desirable goal.[8]

Critics of this client-centered approach raise concerns on two levels. As a descriptive matter, it does not accurately reflect the role that ethical values other than concern for client autonomy in fact play in counseling relationships. Elihu Root is also credited with saying that "about half the practice of a decent lawyer consists of telling would-be clients that they are

2. *Id.* at cmt 2.

3. See Robert F. Cochran, Jr. et al., "Symposium: Client Counseling and Moral Responsibility," 30 *Pepperdine L. Rev.* 591 (2003); Deborah L. Rhode, "Ethics in Counseling," 30 *Pepperdine L. Rev.* 591 (2003).

4. David A. Binder et al., *Lawyers as Counselors: A Client–Centered Approach* (1991); Robert M. Bastress & Joseph D. Harbaugh, *Interviewing, Counseling, and Negotiating: Skills for Effective Representation* (1990); David A. Binder & Susan C. Price, *Legal Interviewing and Counseling: A Client Centered Approach* (1977).

5. 1 Robert Swaine, *The Cravath Firm and Its Predecessors, 1819–1947* (1946) (quot-

ing Elihu Root, one of the founders of Cravath, Swaine & Moore).

6. Immanuel Kant, *Foundations of the Metaphysics of Morals* (1785); often translated under the title *Groundwork of the Metaphysics of Morals* or *Fundamental Principles of the Metaphysics of Morals*.

7. *See generally* J. B. Schneewind, *The Invention of Autonomy: A History of Modern Moral Philosophy* (1998).

8. Stephen L. Pepper, "The Lawyer's Amoral Ethical Role: A Defense, A Problem, and Some Possibilities," 1986 *ABF Res. J.* 613, 617.

damned fools and should stop."[9] And as a normative matter, it does not capture the role that values other than client autonomy *should* play, in order to serve both client and societal interests.

In describing counseling relationships, most client-centered commentary assumes that individuals seek legal assistance to pursue interests that are autonomously determined and that lawyers' basic responsibility is to provide "neutral," "nonjudgmental" assistance.[10] Because clients have the best understanding of their own preferences, an advisor's role should be to enhance their decision-making capacity, not to impose the advisor's own values. Yet even when lawyers strive to be neutral, the manner in which they present information cannot help but shape clients' analysis. Lawyers' own values often unconsciously shape their assessments of legal risks and options. And those assessments in turn shape clients' understandings of their own interests and values. The full autonomy that client-centered theory assumes is seldom realizable in practice.

A second limitation of client-centered approaches is the extent to which they identify client autonomy with helping clients accomplish whatever they desire. Although many philosophers follow Kant in regarding autonomy as a supreme value, Kant meant by "autonomy" something quite different than simply doing whatever one wishes. Kantian autonomy means the power to act on the basis of duty—in other words, the ability to think and act for moral reasons rather than simply following inclinations. Other moral philosophers argue that individual autonomy is not valuable in itself. It derives its importance from other values it fosters, such as personal creativity, initiative, and responsibility.[11] If a particular client objective does not, in fact, promote those values, or does so only at much greater cost to third parties, then deference to that objective lacks ethical justification.[12] Although lawyers generally have less expertise in assessing clients' preferences than clients themselves, lawyers also may have greater capacity to make a disinterested evaluation of third-party concerns. Given the role that self-serving biases play in human decision making, attorneys may be better situated to identify harms that client choices may have on other individuals.[13]

Of course, as a practical matter, lawyers' deference to clients makes perfect sense. Clients are, after all, generally the ones footing the bill for lawyers' services. But from a moral standpoint, placing absolute priority on client autonomy is difficult to justify, particularly when the client is an

---

9. Philip C. Jessup, 1 *Elihu Root* 134 (1964).

10. Binder & Price, *supra* note 4, at 288; Bastress and Harbaugh, *supra* note 4, at 57. For an overview, Katherine R. Kruse, "Fortress in the Sand: The Plural Values of Client–Centered Representation," 12 *Clinical L. Rev.* 369 (2006).

11. David Luban, "Partisanship, Betrayal and Autonomy in the Lawyer–Client Relationship: A Reply to Stephen Ellmann," 90 *Colum. L. Rev.* 1004, 1035–43 (1990).

12. Luban, *supra* note 11; Deborah L. Rhode, *In the Interests of Justice* 66–67 (2000); Deborah L. Rhode, "Moral Counseling," 75 *Fordham L. Rev.* 1317, 1330 (2006).

13. Thomas Gilovich, *How We Know What Isn't So: The Fallacy of Human Reason in Everyday Life* 49 (1990); Paul Tremblay, "Client–Centered Counseling and Moral Activism," 30 *Pepperdine L. Rev.* 615, 623 (2003).

organization rather than an individual. An artificial entity like a corporation or a school district has no personality and no autonomy (except as a figure of speech). A corporation's "right" to maximize profits through unsafe or misleading but imperfectly regulated methods can hardly take ethical precedence over individuals' rights to be free from unreasonable risks. Client-centered representation has led to lawyers' complicity in some of the most socially costly enterprises in recent memory: the distribution of asbestos and Dalkon shields; the suppression of health information about cigarettes; and the financially irresponsible ventures of savings and loan associations and corporations such as Enron.[14]

As officers of the court and gatekeepers in regulatory processes, lawyers have obligations that transcend those owed to any particular client.[15] Honesty, trust, and fairness are collective goods; neither legal nor market systems can function effectively if lawyers lack a basic sense of social responsibility for the consequences of their professional acts. In the corporate scandals of recent decades, client-centered representation was part of the problem, not the solution.

A related difficulty with client-centered approaches is that they reinforce a restrictive role that often ill serves even client interests. The problems are greatest when a client's judgment is impaired. As Chapter XII notes, the impairment may spring from multiple causes: youth, mental health disabilities, peer pressures, economic constraints, or psychological traumas such as divorce. Under such circumstances, individuals may be poorly situated to take a long term view of their interests or live up to their own moral values.

A variety of cognitive biases often prevents even seemingly rational business clients from accurately assessing facts that are economically inconvenient to acknowledge. Situational influences and psychological predispositions often converge to lead managers of organizations to overlook or rationalize unsafe and fraudulent activity.[16] For example, short-term profit incentives tempt decision makers to discount non-quantifiable considerations such as public reaction and the risks of detection. Once managers have committed to particular projects, they are inclined to construe events in ways that confirm prior beliefs, and downplay countervailing evidence. The same optimism and self-confidence that make managers successful

14. See Rhode, "Moral Counseling," *supra* note 12, at 56–57; Lincoln Savings and Loan Association v. Wall, 743 F.Supp. 901 (D.D.C. 1990); Deborah L. Rhode & Paul Paton, "Lawyers, Ethics, and Enron," 8 *Stan. J. Law & Business* 9 (2002).

15. Rhode, "Moral Counseling," *supra* note 12, at 65–66; Robert W. Gordon, "Why Lawyers Can't Just Be Hired Guns," in *Ethics in Practice: Lawyers' Roles, Responsibilities, and Regulation* 42 (Deborah L. Rhode, ed. 2000).

16. See the materials excerpted below and in Chapter VII as well as those in Rhode, "Moral Counseling," *supra* note 12, at 1321–24; Sung Hui Kim, "The Banality of Fraud: Re–Situating the Inside Counsel as Gatekeeper," 74 *Fordham L. Rev.* 983 (2005). Donald C. Langevoort, "The Organizational Psychology of Hyper–Competition: Corporate Irresponsibility and the Lessons of Enron," 70 *Geo. Wash. L. Rev.* 968 (2002); Donald C. Langevoort, "The Epistemology of Corporate–Securities Lawyering: Beliefs, Biases and Organizational Behavior," 63 *Brooklyn L. Rev.* 629 (1997); Richard W. Painter, "Irrationality and Cognitive Bias at a Closing In Arthur Solmssen's *The Comfort Letter*," 69 *Fordham L. Rev.* 1111 (2000).

sometimes lead them to discount risks.[17] Such "cognitive conservatism" and "overconfidence effects" may blind decision makers to evidence of deception or adverse social consequences.[18] Group decision making processes can compound the problem. Diffusion of responsibility and fears (often justifiable) of alienating colleagues may work to suppress unwelcome information.[19] Lawyers no less than clients are subject to such cognitive biases. A definition of professional role that encourages deference to clients' current preference may poorly serve their ultimate interests.

A similar problem arises when clients are entities that can only speak through agents with competing concerns. Managers' desires to maximize their own income, power, or status within an organization may encourage decisions that are not in the broader interest of other stakeholders. Since lawyers' ethical responsibilities run to the entity, not to any particular constituent, their counseling responsibilities need to take account of such conflicting concerns.[20] Yet some client-centered commentary ignores these responsibilities, and assumes a kind of individual counseling relationship that is out of touch with organizational complexities. The Enron case offers a classic illustration of a client who encouraged a race to the bottom by its legal counselors. When one firm didn't provide the answer managers wanted to hear, they retained another.

The second main approach to counseling, which stresses collaboration between lawyers and clients, offers many of the same strengths as client-centered approaches while at least partly compensating for their major limitations. As the term suggests, collaborative counseling envisions lawyers and clients as coventurers in problem solving and jointly responsible for its ethical implications. In general, the client's preferred course of action prevails unless the attorney finds it "morally wrong."[21] Yet collaborative frameworks also recognize that one of lawyers' most valuable contributions is to engage and enlarge their clients' moral vision, and to encourage decisions that express parties' highest principles.[22] By the same token, of course, clients can enlarge lawyers' moral vision; the collaborative approach to counseling favors dialogue that is a genuine two-way street. As

---

17. Langevoort, "Dilemma," *supra* note 16, at 642; Langevoort, "Taking Myths Seriously: An Essay for Lawyers," 74 *Chi.–Kent L. Rev.* 1569 (2000); Painter, *supra* note 12, at 1132; Rhode, *supra* note 1, at 609, and Rhode, *supra* note 8.

18. Painter, *supra* note 16, at 1131; Langevoort, "Dilemma," *supra* note 16, at 641–42; Donald C. Langevoort, "Taking Myths Seriously: An Essay for Lawyers," 74 *Chi. Kent L. Rev.* 1569, 1573 (2000); Susan T. Fisk & Shelley E. Taylor, *Social Cognition*, 149–51 (2d ed. 1991).

19. Chris Argerys, *Overcoming Organizational Defenses: Facilitating Organizational Learning* (1990); Langevoort, "Dilemma," *supra* note 16, at 637, 640, 651–52; Deborah L. Rhode, "If Integrity Is the Answer, What Is

the Question?", 72 *Fordham L. Rev.* 333, 343 (2003).

20. See ABA Model Rules of Professional Conduct, Rule 1.13 (2002), discussed in Chapter VII, *supra,* and William H. Simon, "After Confidentiality: Rethinking the Professional Responsibilities of the Business Lawyer," 75 *Fordham L. Rev.* 1453, 1464 (2006).

21. Thomas L. Shaffer & Robert F. Cochran, *Lawyers, Clients, and Moral Responsibility* 51 (1994).

22. *Id. See also* Kruse, *supra* note 10, at 432–433 (discussing a "client-empowering" view of counseling that aims to connect clients to their deepest values, or higher order desires, which may be obscured by more immediate pressures).

Chapter VIII noted, a promising application of this approach is reflected in the branch of family law practice that has claimed the same term.[23] Under this approach, parties commit to collaborate with each other as well as with their lawyers in seeking fair, out-of-court agreements based on full disclosure. If the parties fail to reach such a settlement, the lawyers may not represent them in further proceedings, a condition designed to give all participants a substantial stake in mutually beneficial problem solving.

This approach has its own limitations. If lawyers must withdraw when unable to achieve a negotiated resolution, the costs of reeducating new counsel may be sufficient to coerce some participants into accepting undesirable agreements. Individuals who are most in need of ethical advice are probably least likely to agree to collaborative approaches. Moreover, under competitive pressures, the risk is that even collaborative lawyers will too closely identify with clients' interests. Many of the lawyers involved in Enron found their client's conduct not so unambiguously illegal or immoral that they were unable to rationalize assistance. Vinson & Elkins, the primary law firm representing Enron, managed to find its highly misleading accounting strategies "creative and aggressive," not deceptive or fraudulent.[24] It is scarcely coincidental that this admiration involved a client that had accounted for a substantial proportion of the firm's annual revenue, and had employed some twenty of the firm's former lawyers. In such circumstances, collaborative approaches that cast lawyers as coventurers with their clients risk understating the need for independent judgment and the economic pressures that get in the way.

A final approach to counseling is more contextual and acknowledges a greater responsibility for the consequences of professional advice. As the label "contextual" indicates, under this approach, lawyers must decide how client-centered their assistance should be under the particular circumstances of their representation. Relevant factors include the significance of the ethical concerns at issue, and the lawyer's information, responsibility, and capacity to affect outcomes. Unlike either the "client-centered" model, which makes the client's autonomous objectives preeminent, or the "collaborative" model, which invites the client, in consultation with the attorney, to "draw on his own moral resources" in resolving issues, contextual approaches acknowledge a significant independent role for the lawyers' own ethical judgments.[25] What this approach entails will vary on the context. A morally justifiable response need not involve imposing values on a client.

---

23. Pauline H. Tesler, *Collaborative Law: Achieving Effective Resolution in Divorce Without Litigation* (2001); James K. Lawrence, "Collaborative Lawyering: A New Development in Conflict Resolution," 17 *Ohio St. J. Dispute Res.* 431 (2002). See http://www.collaborativelaw.com

24. Patti Waldmeir, "Inside Track—A Failure to Squeal," *Financial Times*, Jan. 24, 2002, (quoting Vinson & Elkins memorandum). For discussion of the misleading nature of Enron's conduct, see sources cited in

Rhode & Paton, *supra* note 14; William C. Powers, Report of Investigation by the Special Investigative Committee of the Board of Directors of Enron Corp., Feb. 1, 2002, and sources cited in Chapter VII.

25. Among the theorists commonly included in this school are Rhode, Luban, and Simon. See Rhode, *supra* note 1 and "Moral Counseling," *supra* note 12; David Luban, *Lawyers and Justice: An Ethical Study* 169–74 (1988); William H. Simon, *The Practice of Justice* (1998).

Rather, the lawyer's willingness to take a stance may simply encourage clients to reconsider their position, or to accept the financial and psychological consequences of finding alternative counsel.

Like the other approaches, contextual counseling has its drawbacks. Most obviously, clients may resent overly-intrusive counseling by their lawyers, particularly if the clients have asked what they consider to be a purely legal question. So too, even though Model Rule 2.1 gives substantial leeway for lawyers to engage in moral advice, that role may be an unfamiliar one for which lawyers' training does not necessarily equip them. In the problems that follow, students should consider the implications of each of the three models, in order to determine which seems most appropriate.

B. CORPORATE PRACTICE
PROBLEM 1

You are a litigation partner in a small Midwestern law firm. One of the firm's major clients manufactures a profitable chemical solvent that is currently under investigation by the Environmental Protection Agency (EPA) and Occupational Safety and Health Administration (OSHA). Certain recently published data as well as your client's own preliminary studies suggest that prolonged contact with the solvent during manufacture or use may slightly increase the risks of cancer and birth defects among exposed workers. Total elimination of these risks would be prohibitively expensive. Less toxic substitutes for the solvent are available from competing firms but at substantially higher costs.

Government data also indicate that improper disposal of the product after use could create hazards if significant amounts enter groundwater sources. Current EPA standards prohibit discharges above .050 grams per liter of effluent. Compliance with that standard is quite expensive. You know from informal sources that violations of .075 or less are largely ignored because of a limited enforcement budget, and that inspections are relatively rare in the rural areas where your client's plants are located. EPA officials typically issue a warning before applying sanctions unless the violation is extreme (more than 1.5 grams per liter). Your preliminary investigation reveals that some of the client's plants routinely release the solvent at levels between .75 and 1.00 grams per liter.[26]

In your judgment, the client has a non-frivolous but unconvincing argument that continued manufacture and sale of the solvent is lawful under prevailing statutory standards. You also believe that those standards should, and soon will be, strengthened. However, by pursuing all procedural opportunities, your firm could probably delay application of any standards banning domestic manufacture and sale of the solvent for several years. Even after that point, the company could continue to export stock-

---

26. The discharge limit issues are modeled on a hypothetical problem discussed in Stephen L. Pepper, "Counseling at the Limits of the Law: An Exercise in the Jurisprudence and Ethics of Lawyering," 104 *Yale Law Journal* 1545 (1995).

piled inventory to developing countries with less rigorous safeguards, who need such materials at the lowest possible cost.

Although you oppose continued manufacture or export, neither the other partner working on the case nor the company's top executives share your view. As they point out, the manufacturer's major plant is the mainstay of the local economy and closure would cause severe financial difficulties for the entire community. In their view, employees' risks of cancer are no greater than in many other occupational contexts. Since much of the data on carcinogenic effects are now publicly available, the CEO believes workers should make their own choices about whether to continue employment. Similarly, most of the company's senior managers are convinced that foreign countries should be free to adopt whatever tradeoffs between environmental and economic values they deem advisable. According to the CEO, attempts to impose American standards are a form of cultural imperialism.

QUESTIONS

1. Assume that you believe a neutral tribunal would find that continued domestic manufacture of the solvent is unlawful under existing statutory standards. If the company's in-house counsel disagrees, what are your counseling obligations?

2. Alternatively, suppose that you believe that continued manufacture of the product may be lawful but that it poses an unreasonable risk to public and worker safety. You are also convinced that exporting the solvent to countries without adequate environmental regulation is morally indefensible. How should you proceed? Should, or must you take steps to ensure consideration of the issue by corporate directors, stockholders, or governmental decision makers?

3. Assume that the Board ratifies management's decision to continue domestic manufacture and export while the matter is under EPA and OSHA review. About 15 percent of your firm's litigation profits come from representing this client on a variety of matters. Other partners in your firm strongly oppose withdrawal of representation on the EPA and OSHA cases since it would antagonize management without affecting corporate policy. If you continue to find the client's position objectionable, what is your response?

4. Should you inform your client about what you know concerning the EPA's enforcement of discharge limit? What if you believe that such information might persuade plant managers to continue, or to begin discharging effluents above the 0.050 limit? Would it matter why enforcement was lax in rural areas and whether EPA practices were widely known in the industry? Suppose the .050 discharge limit was set with urban areas in mind, where the mix of other pollutants and the density of population made the harms from contaminated discharge more serious than in rural areas. Alternatively, suppose that the less frequent sanctions in those areas

reflected insufficient agency resources and the greater expense involved in testing at rural sites.

5.   What if you are unsure about the reasons for the EPA's enforcement policy? Does competent representation always require providing clients with information about the likelihood and severity of sanctions?[27]

References:

Model Rules 1.2, 1.4, 1.13, 1.16, 2.1.

NOTES

The issues raised in the preceding problem are not uncommon. As Chapter VII noted, many industrial products and practices involve price/safety tradeoffs. National and international boycotts have also raised questions about the morality of exporting hazards that violate American safety standards but not those of the host country. Consider lawyers' personal and professional responsibilities in light of the readings that follow.

Robert W. Gordon, "The Independence of Lawyers"

68 Boston University Law Rev. 1, 26–28, 71–75 (1988).

Take one of the most routine contexts of business law practice, compliance counseling. The client hopes to seize a profitable opportunity. The plan is routed through the lawyer's office and is seen to pose a potential problem: some legal doctrine or regulation arguably prohibits the plan. What can the lawyer do? Here is a simple, nonexhaustive array of the types of advice a lawyer can give in the context of compliance counseling. The lawyer might advise that a plan:

- may comply with the technical language of the law but not conform to its spirit or to general norms of responsible social conduct, and it should be altered for the sake of appearance; or

- may conform to the general purpose of the law but does not comply with its technical requirements and the company may not wish to take the risk of sanctions;

- may be legal but could be altered to accomplish the same business purpose while also promoting other legal and social objectives.

If the lawyer opposes the plan but is overruled, available courses of action include:

- carrying objections to a higher level of management or the Board of Directors;

- seeking discretely to modify the most objectionable parts of the plan, or insist on recording objections and reservations in Board minutes, opinions or memos to the file;

---

27.   *See* Pepper, *supra* note 26, at 1570–75.

- refusing to participate further in the plan;

- withdrawing from representation;

- warning the client that if the proposed course of action proceeds, the lawyer will make public disclosure....

These are naturally just a tiny handful of the choices to be made regarding the form and content of advice given in the course of compliance counseling, the persons in the organization to whom such advice is given, the tactics one can resort to if one meets opposition. All these choices—except disclosure and withdrawal, which may be regulated—are well within the conventional boundaries of the counselor's role. Which choices are actually made will be a function of the lawyer's situation and convictions, the lawyer's personal courage and confidence, the relations of authority and trust the lawyer has with the managers involved, the lawyer's own position in the hierarchy of the company or outside firm, the importance of the client to the firm, the firm's place in the legal services market, the lawyer's degree of practical knowledge of the business (which will crucially affect the lawyer's ability to suggest alternatives), the form of advice managers prefer to hear from their lawyers, and the general compliance culture of the company (does it walk the line and play hardball with regulators or try to anticipate regulatory problems and initiate its own solutions?).

Obviously most lawyers, or at least lawyers for big, powerful companies, will avoid abrasive and unnecessary confrontations with their clients. They will phrase negative advice as prudential rather than moralistic, supporting their recommendations with reasons that sound much more like statements of technical rules or empirical predictions of risks and results than political or moral judgments....

Probably the most common critique of the independence ideal is that it either conflicts with the ideal of client loyalty or arrogates to lawyers an improper role in political decisionmaking, or both.... Underlying the illegitimacy critique is the central belief that lawyers' roles begin and end with vigorously pursuing their clients' interests within the limits of the law. Rather than injecting any of their own political views into the lawyering process, they should simply function as an extension of their clients' interests, accepting those interests according to the terms the clients use to characterize them....

Although this position is very commonplace, I think it rests on incoherent premises and leads to indefensible conclusions.... [The] position appears to license an untempered adversarial advocacy which when aggregated could easily nullify the purposes of any and every legal regime. Take any simple case of compliance counseling: suppose the legal rule is clear, yet the chance of detecting violations low, the penalties small in relation to the gains from noncompliance, or the terrorizing of regulators into settlement by a deluge of paper predictably easy. The mass of lawyers who advise and then assist with noncompliance in such a situation could, in the vigorous pursuit of their clients' interests, effectively nullify the laws....

[Yet] lawyers do indeed have an official status as licensed fiduciaries for the public interest, charged with encouraging compliance with legal norms. In contexts like counseling, where there is no official third party like a judge to oversee the interaction between the client and the state, the lawyer is not only supposed to predict the empirical consequences of certain behavior, but also to represent the viewpoint of the legal system to the client.... Why should everybody else around the corporation—the engineers, the financial people, the safety and health division—be permitted to deliberate upon and engage in the internal politics of the corporation to promote their views of its best interests, but not the lawyers?

Robert W. Gordon: "A New Role for Lawyers?: The Corporate Counselor after Enron"

35 Conn. L. Rev. 1185 (2003).

[In an opening section of the article, Professor Gordon reports what is publicly known and ethically problematic about lawyers' assistance to Enron.

- Lawyers wrote opinions certifying disguised loans as "true sales" to make it possible for Enron to show debts as earnings;

- Lawyers facilitated management self-dealing by not insisting on disclosure of huge management fees paid by "Special Purpose Entities" to top Enron officials (e.g. over $30 million to Andrew Fastow). Lawyers asserted in SEC filings that such management agreements were negotiated at "arms length" and "on comparable terms" as agreements with other parties but did not seek any factual support for these patently dubious assertions.

- After a vice president warned Enron's chairman about potentially devastating scandals, the Vinson & Elkins law firm agreed to conduct an investigation although its lawyers had participated in some of the transactions at issue and the scope of its investigation was limited to exclude the accounting practices that permitted financial problems to escalate. The firm's report warned that the "bad cosmetics" of the transactions could result in adverse publicity and litigation, but concluded that "no further investigation was necessary." (For additional details, see the materials on the Enron case in Chapter VII, *supra*.)]

II. SOME EXCUSES FOR WHAT THE LAWYERS DID

It is clear that the advice both in-house lawyers and outside law firms gave to the managers of Enron and other companies like it was instrumental in enabling those managers to cream off huge profits for themselves while bringing economic ruin to investors, employees, and the taxpaying public. Although the lawyers were not principally responsible for these acts of waste and fraud, their advice was a contributing (and often necessary) cause of those acts. Such fraud could not have been carried out without the lawyers' active approval, passive acquiescence, or failure to inquire and investigate. Nonetheless, not only the lawyers involved but large numbers of practitioners and bar committees have few or no regrets about the part they played. They vigorously justify their conduct as consistent with the highest conceptions of legal, ethical, and professional propriety, and just as vigorously resist all attempts to change the legal and ethical rules so as to increase their obligations as gatekeepers and monitors of managers' conduct. This attitude is not universal—there are prominent corporate lawyers who dissent from it, and think the profession is failing to live up to its responsibilities; but it is pervasive.

How are we to understand why the lawyers acted as they did, and why they are justifying their actions now? Observers from outside the profession, and even some from within the profession, are tempted to say that the lawyers were simply weak and corrupt, or, for those who prefer to talk this way, that the lawyers were rational economic actors. They want the client's business, in an intensely competitive market, and so they will wish to approve anything senior management of the client firm asks, averting their eyes from signs of trouble and their noses from the smell of fish. . . .

But this is the amoral rational calculator's perspective, and professionals in high-status jobs at respectable blue-chip institutions do not like to think of themselves as amoral maximizers. Like human beings everywhere who want to enjoy self-respect and the esteem of others, they tell stories about how what they do is all right, even admirable; however, some of the stories that the lawyers would like to tell were not available in this situation.

A. Law as the Enemy: Libertarian Antinomianism

In recent years many lawyers have taken on the values of and completely identified with their business clients, some of whom see law as an enemy or a pesky nuisance. Such lawyers say things like, "Helping our clients is good because they create wealth, innovation, and jobs; while their adversaries, the people we help them fight, small-minded vindictive bureaucrats and greedy plaintiffs' lawyers, create nothing and destroy innovation and enterprise. We help our clients work around the constraints on their autonomy and wealth-maximizing activities." . . .

B. Law as Neutral Constraint: The Lawyer as Risk–Manager

This viewpoint is much like the first, but without the negative normative spin. Adverse legal consequences are not an evil, they are just a fact. In this view, law is simply a source of "risk" to the business firm; it is the lawyers' task to assess and, to the extent possible, reduce it. These lawyers do not feel a moral imperative, as libertarians do, to defy or undercut the law; but neither do they feel one to comply. . . .

These two story-lines were not available in the case of Enron, for the obvious reasons that managers were looting the companies for their own benefit while concealing debts and losses from workers and investors. . . .

The lawyers have been relying instead on different stories, somewhat in conflict with one another.

C.   *"We Din' Know Nothin'": The Lawyer as Myopic or Limited–Function Bureaucrat*

These are claims that the lawyers were not at fault because their role was limited: We didn't know, we weren't informed; the accountants said the numbers were okay; management made the decisions; our representation was restricted to problems on the face of the documents or to information submitted to us.

Many of these claims of innocent ignorance now look pretty dubious. Some of the outside law firms, such as V & E and Andrews & Kurth, in fact worked closely with Andersen accountants in structuring many of the transactions.... Some of their claims of limited knowledge are plausible, however, because Enron never trusted any one set of lawyers with extensive information about its operations—it spread legal work out to over 100 law firms.... One question for lawyers—as well as for senior managers and board members—is whether they can conscientiously and ethically do their jobs and exercise their functions as fiduciaries in organizations structured to diffuse responsibility and prevent their access to the big picture.

D.   *The Lawyer as Advocate*

The classic defense of the corporate lawyer's role, both most often advanced and held in reserve if other defenses fail, is of course that we are advocates, whose duty is zealous representation of clients. We are not like auditors, who have duties to the public; our duties are only to our clients. Our job is to help them pursue their interests and put the best construction on their conduct that the law and facts will support without intolerable strain, so as to enable them to pursue any arguably-legal ends by any arguably-legal means....

III.   INADEQUACY OF THE EXCUSES

The Enron and similar scandals illustrate the limits of all these standard stories as adequate accounts of the corporate lawyer's proper role.... It may be that a natural person cannot be compelled to internalize the values promoted by law.... [But] since we are free to construct the character of these artificial [corporate] persons, we should construct them for legal purposes as good citizens, persons who have internalized the public values expressed in law and the obligation to obey even laws they do not like, for the sake of the privileges of the law that generally benefits them as well as the rest of us....

If the corporation should be constructed and presumed to have the interests of a good, law-respecting, citizen, so should its lawyers (even more so). Lawyers are not simply agents of clients—they are also licensed fiduciaries of the legal system, "part of a judicial system charged with upholding the law," to use the ABA's words....

[A]lthough lawyers may take on an assignment that limits the scope of their representation or asks them to accept some facts as given, they may not agree to such limits as will preclude them from competent and ethical representation. They should not, for example, agree to write an opinion certifying the legality of a deal to third parties if they have some reason to be suspicious of the facts or numbers reported to them, without doing some digging to ensure that the facts are accurate. Nor should they give assurances that certain facts are true if they have no independent means of verifying them. . . .

The most important lessons of Enron, et al., for lawyers are the additional clouds of doubt they cast on the most common defense of the corporate lawyer's role, and the one most often invoked by the profession in the current debates over reform. That is the corporate lawyer as adversary-advocate. The usual way in which this role is framed is that the lawyer's loyalty runs to the client and only to the client. The lawyer must help the client realize its goals and desires, recognizing as hard limits only such legal constraints, the "bounds of the law," as the most ingenious interpretations he can construct of fact and law that are most favorable to his client's position. . . .

This idea that the role of the corporate lawyer is really just like the role of the criminal defense lawyer has been criticized so often and so effectively that it always surprises me to see the idea still walking around, hale and hearty, as if nobody had ever laid a glove on it. I will quickly run through some of the strong objections to the analogy and then add another objection: The bar's standard construction of the corporate lawyer's role is deficient in part because it does not take the analogy seriously enough. . . .

The most obvious objection is that legal advice given outside of adversary proceedings is not subject to any of the constraints of such proceedings. The reasons that the lawyer is given so much latitude to fight for his client in court is that the proceedings are open and public, effective mechanisms such as compelled discovery and testimony exist to bring to light suppressed inconvenient facts and make them known to adversaries and adjudicators, adversaries are present to challenge the advocate's arguments of law and his witnesses' and documents' view of facts, and there is an impartial umpire or judge to rule on their sufficiency and validity. . . . Outside of such settings, one-sided advocacy is more likely to help parties overstep the line to violate the law, and to do so in such ways as are likely to evade detection and sanction, and thus frustrate the purposes of law and regulation. . . .

The point I want to add to these standard, but valuable, points is a simple one. Corporate lawyers could actually learn something useful from the role of the criminal defense lawyer. And that is that the adversary-advocate's role—like that of all lawyers—is in large part a public role, designed to fulfill public purposes: The ascertainment of truth and the doing of justice; the protection of the autonomy, dignity and rights of witnesses and especially of the accused; and the monitoring and disciplining of police and prosecutorial conduct. . . .

The real lesson from the defense lawyer's or advocate's role is simply that the [corporate] lawyer is, in addition to being a private agent of his clients, a public agent of the legal system, whose job is to help clients steer their way through the maze of the law, to bring clients' conduct and behavior into conformity with the law—to get the client as much as possible of what the client wants without damaging the framework of the law. He may not act in furtherance of his client's interest in ways that ultimately frustrate, sabotage, or nullify the public purposes of the laws— or that injure the interests of clients, which are hypothetically constructed, as all public corporations should be, as good citizens who internalize legal norms and wish to act in furtherance of the public values they express.

IV. TOWARDS AN ALTERNATIVE CONCEPTION OF THE CORPORATE COUNSELOR'S ROLE

The view that I am pressing here of the corporate counselor's role is neither new nor unorthodox. It is in fact one of the traditional conceptions of the counselor's role in our legal culture, with a pedigree quite as venerable and considerably more respectable than the rival notion of the lawyer as zealous advocate or hired gun. It was regularly invoked by leading lawyers throughout the nineteenth century and surfaced as an express ethical standard in the ABA's first Canons of Ethics, promulgated in 1908:

Canon § 32: No client, corporate or individual, however powerful, nor any cause, civil or political, however important, is entitled to receive, nor should any lawyer render, any service or advice involving disloyalty to the law, whose ministers we are ... or deception or betrayal of the public.... The lawyer ... advances the honor of his profession and the best interests of his client when he renders service or gives advice tending to impress upon the client and his undertaking exact compliance with the strictest principles of moral law. He must also observe and advise his client to observe the statute law, though until a statute shall have been construed and interpreted by competent adjudication, he is free and entitled to advise as to its validity and as to what he conscientiously believes to be its just meaning and extent....

Since the 1970s, this conception of the wise-counselor-lawyer-statesman has been in decay. It is no longer recognized by most corporate lawyers as a norm. It has almost no institutional support in the rules and disciplinary bodies that regulate the profession. Some academic lawyers still support some version of it; and so too do some judges and regulators. It resurfaces on occasion after business disasters such as the savings-and-loan and Enron scandals. The SEC, IRS, banking regulators, and the courts have sporadically revived it and brought enforcement actions in its spirit. Bar commissions on professionalism sometimes nostalgically evoke it. Yet even where it still has some residual influence there are no effective sanctions behind it....

We cannot hope to revive the counselor's role as the profession's dominant role or self-conception or practical way of life. But events like the Enron collapse make one realize that the corporate counselor would still have a useful role to play, if one could revive it as one of the legal profession's many roles, to be deployed on occasions where clients and society would be best served by independent, public-regarding legal advice.... I will limit my job here to trying to spell out what I think would be the essential elements of the counselor's role....

The most basic is this: That the lawyer engaged as a counselor adopt an independent, objective view of the corporate agents' conduct and plans and their legal validity. This emphatically does not mean that the counselor must take up an adversary stance to the client,.... Counselors can and should be as creative as any other good lawyers in devising means to accomplish clients' objectives that will overcome and work around legal objections, and in devising innovative arguments that will alter and expand the boundaries of the existing law. But whatever advice the counselor gives, she should: (a) Construe the facts and law of the client's situation as a sympathetic but objective observer such as a judge, committed to serving the law's spirit and furthering its public purposes, would construe them; (b) impute to the corporate client the character of the good citizen, who has internalized legal norms and wishes to comply with the law's legitimate commands and purposes while pursuing its own interests and goals; and (c) be based on an interpretation and practical application of the law to the client's situation that helps the client, so constructed, to satisfy rather than subvert the purposes of the law....

When the counselor asserts facts or makes a legal claim or argument to authorities or third parties—outside the context of fully adversary proceedings where all interested parties have effective access to relevant facts and legal knowledge necessary to forming the opinion—they should generally be facts and arguments that a fair-minded and fully-informed observer could accept as plausible and correct....

If the counselor perceives that her services have been or are being used to further, or even just to facilitate by providing plausible cover for, corporate strategies that could not be justified to a fully-informed objective observer as conforming to the letter, spirit, and public purposes of the law, she has to take steps to correct the problem and to try to bring the client's agents back into compliance. This means that if she has suspicions she should investigate them; if not satisfied, she should bring the problem to the general counsel, CEO, and if necessary, the board of directors to insist on compliance; and if corrective steps are not taken, she must resign. Finally, if serious damage to outside interests may result from the agents' misconduct, she must signal the problem to people such as regulatory authorities who could prevent it.

I can already hear the cries of protest: "But this is not the lawyer's role!" The obvious answer to that is, yes, I know that it is not the lawyer's role as most corporate lawyers and the bar now see that role; but that is precisely the problem that the savings-and-loan and Enron, etc. scandals have suggested needs to be solved....

[T]he full-scale version of my proposal would have to contain at least two more components. First, there should be government mandates that for some representations and transactions, corporations must hire lawyers who have undertaken the role and accompanying obligation of counselors.

For example: lawyers certifying compliance with laws, regulations, orders, consent decrees, or reporting requirements of official agencies; lawyers giving opinions to satisfy disclosure requirements or filing proxy statements under the securities laws; and lawyers giving opinions on conformity with tax laws on tax-minimization devices. . . .

Second, there should be effective institutionalization of and support for the counselor's role, incentives to perform it, and sanctions for breaches. . . . Obviously, [lawyers] would be subject to special regimes of judicial enforcement, civil liability, and malpractice; and, where practicing before agencies such as the SEC or IRS, to administrative discipline. . . .

NOTES AND QUESTIONS

Geoffrey Hazard writes:

> Many courses of action taken by a client are "wrong" at least in the exacting sense that they are not what would be done by a supremely moral person unconcerned with costs. If this were the standard by which a lawyer should judge whether to continue his association with a client, there would be few of either clients or lawyers.
>
> In recent years, some critics of the legal profession have suggested that a lawyer for a corporation is responsible for its conduct in at least two related respects: his advice to such a client should consist not merely of what the client legally might do but also of what the client morally ought to do; and he should not serve a client who is not disposed to follow advice of that character. . . . It is perfectly possible to think that the lawyer for the criminal accused is not "responsible" for him, while at the same time thinking that the general counsel for a corporation or agency is, in some sense of the word, "responsible" for it. The point is made by suggesting that it is one thing to represent a sometime murderer, quite another to be on retainer to the Mafia. . . .
>
> The obvious answer for the adviser whose advice is ignored is that he can resign. In some circumstances that is the only honorable course to be followed, but it is impractical as a response to all except fundamental disagreements. . . .
>
> There are situations in which it seems proper that the client should suffer that kind of penalty, for example if he insists on fabricating evidence or carrying out a swindle. But if the case is less extreme than this, the sanction of resignation is too severe. It implies that the client should have to function without proper guidance, or perhaps cease functioning at all, because its managers do not see fit to follow the advice of its advisers.
>
> If this were the consequence that should ensue from a client's refusal to follow advice, it would mean that the advice was in effect peremptory—not an informed suggestion but a command. When an adviser's advice is in effect peremptory, however, the result is a reversal of the underlying structure of responsibility for the organiza-

tion's conduct. The adviser becomes the ultimate arbiter and the client a subordinate.[28]

1. How would you assess Hazard's and Gordon's arguments? Whose position do you find more persuasive? Would you support Gordon's proposal for independent counselors?

2. What would you do on the facts of Problem 1? How would it square with Hazard's and Gordon's analyses? Would your responsibilities differ from those of the lawyer in the Ford Pinto case discussed in Chapter VII?

C. FAMILY PRACTICE

PROBLEM 2

a) One of your current clients is an especially anxious and lonely older man. He calls frequently for advice about matters somewhat related to his divorce, but it seems plain that he primarily wants to talk with someone. You have made clear to him that all time spent in telephone conversations will be billed at your standard hourly rates. He says he understands and pays your fees regularly without complaint. The frequency of his calls is increasing, and the press of other work leaves you unwilling to return some of those calls.

How does your conduct square with bar ethical rules and the Matrimonial Lawyers Standards of Conduct? Should you be subject to any sanctions for failing to make prompt responses? What strategies for coping with such a client would be appropriate?[29]

b) You represent a severely depressed woman in a custody dispute over her four-and eight-year-old sons. Her former husband is seeking to reopen the couple's original divorce agreement. That agreement gave the parties joint legal custody and the mother physical custody. The father now claims that your client is unable to cope with the needs of the children and that her vindictiveness toward him has made the joint custody arrangement unworkable. He notes that his older son never does his homework and is not involved in any school activities. His younger son appears deeply conflicted about the divorce, in part because your client makes accusations that undermine the child's relationship with him. Finally, he believes that a man who is now dating your client has abused the children, and is not a good influence in their development. If the father's efforts to obtain physical custody of the boys are unsuccessful, he plans to have no further contact with them. Although he would retain formal custodial rights and would continue to pay child support, the father would stop visiting and calling his sons.

---

28. Geoffrey C. Hazard, Jr., *Ethics in the Practice of Law* 136, 143–45 (1978).

29. This problem is drawn from materials presented by David Chambers at a workshop on Teaching Ethics in Family Law at the Association of American Law Schools' annual meeting.

Your client denies that any physical abuse has taken place, although she concedes that her new partner once spanked the boys under circumstances calling for discipline. While acknowledging that he is not particularly "good with children," your client believes that he will improve over time. Although she knows she has not been spending enough time with the boys since the divorce, she expects that will change as well. She is determined neither to make any concessions concerning custody, nor to suppress her criticism of her former husband in the children's presence. When you indicate that this conduct may be harming the boys, she responds that the real harm was her husband's emotional abuse, which ended their marriage. When you suggest that she might benefit from counseling, she tells you that she has already spent more than she can afford on psychiatrists and that what she needs now is a tough lawyer. Your client also believes that her former husband is now having a closeted relationship with another man, which does not bother her but might bother the judge who will make the custody determination.

How do you proceed? What factors would be relevant to your decision?

References:

Model Rules 1.1, 1.2, 1.4.

American Academy of Matrimonial Lawyers, Bounds of Advocacy: Goals For Family Lawyers

(2000).

Preliminary Statement

. . . The traditional view of the matrimonial lawyer (a view still held by many practitioners) is of the "zealous advocate" whose only job is to win. However, the emphasis on zealous representation of individual clients in criminal and some civil cases is not always appropriate in family law matters. Public opinion (both within and outside the AAML) has increasingly supported other models of lawyering and goals of conflict resolution in appropriate cases. A counseling, problem-solving approach for people in need of help in resolving difficult issues and conflicts within the family is one model; this is sometimes referred to as "constructive advocacy." Mediation and arbitration offer alternative models. . . .

Matrimonial lawyers should recognize the effect that their words and actions have on their client's attitudes about the justice system, not just on the "legal outcome" of their cases. As a counselor, a problem-solving lawyer encourages problem solving in the client. Effective advocacy for a client means considering with the client what is in the client's best interests and determining the most effective means to achieve that result. The client's best interests include the well being of children, family peace, and economic stability.

These Bounds [of Advocacy] reaffirm the attorney's obligation to competently represent individual clients. These Bounds also promote a problem-solving approach that considers the client's children and family as well. In addition, they encourage efforts to reduce the cost, delay and emotional trauma and urge interaction between parties and attorneys on a more reasoned, cooperative level.

1.3 An attorney should refuse to assist in vindictive conduct and should strive to lower the emotional level of a family dispute by treating all other participants with respect.

Comment

... Although the client has the right to determine the "objectives of representation," after consulting with the client the attorney may limit the objectives and the means by which the objectives are to be pursued. The matrimonial lawyer should make every effort to lower the emotional level of the interaction among parties and counsel. Some dissension and bad feelings can be avoided by a frank discussion with the client at the outset of how the attorney handles cases, including what the attorney will and will not do regarding vindictive conduct or actions likely to adversely affect the children's interests. If the client is unwilling to accept the attorney's limitations on objectives or means, the attorney should decline the representation.

1.5 An attorney should attempt to resolve matrimonial disputes by agreement and should consider alternative means of achieving resolution.

2.3 An attorney should keep the client informed of developments in the representation and promptly respond to communications from the client.

Comment

... Frequent communication with the client on important matters (1) empowers the client, (2) satisfies the client's need for information about the progress of the case, (3) helps build a positive attorney-client relationship, and (4) helps the client understand the amount and nature of the work the attorney is performing, thereby reducing concern that nothing is happening and that the attorney's fees are not being earned. While the attorney should understand that a pending divorce is usually the most important matter in the life of the client, the client should understand that a successful lawyer has many clients, all of whom believe their case to be the most important.

2.5 When the client's decision-making ability appears to be impaired, the attorney should try to protect the client from the harmful effects of the impairment.

Comment

The economic and emotional turmoil caused by marital disputes often affects a client's ability to make rational decisions in his own best interest....

The lawyer is not compelled to follow irrational or potentially harmful directives of a client, particularly one who is distraught or impaired, even if the client is legally competent. The lawyer should oppose any client's illegal or improper decision ("I don't care what the court says, I won't pay her a cent"). The attorney should attempt to dissuade the client before accepting any clearly detrimental decision. The attorney should consider consulting others who might have a stabilizing influence on the client such as the client's therapist, doctor or clergy. It would normally be improper for the attorney to seek appointment of a guardian in such a situation because to do so may be expensive, traumatic and adversely affect the client's interest.

When rejection of the attorney's advice is likely to adversely affect the client's interests, the attorney should document both the advice and the client's refusal to follow it. Such documentation emphasizes the risk to the client and protects the attorney from subsequent allegations of complicity in the conduct or failure to properly advise the client of the risks involved. In appropriate cases, the attorney may withdraw from representation.

6.1 An attorney representing a parent should consider the welfare of, and seek to minimize the adverse impact of the divorce on the minor children.

6.2 An attorney should not permit a client to contest child custody, contact or access for either financial leverage or vindictiveness.

Comment

Tactics oriented toward asserting custody rights as leverage toward attaining some other, usually financial, goal are destructive. The matrimonial lawyer should counsel against, and refuse to assist, such conduct. Proper consideration for the welfare of the children requires that they not be used as pawns in the divorce process. . . . If despite the attorney's advice the client persists, the attorney should seek to withdraw.

NOTES

Lawyers in divorce and custody cases play a variety of roles. Which roles a practitioner assumes depend in part on clients' objectives, but also on the attorney's own values.

At one end of the spectrum are "bombers"—lawyers who identify strongly with the neutral partisan function described in Chapter IV. From their perspective, the attorney's job is to get clients the result they want provided it's not illegal.[30] Since divorce rarely brings out the best in the human relationships, what some clients want is for their spouses to suffer as much as they are. For the bomber, the counseling role involves mainly strategic planning and tactical advice about how to gain whatever financial and psychological objectives that their clients identify. According to one lawyer interviewed by a former chair of the ABA Family Section's Ethics

30. See Laura MacFarquhar, "So You Want a Divorce," *New Yorker*, April 23 & 30, 2001, at 88.

Committee, "[n]early all divorce practitioners criticize the bomber ... but in the current moral climate, nothing succeeds like success."[31]

At the other end of the spectrum are lawyers who view themselves as constructive problem solvers and officers of the court with a clear affirmative duty to foster an appropriate resolution for children as well as clients. From this perspective, attorneys' primary counseling obligation is to help divorcing spouses reach durable financial agreements and maintain cooperative parenting relationships. A growing number of these lawyers adopt the collaborative approach described in Chapter VIII.

Some lawyers in both camps place high priority on minimizing the emotional wear and tear of family disputes for themselves as well as the parties. These practitioners often view their clients as "volatile," "irrational," and "unrealistic."[32] For these attorneys, the objective is to avoid emotionally laden discussion and to help parties concentrate on the nuts and bolts aspects of their agreement.

Of course, these role descriptions reflect extreme types; most attorneys' actual behavior relies on a mix of strategies that vary across cases. Much may depend on the needs of clients, their relationships with their spouses, and the interests of children. However, research on family practitioners also reveals significant differences in lawyers' approaches to their role. For example, in one study that asked lawyers to identify their goal in representing matrimonial clients, about a third reported that they sought a fair settlement. A quarter reported that they attempted to get "the most for the client," and about forty percent reported mixed strategies.[33] All of these approaches can raise ethical concerns but some are obviously more problematic than others.

The difficulties with the bomber strategy are readily apparent. A lawyer who helps a client punish a former spouse or obtain a skewed agreement may be undermining the client's long-term interests in establishing sustainable settlements and coparenting relationships. Such interests, although hard to quantify, may have far more enduring value than the financial gain available through hard-ball tactics. Moreover, experts universally agree that open conflict between parents causes significant difficulties for children, and that those adverse effects are likely to be felt by all members of the family.[34]

Lawyers who attempt to avoid dealing with emotional issues also may be ill serving their clients' long-term interests. Family disputes often trigger deep anxiety, stress, anger, and guilt. Yet many individuals who experience such difficulties do not obtain assistance from mental health

31. Richard E. Crouch, "The Matter of Bombers: Unfair Tactics and the Problem of Defending Unethical Behavior in Divorce Litigation," 20 *Fam. L.Q.* 413, 415 (1986).

32. Austin Sarat, "Lawyers and Clients: Putting Professional Service on the Agenda of Legal Education," 41 *J. Legal Educ.* 43, 47 (1991).

33. Richard J. Maiman, Craig A. McEwen, and Lynn Mather, "The Future of Legal Professionalism in Practice," 2 *Legal Ethics* 71, 78 (1999).

34. See Eleanor E. Maccoby & Robert H. Mnookin, *Dividing the Child: Social and Legal Dilemmas of Custody* 248 (1992).

professionals. Clients who are deterred by the cost and perceived stigma of therapy may want or need assistance from their attorneys in coping with the psychological dimensions of divorce. Counsel who have special expertise, experience, or simply distance from the family situation can often provide a crucial perspective. Their assistance may encourage clients to take the long view, to give adequate consideration to their children's welfare, or to obtain support from other sources in the community. By contrast, lawyers who focus on narrow legal and financial issues too often end up talking past concerns that are most central to the well-being of their clients.

Consider the following interchange between a woman and her male lawyer from Austin Sarat's and William Felstiner's study of divorce practitioners:

Client: There was harassment and verbal degradation. No interest at all in furthering my education. None whatsoever ... If there was ever any time when I did not need or want sex, I was subject to, you know, these long verbal whiplashings....

Lawyer: Mmm uh.

Client ... When he undertook to lecturing me and I'd say, "I don't want to hear this. I don't have time right now," I could lock myself in the bathroom and he would break in. And I was just to listen, whether I wanted to or not. And he would lecture me for hours ... There was no escaping him, short of getting in the car and driving away. But then he would stand outside the driveway and yell, anyhow. The man was not well.

Lawyer: Okay. Now how about any courses you took.[35]

As Sarat notes, such interchanges are typical of lawyers who are untrained or unwilling to deal with nonlegal concerns. But most clients "come to the divorce process expecting that their emotions will matter and that lawyers will care;" many come away disappointed.[36] If attorneys lack the necessary counseling skills, then Sarat, like most other experts, argues that the answer is better education, not abdication of the role.

A different set of difficulties arise for lawyers who see themselves as officers of the court with responsibilities to the entire family. Although attractive in principle, that role can be problematic in practice. The interests of parents and children are not always fully consistent. In an ideal world, children would usually remain in close contact with both parents, who would live near enough and have a sufficiently cooperative relationship to make such contact possible. That ideal is often impossible, and hard tradeoffs are sometimes necessary between the needs of clients and unrepresented spouses or children.

---

35. Sarat, *supra* note 32, at 48. **36.** *Id.* at 50.

QUESTIONS

1.   Are such tradeoffs necessary on the facts in Problem 2? What strategies might be effective in counseling the client?

2.   Under what circumstances should the lawyer withdraw from representation? Are there contexts in which the interests of unrepresented children would argue for measures other than withdrawal?

3.   What if a client who suspects infidelity or concealment of financial information wants to put software on the family computer that would enable her to monitor her husband's emails?[37]

D.   TAX PRACTICE

INTRODUCTION

Ethical issues in tax practice reflect both the particular nature of its regulatory framework and the more general tensions arising from lawyers' competing responsibilities. These issues have become increasingly important as the nation has become increasingly dependent on revenue from self-reporting income tax systems. The Internal Revenue Service can afford to audit only about one percent of individual returns and even fewer of corporate returns, and those audits reveal high levels of underpayment. Recent estimates suggest that unreported taxable income averages over $345 billion annually, about 16 percent of taxes owed.[38] Despite recent increases in funds to combat non-compliance, the tax-gap has more than tripled over the past two decades and is expected to continue growing.[39] The low audit rates create a tax cheaters' lottery—the only lottery in which the overwhelming majority of players are winners.[40]

According to recent surveys, noncompliance is becoming more difficult to control, partly as a result of taxpayer dissatisfaction with the complexity and seeming inequities of the tax code, as well as with IRS enforcement practices.[41] Federal tax laws and regulations now exceed 36,000 pages and

---

37. Brad Stone, "Tell All PCs and Phones Transforming Divorce," *N.Y. Times*, Sept. 15, 2007, at A1.

38. When adjusted for taxes paid late or through enforcement efforts, the gap drops, for a compliance rate of about 86 percent IRS and the Tax Gap: Hearings Before the H. Comm. on Budget, 110th Cong. (2007) (Statement of J. Russell George, Treasury Inspector General for Tax Administration). See U.S. Senate Committee on the Budget, Hearings on The Tax Gap and How to Solve It, 109th Cong. (Feb. 15, 2006) (statement of Mark W. Everson, Commission of Internal Revenue); Internal Revenue Service, IRS Updates Tax Gap Estimates (Feb. 14, 2006); Alex Raskolnikov, "Crime and Punishment in Taxation:

Deceit, Deterrence, and the Self–Adjusting Penalty," 106 *Colum. L. Rev.* 569, 574 (2006).

39. Raskolnikov, *supra* note 38, at 574. For continued resource shortages, see U.S. Committee on the Budget, Hearings on IRS and the Tax Gap, 110th Cong. 17–22 (2007) (Statement of the Hon. J. Russell George, Treasury Inspector General for Tax Administration); IRS Oversight Board, Annual Report 2006 17, 21 (2007).

40. Donald L. Barlett & James B. Steele, *The Great American Tax Dodge* 161 (2000).

41. *See* U.S. Committee on Homeland Security and Governmental Affairs, Subcommittee on Federal Financial Management, Government Information, and International

taxpayers frequently receive incorrect answers to questions from taxpayer assistance centers.[42] Widespread criticism has focused on the inadequate share of audit resources that target the richest individuals and largest corporations.[43] These enforcement inequalities and regulatory complexities undermine public confidence and compliance. And once the stigma associated with cheating weakens, evasion spreads and becomes even harder to control.[44]

The role of tax lawyers in widening or narrowing the compliance gap is the subject of the material that follows. To understand these problems, a brief overview of regulatory structures and bar interpretations is helpful.

Taxpayers face penalties for both fraud and accuracy-related violations not rising to the level of fraud. For fraudulent underpayments, taxpayers are subject to penalties of 75 percent of the amount due (26 USC § 6663). For accuracy-related violations, taxpayers are liable for penalties of 20 percent of the resulting underpayment (§ 6662).

Accuracy-related violations take several forms that are relevant to the ethical discussion that follows. The first involves negligence or disregard of applicable rules (§ 6662(c)). "Negligence" encompasses failure to make reasonable attempts at compliance, and "disregard" encompasses careless, reckless, or intentional transgressions. A second accuracy-related penalty applies to "substantial understatement" of income tax. An understatement is substantial if it exceeds 10 percent of the correct tax liability or $5,000, whichever is greater (§ 6662(d)(1)(A)(i) and (ii)). The third accuracy-related penalty concerns "substantial valuation misstatement." This type involves an overstatement of property value or adjusted basis to more than 150 percent of the correct figure (§ 6662(e)(1)(A)) or an understatement of estate or gift tax valuation by at least 65 percent (§ 6662(g)(1)). Most accuracy-related penalties are inapplicable if taxpayers disclose the basis for a position and the position has a reasonable basis. For certain other violations, penalties are avoidable if the taxpayer establishes good faith and reasonable cause (§ 6664(c)(1)).

Preparers of tax returns may also be subject to penalties. A $250 penalty is applicable if a return takes an undisclosed or frivolous position for which "there was not a realistic possibility of being sustained on its

Security, Hearings on Deconstructing the Tax Code: Uncollected Taxes and Issues of Transparency, 109th Congress 9–11 (2006) (statement of Hon. J. Russell George, Treasury Inspector General for Tax Administration); Sagit Leviner, A New Era of Tax Enforcement: From Big Stick to Responsive Regulation 3 (Michigan Law and Economics Research Paper No. 06–007, 2007).

42. Michael R. Phillips, Department of the Treasury, Customer Service at Taxpayer Assistance Centers Showed Improvement During the 2006 Filing Season 3 (2006) (reporting 15 percent error rate); Michael R. Phillips, Department of the Treasury, Over-

sight and Accuracy of Tax Returns Continue to be Problems for the Volunteer Income Tax Assistance Program 8 (2006) (reporting 61 error rate).

43. David Cay Johnston, "I.R.S. Is Spending Less Time Scrutinizing Big Business," *N.Y. Times*, Dec. 21, 2006, at 3; David Cay Johnston, "I.R.S. Will Cut Tax Lawyers Who Audit the Richest," *N.Y. Times*, July 23, 2006, at 16.

44. Luigi Alberto Franzoni, "Tax Evasion and Tax Compliance," in *International Encyclopedia of Law and Economics* 57–58 (Bovdewijn Bouckart & De Geest eds. 1999).

merits," and the preparer knew or reasonably should have known of the position (§ 6694(a)). As with the taxpayer penalties under § 6662, however, the preparer penalty for an unrealistic position under § 6694(a) is inapplicable if there was a reasonable cause for the understatement and the preparer acted in good faith. This exception does not apply to more egregious preparer behavior. For example, preparers are subject to a penalty of $1,000 for willfully attempting to understate the client's liability or for acting with "any reckless or intentional disregard of rules or regulations" (§ 6694(b)). Similarly, under § 6701, a $1,000 penalty ($10,000 for preparers of corporate taxes) applies to practitioners who helped prepare any document that they knew or had reason to believe would be used materially to understate federal tax liability.

Under Circular 230, the IRS may also impose sanctions, including suspension or disbarment from practice before the Service, against any preparers who engage in disreputable conduct. Such conduct includes knowing provision of false or misleading information to the Department of the Treasury, or knowing, reckless, or gross incompetence in provision of false opinions. 31 C.F.R. § 10.51. Circular 230 provides that a practitioner may not sign a return as a preparer if the return has an undisclosed position that lacks "a realistic possibility of being sustained on its merits.... A position is considered to have a realistic possibility ... if a reasonable and well-informed analysis by a person knowledgeable in the tax law would lead such a person to conclude that the position has approximately a one in three, or greater, likelihood of being sustained on its merits." 31 C.F.R. § 10.34. No violation occurs if the position is disclosed and is not frivolous.

Specific statutory efforts to regulate lawyers' tax practice are, for the most part, relatively recent. Although for many years IRS Circular 230 required "due diligence" in preparing or assisting the preparation of tax returns, the Treasury Department offered no interpretive regulations. The ABA filled the gap with Ethics Opinion 314 (1965), which held that a lawyer assisting preparation of a client's tax returns could freely urge the statement of positions most favorable to the client as long as there was a "reasonable basis" for those opinions. In so ruling, the Ethics Committee reasoned that lawyers were acting in a potentially adversarial capacity against the IRS and were not obligated to disclose weaknesses in their clients' position unless the fact indicated beyond a doubt that a crime was being committed. And, the Committee noted, a "wrong or indeed sometimes unjust tax result in the settlement of a controversy is not a crime."

That reasoning provoked considerable criticism. Many commentators challenged the analogy between ex parte administrative filings and adversarial litigation, particularly given the resource constraints and self-reporting aspects of the tax system. Moreover, as a practical matter, the "reasonable basis" standard evolved to what one commentator labeled the "laugh aloud" standard; it would permit any argument you could make with a reasonably straight face.[45]

In response to widespread criticism, the ABA Ethics Committee in 1985 released formal Opinion 85–352, reprinted below. This opinion replaced the "reasonable basis" test with a more stringent standard requiring a "realistic possibility of success." Consider how that standard would apply on the facts of problem 3.

PROBLEM 3

Your client has agreed in principle to pay $1.6 million for an apartment building and the acre of land on which it sits. The building is a wasting asset that may be depreciated. The land is nondepreciable. It is, therefore, in your client's interest to attribute as much of the sale price as possible to the apartment building. The seller is indifferent to how the purchase price is allocated.

You have asked two real estate experts who often work with your firm for appraisals. One values the building at $800,000 and a second at $900,000. These figures strike you as somewhat higher than those that an entirely neutral expert would select, but they do not appear grossly inflated. Your client then finds another appraiser who values the building at $1.2 million. In your client's view, that is a fairer estimate, and he would like you to prepare sales documents and tax returns using that figure. How do you respond? Is your advice affected by past experience indicating that if the IRS audits the return, they are likely to assume some overvaluation and may discount the value allocated to the building by about 10 percent regardless of which figure you use?

NOTES

Problem 3 is a variation on a hypothetical appearing in a landmark survey of tax practitioners before the promulgation of Opinion 85–352, (excerpted below). Under that hypothetical, the lawyer needed to price some stock of a closely-held family corporation in preparing an estate return. Two neutral experts put the value of the stock at about $50 per share. However, its book value was $30, and because it was a minority interest and would be hard to sell, it could be discounted to $22.50. Surveyed practitioners were aware of the IRS's practice of assuming some underreporting and attaching a "mendacity premium" to whatever value the taxpayer selected. Under those hypothesized circumstances, none of the surveyed practitioners would report the value of the shares at $50. About a third would report at $40, and the majority at $30 or less.[46]

Such attitudes have prompted several regulatory responses, including increased penalties for overvaluation and undervaluation of property, requirements concerning the qualifications of appraisers in certain circum-

45. Michael Graetz, "Too Little, Too Late," *Tax Times*, Feb. 1987, at 17.

46. *See* Frederic G. Corneel, "Ethical Guidelines in Tax Practice," 28 *Tax Law Rev.* 1 (1972).

stances, and the "good faith/realistic possibility of success" standard of Opinion 85–352.

In 1990, Frederic G. Corneel published proposed Guidelines to Tax Practice Second with consultation by members of the ABA Section on Taxation's Committee on Standards of Tax Practice. These Guidelines have also attempted to raise practice standards. They provide:

> [W]hile there is nothing wrong in either the appraiser or the preparer giving the client the benefit of the doubt where the value [of property] is uncertain, any valuation involved in a return that we prepare must be responsibly done, make sense, be well-reasoned, and be internally consistent.[47]

QUESTIONS

1. If your firm generally supported the proposed Guidelines to Tax Practice, how would you proceed on the facts in Problem 3?

2. How important to your advice is the IRS practice of attaching a "mendacity premium" to reported values? Does the Service have any realistic alternative, given its resource constraints and the resulting incentives for taxpayers and appraisers? Can you permit a client to undervalue assets as the anticipated IRS premium? Under these circumstances, is all fair in love, war, and IRS valuation disputes?

3. Should you ever discuss with your client the low probability of an audit? Tax law professor Tanina Rostain notes that attorneys

> signal their own attitude toward the legal framework and the posture they believe a client should adopt—respectful, disdainful, alienated or other—through the ways they talk about the law as much as in the specifics they impart . . .
>
> A lawyer who has a socially responsible view of her role can make clear that taking into account a low audit rate is inappropriate in deciding whether to claim a deduction, even while she provides the specific information. When not assuming the persona of "bad men," people are often responsive to the argument that if everyone based their decision to pay taxes on low enforcement rates, government would grind to a halt. Communicating enforcement information is not inconsistent with expressing one's view that it is irrelevant in most circumstances to the issue of compliance.[48]

Do you agree? Are the concerns that should affect lawyers' discussion of enforcement practices in the tax context any different from those involving the environmental issues raised in Problem 1?

4. An experienced corporate tax expert recalls the following situation. A long-time client came to him and said, "I'd like to get your off-the-cuff reaction about whether the deal I'm putting together is legal. I absolutely

---

47. Frederic G. Corneel, "Guidelines for Tax Practice Second," 43 *Tax Law Rev.* 297, 304 (1990).

48. Tanina Rostain, "Ethics Lost," 71 *S. Cal. L. Rev.* 1273, 1356–57 (1998).

don't want you to do any research or get anyone else to do research. I just want to hear what you think. If your gut reaction is that it's legal, I'm willing to bet that the IRS is never going to call me on it." The lawyer understood the client's point: if he researched the law, he might find out that the deal was improper. The client did not really want to know whether the law supported his deal. He wanted to know only whether the deal looked good enough not to raise the suspicions of a first-rate tax lawyer.

Can the lawyer answer the client's question as posed? How should the lawyer proceed with the conversation?[49]

5. Does ABA Formal Opinion 85–352, excerpted below, establish an adequate ethical standard? According to Yale tax professor Michael Graetz, the Opinion's replacement of the "reasonable basis" standard with a "reasonable possibility of success" standard amounts to replacing the "laugh aloud" standard with a "giggle test."[50]

Some commentators have recommended more demanding requirements that would allow lawyers to advance only positions they reasonably believe to be meritorious. By contrast, other commentators believe that if requirements for lawyers extend too far beyond those that seem acceptable to most taxpayers, they will rely on accountants and other service providers instead, or will shop for attorneys willing to skirt their ethical obligations. These commentators believe that other reforms aimed at underreporting would be preferable, such as increased penalties, expanded enforcement resources, or a *qui tam* statute, comparable to the federal False Claims Act, which would provide a bounty to private individuals who report information leading to successful tax enforcement actions.[51]

Are such alternatives politically realistic? The Internal Revenue Service has recently stepped up disciplinary activities against practitioners through its Office of Professional Responsibility, but resources still remain grossly inadequate to the task[52] Consider W. Bradley Wendel's argument that the rule of law in tax practice would be undermined if lawyers refused to interpret it in good faith based on its obvious intent.[53] How would you define the tax counseling role in light of the materials that follow?

ABA Standing Committee on Ethics and Professional Responsibility Formal Opinion 85–352

(1985).

The Committee has been requested by the Section of Taxation of the American Bar Association to reconsider the "reasonable basis" standard in

49. This example comes courtesy of Professor Martin Ginsburg.

50. Graetz, *supra* note 45, at 17.

51. Dennis J. Ventry, Jr., Whistleblowers and *Qui Tam* for Tax, 61 *Tax Lawyer* 355 (2008).

52. Kevin E. Thorn, "A Rare Look Inside the IRS's Office of Professional Responsibility," 18 *Professional Lawyer* 18 (2007).

53. W. Bradley Wendel, "Professionalism as Interpretation," 99 *Nw. U. L. Rev.* 1167, 1215–17 (2005).

the Committee's Formal Opinion 314 governing the position a lawyer may advise a client to take on a tax return. . . .

Rule 3.1 of the Model Rules, which is in essence a restatement of DR 7–102(A)(2) of the Model Code, states in pertinent part:

> A lawyer shall not bring or defend a proceeding, or assert or controvert an issue therein, unless there is a basis for doing so that is not frivolous, which includes a good faith argument for an extension, modification or reversal of existing law. . . .

On the basis of these rules and analogous provisions of the Model Code, a lawyer, in representing a client in the course of the preparation of the client's tax return, may advise the statement of positions most favorable to the client if the lawyer has a good faith belief that those positions are warranted in existing law or can be supported by a good faith argument for an extension, modification or reversal of existing law. A lawyer can have a good faith belief in this context even if the lawyer believes the client's position probably will not prevail. However, good faith requires that there be some realistic possibility of success if the matter is litigated. . . .

Thus, where a lawyer has a good faith belief in the validity of a position in accordance with the standard stated above that a particular transaction does not result in taxable income or that certain expenditures are properly deductible as expenses, the lawyer has no duty to require as a condition of his or her continued representation that riders be attached to the client's tax return explaining the circumstances surrounding the transaction or the expenditures.

Report of the Special Task Force on Formal Opinion 85–352

(1985).

This Report examines Opinion 85–352 and how it will apply to tax practice. It concludes that Opinion 85–352 properly rejects a low standard of tax reporting, reduces some of the potential for misuse of the governing ethical standard, and, properly interpreted and implemented, should work to improve the reliability of tax advice furnished by members of the bar. . . .

"Good Faith" as an Objective Standard

The Opinion restates relevant passages of applicable guidelines to the effect that the lawyer, in advising a client in the course of preparation of the client's tax return, may advise the statement of positions most favorable to the client if the lawyer has a good faith belief that those provisions are warranted in existing law, or can be supported by a good faith argument for an extension, modification, or reversal of existing law. It states expressly that a lawyer can have a good faith belief even if the lawyer believes the client's position probably will not prevail.

The Opinion does not, however, leave "good faith" open to subjective interpretation. It instead applies an objective standard to the determination of whether good faith is present. The Opinion explains: "However, good faith requires that there be some realistic possibility of success if the matter is litigated." The result is an objective standard which can be enforced. . . .

Role of the Audit Lottery

The standard adopted by Opinion 85–352 does not permit taking into account the likelihood of audit or detection in determining whether the ethical standard is met. Whether the return will be audited or not is simply of no consequence to the application of the new standard. The determination of whether there is a realistic possibility of success is made without regard to the reality of the audit lottery, and assumes that the issue is in court and to be decided.

Comparison of "Some Realistic Possibility of Success If Litigated" With "Reasonable Basis"

Doubtless there were some tax practitioners who intended "reasonable basis" to set a relatively high standard of tax reporting. Some have continued to apply such a standard. To more, however, if not most tax practitioners, the ethical standard set by "reasonable basis" had become a low one. To many it had come to permit any colorable claim to be put forth; to permit almost any words that could be strung together to be used to support a tax return position. Such a standard has now been rejected by the ABA Committee. The Opinion expressly states that to the extent "reasonable basis" had been construed to support the use of any colorable claim on a tax return or to justify exploitation of the lottery of the tax return audit selection process, the construction was an improper interpretation and application of what was meant by "reasonable basis."

More important to differentiating between "reasonable basis" and the standard articulated by Opinion 85–352 is that the new standard requires not only that there be some possibility of success, if litigated, rather than merely a construction that can be argued or that seems reasonable, but also that there be more than just any possibility of success. The possibility of success, if litigated, must be "realistic." A possibility of success cannot be "realistic" if it is only theoretical or impracticable. This clearly implies that there must be a substantial possibility of success, which when taken together with the assumption that the matter will be litigated, measurably elevates what had come to be widely accepted as the minimum ethical standard.

A position having only a 5% or 10% likelihood of success, if litigated, should not meet the new standard. A position having a likelihood of success closely approaching one-third should meet the standard. Ordinarily, there would be some realistic possibility of success where the position is supported by "substantial authority," as that term is used in section 6661 of the Code and applicable regulations. A position to be asserted in the return in the expectation that something could be obtained by way of concession in the bargaining process of settlement negotiations would not meet the new standard, unless accompanied by a realistic possibility of success, if litigated. If there is not a realistic possibility of success, if litigated, the new standard could not be met by disclosure or "flagging" of the position in the return.

If the Position Falls Below the Standard

If the standard is not met, the position may be advanced by payment of the tax and claim for refund, which necessarily sets forth in detail each ground upon which a refund is claimed. A position may be advanced in litigation if it is not frivolous. The lawyer may bring a proceeding, and assert an issue therein, if there is a basis for doing so that is not frivolous, which includes a good faith argument for an extension, modification, or reversal of existing law. In such a context good faith does not require that there be a possibility of success that is "realistic." Model Rule 3.1; DR 7–102(A)(2).

If the client determines to proceed to assert a position in a tax return that is not supported by a realistic possibility of success if litigated, the lawyer must withdraw from the engagement, at least to the extent it involves advice as to the position to be taken on the return, subject to usual rules governing withdrawal. Model Rule 1.16(a) provides that a lawyer shall not represent a client, or having done so shall withdraw from the representation of the client, if "the representation will result in violation of the Rules of Professional Conduct or other law. . . ." To avoid conflict with obligations imposed upon tax return preparers, the lawyer should first determine whether the position meets the ethical standard. If not, the lawyer must counsel the taxpayer not to assert the position, and, unless this advice is accepted by the client, the lawyer may not prepare the return, and pursuant to Rule 1.16(a) must withdraw from further representation involving advice as to the position taken on the return. Only if the position meets the standard may the lawyer prepare the return, sign it, and present it to the client. . . .

Opinion 85–352 continues the position of Opinion 314 that if the applicable ethical standard is met, the lawyer has no duty to require as a condition of continued representation that riders be attached to the client's tax return. However, in all cases, and in all dealings with the Internal Revenue Service, "the lawyer is under a duty not to mislead the Internal Revenue Service deliberately, either by misstatements or by silence or by permitting the client to mislead." Thus, although a lawyer has no obligation under the opinion to flag doubtful positions of law as such if they meet the ethical standard, the lawyer has an obligation to counsel that the entries on a tax return must not be misleading. Since many return entries involve explicit or implicit representations of fact, this requirement may result in disclosure obligations beyond those that might be imposed under section 6661.

Tax Returns Are Not Adversarial Proceedings

The Opinion does not state that the general ethical guidelines governing advocacy in litigation are determinative, or suggest that tax returns are adversarial proceedings. To the contrary, a tax return initially serves a disclosure, reporting, and self-assessment function. It is the citizen's report to the government of his or her relevant activities for the year. The Opinion says that because some returns, particularly aggressive ones, may result in an adversary relationship, there is a place for consideration of the ethical considerations regarding advocacy. Thus, the Opinion blends the ethical guidelines governing advocacy with those applicable to advising, from which the new ethical standard is derived.

Matthew C. Ames, "Formal Opinion 352: Professional Integrity and the Tax Audit Lottery"

1 Georgetown Journal of Legal Ethics 411, 421–24 (1987).

RATIONALE: THE ADVERSARIAL RELATIONSHIP

Opinion 352 not only permits playing the lottery, but encourages it. According to the opinion, an attorney who merely believes in good faith that the client has a valid position need not require the client to attach riders to the return explaining the position. This undercuts I.R.C. § 6661, which imposes a penalty for substantial understatement of tax liability without adequate disclosure of a position in the return, or substantial authority for a position. . . .

This position may, in the short run, dissuade some clients from playing the lottery, since the sight of the lawyer balking may shake their confidence. Over time, however, the new standard will not solve the problem. First, many clients will simply say "Thank you," and file the return based on the lawyer's advice, even if the lawyer refuses to sign it. A year later, they will be back, ready for more advice, and the lawyer will be there, ready to give it. As long as the lawyer is permitted to continue representation, the ethical standard will have minimal effect. Second, a great deal depends on the force of the lawyer's warning concerning the consequences. Even if the warning is stated fully and clearly, if the lawyer delivers it with a wink and a nod, or some indication of the low likelihood of an audit, it may not have much of an impact. Finally, and most importantly, the standard will be vitiated, just as "reasonable basis" was. After all, "reasonable basis" once did mean "reasonable"; today the issue has shifted from reasonableness to whether there is any basis. There will always be pressure on the lawyer to give his blessing. . . .

PROBLEM 4

Your client, a full-time physician, raises poodles, which she enters from time to time in local competitions. An acquaintance recently told her that it is possible to deduct the expenses connected with her dogs if she is showing them professionally. She seeks your advice. Although she considers herself "something of a professional," she would never consider selling any of her four dogs, and the prizes at local competitions are far too small to defray her costs.

Under Treasury Regulations § 1.183–2, the costs of an activity are nondeductible if the taxpayer engages in it primarily as a hobby, but are deductible if the taxpayer enters into the activity with the objective of making a profit. Factors relevant in assessing whether the activity is for profit include whether it is carried on in a businesslike fashion with appropriate books and records; the taxpayer's expertise; and the time and effort expended on the activity.

QUESTIONS

1.   How do you advise the taxpayer? If she never kept books and records in the past, may you advise her to begin now and prepare a return claiming the expenses as a deduction?

2.   Where is the dividing line between manufacturing intent and helping clients "put their best foot forward?" Should you ask the client whether she is trying to make a profit before you explain the relevant regulations? If she says no, is she bound by her initial uninformed statement of purpose?

3.   In tax contexts, a recurring question is whether clients should be bound by the way they characterize motives before becoming aware of the tax consequences. For example, a frequently quoted exchange among tax experts involves a hypothetical in which a client indicated that he would like to "save some tax money" by splitting a corporation into two entities after a friend reportedly "divided his business and saved quite a bit."[54] Under regulations then applicable, deductions were not available if the "principal purpose" of the split was to achieve a tax advantage. According to one practitioner, the client's opening statement should not deprive him of the "right to an examination of his factual situation and legal advice as to what his rights are.... [An attorney could appropriately] explore the situation to see whether or not ... there was justifiable basis for proceeding on a basis other than the tax advantage alone."[55] By contrast, David Herwitz, a Harvard Law School tax specialist, observed:

> [W]hen a fellow has come in and stated his objective in the way described here, ... [although] there may well be some other quite adequate business reasons [for the split], there is a real question as to whether one could ever overcome the likelihood of the stated purpose being at least a major purpose, since it is the only one the client starts with on his own.[56]

Ethics professors divide along similar lines. One view is that individuals are naturally inclined to recollect facts in ways that favor their interests, so clients are entitled to know what their interests are before they

---

54.   "Business Planning and Professional Responsibility," 8 *Prac.Law.* 17, 29–30 (1962) (comments of Ross L. Malone).

55.   *Id.* at 30.

56.   *Id.* at 32 (comments of David R. Herwitz).

commit themselves to a particular version of the truth. Any alternative view would penalize less sophisticated clients. Other commentators make similar factual assumptions but arrive at a different conclusion. From their perspective, it is asking too much of human nature to provide a motive for lying and then to ask for the truth. While sophisticated clients may be better able to deceive without assistance, it does not follow that a lawyer's role is to give everyone equal skills in deception.

Where do you fall in this debate? What considerations would be relevant to your decisions to assist the taxpayer in Problem 4?

4.   Would these problems be better addressed by changing Internal Revenue Code provisions to focus solely on objective rather than subjective factors? For many years, a standard ethical dilemma in tax practice involved gifts "made in contemplation of death." IRS rules treated such gifts as taxable parts of the donor's estate in order to prevent avoidance of inheritance taxes. Clients nearing death often wished to avoid taxation by claiming some other motive for their generosity. The difficulties for lawyers and auditors in coping with the IRS standard finally resulted in its replacement with a rule that automatically includes gifts made within three years of death as part of the decedent's estate. Should the tax bar lobby more actively for comparable changes in other IRS provisions that employ subjective tests? What would be the costs of such modifications?

5.   If you advise the client in Problem 4 that the IRS is likely to disallow the proposed exemptions, but she wishes to disregard your advice, should you withdraw from representation?

PROBLEM 5

You are a second-year associate in the tax department of a large law firm. Your firm holds a day-long white water rafting outing that is attended by every lawyer in the firm. Although you hate cold water and boats make you seasick, you feel an obligation to participate. Aside from a discussion of boat safety on shore, no meetings are held during the event. After the outing you learn that the firm plans to deduct the trip as a business expense. As a tax specialist, you know that § 274 of the Internal Revenue Code and the regulations under that section generally disallow deductions for entertainment that does not include meetings.[57] How should you proceed?

Randolph Paul, "The Responsibility of the Tax Adviser"

63 Harvard Law Review 377 (1950).

Tax attorneys know very well that tax avoidance is "in the nature of mortals." Certainly the courts have resigned themselves to the thought

---

57. See Danville Plywood Corp. v. United States, 899 F.2d 3 (Fed.Cir.1990) (finding that a Superbowl outing is not an ordinary business expense under § 162 and that § 274 might also disallow the deduction if it was not directly related to, or associated with, the taxpayer's business).

that it is almost universal. There is nothing reprehensible or illicit in attempts to avoid by legal means some portion of the burden of taxation or in honest efforts "to reduce taxes to the minimum required by law." Tax avoidance has been said to be "above reproach." At the very least, it is a natural product, in terms of human attitude. . . .

I do not mean to give blanket sanction to the many tax avoidance schemes that are constantly being presented to tax advisers. Above all things, a tax attorney must be an indefatigable skeptic; he must discount everything he hears and reads. The market place abounds with unsound avoidance schemes which will not stand the test of objective analysis and litigation. The escaped tax, a favorite topic of conversation at the best clubs and the most sumptuous pleasure resorts, expands with repetition into fantastic legends. But clients want opinions with happy endings, and he smiles best who smiles last. It is wiser to state misgivings at the beginning than to have to acknowledge them ungracefully at the end. The tax adviser has, therefore, to spend a large part of his time advising against schemes of this character. I sometimes think that the most important word in his vocabulary is "No"; certainly he must frequently use this word most emphatically when it will be an unwelcome answer to a valuable client, and even when he knows that the client may shop for a more welcome answer in other offices which are more interested in pleasing clients than they are in rendering sound opinions.

However the question for the tax adviser is not what the law ought to be, but what it is or will become. My point is that in deciding that question the tax adviser must put aside his personal notions of tax policy and make his most intelligent guess as to the meaning of a statute passed by Congress. . . . The tax adviser need not worry about his moral position. It is not his function to improve men's hearts. As Judge Frank has observed, the task of a lawyer is to win specific cases and guide clients to pleasant destinations. . . . Indeed, it is his positive duty to show the client how to avail himself to the full of what the law permits. He is not the keeper of the Congressional conscience. In representing his client in a particular case the tax lawyer must take the law as he finds it.

Joseph Bankman, "An Academic's View of the Tax Shelter Battle," in The Crisis in Tax Administration

(Joel Slemrod & Henry Aaron, eds. 2003).

Tax shelters—structured transactions with little or no independent business purpose—have always been part of the tax landscape . . . There is no single agreed upon definition of a tax shelter. There is certainly no definition of a shelter that can mechanically be applied to any set of transactions and sift out the shelters and only the shelters. That said, the following definition, while incapable of mechanical application, will encompass nearly every transaction commonly described as a tax shelter.

A shelter is (1) A transaction that is marketed and tax-motivated; (2) that under at least one literal reading of the governing statute or regulation; (3) misstates economic income; and (4) in so doing, reduces the tax on capital; (5) in a manner inconsistent with any purposive or intentionalist reading of the statute or regulation. . . .

[In one recent, typical case], prospective purchasers knew that the shelter was likely to be challenged by the IRS if uncovered on audit; that a court was apt to agree with the government's position; and that the government was likely to adopt rules to combat the shelter. They assumed, however, that the shelter was apt to escape detection; that if detected they could settle with the government on favorable terms; and that any rules adopted would be prospective in application.

In fact, it was not until years after the shelter was first marketed that the government announced its opposition to the shelter. No cases involving the shelter have yet been litigated, suggesting that the majority of purchasers won their bet on the "audit lottery" and escaped detection; and that those caught on audit settled on favorable terms. . . .

The Market for Tax Shelters

Tax shelters—sometimes referred to as tax products or structured tax products—are promoted (developed and marketed) by investment banks, smaller tax shelter shops or boutiques and large accounting firms. A large shelter promoter may pay scores of accountants or lawyers to develop shelters and an even larger group to sell shelters. A shelter may cost $1 million to develop and market—a sum that may be recovered in a single sale. There is a competitive market in shelter promotion and little effective intellectual protection. A promoter will often offer its own version of a shelter that was developed by a competitor and proves successful in the marketplaces. At any given time, a large shelter promoter will offer clients a selection of tax products.

For obvious reasons, shelter purchasers do not reveal the shelter sales; purchasers are equally reticent. It is impossible, therefore, to come up with any verified figures of shelter use. . . . Recently, the IRS announced that voluntary disclosures under its tax amnesty provisions had yielded over $30 billion dollars in shelter-related deductions and that it was pursuing leads on newly discovered shelters. . . .

The Problem of Tax Shelters

Shelters impose considerable certain costs in the form of accounting and legal fees, fees paid to promoter and so on. Shelters also impose less easily monitized costs. Shelters redistribute the tax burden, lowering the rate on purchasers and requiring higher rates on everyone else. This raises an obvious fairness problem; it may create inefficiencies as well, as the marginal cost of replacing funds exceeds the cost of raising funds in the no-shelter world.

Perhaps most significantly, shelters threaten to undermine tax compliance. . . . [Their] complexity may be a necessary element of the shelter, but it also serves as a screen against government detection and public scrutiny. Shelters have nonetheless begun to attract attention in the general media. The knowledge that the largest companies and wealthiest individuals are using shelters to reduce tax is likely to infuriate many taxpayers. These taxpayers may view the complexity of the deals as a sign of guilt; or in any event have no sympathy for the technical (and in many cases, implausible) legal arguments upon which the shelter is based. The significant role in shelter promotion played by large accounting firms, still tarnished with their role in recent accounting scandals, is likely to further anger taxpayers. The danger is that some of these taxpayers may respond by reducing their own tax payments—not through tax shelters but through crude measures such as overstated deductions, understated income, and non-filing. The IRS and Justice Department now find themselves hard pressed to pursue current non-compliance. The government would be incapable of responding to any widespread tax revolt . . . [A]nd a decline in compliance from this revenue source would have a dramatic effect on government programs and the economy. . . .

The Political Economy of the Shelter War

The shelter battle, as it were, is fought on one side by [powerful accounting firms that market tax shelters and on the other by] a handful of academics, a handful of practicing lawyers, and a handful of journalists; . . . [T]here are not many taking up the challenge [to shelters] and most of those who do cannot afford to or do not wish to do this full time. The group is further hobbled by the complex nature of the problem; it is difficult to explain the dynamics of the shelter in a way that can be understood by a legislator, let alone a constituent. Of course, that is one reason why there [are] no publicly funded groups that pay a role here.

What of the professions? One can't expect representatives of the Big 4 accounting firms to play a disinterested role here—they are leading sellers of shelters. Smaller national and even regional accounting firms have the same conflict.

Lawyers have somewhat more freedom, and some members of the private bar have done yeoman's duty in this area. However, the lawyers most in the thick of things are conflicted here as well. Those of us in academia who write on the issue frequently get calls from members of the bar who are willing to give the outlines of an argument, or a shelter, but who feel they cannot take a public stand on the matter for fear of alienating clients.

The imbalance here poses a bit of a dilemma for any administration wishing to make high level appointments. Many if not most of the top lawyers and accountants have worked, directly or indirectly, for shelter promoters or taxpayers who bought shelters and need them defended. Of course, experience with industry will in some cases make one a better regulator. . . . [But] it is only natural for someone who has spent a substantial portion of his or her professional life working for one set of clients to identify with those clients. . . .

NOTES AND QUESTIONS

Most tax practice involves three primary roles: structuring transactions to insure compliance and to achieve maximum benefits under applicable regulations; reporting transactions to the IRS; and representing clients in tax disputes. In their reporting function, lawyers often adopt an aggressive posture similar to their adversarial litigating role, partly because the sanction for being wrong are generally low. As noted earlier, the penalties for understating income on a return are modest. Moreover, the vast majority of returns are prepared by accountants, so pressures on tax practitioners to compete for clients further encourages an adversarial stance.

Yet the process of filing returns lacks the safeguards of conventional adversarial procedures, particularly because audits are so infrequent. Some experts believe that the ethical requirements governing tax practice should be comparable to the strict standards of disclosure applicable to SEC work.[58] By contrast, other commentators have maintained that where the law is unclear, individuals should be given a fair degree of latitude in pressing reasonable positions and that the way to increase compliance is through imposing greater penalties on taxpayers, not their advisors. Some prominent associations of tax lawyers have advocated reforms giving clients more incentives to seek the most accurate legal advice, rather than the most aggressive.[59]

1.   Which of these positions do you find most convincing?

2.   Should Congress, the courts, or the Internal Revenue Service seek to impose greater ethical obligations on tax practitioners than the American Bar Association has mandated? Is it reasonable to hold lawyers to higher professional standards than those of other providers of tax-related services, including accountants? If not, does that mean that law, a self-regulating profession, will be hostage to the lowest common denominator accepted by other occupational groups? Do lawyers have a special professional responsibility, along the lines that Robert Gordon suggested, to promote compliance with the law and to respect the values of honesty and fair dealing on which it depends?

3.   Do tax lawyers, as individuals or a group, have any responsibility to help curb abusive tax shelters? As some commentators have noted, the bar has mixed incentives. Tax shelters are promoted primarily by accounting firms, which compete with law firms for tax business. A client who buys shelter-related services from accounting firms may often turn to them for other matters.[60] A crackdown on shelters would erode profits for law

---

58.   "IRS Chief Counsel Calls on Attorneys to Embrace Stricter Ethical Principles," 18 *ABA/BNA Lawyers' Manual on Professional Conduct* 727 (December 4, 2002) (arguing for heightened ethical standards among tax attorneys).

59.   For example, this was the position of the New York State Bar Association Tax Section. See Tanina Rostain, "Sheltering Lawyers: The Organized Tax Bar and the Tax Shelter Industry," 23 *Yale J. Reg.* 77 (2006).

60.   Joseph Bankman, "The Business Purpose Doctrine and the Sociology of Tax," 54 *SMU L. Rev.* 149, 153 (2001).

graduates who work in accounting firms, but would likely benefit other lawyers who are their competitors. Yet as Bankman notes, few of these lawyers have been willing to take an active position in the shelter war for fear of antagonizing clients. Moreover, some attorneys have developed a lucrative speciality in supplying opinions to clients who have bought shelters devised by major accounting firms. Partners at the once prominent firm of Jenkins and Gilchrest charged as much as $2 million for a single opinion.

In response, the IRS has tightened regulations governing tax shelters, 31 C.F.R. part 10, Circular 230 (2005), and pursued some high profile cases against firms that profited from abusive practices. Jenkins and Gilchrest dissolved after paying a $76 million civil penalty to the IRS and settling civil liability claims by shelter clients for $81 million. Another nationally prominent firm, Sidley & Austin LLP, paid a $39 million penalty and $154 million in a civil liability settlement.[61]

The problems caused by tax shelters and similar aggressive practices are unlikely to decline, particularly if competitive pressures continue to increase. Tax work now is more likely to go to accountants than lawyers.[62] Given these market realities, how can a "race to the bottom" in tax ethics be prevented?[63]

PROBLEM 6

Several months ago, the IRS passed a regulation providing that prepayment interest will be tax deductible for certain transactions completed before a specified date. Your firm represents several clients in transactions that almost closed by the prescribed date, and would have done so but for a senior partner's negligence. In order to save those clients from substantial losses and absolve themselves from any malpractice claims, the lawyers working on the case have backdated relevant forms.

a) You are an associate in the firm's tax department. You are not asked to do any backdating personally, although you are working on two transactions in which backdated documents will be submitted. What would you do?

b) Would it matter why the senior partner failed to complete the transactions? Suppose the oversight resulted after the partner's husband had a heart attack?

c) Would it matter what your expectations were about advancement within the firm? Should it?

d) Would your response differ if the clients had themselves backdated forms because of their own oversight? Suppose that after the clients backdate the forms, no one in your firm signs the return or actively assists

---

61. Martin Whittaker, "Specialists Say Lessons of Recent Scandals is that Lawyers Shouldn't Delegate," 23 ABA/BNA *Lawyers' Man. Prof. Conduct* 300, 301 (2007).

62. Bankman, *supra* note 60, at 154.

63. See Randolph W. Thrower, "Is the Tax Bar Going Casual—Ethically?" 54 *Tax Lawyer* 797 (2001).

the backdating. However, you are asked to provide further tax-related representation to those clients. What would you do?

NOTES

Frederic Corneel's proposed Guidelines to Tax Practice Second provide:

1.   It is unethical to assist the client in the preparation of evidence designed to mislead the Service....

2.   At times the client in ignorance of the tax law has taken steps resulting in adverse tax consequences or has failed to take steps to prevent such consequences. It is not unethical to make every effort to correct this result, provided that this can be done without destruction of existing documents, backdating of new documents or other steps intended to mislead the Service as to what in fact happened.[64]

Although the IRS and courts will generally allow correction of clerical, mathematical, or drafting errors that do not reflect the true intent of the parties, they will not permit backdating to obtain favorable tax treatment. Backdating can also lead to criminal liability. See §§ 7201 and 7206.

It is clear that a lawyer cannot ethically assist backdating; it is less clear what an associate under the facts of Problem 6 is obligated to do about it. Consider the materials on supervisory and subordinate attorneys in Chapter VII. Model Rule 5.2 provides that a "lawyer is bound by the rules of professional conduct notwithstanding that the lawyer acted at the direction of another person." However, a subordinate lawyer does not violate the rules by acting "in accordance with a supervisory lawyer's reasonable resolution of an arguable question of professional duty." The Rules also require attorneys to report violations of disciplinary rules that raise a substantial question as to another lawyer's honesty, trustworthiness, or fitness to practice unless their knowledge of such violations is protected as a client confidence. The Code requires reporting of all unprivileged knowledge of violations.

As the materials in Chapter XV indicate, attorneys' reports of collegial misconduct to disciplinary agencies are relatively rare. Disciplinary sanctions against attorneys for failure to report are rarer still. Although the reluctance to "inform" on other lawyers, particularly one's own superiors, is understandable on pragmatic grounds, it is inconsistent with the bar's commitment to self-regulation. At the very least, many experts believe that law firm associates who confront clearly unethical conduct should disclose it to other members of the firm. As the Berkey–Kodak case history in Chapter VII indicates, that strategy may often prove less professionally damaging than silence. In circumstances where the risk of retaliation against the associate is high, many commentators argue that the appropriate response is not to absolve associates from responsibility, but rather to

---

64.   Frederic G. Corneel, "Guidelines to Tax Practice Second," 43 *Tax Law.* 312 (1990).

alter regulatory structures to encourage internal reporting. What is your view?

Are the same considerations applicable where the issue is client rather than collegial fraud, as on the facts of part (d) of Problem 6? Consider Geoffrey Hazard's observations below.

A widespread problem of backdating began in the 1990s, when stock option grants became an increasingly common way of compensating executives. Such options give beneficiaries the right to purchase the stock at a specified "exercise" price.[65] The lower the exercise price in relation to the stock's current market value, the more valuable the right. Widely publicized studies in 2005 and 2006 indicated that as many as 2000 companies may have backdated options to provide the greatest possible returns for the option-holder.[66] In the wake of such reports, over 200 companies have faced adverse consequences connected with backdating, including SEC investigation and shareholder derivative suits.[67] The extent to which lawyers have been involved in misconduct is unclear. In many cases, backdating may have involved ignorance or negligence regarding appropriate accounting and disclosure practices, rather than fraud. In other cases, attorneys may have personally benefitted from backdating, or faced pressure to ignore violations that appeared common in the surrounding business culture.[68] When lawyers are faced with that pressure, what can be done to encourage their resistance?

Panel Discussion on Professional Responsibility and the Model Rules of Professional Conduct

35 University of Miami Law Review 639, 659–60, 662 (1981).

Professor Geoffrey Hazard: There is a critical distinction between giving advice and any further step of facilitation. There is, however, no absolutely clean factual boundary there. The problem of perjury, in my opinion, begins with the fact that the lawyer is presenting the case. It would be one thing if the client asked you, "Look, I left out a lot of income in last year's tax return. What should I do?" In that situation a lawyer can say, "There are severe penalties if they catch up with you; they will be heavy. I have to tell you that the auditing is selective. For someone in your

---

65. If the option price is at the current price when it is issued, it is referred to as "at the money." If it is at a lower price, it is "in the money." Before Sarbanes–Oxley reforms, regulations distinguished between these two options and required only "in the money" options to be recorded as an expense and disclosed to the SEC. That distinction made "in the money" options less desirable because they depressed short term earnings. The temptation, therefore, was to backdate "at the money" options to a date that had lower exercise prices.

66. Erik Lie, "On the Timing of CEO Stock Option Awards," 51 *Management Sci-*ence 802 (2005); Stephanie Saul, "Study Finds Backdating of Options Widespread," *N.Y. Times*, July 17, 2006, at C1.

67. "Options Backdating: Accounting, Tax, and Economics," Part III (NERA Economic Consulting, 2007).

68. Charles Forelle & James Bandler, "McAfee's Ex–Counsel is Charge with Options Fraud," *Wall St. J.*, Feb. 28, 2007, at A3 (describing suit against former general counsel accused of ordering his own option grant to be changed to lower exercise price).

income tax bracket with the kind of income you have, as I understand what they do (and they don't generally tell us), the chances are statistically remote that they will question it. It's for you to decide what you want to do. I consider it my obligation to tell you what the enforcement situation is, as well as what the law is." There is no question what the law is and I can't further the client's purpose, and I haven't done so. There's also no doubt that you don't tell anybody. That's it. If the client wants to do it, that's his problem. The same holds true when you're talking about other kinds of violations.

The problem in practice is often trickier than that, however. Frequently, particularly these days, clients not only have the responsibility of compliance, they also have the responsibility to file reports. They may ask you some questions about the reports. Take the case in which an SEC report requires the lawyer's signature. I just don't see how the lawyer is in any different situation than an income tax preparer signing a tax return. On the other hand, the lawyer can say, "I will look at your report and tell you what the law is." Again what you have done is give advice. You can give advice that tells the client what the law is and what enforcement practices are, as long as you are not involved in executing the purpose. In doing so you do not violate the law and you do not violate legal ethics. . . .

The ethic [of winking at misconduct] leads to the society fairly described in *The Lord of the Flies*, a society of mendacity, irresponsibility, cruelty, and disorder. A system of orderly government presupposes a willingness of its citizens to invoke authority. If you have ever been in a school in which no one "tattled," you know it is as I have described.

So far as what clients think, you have to use good judgment at the margin. You don't go blowing the whistle as your first recourse. One of the things you must have is the courage to tell the client what to do. That brings to mind a good story from the firm I went with. When I was being interviewed, one of the lawyers was writing a resignation letter, firing a client. That impressed the hell out of me. The lawyer was obviously quite distressed by doing it because he had represented the client for quite a while. But this client had been involved in two fraud cases and now had gotten into a third. The lawyer knew these were not accidents. This is just the way the client did business. I'm sure people asked why that firm no longer represented that company, but I believe the firm was far better off without that client. That firm was terribly interested in maintaining its reputation for trustworthiness in its representations. The State Tax Commission and the Internal Revenue Service would believe us if our people made a statement as to what the situation was. That was of great value to the firm; it was of great value to the firm's clients. Most businesses want to be represented by lawyers who have a first-class reputation for integrity because their legal counsel's reputation reflects on them. It's just about that simple.

QUESTIONS

Is it that simple?

E. GOVERNMENT LAWYERS

Government lawyers routinely counsel and advise public officials about their legal responsibilities. Typically, the interpretations of law offered by government lawyers are never tested in court. Government lawyers' advice to officials may be confidential, and it may lead officials to make decisions that do not become public. Even when officials' interpretations of law are challenged, courts may refuse to review executive actions for constitutional reasons grounded in the separation of powers. Sometimes courts regard the issues as political questions, or questions about which the executive deserves deference. When, for one reason or another, judicial review is lacking, the legal interpretations government lawyers provide to officials become for all practical purposes binding law. Arguably, this places a special burden of responsibility on government lawyers. In addition, some have argued that government lawyers have heightened responsibilities of fidelity to law because they are themselves government officials.[69] The materials that follow explore the nature of the government lawyer's counseling role through a case study: the role of executive branch lawyers in the "war on terrorism."

PROBLEM 7

The following excerpt comes from the minutes of a 2002 meeting at Guantanamo Naval Base to discuss the use of harsh interrogation techniques on detainees. Two of the ten participants were lawyers: one, Lieutenant Colonel Diane Beaver, was Staff Judge Advocate to the task force commander at Guantanamo; the other, Jonathan Fredman, was assistant general counsel to the CIA and chief counsel to the CIA's counterterrorism center. The other participants were military and intelligence officers. Nine days after this meeting, LTC Beaver provided a legal memorandum that approved more than a dozen aggressive interrogation techniques, including stress positions, sleep deprivation, intimidation through the use of military working dogs, forced nudity and forced grooming, isolation, and the "wet towel" technique (a form of waterboarding, a technique of near-drowning).[70] Many of these techniques were used on detainees in Guantanamo and Abu Ghraib prison in Iraq.

a) As you read this excerpt, consider the propriety of the lawyers' comments. To what extent are the lawyers providing legal advice? Moral or other advice? Policy recommendations? Which, if any, of their comments exceed the role of a legal advisor?

---

69. For discussion of the heightened public-interest obligations of government lawyers, see, e.g., Steven K. Berenson, "Public Lawyers, Private Values: Can, Should, and Will Government Lawyers Serve the Public Interest?", 41 *B.C. L. Rev.* 789 (2000) and the materials in Chapter X.

70. Legal Brief on Proposed Counter–Resistance Strategies from Diane Beaver to Gen. James T. Hill, Oct. 11, 2002, in *The Torture Papers: The Road to Abu Ghraib* 229 (Karen J. Greenberg & Joshua L. Dratel eds. 2005). The techniques are listed in *id.* at 227–28.

b) After reading the materials following the excerpt, determine the soundness of the legal advice offered by the lawyers.

c) Consider the e-mail from Mark Fallon, deputy commander of DOD's Criminal Investigation Task Force, reproduced directly following the minutes of the meeting. Do you agree or disagree with the concerns Fallon presents there?

For convenience of reading, we identify the comments of the lawyers by placing their names in boldface.

Counter Resistance Strategy Meeting Minutes[71]

The following notes were taken during the aforementioned meeting at 1340 on October 2, 2002. All questions and comments have been paraphrased:

. . .

COL Cummings: We can't do sleep deprivation.

LTC Beaver: Yes we can—with approval.

. . .

LTC Beaver: We may need to curb the harsher operations while ICRC [the International Committee of the Red Cross] is around. It is better not to expose them to any controversial techniques. We must have the support of the DOD.

Becker: We have had many reports from Bagram about sleep deprivation being used.

LTC Beaver: True, but officially it is not happening. It is not being reported officially. The ICRC is a serious concern. They will be in and out, scrutinizing our operations, unless they are displeased and decide to protest and leave. This would draw a lot of negative attention.

. . .

Fredman: The DOJ has provided much guidance on this issue. The CIA is not held to the same rules as the military. In the past when the ICRC has made a big deal about certain detainees, the DOD has "moved" them away from the attention of ICRC. Upon questioning from the ICRC about their whereabouts, the DOD's response has repeatedly been that the detainee merited no status under the Geneva Convention. The CIA has employed aggressive techniques against less than a handful of suspects since 9/11.

Under the Torture Convention, torture has been prohibited under international law, but the language of the statutes is written vaguely. Severe mental and physical pain is prohibited. The mental part is explained as poorly as the physical. Severe physical pain described as anything causing permanent physical damage to major organs or body

---

71. This document was released during Senate hearings on detainee abuse in June 2008, and is available at http://levin.senate. gov/newsroom/supporting/2008/Documents. SASC.061708.pdf, Tab 7.

parts. Mental torture described as anything leading to permanent, profound damage to the senses or personality. It is basically subject to perception. If the detainee dies you're doing it wrong.... Any of the techniques that lie on the harshest end of the spectrum must be performed by a highly trained individual. Medical personnel should be present to treat any possible accidents. The CIA operates without military intervention. When the CIA has wanted to use more aggressive techniques in the past, the FBI has pulled their personnel from theatre. In those rare instances, aggressive techniques have proven very helpful.

LTC Beaver: We will need documentation to protect us.

Fredman: Yes, if someone dies while aggressive techniques are being used, regardless of cause of death, the backlash of attention would be severely detrimental. Everything must be approved and documented.

Becker: LEA [law enforcement agency] personnel will not participate in harsh techniques.

LTC Beaver: There is no legal reason why LEA personnel cannot participate in these operations.... LEA choice not to participate in these types of interrogations is more ethical and moral as opposed to legal.

Fredman: The videotaping of even totally legal techniques will look "ugly." ... The Torture Convention prohibits torture and cruel, inhumane and degrading treatment. The US did not sign up on the second part, because of the 8th amendment (cruel and unusual punishment), but we did sign the part about torture. This gives us more license to use more controversial techniques.

LTC Beaver: Does SERE employ the "wet towel" technique?[72]

Fredman: If a well-trained individual is used to perform this technique it can feel like you're drowning. The lymphatic system will react as if you're suffocating, but your body will not cease to function. It is very effective to identify phobias and use them (ie, insects, snakes, claustrophobia)....

. . .

LTC Beaver: In the BSCT [Behavioral Science Consultation Team] paper it says something about "imminent threat of death", ...

Fredman: The threat of death is also subject to scrutiny, and should be handled on a case by case basis. Mock executions don't work as well as friendly approaches, like letting someone write a letter home, or providing them with an extra book.

---

72. [Editors' note: "SERE" stands for "Survival, Evasion, Resistance, Escape." SERE training is given by the United States to its own special forces to teach resistance to torture and abuse. Several SERE tactics, including waterboarding, were "reverse engineered" to be used by U.S. interrogators against uncooperative detainees.]

Becker: I like the part about ambient noise.

.   .   .

Meeting ended at 1450.

* * *

The approval of the harsh techniques drew some internal criticism at the Department of Defense. Noteworthy is the following e-mail from the deputy commander of DOD's Criminal Investigation Task Force.

From: Fallon Mark

Sent: Monday, October 28, 2002

To: McCahon Sam

Sam:

... This looks like the kinds of stuff Congressional hearings are made of. Quotes from LTC Beaver regarding things that are not being reported give the appearance of impropriety. Other comments like "It is basically subject to perception. If the detainee dies you're doing it wrong" and "Any of the techniques that lie on the harshest end of the spectrum must be performed by a highly trained individual. Medical personnel should be present to treat any possible accidents" seem to stretch beyond the bounds of legal propriety. Talk of "wet towel treatment" which results in the lymphatic gland reacting as if you are suffocating, would in my opinion shock the conscience of any legal body looking at using the results of the interrogations or possibly even the interrogators. Someone needs to be considering how history will look back at this.

R/Mark Fallon

Deputy Commander

Criminal Investigation Task Force [Department of Defense]

NOTES: THE "TORTURE MEMOS"

In the minutes reproduced above, CIA lawyer Fredman remarks that "DOJ has provided much guidance on this issue" of harsh interrogation. He is referring to what have subsequently become known as the "torture memos"—legal opinions on aspects of detainee and interrogation policy written by high-ranking executive branch lawyers.

Shortly after the revelation in 2004 of prisoner torture and humiliation at Abu Ghraib, the Justice Department released a highly controversial memo that approved extremely harsh interrogation tactics that many regard as torture. (Other memos approving specific techniques have not yet been released.) The memos were written by lawyers in Justice's Office of Legal Counsel, or OLC.

The OLC is an elite unit of approximately twenty lawyers whose job is to provide legal advice to the executive branch. OLC alumni include past and present Supreme Court Justices. OLC advisory opinions are generally taken to bind the executive branch, although there is some debate over whether they are binding as a matter of law or of custom.[73] The OLC publishes some of its opinions, but others remain secret. The "torture memos" were among those intended to be secret. The best-known went out over the signature of then-OLC head Jay S. Bybee (now a federal judge), but was written by another OLC lawyer, Berkeley law professor John Yoo. It is often called the "Bybee/Yoo" memo. It analyzes federal statutes making torture a crime, as well as related issues.

The Bybee/Yoo memo, excerpted in the materials below, provided maximum latitude for harsh interrogation tactics. It concluded that inflicting physical pain does not count as torture unless the pain reaches the level associated with organ failure or death; that utilizing techniques known to be painful is not torture unless the interrogator specifically intends the pain to be equivalent to the pain accompanying organ failure or death; that inflicting mental pain or suffering is lawful unless the interrogator specifically intends it to last months or years beyond the interrogation; that enforcing criminal laws against Presidentially-authorized torture would be unconstitutional; that self-defense can include torturing helpless detainees in the name of national defense; and that torture in the name of national security may be legally justifiable as the lesser evil, through the doctrine of necessity. The memo derived its "organ failure or death" definition of "severe pain" from a Medicare statute defining an emergency medical condition as one whose symptoms might include severe pain.

The Bybee/Yoo memo was only one of a series of controversial memos emerging from OLC. An opinion by John Yoo issued two weeks after 9/11 argued for the first time that the President's authority as commander in chief overrides federal statutes.[74] Two memos argued that the Geneva Conventions do not protect either Al Qaeda members or members of the Taliban. This proved to be a crucial argument, because the Geneva Conventions prohibit torture, cruel treatment, and "outrages against personal dignity, including humiliating and degrading treatment" of captives. Although the State Department's legal advisor strongly criticized OLC's reasoning, President Bush adopted its conclusions in February 2002.[75] This decision met with some consternation within the U.S. military: some officers and military lawyers argued that for the U.S. to deny Geneva Convention protections to captives would jeopardize U.S. prisoners of war in the future. Others pointed out that the Army's interrogation schools and its interrogation manual train interrogators according to the Geneva standards.

73. Randolph D. Moss, "Executive Branch Legal Interpretation: A Perspective from the Office of Legal Counsel," 52 *Admin. L. Rev.* 1303, 1318–20 (2000).

74. Memorandum Opinion for the Deputy Counsel to the President, *The President's Constitutional Authority to Conduct Military Operations Against Terrorists and Nations Supporting Them*, Sept. 25, 2001, available at http://www.usdoj.gov/olc/warpowers925.htm.

75. The OLC memos and President Bush' order are reproduced in *The Torture Papers, supra* note 70, at 38–79, 81–117, 134–35. The State Department's critique is Memo from William Howard Taft IV to John Yoo, Jan. 11, 2002, available at http://www.cartoon

A later "torture memo" concerning military interrogators employed reasoning very similar to the Bybee/Yoo memo; it too was written by John Yoo.[76] Two years later, in 2005, the new OLC head, Steven G. Bradbury, reportedly issued additional confidential opinions approving all existing interrogation techniques, singly or in combination.[77]

Some legal background is essential to reading the Bybee/Yoo memorandum. The United States is a party to an international anti-torture treaty, the Convention Against Torture (CAT). CAT defines torture as government agents' intentional infliction of severe mental or physical pain or suffering. It requires parties to criminalize torture, and also requires them to "undertake to prevent" cruel, inhuman, or degrading treatment that does not rise to the level of torture. And it states, "No exceptional circumstances whatsoever, whether a state of war or a threat of war, internal political instability or any other public emergency, may be invoked as a justification of torture." Article 2(2). When the U.S. Senate ratified CAT, it attached a declaration that the United States understands cruel, inhuman, or degrading treatment to be the kind of cruel treatment prohibited by the Constitution—cruel and unusual punishment under the Eighth Amendment, or treatment that violates due process under the Fifth Amendment. The latter is defined in relevant Supreme Court precedent as treatment that "shocks the conscience."

The Senate also added a reservation stating that these clauses of CAT are not self-executing, which means that they are not enforceable U.S. law until Congress implements them through legislation. Congress has implemented the requirement of criminalizing torture by enacting two criminal statutes. (Cruel, inhuman and degrading treatment short of torture has not been criminalized, although in 2005 Congress banned its use.)

18 United States Code § 2340 ("Definitions")

As used in this chapter—

(1) "torture" means an act committed by a person acting under the color of law specifically intended to inflict severe physical or mental pain or suffering (other than pain or suffering incidental to lawful sanctions) upon another person within his custody or physical control;

(2) "severe mental pain or suffering" means the prolonged mental harm caused by or resulting from—

(A) the intentional infliction or threatened infliction of severe physical pain or suffering;

---

bank.com/newyorker/slideshows/01TaftMemo.pdf

76. Memorandum for William J. Haynes II, *Military Interrogation of Alien Unlawful Enemy Combatants Held Outside the United States*, March 14, 2003, available at http://gulcfac.typepad.com/georgetown_u

niversity_law/files/march.14.memo.part1.pdf and http://gulcfac.typepad.com/georgetown_university_law/files/march14.memo.part2.pdf.

77. Scott Shane, David Johnston & James Risen, "Secret U.S. Endorsement of Severe Interrogations," *N.Y. Times*, Oct. 4, 2007, at A1.

(B) the administration or application, or threatened administration or application, of mind-altering substances or other procedures calculated to disrupt profoundly the senses or the personality;

(C) the threat of imminent death; or

(D) the threat that another person will imminently be subjected to death, severe physical pain or suffering, or the administration or application of mind-altering substances or other procedures calculated to disrupt profoundly the senses or personality.

. . .

18 United States Code § 2340A ("Torture")

(a) Offense.—Whoever outside the United States commits or attempts to commit torture shall be fined under this title or imprisoned not more than 20 years, or both, and if death results to any person from conduct prohibited by this subsection, shall be punished by death or imprisoned for any term of years or for life.

Excerpt from the "Bybee/Yoo Memo"

Memorandum from Jay S. Bybee to Alberto Gonzalez (Aug. 1, 2002)

You have asked for our Office's views regarding the standards of conduct under [CAT] as implemented by Sections 2340–2340A of title 18 of the United States Code. As we understand it, this question has arisen in the context of the conduct of interrogations outside of the United States. . . .

We conclude that for an act to constitute torture as defined in Section 2340, it must inflict pain that is difficult to endure. Physical pain amounting to torture must be equivalent in intensity to the pain accompanying serious physical injury, such as organ failure, impairment of bodily function, or even death. For purely mental pain or suffering to amount to torture under Section 2340, it must result in significant psychological harm of significant duration, e.g., lasting for months or even years. . . . We conclude that the statute, taken as a whole, makes plain that it prohibits only extreme acts.

. . .

B. "Severe Pain or Suffering"

The key statutory phrase in the definition of torture is the statement that acts amount to torture if they cause "severe physical or mental pain or suffering." In examining the meaning of a statute, its text must be the starting point. . . . Section 2340 makes plain that the infliction of pain or suffering per se, whether it is physical or mental, is insufficient to amount to torture. Instead, the text provides that pain or suffering must be "severe." The statute does not, however, define the term "severe." "In the absence of such a definition, we construe a statutory term in accordance with its ordinary or natural meaning." FDIC v. Meyer, 510 U.S. 471, 476 (1994). [The memo then sets out several dictionary definitions of "severe."] Thus, the adjective "severe" conveys that the pain or suffering must be of such a high level of intensity that the pain is difficult for the subject to endure.

Congress' use of the phrase "severe pain" elsewhere in the United States Code can shed more light on its meaning. See, e.g., West Va. Univ. Hosps., Inc. v. Casey, 499 U.S. 83, 100 (1991) ("[W]e construe [a statutory term] to contain that permissible meaning which fits most logically and comfortably into the body of both previously and subsequently enacted law.") Significantly, the phrase "severe pain" appears in statutes defining an emergency medical condition for the purpose of providing health benefits. These statutes define an emergency medical condition as one "manifesting itself by acute symptoms of sufficient severity (including *severe pain*) such that a prudent lay person, who possesses an average knowledge of health and medicine, could reasonably expect the absence of immediate medical attention to result in—placing the health of the individual . . . (i) in serious jeopardy; (ii) serious impairment to bodily functions, or (iii) serious dysfunction of any bodily organ or part." (emphasis added). Although these statutes address a substantially different subject from Section 2340, they are nonetheless helpful for understanding what constitutes severe physical pain. They treat severe pain as an indicator of ailments that are likely to result in permanent and serious physical damage in the absence of immediate medical treatment. Such damage must rise to the level of death, organ failure, or the permanent impairment of a significant bodily function. These statutes suggest that "severe pain," as used in Section 2340, must rise to a similarly high level—the level that would ordinarily be associated with a sufficiently serious physical condition or injury such as death, organ failure, or serious impairment of body functions—in order to constitute torture.

. . .

"Prolonged Mental Harm". As an initial matter, Section 2340(2) requires that the severe mental pain must be evidenced by "prolonged mental harm." To prolong is to "lengthen in time" or to "extend the duration of, to draw out." Webster's Third New International Dictionary 1815 (1988); Webster's New International Dictionary 1980 (2d ed. 1935). Accordingly, . . . the acts giving rise to the harm must cause some lasting, though not necessarily permanent, damage. For example the mental strain experienced by an individual during a lengthy and intense interrogation—such as one that state or local police might conduct upon a criminal suspect—would not violate Section 2340(2). On the other hand, the development of a mental disorder such as post-traumatic stress disorder, which can last months or even years, or even chronic depression, which also can last for a considerable period of time if untreated, might satisfy the prolonged harm requirement.

. . .

A defendant must specifically intend to cause prolonged mental harm for the defendant to have committed torture. It could be argued that a defendant needs to have specific intent only to commit the predicate acts that give rise to prolonged mental harm. Under that view, so long as the defendant specifically intended to, for example, threaten a victim with imminent death, he would have had sufficient *mens rea* for a conviction. . . . We believe that this approach is contrary to the text of the statute.

. . .

V.   The President's Commander-in-Chief Power

Even if an interrogation method arguably were to violate Section 2340A, the statute would be unconstitutional if it impermissibly encroached on the President's constitutional power to conduct a military campaign. As Commander-in-Chief, the President has the constitutional authority to order interrogations of enemy combatants to gain intelligence information concerning the military plans of the enemy. . . . Any effort to apply Section 2340A in a manner that interferes with the President's direction of such core war matters as the detention and interrogation of enemy combatants thus would be unconstitutional.

VI.   Defenses

. . .

A.   Necessity

We believe that a defense of necessity could be raised, under the current circumstances, to an allegation of a Section 2340A violation. . . . According to public and governmental reports, al Qaeda has other sleeper cells within the United States that may be planning similar attacks. . . . Clearly, any harm that might occur during an interrogation would pale to insignificance compared to the harm avoided by preventing such an attack, which could take hundreds or thousand of lives. . . .

B.   Self–Defense

Even if a court were to find that a violation of Section 2340A was not justified by necessity, a defendant could still appropriately raise a claim of self-defense. . . . The threat of an impending terrorist attack threatens the lives of hundreds if not thousands of American citizens. . . .

To be sure, this situation is different from the usual self-defense justification. . . . Self-defense as usually discussed involves using force against an individual who is about to conduct the attack. . . . Nonetheless, leading scholarly commentators believe that interrogation of such individuals using methods that might violate Section 2340A would be justified under the doctrine of self-defense, because the combatant by aiding and promoting the terrorist plot "has culpably caused the situation where someone might get hurt. If hurting him is the only means to prevent the death or injury of others put at risk by his actions, such torture should be permissible, and on the same basis that self-defense is permissible." Michael S. Moore, *Torture and the Balance of Evils*, 23 Israel L. Rev. 280, 323 (1989).

. . .

NOTES

The Bybee/Yoo memo attracted a great deal of attention. Among its defenders were Professors Eric Posner and Adrian Vermeule. (Posner is himself an OLC alumnus.) To Posner and Vermeule, "the memorandum's arguments are standard lawyerly fare, routine stuff."[78] They explain:

> The Justice Department memorandum came out of the OLC, whose jurisprudence has traditionally been highly pro-executive.... Not everyone likes OLC's traditional jurisprudence, or its awkward role as both defender and adviser of the executive branch; but former officials who claim that the OLC's function is solely to supply "disinterested" advice, or that it serves as a "conscience" for the government, are providing a sentimental, distorted and self-serving picture of a complex reality.[79]

John Yoo, they add, belongs to "a dynamic generation of younger scholars ... who argue for an expansive conception of presidential power over foreign affairs."[80]

Other commentators were less flattering. Focusing particularly on the interpretation of "severe pain" in the criminal law of torture by drawing on a Medicare statute, Peter Brooks labeled the memo "textual interpretation run amok—less 'lawyering as usual' than the work of some bizarre literary deconstructionist."[81] Anthony Lewis, focusing on the memo's sections on the applicability of criminal defenses like self-defense and necessity if interrogators were accused of torture, claimed that the memo "read like the advice of a mob lawyer to a mafia don on how to skirt the law and stay out of prison."[82] The voluminous academic commentary was almost entirely negative.[83]

Eventually, OLC itself took the highly unusual step of withdrawing the Bybee/Yoo memo, and replacing it with an alternative memo, authored by acting OLC head Daniel Levin.

Excerpt from the "Levin Memo"

Memorandum from Daniel Levin to James B. Comey (Dec. 24, 2004)

Torture is abhorrent both to American law and values and to international norms.... We decided to withdraw the August 2002 Memorandum, a

---

78. Eric Posner & Adrian Vermeule, "A 'Torture' Memo and Its Tortuous Critics," *Wall St. J.*, July 6, 2004.

79. *Id.*

80. *Id.*

81. Peter Brooks, "The Plain Meaning of Torture?," *Slate*, Feb. 9, 2005, available at http://www.slate.com/id/2113314.

82. Anthony Lewis, "Making Torture Legal," *N.Y. Rev. Books*, July 15, 2004.

83. *See, e.g.,* David Luban, "The Torture Lawyers of Washington," in *Legal Ethics and Human Dignity* (2007); Robert K. Vischer, "Legal Advice as Moral Perspective," 19 *Geo. J. Legal Ethics* 225 (2006); Jesselyn Radack, "Tortured Legal Ethics: The Role of the Government Advisor in the War on Terrorism," 77 *U. Colo. L. Rev.* 1 (2006); Kathleen Clark, "Ethical Issues Raised by the OLC Torture Memorandum," 1 *J. Nat'l Security L. & Pol'y* 455 (2005); David Luban, "Liberalism, Torture, and the Ticking Bomb," 91 *Va. L. Rev.* 1425 (2005); Michael D. Ramsey, "Torturing Executive Power," 93 *Geo. L. J.* 1213 (2005); Jeremy Waldron, "Torture and the Common Law: Jurisprudence for the White House," 105 *Colum. L. Rev.* 1681 (2005); W. Bradley Wendel, "Legal Ethics and the Separation of Law and Morals," 91 *Cornell L. Rev.* 67 (2005); Ruth Wedgwood & R. James Woolsey, "Law and Torture," *Wall St. J.*, June 28, 2004; Richard B. Bilder & Detlev A. Vagts, "Speaking Law to Power: Lawyers and Torture," 98 *A.J.I.L.* 689 (2004).

decision you announced in June 2004. At that time, you directed this Office to prepare a replacement memorandum. . . .

This memorandum supersedes the August 2002 Memorandum in its entirety. Because the discussion in that memorandum concerning the President's Commander-in-Chief power and the potential defenses to liability was—and remains—unnecessary, it has been eliminated from the analysis that follows. Considerations of the bounds of any such authority would be inconsistent with the President's unequivocal directive that United States personnel not engage in torture. . . .[84]

. . . [W]e disagree with statements in the August 2002 Memorandum limiting "severe" pain under the statute to "excruciating and agonizing" pain, or to pain "equivalent in intensity to the to the pain accompanying serious physical injury, such as organ failure, impairment of bodily function, or even death."

. . .

Although Congress defined "torture" under sections 2340–2340A to require conduct specifically intended to cause "severe" pain or suffering, we do not believe Congress intended to reach only conduct involving "excruciating or agonizing" pain or suffering. Although there is some support for this formulation in the ratification history of the CAT, a proposed express understanding to that effect was "criticized for setting too high a threshold of pain," and was not adopted. . . .[85]

Drawing distinctions among gradations of pain (for example, severe, mild, moderate, substantial, extreme, intense, excruciating, or agonizing) is obviously not an easy task, especially given the lack of any precise, objective scientific criteria for measuring pain. We are, however, aided in this task by judicial interpretations of the Torture Victims Protection Act ("TVPA"). The TVPA . . . provides a civil remedy to victims of torture. . . .

. . . Cases in which courts have found torture suggest the nature of the extreme conduct that falls within the statutory definition. [The memo then summarizes the conduct constituting torture in four TVPA decisions:] a course of conduct that included, among other things, severe beatings of the plaintiff, repeated threats of death and electric shock, sleep deprivation,

---

84. While we have identified various disagreements with the August 2002 Memorandum, we have reviewed this Office's prior opinions addressing issues involving treatment of detainees and do not believe that any of their conclusions would be different under the standards set forth in this memorandum.

85. . . . The August 2002 Memorandum also looked to the use of "severe pain" in certain other statutes, and concluded that to satisfy the definition in section 2340, pain "must be equivalent in intensity to the pain accompanying serious physical injury, such as organ failure, impairment of bodily function, or even death." We do not agree with those statements. Those other statutes define an "emergency medical condition," for purposes of providing health benefits. . . . They do not define "severe pain" even in that very different context (rather, they use it as an indication of an "emergency medical condition"), and they do not state that death, organ failure, or impairment of bodily function cause "severe pain," but rather that "severe pain" may indicate a condition that, if untreated, could cause one of those results. We do not believe that they provide a proper guide for interpreting "severe pain" in the very different context of the prohibition against torture in sections 2340–2340A. . . .

extended shackling to a cot (at times with a towel over his nose and mouth and water poured down his nostrils), seven months of confinement in a "suffocatingly hot" and cramped cell, and eight years of solitary or near-solitary confinement ...; severe beatings to the genitals, head and other parts of the body with metal pipes, brass knuckles, batons, a baseball bat, and various other items; removal of teeth with pliers; kicking in the face and ribs; breaking of bones and ribs and dislocation of fingers; cutting a figure into the victim's forehead; hanging the victim and beating him; extreme limitations of food and water; and subjection to games of "Russian roulette" ...; "cutting off ... fingers, pulling out ... fingernails," and electric shocks to the testicles ...; frequent beatings, pistol whipping, threats of imminent death, electric shocks, and attempts to force confessions by playing Russian roulette and pulling the trigger at each denial, constituted torture.

. . .

... The inclusion of the words "or suffering" in the phrase "severe physical pain or suffering" suggests that the statutory category of physical torture is not limited to "severe physical pain." ... Exactly what is included in the concept of "severe physical suffering," however, is difficult to ascertain.... We conclude that under some circumstances "physical suffering" may of sufficient intensity and duration to meet the statutory definition of torture even if it does not involve "severe physical pain." To constitute such torture, *"severe* physical suffering" would have to be a condition of some extended duration or persistence as well as intensity....

. . .

Turning to the question of what constitutes "prolonged mental harm caused by or resulting from" a predicate act, we believe that ... [the harm] has some lasting duration....[86]

QUESTIONS

1.   Participants in formulating U.S. interrogation policy emphasize that at the time the torture memos were written, there was a great deal of fear within the government about a possible Al Qaeda attack on or around the anniversary of 9/11. According to General Richard Myers, who chaired the Joint Chiefs of Staff at the time, "There was a sense of urgency that in my forty years of military experience hadn't existed in other contingencies."[87] He explained that there was "the real fear that one of the detainees might know when the next attack would happen, and that they would miss vital information."[88] Should this make a difference in what an executive branch lawyer puts in a legal opinion?

---

86. ... Although we believe that the mental harm must be of some lasting duration to be "prolonged," to the extent that formulation was intended to suggest that the mental harm would have to last for at least "months or even years," we do not agree.

87. Philippe Sands, *The Torture Team: Rumsfeld's Memo and the Betrayal of American Values* 88 (2008).

88. *Id.*

2.   Should a confidential legal opinion take note of adverse legal authority to the position it adopts? Some commentators complained that the Bybee/Yoo memo does not so much as mention the leading case limiting presidential power in wartime, *Youngstown Sheet & Tube v. Sawyer*, 343 U.S. 579 (1952), in which the Court denied President Truman the right to nationalize steel factories in the Korean War.[89] So too, fifteen months before the memo, the Supreme Court's decision in *U.S. v. Oakland Cannabis Buyers' Cooperative* questioned the availability of necessity defenses in federal criminal law:

> [W]e note that it is an open question whether federal courts ever have authority to recognize a necessity defense not provided by statute. A necessity defense "traditionally covered the situation where physical forces beyond the actor's control rendered illegal conduct the lesser of two evils." Even at common law, the defense of necessity was somewhat controversial. And under our constitutional system, in which federal crimes are defined by statute rather than by common law, it is especially so.... Nonetheless, we recognize that this Court has discussed the possibility of a necessity defense without altogether rejecting it.[90]

The Bybee/Yoo memo does not mention *Oakland Cannabis Buyers'* in its discussion of the necessity defense. Nor does it mention that no reported federal case has recognized the necessity defense for crimes of violence. In litigation contexts, Model Rule 3.3(a)(2) stipulates that "a lawyer shall not knowingly fail to disclose to the tribunal legal authority in the controlling jurisdiction known to the lawyer to be directly adverse to the position of the client and not disclosed by opposing counsel." Should the same standard apply when a government lawyer presents a legal opinion?

Along the same lines, the Bybee/Yoo memo cites the legal scholar Michael Moore to support the proposition that "interrogation ... using methods that might violate Section 2340A would be justified under the doctrine of self-defense." The memo omits the following sentence from the page cited from Moore's article: "[T]he literal law of self-defense is not available to justify their torture." Does this omission transcend the bounds of honesty?

3.   Was the Bybee/Yoo memo's "organ failure or death" interpretation of the phrase "severe pain," derived from a Medicare statute, legally frivolous? Was it, as Brooks put it, "textual interpretation run amok," or was it (in Posner and Vermeule's words) "standard lawyerly fare, routine stuff"? Is there any objective way to tell?

4.   Consider the Levin memo's conclusion that " '*severe* physical suffering' would have to be a condition of some extended duration or persistence as well as intensity." Is there language in the statute to support this interpretation? Notice that the statute requires that severe *mental* pain or suffering

---

89. Kathleen Clark & Julie Mertus, "Torturing the Law: The Justice Department's Legal Contortions on Interrogation," *Wash. Post*, June 20, 2004, at B3.

90. *Oakland Cannabis Buyers' Cooperative*, 532 U.S. 483, 490 (2001).

must be prolonged. There is no parallel language regarding physical suffering.

One commentator has speculated that the "extended duration" requirement for severe physical suffering would likely exempt waterboarding from the definition of torture. That is because of widespread news reports that victims of waterboarding invariably break in minutes or even seconds.[91] If an OLC lawyer knows that the government has employed waterboarding and plans to continue doing so, should he try to create a legal argument that waterboarding is not torture?

Acting Assistant Attorney General Daniel Levin, the author of the memo, had himself waterboarded while he was preparing it, in order to experience the technique firsthand.[92] Was Levin's action an instance of heroic conscientiousness, or simply a bizarre misunderstanding of the lawyer's job? How could his experience be relevant to the interpretation of the torture statute? Alternatively, how else could he determine whether the pain or suffering of waterboarding rises to the statutory level of "severe"? What follows about the method of interpreting "severe" used by Bybee and Yoo?

5.   What guidance does the Levin memo offer to interrogators trying to determine whether aggressive tactics are prohibited by the torture statutes? Would it lead them to steer clear of aggressive techniques such as manipulation of room temperature, forcing detainees to stand for long periods of time, stress positions, or waterboarding? Or would it encourage them because these are not as bad as the atrocities canvassed in the TVPA caselaw?

6.   Does the Levin memo reject the Bybee/Yoo conclusions about presidential power and criminal defenses, or merely decline to address the issues? What is the status of those conclusions after the Levin memo?

7.   In footnote 84 (footnote 8 in the Levin memo's original text), Levin states that none of Bybee/Yoo's conclusions about specific interrogation techniques would be different under Levin's analytical framework. Although this was taken by some critics to indicate that the changes between the two memos were merely cosmetic, Levin testified to the contrary before a Senate committee. What he meant by the footnote, he said, was only that the lawyers who had written the Bybee/Yoo memo would not have reached different conclusions about specific techniques based on his analytical framework. The footnote "did not mean, as some have interpreted—and . . . this is my fault, no doubt, in drafting—that we had concluded that we would have reached the same conclusions as those earlier opinions did. We

---

91. Marty Lederman, "Yes, It's a No–Brainer: Waterboarding *Is* Torture," Balkinization, Oct.28, 2006, available at http://balkin.blogspot.com/2006/10/yes-its-no-brainer-waterboarding-is.html.

92. Jan Crawford Greenburg & Ariane deVogue, "Bush Administration Blocked Waterboarding Critic," ABC News, Nov. 2, 2007, available at http://abcnews.go.com/WN/DOJ/story?id=3814076&page=1.

were in fact analyzing that at the time and we never completed that analysis"[93] (because Levin was fired).

8. In the minutes excerpted in Problem 7, Jonathan Federman states, "Severe physical pain described as anything causing permanent physical damage to major organs or body parts. Mental torture described as anything leading to permanent, profound damage to the senses or personality. It is basically subject to perception. If the detainee dies you're doing it wrong." Is this a misuse of the Bybee/Yoo memo?

A Symposium on the OLC Lawyer's Role

The following exchange took place on a listserv. Participants include three former OLC lawyers, Dawn Johnsen (a former head of OLC), Neil Kinkopf, and Marty Lederman. It was compiled by Walter Dellinger, another former head of the OLC. It is reproduced with permission of all the participants.

David Luban

Tuesday, April 11, 2006 2:53 a.m.

... I've been thinking, once again, about how much leeway (ethically speaking) a lawyer writing an opinion for a client has to spin the law in the direction the client desires, as if the opinion were a brief. My view is not much. That's why I was wondering whether John Yoo tacitly agrees with me by continuing to maintain that he wasn't spinning the law. . . .

Carlos Vázquez

Tuesday, April 11, 2006 7:23 a.m.

[John Yoo] has said that many times. Here is one example [from a radio interview]:

> At the Justice Department, I think it's very important not to put in an opinion interpreting a law on what you think the right thing to do is, because I think you don't want to bias the legal advice with these other considerations. Otherwise, I think people will question the validity of the legal advice. They'll say, "Well, the reason they reached that result is that they had certain moral views or certain policy goals they wanted to achieve."

> And actually I think at the Justice Department and this office, there's a long tradition of keeping the law and policy separate. The department is there to interpret the law so that people who make policy know the rules of the game, but you're not telling them what plays to call, essentially. . . .

> I don't feel like lawyers are put on the job to provide moral answers to people when they have to choose what policies to pursue. For example, it's not the Justice Department's job to say: "Here are

---

93. Marty Lederman, "By Contrast, Here's an Administration Attorney Who Takes His Public Service Seriously—Important Revelations from Dan Levin," *Balkiniza-* tion, June 18, 2008, available at http://balkin. blogspot.com/2008/06/by-contrast-heres-admi nistration.html.

the things you should do. We have conducted this examination of interrogation techniques worldwide, and these are the 10 that seem to work best. And so go ahead and do those."[94]

Marty Lederman

Tues. 4/11/06 at 9:03 a.m.

A few disparate reactions to this thread:

Two different (although related) topics afloat here: 1. Was the OLC legal analysis itself in "good faith"? 2. Was OLC right not to include any moral, or policy-based analysis in its opinions? I'll add another, which . . . I find more pressing at this moment: 3. How should the legal profession, and the academy, thereafter treat lawyers who have given wrong, or pernicious, legal advice while in positions of public authority—to the end of ensuring that better legal advice is offered by future OLC lawyers?

1.   Taking [the second question] . . . first:

I think Yoo was correct that OLC should generally try to write its legal opinions without skewing them to a policy-or morality-based end, for at least three reasons: (i) The OLC lawyer's moral and policy judgments are no more worthy of consideration than any of the other numerous government officials who are weighing in on the question—indeed, probably much less so, at least on the policy questions, and it's a mistake (and presumptuous) for OLC lawyers to fancy that they have a better sense of the policy or the morality than do those whose jobs it is to assess those things. (ii) The basic, and unique, function of OLC is to stand apart from the policy and morality debates within the Administration and to give candid, straightforward and reliable legal advice untainted by "extraneous" considerations. And John Yoo was basically correct that it's precisely *because* of this unique role that anyone asks OLC for its advice, and that that advice is generally viewed as definitive and controlling: OLC's views of the law supersede those of everyone else save the AG and the President; its views on policy and morality are not (and should not be) treated with any special solicitude, and the insertion of such matters (at least expressly) in its opinions will, in fact, tend to make those opinions less authoritative on the legal questions, in the eyes of the Executive officials who asked for the legal advice. (iii) As a *general* matter, OLC sees its mission as determining whether the *President's* preferred policy objectives can be implemented consistent with the law. Its job is to advise the President about whether there is a lawful manner of achieving those objectives. As a *general* matter, I think this posture is a good one for OLC to adopt.

Having said that: *Of course* it is impossible to write legal analyses completely without regard to policy or morality, and we should not kid ourselves about that. OLC lawyers, like others, should be humble enough to acknowledge that the law is not an autonomous enterprise, and that there are no objectively "right" answers untainted by such considerations. More-

---

94. *Frontline Interview With John Yoo* (Oct. 18, 2005), available at http://www.pbs. org/wgbh/pages/frontline/torture/interviews/ yoo.html.

over, on those rare occasions—and torture would surely have been one of them—when OLC thinks the preferred policy would be immoral, or wrong-headed, or disastrous, *of course* the head of OLC should feel free (perhaps even ethically or morally obliged) to separately advise the President of that judgment, even if such considerations should not (expressly) appear in the text of the OLC opinion. Whether the President should give substantial weight to the moral or policy views of the AAG for OLC is another question . . .

2.   On to David Luban's focus: Was the torture memo (or others) unethical, or written in "bad faith"? . . . This is a much, much broader topic—no space or time here to address it in any detail—but I think it's a mistake to think about this question in terms of what lawyers must "ethically" do for clients as a general matter. The role of OLC vis-a-vis the President is sui generis, and is not at all analogous to that of other lawyers and their clients. Lawyers have an obligation to give their clients "accurate" legal advice in large part because their clients will suffer very untoward consequences if that advice is wrong: That is to say, private clients *generally* come to their lawyers for advice in order to avoid legal liability or exposure, or criminal culpability, and not because they have a burning desire or moral compulsion to act within the confines of what the law allows, regardless of consequence. Because of this, a lawyer is doing her client a very real disservice by giving bad (or bad-faith) advice—it exposes a client to very serious sanctions.

OLC's advice, on the other hand—especially on criminal statutes such as the Torture Act—generally *determines how the prosecuting authority will construe and enforce the law*. If John's view about the Torture Act was wrong, far from exposing his client to legal liability, such advice will *protect* the client against possible legal exposure. (Indeed, it's increasingly clear that that was the *purpose and function* of the advice in this instance—to immunize torturers against future prosecution—which is a very unfortunate way to view OLC's role.) OLC's obligations are therefore not determined by the ethical rules that generally govern lawyers and their clients, but by a "higher" obligation, and one that is, in some sense, dependent on good and bad "faith" of another kind:

The whole point of OLC is to assist the President in performing his *constitutional* obligation to take care that the laws are *faithfully* executed.

The question we *ought* to be asking, therefore, is the *constitutional* question about what "faithful" execution means in the context of the Take Care Clause. Does it mean acting according to the *best* view of what the law allows? If so, "best" according to whom? The governing Supreme Court doctrine? A prediction of what the current Court would do? What Congress *actually* in some sense "intended" (in the case of a statute such as this one)? The "best" views of the head of OLC, regardless of governing doctrine? The "best" interpretation in light of what is known about the President's own legal judgments and jurisprudence? Very hard questions.

But I don't think John was actually asking that question at all. I know he now insists that the Torture Memo represented his "best" view of what the law requires. But if that's the case, he would be an incompetent lawyer, at least on the statutory question and the questions of "necessity" and "self-defense." (I *do* think he fully believes the Commander-in-Chief arguments, and his arguments about Geneva, other treaties, and [customary international law].) Instead, I think he saw his role as giving the *most pro-presidential advice possible* within the norms of what would be viewed as "reasonable" legal judgment. That is to say, he was asking not "What is the best answer?" but instead "Is there *any* legal analysis, within the bounds of the reasonable, that can support the President's preferred policies?" And if I'm right about this, then the question is whether *that* is "faithful" execution of the law, as the Constitution requires. I think that's a very rich and complex topic. For what it's worth, in answering it I think we should keep in mind that the *President* basically instructed his lawyers to be asking that question: He wasn't asking for the "best" legal answer: He told them he wanted to stretch the envelope, and to determine whether there was *any* legal theory that could reasonably justify what he considered to be absolutely essential policies in the war on terror. Consider, as well, the fact that *most* OLC alums, and observers—but not all—think that on questions of separation of powers, and presidential power generally, OLC's role, or its historical practice, anyway, is to take the strongest pro-presidential view of the law, within the bounds of what's deemed reasonable—and that that "slanted" posture is itself "faithful" to the constitutional scheme, in which the political branches will (and should) each struggle to arrogate power to themselves.

3. Is there anything the legal profession, and the academy, should now be doing to prevent such bad advice from be given in the future? I think the notion of ethics sanctions by bar associations is, frankly, off-base. . . .

. . .

Neil Kinkopf
Tues. 4/11/06 at 10:09 a.m.

Marty, you aptly summarize and agree with John Yoo's position: "I think Yoo was correct that OLC should generally try to write its legal opinions without skewing them to a policy-or morality-based end . . ." But this strikes me as no more useful than the bromide that judges should not legislate from the bench. The context of the OLC/Yoo problem makes the law/morality-and-policy dichotomy a false one. Here the law embodies a moral and policy position: No torture, period. In fact, No torture, exclamation point. It is fair enough that the moral positions of those at OLC should not be employed to vary the moral position embodied in the law. There is of course a potentially tricky legal question as to whether any particular interrogation technique constitutes torture within the meaning of the legal prohibition. But, it seems to me backwards to apologize for taking morality into account in answering that question. The law compels that morality (or policy) come into account, and not just any-old autonomous morality, but a particular morality—the one that regards torture as unqualifiedly immoral. It seems to me that the apology should be offered by those, like John Yoo, who refuse to consider the plain moral sense of statute as written.

As [former OLC lawyer] Nina [Pillard] has so well-observed, OLC will feel pressure to come to conclusions that please the Administration.[95] And, OLC should do what it can to facilitate the policy objectives of the Administration within the law. The only plausible construction of the Torture Memo is that it is driven by an Administration's policy preference for interrogation methods that would fall within a possible definition of torture. But of course, the Administration has refused to recognize this. Whether John Yoo shared those policy objectives is presently unknowable. But it is clear that he saw in the inquiry an opportunity to proffer a view of presidential power that we do know he was deeply committed to. It is a view of executive power that is contrary to a substantial body of precedent and even if we accept that there are occasions where the executive branch appropriately employs legal theories at odds with Supreme Court doctrine (and with some of its own internal precedent), it is improper for OLC to offer such theories without reference to the tension. The Torture Memo itself provides a good example, because once those tensions were aired, the Administration refused to support the Memo and promised its repudiation.

Marty Lederman

Tues. 4/11/06 at 10:30 a.m.

Thanks very much, Neil. You've hit on at least two points that I should have stressed earlier. The first is that, whatever the *conclusion* in the OLC memo, the memo should certainly attempt to accurately and faithfully canvass the questions and the arguments, to deal seriously with the opposing views, and, most importantly, to *acknowledge* when the answer it gives is merely "reasonable" or cutting-edge, and not the "best" answer. What bothered me most about the Torture Memo way back when is precisely that it did none of these things. . . . And you're also correct that this is not merely a process-based objection. As you note, if an opinion does all these things, its unorthodox conclusions will be much less persuasive, and less powerful—which might even make OLC hesitate to reach those conclusions, or other actors hesitate to rely on them . . .

Second, of course many legal texts, including the Constitution, the Geneva Conventions, and the Torture statute, cannot fairly be understood without a full sense of the moral objectives of those texts—and a legal opinion that ignores those objectives is simply bad legal analysis. . . . Nevertheless, having been an OLC attorney for eight years, I can attest that it is often much easier said than done to incorporate the "supra-positive" aspect of such laws into one's legal analysis; or, more to the point, it's extremely difficult to persuade policymakers to act in accord with such "supra-positive" aspects of the laws, when the actual words of the laws contain evident gaps, limitations, and ambiguities—some of which were inserted intentionally by the lawmakers who negotiated, drafted, and ratified such enactments.

.   .   .

---

95. Cornelia T.L. Pillard, "The Unfulfilled Promise of the Constitution in Executive Hands," 103 *Mich. L. Rev.* 676 (2005).

Dawn Johnsen

Tues. 4/11/06 at 10:17 a.m.

I generally agree with Marty, particularly now that he has made clear, in his email below, that he agrees w/Neil's good points. (And of course line between law and policy/morality is not bright, difficult to draw, etc.—I don't have much to add to that right now.) BUT that is only w/ regard to the legal advice OLC gives in its role as final word within EB [the Executive Branch] (subject of course to Pres. or AG override, which almost never happens), which is only part of what the office does. What in my experience actually happens—and definitely should happen—is OLC lawyers (here I am talking primarily about the most senior lawyers, or more junior lawyers working with those heading the office) play critical add'l roles, typically in frequent meetings w/ the AG, WH Counsel, heads of DOJ components, as well as w/ more pure policy types, and in those settings it is entirely appropriate to voice policy/moral views about what the EB should do. I think, for example, of the countless meetings I attended and at which I gave my views, . . . *e.g.*, on the law requiring Clinton to discharge from the military anyone who tested HIV positive, the statutory obstacle we found to compensating African American farmers who had been the victims of official discrimination, . . . FDA regulation of tobacco, the federal abortion ban, the shoot-down of drug-carrying planes, secret service and attorney client privilege in the context of the Starr investigation—the list could go on and on. What is critical is for the OLC lawyer to be very clear about the type of advice he or she is giving.

.   .   .

David Luban

Tues. 4/11/06 at 11:46 a.m.

1.   My own view of lawyers' ethics is that lawyers ought to bring their moral and prudential advice to bear. ABA rules permit it, and I think it's the proper ethical role of the lawyer, other than in certain litigation contexts. (I defend this view—which I labeled "moral activism"—in . . . my 1988 book *Lawyers and Justice* . . . .)

2.   Suppose, as I believe, that John Yoo *was* bringing his own moral views into his opinion; and let's suppose that those moral views are, roughly, that torture in the name of national security is no vice; or even, as [journalist Charles] Krauthammer argued, that torture in the name of national security is a moral obligation of conscientious public servants. In other words, suppose that Yoo's statements "I don't advise about policy, I just state the law as it is" are really [disingenuous]. In that case Yoo would actually be close to my conception of the moral activist . . . .

3.   One way around this dilemma is that a lawyer giving a client a legal opinion ought to state the law in a non-spun way (my proposed rule would be: Make your description of the law more or less the same as it would be if your client wanted the *opposite* result as the one you know your client wants). The lawyer could then confine his or her moral activism to policy advice detached from the law.

4.   But these are CYA opinions. They aren't really "advice" to the client at all. Rather, they are opinions designed to reassure third parties (nervous interrogators, etc.) that they have legal cover. In this respect, they are like opinion letters written by law firms for businesses designed to paper deals by legally koshering them—e.g., designed to reassure potential lenders. In these cases, the client doesn't want the lawyer's candid advice about the law. The client wants the lawyer to say that the deal is just fine. It's really a "brief." My view: if it's a brief, call it a brief. If it's an opinion, it can't be a brief. If you call it an opinion when it's really a brief, you do so at risk of sanction if your "advice" misrepresents the law.... I think the lawyer-advisor' role is to put the "spread" of opinion out candidly for the client.

QUESTIONS

1.   Is Lederman correct that the real questions facing executive branch lawyers are constitutional and not ethical? Should an executive branch lawyer be held to the standard of Model Rule 2.1?

2.   Should OLC lawyers take a pro-presidential tilt? Notice that Posner and Vermeule answer "yes," Lederman answers "only if doing so counts as faithful execution of the law," and Kinkopf answers "OLC should do what it can to facilitate the policy objectives of the Administration within the law." Luban, whose proposed rule is "Make your description of the law more or less the same as it would be if your client wanted the *opposite* result as the one you know your client wants," in effect answers "no." Which is the strongest position?

3.   A few months after the publication of the Bybee/Yoo memo in 2004, nineteen former OLC lawyers issued a set of Principles to Guide the Office of Legal Counsel.[96] Principle One states,

> When providing legal advice to guide contemplated executive branch action, OLC should provide an accurate and honest appraisal of applicable law, even if that advice will constrain the administration's pursuit of desired policies. The advocacy model of lawyering, in which lawyers craft merely plausible legal arguments to support their clients' desired actions, inadequately promotes the President's constitutional obligation to ensure the legality of executive action.[97]

Should this become a formal policy of the OLC?

4.   Lederman writes, "Indeed, it's increasingly clear that that was the *purpose and function* of the advice in this instance—to immunize torturers against future prosecution—which is a very unfortunate way to view OLC's role." Luban agrees, describing the torture memos as "CYA opinions." Is Lederman correct that this is an unfortunate way to view OLC's role? Why?

---

96.   Published as "Guidelines for the President's Legal Advisors," 81 *Ind. L.J.* 1345 (2006).

97.   *Id.* at 1349.

CHAPTER X

CONFLICTS OF INTEREST

A. INTRODUCTION

In his 1836 "Resolutions in Regard to Professional Deportment," David Hoffman proposed the following prohibition against conflicts of interest: "If I have ever had any connection with a cause, I will never permit myself (when that connection is from any reason severed) to be engaged on the side of my former antagonist" (Resolution VIII). Yet the nineteenth century bar was not uniformly opposed to representing conflicting interests. A Georgia lawyer, criticized by acquaintances for representing the plaintiffs one day in a lawsuit and the defendant the following day, replied, "Consistency, thou art a jewel! I am not that jewel."[1] Even so prominent a lawyer as Daniel Webster represented several merchants against a debtor in 1805 while simultaneously representing that debtor in suits to collect overdue notes.[2]

By the late nineteenth century, however, conflicts of interest were generally thought to be improper, and the 1887 Alabama Bar Code of Ethics—the distant ancestor of today's Code and Model Rules—prohibited dual representation unless the parties consented.[3] Today, conflicts of interest are among the most commonly litigated questions in legal ethics.

Why are conflicts of interest such an integral feature of American legal practice? One reason involves the growth in the size of private firms and their organizational clients, together with the expansion of branch offices and corporate subsidiaries. The result has been to increase the possibility of actual, attenuated, or inadvertent conflicts. Similarly, specialization in legal practice within and among firms has generated greater potential for simultaneous or successive representation of competing interests. The more technically complex the matter, the greater the premium placed on prior expertise and the greater the likelihood that the client will seek an attorney who has had some previous involvement with the general subject-matter. So, too, an increase in lateral mobility among lawyers has led to an increase

---

1. Joel Branham, "The Old Court House in Rome [Georgia]" 20, *quoted in* Brian C. Shaw, A Survey of Legal Ethics in the Nineteenth Century 45 (1980) (unpublished paper).

2. Alfred S. Konefsky & Andrew J. King, eds. 1 *The Papers of Daniel Webster* 101–04 (1982).

3. Shaw, *supra* note 1, at 45–46. Rule 25 of the Alabama code read: "An attorney can never represent conflicting interests in

the same suit or transaction, except by express consent of all concerned, with full knowledge of the facts. Even then such a position is embarrassing, and ought to be avoided. An attorney represents conflicting interests within the meaning of this rule, when it is his duty, in behalf of one of his clients, to contend for that which duty to other clients in the transaction requires him to oppose."

in circumstances that permit vicarious disqualification of colleagues under a doctrine that attributes one lawyer's conflicts to others in the firm.

Although conflicts of interest can arise in a wide variety of contexts, the three core situations involve: (1) representing multiple clients in the same matter, some of whose interests conflict; (2) representing one client against a former client in related matters; and (3) representing clients where their interests conflict with those of the attorney. These are, respectively, the problems of *concurrent* (or *simultaneous*) *representation* of conflicting interests, *successive representation* of conflicting interests, and *lawyer-client* conflicts of interest.

Several key features of conflicts doctrine have also increased the likelihood of controversy. First, mentioned above, is the doctrine of *vicarious* or *imputed conflict of interest,* which attributes lawyers' conflicts to their partners and associates unless those conflicts arise from personal interests of the lawyer. Model Rule 1.10. A single lawyer's conflict of interest can disqualify hundreds of colleagues unless they are in one of the minority of jurisdictions that permits firms to screen the conflicted lawyer from others. This means that lawyers who change jobs can become "Typhoid Marys," spreading the "virus" of imputed conflict throughout the firm, a situation explored in the *Silver Chrysler Plymouth* and *Armstrong* cases excerpted below. In a nation where 40 percent of associates leave the firm in which they start within three years, and 78 percent within five years, the impact of the vicarious disqualification rule has become increasingly problematic.[4]

Imputed conflicts are particularly prevalent in large law firms. If a firm includes hundreds of lawyers, representing thousands of clients, it is quite likely that some member of the firm has at some time represented a current client's former adversary, which raises successive representation issues. It is also increasingly possible that other attorneys in the firm, often in a branch office in another city, are providing unrelated services for that adversary at the same time, which raises concurrent representation issues. This was the situation in *Westinghouse v. Kerr-McGee,* excerpted below. Even a quarter of a century ago, a partner from the Wall Street firm of Sullivan & Cromwell warned, "If the top lawyers from the top 10 firms in New York decided to form their own firm they probably would not be able to represent anyone."[5]

This last remark points to another singular feature of conflicts doctrine. The most typical remedy for a conflict of interest in litigation is not, as with most ethics rules, disciplinary proceedings after the fact. Rather, it is the disqualification of the offending attorney before or during the representation. In a typical situation, Plaintiff, represented by Law Firm, sues Defendant. Defendant moves to disqualify Plaintiff's counsel because a lawyer working for Law Firm had previously been part of a team assisting

4. National Association of Law Placement, *Toward Effective Management of Associate Mobility* 21 (2005).

5. Diana Huffman, "Conflicts, Disqualifications Cause Persistent Headaches: Motions Filed for Tactical Reasons," *Legal Times of Wash.,* May 5, 1980, at 1.

Defendant in a related matter; Defendant claims that the lawyer had access to confidential information about Defendant. If the court agrees, Law Firm is disqualified. Then Plaintiff must engage new counsel and bring them up to speed in the case. Moreover, if the court is convinced that Law Firm lawyers have used confidential information about Defendant, it will prohibit Law Firm from turning its work product over to successor counsel, adding further expense and delay.

These two factors—an ethical problem arising frequently in corporate practice and a powerful remedy that is available for tactical use—help account for the proliferation of conflicts cases. Large firms and their clients are especially likely to possess the resources to pursue satellite litigation such as motions to disqualify opposing counsel. These motions often have strategic purposes apart from protecting confidentiality. They can run up the adversary's bill, remove an especially effective antagonist, delay trial, and increase pressures to settle. Courts and commentators have long expressed concerns about this practice. In *Richardson–Merrell, Inc. v. Koller,* 472 U.S. 424, 436 (1985), the United States Supreme Court condemned the "tactical use of disqualification motions to harass opposing counsel," and Justice Brennan's concurring opinion described the strategy as "a deeply disturbing phenomenon in modern civil litigation," 472 U.S. at 441.

Partly in response to tactical abuse, the Supreme Court held in *Firestone Tire & Rubber Co. v. Risjord,* 449 U.S. 368 (1981), that decisions denying disqualification motions could not be appealed immediately. Subsequent cases held that decisions granting disqualification also were not subject to interlocutory appeal, and courts have resisted invitations to provide immediate review except in extraordinary circumstances.[6] Although these decisions have somewhat curtailed the strategic uses of disqualification motions, they remain an important feature of contemporary litigation.

Ethical Rules

Before the Model Rules, the ABA's Code of Professional Responsibility, (DR 5–105©), prohibited concurrent conflicts. However, no Disciplinary Rule explicitly covered conflicts involving former clients. Instead, courts applying the Code often disqualified lawyers where their representation might involve a breach of confidentiality and create an appearance of impropriety. Canon 9 of the Code counsels lawyers to avoid even the appearance of impropriety, and some courts maintained that such an appearance in itself constitutes sufficient ground for disqualification. However, except in cases involving former government lawyers, those decisions typically reveal a colorable violation of confidentiality or other disciplinary rules lurking in the facts.[7] Former government lawyers were subject to an

---

6. Richardson–Merrell, Inc. v. Koller, 472 U.S. 424 (1985) (civil cases); Flanagan v. United States, 465 U.S. 259 (1984) (criminal cases). In many states, courts have also attempted to reduce abuses by finding that a failure to file a timely motion to disqualify will estop parties from raising conflicts objection, or will increase their burden of proof.

7. *See, e.g.,* Hull v. Celanese Corp., 513 F.2d 568 (2d Cir. 1975); Schloetter v. Railoc of Indiana, Inc., 546 F.2d 706, 709 (7th Cir.

appearance-of-impropriety rule barring them from accepting private employment in a matter in which they had substantial responsibility as public servants. See DR 9–101(B) and *Armstrong v. McAlpin, infra.*

The Model Rules, by contrast, includes a separate rule governing former-client conflicts and drops the appearance-of-impropriety standard, which many lawyers found vague and question-begging. Although a concern about appearances figures in justifications for particular conflicts provisions, it is now generally viewed as too indeterminate and ad hominem to constitute a standard itself.[8] The Model Rules' conflict provisions standards were substantially amended in 1989 and again in 2002 based on recommendations by the Ethics 2000 Commission.

The prohibition on concurrent conflicts of interests is grounded in the twin fiduciary duties of loyalty and confidentiality. Concerns about loyalty extend beyond the particular matter for which the lawyer is retained. Thus, a lawyer may not represent a client if the representation would be directly adverse to another client, even if the two matters are legally unrelated, because the effect on attorney-client relationships could be substantial. By contrast, in matters involving former clients, the lawyer owes continuing duties of confidentiality but not loyalty, so representation is impermissible only in circumstances where the matters are sufficiently related to pose a threat of breach of confidences.

Other countries have similar legal ethics provisions governing conflicts of interest. For example, European Union lawyers are subject to the standards of the Council of the Bars and Law Societies of Europe, codified in the CCBE Code. Section § 3.2. provides that a lawyer may not "advise, represent or act on behalf of two or more clients in the same matter if there is a conflict or a significant risk of conflict, between the interests of those clients." Lawyers must also "refrain from acting for a new client if there is a risk of breach of confidence entrusted to the lawyer by a former client or if the knowledge which the lawyer possesses of the affairs of the former client would give an undue advantage to the new client." If one lawyer in a firm has a disabling conflict, it is imputed to other members of the firm. Unlike the Model Rules, European rules generally do not permit clients to waive conflicts.[9] Japan and the Great Britain have rules similar to those in the United States, although Japan also does not permit waivers

---

1976); Fund of Funds, Ltd. v. Arthur Andersen & Co., 567 F.2d 225 (2d Cir.1977); *but cf.* Heelan v. Lockwood, 533 N.Y.S.2d 560 (2d Dep't 1988) (finding appearance of impropriety to be sufficient reason to disqualify attorney who had previously acted as a project consultant in mediating a settlement).

8. Ronald D. Rotunda, "Alleged Conflicts of Interest Because of the Appearance of Impropriety," 33 *Hofstra L. Rev.* 1144, 1145 (2005). The term continues to be used frequently, however. See Id., at 1442 (finding 1698 uses in one year in Westlaw search).

9. For discussion, see James J. Moliterno & George Harris, *Global Issues in Legal Ethics* 104–05 (2007). For the rule on vicarious disqualification, see Code of Conduct for Lawyers in the European Union (1988), excerpted in *id.*, at 109, n.1 ("Where lawyers are practicing in association, paragraphs 3.2.1 to 3.2.3 above shall apply to the association and all its members").

in cases of actual conflict. Australia and New Zealand also prohibit conflicts of interest unless the client gives informed consent.[10]

The following case illustrates the importance that American law attaches to lawyers' undivided loyalty to clients in other factual contexts, beginning with the simultaneous representation of multiple parties in criminal defense.

United States v. Bronston

United States Court of Appeals, Second Circuit, 1981.
658 F.2d 920.

■ MANSFIELD, CIRCUIT JUDGE:

Jack E. Bronston appeals from a judgment of the Southern District of New York entered after a jury trial before Judge Milton Pollack, convicting him of two counts of mail fraud, 18 U.S.C. § 1341, based on the government's allegations that he fraudulently violated his fiduciary duty as an attorney by helping to further the efforts of Convenience and Safety Corporation ("C & S") and Saul Steinberg, chairman of C & S, to obtain a bus stop shelter franchise from the City of New York at the same time when the law firm in which he was a partner, Rosenman, Colin, Freund, Lewis & Cohen ("Rosenman Colin"), was representing a group of investors in BusTop Shelters, Inc. ("BusTop"), the then current holder of the franchise and a participant in the competition for its renewal. We affirm. . . .

[BusTop had an interim franchise with the City of New York to erect and maintain shelters at bus stops. BusTop planned to compete for an extension of the franchise. Investors in BusTop approached Lindenbaum, a partner in Rosenman Colin, to represent them in the deal. At the same time, Saul Steinberg approached Bronston, a state senator and partner in Rosenman Colin, and indicated that he too wished to compete for the bus stop shelter franchise and wished to retain Lindenbaum and Rosenman Colin. Steinberg was Bronston's "friend and client." Bronston broached the matter with Lindenbaum, and subsequently with the firm's management committee. They agreed that representing Steinberg would create an impermissible conflict of interest, because he was competing with BusTop and the firm was representing BusTop's investors. Nevertheless, Bronston asked for permission to create a billing number for Steinberg "just in case at some time in the future something developed in which there was not a conflict." A member of the management committee agreed, but cautioned Bronston against performing any work for Steinberg without permission.

Despite this warning, and without telling his firm, Bronston did substantial work for Steinberg on his bid for the bus stop shelter franchise. Bronston . . . regularly filled out billing tickets for his work for C & S; however, because of the firm's prohibition, none of the work was ever

10. *Id.* at 105–108. *See e.g.* Article 26 of Japan's Code of Ethics for Practicing Attorneys; Rule 104 of the New Zealand Rules of Professional Conduct for Barristers and Solicitors. Few countries allow screening. Moliterno & Harris, *supra* note 9, at 110.

actually billed. Nevertheless, some evidence indicated that Bronston may have been paid $12,500 by Steinberg for his work for C & S. Rosenman Colin billed $52,000 to the BusTop investors.

The mail fraud indictment was based on the sending of two letters. One was a letter announcing C & S's interest in competing for the bus stop franchise. Bronston discussed and reviewed the letter with Steinberg. The other was a letter Bronston himself wrote, on his state senator's stationery, to the city comptroller. In the letter, Bronston expressed concern about BusTop's failure to comply with the terms of its interim agreement. The letter concluded: "Obviously, a renewal of the existing franchise would not appear to be in the public interest since it might be taken for a reward for non-performance."]

DISCUSSION

Bronston's principal contention is that in order to show a violation of the mail fraud statute based on a fraudulent breach of fiduciary duty, the government must prove that the defendant used his breach in some way that would benefit himself or harm the victim of the fraud and that the trial judge erred in failing to instruct the jury accordingly. Under this test, Bronston argues, the conviction must be reversed since the evidence was insufficient to permit the jury to find that he used his fiduciary status as a partner of Rosenman Colin to benefit himself or C & S at the expense of the BusTop investors. We disagree.

Although a mere breach of fiduciary duty, standing alone, may not necessarily constitute a mail fraud, the concealment by a fiduciary of material information which he is under a duty to disclose to another under circumstances where the non-disclosure could or does result in harm to the other is a violation of the statute. *United States v. Von Barta*, 635 F.2d 999 (2d Cir.1980).... As we noted in *Von Barta*, proof that the fiduciary relationship was used or manipulated in some way is not necessary.

> "Thus to make out a mail fraud violation, the Government must show that the scheme was devised with the specific intent to defraud.... The additional element which frequently transforms a mere fiduciary breach into a criminal offense is a violation of the employee's duty to disclose material information to his employer."

In the present case the indictment charged that Bronston, in disregard of the fiduciary duty he owed as a member of the Rosenman Colin firm to the BusTop investors and for the purpose of benefitting Steinberg and C & S to their detriment, promoted the interests of Steinberg and C & S in their efforts to obtain a bus shelter franchise from the City of New York and "did conceal from, and fail to disclose to, the BusTop minority investors and BusTop the fact that he was advising and promoting the interests of Steinberg and C & S." These allegations, coupled with the charge that Rosenman Colin received $50,000 from BusTop for services to it, that Bronston received a check for $12,500 from Steinberg for promoting the interests of Steinberg and C & S with the intent of harming BusTop, and that Bronston caused two letters to be mailed in furtherance of the scheme, were sufficient to state a violation of the mail fraud statute. . . .

Bronston argues that a decision upholding his conviction "would render every disloyal or ethically questionable act which is accompanied by the mailing of a letter a crime." We disagree. Although a hypothetical can be posed in which one could be prosecuted for mail fraud on the basis of a breach of fiduciary duty accompanied by little more than a failure to disclose the breach to the person to whom the duty was owed, without any prospect of substantial economic harm to the victim, this is not such a case. Here we are faced with a straight-forward economic fraud in which the object of the scheme was not merely to deprive the victims of a law firm's undivided loyalty, for which they paid $52,000, but to deprive BusTop and its minority investors of the BusTop franchise. A partner in a law firm used the mails with the specific intent of defrauding one of his firm's own clients of the precise interest which it had been retained to defend. This falls within the ambit of the mail fraud statute. . . .

The conviction is affirmed.

NOTES AND QUESTIONS

1.   Because of Bronston's actions, Rosenman Colin found itself representing both sides of an adversarial transaction. This is hardly a subtle, borderline conflict of interest; it is as blatant as can be. What was Bronston thinking? The opinion is silent about this question, but several possibilities seem plausible.

From the point of view of individual partners, it matters greatly who brings in the business: "finders" or "rainmakers" are critically important to a firm's economic well-being, and they are rewarded accordingly. Many law firms adopt the less than charmingly-named "eat what you kill" compensation system, in which partners' annual income depends partly on how much business each brings in. At the time of this case, Bronston's "friend and client" Saul Steinberg was one of the wealthiest, best-known, and most powerful businessmen in New York, and Bronston may well have been anxious to maintain a lawyer-client relationship with Steinberg, even though for the moment the time could not be billed. Although *Bronston* is an extreme case, internal politicking among large-firm partners occurs regularly over whose client the firm will represent when conflicts of interest preclude representing both. These "conflicts over conflicts" have exacerbated rivalries within firms and sometimes led to significant ethical abuses.[11]

2.   Bronston's chief contention on appeal is that he never abused any fiduciary relationship because he never used his firm's representation of

---

11. Milton C. Regan, *Eat What You Kill: The Fall of a Wall Street Lawyer* 37–39, 304–06 (2004); Mark A. Sargent, "The Moral World of Corporate Lawyers," 19 *Geo. J. Legal Ethics* 289, 290 (2006); Geoffrey C. Hazard, Jr. & Ted Schneyer, "Regulatory Controls in Large Law Firms: A Comparative Perspective," 44 *Ariz. L. Rev.* 593, 602–03 (2002).

the investors to harm them or to benefit himself. His assistance to Steinberg on the C & S bid did not depend on the representation that Bronston's law firm was providing to BusTop investors. Thus, whatever harm to the investors or benefit to Bronston may have resulted, it assertedly did not result from his breach of fiduciary obligations. Matters would have been different if, for example, Bronston had used confidential information from the investors against them in reviewing the C & S letter or writing the anti-BusTop letter. In that case, his breach of the fiduciary obligation would indeed have been the source of benefit to himself and harm to his firm's clients.

The court rejects Bronston's claim that without an abuse of the fiduciary relationship there can be no fraud. According to the court, the fraud lies in Bronston's non-disclosure of his conflict of interest when writing the two letters. How plausible do you find this argument? Is non-disclosure the real evil in this case?

3. Bronston contends that upholding his conviction "would render every disloyal or ethically questionable act which is accompanied by the mailing of a letter a crime." The court disagrees. Do you find its reasoning persuasive? The opinion never mentions whether BusTop got the franchise or not. Should this make a difference to the outcome of the case? Has Bronston been sent to prison for harming the BusTop investors, or merely for a conflict of interest? Under the court's reasoning in *Bronston*, if a lawyer uses the mails in the course of intentionally breaching a fiduciary obligation to a client and fails to disclose the breach, is he guilty of a federal felony?[12] If not, what limiting principle is available?

In another highly-publicized case involving felony charges for a conflict of interest, John G. Gellene pled guilty to bankruptcy fraud and a false sworn declaration. Gellene, a partner in the prestigious Wall Street firm of Millbank, Tweed, represented a company in bankruptcy proceedings without disclosing that he also represented one of the company's secured creditors. He received prison time and was disbarred.[13]

B. CONFLICTS OF INTEREST IN CRIMINAL DEFENSE

1. CONSTITUTIONAL STANDARDS AND CONFLICTS OF INTEREST

In the context of criminal defense, conflicts of interest can raise Fifth and Sixth Amendment issues of due process and effective assistance of counsel. As the following cases indicate, ethical and constitutional standards can sometimes diverge.

---

12. Under 18 USC § 1346, mail and wire fraud include any "scheme or artifice to deprive another of the intangible right of honest services." This "intangible right of honest services" has been held to include fiduciary obligations.

13. See Regan, *supra* note 11.

Cuyler v. Sullivan

Supreme Court of the United States, 1980.
446 U.S. 335, 345–52, 354–58.

[Sullivan, Carchidi, and DiPasquale were indicted for the first-degree murder of a labor official and his companion. Two lawyers, DiBona and Peruto, represented all three defendants, although Sullivan initially had retained separate counsel. Sullivan subsequently accepted joint representation because he could no longer afford to pay his own lawyer. Neither he nor his lawyers objected to the multiple representation at any point. Sullivan went to trial first. The evidence against him was entirely circumstantial, consisting primarily of an eyewitness who saw the three defendants at the scene of the crime. The witness testified that shortly afterward he heard firecracker-like sounds, and was told by Carchidi to leave and say nothing. Sullivan's defense rested without presenting any evidence. Sullivan was convicted, while his codefendants were later acquitted at separate trials. Sullivan appealed, alleging ineffective assistance of counsel because his lawyers represented conflicting interests. On appeal, DiBona and Peruto offered conflicting accounts of who had been Sullivan's lead counsel, as well as of the decision to present no affirmative case. DiBona claimed that he had encouraged Sullivan to testify, while Peruto recalled that he had not "want[ed] the defense to go on because I thought we would only be exposing the [defense] witnesses for the other two trials that were coming up." The Court of Appeals for the Third Circuit held that the possibility of conflict of interest violated Sullivan's Sixth Amendment right to counsel. On appeal by the state, the Supreme Court vacated the court of appeals' decision and remanded the case for further proceedings].

■ [Mr. Justice Powell] delivered the opinion of the Court. . . .

We come at last to Sullivan's claim that he was denied the effective assistance of counsel guaranteed by the Sixth Amendment because his lawyers had a conflict of interest. The claim raises two issues expressly reserved in *Holloway v. Arkansas* [435 U.S. 475, 483–84 (1978)]. The first is whether a state trial judge must inquire into the propriety of multiple representation even though no party lodges an objection. The second is whether the mere possibility of a conflict of interest warrants the conclusion that the defendant was deprived of his right to counsel.

A

In *Holloway,* a single public defender represented three defendants at the same trial. The trial court refused to consider the appointment of separate counsel despite the defense lawyer's timely and repeated assertions that the interests of his clients conflicted. This Court recognized that a lawyer forced to represent codefendants whose interests conflict cannot provide the adequate legal assistance required by the Sixth Amendment. Given the trial court's failure to respond to timely objections, however, the Court did not consider whether the alleged conflict actually existed. It simply held that the trial court's error unconstitutionally endangered the right to counsel.

Holloway requires state trial courts to investigate timely objections to multiple representation. But nothing in our precedents suggests that the Sixth Amendment requires state courts themselves to initiate inquiries into the propriety of multiple representation in every case. Defense counsel have an ethical obligation to avoid conflicting representations and to advise the court promptly when a conflict of interest arises during the course of trial. Absent special circumstances, therefore, trial courts may assume either that multiple representation entails no conflict or that the lawyer and his clients knowingly accept such risk of conflict as may exist. Indeed, as the Court noted in *Holloway,* trial courts necessarily rely in large measure upon the good faith and good judgment of defense counsel. "An 'attorney representing two defendants in a criminal matter is in the best position professionally and ethically to determine when a conflict of interest exists or will probably develop in the course of a trial.' " Unless the trial court knows or reasonably should know that a particular conflict exists, the court need not initiate an inquiry.

Nothing in the circumstances of this case indicates that the trial court had a duty to inquire whether there was a conflict of interest. The provision of separate trials for Sullivan and his codefendants significantly reduced the potential for a divergence in their interests. No participant in Sullivan's trial ever objected to the multiple representation. DiBona's opening argument for Sullivan outlined a defense compatible with the view that none of the defendants was connected with the murders. The opening argument also suggested that counsel was not afraid to call witnesses whose testimony might be needed at the trials of Sullivan's codefendants. Finally, as the Court of Appeals noted, counsel's critical decision to rest Sullivan's defense was on its face a reasonable tactical response to the weakness of the circumstantial evidence presented by the prosecutor. On these facts, we conclude that the Sixth Amendment imposed upon the trial court no affirmative duty to inquire into the propriety of multiple representation.

B

Holloway reaffirmed that multiple representation does not violate the Sixth Amendment unless it gives rise to a conflict of interest. Since a possible conflict inheres in almost every instance of multiple representation, a defendant who objects to multiple representation must have the opportunity to show that potential conflicts impermissibly imperil his right to a fair trial. But unless the trial court fails to afford such an opportunity, a reviewing court cannot presume that the possibility for conflict has resulted in ineffective assistance of counsel. Such a presumption would preclude multiple representation even in cases where " '[a] common defense . . . gives strength against a common attack.' "

In order to establish a violation of the Sixth Amendment, a defendant who raised no objection at trial must demonstrate that an actual conflict of interest adversely affected his lawyer's performance. In *Glasser v. United States,* for example, the record showed that defense counsel failed to cross-examine a prosecution witness whose testimony linked Glasser with the crime and failed to resist the presentation of arguably inadmissible evidence. The Court found that both omissions resulted from counsel's desire to diminish the jury's perception of a codefendant's guilt. Indeed, the evidence of counsel's "struggle to serve two masters [could not] seriously be doubted." Since this actual conflict of interest impaired Glasser's defense, the Court reversed his conviction. . . .

Glasser established that unconstitutional multiple representation is never harmless error. Once the Court concluded that Glasser's lawyer had an actual conflict of interest, it refused "to indulge in nice calculations as to the amount of prejudice" attributable to the conflict. The conflict itself demonstrated a denial of the "right to have the effective assistance of counsel." Thus, a defendant who shows that a conflict of interest actually affected the adequacy of his representation need not demonstrate prejudice in order to obtain relief. But until a defendant shows that his counsel actively represented conflicting interests, he has not established the constitutional predicate for his claim of ineffective assistance.

C

The Court of Appeals granted Sullivan relief because he had shown that the multiple representation in this case involved a possible conflict of interest. We hold that the possibility of conflict is insufficient to impugn a criminal conviction. In order to demonstrate a violation of his Sixth Amendment rights, a defendant must establish that an actual conflict of interest adversely affected his lawyer's performance. Sullivan believes he should prevail even under this standard. He emphasizes Peruto's admission that the decision to rest Sullivan's defense reflected a reluctance to expose witnesses who later might have testified for the other defendants. The petitioner, on the other hand, points to DiBona's contrary testimony and to evidence that Sullivan himself wished to avoid taking the stand. Since the Court of Appeals did not weigh these conflicting contentions under the proper legal standard, its judgment is vacated and the case is remanded for further proceedings consistent with this opinion.

So ordered.

■ [MR. JUSTICE BRENNAN], concurring in Part III of the opinion of the Court and in the result.

Holloway v. Arkansas settled that the Sixth Amendment right to effective assistance of counsel encompasses the right to representation by an attorney who does not owe conflicting duties to other defendants. While *Holloway* also established that defendants usually have the right to share a lawyer if they so choose, that choice must always be knowing and intelligent. The trial judge, therefore, must play a positive role in ensuring that the choice was made intelligently. The court cannot delay until a defendant or an attorney raises a problem, for the Constitution also protects defendants whose attorneys fail to consider, or choose to ignore, potential conflict problems. "Upon the trial judge rests the duty of seeing that the trial is conducted with solicitude for the essential rights of the accused. . . .

The trial court should protect the right of an accused to have the assistance of counsel." *Glasser v. United States*.... "While an accused may waive the right to counsel, whether there is a proper waiver should be clearly determined by the trial court, and it would be fitting and appropriate for that determination to appear upon the record." *Johnson v. Zerbst*....

"[A] possible conflict inheres in almost every instance of multiple representation." *Ante,* at 348. Therefore, upon discovery of joint representation, the duty of the trial court is to ensure that the defendants have not unwittingly given up their constitutional right to effective counsel. This is necessary since it is usually the case that defendants will not know what their rights are or how to raise them. This is surely true of the defendant who may not be receiving the effective assistance of counsel as a result of conflicting duties owed to other defendants. Therefore, the trial court cannot safely assume that silence indicates a knowledgeable choice to proceed jointly. The court must at least affirmatively advise the defendants that joint representation creates potential hazards which the defendants should consider before proceeding with the representation....

■ [MR. JUSTICE MARSHALL] concurring in part and dissenting in part....

I dissent from the Court's formulation of the proper standard for determining whether multiple representation has violated the defendant's right to the effective assistance of counsel. The Court holds that in the absence of an objection at trial, the defendant must show "that an actual conflict of interest adversely affected his lawyer's performance." *Ante,* at 348. If the Court's holding would require a defendant to demonstrate that his attorney's trial performance differed from what it would have been if the defendant had been the attorney's only client, I believe it is inconsistent with our previous cases. Such a test is not only unduly harsh, but incurably speculative as well. The appropriate question under the Sixth Amendment is whether an actual, relevant conflict of interests existed during the proceedings. If it did, the conviction must be reversed....

Our cases make clear that every defendant has a constitutional right to "the assistance of an attorney unhindered by a conflict of interests." *Holloway v. Arkansas* ... Because it is the simultaneous representation of conflicting interests against which the Sixth Amendment protects a defendant, he need go no further than to show the existence of an actual conflict.[3] An actual conflict of interests negates the unimpaired loyalty a defendant is constitutionally entitled to expect and receive from his attorney....

Moreover, a showing that an actual conflict adversely affected counsel's performance is not only unnecessary, it is often an impossible task. As the Court emphasized in *Holloway:*

---

3. "Conflict of interests" is a term that is often used and seldom defined.... There is a possibility of conflict, then, if the interests of the defendants may diverge at some point so as to place the attorney under inconsistent duties. There is an actual, relevant conflict of interests if, during the course of the representation, the defendants' interests do diverge with respect to a material, factual or legal issue, or to a course of action.

"[I]n a case of joint representation of conflicting interests the evil—it bears repeating—is in what the advocate finds himself compelled to *refrain* from doing.... It may be possible in some cases to identify from the record the prejudice resulting from an attorney's failure to undertake certain trial tasks, but even with a record of the sentencing hearing available it would be difficult to judge intelligently the impact of a conflict on the attorney's representation of a client. And to assess the impact of a conflict of interests on the attorney's options, tactics, and decisions in plea negotiations would be virtually impossible."

Accordingly, in *Holloway* we emphatically rejected the suggestion that a defendant must show prejudice in order to be entitled to relief. For the same reasons, it would usually be futile to attempt to determine how counsel's conduct would have been different if he had not been under conflicting duties.

In the present case Peruto's testimony, if credited by the court, would be sufficient to make out a case of ineffective assistance by reason of a conflict of interests under even a restrictive reading of the Court's standard. In the usual case, however, we might expect the attorney to be unwilling to give such supportive testimony, thereby impugning his professional efforts. Moreover, in many cases the effects of the conflict on the attorney's performance will not be discernible from the record. It is plain to me, therefore, that in some instances the defendant will be able to show there was an actual, relevant conflict, but be unable to show that it changed his attorney's conduct.

QUESTIONS

1. The majority and concurring opinions in *Cuyler* implicitly distinguish four conflict-of-interest situations: (1) possible conflicts of interest; (2) actual conflicts that do not impair representation; (3) actual conflicts that impair representation but do not affect the outcome; and (4) actual conflicts that impair representation and do affect the outcome. Neither the majority nor the concurrences assert that the mere possibility of conflicting interests (which exists in all cases of multiple representation) amounts to reversible error. All the opinions also agree that a standard of actual prejudice, which would require proof that the outcome of the defendant's trial would have been different but for the conflicted representation, sets too high a standard. Thus, the argument between the majority and Justice Marshall concerns the difference between (2) and (3). The majority holds that the defendant must establish that the conflict adversely affected representation, while Justice Marshall maintains that any such effort would prove "incurably speculative." Justice Marshall believes that the defendants should need only to establish an actual conflict. Which position do you find most persuasive?

2. David Wasserman describes hypothetical circumstances in which an actual conflict may not impair representation as follows:

> [I]magine an attorney who represents two defendants at a joint trial in which both testify to having been unwitting participants in a robbery conceived by the other. While this obvious conflict may impair her representation of one or both, ... it need not do so[;] for example, she may subject each defendant to a blistering cross-examination on behalf of the other. If so, her representation of each defendant will damage the other just because it is unimpaired, and neither will receive poorer representation as a result of their adverse interests.[10]

Do you agree that the representation has been unimpaired? Would the *Cuyler* majority find any constitutional violation under such circumstances? Should it? Note that this dual representation would be strictly impermissible under Model Rule 1.7(b)(3).

3. In his classic treatment of this issue, John Stewart Geer noted a number of recurrent problems arising in the multiple representation of criminal defendants. These include:

> a) the possibility that the best defense for some clients may be inconsistent with the best defense for others, as in Wasserman's hypothetical;

> b) the possibility that the lawyer will elect to assert only those defense theories that can be raised consistently for all the defendants, thereby "losing" defense theories that might succeed for one defendant at the risk of incriminating others;

> c) the difficulty in advising defendants whether or not to testify because if only one takes the stand, the jury may draw adverse inferences from the other's failure to do so;

> d) the difficulty in handling government evidence that is more damaging for some defendants than others. Emphasizing that a piece of evidence does not inculpate one client may simply underscore the fact that it *does* inculpate others, while failing to emphasize this difference may leave the inaccurate impression that the evidence incriminates all defendants.

> e) the difficulty in constructing a closing argument when any of these conflicts arise.[11]

Such problems lead Geer to recommend a *per se* rule forbidding the multiple representation of criminal defendants. What would be the drawbacks of such a rule? To what extent would separate representation help the defendants in the face of the problems noted above? Consider that issue in light of Kenneth Mann's analysis excerpted below.

Would you prefer the alternative followed by some state courts, which follow Justice Marshall by presuming adverse effects if a defendant can

---

10. David T. Wasserman, *A Sword for the Convicted: Representing Indigent Defendants on Appeal* 164 (1990).

11. John S. Geer, "Representation of Multiple Criminal Defendants: Conflicts of Interest and the Professional Responsibilities of the Defense Attorney," 62 *Minn. L. Rev.* 119 (1978); *see also* Debra Lyn Bassett, "Three's a Crowd: A Proposal to Abolish Joint Representation," 32 *Rutgers L. Rev.* 387 (2001).

establish an actual conflict? Alternatively, consider the California Supreme Court's view that a merely potential conflict might require reversal if the record supports an informed speculation that the defendant's right to effective representation was prejudicially affected. *People v. Mroczko*, 672 P.2d 835, 837 (Cal.1983).

4. To what extent could the risk of prejudicial conflict be avoided through careful inquiry by trial judges? Federal Rule of Criminal Procedure 44(c) requires trial courts to "promptly inquire" into joint representation and to

> personally advise each defendant of his right to the effective assistance of counsel, including separate representation. Unless it appears that there is good cause to believe that no conflict of interest is likely to arise, the court shall take such measures as may be appropriate to protect each defendant's right to counsel.

Should such steps include disqualifying counsel over a defendant's objection? Consider *Wheat v. United States*, 486 U.S. 153 (1988), which represents the mirror-image of *Cuyler*. In *Wheat* the government moved to disqualify attorney Iredale from representing Wheat in a drug conspiracy charge because Iredale was also representing the other alleged co-conspirators, Bravo and Gomez–Barajas. After Iredale had won an acquittal for Gomez–Barajas, the alleged leader of the conspiracy, Gomez–Barajas entered a guilty plea to lesser charges in order to avoid a second trial for other crimes. At the time of Wheat's trial, Gomez–Barajas's plea bargain had not yet been accepted, and the government argued that if it was rejected, Wheat would be called to testify against Gomez–Barajas. The government also stated that Wheat's testimony would be needed against Bravo. The trial court disqualified Iredale, and Wheat was convicted. He appealed, arguing that the trial judge had abused his discretion in balancing the Sixth Amendment right to be represented by counsel of one's choice against the Sixth Amendment right to legal assistance free of conflicts of interest.

Writing for the Court, Chief Justice Rehnquist rejected Wheat's appeal, arguing that the trial judge was legitimately concerned about Iredale's conflict of interest. To hold otherwise would allow trial courts to be " 'whipsawed' by assertions of error no matter which way they rule. If a district court agrees to the multiple representation, and the advocacy of counsel is thereafter impaired as a result, the defendant may well claim that he did not receive effective assistance. On the other hand, a district court's refusal to accede to the multiple representation may result in a challenge" such as Wheat's.

Justice Marshall, dissenting, criticized the district judge and the Court's majority for uncritically accepting the government's theory that Iredale was enmeshed in a conflict of interest. The likelihood that Gomez–Barajas's plea bargain would be refused was minimal, and the record showed that Wheat's testimony had little bearing on Bravo's case. Indeed, the government had added Wheat to its witness list against Bravo only after Wheat attempted to retain Iredale; Marshall therefore suspected that doing so was "a maneuver to prevent Iredale from representing [Wheat] at trial." Justice Marshall quoted the District Court's acknowledgment that Iredale "did a fantastic job in that [Gomez–Barajas] trial." To Marshall, these facts suggested that the prosecution's real reason for wanting Iredale disqualified was the fear that he would be too effective.

Which position do you find more persuasive?[12]

Conflicts Involving Former Clients in Criminal Defense

What if defendant's counsel has a conflict of interest arising from representation of a former client? The U.S. Supreme Court confronted this question in *Mickens v. Taylor*, 535 U.S. 162 (2002), but declined to answer it and instead addressed a narrower question. Mickens was sentenced to death for murdering Timothy Hall "during or following the commission of an attempted forcible sodomy." It was later discovered that Mickens's counsel, Bryan Saunders, was Hall's appointed counsel at the time of the murder in a juvenile-court assault and concealed weapons case. Saunders met Hall once, for about 15 to 30 minutes. Just one business day after the state court judge discharged Saunders because of Hall's death, she appointed Saunders to represent Mickens in Hall's murder case. She did not conduct an inquiry into the possibility that Saunders had a conflict of interest. When the Fourth Circuit Court of Appeals denied Mickens's habeas petition, he appealed.

Mickens v. Taylor

Supreme Court of the United States, 2002.
535 U.S. 162 (2002).

■ JUSTICE SCALIA delivered the opinion of the Court.

The question presented in this case is what a defendant must show in order to demonstrate a Sixth Amendment violation where the trial court fails to inquire into a potential conflict of interest about which it knew or reasonably should have known. . . .

II

The Sixth Amendment provides that a criminal defendant shall have the right to "the assistance of counsel for his defence." This right has been accorded, we have said, "not for its own sake, but because of the effect it has on the ability of the accused to receive a fair trial." It follows from this that assistance which is ineffective in preserving fairness does not meet the constitutional mandate, see *Strickland v. Washington*, 466 U.S. 668, 685–686 (1984); and it also follows that defects in assistance that have no probable effect upon the trial's outcome do not establish a constitutional violation. As a general matter, a defendant alleging a Sixth Amendment violation must demonstrate "a reasonable probability that, but for coun-

---

12. For discussion of *Wheat, see* Bruce A. Green, " 'Through a Glass Darkly': How the Court Sees Motions to Disqualify Crimi- nal Defense Lawyers," 89 *Colum. L. Rev.* 1209 (1989).

sel's unprofessional errors, the result of the proceeding would have been different."

There is an exception to this general rule. We have spared the defendant the need of showing probable effect upon the outcome, and have simply presumed such effect, where assistance of counsel has been denied entirely or during a critical stage of the proceeding. When that has occurred, the likelihood that the verdict is unreliable is so high that a case-by-case inquiry is unnecessary. But only in "circumstances of that magnitude" do we forgo individual inquiry into whether counsel's inadequate performance undermined the reliability of the verdict.

We have held in several cases that "circumstances of that magnitude" may also arise when the defendant's attorney actively represented conflicting interests. The nub of the question before us is whether the principle established by these cases provides an exception to the general rule of *Strickland* under the circumstances of the present case. To answer that question, we must examine those cases in some detail.

In *Holloway v. Arkansas,* 435 U.S. 475, defense counsel had objected that he could not adequately represent the divergent interests of three codefendants. Without inquiry, the trial court had denied counsel's motions for the appointment of separate counsel and had refused to allow counsel to cross-examine any of the defendants on behalf of the other two.... *Holloway* thus creates an automatic reversal rule only where defense counsel is forced to represent codefendants over his timely objection, unless the trial court has determined that there is no conflict.

In *Cuyler v. Sullivan,* the respondent was one of three defendants accused of murder who were tried separately, represented by the same counsel. Neither counsel nor anyone else objected to the multiple representation, and counsel's opening argument at Sullivan's trial suggested that the interests of the defendants were aligned. We declined to extend *Holloway*'s automatic reversal rule to this situation and held that, absent objection, a defendant must demonstrate that "a conflict of interest actually affected the adequacy of his representation." In addition to describing the defendant's burden of proof, *Sullivan* addressed separately a trial court's duty to inquire into the propriety of a multiple representation, construing *Holloway* to require inquiry only when "the trial court knows or reasonably should know that a particular conflict exists"—which is not to be confused with when the trial court is aware of a vague, unspecified possibility of conflict, such as that which "inheres in almost every instance of multiple representation".... In *Sullivan*, no "special circumstances" triggered the trial court's duty to inquire.

Finally, in *Wood v. Georgia*, 450 U.S. 261 (1981), three indigent defendants convicted of distributing obscene materials had their probation revoked for failure to make the requisite $500 monthly payments on their $5,000 fines. We granted certiorari to consider whether this violated the Equal Protection Clause, but during the course of our consideration certain disturbing circumstances came to our attention: At the probation-revocation hearing (as at all times since their arrest) the defendants had been represented by the lawyer for their employer (the owner of the business that purveyed the obscenity), and their employer paid the attorney's fees. The employer had promised his employees he would pay their fines, and had generally kept that promise but had not done so in these defendants' case. This record suggested that the employer's interest in establishing a favorable equal-protection precedent (reducing the fines he would have to pay for his indigent employees in the future) diverged from the defendants' interest in obtaining leniency or paying lesser fines to avoid imprisonment. Moreover, the possibility that counsel was actively representing the conflicting interests of employer and defendants "was sufficiently apparent at the time of the revocation hearing to impose upon the court a duty to inquire further." Because "on the record before us, we [could not] be sure whether counsel was influenced in his basic strategic decisions by the interests of the employer who hired him," we remanded for the trial court "to determine whether the conflict of interest that this record strongly suggests actually existed."

Petitioner argues that the remand instruction in *Wood* established an "unambiguous rule" that where the trial judge neglects a duty to inquire into a potential conflict, the defendant, to obtain reversal of the judgment, need only show that his lawyer was subject to a conflict of interest, and need not show that the conflict adversely affected counsel's performance.... [But t]he notion that *Wood* created a new rule *sub silentio*—and in a case where certiorari had been granted on an entirely different question, and the parties had neither briefed nor argued the conflict-of-interest issue—is implausible.

Petitioner's proposed rule of automatic reversal when there existed a conflict that did not affect counsel's performance, but the trial judge failed to make the *Sullivan*-mandated inquiry, makes little policy sense. As discussed, the rule applied when the trial judge is not aware of the conflict (and thus not obligated to inquire) is that prejudice will be presumed only if the conflict has significantly affected counsel's performance—thereby rendering the verdict unreliable, even though *Strickland* prejudice cannot be shown. The trial court's awareness of a potential conflict neither renders it more likely that counsel's performance was significantly affected nor in any other way renders the verdict unreliable. Nor does the trial judge's failure to make the *Sullivan*-mandated inquiry often make it harder for reviewing courts to determine conflict and effect, particularly since those courts may rely on evidence and testimony whose importance only becomes established at the trial.

Nor, finally, is automatic reversal simply an appropriate means of enforcing *Sullivan*'s mandate of inquiry. Despite JUSTICE SOUTER's belief that there must be a threat of sanction (to-wit, the risk of conferring a windfall upon the defendant) in order to induce "resolutely obdurate" trial judges to follow the law, we do not presume that judges are as careless or as partial as those police officers who need the incentive of the exclusionary rule. And in any event, the *Sullivan* standard, which requires proof of effect upon representation but (once such effect is shown) presumes prejudice, already creates an "incentive" to inquire into a potential conflict. In those cases where the potential conflict is in fact an actual one, only inquiry will enable the judge to avoid all possibility of reversal by either seeking waiver or replacing a conflicted attorney. We doubt that the deterrence of "judicial dereliction" that would be achieved by an automatic reversal rule is significantly greater.

Since this was not a case in which (as in *Holloway*) counsel protested his inability simultaneously to represent multiple defendants; and since the trial court's failure to make the *Sullivan*-mandated inquiry does not reduce the petitioner's burden of proof; it was at least necessary, to void the conviction, for petitioner to establish that the conflict of interest adversely affected his counsel's performance. The Court of Appeals having found no such effect, the denial of habeas relief must be affirmed.

III

Lest today's holding be misconstrued, we note that the only question presented was the effect of a trial court's failure to inquire into a potential conflict upon the *Sullivan* rule that deficient performance of counsel must be shown. The case was presented and argued on the assumption that (absent some exception for failure to inquire) *Sullivan* would be applicable [not Strickland, which requires] a showing of probable effect upon the outcome of trial.... [However, not] all attorney conflicts present comparable difficulties. Thus, the Federal Rules of Criminal Procedure treat concurrent representation and prior representation differently, requiring a trial court to inquire into the likelihood of conflict whenever jointly charged defendants are represented by a single attorney (Rule 44(c)), but not when counsel previously represented another defendant in a substantially related matter, even where the trial court is aware of the prior representation.

This is not to suggest that one ethical duty is more or less important than another. The purpose of our *Holloway* and *Sullivan* exceptions from the ordinary requirements of *Strickland*, however, is not to enforce the Canons of Legal Ethics, but to apply needed prophylaxis in situations where *Strickland* itself is evidently inadequate to assure vindication of the defendant's Sixth Amendment right to counsel.... In resolving this case on the grounds on which it was presented to us, we do not rule upon the need for the *Sullivan* prophylaxis in cases of successive representation. Whether *Sullivan* should be extended to such cases remains, as far as the jurisprudence of this Court is concerned, an open question.

NOTES

Four justices dissented in three separate opinions (and Justice Kennedy concurred in a separate opinion). Justice Stevens argues that Saunders's failure to disclose his prior representation of Hall to Mickens

> would ... make it difficult, if not altogether impossible, to establish the necessary level of trust that should characterize the "delicacy of relation" between attorney and client."

Mickens' habeas counsel garnered evidence suggesting that Hall was a male prostitute; that the area where Hall was killed was known for prostitution; and that there was no evidence that Hall was forced to the secluded area where he was ultimately murdered. An unconflicted attorney could have put forward a defense tending to show that Mickens killed Hall only after the two engaged in consensual sex, but Saunders offered no such defense. This was a crucial omission—a finding of forcible sodomy was an absolute prerequisite to Mickens' eligibility for the death penalty.

Justice Stevens notes that Saunders's duty to keep Hall's confidence did not end with Hall's death, and in this case Saunders did not disclose that Hall's mother had sworn out a warrant for his arrest for assault and battery—a disclosure which might have allowed Mickens to challenge her victim—impact statement that " 'all [she] lived for was that boy.' "

Justice Souter believes that the Court's majority has departed from the leading precedents, and has neglected a crucial similarity between Mickens' case and *Holloway*, namely that in both the judge knew in advance of trial that counsel had a conflict. In Justice Souter's view, the majority has misread *Holloway* in applying its standard only when counsel has objected to the trial court. Judges can learn of a conflict of interest through other means than counsel's objection.

Justices Breyer and Ginsburg focus on the particulars of *Mickens*: the peculiarity of having a murder victim's attorney represent his alleged murderer, the state's role in creating this anomalous situation by appointing the victim's attorney to represent his murderer, and the fact that the death penalty hung in the balance. They believe that these circumstances represent a "breakdown in the criminal justice system ... serious enough to warrant a categorical rule—a rule that does not require proof of prejudice in the individual case."

On a less substantive note, it is striking that none of the nine justices or their clerks appears to know that the rules of professional conduct are not called the "Canons of Legal Ethics." The ABA Code replaced the Canons of Professional Ethics in 1969, thirty-three years before *Mickens,* and replaced the Code with the Model Rules in 1983.

QUESTIONS

1.   Which of the opinions seems most persuasive?

2.   The state asserted in its brief that Mickens's argument of inadequate assistance of counsel "relies heavily on the immediate visceral impact of learning that a lawyer previously represented the victim of his current client." Is that all there is to it? Should the fact that a trial feels fundamentally unfair count for purposes of establishing constitutional standards? Consider the evidence discussed in Chapter IV indicating that people's sense of the fairness of procedures matters more than outcomes in determining whether they believe that justice has been done.

3. In dicta at the end of its opinion, the Court's majority insists that it has not addressed the general question of whether a former-client conflict adversely affecting counsel's performance is per se a constitutional error: the Court has assumed that it is for purposes of inquiring about "the effect of a trial court's failure to inquire into a potential conflict upon the *Sullivan* rule." The majority goes on to suggest that in former-client conflicts, perhaps the rule should be the more stringent *Strickland* standard, which requires the defendant to show prejudice. Would that be an appropriate rule?

2. CONCURRENT CONFLICTS IN CRIMINAL DEFENSE: STRATEGIC CONCERNS

Why might it be advantageous for criminal defendants who could obtain separate counsel to risk the conflicts that may arise with multiple representation? The following materials examine some of the reasons.

Kenneth Mann, Defending White–Collar Crime

166–67, 169–74 (1985).

Representation of Multiple Defendants

At the stage when information control is most important, representation by one attorney of more than one person involved in an investigation may provide him with important influence over how information is dealt with by putative third parties. A typical situation is as follows: an officer and employee of a company is involved in making illegal market control agreements and is being investigated by the antitrust division of the Department of Justice. An associate is also involved in the negotiations, and a secretary has knowledge of meetings and conversations that took place between officers of participating companies. These conversations are inculpatory of the first individual. The secretary also knows where inculpatory records can be found. Where one defense attorney represents all three individuals in an investigation, he can do many things that will affect the readiness of each of these persons to cooperate with the investigator. When the defense attorney uses his position to facilitate noncooperation on the part of more than one person in an investigation, it is said that a "stonewall" strategy has been adopted. Using the colloquialism of the profession in discussing particular cases, it was not uncommon for an attorney to say, "I am stonewalling," meaning that he was conducting a defense in which he was attempting to keep all persons holding inculpatory information from talking to government investigators and thereby defeat the criminal investigation.

There are many benefits to a defense based on multiple representation, including close coordination of statements given to the investigators, early warning of investigatorial contact with third parties, and the making of uniform legal arguments. The major benefit of multiple representation has been described this way:

The sharing of all information regarding both the subject matter and progress of a grand jury investigation may well be the most vital element of a stonewall defense. Certainly it is the element most effectively facilitated by the use of a common attorney. Prior to the witnesses' appearances before the grand jury the attorney is in a position to gather all the relevant facts and to eliminate or at least minimize any inconsistencies produced by faulty memories. Perhaps more important, he is in a good position to assess the progress of the investigation at all stages by virtue of his access not only to the testimony of witnesses but also to information revealed by the prosecutor in his questioning. . . .

While multiple representation is in principle permitted [by codes of professional conduct], not all advice given by an attorney representing more than one person in the same investigation would be ethical. It would be unethical, for instance, for an attorney to advise one client not to make a plea agreement with the prosecution palpably beneficial to the client because of the damage it would cause to another client. On the other hand, when informed consent to multiple representation has been given by all clients and as long as there remains a prima facie benefit to all clients, many courts have chosen not to intervene in multiple representation. There are, however, decisions holding that waiver by a client may be irrelevant. Court rulings in this area have been so far from uniform that there is no clearly recognized standard that attorneys can follow in deciding whether the multiple representation that they want to engage in is ethical or not. . . .

Attorney practices. Where inculpatory information is held by more than one person, it is always to the advantage of the defense attorney for the main target to represent as many of the persons as possible. The usual condition of multiple representation is the belief by more than one of the evidence-carriers that professional legal representation is needed. The coperpetrator situation is the most obvious, but many potential witnesses who are holders of relevant information often feel they need legal representation even though they are not themselves involved in the wrongdoing. A friend or associate of a target may find it easier to stick by his story when he is counseled and accompanied by his friend's or associate's attorney.

Once a multiple representation situation is established, the attorney is faced with the problem of deciding how to represent each client without compromising the interest of the others. In one possible situation, each client holds inculpatory evidence against the other, and the government has just enough evidence to consider asking for an indictment against each, but not enough to dismiss the option of granting immunity to one client in order to get determinative evidence against the other. In this evidentiary context, it is difficult for an attorney to act without compromising one of the clients' interests. If he advises neither to make a deal because he believes that he may be able to win the case for both, he is sacrificing a certain success for one of them. And he clearly cannot advise one to make a deal against the other's interest. Some attorneys are able to obtain informed consent in this situation, after explaining the implications of the multiple representation. They then continue to represent all clients in a strategy based on total noncooperation. It is often the case that no client is willing to voluntarily become an informer against other clients. The stonewall defense continues until the government decides to force immunity on one of the clients, at which time the attorney will then have to divide representation.

In the second situation, each client holds inculpatory information against the other, but the prosecution appears to be far from making its case and completely off track. Here both clients may be able to hold out and save each other the humiliation and embarrassment of becoming either an informant or the subject of a criminal prosecution. In this situation, the position of conflict is less severe for the attorney. The prospect of success for both clients is high. Yet the difference between this situation and the former may disappear quickly. As the government's investigation progresses, one client may be presented with an opportunity to make a good deal with the government, to the detriment of the other client or clients. When an attorney is enthusiastically trying to manage a stonewall defense he may fail to give proper attention to this opportunity and compromise the interest of the client who is the potential beneficiary. An attorney representing multiple clients must constantly reevaluate the relative position of his clients, making certain that each client is well informed of his individual opportunities.

In interviewing, my sense was that many attorneys put a gloss on the situations that raise doubt, while taking as much advantage of control opportunities as possible. Where doubt does exist, the attorney may behave as if it does not. Projection of an attitude of certainty about the propriety of multiple representation is believed by attorneys to be a key factor in preventing the prosecution from asking for disqualification. One attorney explained how he handles multiple representation opportunities:

MANN: How early were you able to get into this case?

ATTY: Very early, before anyone went into the grand jury. . . .

I made my presence known, and the issue was who I would represent. There were many, many people involved here, and the U.S. Attorney wanted lots of lawyers so he could sort of divide and conquer. And I represented everybody at first, and then I broke them off one by one. There was a great deal of argument and discussion over multiple representation here. My own belief is that the more information you control as defense lawyer, the more effective you are, meaning that the only weapon you have as a defense lawyer in my view is control of information. You do not have much else. The prosecution has all the cards—they have the grand jury, they have in effect the presumption, they have all the investigative agencies, they have awesome powers. The only thing you have is sometimes you can stonewall an investigation. Now some people claim that that is obstructing justice. I don't, if you do it ethically and you do it out front, it's not. There are certain things you cannot do. . . . You can't tell people you don't represent to assert the privilege [against self-incrimination], for example. But I operate on the grounds that I can represent as many people whom I can ethically represent, meaning telling them whom else I am representing and discussing with them the conflict-of-interest problems. I say to them, here's what I am doing and I am doing this because I believe that you people have many interests aside from just the case [such as not informing against an associate or friend]. And sometimes they do have just the case, and you have to make that clear to them, too. And when you deal with a prosecutor, I think you have to set a high price, meaning that if he wants information, you want immunity. I've seen cases where, for example, the guy goes in and has his client spill his guts and plead to two felonies, without getting a good deal, where if the client would have gone to trial it would have ended up no worse. The client ends up alienating everybody he ever worked for and his friends. That is stupid. But if you make the prosecutor say, "Well, look, I'll give you immunity," then you may want to cut the client loose. I think the group banding together for defense sometimes has a great advantage, sometimes it is dangerous.

MANN: Well, who were you arguing with in this case about multiple representation?

ATTY: The prosecutor. The prosecutor said I shouldn't do that, it is wrong—

MANN: The assistant U.S. Attorney?

ATTY: The assistant in the office, sure. Their argument is you are obstructing us because you represent everybody; it is unethical; you are not doing them a service, and "We won't talk to you and it's not fair." Usually I say in effect, fuck you. You think it is not fair, I say it is fair. You want to make a motion, you make a motion. I say you have got to establish that what I am doing is wrong. . . .

NOTES: MULTIPLE REPRESENTATION OF CRIMINAL DEFENDANTS

The chief advantages to defendants from multiple representation by the same lawyer are readily apparent. First, and most obviously, the defendants save money, and by pooling their resources, often obtain the services of a high-powered attorney that they otherwise could never afford. In white-collar contexts, defendants' corporate employer may be willing to subsidize a unified defense for several employees. Similarly, in organized crime cases, third parties paying for representation often have a stake in a common defense. As Mann's study makes clear, multiple representation also facilitates control of information and "stonewalling," the tactic of using a common attorney to encourage a united stance of noncooperation by several defendants or targets of investigations.

However, these advantages of multiple representation carry corresponding disadvantages. As *Cuyler v. Sullivan* suggests, the price may be diminished zeal, and loyalty diluted by duties to the other defendants. Recall that one of Sullivan's attorneys testified that he had not "want[ed] the defense to go on because I thought we would only be exposing the [defense] witnesses for the other two trials that were coming up." Moreover, a high-priced lawyer whose fees are paid by a third-party employer may be subject to a less visible but even more pronounced division of loyalty. Mann notes that corporate defense lawyers will sometimes feel pressure to serve their paying client's interest by preventing individual employees from cooperating with prosecutors.

Consider *Pirillo v. Takiff*, 341 A.2d 896 (Pa.1975), *reaffirmed,* 352 A.2d 11 (1975), *cert. denied,* 423 U.S. 1083 (1976). Twelve policemen were subpoenaed to appear before a grand jury investigating police corruption. Pirillo, their lawyer, was paid by the Fraternal Order of Police (F.O.P.), an organization that vigorously opposed the investigation. The F.O.P. openly discouraged individual policemen from cooperating in the inquiry. The state moved to disqualify Pirillo on conflict of interest grounds. Judge Takiff granted the motion, and Pirillo asked for a writ of prohibition to prevent his disqualification. In declining to issue the writ, the Pennsylvania Supreme Court wrote: "Petitioner Pirillo testified that whenever a police officer indicated that he might consider cooperating, he would immediately remove himself as counsel and advise the witness to hire another attorney. This fee arrangement clearly has a chilling effect upon a police witness who is considering cooperation, since his access to F.O.P. paid counsel depends directly on his agreement not to cooperate."

Stonewalling can be a risky proposition even when the attorney attempts in good faith to advance the individual interests of each defendant. If a collective defense works, all is well from the defendants' point of view, but if it doesn't, hindsight may show that an individual client would have been better off cooperating with the authorities.

Consider this fact-pattern described by Mann: "[E]ach client holds inculpatory evidence against the other, and the government has just enough evidence to consider asking for an indictment against each, but not enough to dismiss the option of granting immunity to one client in order to get determinative evidence against the other." Mann concludes that "it is difficult for an attorney to act without compromising one of the client's interests. If he advises neither to make a deal because he believes that he may be able to win the case for both, he is sacrificing certain success for one of them. And he clearly cannot advise one to make a deal against the other's interest."

This fact-pattern describes the well-known "prisoner's dilemma" in game theory. Each client has a choice between stonewalling the prosecution and trying to make a separate immunity deal. If both stonewall, each may stand a better chance of escaping indictment than if both try to make a deal (in which case, we may assume, each has a roughly 50–50 chance that the prosecutor will immunize him rather than the other client). But, from another point of view, each fares better trying for an immunity deal regardless of what the other one does: If the other client stonewalls, the client who makes the deal obtains immunity while the stonewalling partner goes to jail; conversely, if the other client tries for an immunity deal, maintaining the stonewall is suicidal. The prisoner's dilemma makes it rational for each client to seek an immunity deal, even though both can foresee that the other will do the same, and thus that they are better off stonewalling. As two game theorists put it: "True, players will find themselves completely frustrated; nonetheless they have no real alternative."[13]

What advice should defense counsel give? A lawyer who proposes a stonewall defense is asking the clients to trust each other, even though each knows that the other has a strong incentive to deal with the prosecution. Can a defendant trust someone who has such a powerful reason to violate that trust? Moreover, each defendant knows that the other knows about that reason. Each, therefore, has grounds to suspect that the other will undertake a "preemptive" deal. In the words of game theorist Thomas Schelling: "I had to shoot him in self-defense to stop him from shooting me in self-defense."

As a practical matter, the lawyer's role in such contexts may well be to convince each defendant that the other is trustworthy. By breaking the spiral of mutual suspicion, the lawyer may be able to prevent deals that are less desirable than a united defense. But—the point bears repeating—this requires advising defendants to follow a course that is *not* individually rational, and which carries significant risks.

The preceding analysis has focused on the interests of defendants trying to avoid conviction and of lawyers trying to fashion conflict-free advice with this end in view. Yet stonewalling raises other issues as well; the goals of the justice system are obviously compromised when multiple representation enables guilty defendants to escape indictment or conviction. Indeed, this issue was raised in *Pirillo v. Takiff,* discussed above, as an additional ground for the disqualification of attorney Pirillo. The court concluded that Judge Takiff "sought by his order to protect the public function of the grand jury," and agreed that this was a legitimate reason to disqualify Pirillo. But the bar's ethical rules on conflicts do not explicitly provide for disqualification on grounds unrelated—or negatively related—to the interests of the client themselves. Should they? Model Rule 8.4(d) forbid lawyers from engaging in action prejudicial to the administration of justice. Should these rules authorize disqualification "in the interests of justice"? According to the *Restatement (Third) of the Law Governing Lawyers,* § 201, one reason to prevent multiple representation of adverse parties in litigation is to "preserve the integrity of the proceeding." Lawyers with conflicting interests may be unable to provide the forceful advocacy on all issues that is necessary to insure informed decision making.

Does stonewalling also threaten the integrity of proceedings? The leading case, *In re Taylor,* 567 F.2d 1183 (2d Cir.1977), concludes that it does not. *Taylor* turns the reasoning in *Pirillo* on its head. In *Taylor,* a motion to disqualify the defense lawyer was denied because, in the court's view, it was a tactical trick by the prosecution to prevent an effective joint defense.

---

13.   R. Duncan Luce & Howard Raiffa, Games and Decisions *101 (1957).*

"Inquisitorial" systems like Germany's treat the stonewall defense quite differently. The defense emerged in West Germany in the mid–70s in the trial of members of the left-wing Red Army Faction. Members of this anarchist group employed stonewalling tactics in defending charges of bombings and armed robberies. So novel were such tactics in Germany that they were widely denounced as "procedural sabotage," and the German parliament responded by passing a statute prohibiting multiple representation of criminal defendants.[14]

QUESTIONS

1. How should an attorney handle the prisoner's dilemma problem? Do the Model Rules help answer that question? Would clients ever be better off with separate representation?

2. Are there circumstances in which the "interests of justice" call for disqualifying a lawyer for multiple defendants in order to prevent a stonewall defense? In his dissenting opinion in *Pirillo,* Justice Manderino argues that "denying the witnesses their choice of attorneys, is rooted in a presumption that the witnesses are guilty of crimes . . . even though under state and federal law, the witnesses must be presumed innocent—not guilty. I cannot agree with the novel proposition that the *state* can deprive a citizen of his right to be represented by the attorney of his choice by speculating that he may be guilty." Do you agree?

C. CONCURRENT REPRESENTATION OF CONFLICTING INTERESTS IN CIVIL MATTERS

PROBLEM 1

How would you resolve the Case of the Unwanted Will, described by Thomas Shaffer in the following excerpt?

Thomas L. Shaffer "The Legal Ethics of Radical Individualism"

65 Texas Law Review 963, 963–70, 976–78 (1987).

> There's a magnifying glass all cracked and broken, and when you look at broken things through the lens you'd swear they'd turned whole again.
>
> —Anne Tyler

Most of what American lawyers and law teachers call legal ethics is not ethics. Most of what is called legal ethics is similar to rules made by administrative agencies. It is regulatory. Its appeal is not to conscience, but

---

14. "The defense of several accused persons by a collective defender is impermissible." StPO [Code of Criminal Procedure] § 146. Its constitutionality was upheld in the Decision of the Federal Constitutional Court of 11 March 1975, 39 BVerfGE 156.

to sanction. It seeks mandate rather than insight. I argue here that what remains and appropriately is called ethics has been distorted by the weaker side of an old issue in academic moral philosophy. This "weaker side" rests on two doctrines: first, that fact and value are separate; and second, that the moral agent acts alone; as W.H. Auden put it, each of us is alone on a moral planet tamed by terror. The influence of this philosophical position deprives legal ethics of truthfulness and of depth....

I.   The Ethical Context

Ethics properly defined is thinking about morals. It is an intellectual activity and an appropriate academic discipline, but it is valid only to the extent that it truthfully describes what is going on. Those in contemporary ethics who concentrate on the importance of the truthful account argue first that fact and value are not separate—that stating the facts is, as Iris Murdoch put it, a moral act, a moral skill, and a moral art; and second, that organic communities of persons are prior in life and in culture to individuals—in other words, that the moral agent is not alone....

In the practice of estate planning, for example, the facts that are available for moral description are death and property: property seen in the context of mortality, death seen in the context of owning things....

What reconciles death with the ownership of property is the family. The family is the lens through which we understand death as the death of an owner, and property as something owned by dead people. The family is the cracked magnifying glass that shows how things broken by discord and death are whole. The family is normally why people bother with estate planning—"normally" in the sense that, but for the family, estate planning would not be a legal subject. The family is the cultural focus for the realization that estate planning is a worthwhile thing for people to do, because it reflects the hope that none of us will die alone. The human fact that is prior to the moral agency of which moral philosophy usually speaks is the family; the moral art of description in the legal ethics of estate planning is the skill to describe a family....

II.   The Case of the Unwanted Will

I use, in teaching legal ethics, a series of quandaries that were posed in the *American Bar Association Journal* in 1979.[15] One of these quandaries describes John and Mary, a middle-aged couple with adult children. John and Mary want their wills drafted before beginning a vacation trip abroad. Based on John's instructions, the lawyer prepares a set of parallel wills, each leaving all property to the surviving spouse, or, if both are dead, to their children in equal shares. On a second visit to the law office, the lawyer presents the prepared wills to the couple, and John executes his:

> [T]he lawyer [then] suggests to John that he would like to be alone with Mary before she signs. John withdraws to another office. The lawyer asks Mary if the will is as she would have made it had her

---

15. "The Case of the Unwanted Will",
65 *A.B.A.J.* 484 (1979).

husband not been present at the conference and if the will were to be secret from her husband. She says no, that the will as drawn contains several provisions that are contrary to her wishes, and that she would change if her husband were not to know the ultimate disposition of her estate. However, she says that she would not be willing to precipitate the domestic discord and confrontation that would occur if her husband were to learn that she had drawn a will contrary to his wishes and in accordance with her own desires.[16]

You could say that the problem never would have arisen had the lawyer not talked to Mary alone. That description, of course, trivializes the problem, but many law students, and some ponderers of legal ethics, pose the quandary and the solution in just those terms. From that viewpoint, the immediately noticeable premises for the two judgments that there is a problem present, and that the problem is moral, are four. First, a lawyer's proper employment is by or for an individual. Second, employment by or for more than one individual is exceptional. Third, as a consequence, multiple party employment is necessarily superficial. Finally, the means for protecting the superficiality (or, if you like, the means for protecting the principle that employment is ordinarily and properly by or for individuals) is ignorance of any facts known to one of the individuals but not to the other.

It follows from this typical analysis that the lawyer's moral mistake was in talking to Mary alone. Otherwise, Mary's secret intention never would have come to his attention; her thoughts would be hidden, and that is appropriate because John's thoughts are hidden. Now that the lawyer *has* talked to Mary alone, he is in an impossible situation: he cannot allow John to board the plane with the mistaken belief that Mary agreed with what "they" had decided. Nor, for the same reason, can he help Mary to make a different will. And, of course, he cannot allow Mary to execute a will that does not do what she wants it to do.

This principled analysis of *The Case of the Unwanted Will* fails because of what is prior to analysis: the moral art of description. The failure is sad and, I think, corrupting. It is corrupting, first, because it rests on an untruthful account of what is going on. What is present in the law office is a family, and this one-lawyer-for-each-person way of first seeing a moral quandary in this situation and then resolving the quandary with the ethics of autonomy (the ethics of aloneness) leaves the family out of the account. The analysis looks on Mary as a collection of interests and rights that begin and end in radical individuality. Her affiliation with her husband, and with the children they have made and reared, is seen as a product of individuality(!), of contract and consent, of promises and the keeping of promises—all the consensual connections that lonely individuals use when they want circumstantial harmony. The employment of the lawyer is a result, then, of the links, the promises, the contract, the consent, and the need for circumstantial harmony. The family in the office is there only as the product of promise and consent. It is relevant to the legal business at hand

---

16. *Id.*

only because the (radical) individuals, each in momentary and circumstantial harmony with one another, want it to be. The promise and the consent create the family.

This description is offered by the legal ethics of radical individualism. It is sad, corrupting, and untruthful. An alternative argument is that the *family* created the promises, the contract, the consent, and the circumstantial harmony—not the other way around. The family is not the harmony; it is where the harmony (and disharmony) comes from. A truthful description of *The Case of the Unwanted Will* is that the lawyer's employer is a family. I suspect that that proposition will sound unusual in legal ethics, but my argument would be ordinary in other contexts. It treats, sees, and describes the family the way families are treated, seen, and described in the stories we tell, in the television commercials we watch, in the comics, and in our religious tradition. . . .

The lawyer in *The Case of the Unwanted Will,* for example, did not err in turning his attention to Mary, in John's absence. (Nor would it have been a mistake to turn his attention to John, in Mary's absence; if evenhandedness is important, it would have been more evenhanded to talk privately with each of them.) The deep things to be found out about John and Mary, in particular the deep things involved in their will making, are family things. Inquiring into deep family things is not only tolerated, but it is required by common representation, because *the client is the family.* Any other description is incomplete and, thus, untruthful and corrupting. If an adequate account of what is going on in the family (to the extent that it has to do with their will making) requires talking to either or both parents alone, then talking to them alone is appropriate. If the family is well represented, it (that is, each person in it) will learn how to take Mary's purposes into account, because Mary is in the family.

. . . [S]uppose in *The Case of the Unwanted Will* some further facts about Mary's purposes. One of the couple's sons, Henry, was married for ten years to, and is now divorced from, a woman named Susan. Henry and Susan had children who now live with Susan, and Henry lives alone. John and Mary, however, remain fond of Susan and, despite the divorce, continue to be friendly with her. The lawyer's questions to John and Mary have brought this affection to the surface, but John, as is typical, thinks of property and family together, and Susan no longer is in the family. During the joint interview, Mary sits silent while John says that they want "Henry's share" to go to Henry and, if Henry is dead, to his children. In the cases of the other children of John and Mary, says John, the child's share is to go to the child's spouse. What Mary says to the lawyer when they are alone, however, is that she wants her will to provide for Susan. Mary wants some of her family's property to be available for Susan, after Mary dies, when what is left of Mary will be in her family. Mary will be there, not because of a fictional notion about ownership, but because Mary did not die alone.

It is interesting to note how the narrative force of that statement about Mary's property changes as the case is described differently. Does

Mary dispose of *her* property, *her family's* property, *her husband's* property, or *her children's* property? The point is that seeing and saying are moral and legal acts, and moral and legal arts. The law is a language; legal authority will support any one of these ways of speaking of this property, and any of the statements is a moral judgment, as, indeed, the word "property" is a moral judgment. . . .

My argument is that [the lawyer] has begun to do a good thing. It is a good thing because it is a more truthful description of the reality that is the goal of the lawyer's work. . . . The estate planning issue, therefore, is whether this family is equal to the truth of what it is.

NOTES AND QUESTIONS

1.   In analyzing the Case of the Unwanted Will, Shaffer writes that, from an individualist point of view, "[n]ow that the lawyer *has* talked to Mary alone, he is in an impossible situation: he cannot allow John to board the plane with the mistaken belief that Mary agreed with what 'they' decided. Nor, for the same reason, can he help Mary to make a different will. And, of course, he cannot allow Mary to execute a will that does not do what she wants it to do." Do you agree with these three judgments about the lawyer's obligations? What is their basis in the Model Rules? What recommendation should the lawyer make to Mary?

2.   a) *Must* the lawyer disclose to John what Mary has told him? *May* he disclose information that Mary requests him to keep confidential? What if John asks him directly about the conversation with Mary?

b) If Mary requests that their conversation be kept confidential, *must* the lawyer withdraw from the representation? *May* the lawyer withdraw, given that withdrawal is certain to alert John that something unexpected has arisen in the lawyer's conversation with Mary?

3.   According to Shaffer, "[i]nquiring into deep family things is not only tolerated, but it is required by common representation, because *the client is the family.* . . . [M]y argument is that [the lawyer] has begun to do a good thing. It is a good thing because it is a more truthful description of the reality that is the goal of the lawyer's work. . . . The estate planning issue, therefore, is whether this family is equal to the truth of what it is."

a) Do you agree that the lawyer has done a good thing by forcing the family to confront "the truth of what it is"?

b) Suppose the facts are as follows. Mary reveals to the lawyer that as an unmarried teenager, before she met John, she gave birth to a baby girl, who was subsequently adopted by acquaintances of her parents. She tells the lawyer that she would very much have liked to make a bequest to her daughter. John does not know of the daughter's existence, and it seems likely both to Mary and to the lawyer that disclosure of this secret now would jeopardize their relationship. Would these facts affect your answers to part (a) or to the confidentiality issues raised in question 2? Would your answer change if Mary instead wanted to make a bequest to someone with whom she had an affair during her marriage?

Shaffer places a high value on the family "living in truth." Consider this response: "Mary's considered judgment is that 'living in untruth' permits the family to function; she does not think that John can 'handle' full information. In any event, even if she underestimates John in this regard, she is plainly unwilling to take the risk. It is presumptuous and irresponsible for the lawyer to force this family to discover whether (in Shaffer's words) it is equal to the truth of what it is." How might Shaffer answer this argument? How would you?

4. In the *ABA Journal* forum from which Problem 1 is adapted, a specialist in estate work maintained that the lawyer could appropriately counsel Mary how to make subsequent changes. As that commentator pointed out, "[i]f John wanted his will to be conditioned on certain dispositions by Mary, legal mechanisms existed (conditional bequests, or mutual wills, or a joint will) to serve those purposes." However, the commentator also noted that the lawyer had "undoubtedly not outlined these alternatives." If the lawyer did not do so, can he ethically assist Mary in drafting a document that would undermine John's expected estate plan?[17]

Another commentator in the forum argued that the lawyer should not have met with Mary separately in order to execute the will. Rather, the lawyer should have probed for conflicts at the initial joint interview and if he had sensed any undue influence or lack of consensus, he then should have advised separate representation.[18] Do you agree that such an approach would have been preferable and sufficient? Would it have been enough if Mary had also signed a letter waiving conflicts and agreeing to full disclosure of all information obtained from either party?

5. The ABA Special Probate and Trust Division Study Committee on Professional Responsibility has adopted recommendations for joint representation of husbands and wives. The recommendations provide that lawyers need not inquire into the possibility of conflicts at the outset of representation; they may presume that the couple is "unified in goals and interests until shown otherwise."[19] Under these recommendations, if parties disclose information that they do not want revealed to their spouses, lawyers' obligations depend on whether or not these confidences are "adverse" to the other spouse's property interests. Some confidences, such as extra-marital relationships or significant hidden assets, may not be adverse if they would not significantly impair the ignorant spouse's rights

---

17. *Id.* at 486.

18. *Id.*

19. ABA Special Probate and Trust Division Study Committee on Professional Responsibility: Comments and Recommendations on the Lawyers' Duties in Representing Husband and Wife, 8 (May 2, 1993) [hereinafter: Recommendations]; Malcolm M. Moore and Anne K. Hilker, "Representing Both Spouses: The New Section Recommendations," 7 *Probate & Prop.*, July–August 1993, at 26. *But see* American College of Trust and Estate Counsel, *Commentaries on the Model Rules of Professional Conduct* (Oct. 18, 1993) (requiring lawyers to discuss the implications of joint or separate representation).

or expectations. A lawyer who receives an adverse confidence must determine "if the potential for harm from failure to disclose is greater than the harm of disclosure." If so, the lawyer "should, but need not disclose the confidence even without the confiding spouse's consent." If the confiding spouse does not consent, the lawyer may disclose and must eventually withdraw, although the timing of withdrawal may be delayed to prevent tacit disclosure.[20]

Do you agree with this approach? Why shouldn't a lawyer be required to raise the issue of conflicts at the outset of representation?

Family Secrets in Broader Context

Many attorneys sympathetic with Shaffer's approach to the Problem of the Unwanted Will are nevertheless reluctant to inquire too deeply into family matters because of the serious emotional and ethical problems that it may entail. Lawyers are not therapists. It may therefore be useful to consider the strategies of those who *are* trained family therapists. These practitioners often receive confidential disclosures from one or more family members: a spouse has had a secret extramarital affair; a child is adopted and doesn't know it; a son at college is gay and is trying to keep one parent from finding out. Two therapists comment:

> *Ethically,* by colluding with the secret holder to deceive the unaware, the therapist endangers the family's *trust* in him or her.... [T]his clearly runs the risk of undermining the enabling conditions of treatment.... There is an ethical imbalance because the unaware [party] is being asked to trust a therapist whose actions may not ... merit trust.[21]

To avoid such difficulties, these therapists recommend preventive approaches. Most such confidential disclosures will come after family members have requested a private meeting with the therapist or has hinted before or after a therapy session that they have additional important information to discuss. Given such a cue, therapists should discuss with the individual, couple, or family the problems of special confidences and explore how they should handle the situation. During this discussion, therapists should make clear that if keeping secrets at some point undermines their ability to provide adequate assistance for another family member, they will insist on disclosure of the secret, or on terminating the professional relationship. Only after such a discussion can therapists agree to receive confidential information.[22] If and when family members with such information are ready to disclose it to other family members, therapists can strategize about the timing of the disclosure.

This approach (which the authors label "accountability with discretion") does not insist on a blanket policy of either disclosing or keeping

---

20. Recommendations, *supra* note 19, at 14–15.

21. Mark A. Karpel & Eric S. Strauss, *Family Evaluation* 255–56 (1983).

22. *Id.* at 259–60.

secrets. Maintaining confidentiality is justifiable if it does not interfere with the therapist's ability to serve the family. If it does interfere, the therapist should strongly urge the client to disclose. If the client refuses, the therapist should terminate the relationship. According to advocates of this approach, "[i]f the secret holders are unwilling or unable to face the consequences of disclosing the secret, the therapist cannot take responsibility for forcing the situation because all indications are that the necessary resources for minimizing destructive consequences would be insufficient. The therapist can encourage (literally, *give courage to*) family members to face secrets; (s)he cannot do it for them."[23]

6. Would Shaffer agree with this strategy? Families in therapy are likely to be more emotionally fragile than most other families who come to lawyers for estate planning assistance. Thus, when therapists fear that "the necessary resources for minimizing destructive consequences would be insufficient," this judgment may reflect the heightened vulnerability of the families that therapists treat. Does this imply that lawyers may take more "responsibility for forcing the situation" than would be prudent for therapists? Or should lawyers be equally reluctant to impose pressure since they generally lack the therapeutic training that may be necessary to cope with destructive consequences?

7. Russell Pearce argues that it is inappropriately paternalistic for lawyers to impose some single model of the appropriate family on all clients. Such an approach ignores important distinctions in client preferences and power relationships. Rather, Pearce suggests that attorneys should give clients the option of being treated as a marital unit or as individuals after informed discussion. If spouses choose to be treated as a unit, then the lawyer may not keep secrets from either party.[24]

What is your view? What obstacles might stand in the way of parties exercising fully informed and voluntary choices?

8. In another portion of his article, Shaffer notes that many organizations invoke the metaphor of family: "I was, for example, thanked recently for patronizing 'the Piedmont family,' an incorporated airline company. I was for years employed in 'the Notre Dame family,' a not-for-profit Indiana corporation. I worship in what our pastor calls a parish family."[25] Should a lawyer ever take seriously a client's metaphorical claim of family? What implications would taking the metaphor seriously have for organizational representation? Would they be consistent with Model Rule 1.13?

NOTES: "THE LAWYER FOR THE SITUATION"

During the confirmation hearings for Louis D. Brandeis's appointment to the Supreme Court, his opponents made numerous allegations that he had been involved in unethical behavior as a practicing lawyer. One

---

23. *Id.* at 260.

24. Russell G. Pearce, "Family Values and Legal Ethics: Competing Approaches to

Conflicts in Representing Spouses," 62 *Fordham L.Rev.* 1253, 1294, 1304 (1994).

25. *Id.* at 967–68.

prominently featured accusation was that on several occasions he had represented parties with antagonistic interests. For example, Brandeis continued as the lawyer for a family business even after the family members had quarreled and the business needed to be reorganized. In defending this role, Brandeis explained: "I should say that I was counsel for the situation."[26]

The term "lawyer for the situation" has stuck; it refers to lawyers who attempt to mediate between the shifting interests of multiple clients or multiple members of an organizational client—interests that sometimes harmonize, sometimes clash, and sometimes do both. Geoffrey Hazard identifies representative settings in which lawyers serve as "counsel for the situation":

—Acting for a partnership or corporation, not only as legal adviser but also as mediator, go-between, and balance wheel among the principals in the business . . .

—Acting as counsel, board member, and business affairs advisor for charitable organizations such as hospitals, libraries, and foundations.

—Acting as intermediary between a business and its creditors in a period of financial difficulties.

—Acting as intermediary between a corporate chief executive and his board of directors in the face of fundamental differences of policy.

—Acting as something like a marriage broker between clients wanting to settle a complex contract arrangement on terms that would be "fair to everyone."

   Similar functions are performed by lawyers on corporate legal staffs regarding differences between divisions and levels in the corporation, and by lawyers for government agencies that become enmeshed in conflicts of policy. It is safe to say that "ordinary" practitioners do the same sorts of things all the time for small businesses, families, public bodies such as school boards, and local civic and political organizations.[27]

Rita's Case in the Introduction provides another representative example of counsel for the situation. While Maynard acted in the familiar "neutral partisan" role, Kiladis was concerned with the interests of not only her client Gladys, but also Rita and other third parties. Although it is less developed or discussed than the neutral partisan model, the role of "lawyer for the situation" may well describe an equally familiar form of legal assistance. American attorneys spend more time in counseling and negotiation than in litigation. Much of their work requires acting as brokers between various clients.

26.   *Quoted in* John P. Frank, "The Legal Ethics of Louis D. Brandeis," 17 *Stan. L.Rev.* 683, 702 (1965). *See also* Richard W. Painter, "Contracting Around Conflicts in a Family Representation: Louis Brandeis and the Warren Trust," 8 *U. Chi. L. Sch. Roundt-*able 353 (2001); Clyde Spillenger, "Elusive Advocate: Reconsidering Brandeis as People's Lawyer," 105 *Yale L. J.* 1445 (1996).

27.   Geoffrey C. Hazard, Jr., *Ethics in the Practice of Law* 61–62 (1978).

QUESTIONS

1. Is there a difference between Shaffer's "lawyer for the family" and the role of "lawyer for the situation"? Are lawyers for the family advocates of its collective interest—for example, by advocating family unity against the particular interests of an individual family member—or are they mediators among its various members? How would you describe the role of Joan Kiladis in Rita's case? Was it the most effective role under the circumstances?

2. A lawyer for the situation, Hazard notes, is often "advocate, mediator, entrepreneur, and judge, all in one. He could be said to be playing God. Playing God is a tricky business."[28] What ethical difficulties confront lawyers in this role? Is it "riskier" than the zealous advocate role? Recall the similar comment by Frank Armani's (quoted in Chapter V) about his decision not to reveal the locations of victims that his client had murdered. Armani noted, "It's a terrible thing to play God." Was this an unusual case or does advocacy for a particular client often impose risks comparable to those facing counsel for the situation?

3. How well does legal education prepare practitioners for lawyering for the situation? For related discussion, see Chapter VIII, Section B on mediation, and Chapter XVI on legal education.

NOTES: OTHER COMMON SITUATIONS OF CONCURRENT REPRESENTATION

Corporate Practice

Shareholder derivative suits against corporate officers and directors raise similar issues about whether the same lawyer can represent both the corporation and individual defendants. Consent to joint representation is obviously suspect, because the same corporate officers named as individual defendants (and accused of placing their own interests ahead of the corporation's) will make the decision about whether the corporation "consents" to joint representation. For that reason the preferred solution is separate representation unless the complaint is patently frivolous, seeks only minor relief, or does not charge officers and directors with significant wrongdoing.[29] Courts often permit the corporate officers to choose independent counsel for the corporation, but in some contexts judges delegate the choice to outside directors or make the selection themselves.

Separate representation, however, addresses only part of the problem. A more difficult challenge arises from the lack of incentives or capacities for nominal plaintiffs to monitor their counsel's performance or proposed settlements. And as research on derivative actions indicates, corporate officers and directors may be tempted to favor settlements with overly

28. *Id.* at 65.

29. The leading precedent is Cannon v. United States Acoustics Corp., 532 F.2d 1118 (7th Cir.1976). For review of the relevant case law, see Musheno v. Gensemer, 897 F.Supp. 833 (M.D.Pa. 1995).

generous provisions for plaintiffs' counsel in order to avoid adverse judgments that could threaten their own positions. To address such problems, commentators have often urged greater judicial oversight and appointment of lawyers as guardians ad litem for the shareholder class.[30]

Analogous problems may arise in cases where a corporation facing potential criminal or civil liability employs counsel to represent both an organization and its employees who may be individually implicated. Such joint representation has all the advantages of a unified position discussed in the preceding notes on criminal defense, but also all the risks of potential conflicts. Those risks tend to fall disproportionately on the employee, who generally is not paying the lawyer's fee and is not in a position to provide further business. Accordingly, commentators have argued for reforms in code provisions and case law to provide more protection for employees in such circumstances, primarily through requirements of special disclosures and independent advice.

Concurrent representation is also widespread in other corporate contexts such as bankruptcy proceedings, where a lawyer who is particularly knowledgeable about the debtor may represent multiple creditors; and transactional planning, where investors and entrepreneurs may rely on a single lawyer to create a corporation or partnership. At a minimum, clients should receive full disclosure, and when the stakes are substantial, independent advice, before they consent to joint representation.[31]

Divorce

Although conflicts doctrine generally prohibit lawyers from representing both sides in litigation, the rise of no-fault divorce procedures and the public interest in reducing their financial and emotional costs have led to more permissive approaches. An increasing number of jurisdictions permit joint representation of both spouses in limited circumstances of noncontentious separations after full disclosure by the attorney and separate consent of each spouse. Other states maintain that the potential of conflicting interests and the problems of confidentiality are sufficient to bar dual representation.

Taken together, court decisions and expert commentary suggest several rules of thumb for lawyers in multiple representation contexts. Fully informed consent is necessary but not sufficient. Attorneys may be unable to provide adequate assistance to both parties where they have substantially unequal bargaining power, where one spouse dominates the decision-

---

30. For discussion of the inadequacy of ethical rules and proposals for reform, see Janet Cooper Alexander, "Do the Merits Matter? A Study of Settlements in Securities Class Actions," 43 *Stan. L. Rev.* 497 (1991); Jonathan R. Macey & Geoffrey P. Miller, "The Plaintiffs' Attorney's Role in Class Action and Derivative Litigation: Economic Analysis and Recommendations for Reform," 58 *U.Chi.L.Rev.* 1 (1991).

31. Joseph D. Vaccaro and Marc R. Milano, "Section 327(A): A Statute in Conflict: A Proposed Solution to Conflicts of Interest in Bankruptcy," 5 *Am. Bankr. Inst. L. Rev.* 237 (1997); Nancy B. Rappoport, "Wrestling With the Problem of Potential Conflicts of Interest in Bankruptcy," 26 *Viewpoint* (March 7, 1995).

making of the other, or where the attorney's special relationship to one party makes the fact or appearance of neutrality difficult to sustain.[32]

Real Estate Transactions

As courts and commentators have often noted, "a conflict of interest is inherent in the relationship of buyer and seller" of real estate.[33] Price, description of the property, terms of payment, warranties of quality and title, closing date, and risks of interim loss are all matters with potential for controversy. For this reason, some countries prohibit counsel from representing both buyer and seller in real estate transactions.[34] By contrast, American rules generally permit dual representation as long as the parties provide informed consent. Some courts refer to this as the "scrivener" exception: the lawyer is viewed as someone who merely records the terms of a previously agreed-on transaction. However, in certain contexts, such as complex commercial real estate transactions, some courts have held that a bright-line prohibition on multiple representation is necessary. *Baldasarre v. Butler,* 625 A.2d 458 (N.J.1993).

Where joint representation is permissible, recent judicial decisions and bar ethics committee opinions suggest that lawyers should make full disclosure of key facts. They include:

1. Their relationship to all parties, particularly any financial arrangements that might suggest bias;

2. the nature, seriousness, likelihood, and potential consequences of conflicts;

3. the scope of confidentiality protection (i.e., that the attorney-client privilege does not protect communication among multiple clients).

Insurance Defense Work

One of the most controversial contexts of concurrent representation concerns insurance defense. Under the typical indemnity insurance contract, the insurer agrees to pay the insured party's liability and legal costs but retains control of the defense, including the choice of defense counsel and the decision to settle. The traditional view regards the insured as the sole client of defense counsel, and the insurer merely as a third-party payer.[35] Two Model Rules, 1.8(f) and 5.4(c), caution that a third-party payer must not be permitted to influence a lawyer's independent judgment on behalf of the client. According to this traditional view, the ethical obli-

---

32. Deborah L. Rhode, *Professional Responsibility: Ethics by the Pervasive Method* 721–723 (1998).

33. *In re* Kamp, 194 A.2d 236, 240 (N.J. 1963).

34. In other countries, clients can give informed consent. *See e.g.* Moliterno & Har-

ris, *supra* note 9 at 108 (describing Australia's Central Territory rule).

35. Finley v. Home Insurance Co., 975 P.2d 1145 (Hawaii, 1998) citing Douglas Richmond, "Walking a Tightrope: The Tripartite Relation Between Insurer, Insured, and Insurance Defense Counsel," 73 *Neb. L. Rev.* 265 (1994).

gations of defense counsel run solely to the insured, even though the insurance policy confers on the insurer the right to control the defense.

In recent years, however, prominent scholars and lawyers have argued that the insurance company, which retains defense counsel to represent the insured, should be regarded as a co-client.[36] Their argument is straightforward: whether defense counsel has one client (the insured) or two clients (the insured and the insurer) depends on the retainer agreement negotiated between the insurer and defense counsel. Ordinarily, however, there is no written retainer agreement, so the one-client/two-client question must be answered by referring to the insurance contract itself, which typically specifies that the insurer controls the defense. That fact implies that the insurer functions as a co-client of the insured, not just as a third-party payer.

Why does the one-client/two-client debate matter? In brief, the one-client view favors the insured, while the two-client view gives greater control to the insurer. For example, defense counsel may acquire confidential information about the insured that would void the insurance coverage. Under the prevailing one-client view, counsel must keep this information confidential, on the theory that the insured expects such protection and does not have free choice in consenting to joint representation.[37] By contrast, proponents of the two-client view argue that such a result unfairly privileges the interests of the insured, and that such information should be shared with insurers, as in other joint client situation. In a 2008 opinion, the ABA's Standing Committee on Ethics and Professional Representation concluded that in the absence of a valid explicit agreement to the contrary, lawyers must withdraw from representing one or both clients; they cannot reveal confidential information from the insured that would be necessary for effective representation of the insurer. Formal Op. 08–450 (2008).

A related context in which conflicts arise involves settlements. If, for example, the insured insists on defending the case vigorously (at the insurer's expense), and doing so requires thirty five thousand dollars' worth of trial expenses, the one-client model requires counsel to defend, even if the case could be settled for less. According to proponents of the two-client view, such results jeopardize the liability insurance system by unfairly foisting needless costs on insurers, who typically pass along the costs in increased premiums or further restrictions on coverage.[38] Moreover, on the two-client view the insurer may sue a negligent defense counsel for malpractice, which may not be true if the insured is the sole client.

---

36. The leading authorities for this view are Charles Silver, "Does Insurance Defense Counsel Represent the Company or the Insured?," 72 *Tex. L. Rev.* 1583 (1994) and Charles Silver & Kent D. Syverud, "The Professional Responsibilities of Insurance Defense Lawyers," 45 *Duke L. J.* 255 (1995).

37. *See* Geoffrey Hazard & William Hodes, *The Law of Lawyering* § 1.7.303, at 256 (1996 Supp.).

38. Kent D. Syverud, "What Professional Responsibility Scholars Should Know About Insurance," 4 *Conn. Ins. L. J.* 17, 20–24 (1997).

Critics of the two-client view express skepticism that the insurer rather than the insured needs the most protection.[39] Most insurers, after all, are large, sophisticated businesses. Most purchasers of liability insurance are not. Purchasers generally have no choice but to accept contracts that give insurers control over legal defense, and refusing the defense counsel provided by the company typically involves forfeiting their coverage. Critics also point out that the most common conflicts of interest harm the insured, not the insurer. For example, defense counsel (who have clear incentives for favoring the interests of the insurance companies that retain them) will not take positions contrary to the company on contested issues of coverage. So too, in cases where liability is low, the company may not be willing to invest in a vigorous but expensive defense, even if insured parties have strong reasons to contest the claim in order to preserve their reputations—for example, physicians being sued for malpractice.

Other typical conflicts arise when insured parties wish to settle a claim that is within the limits of policy coverage, but insurers prefer to contest the claim, either because of potential liability or because they want to deter similar future suits. If the insurer's preference prevails, the insured runs the risk of losing and being hit with damages that exceed coverage. In such contexts, an insurer is required to exercise good faith judgment on behalf of the insured, and the "duty to settle" doctrine allows recovery for bad faith in decisions that result in judgments over the policy limits and other related damages.[40] This duty-to-settle doctrine does not, however, fully protect the insured in situations of conflict because bad faith can be difficult to prove and generally requires a second lawsuit.

Critics of the two-client view also note that defense counsel remains bound by the requirements of Model Rule 1.7: the joint representation requires a full explanation of the risks and benefits, and consent from the insured. But, critics ask, why would a fully informed insured ever freely consent?

> The insured gains nothing directly from joint representation, and loses access to a lawyer serving only her interests and advising solely from her perspective.... If given candid advice by the lawyer, the insured simply has no reason to accept joint representation with the company other than the altruistic one of saving insureds as a group money on their premiums.[41]

Furthermore, in case of a genuine conflict between insurer and insured, Rule 1.7 and 1.16 require the lawyer to withdraw.

---

39. *See* Stephen L. Pepper, "Applying the Fundamentals of Lawyers' Ethics to Insurance Defense Practice," 4 *Conn. Ins. L. J.* 27, 41–47 (1997).

40. Kent D. Syverud, "The Duty to Settle," 76 *Va.L.Rev.* 1113 (1990). *See generally* Charles Silver, "Does Insurance Defense Counsel Represent the Company or the Insured?," 72 *Tex.L.Rev.* 1583 (1994). For an argument that courts and codes should modify the current dichotomy between clients (to whom almost everything is due) and nonclients (to whom almost nothing is due) and should recognize insurers as "intermediate entities" with reasonable interests to be accommodated, *see* John Leubsdorf, "Pluralizing the Lawyer–Client Relationship," 77 *Cornell L.Rev.* 825 (1992).

41. Pepper, *supra* note 39, at 34.

Finally, critics of the two-client view maintain that it is not necessary to protect insurers' interests. Emerging doctrine already permits non-client beneficiaries such as insurers to sue a negligent defense counsel for malpractice. So too, an insurer would have the right to know information relevant to the case under Model Rule 1.6, which permits "disclosures that are impliedly authorized in order to carry out the representation."[42]

At its most fundamental level, this debate turns on whether defense counsel's obligations should be defined by the principles in bar ethics codes or by the terms of an insurance contract. This dispute led to an acrimonious and hard-fought political battle over which view would be embodied in the *Restatement of the Law Governing Lawyers*.[43] Ultimately, the *Restatement*, § 133, reiterated the traditional view but acknowledged in its comments that resolving the one-client/two-client issue may depend on law outside of bar ethics codes, such as the terms set out in the insurance contract or state statutes. See, e.g. California Civil Code § 2860. So too, the ABA took the position in Formal Opinion 403 (1996) that regardless of whether the insurer is a co-client, defense counsel cannot resolve conflicts in a way that favors the insurer over the insured; instead, counsel confronting an actual conflict of interest must withdraw.

PROBLEM 2

You have been retained by an insurance company to defend the driver in an automobile accident. The driver's wife was injured in the accident, and she files suit against her husband in order to collect on his liability insurance policy. Before trial, the husband tells you that he was driving carefully, but at trial he testifies that he caused the accident by not paying attention. You believe that he is attempting to "take a dive" in order to maximize his wife's recovery on the insurance policy. May you impeach his testimony in order to win the case for him and save the insurer money?[44]

Westinghouse Electric Corporation v. Kerr–Mcgee Corporation

United States Court of Appeals, Seventh Circuit, 1978.
580 F.2d 1311, 1312, 1318–21.

[Due to the rising price of uranium, Westinghouse Electric defaulted on numerous contracts to supply fuel to utilities that had Westinghouse nuclear reactors. The utilities sued Westinghouse for breach of contract.

42. Thomas D. Morgan, "What Insurance Scholars Should Know About Professional Responsibility," 4 *Conn. Ins. L. J.* 1 (1997).

43. Charles W. Wolfram, the Reporter for the *Restatement*, has provided an account of insurance-industry lobbying efforts in "Bismarck's Sausages and the ALI's Restatements," 26 *Hofstra L. Rev.* 817 (1998). *Compare* William T. Barker, "Lobbying and the

American Law Institute: The Example of Insurance Defense," 26 *Hofstra L. Rev.* 573 (1998); Jonathan Groner, "Insurance Lobby Aims at Normally Staid ALI," *Legal Times*, June 10, 1996, at 1.

44. *See* Montanez v. Irizarry–Rodriguez, 641 A.2d 1079 (N.J.Super.Ct.App.Div.1994).

Westinghouse subsequently filed an antitrust suit against its uranium suppliers, alleging a price-fixing conspiracy that had elevated the price of uranium. Kirkland & Ellis, a major Chicago law firm, represented Westinghouse. At the same time, however, Kirkland's Washington office had been retained by the American Petroleum Institute (API), a consortium of oil companies, to aid in lobbying efforts against proposed antitrust legislation directed against the oil industry. In the course of its efforts for API, Kirkland's Washington office confidentially surveyed and interviewed executives of 59 oil companies about aspects of their operations, including the uranium business; three of these companies were defendants in Westinghouse's antitrust suit. As it happened, Kirkland's Washington office released its report for API on the same day that Kirkland's Chicago office filed the antitrust action. Kirkland's Washington office report contended that the energy industry, including the uranium industry, was highly competitive, while Kirkland's Chicago office charged that the uranium industry had engaged in a massive price-fixing conspiracy. The antitrust defendants moved for Kirkland's disqualification. The present case appeals the denial of their disqualification motion.]

■ SPRECHER, CIRCUIT JUDGE.

The novel issues on this appeal are (1) whether an attorney-client relationship arises only when both parties consent to its formation or can it also occur when the lay party submits confidential information to the law party with reasonable belief that the latter is acting as the former's attorney and (2) whether the size and geographical scope of a law firm exempt it from the ordinary ethical considerations applicable to lawyers generally. . . .

III

The client is no longer simply the person who walks into a law office. A lawyer employed by a corporation represents the entity—but that principle does not of itself solve the potential conflicts existing between the entity and its individual participants. . . .

Here we are faced with neither an ordinary commercial corporation nor with an informal or unincorporated association, but instead with a nation-wide trade association [API] with 350 corporate and 7,500 individual members and doing business as a non-profit corporation.

We need not make any generalized pronouncements of whether an attorney for such an organization represents every member because this case can and should be decided on a much more narrow ground.

There are several fairly common situations where, although there is no express attorney-client relationship, there exists nevertheless a fiduciary obligation or an implied professional relation:

(1) The fiduciary relationship existing between lawyer and client extends to preliminary consultation by a prospective client with a view to retention of the lawyer, although actual employment does not result.

(2) When information is exchanged between co-defendants and their attorneys in a criminal case, an attorney who is the recipient of such information breaches his fiduciary duty if he later, in his representation of another client, is able to use this information to the detriment of one of the co-defendants, even though that co-defendant is not the one which he represented in the criminal case.

(3) When an insurer retains an attorney to investigate the circumstances of a claim and the insured, pursuant to a cooperation clause in the policy, cooperates with the attorney, the attorney may not thereafter represent a third party suing the insured nor indeed continue to represent the insurer once a conflict of interest surfaces.

(4) In a recent case, where an auditor's regional counsel was instrumental in hiring a second law firm to represent some plaintiffs suing the auditor and where the second firm through such relationship was in a position to receive privileged information, the second law firm, although having no direct attorney-client relationship with the auditor, was disqualified from representing the plaintiffs.

(5) In a recent case in this circuit, a law firm who represented for many years both the plaintiff in an action and also a corporation which owned 20% of the outstanding stock of the defendant corporation, was permitted to continue its representation of the plaintiff but was directed to disassociate itself from representing or advising the corporation owning 20% of defendant's stock.

In none of the above categories or situations did the disqualified or disadvantaged lawyer or law firm actually represent the "client" in the sense of a formal or even express attorney-client relation. In each of those categories either an implied relation was found or at least the lawyer was found to owe a fiduciary obligation to the laymen.

The professional relationship for purposes of the privilege for attorney-client communications "hinges upon the client's belief that he is consulting a lawyer in that capacity and his manifested intention to seek professional legal advice." The affidavits before the district court established that: the Washington counsel for Gulf "was given to believe that the Kirkland firm was representing both API and Gulf"; Kerr–McGee's vice president understood a Kirkland partner to explain that Kirkland was working on behalf of API and also its members such as Kerr–McGee; and Getty's vice president stated that in submitting data to Kirkland he "acted upon the belief and expectation that such submission was made in order to enable [Kirkland] to render legal service to Getty in furtherance of Getty's interests."

A fiduciary relationship may result because of the nature of the work performed and the circumstances under which confidential information is divulged.... In soliciting confidences from API members, Kirkland did not disavow its capacity as attorneys but came expressly represented as lawyers.

The district court concluded that "the transmission by the oil companies of confidential information on their uranium industries and assets has given rise to justifiable fears that their disclosures will return to haunt them in the present litigation" and "[t]he acquired information appears to be closely related to the subject matter of the Westinghouse complaint." The court did not find violations of Canons 4 or 5 because it could not find an attorney-client relationship on the basis of the narrow agency rules applied. However the court did find a Canon 9 violation, but did not believe that such a violation alone should result in disqualification "especially in a case of the present complexity and magnitude" involving a two-city large law firm which had attempted to segregate the substantial number of lawyers working on each matter.

The lower court perceived that "an attorney should be disqualified under Canon 9 only when 'there is a reasonable possibility of improper professional conduct' and 'the likelihood of public suspicion or obloquy outweighs the social interests which will be served by a lawyer's continued participation in a particular case.' "

Although Kirkland asserted, and the district court agreed, that it constructed a "Chinese wall" between the 8 to 14 Chicago-based attorneys working for Westinghouse and the 6 D.C.-based attorneys working for API, both conceded that William Jentes, one of Kirkland's lead attorneys working on the Westinghouse antitrust complaint, in August 1976 agreed with API task force head Lea, to prepare a legal memorandum analyzing arguments which had been advanced to broaden the scope of existing antitrust laws to outlaw interlocking directorates. Lea forwarded the Kirkland memorandum to the API, which mailed it to its member-company contact officers on September 23, 1976. Despite this breach of the "wall," we do not recognize the wall theory as modifying the presumption that actual knowledge of one or more lawyers in a firm is imputed to each member of that firm. Here there exists a very reasonable possibility of improper professional conduct despite all efforts to segregate the two sizeable groups of lawyers. . . .

Gulf, Kerr–McGee and Getty each entertained a reasonable belief that it was submitting confidential information regarding its involvement in the uranium industry to a law firm which had solicited the information upon a representation that the firm was acting in the undivided interest of each company. Canons 4 and 5, as well as Canon 9, apply. If Kirkland's size and multi-city status had any effect, it was in the direction of encouraging the oil companies to divulge confidential information. Whereas they might show reluctance to entrust their substantial assets and future fortunes to a sole practitioner or small law firm, Kirkland's substance and reputation would tend to comfort any apprehensions and open the lines of communication. In any event, there is no basis for creating separate disqualification rules for large firms even though the burden of complying with ethical considerations will naturally fall more heavily upon their shoulders.

The fact that the two contrary undertakings by Kirkland occurred contemporaneously, with each involving substantial stakes and substantially related to the other, outbalances the client's interest in continuing with its chosen attorney. However, we believe that Westinghouse should have the option and choice of dismissing Gulf, Kerr–McGee and Getty from the antitrust case or discharging Kirkland as its attorney in the case. Substitute counsel has represented Westinghouse in the case since February 17, 1978, so that the impact of any change-over has been somewhat eased.

NOTES AND QUESTIONS

1. *Westinghouse v. Kerr–McGee* was decided under the Code of Professional Responsibility, the predecessor to the Model Rules. It refers to Canon 4 (confidentiality), Canon 5 (no representation of conflicting interests), and Canon 9 (avoiding the appearance of impropriety). How, if at all, would the analysis differ under Model Rule 1.7?

2. The district court opinion denying Kerr–McGee's motion to disqualify Kirkland emphasized the size of the law firm: "With the modern-day proliferation of large law firms representing multi-billion dollar corporations in all segments of the economy and the governmental process, it is becoming increasingly difficult to insist upon absolute fidelity to rules prohibiting attorneys from representing overlapping legal interests." 448 F.Supp. 1284, 1287–88 (N.D.Ill. 1978). By contrast, the Court of Appeals found "no basis for creating separate disqualification rules for large firms...." Should conflicts doctrine take into account the size and geographic locations of law firm offices and branch offices? How would courts apply such a rule? Would such a double standard seem fair to most lawyers in private practice, who are not in large firms? Could or should law firms mitigate their conflicts problems by having cooperative relationships with firms in other cities rather than branch offices?

3. One of the most important holdings in *Kerr–McGee* is its rejection of "Chinese wall" screening techniques to avoid disqualification in simultaneous-representation cases. The term refers to the Great Wall of China, but because its use can be construed as an offensive ethnic stereotype, we avoid it here.[45] Screening originated in large accounting firms in order to protect clients from damaging leaks of information to other clients. The screening process for lawyers involves: (a) physically isolating the screened lawyers from relevant documents, typically by locking up the files and blocking electronic access; (b) forbidding contact, even casual conversations, between groups of lawyers subject to screening; (c) preventing screened lawyers from receiving any financial benefit from the cases from which they are screened, including bonuses or augmented partnership shares; (d) requiring affidavits from the screened lawyers as well as from the lawyers in charge of maintaining the system; and (e) in some cases posting a bond to assure compliance. In general, screening has been rejected in cases involving concurrent representation, but permitted in a growing minority of jurisdictions for successive representation. See Section E.

---

45. For the origin of the term, which refers to the Great Wall of China, *see* Charles W. Wolfram, *Modern Legal Ethics* 401, n. 65 (1986). For judicial criticism of its potential to offend, see Peat, Marwick, & Mitchell & Co. v. Superior Court, 245 Cal.Rptr. 873 (App.1988).

4. In *Kerr–McGee,* the court concluded that the individual oil companies were clients of Kirkland (Washington) even though the nominal client was API. The court's reasoning rests on an extremely broad, functional test to determine whether an attorney-client relationship has formed: "A fiduciary relationship may result because of the nature of the work performed and the circumstances under which confidential information is divulged." Noteworthy among the circumstances that the court identifies is "the client's belief that he is consulting a lawyer in that capacity." How well-founded should that belief be in order to hold the lawyer to fiduciary obligations?

The conclusion that conflicts of interest can arise involving parties other than nominal clients creates a crucial and very expensive problem for law firms: How does the firm track conflicts of interest? After *Kerr–McGee,* a firm considering whether to represent a client against C Corporation cannot merely check whether it is already representing C Corporation; it must also check whether it is representing corporate subsidiaries or parents of C, or trade associations like API to which C belongs. The stakes are high: a firm that unwittingly represents conflicting interests risks substantial malpractice liability if it is forced to withdraw from a representation and successor counsel must educate itself from scratch at the client's expense.

Susan P. Shapiro's landmark study of how law firms handle conflicts found a variety of tracking mechanisms.[46] Lawyers in small firms often rely on nothing more than the memories of the partners or secretaries, who can tick off all the firm's clients and who know the interrelationships among them. Slightly larger firms discuss new business at regular firm meetings. Still-larger firms circulate new-business memos to all lawyers. The largest firms, however, have thousands of current clients and hundreds of thousands of closed cases. Many of them spend tens of thousands of dollars on sophisticated conflict-tracking software, the best of which cross-checks not only the names of clients, adversaries, and corporate relatives, but also plausible misspellings of those names. Software, however, no matter how sophisticated, is only as good as the information it receives. In the volatile world of contemporary business, corporations regularly merge, divide, change their names, and buy and sell each other. Someone must feed these facts to the computer, and that is a time-consuming and quintessentially boring chore. As one lawyer explained, "You have to take reality into account. Lawyers hate all of this.... The real world is you've got a busy lawyer sitting, drowning in paper at his desk.... He or she—90 percent of the time—will not fill out the conflict clearance form.... Garbage in, garbage out."[47] To avoid conflicts, firms often combine several strategies—memory, meetings, memos, and electronic searches—and hope for the best.

---

46. Susan P. Shapiro, *Tangled Loyalties: Conflict of Interest in Legal Practice* (2002). *See* Shapiro, "Everests of the Mundane: Conflict of Interest in Real–World Legal Practice," 69 *Fordham L. Rev.* 1139 (2000); Shapiro, "When You Can't Just Say 'No': Controlling Lawyers' Conflicts of Interest," *in Social Science, Social Policy, and the Law* 322 (Patricia Ewick et al. eds. 1999).

47. Shapiro, *Tangled Loyalties, supra* note 46, at 326.

PROBLEM 3

The law firm of Barnes & Chippe employs over 400 lawyers in its New York office. The following situations have arisen within the last six months.

a) Barnes & Chippe, which represents major chemical and real estate development corporations, has instituted a policy against firm lawyers sitting on boards of public interest environmental groups such as the Natural Resources Defense Council, or providing pro bono assistance to those groups. In an intraoffice memorandum, the management committee explained that such memberships would create conflicts of interest because of the potential misuse of client confidences about controversial environmental decisions. The memorandum mentions that the policy evolved from a request by one of the firm's most important clients.

b) A senior associate in Barnes & Chippe has done pro bono work for several anti-abortion groups, including authorship of an amicus brief for a right-to-life organization in a Supreme Court case. A new partner in the firm, who sometimes works with this senior associate, has different views on reproductive rights. She offers her services to the American Civil Liberties Union to provide pro bono assistance on cases challenging abortion restrictions. An ACLU managing attorney thanks her for the offer, but indicates that the organization does not collaborate with lawyers in reproductive rights work when other members of their firm have represented right-to-life organizations. The ACLU wishes to avoid conflicts of interest and confidentiality concerns. The partner subsequently proposes that the firm establish a committee to screen pro bono cases and to put "controversial" issues to a firm vote before a lawyer undertakes representation.

c) Barnes & Chippe has an active mergers and acquisitions department. In one case, Barnes & Chippe represents corporation P in its hostile takeover attempt to win control of corporation Q. Q has adopted "poison-pill" bylaws that would make the takeover impossible, and Barnes & Chippe is arguing before the Delaware Chancery Court that Q's bylaws are illegal and contrary to public policy. At the same time, Barnes & Chippe is defending corporation X against a takeover attempt by corporation Y. X has poison-pill bylaws very similar to those of corporation Q. In this case, a different team of Barnes & Chippe lawyers is arguing before the same Delaware court that X's poison-pill measures are perfectly legal. There is no connection between X, Y, P, and Q.

d) Barnes & Chippe represents a small biotechnology company in its challenge to a federal regulatory decision. That decision prevents the company from marketing a new product, a genetically-engineered microorganism that "eats" oil slicks, breaking them down into environmentally harmless components. Ecoclean, one of Barnes & Chippe's regular clients, is an environmental disaster-control firm that derives much of its income from cleaning up oil spills by conventional methods. Ecoclean protests to Barnes & Chippe that if the biotechnology company succeeds in bringing its product to market, Ecoclean may lose millions of dollars, and perhaps may even be put out of business. Ecoclean's president sees a conflict of interest in the representation.

Which, if any, of these situations represent genuine conflicts of interest? Which, if any, represent improper interference with an attorney's independence?

NOTES: POSITIONAL CONFLICTS OF INTEREST

A *positional* conflict of interest (sometimes called an issues conflict) arises when a lawyer advocates a position on behalf of one client that is contrary to a position being urged by the lawyer or the lawyer's firm on behalf of another client in an unrelated matter.[48] These conflicts can involve factual or legal questions. An example is the situation in *Federal Defenders of San Diego, Inc. v. United States Sentencing Comm'n*, 680 F.Supp. 26 (D.D.C.1988). There, public defenders attacked the constitutionality of federal sentencing guidelines and based their standing on the ground of positional conflicts. Because the guidelines helped some of their clients and hurt others, the defenders were placed in the untenable position of both challenging and relying on the prescribed sentences. Similar positional conflicts have confronted other public defenders. In the District of Columbia, because only a "handful of trial judges were presiding over these cases, Public Defender Service colleagues found themselves taking inconsistent positions before the same judge."[49]

A related problem, sometimes lumped under the term positional conflict, is what most commentators refer to as "ideological," or "business," conflicts. These involve positions that are likely to offend or adversely affect another client even though they are not inconsistent with a stated factual or legal position of that client.[50] For example, in one widely publicized case, a large firm withdrew from pro bono representation of New York City in a claim against gun manufacturers because, according to a firm statement, the case posed "certain potential positional conflicts." However, as several legal experts noted, the firm's decision seemed to be based on economic, not ethical concerns. The firm was facing clients' disapproval, but not because it was advancing legal or factual claims inconsistent with any positions that it was advocating on those clients' behalf.[51]

48. ABA Committee on Ethics on Professional Responsibility, Formal Op. 93–377 (1993). See Restatement (Third) of the Law Governing Lawyers § 128 (2000); John S. Dzienkowski, "Positional Conflicts of Interest," 71 *Tex. L. Rev.* 457 (1993).

49. Charles J. Ogletree & Randy Hertz, "The Ethical Dilemmas of Public Defenders in Impact Litigation," 14 *N.Y.U.Rev.L. & Soc. Change* 23, 27 (1986). *See* Federal Defenders of San Diego, Inc. v. United States Sentencing Comm'n., 680 F.Supp. 26 (D.D.C.

1988). For a positional conflict that justified the lawyer's withdrawal in a capital case, see Williams v. State, 805 A.2d 880 (Del. 2002).

50. Helen A. Anderson, "Legal Doubletalk and the Concern with Positional Conflicts: A 'Foolish Consistency'?," 11 *Penn. State L. Rev.* 1, 7 (2006).

51. William Glaberson, "New York Loses a Top Legal Ally in Suit Over Guns," *N.Y. Times*, Apr. 17, 2004, at A1, A 7.

A threshold question is whether positional conflicts constitute a breach of ethics. "He is no lawyer who cannot argue both sides of a case," said Charles Lamb. A legendary illustration is that of Matthew Hale Carpenter, one of the nation's leading nineteenth advocates. He achieved widespread recognition and helped build a thriving appellate practice by arguing for two inconsistent interpretations of the 14th Amendment before the U.S. Supreme Court within weeks of each other.[52] Many contemporary lawyers are equally untroubled by such inconsistencies. Neither the Model Rules nor its predecessor, the Code of Professional Responsibility, explicitly forbids positional conflicts of interest. According to Comment [24] to Model Rule 1.7, "Ordinarily, a lawyer may take inconsistent legal positions in different tribunals at different times on behalf of different clients." Yet the Rules, like the Code, also include provisions that implicitly prohibit such conflicts in two situations. First, if it would "materially limit" the representation of one or the other client, a positional conflict is impermissible under Model Rule 1.7(a)(2), and the Code imposes a comparable prohibition.[53] Thus, for example, if prevailing on behalf of one client would set precedent damaging to another client's case, Model Rule 1.7(a)(2) prohibits the representation of both. See Comment [24] to MR 1.7. Second, if a positional conflict risks the misuse of a client's confidences, it is impermissible under Model Rule 1.6, as well as Canon 4 of the Code.

What would impose a "material" limitation on lawyers' representation and who should decide? When must lawyers consult clients about the risks of such conflicts? According to the Model Rule Comment to 1.7:

Factors relevant in determining whether the clients need to be advised of the risk include: where the cases are pending, whether the issue is substantive or procedural, the temporal relationship between the matters, the significance of the issue to the immediate and long-term interests of the clients involved and the clients' reasonable expectations in retaining the lawyer. If there is significant risk of material limitation, then absent informed consent of the affected clients, the lawyer must refuse one of the representations or withdraw from one or both matters.

One disturbing consequence of a broad prohibition on positional conflicts is the effect on law reform and pro bono work. The American bar has long pointed with pride to examples of lawyers who, as advocates for paying clients, exploited loopholes in the law, but who later volunteered their efforts to plug these loopholes.[54] Does this constitute an impermissible conflict? If knowledge of a loophole comes in part from client confidences, should the lawyer be able to provide a plug?

---

52. Carpenter prevailed in the first case, which served as the precedent for his loss in the second. No ethical problem was perceived at the time. Anderson, *supra* note 50, at 3.

53. See also Restatement, *supra* note 48, § 128. If a positional conflict would compromise the lawyer's "independent professional judgment" on behalf of either client, it is impermissible under DR 5–105 of the Code.

54. *See* Lon L. Fuller & John D. Randall, "Professional Responsibility: Report of the Joint Conference of the ABA–AALS," 44 *A.B.A.J.* 1159, 1162 (1958).

Traditionally, the bar has regarded positional conflicts as potentially problematic only in cases of concurrent, not successive representation, unless a breach of confidentiality is involved. Otherwise, a lawyer's independence would be unduly circumscribed. The Model Rules addresses questions of lawyer participation in law reform in two rules, 6.3 and 6.4. Rule 6.3 states that lawyers may participate as directors, officers, or members of a legal services organization, "notwithstanding that the organization serves persons having interests adverse to a client of the lawyer." However, the lawyer may not participate in a decision or action of the organization if doing so creates a concurrent conflict as defined in Rule 1.7. Rule 6.4 permits lawyers to belong to law reform organizations even if the reform may affect a client's interests.[55]

The frequency of positional conflicts is hard to gauge. There are almost no reported decisions, and empirical research is sparse.[56] In the only large scale study, about 40 percent of lawyers were in firms that discouraged pro bono work likely to advance positions inconsistent with client interests or values.[57] Other anecdotal accounts confirm the significance of the problem. As one partner in a Washington, D.C. firm explained:

> The point that has to be honestly faced is that ... most of the firms are being very careful not to step on the toes of their clients' important interests. They want to avoid economic conflicts or conflicts which would put them in a situation where they could be said to be disloyal to their clients. ... We have a system under which the law firms represent companies day in and day out, year in and year out, and the firms develop a sense of loyalty and identification with their clients. That's one of the great problems about the way the Bar is structured.[58]

Another lawyer, reflecting on the increasing impact of business clients to his firm, noted that

> as we represent larger and larger institutions, corporations, we are more identified with the establishment. And, therefore, antiestablishment types of lawsuits are bad for us.... Well, you lose clients, I mean, you just lose clients.... That's the thing that's vexing us.... It won't be the Wild West anymore. It'll be sad. But there you are ... I think it hurts us. But it's reality.[59]

---

55. In the Code, EC 8–1 provides that lawyers "should participate in proposing and supporting legislation and programs to improve the system, without regard to the general interests or desires of clients or former clients," and EC 7–17 advises that a lawyer "may take positions on public issues and espouse legal reforms he favors without regard to the individual views of any client."

56. Anderson, *supra* note 50, at 15. For qualitative data and anecdotal accounts, see Shapiro, *supra* note 46, at 147–68; Norman W. Spaulding, "The Prophet and the Bureaucrat: Positional Conflicts in Service Pro Bono Publico," 50 *Stan. L. Rev.* 1395 (1998).

57. Deborah L. Rhode, *Pro Bono in Principle and in Practice* 146 (2005).

58. *Quoted in* Abe Krash, "Professional Responsibility to Clients and the Public Interest: Is There a Conflict?" 55 *Chi.B.Rec.* 31, 45 (1974). *See* Esther F. Lardent, "Positional Conflicts in the Pro Bono Context: Ethical Considerations and Market Forces," 67 *Fordham L. Rev.* 2279 (1999); and Spaulding, *supra* note 56.

59. *Quoted in* Shapiro, *supra* note 46, at 153.

In practical terms, the possibility of ideological conflicts helps explain why specialty firms typically represent only one side of the specialty: labor law, insurance, environmental and personal injury lawyers typically work only "one side of the street."

Yet these pragmatic concerns run counter to the bar's interest in preserving its independence and protecting lawyers who represent unpopular clients. EC 2–27 points with pride to the "distinguished and sacrificial services by lawyers who have represented unpopular clients and causes." Thus, "regardless of his personal feelings, a lawyer should not decline representation because a client or a cause is unpopular or community reaction is adverse." A recent case in which the bar rose to the challenge involved representation of suspects being held without trial in the military security facility at Guantanamo Bay, Cuba. Some 500 lawyers from 120 of the nation's leading firms committed substantial resources to representing these detainees. And a suggestion by a deputy assistant secretary of defense that business clients should boycott these firms in order to compel them to drop the clients met with widespread condemnation. The official identified a dozen prominent law firms by name in a radio interview, adding: "I think, quite honestly, when corporate CEOs see that those firms are representing the very terrorists who hit their bottom line back in 2001, those CEOs are going to make those law firms choose between representing terrorists or representing reputable firms, and I think that is going to have major play in the next few weeks."[60] The Pentagon hastily disowned his comments, and he publicly apologized for making it (but lost his job anyway). The suggestion actually backfired: one law firm that had been reluctant to take on detainee cases changed its mind because it believed it could not afford *not* to be associated with such a distinguished roster of law firms.[61]

QUESTIONS

1. Suppose that a lawyer learns from client A, an insurance company, about typical practices in some sectors of the insurance industry. That knowledge assists the lawyer in pressing client B's claim against another insurance company in unrelated litigation. If B prevails, the precedent could harm many insurance companies, including A. Should the confidentiality rules prevent the lawyer from representing both clients? What other considerations are relevant?

2. How should law firms handle pro bono matters that may prove unpalatable to important clients? What could bar associations do to support lawyers who provide assistance to unpopular clients and causes?

60. Interview with Charles "Cully" Stimson, Federal News Radio, Jan. 11, 2007, audio available at http://www.federalnewsradio.com/index.php?sid=1029698&nid=250.

61. David Luban, "Lawfare and Legal Ethics at Guantanamo," 60 *Stan. L. Rev.* 1981 (2008).

D.   CONFLICTS INVOLVING FORMER CLIENTS

PROBLEM 4

You are a business lawyer with an expertise in corporate mergers and acquisitions. Executives from Insatiable Industries approach you to represent Insatiable in a forthcoming hostile takeover attempt of Tidbit Technologies. One of the crucial decisions in any hostile takeover is how much to offer stockholders of the target for their shares; the amount must be large enough to induce them to sell, but not so large that acquiring the target becomes unprofitable. To set the share price of the tender offer, corporate raiders carefully evaluate the profitability of the target, a task for which information about the target is crucial. Bearing this in mind, consider four alternative scenarios:

a) Tidbit Technologies has a unionized workforce, and several years ago your firm represented Tidbit in negotiating a labor contract with the union.

b) Several years ago, Tidbit Technologies fended off another hostile takeover, by a company unrelated to Insatiable Industries. A different law firm than yours handled Tidbit's takeover defense, which included lawsuits in state and federal courts. However, after losing on an intricate choice-of-law issue, Tidbit retained your firm to draft a petition for certiorari to the U.S. Supreme Court. The cert petition was denied, and that ended the representation. No lawyer in your firm acquired confidential information from Tidbit.

c) Several years ago you drafted "poison pill" anti-takeover bylaws for Tidbit Technologies. No lawyer in your firm acquired confidential information from Tidbit. However, if you represent Insatiable Industries in its takeover of Tidbit, you may be forced to argue in court that the poison pill provisions you drafted violate state law.

d) Several months ago Tidbit Technologies came to your firm for advice on legal aspects of a contemplated expansion into European markets. No lawyer in your firm acquired confidential information from Tidbit. Tidbit executives stated that they would continue to use your firm if they decided to proceed with the European expansion. Since then, there has been no further contact between Tidbit and your law firm. The *Wall Street Journal* reports that Tidbit has put its European plans on hold.

Under which, if any, of these scenarios may you represent Insatiable Industries in the hostile takeover of Tidbit Technologies?

e) At the time Insatiable Industries approaches you about the Tidbit takeover, your firm is representing Tidbit in a minor piece of trademark-infringement litigation against a snack-food company with a similar name. The litigation is expected to generate less than $100,000 in fees, while the Insatiable Industries takeover would bring in millions. May your firm withdraw from the trademark case in order to represent Insatiable? The trademark case is at an early enough stage that withdrawal would not obviously affect trial preparation or expense.

f) You suspect that Tidbit Technologies retained your firm for the trademark litigation only because it anticipated a hostile takeover attempt, and wanted to create a conflict that would prevent your firm from representing potential corporate raiders. In effect, Tidbit's savvy general counsel appears to have "planted" the trademark case in order to neutralize you. May that affect your decision whether to withdraw?

g) When Tidbit Technologies engaged your firm for the trademark case, the retainer agreement included a clause in which Tidbit waived any conflicts of interest with "existing or new clients in any matter that is not substantially related to our work for you even if the interests of such clients in those other matters are directly adverse." Does this permit you to represent Insatiable Industries in its attempt to take Tidbit over?

References: Model Rules 1.7, 1.9, 1.10, 1.16.

1.   The Rationale for Disqualification

Model Rule 1.7 forbids a lawyer from accepting any concurrent representation that might be "directly adverse" to, or "materially interfere" with interfere with another client relationship. As noted earlier, the justification for these rules rests on the twin rationales of loyalty and confidentiality. The loyalty runs to the client individually and extends beyond the subject matter of the representation. In effect, to borrow Charles Fried's metaphor, the "lawyer as friend" in one case must be a friend in others and may not compromise a client's interest even on unrelated matters. In general, personal loyalty to current clients ends when the representation ends. If lawyers were unable to accept new matters adverse to past as well as current clients, the rules would be unworkable. As attorneys' careers progressed, and their number of past clients increased, their ability to accept new cases could dramatically decrease. Lawyers would become totally identified with their previous clients, and the concept of an independent profession would be threatened. By contrast with the obligation of loyalty, obligations of confidentiality continue even after a client relationship terminates, and adverse representation is impermissible if it would risk misuse of confidential information.

In short, it is often said that the rules governing concurrent representation of conflicting interests are based on loyalty and confidentiality, while the rules governing successive representation are based on confidentiality alone.[62] If confidentiality is not an issue, lawyers may represent current clients against former clients. The principal exception occurs when a lawyer, on behalf of the current client, attacks work done on behalf of a

---

62. *See* Charles W. Wolfram, "Former-Client Conflicts," 9 *Geo. J. Legal Ethics* 677, 685–96 (1997). For a case to the contrary, however, *see* In re American Airlines, 972 F.2d 605, 616 (5th Cir. 1992)("we adhere to our precedents in refusing to reduce the con-cerns underlying the substantial relationship test to a client's interest in preserving his confidential information. The second fundamental concern protected by the test is . . . the client's interest in the loyalty of his attorney").

former client, for example by litigating to declare a contract unenforceable even though the lawyer had drafted the contract in the earlier representation. Here, disqualification results whether or not the lawyer acquired confidences from the former client. The rationale for this exception is given in the *Restatement*, § 132, cmt. b.: "[A]t the time the lawyer represented the former client, the lawyer should have no incentive to lay the basis for subsequent representation against that client, such as by drafting provisions in a contract that could later be construed against the former client."

2. CONFIDENTIALITY AND THE "SUBSTANTIAL RELATION" STANDARD

To determine when representation adverse to a former client poses substantial confidentiality concerns, courts and ethical codes have focused on whether there is a substantial relationship between the current and former matters. The following case is a leading precedent on point.

Westinghouse Electric Corporation v. Gulf Oil Corporation

United States Court of Appeals, Seventh Circuit, 1978.
588 F.2d 221, 222–25, 227–29.

[Like *Westinghouse Electric Corp. v. Kerr–McGee Corp., supra,* this case arose out of Westinghouse's antitrust suit against uranium suppliers. Although Gulf Oil Corporation and United Nuclear Corporation (UNC) were both defendants in this action, their interests were adverse: UNC was trying to exculpate itself by inculpating Gulf. UNC was represented by the Bigbee law firm, which had previously represented Gulf. Gulf therefore moved for Bigbee's disqualification. From 1971 through 1976, Bigbee had represented Gulf on legal matters concerning Gulf's uranium operations in New Mexico. Gulf obtained uranium reserves at Mt. Taylor, and Bigbee drafted mining patents for this property and litigated conflicting claims to the property. Gulf alleged that it had given Bigbee detailed information about the quality and quantity of uranium at Mt. Taylor, together with information concerning Gulf's reasons for delaying production of that uranium. Such information, Gulf argued, was directly relevant to Westinghouse's allegation that Gulf had withheld uranium in restraint of trade. Accordingly, Gulf claimed that Bigbee's access to confidential communications could aid UNC in its effort to inculpate Gulf.]

■ SPRECHER, CIRCUIT JUDGE.

In this case we review the propriety of a district court's refusal to grant a motion to disqualify opposing counsel. The issues presented are whether there is a sufficient relationship between matters presented by the pending litigation and matters which the lawyers in question worked on in behalf of the party now seeking disqualification and whether the party seeking disqualification has given legally sufficient consent to the dual representation. . . .

II

The district court set out and attempted to apply what is clearly settled as the relevant test in disqualification matters: where an attorney represents a party in a matter in which the adverse party is that attorney's former client, the attorney will be disqualified if the subject matter of the two representations are "substantially related." . . .

The substantial relationship rule embodies the substance of Canons 4 and 9 of the A.B.A. Code of Professional Responsibility. Canon 4 provides that "a lawyer should preserve the confidences and secrets of a client," and Canon 9 provides that "a lawyer should avoid even the appearance of professional impropriety." As a result it is clear that the determination of whether there is a substantial relationship turns on the possibility, or appearance thereof, that confidential information might have been given to the attorney in relation to the subsequent matter in which disqualification is sought. The rule thus does not necessarily involve any inquiry into the imponderables involved in the degree of relationship between the two matters but instead involves a realistic appraisal of the possibility that confidences had been disclosed in the one matter which will be harmful to the client in the other. The effect of the Canons is necessarily to restrict the inquiry to the possibility of disclosure; it is not appropriate for the court to inquire into whether actual confidences were disclosed.[63] . . .

Doubts as to the existence of an asserted conflict of interest should be resolved in favor of disqualification. . . . In Judge Marshall's opinion in *Cannon,* adopted and affirmed by us, he paraphrased the *T.C. Theatre* formulation that substantial relationship "is determined by asking whether it could reasonably be said that during the former representation [that] attorney might have acquired information related to the subject matter of the subsequent representation." The opinion in *T.C. Theatre* continued "[i]f so, then the relationship between the two matters is sufficiently close to bring the later representation within the prohibition of . . . [the canons]." Essentially then, disqualification questions require three levels of inquiry. Initially, the trial judge must make a factual reconstruction of the scope of the prior legal representation. Second, it must be determined whether it is reasonable to infer that the confidential information allegedly given would have been given to a lawyer representing a client in those matters. Finally, it must be determined whether that information is relevant to the issues raised in the litigation pending against the former client.

---

63. In addition, such an inquiry should be avoided whenever a presumption can be utilized due to the unsatisfactory nature of the potential evidence. This inquiry might for example consist of the questionable reliance on *ex parte* representations made *in camera* by the party seeking disqualification as to communicated confidences. Further, as the court in *T.C. Theatre Corp.* stated:

> To compel the client to show, in addition to establishing that the subject of the present adverse representation is related to the former, the actual confidential matters previously entrusted to the attorney and their possible value to the present client would tear aside the protective cloak drawn about the lawyer-client relationship. For the Court to probe further and sift the confidences in fact revealed would require the disclosure of the very matters intended to be protected by the rule.

113 F.Supp. at 269.

Although the district court properly identified this rule of law, it erred in its application . . . . . Here it could reasonably be said that during the former representation the attorneys might have acquired information related to the subject matter of the subsequent representation, that the former representation was lengthy and pervasive, that the former representation was more than peripheral, and that the relationship between the two matters is sufficiently close to bring the later representation within the prohibition of the canons. Therefore there was clearly a substantial relationship between the two representations.

III

Given the conclusion that the Bigbee firm's prior work for Gulf was sufficiently related to issues raised in the present litigation, it is necessary to address UNC's argument that Gulf waived any right it might have had to seek disqualification. Although this issue was not addressed by the district court, we hold that, even accepting completely UNC's account of the facts supporting waiver, these facts are legally insufficient to demonstrate a waiver that would prevent disqualification in the present case.

UNC now claims that in 1971, as Gulf began development of its New Mexico properties and sought to retain the Bigbee firm, Gulf was informed that the Bigbee firm had a prior relationship with UNC, which like Gulf was involved in the mining of uranium. UNC further claims that Bigbee informed Gulf that due to this relationship the Bigbee firm could only represent Gulf if Gulf consented that should a conflict arise between Gulf and UNC, Bigbee would not be precluded from representing UNC. Although this forms the basis of UNC's argument of waiver, it also argues that the waiver was subsequently reaffirmed by Gulf on two other occasions. . . . Ultimately UNC's waiver argument depends on the underlying proposition that a client would, or even may, authorize an attorney to utilize against him information given to the attorney in confidence.

As we noted earlier, disqualification in this case is required by the application of Canon 4. . . . Of particular relevance is the following passage:

> A lawyer should not use information acquired in the course of the representation of a client to the disadvantage of the client and a lawyer should not use, except with the consent of the client after full disclosure, such information for his own purposes.

EC 4–5. We believe it significant that the language of this ethical consideration is carefully constructed so that the consent clause only applies to the portion of the sentence dealing with the lawyer's personal use of confidential information. The omission of this phrase from the first half of the sentence leads to the conclusion that a client's consent will not justify the use of confidential information against the client. . . .

[I]t is impossible to conclude that a client could ever have any reason to desire that information disclosed in confidence should be utilized against him. . . . Accordingly, we hold that a simple consent by a client to representation of an adverse party is not a defense to that former client's motion for disqualification, such as the one under review here, based on the possibility that confidential information will be used against the former client.

The district court is reversed and the motion of Gulf Oil Corporation to disqualify Bigbee, Stephenson, Carpenter & Crout from representing United Nuclear Corporation in *Westinghouse Electric Corporation v. Rio Algom Limited, et al.,* is granted.

Reversed and remanded.

NOTES

The Substantial Relation Standard

The "substantial relationship" test originated in Judge Weinfeld's opinion in *T.C. Theatre Corp. v. Warner Bros. Pictures,* 113 F.Supp. 265, 268 (S.D.N.Y.1953):

> [T]he former client need show no more than that the matters embraced within the pending suit wherein his former attorney appears on behalf of his adversary are substantially related to the matters or cause of action wherein the attorney previously represented him, the former client. The Court will assume that during the course of the former representation confidences were disclosed to the attorney bearing on the subject matter of the representation.

Westinghouse v. Gulf Oil adopts this test, but adds to it Judge Marshall's explanation in *Cannon v. U.S. Acoustics Corp.,* 398 F.Supp. 209, 228–29 (N.D.Ill.1975), that a substantial relationship "is determined by asking whether it could reasonably be said that during the former representation [that] attorney might have acquired information related to the subject matter of the subsequent representation." Under *Westinghouse,* if confidences *might have* passed, the court will irrebuttably presume that they *have* passed.

Model Rule 1.9(a) codifies this body of decisional law, prohibiting lawyers from representing a person "in the same or a substantially related matter in which that person's interests are materially adverse to the interests of the former client unless the former client gives informed consent, confirmed in writing." Comment [3] defines "substantial relationship" in terms slightly different from Judge Sprecher's *Westinghouse* test: matters are substantially related if there is "a substantial risk that confidential factual information as would normally have been obtained in the prior representation would materially advance the client's position in the subsequent matter." According to this test, not only must the confidential information that presumptively passed from the former client to the attorney be relevant to the present case, it must materially advance the present client's position. In practice, however, the two versions of substantial relationship are hard to distinguish: if the information is relevant to the present case, presumably that is because it would materially advance one party's interests against the other.

Why make the presumption that confidences have passed irrebuttable? In the passage quoted in footnote 3 of *Westinghouse v. Gulf Oil*, Judge Weinfeld explained that making the former client demonstrate that confidences had actually passed to the attorney would be self-defeating, for it would require disclosure of the very confidences that disqualification is meant to preserve. This would not always be avoided by having a court review the evidence *in camera* because many cases settle before that stage.

In *Analytica, Inc. v. NPD Research, Inc.,* 708 F.2d 1263, 1266 (7th Cir.1983), Judge Posner wrote: "It is irrelevant whether [the lawyer] actually obtained [confidential] information and used it against his former client, or whether—if the lawyer is a firm rather than an individual practitioner—different people in the firm handled the two matters and scrupulously avoided discussing them." Judge Posner acknowledges that "[t]he 'substantial relationship' test has its problems, but conducting a factual inquiry in every case into whether confidences had actually been revealed would not be a satisfactory alternative...." *Id.* at 1269.

It is not always easy to determine which facts about a former client are relevant in a current litigation. Consider the so-called "playbook problem." As explained by Charles Wolfram, "Playbook involves the claim that although the lawyer doesn't know anything specific about the matter, the lawyer knows a lot of generalities about the former client and therefore the lawyer is disqualified."[64] Wolfram elaborates:

> There have been cases suggesting that if you know something about the way the client's head works you know something that's relevant for purposes of applying the substantial relationship test.... I think ... it will turn out that some of them indeed are cases of substantial relationship, but some of them have not been. Those cases that are cases of substantial relationship would be cases where what you probably learn about the client's inclination, the client's willingness to settle, the client's unwillingness ever to be deposed is both relevant and unknown to others in the second litigation. That is to say it's still a secret. It was a secret obviously when you obtained it but it's still a secret that others don't know it.[65]

Thus, Wendy Fleishman, a lawyer who had previously represented the insurance company MetLife in personnel matters, was disqualified when she joined a law firm representing MetLife employees suing the company for gender discrimination. The court concluded that she knew too much about MetLife's personnel department and its procedures; furthermore, she "was privy to highly privileged communications originating with MetLife's corporate law department regarding settlement strategies in class action litigations." *Mitchell v. Metropolitan Life Insurance Co.*, 2002 WL 441194 (S.D.N.Y.), at *23. In other words, even if Fleishman knew nothing specific about the gender discrimination cases, she knew MetLife's playbook, and

64. Charles W. Wolfram, "The Vaporous and the Real in Former-client Conflicts," 1 *J. Inst. Stud. Leg. Eth.* 133, 135 (1996).

65. *Id.* at 138.

that made her past cases and the present case "substantially related." Interestingly, Prof. Wolfram served as an expert witness on the side of Fleishman's new firm; in response, the judge cited the paragraph quoted above from his article to explain why she must be disqualified.

Sideswitching Exceptions and Lateral Mobility

What if a lawyer did not personally represent the former client, but the lawyer's former firm did? Ordinarily, one lawyer's conflicts of interest are imputed to all lawyers in the firm, but this imputation may end when the lawyer leaves the firm, provided the lawyer acquired no confidential information about the former client.[66] Under those circumstances, if the lawyer's new firm seeks to represent a party against the previous firm's former client, the new firm may rebut the presumption that the lawyer had obtained confidences. This exception is analyzed in *Silver Chrysler Plymouth,* below, and is governed by Model Rules 1.9(b)–(c). They provide:

Rule 1.9 Duties to Former Clients

(b) A lawyer shall not knowingly represent a person in the same or a substantially related matter in which a firm with which the lawyer formerly was associated had previously represented a client

(1) whose interests are materially adverse to that person; and

(2) about whom the lawyer had acquired information protected by Rules 1.6 and 1.9(c) that is material to the matter;

unless the former client gives informed consent, confirmed in writing.

(c) A lawyer who has formerly represented a client in a matter or whose present or former firm has formerly represented a client in a matter shall not thereafter:

(1) use information relating to the representation to the disadvantage of the former client except as these Rules would permit or require with respect to a client, or when the information has become generally known; or

(2) reveal information relating to the representation except as these Rules would permit or require with respect to a client.

Furthermore, just as Model Rule 1.9(b) allows lawyers who have moved to a new firm to rebut the presumption that they acquired confidential information about the former firm's client, Model Rule 1.10(b) allows the former firm to rebut the presumption that any of its lawyers retain confidential information about the former client after the lawyers who represented that client depart.

It provides:

Rule 1.10 Imputation of Conflicts of Interest: General Rule

(b) When a lawyer has terminated an association with a firm, the firm is not prohibited from thereafter representing a person with

---

66. *See generally* Lynda C. Shely, "Law Firm Changes: The Ethical Obligations When Lawyers Switch Firms," 2006 *Professional Lawyer* 69.

interests materially adverse to those of a client represented by the formerly associated lawyer and not currently represented by the firm, unless:

(1) the matter is the same or substantially related to that in which the formerly associated lawyer represented the client; and

(2) any lawyer remaining in the firm has information protected by Rules 1.6 and 1.9(c) that is material to the matter.

(c) A disqualification prescribed by this rule may be waived by the affected client under the conditions stated in Rule 1.7.

(d) The disqualification of lawyers associated in a firm with former or current government lawyers is governed by Rule 1.11.

Factual Versus Legal Relationships

Notice that *T.C. Theatre* refers to a substantial relationship between "the matters or cause of action," which suggests that the relationship can exist between the *facts* ("matters") of the two cases or between the *legal issues* ("cause of action") of the two cases. Focusing on legal issues generally results in a considerably narrower range of disabling conflicts than focusing on factual questions. Thus, for example, a lawyer may represent a client in a series of real estate transactions, and then attempt to represent the client's spouse in a divorce action where the value of the former client's property is a contested issue. Model Rule 1.9, cmt 3. The legal questions are completely unrelated, but the factual questions overlap and the potential for misusing the former client's confidences is significant. Thus, the two matters would be substantially related under Model Rule 1.9 and *Westinghouse v. Gulf*. In a small minority of opinions, courts have refused to disqualify lawyers unless the past and present issues were "identical" or "essentially the same." *Government of India v. Cook Industries, Inc.*, 569 F.2d 737, 739–40 (2d Cir. 1978). But the basis for these opinions was the practical burdens disqualification would impose on clients, rather than a principled disagreement with the proposition that substantial relation primarily has to do with facts, not legal issues.

Waivers

One final issue raised in *Westinghouse v. Gulf Oil* and in similar conflicts cases involves waivers. Under the Seventh Circuit's analysis, client waivers of conflicts prohibitions may be binding in cases of concurrent representation because clients are in an "adequate position to judge the effects of divided loyalties." By contrast, in cases of successive representation

[d]isqualification based on the potential for abuse of confidential information ... involves different considerations which preclude the effectiveness of consent, particularly a vague, general consent given or implied prior to the threat of disclosure or adverse litigation. In that instance it is impossible to conclude that a client could ever have any

reasons to desire that information disclosed in confidence should be utilized against him. 588 F.2d at 229.

Yet as other courts and commentators have noted, waivers consisting of "a vague, general consent given or implied prior to the threat of disclosure or adverse litigation" may be equally suspect in concurrent representation. In the words of the *Restatement*, § 122, cmt. d, "A client's open-ended agreement to consent to all conflicts normally should be ineffective unless the client possesses sophistication in the matter in question and has had the opportunity to receive independent legal advice about the consent."[67]

Nevertheless, what little empirical information is available suggests that law firms frequently request waivers of conflicts of interest from clients. In one study of Illinois attorneys, over two thirds indicated that they informed clients that conflicts were waivable 90 percent of the time. Interestingly, a smaller number of attorneys, 44 percent, told clients that they could do a good job despite the conflict.[68] Anecdotal evidence also suggests that blanket advance waivers are common, particularly among large law firms with long client lists. Firms often fear that accepting a new client, or even a new matter for an existing client, risks preempting so many other potential matters that the new engagement may become more a burden than a benefit. A typical waiver clause in a retainer agreement provides:

> "As we have discussed, you are aware that the firm represents many other companies and individuals. It is possible that during the time that we are representing the Company, some of our present or future clients will have [disputes or transactions] with the Company.... The Company agrees that we may continue to represent or may undertake in the future to represent existing or new clients in any matter that is not substantially related to our work for you even if the interests of such clients in those other matters are directly adverse. We agree, however, that your prospective consent to conflicting representation contained in the preceding sentence shall not apply in any instance where, as a result of our representation of you, we have obtained proprietary or other confidential information of a nonpublic nature, that, if known to such other client, could be used in any such other matter by such client to your material disadvantage. [You should know that, in similar engagement letters with many of our other clients, we have asked for similar agreements to preserve our ability to represent you.]"[69]

67. For general discussion, see Richard Painter, "Advance Waivers of Conflicts," 13 *Geo. J. Legal Ethics* 289 (2000).

68. Leonard Gross, "Are Differences Among the Attorney Conflict of Interest Rules Consistent with Principles of Behavioral Economics?," 19 *Geo. J. Legal Ethics* 111, 128 (2006).

69. Robert O'Malley et al., "Selected Conflict of Interest Issues," 2 *ALI–ABA Course of Study Materials, Qualified Plans, Professional Organizations, Health Care, and Welfare Benefits* (Feb. 1997). *See also* Richard W. Painter, "Rules Lawyers Play By," 76 *N.Y.U. L. Rev.* 665, 703–08 (2001).

ABA Formal Opinion 93–372 (1993) finds that such advance waivers are not unethical, but it warns that their validity cannot be determined until an imminent conflict actually arises. At that point, the adequacy of any advance waiver must be revisited. "Even though one might think that the very purpose of a prospective waiver is to eliminate the need to return to the client to secure a 'present' second waiver when what was once an inchoate matter ripens into an immediate conflict, there is no doubt that in many cases that is what will be ethically required." *Id.*

As the frequency of conflicts of interest have increased, so too has the frequency and importance of waivers. Yet research on informed consent strategies reveal that they are highly imperfect responses to conflicts.[70] Various cognitive biases prevent individuals from adequately adjusting for misleading information even when conflicts are fully disclosed. Because so much self-serving bias operates at unconscious levels, neither those who give, nor those who receive, skewed advice may appreciate the extent of the problem. A further problem is that informed consent strategies may reduce professionals' feelings of concern about potentially adverse affects, and encourage them to merely disclose, rather than avoid, compromising influences.[71]

Games Lawyers and Clients Play: "Sabotage," "Protection," and "Hot Potatoes"

One reason law firms seek advance waivers from clients is apparent from part (f) of Problem 4. Sophisticated corporate clients sometimes distribute small amounts of legal work among law firms in order to ensure that they will be unavailable to potential adversaries in upcoming major deals or litigation—a tactic that some lawyers describe as "sabotage."[72] This is one of several conflict-of-interest games that shrewd businesses and law firms play with each other. A related practice is to place highly feared lawyers on retainer so that they cannot represent adversaries. Prominent lawyers may, in turn, exploit their reputations to extract generous nonrefundable retainers from cautious corporations.

A well-publicized example involves Skadden, Arps, Slate, Meagher & Flom. For many years, named partner Joseph Flom has been among the premier mergers-and-acquisitions lawyers in New York City, and at one point nearly 300 corporations were paying $150,000 annual retainers to Skadden Arps for the purpose of "sterilizing Joe," that is, ensuring that Flom would not end up representing the enemy in a takeover battle.

70. Daylian M. Cain, George Loewenstein, & Don A. Moore, "The Dirt on Coming Clean: Perverse Effects of Disclosing Conflicts of Interest," 34 *J. Legal Studies* 1, 2 (2005); Paul M. Healy and Krishna G. Palepu, "Information Assymetry: Corporate Disclosure and the Capital Markets: A Review of the Empirical Disclosure Literature," 31 *J. Accounting & Econ.* 405 (2001).

71. Cain, Loewenstein & Moore, *supra* note 65, at 16–22.

72. Lincoln Caplan, *Skadden: Power, Money, and the Rise of a Legal Empire* 84 (1993). For further discussion, *see* Richard W. Painter, "Advance Waiver of Conflicts," 13 *Geo. J. Legal Ethics* 289 (2000); Fred C. Zacharias, "Waiving Conflicts of Interest," 108 *Yale L.J.* 407 (1998); Lawrence J. Fox, "All's O.K. Between Consenting Adults: Enlightened Rule on Privacy, Obscene Rule on Ethics," 29 *Hofstra L. Rev.* 701 (2001).

Retainers during this period sometimes accounted for more than 40% of Skadden's income.[73] Although critics charged that the retainers were little more than protection money, Skadden justified its practice as a safeguard against sabotage. In Flom's words, "If you didn't have some way of assuring a guy was serious about hiring you, everybody would talk to you about some tiny problem and you'd be conflicted out of everything."[74] Skadden nevertheless came under fire for its policy of declining legitimate (not "sabotage") matters in order to escape being conflicted out of more lucrative work later. To address these difficulties, the firm made a short-lived effort to "have its cake and eat it too" by accepting non-refundable retainers from clients but also asking them to waive conflicts of interest. This would permit Skadden to drop their matters, represent an adversary, and keep the money. In the face of public criticism, Skadden announced that it would change its practice and refund the year's retainer if it invoked the waiver clause against a client. Skadden also encouraged retainer clients to utilize the firm rather than merely buying its inactivity.[75]

Chapter XII discusses the ethical issues arising from non-refundable retainers. For present purposes, it is sufficient to note that the practices described above generally violate no provisions of bar ethics codes.[76] Matters stand differently, however, in scenarios such as Problem 4(e), in which a lawyer withdraws from an active case in order to represent the adversary in a more profitable matter. Model Rule 1.16(b) permits withdrawal if it "can be accomplished without material adverse effect on the interests of the client." Yet courts have consistently forbidden withdrawal for purposes of representing the client's adversary. See *Restatement*, § 132, cmt. c. The prohibition on withdrawal in such cases has become known as the "hot potato rule," so named because of language in *Picker International, Inc. v. Varian Associates*, 670 F.Supp. 1363, 1365 (N.D.Ohio 1987): "A firm may not drop a client like a hot potato, especially if it is in order to keep happy a far more lucrative client."

All these practices carry a whiff of pure amoral gamesmanship, which some find repugnant and others see as a breath of fresh air. The conflicts games between large law firms and large corporations involve sophisticated players with business calculations on both sides. Yet many bar leaders, equally schooled in the economic realities of practice, maintain that lawyers should be held to a higher standard. Are they right?

E. IMPUTED DISQUALIFICATION
PROBLEM 5

Senior Partner, an attorney at the law firm of Adams & Adams, represents Client One in Matter One. Junior Partner, another attorney in

---

73. Caplan, *supra* note 72, at 81–82.
74. *Id.* at 84.
75. *Id.*, at 83–85, 137.
76. *See* Lester Brickman & Lawrence A. Cunningham, "Nonrefundable Retainers: Impermissible Under Fiduciary, Statutory and Contract Law," 57 *Fordham L. Rev.* 149 (1988). *See also* the discussion of fees in Chapter XII.

Adams & Adams, has acquired confidential information about Matter One and Client One, although Junior Partner has done no work on Matter One. Associate, a third attorney at Adams & Adams, has researched a purely legal issue connected with Matter One, but has acquired no confidential information about it.

Assume that your jurisdiction has adopted Model Rules 1.9 and 1.10, and answer the following questions:

1.   a) Suppose Senior Partner moves to law firm Baker & Baker. Baker & Baker wishes to represent Client Two against Client One in Matter Two, which is substantially related to Matter One. May Senior Partner undertake the representation? May any lawyer in Baker & Baker undertake the representation? May Baker & Baker undertake the representation if Senior Partner is screened from the case?

b) Alternatively, suppose Junior Partner moves to Baker & Baker. As in the previous question, Baker & Baker wishes to represent Client Two against Client One in Matter Two, which is substantially related to Matter One. May Junior Partner undertake the representation? May any lawyer in Baker & Baker undertake the representation? May Baker & Baker undertake the representation if Junior Partner is screened from the case?

c) Alternatively, suppose Associate moves to Baker & Baker. As in the previous questions, Baker & Baker wishes to represent Client Two against Client One in Matter Two, which is substantially related to Matter One. May Associate undertake the representation? May any lawyer in Baker & Baker undertake the representation? May Baker & Baker undertake the representation if Associate is screened from the case?

2.   Do any of your answers to the preceding question change if Baker & Baker was already representing Client Two against Client One in Matter Two at the time that the Adams & Adams lawyer moved to Baker & Baker?

3.   Alternatively, suppose Senior Partner and Junior Partner both move to Baker & Baker. Their former firm, Adams & Adams, wishes to represent Client Two against former Client One in Matter Three, which is substantially related to Matter One. Senior Partner and Junior Partner were the only lawyers in Adams & Adams who acquired confidential information from Client One about Matter One.

a) May Adams & Adams undertake Matter Three?

b) For its own protection, Adams & Adams retains copies of all case files, including those of lawyers who have left the firm. When lawyers leave the firm, their case files are electronically sequestered and hard copies are transferred to a locked file cabinet to which only the managing partner of Adams & Adams has access. The managing partner's responsibilities do not include representing clients. The firm's file on Matter One includes case memoranda written by the firm's lawyers, itemized billing sheets and time records, correspondence between Senior Partner and Client One as well as between Senior Partner and other parties involved in Matter One, and receipts for confidential client documents that have subsequently been returned to Client One. These receipts include identifying descriptions of the documents.

Do these facts affect your answer about whether Adams & Adams can accept Matter Three?

Silver Chrysler Plymouth, Inc. v. Chrysler Motors Corporation

United States Court of Appeals, Second Circuit, 1975.
518 F.2d 751.

■ MOORE, CIRCUIT JUDGE:

An action is pending before Judge Weinstein in the Eastern District of New York entitled *Silver Chrysler Plymouth, Inc. v. Chrysler Motors Corporation and Chrysler Realty Corporation*. It awaits trial.... [T]he issue on this appeal . . . is disqualification of counsel.

Chrysler for many years has been represented by the law firm of Kelley Drye Warren Clark Carr & Ellis (Kelley Drye) and its predecessors, which also represents Chrysler in this action. Although many other law firms represent Chrysler on various matters throughout the country, only Kelley Drye is listed on Chrysler's annual reports as "Counsel." Silver Chrysler is represented by the firm of Hammond & Schreiber, P.C. Dale Schreiber of that firm had been employed as an associate by Kelley Drye, and while there worked on certain Chrysler matters. Because of this fact Kelley Drye by motion sought to disqualify both Schreiber and his firm from representing Silver Chrysler in this action. In support of, and in opposition to, the motion respectively, the parties submitted voluminous affidavits, copies of pleadings in cases in which Schreiber had allegedly worked, and extensive memoranda of law. With this material before him and after oral argument, the Judge proceeded to analyze the motion on the theory that "[d]ecision turns on whether, in the course of the former 'representation,' the associate acquired information reasonably related to the particular subject matter of the subsequent representation." The Judge reviewed the subject matter of the cases on which Schreiber was claimed to have worked and the law as it appears in this Circuit from decided cases and in a comprehensive opinion, concluded that "[d]isqualification of plaintiff's counsel is not warranted." From this decision Chrysler appeals....

Upon graduation from law school in 1965, Dale Schreiber was hired by Kelley Drye to commence work in September 1965. He worked at the firm briefly before accepting a position as a law clerk to a federal judge. His work at Kelley Drye began again in September 1966 and continued to February 1969.

Kelley Drye is one of New York's larger law firms, having had at the time some 30 partners and 50 associates.... Many firms hire a dozen or more law graduates each year and it has now become the practice to hire for summer work (usually between their second and third years at law school) a substantial number of law students. These "summer associates" most frequently perform tasks assigned to them by supervising associates or partners. Many of the summer students do not return to the same firms with which they have been associated or even remain in New York City. Even after an initial association with a firm upon graduation, it is not uncommon for young lawyers to change their affiliation once or even several times. It is equally well known that the larger firms in the metropolitan areas have hundreds (collectively thousands) of clients. It is unquestionably true that in the course of their work at large law firms, associates are entrusted with the confidences of some of their clients. But it would be absurd to conclude that immediately upon their entry on duty they become the recipients of knowledge as to the names of all the firm's clients, the contents of all files relating to such clients, and all confidential disclosures by client officers or employees to any lawyer in the firm. Obviously such legal osmosis does not occur. The mere recital of such a proposition should be self-refuting. And a rational interpretation of the Code of Professional Responsibility does not call for disqualification on the basis of such an unrealistic perception of the practice of law in large firms.

Fulfilling the purpose of the disqualification remedy, "namely the need to enforce the lawyer's duty of absolute fidelity and to guard against the danger of inadvertent use of confidential information" does not require such a blanket approach. Nor are such broad measures required to maintain "in the public mind, a high regard for the legal profession." Thus, while this Circuit has recognized that an inference may arise that an attorney formerly associated with a firm himself received confidential information transmitted by a client to the firm, that inference is a rebuttable one. And in *Laskey,* the court cautioned that:

> It will not do to make the presumption of confidential information rebuttable and then to make the standard of proof for rebuttal unattainably high. This is particularly true where, as here, the attorney must prove a negative, which is always a difficult burden to meet.

The importance of not unnecessarily constricting the careers of lawyers who started their practice of law at large firms simply on the basis of their former association underscores the significance of this language.

The Circuit has also adhered to the rule enunciated by Judge Weinfeld in *T.C. Theatre Corp. v. Warner Bros. Pictures, Inc.,* that "where any substantial relationship can be shown between the subject matter of a former representation and that of a subsequent adverse representation, the latter will be prohibited." . . .

In contrast to [prior cases finding substantial relationships], quite a different situation is presented here. Schreiber was not counsel for Chrysler in the sense that the disqualified attorneys were in those cases. Although Kelley Drye had pervasive contacts with Chrysler, Schreiber's relationship cannot be considered co-extensive with that of his firm. The evidence submitted to Judge Weinstein on the motion was admittedly somewhat conflicting. By affidavits submitted by the head of the litigation department at Kelley Drye, Chrysler sought to show not only the purportedly "substantially related" cases upon which Schreiber worked but also the extensive amount of Chrysler-dealer litigation in the office and in which Schreiber was concededly not involved. Schreiber responded by affidavit, detailing his responsibilities in Chrysler matters upon which he recalled working. Schreiber also obtained, amongst other things, supporting affidavits of Clark J. Gurney (the associate who handled the bulk of Chrysler dealer matters) and Hugh M. Baum, two former colleagues at Kelley Drye (presently employed elsewhere).

As we recently recognized in *Hull v. Celanese Corp.:*

> The district court bears the responsibility for the supervision of the members of its bar. . . . The dispatch of this duty is discretionary in nature and the finding of the district court will be upset only upon a showing that an abuse of discretion has taken place.

Judge Weinstein was well aware of the tests to be applied. He examined *Checker v. Chrysler,* an antitrust action and Schreiber's principal Chrysler case while at Kelley Drye, and concluded that the case was not substantially related to this litigation. As to other matters that Schreiber recalled working on, the judge was entitled to conclude that they also were not substantially related. . . . [T]here was ample basis for crediting Schreiber's denial of having worked on them and concluding that Schreiber's involvement was, at most, limited to brief, informal discussions on a procedural matter or research on a specific point of law. The affidavits of Gurney and Baum provided support for such a conclusion. In this respect we do not believe that there is any basis for distinguishing between partners and associates on the basis of title alone—both are members of the bar and are bound by the same Code of Professional Responsibility. But there is reason to differentiate for disqualification purposes between lawyers who become heavily involved in the facts of a particular matter and those who enter briefly on the periphery for a limited and specific purpose relating solely to legal questions. In large firms at least, the former are normally the more seasoned lawyers and the latter the more junior. This is not to say that young attorneys in large firms never become important figures in certain matters but merely to recognize that some of their work is often of a far more limited variety. Under the latter circumstances the attorney's role cannot be considered "representation" within the meaning of *T.C. Theatre Corp.* and *Emle* so as to require disqualification. Those cases and the Canons on which they are based are intended to protect the confidences of former clients when an attorney has been in a position to learn them. To apply the remedy when there is no realistic chance that confidences were disclosed would go far beyond the purpose of those decisions. Chrysler was in a position here conclusively to refute Schreiber's position that his role in these cases had been non-existent or fleeting. Through affidavits of those who supervised Schreiber on particular matters or perhaps through time records, the issue was capable of proof. Chrysler instead chose to approach the matter in largely conclusory terms.[77] We cannot realistically subscribe

---

77. Example from a Kelley Drye (Chrysler) affidavit:

"[Schreiber] obtained unmeasurable confidential information regarding the prac-to the contention that proof submitted for this limited purpose, by time records or otherwise, would have necessitated disclosure of any confidences entrusted to Kelley Drye.

Judge Weinstein also concluded that Schreiber had rebutted any inference, arising merely from his former association with Kelley Drye, that he possessed confidences that can be used against Chrysler in this lawsuit. We think the district judge was plainly correct. There may have been matters within the firm which, had Schreiber worked on them, would have compelled disqualification here. But Schreiber denied having been entrusted with any such confidences. He was supported in this respect by the affidavits of Gurney and Baum. This was sufficient.

Finally, in view of the conclusion that Schreiber's work at Kelley Drye does not necessitate disqualification, we agree with the district court that refusal to disqualify Schreiber and his firm will not create an appearance of impropriety. Neither Chrysler nor any other client of a law firm can reasonably expect to foreclose either all lawyers formerly at the firm or even those who have represented it on unrelated matters from subsequently representing an opposing party. Although Canon 9 dictates that doubts should be resolved in favor of disqualification, it is not intended completely to override the delicate balance created by Canon 4 and the decisions thereunder....

Order affirmed.

NOTES

Contemporary American lawyers work in an era of increasing lateral mobility. Firms split, merge, and compete for lateral hires. Partners switch firms and bring colleagues or even whole departments with them. The vast majority of associates do not stay in the firms where they start. As a result, many lawyers now find themselves in situations similar to that of Dale Schreiber in *Silver Chrysler Plymouth.* That decision's approach has been codified in Model Rule 1.9(b), reprinted above. It provides that unless a client gives informed written consent a lawyer "shall not knowingly represent a person in the same or a substantially related matter in which a firm with which the lawyer formerly was associated had previously represented a client

    1) whose interests are materially adverse to that person and

    2) about whom the lawyer had acquired [confidential] information...."

The comments to the Rule add that "a conclusion about the possession of [confidential] information may be based on the general nature of the services the lawyer provided ..." In essence, the effect of the Rule is that: (1) lawyers are presumed to have acquired confidential information about

tices, procedures, methods of operation, activities, contemplated conduct, legal problems, and litigations of [Chrysler]."

their former firm's clients; (2) this presumption is rebuttable; (3) if the presumption is successfully rebutted, lawyers who switch firms and their new colleagues may represent interests adverse to their former firm's clients, even when the present and past matters are substantially related; (4) if lawyers who switch firms cannot rebut the presumption, neither they nor their new partners and associates may represent interests adverse to the former firm's client in substantially related matters unless, after consultation, the former client consents. Screening the personally-disqualified lawyer will not prevent vicarious disqualification except in the case of former government lawyers, discussed in Section F below.

The ABA Ethics 2000 Commission recommended that screening be permitted, with notice to any affected clients, when a disqualified lawyer makes a lateral move to a new firm, as long as any confidential information is not likely to be significant in the future representation. The Commission based its recommendation on the absence of virtually any complaints of harm in the jurisdictions that have permitted screening, some of which have allowed the practice for over a decade. The Commission also heard substantial evidence concerning problems with the current rule: undue restraints on the mobility of lawyers, excessive costs to parties, and unreasonable assumptions that screening can work for former government lawyers but not for anyone else. Although a divided ABA House of Delegates rejected the Commission's proposed rule on screening, it is likely to remain a subject of ongoing debate and a model for adoption by some jurisdictions. About half of states currently permit screening of lateral hires under some circumstances.[78]

QUESTIONS

1.   Charles Wolfram has observed that "[i]n the end there is little but the self-serving assurance of the screening-lawyer foxes that they will carefully guard the screened-lawyer chickens."[79] Lawrence Fox, who led the fight against screening in the ABA House of Delegates, adds: "You tell me how an individual client is going to feel when that client learns that the lawyer is now working for the other side ... I think this is the place where we've got to make a stand for loyalty."[80] Do you agree? What are the incentives for law firms to violate or to comply with screening procedures? Would any external monitoring be effective in enforcement of screening procedures? Is it significant that in states like Oregon and Washington, which have had screening for decades, disciplinary agencies report no complaints or malpractice claims arising from the practice?[81]

78. "Conflicts of Interest: Imputed Disqualification," 23 ABA/BNA *Lawyers' Man. Prof. Conduct* 647, 649 (2007).

79. Wolfram, *supra* note 45, at 402. See Charles W. Wolfram, "Ethics 2000 and Conflicts of Interest: The More Things Change ..." 70 *Tenn. L. Rev.* 27 (2002).

80. Lance J. Rogers, "Speakers, Audience Debate Screening As Tool to Forestall Imputed Conflicts," 22 ABA/BNA *Lawyers' Man. Prof. Conduct* 290, 291 (2006)(quoting Fox).

81. *Id.* at 290.

Based on her empirical study, Susan Shapiro argues that more liberal rules on screening may in fact provide better protection for clients than current approaches. In jurisdictions that generally allow screens, they are subject to more stringent internal and external regulation than in jurisdictions that generally do not permit them unless the client consents.[82] As Shapiro also notes, her data do not resolve the most crucial issues: whether the additional regulation makes the screens sufficiently effective; and which rule best protects relatively powerless and unsophisticated clients who are most in need of protection. But she aptly concludes that sensible rule-making on this issue should be informed by better information about how screening and consent standards actually operate.

2.   *Silver Chrysler Plymouth* reaches its no-disqualification result by holding that Dale Schreiber "was not counsel for Chrysler in the sense that the disqualified attorneys were in [prior cases]." The limited responsibilities of young lawyers "cannot be considered 'representation' within the meaning of [previous cases] so as to require disqualification." What if Schreiber had unquestionably represented Chrysler in the past—if, for example, he had been Chrysler's attorney of record in a previous case—but was prepared to show by affidavits or other evidence that he had received no confidential information bearing on the present litigation? Should he be permitted to offer this evidence under *T.C. Theatre* or *Westinghouse v. Gulf Oil?* Under Model Rule 1.10(b)?

3.   If you were a member of your state bar committee or supreme court considering whether to allow screening, which approach would you support? Why?

F.   THE FORMER GOVERNMENT LAWYER
PROBLEM 6

You are a fifth year associate with a large Washington, D.C. law firm. Before joining the firm, you served for two years as a special assistant to the Assistant Attorney General in charge of the Antitrust Division. Your major responsibility during that time was completion of a special position paper outlining the Administration's views on the oil industry. In particular, the paper's objective was to justify a more permissive policy regarding vertical combinations in the industry. To complete the paper, you reviewed a broad range of economic and legal literature, interviewed various oil company executives, and consulted with several government economists.

The arrival of a new Assistant Attorney General prompted your departure from the Division. The current leadership has inaugurated certain changes in policy regarding antitrust in general and the oil industry in particular. Accordingly, the Antitrust Division recently filed suit against

---

82.   Susan P. Shapiro, "If It Ain't Broke . . . An Empirical Perspective on Ethics 2000, Screening and the Conflict-of-Interest Rules," 2003 *U. Ill. L. Rev.* 1299; and Susan P. Shapiro, "Bushwacking the Ethical High Road: Conflict of Interest in the Practice of Law and Real Life," 28 *Law & Soc. Inquiry* 87 (2003).

a number of major oil companies, two of which have expressed interest in retaining your firm.

a) Under what circumstances may you participate in the litigation? Under what circumstances may your firm do so?

b) If you became involved in the case, what, if any, *ex parte* calls to friends in the Antitrust Division would be permissible?

c) What constraints should guide former government lawyers when lobbying and appearing before a public body in which they previously held a position?

References:

Model Rules 1.11; 3.5; 3.9. *See also* Rules 1.9; 1.10; and 8.4, and ABA Code of Professional Responsibility, DR 5–105(D); DR 9–101; ECs 9–3 & 9–4.

Armstrong v. McAlpin

United States Court of Appeals, Second Circuit, 1980.
625 F.2d 433, 443–46, 452–54 (en banc) *vacated*, 449 U.S. 1106 (1981).

[As a lawyer for the Securities and Exchange Commission (SEC), Altman supervised a 1974 investigation and litigation against Capital Growth Fund. Clovis McAlpin was accused of looting millions of dollars from that Fund before fleeing to Costa Rica. Altman left the SEC in 1975 and went into private practice for the Gordon firm. In 1974, Michael Armstrong was appointed receiver of Capital Growth; one of his principal duties was recovering the looted assets from McAlpin. Armstrong retained the Gordon firm in 1976 as litigation counsel against McAlpin. Concerned about Altman's prior participation, the Gordon firm obtained the SEC's consent to the representation, and screened Altman from the case. Nevertheless, in 1978 McAlpin moved to disqualify the Gordon firm because of Altman's prior participation in the case. In ruling on this motion, Judge Werker noted that Altman would be disqualified under DR 9–101(B) of the ABA Code, which provides that "a lawyer shall not accept private employment in a matter in which he had substantial responsibility while he was a public employee," and that the Gordon firm would then be vicariously disqualified under DR 5–105(D). However, he also noted that ABA Formal Opinion 342 (1976) states that when a former government lawyer is personally disqualified under DR 9–101(B), screening that lawyer will suffice to avoid the vicarious disqualification of the lawyer's firm. Applying the latter approach, Judge Werker denied the disqualification motion. On appeal, Judge Newman, writing for a panel of the Second Circuit, reversed and disqualified the Gordon firm. The Second Circuit voted to rehear the case *en banc,* and reversed the panel in the following decision. The Supreme Court rejected McAlpin's appeal on other grounds, 449 U.S. 1106 (1981).]

■ FEINBERG, CIRCUIT JUDGE:

On this rehearing en banc, we are favored with briefs not only from the parties but also from the United States, the Securities and Exchange

Commission, the Interstate Commerce Commission, the Federal Maritime Commission, the Commodities Futures Trading Commission and twenty-six distinguished former government lawyers now employed as practicing attorneys, corporate officers, or law professors, all attesting to the importance of the issues raised on appeal. Thus, the United States asserts that a "decision to reject screening procedures is certain to have a serious, adverse effect on the ability of Government legal offices to recruit and retain well-qualified attorneys"; this view is seconded by the other government amici. And the former government lawyers, including two former Attorneys General of the United States and two former Solicitors General of the United States, state that they are all "affected at least indirectly, by the panel opinion's underlying assumption that government lawyers cannot be trusted—trusted to discharge their public responsibilities faithfully while in office, or to abide fully by screening procedures afterwards." While the tone of these assertions may be overly apocalyptic, it is true that a decision rejecting the efficacy of screening procedures in this context may have significant adverse consequences. Thus, such disapproval may hamper the government's efforts to hire qualified attorneys; the latter may fear that government service will transform them into legal "Typhoid Marys," shunned by prospective private employers because hiring them may result in the disqualification of an entire firm in a possibly wide range of cases. The amici also contend that those already employed by the government may be unwilling to assume positions of greater responsibility within the government that might serve to heighten their undesirability to future private employers. Certainly such trends, if carried to an extreme, may ultimately affect adversely the quality of the services of government attorneys.

Not only is the panel decision possibly of great practical importance, the ethical issues it addresses are also complex and are currently being hotly contested by various groups. . . . We do not believe that it is necessary or appropriate for this court to enter fully into the fray, as the panel opinion did. Indeed, the current uncertainty over what is "ethical" underscores for us the wisdom, when considering such issues, of adopting a restrained approach that focuses primarily on preserving the integrity of the trial process. . . .

We believe that this approach is dispositive here and requires our affirmance of the ruling of the district court. It is apparent from a close reading of Judge Werker's opinion that he saw no threat of taint of the trial by the Gordon firm's continued representation of the receiver. Nor did the panel opinion in this case challenge that view. Although appellants assert that the trial will be tainted by the use of information from Altman, we see no basis on the record before us for overruling the district court's rejection of that claim. Using the *Nyquist* analysis, there is certainly no reason to fear any lack of "vigor" by the Gordon firm in representing the receiver; this is not a case where a law firm, by use of a "Chinese wall," is attempting to justify representation of conflicting interests at the same time. Nor is the Gordon firm "potentially in a position to use privileged information" obtained through prior representation of the other side. And finally, the receiver will not be making unfair use of information obtained by Altman as a government official, since the SEC files were turned over to the receiver long before he retained the Gordon firm and Altman has been entirely screened from all participation in the case, to the satisfaction of the district court and the SEC. Nor is there any reason to believe that the receiver retained the Gordon firm because Altman was connected with it or that Altman had anything to do with the retention. If anything, the presence of Altman as an associate at that time was a problem, not a benefit, for the Gordon firm, as the district court, the receiver and the Gordon firm all apparently recognized.

Thus, because the district court justifiably held that the Gordon firm's representation of the receiver posed no threat to the integrity of the trial process, disqualification of the firm can only be based on the possible appearance of impropriety stemming from Altman's association with the firm. However, as previously noted, reasonable minds may and do differ on the ethical propriety of screening in this context. But there can be no doubt that disqualification of the Gordon firm will have serious consequences for this litigation; separating the receiver from his counsel at this late date will seriously delay and impede, and perhaps altogether thwart, his attempt to obtain redress for defendants' alleged frauds. Under the circumstances, the possible "appearance of impropriety is simply too slender a reed on which to rest a disqualification order ... particularly ... where ... the appearance of impropriety is not very clear." Thus, we need not resolve the ethical propriety of the screening procedure used here at this time as long as the district court justifiably regarded it as effective in isolating Altman from the litigation. . . .

. . .

Accordingly, we vacate the panel opinion in this case and affirm the judgment of the district court. . . .

■ NEWMAN, CIRCUIT JUDGE, concurring in part and dissenting in part. . . .

... DR 9–101(B) is not concerned solely with the trial taint that may occur if an attorney handles a matter for which he previously had substantial responsibility as a government lawyer. It also seeks to avoid "the manifest possibility that ... [a former Government lawyer's] action as a public legal officer might be influenced (or open to the charge that it had been influenced) by the hope of later being employed privately to uphold or upset what he had done." Courts traditionally have been most sensitive to the enforcement of standards designed to limit governmental power. They should be at least as sensitive to the enforcement of standards specifically designed to protect against the misuse of such power. The purposes of DR 9–101(B) cannot be fully achieved unless there is no possibility that the government attorney can be (or seem to be) influenced by the prospect of later private employment. To remove that possibility requires disqualification not only of the attorney, when handling a related matter, but also of his firm.

NOTES: THE REVOLVING DOOR

Armstrong v. McAlpin concerns an issue of considerable public importance: the "revolving door" between government and the private sector. For a substantial and increasing number of attorneys, a common career path involves acquiring expertise on the workings *of* government by working *in* government. With this expertise, many individuals leave public sector employment for positions as lobbyists, consultants, or practitioners in areas involving their prior government employer. Over the last half century, an increasing number of top ranking government officials have become "in-and-outers" rather than "sitters and stayers."[83]

The importance of lobbying has increased dramatically over the last half century, and so also has the role of lawyers involved in such activities. Before the 1950s, only a few corporations or public interest organizations and a few thousand unions and trade associations had offices in the nation's capitol. Today, over 500 corporations, 2000 public interest organizations, and 85,000 unions and trade associations have such offices.[84] Groups range in size and importance from the American Bar Association, with some 400,000 members, to the National Frozen Pizza Institute. Lobbying activities have similarly increased at the state and local level. The number of lawyers assisting these and other organizations has correspondingly escalated. "Governmental relations" work for private clients involves a broad variety of activities, such as providing advice about political and legislative developments; preparing testimony for legislative and administrative hearings; drafting statutes, regulations, and comments; negotiating government contracts; suing governmental bodies; maintaining contacts with public officials and agencies; and coordinating legal, political, and public relations strategies at state, local, and national levels.[85] Lawyers who cycle in and out of government form an important link between the public and private sectors.

Yet this linkage also poses obvious risks of conflicts of interest. *McAlpin*'s approach, derived from ABA Formal Opinion 342, forbids the former government lawyer from representing private clients on matters in which the lawyer had participated personally and substantially while in government, but permits other lawyers in the firm to do so provided that former government lawyer is screened. Although controversial at the time,

83. John D. Donahue, "In-and-Outers: Up or Down?," in *For the People: Can We Fix Public Service*, 60, 62 (John D. Donahue and Joseph S. Nye, Jr. eds. 2003). A representative survey by the Public Interest Research Group found that of some 300 federal government employees who left office during one change in administration, about a third went directly into lobbying and another fifth joined law firms that were involved in lobbying. Catherine Crier, *The Case Against Lawyers* 169 (2002).

84. Congressional Research Service, *Lobbyist and Interest Groups: Sources of Information* (2006); Ronald G. Shaiko, "Lobby-

ing in Washington: A Contemporary Perspective," in *The Interest Group Connection: Electioneering, Lobbying, and Policymaking in Washington* 3, 7–8 (Paul S. Hernson, Ronald G. Shaiko, & Clyde Wilcox eds. 1998).

85. Shaiko, *supra* note 79, at 9. For the expansion of lobbying activities, see Congressional Research Service, *Lobbying Reform: Background and Legislative Proposals* (2006); Mark J. Green, *The Other Government: The Unseen Power of Washington Lawyers* (1975); Edward O. Laumann, et al., "Washington Lawyers and Others: The Structure of Washington Representation," 37 *Stan. L. Rev.* 465 (1985).

the *McAlpin* doctrine has become settled law, embodied in Model Rule 1.11 and in §§ 124(3) and 133 of the *Restatement*.

At first glance, *McAlpin* appears to involve merely a special case of the more general problem of successive representation. If so, it seems puzzling that the solution differs so dramatically from other cases of former-client conflicts, in which screening the affected lawyer will not remove an imputed conflict of interest. The explanation is that the revolving door between public and private sectors raises a distinct set of issues concerning not just the ethics of lawyers but the demands of public service. At issue are competing needs. One is to prevent the promise of future private employment from improperly influencing government officials. A second is to avoid restrictions that will unduly discourage qualified lawyers from entering public service. Model Rule 1.11, like its predecessor DR 9–101(B), seeks to maintain public confidence not merely in the legal profession, but in government itself, without hampering its ability to attract capable counsel.

Possibilities for compromised loyalties are a common spinoff of the revolving door. In recent years, prominent Washington lobbyists, White House aides, members of Congress, and federal agency officials have been dismissed or prosecuted for ethics violations, and these highly visible cases have had their less visible counterparts in state and local government as well. In the wake of these scandals, nearly 90 percent of surveyed Americans believe that there is a serious, or very serious problem of corruption in the nation's capital.[86]

Such abuses have prompted an increasing array of statutory and administrative regulation. Federal officials, including lawyers, are governed by a detailed set of regulations in the Ethics in Government Act, 18 U.S.C. §§ 201–19, strengthened in 2007 by the Honest Leadership and Open Government Act. Virtually every state and locality has conflicts rules for its own employees. Under the federal framework, 18 U.S.C. § 207 prohibits certain post-executive and legislative branch representation activities for a specified period of time. Section 207(a)(1) permanently prohibits former executive branch employees from engaging in representation regarding any matter in which they participated "personally and substantially," while employed by the government. Section 207(a)(2) provides for a two-year "cooling-off" period by prohibiting a former executive branch employee from making any communication to or appearance before a federal agency or court, with the intent to influence, respecting any matter "actually pending" within a year preceding the employee's termination of employment. Sections 207(c) and (d) apply to high level executive department employees such as cabinet officers and agency heads, who are restricted for two years from representing a client before, or communicating so as to influence, the government entity for which they served, in connection with any matter in which the former high level employee seeks official action. In addition, 18 U.S.C. § 1905 makes it a criminal offense to divulge confiden-

---

86. Edward Alden, "Abramoff Adds to Pressures for Clean–Up in Washington," *Fi-* *nancial Times* (London), January 5, 2006, at 5 (citing AP–Ipos poll).

tial information obtained in government service, although other statutory provisions protect disclosure of illegal conduct. See Federal Bar Association Opinion 73–1, 32 Fed.B.J. 71 (1973) and the materials on whistleblowing below and in Chapter VII.

Government officials and influential policy advisors often complain that broad ethical prohibitions discourage qualified individuals from accepting public sector employment. This view figured prominently in the various amicus briefs that Judge Feinberg describes in the *McAlpin* opinion. Their concern is that lawyers with ambitions beyond civil service will not seek government employment if they know that they will be unable to practice their specialty in the private sector soon afterward and that private firms may be unwilling to hire a government employee who might vicariously disqualify the firm in many cases. Relatively low salaries and an increasingly intrusive appointments process for public officials, involving extensive background checks and financial disclosure requirements, have already compromised government's ability to recruit the "best and brightest."[87] Strict conflict of interest rules might contribute to a semi-permanent bifurcation of the bar, with a public service sector less qualified than its private counterpart.[88]

Such a bifurcation would deprive both constituencies of what many observers view as a useful exchange of perspectives that may enhance the government's ability to regulate effectively and the private sector's tendencies towards regulatory compliance. Finally, career mobility may also increase the quality of government by ensuring some measure of independence and fresh perspectives among government officials. Civil servants who have alternative job possibilities may be more willing to challenge a position that they believe is erroneous.

By contrast, public interest groups worry about the consequences of a wide-open revolving door: government by a relatively small group of insiders who move back and forth, developing an unhealthy level of cronyism and government-by-connections, and permitting exploitation of confidential information. Opponents of the revolving door also challenge assertions that strict ethics rules will prevent recruitment of talented individuals for government service. From these commentators' perspective, such claims inaccurately assume that the only competent public servants available are individuals hoping to cash in on their public service immediately afterward. To the extent that the government would have problems attracting qualified lawyers under stringent conflicts rules, the solution is to improve the pay and working conditions of public sector employment, not relax ethical requirements.

Underlying much of this discussion is an idealized vision: the private citizen who enters government without attempting to exploit his public service for private gain, serves with selfless distinction, and then retires to

---

87. Donahue, *supra* note 83, at 67.

88. Daniel Schwartz, "The 'New' Legal Ethics and the Administrative Law Bar," in *The Good Lawyer: Lawyers' Roles and Lawyers' Ethics* 251 (David Luban ed. 1983).

a quiet private life. The historical archetype of such a figure is the legendary Roman general Cincinnatus, who was pulled from his small farm to rule Rome during an emergency. He defeated the Aequians in a single day in 458 B.C., and, after entering Rome in triumph, his fellow citizens begged him to remain as dictator. Instead, Cincinnatus returned to his farm. Pulled from his plow a second time in 439, Cincinnatus again returned when the menace had passed.

Cincinnatus was a figure of great significance in our nation's founding era, because many people viewed George Washington as an American reincarnation of the legend. In 1783, Washington voluntarily resigned his commission as commander-in-chief of the army with the celebrated declaration:

> Having now finished the work assigned me, I retire from the great theater of Action; and bidding an Affectionate farewell to this August body under whose orders I have so long acted, I here offer my Commission, and take my leave of all the employments of public life.[89]

Admiring artists began depicting Washington as Cincinnatus. After his return to public life as president, Washington again renounced invitations to continue service. Following a Farewell Address in 1796, Washington retired to his farm. His example epitomized the "republican virtue" that political theorists in the founding era insisted was essential for a democratic social order.

Is this vision of public service hopelessly romantic and utopian? Some historians believe it is, and was so even in Washington's time. The painter John Trumbull (who later portrayed Washington as Cincinnatus) wrote his brother from London in 1784 about Washington's first resignation: " 'Tis a Conduct so novel, so inconceivable to People, who, far from giving up powers they possess, are willing to convulse the Empire to acquire more."[90] However, many of the founders believed that public service should be an avocation, not a vocation. According to John Adams, the true government servant "should make it a rule never to become dependent on public employment for subsistence. Let him have a trade, a profession, a farm, a shop, something where he can honestly live, and then he may engage in public affairs, if invited, upon independent principles."[91] Ironically, Adams himself violated his own advice. Almost his entire adult life was spent in public service. And many other eighteenth-century leaders were full-time government officials, with only side interests in farming, law, or business. But certainly during America's early decades, few full-time public positions were available. Government remained a small, largely local, and relatively simple pursuit, and the handful of appointive positions available were usually viewed as political spoils, to be allocated by elected officials on the basis of loyalty and integrity, not specialized skills.

89. Quoted in Garry Wills, *Cincinnatus: George Washington and the Enlightenment* 13 (1984).

90. Quoted in *id.* at 13.

91. Joseph S. Nye, Jr. and John D. Donahue, "Introduction," in *For the People, supra* note 83.

This model became unworkable as the economy grew in size and complexity and the need for centralized government increased.[92] The number of lawyers in public service increased as well, with a large influx occurring during the New Deal. But most did not stay permanently. About two-thirds of those surveyed subsequently went into private practice, and some wound up as paradigmatic Washington insiders.[93] Similar career paths now occur with regularity. Whether this is an entirely healthy development is open to question. Government has become increasingly complicated, and it may be naive to think that an inexperienced Cincinnatus could do even a minimally competent job in any high-level public sector position. At the same time, however, it is appropriate to ask whether government by insiders is consistent with democratic premises, and to note that the most fervent defenders of the revolving door are typically those who are passing through it.

QUESTIONS

1. In his *McAlpin* dissent, Judge Newman argues that the real reason for tightening conflicts rules is to prevent private law firms from attempting to influence agency lawyers by holding out the prospect of private employment. How significant is this concern on the facts of *McAlpin* or of Problem 6? For example, is it relevant that Altman had left government service for private practice well before Armstrong approached the Gordon firm? Can Model Rule 1.11(d) provide an effective cure for the problem worrying Judge Newman and other commentators by banning representation of a private client in matters in which the lawyer "participated personally and substantially as a public officer or employee," absent informed consent by the government agency?

2. Is it likely that most private firms would want to hire lawyers who had shown disloyalty to their government "client" in order to curry favor with potential private employers? Wouldn't many government lawyers try to market themselves by being tough, incorruptible adversaries? Alternatively, would at least some public sector employees believe that they could enhance their reputation by appearing reasonable and responsive to private-sector concerns? And wouldn't private firms gladly encourage such expectations if that could benefit their clients? If a government lawyer hopes to move into an attractive private sector position, is it inevitable that some of his work will be influenced, consciously or unconsciously, by a desire to impress potential employers, whatever that requires?

3. How should the problem of networking and informal contacts between current and former government employees be handled? The Ethics in Government Act specifically allows senior employees to communicate with their former colleagues on matters of a "personal and individual nature." Is this a context where prohibitions against the "appearance of improprie-

---

92. *Id.*, 2.

93. Peter H. Irons, *The New Deal Lawyers* 298–300 (1982). For examples, see Robert L. Nelson and John P. Heinz, "Lawyers and the Structure of Influence in Washington," 22 *Law & Soc. Rev.* 237 (1988).

ty" should have bite? Or are such informal contacts a natural and often constructive way of maintaining effective working relationships between public and private sector employees? Can the prohibition on substantive communications be partially circumvented by coaching colleagues on how to make such contacts?

To what extent does the problem of the revolving door stem from ambivalence in our objectives for government service? We want a public sector that is insulated from private pressure but not too insulated. Our goals are independence and responsiveness, quality and economy; we hope to attract the "best and brightest," to public service, but we don't want to pay the cost of salaries competitive with the private sector.

4.   *McAlpin* follows ABA Formal Opinion 342 by disqualifying Altman but not vicariously disqualifying other Gordon firm lawyers, provided that Altman is screened. This is also the approach of Model Rule 1.11(b), which permits other lawyers to provide representation provided that the disqualified lawyer is (1) "timely screened from participating in the matter and is apportioned no part of the fee; and (2) written notice is promptly given to the appropriate government agency to enable it to ascertain compliance with the provisions of this rule." Since the court acknowledges that Altman possessed no confidential information about Capital Growth, because all the SEC files had been turned over to Armstrong, what is the rationale for disqualifying Altman?

Note that Model Rule 1.11(a) bars lawyers from accepting private employment in a matter in which they participated personally and substantially as public employees even if their representation would not be adverse to their former employer's. This prohibition is broader than the general conflicts rules regarding successive representation. What is the rationale for broader coverage?

5.   Presumably, Clovis McAlpin, living in Costa Rica with $24 million in ill-gotten gains, did not move to disqualify the Gordon firm out of altruistic concerns for the integrity of the federal bar. Should private parties like McAlpin have standing to move for disqualification or should it be up to the former government "client" to object or consent to the conflict? Would agency lawyers be too indulgent of practices that they might wish to replicate? Who constitutes the client for these purposes?[94]

6.   Should special screening rules apply to government bodies? When lawyers leave private practice to take public service positions, should their prior involvement with a case require disqualification of all government attorneys in their office? In *City of Santa Barbara v. Superior Court*, 122 Cal.App.4th 17 (2004), water and sewerage from a municipal line flooded

---

94.   For a general overview of problems on identifying the client, see Geoffrey P. Miller, "Government Lawyers' Ethics in a System of Checks and Balances," 54 *U.Chi. L.Rev.* 1293, 1294, n. 1 (1987); Keith W. Donahoe, "The Model Rules and the Government Lawyer: A Sword or Shield? A Response to the D.C. Bar Special Committee on Gov- ernment Lawyers and the Model Rules of Professional Conduct," 2 *Geo.J.Legal Ethics* 987 (1989). For other issues see Andrew Stark, *Conflict of Interest in American Public Life* (2000); the symposium on "Government Lawyering," 61 *Law & Contemp. Probs.* 1 (1998).

portions of a private residence. The homeowners retained a firm to pursue a claim against the city. One of the firm's lawyers who worked on the case subsequently joined the City Attorney's office, which was defending the suit. The lawyer was screened but the homeowners moved to disqualify the office. Prior to this case, California courts had not allowed screening for lateral hires, and the state trial court granted their motion. An appellate panel reversed. In justifying a special rule for government offices, the court reasoned first that: "Unlike their private sector counterparts, public sector lawyers do not have a financial interest in the matters on which they work. As a result, they may have less, if any, incentive to breach client confidences." A further consideration was that strict rules on vicarious disqualification might force public entities "to avoid hiring lawyers with relevant private-sector experience."[95] An article critical of the decision ran under the title, "Are Public Lawyers More Honorable Than Private Ones?"[96] Is that the relevant question? Do you agree that the opinion "appears to deeply malign and offend every lawyer in private practice"?[97]

7. Although government lawyers are under both ethical and statutory obligations to maintain confidential information, they are also subject to legislation requiring them to report fraud or criminal conduct by other public servants.[98] As noted earlier, they are also subject to whistleblower protection for such reports. One consequence, particularly in this era of electronic communication, is that leaks of compromising information by government attorneys are not uncommon, particularly in the nation's capitol.

What about disclosures that do not involve illegal conduct, but that may expose ethical concerns? Consider the statement by Michael Stokes Paulsen: "I am responsible indirectly, remotely, only contributorily, and perhaps excusably, but nonetheless partially responsible—for the deaths of one and half million innocent unborn children per year."[99] The basis for this assertion was his decision not to leak information concerning the nomination of David Souter to the United States Supreme Court. As a lawyer in the Office of the Legal Counsel in the Department of Justice during the administration of George H. W. Bush, Paulsen helped to research Souter's record and concluded that he was likely to uphold *Roe v. Wade's* protection of women's right to abortions. In failing to leak information to a prominent conservative columnist, or to friends in anti-abortion groups, Paulsen believes that he enabled Souter to receive the nomination

---

95. City of Santa Barbara v. Superior Court, 122 Cal.App.4th 17, 24, 25 (2004).

96. Kurt W. Melchior, "Are Public Lawyers More Honorable than Private Ones?," 15 *Professional Lawyer* 26 (2005).

97. *Id*. In a subsequent decision, the California Supreme Court endorsed screening in government offices under circumstances like those in *City of Santa Barbara,* but not in contexts where the disqualified attorney is the head of the office. See City and County of San Francisco v. Cobra Solutions, Inc., 135 P.3d 20 (Cal. Sup. Ct. 2006).

98. *See* 28 U.S.C. § 535(b) (2002); James E. Moliterno, "The Federal Government Lawyer's Duty to Breach Confidentiality," 14 *Temple Pol. & Civil Rights L. Rev.* 633, 636, 643–44.

99. Michael Stokes Paulsen, "Hell, Handbaskets, and Government Lawyers: The Duty of Loyalty and its Limits," 61 *Law & Contemp. Probs*. 1 (1998).

and to later cast a decisive vote sustaining *Roe*. As Paulsen now sees it, he did the *"wrong* thing."[100] What is your view? Does it depend on your position on abortion? How would you analyze the government attorney's responsibility in matters of conscience?

On the other hand, when former OLC lawyer Jack Goldsmith wrote a memoir revealing improper behavior by lawyers in the administration of George W. Bush, Paulsen harshly criticized him for revealing client confidences—and added that he now wonders whether "my own minor league storytelling [in the article discussed above] might have been too close to the line, or even just over it."[101] He asks, "Has the tell-all book phenomenon succeeded in Defining Duty Down, for government lawyers, so that the operative ethical standard is less than the one described in the texts of the legal ethics rules?"[102]

8. What, if any, special ethical constraints should inform the work of lawyers as lobbyists? Do the differences between advocacy in courtrooms and in legislative corridors demand recognition? A lobbyist typically does not work under the procedural safeguards of adversarial processes. Nor is the decision maker systematically protected from influences that might produce a biased result.[103] What follows from this fact? Leaders of the bar have long emphasized that when lawyers are advising on matters of public policy in a non-adversarial context, they have a special responsibility to consider public welfare. As Professor Paul Freund once put it, an attorney in this setting has a "wider scope and obligation to see around a problem unconstrained by what may be too parochial concerns of his clients, and to advise accordingly."[104] Lawyers' own reputational interests often push in similar directions. Many practitioners who specialize in governmental relations have invested a substantial part of their careers either in serving in public office or in establishing good working relations with those who do. Their effectiveness usually depends on maintaining a reputation for candor, fairness, integrity, and reasonableness among those with whom they will have continued dealings.[105] Yet some issues involve intense conflict among interest groups, and between those groups and government regulators. In such contexts, the limited research available suggests that lawyer/lobbyists are no less partisan than advocates in other settings.[106] Such partisanship in pursuit of socially dubious interests fuels widespread public distrust. Indeed, in one Colorado Senate election involving an attorney who had previously worked in lobbying, a media strategist reported that he had "never tested anything that tested worse" on public image than "lawyer-lobbyist."[107]

100. *Id.*, at 92.

101. Michael Stokes Paulsen, "Jack Goldsmith, Legal Ethics, and 'the Cover-Your–Ass Syndrome'," *Balkinization*, Sept. 10, 2007, available at http://balkin.blogspot.com/2007/09/jack-goldsmith-legal-ethics-and-cover.html.

102. *Id.*

103. Wolfram, *supra* note 45, at 749.

104. Green, *supra* note 85, at 12 (quoting Paul Freund).

105. Laumann, et al., *supra* note 80, at 490–95.

106. *Id.*

107. Mike Soraghan, "Strickland Changes Tack on 'Lawyer Lobbyist' Label," *Denver Post*, Sep. 4, 2001, at A10 (quoting Bob Klein).

It is perhaps inevitable that lawyers acting in a lobbying role will be tainted by association with unpopular positions taken by their clients. But it is also fair to ask whether the profession as well as society would benefit if private practitioners seeking to influence public policy accepted greater responsibility to consider the public interest. Many highly successful government relations attorneys do so, and have withdrawn from celebrated cases such as those involving tobacco companies' resistance to warning labels.

9. What are the obligations of government lawyers if they perceive a conflict between the public's interest and the position of an agency that they are asked to defend? Are agency officials entitled to have their "day in court" and to have the merits of their policies determined by a court? Alternatively, does a lawyer representing "the public" have an independent obligation to assess its interests?[108]

Such issues raise a broader conceptual question: who is "the client" of the government lawyer? Theoretically, the client could be the public, the government as a whole, the branch of government in which the lawyer is employed, the agency in which the lawyer works, or the officials responsible for the lawyer's actions. Courts, commentators, and bar ethical codes have taken different views, although they all maintain that lawyers in public office owe special responsibilities to the public.[109] The difficulty lies in determining what constitutes the public's interest and what it requires when members of the government disagree.

That difficulty arises in a wide variety of factual settings. In some instances, lawyers in one agency, like the Department of Justice or a state attorney general's office, are responsible for representing another agency's position but find that position inconsistent with applicable laws, policies, or societal concerns. In other contexts, higher authorities within the lawyers' own agency or the central administration may direct them to act in ways that they find similarly problematic. For example, a change in administration during the pendency of litigation may result in directives for a government lawyer to "switch sides," although the lawyer believes that the new position is unsupported by the law or facts. Dilemmas also arise when the legislative or executive branch is unwilling to provide adequate funding for government institutions, such as prisons or mental health facilities. Government attorneys may then be in the position of defending conditions that they believe violate constitutional standards or individual rights. Another common problem involves confidential information that lawyers

---

108. *See* Catherine J. Lanctot, "The Duty of Zealous Advocacy and the Ethics of the Federal Government Lawyer: The Three Hardest Questions," 64 *S.Cal.L.Rev.* 951 (1991); Kathleen Clark, "Government Lawyering: The Ethics of Representing Elected Representatives," 61 *Law & Contemp. Prob.* 31 (1998).

109. Steven K. Berenson, "Public Lawyers, Private Values: Can, Should, and Will Government Lawyers Serve the Public Interest?" 41 *B. C. L. Rev.* 789 (2000); Jack B. Weinstein & Gay A. Crosthwait, "Some Reflections on Conflicts Between Government Attorneys and Clients," 1 *Touro L. Rev.* 1 (1985); William Josephson & Russell Pearce, "To Whom Does the Government Lawyer Owe the Duty of Loyalty When Clients Are in Conflict?" 29 *How. L. J.* 539 (1986).

believe should be shared with other legislative, executive, or judicial decision makers or with the general public.

Very little case law is available to help identify the "client" in such circumstances. Commentators and bar ethics codes have taken several approaches. One position is that the client is normally the government agency that employs the lawyer. This "agency approach" is reflected in Rule 1.13 of the Federal Bar Associations' Model Rules of Professional Conduct for Federal Lawyers. However, the Rule includes the caveat that a government lawyer may have "authority to question [agency] . . . conduct more extensively than . . . a lawyer for a private organization in similar circumstances." The *Restatement (Third) of the Law Governing Lawyers* offers a variation of the agency approach. The Comment to § 156 suggests that in most cases, the client of the government lawyer is the agency involved in the underlying dispute, but that the lawyer's responsibility may differ depending on the circumstances. The primary advantages of the agency approach are clarity and political accountability. By limiting the government lawyer's discretion to make independent judgments of the public's interest, this approach vests decision-making authority with elected officials who are more directly responsible to the public.[110]

Yet in some contexts, an agency framework reflects an unrealistic assumption of political oversight and an impoverished conception of the government lawyer's social responsibilities. After all, most government decisions are made by middle level bureaucrats who are not in any direct sense subject to majoritarian control. Even senior agency officials have attenuated democratic accountability. High-ranking federal officials can owe their appointment to a single election where no candidate has even received a majority of the popular vote.[111] More fundamentally, the agency-as-client framework may unduly restrict the lawyer's obligation as a government employee to ensure that government policy is appropriately carried out. Where, for example, higher level officials are directing a lawyer to act in ways that defy applicable law, regulations, or well-established legal principles, some effort to challenge that decision is consistent with democratic values.

To that end, a second approach identifies the client of the government lawyer as the government as a whole. The Model Rules take that view. The Comment to Rule 1.13 notes:

> Defining precisely the identity of the client and prescribing the resulting obligations of such lawyers may be more difficult in the government context and is a matter beyond the scope of these Rules. . . . Although in some circumstances the client may be a specific agency, it may also be a branch of government, such as the executive branch, or

---

110.   *See, e.g.,* Lanctot, *supra* note 103; Jonathan R. Macey & Geoffrey P. Miller, "Reflections on Professional Responsibility in a Regulatory State," 63 *Geo. Wash. L. Rev.* 1105, 1116 (1995); Paulsen, *supra* note 94, at, 83, 85–86.

111.   Note, "Rethinking the Professional Responsibilities of Federal Agency Lawyers," 115 *Harv. L. Rev.* 1170, 1175 (2002). *See also* Berenson, *supra* note 109, at 823.

the government as a whole. For example, if the action or failure to act involves the head of a bureau, either the department of which the bureau is a part or the relevant branch of government may be the client for purposes of this Rule. Moreover, in a matter involving the conduct of government officials, a government lawyer may have authority under applicable law to question such conduct more extensively than that of a lawyer for a private organization in similar circumstances. . . .

This approach, however, raises as many questions as it answers. Indeed, the Rule itself recognizes as much, by placing beyond its scope the question of what concrete actions lawyers should take in the face of wrongful conduct.

Other efforts to define the government lawyer's obligations in particular contexts have been equally vague. For example, EC 7–14 of the Code states:

A government lawyer in a civil action or administrative proceeding has the responsibility to seek justice and to develop a full and fair record, and he should not use his position or the economic power of the government to harass parties or to bring about unjust settlements or results.

Yet what constitutes an "unjust" settlement is often open to dispute. Agency lawyers have taken different views on such questions as whether the government should disclose adverse material facts, assert a statute of limitations, or fail to inform opposing counsel of impending procedural defects in order to defeat an otherwise meritorious claim.[112]

In addressing the government lawyers's responsibility to seek justice, Federal District Judge Jack Weinstein gives an example from his experience as counsel for a New York county. The case involved a condemnation proceeding in which government negotiators had worked out a property valuation settlement with an elderly couple who were unrepresented by counsel. The offer was about a third of what county appraisers had estimated the property to be worth, and the couple was unaware of its value. Weinstein believed that it was inappropriate for a public servant to exploit the landowner's ignorance, even though it would save taxpayers money.[113] On similar reasoning, a state bar ethics committee concluded that it was appropriate for a municipal lawyer to inform an unrepresented civil opponent that he faced risks of self incrimination and might profit from advice of counsel.[114]

To the extent that such cases suggest generalizable principles, they imply an obligation on the part of attorneys to preserve governmental

112. Bruce A. Green, "Must Government Lawyers 'Seek Justice' in Civil Litigation?," 9 *Widener J. Public Law* 235 (2000).

113. Jack B. Weinstein, "Some Ethical and Political Problems of a Government Attorney," 18 *Me. L. Rev.* 156, 169 (1966).

114. N.Y. State Bar Association, Committee on Professional Ethics, Op. 728 (2000).

legitimacy by promoting compliance with applicable laws and ensuring fairness in substantive and procedural decisions. When a proposed governmental action appears inconsistent with these principles, attorneys have, at minimum, a responsibility to seek internal review and reconsideration. If such internal efforts are unsuccessful, a further strategy involves disclosure of information to others, such as the legislature, the courts, or the public.[115] These bodies may or may not secure reversal of the decision in the case at issue, but they may be able to alter future policy.

A related question concerns the role of government lawyers called on to render advice or provide legal opinions to officials, who may have very definite ideas of what advice they wish to receive. For material on the government lawyer's counseling role, see Chapter IX, *supra*.

G. CONFLICTS OF INTEREST IN CLASS ACTIONS

Some of the most complex and challenging conflict-of-interest problems arise in the context of class action lawsuits. The interests of class members seldom coincide exactly, and the ideological and financial interests of lawyers and clients may diverge dramatically. In many contexts, parties may not even be aware of what counsel are doing in their names—or even that they are part of a class action.

During the 1960s and 1970s, national attention focused on civil rights class actions that sought to restructure major public institutions such as school systems and prisons. These "structural reform" class actions were widely perceived by both critics and supporters as invitations to judicial activism on behalf of progressive causes. By the late twentieth century, however, such litigation was in steep decline. Between 1977 and 1999 the number of federal class actions shrunk from 2.4% of the docket to 0.8%, and the number of civil rights class actions dropped from 1.4% of the docket to .08%. In 2006, the number of civil rights class actions in surveyed districts totaled 185 out of a total federal docket including a quarter of a million civil cases.[116] The reasons for this decline include tighter (and thus more expensive) notice requirements, doctrinal and statutory restrictions on recovery of attorneys' fees, tightened requirements of standing, bans on class actions by federally funded legal aid lawyers, a less receptive judiciary, and the reduction in clear civil rights abuses that can be addressed through

---

115. A celebrated case involved acting Solicitor General Lawrence Wallace's Supreme Court brief involving the IRS's denial of tax exemptions for racially segregated Bob Jones University. Wallace, who served for twenty five years with distinction in the Solicitor General's office, filed a brief arguing the position of the administration but inserted a footnote indicating that his own different view on the merits had been set forth in an earlier brief supporting the petition for certiorari. See Philip B. Heyman & Lance Liebman, *The Social Responsibilities of Lawyers* 136–82 (1986); Marcia E. Mulkey, "A Crisis of Conscience and the Government Lawyer," 14 *Temple Pol. & Civ. Rights L. Rev.* 649, 653–58 (2005).

116. Thomas E. Willging & Emery G. Lee, Third Interim Report to the Judicial Conference Advisory Committee on Civil Rules, *The Impact of the Class Action Fairness Act of 2005 on the Federal Courts* (Federal Judicial Center, 2007).

litigation. As a consequence, structural reform class actions have become an endangered species, the giant pandas of the legal world—fascinating, charismatic, and rare.

This does not mean, however, that class actions have lost their importance. The reform cases that continue to be brought generally have substantial social importance and serve as a deterrent to future abuses. Moreover, class actions in other contexts, primarily involving consumer and personal injury claims, have grown in scope and significance, sometimes involving billions of dollars. In these class actions, the attorneys are often ambitious, wealthy entrepreneurs rather than underfinanced public interest lawyers, the defendants are corporations rather than governmental units, and the remedy sought is damages rather than injunctions. Yet despite these contrasts, many consumer and personal injury class actions raise the same kind of conflicts as their public interest predecessors.

The materials that follow are grouped accordingly. Problem 7, the excerpt from "Class Conflicts" and *Fiandaca v. Cunningham* all involve structural reform litigation. Problem 8 and the accompanying notes study mass tort and consumer class actions. The basic framework for both, however, is Rule 23 of the Federal Rules of Civil Procedure.

Federal Rules of Civil Procedure, Rule 23
CLASS ACTIONS

(a) Prerequisites to a Class Action. One or more members of a class may sue or be sued as representative parties on behalf of all only if (1) the class is so numerous that joinder of all members is impracticable, (2) there are questions of law or fact common to the class, (3) the claims or defenses of the representative parties are typical of the claims or defenses of the class, and (4) the representative parties will fairly and adequately protect the interests of the class.

(b) Class Actions Maintainable. An action may be maintained as a class action if the prerequisites of subdivision (a) are satisfied, and in addition:

(1) the prosecution of separate actions by or against individual members of the class would create a risk of

(A) inconsistent or varying adjudications with respect to individual members of the class which would establish incompatible standards of conduct for the party opposing the class, or

(B) adjudications with respect to individual members of the class which would as a practical matter be dispositive of the interests of the other members not parties to the adjudications or substantially impair or impede their ability to protect their interests; or

(2) the party opposing the class has acted or refused to act on grounds generally applicable to the class, thereby making appropriate final injunctive relief or corresponding declaratory relief with respect to the class as a whole; or

(3) the court finds that the questions of law or fact common to the members of the class predominate over any questions affecting only indi-

vidual members, and that a class action is superior to other available methods for the fair and efficient adjudication of the controversy. The matters pertinent to the findings include: (A) the interest of members of the class in individually controlling the prosecution or defense of separate actions; (B) the extent and nature of any litigation concerning the controversy already commenced by or against members of the class; (C) the desirability or undesirability of concentrating the litigation of the claims in the particular forum; (D) the difficulties likely to be encountered in the management of a class action. . . .

(c)(3). (3) The judgment in an action maintained as a class action under subdivision (b)(1) or (b)(2), whether or not favorable to the class, shall include and describe those whom the court finds to be members of the class. The judgment in an action maintained as a class action under subdivision (b)(3), whether or not favorable to the class, shall include and specify or describe those to whom the notice provided in subdivision (c)(2) was directed, and who have not requested exclusion, and whom the court finds to be members of the class. . . .

(e) Settlement, Voluntary Dismissal, or Compromise.

(1) (A) The court must approve any settlement, voluntary dismissal, or compromise of the claims, issues, or defenses of a certified class.

(B) The court must direct notice in a reasonable manner to all class members who would be bound by a proposed settlement, voluntary dismissal, or compromise.

(C) The court may approve a settlement, voluntary dismissal, or compromise that would bind class members only after a hearing and on finding that the settlement, voluntary dismissal, or compromise is fair, reasonable, and adequate.

(2) The parties seeking approval of a settlement, voluntary dismissal, or compromise under Rule 23(e)(1) must file a statement identifying any agreement made in connection with the proposed settlement, voluntary dismissal, or compromise.

(3) In an action previously certified as a class action under Rule 23(b)(3), the court may refuse to approve a settlement unless it affords a new opportunity to request exclusion to individual class members who had an earlier opportunity to request exclusion but did not do so.

(4) (A) Any class member may object to a proposed settlement, voluntary dismissal, or compromise that requires court approval under Rule 23(e)(1)(A).

(B) An objection made under Rule 23(e)(4)(A) may be withdrawn only with the court's approval.

1.   PUBLIC INTEREST CLASS ACTIONS

PROBLEM 7

You are an attorney working for the Disability Rights Defense Fund (DRDF), a public interest organization. You have filed a class action in state court against officials who operate Pennhurst, a state institution for the mentally retarded. The class as certified consists of present and future residents of Pennhurst, speaking through their guardians or next friends. For years, Pennhurst has been overcrowded and underfunded, and as a result it provides almost no opportunities for its 1,200 residents to receive the occupational and special education programs that might enable them to move to assisted living in the community. Instead, residents are frequently given high levels of medication and inadequate staff attention, and an independent study has found that their intellectual, physical, and emotional skills are deteriorating. Your complaint alleges that Pennhurst's treatment of its residents violates state statutes and the state constitution, which, you are arguing, require minimally adequate treatment in the least restrictive environment consistent with the individual's needs. As a result, you are seeking an injunction to close Pennhurst and to place the residents in community facilities.[117]

During the course of litigation, however, it becomes clear that many of the families of Pennhurst residents oppose deinstitutionalization. These families question the adequacy of community facilities and do not believe that they can provide appropriate care in their homes. Their preference is for Pennhurst to stay open, with improved funding and programs. State officials have promised to upgrade Pennhurst, but they have made and broken such promises in the past, and you are skeptical that the legislature will ever appropriate sufficient funds for the upgrade. Moreover, studies of deinstitutionalization in other states have shown that placements of mentally disabled persons in community facilities often have excellent results, and that families who were initially skeptical have generally been pleased with the placements. DRDF's consistent position has been that community care offers a superior alternative to institutionalization.

The present lawsuit is being closely watched by officials and activists in other states. A shift in strategy away from community placements would look like surrender in the face of recalcitrant government officials. Accordingly, you believe it would be a great disservice to Pennhurst residents and to disabled persons generally if the litigation focused on upgrading large state institutions rather than moving their patients into alternative treatment centers.

What are your obligations to the class and to the court?

References:

Model Rules: 1.2, 1.7; Federal Rules of Civil Procedure, Rule 23.

QUESTIONS

1. Under the Federal Rules of Civil Procedure, *supra,* and bar ethical provisions governing conflict of interest, can the lawyer adequately represent this class? What is the "interest" of class members and who should

---

117. This problem is based loosely on the facts of a landmark structural reform case, Pennhurst State School & Hospital v. Halderman, 465 U.S. 89, 92–93 (1984).

decide? By what means? What if the short-term desires of parents and guardians are unlikely to promote the best long-term results for institutionalized residents?

2. Would it make any difference if the named plaintiffs had signed a retainer agreement specifying deinstitutionalization and community placement as the objectives of the suit, or authorizing representation "consistent with the goals of the Disability Rights Defense Fund?" What role should "informed consent" play in the context of large classes, whose memberships will shift over time? If named plaintiffs lack adequate information or incentives to monitor counsel, or to address other class members' competing preferences, how should the legal system respond?

Could the lawyer solve the problem of conflicting interests by bringing suit on behalf of a single individual or an organization of some affected parties rather than a class? Would that procedural strategy create its own problems by seeking class relief without class responsibilities? When should conflicts between clients or between lawyers and clients give rise to separate representation? How should it be financed?

3. Difficulties similar to those in the Pennhurst problem have emerged in many other contexts. Some widely publicized examples involved large school desegregation lawsuits filed by the NAACP Legal Defense Fund in Boston and other major cities. As certified, the classes included all black children who were then or would be attending public schools. Conflicts arose between the parents who favored integration through busing and those who preferred improvements in their de-facto segregated neighborhood schools. Derrick Bell, then a prominent litigator for the NAACP, published a landmark law review article criticizing NAACP lawyers for "serving two masters," and placing their own integration ideals over the desires of class members. "Idealism," he maintained, "though perhaps rarer than greed, is harder to control."[118] Similar remedial controversies continued to emerge over the next several decades in both desegregation and school finance cases.

Are there significant differences between representation of a relatively small and discrete class, as in Pennhurst, and a very large class with a membership constantly changing over the long duration of a lawsuit? Do such differences matter in defining the ethical responsibilities of their lawyers?

Deborah L. Rhode, "Class Conflicts in Class Actions"

34 Stanford Law Review 1183, 1183–91, 1204–07, 1209–12, 1258, 1261–62 (1982).

A fundamental premise of American adjudicative structures is that clients, not their counsel, define litigation objectives. Thus, the American Bar Association's . . . ethical codes both emphasize that an attorney must defer to the client's wishes on matters affecting the merits of legal action.

---

118. Derrick Bell, "Serving Two Masters: Integration Ideals and Client Interests in School Desegregation Litigation," 85 *Yale L. J.* 470 (1976).

However, by presupposing an individual client with clearly identifiable views, these codes elide a frequent and fundamental difficulty in class action proceedings. In many such cases, the lawyer represents an aggregation of litigants with unstable, inchoate, or conflicting preferences. The more diffuse and divided the class, the greater the problems in defining its objectives . . . . .

[To cope with these problems,] we need a more coherent theory of class interests and of the role plaintiff preferences should play in defining class objectives. As a first cut at reconceptualization, this article posits a theory of representation mandating full disclosure of, although not necessarily deference to, class sentiment. A central premise is that the class as an entity has interests that may not be coextensive with the preferences of its current membership. Often those able to register views will be insufficiently disinterested or informed to speak for the entire constituency of present and future class members who will be affected by the court's decree. Nonetheless, preferences matter, not because they are conclusive of class interests, but because their disclosure is critical to the efficacy and legitimacy of judicial intervention. . . .

I. Intra–Class Conflicts and Disclosure Obligations

. . . The importance, complexity, and protracted character of structural reform lawsuits create opportunities for conflict at every stage of litigation. Class members who prefer the certainty of the status quo to the risks of judicial rearrangement may oppose litigation from the outset. For example, some parents who anticipate busing or closure of institutional facilities as a consequence of legal intervention will prefer to never initiate proceedings. So too, minority employees have feared retaliation by coworkers and management, or loss of job-related advantages in the aftermath of Title VII actions. . . .

Far more common, however, are schisms that surface during settlement or remedial deliberations. Often when a suit is filed, plaintiffs will not have focused on issues of relief. The impetus for the action will be a general sense that rights have been infringed or needs ignored, rather than a shared conviction about the appropriate remedy. Thus, there may be consensus only on relatively abstract questions—that ghetto schools are bad, institutional conditions unbearable, or special education programs inadequate. During the liability phase of litigation, class members may not be sufficiently informed or interested to participate in decisionmaking. However, once it becomes clear that some relief will be forthcoming, factions emerge. Also, where proceedings are protracted, changes in legal doctrine, contested practices, or plaintiff preferences can create new sources of dissension.

School desegregation cases provide the most well-documented instances of conflict. Both commentators and litigators have described in some detail the balkanization within minority communities over fundamental questions of educational policy. Dispute has centered on the relative importance of integration, financial resources, minority control, and ethnic identification in enriching school environments. Constituencies that support integration in principle have disputed its value in particular settings where extended bus rides, racial tension, or white flight seem likely concomitants of judicial redistricting. . . .

Comparable cleavages arise in various other institutional reform contexts. Parents challenging the adequacy of existing bilingual or special education programs have differed over whether mainstreaming or upgrading separate classes represents the better solution. Suits involving rights of the disabled have divided their families over whether to demand institutional improvement or creation of community care alternatives. . . . In employment cases, controversy has centered on tradeoffs between back-pay awards and prospective relief, the formula used to compute damages, and the means chosen to restructure hiring, promotion, and transfer systems.

Moreover, as with any form of collective litigation, parties often differ in their amenability to compromise and their assessment of particular proposals. Given the uncertainty of outcome and indeterminacy of relief in many institutional reform class actions, risk-averse plaintiffs will often be prepared to make substantial concessions. Other class members will prefer to fight, if not to the death, at least until the Supreme Court denies certiorari. Particularly where the proffered settlement provides generously for a few named plaintiffs, or where some individuals have special reasons for wanting expeditious relief, dissension may arise within the ranks. And, as the following discussion will suggest, all of these problems are compounded by class counsels' own interests and by a doctrinal framework that fails to raise, let alone resolve, the most difficult issues. . . .

II.   The Participants' Roles in Disclosing
Conflict: Rules and Realities . . .

B. Class Counsel

A familiar refrain among courts and commentators is that lawyers assume special responsibilities in class litigation. According to one circuit court of appeals, the duty to ensure adequate representation rests "primarily upon counsel for the class . . . in addition to the normal obligations of an officer of the court, and . . . counsel to parties of the litigation, class action counsel possess, in a very real sense, fiduciary obligations to those not before the court." Principal among those duties is the responsibility to apprise the trial judge of conflicting interests that may warrant separate representation or other corrective measures.

Although unobjectionable in concept, that role definition has frequently proved unworkable in practice. To be sure, many attorneys make considerable efforts to appreciate and accommodate the broadest possible spectrum of class sentiment. . . . [But] where the range and intensity of divergent preferences within the class are unlikely to surface without counsel's assistance, he often has strong prudential and ideological reasons not to provide it. . . .

1.   Prudential Interests.

An attorney active in institutional reform class actions is subject to a variety of financial, tactical, and professional pressures that constrain his response to class conflicts. Of course, none of these constraints is unique to this form of litigation. And the intensity of such pressures varies considerably.... [F]lushing out dissension among class members can prove costly in several respects.

For example, opposing parties often seek to capitalize on class dissension by filing motions for decertification. If such efforts prove successful, class counsel may lose a substantial investment that he cannot, as a practical matter, recoup from former class members. At a minimum, such motions result in expense, delay, and loss of bargaining leverage, and deflect resources from trial preparation. Certification disputes may also trigger involvement of additional lawyers, who would share the limelight, the control over litigation decisions and, under some circumstances, the resources available for attorneys' fees.

Exposing conflict can also impede settlement arrangements that are attractive to class counsel on a number of grounds. As in many other litigation contexts, attorneys often have a bias to settle not shared by their clients. Since institutional reform plaintiffs generally do not underwrite the costs of litigation, their primary interest is in the result attained; the time and effort necessary to attain it are of less concern. Yet from the attorney's perspective, a modest settlement may generate a result "bearing a higher ratio to the cost of the work than a much larger recovery obtained only after extensive discovery, a long trial and an appeal." For example, if the prospects for prevailing on the merits are uncertain, some plaintiffs will see little to lose and everything to gain from persistence. That viewpoint may be inadequately aired by class counsel, who has concerns for his reputation as well as competing claims on his time and his organization's resources to consider.

The potential for attorney-client conflicts is compounded when a proposed settlement makes extremely generous, or totally inadequate, provision for class counsel. Of course a lawyer may attempt to avoid compromising influences by refusing to discuss fees until agreement on all other issues is final. However, that strategy is not necessarily in anyone's interest if it inhibits favorable settlement offers, and many defendants are reluctant to compromise without some understanding of their total liability. Moreover, in an escalating number of civil rights cases, defendants have sought to make settlement on the merits conditional on counsel's waiver or curtailment of claims to statutory compensation....

A final set of problems emerges in test-case litigation. In some instances, counsel may be reluctant to espouse positions that are at odds with those he has taken or intends to take in other proceedings or that could establish an unwelcome precedent. Moreover, test-case litigation often generates settlement biases directly converse to those discussed above. Once a lawyer has prepared a claim with potentially significant impact, he may be disinclined to settle. He almost certainly would not share some plaintiffs' enthusiasm for pre-or post-trial agreements promising generous terms for the litigants but little recognition and no precedential value for similarly situated victims. Few professionals, class attorneys included, can make decisions wholly independent of concerns about their careers and reputations among peers, potential clients, and funding sources. Litigating well-publicized institutional reform cases can provide desirable trial experience, generate attractive new cases, legitimate organizational objectives in the eyes of private donors, and enhance attorneys' personal standing in the legal community. Where such rewards are likely, counsel may tend to discount preferences for a low-visibility settlement, particularly if it falls short of achieving ideological objectives to which he is strongly committed. . . .

2.   Ideological Interests.

. . . Relying on case histories from Boston, Atlanta, and Detroit, Derrick Bell submits that NAACP attorneys' "single-minded commitment" to maximum integration has led them to ignore a shift in priorities among many black parents from racial balance to quality education.

Similar indictments have been leveled against attorneys in other civil rights contexts. For example, . . . a number of parents and guardians brought suit in behalf of all present and future residents of Pennsylvania's Pennhurst facility for the retarded. Class counsel took the position that his obligations ran solely to the residents, and that their interests dictated Pennhurst's closure and replacement with community facilities. Accordingly, counsel made little effort to expose or espouse the views of parents and guardians preferring institutionalization. Indeed, according to one of the lawyers subsequently involved, class counsel sought to avoid "stir[ring] people up" by deemphasizing the possibility of Pennhurst's closure in his out-of-court statements. After the district judge ordered removal of Pennhurst residents to community facilities, a systematic survey of their parents and guardians revealed that only 19% of respondents favored deinstitutionalization. Accounts of other civil rights litigation suggest that Pennhurst is not an isolated example.

It does not follow, of course, that attorneys in these and comparable cases failed to represent class interests. Much depends on who one views as appropriate spokesmen for the class and how broadly one defines "interest." . . . [P]arents are often poorly situated to speak for all children who will be affected by judicial decree. But neither is an attorney with strong prudential or ideological preferences well positioned to decide which class members or guardians deserve a hearing and which do not. And one critical problem with existing class action procedures is that they fail to assure adequate disclosure of counsel's own interests or of countervailing client concerns. . . .

[Discussion is omitted concerning limitations in the two most common procedural approaches to class conflicts. The current pluralist approach—which is to rely on separate counsel for separate interests—may, in some instances, exacerbate problems of delay, expense, manageability, and accountability. In other contexts, that strategy can bias results toward those with the organizational and financial resources to make themselves heard. The majoritarian alternative is to provide for direct class participation through polls and public hearings. Yet that approach cannot adequately respond to circumstances where those registering preferences are uninformed, unrepresentative, or unresponsive to the needs of most current or future class members. For example, the complexity of remedial tradeoffs may be difficult to convey to large constituencies. And parents whose children will bear the short term costs of certain desegregation and deinstitutionalization remedies may be poorly situated to evaluate their long-range benefits.

However, granting these difficulties, the article considers various ways to increase responsiveness to class conflicts. Among other things, courts could be required to make a record concerning their efforts to address conflicts. To assist judicial determinations, counsel could submit statements detailing contacts with class members, and attorneys' fee awards might be structured to create greater incentives for lawyer-client communication.]

C.   The Bounded Potential of Procedural Solutions . . .

The ultimate effect of procedural reforms is difficult to predict. . . . [Yet] clearer mandates to class counsel than those provided by existing procedural and ethical rules could serve important socialization functions. . . . Requiring attorneys to record contacts with the class and perceptions of conflict would, if nothing else, narrow their capacity for self-delusion about whose views they were or were not representing. Explicit professional obligations, even those unlikely to trigger any formal sanction, often affect behavioral norms simply by sensitizing individuals to the full implications of their conduct. . . .

To be sure, none of the proposals outlined here can guarantee better results in [institutional reform cases]. But that conclusion, if disconcerting, is not necessarily damning. Given the values at issue in institutional reform cases, conflicts are an ineradicable feature of the legal landscape. Virtually all of the pluralist and majoritarian deficiencies that impede judicial management of such conflicts would arise with equal force if the underlying issues were addressed in legislative or bureaucratic settings. Indeed, one of the strongest justifications for those governance structures is equally available to class actions: While we cannot depend on disinterested and informed judgment by any single group of decisionmakers, we can at least create sufficient procedural checks and balances to prevent the worst abuses.

NOTES

Class action attorneys often take the position that the responsibility for airing conflicts of interest lies elsewhere: with named class representatives, with dissatisfied class members, with opposing parties, or with trial courts. In some contexts, however, none of these participants has the necessary information or incentives to monitor the adequacy of representation. Named representatives or dissenting members may be uninformed, unaccountable, or unrepresentative of the class as a whole; they may also be unwilling to assume the costs of complaining about counsel's performance. Opposing parties may not always be able to discover the extent of conflict within a class. Nor will they always be interested in drawing the problem to a court's attention if the likely result is to multiply counsel. That is particularly true where opponents could be liable for prevailing parties' attorneys' fees under state or federal statutes.

Although procedural rules and due process standards require judges to ensure adequate class representation, practical constraints often discourage active oversight. In many cases, finding class representatives or their counsel inadequate will not terminate proceedings; it will prolong them. From a trial court's perspective, "more is seldom merrier.... Multiple representation generally multiplies problems.... More parties means more papers, more scheduling difficulties, and more potential for objection to any given ruling or settlement proposal...."[119]

QUESTIONS

1.   How should courts and counsel respond to these incentive structures? Would you support measures such as requiring a record concerning conflicts and the measures taken to address them, expanding resources for separate counsel, and making greater use of notice and survey procedures to determine class views?[120]

2.   Would any of these measures help on the facts of Problem 7? Suppose there are substantial differences in remedial preferences within both the institutionalization and community treatment camps? Must all the factions be heard? Who should decide? And who should pay? In complex class actions where lawyers represent coalitions with distinct interests, the result has sometimes been a trial with 25 to 30 attorneys. Every time one of them sneezes, "the gesundheits [will take] ten pages of transcript."[121] Critics of this approach question how much it helps to have "lawyers representing ten different interest groups objecting to ten different aspects of a proposed decree if the court has no sense of how substantial a constituency each represents."[122]

3.   Would a preferable alternative be to survey class membership? If so, how should information be gathered? Neither town meetings nor written questionnaires will necessarily ensure a cross-section of views, and efforts are rarely undertaken to assess the representativeness of responses. Deferring to majority preferences may provide inadequate protection for minori-

119.   *See* Deborah L. Rhode: "Class Conflicts in Class Actions," 34 *Stan.L.Rev.* 1183, 1219 (1982).

120.   *Id.* For an argument favoring this approach in gay rights litigation, *see* William B. Rubenstein, "United We Stand, Divided We Litigate: Addressing Disputes Among Group Members and Lawyers in Civil Rights Campaigns," 106 *Yale L. J.* 1623 (1997).

121.   Rhode, *supra* note 119, at 1228.

122.   *Id.* at 1224.

ties and may be impractical where choices are too numerous and complicated for simple explanation.[123]

4.   Consider recommendations by Jonathan Macey and Geoffrey Miller, including experimentation with guardians *ad litem* who represent absent class members at the settlement phase of litigation, and auctions among attorneys for rights to represent a class. Under such a system, no figurehead plaintiff would be necessary; the action would proceed on behalf of John or Jane Doe, and attorneys would compete among themselves in terms of fees, competence, and resources for financing litigation.[124] Would you support such a proposal?

5.   Given the difficulties detailed in the "Class Conflicts" excerpt, can lawyers representing plaintiffs with different interests or preferences comply with Model Rule 1.7? The Second Circuit Court of Appeals has noted that "traditional principles governing disqualification of attorneys on grounds of conflict of interest would seemingly dictate that whenever a rift arises in the class, ... the attorney who has represented the class should withdraw entirely and take no position."[125] However, in declining to disqualify plaintiffs' attorneys under such circumstances, the court noted:

> [o]ur system of justice demands that the interests of all concerned be accommodated as fairly as possible, and this accommodation includes the preservation of the class action form of litigation without a wasteful multiplication of costs.... Thus, we conclude that the traditional rules ... should not be mechanically applied to the problems that arise in the settlement of class action litigation.[126]

Does this mean that lawyers in class actions are not subject to the general conflicts rules? If so, under what circumstances should a class's lawyers be subject to disqualification for conflict of interest? Are these the same circumstances that should lead to decertification of the class under Rule 23?

The following case concerns a different sort of class conflict—a conflict between classes rather than within a class.

Fiandaca v. Cunningham

First Circuit Court of Appeals, 1987.
827 F.2d 825.

■ COFFIN, CIRCUIT JUDGE:

This opinion discusses two consolidated appeals related to a class action brought by twenty-three female prison inmates sentenced to the custody of the warden of the New Hampshire State Prison. The suit

---

123. Nancy Morawetz, "Bargaining, Class Representation, and Fairness", 54 *Ohio St.L.J.* 1, 37–38 (1993). *See also* Geoffrey P. Miller, "Conflicts of Interest in Class Action Litigation: An Inquiry into the Appropriate Standard," 2003. *U. Chi. L. Forum* 581.

124. Macey & Miller, *supra* note 30.

125. *In re* "Agent Orange" Product Liability Litigation, 800 F.2d 14, 18 (2d Cir. 1986).

126. *Id.* at 19.

challenges the state of New Hampshire's failure to establish a facility for the incarceration of female inmates with programs and services equivalent to those provided to male inmates at the state prison. After a bench trial on the merits, the district court held that the state had violated plaintiffs' right to equal protection of the laws and ordered the construction of a permanent in-state facility for plaintiffs no later than July 1, 1989. It also required the state to provide a temporary facility for plaintiffs on or before November 1, 1987, but prohibited the state from establishing this facility on the grounds of the Laconia State School and Training Center ("Laconia State School" or "LSS"), New Hampshire's lone institution for the care and treatment of mentally retarded citizens.

One set of appellants consists of Michael Cunningham, warden of the New Hampshire State Prison, and various executive branch officials responsible for the operation of the New Hampshire Department of Corrections ("state"). They challenge the district court's refusal to disqualify plaintiffs' class counsel, New Hampshire Legal Assistance ("NHLA"), due to an unresolvable conflict of interest. See N.H. Rules of Professional Conduct, Rule 1.7(b). . . .

The other group of appellants is comprised of the plaintiffs in a separate class action challenging the conditions and practices at the Laconia State School, *Garrity v. Sununu*, including the New Hampshire Association for Retarded Citizens ("NHARC") and the mentally retarded citizens who currently reside at LSS (the *"Garrity* class"). This group sought unsuccessfully to intervene in the relief phase of the instant litigation after the conclusion of the trial, but prior to the issuance of the court's final memorandum order. On appeal, these prospective intervenors argue that the district court abused its discretion in denying their motion.

We begin by presenting the relevant facts and then turn to our analysis of the legal issues raised by each of these appeals.

I. Factual Setting.

This case began in June, 1983, when plaintiffs' appellate counsel, Bertram Astles, filed a complaint on behalf of several female inmates sentenced to the custody of the state prison warden and incarcerated at the Rockingham County House of Corrections. NHLA subsequently became co-counsel for plaintiffs and filed an amended complaint expanding the plaintiff class to include all female inmates who are or will be incarcerated in the custody of the warden. In the years that followed, NHLA assumed the role of lead counsel for the class, engaging in extensive discovery and performing all other legal tasks through the completion of the trial before the district court. Among other things, NHLA attorneys and their trial expert, Dr. Edyth Flynn, twice toured and examined potential facilities at which to house plaintiffs, including buildings at the Laconia State School, the New Hampshire Hospital in Concord, and the Youth Development Center in Manchester. Pursuant to Fed. R. Civ. P. 68, the state offered to settle the litigation on August 1, 1986, in exchange for the establishment of a facility for female inmates at the current Hillsborough County House of Corrections in Goffstown. The state had already negotiated an agreement with Hillsborough County to lease this facility and expected to have it ready for use by the end of 1989. Plaintiffs rejected this offer, however, primarily because the relief would not be available for over three years and because the plan was contingent on Hillsborough County's ability to complete construction of a new facility for the relocation of its prisoners. Plaintiffs desired an in-state facility within six to nine months at the latest and apparently would not settle for less.

The state extended a second offer of judgment to plaintiffs on October 21, 1986. This offer proposed to establish an in-state facility for the incarceration of female inmates at an existing state building by June 1, 1987. Although the formal offer of judgment did not specify a particular location for this facility, the state informed NHLA that it planned to use the Speare Cottage at the Laconia State School. NHLA, which also represented the plaintiff class in the ongoing *Garrity* litigation, rejected the offer on November 10, stating in part that "plaintiffs do not want to agree to an offer which is against the stated interests of the plaintiffs in the *Garrity* class." The state countered by moving immediately for the disqualification of NHLA as class counsel in the case at bar due to the unresolvable conflict of interest inherent in NHLA's representation of two classes with directly adverse interests. The court, despite recognizing that a conflict of interest probably existed, denied the state's motion on November 20 because NHLA's disqualification would further delay the trial of an important matter that had been pending for over three years. It began to try the case four days later.

The *Garrity* class filed its motion to intervene on December 11, ten days after the conclusion of the trial on the merits. The group alleged that it had only recently learned of the state's proposal to develop a correctional facility for women at the Laconia State School. The members of the class were concerned that the establishment of this facility at the school's Speare Cottage, which they understood to be the primary building under consideration, would displace 28 residents of the school and violate the remedial orders issued by Chief Judge Devine in *Garrity*. The district court denied the motion to intervene on December 23, assuring the applicant-intervenors that it would "never approve a settlement which in any way disenfranchises patients of LSS or contravenes the letter or intent of [Chief Judge] Devine's order in *Garrity*."

Meanwhile, the court agreed to hold up its decision on the merits pending the conclusion of ongoing settlement negotiations, permitting the principal parties to spend the month of December, 1986, engaged in further efforts to settle the case. Within approximately one week after the conclusion of the trial, the parties reached an understanding with regard to a settlement agreement which called for the establishment of a "fully operational facility at the present site of the Laconia State School for the incarceration of female inmates by November 1, 1987." The agreement also provided that all affected residents of LSS would receive appropriate placements at least two months prior to the opening of the correctional facility. After negotiating this agreement, NHLA moved to withdraw as class co-counsel on December 11 and attorney Astles signed the settlement agreement on plaintiffs' behalf. The state, however, refused to sign the agreement.

This collapse of the post-trial settlement efforts prompted Judge Loughlin, the district judge in the instant case, and Chief Judge Devine, the *Garrity* trial judge, to convene a joint settlement conference on December 22, 1986. At this conference, plaintiffs formally withdrew their consent to the original settlement agreement in light of the state's refusal to abide by the agreement. . . .

The district court finally announced its decision on the merits on January 13, 1987. Finding that the conditions of confinement, programs, and services available to New Hampshire female prisoners are not on par with the conditions, programs, and services afforded male inmates at the New Hampshire State Prison, the court held that such gender-based, inferior treatment violates the Equal Protection clause of the Fourteenth Amendment. As a primary remedy, it ordered the state to establish "a permanent facility comparable to all of the facilities encompassed at the New Hampshire State Prison . . . to be inhabited no later than July 1, 1989." In crafting a temporary remedy, it reiterated that "there shall not be a scintilla of infringement upon the rights and privileges of the *Garrity* class," and proceeded to rule that the state had to provide plaintiffs with "a building comparable to the Speare Building," but that such facility "shall not be located at the Laconia State School or its environs." This appeal resulted. . . .

The state's first argument is that the district court erred in permitting NHLA to represent the plaintiff class at trial after its conflict of interest had become apparent. . . . We must determine, therefore, whether the court's denial of the state's disqualification motion amounts to an abuse of discretion in this instance.

The state's theory is that NHLA faced an unresolvable conflict because the interests of two of its clients were directly adverse after the state extended its second offer of judgment on October 21, 1986. . . . In this case, it is the state's contention that the court should have disqualified NHLA as class counsel pursuant to Rule 1.7 because, at least with respect to the state's second offer of judgment, NHLA's representation of the plaintiff class in this litigation was materially limited by its responsibilities to the *Garrity* class.

We find considerable merit in this argument. The state's offer to establish a facility for the incarceration of female inmates at the Laconia State School, and to use its "best efforts" to make such a facility available for occupancy by June 1, 1987, presented plaintiffs with a legitimate opportunity to settle a protracted legal dispute on highly favorable terms. As class counsel, NHLA owed plaintiffs a duty of undivided loyalty: it was obligated to present the offer to plaintiffs, to explain its costs and benefits, and to ensure that the offer received full and fair consideration by the members of the class. Beyond all else, NHLA had an ethical duty to prevent its loyalties to other clients from coloring its representation of the plaintiffs in this action and from infringing upon the exercise of its professional judgment and responsibilities.

NHLA, however, also represents the residents of the Laconia State School who are members of the plaintiff class in *Garrity*. Quite understandably, this group vehemently opposes the idea of establishing a correctional facility for female inmates anywhere on the grounds of LSS. As counsel for the *Garrity* class, NHLA had an ethical duty to advance the interests of the class to the fullest possible extent and to oppose any settlement of the instant case that would compromise those interests. In short, the combination of clients and circumstances placed NHLA in the untenable position of being simultaneously obligated to represent vigorously the interests of two conflicting clients. It is inconceivable that NHLA, or any other counsel, could have properly performed the role of "advocate" for both plaintiffs and the *Garrity* class, regardless of its good faith or high intentions. Indeed, this is precisely the sort of situation that Rule 1.7 is designed to prevent.

Plaintiffs argue on appeal that there really was no conflict of interest for NHLA because the state's second offer of judgment was unlikely to lead to a completed settlement for reasons other than NHLA's loyalties to the *Garrity* class. We acknowledge that the record contains strong indications that settlement would not have occurred even if plaintiffs had been represented by another counsel. For instance, in ruling on the intervention motion, the district court stated that, pursuant to its duties under Fed. R. Civ. P. 23(e), it would not approve a settlement that infringed in any way on the rights of the LSS residents. Furthermore, as plaintiffs contend, the second offer of judgment was unattractive because it was phrased in "best efforts" language and did not set a firm date for establishment of the facility. The question, however, is not whether the state's second offer of judgment would have resulted in a settlement had plaintiffs' counsel not been encumbered by a conflict of interest. Rather, the inquiry we must make is whether plaintiffs' counsel was able to represent the plaintiff class unaffected by divided loyalties, or as stated in Rule 1.7(b), whether NHLA could have reasonably believed that its representation would not be adversely affected by the conflict. Our review of the record and the history of this litigation—especially NHLA's response to the state's second offer, in which it stated that "plaintiffs do not want to agree to an offer which is against the stated interests of plaintiffs in the *Garrity* case"—persuade us that NHLA's representation of plaintiffs could not escape the adverse effects of NHLA's loyalties to the *Garrity* class. . . .

Absent some evidence of true necessity, we will not permit a meritorious disqualification motion to be denied in the interest of expediency unless it can be shown that the movant strategically sought disqualification in an effort to advance some improper purpose. Thus, the state's motivation in bringing the motion is not irrelevant; as we recognized in *Kevlik*, "disqualification motions can be tactical in nature, designed to harass opposing counsel." However, the mere fact that the state moved for NHLA's disqualification just prior to the commencement of the trial is not, without more, cause for denying its motion. There is simply no evidence to support plaintiffs' suggestion that the state "created" the conflict by intentionally offering plaintiffs a building at LSS in an effort "to dodge the bullet again" with regard to its "failure to provide in-state housing for the plaintiff class." We do not believe, therefore, that the state's second offer of judgment and subsequent disqualification motion were intended to harass plaintiffs. Rather, our reading of the record indicates that a more benign scenario is more probable: the state made a good faith attempt to accommodate plaintiffs by offering to establish a correctional facility in an existing building at the Laconia State School and, once NHLA's conflict of interest with regard to this offer became apparent, the state moved for NHLA's disqualification to preserve this settlement option.

As we are unable to identify a reasoned basis for the district court's denial of the state's pre-trial motion to disqualify NHLA from serving as plaintiffs' class counsel, we hold that its order amounts to an abuse of discretion and must be reversed....

NOTES AND QUESTIONS

1. Although the Court of Appeals agreed that the trial judge erred by failing to disqualify NHLA, it found that the error was harmless in the proceedings on the merits, because of the "overwhelming evidence of inequitable treatment" of female inmates in the state prison. The Court of Appeals therefore declined to remand for a new hearing on the merits. The court did, however, remand for new proceedings on the appropriate remedy. It also granted the *Garrity* class's motion to intervene.

2. NHLA charged that the state offered Laconia State School to the plaintiffs solely for the strategic purpose of generating a conflict of interest that would disqualify NHLA and delay the proceedings. Notice that if the state had offered some other facility rather than LSS, there would have been no conflict of interest—and that the offer was made just two weeks before trial. The appellate court, however, finds that the state offered LSS to the plaintiffs in good faith. What evidence cited in the opinion supports that conclusion? What evidence might lead to the opposite finding?

3. The court points out that NHLA attorneys and their expert had examined several facilities, including LSS, as potential sites for a women's correctional facility. Assuming that NHLA was already representing the *Garrity* class at the time, should they have realized then that they were embroiled in a potential conflict of interest? What should they have done about it? NHLA was, at the time, the only legal aid organization in New Hampshire.

4. Does it matter that the party raising the conflicts issue was the defendant, not one of the clients ostensibly affected? Courts are divided about the standing of non-clients to raise such concerns. See *Dawson v. City of Bartlesville*, 901 F.Supp. 314 (N.D.Okla.1995).

2.   MASS TORTS

PROBLEM 8

You are a plaintiffs' personal injury lawyer. Your firm has developed an expertise in products liability litigation over a chemical called UC–55. For more than thirty years, UC–55 was among the most widely-marketed solvents in the U.S., used in industrial processes that employed millions of people, as well as in many homes where its diluted form was a component of grease-cutting cleansers. UC–55 has now been found to cause serious health problems. These include: irregularities in skin pigmentation (blotchiness); skin cancers; inability to digest certain foods; and, in a small percentage of cases, stomach cancer. The latency period between UC–55 use and the development of symptoms varies widely, from months in cases of blotchiness, to periods up to ten years in cases of stomach cancer. A wave of products-liability litigation has started, potentially involving millions of people. Your own firm currently handles an inventory of almost 10,000 UC–55 cases.

UC–55 was manufactured by four chemical companies. During the early years of UC–55 use, one of the manufacturers (Consolidated Alchemists) discovered evidence of UC–55's health effects but concealed this evidence. This has led to some large punitive awards against Consolidated Alchemists, and the size of awards and settlements often turns on which company's product plaintiffs used at which times. However, the harmful effects of UC–55 have now been scientifically established, and the settlement value of most cases falls within a predictable range. Defendants' financial exposure is large, and new cases continue to be filed as victims develop symptoms.

Together, the four chemical companies approach your law firm with a proposal. The companies would like to negotiate a global settlement with you and several other expert UC–55 lawyers, in order to obtain some finality and to cap their annual financial exposure. The settlement they envision would establish standardized payouts for different levels of illness. In essence, it would substitute a predictable insurance plan for the expensive and capricious litigation process. It would specify medical criteria of eligibility for these payouts, and set "case flow maximums" that would limit the number of payouts per year (with eligible plaintiffs who exceed that number being bumped to a later year). Class members will receive payouts ranging from $7,500 (for blotchiness) up to a maximum of $75,000 (for stomach cancer). This is lower than typical settlements of individually-litigated cases, which average ten to twenty percent higher. Under the terms of the settlement, plaintiffs' counsel will receive fees capped at 25% of the client's recovery.

The plan is to file a complaint asking for the certification under Rule 23(b)(3) of a number of subclasses to encompass everyone injured by or exposed to UC–55 simultaneously with the settlement itself. You and the other plaintiffs' lawyers in the negotiation will be designated as class counsel. This procedure of negotiating a settlement before filing a class action suit, and then filing the suit solely for purposes of settling it whether or not the case could actually be tried, is known as a "settlement class action." You agree to participate in the negotiations.

a) What are your responsibilities to your current UC–55 clients, many of whom might be able to get better deals than the global settlement provides? May you negotiate separate settlements for your current clients and the "futures class" of those who have not yet filed UC–55 lawsuits, perhaps because they have not yet manifested symptoms of UC–55–related illness ("exposure-only" cases)? On what terms?

b) Can you adequately represent the class? Specifically, consider the following possible conflicts of interest:

- Those class members who are currently afflicted prefer larger immediate payouts. Exposure-only class members would prefer lower payouts now in order to reserve more money in the settlement fund as a hedge against inflation.

- Class members from different states have different causes of action because tort law and statutes of limitations vary across jurisdictions. Some states also disallow or impose caps on punitive damages. Some states permit exposure-only claimants to recover for emotional distress, while others do not.

- In addition, different jurisdictions have different legal cultures, which result in different settlement-values for otherwise identical cases. On average, for example, plaintiffs in three counties in Alabama recover twice as much as the national average.

- The four manufacturers have had different levels and kinds of insurance coverage, which have changed over time. In individually-litigated cases, settlement levels have depended on how long the plaintiff was exposed to UC–55 and which manufacturer's UC–55 was involved.

c) The chemical companies worry that many class members will opt out of the settlement, as permitted by Rule 23(c)(3), and file their own individual suits. At their insistence, the settlement agreement specifies that if more than 15 percent of class-members opt out, the agreement is void. In addition to this provision, the defendants insist that you and the other class attorneys agree to counsel your own UC–55 clients to enroll in the settlement program rather than opting out, and to explain that if they opt out you will withdraw from representing them. Can you accept this condition? Even without such a requirement, is your own judgment impermissibly compromised by the desire not to have the settlement unravel?

d) Assume that a negotiated settlement is filed along with the class action. You then receive notice that numerous individuals will appear to voice objections at the upcoming fairness hearing. Some of these objectors appear to be class members who do not fare well under the settlement. Others are clients of some well-known UC–55 plaintiffs' lawyers who were not invited to participate in the settlement, and who are hoping that it will be rejected and that they can get in on the action in the next round.

Your fellow class counsel have a simple solution to the problem of the objectors: pay them off. They propose that the chemical companies negotiate side settlements with the objectors, offering them highly favorable terms in order to persuade them to withdraw their objections. You have qualms about giving these objectors a better deal than other class members will receive. What should you do?

References

Model Rules 1.4, 1.6, 1.7, 3.3, 5.6(b); Federal Rule of Civil Procedure 23.

NOTES

When Rule 23 was adopted in its present form in 1966, the Rules Advisory Committee warned that mass torts are "ordinarily not appropriate" for class treatment. Rule 23(b)(3) requires that common questions predominate over questions affecting only individual members, and in the Committee's opinion this would seldom be true in tort cases, which are highly fact-specific. During the 1970s, however, this view began to fade and Rule 23(b)(3) mass tort actions became an important part of the legal landscape.

The device of settlement class actions originated in the mid–1980s, and attracted widespread attention through asbestos products liability suits.[127] During the peak of asbestos use, between 13 and 20 million Americans were exposed to the substance, with health effects that ranged from a slight thickening of the lung walls that causes no immediate symptoms, to debilitating asbestosis and fatal cancers. Hundreds of thousands of asbestos cases were filed, and for many years they clogged the dockets of federal courts. In the mid–1980s, for example, asbestos claims amounted to one-third of the federal tort caseload. These claims were widely perceived as causing a crisis-level strain on the judicial system.

The Center for Claims Resolution (CCR) is an asbestos-settlement organization created by twenty defendant manufacturers. CCR approached a group of plaintiffs' lawyers with large inventories of asbestos cases to negotiate a settlement class action on terms similar to those of the hypothetical settlement in Problem 8. This vast settlement attracted controversies from start to finish. A basic question was whether a class including individuals with so many different diseases, many of whom had yet to manifest symptoms, could be represented by class counsel without a conflict of interest. But this was hardly the only issue.

The plaintiffs' counsel insisted on negotiating not one settlement but two: one on behalf of the futures class, defined as all claimants who had not filed suit against the companies by a specified date, and a side-settlement on behalf of their current clients ("present claimants" or "inventory clients"). Present claimants received more generous recoveries than those

---

127. A brief history of the settlement class action appears in Jay Tidmarsh, *Mass Tort Settlement Class Actions: Five Case Studies* 19–31 (Federal Judicial Center, 1998).

in the global settlement; moreover, the present claimants' lawyers received contingency fees of one-third of recovery, rather than the one-fourth of recovery granted by the settlement. This led some critics to charge that the classes had been artfully gerrymandered to maximize profits for class counsel. According to one expert, class counsel enhanced their fees for the inventory cases between 54% and 72% over what the class settlement would have granted them.[128] These critics charged that the entire global settlement was collusive—an effort by the defendants to buy closure as cheaply as possible from plaintiffs' lawyers eager to line their own pockets, with little critical oversight by judges anxious to relieve the court system of the asbestos burden as expeditiously as possible.[129]

Early versions of the settlement included a clause obligating class counsel not to represent opt-out clients. However, the ABA Committee on Professional Ethics held in Formal Opinion 371 (1993) that such a clause violated Model Rule 5.6(b), "A lawyer shall not participate in offering or making an agreement in which a restriction on the lawyer's right to practice is part of the settlement of a controversy between private parties."[130] The parties modified the agreement to a form similar to that given in Problem 8(c). Although legal ethics experts continued to differ over whether the new agreement violated Rule 5.6(b), the judge presiding over the fairness hearing found that the agreement was ethical. He also found that the settlement as a whole was fair—neither collusive nor impermissible due to lawyers' conflicts of interest.[131]

However, the Third Circuit Court of Appeals and the Supreme Court disagreed. In *Amchem Products, Inc. v. Windsor*, 521 U.S. 591 (1997), the Court rejected the global asbestos settlement, finding that the "sprawling" class included too many different subclasses of individuals with differing interests. *Windsor* was a narrow opinion, however, and left unsettled crucial questions about whether less inclusive classes might be suitable candidates for settlement class actions. The Court did not address whether the side-settlement of inventory cases created a conflict of interest for class counsel. Nor did it address some of the basic, structural conflicts that the asbestos settlement shares with many other mass torts, especially the question whether already-ailing class members and exposure-only class members constitute interests so opposed that no class counsel could adequately represent both.

In a subsequent opinion, the Supreme Court rejected another asbestos settlement that had tried to solve defendants' opt-out problem by making the class action mandatory under a "limited fund theory" based on Rule

---

128. Susan P. Koniak, "Feasting While the Widow Weeps: *Georgine v. Amchem Products, Inc.*," 80 *Cornell L. Rev.* 1045, 1067–78 (1995).

129. *Id.* This article, perhaps the harshest published critique of the asbestos settlement, also provides the most detailed examination of it. For a less critical view, see Deborah Hensler, "As Time Goes By: Asbes-

tos Litigation After *Amchem* and *Ortiz*," 80 *Tex. L. Rev.* 1899 (2002) and sources cited therein.

130. For further discussion, see the materials on "attorney buyout" in Section H 2, *infra*.

131. Georgine v. Amchem Products, Inc., 157 F.R.D. 246 (E.D.Pa.1994).

23(b)(1): *Ortiz v. Fibreboard Corp.*, 527 U.S. 815 (1999). Between *Windsor's* rejection of the global settlement with opt-outs and *Ortiz's* rejection of mandatory settlements, the Supreme Court placed formidable tools in the hands of those challenging settlement class actions.

Nevertheless, many settlement class actions continue to thrive because class counsel frequently buy off objectors through side-settlements, generally on terms more generous than the class settlement itself. For class counsel, this strategy can be worth tens of millions of dollars of lawyers' fees. Until recently, the terms of these side-deals have usually been kept secret. In 1999, the First Circuit Court of Appeals held that federal courts have no authority to review side-settlements, and denied an effort by an objector to obtain discovery about side-settlements that caused other objectors to withdraw their objections.[132] Reportedly, some plaintiffs' lawyers have now become "professional objectors," who challenge class action settlements solely for the purpose of extorting lucrative side-deals. In response to this phenomenon, Rule 23 was revised in 2003, and a new section (e)(2) requires settling parties to file a notice of any agreement made in connection with the settlement.

At bottom, the arguments for and against settlement class actions are straightforward. Critics point to the fact that a settlement class action is, in effect, a *reverse auction*: the defendants auction off the right to be class counsel to those plaintiffs' lawyers prepared to offer them the best deal.[133] This raises the concern that defendants will "offer a bribe to plaintiffs' counsel to take a dive and sell res judicata."[134] Plaintiffs' lawyers negotiate the settlement before the class action is filed, and thus they negotiate terms for individuals who are not yet their clients. The result is a kind of collusion in which the defendants get a favorable settlement, class counsel get a lot of money, the courts get rid of burdensome cases—and the class members get compensation more quickly and surely, but at significantly lower levels, than litigating their cases would provide.

Those who support settlement class actions claim that this is likely to be the best deal the victims can get. Individual litigation is riskier, lengthier, and more expensive than the administrative mechanisms that the settlements establish. Furthermore, individual litigation runs the risk that earlier, higher awards will leave nothing for the last plaintiffs in the queue, particularly if defendants may land in bankruptcy. This is, in fact, what has happened following *Amchem*. At least seventeen asbestos companies have filed for bankruptcy since the Court's decision. The pool available for payments has been dwindling and individuals with severe impairments that materialized late are likely to get far less adequate recoveries than claimants with less severe injuries who settled early.[135] Moreover, plaintiffs'

132. Duhaime v. John Hancock Mutual Life Ins., 183 F.3d 1 (1st Cir.1999).

133. John C. Coffee, Jr., "Class Wars: The Dilemma of the Mass Tort Class Action," 95 *Colum. L. Rev.* 1343, 1367–84 (1995).

134. Comm. on Rules of Practice and Procedure of the Judicial Conference of the U.S., 104th Cong. Preliminary Draft of Proposed Amendments to the Federal Rules of Appellate, Civil, and Criminal Procedure: Request for Comment 35 (Comm. Print 1996).

135. Hensler, *supra* note 129, at 1908, 1918–19. For example, the Manville Trust, which pays claims against a leading asbestos

lawyers are still negotiating aggregate settlements for clients with different degrees of disability, but these negotiations are now proceeding as individual cases without the judicial approval required for settlements of class actions.[136] Is this an improvement? Given these options, should courts strictly apply conflicts standards that were not designed for mass justice? As seasoned federal judge Jack Weinstein puts it, the law "does not insist on its own inutility. When rules ... break down in application, we do not ignore their lack of congruency with life. We try to change them."[137] Does Weinstein's observation argue for reforming the conflict of interest rules applicable in class action contexts? What changes would be appropriate?

Analogous issues can arise in mass torts even if there is no class action. A prominent example is a 2007 settlement between Merck, a pharmaceutical company, and plaintiffs' lawyers representing clients claiming injury from the drug Vioxx.[138] Vioxx was a highly successful painkiller, which Merck withdrew from the market after revelations that Vioxx quintupled the risk of heart attacks and strokes among users. Evidence indicated that Merck was aware of the risks, which it failed to disclose. Up to 47,000 people filed claims against Merck, and financial analysts predicted a potential liability of tens of billions of dollars. Both sides faced substantial legal risks. Plaintiffs face an uphill battle establishing causation, because most Vioxx users have not suffered heart attacks or strokes, and many elderly arthritis sufferers who used Vioxx might have had heart attacks or strokes even without taking the drug. Of the first 17 cases to go to trial, the plaintiffs won only five. So too, at the time of the settlement, the Supreme Court had granted certiorari on a case that might have foreclosed plaintiffs' claims by finding that federal regulations preempt state tort law. On the other hand, evidence of Merck's concealment of Vioxx risks was strong, and the five plaintiffs who won all collected punitive damages.

With risks on both sides, Merck negotiated a settlement. The company would pay $4.85 billion dollars into a compensation fund. Clients who accepted the settlement would receive payment based on the severity of their heart attack or stroke, the length of time they had taken Vioxx, and the presence of other risk factors. They would be unable to know in advance of the settlement how much money they would receive, because the amount would be contingent on the overall composition of the class.

---

manufacturer, now bankrupt, is reportedly paying serious cancer victims $10,000 or less. *Id.* at 1919.

136. The Model Rules permit aggregate settlement if the clients consent after receiving information about what other clients are receiving under the terms of the agreement. Model Rule 1.8 Comment. *See* Charles Silver & Lynn A. Baker, "Mass Lawsuits and the Aggregate Settlement Rule," 32 *Wake Forest L. Rev.* 733 (1997). Not all clients want to allow disclosure of private details about their cases, which presents difficulties for attorneys seeking aggregate settlements. See Di-

ane Karpman, "Multiple Clients May Present Multiple Conflicts," *Cal. Bar J.*, August, 2007, at 16.

137. Jack B. Weinstein, *Individual Justice in Mass Tort Litigation: The Effect of Class Actions, Consolidations, and Other Multiparty Devices* 46 (1995). *See also* Carrie Menkel–Meadow, "Ethics and the Settlements of Mass Torts: When the Rules Meet the Road," 80 *Cornell L. Rev.* 1159 (1995).

138. The discussion that follows draws on on Benjamin Zipursky, "The Vioxx Settlement Agreement and Some Problems in Legal Ethics," draft of May 2008.

Other aspects of the settlement agreement followed Problem 8(c): the agreement is void unless at least 85% of plaintiffs opt in; lawyers must counsel their clients to opt in, and must warn the clients that they will withdraw if the client does not do so. Plaintiffs' lawyers would collect approximately a billion dollars.

Benjamin Zipursky, a scholar of ethics and tort law, asks several pertinent questions about settlements structured this way:

1) Model Rule 1.2(a) states, "A lawyer shall abide by a client's decision whether to settle a matter." Does the Vioxx settlement violate this rule? As Zipursky observes, "A lawyer who tells the client 'Settle or you're fired!' is hardly abiding by or deferring to the client's decision."[139]

2) Model Rule 2.1 requires lawyers to offer clients independent and candid advice. If the lawyer has signed a settlement agreement specifying the advice he or she must give, does that violate the rule? What if the lawyer is convinced that the settlement agreement is undoubtedly better for all clients than pursuing lengthy litigation against long odds?

3) Model Rule 1.7(a)(2) forbids lawyers from representations that might be materially limited by responsibilities to a third person. In this settlement, the lawyer has obligations to Merck to counsel the client as specified in the settlement agreement. On the other hand, Model Rule 1.8(g) permits an aggregate settlement if all clients give informed consent. Which rule predominates in this case?

4) Does the requirement that the attorney withdraw if the client refuses to enter the agreement violate Model Rule 5.6, which forbids the negotiation of settlements that limit attorneys' right to practice? Does it matter that the settlement agreement contains language stating that its terms apply only to the extent consistent with Rule 5.6 and 1.16?

5) For that matter, on what basis can attorneys withdraw? Rule 1.16(b)(4) allows attorneys to withdraw if the client insists on action that the lawyer finds repugnant; but, as Zipursky notes, the decision whether or not to accept a settlement belongs to the client. Rule 1.16(b)(7) allows the lawyer to withdraw for "other good cause." The lawyer's agreement with Merck would not be a "good cause" if it violates ethics rules. What about Rule 1.16(b)(6), which allows withdrawal if continuing would place an unreasonable financial burden on the attorney?

An American Law Institute draft proposes a rule that permits lawyers to negotiate aggregate settlements conditioned on 75% of the plaintiffs accepting the settlement. However, the proposal was tabled for further study in response to objections that the rule undermines traditional legal ethics.[140]

---

139. *Id.*

140. Am. Law Inst., Principles of the Law of Aggregate Litigation (Discussion Draft No. 2, April 6, 2007) 3.17, cited and discussed in Nancy J. Moore, "The American Law Institute's Draft Proposal to Bypass the Aggregate Settlement Rule: Do Mass Torts Plaintiffs Need (or Want) Group Decision Making?" 57 *DePaul L. Rev.* 395 (2008).

PROBLEM 9

How would you answer Zipursky's questions?

H.   Fee–Related Conflicts of Interest

1.   Conflicts in Public Interest Representation

PROBLEM 10

Your firm represents a migrant farmworker's organization in a lawsuit against the U.S. Labor Department for failure to enforce certain protective legislation. You personally believe that the odds of obtaining any relief in court are about 70% against you, but hope that the costs and adverse publicity involved in litigation will prod the Department into reassessing its enforcement priorities and settling the case on favorable terms. Your firm is currently subsidizing the lawsuit on a pro bono basis but hopes to recoup some of its expenses under a federal fee-shifting statute. That statute has been construed to authorize recovery of reasonable attorneys' fees and litigation costs for a party who "prevails" in litigation, or who obtains substantial relief through settlement.

a) Your fondest hopes are realized. After two years of pretrial maneuvers, the Department comes up with what you believe to be a reasonably adequate enforcement policy in light of its budget constraints. The changes exceed what you believe a court would order and the defendant's lawyers assure you that if the case goes to trial, they will challenge the legal authority of any group to question Department priorities. As part of the proposed agreement, the defendants agree to a substantial attorney's fee award. They also invite your firm to serve as a paid consultant to the government in its development of future enforcement policy.

The leaders of your client organization remain unwilling to compromise in any respect and want to pursue their claim for full enforcement. The senior partners in your firm point out that they already have been subsidizing this litigation for an extended interval. If the client refuses to settle, they wish to withdraw. When you convey this to your client's leaders, they are incensed and intransigent. At this stage, they believe that withdrawal would substantially prejudice their interests. You have been unable to find qualified counsel willing to replace you. What are your options?

b) Alternatively, your fondest hopes are not realized. Rather, the Department proposes to satisfy your client by vigorously enforcing regulations in only the regions that affect its members. Such a policy would leave 90% of the migrant work force unprotected. Moreover, as part of the proposed agreement, defendants insist that you waive attorneys' fees, agree not to represent other migrant groups, and return key documents related to the case.

Since you already have invested substantial efforts in trying to effect policy changes that will help migrant workers generally, you strongly oppose this settlement. You also believe that agreement to the fee waiver will jeopardize funding for other pro bono matters at your firm. However, you suspect that the leaders of your client organization, if told that the odds of ultimately gaining judicial relief are strongly against them, may prefer the settlement. A victory against the Department could build support for their organizing campaign and serve as a catalyst to further collective efforts.

What are your obligations to the client leadership, your law firm, and to migrant workers generally?

References

Model Rules 1.2, 1.7, 1.8(e), 1.16, 5.1; Federal Rules of Civil Procedure, Rule 23.

QUESTIONS

1.   Once you have agreed to represent the farm workers in this matter, are you obligated to press their claim until death do you part or the Supreme Court denies certiorari? Could, or should, you have dealt with the problem by drafting a retainer agreement limiting your firm's commitment? Would such a strategy institutionalize a double standard of representation, which reserves zealous advocacy only for clients who can afford it? Alternatively, would such retainers be the most practical way of encouraging private attorneys to accept pro bono cases that could become unexpectedly expensive? Under Model Rule 1.16(b)(6) a lawyer may withdraw from representation that will result in an "unreasonable financial burden." How should reasonableness be assessed?

2.   Consider Model Rule 1.7, which prohibits representation that may be materially limited by the lawyer's own interests or responsibilities to a third person unless the lawyer reasonably believes such representation will not be adversely affected and the client consents after full disclosure. Should "adverse affect" be determined by reference to some hypothesized ideal or to the practical alternatives available for the client? Is informed consent a meaningful standard where the client has no alternative means of securing representation?

Evans v. Jeff D.

Supreme Court of the United States, 1986.
475 U.S. 717.

■ Justice Stevens delivered the opinion of the Court.

The Civil Rights Attorney's Fees Awards Act of 1976 (Fees Act) provides that "the court, in its discretion, may allow the prevailing party ... a reasonable attorney's fee" in enumerated civil rights actions.... In this case, we consider the question whether attorney's fees *must* be assessed when the case has been settled by a consent decree granting prospective relief to the plaintiff class but providing that the defendants shall not pay any part of the prevailing party's fees or costs. We hold that the District Court has the power, in its sound discretion, to refuse to award fees.

I

The petitioners are the Governor and other public officials of the State of Idaho responsible for the education and treatment of children who suffer from emotional and mental handicaps. Respondents are a class of such children who have been or will be placed in petitioners' care.

On August 4, 1980, respondents commenced this action by filing a complaint against petitioners in the United States District Court for the District of Idaho. The factual allegations in the complaint described deficiencies in both the educational programs and the health care services provided respondents. . . . The complaint prayed for injunctive relief and for an award of costs and attorney's fees, but it did not seek damages.

On the day the complaint was filed, the District Court . . . appoint[ed] Charles Johnson as [respondents'] next friend for the sole purpose of instituting and prosecuting the action. At that time Johnson was employed by the Idaho Legal Aid Society, Inc., a private, nonprofit corporation that provides free legal services to qualified low-income persons. Because the Idaho Legal Aid Society is prohibited from representing clients who are capable of paying their own fees, it made no agreement requiring any of the respondents to pay for the costs of litigation or the legal services it provided through Johnson. Moreover, the special character of both the class and its attorney-client relationship with Johnson explains why it did not enter into any agreement covering the various contingencies that might arise during the course of settlement negotiations of a class action of this kind.

In March 1983, one week before trial, petitioners presented respondents with a new settlement proposal. As respondents themselves characterize it, the proposal "offered virtually all of the injunctive relief [they] had sought in their complaint". . . . The Court of Appeals agreed with this characterization, and further noted that the proposed relief was "more than the district court in earlier hearings had indicated it was willing to grant." As was true of the earlier partial settlement, however, petitioners' offer included a provision for a waiver by respondents of any claim to fees or costs. Originally, this waiver was unacceptable to the Idaho Legal Aid Society, which had instructed Johnson to reject any settlement offer conditioned upon a waiver of fees, but Johnson ultimately determined that his ethical obligation to his clients mandated acceptance of the proposal. The parties conditioned the waiver on approval by the District Court.

After the stipulation was signed, Johnson filed a written motion requesting the District Court to approve the settlement "except for the provision on costs and attorney's fees," and to allow respondents to present a bill of costs and fees for consideration by the court. App. 87. At the oral argument on that motion, Johnson contended that petitioners' offer had exploited his ethical duty to his clients—that he was "forced," by an offer giving his clients "the best result [they] could have gotten in this court or any other court," to waive his attorney's fees. The District Court, however, evaluated the waiver in the context of the entire settlement and rejected the ethical underpinnings of Johnson's argument. . . . The Court of Appeals . . . after ordering preliminary relief . . . invalidated the fee waiver and left standing the remainder of the settlement; it then instructed the District Court to "make its own determination of the fees that are reasonable" and remanded for that limited purpose.

In explaining its holding, the Court of Appeals emphasized that Rule 23(e) of the Federal Rules of Civil Procedure gives the court the power to approve the terms of all settlements of class actions. . . . The court added that "[w]hen attorney's fees are negotiated as part of a class action settlement, a conflict frequently exists between the class lawyers' interest in compensation and the class members' interest in relief." "To avoid this conflict," the Court of Appeals relied on Circuit precedent which had "disapproved simultaneous negotiation of settlements and attorney's fees" absent a showing of "unusual circumstances." In this case, the Court of Appeals found no such "unusual circumstances" and therefore held that an agreement on fees "should not have been a part of the settlement of the claims of the class." . . . We now reverse.

II

. . . To begin with, the Court of Appeals' decision rested on an erroneous view of the District Court's power to approve settlements in class actions. Rule 23(e) wisely requires court approval of the terms of any settlement of a class action, but the power to approve or reject a settlement negotiated by the parties before trial does not authorize the court to require the parties to accept a settlement to which they have not agreed. . . . The question we must decide, therefore, is whether the District Court had a duty to reject the proposed settlement because it included a waiver of statutorily authorized attorney's fees.

That duty, whether it takes the form of a general prophylactic rule or arises out of the special circumstances of this case, derives ultimately from the Fees Act rather than from the strictures of professional ethics. Although respondents contend that Johnson, as counsel for the class, was faced with an "ethical dilemma" when petitioners offered him relief greater than that which he could reasonably have expected to obtain for his clients at trial (if only he would stipulate to a waiver of the statutory fee award), and although we recognize Johnson's conflicting interests between pursuing relief for the class and a fee for the Idaho Legal Aid Society, we do not believe that the "dilemma" was an "ethical" one in the sense that Johnson had to choose between conflicting duties under the prevailing norms of professional conduct. Plainly, Johnson had no *ethical* obligation to seek a statutory fee award. His ethical duty was to serve his clients loyally and competently. Since the proposal to settle the merits was more favorable than the probable outcome of the trial, Johnson's decision to recommend acceptance was consistent with the highest standards of our profession. The District Court, therefore, correctly concluded that approval of the settlement involved no breach of ethics in this case. . . . For reasons set out below, we are not persuaded that Congress has commanded that all such settlements must be rejected by the District Court. Moreover, on the facts of record in this case, we are satisfied that the District Court did not abuse its discretion by approving the fee waiver.

III

The text of the Fees Act provides no support for the proposition that Congress intended to ban all fee waivers offered in connection with substantial relief on the merits. In fact, we believe that a general proscription against negotiated waiver of attorney's fees in exchange for a settlement on the merits would itself impede vindication of civil rights, at least in some cases, by reducing the attractiveness of settlement. . . .

Most defendants are unlikely to settle unless the cost of the predicted judgment, discounted by its probability, plus the transaction costs of further litigation, are greater than the cost of the settlement package. If fee waivers cannot be negotiated, the settlement package must either contain an attorney's fee component of potentially large and typically uncertain magnitude, or else the parties must agree to have the fee fixed by the court. Although either of these alternatives may well be acceptable in many cases, there surely is a significant number in which neither alternative will be as satisfactory as a decision to try the entire case. . . .[141] Petitioners and the *amici* who support them never suggest that the district court is obligated to place its stamp of approval on every settlement in which the plaintiffs' attorneys have agreed to a fee waiver. The Solicitor General, for example, has suggested that a fee waiver need not be approved when the defendant had "no realistic defense on the merits," or if the waiver was part of a "vindictive effort . . . to teach counsel that they had better not bring such cases."

We find it unnecessary to evaluate this argument, however, because the record in this case does not indicate that Idaho has adopted such a statute, policy, or practice. Nor does the record support the narrower proposition that petitioners' request to waive fees was a vindictive effort to deter attorneys from representing plaintiffs in civil rights suits against

---

141. . . . Although the dissent would allow simultaneous negotiations, it would require that "whatever fee the parties agree to" be "found by the court to be a 'reasonable' one under the Fees Act." The dissent's proposal is imaginative, but not very practical. Of the 10,757 "other civil rights" cases filed in federal court last year—most of which were 42 U.S.C. § 1983 actions for which § 1988 authorizes an award of fees—only 111 sought class relief. Assuming that of the approximately 99% of these civil rights actions that are not class actions, a further 90% would settle rather than go to trial, the dissent's proposal would require district courts to evaluate the reasonableness of fee agreements in several thousand civil rights cases annually while they make that determination in slightly over 100 civil rights class actions now. Moreover, if this novel procedure really is necessary to carry out the purposes of the Fees Act, presumably it should be applied to all cases arising under federal statutes that provide for fee shifting.

Idaho.[142] . . . In this case, the District Court did not abuse its discretion in upholding the settlement.

The judgment of the Court of Appeals is reversed.

■ Justice Brennan, with whom Justice Marshall and Justice Blackmun join, dissenting.

Ultimately, enforcement of the laws is what really counts. It was with this in mind that Congress enacted the Civil Rights Attorney's Fees Awards Act of 1976. Congress authorized fee shifting to improve enforcement of civil rights legislation by making it easier for victims of civil rights violations to find lawyers willing to take their cases. Because today's decision will make it more difficult for civil rights plaintiffs to obtain legal assistance, a result plainly contrary to Congress' purpose, I dissent.

I

The Court begins its analysis by emphasizing that neither the language nor the legislative history of the Fees Act supports "the proposition that Congress intended to ban all fee waivers offered in connection with substantial relief on the merits." I agree. There is no evidence that Congress gave the question of fee waivers any thought at all. However, the Court mistakenly assumes that this omission somehow supports the conclusion that fee waivers are permissible. . . . However, the legislative history of the Fees Act discloses that this is not the case. Rather, Congress provided fee awards to ensure that there would be lawyers available to plaintiffs who could not otherwise afford counsel, so that these plaintiffs could fulfill their role in the federal enforcement scheme as "private attorneys general," vindicating the public interest.

It seems obvious that allowing defendants in civil rights cases to condition settlement of the merits on a waiver of statutory attorney's fees will diminish lawyers' expectations of receiving fees and decrease the willingness of lawyers to accept civil rights cases. Even the Court acknowledges "the possibility that decisions by individual clients to bargain away fee awards may, in the aggregate and in the long run, diminish lawyers' expectations of statutory fees in civil rights cases." The Court tells us, however, that "[c]omment on this issue" is "premature at this juncture" because there is not yet supporting "documentation." The Court then goes on anyway to observe that "as a practical matter the likelihood of this circumstance arising is remote."

142. We are cognizant of the possibility that decisions by individual clients to bargain away fee awards may, in the aggregate and in the long run, diminish lawyers' expectations of statutory fees in civil rights cases. If this occurred, the pool of lawyers willing to represent plaintiffs in such cases might shrink, constricting the "effective access to the judicial process" for persons with civil rights grievances which the Fees Act was intended to provide. H.R.Rep. No. 94–1558, p. 1 (1976). That the "tyranny of small decisions" may operate in this fashion is not to say that there is any reason or documentation to support such a concern at the present time. Comment on this issue is therefore premature at this juncture. We believe, however, that as a practical matter the likelihood of this circumstance arising is remote.

I must say that I find the Court's assertions somewhat difficult to understand. To be sure, the impact of conditional fee waivers on the availability of attorneys will be less severe than was the restriction on fee awards created in *Alyeska*. However, that experience surely provides an indication of the immediate hardship suffered by civil rights claimants whenever there is a reduction in the availability of attorney's fee awards. . . . And, of course, once fee waivers are permitted, defendants will seek them as a matter of course, since this is a logical way to minimize liability. . . .

This all seems so obvious that it is puzzling that the Court reaches a different result. The Court's rationale is that, unless fee waivers are permitted, "parties to a significant number of civil rights cases will refuse to settle. . . ." This is a wholly inadequate justification for the Court's result.

First, the effect of prohibiting fee waivers on settlement offers is just not an important concern in the context of the Fees Act. I agree with the Court that encouraging settlements is desirable policy. But it is *judicially* created policy, applicable to litigation of any kind and having no special force in the context of civil rights cases. The *congressional* policy underlying the Fees Act is, as I have argued throughout, to create incentives for lawyers to devote time to civil rights cases by making it economically feasible for them to do so. . . .

Second, even assuming that settlement practices are relevant, the Court greatly exaggerates the effect that prohibiting fee waivers will have on defendants' willingness to make settlement offers. This is largely due to the Court's failure to distinguish the fee waiver issue from the issue of simultaneous negotiation of fees and merits claims. The Court's discussion mixes concerns over a defendant's reluctance to settle because total liability remains uncertain with reluctance to settle because the cost of settling is too high. However, it is a prohibition on simultaneous negotiation, not a prohibition on fee waivers, that makes it difficult for the defendant to ascertain his total liability at the time he agrees to settle the merits. . . .

The Court asserts, without factual support, that requiring defendants to pay statutory fee awards will prevent a "significant number" of settlements. It is, of course, ironic that the same absence of "documentation" which makes comment on the effects of *permitting* fee waivers "premature at this juncture," does not similarly affect the Court's willingness to speculate about what to expect if fee waivers are *prohibited*. Be that as it may, I believe that the Court overstates the extent to which prohibiting fee waivers will deter defendants from making settlement offers. Because the parties can negotiate a fee (or a range of fees) that is not unduly high and condition their settlement on the court's approval of this fee, the magnitude of a defendant's liability for fees in the settlement context need be neither uncertain nor particularly great. . . .

[In any event] an actual disincentive to settling exists only where three things are true: (1) the defendant feels he is likely to win if he goes to trial, in which case the plaintiff will recover no fees; (2) the plaintiff will agree to relief on the merits that is less costly to the defendant than litigating the case; and (3) adding the cost of a negotiated attorneys fee makes it less costly for the defendant to litigate. I believe this describes a very small class of cases—although like the Court, I cannot document the assertion. . . .

I would, on the other hand, permit simultaneous negotiation of fees and merits claims, since this would not contravene the purposes of the Fees Act. . . .

NOTES AND QUESTIONS

1.   How should public interest attorneys handle fee negotiations? According to the majority in *Evans v. Jeff D.*, a settlement offer requiring a waiver of attorney fees presents no ethical conflict since lawyers are under no ethical obligation to seek statutory fees. Is this view convincing, or should the Court have considered lawyers' responsibilities to their employers or to other nonpaying clients, whose representation is subsidized in part by statutory fee awards? For example, Charles Silver argues that the fee-waiver issue reflects a tradeoff: some victims who can sue do better if waivers are allowed, while others denied representation do worse. In Silver's view, the majority opinion in *Jeff D.* is problematic in that it "cites no evidence tending to show that the former [victims] gain more than the latter lose, and offers no guidance on how to compare the effects on the two groups."[143] If Silver is right, how could the effects be compared?

2.   At the close of his dissent in *Evans v. Jeff D.*, Justice Marshall urges more state bars to prohibit defendants from demanding fee waivers as a condition of settlement. He also suggests that public interest organizations might obtain agreements from their clients not to waive fees. If you were a member of a state bar ethics committee or a public interest lawyer, would you follow such advice? Committees that have ruled on the issue have reached mixed results.[144]

If attorneys may be pressured into accepting fee waivers in some cases, should they be allowed to seek additional payments in other cases as compensation for the risk of nonpayment? In determining statutory fees, courts generally take as a starting point the number of hours reasonably expended on the litigation multiplied by a reasonable hourly rate. This "lodestar" amount is then sometimes adjusted by a "multiplier." The award may be decreased if the prevailing parties' success is limited in comparison to the scope of the litigation as a whole, or increased in instances of exceptional success. See e.g., *Hensley v. Eckerhart*, 461 U.S.

---

143.   Charles Silver, "A Restitutionary Theory of Attorneys' Fees in Class Actions," 76 *Cornell L.Rev.* 656, 700 (1991).

144.   *Compare* Utah State Bar Ethics Advisory Comm., Op. 98–05 (1998)(attorneys cannot deny through contract clients right to determine whether to adopt a settlement that waives fees); D.C. Bar Legal Ethics Comm. Op. 289 (1999) (citing opinions); *with* State Bar of California Standing Comm. On Professional Responsibility and Conduct, Formal Op. 1994–136 (1994) (clients may assign to attorneys the right to recover fees, and retainer contracts may bar waiver of fees provided that the terms are fully disclosed and are fair and reasonable to the client).

424, 434 (1983); *Blum v. Stenson*, 465 U.S. 886 (1984). In *Pennsylvania v. Delaware Valley Citizens' Council for Clean Air*, 483 U.S. 711 (1987), a divided Court declined to allow a "risk multiplier" that would provide increased compensation above the lodestar amount. Does that holding make sense from a policy perspective?

More recent Supreme Court decisions have, like *Jeff D.*, made it difficult for civil rights attorneys to recover statutory fees. In *Farrar v. Hobby*, 506 U.S. 103 (1992), the Court confronted a case in which the prevailing plaintiff recovered only nominal damages. The Court held that in such cases reviewing courts may award low fees or no fees without calculating a lodestar amount. However, *Farrar* does not limit its holding to cases where the plaintiff obtains only a de minimis recovery. The decision also permits reviewing courts in all cases to "consider the amount and nature of damages awarded" and assign minimal attorney's fees without ever calculating hourly rates. *Id.* at 115.

In *Buckhannon Bd. & Care Home, Inc. v. West Virginia Dep't. of Health and Human Resources*, 532 U.S. 598 (2001), the Court further held that if a defendant voluntarily grants relief before judgment has been entered, the plaintiff is not entitled to attorney's fees under statutes authorizing such recoveries for "prevailing parties." This decision rejected the catalyst theory, previously endorsed by all nine circuit courts, which had authorized attorney's fees if the litigation was the catalyst to relief or a settlement. As many commentators have noted, that theory seemed more consistent with the legislative history and purpose of the fee-shifting statute than the formalistic dictionary definition of "prevailing" party on which the *Buckhannon* majority relied.[145] In reaching its decision, the majority reasoned that eliminating the catalyst theory would encourage settlement and reduce satellite litigation over fees. 532 U.S. at 608–10. The dissent, by contrast, worried that the result instead would be strategic capitulation; defendants could force their opposing counsel to engage in expensive pretrial work and then, if it appeared that they would lose, they could agree on the eve of trial to a settlement that would moot the plaintiff's claim and deprive the attorneys of fees. Reducing the possibilities of fee awards would, in the long term, then "impede access to the court for the less well heeled" and discourage suits by plaintiffs with claims that were meritorious but expensive to litigate. 532 U.S. at 633 (dissenting).

Although the majority in *Buckhannon* dismissed dissenters' concerns as "speculative and unsupported by any empirical evidence," 532 U.S. at 608, subsequent research has demonstrated precisely the results that the dissent feared. A systematic survey of some 222 public interest organizations found that over a third reported that the decision had made it more difficult to pursue their goals. Conservative, no less than progressive

---

145. David Luban, "Taking Out the Adversary: The Assault on Progressive Public–Interest Lawyers," 91 *Cal. L. Rev.* 209, 243–44 (2003); Deborah M. Weissman,"Law as Largess: Shifting Paradigms of Law for the Poor," 44 *Will. & Mary L. Rev.* 737, 781–82 (2002) (discussing legislative history).

organizations, experienced difficulties.[146] That study also reviewed a significant number of reported cases in which the defendants' strategic capitulation deprived attorneys of fees and discouraged future enforcement actions.

So too, *Buckhannon* has adversely affected private attorneys in contexts like representation of government contractors before the Federal Court of Claims. Small businesses complaining of an unfair bidding process for government contracts can seldom afford to pay counsel to bring these claims, because the only remedy to which they are entitled is a repeat of the bidding process, with no guarantees that they will get the contract the second time around. It would rarely be worth their while to bring these actions without the availability of statutory attorney's fees, which the government can deny simply by conceding that its bidding process was faulty.[147]

How should the legal profession respond to the adverse affects of *Buckhannon*?

Is there any remedy apart from legislative modification of fee shifting statutes?

2.   ATTORNEY BUYOUTS AND SECRET SETTLEMENTS

PROBLEM 11

You represent the plaintiff in what you believe to be the first product liability suit involving a new form of breast implants. Your client is alleging that the implants leaked and caused a life-threatening reaction by her auto-immune system. During the discovery process, the defendant offers to let you review certain internal memoranda and unpublished studies on condition that you agree to a judicial order not to reveal any of their contents. If you refuse to accept that condition, the defendant will fight your discovery request. After consultation with your client, you agree to the nondisclosure provision. The documents at issue reveal safety risks from the implants that you believe are not generally known, even by the Food and Drug Administration.

a) The defendant has now offered your client an extremely generous settlement. One of its conditions is that you not disclose any information about the implants or rely on it in any future legal actions. Your client, who badly needs the money to cover her medical expenses, wants to accept the settlement. What should you do?[148]

---

146. Catherine R. Albiston & Laura Beth Nielsen, "The Procedural Attack on Civil Rights: The Empirical Reality of *Buckhannon* for the Private Attorney General," 59 *U.C.L.A. L. Rev.* 1087 (2007).

147. *See Brickwood Contractors, Inc. v. United States*, 49 Fed. Cl. 738 (2001), *reversed* 288 F.3d 1371 (Fed. Cir. 2002).

148. This problem is based on the dilemma that reportedly faced the lawyer and client in the first product liability lawsuit involving silicone breast implants, against Dow Corning Corporation. Gina Kolata, "Secrecy Orders in Lawsuits Prompt States' Efforts to Restrict Their Use," *N.Y. Times*, Feb. 18, 1992, at D10. Subsequent litigation has generally failed to find liability. *See* Marcia Angell, *Science on Trial*, 99–110, 195–96 (1996). For other examples, *see* David Hechler, "Secrecy in Settlements as a Public Issue," *Nat'l L. J.* Jan. 12, 2004, at A1.

b) Shortly after the conclusion of the lawsuit, the defendant offers to retain you as an "expert consultant" in any future silicone-implant product liability suits. You will receive a generous annual retainer for nominal responsibilities. Such an arrangement will prevent you from using your knowledge on behalf of future plaintiffs in breast implant cases. What considerations would affect your decision whether to accept the offer?

c) Alternatively, suppose that the original settlement proposal provides that, in addition to not disclosing information you have discovered, you will not handle breast implant product liability suits in the future. What do you do?

NOTES

The practice of attorney buyouts, i.e., preempting an attorney's participation in similar lawsuits as a condition of settlement, has an extended and unbecoming history.[149] For example, during the 1930s, plaintiffs' lawyers in a notorious industrial disaster claim and in an early asbestos lawsuit accepted settlements with generous attorneys' fees conditioned on their agreements to forego further legal actions against defendants.[150] Rule 5.6 of the Model Rules, like DR 2–108 of the Code of Professional Conduct, prohibits lawyers from accepting settlements that restrict their right to practice law. However, case studies indicate that these prohibitions are sometimes evaded.[151] A practice more consistent with the letter if not the spirit of ethical codes is for a party to hire the lawyer for a successful opponent as a "consultant" after the case terminates, which effectively preempts the lawyer's future involvement as an adversary in similar matters. And, as previous discussion noted, the global asbestos settlement in *Georgine v. Amchem* initially included an attorney buyout clause specifying that class counsel would not represent plaintiffs who opted out of the settlement. After ABA Formal Opinion 93–371 (1993) ruled that this clause violates Rule 5.6(b), the provision was modified to require class counsel to advise future clients against opting out unless "in the exercise of . . . professional judgment given some unforseen circumstances," the lawyer felt obligated to recommend otherwise. Does this modification avoid an ethical violation? Should it?

QUESTIONS

1. To what extent should the bar seek to regulate restrictions on attorneys' practice? Are such rules primarily designed to protect counsel, future claimants, or both?

---

149. The term comes from Marc Galanter, "A Note on Lawyer Buyout" (1990) (unpublished manuscript).

150. A well-publicized illustration involved personal injury suits against the manufacturers of Dalkon Shields; some plaintiffs' attorneys accepted settlements barring their representation of similar claims Martin Cher-

niack, *The Hawk's Nest Incident: America's Worst Industrial Disaster* 66–72 (1986); Paul Brodeur, *Outrageous Misconduct: The Asbestos Industry on Trial* 113–14 (1985).

151. Morton Mintz, *At Any Cost: Corporate Greed, Women, and the Dalkon Shield* 197–98 (1985).

2.   According to Marc Galanter:

> Our intuition that buyout is bad points to a hard-to-articulate dimension of the distinctive "professional" character of law. Practicing a profession means taking on not only duties to specific clients, but sharing in a collective responsibility to the general public. Part of this responsibility is to serve as trustee of a body of skills and knowledge, to various classes, defined and as yet undefined, within that public. This knowledge can be used for private gain, but there are corresponding obligations to maintain its integrity, to have it grow and adapt to encompass new situations.[152]

Do you agree?

3.   Should attorneys who offer prohibited buyouts be subject to discipline? Note that under Model Rule 8.4(a), it is professional misconduct for a lawyer to "knowingly assist or induce another" lawyer to violate the Rules. In a highly publicized case, a law professor handling a tort case was suspended for a number of infractions, including violating Rule 5.6(b) by accepting a settlement in which he agreed not to represent future claimants against the defendant. *In re Hager*, 812 A.2d 904 (D.C. App. 2002). So too, the defendant's lawyer who made the buyout offer was suspended for one year in New Jersey, on the basis of Rule 8.4(a) as well as the fact that Rule 5.6(b) prohibits "offering" as well as "making" a buyout agreement. *In the Matter of Zaruba*, 832 A.2d 317 (N.J.2003).

4.   Do secrecy orders pose similar concerns? Surveyed public interest lawyers report sometimes feeling obligated to accept settlements that required documents to be sealed.[153] In the case on which Problem 11(a) is based, the lawyer for the plaintiff felt that he had no choice but to accept the discovery agreement:

> There are only so many battles you can fight in a lawsuit. Getting the documents was more important than debating whether they should be under a protective order. I needed the documents to represent my client.... [I have] very strong feelings that this is information that the public needs to know, but my first obligation is to my client.[154]

In other similar cases, plaintiffs have agreed as part of their settlements not to disclose product defects, not to identify doctors accused of malpractice, and not to discuss sexual abuse of children.[155]

Should attorneys be able to protect against such requirements in their retainer agreements? Should the bar's ethical codes be amended to prohibit secrecy clauses? The ABA Ethics 2000 Commission considered but rejected

---

152.   Galanter, *supra* note 149.

153.   Joel S. Newman, "Gagging on the Public Interest," 4 *Geo. J. Legal Ethics* 371 (1990).

154.   Kolata, *supra* note 148.

155.   *Id.*; Alex Berenson, "Eli Lilly Said to Play Down Risk of Top Pill," *N. Y. Times*, December 17, 2006, at A1; Richard A Zitrin,

"Secrecy's Dangerous Side Effects: When Legal Settlements Allow Companies to Hide Their Mistakes, What We Don't Know Can Hurt Us," *L.A. Times*, February 8, 2007, at A21; Stephen Gillers, "Court–Sanctioned Secrets Can Kill," *Los Angeles Times*, May 14, 2003, at A13; Ellen McNamera, "Courts Must End Secrecy," *Boston Globe*, Feb. 27, 2002, at B1.

such a rule. Many legal ethics experts support such prohibitions. Richard A. Zitrin proposes the following addition to Model Rule 3.2:

> Rule 3.2(b): A lawyer shall not participate in offering or making an agreement, whether in connection with a lawsuit or otherwise, to prevent or restrict the availability to the public of information that the lawyer reasonably believes directly concerns a substantial danger to the public health or safety, or to the health or safety of any particular individual(s).[156]

Would you support such a rule? Would it prevent secrecy agreements, or would it merely encourage litigants to negotiate such agreements without involving lawyers?

Alternatively, would you support statutes limiting a party's right to seal documents involving health, safety, or other pressing public concerns? For example, several states have enacted "sunshine in litigation" legislation prohibiting courts from granting secrecy orders in cases involving public hazards, such as product defects, medical malpractice or environmental dangers.[157] A district court in South Carolina set a new precedent by banning sealed settlements, and Congress has considered federal legislation that would prohibit privacy secrecy agreements and judicial orders that bar disclosure of information relevant to public health or safety.[158]

Opponents of such measures claim that they are unnecessary and inefficient; few secrecy orders result in public harm; safety risks eventually come to light despite settlements incorporating secrecy orders, and preventing such orders assertedly will deter settlements, fuel lengthy discovery fights, expose trade secrets, and encourage document destruction.[159] Proponents respond that such adverse consequences have not been demonstrated in states with legislative prohibitions, that substantial harms often occur before certain risks become public, and that secrecy provisions burden the legal system with unnecessarily duplicative suits and discovery.[160] What is your view? Should the issue be left to politically accountable legislatures? Or if well-financed special interests prevent legislative action, should courts and bar associations impose ethical prohibitions on lawyers?

5. A related issue involves gag orders. Should attorneys be allowed to waive their rights to comment on litigation as a condition of settlement? What, if any, remedies should be available to enforce such provisions?

---

156. Richard A. Zitrin, "The Case Against Secret Settlements (Or, What You Don't Know *Can* Hurt You)," 2 *J. Inst. for the Study of Legal Ethics* 115, 116 (1999); David Luban, "Limiting Secret Settlements By Law," 2 *J. Inst. Stud. Leg. Eth.* 125 (1999).

157. For references, see Susan Koniak, "Are Agreements to Keep Secret Information Learned in Discovery Legal, Illegal, or Something In Between?" 30 *Hofstra L. Rev.* 783 (2002); David Luban, "Settlements and the Public Realm," 83 *Geo. L.J.* 2619, 2651 n. 126–29 (1995); Martha Neil, "Confidential

Settlements Scrutinized," *ABA J*, July 2002, at 20–21.

158. D.S.C. Local R. 5.03(E); Proposed Sunshine in Litigation Act of 2005, S. 1348, 109th Cong. (1st Sess. 2005).

159. Eric Frazier, "Judges Veto Sealed Deals," Nat'l Law J., August 12, 2002, at A1; Hechler, *supra* note 136, at 1, 33; Kevin Livingston, "Open Secrets," *The Recorder*, May 8, 2001, at 1.

160. Zitrin, *supra* note 152; Luban, *supra* note 157, at 2652–59; Gillers, *supra* note 155, at A13.

Consider the conduct of four staff attorneys who, in settling their sex discrimination claims against Pacific Gas & Electric, agreed to a provision stating that the company had not engaged in discrimination. In subsequent statements to the press, three of the attorneys claimed that they had been victims of gender bias. According to one of them, the "no discrimination" provision was not made under oath, and was essential to the settlement: "I can't say I'm proud of . . . [agreeing to the clause] but I felt this was a deal breaker. It was simply something I felt I had to agree to to get all this behind me and get on with my life."[161] Once the attorney had made such an agreement, was her subsequent conduct ethically defensible? If you had been counsel for P G & E, how would you have advised your client to respond?

3.   Consumer Class Action Abuses

The frequent inadequacy in class action oversight has generated a range of other problems. One involves settlements in which plaintiffs receive non-monetary payments in the form of coupons (also known as "scrip") good for discounts on the defendant's products. Few of these coupons are ever redeemed, either because the amounts are too small to justify the trouble, or the plaintiffs don't want to buy another product from the defendant within the redemption period. Experts have estimated the redemption rates to be as low as 3 percent; in one celebrated case, only two of some 96,000 coupons were used (a rate of .002 percent).[162] Needless to say, the plaintiffs' attorneys who negotiate in-kind settlements are paid in cash, not in kind. Some claims have yielded counsel millions and individual consumers less than 50 cents.[163]

Related problems involve distributions to charity. Under a proposed settlement of a price-fixing class action involving the matzo industry, the plaintiff distributors of matzo products would have received no financial recovery. Instead, the defendant proposed to distribute $1.8 million worth of matzo product to various charities, while the plaintiff's lawyers would receive close to $500,000. There was some indication that the distributors may have been reluctant to press further demands against the defendant for fear of "biting the hand that feeds them or supplies them with needed goods."[164] In refusing to approve the settlement, the district trial judge complained that "class counsel are litigating this case without any clients," and that the proposed agreement was a "thinly disguised ploy" for the attorneys' benefit.[165] Even more egregious conduct surfaced in litigation

161. John E. Morris, "Women: PG & E Ignored Sex Bias," *Recorder,* June 18, 1991, at 15 (quoting Jo Ann Shaffer).

162. Christopher R. Leslie, "The Need to Study Coupon Settlements in Class Action Litigation," 18 *Geo. J. Legal Ethics* 1395, 1397 (2005); Catherine Crier, *The Case Against Lawyers* 194 (2002).

163. Deborah L. Rhode, *In the Interests of Justice* 176 (2001)(describing 28 cent recovery); Doug Smith, "A Suit That Makes More Cents for the Lawyers," *L. A. Times,* April 11, 2005, at B1 (describing suit against Bank of America that yielded 49 cents for consumers while lawyers received half of the $4.2 million judgment).

164. *In re* Matzo Food Products Litigation, 156 F.R.D. 600, 608 (D.N.J.1994).

165. *Id.* at 606. See Jonathan D. Glater, "Game's Hidden Sex Scene Draw Ho–Hum, Except From Lawyers," *N.Y. Times,* June 25, 2008, at C1 (describing proposed

involving the diet drug, Fen–Phen, which was ultimately removed from the market because of links to heart disease. The class of 400 plaintiffs received only $74 million of a $200 million negotiated settlement. Over half the judgment went to four lawyers and $20 million went into a charity fund, the Kentucky Fund for Healthy Living, Inc., which employed the lawyers as directors at $5000 a month. The judge who approved the settlement also became a director at the same pay rate. His defense was that he had approved the settlement without reading it, and he later resigned rather than face removal.[166]

In response to such abuses, Congress passed the Class Action Fairness Act of 2005. It links the size of attorneys' fees not to the face value of coupons, but to the amounts actually redeemed, and prohibits class counsel from designating charities to receive part of any recovery.

QUESTIONS

1. What persuades judges to approve settlements that enrich lawyers while providing little of value to their clients? One obvious factor is the crushing caseload in most court systems, which encourages agreements that will avoid trial. Another explanation is the difficulty that judges often face in determining whether a settlement is in fact fair, reasonable, and in the best interests of the members of the class. This inquiry in turn requires the court to balance the strength of the plaintiffs' case against the terms of the defendant's offer, which requires more knowledge of the law and facts than many overburdened trial judges are willing to acquire for disputes that are settling. If a case has difficult problems of proof, a small recovery may be the best plaintiffs can realistically hope for. Does this balancing test create a perverse incentive for entrepreneurial lawyers to troll for attorneys' fees by bringing dubious cases that defendants will settle on the cheap? Should fairness hearings include causes of action by aggrieved class members for malpractice or fraud, as Susan Koniak and George Cohen recommend?[167]

2. Plaintiffs' class action lawyers sometimes cast themselves as modern "bounty hunters, riding the range in search of outlaw corporations and collecting fees for the service. When they find wrongdoing, they expose it and force change...."[168] From this perspective, the primary social value of such cases lies not in the benefits to the plaintiff class, but in the

settlement of video game with hidden sex scenes that would net lawyers $1.3 million, charity, $860,000, and buyers $30,000 in new games).

166. Adam Liptak, "Lawyers' Payday in Diet–Pill Case Is Called Fraud," *N.Y. Times*, March 24, 2007, at A1; Ted Frank, "Fen–Phen Zen," *American.Com*, April 4, 2007; Robert Alford, "Judge Resigns Amid Accusations He Profited from Fen–Phen Case," Associated Press, Feb. 28, 2006.

167. Susan P. Koniak & George M. Cohen, "Under Cloak of Settlement," 82 *Virg. L. Rev.* 1053 (1996). See Susan P. Koniak & George M. Cohen, "In Hell There Will Be Lawyers Without Clients or Law," in *Ethics in Practice* 177–206 (Deborah L. Rhode, ed. 2000).

168. Joe Stephens, "Coupons Create Cash for Lawyers," *Washington Post*, November 14, 1999, at A1, A20 (quoting Daniel Edelman).

deterrence of wrongful conduct. In approving one such settlement, a federal court noted, "In spite of the small monetary return to the class, the court does not find the case frivolous or merely a fee generating tool for class counsel. Through the accumulation of small claims, class actions can effect reform of improper practices and thereby benefit consumers."[169] How convincing is this argument? How should courts and bar ethical codes balance the competing concerns?

I.   Conflicts of Interest in Context

The eighteenth century philosopher Helvétius wrote: "[A]s the physical world is ruled by the laws of movement so is the moral universe ruled by laws of interest."[170] Since our interests include concerns about other people as well as ourselves, Helvétius was certainly right. Small wonder, then, that the possibilities for conflicting interests in legal practices are almost without limits. A wide range of concerns may deflect a lawyer's attention from single-minded loyalty to the client. The following overview summarize some of the conflicts that arise in particular factual settings.

BUSINESS TRANSACTIONS BETWEEN ATTORNEYS AND CLIENTS

PROBLEM 12

You are a lawyer in a firm that specializes in representing high-technology startups. A group of scientists and genetic engineers seeks your assistance in launching a biotechnology firm. They ask you to accept shares in the company in lieu of your fee. Their expectation is that once they make an initial public offering, the stock will become highly profitable and share prices will rise dramatically.

a) Is this arrangement appropriate under the Model Rules? Under what circumstances could this compensation scheme compromise your independent judgment?

b) Assume that you agree to the arrangement. How do you determine the fair market value of the shares in order to comply with Model Rule 1.5's requirement that fees be "reasonable"?

c) After the company is launched, the biotechnology partners invite you to leave your law firm and become general counsel. You accept the offer. Some years later, after you have become a member of the board of directors and a large shareholder, the company becomes the target of a hostile takeover. A lucrative tender offer is likely to make you rich by boosting the value of your shares; a successful takeover could also deprive you of your job. In either case, are you capable of rendering independent legal judgment to the company? What should you do?

169. Williams v. General Electric Capital Auto Lease, 1995 WL 765266.

170. Claude–Adrien Helvétius, *De L'Esprit* (1758), *quoted in* Albert O. Hirschman, *The Passions and the Interests: Political Arguments for Capitalism Before Its Triumph* 43 (1977).

d) Assume that during the course of the takeover battle, the directors vote to set up "golden parachutes" for themselves and top management. These lucrative severance packages will become available if management changes hands. In one sense, such arrangements serve the corporation's interest because they reduce financial incentives that might bias the judgment of its decision-makers. In another sense, these provisions look like crass self-dealing. How should you proceed? Can you draft a golden parachute for yourself?[171]

References:

Model Rules 1.5, 1.8(c).

NOTES: BUSINESS TRANSACTIONS BETWEEN ATTORNEYS AND CLIENTS

Model Rule 1.8(a) requires that business transactions be "fair and reasonable to the client" and be "fully disclosed and transmitted in writing in a manner that can be reasonably understood by the client." A revision to the Rule based on the Ethics 2000 Commission recommendations also requires lawyers to advise clients in writing of the desirability of seeking independent advice and to provide reasonable opportunities for clients to obtain such advice before they consent in writing to the transaction. Model Rule 1.7(a)(2) also provides that a lawyer shall not represent a client if "there is a significant risk that the representation of one or more clients will be materially limited by . . . a personal interest of the lawyer," unless the client gives written informed consent and "the lawyer reasonably believes that the lawyer will be able to provide competent and diligent representation. . . ." Do Rules 1.7 and 1.8 appropriately assume that the clients can recognize a conflict when they see it, and do not need protection against arrangements that might compromise the lawyer's independent judgment?

During the boom in internet and other high-technology companies in the late 1990s, many prominent law firms pioneered fee arrangements in which cash-strapped entrepreneurs compensated lawyers with shares or investments in their start-up companies. This practice has proven controversial within the bar, both because it threatens to compromise lawyers' independent judgment and because, when some high-tech bubbles expand, lawyers can make fortunes, raising questions about whether their fees are excessive.[172]

---

171. Thomas D. Terry, American Law Institute—American Bar Association Continuing Legal Education, Executive Compensation: Strategy, Design, and Implementation: Golden Parachute Payments, June 8–9, 2000, at 117–118, 136–138.

172. See Passante v. McWilliams, 62 Cal.Rptr.2d 298 (App. Ct. 1997) (invalidating a fee contract where lawyers' 3 percent share in company stock came to be worth $33 million, not because the fee was excessive but because the lawyer failed to comply with informed consent rules). See Debra Baker, "Who Wants to Be a Millionaire?" ABA J, February 2000, at 36; John S. Dzienkowski and Robert J. Peroni, "The Decline in Lawyer Independence: Lawyer Equity Investments in Clients," 81 Tex. L. Rev. 405 (2002).

ABA Formal Opinion 00–418 (2000) concluded that compensation in the form of client shares need not violate either Model Rule 1.8(a) or 1.5. According to the Opinion, "when assessing the reasonableness of a contingent fee, only the circumstances reasonably ascertainable at the time of the transaction should be considered." The opinion does not, however, elaborate on what "reasonably ascertainable" means. According to New York City's Committee on Professional Ethics, "A lawyer accepting payment in the form of client securities should seriously consider engaging an investment professional to advise as to the value of the securities as given." Formal Opinion 2000–3. Should this be a requirement in such arrangements? What other considerations should guide courts, clients, and bar ethical decisions?[173]

The ABA Opinion also directed lawyers to advise clients that events might arise after acquisition of stock ownership that would create conflicts between the lawyer's personal financial interests and the duty of independent judgment. Lawyers whose objectivity might reasonably be questioned would need to withdraw or to obtain consent to continued representation. Could such problems be mitigated by pooling arrangements in which firms that accept fees in the form of equity hold the securities in a joint fund, in which all firm lawyers may invest? Such arrangements may reduce an individual lawyer's direct interest in the value of any particular corporate holding. Would you advise your firm to establish such arrangements, or would you follow the policy of some Wall Street firms and bar direct investment in clients?

NOTES: MEDIA CONTRACTS

A business conflict of a different sort arises when a lawyer agrees to represent a litigant in a sensational case in return for media rights to the story. In many cases, this is the only way that the client can afford the services of a highly qualified lawyer. Yet Model Rule 1.8(d) forbids lawyers from negotiating or entering into a contract before the end of representation giving the lawyer media or literary rights to an account based in substantial part on information related to the representation. What possible conflicts might arise? Are they severe enough to warrant a *per se* rule forbidding such arrangements? Can clients anticipate at the outset of representation what impact a "tell all" media arrangement might have on lawyers' tactical choices or on their own lives following litigation? See *Restatement (Third) of the Law Governing Lawyers* § 48.

In a landmark decision, *Maxwell v. Superior Court*, 639 P.2d 248 (Cal.1982), the California Supreme Court held that a criminal defendant has a due process right to promise his counsel media rights, provided that he knowingly waives the possible conflicts of interest. Is that approach preferable to the *per se* prohibition in the Code and Model Rules? Can the

173. *See* Brian J. Redding, "Investing In or Doing Business With Clients: Some Thoughts on Lawyer Liability and Legal Ethics Issues," *Professional Lawyer* 113 (2000).

current prohibition fully protect clients from lawyers whose judgments are made with an eye to their media value?

Do similar concerns arise with prosecutors? Should they be subject to any restrictions on sales of media rights once a case has ended? See N.Y. Opinion 606 (1990) (upholding rights). Do the profession and the public also have an interest in mitigating the effects of lawyers' exploitation of celebrity trials or of confidential information even where clients have consented? If so, how should that interest be protected?

NOTES: THE ADVOCATE–WITNESS RULE

Model Rule 3.7 generally forbids lawyers from representing a client in litigation if they know or it is obvious that they should be called as witnesses. This "advocate-witness rule" includes several common-sense exceptions. The most significant is that disqualification will not be required if it "would work substantial hardship on the client." What hardships should this exception encompass? In a typical case, a lawyer representing a long-standing client in business matters negotiates a contract that subsequently becomes a subject of litigation. The client may greatly desire the lawyer's services as trial counsel, because their extended relationship gives the lawyer detailed knowledge of the client's affairs. Yet a strict application of the advocate-witness rule would prevent the lawyer from assuming that role because of the likelihood that he will have to testify about the negotiation.[174]

The most often-stated rationale for this rule—that the role of witness and the role of advocate are inconsistent—seems to beg the question. What, exactly, makes them inconsistent and why is a prohibition rather than informed consent the appropriate response? One justification for the current rules focuses on the client. The underlying assumption is that advocates will have diminished credibility as witnesses. According to EC 5–9, combining roles places the lawyer "in the unseemly and ineffective position of arguing his own credibility." But if the primary purpose of the advocate-witness rule is to protect clients, should they have the option to waive that protection through informed consent?

Many jurisdictions' unwillingness to abide by clients' preferences suggests a different justification for the rule: it protects adversaries and enhances public confidence in the justice system. According to this line of argument, the advocate-witness may be *too* credible, either because of lawyers' special prestige in courtroom settings, or because adversaries will hesitate to subject a fellow-lawyer to withering cross-examination out of professional courtesy. Do you find either argument plausible? Another

---

174. Comden v. Superior Court, 576 P.2d 971 (Cal.1978), *cert. denied*, 439 U.S. 981 (1978). Following the *Comden* case, which barred attorneys from serving as both advocates and witnesses in the same matter, California amended its ethical rules to permit client consent to such representation. Some courts have permitted clients to consent. See Nolte v. Pearson, 133 F.R.D. 585 (D.Neb. 1990). Others have disqualified the lawyer even when the defendant is willing to waive the testimony. Gonzalez v. State, 117 S.W.3d 831 (Tex.Crim.App.2003).

concern is that combining roles threatens the fact or appearance of justice. Lawyers may be tempted to distort the truth in their testimony, the public may suspect such distortions, or jurors may be confused about whether particular statements by lawyers reflect fact or advocacy.[175] How significant are these concerns? Are the pressures on lawyer advocates to skew their testimony much greater than the pressures lawyer witnesses would feel in order to assist a former (and possibly future) client even if they were not serving in an advocacy role?

The Model Rules do not require vicarious disqualification except in circumstances creating other conflicts under Model Rules 1.7 or 1.9. Which approach best serves the purposes of the advocate-witness rule?

NOTES: CONFLICTS OF INTEREST INVOLVING PROSPECTIVE CLIENTS

The 2002 revisions of the Model Rules added a new Rule 1.18, governing prospective clients. The rule guarantees confidentiality to information given by a prospective client; furthermore, it prohibits lawyers from representing clients against prospective clients "in the same or a substantially related matter if the lawyer received information from the prospective client that could be significantly harmful to that person in the matter...." Model Rule 1.18(c). Furthermore, any such disqualification will be imputed to other lawyers in the firm. Although the rule is new, it seems to codify longstanding practice. As one lawyer explained, in initial interviews "you have to cut people off: 'Stop! Don't tell me anything. Let's not get into the facts right now. Give me names and nothing more.' "[176] Another lawyer confirms that "we have ... [a] process to try to prevent learning too much information right off the bat until we found out whether there's a conflict involved."[177]

NOTES: CONFLICTS BASED ON PERSONAL AND FAMILY RELATIONSHIPS

The conflicts of interest arising from lawyers' personal and family relationships are by no means recent phenomena, but changes in the demographics of the profession have given such conflicts a greater dimension. Approximately half of new entrants to the bar are women, half of female practitioners are married to attorneys, and many lawyers have other close relationships with lawyers.

Until the 1980s, little attention focused on conflicts created by family or personal relationships. Early opinions addressing the issue generally

---

175. Wolfram, *supra* note 45, at 378–79 (1986); *See* United States v. Johnston, 690 F.2d 638 (7th Cir.1982) (holding advocate-witness rule applicable to prosecutors).

176. Quoted in Shapiro, *supra* note 46, at 283.

177. *Id.*, at 408; Non–Punitive Segregation Inmates v. Kelly, 589 F.Supp. 1330, 1339 (E.D.Pa. 1984), *aff'd*, 845 F.2d 1014 (3d Cir. 1988).

held that husbands and wives could not represent opposing interests and that vicarious disqualification was appropriate for a firm if the spouse of one of its lawyers had personally assisted a matter adverse to the firm's client. By contrast, other family relationships, such as those between siblings or parents and children, were not typically grounds for disqualification unless some closer financial connection tied their interests together.[178] Underlying these different ethical rules were certain obvious differences. The degree of intimacy and pooling of assets common in most marriages or domestic partnerships is uncommon in other family relationships. Yet as has become increasingly apparent, rigid conflicts rules have a severe effect on career opportunities, particularly those of women. Prohibitions that turn a spouse into a "Typhoid Mary" would not only be unfair to lawyers and their potential clients, but would also compromise the profession's commitment to equal opportunity.[179] Married lawyers in relatively small communities or practice specialties would face recurring conflicts, and this would create pressure for one spouse (usually the younger or lower-earning wife) to change employment.

In recognition of this fact, Formal Opinion 340 of the American Bar Association's Committee on Ethics established the foundations for a new approach. While recognizing that the unique nature of the marital relationship might require special caution, the opinion declined to subject married lawyers to special rules. Under the committee's analysis, it is not necessarily improper for husbands and wives to represent differing interests in a legal matter, or for organizations employing married lawyers to take opposing positions. Rather, the potential application of disciplinary rules should be evaluated in light of the particular facts of each case. As in other contexts, lawyers should decline employment in a matter where their personal or financial interests might reasonably affect judgment and loyalty to a client.

Such considerations also prompted the American Bar Association to include a more permissive approach to spousal conflicts in drafting its Model Rules of Professional Conduct. Until revision in 2002, Model Rule 1.8(i) provided that: "A lawyer related to another lawyer as parent, child, sibling or spouse shall not represent a client in a representation directly adverse to a person who the lawyer knows is represented by the other lawyer except upon consent by the client after consultation regarding the relationship." In 2002, the ABA deleted this rule, on the theory that familial conflicts are simply one species of concurrent conflicts based on a lawyer's personal interest, and these conflicts are already regulated by Rule 1.7. Comment [11] to Rule 1.7 asserts that lawyers "ordinarily may not represent a client in a matter where [another lawyer in the lawyer's immediate family] is representing another party, unless each client gives informed consent." Although some states still prohibit lawyers from directly opposing their spouse in a legal matter, the weight of authority follows

---

178. Wolfram, *supra* note 45, at 407.

179. *Id.*, at 408; Non–Punitive Segregation Inmates v. Kelly, 589 F.Supp. 1330, 1339 (E.D.Pa.1984), *aff'd,* 845 F.2d 1014 (3d Cir. 1988).

Model Rule 1.7. The Model Rules also decline to require disqualification of other lawyers in a firm where a conflict arises from a personal or family relationship. See Model Rule 1.7, Comment [11] and Rule 1.10.

Some bar ethics rules and committees have held that lawyers representing adverse parties who are not married but who are living together or are having an intimate relationship must also seek client consent. See Cal. Rules of Professional Conduct, Rule 3.320; Michigan Op. 123 (1989). Should the Model Rules include such a provision? Would it be unduly intrusive for couples in same-sex relationships?

PROBLEM 13

Lawyer A is a 30–year–old associate in a large law firm, working on intellectual property issues. One of the firm's long-term clients is Consolidated Corporation. A frequently works on teams representing Consolidated, which requires frequent collaboration with in-house lawyers. For several months, A works side-by-side with B, a young Consolidated attorney. B occasionally directs A concerning the company's legal matters. The two become attracted and begin a sexual relationship. Their state has recently adopted Model Rule 1.8(j), forbidding lawyer-client sexual relationships except those that pre-exist the legal representation. Besides their mutual attraction, A and B share libertarian political convictions, and both of them are outraged at the bar's efforts to ban consensual sexual relationships. They decide to bring a test case by reporting themselves to bar counsel. Their local bar counsel harbors his own doubts about the legality of enforcing Rule 1.8(j) against lawyers in A and B's circumstances, and decides to proceed with the test case.

A and B are represented by a well-known public interest law firm. Their argument relies on the Supreme Court's 2003 decision in *Lawrence v. Texas*, invalidating a criminal sodomy statute directed against homosexuality. They argue that the same considerations should invalidate Rule 1.8(j), regardless of whether the relationship is homosexual or heterosexual. In support of this argument, they point to two passages in *Lawrence*:

First, according to the Court, sexual relations, " 'involving the most intimate and personal choices a person may make in a lifetime, choices central to personal dignity and autonomy, are central to the liberty protected by the Fourteenth Amendment. . . .' Persons in a homosexual relationship may seek autonomy for these purposes, just as heterosexual persons do." *Lawrence v. Texas*, 539 U.S. 558, 574 (2003). The Court also stated:

> The present case does not involve minors. It does not involve persons who might be injured or coerced or who are situated in relationships where consent might not easily be refused. It does not involve public conduct or prostitution. . . . The case does involve two adults who, with full and mutual consent from each other, engaged in sexual practices common to a homosexual lifestyle. The petitioners are entitled to respect for their private lives. The . . . statute furthers no state

interest which can justify its intrusion into the personal and private life of the individual.

Lawrence, 539 U.S., at 578.

The bar's response to A and B's argument is straightforward. First, disciplinary rules are not criminal statutes, but protections for the public. Second, there is a legitimate state interest in barring sexual relationships between lawyers and clients because such relationships may often interfere with the lawyer's independent professional judgment. Third, the rule addresses a genuine problem: the potential for sexual exploitation of emotionally vulnerable clients by their lawyers, particularly in matrimonial contexts.

Understandably, the case attracts substantial public attention. In a press conference, A points out that, "When you're billing 2,000 hours a year, you don't have a lot of time to meet people outside of work. Under this rule, there wouldn't be much of a dating scene for law firm associates. When I took my bar oath, no-one ever told me it would be an oath of celibacy."

How should the case be decided?

NOTES AND QUESTIONS: ATTORNEY–CLIENT SEXUAL RELATIONS

Lawyers' sexual exploitation of clients constitutes what commentator have called "the profession's dirty little secret."[180] The ABA, in the only Formal Opinion on the subject, identified several practice areas where the vulnerability of the client raises substantial danger of coercive sexual relations or impaired professional judgment.

An individual client, in particular, is likely to have retained a lawyer at a time of crisis. The divorce client's marriage is disintegrating. The criminal client may have just been arrested and could be facing the possibility of jail. The probate client is dealing with the loss of a loved one. The immigration client may be in fear of deportation. Other clients may be trying to save a business or salvage a reputation.[181]

In some reported cases, attorneys have threatened to withhold legal services from clients (who could not readily change counsel) unless the clients acceded to the lawyers' sexual advances.[182] In other cases, attorneys have offered to reduce their legal fees in exchange for sexual favors.[183] That such

---

180. William K. Shirey, "Note: Dealing With the Profession's Dirty Little Secret: A Proposal for Regulating Attorney–Client Sexual Relations," 13 *Geo. J. Leg. Ethics* 131 (1999). *See also* Thomas Lyon, "Sexual Exploitations of Divorce Clients: The Lawyer's Prerogative?" 10 *Harv. Women's L.J.* 159 (1987). For a critique of rules banning sex between domestic relations lawyers and their clients, *see* Linda Fitts Mischler, "Personal Morals Masquerading as Professional Ethics:

Regulations Banning Sex Between Domestic Relations Attorneys and their Clients," 23 *Harv. Women's L. J.* 1 (2000).

181. ABA Formal Op. 92–364 (1992).

182. McDaniel v. Gile, 281 Cal.Rptr. 242 (Cal. Ct. App. 1991); *In re* Rinella, 677 N.E.2d 909 (Ill. 1997); *In re* Howard, 912 S.W.2d 61 (Mo.1995).

183. People v. Crossman, 850 P.2d 708 (Colo. 1993).

behavior constitutes unethical behavior has never been controversial. As one commentator notes, "It is hard not to be disgusted by lawyers who would turn their own clients into prostitutes."[184] However, even in cases with no explicit quid pro quo, psychologists point to the phenomenon of transference, in which clients in times of stress temporarily transfer feelings of affection to trusted professionals because of the intimacy and dependence inherent in their relationship.[185] Transference, like economic distress, can readily be exploited. Attorneys looking for validation of their own attractiveness often have difficulty seeing a sexual relationship under such circumstances as anything but consensual.

In 1992, California became the first state to establish a rule against attorney-client sexual relationships, and ten years later, the ABA adopted Model Rule 1.8(j). States that have not adopted some version of this rule have often disciplined attorneys under Model Rule 1.7, and have treated coercive sexual relationships as a breach of fiduciary obligations. See *Bezold v. Kentucky Bar Association*, 134 S.W.3d 556, 566 (Ky.2004). Note, however, that Rule 1.8(j) takes a broader approach and imposes a per se prohibition on all sexual relationships. Why? Comment [17] to Model Rule 1.8(j) explains that, in addition to the possible violation of the lawyer's fiduciary obligations to the client, "such a relationship presents a significant danger that, because of the lawyer's emotional involvement, the lawyer will be unable to represent the client without impairment of the exercise of independent professional judgment." The Comment adds that the blurring of the line between personal and professional relationships endangers attorney-client confidences, because it may be difficult to tell whether information has been given in the course of legal representation, as required to establish the attorney-client privilege. More controversially, the Comment asserts that "the client's own emotional involvement renders it unlikely that the client could give adequate informed consent" to combining a sexual with a professional relationship. When the client is an organization, Comment [19] adds that the rule prohibits both inside and outside counsel "from having a sexual relationship with a constituent of the organization who supervises, directs or regularly consults with that lawyer concerning the organization's legal matters." In this context, ABA Formal Opinion 364 has acknowledged that the danger of sexual exploitation is slight. Presumably, then, the rationale for Comment [19] is entirely based on the possible impairment of the lawyer's independent professional judgment. How plausible is this rationale?

Some commentators have criticized Rule 1.8(j) on the grounds that a *per se* ban demeans women clients by assuming their incompetence, and deprives female lawyers of opportunities for relationships that pose little

---

184. Christian F. Southwick, "Ardor and Advocacy: Attorney–Client Sexual Relations and the Regulatory Impulse in Texas and Across the Nation," 44 *S. Tex. L. Rev.* 307, 316 (2002).

185. For a discussion of transference in lawyer-client relationships, *see* Marjorie A. Silver, "Love, Hate, and Other Emotional Interference in the Lawyer/Client Relationship," 6 *Clinical L. Rev.* 259 (1999).

threat of coercion or impaired judgment.[186] Another commentator questions why the Model Rules have a *per se* ban on sexual but not business relationships with clients: "none of the principles of behavioral economics would suggest that lawyers are more inclined to put their interests ahead of their clients in the personal rather than the financial realm."[187] Do you agree? What approach would you support?

186. For criticism of ethics rules and theories of transference that presume female clients to be incapable of informed consent to sexual relations, *see* Southwick, *supra* note 184, at 344–51. For an alternative view, see Malinda L. Seymore, "Attorney–Client Sex: A Feminist Critique of the Absence of Regulation," 15 *Yale J. L. & Feminism* 175 (2003).

187. Gross, *supra* note 68, at 134.

CHAPTER XI

LAWYER–CLIENT DECISION MAKING

A. THE DEFINITION OF THE PROBLEM

INTRODUCTION

The preceding chapter focused on contexts in which the interests of attorneys, ideological as well as financial, clash with those of clients. The present chapter concerns conflicts that arise when lawyers are altruistic, intent on pursuing the best interests of their clients, but are convinced that clients misunderstand their own interests. In such cases, lawyers may be tempted to act paternalistically, by interfering with the client's choices for the client's own good.

Such ethical dilemmas are longstanding, but during the last quarter century they have come into sharper focus. Part of the reason involves the rise of public interest and legal services practice. Many lawyers in such practice settings have found themselves talking across cultural divides; differences in social, economic, racial, and ethnic backgrounds have sometimes made it hard to understand the full range of concerns and needs of clients. Just as importantly, clients have often viewed their problems in terms that are not readily translatable into legal categories or resolvable by the legal system. When lawyers have reformulated the goals of representation in ways that the lawyers knew how to address, it has been hard for clients to keep control over the terms of representation.

Public interest, legal services, and criminal defense attorneys have been sensitive to such problems, because many of them are committed as a matter of principle to client empowerment and "democracy from the bottom up." However, the issues of paternalism are by no means limited to these contexts. Attorneys who represent clients with impaired capacity have long struggled with these concerns. Juveniles, mental health patients, or individuals going through a traumatic life event may have difficulty evaluating their long-term interests. In other situations, individuals with little experience or interest in legal matters will often be tempted to leave crucial decisions up to their attorneys. The result may sometimes to be the clients' practical advantage, but the price will be losing control over their own affairs. As John Dewey and James H. Tufts wrote in 1932, there is a danger in the actions "of reformers and philanthropists when they try to do good to others in ways which leave passive those to be benefitted. There is a moral tragedy inherent in efforts to further the common good which prevent the result from being either good or common—not good, because it is at the expense of the active growth of those to be helped, and not common because these have no share in bringing the result about."[1]

The problem of attorneys defining client goals—or rather, attorneys assuming that client goals must be redefined to fit the limitations of the law or of their own capabilities and resources—is only one part of the paternalism problem. Other difficulties arise when lawyers consciously or unconsciously override or manipulate clients for "the client's own good." Consider the rather extreme example of Gary Gilmore, a convicted murderer, sentenced to death, who asked his lawyers to drop all appeals because he wanted to be executed:

Gilmore said, "Now, don't I have the right to die?" ...

Gary told [his lawyers] of his belief that he had been executed once before, in eighteenth-century England. He said, "I feel like I've been here before. There is some crime from my past." He got quiet, and said, "I feel I have to atone for the thing I did then." Esplin couldn't help thinking that this stuff about eighteenth-century England would sure have made a difference with the psychiatrists if they had heard it.

Gilmore now began to say that his life wouldn't end with this life. He would still be in existence after he was dead. It all seemed part of a logical discussion. Esplin finally said, "Gary, we can see your point of view, but we still feel duty bound to go ahead on that appeal."

When Gary said again, "What can I do about it?" Snyder answered, "Well, I don't know."

Gary then said, "Can I fire you?"

Esplin said, "Gary, we'll make the judge aware that you want to can us, but we're going to file anyway." ...

On the 3rd of November, Esplin got a letter from Gary. It read: *"Mike, butt out. Quit fucking around with my life. You're fired."* ...

Despite being dismissed, the two defense attorneys later Wednesday filed a notice of appeal—in their names. . . .

They said it was "in the best interest" of the defendant.[2]

Esplin and Snyder found Gilmore's belief in reincarnation irrational. But millions of people around the globe hold such beliefs. This case, like some of those addressed in Chapter X on public interest representation,

---

1. John Dewey & James H. Tufts, *Ethics* 385 (rev.ed. 1986).

2. Norman Mailer, *The Executioner's Song* 482, 505–06 (1979). See State v. Berry, 706 N.E.2d 1273 (Ohio 1999) (denying defender's motion to review competency of death-row inmate who desires to abandon all appeals). For cases and lawyers' motivations, see Anthony V. Alfieri, "Mitigation, Mercy, and Delay: The Moral Politics of Death Penalty Abolitionists," 31 *Harv. C.R.C.L.L. Rev.*

325 (1996); Richard W. Garnett, "Sectarian Reflections on Lawyers' Ethics and Death Row Volunteers," 77 *Notre Dame L. Rev.* 795, 801 (2002). For discussion of the reasons for defendants' decisions, including prison conditions, mental health impairments, and the anxieties of a prolonged appellate process, see *id.*, at 803, 816, and Michael Mello, "A Letter on a Lawyer's Life of Death," 38 *S. Tex. L. Rev.* 121, 166 (1997).

raise questions about when lawyers may justifiably impose their own views about the clients best interest and the objectives of representation.

PROBLEM 1

a) You represent an elderly client of limited means. He has been pressured by his former wife into signing a promissory note secured by his house in order to help his stepson start a new business. Fraudulent representations were made about the state of the company's finances and it has now gone bankrupt. The note has come due and the house will be subject to foreclosure unless the client contests the transaction. He is unwilling to do so, both because it would trigger an acrimonious dispute and because everyone would learn that he had allowed himself to be cheated. He is, however, concerned about losing his home. Are you free to disregard your client's short-term instruction not to file suit in favor of his long-term value of keeping his house?[3]

Suppose that your client remains adamant about not contesting the foreclosure. Then suddenly one afternoon, he calls to announce that he has changed his mind because spirits in the house have begun talking to him at night and asking him not to leave the house. In other respects, your client appears quite functional. How do you proceed?

b) Your client, a wealthy newspaper owner, is suffering from a terminal illness and is deeply depressed. He suddenly tells you that he wishes to redraft his will to cut out his wife of many years. He does not wish to discuss the reasons, apart from expressing general bitterness concerning their current relationship. Would it be permissible, or appropriate, to question this decision and delay carrying out your client's instructions to provide time for further consideration? Suppose that you have been a friend and advisor to the wife in the past, although you have not had recent contact. What if your client dies without changing his mind before the new will is executed?[4]

c) Your client was involved in a car accident in which one of his close college friends was killed. He is charged with driving while intoxicated and vehicular homicide, but some of the circumstances are unclear and you believe that if he contests the charges, the prosecutor might ultimately accept a plea to reckless operation of a vehicle. The client, however, insists that he should plead guilty to homicide, and in an emotional scene tells you that he cannot live with himself unless he publicly acknowledges his guilt.

---

3. Peter Margulies, "Access, Connection, and Voice: A Contextual Approach to Representing Senior Citizens of Questionable Capacity," 62 *Fordham L.Rev.* 1073, 1084–85 (1994). For the influence of stress on cognitive capacity, *see* Robert S. Stawski, Martin J. Sliwinski, & Soshua M. Smth, "Stress–Related Cognitive Interference Predicts Cognitive Function in Old Age," 21 *Psych. & Aging* 535 (2006).

4. This hypothetical is modeled on Edward Bennett Williams' refusal to immediately redraft the will of Philip Graham, owner of the *Washington Post.* Graham died before the will was changed. His wife Katherine inherited the paper and gave its legal business to Williams. *See* Evan Thomas, *The Man to See: Edward Bennett Williams: Ultimate Insider, Legendary Trial Lawyer* 178–80 (1991); Peter Margulies, *supra* note 3, at 1085–86.

You do not think he has a realistic understanding of prison conditions or the effect of such a conviction on his long term career options. Should you enlist the client's family and friends in trying to convince him not to plead guilty unless the prosecutor offers to reduce the charges? Would it be preferable simply to provide your best assessment of the likely consequences? Would you respond differently if the crime carried the death penalty and the client wants to accept that punishment?

Alternatively, suppose that the facts are strongly against your client, but that the prosecutor is willing to offer a plea to reckless operation of a vehicle. You advise your client that he would be extremely foolish not to take the plea because if, as is likely, he is convicted on the greater charge, the judge would doubtless impose the maximum penalty. Your client still wants to take his chances. If neither you nor his family can change his mind, can you threaten to withdraw?[5]

d) The Long Black Veil case:

The judge said, "Son, what is your alibi?

"If you were somewhere else then you won't have to die."

I spoke not a word, though it meant my life.

For I had been in the arms of my best friend's wife.[6]

If your client is unwilling to invoke the alibi defense, are there considerations that might cause you to override his preferences? He is prepared to die rather than expose the wife's infidelity and his own betrayal of his best friend. As his lawyer, do you argue with him about his priorities? Consider analogous cases in which women charged with low-level drug offenses carrying long sentences refuse favorable plea bargains that would require them to give evidence against abusive boyfriends. Consider as well the following example:

e) You are representing a refugee from a brutal military dictatorship in a deportation hearing. The immigration authorities found his story of political persecution not credible and denied his application for political asylum. In order to document his story, you wish to contact a former colleague, who remains in their native country. Your client, however, resists that strategy for fear of jeopardizing her safety. You have contacts with human rights groups who believe they can get a message through to her safely and that can smuggle out the documents necessary to prove your client's story. He is unwilling to take the risk, even though obtaining these documents offers his only chance of victory in the asylum hearing. May you contact her despite his unwillingness if you believe it will save his life?

References:

Model Rules 1.2(a), 1.14.

5. See Steven Zeidman, "To Plead or Not to Plead: Effective Assistance and Client–Centered Counseling," 39 *B.C. L. Rev.* 841 (1998).

6. M.J. Wilkin & D. Dill, "Long Black Veil" (song).

Richard Wasserstrom, "Lawyers as Professionals: Some Moral Issues"

5 Human Rights 1, 15–24 (1975).

One . . . pervasive, and I think necessary, feature of the relationship between any professional and the client or patient is that it is in some sense a relationship of inequality. This relationship of inequality is intrinsic to the existence of professionalism. For the professional is, in some respects at least, always in a position of dominance vis-à-vis the client, and the client in a position of dependence vis-à-vis the professional. To be sure, the client can often decide whether or not to enter into a relationship with a professional. And often, too, the client has the power to decide whether to terminate the relationship. But the significant thing I want to focus upon is that while the relationship exists, there are important respects in which the relationship cannot be a relationship between equals and must be one in which it is the professional who is in control. . . .

To begin with, there is the fact that one characteristic of professions is that the professional is the possessor of expert knowledge of a sort not readily or easily attainable by members of the community at large. . . . Moreover, virtually every profession has its own technical language, a private terminology which can only be fully understood by the members of the profession. . . . These circumstances, together with others, produce the added consequence that the client is in a poor position effectively to evaluate how well or badly the professional performs. In the professions, the professional does not look primarily to the client to evaluate the professional's work. . . . In addition, because the matters for which professional assistance is sought usually involve things of great personal concern to the client, it is the received wisdom within the professions that the client lacks the perspective necessary to pursue in a satisfactory way his or her own best interests, and that the client requires a detached, disinterested representative to look after his or her interests. . . .

Finally, as I have indicated, to be a professional is to have been acculturated in a certain way. It is to have satisfactorily passed through a lengthy and allegedly difficult period of study and training. It is to have done something hard. Something that not everyone can do. Almost all professions encourage this way of viewing oneself; as having joined an elect group by virtue of hard work and mastery of the mysteries of the profession. In addition, the society at large treats members of a profession as members of an elite by paying them more than most people for the work they do with their heads rather than their hands, and by according them a substantial amount of social prestige and power by virtue of their membership in a profession. It is hard, I think, if not impossible, for a person to emerge from professional training and participate in a profession without the belief that he or she is a special kind of person, both different from and somewhat better than those nonprofessional members of the social order. It is equally hard for the other members of society not to hold an analogous view of the professionals. And these beliefs surely contribute, too, to the dominant role played by a professional in any professional-client relationship.

[The criticism of professionals I want to consider] might begin by conceding, at least for purposes of argument, that some inequality may be inevitable in any professional-client relationship. It might concede, too, that a measure of this kind of inequality may even on occasion be desirable. But it sees the relationship between the professional and the client as typically flawed in a more fundamental way, as involving far more than the kind of relatively benign inequality delineated above. This criticism focuses upon the fact that the professional often, if not systematically, interacts with the client in both a manipulative and a paternalistic fashion. The point is not that the professional is merely dominant within the relationship. Rather, it is that from the professional's point of view the client is seen and responded to more like an object than a human being, and more like a child than an adult. . . .

Desirable change could be brought about in part by a sustained effort to simplify legal language and to make the legal processes less mysterious and more directly available to lay persons. The way the law works now, it is very hard for lay persons either to understand it or to evaluate or solve legal problems more on their own. But it is not at all clear that substantial revisions could not occur along these lines. Divorce, probate, and personal injury are only three fairly obvious areas where the lawyers' economic self-interest says a good deal more about resistance to change and simplification than does a consideration on the merits.

The more fundamental changes, though, would, I think, have to await an explicit effort to alter the ways in which lawyers are educated and acculturated to view themselves, their clients, and the relationships that ought to exist between them. It is, I believe, indicative of the state of legal education and of the profession that there has been to date extremely little self-conscious concern even with the possibility that these dimensions of the attorney-client relationship are worth examining—to say nothing of being capable of alteration. That awareness is, surely, the prerequisite to any serious assessment of the moral character of the attorney-client relationship as a relationship among adult human beings.

NOTES

Wasserstrom poses two related problems. First, he argues that the attorney-client relationship is structurally flawed, placing far too much power in the hands of the attorney. In effect, the lawyer rather than the client defines the strategies of representation, which typically leads lawyers to act in a paternalistic fashion toward their clients. Second, he suggests that paternalism is morally wrong. "The professional does not . . . treat the client like a person; the professional does not accord the client the respect that he or she deserves." Who is the client that Wasserstrom envisions? Does the description fit the typical business client or wealthy individual seeking advice on tax or other financial issues? If Wasserstrom's focus is on less sophisticated and powerful clients, is his criticism well taken?

A study by William Felstiner and Austin Sarat of divorce cases documented some of the patterns Wasserstrom described. Many lawyers attempted to "control clients and maintain professional authority" by suggesting that only insiders such as themselves would be able to deal with the "chaotic 'anti-system'" in which the client was embroiled.[7] In some cases, attorneys appeared to find it in their interest to maintain dominance: a dependent client was a more compliant client.

On the other hand, in most private practice power flows in both directions:

> Lawyers, to be sure, exercise considerable leverage over their clients, who need their expertise, and that leverage can be abused. But we must not forget that private practitioners depend wholly on their clients for their livelihood, and this dependence is fundamental in the distribution of power. Lawyers may try to manipulate their clients, but such phenomena are of necessity relatively slight ripples on a vast ocean of lawyers' economic dependence upon their clients.[8]

How might Wasserstrom reply? How would you?

A related issue involves the allocation of decision-making authority between lawyer and client under bar ethical rules. Model Rule 1.2(a) states that a "lawyer shall abide by a client's decisions concerning the objectives of representation ... and shall consult with the client as to the means by which they are to be pursued. A lawyer may take such action on behalf of the client as is impliedly authorized to carry out the representation." The Comment to the Rule explains:

> On occasion, however, a lawyer and a client may disagree about the means to be used to accomplish the client's objectives. Clients normally defer to the special knowledge and skill of their lawyer with respect to the means to be used to accomplish their objectives, particularly with respect to technical, legal and tactical matters. Conversely, lawyers usually defer to the client regarding such questions as the expense to be incurred and concern for third persons who might be adversely affected. Because of the varied nature of the matters about which a lawyer and client might disagree and because the actions in question

---

7. Austin Sarat & William L.F. Felstiner, "Lawyers and Legal Consciousness: Law Talk in the Divorce Lawyer's Office," 98 *Yale L.J.* 1663 (1989).

8. David Luban, "Partisanship, Betrayal and Autonomy in the Lawyer–Client Relationship: A Reply to Stephen Ellmann," 90 *Colum.L.Rev.* 1004, 1036–37 (1990). For discussion of the complexity of power relationships, see William L.F. Felstiner & Austin Sarat, "Enactments of Power: Negotiating Reality and Responsibility in Lawyer–Client Interactions," 77 *Cornell L.Rev.* 1447 (1992).

may implicate the interests of a tribunal or other persons, this Rule does not prescribe how such disagreements are to be resolved.

However, the Comment further notes that if "no mutually acceptable resolution" of the matter is possible, the lawyer may withdraw or the client may discharge the lawyer.[9]

Judicial decisions typically concur with Model Rule 1.2's allocation of authority over tactical choices to lawyers. Even over the client's objections, a lawyer can:

> present or refuse to present certain witnesses, stipulate to the use of testimony from a prior trial, withdraw or refuse to submit a defense as a matter of trial expediency or tactics, agree to proceed without a court reporter, stipulate to certain facts, decline cross-examination, agree to a continuance, . . . waive or insist upon a trial by jury in a civil case, . . . and . . . stipulate to proceed on the basis of pleadings and depositions.[10]

Only when tactical choices unquestionably compromise a substantive right must the lawyer obtain the client's consent. Such situations may include decisions to:

> stipulate to facts that will foreclose an essential defense or stipulate to facts in such a manner as to materially prejudice the client's interest; stipulate to a legal conclusion contrary to the client's rights at law; refuse to assert a statutory right that would constitute a complete defense; stipulate to summary judgment against the client; agree to accept nominal damages only; agree to increase the judgment against the client; waive findings so that no appeal may be taken; grant an extension of time, waive a forfeiture, or otherwise alter the terms of a contract.[11]

However, as Chapter VII noted, lawyers may decide not to take advantage of a scrivener's error without consulting the client even when doing so would materially advance the client's interests.

Jones v. Barnes is a leading case on the allocation of authority over tactical choices.

---

9. The ABA Code vests virtually all authority in the client: Ethical Consideration 7–7 provides: "In certain areas of legal representation not affecting the merits of the cause or substantially prejudicing the rights of a client, a lawyer is entitled to make decisions on his own. But otherwise the authority to make decisions is exclusively that of the client and, if made within the framework of the law, such decisions are binding on his lawyer." Yet this rule raises difficult questions. What counts as "affecting the merits of the cause" or "substantially prejudicing the rights of a client"? Lawyers may define the "cause" narrowly, for example obtaining a favorable legal result in the deportation proceeding in Problem 1(e). From this perspective, tactical choices that improve a client's prospects are up to the lawyer, because they do not affect the merits of the cause. Clients, on the other hand, may define "the cause" broadly—obtaining a favorable result without exposing a former colleague to undue risks. EC 7–7 does, however, include exceptions, as does EC 7–12, which states that a lawyer's responsibilities increase when the client is afflicted with a "mental or physical condition . . . that renders him incapable of making a considered judgment on his own behalf."

10. *ABA/BNA Lawyer's Manual on Professional Conduct* at 31:304 (citations omitted).

11. *Id.* at 31:306.

Jones v. Barnes

Supreme Court of the United States, 1983.
463 U.S. 745, 750–55, 758–64.

[Barnes was convicted in state court of robbery and assault. He instructed Melinger, his assigned counsel, to raise several issues on appeal. Though the issues were nonfrivolous, Melinger omitted several that he believed would not succeed. Barnes submitted a pro se brief presenting the issues that Melinger omitted, but his conviction was affirmed. Based on Melinger's failure to raise the issues that Barnes had requested, Barnes filed for federal habeas relief, which was granted by the Second Circuit Court of Appeals, 665 F.2d 427 (2d Cir.1981). The Supreme Court reversed.]

■ [CHIEF JUSTICE BURGER] delivered the opinion of the Court. . . .

In announcing a new *per se* rule that appellate counsel must raise every nonfrivolous issue requested by the client, the Court of Appeals relied primarily upon *Anders v. California.* There is, of course, no constitutional right to an appeal, but in *Griffin v. Illinois,* 351 U.S. 12, 18 (1956), and *Douglas v. California,* 372 U.S. 353 (1963), the Court held that if an appeal is open to those who can pay for it, an appeal must be provided for an indigent. It is also recognized that the accused has the ultimate authority to make certain fundamental decisions regarding the case, as to whether to plead guilty, waive a jury, testify in his or her own behalf, or take an appeal. In addition, we have held that, with some limitations, a defendant may elect to act as his or her own advocate. Neither *Anders* nor any other decision of this Court suggests, however, that the indigent defendant has a constitutional right to compel appointed counsel to press nonfrivolous points requested by the client, if counsel, as a matter of professional judgment, decides not to present those points.

This Court, in holding that a state must provide counsel for an indigent appellant on his first appeal as of right, recognized the superior ability of trained counsel in the "examination into the record, research of the law, and marshaling of arguments on [the appellant's] behalf," *Douglas v. California.* Yet by promulgating a *per se* rule that the client, not the professional advocate, must be allowed to decide what issues are to be pressed, the Court of Appeals seriously undermines the ability of counsel to present the client's case in accord with counsel's professional evaluation.

Experienced advocates since time beyond memory have emphasized the importance of winnowing out weaker arguments on appeal and focusing on one central issue if possible, or at most on a few key issues. Justice Jackson, after observing appellate advocates for many years, stated:

> One of the first tests of a discriminating advocate is to select the question, or questions, that he will present orally. Legal contentions, like the currency, depreciate through over-issue. The mind of an appellate judge is habitually receptive to the suggestion that a lower court committed an error. But receptiveness declines as the number of assigned errors increases. Multiplicity hints at lack of confidence in any one. . . . "[E]xperience on the bench convinces me that multiplying

assignments of error will dilute and weaken a good case and will not save a bad one." . . .

There can hardly be any question about the importance of having the appellate advocate examine the record with a view to selecting the most promising issues for review. This has assumed a greater importance in an era when oral argument is strictly limited in most courts—often to as little as 15 minutes—and when page limits on briefs are widely imposed. Even in a court that imposes no time or page limits, however, the new *per se* rule laid down by the Court of Appeals is contrary to all experience and logic. A brief that raises every colorable issue runs the risk of burying good arguments—those that, in the words of the great advocate John W. Davis, "go for the jugular," in a verbal mound made up of strong and weak contentions.

This Court's decision in *Anders,* far from giving support to the new *per se* rule announced by the Court of Appeals, is to the contrary. *Anders* recognized that the role of the advocate "requires that he support his client's appeal to the best of his ability." Here the appointed counsel did just that. For judges to second-guess reasonable professional judgments and impose on appointed counsel a duty to raise every "colorable" claim suggested by a client would disserve the very goal of vigorous and effective advocacy that underlies *Anders.* Nothing in the Constitution or our interpretation of that document requires such a standard. The judgment of the Court of Appeals is accordingly

Reversed.

■ [Justice Brennan] with whom [Justice Marshall] joins, dissenting. . . .

What is at issue here is the relationship between lawyer and client— who has ultimate authority to decide which nonfrivolous issues should be presented on appeal? I believe the right to "the assistance of counsel" carries with it a right, personal to the defendant, to make that decision, against the advice of counsel if he chooses.

If all the Sixth Amendment protected was the State's interest in substantial justice, it would not include such a right. However, in *Faretta v. California,* 422 U.S. 806 (1975), we decisively rejected that view of the Constitution. . . .

Faretta establishes that the right to counsel is more than a right to have one's case presented competently and effectively. It is predicated on the view that the function of counsel under the Sixth Amendment is to protect the dignity and autonomy of a person on trial by *assisting* him in making choices that are his to make, not to make choices for him, although counsel may be better able to decide which tactics will be most effective for the defendant. *Anders v. California* also reflects that view. Even when appointed counsel believes an appeal has no merit, he must furnish his client a brief covering all arguable grounds for appeal so that the client may "raise any points that he chooses."

The right to counsel as *Faretta* and *Anders* conceive it is not an all-or-nothing right, under which a defendant must choose between forgoing the assistance of counsel altogether or relinquishing control over every aspect of his case beyond its most basic structure (*i.e.,* how to plead, whether to present a defense, whether to appeal). A defendant's interest in his case clearly extends to other matters. Absent exceptional circumstances, he is bound by the tactics used by his counsel at trial and on appeal. He may want to press the argument that he is innocent, even if other stratagems are more likely to result in the dismissal of charges or in a reduction of punishment. He may want to insist on certain arguments for political reasons. He may want to protect third parties. This is just as true on appeal as at trial, and the proper role of counsel is to *assist* him in these efforts, insofar as that is possible consistent with the lawyer's conscience, the law, and his duties to the court.

I find further support for my position in the legal profession's own conception of its proper role. The American Bar Association has taken the position that

> when, in the estimate of counsel, the decision of the client to take an appeal, *or the client's decision to press a particular contention on appeal,* is incorrect[, c]ounsel has the professional duty to give to the client fully and forcefully an opinion concerning the case and its probable outcome. *Counsel's role however, is to advise. The decision is made by the client.* ABA Standards for Criminal Justice, Criminal Appeals, Standard 21–3.2, Comment, at 21–42 (2nd ed., 1980) (emphasis added).

The Court disregards this clear statement of how the profession defines the "assistance of counsel" at the appellate stage of a criminal defense by referring to standards governing the allocation of authority between attorney and client at trial. See ABA Standards for Criminal Justice, The Defense Function, Standard 4–5.2 (1980). In the course of a trial, however, decisions must often be made in a matter of hours, if not minutes or seconds. From the standpoint of effective administration of justice, the need to confer decisive authority on the attorney is paramount with regard to the hundreds of decisions that must be made quickly in the course of a trial. Decisions regarding which issues to press on appeal, in contrast, can and should be made more deliberately, in the course of deciding whether to appeal at all.

. . . [T]he Court argues that good appellate advocacy demands selectivity among arguments. That is certainly true—the Court's advice is good. It ought to be taken to heart by every lawyer called upon to argue an appeal in this or any other court, and by his client. It should take little or no persuasion to get a wise client to understand that, if staying out of prison is what he values most, he should encourage his lawyer to raise only his two or three best arguments on appeal, and he should defer to his lawyer's advice as to which are the best arguments. The Constitution, however, does not require clients to be wise, and other policies should be weighed in the balance as well.

It is no secret that indigent clients often mistrust the lawyers appointed to represent them. There are many reasons for this, some perhaps unavoidable even under perfect conditions—differences in education, disposition, and socio-economic class—and some that should (but may not always) be zealously avoided. A lawyer and his client do not always have the same interests. Even with paying clients, a lawyer may have a strong interest in having judges and prosecutors think well of him, and, if he is working for a flat fee—a common arrangement for criminal defense attorneys—or if his fees for court appointments are lower than he would receive for other work, he has an obvious financial incentive to conclude cases on his criminal docket swiftly. Good lawyers undoubtedly recognize these temptations and resist them, and they endeavor to convince their clients that they will. It would be naive, however, to suggest that they always succeed in either task. A constitutional rule that encourages lawyers to disregard their clients' wishes without compelling need can only exacerbate the clients' suspicion of their lawyers. As in *Faretta,* to force a lawyer's *decisions* on a defendant "can only lead him to believe that the law contrives against him." In the end, what the Court hopes to gain in effectiveness of appellate representation by the rule it imposes today may well be lost to decreased effectiveness in other areas of representation....

Finally, today's ruling denigrates the values of individual autonomy and dignity central to many constitutional rights, especially those Fifth and Sixth Amendment rights that come into play in the criminal process. Certainly a person's life changes when he is charged with a crime and brought to trial. He must, if he harbors any hope of success, defend himself on terms—often technical and hard to understand—that are the State's, not his own. As a practical matter, the assistance of counsel is necessary to that defense. Yet, until his conviction becomes final and he has had an opportunity to appeal, any restrictions on individual autonomy and dignity should be limited to the minimum necessary to vindicate the State's interest in a speedy, effective prosecution. The role of the defense lawyer should be above all to function as the instrument and defender of the client's autonomy and dignity in all phases of the criminal process....

The Court subtly but unmistakably adopts a different conception of the defense lawyer's role—he need do nothing beyond what the State, not his client, considers most important. In many ways, having a lawyer becomes one of the many indignities visited upon someone who has the ill fortune to run afoul of the criminal justice system.

I cannot accept the notion that lawyers are one of the punishments a person receives merely for being accused of a crime. Clients, if they wish, are capable of making informed judgments about which issues to appeal, and when they exercise that prerogative their choices should be respected unless they would require lawyers to violate their consciences, the law, or their duties to the court. On the other hand, I would not presume lightly that, in a particular case, a defendant has disregarded his lawyer's obviously sound advice. The Court of Appeals, in reversing the District Court, did not address the factual question whether respondent, having been advised by his lawyer that it would not be wise to appeal on all the issues respondent had suggested, actually insisted in a timely fashion that his lawyer brief the nonfrivolous issues identified by the Court of Appeals. If he did not, or if he was content with filing his *pro se* brief, then there would be no deprivation of the right to the assistance of counsel. I would remand for a hearing on this question.

NOTES AND QUESTIONS

1.   The majority in *Jones* employs reasoning that is overtly paternalistic: it justifies the attorney's authority to override a client's desires for the client's own good. After noting that it is often counterproductive to barrage an appellate court with too many arguments, the majority concludes: "For judges to ... impose on appointed counsel a duty to raise every 'colorable' claim suggested by a client would disserve the very goal of vigorous and effective advocacy...."

a) Does the fact that Barnes submitted a *pro se* brief presenting "his" issues undercut or support the outcome? One might argue that if the appellate court was going to be barraged with the same arguments in any event, then the client had a right to have them presented by his attorney rather than *pro se*. The tactical choice was not whether to inundate the appellate court with arguments; rather, it was whether to inundate the appellate court with arguments presented by Barnes rather than the same arguments presented by Melinger. From this perspective, Barnes had the worst of both worlds: too many arguments and too little expert presentation. Conversely, one might argue that since the issues were presented by Barnes's *pro se* brief, the appellate court was not denied an opportunity to consider them; Melinger's omission was therefore harmless. Which position is most persuasive?

b) Would the *Jones* decision have come out differently if Barnes had not submitted a *pro se* brief? Suppose that the appellate court, in affirming the conviction, had noted in dicta or during oral argument that it was not reaching certain issues because the defendant had not raised them. If these were the very issues that Barnes had wanted Melinger to raise, should it alter the result?

2.   Commentators note that lawyers' counseling falls on a spectrum: neutral information—suggestion—advice—urging.[12] What limited empirical research is available indicates that lawyers vary greatly in terms of where they fall on this spectrum and how much they defer to clients on strategies that could determine outcomes. For example, one study of criminal defense lawyers found that only about a third believed that clients should make all important decisions and that about three quarters thought that counsel should have the final say over whether to waive an affirmative defense. Lawyers divided over whether to obtain client consent before asking for a lesser included offense.[13] Courts have also divided about what constitutes

---

12.   Zeidman, *supra* note 5, at 888.

13.   Rodney J. Uphoff & Peter V. Wood, "The Allocation of Decisionmaking Between Defense Counsel and Criminal Defendant: An Empirical Study of Attorney–Client Decision-making," 47 *Kan. L. Rev.* 1 (1998).

undue neutrality or coercion. Although most judges give considerable deference to a defense attorney's decisions, they are split on some issues, such as whether a lawyer's failure to provide advice about accepting a plea constitutes ineffective assistance of counsel.[14]

Attorneys who fall on the neutrality end of the spectrum see their role as empowering clients and are reluctant to provide guidance that may unduly influence their decisions. As one public defender put it, "the defendant does the time, not me."[15] By contrast, other lawyers argue that such attitudes are likely to result in more defendants doing more time in prison than if attorneys attempted to guide plea bargaining decisions. As these lawyers note, many criminal defendants suffer from mental health impairments, and the stress and time pressures of the process may make rational decision making difficult.[16] The problems are compounded by cognitive biases that encourage individuals to make overly optimistic assessments of their own circumstances and capabilities.[17] Some commentators argue further that withholding advice is itself a form of paternalism, because it assumes that clients are incapable of weighing their attorney's views and then making an autonomous judgment.[18] Where would you put yourself on the counseling spectrum? Would it matter whether the case was civil or criminal or whether you were retained by the client or appointed by the court?

3.   Can attorneys take into account their own credibility in determining whether to advance a weak claim? Criminal defense lawyers routinely face issues about how to spend their "credibility capital" if they appear repeatedly before the same judges or bargain frequently with the same prosecutors.[19]

4.   The dissenters in *Jones v. Barnes* emphasize "the dignity and autonomy of a person on trial," and suggest that these values argue for deferring to a defendant's choices even if they are not ones that experienced counsel would find prudent. How far does this argument extend? Is it consistent with *Martinez v. Court of Appeal*, 528 U.S. 152 (2000), in which the Supreme Court found no constitutional right to self-representation on a direct appeal of a criminal conviction? *Martinez* upheld a decision of the California Court of Appeal requiring a self-taught paralegal to accept a court-appointed lawyer for his appeal, although he had represented himself

---

14. See cases discussed in Zeidman, *supra* note 5, at 891.

15. *Id.*, at 904 (quoting public defender).

16. A majority of prison and jail inmates have mental health problems, and an additional number of clients facing criminal charges end up in state mental institutions. Doris J. James & Lauren E.Glaze, Mental Health Problems of Prison and Jail Inmates, U.S. Department of Justice, Bureau of Justice Statistics, Special Report (December 14, 2006).

17. For impairments, see sources cited in Zeidman, *supra* note 5, at 902. For overoptimism, see sources cited in Jeffrey J. Rachlinski, "The Uncertain Psychological Case for Paternalism," 97 *N.W. L. Rev.* 1165, 1172, 1192 (2003); Richard Birke, "Reconciling Loss Aversion and Guilty Pleas," 1999 *Utah L. Rev.* 205.

18. *Id.*, at 902, 908.

19. Margareth Etienne, "The Ethics of Cause Lawyering: An Empirical Examination of Criminal Defense Lawyers as Cause Lawyers," 95 *J. Crim. L. & Criminology* 1195, 1245 (2005) (quoting unnamed lawyer).

at his jury trial and had wished to do so again on appeal. Do *Martinez* and *Jones v. Barnes* together imply that a lawyer who is forced on an appellant may then decline to brief arguments that the client wants to raise? Or should appellate lawyers who are appointed over defendants' objections give greater deference to their clients than *Jones v. Barnes* requires?

Although the right to self-representation extends only to trial proceedings, that includes the sentencing phase of trial; thus a defendant cannot be compelled to accept the assistance of counsel in asserting mitigation claims. In *United States v. Davis*, 285 F.3d 378, 380 (5th Cir. 2002), the court held that it was erroneous for the trial judge to appoint an "independent counsel" to "represent the interest of the public" in presenting mitigation evidence in a death penalty case, so as to ensure a "full and fair" penalty proceeding. If defendants accept legal representation, are they bound to defer to their attorneys' judgment about which arguments to present? Thus, for example, if a convicted defendant would find it humiliating to have facts about his abusive upbringing introduced as mitigating factors, must his counsel defer to the defendant's priorities? See the Kaczynski case *infra*.

5.   One commonly cited purpose of criminal punishment is to make defendants understand the seriousness and importance of the social norms that they have violated. Moreover, a wide array of criminal justice research indicates that procedural fairness and an opportunity to be heard are more important than the substantive outcome in shaping litigants' perceptions of the justness of the legal system.[20] Guilty defendants do not acknowledge the legitimacy of their punishment if the process appears unfair. Does this research undermine the view of the majority in *Jones* that choices about which arguments to raise on appeal are purely tactical? Are concerns about the effectiveness and moral justification of criminal punishment better served by the dissenters' position? Or are the client's overriding interests in reducing the risks or severity of punishment best served by giving lawyers authority to mount the most effective defense?

6.   Consider the following case, in which you are a court-appointed appellate lawyer representing an inmate taking a first appeal from a felony conviction. Your client appears bitter about the fact that he was not permitted to "tell his side of the story" at his trial. The transcript shows that he initially insisted that he wanted to testify, then withdrew his request after conferring with his lawyer. According to the lawyer, she had strongly and repeatedly resisted allowing the client to testify because of an admissible prior record, a transparently false alibi, and a rambling, incoherent speaking style. You explain to your client that the only way to raise the issue on appeal is to argue that the lawyer offered ineffective assistance by so exaggerating the risks of testifying that his will was "overbourne."[21]

---

20. *See, e.g.,* Tom Tyler, *Why People Obey the Law: Procedural Justice, Legitimacy, and Compliance* (1990); Robert J. MacCoun, "Voice, Control, and Belonging: The Double Edged Sword of Procedural Fairness," 1 *Ann. Rev. Law & Soc. Science* 171 (2006).

21. See cases discussed in Zeidman, *supra* note 5, at 841–42, 887.

This argument is a sure loser, and is likely to distract the court's attention from the more promising issues you wish to raise on appeal. Yet the client is presenting a grievance that appears to be of considerable personal importance.

a) One possible solution is to raise this issue in the appellate brief without arguing it at any length. Is this an adequate compromise, or does it undercut both the lawyer's and the client's objectives?

b) Is an issue that is certain to lose under prevailing doctrine, but one that raises real concerns, "frivolous" within the meaning of bar ethical rules? Model Rule 3.1 forbids the lawyer from presenting frivolous claims, and if there are no non-frivolous issues, the lawyer must attempt to withdraw. However, in *Anders v. California*, 386 U.S. 738 (1967), the Court held that states must put safeguards in place to protect clients from erroneous withdrawal by their appellate lawyers. Under the procedure that *Anders* proposed, attorneys who believed that the appeal was frivolous would move to withdraw. In addition, they would file an "*Anders* brief" setting forth "anything in the record that might arguably support the appeal." 386 U.S., at 744. But in *Smith v. Robbins*, 528 U.S. 259 (2000), the Court held that the *Anders* brief is not a constitutional requirement; alternative procedures, such as independent review of the record by the appeals court, are permissible. If the only argument that the client wishes to press on appeal involves the coercive counseling issue, and the appellate court has rejected similar claims, should you file an *Anders* brief?

Some criminal defense lawyers do not file *Anders* briefs. One reason is that it seems disloyal. As one surveyed attorney explained: "[T]o me an Anders Brief is almost like a slap in the face to the client. Why are you even bothering to write the brief, if all you are going to say is here is all the reasons to deny relief. To me it sort of inherently conflicts with your obligation to represent your client zealously . . . [to say in a public document] my client is a loser, or his issues are loser issues."[22] Another reason attorneys resist filing such briefs is that they turn out to be more work than the standard appellate brief. Another surveyed lawyer noted, "you have to argue why all these issues are not issues."[23] Then, if an appellate panel disagrees, the lawyer has to brief and argue a claim that the court almost always denies anyway.

What is your view? Is an *Anders* brief a useful compromise because it enables attorneys to maintain their credibility without totally foreclosing review of possible grounds for appeal? Or is it a largely formalistic exercise that undermines fundamental principles of client loyalty and effective assistance of counsel?

7.   International criminal courts do not invariably recognize defendants' right to represent themselves at trial. What should lawyers do if they are appointed for clients who object to the proceedings and who instruct their counsel not to conduct a defense? That issue has arisen in two prominent

---

22. Etienne, *supra* note 19, at 1231 (quoting unnamed lawyer).

23. *Id.*, at 1232.

proceedings. One involved Jean–Bosco Barayagwiza, a senior official in the Rwanda Ministry of Foreign Affairs, who was tried for genocide and crimes against humanity by the International Criminal Tribunal for Rwanda. He challenged the impartiality of the tribunal and instructed his assigned counsel not to participate in the proceedings. His two lawyers, one from Canada and one from the United States, sought to withdraw, and cited ethical codes from their respective bars that prohibited attorneys from acting contrary to their clients' instructions. The rules of the tribunal, however, permitted withdrawal only under "exceptional circumstances," which were found lacking. In denying counsels' request, the tribunal reasoned that the client was attempting to obstruct a proceeding that was in accordance with international law, and that lawyers owed an obligation to the court "to ensure that the Accused receives a fair trial."[24]

In a similar case, Slobodan Milosevic, former President of Yugoslavia, challenged the proceedings against him by the International Criminal Tribunal for the former Yugoslavia. He informed the Tribunal that he did not intend to participate and did not want counsel appointed to represent him. The Tribunal compromised by appointing counsel as amicus curiae to assist its fact-finding functions. In effect, counsel were instructed to perform the functions of a defense lawyer, including presentation of exculpatory evidence and cross examination of witnesses.[25]

Do you find either of these Tribunal rulings defensible? What would you have done if you had been appointed as counsel in one of these cases?

The issue has also arisen in Guantanamo detainee proceedings before military commissions. A number of detainees who do not trust American lawyers have sought representation by Muslim lawyers from their home countries; in the alternative, they prefer to represent themselves. However, commission rules require primary representation by U.S. military lawyers, and in any case the foreign lawyers preferred by detainees would be unable to obtain necessary security clearances. After the presiding judge in one such case refused to allow military defense counsel to withdraw, the Defense Department issued a ruling requiring counsel to serve over a detainee's objection. That ruling was superceded by the Military Commissions Act of 2006, which authorizes a defendant to represent himself as long as he conforms to rules of "evidence, procedure, and decorum applicable to trials by military commission." If he fails to do so, the judge may partially or totally revoke the right to self representation. 10 U.S.C. Section 949(b) (2007). The issue is complicated in two ways: some detainees want no representation because they have chosen to boycott their trials as a protest against the military commissions. Others, however, have chosen self-representation only as a second-best alternative to representation by

24. Prosecutor v. Barayagwiza (Case No. ICTR 97–19–T), Decision on Defense Counsel Motion to Withdraw, 2 November 2000, paragraph 21. The case is discussed in Daniel D. Ntanda Nsereko, "Ethical Obligations of Counsel in Criminal Proceedings: Representing an Unwilling Client," 12 *Crim. L Forum* 487, 500–504 (2001).

25. Prosecutor v. Milosevic (Case No. IT–99–37–PT), Order Inviting Designation of Amicus Curiae, 30 August 2000, discussed in Nsereko, *supra* note 24, at 505–06. Milosevic conducted much of the cross-examination himself; the appointed counsel cross-examined the remaining witnesses and filed a number of motions.

the lawyers of their choice.[26] How should tribunals respond to detainees' concerns?

One strategy courts have employed in cases where a defendant insists on proceeding pro se is to appoint standby counsel in case the defendant later realizes the need for legal advice or forfeits his right by disrupting the proceedings. In the latter circumstances, appointed counsel does not have a lawyer-client relationship with the defendant. ABA Standing Committee on Ethics and Professional Responsibility, Formal Opinion 07–448 (2007).

8. How should lawyers deal with clients who are judged competent to stand trial but who have some mental health difficulties that seem to impair their decision-making ability? The United States Supreme Court confronted that issue in *Florida v. Nixon*, 543 U.S. 175 (2004). The defendant, Joe Nixon, was charged with kidnapping a woman he asked for assistance in a parking lot, and then burning her to death. The evidence of guilt was overwhelming. Nixon confessed to police investigators and bragged about the crime to his brother and girlfriend. Numerous witnesses saw Nixon driving the victim's automobile, his fingerprints appeared on its trunk, and pawnshop receipts for the woman's ring had his signature. The defense attorney, Michael Corin, attempted unsuccessfully to negotiate a plea with prosecutors that would avoid the death penalty. He also had difficulty communicating with Nixon and could not get him to discuss a proposed strategy of conceding guilt and urging leniency during the penalty phase of the trial based on mental and emotional impairments. Nixon was African–American, and he demanded a different attorney and judge who were also African–American.

The trial judge denied those requests, and Nixon refused to attend trial. When questioned by the judge, he stated:

> Y'all go ahead and have your trial if you want, but leave me out of it. You can sentence me, hang me, do what you want but leave me out of it. If you don't give me no other lawyer.... Take me back to the jail and have Court without me. I don't care.

The trial court found that Nixon knowingly waived his right to attend trial and Corin proceeded with his strategy of conceding guilt and claiming mitigating circumstances. The jury imposed the death penalty.

A different lawyer represented Nixon in habeas proceedings, arguing ineffective assistance of counsel. The Florida Supreme Court agreed, on grounds that the concession of guilt was tantamount to a guilty plea and required the defendant's affirmative consent. In so ruling, the court relied on *United States v. Cronic*, 466 U.S. 648 (1984), which held that counsel's "failure to subject the prosecution's case to meaningful adversarial testing" required automatic reversal.

In a unanimous opinion, the United States Supreme Court reversed. In its view:

---

26. *See* Matthew Bloom, " 'I Did Not Come Here To Defend Myself': Responding to War on Terror Detainees' Attempts To Dismiss Counsel and Boycott the Trial," 117 *Yale L.J.* 70 (2007); Clive Stafford Smith, *Eight O'Clock Ferry to the Windward Side* (2007).

When counsel informs the defendant of the strategy counsel believes to be in the defendant's best interest and the defendant is unresponsive, counsel's strategic choice is not impeded by any blanket rule demanding the defendant's explicit consent. Instead, if counsel's strategy, given the evidence bearing on the defendant's guilt, satisfies the *Strickland* standard, that is the end of the matter; no tenable claim of ineffective assistance would remain. 543 U.S., at 192.

What would you have done if you had been in Corin's situation, or on one of the courts reviewing the adequacy of his representation? One commentator described the case as involving "a mentally retarded black man with an appointed white lawyer on trial before a white judge in Leon County, Florida for killing a white woman."[27] Do the racial dynamics of the case affect your assessment? Lawrence Fox argues that Corin's conduct was inconsistent with bar ethical rules because his concession of guilt relied on confidential information and the client had not consented to disclosure. In addition, Fox argues, Corin failed to adhere to Model Rule 1.14 concerning clients under a disability, discussed in Section C (2) *infra*.[28] It requires lawyers to maintain a normal lawyer-client relationship "as far as reasonably possible" with clients whose decision making is impaired. Lawyers may also "seek the appointment of a guardian or take other protective measures" when they reasonably believe that the client "cannot adequately act in the client's own interest." What kind of relationship was "reasonably possible" with Nixon? Should Corin have sought to withdraw from the case or should he have requested appointment of a guardian with whom to communicate on trial strategy? Should the trial court have granted a motion to withdraw and looked for an African–American lawyer to represent Nixon?

A related issue arose in *Indiana v. Edwards*, 128 S.Ct. 2379 (2008). There, after lengthy competency proceedings, the state trial judge found that the defendant suffered from schizophrenia, that he was competent to stand trial for attempted murder, but that he was not competent to represent himself. At a trial with court-appointed counsel, the defendant was convicted and sentenced to thirty years. The Indiana Supreme Court reversed on the ground that prior federal decisions had made the standard for self-representation the same as the standard for competency to stand trial. The Supreme Court reversed and remanded, holding that the standards should be different. Competency to stand trial required only that the individual have a rational and factual understanding of the proceedings, and an ability to consult with counsel with a reasonable degree of rational understanding. *Dusky v. United States*, 362 U.S. 402 (1960) (per curiam). In the Court's view, an individual could satisfy that standard while still being "unable to carry out the basic tasks needed to present his own defense without the help of counsel." However, the majority declined to endorse the standard proposed by the state, which would deny self-repre-

---

27. Thomas Adcock, "A Matter of Death," *N.Y. L. J*, November 12, 2004, at 16.

28. Lawrence J. Fox, "No Ethics for Capital Defendants," *16 Professional Lawyer* 2 (2005).

sentation if a defendant "could not communicate coherently with the jury or court," because it was unclear how such a standard would work in practice. The Court also declined to overturn *Faretta v. California*'s guarantee of the right of self-representation, which the state claimed had led to unfair trials. In fact, the majority noted, a 2007 study indicated that of the small number of defendants who chose to proceed pro se—roughly 0.3% to 0.5% of the total—state felony defendants achieved higher felony acquittals than their represented counterparts.

Do you agree with the Court's reasoning? Similar questions surfaced in the celebrated case involving the "Unabomber," described in the decision below. Judge Reinhardt, in his dissenting opinion included below, summarizes the background facts of the case:

> By the time of his arrest in a remote Montana cabin on April 3, 1996, Ted Kaczynski had become one of the most notorious and wanted criminals in our nation's history. For nearly two decades, beginning in 1978, the "Unabomber"—so designated by the FBI when his primary targets appeared to be universities and airlines—had carried out a bizarre ideological campaign of mail-bomb terror aimed at the "industrial-technological system" and its principal adherents: computer scientists, geneticists, behavioral psychologists, and public-relations executives. Three men—Hugh Scrutton, Gilbert Murray, and Thomas Mosser—were killed by Kaczynski's devices, and many other people were injured, some severely.
>
> In 1995, Kaczynski made what has been aptly described as "the most extraordinary manuscript submission in the history of publishing." Kaczynski proposed to halt all his killings on the condition that major American newspapers agree to publish his manifesto, "Industrial Society and Its Future." The *New York Times* and *Washington Post* accepted the offer, and that most unusual document, with its "dream . . . of a green and pleasant land liberated from the curse of technological proliferation," revealed to the world the utopian vision that had inspired Kaczynski's cruel and inhumane acts. Among the readers of the manifesto was David Kaczynski, who came to suspect that its author was his brother Ted, a former mathematics professor at Berkeley who had isolated himself from society some quarter-century before. David very reluctantly resolved to inform the FBI of his suspicions, although he sought assurances that the government would not seek the death penalty and expressed his strong view that his brother was mentally ill. On the basis of information provided by David, the FBI arrested Kaczynski and, despite David's anguished opposition, the government gave notice of its intent to seek the death penalty.

U.S. v. Kaczynski, 239 F.3d 1108, 1120 (2001) (Reinhardt, J., dissenting).

United States v. Kaczynski

United States Court of Appeals, Ninth Circuit, 2001.
239 F.3d 1108.

■ RYMER, CIRCUIT JUDGE:

Theodore John Kaczynski, a federal prisoner, appeals the district court's denial of his motion under 28 U.S.C. § 2255 to vacate his conviction. In that motion, Kaczynski alleges that his guilty plea to indictments returned against him as the "Unabomber" in the Eastern District of California and in the District of New Jersey, in exchange for the United States renouncing its intention to seek the death penalty, was involuntary because his counsel insisted on presenting evidence of his mental condition, contrary to his wishes, and the court denied his *Faretta* request to represent himself. Having found that the *Faretta* request was untimely and not in good faith, that counsel could control the presentation of evidence, and that the plea was voluntary, the district court denied the § 2255 motion without calling for a response or holding a hearing....

I

The facts underlying Kaczynski's arrest (April 3, 1996) and indictment for mailing or placing sixteen bombs that killed three people, and injured nine others, are well known and we do not repeat them here. Rather, we summarize the pre-trial proceedings that bear on the voluntariness of Kaczynski's plea.

[Kaczynski's capital case was assigned to Judge Garland Burrell, and Kaczynski was represented by Judy Clarke, Quin Denvir, and Gary Sowards, all highly experienced federal public defenders. They filed a notice under F.R.Crim.P. 12.2(b) that they intended to introduce psychiatric evidence for an impaired mental state defense of Kaczynski. Kaczynski himself made it clear that he was extremely reluctant to agree to this notice, and that he strongly opposed any form of mental state defense. Instead, he favored a combination of a necessity defense (arguing that his bombings were self-defense against technological society) and a motion to suppress all the evidence seized from his Montana cabin by the FBI. After jury selection, Kaczynski learned that his defenders intended to go ahead with the mental defense. In mid-December, Kaczynski agreed that evidence of his mental state could be introduced at the penalty stage of the trial but not at the guilt stage. Subsequently, however, Kaczynski announced that he wished to replace his counsel with Tony Serra, another lawyer with whom he had been in contact, because Serra would not use a mental status defense, and would defend the case along Kaczynski's preferred lines. When the judge denied that motion because it would delay trial, Kaczynski asked to represent himself. The judge denied this motion as well, on the ground that it was untimely and made in a bad-faith attempt to delay the trial. Kaczynski attempted suicide, and the trial was postponed until he could be examined for competence. The court determined that he was competent to stand trial, and that despite his desire to represent himself, he would be represented by Clarke and Denvir, who would present a mental state defense. The court noted that permitting Kaczynski to represent himself would mean foregoing "the only defense that is likely to prevent his conviction and execution." Kaczynski immediately agreed to plead guilty in return for no death sentence. He was sentenced to life without parole. He appealed.]

On the merits, Kaczynski contends that his plea was involuntary because he was improperly denied his *Faretta* right, or because he had a constitutional right to prevent his counsel from presenting mental state evidence. Even if neither deprivation suffices, still the plea was involuntary in his view because it was induced by the threat of a mental state defense that Kaczynski would have found unendurable.

It goes without saying that a plea must be voluntary to be constitutional.... The general principles are well settled.... In sum, "a guilty plea is void if it was 'induced by promises or threats which deprive it of the character of a voluntary act.'"

A

[The court finds, on the basis of Kaczynski's written and oral statements, his responses to questions at the time his guilty plea was entered, and his demeanor, that the plea was entered voluntarily.]

This would normally end the enquiry, for being forced to choose between unpleasant alternatives is not unconstitutional. However, since the district court ruled on Kaczynski's § 2255 motion, we held in *United States v. Hernandez*, 203 F.3d 614 (9th Cir.2000), that the erroneous denial of a *Faretta* request renders a guilty plea involuntary. We reasoned that wrongly denying a defendant's request to represent himself forces him "to choose between pleading guilty and submitting to a trial the very structure of which would be unconstitutional." Because this deprives the defendant "of the choice between the only two constitutional alternatives—a plea and a fair trial," we concluded that a district court's improper *Faretta* ruling "imposed unreasonable constraints" on the defendant's decision making, thus making a guilty plea involuntary. Therefore, we must consider whether Kaczynski's plea was rendered involuntary on account of a wrongful refusal to grant his request for self-representation.

B

Following *Faretta*, our court has developed the rule that "[a] criminal defendant's assertion of his right to self-representation must be timely and not for purposes of delay; it must also be unequivocal, as well as voluntary and intelligent."

Kaczynski argues that there must be an affirmative showing that he intended to delay the trial by asking to represent himself, and that none was made here. Rather, he asserts, the facts show that his purpose was to avoid the mental state defense. Kaczynski also contends that his *Faretta* request was timely, which we assume (without deciding) that it was for purposes of appeal....

The court found that Kaczynski "clearly and unambiguously permitted his lawyers to adduce mental status evidence at trial, and his complaints to the contrary, asserted on the day trial was set to commence, evidence his attempt to disrupt the trial process." Further, the court found that although Kaczynski contended he made his January 8 request to represent himself only because he could not endure his attorneys' strategy of presenting mental status evidence in his defense, the record belied this contention because Kaczynski had authorized its use. The court also found that Kaczynski was well aware before January 8 that evidence of his mental status would be adduced at trial. In addition to the December 22 accord, Kaczynski was present during all but one day of the seventeen days of voir dire, during which the court observed that he conferred amicably with his attorneys while they openly and obviously selected jurors appearing receptive to mental health evidence about him. Finally, the court found that Kaczynski could not have immediately assumed his own defense without considerable delay, given the large amount of technical evidence and more than 1300 exhibits that the government intended to offer. . . .

Kaczynski contends that he could not have been influenced by delay, given that he was incarcerated for the long haul in any event. However, the district court found that he was simultaneously pursuing strategies to delay the trial, to project a desired image of himself, and to improve his settlement prospects with the government. Kaczynski also argues that it should not matter whether he agreed to let evidence of his mental state be presented in the penalty phase, because the trial might never have gotten that far. We disagree, for Kaczynski never did—and does not now suggest—that he is actually innocent or that there was any realistic chance that the jury would not unanimously find him guilty beyond a reasonable doubt
. . . . .

AFFIRMED.

■ Reinhardt, Circuit Judge, dissenting:

I disagree strongly with the majority's decision and regretfully must dissent.

This case involves the right of a seriously disturbed individual to insist upon representing himself at trial, even when the end result is likely to be his execution. It presents a direct clash between the right of self-representation and the state's obligation to provide a fair trial to criminal defendants, especially capital defendants. It raises the question whether we should execute emotionally disturbed people whose crimes may be the product of mental disease or defect and, if so, whether they should be allowed to forego defenses or appeals that might prevent their execution. In fact, it raises, albeit indirectly, the question whether anyone should be permitted to waive his right to contest his execution by the state if that execution might be unlawful.

The case of Ted Kaczynski not only brings together a host of legal issues basic to our system of justice, it also presents a compelling individual problem: what should be the fate of a man, undoubtedly learned and brilliant, who determines, on the basis of a pattern of reasoning that can only be described as perverse, that in order to save society he must commit a series of horrendous crimes? What is the proper response of the legal system when such an individual demands that he be allowed to offer those perverse theories to a jury as his only defense in a capital case—a defense that obviously has no legal merit and certainly has no chance of success?

What should the response be when he also insists on serving as his own lawyer, not for the purpose of pursuing a proper legal defense, but in order to ensure that no evidence will be presented that exposes the nature and extent of his mental problems? The district judge faced these questions and, understandably, blinked. He quite clearly did so out of compassionate and humanitarian concerns. Nevertheless, in denying Kaczynski's request to represent himself, the district court unquestionably failed to follow the law. Notwithstanding the majority's arguments in defense of the district judge's actions, they simply cannot be supported on the ground he offered, or on any other ground available under the law as it now stands.

Whether Theodore Kaczynski suffers from severe mental illness, and which of the various psychiatric diagnoses that have been put forth is the most accurate, are questions that we cannot answer here. However, it is not now, nor has it ever been, disputed that under the governing legal standards, he was competent to waive his right to the assistance of counsel. Therefore, whatever we may think about the wisdom of his choice, or of the doctrine that affords a defendant like Kaczynski the right to make that choice, he was entitled, under the law as enunciated by the Supreme Court, to represent himself at trial. A review of the transcript makes startlingly clear that, under the law that controls our decision, the denial of Kaczynski's request violated his Sixth Amendment rights. There is simply no basis for the district court's assertion that the request was made in bad faith or for purposes of delay. Because, as the majority acknowledges, the erroneous denial of a self-representation request renders a subsequent guilty plea involuntary as a matter of law, I must respectfully dissent from the majority's holding that Kaczynski's plea was voluntary.[4]

I.

. . .

Following Kaczynski's indictment, Federal Defenders Quin Denvir and Judy Clarke were appointed to represent him. Attorney Gary Sowards joined the defense team some time later. All three are superb attorneys, and Kaczynski could not have had more able legal representatives. From the outset, however, Kaczynski made clear that a defense based on mental illness would be unacceptable to him, and his bitter opposition to the only defense that his lawyers believed might save his life created acute tension between counsel and client. That tension persisted, and periodically erupted, throughout the many months leading up to Kaczynski's guilty plea, and the dispute was not definitively resolved until Judge Burrell ruled on January 7, 1998, that Kaczynski's attorneys could present mental-health evidence even over his vehement objection. It was that ruling, Kaczynski maintains—and the record indisputably reflects—that compelled him to request self-representation the very next day as the only means of prevent-

---

4. Because I conclude that the denial of Kaczynski's right of self-representation rendered his plea involuntary, I do not consider his alternative argument that the plea was rendered involuntary by the court's ruling that his counsel, not he, would decide whether a mental-health defense would be offered in the guilt phase of his trial.

ing his portrayal as a "grotesque and repellent lunatic." In doing so, Kaczynski was merely exercising the right that Judge Burrell had recognized he possessed the day before, immediately after he issued his controversial ruling that counsel, not client, would control the presentation of mental-health evidence.[8]

Whether Kaczynski's self-representation request was made in good faith, as Judge Burrell repeatedly stated on January 8, or whether it was a "deliberate attempt to manipulate the trial process for the purpose of causing delay," as Judge Burrell subsequently held when explaining his reason for denying the request, is the issue before us. Although the answer is absolutely clear from the record, it is helpful to set forth a number of colloquies that demonstrate that everyone involved—including counsel for both sides and the district judge—was fully aware that Kaczynski's request was made in good faith and not for purposes of delay. The record reveals that Kaczynski's aversion to a mental-health defense was, indisputably, heartfelt, and that no one—least of all Judge Burrell—ever questioned Kaczynski's sincerity prior to the time the judge commenced formulating his January 22 ruling.

II.

[Judge Reinhardt summarizes various evidence, including dozens of notes that Kaczynski wrote to his attorney, in which he expressed his unwillingness to present a mental-health defense at trial. For example, in 1997 he wrote: "I categorically refuse to use a mental-status defense." He submitted to psychiatric evaluations only after receiving what he described as "false promises and intense pressure" from his attorneys, who understood that his primary concern was, as he wrote them in June 1997, "to get reliable psychological data about myself before the public in order to counteract all this silly stuff about me that the media have been pushing."]

When, on November 25, 1997, Kaczynski learned that defense experts had diagnosed him as suffering from paranoid schizophrenia, and that the results of those examinations had been released to the government and to the public, he felt "shock and dismay." In the courtroom on that day, Kaczynski wrote to Denvir and Clarke:

> Did Gary [Sowards] give that info to the prosecutors with your knowledge and consent? If you all assume responsibility for revealing what is being revealed now, then this is the end between us. I will not work with you guys any more, because I can't trust you....
>
> This case is developing in a direction that I certainly did not expect. I was lead [sic] to believe that this was not really a "mental health" kind of defense, but that you would try to show that my actions were a kind of "self defense." Gary [Sowards] gave me the impression that we

---

8. The government agreed with Kaczynski that he, not counsel, had the right to decide whether mental-health evidence should be presented and warned the court of "grave appellate error" if it ruled otherwise.

would use only Dr. Kriegler, and would use her only to show I would not "do it again."

In the weeks that followed, Kaczynski also wrote three separate letters to Judge Burrell in which he explained his conflict with his attorneys and sought replacement of counsel. However, Denvir and Clarke prevailed upon him to delay bringing the conflict to the attention of the judge while they were engaged in negotiations with the Justice Department aimed at allowing him to plead guilty conditionally while preserving his suppression issues for appeal.[11] When those negotiations failed, Denvir and Clarke agreed to deliver Kaczynski's letters to Judge Burrell, and they did so on December 18.

The letters reveal the depth of the rift that had developed between Kaczynski and his attorneys regarding the issue of mental-health evidence. The first letter, dated December 1, 1997 begins: "Last Tuesday, November 25, I unexpectedly learned for the first time in this courtroom that my attorneys had deceived me." Kaczynski explained that he had been assured by his attorneys that the results of psychiatric examinations that he reluctantly agreed to undergo—and even the fact that he had been examined at all—would be protected by attorney-client privilege and would not be disclosed absent his approval. Moreover, he had been "led to believe that [he] would not be portrayed as mentally ill without [his] consent...."

In a letter dated December 18, Kaczynski offered his reasons for objecting to a defense based on mental-health evidence:

> I do not believe that science has any business probing the workings of the human mind, and ... my personal ideology and that of the mental-health professions are mutually antagonistic.... It is humiliating to have one's mind probed by a person whose ideology and values are alien to one's own.... [My lawyers] calculatedly deceived me in order to get me to reveal my private thoughts, and then without warning they made accessible to the public the cold and heartless assessments of their experts.... To me this was a stunning blow ... [and] the worst experience I ever underwent in my life.... I would rather die, or suffer prolonged physical torture, than have the 12.2b defense imposed on me in this way by my present attorneys.

Previous consent to such a defense was, Kaczynski contended, "meaningless because my attorneys misled me as to what that defense involved."
...

On the morning of January 5, Kaczynski informed Judge Burrell of his continuing conflict with counsel, and the judge appointed attorney Kevin Clymo as "conflicts counsel" to represent Kaczynski's interests. Proceedings were postponed until January 7. On that day, Judge Burrell ruled that Kaczynski's counsel could present mental-state testimony even if Kaczynski objected. Judge Burrell then offered Kaczynski the option of self-represen-

---

11. Kaczynski's motion to suppress evidence seized from his Montana cabin had been denied by the district court.

tation, warning: "I don't advise it, but if you want to, I've got to give you certain rights." At the time of the court's offer, Kaczynski declined to accept it, explaining that he was "too tired . . . [to] take on such a difficult task," and that he did not feel "up to taking that challenge at the moment." By then, according to his section 2255 motion, "Kaczynski was already contemplating suicide as the most probable way out of this cul-de-sac." Later that same day, the court was informed that Tony Serra would, after all, be willing to represent Kaczynski. Kaczynski promptly requested a change of counsel, but Judge Burrell denied the request on the ground that substituting counsel would require a significant delay before trial could commence.

On January 8, Kaczynski decided to accept the court's offer of the previous day and informed the court that he wished to represent himself.[15] Kaczynski's counsel conveyed his request to the court with great reluctance:

> Your Honor, if I may address the Court, Mr. Kaczynski had a request that we alert the Court to, on his behalf—it is his request that he be permitted to proceed in this case as his own counsel. This is a very difficult position for him. He believes that he has no choice but to go forward as his own lawyer. It is a very heartfelt reaction, I believe, to the presentation of a mental illness defense, a situation in which he simply cannot endure.

Kaczynski's attorneys made clear that he was not seeking any delay in proceedings and that he was prepared to proceed pro se immediately. On that day, as before, Judge Burrell did not intimate that he perceived any bad-faith motive on Kaczynski's part. To the contrary, he made numerous comments demonstrating his belief that Kaczynski sought self-representation solely because of the conflict over control of the mental-health defense. . . .

The court repeatedly asserted that the key to the self-representation issue was whether Kaczynski was "competent," and did not even hint at the possibility of a bad-faith motive. Ultimately, Kaczynski's own attorneys called their client's competency into question, expressing the view that his efforts to waive what appeared to be his only meritorious defense attested to the need for a competency evaluation. At that point, all counsel (including the court-appointed conflicts counsel) and Judge Burrell agreed that Kaczynski should undergo a psychiatric evaluation to determine his competency to exercise his right to self-representation, and the next day the judge issued an order for the necessary medical examinations.

The competency evaluation would, of course, have been altogether unnecessary had Judge Burrell believed on January 8 that Kaczynski's request to represent himself was made in bad faith. The judge could simply have denied the request on that ground. Nevertheless, two weeks later,

---

15. The night before, Kaczynski apparently attempted suicide, although the record shows that Judge Burrell was unaware of that fact until after the January 8 hearing was over.

after Kaczynski had been determined to be competent by a government psychiatrist, Judge Burrell denied the self-representation request, characterizing it—in a manner that directly contradicted the numerous statements he had made at the prior proceedings—as a "deliberate attempt to manipulate the trial process for the purpose of causing delay."

III.

It is impossible to read the transcripts of the proceedings without being struck by Judge Burrell's exceptional patience, sound judgment, and sincere commitment to protecting Kaczynski's right to a fair trial—and his life. Judge Burrell's commendable concern about preventing Kaczynski from pursuing a strategy that would almost certainly result in his execution is reflected most dramatically in statements made in connection with the judge's January 22, 1998 oral ruling denying Kaczynski's self-representation request. The judge observed that by abandoning a mental-health defense and proceeding as his own counsel, Kaczynski would be foregoing "the only defense that is likely to prevent his conviction and execution.... That ill-advised objective is counterproductive to the justice sought to be served through the adversary judicial system, which is designed to allow a jury to determine the merits of the defense he seeks to abandon." Judge Burrell was unwilling to permit Kaczynski to use the criminal justice system "as an instrument of self-destruction," explaining that "a contrary ruling risks impugning the integrity of our criminal justice system, since it would simply serve as a suicide forum for a criminal defendant." He contended, in effect, that society had an interest in preventing capital defendants from using the instrument of the state to commit suicide. As legal support for his reasoning, Judge Burrell cited Chief Justice Burger's dissenting opinion in *Faretta*.

Nevertheless, Judge Burrell did not base his decision denying Kaczynski's *Faretta* rights on his views of the role of the criminal justice system in capital cases; he was not free to do so under controlling law.... Because Kaczynski's psychiatric evaluation resulted in a declaration that he was competent, the only available basis for denying his request was to find that it was not made in good faith—but rather for the purpose of delay—even though the record squarely refuted that conclusion.

There can be no doubt that Judge Burrell's admirable desire to prevent an uncounseled, and seriously disturbed, defendant from confronting, on his own, the "prosecutorial forces of organized society"—in this case, three experienced federal prosecutors aggressively seeking that defendant's execution—lay at the heart of his denial of Kaczynski's request for self-representation. A fair reading of the record provides no support for the finding that Kaczynski's purpose was delay.... Yet it is easy to appreciate why, as one commentator has suggested, "the judicial system breathed a collective sigh of relief when the Unabomber pled guilty." Indeed, all the players in this unfortunate drama—all except Kaczynski, that is—had reason to celebrate Kaczynski's unconditional guilty plea. His attorneys had achieved their principal and worthy objective by preventing his execution. The government had been spared the awkwardness of pitting three experienced prosecutors against an untrained, and mentally unsound, defendant, and conducting an execution following a trial that lacked the fundamental elements of due process at best, and was farcical at worst. Judge Burrell, as noted, had narrowly avoided having to preside over such a debacle and to impose a death penalty he would have considered improper in the absence of a fair trial. It is no wonder that today's majority is not eager to disturb so delicate a balance.

The problem with this "happy" solution, of course, is that it violates the core principle of *Faretta v. California*—that a defendant who objects to his counsel's strategic choices has the option of going to trial alone. Personally, I believe that the right of self-representation should in some instances yield to the more fundamental constitutional guarantee of a fair trial. Here, the district court understood that giving effect to *Faretta*'s guarantee would likely result in a proceeding that was fundamentally unfair. However, *Faretta* does not permit the courts to take account of such considerations. Under the law as it now stands, there was no legitimate basis for denying Kaczynski the right to be his own lawyer in his capital murder trial.

IV.

I do not suggest that the result the majority reaches is unfair or unjust. It is neither. I would prefer to be free to uphold the district judge's denial of Kaczynski's request on the basis of the societal interest in due process for all defendants, and particularly capital defendants. Unfortunately, I am not permitted by precedent to do so. Because I am bound by the law, I am also unable to vote to affirm on the basis the district court relied on: that Kaczynski's request was made in bad faith. Thus, with much regret, I must conclude that Kaczynski's plea of guilty was not voluntary and that he was entitled to withdraw it. Accordingly, I must respectfully dissent.

NOTES AND QUESTIONS

1.   Lawyer Michael Mello assisted Kaczynski in preparing his pro se appeal to the Ninth Circuit; he also wrote a book about the Unabomber case.[24] Mello describes Kaczynski as follows:

> Like most psychopaths I've encountered in my travels as a capital defense lawyer, Kaczynski is wildly manipulative of people. He is the most selfish person I've ever known. He is a control freak.... He's fixated as Nixon was with rehabilitating his public image, to correcting perceived "lies" others have said about him; he has even written a book to that end, tellingly and pretentiously (if inaccurately) titled *Truth versus Lies*. (The alleged "liars" are Kaczynski's brother and

24. Michael Mello, *The United States Versus Theodore John Kaczynski: Ethics,* *Power and the Invention of the Unabomber* (1999).

mother, the media, etc, and guess who the "truth" teller is?). He desperately tries to control what people say or write about him.[28]

Does this describe a form of psychopathology, or merely a strongly-felt value placed by Kaczynski on his own image—different in degree, but not in kind, from the value that most individuals place on their own reputations? If his public image matters so much to Kaczynski, is the decision to use a mental status defense merely a tactical choice, or is it a basic decision about the aims of the representation? How would you analyze this case in terms of Model Rule 1.2(a)?

From another perspective, Kaczynski may have been desperate to avoid having doubts cast on his sanity for fear that the public would discount the arguments in his manifesto—a work that in his eyes provided the justification for his campaign of terrorism. Should his lawyers have taken this into account?

Mello believes that most people desperately wish to view the Unabomber as insane because that is more comforting than believing that inexplicable crimes can be the product of a healthy mind. Yet as Mello notes:

> If you think Kaczynski is a paranoid schizophrenic, I have a question for you: What are his delusions? . . . That the Industrial Revolution has been a mixed blessing? Hardly a delusion. That technology is chipping away at our freedoms and privacy? Hardly a delusion. That committing murder—and threatening to commit more—was the only way to force the *New York Times* and *Washington Post* into publishing, in full and unedited form, the 35,000–word Unabomber Manifesto? Hardly delusion. That the powers that be in our culture would define the Unabomber as a pathetic lunatic? Hardly a delusion. That a simple, self-sufficient life, in one of the most physically beautiful places in America, is preferable to the rat-race of academia? Hardly a delusion.[29]

One of the psychiatrists who examined Kaczynski explained that his paranoid delusion was "[h]is view of technology as the vehicle by which people are destroying themselves and the world." In what sense is this a delusion? Wouldn't many "normal" Americans agree? Another psychiatrist submitted a report asserting that Kaczynski's unawareness of his psychiatric illness was itself a sign of illness.[30] Is there any way for Kaczynski to avoid confirming this diagnosis? Is it legitimate for lawyers to submit such evidence against the client's will?

2. After Kaczynski's trial, journalist William Finnegan published an article strongly condemning the Unabomber defense. According to Finnegan, Kaczynski was spared the death penalty "by a bizarre alliance of lawyers he was trying to fire, a family he had renounced, psychiatrists he did not trust or respect (and in some cases had never met), a federal judge who had drastically restricted his right to counsel and seemed to fear (with reason)

---

28. Michael Mello, "The Non–Trial of the Century: Representations of the Unabomber," 24 *Vt. L. Rev.* 417, 435 (2000).

29. *Id.* at 472.

30. William Finnegan, "Defending the Unabomber," *The New Yorker*, March 16, 1998, at 55–56.

the trial to come, a press convinced that he was a paranoid schizophrenic, and, finally, a legendary death-penalty opponent skilled at 'client management' (management, that is, of Kaczynski)."[31] As Finnegan tells the story, the defense team worked closely with Kaczynski's mother and brother to popularize the image of Kaczynski as a madman in order to pressure the prosecution into dropping its demand for the death penalty. The press was more than happy to oblige, and the "client management" consultant succeeded in keeping Kaczynski in the dark about the mental defense his lawyers planned.

As Finnegan relates the story, Kaczynski's opposition to the mental defense did not represent a preference for death over dishonor, because Kaczynski did not see these as the only choices. He was focused on the possibility of a successful motion to suppress all the evidence seized from his cabin—essentially, the prosecution's entire case. He wanted acquittal, not death. Finnegan comments: "If he did, in fact, believe that he had a chance of walking free from jail, he was, of course, severely deluded (not clinically deluded but blinded by unrealistic hopes, however conceived and encouraged). No judge in America would have set him free."[32]

Does this mean that Kaczynski's rejection of a psychiatric defense was based on faulty legal judgment rather than fundamental values? If so, does it justify the defenders' taking matters out of his hands? Consider a conversation recounted by Judy Scheindlin—television's "Judge Judy." It involved a seasoned defense lawyer and his youthful client, who had been arrested for selling drugs to an undercover policeman. When the lawyer stated that his client was prepared to plead guilty, the client objected. "Whereupon his lawyer looked at him and said, 'Listen, pal, I don't tell you how to sell drugs. Don't tell me how to practice law!'"[33]

3.   Did Clarke and Denvir act improperly by insisting on a mental impairment defense? By plea bargaining on terms that Kaczynski detested (even though he was mistaken to think that he could get better terms)? In a brief to the court, Clark and Denvir asserted:

> The decisions whether and how to present a mental status defense in the guilt phase (other than in an insanity defense) and what witnesses to call in the penalty phase of capital trial fall squarely within the category of strategic decisions that ultimately must be decided by trial counsel.... It is unconscionable for the government to ask to the court—in a capital case—to order defense counsel to forgo the only defense that is likely to prevent the defendant's conviction and execution.[34]

Do you agree? What would you have done?

31. *Id.* at 54.

32. *Id.* at 59.

33. Judy Scheindlin, *Don't Pee on My Leg and Tell Me It's Raining* 44 (1996).

34. Michael Mello, "United States v. Kaczynski: Representing the Unabomber," in *Legal Ethics: Law Stories* 139, 165 (Deborah L. Rhode & David Luban, 2006).

4. According to one of the Moslem fundamentalist defendants in the 1994 World Trade Center bombing trial, his court-appointed lawyer violated his expressed wishes during closing argument. At issue was the lawyer's characterization of one co-defendant as a "devious and evil" person who had duped the client into participating in the terrorist bombing. Would it matter whether observers believed that the tactic had aided the client but had seriously damaged the defenses of the co-defendants by acknowledging that there had been a terrorist conspiracy? Does this case differ from Kaczynski's?[35]

5. In the aftermath of his trial, Kaczynski wrote:

> Perhaps I ought to hate my attorneys for what they have done to me, but I do not. Their motives were in no way malicious. They are essentially conventional people who are blind to some of the implications of this case, and they acted as they did because they subscribe to certain professional principles that they believe left them no alternative. These principles may seem rigid and even ruthless to a nonlawyer, but there is no doubt my attorneys believe in them sincerely.[36]

Suppose that the principles to which Kaczynski refers are a fundamental commitment to zealous advocacy and a belief that the responsibility of a defense lawyer in a capital case is to save the client's life. Would you agree that these principles were "rigid and ruthless" as applied in Kaczynski's case?

B. The Justification of Paternalism

INTRODUCTION

To some commentators, paternalism is inappropriate under most circumstances on both deontological and utilitarian grounds. From a deontological rights-based perspective, respect for individual autonomy counsels deference to freely-made choices concerning the conduct of one's own life. And from a utilitarian perspective, evidence from a wide range of contexts suggests that people who exercise control over decisions are more likely to be satisfied with the outcome, and that clients who participate actively in the decision making process often achieve better results.[37] Other commentators, while acknowledging that clients' involvement should be encouraged and their decisions generally respected, nonetheless believe that paternalism is sometimes morally justified. The materials that follow explore these views.

---

35. Monroe Freedman, "Whose Case Is It Anyway?" *Legal Times*, March 28, 1994, at 26.

36. Mello, *supra* note 28, at 502.

37. *See* MacCoun, *supra* note 20; Stephen Ellmann, "Lawyers and Clients," 34 *UCLA L.Rev.* 717 (1987); Marcy Strauss, "Toward a Revised Model of Attorney–Client Relationship: The Argument for Autonomy," 65 *N.C.L.Rev.* 315, 338–339 (1987).

PROBLEM 2

You are a tax and estate planning attorney. Two men in their forties approach you to alter their wills. They explain that they are long-time partners, and that one of them is terminally ill. The other is in excellent health.

They want their wills altered quickly, they explain, because they have decided to end their lives in a suicide pact. They ask you to write new wills removing each other as beneficiaries and substituting third parties. You tell them that you need time to examine the law and to determine whether you are willing to take the case. In the interim, you strongly urge them to discuss their decision with a mental health professional or some other trustworthy counselor, such as a minister.

Your research reveals that suicide is no longer a crime in your state. However, directly assisting another's suicide is a criminal offense, and you are concerned that the partners will be engaging in mutual assisted suicide or even mutual murder. In that case, drawing up their wills may run afoul of Model Rule 1.2(d), "A lawyer shall not . . . assist a client in conduct that the lawyer knows is criminal. . . ." Furthermore, your state's version of Rule 1.6 requires you to reveal confidential information in order to prevent a criminal act that you reasonably believe will result in death or substantial bodily injury. A colleague whom you ask for advice suggests that these legal concerns are not what really bothers you about the case. In your friend's opinion, your worries about the law and the ethics rules really show your more fundamental ambivalence about whether to take steps to prevent the double suicide.[38] You do not disagree.

References:

Model Rules 1.2, 1.6.

QUESTIONS

1.   Should you draw up the new wills? What information from the partners might assist your decision? Would it be proper for you to speak to either of them separately? What, if any, advice would you offer these clients?

2.   If the partners choose not to seek counseling, should you report their intentions in order to force them to obtain mental health assistance? Must you make such disclosures under Rule 1.6? If the version of Rule 1.6 in effect in your state permits but does not require disclosure of confidential information in order to prevent a criminal act that you reasonably believe will result in death or substantial bodily injury, would you disclose their intentions?

3.   What role should, or would, your own moral and religious convictions about suicide, assisted suicide, and euthanasia play in your deliberations?

---

38.   This problem is drawn from a case occurring in New Jersey, a state with a mandatory-disclosure rule as in the problem. See Richard Pliskin, "The Ethics of Suicide," *New Jersey L.J.,* June 20, 1994, at 1.

4. Would you distinguish between the requests of the healthy and the ill partner? Why or why not?

5. How should lawyers respond if clients request more active assistance in life-threatening actions? Consider the role of counsel who represented detainees in Guantanamo Bay. According to U.S. military reports, 84 detainees went on a hunger strike to protest the facility's failure to comply with Geneva Conventions and to afford them a fair hearing. At least 32 were being force fed. (Detainees' lawyers claimed that the strike involved 250 prisoners.) If those prisoners asked their lawyers to sue to halt the forced feeding, should the lawyers do so even if a legal victory might mean death for their clients?[39] The force-feeding of mentally competent prison hunger strikers who are striking voluntarily violates principles of the World Medical Association.[40] However, U.S. law concerning federal prisons permits non-consensual "immediate treatment of a life or health threatening situation," and the Supreme Court has permitted compulsory medical treatment of inmates if it is "reasonably related" to legitimate penological interests.[41] Some state courts do not permit force-feeding of hunger strikers.[42]

Experts on hunger strikes note that sometimes prisoners may be participating involuntarily, because of peer group pressure or even threats of violence from other strikers; interviewed out of earshot of other strikers, such strikers may actually request force-feeding. (However, there has been no allegation of this phenomenon at Guantanamo.) Others may have fallen into depression or other psychological conditions that call into question their competence to decide life-and-death matters. Such experts recommend individualized interviews with hunger strikers to determine their competency and the voluntariness of their strike.[43] What implications do these recommendations carry for lawyers whose access to their clients is extremely limited, as at Guantanamo?

Force-feeding can be carried out in extremely brutal ways, by restraining the striker and feeding him through a nasal tube that is inserted and removed, painfully, at each feeding. The European Court of Human Rights has found the procedure to constitute cruel treatment or torture unless it is medically necessary.[44] Some critics have charged that U.S. authorities at

---

39. "US Reports Surge in Guantanamo Hunger Strike," *N.Y. Times.com*, Dec. 29, 2005. Clive Stafford Smith, *Eight O'Clock Ferry to the Windward Side* 190–204 (2007) (description of hunger strike by detainee's lawyer).

40. World Medical Association, World Medical Association Declaration on Hunger Strikers (Declaration of Malta) (2006), available at http://www.wma.net/e/policy/h31.htm.

41. 28 C.F.R. 549.65(b); Washington v. Harper, 494 U.S. 210, 223 (1990).

42. Singletary v. Costello, 665 So.2d 1099 (Fla.App.1996) (competent inmate who voluntarily took up hunger strike cannot be

forced to receive medical care); Thor v. Superior Court, 855 P.2d 375 (Cal. 1993) (inmate has a right to refuse medical treatment, even if it is force-feeding; Zant v. Prevatte, 286 S.E.2d 715 (Ga. 1982) (no force-feeding of competent hunger striker).

43. Hernan Reyes, "Medical and Ethical Aspects of Hunger Strikes in Custody and the Issue of Torture", in Maltreatment and Torture, 19 *Research in Legal Medicine* (1998), available at http://www.icrc.org/web/eng/siteeng0.nsf/htmlall/health-article–0 10198?opendocument.

44. Nevmerzhitsky v. Ukraine, [2005] ECHR 54825/00.

Guantanamo use the force-feeding procedure well before the point of medical necessity, as a strike breaking tool.[45]

NOTES: THE MORAL PROBLEM OF PATERNALISM

Wasserstrom argues that lawyers' paternalism toward their clients is at best morally problematic, and at worst indefensibly dismissive of individual dignity and autonomy. Yet paternalism is a persistent feature of our legal landscape, as Duncan Kennedy reminds us:

> [Lawmakers] have regulated the safety features of food and drugs, airplanes, railroads and boats, automobiles, fabrics for children's clothing, and building materials. They have regulated the design of residential buildings, and of public buildings, in each case indirectly controlling what arrangements the owners of property could make with willing paying customers. They have regulated interest rates, the sale of securities, the structure of financial intermediaries and the contracts between corporations and their shareholders (both in and out of bankruptcy). They have developed whole panoplies of required terms for insurance contracts, the wages and hours of employment, occupational safety and health, occupational licensing, conditions of rental housing, terms of payment and non-payment of rent, consumer credit (truth in lending), security arrangements, door-to-door sales, franchising, sales of condominiums, condominium conversion, mine safety, pension and annuity contracts, union pension funds. They have required workers, as a condition of employment, to lay aside money for their old age, and required employers to join workmen's compensation schemes.[46]

Bar ethical codes similarly include a broad array of provisions that prohibit lawyers from engaging in conduct that might be harmful to clients irrespective of their desires or consent. Examples include accepting an unreasonable fee; initiating a sexual relationship; handling a divorce case on a contingent fee basis; acquiring a financial interest in litigation; or preparing an instrument giving a lawyer a gift.[47] Each is an instance of paternalism, which Dennis Thompson has defined as "the imposing of constraints on an individual's liberty for the purpose of promoting his or her own good."[48]

This definition highlights the moral problem posed by paternalism:

---

45. Al–Joudi v. Bush, 406 F.Supp.2d 13, 16–17 (D.D.C.2005) (summarizing declaration of detainees' counsel about brutal force-feeding); Stafford Smith, *supra* note 39, at 215.

46. Duncan Kennedy, "Distributive and Paternalist Motives in Contract and Tort Law, With Special Reference to Compulsory Terms and Unequal Bargaining Power," 41 *Md.L.Rev.* 563, 594 (1982).

47. See Model Rules of Professional Conduct, Rules 1.5 and 1.8; Fred Zacharias, "Limits on Client Autonomy," 81 *B.U. L. Rev.* 198, 212 (2001).

48. Dennis F. Thompson, "Paternalism in Medicine, Law, and Public Policy," in *Ethics Teaching in Higher Education* 246 (Daniel Callahan & Sissela Bok eds. 1980).

"paternalism needs justification because it is a restriction of liberty."[49] As philosopher Samuel Gorovitz puts it:

> Because we respect individuals, we subscribe to what has been called the Principle of Autonomy, the view that individuals are entitled to be and do as they see fit, so long as they do not violate the comparable rights of others. . . .
>
> Because we care about the well-being of individual persons, we also grant a prominent place in the structure of our moral outlook to a second principle, often called the Principle of Beneficence. That principle, simply stated, holds that one ought to do good. . . . It is this principle that is typically invoked as the justification for overriding the Principle of Autonomy, when we limit someone else's freedom in order to achieve what we see as being his or her own good.[50]

In these terms, the problem of paternalism is not *whether* paternalism is ever permissible (or required), but *when*: when does the Principle of Beneficence override the Principle of Autonomy, and when does it fail to override it? Three approaches are common.

1. Objective conditions

Dennis Thompson proposes a three-part objective test for justifiable paternalism:

> First, the decision of the person who is to be constrained must be *impaired*. . . . Second, the restriction is as *limited* as possible. . . . Finally, the restriction prevents a serious and irreversible *harm*.[51]

The first condition assures us that paternalistic intervention will not seriously offend the Principle of Autonomy, for a person whose decision-making is impaired is not acting in a fully autonomous way. The second condition requires consideration of less restrictive alternatives. The third condition acknowledges the Principle of Beneficence under circumstances that most individuals would find compelling. Yet each of the highlighted terms—*impaired* decision, *limited* restriction, and *serious, irreversible harm*—clearly requires further analysis, and can provoke significant dispute. Is a demonstrably foolish decision "impaired"? Under what circumstances might an imprudent gift or selfless act constitute a "harm"?[52]

2. Hypothetical consent

The preceding objective conditions may not explain all the instances of paternalistic intervention that most Americans find justifiable. The laws that Kennedy cites typically serve to protect the general public, whose members are not presumed to have impaired decision-making. To explain

49. *Id.* at 247.

50. Samuel Gorovitz, *Doctors' Dilemmas: Moral Conflict and Medical Care* 36–37 (1982).

51. Thompson, *supra* note 48, at 250–51.

52. For further discussion *see* John Kleinig, *Paternalism* (1982) and Donald VanDeVeer, *Paternalistic Intervention: The Moral Bounds of Benevolence* (1986); *Paternalism* (Rolf Sartorius ed. 1983).

paternalism under these circumstances, a second prominent approach emphasizes situation-specific justifications. In some contexts anyone's decision-making may be impaired, and reasonable individuals will consent to benign interventions in these cases. As Kennedy explains the origin of securities regulations:

> [E]veryone knew that what was really at work was greed, gullibility, incurable optimism, the gambler's itch, the allure of something for nothing, all followed by addiction to the ticker, the secret diversion of the family's savings, the mortgaging of a small business, and then, when things turned down, increasing margin requirements, a desperate scramble to stay in the game just a little longer ... ruin and a swan dive from a high window.... People are idiots.[53]

All people are idiots sometimes, ourselves included. Or as psychologists more diplomatically put it, all human decision-making is subject to certain cognitive biases, such as overoptimism or reduction of dissonant information, that may prevent rational judgments.[54] Like Odysseus ordering himself bound to the mast while the Sirens sang, we accept paternalism to protect ourselves from ourselves. As Gerald Dworkin notes:

> since we are all aware of our irrational propensities, deficiencies in cognitive and emotive capacities, and avoidable and unavoidable ignorance it is rational and prudent for us to in effect take out "social insurance policies." We may argue for and against proposed paternalistic measures in terms of what fully rational individuals would accept as forms of protection.[55]

That is, we ask what one *would* consent to if one were fully rational. Under this approach, hypothetical consent becomes the touchstone of justifiable paternalism.

However, we do not know exactly what "the fully rational individual" is or would consent to. None of us, after all, is fully rational under all circumstances; perhaps not under *any* circumstances.[56] In Problem 2, for example, consider the difficult questions that a lawyer must resolve in applying the hypothetical consent test: Is it irrational for someone with a painful terminal illness to commit suicide? Is it irrational for a partner to commit suicide if he or she is convinced that life alone is not worth living? These are questions about ultimate values—life, death, dignity, and love—which often have deep religious foundations. Such questions cannot be resolved through a value-free concept like "rationality."

3. Ad hoc paternalism

The preceding critiques suggest the difficulties in attempting to justify paternalism by some unitary principle. Building on this insight, Kennedy

---

53. Kennedy, *supra* note 46, at 632–33.

54. Rachlinski, *supra* note 17, at 170–73.

55. Gerald Dworkin, "Paternalism," in *Morality and the Law* 120 (Richard A. Wasserstrom ed. 1971).

56. For a critique of hypothetical consent, *see* David Luban, "Paternalism and the Legal Profession," 1981 *Wisc. L. Rev.* 454, 463–67.

argues that there is no such thing as capacity in the abstract; there is only capacity to make particular decisions, and the real basis of paternalism is empathy:

> The actor feels he has intuitive access to the other's feelings and perceptions about the world, and that he participates directly in the suffering and the happiness of the other.... It feels like unity.
>
> In this condition of unity, the actor comes to believe that the other is suffering from some form of false consciousness that will cause him to do something that will hurt him, physically or financially or morally or in some other way.... The basis of this kind of intuition is one's own experience of being mistaken, and of having other people sense one's mistake.[57]

Kennedy acknowledges, however, that such intuitions may well be erroneous.

> Paternalist action is inherently risky because it will make [individuals with whom you empathize] furious at you, and they may be right. If they are right, you will suffer twice: you will suffer with them the pain of the frustration of a valid project, and you will suffer on your own behalf ... guilt that you have done them not just an injury, but an injustice. Even if it turns out that they were indeed suffering from false consciousness and that your intervention spared them a serious evil, they may not forgive you for taking things into your own hands.[58]

In the end, on this view, we are forced into purely "ad hoc paternalism,"

> by which I mean that in fear and trembling you approach each case determined to act if that's the best thing to do, recognizing that influencing another's choice—another's life—in the wrong direction, or so as to reinforce their condition of dependence, is a crime against them.[59]

From this perspective, the problem of when paternalism is justified has no general "bright line" solution, because while we can often empathize with others, we can never be certain that our intuitions about their values, needs, and concerns are correct.

According to many commentators including Kennedy, paternalism is justified when we "believe that the other is suffering from some form of false consciousness that will cause him to do something that will hurt him, physically or financially or morally or in some other way...."[60] In other words, the need for paternalistic protection arises because we are all prone to confusion between our deeply-held values, our immediate whims or wants, and our "objective" best interests. The following excerpt analyzes the distinction between values, wants, and interests, and argues that paternalism is unjustifiable if an action seemingly against a client's self

---

57.   Kennedy, *supra* note 46, at 638–39. Many feminist writers similarly stress the importance of empathy. *See* Robin L. West, *Caring for Justice* (1997).

58.   Kennedy, *supra* note 46, at 641.

59.   *Id.* at 644.

60.   *Id.*

interest comes from that individual's deeply-held values, whereas paternalism can be justified to protect the client's long-term values or objective interests against momentary whims.

David Luban, "Paternalism and the Legal Profession"

1981 Wisconsin Law Review 454, 467–74.

1. Values, Wants and Interests

Paternalism imposes constraints on an individual's liberty for his or her own good. But what does this mean? How should we construe "liberty" or "an individual's own good"?

Liberty may be described as the ability to act as one chooses. But "as one chooses" is ambiguous: sometimes choosing refers to *wants,* and sometimes to *values.* The difference, as we shall see, is crucial.

The distinction is a simple and familiar one, which operates (to give the simplest instance) whenever we wish to do something but judge that it is wrong. The judgment is an expression of our system of values, while the wish is an expression of our system of wants. Of course these systems frequently direct us toward the same objects, when what we want we also value.... My point is not to deny a connection between wants and values, but to point out that, connected or not, they are different from each other. The distinction between wants and values lies at the root of such phenomena as temptation (our wants clash with our values), weakness of the will or "incontinence" (our wants defeat our values), and compulsion (one set of wants always defeats our values)....

Values and wants, then, are different sorts of things. Briefly, values are *reasons for acting,* while wants are not.... Values are in principle intersubjective, and susceptible to argument and disputation. A want, on the other hand, such as lust in one's heart, is a subjective event and is not to be refuted....

Our values are obviously not our only reasons for acting, however. Reasons for acting are the genus, values the species. What sort of reasons for acting are values? ... I suggest that they are differentiated by their role in the agent's personality. Values ... are those reasons with which the agent most closely identifies—those that form the core of his personality, that make him who he is. This is why we feel that we understand a person's actions when we comprehend them as "flowing from" his values— why, conversely, we do not really know a person without knowing his values. A value system, therefore, has two aspects. On the one hand, values are reasons, and thus intersubjective and open to criticism and public assessment. On the other hand, values are definitive of the person who holds them. Both aspects are crucial. Because of the former aspect, we feel entitled to judge a person as having *wrong* values, *inadequate* values, *irrational* values, and so on. Because of the latter aspect, we nevertheless sense that attempting to change a person's values by main force, or to override them, directly assaults the integrity of his or her personality. I suggest that the former aspect is the deep reason for our temptation to act paternalistically toward someone whose values are weirdly different from our own; the latter aspect explains why we find paternalism offensive. The account I am offering helps to explain our conflicting intuitions toward paternalism.

Different from both a person's values and wants are his *interests*. I will use this term in a somewhat special way—a lawyerly way, if I may say so— to refer to freedom, money, health and control over other people's actions: what I have earlier called "generalized means to any ultimate ends." (These are the interests that our laws protect and regulate, and that lawyers are trained to obtain for clients.) The concept of interests that I am employing is meant to be an objective concept. A person's interests can be understood as those goods that enable the person to undertake the normal range of socially available actions. . . .

This objective sense of "interests" is meant to capture the meaning of the concept in sentences such as "Like it or not, I'm going to look out for your best interests." Whether or not a person wants money or values freedom, in our society it is in the person's *interest* to have money and freedom. And just as the concept of liberty is ambiguous, in that it can mean either liberty to act on your values or liberty to do what you want, so the concept of *a person's own good* is ambiguous: it can refer either to what is good according to a person's own values, or to what is in the person's best interest. Sometimes these coincide, but often they do not.

2.   Varieties of Paternalistic Intervention

Bearing in mind these distinctions, we find four formally different conceptions of paternalism emerging, depending on how we interpret "liberty" and "an individual's own good" in the formula "imposing constraints on another's liberty for his or her own good."

1.   *Values Over Values:* constraining, on behalf of another's values, his liberty to act according to his values.

2.   *Values Over Wants:* constraining, on behalf of another's values, his liberty to do what he wants.

3.   *Interests Over Values:* constraining, in another's own best interest, his liberty to act according to his values.

4.   *Interests Over Wants:* constraining, in another's own best interest, his liberty to do what he wants.

.   .   .

[Values Over Wants] is the classic sort of justifiable paternalism: knowing your values, and seeing you about to give in to an impulse that violates those values, I restrain you: I force you to be free. Because I am helping you act on your own values I am entitled to presume your consent. . . .

I must be sure, however, that I know your values before overriding your wants in their name. If I don't, I am merely assuming that your stated preference does not reflect your genuine values; if I am wrong, I am overriding your real values in the name of values I impute to you. And this, because your values form the core of your personality, attacks your integrity.

Precisely this is the situation in the Interests Over Values case, in which the paternalist overrides an agent's values because they are costing the agent money, or freedom, or health, or leverage over others.... [M]any people, because they are self-sacrificing, or high rollers, or ideologically committed, pursue goals that are flatly incompatible with their interests. It is absurd, then, to assume that interests constitute the dominant values in a normal human life. Thus, if an individual adduces reasons for acting in non-self-interested ways, paternalism is unjustifiable—it is an assault on the individual's integrity.

It is important, though, that the individual have reasons for non-self-interested preferences. Otherwise, we may be forced to conclude that these preferences are irrational wants, the product of impaired capacities. In that case, ... paternalism is (once again) justifiable. Thus, Interests Over Wants paternalism is justifiable only if we have evidence that the individual's non-self-interested wants do not express his genuine values.

QUESTIONS

1. To what extent does Luban's distinction among interests, wants, and values help in resolving the issues in Problems 1 and 2?

2. How should lawyers respond when clients appear to misjudge their wants and interests or wants and values? How would you classify the objectives of Gilmore, Joe Nixon (see note 7 to *Jones v. Barnes, supra*), and Kaczynski?

C. Informed Consent and the Partially Competent Client

NOTES AND QUESTIONS: INFORMED CONSENT

One obvious way for attorneys to avoid acting paternalistically is to inform their clients of the risks and benefits of different options, and then to accept their clients' choices—or at least obtain their clients' consent to the option recommended.

The moral significance of informed consent surfaced first in medical ethics. Three decades ago, the unquestioned norm among physicians was paternalism toward patients. The Hippocratic oath enjoins physicians to "Do no harm", and it was assumed that trained professionals were in a better position than patients to know what constituted harm. Many physicians believed that patients and their families were too anxious or ill-informed to be entrusted with life-and-death decisions. Moreover, the conventional wisdom was that giving patients bad news might itself jeopardize their health. Today the prevailing norm is quite different. Physicians expect to inform their patients about their illnesses and options, and will not undertake even routine treatment without obtaining the patient's consent.

Informed consent standards have been advocated, and in some instances adopted, for legal practice as well. The Model Rules define informed consent as "the agreement by a person to a proposed course of conduct after the lawyer has communicated adequate information and explanation about the material risks of reasonably available alternatives to the proposed course of conduct." Model Rule 1.0(e). The 2002 revision of the Model Rules incorporates informed consent requirements in several rules. Such standards appear in various conflict of interest provisions requiring that lawyers shall not represent clients in situations unless "each client consents after consultation."[61]

In principle, informed consent seems like an attractive alternative to paternalism; in practice it is often difficult to apply. Some matters, such as the risks and benefits of representation that present a potential conflict of interest, may be too complex for inexperienced clients to assess. The difficulty is graphically illustrated by an antitrust class action involving claims against drug companies on behalf of antibiotics purchasers. Members of the class received notification that they would be bound by the result of the litigation unless they opted out. Letters that the attorney general received in response included the following:

Dear Sir:

I received your pamphlet on drugs, which I think will be of great value to me in the future.

Due to circumstances beyond my control I will not be able to attend this class at the time prescribed on your letter due to the fact that my working hours are from 7:00 until 4:30.

Dear Sir:

Our son is in the Navy, stationed in the Caribbean some place. Please let us know exactly what kind of drugs he is accused of taking. From a mother who will help if properly informed.

A worried mother,

Jane Doe

Dear Attorney General:

Holy greetings to you in Jesus name. I received a card from you and I don't understand it, and my husband can't read his. Most of the

---

61. Model   Rules   1.6(a),   1.7(b)(4), 1.8(a)(3),   1.8(b),   1.8(f)(1),   1.8(g),   1.9(a), 1.9(b)(2).

time all I buy is olive oil for healing oil after praying over it, it is anointed with God's power and ain't nothing like dope.[62]

In some cases, informing clients about technical matters may require a great deal of time and expense for which clients (or lawyers with fixed or contingent fee agreements) may be reluctant to pay.

Power asymmetries in many attorney-client relationships also may raise problems in determining if a client's consent is truly autonomous. Even when lawyers are attempting to remain neutral and objective, the way that they describe options and their likely consequences can preempt certain choices. Moreover, attorneys are trained to advocate positions and to persuade decisionmakers to reach what the attorney believes are the right results. In many instances, attorneys may not even realize the extent to which they are pressuring or manipulating clients.[63]

Consider an example that William Simon encountered as an inexperienced attorney. His client, Mrs. Jones, was a 65–year–old black woman charged with leaving the scene of an accident. He obtained strong evidence that the charge was unfounded; remarks made to her by police officers also suggested that her arrest was racially motivated. Given the strength of that evidence, Simon believed they would prevail at trial. Concerned about his own inexperience, however, he enlisted the aid of an experienced criminal defense lawyer. That lawyer promptly negotiated a plea bargain that would result in six months probation for the client. Simon, however, was unhappy that his client would lose her opportunity for vindication and for exposure of police misconduct. He presented the plea agreement to the defendant and her minister (who had accompanied her to the courthouse to serve as a character witness):

> I insisted that, because the decision was hers, I couldn't tell her what to do. I then spelled out the pros and cons.... However, I mentioned the cons last, and the final thing I said was, "If you took their offer, there probably wouldn't be any bad practical consequences, but it wouldn't be total justice." Up to that point, Mrs. Jones and her minister seemed anxiously ambivalent, but that last phrase seemed to have a dramatic effect on them. In unison, they said, "We want justice."
>
> I went back to my friend and said, "No deal. She wants justice." My friend stared in disbelief and then said, "Let me talk to her."
>
> He then proceeded to give her his advice. He didn't tell her what he thought she should do, and he went over the same considerations I did. The main differences in his presentation were that he discussed the disadvantages of trial last, while I had gone over them first; he described the remote possibility of jail in slightly more detail than I had; and he didn't conclude by saying, "It wouldn't be total justice."

---

62. Quoted in Deborah L. Rhode, "Class Conflicts in Class Actions," 34 *Stan. L.Rev.* 1183, 1235 & n. 212 (1982).

63. For legal contexts, see Deborah L. Rhode, "Ethics in Counseling," 30 *Pepperdine L. Rev.* 591 (2003). For medical contexts, *see* Gorovitz, *supra* note 50, at 38–54.

At the end of his presentation, Mrs. Jones and her minister decided to accept the plea bargain. As I said nothing further, that's what they did.[64]

Based on such examples, Simon questions how often clients can make the fully autonomous choices necessary for informed consent. In commenting on the case, he adds:

My guess is that most people will have some doubts about whether Mrs. Jones's ultimate decision was autonomous. Before we explore these doubts, however, we should consider a prior set of circumstances that seems to represent a paradox for the autonomy view.

Mrs. Jones did not want to be autonomous in the way that the autonomy view contemplates. She asked me to make the decision for her. She would have been immensely relieved if I had told her without explanation what to do, and she would have done it.

Now most people recognize that a commitment to individual autonomy requires the condemnation of some individual choices that, however seemingly autonomous in themselves, would preclude capacity for further autonomous choice. Choosing to sell yourself into slavery is the classic example. So long as these choices seem crazy or highly unusual, the contradiction they pose for the commitment to autonomy is not that serious.

However, I don't think that Mrs. Jones's desire for an "escape from freedom" was crazy or highly unusual. Decision making of this kind involves anxiety. Moreover, some people may reasonably believe that they are not very good at it. In such circumstances, the opportunity to put your fate in the hands of an apparently benevolent expert may seem attractive....

Proponents of the autonomy view are likely to respond that the problem illustrated by Mrs. Jones's case is not the implausibility of the autonomy ideal, but the failure to implement it competently on the part of her lawyers. They would suggest that the discussion was too hurried and pressured and the advice was less informative and neutral than it should have been. Although such criticisms have substance, they tend to underestimate some intractable problems. Time is scarce in nearly all practice situations, and the difficulties of framing unbiased advice are often overwhelming.

[In Mrs. Jones's case, my] friend and I made clear to her that there was a theoretical possibility of a jail term if she were convicted, even though we both thought this probability tiny, and this knowledge visibly evoked anxiety and fear in Mrs. Jones....

Most practicing lawyers would probably approve our conduct. Such judgments are based on assumptions that lawyers necessarily rely on

64. William H. Simon, "Lawyer Advice and Client Autonomy: Mrs. Jones's Case," in *Ethics in Practice: Lawyers' Roles, Responsibilities, and Regulation,* 165, 167 (Deborah L. Rhode, ed. 2000).

about what a client's goals are likely to be. Most lawyers would assume that even a small probability of jail would be important to most clients.... The compatibility of such assumptions with the autonomy view depends on the extent to which the assumption accurately reflects client ends. My own impression is that they are often too crude to serve as reliable guides. For example, in Mrs. Jones's case, I think the conventional assumptions about the jail penalty ... were wrong.

Going to jail would have been a disastrous outcome for Mrs. Jones. However, it was also a very unlikely outcome. As a purely cognitive matter, most people have difficulty rationally (that is, consistently) making decisions about risk. When the decision involves an outcome that evokes strong emotions and vivid images, the difficulty is compounded....

In Mrs. Jones's case, I think my friend and I should have either omitted mention of jail entirely or characterized it [as a negligible risk].... I think she was bound to be disabled by any description of jail as a real, even if small, possibility.[65]

Do you agree? Consider the discussion of paternalism in criminal contexts in Part A. How would you have advised Mrs. Jones?

Abbe Smith notes that one of the most difficult but crucial jobs of a defense attorney arises in cases with the opposite problem of that confronting Simon—cases where any experienced criminal defense lawyer would advise a plea but the defendant insists on trial. Smith believes that the role of counsel in these cases is to "convince a client to hang on to as much liberty as he or she can—not to take an ill-considered, irrational, or immature 'no' for an answer.... [Lawyers] have to be willing to plead, argue, cajole ... yell [and] badger ... [and] to bring in family...."[66]

How far should badgering extend? Does it differ for privately-retained and court-appointed lawyers? How will defendants feel if they are railroaded into accepting pleas by defense counsel whom they have not chosen? Does it matter, if the result is to spare the defendant an extended sentence?

1. DEFINING COMPETENCE

INTRODUCTION

The difficulties concerning informed consent are compounded in cases where clients are, to a greater or lesser degree, *incompetent*. If a client is comatose or otherwise wholly incompetent, informed consent is obviously impossible. In such cases, the lawyer has only two alternatives: to "play God" or to take instructions from an alternative decision-maker, such as a guardian.

More difficult ethical problems arise with partially competent clients. Two paradigmatic circumstances involve juveniles and mentally disabled or

---

65. *Id.*, at 167–70.

66. Abbe Smith, "The Lawyer's Conscience and the Limits of Persuasion," 36 *Hofstra L. Rev.* 479, 491 (2007).

unstable adults. However, issues of relative incompetence are by no means unique to such settings.[67] Even highly sophisticated decision-makers can sometimes become irrational and fail to realize that their judgment is slipping. Clients can be "too smart for their own good," or too indecisive about what their own good is. Problems 3 and 4, *infra,* concern such cases.

A threshold question is what "competence" means. Experts generally agree that mental illness should not be equated with incompetence; many individuals suffering impairment in some areas retain decision making capacity in others.[68] Nor is eccentricity the same as incompetence, and in many situations there is no value-neutral standpoint from which to assess the rationality of another's convictions. For example, a person may decide to give all his money to his church. If the church is part of a mainstream religion, observers may call the person a saint; if the church is a "cult," observers may assume that the person has been brainwashed and take legal steps to freeze the assets. Yet almost every mainstream religion began as a cult, scorned by popular opinion. An outsider's judgment that a "cultist" is incompetent may reveal more about the outsider's biases than about the believer's incapacity.

A further difficulty is that evaluations of competence may be influenced by ulterior motives. A typical situation arises when an elderly individual begins making extravagant expenditures, charitable contributions, or gifts to companions that will shrink the estate of potential heirs. They may respond by threatening or initiating involuntary guardianship proceedings, or pressuring the individual's lawyer to intervene.[69] Alternatively, disappointed heirs who learn that a deceased relative has made substantial charitable bequests may attack the testator's competence and ask that the will be set aside—a form of after-the-fact "paternalism" that is particularly problematic because the other heirs are scarcely disinterested and the deceased is no longer around to defend his competency.[70] Dennis Thompson warns of the circular reasoning that bases judgments of incompetency solely on a person's "eccentric" choices, and then overrules those choices because the person is incompetent. Recall that one of the psychiatrists who examined the Unabomber concluded that his anti-technology beliefs were the product of mental illness, and that the evidence of his mental illness consisted of his failure to recognize that he was mentally ill.

---

67. Estimates suggest that at least half of Americans will suffer from a mental health problem at some point in their lives. Ronald C. Kessler, et al., "Lifetime Prevalence and Age of Onset Distributions of DSM–IV Disorders in the National Comorbidity Survey Replication," 62 *Arch. Gen. Psychiatry* 593 (June, 2005). Many others will be situationally impaired due to the stress or emotional difficulties that arise in particular contexts.

68. Phyllis Coleman & Ronald A. Shellow, "Ineffective Assistance of Counsel: A Call for a Stricter Test in Civil Commitments," 27 *J. Legal Profession* 37, 56 n. 172 (2003).

69. Robert Fleming & Rebecca C. Morgan, "Lawyers' Ethical Dilemmas: A 'Normal' Relationship When Representing Demented Clients and Their Families," 25 *Ga. L. Rev.* 735 (2001).

70. For classic discussions of this problem is Milton D. Green, "Proof of Mental Incompetency and the Unexpressed Major Premise," 53 *Yale L.J.* 171, 301 (1944) and Alexander M. Meiklejohn, "Contractual and Donative Capacity," 39 *Case W.Res.L.Rev.* 307, 314–29 (1989).

An adequate justification of paternalism requires us to "identify some impairment that can be described independently of the end or good an individual chooses."[71]

To avoid such circular analysis, some commentators propose focusing on the process rather than the substance of a decision. For example, do individuals understand the consequences of a choice, the alternatives available, and the likelihood that the particular choice will advance their objectives? Can they give reasons for their decision? However, as other experts note, it is often impossible to evaluate process without some background assumptions about substance. We evaluate an individual's understanding and reasoning by reference to what we consider rational goals.[72] Moreover, as a practical matter, most of us will be willing to defer to people's choices that appear consistent with their objectives even if their reasoning process seems questionable. On the facts of Problem 1(a), most lawyers would be inclined to follow a client's instructions to challenge a foreclosure even if what motivated the instructions was a message from the spirit world. A harder question arises when clients' short-term preferences seem clearly inconsistent with their long-term well being.

Although the difficulties in objectively assessing competence cannot be entirely escaped, they can be addressed by examining factors such as: the ability to articulate the reasons behind a decision; the variability in the decision-maker's mental state; the appreciation of the consequences of a particular decision; the substantive fairness of the outcome; and its consistency with the decision-maker's long-term values.[73]

Alternatively, David Luban proposes adopting a test of competency articulated in *Matter of Will of White,* a nineteenth-century estates case:

> [I]f there are facts, however insufficient they may in reality be, from which a prejudiced or a narrow ... mind might derive a particular idea or belief, it cannot be said that the mind is diseased in that respect.[74]

Luban comments, "All that we can reasonably require is that the person be connecting beliefs to real facts by *some* recognizable inferential process...."[75] When the individual's potentially harmful choice arises from membership in some recognizable group, such as a religious cult or political movement, Luban believes that viewing the individual as incompetent

---

71.   Thompson, *supra* note 48, at 252.

72.   *See* Margulies, *supra* note 3, at 1083–84. See also Nancy M. Maurer & Patricia W. Johnson, "Ethical Conflicts in in Representing Capacity," 96 *Practicing L. Institute* 1143, 1158 (2001).

73.   Margulies, *supra* note 3, at 1085. *See* Anthony T. Kronman, "Paternalism and the Law of Contracts," 92 *Yale L.J.* 763, 790 (1983) (defining judgment as "the faculty of moral imagination, the capacity to form an imaginative conception of the moral consequences of a proposed course of action and to anticipate its effect on one's character. A

person has good judgment if this faculty is developed and strong, poor judgment if it is not").

74.   24 N.E. 935, 937 (N.Y.1890).

75.   Luban, *supra* note 56, at 479. Compare the test for competency to stand trial in Dusky v. United States, 362 U.S. 402 (1960): whether a defendant has "sufficient present ability to consult with his lawyer with a reasonable degree of rational understanding and whether he has a rational as well as a factual understanding of the proceedings against him."

would be inconsistent with associational freedom.[76] This approach would rule out a great deal of paternalistic intervention.

QUESTIONS

How would the tests that Margulies and Luban propose resolve Problems 1 and 2? Is the *White* test too "permissive" in what counts as competent? Is there a preferable alternative?

2. Representing Clients Under a Disability

Ethical questions routinely confront attorneys whose clients are under disabilities related to age, youth, retardation or mental illness. Prior to the adoption of the Model Rules of Professional Conduct, the bar's ethical codes provided no explicit guidance for such representation. Now, Model Rule 1.14 provides:

(a) When a client's capacity to make adequately considered decisions in connection with a representation is diminished, whether because of minority, mental impairment or for some other reason, the lawyer shall, as far as reasonably possible, maintain a normal client-lawyer relationship with the client.

(b) When the lawyer reasonably believes that the client has diminished capacity, is at risk of substantial physical, financial or other harm unless action is taken and cannot adequately act in the client's own interest, the lawyer may take reasonably necessary protective action, including consulting with individuals or entities that have the ability to take action to protect the client and, in appropriate cases, seeking the appointment of a guardian ad litem, conservator, or guardian.

What constitutes a "considered decision" or appropriate "protective action" are matters open to dispute. Courts have divided over how far lawyers should depart from the typical advocacy role in representing clients under a disability. Some judges have applauded attorneys for acting in clients' "best interest;" other judges have criticized attorneys for making judgments about medical treatment that are beyond their expertise and that usurp the judicial role.[77] The trend, both among courts and experts in the field, is toward deference to clients' expressed preferences. The fact that a client disagrees with mental health experts concerning his condition does not always mean that he is incompetent to make his own decisions and to direct his lawyer accordingly. For obvious reasons, psychiatric professionals are often highly risk averse when any possibility of harm to the patient or to third parties is at stake; individuals whose liberty is at

---

76. Luban, *supra* note 56, at 478–79. For further discussion, *see* Linda F. Smith, "Representing the Elderly Client and Addressing the Question of Competence," 14 *J.Contemp.L.* 61 (1988); Paul R. Tremblay, "On Persuasion and Paternalism: Lawyer Decisionmaking and the Questionably Competent Client," 1987 *Utah L.Rev.* 515.

77. Coleman & Shellow, *supra* note 68, at 57; Maurer & Johnson, *supra* note 72, at 1159–60.

issue or who suffer significant side effects from medication, may have a different assessment of their own best interests.

In some instances, the issue is complicated by the inadequacies of the options available. For example, some mental health institutions may be too understaffed to offer more than custodial care, coupled with heavy medication of patients who would otherwise prove difficult to control. Adequate outplacement programs may be unavailable or unaffordable, and patients' families may be unable or unwilling to fill the gaps. Related problems figure in the guardianship system. Appointment of a guardian or conservator is not always appropriate for individuals of diminished capacity. Elderly individuals may be competent to handle certain decisions but not others. These individuals may justifiably fear that guardianship would mean the loss of control over crucial aspects of their lives. Moreover, the frequently inadequate oversight of guardians, and the undue costs of providing them for individuals with little property or only temporary disabilities, may make their appointment less desirable than relying on family attorneys to function as "de facto" guardians.[78]

That role frequently presents difficult choices. When should attorneys follow a client's wishes that are contrary to recommendations of mental health experts? Either strategy runs significant risks of harm. For example, in the context of civil commitments, to agree with experts that institutionalization is beneficial may "fail to take into account ... the conditions prevalent in many of the public psychiatric facilities to which patients are regularly committed and the severity of the side effects often caused by the administration of psychotropic medication."[79] If the lawyers who are appointed to represent individuals at commitment hearings are encouraged to follow doctors' rather than clients' wishes, they may end up failing to provide the kind of check on the system that their presence was meant to secure.[80] Given the loss of liberty and stigma associated with involuntary commitment, individuals deserve an advocate who will speak for their interest as they perceive it.

On the other side of the issue, one commentator cautions:

> The patient-hospital relationship is not a simple adversarial one. It is not approached as such by the institution. To approach it that way from the patient's side would, if nothing else, be incongruous. All the elements that argue for the broader fact-finder-counselor role are present, and pursuit of the objectives of improving the decision-making process, getting the full facts, promoting serious reflection on all options and their consequences, and of serving interests less narrow

---

78. For representative illustrations of problems in the guardianship system, see Carol D. Leonnig, Lena H. Sun, & Sarah Cohen, "Under Court, Vulnerable Became Victims: Attorneys Who Ignored Clients or Misspent Funds Rarely Sanctioned," *Washington Post*, June 15, 2003, at A1; and Carol D. Leonnig, Lena H. Sun, & Sarah Cohen, "Rights and Funds Can Evaporate Quickly: Attorney's Power Thwarted D.C. Residents Trying to Remain Independent," *Washington Post*, June 16, 2003, at A1.

79. Michael L. Perlin, *Mental Disability Law: Civil and Criminal* § 8.17 (1989).

80. Michael L. Perlin, "A Critical Evaluation of the Role of Counsel in Mental Disability Cases," 16 *Law and Hum. Beh.* 39 (1992).

than those announced in mental confusion by the patient or perceived at first blush by the lawyer would appear to be the essence of good lawyering in the mental institution. To extend without thought the dictates or folklore of "traditional litigation" to the mental hospital situation is unlikely to benefit anyone other than the lawyer who measures success in terms of "beating" imagined adversaries....[81]

Complicating matters are the participants' own self interests. As numerous studies have documented, appointed counsel often lack the time and resources to prepare adequately.[82] Efforts to do so may arouse resistance from mental health personnel who are equally overburdened and who view attorneys' intervention as counterproductive. Moreover, as Jan Costello notes,

> [s]ome lawyers struggle with wanting to appear credible in the eyes of the judge and court personnel. If the client is behaving in a way that indicates severe mental illness, a lawyer advocating for the client's release may feel foolish. There is a temptation to dissociate him or herself from the client's "craziness," by adopting a compassionate but condescending manner toward the client, or by stating the client's position, but in a tone that conveys a different message to the court. Lawyers may justify this in individual cases by saying they made a pragmatic assessment that the client could not win, and by "rolling over" in this case are gaining credibility for a future client with a stronger case.[83]

One final difficulty is that the choice of which role to adopt is generally up to lawyers themselves. Client oversight, the normal check on attorney conduct, is insufficient because the point at issue is how much direction to take from the client. The problem is exacerbated by many clients' difficulties in communicating with their attorneys or in replacing them if the relationship is unsatisfactory.

Does Model Rule 1.14 provide adequate guidance? How would you respond as an attorney in Problems 1 and in cases like *Nixon* and *Kaczynski*?

3. Representing Juveniles

PROBLEM 3

a) The mother and step father of a 15–year–old girl have retained you to defend their daughter on charges of vandalism and burglary. She comes from a troubled home and has a history of drug abuse. If she is willing to identify the other participant in the crime, the prosecutor will allow her to

---

81. Samuel Brakel, "Legal Aid in Mental Hospitals," 1981 *Am.B.Found.Res.J.* 23, 81, 84–85; *see also* John R. Murphy, "Older Clients of Questionable Competency: Making Accurate Competency Determinations Through the Utilization of Medical Professionals," 4 *Geo. J. Legal Ethics* 899 (1991).

82. Coleman & Shellow, *supra* note 68, at 40.

83. Jan C. Costello, "Why Would I Need a Lawyer?: Legal Counsel and Advocacy for People With Mental Disabilities," in *Law, Mental Health, and Mental Disorder* (Bruce D. Sales & Daniel W. Schuman eds. 1996).

plead to vandalism and will support her placement in a local halfway house with an excellent therapeutic counseling program. If she refuses, you believe that it might still be possible, on the eve of trial, to talk the prosecutor into a diversion program. Under that program, all charges will be dropped if your client successfully completes two years of probation, including participation in a youth-center counseling program. If your client fails to complete the program, the prosecutor can reinstate both charges and proceed against her as an adult-felony offender. If you take the case to a bench trial in juvenile court, you estimate that the chances of acquittal are about 40 percent. A conviction would probably result in a sentence of anywhere from 6 to 18 months at the state's correctional facility, an outcome that is likely to compound your client's problems.

You believe that the halfway house is by far the best option. Given your client's current attitudes and closest friends, you doubt that she could manage to stay out of trouble for a two-year probation term. Since failure to complete that term might well result in a felony record, you believe that diversion is not a particularly desirable strategy.

b) Your client's parents agree. They would like their daughter to live in the halfway house, since it would provide the supervision that they are finding difficult and unpleasant to impose. After preliminary conversations, your client appears adamantly opposed to the idea. She is unwilling to identify her accomplice, who appears responsible for supplying her occasional drug habit. She also appears more concerned about losing the ability to stay out late with friends if she moves to the halfway house than about the possibility of acquiring a felony record. She is frightened by the prospect of the state correctional facility, but has an unrealistic faith that she could talk her way out of a conviction if the case goes to trial. How should you proceed? Should you raise the possibility of a diversion program if the prosecutor does not propose it? If the prosecutor mentions the possibility but does not make a formal offer, must you present that option to your client?

c) The facts are the same as in Part (a) except that the parents oppose the halfway house. The step father is convinced that the daughter does not need therapy; she just has a "bad attitude" and needs more discipline. The mother, who is deeply religious, thinks that greater involvement in their a local church is the answer. She has already enlisted the minister to talk with her daughter about part time work and participation in the church choir and youth group. Your client agrees, but you suspect that she is simply doing whatever is necessary to avoid the halfway house. What should you do?[84]

d) The facts are the same as in Part (a), except that your client, after obtaining assurances of confidentiality, tells you that her stepfather has sexually abused her and that her mother refuses to believe it. The daughter doesn't want to "destroy the family" by reporting the abuse, and believes

84. For a similar hypothetical, see Jan C. Costello, " 'The Trouble Is They're Growing, The Trouble Is They're Grown': Therapeutic Jurisprudence and Adolescents' Participation in Mental Health Care Decisions," 29 *Ohio Northern U. L. Rev.* 607, 609–12 (2003).

that she has the situation under control by locking her door and managing not to be in the house alone with her stepfather. Your state has laws requiring health professionals, but not lawyers, to report any suspicion of child abuse. How do you proceed?

References: Model Rules 1.2, 1.6, 1.14, 1.8(f)(2).

NOTES AND QUESTIONS

Experts disagree about the role of lawyers representing minors, and the relevant statutory and common law provides little clarification. Typically, provisions governing appointment of counsel for juveniles in family, civil commitment, or delinquency proceedings refer to representation of their rights, interests, welfare, or well-being. What that means when lawyers and their clients disagree is a matter largely unresolved in law and highly controversial in practice. As noted earlier, Model Rule 1.14 is phrased in highly abstract terms. It directs lawyers to maintain as "normal" a relationship as is "reasonably possible" with clients unable to make "adequately considered decisions." With respect to confidentiality, 1.14(c) provides:

> Information relating to the representation of a client with diminished capacity is protected by Rule 1.6. When taking protective action pursuant to paragraph (b), the lawyer is impliedly authorized under Rule 1.6(a) to reveal information about the client, but only to the extent reasonably necessary to protect the client's interests

According to some commentators, these provisions are so "riddled with ambiguity" that the rule is "virtually unenforceable."[85]

The ambiguity is longstanding. In earlier eras, appointment of a guardian ad litem generally signified that the client was not competent to identify his or her own interests; it was the guardian's responsibility to determine those interests and to advocate them in legal proceedings. Under current usage, the term "guardian ad litem" is often used interchangeably with "court-appointed counsel." However, some courts and commentators, in recognition of this historical legacy, use the guardian description to identify individuals including lawyers who represent what they consider to be the client's best interest. A variation on this approach is an amicus curiae role, in which the lawyer places before the judge any information that would further the decision-making process and acts as an intermediary between the client and the legal system.[86]

However, in most contexts, the preferred role for attorneys representing juveniles is the conventional advocacy role. This approach, endorsed by the ABA Juvenile Justice Standards and other children's rights groups, defers to the client's own preferences unless the client is impaired (i.e.,

85. David R. Katner, "Coming to Praise, Not to Bury, the New ABA Standards of Practice for Lawyers Who Represent Children in Abuse and Neglect Cases," 14 *Geo. J. Legal Ethics* 103, 112 (2000).

86. Institute of Judicial Administration, American Bar Association, *Juvenile Justice Standards* (1979).

lacks "capacity to direct the representation").[87] At the foundation of this approach is the Supreme Court's decision in *In re Gault*, 387 U.S. 1 (1967), which found that juvenile hearings must meet basic due-process standards of adult trials, including the right to counsel. Proponents of the conventional advocacy role for lawyers representing juveniles argue that anything less would violate the principles *Gault* establishes, even though *Gault* specifically concerns only criminal cases, not the full range of cases involving juveniles.[88] Even in the conventional advocacy role, questions of paternalism arise. Thus, one experienced defender writes, "I am focused . . . on how to convince a young person to take a favorable plea rather than go to trial when the chances of prevailing are low and the stakes are high. . . . [W]hen there is no question that going to trial will be ruinous, and the client does not understand this, it is incumbent upon the lawyer to get through to the client. This is especially true when the client is developmentally immature and emotionally traumatized."[89] She adds that this quintessentially paternalistic issue arises with adult clients as well as juveniles, and comments wryly that "the client invariably gets in the way."[90]

Each of these approaches has been subject to considerable criticism. The conventional advocacy model gives priority to individual dignity and autonomy by allowing persons to make their own choices. And as Martin Guggenheim notes, it seems "both inconsistent and unfair to treat the child as a morally responsible actor who must suffer the legal consequences of his own . . . acts and yet, at the same time, deny that he is autonomous enough to be capable or entitled to instruct counsel."[91] So too, in abuse and neglect proceedings, where "what happens in court will fundamentally alter a child's life," many legal experts believe that the child's perspective needs to be heard.[92] However, as Sarah Ramsey argues, the value of autonomy has little meaning "without some consideration of the individual's capacity to understand the significance of the choice he is making. . . . The ideal of autonomy depends upon the individual's being capable of shaping his life through his own choices . . . [but] the ability to express a preference is not a sufficient test of capacity."[93]

87. ABA Juvenile Justice Standards, *supra* note 86. These standards provide that where juvenile clients are capable of considered judgment, they are responsible for defining their own interests. *See also* "Recommendations of the Conference on Ethical Issues in the Legal Representation of Children," 64 *Fordham L. Rev.* 1301, 1302 (1996). For discussion of variations among the Model Rules, the ABA Standards, and the Fordham Conference recommendations, see Linda Elrod, "An Analysis of Proposed Standards of Practice for Lawyers Representing Children in Abuse and Neglect Cases," 83 *Fordham L. Rev.* 1999 (1996).

88. Two law review symposia consider the legacy of *Gault* on its fortieth anniversary: "Symposium, *In re Gault*," 9 *Barry L. Rev.* 1 (2007); "The Promise of In re Gault: Promoting and Protecting the Right to Coun-

sel in Juvenile Court: Symposium 2007," 60 *Rutgers L. Rev.* 1 (2007).

89. Abbe Smith, " 'I Ain't Takin' No Plea": The Challenges in Counseling Young People Facing Serious Time, 60 *Rutgers L. Rev.* 11, 12 (2007).

90. *Id.*

91. Martin Guggenheim, "The Right to be Represented but not Heard: Reflections on Legal Representation for Children," 59 *N.Y. L. Rev.* 76, 87 (1984).

92. Margaret Graham Tebo, "The Youngest Clients," *ABA J.*, April, 2007, at 56, 57 (quoting Miriam A. Krinsky of the Children's Law Center).

93. Sarah H. Ramsey, "Representation of the Child in Protection Proceedings: The Determination of Decision–Making Capacity," 17 *Fam. L.Q.* 287, 306 (1983).

According to many commentators, the distinctive features of childhood and adolescence make paternalism especially appropriate. Compared with adults, adolescents tend to be more subject to peer influences, more likely to engage in risky behavior, and more inclined to overvalue short-term concerns and undervalue long-term consequences.[94] They may also lack sufficient experience to understand the full implications of certain choices. Younger clients are particularly vulnerable; by the same token, opportunities for positive intervention are correspondingly greater than with most adults.

What should lawyers do when their efforts at persuasion fail? Some experts believe that their fundamental responsibility is to present the child's perspective. Why should attorneys be involved in a case if they function just like a judge or a social worker? What in lawyers' training equips them to determine children's best interests and what oversight structures are available if they are wrong? If lawyers function as de facto guardians or amicus curiae, who will voice the concerns of the client as the client perceives them? After all, it is the client who will have to live with the consequences. As these commentators also note, much of the empirical literature does not find strong differences in the decision-making capacity of adults and of older minors, particularly those over age 14.[95] Nor does the history of juvenile and family courts suggest that experts are generally able to determine the "best interest" of children in any objective sense.[96]

From this perspective, once minors reach a certain age, or demonstrate what the ABA Standards refer to as "considered judgment," their decisions should be controlling for the attorney. When representing adults, lawyers do not equate competence with an ability to weigh accurately all the costs and benefits of available options. It is, as the ABA Standards note, "ordinarily sufficient that clients understand the nature and purposes of the proceedings and its general consequences and be able to formulate their desires ... with some degree of clarity. Most adolescents can meet this standard, and more ought not to be required of them."[97]

An alternative, amicus curiae approach attempts to accommodate concerns of both autonomy and protection by presenting all information to the decision-maker, including the client's preferences and the lawyer's assessments. This strategy, however, risks compromising both concerns. An

94. Elizabeth S. Scott, N. Dickon Reppucci, and Jennifer L. Woolard, "Evaluating Adolescent Decision Making in Legal Contexts," 19 *Law & Human Behav.* 221 (1995).

95. Shannan L. Wilber, "Independent Counsel for Children," 27 *Fam. L. Q.* 349, 356 (1993); David G. Scherer, "The Capacities of Minors to Exercise Voluntariness in Medical Treatment Decisions," 15 *Law & Hum. Behav.* 431 (1991). *See also* Scott et al., *supra* note 94, at 220–231 (discussing research finding similarities in the understanding and reasoning capacities of adults and adolescents, but differences in capacities for judgment).

96. Jean Koh Peters, "The Roles and Content of Best Interests in Client–Directed Lawyering for Children in Child Protective Proceedings," 64 *Fordham L. Rev.* 1505 (1996). *See generally* Jean Koh Peters, *Representing Children in Child Protective Proceedings: Ethical and Practical Dimensions* (1997; Supp. 2000).

97. ABA Juvenile Justice Standards, *supra* note 86. *See also* Martin Guggenheim, "A Paradigm for Determining the Role of Counsel for Children," 64 *Ford. L. Rev.* 1399, 1424 (1996).

attorney who reports the juvenile's desires but then proceeds to undermine them by disclosing further, often confidential, information has hardly respected individual dignity and autonomy. Yet an attorney who fails to make such disclosures or who attempts to present all facts neutrally may be unable to provide the guidance that an overburdened and understaffed court requires.

In recognition of these difficulties, some commentators have advocated a more contextual approach. This framework recognizes that age is not an adequate proxy for competence, and that a minor who is able to make considered decisions in some circumstances may be unable to do so in others. Under this approach, an attorney should focus on factors such as the risks of a "wrong" decision and the minor's age, mental capacity, psychological stability, strength of preferences, and ability to make rational, consistent judgments without undue influence by others.[98]

QUESTIONS

1. Which of these frameworks do you find most helpful? Given the facts of Problem 4(a), would it be justifiable to omit mentioning the diversion program?

2. In addressing the issues in Problem 4(c), recall the materials on confidentiality in Chapter V, section G. What information would you need about incest and abuse victims in general, or about this family situation in particular, before you decide how to proceed?

3. Consider the ABA's Standards of Practice for Lawyers who Represent Children in Abuse and Neglect Cases (1996). Standard B–4 provides that the attorney generally should "respect the child's expressed preference and follow the child's directions throughout the course of litigation." However, Standard B–4(3) adds:

> If the child's attorney determines that the child's expressed preference would be seriously injurious to the child (as opposed to merely being contrary to the lawyer's opinion of what would be in the child's interest), the lawyer may request appointment of a separate guardian ad litem and continue to represent the child's expressed preference.... The child's attorney shall not reveal the basis of the request for appointment of a guardian ad litem which would compromise the client's position.

The Comment notes that one of the "most difficult ethical issues for lawyers representing children occurs when the child is able to express a position ... that could result in serious injury." This is particularly likely when the child desires to "live in a dangerous situation because it is all he or she knows, because of a feeling of blame or of responsibility to take care

---

98. Peter Margulies, "The Lawyer as Caregiver: Child Clients' Competence in Context," 64 *Ford. L. Rev.* 1473, 1487–1493 (1996);. *See also* Peters, "The Roles and Con-tent of Best Interests I Client–Directed Law-yering for Children in Child Protective Pro-ceedings," *supra* note 96.

of the parents, or because of threats. The child may choose to deal with a known situation rather than risk the unknown world of a foster home or other out-of-home placement." In most cases, the Comment suggests that this dilemma can be resolved by effective counseling. However, if the child "cannot be persuaded [to abandon a dangerous position], the attorney has a duty to safeguard the child's interests by requesting appointment of a guardian ad litem, who will be charged with advocating the child's best interest." Yet as the Comment also acknowledges, "as a practical matter, this may not adequately protect the child if the danger to the child was revealed only in a confidential disclosure to the lawyer because the guardian ad litem may never learn of the disclosed danger."

Does this Standard provide appropriate guidance on the facts of Problem 4(c)? If not, what would you propose?

A Law Student's Response

The dilemma posed in Problem 3 is not only difficult, it may also be personally wrenching for the lawyer. The following is excerpted from a case-report written by a third-year law student working in the clinic of an urban law school:

> A child can't sue, a child can't enter into a contract, a child isn't considered able to consent to sex, but yet, for the purpose of legal ethics, a lawyer must treat a child just like an adult client: she must advocate for the child's stated interests, no matter how obvious it is to her that the stated interests are not in the best interests of the child.
>
> Monday I picked up the case of A.B. She is a thirteen year old girl who was arrested for Theft II. She apparently had no prior record (later I discovered she had a shoplifting record in [another state]). When I saw her in the cellblock, the first thing that struck me was the way she was dressed—like a prostitute. I expected her to be scared, upset ... instead she laughed at nearly everything. She told me she had only missed two days of school this year and that she participates in track, choir, and cheerleading! Nearly everything she said was a lie, but it was amazing how quickly she would think of such things and how easily they would roll off her tongue, with such conviction (she could be president someday)....
>
> When I went into the hallway to interview her parents, they informed me that they refused to have her released to them. Parents: She constantly runs away, spends all of her time on the streets with twenty-one year olds (the age of some first year law students), never goes to school, does drugs, is completely out of control. The parents are not married or [living] together but they both showed up in court together and stood firm in their decision. It was clear that they believed that this girl desperately needs help and that getting it through the system was in A.B.'s best interests. I thought they were well-meaning but misguided at the time.

The government hadn't been looking to detain her but when they found out the parents didn't want her released the intake worker and prosecutor both recommended that she be placed in a shelter home until trial. The government did not file a petition (formal charge) and the statute says filing of petition may be delayed for 5 days upon good cause shown. The prosecutor's showing of good cause consisted of an assertion that they haven't been able to contact the Complainant. The judge denied my motion to dismiss the case for lack of good cause for the five-day hold. The probable cause hearing consisted of the arresting officer testifying as follows: The Complainant called him and said that she had given A.B. $100 to hold for her in her bag. When she asked for it back the next day, A.B. wouldn't give it to her. A.B. was then arrested and there was no money in her bag. I only asked three questions on cross because it was so obvious to me that they hadn't established probable cause that I didn't want to mess it up. The government apparently had no information about the Complainant (thus the request for a five day hold in filing the petition). It was just a hearsay account of an anonymous Complainant with no evidence as to why this mystery person (that the government did not know enough about to even contact) should be believed. If she had called and said I took her money would there be probable cause to hold me for theft? The judge found probable cause.

Then the detention argument. Pretrial detention is for kids who are a danger to themselves or others or unlikely to show up at their hearing otherwise. The ONLY reason they were looking to detain her (as conceded by the prosecutor) was that the parents didn't want her back. She was ordered into a shelter home. She was crying her eyes out as she heard in open court that her parents did not want her back. Afterwards I went back to the cellblock to talk to her and she was not laughing or smiling anymore. "I have no parents," she said with tears streaming down her face. I felt really bad for her at the time although in the back of my mind I knew that the parents were doing what is best for her and I was arguing for something not in her best interest: for her to be put back on the street with her twenty-one year old boyfriends, drugs, etc. rather than getting help that she desperately needs.

The next day, feeling that my client got railroaded, I filed an emergency motion to review the findings on good cause for the five day hold and probable cause to detain. Today the prosecutor called and said the government has decided to drop the case. Though I don't know why, it is probably because they couldn't contact the complaining witness. The motion may have helped. Tomorrow she is to be released. The question is: released to whom? Social services contacted her aunt and secured a promise that the aunt would take her if the parents won't.

Tonight I called A.B.'s mother to tell her A.B. will be released and find out if she plans to take her tomorrow. . . . The mother still refuses to take her. She asked me what was the point of this whole thing if she is just going to be released. She asked what she is supposed to do when she has tried counseling and tried having her live with family members and A.B. is just completely out of control and nobody will see that she needs help. She asked why the law doesn't protect her right as a parent who tries hard and cares about her child, but gives lawyers and all sorts of rights to children so they can be released back out onto the street. She asked what kind of a threat she can use on A.B. now that "they'll lock your ass up if you commit a crime" has been proven idle. She said she refuses to take A.B. back if that's what it takes to get somebody to listen to her and get help for A.B. before she gets pregnant, gets AIDS or ends up dead. The mother was very upset but was also respectful to me throughout the conversation and even thanked me for calling her when it was over. She pointed out how the system has failed and pointed out my role in that.

I really didn't have any answers for her. It is a little too much reality for me—I will be happy next fall to go off into the world of faceless corporations squabbling over obscure language in contracts, where the immorality of lawyering is a bit more innocuous.

4. Representing Sophisticated Clients

PROBLEM 4

a) You are an experienced white-collar defense attorney representing John Buckley, a nationally-famous securities broker who has been charged with insider trading and mail fraud. You have negotiated a plea agreement with the prosecution that would involve a large but not catastrophic fine, less than a year in jail, and a lifetime ban from securities trading, in return for assistance in the prosecution of others in the securities industry. In your view, the agreement is an excellent one for Buckley, who otherwise faces years in prison. Buckley, however, is convinced that he will be acquitted at trial. In his opinion, the prosecution's case is not strong, and the prosecutor is not smart. He is also convinced that the same charm and charisma that have advanced him for his entire career are sure to win over the jury.

That is not how you see the case. You know that the prosecution's evidence is very strong, and your trial experience convinces you that Buckley will impress jurors as glib, arrogant, and unlikable. Buckley strikes you as a man who has beaten the system so often that he has persuaded himself the system can always be beaten, but there is little doubt in your mind that he will be convicted. You have repeatedly explained your assessment of the case, discreetly at first, then quite bluntly. Buckley's response has invariably been the same: "I've made a hundred million dollars selling myself to the hardest guys on Wall Street, and no lawyer is going to tell me that I can't sell myself to a jury." He has threatened to fire you. You have considered quitting.

You are now contemplating alternative strategies. One is to propose that Buckley give a "dress rehearsal" of his testimony before a jury composed of secretaries and paralegals from your firm; one of your partners would do the direct examination and you would do the cross. Afterwards, the mock jurors would give Buckley their candid opinion of his performance. You would select jurors likely to agree with your assessment of the case. Another possibility is to enlist Buckley's wife to place pressure on him to accept the plea.

b) Assume also that you have just received information that will enable you to discredit one of the prosecution's witnesses. In your view, the prosecution's case will remain strong enough to convict Buckley. You are convinced, however, that if you inform Buckley about the new information, his resolve to reject the plea agreement will be even greater. You plan not to tell him about the information.

Would any of these strategies be proper? Can, or should you withdraw if Buckley insists on going to trial?

References:

Model Rules 1.2(a), 1.4, 8.4(c).

NOTES

Most of the problems of paternalism we have examined in this chapter involved clients who are less competent, mature, well-educated, or well-off than their lawyers. This is scarcely surprising, because opportunities for paternalism arise only when lawyers believe they know better than their clients and have the power to put that belief into practice. Lawyers are less likely to have the confidence or the opportunity to second-guess wealthy, powerful, or sophisticated clients. Yet these clients also can have bad judgment or selective blind-spots. It frequently happens that the more canny the clients, the more difficult it is to dissuade them from mistakes because "[c]lients who've spent a lifetime outsmarting their opponents always think they know more about being a lawyer than their lawyer."[99] In the words of one Washington, D.C. white-collar defender, a powerful client who "has been in charge of his own life ... is not used to releasing control" to his lawyer.[100] If the lawyer is to do the job successfully, it will often be necessary to manipulate or "manage" the client for his own good—and that raises the problem of paternalism.

Such problems can arise in connection with a sophisticated client's non-legal judgment as well. Examples of clients who are extremely successful in one line of business but prone to disastrous misjudgments in another are, unfortunately, all too common. The savings-and-loan disasters in the late 1980s and 1990s came about in large part because many of these institutions were acquired by builders and developers whose lifelong busi-

99. Saundra Torry, "In the Land of the Mighty, Titans Often Tussle," *Wash. Post,* June 6, 1994, at F7.

100. *Id.*

ness habits were unsuited to the thrift industry. One bank regulator explained that, in the wake of deregulation, the S & Ls were taken over by "the guys who want to hit home runs. But the cardinal rule of financial services is that there are no home runs."[101] The result was speculative investments that yielded a few gains but many losses, leading to spiraling capital needs that could be satisfied only by further speculative investments. As Chapter VII noted, the recent spate of corporate scandals involving Enron et al. reflect similar cognitive biases.

Under what circumstances might paternalism be proper for lawyers representing clients with no "disability" other than bad judgment? Consider the ABA Section on Litigation's Ethical Guidelines for Settlement Negotiations (2002). Standard 3.2.4 provides:

> A lawyer should provide a client with a professional assessment of the advantages and disadvantages of a proposed settlement, so that the client can make a fully-informed decision about settlement. Any effort to assist the client in reaching a decision should avoid interference with the client's ultimate decisionmaking authority.

The Committee Notes on that Standard add:

> The lawyer's role in connection with settlement negotiations is one of advisor to and agent of the client. The lawyer should adhere to that relationship even when the lawyer's judgment or experience leads the lawyer to believe that the lawyer more fully appreciates the wisdom of a proposed course of action than the client does. While a lawyer can and often should vigorously advise the client of the lawyer's views respecting proposed settlement strategies and terms, that advice should not override or intrude into the client's ultimate decisionmaking authority.... A lawyer should not threaten to take actions that may ... induce the client's assent to the lawyer's position respecting a proposed settlement. Efforts to persuade should be pursued with attention to ensuring that ultimate decisionmaking power remains with the client.

Does that standard strike the appropriate balance for cases like those presented in Problem 4? What if a client's foolish decisions could have disastrous effects on other corporate stakeholders, such as employees and investors, as well as the client's reputation in the business community? Would the strategies considered in Problem 4 ever be justified?

---

101. Martin Mayer, *The Greatest–Ever Bank Robbery 63 (1992).*

CHAPTER XII

MARKET REGULATION

INTRODUCTION

As the materials in Chapter III indicate, much of the early impetus for bar ethical codes arose from concerns about lawyers' marketing practices. The readings that follow explore these concerns in the context of current rules and policies. Standard justifications for bar regulation of the legal services market rest on two central assumptions. One involves the need for regulatory structures; a second involves the appropriateness of professional control over regulatory processes.

The first assumption is that certain imperfections in the market for legal services justify external oversight. Such imperfections include what economists variously describe as information barriers, adverse selection, free riders, and externalities.

Information Barriers

An initial difficulty stems from many consumers' inability to make accurate assessments about the services they receive, either before or after purchase. Most individual (as opposed to business) clients are one-shot purchasers; they will not consult the same attorney more than once. This lack of experience, coupled with the expense and difficulties of comparative shopping for professional services, makes it hard for such consumers to identify cost-effective practices. In a survey by Yankelovich Partners for Martindale–Hubbell, three quarters of consumers indicated that it was hard to know who to trust when choosing a lawyer. Over two in five Americans (44 percent) agree that it is hard to find a good lawyer and almost three out of ten (28 percent) report that their inability to compare information about different attorneys would limit their ability to research options for representation. Consumers who have hired a lawyer spent less time researching their choices than they spent researching purchases of furniture or major appliances.[1] Even sophisticated corporate clients report problems in assessing the necessity or efficiency of certain services. In the absence of some external regulation, too many purchasers may end up with incompetent, overpriced, or unethical practitioners.

Adverse Selection

A related problem involves the adverse effects of information barriers on the quality of professional services. If clients cannot accurately discrimi-

---

1. Yankelovich Partners for Martindale Hubbell, *Consumers Attitudes Toward Choosing Legal Counsel* (2000), available at http:// research.lawyers.com/Consumers–Attitudes– Toward–Choosing–Legal–Counsel.html (reporting an average of 19 hours researching

nate among the services available, and no regulatory body enforces minimum standards, lawyers will lack adequate incentives to invest time, education, and resources in providing quality services. Competition may encourage attorneys to cut corners and a "market for lemons" may develop, in which bad lawyering drives out good and the public pays the price.

Free Riders

An additional difficulty involves "free riders," that is, those who gain from bar standards without personally observing them. For example, the bar collectively has an interest in securing the public's trust, and in having lawyers conduct themselves in such a way as to maintain that trust. However, absent effective regulatory structures, individual attorneys will have inadequate economic incentives to avoid cheating; they can benefit as free riders from the bar's general reputation without adhering to the rules that maintain it.

Externalities

A final category of problems calling for regulatory responses involves external costs to society and third parties from conduct that may be advantageous to particular clients and their lawyers. For example, the public generally has an interest in seeing prompt and just resolution of disputes in circumstances where individual clients would be willing to pay lawyers to delay or obstruct truth-finding processes.

Although these problems call for some regulation, there is no comparable consensus about the forms it should take and who should make these decisions. The following materials explore such disputes concerning lawyers' advertising, solicitation, specialization, group services, and fee arrangements.

A.   ADVERTISING

INTRODUCTION

Although many lawyers view advertising of legal services as a recent and regrettable development, it is restrictions on advertising that are recent. Practitioners in ancient Rome, for example, employed various techniques for self-promotion; some hawked their services on the street and others hired clappers to applaud presentations before judges.[2] Advertising in circulars and newspapers remained common in this country throughout most of the nineteenth century. Self-promotion was not infrequent among even the most distinguished attorneys, including Abraham Lincoln and David Hoffman, the author of one of the first ethical treatises (*Fifty Resolutions in Regard to Professional Deportment*). The first state ethical code (Alabama, 1887) explicitly permitted newspaper advertisements that

---

lawyers, compared with 33 hours for furniture and 23 hours on a major appliance).

2. William Forsyth, *The History of Lawyers* 172 (1875).

did not involve "laudation." While other jurisdictions were less tolerant, formal sanctions for such conduct remained rare.[3]

However, as the materials in Chapter III indicate, bar leaders after the turn of the century became increasingly concerned about commercial practices within the profession. The ABA's 1908 Canons of Ethics included broad prohibitions on advertisements that included furnishing or inspiring newspaper comments and engaging in "self-laudation [which] offends the traditions and lowers the tone of our profession."[4] According to prominent early commentators on ethics such as George Sharswood, "business [should] seek the young attorney," rather than the converse.[5] By and large, that remained the bar's position until the 1970s. Legal ethics committees spent more time refining and enforcing restrictions on advertising and solicitation than on any other subject.[6]

Few forms of self-promotion, however insignificant, were beneath bar concern. In the six decades between promulgation of the Canons of Ethics and enactment of the Code of Professional Responsibility, courts and committees condemned practices such as: distributing embossed matchbooks or Christmas cards with a lawyer's name and profession; using neon lighting or ostentatious lettering in law office signs; endorsing a particular brand of Scotch; wearing jewelry with the state bar insignia; and using boldface type in telephone books.[7]

The seemingly trivial preoccupations of some ethics opinions should not, however, obscure the serious concerns at issue. To leaders of the organized bar, the prohibitions on advertising and solicitation expressed deeply felt understandings about law as a profession rather than a business. From their perspective, allowing overt self-promotion would erode professionalism, invite deception, and "lower the whole tone of the administration of justice."[8]

By the late 1960s and early 70s, a growing constituency both within and outside the profession began to challenge those assertions. The increasing diversity of the profession, the rise of the consumer movement, the emergence of low-cost legal clinics, and the growth of concerns about unmet legal needs helped fuel criticisms about the bar's anti-competitive

---

3. Lori B. Andrews, *Birth of a Salesman: Lawyer Advertising and Solicitation* (1980); Federal Trade Commission, *Improving Consumer Access to Legal Services: The Case for Removing Restrictions on Truthful Advertising* 21–24 (1984).

4. ABA, *Canons of Ethics*, Canon 27.

5. George Sharswood, *Essay on Professional Ethics* (1854) *quoted in* Jerold Auerbach, *Unequal Justice: Lawyers and Social Change in Modern America* 41 (1976).

6. James Willard Hurst, *The Growth of American Law: The Law Makers* 331 (1950); Philip Shuchman, "Ethics and Legal Ethics: The Propriety of the Canons as a Group

Moral Code," 37 *Geo. Wash. L. Rev.* 244, 255–56 (1968).

7. *In re* Maltby, 202 P.2d 902 (Ariz. 1949) (matchbooks); ABA Comm. on Professional Ethics, Formal Op. 309 (1963) (Christmas cards); *In re* Duffy, 19 A.D.2d 177, 242 N.Y.S.2d 665 (1963) (neon sign); Henry S. Drinker, *Legal Ethics* 289, App. A No. 132 (1953) (size of sign); Belli v. State Bar, 519 P.2d 575 (Cal.1974) (Scotch); ABA Informal Decision C–747 (1964) (state bar jewelry); ABA Formal Op. 284 (1951) (phone book); *but see* ABA Informal Op. 1222 (1972) (jewelry with ABA insignia permissible under DR 2–101(A)).

8. Drinker, *supra* note 7, at 210–12.

policies. Many commentators viewed such policies as anachronistic; they seemed premised on the model of a small-town legal practice in which reputation was a matter of common knowledge and information about the cost and quality of services was readily accessible. In addition, critics objected to the elitist biases underpinning bar policy. Lawyers representing wealthy individuals and corporations had various opportunities for genteel promotion; their firms often subsidized social events and memberships in private clubs, as well as purchased listings in bar-approved law directories available to major businesses. By contrast, attorneys representing poor and middle-income individuals had fewer chances to publicize their services and their potential clients were less likely to have adequate sources of information.

These concerns set the stage for legal challenges that eventually reached the Supreme Court. In 1975, the Supreme Court struck down mandatory minimum fees for lawyers as an antitrust violation, and thereby made price competition possible. (The case was *Goldfarb v. Virginia State Bar*, 421 U.S. 773 (1975). See discussion in Section F, *supra*.) The first low-cost legal clinics appeared shortly afterward, but their founders quickly realized that to survive they needed to advertise. The first challenge to prohibitions on advertising, *Bates v. State Bar of Arizona*, 433 U.S. 350 (1977), involved a somewhat colorless advertisement for a legal clinic offering "legal services at very reasonable fees." The ad also listed charges for certain routine services such as uncontested divorces, adoptions, and simple personal bankruptcies. The Supreme Court held that lawyer advertising could not be subjected to blanket suppression, and that the advertisement at issue fell within First Amendment protections. In a subsequent decision, *In re R.M.J.*, 455 U.S. 191, 203 (1982), the Court again struck down content restrictions on non-misleading commercial speech and summarized its approach as follows:

> Truthful advertising related to lawful activities is entitled to the protections of the First Amendment. But when the particular content or method of the advertising suggests that it is inherently misleading or when experience has proved that in fact such advertising is subject to abuse, the States may impose appropriate restrictions. Misleading advertising may be prohibited entirely. But the States may not place an absolute prohibition on certain types of potentially misleading information, e.g., a listing of areas of practice, if the information also may be presented in a way that is not deceptive.... Although the potential for deception and confusion is particularly strong in the context of advertising professional services, restrictions upon such advertising may be no broader than reasonably necessary to prevent the deception.
>
> Even when a communication is not misleading, the State retains some authority to regulate. But the State must assert a substantial interest and the interference with speech must be in proportion to the interest served.... Restrictions must be narrowly drawn and the State lawfully

may regulate only to the extent regulation furthers the State's substantial interest.[9]

Subsequent cases held that states could not prohibit nondeceptive graphic illustrations or descriptions of ongoing litigation, *Zauderer v. Office of Disciplinary Counsel*, 471 U.S. 626 (1985);[10] mailings targeted to a specific recipient rather than members of the general public, *Shapero v. Kentucky Bar Assn.*, 486 U.S. 466 (1988);[11] or accurate identification of an attorney as a certified trial specialist, *Peel v. Attorney Registration and Disciplinary Comm'n.*, 496 U.S. 91 (1990).[12]

All these decisions provoked strong dissension within the Court and widespread opposition within the bar. According to the chair of the ABA's Commission on Advertising, *Bates* and the resulting reforms in ethical rules were "about as popular with the legal profession as venereal disease."[13] Surveys in the first two decades following the opinion generally found that most lawyers opposed mass media advertising and that a significant number of practitioners agreed with former Chief Justice Warren Burger that such self-promotion was one of the most "unethical things a lawyer can do."[14] By contrast, according to most surveys, the majority of non-lawyer consumers agreed that mass media advertising was professionally acceptable.[15]

9. The case involved a successful challenge to Missouri regulations that narrowly limited advertising to certain specified categories of information and designated areas of practice.

10. At issue was an advertisement featuring a drawing of the Dalkon Shield contraceptive device, accompanied by the question, "Did you use this iud?" The ad stated that the device was alleged to cause certain serious complications, that the law firm was representing women with claims against the manufacturer, and that "the cases are handled on a contingent fee basis of the amount recovered. If there is no recovery, no legal fees are paid by our clients." The Court held that the state bar could impose discipline for only the last sentence of the advertisement, which did not distinguish between fees and costs and which therefore might mislead lay persons to believe they had no liability in a losing cause. 471 U.S. at 652–653. The Court also found reasonable the Ohio Supreme Court's suggestion that attorneys advertising their availability on a contingency fee basis must also disclose their rates. *Id.* at 653 n. 15.

11. The mailing at issue was directed to individuals subject to mortgage foreclosure proceedings.

12. The attorney's letterhead stated that he was a "certified civil trial specialist by the National Board of Trial Advocacy [NBTA]." The lower court made no finding of

actual deception, and because the NBTA standards were verifiable and rigorous, the Supreme Court did not find the advertisement inherently misleading despite the absence of an official state certification program.

13. William Hornsby, "Clashes of Class and Cash: Battles from the 150 Years War to Govern Client Development," 37 *Ariz. State L. J.* 255, 271 (2005).

14. Archer W. Honeycutt & Elizabeth A. Wibker, "Consumers' Perceptions of Selected Issues Relating to Advertising by Lawyers," 7 *J. of Prof. Services Marketing* 119, 120 (1991). Then Chief Justice Burger had difficulty finding appropriate language for lawyers who advertised. "Perhaps huckster is not strong enough a word; shyster is more appropriate, but I find on consulting the dictionary that even 'shyster' is not strong enough. I will settle for huckster-shyster advertising." Hornsby, *supra* note 13, at 260 (quoting Warren Burger). Almost 90% of surveyed ABA members believe that advertising harms the profession's image. *See* Mary Hladky, "High Court Case to Test Limits on Lawyer Ads," *Legal Times*, Jan. 9, 1995, at 18.

15. Milo Geyelin, "Debate Intensifies Over State Regulations That Restrict TV Advertising by Lawyers," *Wall St.J.*, Aug. 31, 1992, at B1, B4; Diane B. MacDonald & Mary Anne Raymond, "Attorney Advertising: Do

Although the bar has proved increasingly receptive toward marketing, the number of practitioners who advertise in major media has remained small. The American Bar Association estimates that only about two percent of the nation's attorneys advertise on television and five percent on radio. Only a few large firms have used mass media marketing; most rely instead on more indirect public relations and business development strategies such as press releases, promotional literature, special events, and client education seminars. A majority of lawyers use brochures or yellow page listings, and about 12 percent use direct mail. A large and growing number have websites, and many are beginning to affiliate with web-based lawyer-client matching services.[16] Overall, legal advertising now accounts for over $575 million in revenue annually.[17]

The increase in marketing strategies, together with divisions within the bar concerning their acceptability, have led to continuing reassessment of bar ethical rules. State requirements are often more restrictive than those specified in the ABA's Model Rules, and differ considerably across jurisdictions concerning matters such as testimonials, dramatizations, and claims concerning past performance or comparative advantages.[18] Consider what regulations you would support concerning such advertisements in light of the policy considerations discussed below.

PROBLEM 1

You are the chair of a committee appointed by your state supreme court to consider revising ethical rules on attorney advertising. Your current code bans testimonial endorsements, lyrics, jingles, dramatizations, animations, and undignified claims. Most lawyers on your committee, including members of various trial lawyers' associations, want to retain these prohibitions. The non-lawyer members support the proposal of a Federal Trade Commission study, which would ban only false or deceptive communications. How would you vote? Would any compromise proposal be preferable?

Committee members have collected the following examples from various jurisdictions that suggest areas where guidance would be useful. Under the standard that you favor, how would you rule on the following advertisements?

Attorneys Know Their Clients?," 7 *J. of Prof. Services Marketing* 99 (1991). *See generally* American Bar Association, *Lawyer Advertising at the Crossroads* (1995).

16. Terry Carter, "Casting for Clients," *ABA Journal*, March 2004, at 35; Leigh Jones, "A Tough Sell: Lawyer Ads Show Glacial Evolution," *Nat'l L. J.*, June 4, 2007, at A1; Geeta Kharkar, "Googling for Help: Lawyer Referral Services and the Internet," 20 *Geo. J. Legal Ethics* 769 (2007).

17. Maria Aspan, "Getting Law Firms to Like Commercials," *N.Y. Times*, June 19, 2007, at C5.

18. See Emily Olson, "The Ethics of Attorney Advertising: The Effects of Different State Regulatory Regimes," 18 *Geo. J. Legal Ethics* 1055 (2006). For online links to the specific state ethics provisions governing the communications of legal services, see ABA Comm'n. On Responsibility in Client Dev., Links to State Ethics Rules Governing Lawyer Advertising, Solicitation, and Marketing, ABA Network, at htttp://www.abanet.org/legalservices/clientdevelopment/adrules.

Advertisements Questionable as to Substance

a) A television advertisement in which a casually dressed man announces that his lawyer "got me $175,000 even though the police report said I was totally at fault."[19]

b) Print advertisements that use the terms "expert," "competent," "unique," "tough," "revolutionary," "specializes," "heavy hitter," "Super Lawyer," and "Best Lawyer," and a web address "bestpersonalinjury.com."[20]

c) A full-page advertisement with a picture of a taxi fare meter, with a headline "How to Hire a Lawyer Without Getting Taken for a Ride," and text that states, "Few things are as frustrating as retaining an attorney. Because the minute you walk into their office the meter starts to run. For reasonable fees for routine services, call [F]".[21]

d) An advertisement for services at a 20% discount, and a claim, "Best Possible Settlement in Least Amount of Time." The advertisement also states, "My reputation, experience, and integrity result in most of our cases being settled without a complaint or lengthy trial."[22]

e) A television advertisement in which a man truthfully states that after his third arrest for drunk driving, "They wanted to put me in jail for a year and take away my driver's license for ten years. That's when I called the lawyers at the Ticket Center. They got my case thrown out of court. No jail. No suspension. Nothing."[23]

f) A television advertisement showing insurance adjusters planning to delay payments to an accident victim. One of them asks who is representing the defendant. When the answer is Keller & Keller, he says, "Let's settle this one." A Florida television ad that advises: "Don't settle for less than you deserve[24]

Advertisements Questionable as to Manner of Presentation

g) A thirty second television ad in which a prominent football player advises viewers that, "I don't like to get hurt or to lose and I don't think you do either," and that a phone call to E's personal injury firm may be "the most important one" they'll ever make.[25]

---

19. Brae Canlen, "Injured? Call Now," *California Lawyer*, January 1995, at 51.

20. *See* Louise L. Hill, *Lawyer Advertising*, 93, 99 (1993); Alexander v. Cahill, F. Supp. (N.D.N.Y. 2007) (heavy hitter); "Advertising May Tout 'Super Lawyer' Listing and Other Ratings that Meet Certain Criteria," 23 *ABA/BNA Lawyer's Man. Prof. Conduct* 407, 408 (2007) (discussing various state bar opinions on best and super lawyer designations); Jill Schachner Chanen, "Watch What You Say," *ABA J.*, Oct. 2005, at 59–60 (discussing web address).

21. *See* Matter of Marcus, 320 N.W.2d 806, 809 (Wis. 1982); Linda Ewald, "Content Regulation of Lawyer Advertising: An Era of Change," 3 *Geo. J. Legal Ethics* 429, 463 (1990).

22. Kentucky Bar Ass'n v. Gangwish, 630 S.W.2d 66 (Ky.1982) (discount); In Matter of Wamsley, 725 N.E.2d 75 (Ind. 2000).

23. Geyelin, *supra* note 15, at B1.

24. Matter of Keller, 792 N.E.2d 865 (Ind. 2003); Harrell v. Florida Bar, 2008 WL 596086 (M.D. Fla. 2008).

25. *See* Martha Middleton, "Ads Pay Off—In Image and Income," *Nat'l L.J.*, March 5, 1984, at 1, 24. See also Leonard Post, "Kentucky Bar Rewrites Ad Rules,"

h) A suggestive picture of an attractive blonde attorney wearing a miniskirt and spiked heels, lying prone across her desk, with a caption stating: "Does this firm have a reputation? You bet it does." Another features a model in a bikini and boxing gloves with the caption, "Protect yourself at all times."[26]

i) A bill board featuring a woman's body in racy lingerie and a half-naked man's chiseled torso, with the caption: "Life's Short: Get a Divorce," and an ad announcing "HOLIDAY SPECIAL ... get that spouse some'in she's been wanting for a long time ... A Deeeevorce.... $150 Bucks," followed by the lawyers, name, phone number and "Happy Holidays."[27]

j) An ad showing lawyers as giants leaping over large buildings and giving legal assistance to space aliens. Ads featuring pitbulls, sharks, panthers, or lions.[28]

k) A hearse with a sign promising "No Frill Wills" driven by lawyer K's son in a moderate-sized midwestern city.[29]

l) A larger-than-life portrait of an attorney on billboards that announce "I Sue Drunk Drivers;" a television ad picturing a recent ferry accident with a tidal wave of green dollar signs; and a promise that the firm settles most cases quickly and "$ucessfully," followed by a phone number "1–800–Sue–Them."[30]

m) An ad with the following limerick:

A careless roadrunner named Fred

Slipped under a light that was red.

He thought he'd go free

With a "No Contest" plea

But now he's a jailbird instead.[31]

NOTES

What are the justifications for the bar's restrictions on advertising? Consider the following justifications in light of Problem 1.

Nat'l L.J. May 12, 2003 (discussing bans on testimonials and actors posing as lawyers and clients).

26. Evelyn Nieves, "Using a Feminine Edge to Open a Man's World," *N.Y. Times*, Nov. 28, 1995, at 1, 3; Hornsby, *supra* note 13, at 265.

27. Jones, *supra* note 16; Hornsby, *supra* note 13, at 265. The lawyer herself was the partly-undressed woman in the billboard ad; in the wake of the notoriety it gave her, she also posed in *Playboy* in a profile titled "Lawyer of Love."

28. Alexander v. Cahill, 2007 WL 1202402 (N.D.N.Y. 2007); Nathan Koppell,

"Objection: Funny Legal Ads Draw Censure," *Wall St. J.*, Feb. 7, 2008, at A1.

29. *See* Hornsby, *supra* note 13, at 265. The lawyer also offered a free 10–speed bicycle to any client whose drunk driving case he lost. 4 *Bar Leader*, Nov.–Dec. 1978, at 7.

30. "The Billboard Wars," *The Legal Reformer*, Jan.–March 1990, at 9; Susan Saulny, "Lawyers' Ads Seeking Clients in Ferry Crash," *N.Y. Times* Nov. 4, 2003, at A1; Hornsby, *supra* note 13, at 265.

31. Lori Andrews, "The Selling of a Precedent," 10 *Student Law.*, March 1982, at 12, 49.

Deception

As the majority in *Bates* noted, opponents of advertising often claim that it "inevitably will be misleading (a) because such services are so individualized with regard to content and quality as to prevent informed comparison on the basis of advertisement, (b) because the consumer of legal services is unable to determine in advance just what services are required, and (c) because advertising by attorneys will highlight irrelevant factors and fail to show the relevant factor or skill." 433 U.S. at 372. Although acknowledging the force of this objection, the *Bates* majority felt that the preferred remedy was "more disclosure rather than less." *Id.* at 375. Advertising "does not provide a complete foundation on which to select an attorney. But it seems peculiar to deny the consumer, on the ground that the information is incomplete, at least some of the relevant information needed to reach an informed decision." *Id.* at 374.

Cost and Quality

Opponents of advertising claim that its likely result will be to raise the price and lower the quality of services. Attorneys assertedly will pass on their additional costs of marketing in the form of higher fees, and practitioners who advertise prices also will be inclined to provide a "standard package [of services] regardless of whether it fits the client's needs." *Bates v. State Bar of Arizona*, 433 U.S. at 378. The Court in *Bates* rejected these arguments as empirically "dubious" and constitutionally "[ir]relevant." *Id.* at 377. As the majority pointed out, the bar's own support for prepaid group legal services programs with fixed fee schedules somewhat undercut its opposition to standardized price competition. *Id.* at 378. Moreover, the majority noted, such competition generally results in lower fees. Subsequent research, including a Federal Trade Commission study, has suggested that this is in fact the case for legal services.[32]

Some analysts also believe that greater competition, by decreasing charges, will increase demand, expand volume, and encourage economies of scale through specialization and more efficient use of paralegals and technology.[33] What limited data are available suggest that advertising has a favorable effect on price and no demonstrably unfavorable effect on quality.[34] In any event, many commentators agree with the *Bates* majority that restraints on advertising are an "ineffective way of deterring shoddy work." 433 U.S. at 378.

32. Federal Trade Commission, *supra* note 3; Geoffrey Hazard, Jr., Russell Pearce & Jeffrey Stempel, "Why Lawyers Should Be Allowed to Advertise: A Market Analysis of Legal Services," 58 *N.Y.U.L.Rev.* 1084 (1983).

33. Hazard, Pearce & Stempel, *supra* note 32; ABA, *Lawyer Advertising at the Crossroads, supra* note 15.

34. One of the few studies on point found that a legal clinic that advertised aggressively produced better objectives and subjective client ratings in divorce cases than local firms that did not advertise. For discussion of the quality studies, see Van O'Steen, "Bates v. State Bar of Arizona: The Personal Account of a Party and the Consumer Benefits of Lawyer Advertising," 37 *Ariz. St. L. J.* 245, 252–53 (2005).

Professionalism and Administration of Justice

Critics of advertising claim that it may stir up unnecessary litigation, undermine attorneys' "sense of dignity and self-worth," erode client trust, and cheapen the public image of the profession. *Bates v. State Bar of Arizona*, 433 U.S. at 368. In rejecting such claims, the *Bates* majority responded:

> At its core, the argument presumes that attorneys must conceal from themselves and from their clients the real-life fact that lawyers earn their livelihood at the bar. We suspect that few attorneys engage in such self-deception. . . . Bankers and engineers advertise, and yet these professions are not regarded as undignified. . . . Since the belief that lawyers are somehow "above" trade has become an anachronism, the historical foundation for the advertising restraint has crumbled. . . . Although advertising might increase the use of judicial machinery, we cannot accept the notion that it is always better for a person to suffer a wrong silently than to redress it by legal action.

433 U.S. at 368–376. In *Zauderer v. Office of Disciplinary Counsel*, 471 U.S. at 648, the majority added:

> [W]e are unsure that the State's desire that attorneys maintain their dignity in their communications with the public is an interest substantial enough to justify the abridgment of their First Amendment rights. . . . As we held in *Carey v. Population Services International*, the mere possibility that some members of the population might find advertising embarrassing or offensive cannot justify suppressing it. The same must hold true for advertising that some members of the bar might find beneath their dignity.

Is this an adequate response to concerns (in former Chief Justice Burger's phrase) about selling law like laxatives? Survey evidence on this point is mixed. Some bar studies which have relied on small samples and problematic methodologies have found adverse effects from advertising. For example, in one survey consumers who were aware of lawyers' ads rated the profession lower on characteristics such as trustworthiness, professionalism, honesty, and integrity.[35] In another study, exposure to the advertisements such as the ticket clinic in Problem 1(e) "heightened pre-existing biases that jury awards are too high, [that] justice can be 'bought and sold,' [and] that most lawyers will help clients win 'even if they know they are lying.' "[36] However, other research using accepted methodologies indicated that "dignified" advertisements reflect favorably on the profession and on attorneys who advertise.[37] A review of research by the ABA's Commission

---

35. W. Ward Reynoldson, "The Case Against Lawyer Advertising," 75 *ABA J.*, Jan. 1989, at 60; Jim Rossi & Mollie Weighner, "An Empirical Examination of the Iowa Bar's Approach to Regulating Lawyer Advertising," 77 *Iowa L.Rev.* 179, 223, 253–255, n. 4 (1991). Ronald Rotunda, "Professionalism, Legal Advertising and Free Speech in the Wake of Florida Bar v. Went For It," 49 *Ark. L. Rev.* 703 (1997) (noting methodological problems in bar studies).

36. Geyelin, *supra* note 15, at B1.

37. Honeycutt & Wibker, *supra* note 14, at 124; ABA Commission on Advertising, *Report on the Survey on the Image of Lawyers in Advertising* (Jan. 1990).

on Advertising found no convincing evidence that legal advertising significantly affects public attitudes about lawyers. Rather, the dominant influences are personal contact, news stories of inappropriate conduct by attorneys and judges, and fictional portrayals of attorneys on television, in movies, and in books.[38] Most members of the public believe that lawyers should be allowed to advertise.[39] In states such as California, more than 90% of the complaints made to the bar about attorneys' advertisements come from other attorneys.[40]

Still, according to Adrian Foley, former chair of the ABA Commission on Advertising, "Ensuring dignity is very important if advertising is to become more widely accepted." Tasteless advertisements like some of those in Problem 1 "demean the dedication of a great many lawyers whose professionalism is the result of years of study and hard work"[41]

References: Model Rules 7.1, 7.2.

QUESTIONS

1. Consider the advertisements in Problem 1 in light of these Supreme Court precedents. By whose standard should the bar evaluate whether lawyers' representations are misleading? The question, of course, is "misleading to whom?" If the test is a "reasonable person" standard, how much knowledge of legal services should be assumed? How much tolerance of "puffing?" What kind of evidence is necessary to show that consumers might be misled? Should surveys or consumer complaints be required?[42]

For example, how would you evaluate advertising that highlights an attorney's designation as a "Super Lawyer" or "Best Lawyer" by a commercial rating service? *Super Lawyers* is a magazine or a magazine supplement that claims to base its ratings on peer review. Lawyers who are chosen are encouraged to purchase advertisements in the magazine or supplement. The methodology for selection is not available. "Best Lawyers" ratings follow a similar model in some states; in others, selections are not focused on encouraging purchase of advertising. See New Jersey Supreme Court Committee on Lawyer Advertising, Op. 39 (July 17, 2006). In an opinion stayed by the New Jersey Supreme Court, its Committee on Advertising barred lawyers from advertising these "self-aggrandizing titles," which cannot be objectively verified and may "lead an unwary

---

38. American Bar Association, *Lawyer Advertising at the Crossroads, supra* note 15, at 3.

39. David A. Grey, "Ads Lift the Profession's Image," *San Francisco Daily Journal*, August 24, 1994, at 4 (1993 poll found that only 28% of those surveyed believed that lawyers should not be allowed to advertise).

40. Canlen, *supra* note 19, at 30.

41. "Is Dignity Important in Legal Advertising?," 73 *ABA J.*, Aug. 1987, at 52, 53 (quoting Foley).

42. In Alexander v. Cahill, 2007 WL 2120024 (N.D.N.Y. 2007), the court noted the absence of such evidence in support of New York's prohibitions on client testimonials, portrayals of judges or fictitious law firms, and nick-names or trade names that implied an "ability to obtain results in a matter." Without such evidence, or a showing that disclaimers would be inadequate, the court found that such prohibitions violated the First Amendment.

consumer to believe that the lawyers so described are … superior to their colleagues who practice in the same area of law." By contrast, other state bars have permitted advertising of "Best" or "Super Lawyer" designations, sometimes subject to specified conditions. For example, Michigan requires that the certifying organization consider the lawyers' qualifications, issue ratings "discriminately," refrain from conditioning ratings on purchases, and provide information about the basis for judgment. Michigan State Bar Comm. On Professional and Judicial Ethics, Informal Op. RI–341 (June 8, 2007).[43] What approach would you support?

2. The Supreme Court suggested in *RMJ* that a state's "substantial interest" might justify restrictions on advertisements that are not false or misleading. What interests are sufficiently substantial to justify such restraints? Are prohibitions on "self-laudatory" statements constitutional? Do most advertisements that do more than list available services intend implicitly, if not explicitly, to be self-laudatory? Can states ban representations that may create "unjustified expectations?" Are any of the advertisements in Problem 1 impermissible on that ground?

3. Should "undignified" techniques also be subject to prohibition? Undignified by whose standards? In comparison to what? How should the bar's concern in maintaining its public image be weighed against the benefits of unrestricted speech? How substantial are these benefits in cases such as those in Problem 1? In a nation where the average consumer receives close to a thousand messages a day, are tasteless but attention-getting advertisements justified? Or does the bar have a legitimate interest in preventing a race to the bottom? In most European countries, advertising is much more tightly regulated than in the United States, and according to the Charter of the Council of Bars and Law Societies of Europe (CCBE) a core principle is that courts, legislators, and regulatory bodies should seek to uphold the "dignity and honour of the legal profession."[44]

If rules on advertising require some trade-offs among competing values—such as broadening access to information, encouraging more cost-effective services, and preserving the profession's image—which values should take precedence? How should that decision be made and by whom? Should there be a greater role for consumer protection agencies?

In 2007, after a widely publicized debate, New York's Appellate Court adopted revisions to its rules on advertising. They were immediately subject to First Amendment challenge. Two controversial provisions involved matters of taste. One was the prohibition on portrayals of fictitious law firms. Another was the ban on "techniques to obtain attention that demonstrate a clear and intentional lack of relevance to the selection of counsel including the portrayal of lawyers exhibiting characteristics clearly unrelated to legal competence." N.Y. Comp. Codes R. & Regs. Title 22, § 1200.6. The latter

43. The opinion also discusses other state bar rulings. See also "Advertising," *supra* note 20, at 407. See William W. Yavinsky, "A Comparative Look at Comparative Attorney Advertising: Why Efforts to Prohibit Evaluative Rankings Spark Debate from Buffalo to Buenos Aires," 20 *Geo. J. Legal Ethics* 969 (2007).

44. CCBE Charter, paragraph (d). For various countries' approaches, see European Union Report on Competition 15 Paragraph 46 (2004).

provision was a response to advertisements with images like the provocative blonde with a "reputation" in Problem 1. In evaluating these prohibitions, a federal district court took notice of the "proliferation of tasteless and at times obnoxious attorney advertising in recent years." "As a result," the court concluded, "the public perception of the legal profession has been greatly diminished." *Alexander v. Cahill*, 2007 WL 2120024 (N.D.N.Y. July 23, 2007). The court also found that the state has a substantial interest in maintaining "professionalism and respect for members of the bar." *Id.*, at n. 6. However, the court also noted that regulation of advertising had to be "consistent with established First Amendment jurisprudence," and New York had introduced no evidence that the challenged prohibitions "materially advance the State's interests." *Id.*

What evidence would be sufficient? Would you allow the advertisements in Problem 1 (g)-(m) ? Are the public opinion surveys summarized above relevant to your analysis?

4. Consider the rule approved by a referendum of Texas lawyers that requires advertising to be presented "without appeals primarily to emotions" and prohibits portrayals of lawyers by nonlawyer actors or narrators. What about commentary in Florida's rule that advertisements should include "only useful, factual information" presented in a "nonsensational manner," without "slogans or jingles."[45] All Texas advertisements that include more than certain minimal information must be sent to the state bar's Lawyer Advertisement and Solicitation Review Committee. Would you support such rules? What about a Florida Supreme Court decision prohibiting an illustration of a "pit bull terrier," *Florida Bar v. Pape*, 918 So.2d 240, 241 (Fla. 2005), reh'g granted (2006), cert. denied, 547 U.S. 1041 (2006). Would you prefer California's approach, which presumes certain kinds of advertising such as testimonials to be misleading, and requires that if such advertisements are challenged, a lawyer withdraw them or prove that they are not false and misleading? Or would you agree with Jeffrey Zuckerman, then Director of the FTC Bureau of Competition: "[If] testimonials are true, why not permit them? Have a little respect for the intelligence of adults."[46]

5. How strictly should lawyer advertising be monitored? Recent research suggests that bar regulations are grossly underenforced. Since *Bates*, surveyed jurisdictions have averaged fewer than one reported disciplinary case per year for advertising violations.[47] Formal enforcement actions are rare even in jurisdictions where non-compliance with specific rules is common.[48] A number of factors may account for this pattern:

45. Rules 704, 707, "Texas Lawyers Approve Changes to Advertising Rules," *ABA/BNA Manual on Professional Conduct*, June 15, 1994, at 162–63; Florida Rule 4–7.1, challenged in Harrell v. Florida Bar, 2008 WL 596086 (M.D. Fla. 2008).

46. "Is Dignity Important?," *supra* note 41, at 53 (quoting Zuckerman).

47. Fred C. Zacharias, "What Lawyers Do When Nobody's Watching: Legal Advertising as a Case Study of the Impact of Underenforced Professional Rules," 87 *Iowa L. Rev.* 971, 992 (2002).

48. In San Diego during a one year period, there were 257 cases of actual or presumptive noncompliance. In the state as a whole, there were only 3 disciplinary cases

- a lack of resources within disciplinary agencies;

- a lack of client complaints and demonstrable harm from violations;

- a lack of consensus within the bar about the appropriateness of many advertising restrictions; and

- a lack of confidence among regulatory officials that rules can be fully and fairly enforced.

Does the high visibility of unsanctioned rule violations raise concern? According to some commentators, a refusal to enforce ethical standards erodes respect for bar regulatory processes and shields judgments about commercial speech from open debate and review. At the very least, these commentators argue, disciplinary authorities should define and defend their enforcement policies, and work to bring formal rules in line with actual practices. Do you agree? If so, should rules be liberalized or should sanctions be more frequent?

6. Advertising on the internet poses particular challenges for bar enforcement agencies. The number of attorneys with website listings and promotional materials has been growing rapidly and bar disciplinary agencies have been unable to keep pace. Their efforts have been limited by inadequacies in enforcement resources, ambiguities in the application of ethical standards to electronic communication, and lack of authority over out-of-state lawyers.[49] Advertising rules were generally not written with websites, blogs, or promotional emails in mind, and a host of questions have arisen with respect to disclaimers, bar approval, and related issues.[50] Given recent trends toward multijurisdictional practice, state-based regulatory structures with inconsistent standards present obvious problems. For many lawyers, full compliance with advertising requirements in all the jurisdictions that their electronic communications reach will severely hamper promotional efforts and limit their "ability to compete in the global marketplace."[51] What follows from this fact?

7. Should the legal profession more actively support forms of public communication apart from advertising by individual attorneys? Should it, for example, attempt to develop directories or clearinghouses of information that might provide centralized data about attorneys' specialties, experience, education, discipline, malpractice complaints, and so forth? Before the *Bates* decision, the ABA opposed an attempt by Consumers Union to publish such a directory in Virginia. Should its position now be to encourage or subsidize such efforts? What other alternatives to increase informed selection of attorneys might be desirable?

involving predominantly advertising violations. *Id.*, at 978–88.

49. Richard B. Schmitt, "Lowering the Bar: Lawyers Flood Web, But Many Ads Fail to Tell Whole Truth," *Wall St. J.* Jan 15, 2001, at A1; Chanen, *supra* note 9, at 59–60.

50. See Chanen, *supra* note 9, at 59–61; Fred C. Zacharias, "What Direction Should Legal Advertising Regulation Take, *Professional Lawyer* 49 (2005); ABA eLawyering Task Force in the Law Management Section and the Delivery of Legal Services Committee, Best Practices for Legal Websites, available at www.elawyering.org/tools/practices.shtml; Melissa Blades & Sarah Vermylen, "Virtual Ethics for A New Age: The Internet and the Ethical Lawyer," 17 *Geo. J. Legal Ethics* 637 (2004); Louise Hill, "Change Is in the Air: Lawyer Advertising and the Internet," 36 *U. Rich. L. Rev.* 21 (2002).

51. Hill, *supra* note 50, at 50.

About half the states offer "practitioner profiles" for all licensed doctors that include information such as education, practice area, professional affiliations, criminal convictions, disciplinary and malpractice actions, and liability insurance. More states are expected to follow, and a national consumer organization, Public Citizen, also maintains a publicly available directory of disciplined doctors. No comparable, readily accessible databases have been available for lawyers. Legal directories and referral services do not provide information concerning disciplinary, criminal, and malpractice histories and many consumers who are "one shot" purchasers lack reliable sources of information.[52] According to the most systematic research available, four-fifths of surveyed Americans express a desire for a resource that they could consult concerning the records of particular lawyers.[53]

In 2007, Avvo, a for-profit company, launched the first effort to make such data broadly available. It provided profiles and ratings of lawyers in several of the largest states, and included information on disciplinary histories that was publicly accessible. A suit by a disgruntled lawyer claiming that his profile was inaccurate and misleading was rejected by a federal court on first amendment grounds.[54]

Attorneys often object to providing such a clearinghouse on the grounds that potential clients may attach undue importance to partial information or to minor transgressions, and that the reputation of practitioners would be unjustly impaired. However, no evidence for that claim has been forthcoming, and as Chapter XV notes, minor indiscretions rarely trigger public disciplinary action or malpractice judgments. And by identifying lawyers with good records and adequate malpractice insurance, such clearinghouses would create additional incentives for appropriate conduct.[55] What is your view? How would you balance the public's interest in disclosure against lawyers' interest in preserving their privacy and reputations? What other strategies might promote more informed selection of attorneys?

B. SOLICITATION

INTRODUCTION

Prohibitions on lawyers' in-person solicitation of clients date to medieval England. During a time when tribunals were all too easily corrupted,

52. Martindale Hubbell provides ratings based on peer review and Nolo.com profiles lawyers by geographic and practice specialty, and verifies that they are currently in good standing. Paul Davies, "Need A Lawyer? Online Services Speed the Search," *Wall St. J.*, July 21–22, 2007, at B1.

53. Steven K. Berenson, "Is It Time for Lawyer Profiles?," 70 *Fordham L. R.* 645, 651–57, 680 (2001); Deborah L. Rhode, *In the Interests of Justice*, 163–64 (2000).

54. Brown v. Avvo, Inc., CO7–0920RSL (W.D. Wash., December 18, 2007). The court dismissed the claim that the ratings were misleading because the website fairly describes the information on which the ratings are based and acknowledges the relevance of other factors.

55. Berenson, *supra* note 53, at 680–81; Deborah L. Rhode, *Access to Justice* 99 (2004).

leaders of the profession sought to discourage certain entrepreneurial practices associated with solicitation: maintenance (assisting others to prosecute or defend a suit without just cause); champerty (supporting a suit in return for a share of the recovery); and barratry (stirring up quarrels and litigation). All three of these were criminal offenses. In this country, experience with solicitation has been mixed. Prominent attorneys have openly or not so openly approached potential clients, and many socially important cases have arisen in that fashion.[56] The practice has also had a seamier side, known colloquially as ambulance chasing. This mixed record in promoting the public interest and exploiting vulnerable parties is explored in the readings below.

Jerold S. Auerbach, Unequal Justice: Lawyers and Social Change in Modern America

41–50 (1976).

The [1908 Canons of Professional Ethics] drew heavily upon George Sharswood's *Essay on Professional Ethics*, published in 1854. Sharswood's *Essay* was at best, antiquated; at worst, irrelevant. He had addressed it to a generation accustomed to moral exhortation and confident that its own definitions of character, honor, and duty were eternal verities. Warning even in the 1850s of "a horde of pettifogging, barratrous, money-making lawyers," Sharswood had urged "high moral principle" as the bedrock of professional dignity. Passivity and patience were his cardinal virtues. Like young maidens awaiting suitors, aspiring lawyers must await clients. "Let business seek the young attorney," Sharswood insisted. It might come too slowly for profit or fame (or never come at all), but if the lawyer cultivated "habits of neatness, accuracy, punctuality, and despatch, candor toward his client, and strict honor toward his adversary, it may be safely prophesied that his business will grow as fast as it is good for him that it should grow." Sharswood's safe prophecy may have comforted a young nineteenth-century attorney in a homogeneous small town, apprenticed to an established practitioner, known in his community, and without many competitors. It could hardly reassure his twentieth-century counterpart, the new-immigrant neophyte in a large city where restricted firms monopolized the most lucrative business and thousands of attorneys scrambled for a share of the remainder. He could draw scant comfort from Sharswood's confident assertion that some preordained rule determined that his practice grew no faster than was good for him. He either hustled or starved....

[The bar's ethical prohibitions] rewarded the lawyer whose law-firm partners and social contacts made advertising unnecessary at the same time that it attributed inferior character and unethical behavior to attorneys who could not afford to sit passively in their offices awaiting clients; it

---

56. *See* Charles W. Wolfram, *Modern Legal Ethics* 786 (1986) (discussing, for example Abraham Lincoln, the Aaron Burr litigation, and the Dred Scott Case); Deborah L. Rhode, "Solicitation," 36 *J. Leg. Ed.* 317, 325–29 (1986) (discussing Brown v. Board of Education).

thus penalized both them and their potential clients, who might not know whether they had a valid legal claim or where, if they did, to obtain legal assistance. The canon prohibiting solicitation discriminated against those in personal injury practice, who bore the pejorative label "ambulance chasers." . . .

The consequences were starkly exposed in Crystal Eastman's study *Work–Accidents and the Law*, conducted for the Russell Sage Foundation and published in 1910 as part of the landmark Pittsburgh Survey. In more than half of all work-accident fatalities in Allegheny County, widows and children bore the entire income loss. . . . Similarly, more than half of all injured workers received no compensation: only 5 percent were fully compensated for their lost working time while disabled. . . .

"Ambulance chasing" was never precisely defined. As a term of art it ostracized plaintiffs' lawyers who, representing outsiders to the economic system, solicited certain types of business. Once fee-hungry ambulance chasers were isolated, they could be excluded from professional respectability by a series of discriminatory ethical judgments. Their methods of solicitation were condemned, but nothing was said about company claim agents who visited hospitalized workers to urge a quick and inexpensive settlement. Their [contingent] fees were isolated for judicial scrutiny, but larger corporate retainers were ignored by professional associations. . . . Not only were [personal injury lawyers] they criticized for professional malfeasance; their speech was mocked (many were recent immigrants) and their perseverance was denigrated as aggressiveness (many were Jewish). Commercialization, speculation, solicitation, and excessive litigation were decried, but there was no mention of the contribution of contingent fees to the enforcement of legitimate claims otherwise denied by the victim's poverty.

Ohralik v. Ohio State Bar Association

Supreme Court of the United States, 1978.
436 U.S. 447.

■ MR. JUSTICE POWELL delivered the opinion of the Court. . . .

I

Appellant, a member of the Ohio Bar, lives in Montville, Ohio. Until recently he practiced law in Montville and Cleveland. On February 13, 1974, while picking up his mail at the Montville Post Office, appellant learned from the postmaster's brother about an automobile accident that had taken place on February 2 in which Carol McClintock, a young woman with whom appellant was casually acquainted, had been injured. Appellant made a telephone call to Ms. McClintock's parents, who informed him that their daughter was in the hospital. Appellant suggested that he might visit Carol in the hospital. Mrs. McClintock assented to the idea, but requested that appellant first stop by at her home.

During appellant's visit with the McClintocks, they explained that their daughter had been driving the family automobile on a local road when she was hit by an uninsured motorist. Both Carol and her passenger, Wanda Lou Holbert, were injured and hospitalized. In response to the McClintocks' expression of apprehension that they might be sued by Holbert, appellant explained that Ohio's guest statute would preclude such a suit. When appellant suggested to the McClintocks that they hire a lawyer, Mrs. McClintock retorted that such a decision would be up to Carol, who was 18 years old and would be the beneficiary of a successful claim.

Appellant proceeded to the hospital, where he found Carol lying in traction in her room. After a brief conversation about her condition, appellant told Carol he would represent her and asked her to sign an agreement. Carol said she would have to discuss the matter with her parents. She did not sign the agreement, but asked appellant to have her parents come to see her. Appellant also attempted to see Wanda Lou Holbert, but learned that she had just been released from the hospital. He then departed for another visit with the McClintocks.

On his way appellant detoured to the scene of the accident, where he took a set of photographs. He also picked up a tape recorder, which he concealed under his raincoat before arriving at the McClintocks' residence. Once there, he re-examined their automobile insurance policy, discussed with them the law applicable to passengers, and explained the consequences of the fact that the driver who struck Carol's car was an uninsured motorist. Appellant discovered that the McClintocks' insurance policy would provide benefits of up to $12,500 each for Carol and Wanda Lou under an uninsured-motorist clause. Mrs. McClintock acknowledged that both Carol and Wanda Lou could sue for their injuries, but recounted to appellant that "Wanda Lou swore up and down she would not do it." The McClintocks also told appellant that Carol had phoned to say that appellant could "go ahead" with her representation. Two days later appellant returned to Carol's hospital room to have her sign a contract, which provided that he would receive one-third of her recovery.

In the meantime, appellant obtained Wanda Lou's name and address from the McClintocks after telling them he wanted to ask her some questions about the accident. He then visited Wanda Lou at her home, without having been invited. He again concealed his tape recorder and recorded most of the conversation with Wanda Lou. After a brief, unproductive inquiry about the facts of the accident, appellant told Wanda Lou that he was representing Carol and that he had a "little tip" for Wanda Lou: the McClintocks' insurance policy contained an uninsured-motorist clause which might provide her with a recovery of up to $12,500. The young woman, who was 18 years of age and not a high school graduate at the time, replied to appellant's query about whether she was going to file a claim by stating that she really did not understand what was going on. Appellant offered to represent her, also, for a contingent fee of one-third of any recovery, and Wanda Lou stated "O.K."

Wanda Lou's mother attempted to repudiate her daughter's oral assent the following day, when appellant called on the telephone to speak to Wanda Lou. Mrs. Holbert informed appellant that she and her daughter did not want to sue anyone or to have appellant represent them, and that if they decided to sue they would consult their own lawyer. Appellant insisted that Wanda Lou had entered into a binding agreement. A month later Wanda Lou confirmed in writing that she wanted neither to sue nor to be represented by appellant. She requested that appellant notify the insurance company that he was not her lawyer, as the company would not release a check to her until he did so. Carol also eventually discharged appellant. Although another lawyer represented her in concluding a settlement with the insurance company, she paid appellant one-third of her recovery in settlement of his lawsuit against her for breach of contract. . . .

After a hearing, the Board found that appellant had violated Disciplinary Rules (DR) 2–103(A) and 2–104(A) of the Ohio Code of Professional Responsibility [forbidding solicitation]. The Board rejected appellant's defense that his conduct was protected under the First and Fourteenth Amendments. The Supreme Court of Ohio adopted the findings of the Board, reiterated that appellant's conduct was not constitutionally protected, and increased the sanction of a public reprimand recommended by the Board to indefinite suspension. . . .

II

The solicitation of business by a lawyer through direct, in-person communication with the prospective client has long been viewed as inconsistent with the profession's ideal of the attorney-client relationship and as posing a significant potential for harm to the prospective client. It has been proscribed by the organized Bar for many years. . . .

In-person solicitation by a lawyer of remunerative employment is a business transaction in which speech is an essential but subordinate component. While this does not remove the speech from the protection of the First Amendment, as was held in *Bates* and *Virginia Pharmacy*, it lowers the level of appropriate judicial scrutiny.

. . . Unlike a public advertisement, which simply provides information and leaves the recipient free to act upon it or not, in-person solicitation may exert pressure and often demands an immediate response, without providing an opportunity for comparison or reflection. The aim and effect of in-person solicitation may be to provide a one-sided presentation and to encourage speedy and perhaps uninformed decisionmaking: there is no opportunity for intervention or counter-education by agencies of the Bar, supervisory authorities, or persons close to the solicited individual. The admonition that "the fitting remedy for evil counsels is good ones" is of little value when the circumstances provide no opportunity for any remedy at all. In-person solicitation is as likely as not to discourage persons needing counsel from engaging in a critical comparison of the "availability, nature, and prices" of legal services, . . . it actually may disserve the individual and societal interest, identified in *Bates*, in facilitating "informed and reliable decisionmaking."

It also is argued that in-person solicitation may provide the solicited individual with information about his or her legal rights and remedies. In this case, appellant gave Wanda Lou a "tip" about the prospect of recovery based on the uninsured-motorist clause in the McClintocks' insurance policy, and he explained that clause and Ohio's guest statute to Carol McClintock's parents. But neither of the Disciplinary Rules here at issue prohibited appellant from communicating information to these young women about their legal rights and the prospects of obtaining a monetary recovery, or from recommending that they obtain counsel. DR 2–104(A) merely prohibited him from using the information as bait with which to obtain an agreement to represent them for a fee. The Rule does not prohibit a lawyer from giving unsolicited legal advice; it proscribes the acceptance of employment resulting from such advice. . . .

A lawyer's procurement of remunerative employment is a subject only marginally affected with First Amendment concerns. It falls within the State's proper sphere of economic and professional regulation. . . . While entitled to some constitutional protection, appellant's conduct is subject to regulation in furtherance of important state interests.[16]

B

The substantive evils of solicitation have been stated over the years in sweeping terms: stirring up litigation, assertion of fraudulent claims, debasing the legal profession, and potential harm to the solicited client in the form of overreaching, overcharging, underrepresentation, and misrepresentation. The American Bar Association, as *amicus curiae*, defends the rule against solicitation primarily on three broad grounds: It is said that the prohibitions embodied in DR 2–103(A) and 2–104(A) serve to reduce the likelihood of overreaching and the exertion of undue influence on lay persons, to protect the privacy of individuals, and to avoid situations where the lawyer's exercise of judgment on behalf of the client will be clouded by his own pecuniary self-interest.[19]

16. . . . In recognizing the importance of the State's interest in regulating solicitation of paying clients by lawyers, we are not unmindful of the problem of the related practice, described in *Railroad Trainmen*, of the solicitation of releases of liability by claims agents or adjusters of prospective defendants or their insurers. Such solicitations frequently occur prior to the employment of counsel by the injured person and during circumstances posing many of the dangers of overreaching we address in this case. Where lay agents or adjusters are involved, these practices for the most part fall outside the scope of regulation by the organized Bar, but releases of settlements so obtained are viewed critically by the courts.

19. A lawyer who engages in personal solicitation of clients may be inclined to subordinate the best interests of the client to his own pecuniary interests. Even if unintentionally, the lawyer's ability to evaluate the legal merit of his client's claims may falter when the conclusion will affect the lawyer's income. A valid claim might be settled too quickly, or a claim with little merit pursued beyond the point of reason. These lapses of judgment can occur in any legal representation, but we cannot say that the pecuniary motivation of the lawyer who solicits a particular representation does not create special problems of conflict of interest.

We need not discuss or evaluate each of these interests in detail as appellant has conceded that the State has a legitimate and indeed "compelling" interest in preventing those aspects of solicitation that involve fraud, undue influence, intimidation, overreaching, and other forms of "vexatious conduct." We agree that protection of the public from these aspects of solicitation is a legitimate and important state interest.

III

Appellant's concession that strong state interests justify regulation to prevent the evils he enumerates would end this case but for his insistence that none of these evils was found to be present in his acts of solicitation. . . .

Appellant's argument misconceives the nature of the State's interest. The Rules prohibiting solicitation are prophylactic measures whose objective is the prevention of harm before it occurs. The Rules were applied in this case to discipline a lawyer for soliciting employment for pecuniary gain under circumstances likely to result in the adverse consequences the State seeks to avert. In such a situation, which is inherently conducive to overreaching and other forms of misconduct, the State has a strong interest in adopting and enforcing rules of conduct designed to protect the public from harmful solicitation by lawyers whom it has licensed.

The State's perception of the potential for harm in circumstances such as those presented in this case is well founded. The detrimental aspects of face-to-face selling even of ordinary consumer products have been recognized and addressed by the Federal Trade Commission, and it hardly need be said that the potential for overreaching is significantly greater when a lawyer, a professional trained in the art of persuasion, personally solicits an unsophisticated, injured, or distressed lay person. Such an individual may place his trust in a lawyer, regardless of the latter's qualifications or the individual's actual need for legal representation, simply in response to persuasion under circumstances conducive to uninformed acquiescence. Although it is argued that personal solicitation is valuable because it may apprise a victim of misfortune of his legal rights, the very plight of that person not only makes him more vulnerable to influence but also may make advice all the more intrusive. Thus, under these adverse conditions the overtures of an uninvited lawyer may distress the solicited individual simply because of their obtrusiveness and the invasion of the individual's privacy, even when no other harm materializes. Under such circumstances, it is not unreasonable for the State to presume that in-person solicitation by lawyers more often than not will be injurious to the person solicited.

The efficacy of the State's effort to prevent such harm to prospective clients would be substantially diminished if, having proved a solicitation in circumstances like those of this case, the State were required in addition to prove actual injury. Unlike the advertising in *Bates*, in-person solicitation is not visible or otherwise open to public scrutiny. Often there is no witness other than the lawyer and the lay person whom he has solicited, rendering it difficult or impossible to obtain reliable proof of what actually took place....

Under our view of the State's interest in averting harm by prohibiting solicitation in circumstances where it is likely to occur, the absence of explicit proof or findings of harm or injury is immaterial. The facts in this case present a striking example of the potential for overreaching that is inherent in a lawyer's in-person solicitation of professional employment. They also demonstrate the need for prophylactic regulation in furtherance of the State's interest in protecting the lay public. We hold that the application of DR 2–103(A) and 2–104(A) to appellant does not offend the Constitution....

■ MR. JUSTICE MARSHALL, concurring in part and concurring in the judgments....

What is objectionable about Ohralik's behavior here is not so much that he solicited business for himself, but rather the circumstances in which he performed that solicitation and the means by which he accomplished it. Appropriately, the Court's actual holding in *Ohralik* is a limited one: that the solicitation of business, under circumstances—such as those found in this record—presenting substantial dangers of harm to society or the client independent of the solicitation itself, may constitutionally be prohibited by the State. In this much of the Court's opinion in *Ohralik*, I join fully....

Notwithstanding the injurious aspects of Ohralik's conduct, even his case illustrates the potentially useful, information-providing aspects of attorney solicitation: Motivated by the desire for pecuniary gain, but informed with the special training and knowledge of an attorney, Ohralik advised both his clients (apparently correctly) that, although they had been injured by an uninsured motorist, they could nonetheless recover on the McClintocks' insurance policy. The provision of such information about legal rights and remedies is an important function, even where the rights and remedies are of a private and commercial nature involving no constitutional or political overtones.

In view of the similar functions performed by advertising and solicitation by attorneys, I find somewhat disturbing the Court's suggestion in *Ohralik* that in-person solicitation of business, though entitled to some degree of constitutional protection as "commercial speech," is entitled to less protection under the First Amendment than is "the kind of advertising approved in *Bates*." The First Amendment informational interests served by solicitation, whether or not it occurs in a purely commercial context, are substantial, and they are entitled to as much protection as the interests we found to be protected in *Bates*.

B

Not only do prohibitions on solicitation interfere with the free flow of information protected by the First Amendment, but by origin and in practice they operate in a discriminatory manner. As we have noted, these constraints developed as rules of "etiquette" and came to rest on the notion that a lawyer's reputation in his community would spread by word of mouth and bring business to the worthy lawyer. *Bates v. State Bar of Arizona.* The social model on which this conception depends is that of the small, cohesive, and homogeneous community; the anachronistic nature of this model has long been recognized. If ever this conception were more generally true, it is now valid only with respect to those persons who move in the relatively elite social and educational circles in which knowledge about legal problems, legal remedies, and lawyers is widely shared.

The impact of the nonsolicitation rules, moreover, is discriminatory with respect to the suppliers as well as the consumers of legal services. Just as the persons who suffer most from lack of knowledge about lawyers' availability belong to the less privileged classes of society, ... so the disciplinary rules against solicitation fall most heavily on those attorneys engaged in a single-practitioner or small-partnership form of practice—attorneys who typically earn less than their fellow practitioners in larger, corporate-oriented firms. Indeed, some scholars have suggested that the rules against solicitation were developed by the professional bar to keep recently immigrated lawyers, who gravitated toward the smaller, personal injury practice, from effective entry into the profession. See J. Auerbach, Unequal Justice 42–62, 126–129 (1976). In light of this history, I am less inclined than the majority appears to be, *ante,* to weigh favorably in the balance of the State's interests here the longevity of the ban on attorney solicitation.

C

By discussing the origin and impact of the nonsolicitation rules, I do not mean to belittle those obviously substantial interests that the State has in regulating attorneys to protect the public from fraud, deceit, misrepresentation, overreaching, undue influence, and invasions of privacy. But where honest, unpressured "commercial" solicitation is involved—a situation not presented in either of these cases—I believe it is open to doubt whether the State's interests are sufficiently compelling to warrant the restriction on the free flow of information which results from a sweeping nonsolicitation rule and against which the First Amendment ordinarily protects. While the State's interest in regulating in-person solicitation may, for reasons explained *ante,* ... be somewhat greater than its interest in regulating printed advertisements, these concededly legitimate interests might well be served by more specific and less restrictive rules than a total ban on pecuniary solicitation. For example, the Justice Department has suggested that the disciplinary rules be reworded "so as to *permit* all solicitation and advertising except the kinds that are false, misleading, undignified or champertous."

To the extent that in-person solicitation of business may constitutionally be subjected to more substantial state regulation as to time, place, and manner than printed advertising of legal services, it is not because such solicitation has "traditionally" been banned, nor because one form of commercial speech is of less value than another under the First Amendment. Rather, any additional restrictions can be justified only to the degree that dangers which the State has a right to prevent are actually presented by conduct attendant to such speech, thus increasing the relative "strength of the State's countervailing interest in prohibition." As the majority notes, and I wholeheartedly agree, these dangers are amply present in the *Ohralik* case.

Accordingly, while I concur in the judgments of the Court in both of these cases, I join in the Court's opinions only to the extent and with the exceptions noted above.

In re Primus

Supreme Court of the United States, 1978.
436 U.S. 412.

[*In re Primus* was a companion case to *Ohralik*. It involved a South Carolina attorney who provided pro bono services for the American Civil Liberties Union and paid assistance to the South Carolina Council on Human Relations. During the early 1970s, Gary Allen, a representative of an organization serving low-income communities, requested that the Council provide information to pregnant welfare recipients who were being sterilized or threatened with sterilization as a condition of receiving Medicaid funds. At a meeting with some of these women in Allen's office, Primus provided advice about their legal rights and suggested the possibility of a lawsuit.

A month later, Primus learned from the ACLU that it was willing to provide representation to mothers who had been sterilized, and learned from Allen that one woman, Mary Williams, was interested in taking legal action. Primus then wrote Williams as follows:

> You will probably remember me from talking with you at Mr. Allen's office in July about the sterilization performed on you. The American Civil Liberties Union would like to file a lawsuit on your behalf for money against the doctor who performed the operation. We will be coming to Aiken [South Carolina] in the near future and would like to explain what is involved so you can understand what is going on. . . . About the lawsuit, if you are interested, let me know, and I'll let you know when we will come down to talk to you about it. We will be coming to talk to Mrs. Waters at the same time; she has already asked the American Civil Liberties Union to file a suit on her behalf.

436 U.S. 412, 417 n. 6 (1978).

Shortly after receiving this letter, Williams visited the doctor who had performed the sterilization to discuss her third child, who was then ill. At the doctor's office, she encountered his attorney and, at the latter's request, signed a release of liability for the sterilization. She also provided them a copy of Primus' letter and called Primus from the doctor's office to communicate the decision not to file suit. There was no further contact between Williams and Primus.

The South Carolina Board of Commissions on Grievances and Discipline subsequently found that Primus had solicited a client on behalf of the ACLU in violation of DR 2–103(D)(5)(a) and (c) and DR 2–104(A)(5) of the Code and recommended a private reprimand. The Supreme Court of South Carolina accepted those findings and increased the sanction to a public reprimand. The Supreme Court reversed.]

■ MR. JUSTICE POWELL delivered the opinion of the Court.

[W]e decide today in *Ohralik v. Ohio State Bar Assn.*, that the States may vindicate legitimate regulatory interests through proscription, in certain circumstances, of in-person solicitation by lawyers who seek to communicate purely commercial offers of legal assistance to lay persons.

Unlike the situation in *Ohralik*, however, appellant's act of solicitation took the form of a letter to a woman with whom appellant had discussed the possibility of seeking redress for an allegedly unconstitutional sterilization. This was not in-person solicitation for pecuniary gain. Appellant was communicating an offer of free assistance by attorneys associated with the ACLU, not an offer predicated on entitlement to a share of any monetary recovery. And her actions were undertaken to express personal political beliefs and to advance the civil-liberties objectives of the ACLU, rather than to derive financial gain. The question presented in this case is whether, in light of the values protected by the First and Fourteenth Amendments, these differences materially affect the scope of state regulation of the conduct of lawyers. . . .

We find . . . unpersuasive any suggestion that the level of constitutional scrutiny in this case should be lowered because of a possible benefit to the ACLU. The discipline administered to appellant was premised solely on the possibility of financial benefit to the organization, rather than any possibility of pecuniary gain to herself, her associates, or the lawyers representing the plaintiffs in the *Walker v. Pierce* litigation. It is conceded that appellant received no compensation for any of the activities in question. It is also undisputed that neither the ACLU nor any lawyer associated with it would have shared in any monetary recovery by the plaintiffs in *Walker v. Pierce*. . . .

Contrary to appellee's suggestion, the ACLU's policy of requesting an award of counsel fees does not take this case outside the protection of [*NAACP v.*] *Button*. Although the Court in *Button* did not consider whether the NAACP seeks counsel fees, such requests are often made by that organization. In any event in a case of this kind there are differences between counsel fees awarded by a court and traditional fee-paying arrangements which militate against a presumption that ACLU sponsorship of litigation is motivated by considerations of pecuniary gain rather than by its widely recognized goal of vindicating civil liberties. Counsel fees are awarded in the discretion of the court; awards are not drawn from the plaintiff's recovery, and are usually premised on a successful outcome; and the amounts awarded often may not correspond to fees generally obtainable in private litigation. Moreover, under prevailing law during the events in question, an award of counsel fees in federal litigation was available only in limited circumstances. And even if there had been an award during the period in question, it would have gone to the central fund of the ACLU.[24] Although such benefit to the organization may increase with the maintenance of successful litigation, the same situation obtains with voluntary contributions and foundation support, which also may rise with ACLU victories in important areas of the law. That possibility, standing alone, offers no basis for equating the work of lawyers associated with the ACLU or the NAACP with that of a group that exists for the primary purpose of financial gain through the recovery of counsel fees.

Appellant's letter of August 30, 1973, to Mrs. Williams thus comes within the generous zone of First Amendment protection reserved for associational freedoms....

V

South Carolina's action in punishing appellant for soliciting a prospective litigant by mail, on behalf of the ACLU, must withstand the "exacting scrutiny applicable to limitations on core First Amendment rights...." *Buckley v. Valeo.* South Carolina must demonstrate "a subordinating interest which is compelling," [*Bates*] and that the means employed in furtherance of that interest are "closely drawn to avoid unnecessary abridgment of associational freedoms." [*Buckley*]

Where political expression or association is at issue, this Court has not tolerated the degree of imprecision that often characterizes government regulation of the conduct of commercial affairs. The approach we adopt today in *Ohralik*, that the State may proscribe in-person solicitation for pecuniary gain under circumstances likely to result in adverse consequences, cannot be applied to appellant's activity on behalf of the ACLU. Although a showing of potential danger may suffice in the former context, appellant may not be disciplined unless her activity in fact involved the type of misconduct at which South Carolina's broad prohibition is said to be directed.

The record does not support appellee's contention that undue influence, overreaching, misrepresentation, or invasion of privacy actually occurred in this case. Appellant's letter of August 30, 1973, followed up the earlier meeting—one concededly protected by the First and Fourteenth Amendments—by notifying Williams that the ACLU would be interested in supporting possible litigation. The letter imparted additional information

---

24. Appellant informs us that the ACLU policy then in effect provided that cooperating lawyers associated with the ACLU or with an affiliate could not receive an award of counsel fees for services rendered in an ACLU-sponsored litigation. Reply Brief for Appellant 4–5. Apparently it was feared that allowing acceptance of such fees might lead to selection of clients and cases for pecuniary reasons. See App. 182.... This policy was changed in 1977 to permit local experimentation with the sharing of court-awarded fees between state affiliates and cooperating attorneys. The South Carolina chapter has not exercised that option. Reply Brief for Appellant 5–6. We express no opinion whether our analysis in this case would be different had the latter policy been in effect during the period in question.

material to making an informed decision about whether to authorize litigation, and permitted Williams an opportunity, which she exercised, for arriving at a deliberate decision. The letter was not facially misleading, indeed, it offered "to explain what is involved so you can understand what is going on." The transmittal of this letter—as contrasted with in-person solicitation—involved no appreciable invasion of privacy; nor did it afford any significant opportunity for overreaching or coercion. Moreover, the fact that there was a written communication lessens substantially the difficulty of policing solicitation practices that do offend valid rules of professional conduct.

The State is free to fashion reasonable restrictions with respect to the time, place, and manner of solicitation by members of its Bar.... The State's special interest in regulating members whose profession it licenses, and who serve as officers of its courts, amply justifies the application of narrowly drawn rules to proscribe solicitation that in fact is misleading, overbearing, or involves other features of deception or improper influence. As we decide today in *Ohralik*, a State also may forbid in-person solicitation for pecuniary gain under circumstances likely to result in these evils. And a State may insist that lawyers not solicit on behalf of lay organizations that exert control over the actual conduct of any ensuing litigation.... Accordingly, nothing in this opinion should be read to foreclose carefully tailored regulation that does not abridge unnecessarily the associational freedom of nonprofit organizations or their members, having characteristics like those of the NAACP or the ACLU.

We conclude that South Carolina's application of its DR 2–103(D)(5)(a) and (c) and 2–104(A)(5) to appellant's solicitation by letter on behalf of the ACLU violates the First and Fourteenth Amendments. The judgment of the Supreme Court of South Carolina is

Reversed.

■ Mr. Justice Rehnquist (dissenting)....

In distinguishing between Primus' protected solicitation and Ohralik's unprotected solicitation, the Court lamely declares: "We have not discarded the 'common-sense' distinction between speech proposing a commercial transaction, which occurs in an area traditionally subject to government regulation, and other varieties of speech." Yet to the extent that this "common-sense" distinction focuses on the content of the speech, it is at least suspect under many of this Court's First Amendment cases, and to the extent it focuses upon the motive of the speaker, it is subject to manipulation by clever practitioners. If Albert Ohralik, like Edna Primus, viewed litigation " 'not [as] a technique of resolving private differences,' " but as " 'a form of political expression' and 'political association,' " for all that appears he would be restored to his right to practice. And we may be sure that the next lawyer in Ohralik's shoes who is disciplined for similar conduct will come here cloaked in the prescribed mantle of "political association" to assure that insurance companies do not take unfair advantage of policyholders.

This absence of any principled distinction between the two cases is made all the more unfortunate by the radical difference in scrutiny brought to bear upon state regulation in each area. Where solicitation proposes merely a commercial transaction, the Court recognizes "the need for prophylactic regulation in furtherance of the State's interest in protecting the lay public." On the other hand, in some circumstances (at least in those identical to the instant case)[1] "[w]here political expression or association is at issue," a member of the Bar "may not be disciplined unless her activity in fact involve[s] the type of misconduct at which South Carolina's broad prohibition is said to be directed."

As the Court understands the Disciplinary Rule enforced by South Carolina, "a lawyer employed by the ACLU or a similar organization may never give unsolicited advice to a lay person that he or she retain the organization's free services." That prohibition seems to me entirely reasonable. A State may rightly fear that members of its Bar have powers of persuasion not possessed by laymen, and it may also fear that such persuasion may be as potent in writing as it is in person. Such persuasion may draw an unsophisticated layman into litigation contrary to his own best interests, and it may force other citizens of South Carolina to defend against baseless litigation which would not otherwise have been brought. I cannot agree that a State must prove such harmful consequences in each case simply because an organization such as the ACLU or the NAACP is involved.

I cannot share the Court's confidence that the danger of such consequences is minimized simply because a lawyer proceeds from political conviction rather than for pecuniary gain. A State may reasonably fear that a lawyer's desire to resolve "substantial civil liberties questions," may occasionally take precedence over his duty to advance the interests of his client. It is even more reasonable to fear that a lawyer in such circumstances will be inclined to pursue both culpable and blameless defendants to the last ditch in order to achieve his ideological goals. Although individual litigants, including the ACLU, may be free to use the courts for such purposes, South Carolina is likewise free to restrict the activities of the members of its Bar who attempt to persuade them to do so.

QUESTIONS

1. The majority opinion in *Primus* refers to the case *NAACP v. Button*, 371 U.S. 415 (1963). *Button* held that the NAACP's solicitation of clients

---

1. The Court carefully reserves judgment on factual circumstances in any way distinguishable from those presented here. For instance, the Court suggests that different considerations would arise if Primus herself had received any benefit from the solicitation, or if her income depended in any way on the outcome of the litigation. Likewise, the Court emphasizes that the lawyers conducting the litigation would have taken no share had attorney's fees been awarded by the court. Finally, the Court points out that Williams had not "communicated unambiguously a decision against litigation," that the solicitation was not effected in person, and that legal services were offered free of charge. All these reservations seem to imply that a State might be able to raise an absolute prohibition against any of these factual variations, even "[i]n the context of political expression and association." On the other hand, in *Ohralik*, the Court appears to give a broader reading to today's holding. "We hold today in *Primus* that a lawyer who engages in solicitation as a form of protected political association generally may not be disciplined without proof of actual wrongdoing that the State constitutionally may proscribe."

for litigation of constitutional rights is a form of expression and political association protected by the First Amendment. Notice that *Primus* extends *Button* because Edna Primus solicited a client for a private suit for damages rather than for a constitutional claim. However, unlike Ohralik, her interest was not financial. Under the Court's analysis, how crucial should attorneys' motives be in determining whether their conduct is constitutionally protected? If Primus had been a self-supporting civil rights practitioner entitled to attorney's fees, should she have been subject to disciplinary action?

2.   Consider the harms that the *Ohralik* decision associated with solicitation, such as overreaching, undue influence, conflicts of interest, and invasion of privacy. To what extent can these occur irrespective of who initiates contact? What evidence supports the Court's assumption that these harms are particularly likely to accompany fee-generating cases that result from personal solicitation? Suppose that Ohralik's only in-person contact had been with Carol McClintock's parents, following his telephone call and their invitation to stop by their home. Note the frequency of terms such as "may" and "likely" in the majority decision in *Ohralik*. In contexts involving First Amendment interests, should the state be required to establish a firmer causal relationship between prohibited expression and the harms that assertedly follow from it?

In re Marshall I. Teichner

Supreme Court of Illinois, 1979.
387 N.E.2d 265.

[An Illinois Disciplinary Commission filed a complaint against Marshall Teichner, a Chicago attorney, in connection with his solicitation of employment following a railroad crash in Laurel, Mississippi. The accident involved the derailment and explosion of a train operated by a subsidiary of the Southern Railway System. Among the killed and injured were many members of a predominantly Black Presbyterian Church. Allan Johnson, the Reverend at that church, established a relief program for the injured. Through a cousin living in Chicago, he also asked Teichner to come to Laurel. Johnson was concerned that Southern Railway agents were negotiating immediate and inadequate settlements with injury victims and their families. After a Church meeting that Teichner attended, Reverend Johnson assigned some of his aides to accompany the lawyer in visiting injured persons and their families.]

Counsel for the railroad lost little time in responding to this counterattack upon the railroad's settlement practices. The railroad's Chicago attorney wrote the following letter to the president of the Chicago Bar Association.

"Dear Joe:

We represent the Southern Railway System. We are informed that in mid-January, 1969, the Southern had a serious derailment at

Laurel, Mississippi, that destroyed some 35 houses, injured about 40 people and caused one death. To provide prompt relief for those harmed, many of whom were poor, the Southern promptly sent a large number of claim agents who worked around the clock with a board to make immediate settlements. A few days after the accident, Marshall I. Teichner, an attorney of 100 N. LaSalle Street, Chicago, Illinois, appeared in Laurel and went driving around, passing out business cards and seeking clients.

This information is passed along to you for such investigation and possible disciplinary action as may seem appropriate. If further information is desired from the Southern, we will be glad to supply it.

With warmest regards." . . .

The record indicates that the respondent, accompanied by Wallace Dillon, a teacher at a local junior high school and aide to Rev. Johnson, visited Ward at a store he operated in Laurel. Although Ward was not a member of Rev. Johnson's congregation, he knew both Rev. Johnson and Dillon, was aware of Rev. Johnson's relief efforts, and agreed to talk with the respondent.

Ward's parents had been injured in the derailment and the respondent asked Ward's permission to speak with them in the hospital where they were being treated, and to offer them his services. There is no evidence that respondent asked Ward to request that his parents retain the respondent, although there is some evidence that either the respondent or Dillon offered to advance money to Ward's parents for their medical needs. Respondent also inquired as to whether the Wards were receiving proper medical attention. Ward nonetheless declined to give respondent permission to visit Ward's parents in the hospital. Respondent returned to Ward's store on a subsequent occasion, ostensibly to use a public telephone, at which time respondent again asked permission to visit Ward's parents to discuss his representation of them and Ward again refused.

Respondent denies that the foregoing conduct constituted the "improper solicitation of a client," and, alternatively, argues that his conduct was constitutionally protected.

The record clearly and convincingly demonstrates that respondent solicited employment by the elder Wards. . . . However, we also agree with the respondent that his conduct was constitutionally protected.We find it crucial that, in turning to the respondent for help, Rev. Johnson was not attempting to create a facade or device designed to facilitate the respondent's solicitation of remunerative employment (*cf. In re Primus* (1978) n. 20 (no evidence of "sham")), but rather was acting as part of a *bona fide* relief effort created to further interests independent of the respondent's interest in remunerative employment. Thus, even though the respondent's motives were predominantly pecuniary, his conduct served to further the interests of Rev. Johnson's community, and a blanket prohibition of all contact between respondent and that community would not pass constitutional muster. . . .

■ RYAN, JUSTICE, specially concurring:

. . . The majority opinion finds that the respondent's solicitation activities in Mississippi were tinged with associational values protected by the first and fourteenth amendments. I do not agree. . . . The only difference between our respondent's activities in Mississippi and those of the attorney in *Ohralik* is the nebulous associational relationship which the majority finds present in our case. This relationship is apparently not with Rev. Johnson's church, nor was the solicitation to further its ends, because some of those solicited were not members of the church. The association which the majority finds renders this otherwise improper solicitation permissible is indefinitely defined as "Rev. Johnson's community." There is no organization in existence with which the respondent was associated. Rev. Johnson stood as a self-appointed person in the community conducting what he thought was a helpful effort. The opinion in this case fulfills the prophetic statement of Mr. Justice Rehnquist in his dissent in *Primus*:

> "And we may be sure that the next lawyer in Ohralik's shoes who is disciplined for similar conduct will come here cloaked in the prescribed mantle of 'political association' to assure that insurance companies do not take unfair advantage of policyholders."

PROBLEM 2

You are an attorney with a small civil rights firm that specializes in plaintiffs' employment discrimination and sex harassment suits. Your litigation is now supported primarily by contingent fee recoveries and fee awards, although you have sometimes received project grants from foundations for public education.

Last month, while attending a reception for a local artist, you met one of the few women welders at Allard, Inc., a large manufacturing firm. You expressed admiration for her ability to survive in a such a sex-segregated workplace. Her response suggested that the company's attitude toward women in general, and her, in particular, may provide grounds for liability. You then explain the nature of your legal practice and suggest that if she is interested in pursuing the matter, she should contact your firm.

She does so. Although she is interested in filing suit, she is unable to underwrite the costs of the litigation. You explain that although she must agree to be nominally liable for litigation expenses, your firm would never seek to recover costs from her if the claim is unsuccessful. She wants you to put that representation into your retainer agreement or to drop the clause holding her financially responsible.

a) You seek advice from a fellow attorney. She believes that the solicitation-maintenance issue could become sticky and advises you to refer the client to another lawyer. You are reluctant to pass up this opportunity for a suit likely to generate substantial publicity and fees. How do you proceed?

b) If you decide to accept the case, may you call, write, or hold a meeting for other female Allard employees describing the litigation? If they contact your firm later with questions about their own situation, may you represent them ? Alternatively, may you suggest that your client contact them? Could you accept those other employees as clients or refer them to another lawyer who would serve as co-counsel in a class action?

c) While the suit is pending, your client suffers a disabling injury. Can you advance her modest sums to pay medical and living expenses in order to prevent her from accepting an inadequate settlement?

d) Would the results be different if you worked for a non-profit civil rights organization that gets 5 percent of its support through attorney's fees?

References:

Model Rules 1.8, 7.3.

PROBLEM 3

Three years ago, one of your law school friends opened a small firm that specializes in personal injury matters. He and several attorneys in his firm are facing charges involving various forms of allegedly prohibited solicitation and maintenance. They seek your assistance. The charges at issue are as follows.

a) A firm lawyer arrived at an accident scene, identified himself as a personal injury attorney, advised those present how to preserve evidence, and later accepted representation from one of the victims.[57]

b) Firm staff sent a wreath to the funeral of a child killed in a widely publicized local accident. The wreath included a firm brochure and a letter to the family stating: "Please accept our deepest sympathy in the loss of Randy. We know that you are presently being faced with many difficult decisions and will soon be faced with others. If we may be of assistance to you in any regard, do not hesitate to contact us." The state's prohibitions against solicitation refer only to contact made in person or by phone.[58]

c) The firm accepts clients who make contact through on-line chat rooms and a website, minesafety.com, which includes information about the legal rights of miners as well as the firm's expertise in handling cases related to mine safety.

d) Firm attorneys sign agreements guaranteeing bank loans to clients in order to cover their medical and living expenses during litigation.[59]

e) Firm attorneys provide "pro bono" legal services to friends in the medical profession who have referred patients with personal injury claims.

57. Maura Dolan, "Fresh on the Heels of Trouble," *L.A. Times*, October 13, 1993, at A1.

58. Mark Hansen, "Solicitation or Sympathy?," *A.B.A.J.*, Sept., 1991, at 34. *See also* Norris v. Alabama State Bar, ABA/BNA Manual on Professional Conduct, 7 *BNA Reports* 107 (1991).

59. Toledo Bar Association v. McGill, 597 N.E.2d 1104 (Ohio 1992).

No clients have complained to the bar concerning the adequacy of the firm's representation. What do you advise its lawyers on the merits of these charges?

f) Your friends plan to organize a group of lawyers interested in liberalizing the state's rules on solicitation and maintenance. Do you agree to assist this effort? They are, for example, opposed to a provision along the lines upheld in *Florida Bar v. Went for It*, 515 U.S. 618 (1995); it prohibits lawyers' targeted mailings to accident victims for 30 days following their accident. In opposing that provision, your friend hopes to enlist a national public interest organization, the Public Citizen Litigation Group, which filed an amicus brief in the *Florida Bar* case. According to the Group's director, David Vladeck, the moratorium cuts off "an important avenue of information when [accident victims] are most vulnerable" to inadequate settlement offers. In his view, "Just because there are a few lawyers that are out of control doesn't mean you should burn an important bridge."[60]

g) Your friend's firm would also like your help in filing a complaint with the state bar and consumer protection agency against Allstate Insurance Company. For the last several years, the company has been sending letters headed "Do I Need an Attorney" to individuals involved in accidents with Allstate policy holders. The letters include the following statements.

● Claims are settled faster when no lawyer is involved.

● Lawyers typically charge a percentage of the recovery plus expenses. Victims who settle directly with Allstate keep the entire amount.

● Victims can hire a lawyer at a later date if they are not satisfied after negotiating directly with Allstate. The letter includes the statute of limitations for filing a legal claim.

Lawyers in several other states have filed unsuccessful complaints charging that the letter is misleading and constitutes the unauthorized practice of law. One basis for those claims is the insurance industry's own research, which shows that individuals who hire lawyers do substantially better than those who negotiate themselves, even after deducting attorneys fees.[61] What advice do you provide concerning the merits of the complaints?

References:

Model Rules 1.8, 7.2, 7.3.

For discussion of maintenance, see Section F, Notes on Attorneys' Fees, and Section G, Notes: Acquiring an Interest in Litigation, For discussion of unauthorized practice, see Section D.

60. Hladky, *supra* note 14, at 18.

61. Bill Ibelle, "Allstate Tells Car Crash Victims, 'You Don't Need a Lawyer,'" *Lawyers Weekly*, March 24, 1997, B1, 2 (noting study finding that average settlement for claimants without lawyers was $3,262 compared to $11,939 for claimants with legal representation).

Deborah L. Rhode, "Solicitation"

36 Journal of Legal Education 317, 317–321, 321–330 (1986).

I.

Much of the commentary surrounding solicitation has had all the trappings of a medieval morality play. Lawyers generally emerge as either heroes or villains in plots that rarely thicken enough to admit any narrative complexity. All too often, the result has been a rhetorical standoff that fails to capture the competing values at issue.

To many commentators in both the press and the profession, recent experience with mass disasters provides ample justification for the bar's traditional view of solicitation.... Particular opprobrium [has been] ... reserved for "ambulance chasers," the "ghoulish" and "nefarious" souls who lurked about scenes of human distress where tort actions might be waiting to be born.... Except under certain limited circumstances, involving for example, *pro bono* representation or advice to friends and relatives, the bar's official codes have prohibited in-person solicitation. The stated rationale for such prohibitions has rested on concerns about underrepresentation and overreaching that have been historically associated with solicitation....

Underrepresentation in this context has generally assumed two forms. The most obvious has involved attempts to minimize risks and maximize profits through high volume caseloads.... Another cluster of evils historically associated with solicitation has included [overreaching: e.g.] misrepresentation, overcharging, and intrusiveness. Although systematic evidence is lacking, ethical violations in pursuit of personal injury clients have unquestionably been coupled with ethical violations in pursuit of their claims ..., including fraud, bribery, perjury, and fabricated evidence. More common problems have involved indelicate or exploitative forms of client contact. Enterprising attorneys with retainer agreements in tow have too often appeared in emergency wards and funeral parlors. For victims of mass disasters, the period following their release from the hospital has sometimes been anything but restful; on her first day home, one victim of ... [a] Hyatt Regency hotel fire received seven calls from local practitioners interested in her legal health. Relationships forged under many such circumstances are unlikely to reflect the kind of informed consideration of alternatives that the free market paradigm presupposes....

[It is also the case, however, that legal entrepreneurs have prevented as well as profited from exploitation.] ... [M]any civil rights attorneys during the last quarter century have found personal persuasion to be the most effective means of rousing relevant constituencies. To cite only the most notable example, the named plaintiff in *Brown v. Board of Education* was initially "anything but eager" to incur the risks of legal proceedings. As the facts in *Primus* similarly suggested, the retiring posture contemplated by conventional bar etiquette is ill-suited to the realities of much public interest litigation. Without personal contact, many victims of constitutional violations will remain unaware of potential remedies or means to pursue them.

Lawyers willing to skirt the official rules on decorum have made for a more humane social order in both public and private law contexts. By helping to redistribute the costs of accidents, the personal injury bar has increased incentives for reducing accidents while ameliorating the conditions of victims and their dependents. Similarly, by raising the costs and consciousness of various constitutional and statutory violations, entrepreneurial public interest attorneys have helped produce some of the most progressive social changes in this nation's history. . . .

So too, the intrusiveness of personal injury lawyers in the wake of mass disasters is frequently related to, and/or dwarfed by, the intrusiveness of insurance claims adjusters, who are not subject to the same professional prescriptions regarding decorum. . . . [R]ecent mass disasters have witnessed industrious industry representatives waylaying family members en route from the funeral. Uninformed consent, while too often reflected in solicited lawyer-client agreements, is also too often evident in insurance adjusters' settlements. The conditions of legal ignorance and economic necessity that have permitted exploitation by plaintiffs' counsel have presented equal opportunities for their adversaries. . . .

Prevailing constitutional doctrine and codified standards, by focusing on attorneys' motives rather than conduct, have misconstrued the problem and misconceived the solution. The kind of pure [charitable] intent ostensibly present in *Primus* has become increasingly unusual given recent legislation expanding the potential for fee recoveries in public interest litigation. Since unalloyed altruism is rare, to prohibit personal contact except in the highly atypical circumstances where lawyers have no conceivable financial interest in the outcome is both over-and underinclusive. Such an approach bans conduct that need not result in overreaching or underrepresentation, and it ignores the ways in which nonmonetary concerns can compromise counsels' fiduciary obligations. Attorneys' personal interests and ideologies are often implicated in pro bono contexts. . . .

A constituency more concerned with the fact than the image of impropriety should seek a different regulatory framework. . . . One possible approach would be the kind of time, place, and manner restrictions suggested in an earlier draft of the ABA Model Rules and in other proposals submitted to state and national bar officials. Rather than imposing a categorical ban on personal contact, the profession could proscribe specific forms of abuse, such as coercive or harassing conduct, or communications where the lawyer reasonably should know that the client's physical or psychological state prevents informed deliberation. Curtailment of prohibitions on direct attorney-client contact could be coupled with expanded protections from other forms of abuse. . . . Attorney incompetence should be subject to more effective remedies, and overreaching by insurance claims agents should result in more stringent sanctions.

These regulatory strategies cannot, of course, provide wholly adequate protection against the cupidity and callousness that has accompanied some solicitation. But too much outrage has been directed at intractable individual frailties and too little at institutional failures. Ultimately, the most effective way to minimize attorney overreaching is to minimize the profit incentives that encourage it. To that end, we should be designing remedial structures that rely less on lawyers in general and on privately subsidized lawyers in particular. Our present legal procedures, rather than focusing on restitution for victims, divert an inordinate percentage of compensation to attorneys. Yet there has been no lack of models for no-fault insurance schemes and alternative dispute resolution systems that promise some improvement. Nor has there been an absence of innovative pro bono models for delivering emergency legal aid for mass disaster victims. What has been notably lacking, however, is support from the bar. . . . [It is that constituency which must rethink the premises and processes by which we distribute legal services.]

NOTES AND QUESTIONS

1. In *Edenfield v. Fane*, 507 U.S. 761 (1993), the Court struck down Florida's ban on personal solicitation by certified public accountants. The case involved a declaratory action by Scott Fane, a CPA who previously had built a practice in New Jersey by making unsolicited telephone calls to business executives and arranging meetings to explain his services and expertise. New Jersey, along with some twenty other states, permitted such solicitation. The absence of demonstrated harm from these permissive state rules helped convince the Court to invalidate Florida's ban.

In the majority's view, personal solicitation by CPAs differed from personal solicitation by lawyers. Cases like *Ohralik* involve unsophisticated clients at moments of "high stress and vulnerability." By contrast, CPAs' solicitation methods are generally conducive to "rational and considered decision making" by experienced executives. Moreover, "the importance of repeat business and referrals gives the CPA a strong incentive to act in a responsible and decorous manner." Finally, the dangers of overreaching by lawyers are greater than in the case of accountants, since lawyers are trained in the art of advocacy.

In speaking for the majority, Justice Kennedy also emphasized the positive aspects of solicitation:

> A seller has a strong financial incentive to educate the market and stimulate demand for his product or service, so solicitation produces more personal interchange between buyer and seller than would occur if only buyers were permitted to initiate contact. Personal interchange enables a potential buyer to meet and evaluate the person offering the product or service, and allows both parties to discuss and negotiate the desired form for the transaction or professional relation. Solicitation also enables the seller to direct his proposals toward those consumers whom he has a reason to believe would be most interested in what he has to sell. For the buyer, it provides an opportunity to explore in

detail the way in which a particular product or service compares to its alternatives in the market.

Do similar considerations argue for more liberal rules on solicitation in at least some legal contexts, where clients are not approached at times of special stress and vulnerability? Does lawyers' advocacy training put them in an entirely different category than other sellers of professional service?

2.   In *Florida Bar v. Went For It*, 515 U.S. 618 (1995), the Court upheld a Florida rule prohibiting lawyers from soliciting accident victims or other families by mail for 30 days after the accident. The bar's justification for that prohibition rested primarily on the interest in protecting lawyers' public image:

> Because direct mail solicitations in the wake of accidents are perceived by the public as intrusive, the Bar argues, the reputation of the legal profession has suffered commensurably. The regulation, then, is an effort to protect the flagging reputation of Florida lawyers by preventing them from engaging in conduct that the Bar maintains, "is universally regarded as deplorable and beneath common decency because of its intrusion upon the special vulnerability and private grief of victims or their families."

In supporting that claim, the bar cited a public opinion survey and journalistic accounts of victims who had been offended by lawyers' letters. The survey found that about a quarter of consumers reported lower regard for the profession as a result of solicitation.

Would that same rationale support a ban on lawyers' television advertisements following an accident advising potential victims that they "may be entitled to compensation and there may be insurance that covers your injuries"?[62] Is protecting the bar's image an adequate basis for prohibiting truthful speech? Should the Court also have taken into account the benefits to some individuals in receiving prompt information and the possibility of less restrictive strategies for achieving the state's interest? Would your view be affected by knowing that accident victims who are represented by counsel receive much higher awards on average than those who negotiate directly with insurance agents?[63]

3.   In *Central Hudson Gas & Electric Corp. v. Public Service Commission*, 447 U.S. 557, 572 (1980), the Court held that restrictions on commercial speech should be "no more extensive than is necessary to serve the state interest." Does that test argue against a categorical ban on solicitation? Florida, like other jurisdictions, requires that all written solicitation letters have the word "advertisement" in red ink on the outside envelope. Should the Court require evidence that such a disclosure is generally inadequate to protect consumers who might find mailings offensive?

---

62. Solomon Moore, "Lawyers Seek Out Victims of Crash," *L.A. Times,* February 7, 2005, at B3 (describing ad by Jacoby & Meyers following a California train crash).

63. Peter A. Bell & Jeffrey O'Connell, *Accidental Justice: The Dilemma of Tort Law* 165–166 (1997); Richard Zitrin & Carol M. Langford, *The Moral Compass of the American Lawyers* 129, 135 (1999).

Consider the alternative proposed by the Federal Trade Commission, which would prohibit only in-person solicitation that

1) involves harassment, coercion, or undue influence;

2) involves communication with persons who have expressed a desire not to be contacted; or

3) occurs when a potential client is unable to exercise reasonable, considered judgment.[64]

Would such a prohibition, coupled with strict enforcement of existing rules on fraud and unreasonable fees, be preferable to the Model Rules approach?

4.   Under such an approach, would too much invasion of privacy go unregulated? In other contexts, for example door-to-door solicitation of charitable contributions, the Court has found privacy interests insufficient to justify broad prohibitions.[65] Are you persuaded that all personal solicitation by lawyers stand on different footing? Does such solicitation pose greater risks than solicitation by insurance or sports agents? Would a preferable approach be the legislation Congress enacted to protect victims of airline accidents and their families from any unsolicited communication either by an attorney or by "any potential party to the litigation" for 30 days following the accident? 49 U.S.C.A. § 1136 (g)(2) (1999). If states barred solicitation by agents of defendants and their insurers, would that remove the consumer's need for attorney solicitation as well? Why do you suppose more states haven't adopted such an approach? Would another useful strategy be for more bar associations to provide free legal advice to mass disaster victims by volunteer lawyers who agree not to accept cases arising from the accident?[66]

5.   What rules should apply to solicitation of law firm clients by lawyers who are leaving the firm? Compare DR 2–104(A) and Model Rule 7.3. ABA Informal Opinion No. 1457 (1980) and Informal Opinion 1466 (1981) conclude that lawyers may send announcements of their departure to clients with whom they had an active lawyer-client relationship, provided that the notice is related to open and pending matters for which the lawyer had direct responsibility, and that it does not urge the client to sever relations with the firm. The notice may, however, make clear that the client has the right to determine which lawyer will provide further representation.

Should law firms be allowed to restrict departing members' right to take clients with them through noncompetition contractual penalties? Reasonable restrictions are generally enforceable for other professions such

64. Federal Trade Commission, *supra* note 3, at 151.

65. Village of Schaumburg v. Citizens for a Better Environment, 444 U.S. 620 (1980).

66. See Louisiana State Bar Association Rules of Professional Conduct Committee, Opinion 005–RPPC–005 (September 27, 2005) (noting that "profit-motivated" solici-

tation by volunteer lawyers will not be tolerated, either directly or for the benefit of others through systematic referrals). For general discussion see Robert Kirby, "Direct Client Solicitation: When Does Informing Someone of Available Legal Services and Remedies Become Ambulance Chasing?," 14 *Geo. J. Legal Ethics* 757 (2006).

as accounting and medicine, but not for law. See Model Rule 5.6 and Model Code DR 2–108. Is such different treatment justifiable? Is it enough to provide law firms with an action for breach of fiduciary obligation or tortious interference with business if members lure clients away in secret?[67]

C.   Specialization and Group Legal Services Plans

PROBLEM 4

a) You are the chair of a committee established by your state supreme court to formulate recommendations concerning specialization and group legal services. Committee members are evenly divided among those who favor no specialization program, those who support a state certification plan, and those who prefer allowing individual practitioners to designate themselves as specialists after a minimum number of years of experience in their specialty or satisfaction of certification requirements by ABA-approved private programs such as the National Board of Trial Advocacy. What is your view?

b) Your committee is also reassessing rules concerning group legal services. Three kinds of plans are common. One model involves an organization that selects attorneys to provide specified services for its members. Members pay an annual premium for coverage. In exchange for receiving client referrals, lawyers agree to certain terms and conditions, including fixed fees at a discount from normal rates. A second model involves a consortium that provides an advertising and referral service for attorneys at a specified monthly rate. In essence, the consortium sponsors advertisements as well as screens and refers potential clients. Lawyer participants in the plan carry malpractice insurance and agree to arbitration of client complaints. A third model involves an online matching service that recruits lawyers to participate. Lawyers pay a fee to the service, which markets itself to individuals with legal needs. Those individuals post a description of the service they require, the jurisdiction involved, the amount of expertise they desire, and their requested fee range. The service then sends that information to lawyers who qualify without identifying the potential client. Lawyers can then post a response on line and the individual can determine whether to contact any of them regarding representation.

What ethical issues do these plans raise? Would it matter if the organization running the program is non-profit or is owned by lawyers? Should it matter? What are the advantages and disadvantages of each plan for lawyers and clients?

References:

Model Rules 5.4, 7.2, 7.3.

---

67. Dowd & Dowd v. Gleason, 693 N.E.2d 358 (Ill. 1998); Robert W. Hillman, *Hillman on Lawyer Mobility: The Law and Ethics of Partner Withdrawals and Law Firm* *Breakups*, 2:47 (2d ed. 1999); Milton C. Regan, Jr., "Law Firms, Competition Penalties, and the Values of Professionalism," 13 *Geo. J. Legal Ethics* 1 (1999).

NOTES ON SPECIALIZATION

Since the early 1950s, state and national bar associations have been wrestling with the issue of specialization. A large number of committees have come and gone, leaving in their wake a series of conflicting rules and recommendations. The ABA accredits the certification programs of a number of national organizations, and 22 states allow lawyers to advertise their certification by these organizations. Another 8 states also have their own process for accreditation and 12 run their own certification programs. At latest count, about 32,000 lawyers are certified specialists.[68] Common areas of certification include litigation, family law, real property law, estate planning and probate law, elder law, and health care law. These programs are voluntary in two important respects: no attorneys certified as specialists are required to limit their practice to their areas of specialty, and no attorneys lacking certification are foreclosed from practicing in areas where certification is available. Under ABA accreditation standards, specialist certification programs should require that candidates pass an exam, provide five peer references and demonstrate 25 percent of practice time and 36 hours of continuing legal education in their specialty over the preceding three years.[69]

Although most lawyers consider themselves specialists, the issue of certification remains divisive. Advocates of specialization programs generally stress advantages of competence and efficiency. A plan that insures some minimum level of expertise among its participants can reduce consumers' search costs and risks of inadequate assistance. It can also bring down the price of certain services by eliminating referral fees and by decreasing the number of hours attorneys will need to spend acquainting themselves with new fields. Such a program might also prevent clients from drawing unwarranted inferences about the capabilities of uncertified lawyers who currently advertise their practice as limited to particular fields.

In response to such claims, critics of specialization plans have questioned whether they provide sufficient guarantees of competence or are cost-effective for clients. In these commentators' view, requirements such as three years of practice in a particular area, ability to memorize enough facts to pass a single exam, and passive attendance at continuing legal education courses, may not afford adequate protection to consumers. Even the most rigorous programs, critics note, have had exams with high pass rates and generous grandparent provisions exempting current practitioners from exam requirements. Less rigorous programs may mislead clients into believing that specialists have more expertise than the program require-

---

68. Dick Dahl, "Lawyers Describing Themselves as Specialists," *S. Carolina Lawyers' Weekly,* June 18, 2007, at 1.

69. An alternative approach allows attorneys to designate themselves as specialists. Under the system pioneered by New Mexico, lawyers submit affidavits stating that they have spent at least 60% of their time in one of various recognized specialties during the five years preceding application, and will attend continuing legal education courses in that area. This entitles applicants to continue identifying themselves as specialists as long as they continue to meet those requirements. Under this approach, the state makes no further effort to ascertain the competence of applicants.

ments guarantee. As a result, these critics contend, formal specialization could allow participants to charge a premium for services that will often be no better than those available from noncertified attorneys. An additional concern is that programs that begin as voluntary will end up as compulsory. Analogizing to other fields such as medicine and accounting, some critics have warned that consumers' desire to minimize risks in areas where they cannot adequately judge services will encourage reliance exclusively on certified professionals. Ultimately, general practitioners might lose status, face greater risks of malpractice claims, and find themselves without a substantial market. The resulting oligopoly could produce not only higher prices but greater political cohesion among specialists.[70] Certified practitioners could form a powerful unified lobbying group in opposition to regulation that might challenge their own or their clients' interests.

In sorting out these arguments, commentators generally share two assumptions. First, the trend toward specialization is unlikely to reverse itself, given the growing complexity of the law and the increasing competition among lawyers. Second, consumers will inevitably draw conclusions about the relative competence of those who limit their fields of work, no matter what policy the bar adopts. In a survey by the Social Science Research Institute, a majority of Americans indicated that they would be more likely to use a lawyer who was board certified. However, a majority also incorrectly assumed that lawyers already were board certified.[71] If de facto specialization is inescapable, and consumers are misinformed about the role of formal programs, should more attention focus on designing an appropriate certification system?

QUESTIONS

1. Should more states adopt certification programs? Would a national system be preferable?

2. If states adopt a program, should they establish their own standards or defer to ABA-approved specialty organizations like the National Board of Trial Advocacy, which would avoid the inconsistency and duplication of efforts inevitable under current decentralized approaches?

NOTES ON GROUP LEGAL SERVICES, REFERRAL PLANS, AND LEGAL INSURANCE

Group legal services include any type of plan by which a group makes legal assistance available to its members. Some plans involve prepayment (i.e., insurance) programs in which premiums are paid by individuals or third parties such as employers in order to cover future services. Such programs are marketed to groups or to individuals. Under some prepaid

---

70. Herbert M. Kritzer, "The Future Role of 'Law Workers': Rethinking the Forms of Legal Practice and the Scope of Legal Education," 44 *Ariz. L.R.* 917, 930 (2002).

71. Jeremy Perlin, "Special Recognition," *ABA J.*, May 1998, at 76.

programs, members receive "comprehensive" coverage; that is, coverage for 80–90% of an average person's legal needs in a given year. Under other prepaid "access" programs, members receive unlimited advice but pay separately for other services, and not all needs are covered. Costs vary accordingly, but generally range between $6 and $25 a month.[72]

Other group legal service plans do not involve prepayment but rather provide referrals to cooperating attorneys or employ lawyers to handle members' claims. Referral arrangements are sponsored by bar associations as well as private organizations. Bar plans generally permit participation by all licensed attorneys within the jurisdiction who agree to abide by the requirements of the plan, such as low initial consultation fees or, in some cases, arbitration of certain disputes. Group referral systems are generally classified as either "closed" (limited to attorneys selected by the group) or "open" (available to all attorneys who accept the terms of the group, such as specified fees for certain services).

Group legal services plans began around the start of the twentieth century. Most were sponsored by employers, unions, automobile clubs, and insurance companies. The organized bar initially opposed the entire concept of group services and sued, often successfully, to shut them down entirely or limit their development through a variety of marketing and ownership restrictions. Bar leaders objected that such plans violated ethical rules prohibiting the practice of law by corporations, fee-sharing with nonlawyers, and solicitation of clients. In effect, early bar ethical codes allowed lawyers to provide services to an organization but not to its members. The stated rationales for this restriction were that corporations were not subject to bar ethical regulation, that nonlawyers should not exercise control over lawyers' professional judgment, and that conflicts of interest might arise between organizations and their members. A less altruistic concern, but one repeatedly expressed by bar members, was that group plans restricted access to clients by lawyers who were not part of the plan, and limited the fees available to attorneys who were participants.[73]

The profession's preferred alternative was a referral system run under bar auspices. Los Angeles established the first of these systems in 1937, and by the turn of the 21st century, about three hundred and fifty were handling some five to six million requests for information a year. From a consumer standpoint, however, these systems have significant limitations. Only about half comply with ABA model standards, and even those that do provide relatively little price and quality information. Typically, any lawyer may receive referrals as long as he or she accepts a few basic terms, such as maintaining malpractice insurance and limiting fees for the first half hour of consultation. No information is available concerning the participants' prior performance, average fees, or complaint record. Moreover, many

---

72. Mary Flood, "More Workers get Legal Perk: A Lawyer," *Houston Chronicle,* July 2, 2007, at B1.

73. For early plans and ethical restrictions, *see* Alec M. Schwartz, *A Lawyer's*

Guide to Prepaid Legal Services: A Handbook for the Small Firm (Chicago: American Bar Association, 1998); ABA Canons of Ethics, Canons 12, 34, 35, 47.

consumers worry about the quality of services that would be available from lawyers who need to place themselves on bar panels in order to obtain work. As a consequence, only about six percent of surveyed clients have relied on such referral systems.[74]

By contrast, group services can offer additional benefits along several dimensions, depending on the nature of the plan. First, any prepaid system has the advantage of spreading costs; individuals can protect themselves from incurring substantial legal expenses in any given year through modest premiums. Sponsoring organizations can also provide some control over the cost and quality of services. Such control is greatest in closed panel systems, where the organization hires or selects attorneys whom its members consult for covered services. Under such plans, participating attorneys are either on salary to the organization or agree to provide services at reduced rates. In both cases, participants can develop special expertise in members' problems and performance can be monitored. Clients also have fewer search costs and run no risk of referral fees. Even open panel plans, in which members choose their own attorney, give participating professionals incentives to limit charges along lines specified by the plan. Both types of programs help to reduce what surveys have revealed as a major barrier to the use of legal services—unrealistic fears about the costs of routine services.

Such advantages have prompted various challenges to bar ethical restrictions. In a series of cases in the 1960s, the Supreme Court extended First Amendment protection for group legal services. The first of these cases, *NAACP v. Button*, 371 U.S. 415 (1963), recognized the NAACP's right to seek plaintiffs and provide them with counsel for civil rights suits. Subsequent decisions in *Brotherhood of Railroad Trainmen v. Virginia State Bar*, 377 U.S. 1 (1964), *reh'g denied*, 377 U.S. 960 (1964), and *United Mine Workers Dist. 12 v. Illinois State Bar Association*, 389 U.S. 217 (1967), extended *Button* to protect union practices of referring members to selected lawyers or employing attorneys to handle members' workers' compensation claims. As the Court subsequently summarized its holdings, the "common thread" running through these decisions was that "collective activity undertaken to obtain meaningful access to the courts is a fundamental right within the protection of the First Amendment." *United Transportation Union v. State Bar of Michigan*, 401 U.S. 576, 585 (1971).

In response to these decisions, the ABA adopted a set of amendments to the Code that liberalized treatment for group legal services. However, DR 2–103 still retains restrictions on for-profit closed panel plans, as well as on plans initiated by lawyers for their own financial benefit. These restrictions have been largely abandoned in the Model Rules. Under ABA Formal Opinion 355, lawyers may participate in a group plan provided that they: exercise independent professional judgment on behalf of clients;

74. Kristin Choo, "Linking Lawyers and Clients," *ABA Journal* February 2001, 83; American Bar Association Standing Committee on Lawyer Referral and Information Service, *Report to the House of Delegates* (1993); ABA Model Lawyer Referral and Information Service Quality Assistance Act (1993).

maintain client confidences; provide competent services; avoid conflicts of interest; and refrain from improper solicitation, advertising, fee sharing, or violations of applicable laws. However, as subsequent discussion on multidisciplinary practice notes, prohibitions on lay ownership of legal service providers or fee-sharing with non-lawyers have remained significant limitations.

Despite these constraints, group legal service programs have experienced substantial growth, partly due to changes in federal tax, labor, and insurance laws, as well as more permissive policies toward lawyer advertising. An estimated 18 million Americans have some form of coverage, and about a quarter of surveyed employers offer legal insurance plans as one of the benefits that employees can elect.[75] Still, a far smaller proportion of the population has legal insurance compared to European countries such as Germany and Sweden, where a majority of adults have some form of coverage. Whether the United States follows that pattern may be influenced in part by the profession's attitudes toward the regulation and the marketing of insurance plans.

What are the primary risks of for-profit plans from the public's standpoint? What about from the profession's standpoint? An earlier draft of the Model Rules included a provision that would have allowed lawyers to practice with a firm owned or managed by nonlawyers if the firm met requirements similar to those set forth in Opinion 355. According to Geoffrey Hazard, reporter for the Model Rules Commission, "[d]uring the debate [in the ABA's House of Delegates] someone asked if [this provision] would allow Sears Roebuck to open a law office. When [bar members] found out it would, that was the end of the debate."[76] Under the Rules ultimately adopted, lawyers can affiliate with a prepaid plan offered by Sears, they can provide legal services to Sears as in-house counsel, but they cannot provide services to Sears' customers or practice in a firm that Sears runs in whole or in part.

QUESTIONS

1. Does this result make sense? Australia and the United Kingdom now permit non-lawyer equity investments in law firms, although in Australia to date only personal injury plaintiffs' firms have taken advantage of this method for raising capital.[77] Should the United States move in a similar direction? Would such investment offer a useful spur to innovation and

---

75. Randi Bojornstad, "Legal Insurance Business Gains Momentum in U.S.," *Register–Guard*, June 22, 1999, at A1; Karen Pallarito, "Group Legal Coverage Grows in Popularity as Valued Benefit," *Business Insurance*, June 25, 2007, at 14. Where employers offer such coverage as a benefit paid by employees, about 10 to 20 percent elect coverage. *Id.*

76. David Kaplan, "Want to Invest in a Law Firm?," *Nat'l L.J.*, Jan. 19, 1987, at 28.

77. United Kingdom Legal Services Act of 2007; Jason Kirause, "Selling Law on an Open Market," *ABA J.*, July 2007, at 34; Martin W. Whitaker, "Nonlawyer Ownership of Law Firms Is Here: Many Question Whether It Is Right for U.S.," 23 *ABA/BNA Lawyers' Manual on Professional Conduct* 439 (2007); Bruce MacEwen, Milton C. Regan, Jr. & Larry Ribstein, "Law Firms, Ethics, and Equity Capital," 21 *Geo. J. Legal Ethics* 61 (2008).

managerial efficiency? Are there ways of protecting public interests apart from a categorical ban on lay ownership or investment? For example, states could develop more targeted safeguards, such as protection of attorneys' independent professional judgment, and requirements that nonlawyers observe bar ethical rules concerning competence, confidentiality, and conflicts of interest. The Australian law firms warn investors that in the event of conflicts between client interests and investor interests, the client interests must take precedence. Additional quality controls could be imposed by statute or by standards adopted by consumer protection agencies, insurance commissioners, and employers' benefit managers.[78] Would those protections be sufficient? Consider that issue in light of the discussion on multidisciplinary legal practice below.

2. Should the bar develop special rules for online matching services? If so, what should they require? For useful discussion of advertising, solicitation, and fee issues, see D.C. Bar Ethics Opinion 342 ("Participation in Internet-Based Lawyer Referral Services Requiring Payment of Fees") (2007).

3. Which state bars should be able to exercise regulatory jurisdiction over lawyers who run online matching services in multiple states? Does Model Rule 8.5 offer useful guidance for the regulation of online referral services?

D. UNAUTHORIZED PRACTICE OF LAW: NONLAWYER SERVICES AND MULTIJURISDICTIONAL PRACTICE

Orison S. Marden, "The American Bar and Unauthorized Practice"

33 Unauthorized Practice News 1–2 (Spring–Summer 1967).[79]

There are numerous other groups whose activities touch on the practice of law [including] accountants, auditors, real estate agents, architects, life insurance salesmen, chartered life underwriters, labor consultants, patent agents, tax specialists and so on, almost ad infinitum.

Now, if it is in the interest of our entire society that lawyers and lawyers alone are to be licensed to practice law, it then follows that there must be a line drawn between lawyers and other groups whose work touches on the practice of law.

That is why we are here today, to talk about the way the lines are currently being drawn between lawyers and others. Our concern in this subject matter is governed by broad considerations of social policy and the public interest. It must not be motivated by selfishness, by competition-for-competition's sake, or by avaricious materialism. The lawyer who thinks

---

78. Brian Heid & Eitan Misulovin, "The Group Legal Plan Revolution: Bright Horizon or Dark Future?," 18 *Hofstra Labor and Employment Law Journal* 3612 (2000).

79. Marden was then president of the American Bar Association.

that unauthorized practice work is simply a means for increasing his own income has no place in this discussion.

We are here to protect the public from the hidden dangers of dealing with the unlicensed and unauthorized practitioner; not to protect the lawyer from competition. We are not a trade union, and we must beware of giving the appearance of acting for our selfish interests when we attack the illegal practitioner.

Florida Bar v. Brumbaugh

Supreme Court of Florida, 1978.
355 So.2d 1186.

■ Per Curiam.

The Florida Bar has filed a petition charging Marilyn Brumbaugh with engaging in the unauthorized practice of law. . . .

Respondent, Marilyn Brumbaugh, is not and has never been a member of the Florida Bar, and is, therefore, not licensed to practice law within this state. She has advertised in various local newspapers as "Marilyn's Secretarial Service" offering to perform typing services for "Do–It–Yourself" divorces, wills, resumes, and bankruptcies. The Florida Bar charges that she performed unauthorized legal services by preparing for her customers those legal documents necessary in an uncontested dissolution of marriage proceeding and by advising her customers as to the costs involved and the procedures which should be followed in order to obtain a dissolution of marriage. For this service, Ms. Brumbaugh charges a fee of $50. . . .

With regard to the charges made against Marilyn Brumbaugh, this Court appointed a referee to receive evidence and to make findings of fact, conclusions of law, and recommendations as to the disposition of the case. The referee found that respondent, under the guise of a "secretarial" or "typing" service prepares, for a fee, all papers deemed by her to be needed for the pleading, filing, and securing of a dissolution of marriage, as well as detailed instructions as to how the suit should be filed, notice served, hearings set, trial conducted, and the final decree secured. The referee also found that in one instance, respondent prepared a quit claim deed in reference to the marital property of the parties. The referee determined that respondent's contention that she merely operates a typing service is rebutted by numerous facts in evidence. Ms. Brumbaugh has no blank forms either to sell or to fill out. Rather, she types up the documents for her customers after they have asked her to prepare a petition or an entire set of dissolution of marriage papers. Prior to typing up the papers, respondent asks her customers whether custody, child support, or alimony is involved. Respondent has four sets of dissolution of marriage papers, and she chooses which set is appropriate for the particular customer. She then types out those papers, filling in the blank spaces with the appropriate information. Respondent instructs her customers how the papers are to be signed, where they are to be filed, and how the customer should arrange for a final hearing. . . .

This case does not arise out of a complaint by any of Ms. Brumbaugh's customers as to improper advice or unethical conduct. It has been initiated by members of The Florida Bar who believe her to be practicing law without a license. The evidence introduced at the hearing below shows that none of respondent's customers believed that she was an attorney, or that she was acting as an attorney in their behalf. Respondent's advertisements clearly addressed themselves to people who wish to do their own divorces. These customers knew that they had to have "some type of papers" to file in order to obtain their dissolution of marriage. Respondent never handled contested divorces. During the past two years respondent has assisted several hundred customers in obtaining their own divorces. The record shows that while some of her customers told respondent exactly what they wanted, generally respondent would ask her customers for the necessary information needed to fill out the divorce papers, such as the names and addresses of the parties, the place and duration of residency in this state, whether there was any property settlement to be resolved, or any determination as to custody and support of children. Finally, each petition contained the bare allegation that the marriage was irretrievably broken. Respondent would then inform the parties as to which documents needed to be signed, by whom, how many copies of each paper should be filed, where and when they should be filed, the costs involved, and what witness testimony is necessary at the court hearing. Apparently, Ms. Brumbaugh no longer informs the parties verbally as to the proper procedures for the filing of the papers, but offers to let them copy papers described as "suggested procedural education."

The Florida Bar argues that the above activities of respondent violate the rulings of this Court in *The Florida Bar v. American Legal and Business Forms, Inc.*, 274 So.2d 225 (Fla.1973), and *The Florida Bar v. Stupica*, 300 So.2d 683 (Fla.1974). In those decisions we held that it is lawful to sell to the public printed legal forms, provided they do not carry with them what purports to be instructions on how to fill out such forms or how to use them. We stated that legal advice is inextricably involved in the filling out and advice as to how to use such legal forms, and therein lies the danger of injury or damage to the public if not properly performed in accordance with law. . . .

Although Marilyn Brumbaugh never held herself out as an attorney, it is clear that her clients placed some reliance upon her to properly prepare the necessary legal forms for their dissolution proceedings. To this extent we believe that Ms. Brumbaugh overstepped proper bounds and engaged in the unauthorized practice of law. We hold that Ms. Brumbaugh, and others in similar situations, may sell printed material purporting to explain legal practice and procedure to the public in general and she may sell sample legal forms. . . . Further, we hold that it is not improper for Marilyn Brumbaugh to engage in a secretarial service, typing such forms for her clients, provided that she only copy the information given to her in writing by her clients. In addition, Ms. Brumbaugh may advertise her business activities of providing secretarial and notary services and selling legal forms and general printed information. However, Marilyn Brumbaugh must not, in conjunction with her business, engage in advising clients as to the various remedies available to them, or otherwise assist them in preparing those forms necessary for a dissolution proceeding. More specifically, Marilyn Brumbaugh may not make inquiries nor answer questions from her clients as to the particular forms which might be necessary, how best to fill out such forms, where to properly file such forms, and how to present necessary evidence at the court hearings. Our specific holding with regard to the dissolution of marriage also applies to other unauthorized legal assistance such as the preparation of wills or real estate transaction documents. While Marilyn Brumbaugh may legally sell forms in these areas, and type up instruments which have been completed by clients, she must not engage in personal legal assistance in conjunction with her business activities, including the correction of errors and omissions. . . .

It is so ordered.

QUESTIONS

1. What constitutes the "practice of law"? Do bar ethical codes provide adequate notice as to what activities may be performed only by lawyers? If the practice of law encompasses giving advice on matters involving legal issues, are individuals such as accountants, real estate brokers, investment counselors, and insurance agents engaged in prohibited practices? Many of these competitors are members of regulated occupational groups. Does restricting their competition with lawyers serve more to protect the profession than the public?

In 2002, the ABA created a Task Force on the Model Definition of the Practice of Law. The Task Force proposed that all states and territories adopt a definition of the practice of law including "the basic premise that the practice of law is the application of legal principles and judgment to the circumstances or objectives of another person or entity." The Task Force further proposed that states and territories should "determine who may provide services that are included within the state's or territory's definition of the practice of law and under what circumstances, based upon the potential harm and benefit to the public." The proposal received harsh criticism from the Federal Trade Commission and the Justice Department's Antitrust Division. Their joint letter to the ABA argued that the proposed definition is so broad that it could preclude tax preparers from interpreting clauses of the tax code and real estate agents from explaining smoke detector ordinances. In response to that criticism, the ABA's Task Force abandoned the attempt to craft a national standard on what constitutes the practice of law, and recommended simply that every jurisdiction devise its own standard. If you were a state bar official charged with drafting a rule, what would you propose?

2. Courts and ethics committees that have considered the issue have generally followed the approach in *Brumbaugh*, and prohibited non-lawyers from offering personalized assistance, including the corrections of errors and omissions in standardized forms. Are such prohibitions appropriate? Should all personalized advice be impermissible however accurate or routine?

3. A typical case under prevailing rules is *Fifteenth Judicial District Unified Bar Ass'n v. Glasgow*, 1999 WL 1128847 (Tenn. App. 1999), which found that a typing service had engaged in unauthorized practice by informing low-income customers where and when papers should be filed and by preparing some quit claim deeds necessary to divide real property. If you were the lawyer representing the typing service on appeal in that case, what arguments would you make? If you were counsel for the bar, how would you respond? If you were a judge hearing that appeal, what would you decide?

PROBLEM 5

a) You are a lawyer representing "Pro Se Legal Services," which provides form-preparation assistance to individuals who are attempting to represent themselves in uncontested divorces, bankruptcy proceedings, and landlord-tenant cases. Your client employs independent paralegals, and is concerned about what to do when a customer asks them simple questions or makes obvious errors on the forms. It obviously does not help business for employees to prepare forms with clear mistakes. But neither will it help if paralegals are charged with unauthorized practice of law. Your client wonders if it would solve the problem to have you provide nominal supervision of the employees by being available for consultation if questions arise. Would this arrangement place you in violation of the Model Rules?

b) Your client also asks whether she could market a "bankruptcy assistant" computer program. With this software, users fill out basic personal and financial information. The software then aids users to complete bankruptcy forms by selecting exemptions and appropriate schedules.[80]

c) Could you propose legislation that would permit Pro Se Legal Services to function effectively and legally?

Deborah L. Rhode, Access to Justice

87–91 (2004).

Recent technological advances, coupled with Americans' escalating interest in legal self help, have expanded opportunities for such nonlawyer practice. A celebrated recent case involved a fifteen year old, Marcus Arnold, who presented himself as a "legal expert" on a website that allows anyone to volunteer answers to posted questions. By his own account,

---

80. In re Reynoso, 477 F.3d 1117 (9th Cir. 2007).

Arnold had never read a law book; his answers were based on information from Court TV and the Net, or common sense. Users of the site rated the answers and ranked Arnold number three, ahead of many lawyers. After Arnold revealed that he was only a high school student without legal training, his popularity initially dipped, but he eventually gained the number one spot, and was inundated with requests to represent parties in legal matters.

From the profession's standpoint, such examples are cautionary tales of what can happen without vigorous unauthorized practice enforcement. State bar leaders repeatedly sound alarms along the lines issued by one Arizona committee that nonlawyer services are causing "a crisis of faith" in the legal system. Over four-fifths of surveyed attorneys have supported prosecution of lay practitioners, and the profession has consistently blocked licensing proposals that would enable independent paralegals to offer routine services. Many local, state, and national bar associations have recently launched initiatives to broaden the definition, raise the penalties, and increase the enforcement of unauthorized practice prohibitions. In 2001, the ABA voted to strengthen enforcement efforts and in 2003 it considered a task force proposal for a stringent model definition of unauthorized practice. When the Justice Department, Federal Trade Commission, and the ABA's own antitrust division protested that the proposal would inappropriately restrict client choices and increase prices, the Association's President flatly denied any such effects. The ABA's sole objective, he assured his critics, was providing a clearer definition of permissible and impermissible activities, thus "enhancing consumer access and protection, not limiting competition."

Occasionally, however, a bar leader will go off message. One former President of the New Jersey Bar expressed common views with uncommon candor when he acknowledged "no difficulty saying my position is protecting the interests of lawyers." Why should the ABA pretend that it is willing to "find work for nonlawyers[?] . . . This is the American Bar Association, not the American Paralegal Association."

That fact is not lost on the public, which seems largely unsupportive of the protective efforts ostensibly launched in its behalf. On one of the rare occasions when bar researchers consulted consumer views, over four-fifths agreed that many matters lawyers handled could be "done as well and less expensively by non-lawyers." In the only reported bar survey of consumer satisfaction, nonlawyer specialists got higher ratings than lawyers. Some efforts to broaden prohibitions on unauthorized practice have resulted in political reversals. In one state constitutional referendum, Arizona voters reversed a decision giving lawyers a monopoly over routine real estate closings. And the Texas legislature amended its unauthorized practice statutes to exempt computer software that the bar had succeeded in suppressing as impermissible legal advice.

The public's support for greater access to lay legal services is well founded. Other nations generally permit nonlawyers to provide legal advice and assist with routine documents, and no evidence suggests that their performance has been inadequate. In this country, the American Law Institute's Restatement of the Law Governing Lawyers notes that "experience in several states with extensive nonlawyer provision of traditional legal services indicates no significant risk of harm to consumers...." So too, studies of lay specialists who provide legal representation in bankruptcy and administrative agency hearings find that they generally perform as well or better than attorneys. In the most systematic bar survey to date, a majority of states did not report unauthorized practice complaints from consumers; the vast majority came from lawyers and involved no claims of specific injury. Such findings should come as no surprise. Three years in law school and passage of a bar exam are neither necessary nor sufficient to ensure expertise in the specialized areas where nonlawyer services flourish; lay specialists may be better able to provide cost-effective services than lawyers who dabble in multiple areas

This is not to discount the problems that can result from unqualified or unethical nonlawyer assistance. Some unlicensed practitioners, including disbarred attorneys, misrepresent their status and exploit vulnerable consumers. Immigrants are particularly common targets, both because they are often unfamiliar with the American legal system and because they are unlikely to approach law enforcement agencies to report abuses. However, the appropriate response to these problems is regulation, not prohibition. Consumers need an approach that balances their need for protection with their interests in competition and affordable services.

Unauthorized practice restrictions are ill-suited to that task, because they focus only on whether nonlawyers are providing legal assistance, not whether they are doing so effectively. Strong consumer demand for low-cost services makes such restrictions difficult to enforce. As a result, most lay practice goes unregulated, and when abuses occur, the public has inadequate remedies. A preferable regulatory structure would provide both less and more protection—less for attorneys and more for consumers. Nonlawyers like accountants or real estate brokers who are already licensed by the state should be allowed to provide legal assistance related to their specialties. For currently unlicensed service providers, states should develop regulatory frameworks responsive to public needs, which may vary across different practice areas. Where the risk of injury is substantial, in contexts such as immigration, consumers may benefit from licensing systems that impose minimum qualifications and offer proactive enforcement. In other fields, it could be sufficient to register practitioners and permit voluntary certification of those who meet specified standards. States also could require all lay practitioners to carry malpractice insurance, and observe basic ethical obligations governing confidentiality, competence, and conflicts of interest. Similar protections could extend to internet services. Enforcement, of course, poses substantial challenges, but the problems are not unique to lay legal assistance. As discussion below indicates, the bar's current state-based framework for lawyer regulation is highly inadequate for services that observe no geographic borders. Devising an appropriate oversight strategy for all forms of legal practice demands national efforts.

In general, however, an approach that seeks to regulate rather than preempt lay competition, would offer a number of advantages. Experience here and abroad suggests that increased competition between lawyers and nonlawyers is likely to result in lower prices, greater efficiency, and more consumer satisfaction. Regulating the activities of lay practitioners should help curb abuses that currently go unremedied, while encouraging innovative partnerships between lawyer and nonlawyer specialists.

NOTES AND QUESTIONS ON NONLAWYER SERVICES

1.   Over the last two decades, courts, bar associations, and legislatures have faced increasing pressure to increase access to nonlawyer providers of legal services. Such pressure has come from several trends, including cutbacks in funds for civil legal aid, and the growing availability of self-help publications, services, and computer software, legal information websites, standardized forms, and simplified or alternative dispute resolution procedures. The number of pro se litigants has increased accordingly. They appear in 60 to 90 percent of cases in some family, probate and landlord/tenant courts, and in a substantial number of other routine proceedings.[81]

One response to these trends has been an increase in court-based services such as free pro se resource centers, ombudsmen, or on-line resources to help individuals complete routine forms. However, many jurisdictions still lack organized pro se assistance programs, and those that are available are often inaccessible to those who need help most: individuals with limited literacy, English language and computer skills.[82] Many other nations have far more extensive systems of nonlawyer assistance for ordinary legal needs and find that lay advocates perform effectively.[83]

To address these needs, some states have liberalized rules on nonlawyer assistance. For example, several years after the *Brumbaugh* case, the Florida Supreme Court adopted a rule permitting nonlawyers to provide limited oral advice concerning the completion of legal forms approved by the Supreme Court of Florida. Oral communications by nonlawyers are restricted to those "reasonably necessary to elicit factual information to complete the form(s)" and inform the individuals how to file such forms. *In re Amendment to Rules Regulating the Florida Bar*, 510 So.2d 596 (Fla. 1987).

Another strategy has been to license lay providers of certain routine legal services. The Washington Supreme Court has established a licensing

81.   Deborah L. Rhode, *Access to Justice* (2004); Pamela A. MacLean, "Self–Help Centers Meet Pro Se Flood," *Nat'l L. J.,* June 26, 2006, at A1, A5.

82.   Rhode, *supra* note 81, at 83; MacLean, *supra* note 81, at A15 (noting that 150 self-help centers operate nationwide).

83.   See United Kingdom, Department for Constitutional Affairs, The Legal Profes-sions,   http://www.dca.gov.uk/legalsys/profs. htm#sectors (last visited July 2008); Citizen's Advice Bureau, Annual Report (2005–06): Richard Moorhead, Alan Paterson, & Avrom Sherr, "Contesting Professionalism: Legal Aid and Nonlawyers in England and Wales," 37 *Law & Soc'y Rev.* 765 (2003) (finding that in some settings, lay advocates performed better than solicitors).

system for "limited practice officers" who prepare real estate documents. In California, after the state bar rejected a proposal by its own expert commission to license legal technicians in specified areas, the California state legislature ultimately passed a "Legal Document Assistant" statute. It allows registered assistants to complete, file, and serve forms, but as a concession to the bar, prohibits them from providing any "advice, explanation, opinion, or recommendation" about "possible legal rights, remedies, defenses, options, selection of forms, or strategies." Arizona similarly permits "certified legal document preparers" to complete and file documents and provide "general legal information" but not "specific advice . . . about legal rights, remedies, defenses, options or strategies." Arizona Code of Judicial Administration Section 7–208 (effective January 2003). In Texas, after a federal district court held that a computer software program, *Quicken Family Lawyer*, constituted the unauthorized practice of law, the Texas Legislature passed a statute excluding such software from prohibited activities if it "clearly and conspicuously" states that it is not a "substitute for the advice of an attorney."[84]

If you were a member of one of these bar commissions or state legislatures, what position would you take on nonlawyer services?

2. Defenders of unauthorized practice prohibitions marshal several arguments to support their view. The first and most important is that lawyers possess skills that even very knowledgeable non-lawyers lack. Virtually every law school graduate recognizes that the first year or two of law school teaches the hard-to-define knack of "thinking like a lawyer." Thinking like a lawyer does not lie in acquiring a definite body of legal knowledge. Rather, it lies in the abilities (a) to view fact situations as "the law" understands them, and (b) to differentiate strong from weak legal arguments. These are forms of judgment that come from full and prolonged immersion in the law—and, lawyers argue, there is no short-cut to learning to think like a lawyer. Furthermore, even if a non-lawyer acquires substantial expertise in some corner of the law, he or she is likely to miss other aspects that a trained lawyer, with a broad knowledge of many fields of law, will catch. Second, the bar exam offers a screening method intended to ensure a measure of proficiency among lawyers that non-lawyers may lack. Third, the fact that lawyers are governed by an enforceable code of ethics offers clients an extra measure of protection; so does the existence of an attorney-client privilege. A great many lawyers also carry malpractice insurance, and clients who lose money to dishonest lawyers can often be indemnified by state client security trust funds. Finally, the legal system as a whole benefits by having legal transactions done at a high level of proficiency—a public good over and above the benefit to clients.

How persuasive are these arguments? Do they make sense when legal services consist of routine paperwork or elementary research tasks? Or when, as in most jurisdictions, bar discipline is lax and the rules of conduct

---

84. Unauthorized Practice of Law Committee v. Parsons Technology, 1999 WL 47235 (N.D.Tex.), vacated and remanded, 179 F.3d 956 (1999); Randall Samborn, "So What Is a Lawyer, Anyway?" *Nat'l L.J.*, June 21, 1993, at 1, 12.

are underenforced? Could most of the advantages of licensing for lawyers be achieved by a licensing system for independent paralegals, who could be required to carry malpractice insurance, contribute to a client indemnity fund, and demonstrate competence in their area of practice?

3. Efforts to challenge unauthorized practice statutes in the courts have rarely been successful. In a typical ruling analogous to *Brumbaugh*, the Oregon Supreme Court affirmed an order enjoining a form preparation service from providing oral advice. In so ruling, the court summarily rejected a claim that the prohibition impaired constitutionally protected expression. Such an argument, the court reasoned, would call into question many professional licensing and regulatory schemes. *Oregon State Bar v. Smith*, 942 P.2d 793 (Or.App.1997). By contrast, in *In re Opinion No. 26*, 654 A.2d 1344 (N.J.1995), the New Jersey Supreme Court rejected bar efforts to restrict preparation of real estate closing documents to lawyers. Although acknowledging its view that parties would be well served by hiring lawyers, the court noted that the record reflected no proof of significant harm to buyers and sellers in parts of New Jersey where realtors performed such services. As the court further pointed out, the absence of proof was "particularly impressive . . . [because] the dispute between the realtors and the bar is of long duration with the parties and their counsel singularly able and highly motivated to supply such proof as may exist. . . ." *Id.* Is this holding consistent with cases like *Brumbaugh* and *Oregon State Bar*? If not, which approach is preferable?[85]

4. How should unauthorized practice rules apply to on line assistance? In *In re Reynoso*, 477 F.3d 1117 (9th Cir. 2007), the 9th Circuit Court of Appeals held that Frankfort Digital Services had engaged in prohibited practices by supplying software aid that went "far beyond providing clerical service." In essence, the program took information supplied by the customer and determined where to place it on bankruptcy forms and selected appropriate exemptions. The company's website "offered customers extensive advice on how to take advantage of so-called loopholes in the bankruptcy code, promised services comparable to those of a 'top notch bankruptcy lawyer,' and described its software as an 'expert system' that would do more than function as a 'customized word processor.' " 477 F.3d, at 1125. The court did not consider any First Amendment or public policy arguments that might have argued for a different approach. Should it have considered such issues? Should it matter whether the program's work was in fact comparable to that of a bankruptcy lawyer and superior to that of a bankruptcy petition preparer permitted under 11 USCA § 110?

---

85. Nationally, about 80 percent of real estate closings are conducted by nonlawyers. About ten states require lawyers' assistance. Adam Liptak, "U.S. Opposes Proposal to Limit Who May Give Legal Advice," *N. Y. Times*, Feb. 3, 2003 at A11. For an opinion requiring lawyers' assistance, see In re UPL Advisory Opinion 2003–2, 588 S.E.2d 741 (Ga.2003). For analysis of conflicting unauthorized practice doctrine on real estate services, and challenges by the Federal Trade Commission and Department of Justice to restrictive practices, *see* Robert R. Keatinge, "Multidimensional Practice in a World of Invincible Ignorance: MDP, MJP, and Ancillary Business After Enron," 44 *Ariz. L. Rev.* 717, 758–59 (2002). For an argument favoring free market approaches, see George C. Leef, "The Case for a Free Market in Legal Services," 322 *Policy Analysis* 1 (1998).

5. The preceding excerpt from *Access to Justice* argues that a "sensible regulatory framework would provide both less and more protection—less for attorneys and more for consumers." To that end, many commentators endorse registration or licensing structures for nonlawyers, along the lines proposed in the excerpt. Would you support such a regulatory system? If not, what alternative would you favor? In the absence of such a system, how should courts decide what constitutes unauthorized practice of law?

NOTES AND QUESTIONS ON MULTIJURISDICTIONAL PRACTICE

As noted in Chapter III, many legal problems do not observe state lines. What implications does current unauthorized practice doctrine have in an era of increasing geographic mobility and multistate transactions? The bar's longstanding position, codified in the Model Rules of Professional Conduct and the Code of Professional Responsibility, is that a "lawyer shall not . . . practice law in a jurisdiction in violation of regulation of the legal profession in that jurisdiction. . . ." Model Rule 5.5(a). Accord DR 3–101(B). Violation of this rule counts as unauthorized practice of law in the same way that practice by non-lawyers does. Under Model Rule 8.5(a), lawyers are subject to discipline in any jurisdiction where they provide legal services, including, of course, services in violation of local unauthorized practice rules.

Traditionally, attorneys who wished to represent a client outside of the jurisdiction in which they were licensed had to affiliate local counsel, or, if the matter involved litigation, request the court to admit them temporarily, *pro hac vice* ("for this occasion"). Courts are not constitutionally obligated to extend *pro hac vice* admission, and may impose requirements such as affiliation of local counsel.[86] A few jurisdictions permitted in-house lawyers to provide legal services on behalf of their employer from an office outside of the state if they register and submit to the local bar's regulatory authority.[87] Many states also allow members of a foreign bar to be licensed without examination as legal consultants, who may practice on a restricted basis, typically involving advice on the law of the country in which they are admitted. See ABA Model Rule for the Licensing of Legal Consultants.[88]

The traditional approaches to unauthorized practice have grown increasingly out of step with the needs of contemporary practice. Many legal matters and attorney communications by phone, e-mail, fax, and internet web sites do not remain within jurisdictions where the attorneys are licensed to practice law. As an ABA Commission on Multijurisdictional Practice noted:

86. Leis v. Flynt, 441 U.S. 956 (1979).

87. ABA Report of the Commission on Multijurisdictional Practice (Aug. 2002) available at http://www.abanet.org/cpr/mjp/final_mjp_rpt_5–13.pdf.

88. About half the states license foreign legal consultants. Others are considering such licenses, over a third are considering allowing temporary practice by foreign lawyers. Vesna Jaksic, "States Review Licenses for Foreign Attorneys," *Nat'l L. J.*, June 4, 2007, at A4.

Testimony before the Commission was unanimous in recognizing that lawyers commonly engage in cross-border legal practice. Further, there was general consensus that such practice is on the increase and that this trend is not only inevitable, but necessary. The explosion of technology and the increasing complexity of legal practice have resulted in the need for lawyers to cross state borders to afford clients competent representation....

The existing system of lawyer regulation is and should be a matter of serious concern for many lawyers. Even in contexts where jurisdictional restrictions clearly apply, as in state-court proceedings, problems are caused by the lack of uniformity among the *pro hac vice* provisions of different states, unpredictability about how some of the provisions will be applied by the courts in individual cases, and, in some cases, the provisions' excessive restrictiveness. Of even greater concern, however, is that, outside the context of litigation, the reach of the jurisdictional restrictions is vastly uncertain as well as, potentially, far too restrictive.... The existing system of lawyer regulation has costs for clients. For example, out of concern for jurisdictional restrictions, lawyers may decline to provide services that they are able to render skillfully and ethically....[89]

The problems inherent in current unauthorized practice rules are illustrated by a leading decision, *Ranta v. McCarney*, 391 N.W.2d 161 (N.D.1986), where the court held that a client need not pay for work done in North Dakota by a lawyer who was licensed only in Minnesota, but who provided federal tax advice in connection with the sale of a North Dakota business. The dissent argued that the point of unauthorized practice statutes was to protect the public, and that the only protection offered by the majority's ruling was of the economic interests of North Dakota attorneys and a client who had profited from the assistance.

How would you have decided the case? May a lawyer admitted only in North Dakota give advice by telephone or e–mail to a client living in Minnesota? What if it involves North Dakota or federal law? Does it matter whether the lawyer provides that advice while in Minnesota? Suppose the client has a branch office in North Dakota. May the lawyer representing that office negotiate a claim in Minnesota or give advice while conducting discovery outside of North Dakota?[90]

This is an area of growing confusion and change, as is apparent from Chapter III's discussion of choice of law issues and Chapter XIV's analysis

---

89. *Id*. at 10–12.

90. For representative decisions see Spivak v. Sachs, 16 N.Y.2d 163, 263 N.Y.S.2d 953, 211 N.E.2d 329 (1965) (disallowing fees of California lawyer for advice given in New York on Connecticut divorce, but acknowledging that it would be inappropriate to penalize every instance in which an out-of-state attorney came into New York to work on transactions somehow tied to the state); and cases discussed in Anthony E. Davis, "Multi-

jurisdictional Practice by Transnational Lawyers," 70 *Bar Examiner* 15 (February 2001); Gould v. Harkness, 470 F.Supp.2d 1357 (S.D.Fla. 2006) denying a constitutional challenge to a possible discipline for an advertisement claiming his availability to work on New York and Federal matters from a Florida office since he was not licensed to practice in Florida and practice from that office would be unlawful.

of interstate regulation and admissions. The California Supreme Court added to the confusion with its decision in *Birbrower, Montalbano, Condon & Frank v. Superior Court*, 949 P.2d 1 (Cal.), *cert. denied*, 525 U.S. 920 (1998). Birbrower was a New York firm that had represented the Sandhu family in various business matters since 1986. One such matter involved a marketing agreement between Tandem Corporation and ESQ Business Services (ESQ–NY), a New York business software producer owned by Kamal Sandhu. Sandhu's brother subsequently became the primary shareholder of a California corporation with the same name (ESQ–Cal). In 1992, the two corporations hired Birbrower to resolve a dispute with Tandem. The original fee agreement was made in New York and modified in California over the next two years. Birbrower's lawyer made three brief trips of several days each to California to confer with ESQ officers, to negotiate with Tandem representatives, and to initiate arbitration proceedings. The dispute was settled before arbitration, but ESQ–Cal then sued Birbrower for malpractice. Birbrower cross-claimed to recover its fee. The trial court granted the plaintiff's motion for summary judgment on the ground that the fee agreement was unenforceable because Birbrower had engaged in the unauthorized practice of law. The California Supreme Court affirmed. Under its analysis, the "primary inquiry is whether the unlicensed lawyer engaged in sufficient activities in the state or created a continuing relationship with the California client that included legal duties and obligations." Physical presence, according to the court, was a relevant but not conclusive factor. Lawyers could engage in unauthorized practice by providing legal advice by telephone, fax, or other means. In the court's view, the Birbrower lawyers "extensive practice" in the state was sufficient to establish a violation.

The *Birbrower* decision attracted widespread criticism, which the California legislature partially addressed by creating a statutory exemption from unauthorized practice prohibitions for arbitration proceedings. California Rules of Court Rule 9.43. The California Supreme Court also appointed a committee to recommend further changes, and ultimately enacted rules that allow limited practice by registered in-house and legal aid attorneys licensed in another jurisdiction, and out-of-state attorneys temporarily in California for litigation or transactional matters. California Rules of Court 9.45–9.48. To qualify for the temporary legal assistance exemption, the attorney must not maintain an office or a "continuous presence in California for the practice of law" or "regularly engage in substantial business or professional activities in California." Rule 9.47 (d) (2) and (5) and Rule 9.48 (d) (2) and (5).

Other states are moving in similar directions. In response to growing concerns, the ABA established a Commission on Multijurisdictional Practice and approved its recommended amendments to the Model Rules. As revised, Model Rule 5.5 provides certain "safe havens" from unauthorized practice prohibitions for an out-of-state lawyer who provides legal services on a temporary basis. The Rule protects services that:

(c)(1) are undertaken in association with a lawyer who is admitted to practice in this jurisdiction and who actively participates in the matter;

(2) are in or reasonably related to a pending or potential proceeding before a tribunal in this or another jurisdiction, if the lawyer, or a person the lawyer is assisting, is authorized by law or order to appear in such proceeding or reasonably expects to be so authorized; [or]

(3) are in or reasonably related to a pending or potential arbitration, mediation, or other alternate dispute resolution proceeding in [the] . . . jurisdiction, if the services arise out of or are reasonably related to the lawyer's practice in a jurisdiction in which the lawyer is admitted to practice and are not services for which the forum requires *pro hac vice* admission; . . .

(d)(1) are provided to the lawyer's employer or its organizational affiliates and are not services for which the forum requires *pro hac vice* admission; or

(2) are services that the lawyer is authorized to provide by federal law or other law of this jurisdiction.

How workable this approach will prove in practice is not yet clear. Its inadequacy in the wake of Hurricane Katrina prompted the ABA in 2007 to adopt a Model Court Rule on Provision of Legal Services Following Determination of Major Disaster. That Rule, if adopted by state supreme courts, would ease unauthorized practice restrictions for displaced lawyers and out of state lawyers providing pro bono assistance following the supreme court's determination of a major disaster.

Some commentators believe that even with such an addition, the approach of Model Rule 5.5 is unduly complex and restrictive. A variety of other possibilities have been proposed. One option is to follow Section 3 of the *Restatement (Third) of the Law Governing Lawyers*, which permits legal work that "arises out of or is otherwise related to the lawyer's practice" in a jurisdiction in which the lawyer is licensed. Other possibilities include: a national system of bar admission, discussed in Chapter XIV; more permissive state-based reciprocity rules modeled on the European Union system; or a "Common Sense Proposal" to permit legal services on a temporary basis by out of state attorneys.[91] Under a national bar admission system, a license to practice law would be similar to a driver's license; the attorney's state of residence would test for competence, and other jurisdictions would honor its judgment as long as the attorney's presence is temporary. Under a system like that of the European Union, discussed in Chapter XIV, lawyers could provide legal services in another jurisdiction if they register to do so, limit their practice to occasional activity, agree to comply with local ethics rules and enforcement processes, and maintain legal malpractice insurance.[92] Do any of these approaches appear preferable to the current system?

NOTES ON GATS

The General Agreement on Trade in Services (GATS) is a multilateral treaty. GATS is an outgrowth of the agreement that created the World Trade Organization, and applies to cross-border services that participating countries (all 152 WTO members) list in their Schedule of Special Commitments. In 1995, when GATS was finalized, approximately 45 countries, including the United States, listed legal services on their Schedule. When a country lists services, it must disclose any limits placed on foreign service providers and it must base any qualifications and licensing standards "on objective and transparent criteria" that are "not more burdensome than necessary." Article XIX of GATS also requires WTO countries, within five years of signing the Agreement, to begin negotiations to further liberalize trade in services. Those negotiations are proceeding slowly. In this country, efforts have included expansion of rules allowing foreign legal consultants. About 29 states have such rules, which enable lawyers from other countries who are not licensed in the United States to provide services related to the laws of their home country (or in some jurisdictions, international law as well). The European Union has not only liberalized rules on admission of foreign attorneys, it has also begun discussion of ways to harmonize codes of conduct. GATS-related initiatives are likely to have growing influence as increasing numbers of lawyers engage in transnational practice.

NOTES AND QUESTIONS ON OUTSOURCING

PROBLEM 6

You are a partner in a two-lawyer Seattle litigation firm. A business acquaintance asks you to defend a complex intellectual property dispute in Seattle Superior Court. You accept the case although you have limited experience in this area. Without telling the client, you contract on an hourly basis with a firm in India that has expertise in this area. None of that firm's lawyers are licensed in the United States. You review the work you receive and sign all court submissions and communications. You bill the client at cost under broad categories such as "legal research" and "preparation of pleadings." You ultimately obtain dismissal of the case on a summary judgment motion.

Have you violated any ethical rules or responsibilities?[93]

---

92. *See* Geoffrey C. Hazard Jr., "New Shape of Lawyering," *Nat'l. L. J.*, July 23, 2001, at A21; Stephen Gillers, "Protecting Their Own," *American Lawyer*, Nov. 1998, at 118.

93. This problem is based on facts reviewed in San Diego County Bar Association Ethics Opinion 2007–1 (2007). Because California's rules of conduct are not based on the Model Rules, we have "moved" the problem to the State of Washington.

"Do you hear that loud sucking sound?," asks an article on outsourcing in *The American Jurist*. "[I]t is the value of a $120,000 legal education going down the toilet."[94] Estimates suggest that about 29,000 legal jobs will leave the United States by 2008 and over 79,000 by 2015.[95] A greater number of paralegal and other legal support jobs are also moving overseas, where labor costs are far cheaper. The ad for a typical offshore provider, Economical Services, India, states:

> Whether it is a minor research project, cite checking an adversary's brief, or if you simply don't have the resources, we are here to assist you. We will investigate the latest case law, statutes, administrative pronouncements and rulings, law review articles, and many other sources to find information you need. In addition, we handle Federal tax matters, Federal document location, and extensive researching of secondary sources. A few members of our team have been specially trained by US attorneys for handling legal assignments. ... [We] ensure that all projects undertaken by us are completed within the stipulated time period with complete confidentiality, accuracy, and quality. Our legal services are priced nominally at US $25 an hour ... We shall return the completed report to you within 72 hours, or earlier if you require.

Despite the growth of outsourcing, the bar has provided relatively little guidance on the issues that it raises. The ABA has taken no formal position on the practice, and only a few state bar ethics committees have issued opinions on point. However, these opinions, together with other rulings on the use of domestic contract attorneys, suggest certain precautions.

Competence and Supervision

As a general matter, lawyers do not violate unauthorized practice rules if they rely on the work of an unlicensed legal services provider under their supervision. San Diego County Bar Association Ethics Opinion 2007–1 (2007). Adequate supervision, however, requires that the lawyer have sufficient expertise to evaluate the quality of outsourced work. *Id.* In the case of offshore providers where direct contact is limited, attorneys should obtain adequate background information about providers, and have sufficient communication to ensure that they are acting competently and ethically in discharging their responsibilities. Association of the Bar of the City of New York Committee on Professional and Judicial Ethics, Formal Op 2006–3 (2006).

Confidentiality

Other nations have different rules and practices concerning confidentiality, and it is not entirely clear how American rules governing the

---

94. Brian O'Neill, "Outsourcing Legal Work to India: The Giant Sucking Sound from the East," *The American Jurist Online,* November 1, 2005.

95. John C. McCarthy & Forrester Research, "Near Term Growth of Offshoring Accelerating," (2004); Ursula Furi–Perry, "Law Jobs Go to Asia, Eastern Europe," *The National Jurist,* Nov. 2005, at 38.

attorney-client privilege would apply to threatened breaches.[96] Lawyers who outsource work need to take special measures to safeguard information. These include "restricting access to confidences and secrets, contractual provisions addressing confidentiality and remedies in the event of breach, and period reminders concerning confidentiality." *Id.*

Conflicts of Interest

In cases involving temporary attorneys, the ABA Committee on Professional Ethics and Professional Responsibility concluded that temporary contract attorneys were subject to ethical rules governing conflicts of interest involving current and former clients (Model Rules 1.7 and 1.9). Formal Opinion 88–356 (1988). Whether Rule 1.10 and prevailing court opinions would require vicarious disqualification would depend on factual circumstances, such as the temporary attorney's access to confidential information and extent of involvement with the employing law firm. In cases involving outsourcing, the New York City Bar Ethics Committee advised that the employing lawyer should "ordinarily ask both the intermediary and the non-lawyer performing the legal support service whether either is performing, or has performed, services for any parties adverse to the lawyer's client." Formal Opinion 2006–3.

Disclosure and Consent

A final issue involves whether lawyers must obtain informed consent from clients before outsourcing their work. Differing opinions have emerged from courts and bar ethics committees that have considered this issue or analogous issues involving temporary domestic lawyers. Some opinions have required consent in all cases involving temporary attorneys. See sources summarized in New York City Formal Opinion 2006–3. By contrast, the San Diego Bar Ethics Committee concluded that the test should be whether clients had a "reasonable expectation" that the work would be performed by the attorney they retained. In the Committee's view, clients would reasonably expect, absent a specific understanding to the contrary, that attorneys would perform work using their own or their firm's resources in order to develop legal theories and arguments, and prepare correspondence and court filings. Ethics Op 2007–1. The New York City Bar Ethics Committee took a more contextual view and specified several factors that would be relevant in determining whether consent is necessary. If confidences would be shared or the services would be billed on any basis other than cost, then clients should be asked for consent. In other cases, relevant factors would include the significance of the offshore provider's role and the client's expectation. Formal Opinion 2006–3.

Which approach makes most sense? What factors should attorneys take into account in determining whether to outsource legal work?

---

96. See San Diego County Bar Association Ethics Opinion 2007–1 (2007); Alison M. Kadzik, "The Current Trend to Outsource Legal Work Abroad and the Ethical Issues Related to Such Practices," 19 *Geo. J. Legal Ethics* 731, 735 (2006).

E. Multidisciplinary Practice

NOTES

Over the last quarter century, two related issues have assumed increasing importance: lawyers' involvement in nonlegal "ancillary" businesses, and multidisciplinary practice (MDP). Neither form of involvement is an entirely new development. Some attorneys have long engaged in activities tangential to legal practice, such as selling insurance or providing investment advice. And lawyers have long worked for multidisciplinary accounting firms and other providers of legal services owned by nonlawyers. But recent trends reveal cross-professional alliances on a larger scale. Faced with increasing competition for clients and increasing needs for multiple specialties in certain practice areas, more lawyers have forged closer relationships with other professionals. In the District of Columbia, which pioneered liberalized rules on ancillary business, prominent law firms have formed subsidiaries or quasi-independent business groups within the firm. Major areas of concentration have included financial management and investment, international trade, lobbying, real estate, and employee benefits. Increasing numbers of lawyers have also begun experimenting with "one-stop" services for individual as well as corporate clients; a representative example is a law office that employs or affiliates with medical and social workers to assist senior citizens.

Such arrangements have had a mixed reception within the organized bar. As noted in the preceding materials on group legal services, one controversy involved a proposed Model Rule that would have permitted nonlawyer ownership or participation in firm management. Although the ABA House of Delegates rejected that rule, debates within the bar continued. In 1990, the District of Columbia adopted a rule permitting nonlawyers to become partners under specified circumstances. This rule, and the broader trends it reflected, prompted continued disputes within the ABA and other bar organizations. One such controversy erupted in the early 1990s when the American Bar Association's House of Delegates first voted to prohibit lawyers' ownership of ancillary non-legal businesses and then repealed the ban. The ABA's current approach, reflected in Rule 5.7, is to require that lawyers adhere to bar ethical rules for ancillary services "not distinct" from their legal practice or services controlled by the lawyer if clients are not made aware that the protections of a lawyer-client relationship are unavailable. Only about ten states have adopted the rule, although other jurisdictions permit the practice. Only a relatively small number of firms have developed formal affiliations with ancillary law-related businesses.[97]

97. "Firms Ancillary Businesses Can Flourish Even Though Most States Have Rule 5.7," 19 *ABA/BNA Manual on Professional Conduct* 329 (June 4, 2003).

Underlying these disputes are a range of issues about quality, efficiency, commercialization, and professionalism. Proponents of lawyers' ancillary business activities argue that they encourage cost-effective collaborations between lawyers and non-law experts; decrease search costs in hiring such experts; and give lawyers incentives to monitor the services of affiliated practitioners. By contrast, critics worry that diversification into nonlegal activity distracts lawyers from the practice of law; impairs their objectivity in recommending experts; invites misuse of confidential information; introduces too much profit-oriented, non-lawyer influence into law firm management; and erodes the distinctiveness of law as a profession rather than a business.

Multidisciplinary practice poses similar concerns. How best to respond has attracted increasing attention largely due to increasing competition from accounting firms. Other western industrialized nations generally permit nonlawyers to provide out-of-court law-related services and to employ or form partnerships with lawyers.[98] As a consequence, large accounting firms dominate the global legal market. They have a presence in 138 countries and are making increased inroads in the American market. Federal law provides that tax advice and representation in tax court does not constitute the practice of law. This exception to traditional unauthorized practice prohibitions enables lawyers to provide services for clients of accounting firms as long as the work can be defined as tax, not legal, assistance. Over the past decade, accounting firms have taken increasing liberties with the definition, and have expanded their in-house legal staff to provide much the same services as law firms on matters such as tax, financial, and estate planning, intellectual property, ADR, and litigation support. The American legal profession faces growing difficulties competing with these accounting organizations, which generally offer a wider range of services, greater economies of scale, and more effective marketing and managerial capacities. An ABA report found that in 2000, two of the four largest "law firms" in the world were accounting firms.

Supporters of multidisciplinary practice (MDP) stress the advantages to clients of "one stop" shopping and the advantages to lawyers of being able to attract additional capital and expertise, and thus becoming more competitive with other well-financed service providers. The benefits would extend not just to large firms and business clients, but to small firms and sole practitioners serving individuals whose needs cut across multiple fields. By contrast, opponents worry that lawyers will become accountable to supervisors from a different tradition with less rigorous standards governing confidentiality, conflicts of interest, and pro bono service. In critics' view, as disciplinary boundaries blur and thin, law will become just

---

98. The CCBE Code does not mention multidisciplinary practice, but provides simply that fee splitting with nonlawyers is prohibited except in jurisdictions where permitted by local law and ethical rules. For an overview of European practice, see Rees M.

Hawkins, "Not 'If,' but 'When' and 'How': A Look at Existing De Facto Multidisciplinary Practices and What They Can Teach Us About the Ongoing Debate," 83 *N.C. L. Rev.* 481, 494–96 (2005).

another business, and clients will pay the price as professional judgments are driven by the bottom line.

In 1999, an ABA Commission on Multidisciplinary Practice issued a report acknowledging these ethical concerns but proposing strategies short of prohibition. The Commission recommended holding nonlawyers in multidisciplinary firms to the same ethical standards governing conflicts and confidentiality as those applicable to the bar generally. In addition, the Commission proposed special audit provisions to prevent nonlawyers from interfering with lawyers' professional judgments. Under this framework, the attorney-client privilege could be extended to cover nonlawyers, or clients could be warned about its unavailability.[99] An alternative approach, proposed by accounting firms, would be to follow their less stringent conflict of interest procedures. These procedures create screens between professionals representing competing concerns and seek informed client consent to the dual representation. Sophisticated clients appear satisfied with this approach; they have not pressed for reforms or alternatives.

The ABA House of Delegates twice rejected the Commission's recommendations. House members voted against relaxing prohibitions on multidisciplinary partnerships in the absence of evidence that they would serve the public interest and would not compromise the profession's independence or loyalty to clients. However, as the Commission responded, it will be impossible to assess the public interest in such arrangements until the "taint of illegality" is removed. And the support expressed by consumer groups and the market demand for lawyers in multidisciplinary settings was, in the Commission's view, at least some evidence of the social value of these arrangements.[100]

After the ABA's second vote in 2000, controversy shifted to the states. By the turn of the twenty-first century, virtually every jurisdiction was considering the issue. A cottage industry of commentary also emerged.[101] Recent scandals involving accounting practices fueled further disputes. To some commentators, the misconduct in cases like Enron reflected conflicts of interest between accountants' audit and consulting functions and demonstrated why lawyers should not participate in partnerships providing such services.[102] To other commentators, these conflicts of interest underscored the need for tighter regulation of competing professionals who were employing a growing number of lawyers and supplying an increasing volume of law-related services.

---

99. American Bar Association Commission on Multidisciplinary Practice, Report to the ABA House of Delegates, reprinted in 10 *Professional Lawyer* (1999).

100. "MDP Rides Again," *ABA J.* Feb. 2000, at 96.

101. See sources cited in Hawkins, *supra* note 98;. Symposia on the subject include: "The Brave New World of Multidisciplinary Practice," 50 *J. Leg. Ed.* 469 (2000); "Future of the Profession: A Symposium on Multidisciplinary Practice," 84 *Minn. L. Rev.*

1083 (2000). For an overview by the ABA Commission reporter, *see* Mary C. Daly, "Choosing Wise Men Wisely: The Risks and Rewards of Purchasing Legal Services From Lawyers in a Multidisciplinary Partnership," 13 *Geo. J. Legal Ethics* 217 (2000).

102. Geanne Rosenberg, "Scandal Seen as Blow to Outlook for MDP," *Nat'l. L. J.*, Jan. 21, 2002, at A1; Steven C. Krane, "Let Lawyers Practice Law," *Nat'l. L. J.*, Jan. 28, 2002, at A16.

Part of the difficulty in resolving these disputes involves the lack of systematic information about the extent of ethical problems in multidisciplinary organizations and the likely effectiveness of proposed responses. Lawyers who have worked in both law firms and MDPs testified before the Commission that there were not significant differences in the ethical cultures of the two kinds of organization, apart from the rules about imputed conflicts of interest. Many of the MDPs that presented testimony also pointed to records of pro bono service that rivaled those of law firms. In any event, even if it could be established that conflicts and confidentiality problems were somewhat more likely to arise in multidisciplinary firms, and that those firms were somewhat less likely to provide institutional support for public service than law firms, it would not be self evident that total prohibition is the best response. Many experts believe that clients should have the option of weighing the risks and benefits of MDPs, and that ethical restrictions should be narrowly tailored to address demonstrated abuses.[103]

However these issues are resolved, multidisciplinary collaborations of some form are likely here to stay. There is a strong market demand and legitimate societal need for integrated legal and nonlegal advice. Where state bars prohibit multidisciplinary partnerships, multidisciplinary practice may take other forms. For example, New York now permits, and some American law firms are developing, "strategic alliances" with professional services firms. Under these arrangements, the firms agree to share clients and sometimes capital and marketing capacities.[104] In other jurisdictions, lawyers and non lawyers are providing holistic services through collaborative arrangements that do not involve fee sharing.[105] Whether these arrangements can address client needs as effectively as fully integrated MDPs remains to be seen. If experience is any guide, the only viable long term strategy for regulating the legal services market is one that can adequately adapt to competitive forces.

In devising such regulations, many commentators argue for a shift in focus beyond what recent debates have emphasized. The most relevant question may not be the one that either supporters or opponents of multidisciplinary practice are most often asking: "Is this good for lawyers?" or "Is this good for clients?" On those issues, the market can decide. Clients can vote with their feet, and lawyers can choose whether to follow. The more important question is whether multidisciplinary practice is "good for the rest of us, 'us' being citizens who count on lawyers to be guardians of the law and who cannot always count on market forces for protec-

103. For discussion of these arguments, *see* David Luban, "Asking the Right Questions," 72 *Temple L. R.* 839 (1999).

104. New York State Bar Association Committee on Professional Ethics, Op. 765 (July 22, 2003) (approving nonexclusive reciprocal referral arrangements). See Hawkins, *supra* note 98, at 498.

105. See Hawkins, *supra* note 98, at 511–12 (describing Boston Legal Collaborative, which employs 7 attorneys, a psychologist, a financial planner, and a work consultant in handling employment, family and business matters).

tion.''[106] If this is the right question, what evidence will be necessary to answer it? Does a law firm in which attorneys share control with nonlawyers present qualitatively different problems than a corporate in-house counsel's office or an accounting firm in which attorneys are under the authority of nonlawyers? Do the bar's rules on vicarious disqualification make sense for large multidisciplinary law firms? What approach toward multidisciplinary practice would you support?

F.   ATTORNEYS' FEES

INTRODUCTION

Of all the public's complaints about lawyers, expense is at the top of the list. About three-fifths of Americans describe attorneys as greedy and fewer than 5 percent believe that clients get good value for the price of legal services.[107] Such perceptions are longstanding and most societies have, at least intermittently, made efforts to control attorneys' fees. Roman, English, American, and Chinese societies all attempted at some point to prohibit any charges for legal services.[108] Although such policies tended to be short-lived, some forms of fee regulation have remained common. Many countries now set attorneys' fees by statutes that carefully graduate the amount of payment for specified actions or specified stakes. See CCBE Code of Conduct, Rule 3.3.

America's history of fee regulation reveals a checkered pattern of deference to market forces, price-fixing agreements among lawyers, and occasional legislative and judicial oversight. In evaluating this regulatory pattern, it is appropriate to consider what approaches will best accommodate an array of interests: protecting clients against overreaching, encouraging competent and efficient professional services, and maximizing access to the law.

Practices surrounding the collection of legal fees have long aroused discomfort among both lawyers and clients. In England, early traditions had it that gentlemen did not pay other gentlemen for their services.[109] Accordingly barristers, the elite of the profession, never discussed fees with their clients; all commercial matters were handled through solicitors and clerks. In this country, the absence of a comparable status division among practitioners made analogous fee conventions impractical. However, many attorneys attempted to distance themselves somewhat from the more

---

106. Luban, *supra* note 103, at 839.

107. Gary A. Hengstler, "Vox Populi: The Public Perception of Lawyers," *ABA J.* Sept. 1993, at 63; Marc Galanter, "Anyone Can Fall Down a Manhole: The Contingency Fee and Its Discontents," 42 *DePaul Law Review* 457, 459 (1994). *See also* ABA Section on Litigation, *Public Perception of Lawyers: Consumer Research Findings* 14 (2002).

108. William Howard Taft, *Ethics in Service* 4–8, 15 (1915); Charles Warren, *A History of the American Bar* 112–113 (1911); Dennis Nolan, *Readings in the History of the American Legal Profession* 103–05 (1980).

109. William J. Reader, *Professional Men: The Rise of the Professional Classes in Nineteenth–Century England* 36–37 (1966); Robert E. Megarry, *Lawyer and Litigant in England* 56–60 (1962).

sordid commercial aspects of their profession by declining to "haggle" with their clients over money. This necessity could be avoided by adhering to collectively established minimum fees and by attempting not to sue their clients publicly for non-payment. In cases where lawyers anticipated or experienced reluctance to settle accounts, they resorted to a variety of alternative measures: substantial non-refundable retainers, refusals to complete work or relinquish client papers, adjustments of their bill, or threats to reveal confidential information in the course of establishing the client's liability for fees.

The profession's distaste for bargaining over fees was apparent in its earliest Canons of Ethics' condemnation of "underbidding" and the bar's subsequent encouragement of minimum fee schedules.[110] According to the ABA's 1961 Committee on Professional Ethics, "[t]he evils of fee cutting ought to be apparent to all members of the Bar," and "habitual charging of fees less than those established in suggested or recommended minimum fee schedules, or the charging of such fees without proper justification, may be evidence of unethical conduct."[111] Other bar leaders took a similar view. An ABA Practice Manual recommended, for example, that lawyers initiate fee discussions by presenting minimum fee schedules in attractive folders, preferably evidencing a "degree of dignity and substance." A black leather cover with gold lettering was recommended, although a plain but neat paper cover was acceptable.[112] However packaged, such schedules were designed to discourage comparison shopping and competitive pricing.

During the early 1970s, minimum fees came under increasing challenge. The decisive battle occurred in a case against the Fairfax County and Virginia state bars by Lewis and Ruth Goldfarb. After unsuccessfully attempting to find an attorney who would perform a title examination for less than the minimum fee set forth in the county bar's schedule, the Goldfarbs filed suit. They claimed that the fee schedule constituted price fixing in violation of Section 1 of the Sherman Act. The Supreme Court agreed. Speaking through Chief Justice Burger, the Court held that "learned professions" involved "trade or commerce" within the scope of federal antitrust legislation. In the Court's view, a profession's promulgation of a minimum fee schedule, enforced through disciplinary action, was an unlawful restraint of trade.[113] *Goldfarb v. Virginia State Bar*, 421 U.S. 773, 787 (1975). After that decision, bar associations ceased promulgating minimum fee schedules, although some information concerning standard charges remained accessible through various publications for practitioners.

Four types of fee arrangements are now common. The predominant billing method is the hourly fee. Other options are a flat fee for a particular matter; a proportional fee (such as a percentage of an estate or property

---

110. ABA Canons of Ethics, Canons 27 and 28.

111. ABA Committee on Professional Ethics, Formal Op. 302 (1961). *See also id.,* Formal Op. 323 (1970).

112. *See* Philip Stern, *Lawyers on Trial* 55 (1980).

113. Goldfarb v. Virginia State Bar, 421 U.S. 773, 787 (1975).

involved in a transaction); or a contingent fee, which gives the lawyer a specified fee or a proportion of the recovery if the matter is successfully resolved. Such billing methods can also be used in combination (i.e. a "blended fee"), or adjusted to incorporate certain incentives (e.g., a flat fee with a bonus for a particular result).[114]

Bar ethics rules require lawyers' fees to be not "unreasonable" (Model Rule 1.5) or not "clearly excessive," (DR 2–106). However, bar ethics committees and disciplinary authorities generally have not enforced these rules in individual cases unless the amount charged is so excessive as to appear unconscionable or equivalent to a misappropriation of funds.[115] Rather, bar ethics authorities usually confine their focus to the general propriety of certain billing practices. For example, in Formal Opinion 93–379 (1993), the ABA Ethics Committee concluded that a lawyer should not bill more than one client for the same hours, or work product; should not charge a client for overhead expenses generally associated with equipping an office; and should not impose surcharges on services such as photocopying beyond the costs actually incurred.[116]

On the whole, however, bar regulatory authorities have viewed the appropriate remedy for unreasonable charges to be malpractice claims, breach of contract actions, or defenses in litigation by attorneys to collect their fees. To many committees, the criteria for deciding what constitutes an excessive fee are too indeterminate to justify disciplinary proceedings, except in egregious cases. However, as Chapter XV notes, malpractice and contractual actions are often inadequate means of deterring or remedying excessive fees. For many individuals who feel aggrieved by the costs of legal proceedings, hiring a second attorney to challenge the charges of the first is not an appealing option, particularly if the amount at issue is modest. Although corporate clients may have sufficient knowledge, experience, and leverage to protect themselves from excessive charges, many individual clients do not. And even sophisticated clients may not always have sufficient information to insure fairness, as is clear from the frequency of problems concerning excessive charges, nonrefundable retainers, and contingent fees noted below.

The limitations of contractual and malpractice proceedings have prompted a growing number of bar associations to establish fee arbitration systems and a few disciplinary authorities to become more involved in overseeing fees. The following case is the first Massachusetts decision disciplining a lawyer for an excessive fee.

114. See *ABA Commission on Billable Hours Report* 16–18 (2002). Http://www/aba net.org/careercounsel/billable/tool kit/bib.html.

115. American Bar Foundation, *Annotated Code of Professional Responsibility* 101–102, 104–105 (1979).

116. A lawyer may charge direct costs as well as a reasonable allocation of overhead expenses directly attributable to provision of the services (e.g. the salary of a photocopy machine operator). However, any attempt to create an additional source of profit for the firm in providing such services would be impermissible. In the Committee's view, the "lawyer's stock in trade is the sale of legal services, not photocopy paper [or] tuna fish sandwiches. . . ." *Id.*

1. EXCESSIVE FEES

In the Matter of Laurence S. Fordham

Supreme Court of Massachusetts, 1996.
668 N.E.2d 816.

This is an appeal from the Board of Bar Overseers' (board's) dismissal of a petition for discipline filed by bar counsel against attorney Laurence S. Fordham. On March 11, 1992, bar counsel served Fordham with a petition for discipline alleging that Fordham had charged a clearly excessive fee in violation of S.J.C. Rule 3:07, DR 2–106 ... for defending Timothy Clark (Timothy) in the District Court against a charge that he operated a motor vehicle while under the influence of intoxicating liquor (OUI) and against other related charges....

After five days of hearings, and with "serious reservations," the hearing committee concluded that Fordham's fee was not substantially in excess of a reasonable fee and that, therefore, the committee recommended against bar discipline. Bar counsel appealed from that determination to the board. By a vote of six to five, with one abstention, that board accepted the recommendation of the hearing committee and dismissed the petition for discipline. Bar counsel then filed in the Supreme Judicial Court for Suffolk County (county court) a claim of appeal from the board's action.... We conclude ... that the board erred in dismissing bar counsel's petition for discipline. We direct a judgment ordering public censure be entered in the county court.

We summarize the hearing committee's findings. On March 4, 1989, the Acton police department arrested Timothy, then twenty-one years old, and charged him with OUI, operating a motor vehicle after suspension, speeding, and operating an unregistered motor vehicle. At the time of the arrest, the police discovered a partially full quart of vodka in the vehicle. After failing a field sobriety test, Timothy was taken to the Acton police station where he submitted to two breathalyzer tests which registered .10 and .12 respectively.

Subsequent to Timothy's arraignment, he and his father, Laurence Clark (Clark) consulted with three lawyers, who offered to represent Timothy for fees between $3,000 and $10,000. Shortly after the arrest, Clark went to Fordham's home to service an alarm system which he had installed several years before. While there, Clark discussed Timothy's arrest with Fordham's wife who invited Clark to discuss the case with Fordham. Fordham then met with Clark and Timothy.

At this meeting, Timothy described the incidents leading to his arrest and the charges against him. Fordham, whom the hearing committee described as a "very experienced senior trial attorney with impressive credentials," told Clark and Timothy that he had never represented a client in a driving while under the influence case or in any criminal matter, and he had never tried a case in the District Court. The hearing committee found that "Fordham explained that although he lacked experience in this area, he was a knowledgeable and hard-working attorney and that he believed he could competently represent Timothy." Fordham, described himself as "efficient and economic in the use of [his] time." ... Towards the end of the meeting, Fordham told the Clarks that he worked on [a] time charge basis and that he billed monthly.... After the meeting, Clark hired Fordham to represent Timothy.

According to the hearing committee's findings, Fordham filed four pretrial motions on Timothy's behalf, two of which were allowed.... [At the bench trial] [t]he judge found Timothy not guilty of driving while under the influence.... [Fordham sent six monthly bills.] The bills totaled $50,022.25, reflecting 227 hours of billed time, 153 hours of which were expended by Fordham and seventy-four of which were his associates' time. Clark did not pay the first two bills when they became due and expressed to Fordham his concern about their amount. Clark paid Fordham $10,000 on June 20, 1989. At that time, Fordham assured Clark that most of the work had been completed, "other than taking [the case] to trial." Clark did not make any subsequent payments. Fordham requested Clark to sign a promissory note evidencing his debt to Fordham and, on October 7, 1989, Clark did so. In the October 13, 1989 bill, Fordham added a charge of $5,000 as a "retroactive increase" in fees. On November Fordham, sent Clark a bill for $15,000....

In concluding that Fordham did not charge a clearly excessive fee, the board adopted, with limited exception, the hearing committee's report. The board's and the hearing committee's reasons for dismissing the petition are as follows: Bar counsel and Fordham stipulated that Fordham acted conscientiously, diligently, and in good faith in his representation of the client and his billing on the case. Although Fordham lacked experience in criminal law, he is a "seasoned and well-respected civil lawyer." The more than 200 hours spent preparing the OUI case were necessary "in part to educate [Fordham] in the relevant substantive law and court procedures," because he had never tried an OUI case or appeared in the District Court. The board noted that "[al]though none of the experts who testified at the disciplinary hearing had ever heard of a fee in excess of $15,000 for a first-offense OUI case, the hearing committee found that [Clark] had entered into the transaction with open eyes after interviewing other lawyers with more experience in such matters." The board also thought significant that Clark "later acquiesced, despite mild expressions of concern, in [Fordham's] billing practices." Moreover, the Clarks specifically instructed Fordham that they would not consider a guilty plea by Timothy. Rather they were interested only in pursuing the case to trial. Finally, Timothy obtained the result he sought: an acquittal.... "In the instant case we are persuaded that the hearing committee's and the board's determinations that a clearly excessive fee was not charged are not warranted."

The first factor listed in DR 2–106(B) requires examining "[t]he time and labor required, the novelty and difficulty of the questions involved, and the skill requisite to perform the legal service properly." Although the hearing committee determined that Fordham "spent a large number of hours on [the] matter, in essence learning from scratch what others ... already knew," it "[did] not credit Bar Counsel's argument that Fordham violated DR 2–106 by spending too many hours." ... We disagree.

Four witnesses testified before the hearing committee as experts on OUI cases. One of the experts, testifying on behalf of bar counsel, opined that "the amount of time spent in this case is clearly excessive." He testified that there were no unusual circumstances in the OUI charge against Timothy and that it was a "standard operating under the influence case." The witness did agree that Fordham's argument for suppression of the breathalyzer test results, which was successful, was novel and would have justified additional time and labor. He also acknowledged that the acquittal was a good result; even with the suppression of the breathalyzer tests, he testified, the chances of an acquittal would have been "[n]ot likely at a bench trial." The witness estimated that it would have been necessary, for thorough preparation of the case including the novel breathalyzer suppression argument, to have billed twenty to thirty hours for preparation, not including trial time.

A second expert, testifying on behalf of bar counsel, expressed his belief that the issues presented in this case were not particularly difficult, nor novel, and that "[t]he degree of skill required to defend a case such as this ... was not that high." He did recognize, however, that the theory that Fordham utilized to suppress the breathalyzer tests was impressive and one of which he had previously never heard. Nonetheless, the witness concluded that "clearly there is no way that [he] could justify these kind of hours to do this kind of work." He estimated that an OUI case involving these types of issues would require sixteen hours of trial preparation and approximately fifteen hours of trial time....

An expert called by Fordham testified that the facts of Timothy's case presented a challenge and that without the suppression of the breathalyzer test results it would have been "an almost impossible situation in terms of prevailing on the trier of fact." He further stated that, based on the particulars in Timothy's case, he believed that Fordham's hours were not excessive and, in fact, he, the witness, would have spent a comparable amount of time. The witness later admitted, however, that within the past five years, the OUI cases which he had brought to trial required no more than a total of forty billed hours, which encompassed all preparation and court appearances....

The fourth expert witness, called by Fordham, testified that she believed the case was "extremely tough" and that the breathalyzer suppression theory was novel. She testified that, although the time and labor consumed on the case was more than usual in defending an OUI charge, the hours were not excessive. They were not excessive, she explained, because the case was particularly difficult due to the "stakes [and] the evidence." She conceded, however, that legal issues in defending OUI charges are "pretty standard" and that the issues presented in this case were not unusual. Furthermore, the witness testified that challenging the breathalyzer test due to the .02 discrepancy was not unusual, but the theory on which Fordham proceeded was novel. Finally, she stated that she thought she may have known of one person who might have spent close to one hundred hours on a difficult OUI case; she was not sure; but she had never heard of a fee in excess of $10,000 for a bench trial.

In considering whether a fee is "clearly excessive" within the meaning of S.J.C. Rule 3:07, DR 2–106(B), the first factor to be considered pursuant to that rule is "the novelty and difficulty of the questions involved, and the skill requisite to perform the legal service properly." DR 2–106 (B) (1).... Based on the testimony of the four experts, the number of hours devoted in Timothy's OUI case by Fordham and his associates was substantially in excess of the hours that a prudent experienced lawyer would have spent. According to the evidence, the number of hours spent was several times the amount of time any of the witnesses had ever spent on a similar case. We are not unmindful of the novel and successful motion to suppress the breathalyzer test results, but that effort cannot justify a $50,000 fee in a type of case in which the usual fee is less than one-third of that amount.... [Under Ethical Consideration 6–3] a lawyer should not accept employment in any area of the law in which he is not qualified. However, he may accept such employment if in good faith he expects to become qualified through study and investigation, as long as such preparation would not result in unreasonable delay or expense to his client....

DR2–106(B) provides that the third factor to be considered in ascertaining the reasonableness of a fee is its comparability to "[t]he fee customarily charged in the locality for similar legal services." The hearing committee made no finding as to the comparability of Fordham's fee with the fees customarily charged in the locality for similar services. However, one of bar counsel's expert witnesses testified that he had never heard of a fee in excess of $15,000 to defend a first OUI charge, and the customary flat fee in an OUI case, including trial, "runs from $1,000 to $7,500." Bar counsel's other expert testified that he had never heard of a fee in excess of $10,000 for a bench trial. In his view, the customary charge for a case similar to Timothy's would vary between $1,500 and $5,000. One of Fordham's experts testified that she considered a $40,000 or $50,000 fee for defending an OUI charge "unusual and certainly higher by far than any I've ever seen before." The witness had never charged a fee of more than $3,500 for representing a client at a bench trial to defend a first offense OUI charge. She further testified that she believed an "average OUI in the bench session is two thousand [dollars] and sometimes less." Finally, that witness testified that she had "heard a rumor" that one attorney charged $10,000 for a bench trial involving an OUI charge; this fee represented the highest fee of which she was aware. The other expert witness called by Fordham testified that he had heard of a $35,000 fee for defending OUI charges, but he had never charged more than $12,000 (less than twenty-five per cent of Fordham's fee).

Although finding that Fordham's fee was "much higher than the fee charged by many attorneys with more experience litigating driving under the influence cases," the hearing committee nevertheless determined that the fee charged by Fordham was not clearly excessive because Clark "went into the relationship with Fordham with open eyes," Fordham's fee fell within a "safe harbor," and Clark acquiesced in Fordham's fee by not strenuously objecting to his bills. The board accepted the hearing committee's analysis apart from the committee's reliance on the "safe harbor" rule....

It is also significant, however, that the hearing committee found that "[d]espite Fordham's disclaimers concerning his experience, Clark did not appear to have understood in any real sense the implications of choosing Fordham to represent Timothy. Fordham did not give Clark any estimate of the total expected fee or the number of $200 hours that would be required." The express finding of the hearing committee that Clark "did not appear to have understood in any real sense the implications of choosing Fordham to represent Timothy" directly militates against the finding that Clark entered into the agreement "with open eyes." ...

Finally, bar counsel challenges the hearing committee's finding that "if Clark objected to the numbers of hours being spent by Fordham, he could have spoken up with some force when he began receiving bills." Bar counsel notes, and we agree, that "[t]he test as stated in the DR 2–106(A) is whether the fee 'charged' is clearly excessive, not whether the fee is accepted as valid or acquiesced in by the client." Therefore, we conclude that the hearing committee and the board erred in not concluding that Fordham's fee was clearly excessive.

Fordham argues that our imposition of discipline would offend his right to due process.... Fordham contends that the bar and, therefore, he, have not been given fair notice through prior decisions of this court or the express language of DR 2–106 that discipline may be imposed for billing excessive hours that were nonetheless spent diligently and in good faith.... [However,] charging a clearly excessive fee, Fordham departed substantially from the obligation of professional responsibility that he owed to his client. The ABA Model Standards for Imposing Lawyer Sanctions § 7.3 (1992) endorses a public reprimand as the appropriate sanction for charging a clearly excessive fee. We deem such a sanction appropriate in this case.

QUESTIONS

1. Under what circumstances should courts and ethics committees protect clients from fee agreements that they freely accept but that turn out to be extremely bad bargains? Do Code and Model Rule provisions provide sufficiently determinate criteria to assess the fairness of attorneys' charges? Under Disciplinary Rule 2–106(B) and many judicial and bar ethics opinions, a fee is impermissibly excessive when a "lawyer of ordinary prudence would be left with a definite and firm conviction that the fee is in excess of a reasonable fee." Is this standard too vague to be applied? Does it reflect a fair accommodation of the competing interests at issue? Why is the

test a lawyer of ordinary prudence rather than the usual "reasonable person" standard?

Model Rule 1.5 lists the following factors as relevant in determining the reasonableness of a fee:

(1) the time and labor required, the novelty and difficulty of the questions involved, and the skill requisite to perform the legal service properly;

(2) the likelihood, if apparent to the client, that the acceptance of the particular employment will preclude other employment by the lawyer;

(3) the fee customarily charged in the locality for similar legal services;

(4) the amount involved and the results obtained;

(5) the time limitations imposed by the client or by the circumstances;

(6) the nature and length of the professional relationship with the client;

(7) the experience, reputation, and ability of the lawyer or lawyers performing the services; and

(8) whether the fee is fixed or contingent.

Courts and commentators generally agree with this list, although some would add the client's ability to pay and two further considerations set forth in the *Restatement (Third) of Law Governing Lawyers*, § 46, Comment: "when the agreement was made, did the lawyer afford the client a free and informed choice?; [and] ... was there a subsequent change in circumstances that made the fee agreement unreasonable?" Does this list omit any important considerations, such as the client's ability to pay?[117]

The ABA Ethics 2000 Commission recommended that Rule 1.5 require lawyers to communicate the scope of their responsibility and arrangements for fees and expenses in writing at the outset of representation except where lawyers will charge regularly represented clients at their regular rate. The version of the Rule adopted by the ABA House of Delegates provided rather that this communication "preferably" be in writing. Which version of the Rule was better?

2. If you had been a member of the Massachusetts Supreme Court, what would you have decided in *Fordham?* What could, or should, Fordham have done differently?

3. Is it unfair to single out lawyers for special regulation? Consider the following claim:

one searches ... in vain to discover precisely why a lawyer, acting without deceit, without coercion, and without any other form of untoward conduct is not free to price legal services at what a client is willing to pay, reasonable or otherwise. Most other actors in the

---

117. For a summary of cases finding clients' lack of resources relevant, *see* Wolfram, *supra* note 56, at 518–22. *See also* former Canon 12 of the ABA *Canons of Ethics,* which provided that a client's ability to pay could not justify charges in "excess of the value of ... services," but poverty could justify lower charges.

marketplace can do that—why not lawyers? When professional rhetoric is set aside all that is left is an extraordinary, socialist maxim that lawyers should be ashamed of making "too much" money. . . .

Some plausible reasons do exist for a pricing norm for lawyers: legal services are apt to be more widely available when reasonably priced; charging an "excessive" fee would exploit the relationship of attorney and client; and there is a certain public relations value for the profession in avoiding price gouging. Although each of these reasons has some appeal, that appeal is surely not limited to the legal profession.[118]

Do you agree? If so, are there any circumstances in which courts should set aside agreements that clients negotiated with "open eyes?"

Another commentator criticizes courts' willingness to police fee agreements in order to protect the public reputation of lawyers. His view, widely shared among practitioners, is that the "public already thinks that lawyers often gouge their clients. Whether courts reduce or eliminate fees in a few selected cases will hardly make a difference. Second, it does not matter whether the public thinks that lawyers in general overcharge. What matters is how that opinion might impact people's conduct," for example, by discouraging them from hiring counsel in the first instance.[119] But as the preceding material on unauthorized practice of law indicated, a growing number of consumers are resorting to self-help largely because of the perceived high costs of lawyers' services. Does this suggest a justification for more active regulation of unreasonable fees?

4.   Should non-refundable retainer fees be prohibited? Such fees generally take two forms. One is an "engagement" fee or "general retainer," which is a deposit by the client to assure that the attorney will handle the case. Lawyers earn this fee when they lend their names to the case, and it bears no relation to the charge for hours subsequently spent on the matter. Such a fee is intended to compensate for the attorney's reputation, commitment to a specific client, and reservation of future time to be spent on that client. A second type of non-refundable fee is a "special" retainer; services are billed against that initial amount but at the conclusion of the case, the attorney keeps any part of the retainer that has not yet been charged.

Several jurisdictions prohibit certain types of non-refundable fees. In one leading case, the New York Court of Appeals disallowed a "special retainer" agreement that would have enabled a divorce lawyer to collect substantial sums for little or no work. *In re Cooperman*, 633 N.E.2d 1069 (N.Y.1994). In the Court's view, if such agreements were "allowed to

---

118. Roy R. Anderson & Walter W. Steele, Jr., "Ethics and the Law of Contract Juxtaposed: A Jaundiced View of Professional Responsibility Considerations in the Attorney–Client Relationship," 4 *Geo. J. Leg. Ethics* 791 (1991).

119. Leonard Gross, "The Public Hates Lawyers: Why Should We Care?", 29 *Seton Hall L. Rev.* 1405, 1445 (1999).

flourish, clients would be relegated to hostage status," because they would find it prohibitively expensive to fire their counsel.[120]

Do you agree with that reasoning? One New York study found that over a quarter of all complaints to a New York state oversight panel concerned non-refundable retainers. If the experience in other states is comparable, what responses would you recommend?[121]

5. Should the standard for enforcing fee agreements be different than for disciplining lawyers? In *McKenzie Construction, Inc. v. Maynard*, 758 F.2d 97, 101 (3d Cir.1985), a panel of the Third Circuit concluded that a less stringent standard is appropriate in enforcement proceedings and that the test there is whether the amount "offends a court's sense of fundamental fairness and equity." Should that also be the test in bar-sponsored fee arbitration proceedings?

6. Under what, if any, circumstances, should courts set aside fee agreements where the client is a sophisticated commercial player? In a frequently cited opinion, *Brobeck, Phleger & Harrison v. Telex Corp.*, 602 F.2d 866 (9th Cir.1979), the court enforced a $1 million fee for services that turned out to involve only filing one petition for certiorari. The case arose from antitrust proceedings in which Telex obtained a $259 million judgment against IBM, but lost an $18 million counterclaim. On appeal, IBM won reversal of the judgment and affirmance of its counterclaim. In the face of liability substantial enough to bankrupt the company, Telex sought the best available lawyer for its petition to the Supreme Court. The company settled on a partner at Brobeck, and agreed to a complicated contract specifying different fees contingent on different outcomes. After the Supreme Court granted certiorari, Telex and IBM reached a settlement in which each dropped their claims. In rejecting Telex's claim that the $1 million fee was unconscionable, the court concluded that the contract must be reviewed "with reference to the time it was made and cannot be resolved by hindsight." *Id.* at 875.

Do you agree? Note that the fee, if translated into current dollars, would be considerably greater. If the Massachusetts Court had taken a similar approach, would, or should, it have reached a different result in *Fordham?* Would the result be an unacceptable double standard: "[l]aissez-faire for the rich, paternalism for the little guy...."[122] ?

References:

Model Rule 1.5.

---

120. The court did not, however, prohibit general retainer agreements. Section 34 of the ALI's *Restatement (Third) of the Law Governing Lawyers* views engagement retainer fees as legitimate to the extent that they bear a reasonable relationship to income that lawyers sacrifice or expenses that they incur.

121. Lester Brickman & Lawrence A. Cunningham, "Nonrefundable Retainers Re-

visited," 72 *North Car. L. Rev.* 1 (1993); Ian Fisher, "No-refund Retainer Fees Are Outlawed in New York," *N.Y. Times*, March 18, 1994, at B12.

122. Stephen Gillers, *Regulation of Lawyers: Problems of Law and Ethics* 139 (5th ed. 1998).

NOTES

Fee-related abuses fall across a spectrum, reflecting everything from flagrant fraud and "creative timekeeping," to sloppy accounting and inefficient staffing. Their frequency is difficult to gauge, since many abuses constitute the "perfect crime." Although sophisticated business clients have become increasingly adept at monitoring charges, it is often impossible to verify whether certain tasks are essential and whether they take, or should take, the time that lawyers charge for completing them. However, auditors find demonstrable fraud in about 5–10 percent of the bills they review and questionable practices in another 25–35 percent. Such practices include inflating hours, overstaffing cases, performing unnecessary work, and double billing two clients for the same task or time. Forty percent of surveyed lawyers acknowledge that some of their work is influenced by a desire to bill additional hours. About 15 percent report engaging in practices such as double billing and charging more than one client for the same work product. And two thirds agree that lawyers rationalize questionable fee-related practices such as overbilling.[123]

The basic problem arises from the difference in lawyers' and clients' interests. An attorney's goal is often to maximize profits, while a client's goal is to maximize value and minimize costs. If lawyers are charging by the hour and lack other equally profitable uses for their time, they have an incentive to prolong projects. When billings also affect power, promotion, and compensation within law firms, those incentives intensify. Yet as Scott Turow notes, lawyers rarely acknowledge, let alone disclose, the obvious conflicts of interest that the billable hour system creates. "Who ever says to a client that my billing system on its face rewards me at your expense for slow problem-solving, duplication of effort, featherbedding the workforce, and compulsiveness—not to mention fuzzy math?"[124]

The problem is compounded by the amount of work that firms increasingly demand. Current billable hour quotas in major metropolitan areas are generally around 2000 a year and the averages are higher in many large firms. Most estimates indicate that about a third of lawyers' office time cannot be billed honestly to clients; administrative matters, firm meetings, personal needs, and keeping current with legal developments all require attention. To generate 2000 billable hours, attorneys typically need to work 10 hours a day, six days a week. As then Chief Justice Rehnquist has noted, if lawyers are expected to bill at current levels, "there are bound to be temptations to exaggerate the hours put in."[125] Or as associates at Clifford Chance less diplomatically observed in an internal memorandum leaked to the press, the firm's "profoundly unrealistic" billable hour requirements

123. William G. Ross, The *Honest Hour: The Ethics of Time Based Billing* by *Attorneys* 65 (1996); John J. Marquess, "Legal Audits and Dishonest Legal Bills," 22 *Hofstra L. R.* 637, 643–44 (1994); Susan Saab Fortney, "Ethics Counsel's Role in Combating the Ostrich Tendency," *Professional Law.* 131, 139 (2002).

124. Scott Turow, "The Billable Hour Must Die," *ABA J.*, August 2007, at 35.

125. Ross, *supra* note 123, at 3, 27; William H. Rehnquist, "The Legal Profession Today," 62 *Ind. L. J.* 151, 153 (1987). *See also ABA Commission Report, supra* note 114, at 5–6.

encouraged "padding of hours, inefficient work, repetition of tasks, and other problems."[126]

In the face of such pressures, rationalizations for inflating charges come readily to hand. Studies of billing abuses find that lawyers often insist that their work really was "worth more" than the time that it required. Others use upward "adjustments" to compensate for hours and expenses that they assume they forget to claim or that the client won't reimburse. Some associates acknowledge padding if the client is "a jerk," has deep pockets, or has agreed to an estimated charge.[127] In especially egregious cases, running shoes have been billed as "ground transportation," and dry cleaning for a toupee has been labeled a litigation expense.[128] These, and related forms of fee-related deception not only erode client trust and attorney integrity, they may deflect attention from the problems that contribute to overbilling, such as lack of expertise, poor organization, or excessive overhead expenses.

Internal law firm procedures and bar disciplinary processes are often poorly structured to police fee-related misconduct. In surveys of associates, only 40 percent indicated that their firms had written billing guidelines; and roughly a third to a half received little or no instruction on fee-related practices.[129] As noted earlier, most bar disciplinary authorities are unwilling to intervene in the absence of egregious abuses and these are often difficult for clients to prove. Most lawyers are reluctant to second guess their colleagues' charges, or to support a regulatory approach that might subject their own fees to more frequent oversight. Only a minority of jurisdictions have fee arbitration systems, and even fewer require lawyers to participate. Arbitrators are not generally required to follow substantive law and their findings are largely insulated from review. Most programs also exclude issues regarding the quality of services, which underlie many fee disputes. Unsurprisingly, clients are significantly less satisfied than lawyers with bar arbitration procedures.[130]

How might these problems be addressed? Over a decade ago, the Report of the American Bar Association Commission on Evaluation of Disciplinary Enforcement (1991) proposed that all states establish a mandatory fee arbitration system; most still have not done so. Ethics experts generally believe that bar rules should require written fee agreements. At

---

126. Adam Liptak, "Stop the Clock? Critics Call the Billable Hour a Legal Fiction," *N.Y. Times*, Oct. 29, 2002, at E7 (quoting memo). To qualify for a bonus, associates needed to bill 2400 hours. *Id.*

127. Helen Coster, "The Inflation Temptation," *Am. Lawyer*, Oct. 2004, at 129.

128. Rhode, *supra* note 43, at 171–72; Lisa Lerman, "Blue–Chip Bilking: Regulation of Billing and Expense Fraud by Lawyers," 12 *Geo. J. Legal Ethics* 205 (1999). For an example, *see* Nathan Koppel, "Lawyer's Charge Opens Window on Bill Padding," *Wall St. J.*, Aug. 30, 2006, at B1.

129. Fortney, *supra* note 123, at 135 (over half); Coster, *supra* note 127, at 129 (over a third). However, only 4 percent reported that inflating hours on time sheets was an accepted practice at their firm. *Id.*

130. Rhode, *supra* note 43, at 181. According to HALT's 2007 Fee Arbitration Report Card, 38 states failed to provide an adequate fee arbitration system based on criteria such as whether the system was mandatory, well-publicized, and readily accessible, and whether it included non-lawyer arbitrators and effective enforcement of awards.

the very least, they should mandate, as the Commission recommended, that where no written fee agreement exists, lawyers should bear the burden of proof on all facts, including competence and absence of neglect or delay. Arbitration programs could be made mandatory and independent of the organized bar. Bar disciplinary systems could expand their jurisdiction, enforce fiduciary standards, address issues of performance, include greater lay representation, and provide outreach to consumers through media publicity and disclosure requirements. Bar ethical codes could require that lawyers indicate the availability of arbitration in written fee agreements or in notices issued prior to instituting fee collection proceedings.

Better monitoring by law firms is equally crucial. Recent studies illustrate common patterns of institutional indifference. When the issue is padding or meter running, supervising lawyers often look the other way or fail to look at all. And when significant misconduct comes to light, significant responses seldom follow. In one survey of lawyers convicted of billing fraud, fewer than half the firms reported criminal conduct of their members to bar disciplinary authorities or prosecutors.[131] In most cases, the only penalty for excessive fees is a reduction of charges or reimbursement for overpayments, coupled with a loss of future business or favorable recommendations from the client. Given the low probability of detection and formal complaints, and the inadequate leverage of many consumers, such sanctions provide inadequate deterrence. At the same time, however, the mistrust surrounding the billing process has often strained lawyer-client relationships. As Turow notes, there are now firms that specialize in "disputing others' bills–and in-house nudniks who demand copious details and then flyspeck them."[132]

In response to these problems, commentators generally recommend more stringent oversight, stiffer penalties, and greater experimentation with alternative billing. Some courts have agreed and have required lawyers to forfeit all or most of their fees in cases of serious ethical abuse. See *Restatement (Third) of the Law Governing Lawyers*, § 49, and *Burrow v. Arce*, 997 S.W.2d 229 (Tex.1999). Most experts also recommend that all firms establish policies, training, and oversight structures for billing issues. The ABA's recent Commission Report on Billable Hours identifies best and worst practices to guide that effort. Among the best practices are a policy emphasizing that an "absolute requirement and condition of continued employment [is] that lawyers be scrupulously honest in recording time" and that "violators will be terminated." Among the worst practices are policies that tie lawyers' compensation to hours worked, irrespective of quality or other contributions.[133] Many experts further recommend that firms found guilty of billing abuse should be required to develop appropriate oversight procedures, including random billing audits. Lawyers who

---

131. Lerman, *supra* note 128, at 278; *see also* Ross, *supra* note 123, at 199–219; Fortney, *supra* note 123. Billing fraud involving the use of wire or mail (including to transmit the bill) is a federal felony under 18 U.S.C. §§ 1341, 1343, 1346.

132. Turow, *supra* note 124, at 36.

133. *ABA Commission Report, supra* note 114, at 46–47.

knowingly fail to report billing fraud should be subject to disciplinary sanctions. Firms also need to create internal cultures of billing integrity, which are likely to be more effective than sanctions in dealing with hard-to-detect abuses.[134]

QUESTIONS

1. Which, if any, of these reform proposals would you support? How effective do you believe they would be in addressing the problems raised by the preceding readings?

2. Are more innovative billing structures necessary? The last decade has witnessed increasing efforts to focus less on hourly rates and more on the value of services provided. One common option is flat fees for service, sometimes combined with an hourly rate. Other possibilities are discounts, blended rates, and a reduced hourly fee plus a contingency bonus based on results. Such arrangements can accommodate different client concerns, such as the desire to increase predictability, encourage efficiency, or share risks.

Many experts and general counsel believe that alternative billing methods can help combat the most corrosive aspects of hourly fees, particularly padding, inefficiency, and devaluation of nonbillable activities.[135] However, as the recent ABA Commission survey found, most lawyers are reluctant to abandon time-based billing, which has the apparent advantages of simplicity, familiarity, objectivity, and profitability. Alternative billing, by contrast, seems to pose more difficult and contentious issues about value, and may encourage shoddy service if lawyers agree to flat fees for work that is unexpectedly time consuming.[136]

Another way to increase the efficient use of lawyers' time is an online collaborative database involving in-house corporate lawyers and outside law

---

134. Rhode, *supra* note 43 at 182; Lerman, *supra* note 128, at 297–300. One study based on hypothetical problems of billing abuse suggested that strong reinforcement of an honor system would work better than threatening a random audit of bills of 5 percent of firm lawyers, coupled with sanctions for abuse. The reason is that once an audit system is put in place, the ethical dimensions of the practice "fade" into the background, and are supplanted y cost-benefit judgments about the risks and costs of noncompliance. See study by Ann Tenbrunsel discussed in "Center Update," 18 *Professional Lawyer* 2 (2007).

135. *ABA Commission Report, supra* note 119, at 5–6; Turow, *supra* note 124, at 129; Susan Saab Fortney, "I Don't Have Time to Be Ethical: Addressing the Effects of

Billable Hour Pressure," 39 *Idaho L. Rev.* 305 (2003). In one survey, more than 85 percent of in-house counsel were testing alternative billing arrangements. Leigh Jones, "Firms Learn to Cope with Alternative Billing Plans," *Nat'l. L. J.*, Sep. 10, 2007, at A1, A10. For an argument that fee-related abuses are attributable to "dishonest and incompetent lawyers who bill by the hour," not the hourly billing system itself, *see* Douglas R. Richmond, "In Defense of the Billable Hour," 24 *Prof. Lawyer* 1, 5 (Winter 2003).

136. *ABA Commission Report, supra* note 114, at 7–10; Daniel Lee Jacobson, "Is the Billable Hour Running Out of Time?," *Cal. Law.* 36, 39 (April 2006); Douglas McCollam, "The Billable Hour: Are Its Days Numbered?" *The American Lawyer* November 28, 2005.

firms. Participants share legal knowledge and strategies, and pitch requests and responses regarding assistance.[137]

How would you evaluate these risks and desirability of alternative billing systems? Would your views differ if you were the in-house counsel or the outside lawyer in cases involving, for example, antitrust litigation or tax counseling?

PROBLEM 6

As chair of your state bar ethics committee, you have been asked by the state supreme court to recommend regulations concerning referral fees, contingent fees, and nonlawyer financing of legal claims. Your committee has received position papers from various consumer groups, bar organizations, insurance companies, and scholars that are evaluated in the following notes. What are your recommendations?

2. REFERRAL FEES

NOTES AND QUESTIONS

In theory, the American bar has long prohibited fees to other lawyers and nonlawyers who refer business, except under carefully limited circumstances. In practice, these prohibitions have been widely ignored and rarely enforced. In many contexts, lawyers who forward a case and agree to assume nominal responsibility for its progress routinely receive one-third of the total attorney's fee. The reasons for both the theory and practice are fairly straightforward. As an ethical matter, fees for referring a client are difficult to justify: why should a lawyer "get paid for no work?"[138] As a practical matter, however, enforcing rules against referral fees could encourage attorneys to retain matters that they cannot effectively or efficiently pursue rather than directing the client toward a more qualified practitioner. Some commentators also argue that as long as lawyers within the same firm can share fees irrespective of how their work is divided, it is hypocritical to ban fee-splitting outside of firms.

1. Model Rule 1.5, like its predecessor in the Code, permits referral fees if clients consent and the total fee is reasonable. Amendments to the Rule following the Ethics 2000 Commission, also required that the consent be in writing, that lawyers disclose the fee that each will receive, and that the division be proportional to the services each performs or that they will be jointly responsible for in the representation. The Code includes no requirement that the amount of each fee be disclosed, but it mandates that the division be proportional to "the services performed and the responsibility

---

137. Terry Carter, "New Routes to the Corporate Door," *ABA J.*, August 2007, at 36–37.

138. Geoffrey Hazard, Jr., *quoted in* Larry Bodine, "Forwarding Fees: Ethical?," *Nat'l. L. J.*, Feb. 5, 1979, at 1. According to Hazard, paying lawyers for referrals "amounts to saying that a lawyer should be bribed to act ethically. For it happens to be the unambiguous rule ... that lawyers not competent to handle cases should not handle them.... [I]f a lawyer can afford to forego some percentage of his fee in favor of a lawyer who does no work on the case, then that lawyer ... is charging too much." *Id.*

assumed by each." DR 2–107(A)(2). Which approach makes most sense? Should state bars attempt to prevent substantial fees for referring lawyers who do no real work?

A related issue that has attracted increasing attention involves reciprocal referral agreements between lawyers and other service providers. As Part E noted, a growing number of lawyers are entering into such arrangements as an alternative to multidisciplinary partnerships. To provide guidance concerning these reciprocity agreements, the ABA House of Delegates recently adopted an addition to Rule 7.2 recommended by its Ethics 2000 Commission. As amended, the Rule provides:

(b) A lawyer shall not give anything of value to a person for recommending the lawyer's services except that a lawyer may . . .

(4) refer clients to another lawyer or a nonlawyer professional pursuant to an agreement not otherwise prohibited under these Rules that provides for the other person to refer clients or customers to the lawyer, if

(i) the reciprocal agreement is not exclusive, and

(ii) the client is informed of the existence and nature of the agreement.

The Comment to the Rule adds that such reciprocal agreements must not interfere with "the lawyer's professional judgment as to making referrals or providing substantive legal services," and are subject to the conflicts of interest provisions of Rule 1.7.

What kinds of ethical problems might arise under such reciprocity agreements? As a practical matter, are the requirements of non-exclusivity and non-interference with professional judgment enforceable? Would any other protection be appropriate?

3. CONTINGENT FEES

INTRODUCTION

One of the most longstanding controversies surrounding fee regulation involves fees whose payment is conditional on a certain outcome. Contingency agreements are almost universal in personal injury litigation and widespread in other areas such as professional malpractice, tax refunds, employment discrimination, eminent domain, debt collection, shareholder's derivative claims, and private antitrust actions. The size of the fee often varies, but one-third of the total client recovery is a common rate.

Such arrangements have prompted continuing criticism and intermittent restrictions. Early English common law banned contingent fees entirely as a form of unlawful maintenance, barratry, and champerty (i.e., selling shares in the subject matter of a lawsuit and stirring up frivolous litigation). Although some American jurisdictions initially retained such prohibitions, by the early twentieth century contingency arrangements under court supervision were generally permissible.[139] By contrast, most other countries' legal systems traditionally banned contingent fees, not only because of concerns about "speculative" non-meritorious suits but also because of potential lawyer-client conflicts of interest. CCBE Code of Conduct Rule 3.3 and Explanatory Memorandum. However, a growing trend is to permit contingent fees in some form in at least some categories of cases. For example, since the 1990s, the United Kingdom has permitted "conditional fees," which are based on hourly rates plus a premium for success that parties agree to in advance. Like the contingent fee, the conditional fee rewards favorable outcomes, but determines the amount by the effort expended rather than the recovery obtained.[140] Other countries allow counsel to receive a premium based on results.

Defenders of contingent fees generally emphasize three main advantages of America's permissive rules. Such arrangements:

1) give lawyers an incentive to pursue a case vigorously in contexts where clients would have difficulty evaluating the quality of professional services;

2) allow clients with limited financial resources to afford competent legal assistance by borrowing against the value of their claims; and

3) enable such clients to shift most of the risk of an unsuccessful suit to attorneys, who can spread the costs among other claimants.

By contrast, critics of prevailing contingency agreements object to the conflict of interest they create between lawyers and clients. Attorneys' economic interest lies in maximizing the return on their work; clients' interest lies in gaining the highest possible settlement. Depending on lawyers' degree of risk aversion, the amount of effort and expense they have invested in preparation, and the alternative uses of their time, they may be more or less disposed to settle than their clients. Most commentators have concluded that for claims with low or modest stakes, contingent fee lawyers have inadequate incentives to prepare a case thoroughly and to hold out for the highest possible settlement. Conversely, in high stakes cases, once lawyers have spent substantial time in preparation, they may be more inclined to gamble for a large recovery than clients with modest incomes and pressing economic needs. Lawyers also have to consider whether acceptance of a quick settlement will risk their future bargaining credibility. Insurance companies may offer less to those represented by attorneys who are known to avoid trials.[141]

In addition, critics of contingency arrangements object to fee structures in which a lawyer's return bears no necessary relationship to the amount of

---

139. After heated debate, the ABA adopted that position in its 1908 *Canons of Ethics*. For a critical analysis of the organized bar's hostility toward contingent fees, and the class, religious, and ethnic biases that helped explain such animosity, *see* Auerbach, *supra* note 5, at 45–51.

140. Geoffrey C. Hazard Jr., and Angelo Dondi, Legal Ethics: A Comparative Study 265 (2004).

141. Herbert M. Kritzer, *Contingent–Fee Lawyers and Their Clients: Settlement Expectations, Settlement Realities, and Issues of Control in the Lawyer–Client Relationship*, 23 *Law & Soc. Inquiry* 795, 812 (1998).

work performed or to the risk actually assumed. In cases with easy facts and large damages, a standard one-third percentage recovery will provide windfalls for the attorney. In some widely publicized examples, the amount of work done was so insignificant that it would amount to hourly returns estimated at between $12,500 and $30,000 an hour. Fees for the plaintiffs' lawyers in tobacco litigation have run substantially higher, sometimes exceeding $150,000 an hour.[142] In one widely discussed case, a plaintiffs' firm in Massachusetts tobacco litigation received $178 million in fees, amounting to $7,700 per hour; each partner would have received $140,000 per year from the case, and the firm's litigation chief would receive $14 million for seventy hours' work, a rate of $200,000 per hour. The firm nevertheless sued the state for an additional $1.3 billion in fees because their initial fee allotment was less than the contingency agreement specified—9.3% of the $8.3 billion tobacco settlement, rather than the 25% in the contingency agreement. (One partner testified that $140,000 a year was "not enough for anyone to retire on.") The state argued that the higher amount would violate the ethical requirement that fees be reasonable; the jury eventually awarded the firm an additional 1.2 %, less than a tenth of what the firm had demanded, but an additional $100 million nevertheless.[143]

Lawyers frequently defend such recovery as essential to subsidize other cases with higher risks. Evidence on this point is mixed. Some research finds that personal injury cases have somewhat lower litigation success rates than other cases, which suggests that plaintiffs' lawyers are indeed accepting the riskier claims that justify contingency fees.[144] Other evidence suggests that, outside the large metropolitan areas where high stakes litigation centers, the average earnings of contingent fee attorneys are not significantly higher than those of counsel who bill hourly.[145] But as critics also note, in too many cases, lawyers' windfall recoveries far exceed a reasonable return or a necessary incentive to bring socially useful lawsuits.[146] Moreover, many clients' consent to such excessive fees is anything but informed. They do not receive an option of an hourly fee, an indication of how much work their case is likely to require, or a statement at the

---

142. Lester Brickman *et al., Rethinking Contingency Fees* 20–23 (1994). Marcia Coyle, "Bill Targets Class Action Fees, Sparked by Ire Over Tobacco Money," *Nat'l L. J.* May 19, 2003, at A1.

143. Alex Beam, "Greed on Trial," in *Legal Ethics Stories* 286–87, 292, 301 (Deborah L. Rhode & David Luban eds. 2006).

144. Samuel D. Gross & Kent D. Syverud, "Getting to No: A Study of Settlement Negotiations and the Selection of Cases for Trial," 90 *Mich. L. Rev.* 319, 337 (1991). *See also* David Luban, "Speculating on Justice: The Ethics and Jurisprudence of the Contingency Fee," in *Legal Ethics and Legal Practice* 89 (Stephen Parker & Charles Samford

eds. 1995). For conflicting research *see* Adam Liptak, "In 13 States, A Push to Limit Lawyers' Fees," *N.Y. Times*, May 26, 2003, at A1.

145. Herbert Kritzer, "The Wages of Risk: The Returns of Contingency Fee Legal Practice," *DePaul Law Review* 267, 302 (1998); Lester A. Brickman, "Contingency Fee Abuses, Ethical Mandates and the Disciplinary System: The Case Against Case-by-Case Enforcement," *Wash. & Lee L. Rev.* 1339, 1345 (1996).

146. Alison Frankel, "Greedy, Greedy, Greedy," *American Lawyer*, November 1996, at 71; Brickman, *supra* note 145; Coyle, *supra*, note 142, at A1.

conclusion of the case indicating the hours worked and the effective hourly fee.[147]

As Chapter X noted, the potential for abuse is especially great in class action litigation because most members of large plaintiff classes lack sufficient information or incentive to monitor lawyers' fees. The same is true of trial judges, despite their formal responsibility to ensure the reasonableness of fee agreements in class action settlements and to award fees under statutes authorizing such remedies. Effective oversight of compensation often requires more time-consuming review than overburdened judges can readily supply. Many courts face staggering caseloads, and the prospect of prolonging a case by overturning a fee agreement is seldom appealing.[148] Adequate judicial review is particularly difficult when defense counsel acquiesce in excessive fee requests. Although defendants often have an interest in challenging such requests in order to discourage nonmeritorious claims, the path of least resistance is sometimes a cheap settlement with generous fees. In other contexts involving mass torts, the judgments are so enormous that a standard contingency arrangement delivers returns out of all proportion to the work performed or the risks assumed.

To address the problem of excessive fees, a number of approaches are possible. One is to require attorneys to disclose in writing the actual services performed and the number of hours spent on a contingent fee case. Courts could also more actively review awards and require a detailed record to support them.[149] Another strategy is to set statutory caps on fees, with advancing percentage formulas. Under this approach, lawyers receive a larger portion of the total recovery as the case progresses and presumably becomes more time consuming. So, for example, in a matter settled without filing suit, the lawyer receives 25% of the recovery; in a case settled after filing, 33%; in a case that goes to trial, 40%; and in a case won on appeal, 50%. An obvious problem with such a formula, however, is that it may encourage lawyers to prolong proceedings where the stakes are sufficiently high. Also, some jurisdictions permit clients to waive caps with court approval, which can undermine their effectiveness.[150] An alternative that some jurisdictions have adopted sets a graduated scale giving lawyers a smaller percentage of recovery as clients' claims grow larger. This approach prevents windfall fees but at the cost of discouraging lawyers from accepting large, complex claims. A number of jurisdictions have also considered a proposal developed by the Manhattan Institute, which limits contingency awards where the plaintiff accepts an early settlement, and uses a settlement that is declined to gauge the reasonableness of other contingency fees.

147. Leonard Gross, "Are Differences Among the Attorney Conflict of Interest Rules Consistent with Principles of Behavioral Economics?," 19 *Geo. J. Legal Ethics* 11, 140 (2006).

148. Jonathan Molot, "An Old Judicial Role for a New Litigation Era," 113 *Yale L. J.* 27, 52–53 (2003); John C. Coffee, Jr., "The Corruption of the Class Action: The New Technology of Collusion," 80 *Cornell L.Rev.* 851, 855 (1995); Samuel Issacharoff, "Class Action Conflicts," 30 *University of California at Davis L.Rev.* 805, 829 (1998).

149. Molot, *supra* note 148, at 112.

150. David Horrigan, "Lawyers, Doctors, Class on Fee Caps," *Nat'l Law J.*, Aug. 8, 2005, at A5.

QUESTIONS

1. Which, if any, of these reform initiatives would you favor? If the result is to curb windfall fees, but somewhat diminish lawyers' willingness to take risky contingent-fee cases, would the trade off be worthwhile? Who should decide?

2. Do you support current ethical prohibitions on contingent fees in domestic relations? Model Rule 1.5(d)(1) The rationale for banning such fees is that lawyers should not have an economic incentive to prevent reconciliation or to negotiate a property settlement that advances their own but not necessarily the family's long term interests. Since courts can require a spouse to pay the other's fees out of marital assets, the need for contingency fees is not as pressing as in other civil contexts.

However, the American Academy of Matrimonial Lawyers has urged that the prohibition be limited to fees contingent on getting a divorce of "specified amount of support or custody and visitation rights." With respect to other matters relating to divorce, the Academy recommends that contingent fees be allowed. Otherwise clients might need to forego assistance in complex cases in which courts often decline to require payment by the opposing spouse. Alternatively, attorneys might feel obligated to forego collecting their bill if the results were unfavorable—a result "indistinguishable" on policy grounds from a contingent fee agreement.[151] What is your view?

3. Do you see a convincing rationale for prohibiting contingency fees in criminal cases? Model Rule 1.5(d)(2) and DR 2–106(C). The Model Rule Comment offers no justification. Ethical Consideration 2–20 of the Code explains that contingency agreements are impermissible because the lawyers' services "do not produce a *res* with which to pay the fee."[152] Yet courts have often approved the use of contingency arrangements in defense of civil suits that do not create a *res*. Moreover, in criminal matters, legal representation that prevents forfeiture of assets or incarceration could increase defendants' ability to pay attorneys.

An alternative rationale for the prohibition on contingent fees in criminal matters is that it prevents incentives that might result in corruption of justice. However, some commentators question whether the risks of such corruption are significantly greater among the criminal defense than civil litigation bar. As they also note, the current practice of requiring poor defendants to pay a large retainer in advance may encourage them to commit other income-producing offenses or, in organized crime cases, rely on third-party payments. Moreover, since such retainers are unrelated to result, they may also foster underpreparation.

Given these considerations, some commentators have suggested that the most significant function of banning contingent fees in criminal cases is

151. American Academy of Matrimonial Lawyers, *Bounds of Advocacy*, 4.5, Comment (2000).

152. Peyton v. Margiotti, 398 Pa. 86, 156 A.2d 865, 867 (1959), *quoted in* DR 2–106(C), n. 90.

not to protect clients or the public, but rather to protect the bar. For many criminal defendants, full "success" is unrealistic. Yet in the absence of bar prohibitions, many clients might place considerable pressure on attorneys to enter contingency agreements that would be based on unrealistic expectations or that would prove impossible to enforce. Current ethical prohibitions give lawyers a diplomatic means of resisting such pressure. Those prohibitions may also reflect an implicit judgment that criminal defendants generally have greater incentives to deceive their counsel and the courts than do civil litigants and that the need for protection against such abuses is correspondingly greater.[153] A crucial question is whether such considerations are sufficient to outweigh the advantages to defendants from contingency arrangements.[154]

4.   How would you assess the reasonableness of "reverse" contingent fees for defense counsel in civil cases? In such contexts, the contingency rests on the amount of money that a client saves, which is generally far more difficult to calculate than the amount that a client recovers. In Formal Opinion 93–373 (1993), the ABA Committee on Professional Ethics acknowledged the problems in calculation, but held that such contingency agreements were permissible if the amount saved is "reasonably determinable," the fee is "reasonable in amount" and the client's agreement is "fully informed." In addition, the Committee emphasized, "it is incumbent on the defendant's lawyer to fairly evaluate [a] plaintiff's claim" and to provide a reasonable estimate of potential liability from which to assess any savings. What problems do you anticipate under such an approach? Is the potential for abuse greater than with other fee arrangements? Are the risks off set by the incentive for efficiency that a contingency agreement supplies?[155]

5.   A related question is whether the ban on contingent fee payments to expert witnesses should be relaxed. In *Person v. Association of the Bar of City of New York*, 554 F.2d 534 (2d Cir.1977), *cert. denied*, 434 U.S. 924 (1977), a federal court of appeals rejected constitutional challenges to the ban on such fee arrangements in DR 7–109(C). Although the court acknowledged policy reasons for permitting such fees, it believed that the initiative should come from the legislature. According to some commentators, the current system not only disadvantages litigants of limited means, it also does a poor job of exposing expert bias because it encourages *de facto* rather than explicit contingent arrangements and such tacit understandings are harder to expose in cross examination. Do you agree?

153. Pamela S. Karlan, "Contingent Fees and Criminal Codes," 93 *Colum. L. Rev.* 593, 620 (1993).

154. For example, Pamela Karlan argues that contingency arrangements might make sense in certain criminal cases, particularly if the reward is provided by the government rather than the defendant. Such a fee structure might give prosecutors less incentive to overcharge and defense attorneys more incentive to prepare and litigate a case fully. *See* Karlan, *supra* note 153, at 637.

155. Jim O. Stuckey, II, " 'Reverse Contingency Fees': A Potentially Profitable and Professional Solution to the Billable Hour Trap," 16 *Prof. Lawyer* 25 (2005).

6.   Evaluate the following analysis and criticism of contingency fees.

[T]he essence of the contingency fee is that it represents a kind of litigation insurance.... The crucial point ... is that successful clients will pay their lawyers more than they would under alternative [hourly] fee arrangements, while unsuccessful clients pay their lawyers nothing. In effect, then, the lawyer—like an insurance company—subsidizes unsuccessful litigants out of premium revenues collected from successful clients. The extra emoluments paid by successful litigants amount to insurance premiums, insuring them against the possibility of failure. The contingency fee is at bottom a risk-spreading device....

[However, t]he American-style percentage contingency fee ... is an irrational method of distributing risk. Clients with higher awards pay higher fees to subsidize losers' losses. If we assume that higher awards are entirely compensatory—no punitive damages—and that they represent the client's actual damages, then the situation is this: the client who has suffered the greatest damages pays the largest number of dollars to subsidize unsuccessful litigants. He who has suffered the most pays the most—it is hard to imagine a justification for such a distributive principle.[156]

G.   FINANCING LITIGATION

NOTES AND QUESTIONS

A related set of questions involves whether attorneys or third parties should be able to purchase interests in litigation, and underwrite its costs. Current ethical prohibitions derive from the old common law crimes of champerty and maintenance. Maintenance, according to Blackstone, is "an officious intermeddling ... by maintaining or assisting either party with money or otherwise, to prosecute or defend it;" champerty, "a species of maintenance," is "a bargain with a plaintiff or defendant ... to divide the ... matter sued for between them, if they prevail at law; whereupon the champertor is to carry on the party's suit at his own expense."[157]

As discussion in Part B on Solicitation noted, these prohibitions were originally designed to address widespread corruption in the judicial process. They have persisted in order to discourage frivolous litigation and to prevent the conflicts of interest that can arise when attorneys have a financial stake in litigation. The prohibition on purchasing a claim also seeks to prevent lawyers from taking advantage of clients who are ignorant of its value or in need of an immediate recovery.

Yet the same concerns arise with contingency fees, the one method of "acquiring an interest in litigation" that the Code and Model Rules do permit. As the preceding materials indicated, lawyers with contingency agreements often have different interests than their clients concerning

---

156.   Luban, *supra* note 144, at 109–12.   **157.**   4 W. Blackstone, *Commentaries*, ch x, §§ 12 and 13, 135 (Tucker ed. 1803).

proposed settlements. If the potential conflicts that arise from contingency fees and from acquiring an interest in litigation are similar, should both forms of conduct be subject to similar regulation? If so, should the bar take a more permissive view of investments in litigation, or a less permissive view of contingency agreements? Is it likely that allowing lawyers to have a greater stake in lawsuits would encourage frivolous claims?[158]

According to some commentators, if rules against maintenance were "strictly enforced, it would paralyze class and [shareholder] derivative litigation," because no individual plaintiff has a sufficient economic incentive to subsidize the costs of litigation.[159] Some lawyers inform clients that they must agree to be formally liable for litigation expenses but that no effort will be made to collect those costs if the suit is unsuccessful. Should it be permissible for attorneys to do directly what they now do indirectly?

This issue arises with particular force in the context of mass tort actions—for example, cases involving asbestos, Agent Orange, tobacco, guns, and pharmaceuticals. Contemporary products liability litigation increasingly requires multi-million dollar capital investments, which clients cannot afford. The following selections from Peter H. Schuck's *Agent Orange on Trial: Mass Toxic Disasters in the Courts* (1987) concern the methods by which the plaintiffs' lawyers—the "Plaintiff's Management Committee," or "PMC"—attempted to finance their multi-million dollar class action suit against seven chemical companies. The case was ultimately settled for $180 million, at that time the largest settlement ever achieved in a tort action.

Agent Orange was a chemical defoliant used by the U.S. military during the Vietnam War. It contained dioxin, a powerful carcinogen. The class action was filed on behalf of veterans who had been exposed to Agent Orange.

Peter H. Schuck, Agent Orange on Trial: Mass Toxic Disasters in the Courts

120–21, 202–04 (1987).

[Judge Jack] Weinstein's renovation of the Agent Orange litigation created a mood of near-panic among the plaintiffs' lawyers. They knew, first of all, that even the recent infusions of new capital and manpower would be inadequate to meet the judge's extremely demanding schedule. Their efforts to recruit additional financiers and lawyers, [. . . ultimately] succeeded.

---

158. *See* James E. Moliterno, "Broad Prohibition, Thin Rationale: The 'Acquisition of an Interest and Financial Assistance in Litigation" Rules, 16 *Geo. J. Legal Ethics* 223, 251 (2003) (arguing that lawyers are unlikely to invest their own assets in non-meritorious claims).

159. *See* Jonathan Macey & Geoffrey Miller, "The Plaintiffs' Attorney's Role in Class Action and Derivative Litigation: Economic Analysis and Recommendations for Reform," 58 *U. Chi. L. Rev.* 1, 98 (1991).

Musslewhite [one of the plaintiffs' lead trial lawyers] recruited Newton Schwartz and John O'Quinn, Houston practitioners, but only after Musslewhite had agreed to sell them a share of his interest in a fee award. (Dean, jokingly referring to the financially pressed character in Mel Brooks's film "The Producers," called Musslewhite "the Max Bialystok of the legal profession; he sold 10,000 percent of his case.")

The new PMC, now consisting of nine members, set its internal finances on a new footing by negotiating a fresh arrangement for defraying expenses and sharing whatever fees the court might ultimately award. Under the agreement, as the court later interpreted it, five of them (Brown, Chesley, Locks, O'Quinn, and Schwartz) each contributed $250,000 for litigation expenses, Henderson contributed $200,000, and the three others (Dean, Musslewhite, and Schlegel) contributed their time but no cash for general expenses. In the event of an award, however, the cash contributors would receive "off the top" three times the amount they had advanced. Half of the remainder of the award would be allocated in equal shares among all PMC members, 30 percent in proportion to hours worked and 20 percent based on certain conventional "merit" factors (what Musslewhite calls "the golden spike").

This new fee-sharing arrangement created yet another fissure within the PMC, dividing the financial interests of the litigators from those of the financiers (there was, of course, some overlap between the two categories). The financiers, who now stood to obtain their profit even if the fee award were relatively low and without regard to their time contributions, might find settlement at a relatively low figure more attractive than the litigators. If a settlement did take place, even the appearance of such conflicts might be used to impugn the integrity of the settlement. In the event, this is precisely what transpired. . . .

A final significant aspect of Weinstein's initial fee opinion concerned his review of the PMC's internal fee-splitting agreement. The initial arrangement, signed during the group's most financially desperate hours, was described [earlier]; under its terms (in Weinstein's words), "those who advanced money would be advantaged to an extraordinary degree over those who gave their time and skill to the enterprise." The arrangement raised a number of important and little-explored legal and ethical issues. First, this "banker's approach" (as Sol Schreiber calls it) might amount to champerty (the fomenting and maintenance by lawyers of litigation in which they have a proprietary interest), a practice that the courts have long regarded as unethical and illegal.

Second, as noted above, the arrangement created the potential for serious conflicts of interest between the financiers and the litigators on the PMC and exacerbated similar conflicts between the lawyers and their clients. A financier who knows that he will receive a profitable return on his investment "off the top" of any fee award has a strong incentive to settle the case quickly, even if the settlement amount is far below what might be obtained by holding out for a higher figure or by proceeding to trial (at the risk of losing everything). By the same token, a litigator who

knows that such a settlement will siphon off the bulk of the fee award for the financiers, leaving relatively little to be divided up among the litigators, has a strong incentive to resist such a settlement. The clients' interests may well be lost in the crossfire. In such a situation mistrust flourishes; for example, some saw Chesley's eagerness to lead the settlement talks, his readiness to compromise at the $180 million figure, his assurance that even with a very small fee award he would receive a quick $600,000 on his $200,000 investment, as predictable signs of this logic at work. (Also contributing to these suspicions was Chesley's well-established reputation for settling huge class action cases, securing handsome fees in the process.)
. . .

Third, the PMC agreement placed the court in the awkward position of awarding fees that it knew would actually be allocated among the lawyers in an entirely different manner and without regard to the traditional, legally sanctioned criteria—work performed, professional value conferred, or responsibility assumed. . . .

[These] arguments have some force, yet the ethical strictures they embody seem curiously anachronistic, quaint reminders of bygone attitudes toward the social functions of adjudication. The legal system cannot have it both ways. If it desires the end, then it must desire (or at least accept) the only practical means to that end. If it wishes to encourage so-called public interest tort litigation on behalf of diffuse, poorly financed interests over extremely complex issues of scientific or technical uncertainty, then it must either transform the government into a tort litigator on behalf of these interests (a solution with enormous problems of its own), or it must countenance, indeed welcome, private arrangements for securing the resources necessary for effectively prosecuting such cases. The truth is that in the fall of 1983, if the Agent Orange litigation was to go forward, the resources of the financiers were desperately needed; it is no exaggeration to say that at that critical moment and thereafter, they were needed far more than the services of the chief trial counsel, valuable as his services were. . . . Although the opportunism of investors is not a pretty or edifying sight, the prospect of meritorious cases failing for want of resources is even less appealing. Any set of principles that affirms the importance of litigating very costly cases while denying the means for doing so seems more hypocritical than ethical, more delusive than just.

NOTES

Shuck concludes: "The legal system cannot have it both ways. . . . If it wishes to encourage so-called public interest tort litigation on behalf of diffuse, poorly financed interests . . . it must countenance, indeed welcome, private arrangements for securing the resources necessary for effectively prosecuting such cases." Is he right?

On appeal from a judgment of the district court, the Second Circuit held that the distribution of fees in a class action "must bear some relationship to the services rendered." *In re Agent Orange Product Liability*

Litigation, 818 F.2d 216 (2d Cir.), *cert. denied*, 484 U.S. 926 (1987). In the appellate court's view, agreements allocating fees based on the amount of funds advanced rather than work performed would give investors an undue incentive to accept an early settlement not in the best interests of the class. Judge Weinstein also had second thoughts about his decision to accept the proposed fee arrangement. In a subsequent article, "Ethical Dilemmas in Mass Tort Litigation," he states:

> I believe I gave too little attention to this subject in "Agent Orange" and did not fairly compensate the attorneys who represented individuals. All the fees went to members of the central committee who had almost no individual client contact. Many attorneys had spent time with individual clients and should have received compensation for this important personal relationship aspect of the litigation.[160]

QUESTIONS

1.   If you agree with Judge Weinstein, what criteria should courts use to assess the fairness of fee agreements between lawyers?

2.   Note that if the Agent Orange attorneys had been partners in a firm, they could have reached any agreement about the appropriate distribution of work, investment, and profit. Should lawyers who form an *ad hoc* partnership be treated differently? The Second Circuit reasoned that they should because they lacked an "ongoing relationship that is the essential element of attorneys practicing as partners." 818 F.2d, at 226. Should that difference be conclusive?

3.   Shuck seems willing to endorse lawyer financing of litigation, even where lawyers are brought in for their capital and not for their legal skills. How far should this argument be carried? Why not include nonlawyers with capital? Recall prior discussion of Australian rules permitting law firms to raise capital by selling shares, discussed in Section C, *supra*. Should investors be allowed to purchase shares of a major products liability case? Should litigants be able to incorporate ("Agent Orange Products Liability Litigations, Inc.") and offer stock in their lawsuit? Suppose that is the only way they will be able to afford their "day in court"?[161] Would broadening the pool of potential investors in litigation also serve the public interest by decreasing the "economic rent" available to lawyers when they have close to a monopoly over the market?[162]

The practice of "syndicating" lawsuits began during the 1980s, and has met with a mixed reception in the courts. In effect, the practice involves selling shares in a prospective recovery to finance litigation ex-

160. Jack B. Weinstein, "Ethical Dilemmas in Mass Tort Litigation," 88 *Northwestern Univ. L. Rev.* 469, 531 (1994).

161. *See* Macey and Miller, *supra* note 159; Douglas R. Richmond, "Litigation Funding: Investing, Lending or Loan Sharking?," *Prof. Lawyer* 17 (2005).

162. Rudy Santore & Alan D. Viard, "Legal Fee Restrictions, Moral Hazard, and Attorney Rents," 44 *J. L. & Econ.* 549 (2001).

penses.[163] This form of financing has grown substantially in recent years, and most often involves victims of automobile or work accidents who receive relatively small amounts, typically between $2500 to $3000 or 10 percent of their expected settlement.[164]

Is this practice different from allowing attorneys to use forthcoming claims as collateral to secure loans? Consider *Rancman v. Interim Settlement Funding Corp.*, 789 N.E.2d 217 (Ohio 2003). The plaintiff sued State Farm Insurance Company for uninsured motorist benefits, and received an advance of $6,000 from an affiliate of the defendant, Interim Settlement, to finance the claim. Under the terms of the contract, the defendant would receive the first $16,800 she would recover if the case was resolved in twelve months, $22,200 if the case was resolved within eighteen months, or $27,600 if the case was resolved within twenty-four months. She had no obligation to repay the advance if the case was unsuccessful. Rancman subsequently received an additional $1,000 secured by the next $2,800 she might recover. Ultimately, she settled her suit within twelve months for $100,000, but refused to honor her agreement with the defendant. Her claim was that the financing companies had incurred virtually no risk and the terms were "unfair, deceptive and unconscionable" and in violation of Ohio's usury law. The defendants countered that because the advance was an investment, not a loan, it did not fall under the Ohio's statute. The Ohio Supreme Court did not reach the usury issue, but determined instead that the advances were "void as champerty and maintenance." 789 N.E.2d, at 219. In the court's view "a lawsuit is not an investment vehicle," and the terms of the contract gave Rancman a disincentive to settle. *Id.*, at 221.

Do you agree? Would you allow third party investments in any circumstances? What restrictions might you impose? If you were a judge in *Rancman* or *Agent Orange*, how would you balance the competing concerns?

4. Should lawyers be allowed to make or guarantee loans to clients for medical and living expenses to enable them to withstand inadequate settlement offers? This was the issue in Problem 3(d) above. Model Rule 1.8 (e) prohibits such aid. Under its terms:

> A lawyer shall not provide financial assistance to a client in connection with pending or contemplated litigation, except that:
>
> (1) a lawyer may advance court costs and expenses of litigation, the repayment of which may be contingent on the outcome of the matter; and

---

163. Susan Lorde Martin, "Financing Plaintiffs' Lawsuits: An Increasingly Popular (and Legal) Business," 33 *U. Mich. J. L. Reform* 57 (2000); Margaret Crown Fisk, "Large Verdicts For Sale," *National Law J.*, Jan. 11, 1999 at 1. A related practice is to sell future claims to attorneys' fees in lawsuits that are settled in exchange for cash that can be used to finance other litigation. *See* James Wooton, "Litigation Bonds Are a Risky Investment," *Wall St. J.*, March 14, 2001, at A22 (describing litigation bonds in tobacco fee cases).

164. Tresa Baldas, "Some States Regulate Lawsuit Funding Laws," *Nat'l L. J.*, Nov. 12, 2007, at 4.

(2) a lawyer representing an indigent client may advance court costs and expenses of litigation on behalf of the client.

The comment explains that lawyers may not make or guarantee loans covering clients' living expenses "because to do so would encourage clients to pursue lawsuits that might not otherwise be brought and because such assistance gives lawyers too great a financial stake in the litigation." Accord, DR 5–103(B) and ABA Committee on Professional Ethics and Grievances, Formal Op. 288 (1955). A further rationale for the prohibition figured prominently in debates over the Restatement of the Law Governing Lawyers. Without such a ban, attorneys would have to compete for clients based on the amount of their assistance rather than the quality of their representation.[165]

Critics of the bar's traditional position argue that humanitarian assistance is necessary to prevent inadequate compensation of needy claimants, and that it creates no greater dangers of conflict of interest or non meritorious claims than contingent fees.[166] A minority of states agree, and allow lawyers to advance or guarantee loans for living expenses under certain circumstances. Typically, the lawyer may not advertise the practice or promise to provide such assistance in order to obtain or maintain employment.[167]

---

165. See the 1996 proceedings relating to the ALI, Restatement of the Law Governing Lawyers, § 48(2); Fred C. Zacharias, "Limits on Client Autonomy in Legal Ethics Representation," 81 B.U.L. Rev. 199, 237 (2001).

166. Danielle Z. Cohen, "Advancing Funds, Advancing Justice: Adopting the Louisiana Approach," 19 *Geo. J. Legal Ethics* 613 (2006); Moliterno, note 158, at 138–40; Jack P. Sahl, "The Cost of Humanitarian Assis-

tance: Ethical Rules and the First Amendment," 34 *St. Mary's L. J.* 795 (2003).

167. The landmark decision was *Louisiana State Bar Association v. Edwins*, 329 So.2d 437 (La. 1976). For other decisions, *see* Cohen, *supra* note 166, at 625–26; Sahl, *supra* note 166, at 820–26. For the similar *Restatement* position, *see Restatement, supra* note 165, at § 48.

CHAPTER XIII

THE DISTRIBUTION OF LEGAL SERVICES

A. PROBLEMS OF LITIGIOUSNESS: THE OVERLAWYERED SOCIETY

Charles Dickens, Bleak House

(Ed. 1858).

The raw afternoon is rawest, and the dense fog is densest, and the muddy streets are muddiest, near that leaden-headed old obstruction, appropriate ornament for the threshold of a leaden-headed old corporation: Temple Bar. And hard by Temple Bar, in Lincoln's Inn Hall, at the very heart of the fog, sits the Lord High Chancellor in his High Court of Chancery.

Never can there come fog too thick, never can there come mud and mire too deep, to assort with the groping and floundering condition which this High Court of Chancery, most pestilent of hoary sinners, holds, this day, in the sight of heaven and earth.

On such an afternoon, if ever, the Lord High Chancellor ought to be sitting here—as here he is—with a foggy glory round his head, softly fenced in with crimson cloth and curtains, addressed by a large advocate with great whiskers, a little voice, and an interminable brief, and outwardly directing his contemplation to the lantern in the roof, where he can see nothing but fog. On such an afternoon, some score of members of the High Court of Chancery bar ought to be—as here they are—mistily engaged in one of the ten thousand stages of an endless cause, tripping one another up on slippery precedents, groping knee-deep in technicalities, running their goat-hair and horsehair warded heads against walls of words, and making a pretence of equity with serious faces, as players might. On such an afternoon, the various solicitors in the cause, some two or three of whom have inherited it from their fathers, who made a fortune by it, ought to be—as are they not?—ranged in a line, in a long matted well (but you might look in vain for Truth at the bottom of it), between the registrar's red table and the silk gowns, with bills, cross-bills, answers, rejoinders, injunctions, affidavits, issues, references to masters, masters' reports, mountains of costly nonsense, piled before them. Well may the court be dim, with wasting candles here and there; well may the fog hang heavy in it, as if it would never get out; well may the stained-glass windows lose their colour, and admit no light of day into the place; well may the uninitiated from the streets, who peep in through the glass panes in the door, be deterred from entrance by its owlish aspect, and by the drawl languidly echoing to the roof from the padded dais where the Lord High Chancellor looks into the lantern that has no light in it, and where the attendant wigs are all stuck in a fog-bank! This is the Court of Chancery; which has its decaying houses and its blighted lands in every shire; which has its worn-out lunatic in every madhouse, and its dead in every church-yard; which has its ruined suitor, with his slipshod heels and threadbare dress, borrowing and begging through the round of every man's acquaintance; which gives to monied might the means abundantly of wearying out the right; which so exhausts finances, patience, courage, hope; so over-throws the brain and breaks the heart; that there is not an honourable man among its practitioners who would not give—who does not often give—the warning, "Suffer any wrong that can be done you, rather than come here!"

Who happen to be in the Lord Chancellor's court this murky afternoon besides the Lord Chancellor, the counsel in the cause, two or three counsel who are never in any cause, and the well of solicitors before mentioned? There is the registrar below the Judge, in wig and gown; and there are two or three maces, or petty-bags, or privy-purses, or whatever they may be, in legal court suits. These are all yawning; for no crumb of amusement ever falls from JARNDYCE AND JARNDYCE (the cause in hand), which was squeezed dry years upon years ago. The short-hand writers, the reporters of the court, and the reporters of the newspapers, invariably decamp with the rest of the regulars when Jarndyce and Jarndyce comes on.

Jarndyce and Jarndyce drones on. This scarecrow of a suit has, in course of time, become so complicated that no man alive knows what it means. The parties to it understand it least; but it has been observed that no two Chancery lawyers can talk about it for five minutes without coming to a total disagreement as to all the premises. Innumerable children have been born into the cause; innumerable young people have married into it; innumerable old people have died out of it. Scores of persons have deliriously found themselves made parties in Jarndyce and Jarndyce, without knowing how or why; whole families have inherited legendary hatreds with the suit. The little plaintiff or defendant, who was promised a new rocking-horse when Jarndyce and Jarndyce should be settled, has grown up, possessed himself of a real horse, and trotted away into the other world. Fair wards of court have faded into mothers and grandmothers; a long procession of Chancellors has come in and gone out; the legion of bills in the suit have been transformed into mere bills of mortality; there are not three Jarndyces left upon the earth perhaps, since old Tom Jarndyce in despair blew his brains out at a coffee-house in Chancery Lane; but Jarndyce and Jarndyce still drags its dreary length before the Court, perennially hopeless.

Jarndyce and Jarndyce has passed into a joke. That is the only good that has ever come of it. It has been death to many, but it is a joke in the profession. Every master in Chancery has had a reference out of it.... The last Lord Chancellor handled it neatly, when, correcting Mr Blowers the eminent silk gown who said that such a thing might happen when the sky rained potatoes, he observed, "or when we get through Jarndyce and Jarndyce, Mr Blowers"—a pleasantry that particularly tickled the maces, bags, and purses.

How many people out of the suit, Jarndyce and Jarndyce has stretched forth its unwholesome hand to spoil and corrupt, would be a very wide question. From the master, upon whose impaling files reams of dusty warrants in Jarndyce and Jarndyce have grimly writhed into many shapes; down to the copying-clerk in the Six Clerk's Office, who has copied his tens of thousands of Chancery-folio-pages under that eternal heading; no man's nature has been made the better by it. In trickery, evasion, procrastination, spoliation, botheration, under false pretences of all sorts, there are influences that can never come to good. The very solicitors' boys who have kept the wretched suitors at bay, by protesting time out of mind that Mr Chizzle, Mizzle, or otherwise, was particularly engaged and had appointments until dinner, may have got an extra moral twist and shuffle into themselves out of Jarndyce and Jarndyce. The receiver in the cause has acquired a goodly sum of money by it, but has acquired too a distrust of his own mother, and a contempt of his own kind. Chizzle, Mizzle, and otherwise, have lapsed into a habit of vaguely promising themselves that they will look into that outstanding little matter, and see what can be done for Drizzle—who was not well used—when Jarndyce and Jarndyce shall be got out of the office. Shirking and sharking, in all their many varieties, have been sown broadcast by the ill-fated cause; and even those who have contemplated its history from the outermost circle of such evil, have been insensibly tempted into a loose way of letting bad things alone to take their own bad course, and a loose belief that if the world go wrong, it was, in some offhand manner, never meant to go right.

Thus, in the midst of the mud and at the heart of the fog, sits the Lord High Chancellor in his High Court of Chancery....

"Several members of the bar are still to be heard, I believe?" says the Chancellor, with a slight smile.

Eighteen of Mr Tangle's learned friends, each armed with a little summary of eighteen hundred sheets, bob up like eighteen hammers in a pianoforte, make eighteen bows, and drop into their eighteen places of obscurity.

"We will proceed with the hearing on Wednesday fortnight," says the Chancellor. For the question at issue is only a question of costs, a mere bud on the forest tree of the parent suit, and really will come to a settlement one of these days.

Dave Barry, "Here's Proof That the Law Has Teeth"

Miami Herald Sun, Nov. 21, 1993, at 5.

I am sick and tired of all this lawyer-bashing. When I hear somebody say something bad about lawyers, it makes me want to walk up and spit in his face, thereby causing him to shove me, so I can fall down and file a $17 million personal-injury lawsuit against him.

Because I happen to think lawyers are great. I am darned grateful that I live in a country that has, pound for pound, more lawyers than any other country in the entire world. We *need* a lot of lawyers, to protect all these rights we have as Americans. . . .

We have so many rights that we cannot possibly keep track of them all with our primitive non-legal minds. This is why we need all these lawyers out there fighting for us, even when we are not aware of it.

A fine example of this, brought to my attention by alert reader Leon Rothman, is the Case of the Denture Adhesive Menace. . . . Let me review the facts of the case:

From 1985 to 1990, a company named SmithKline Beecham manufactured denture adhesives sold under the names "Orafix Special" and "Brace." SmithKline recalled these products in 1990 after they were found to contain trace amounts of benzene, a carcinogen. SmithKline contends that the products were not harmful. There is no evidence anybody got cancer from using them.

Then a retired Philadelphia auto-supplies dealer named Meyer E. Duboff, who used SmithKline denture products, contacted his lawyer, Jay S. Cohen.

"He called me and said, 'I've been using this stuff for years. Can you check it out?' " Cohen told The Miami Herald.

OK, is everybody following this so far? *One guy* has called his lawyer. This guy does *not* have cancer. *Nobody* has cancer. Nobody is claiming *anybody* actually got hurt.

So the lawyer told the guy: "Gosh, Meyer, nothing really happened. Why don't you just forget about it?"

No! Just kidding! That might happen in some backward, under-lawyered nation like Japan, but not here in the U.S.A.! What happened here, of course, was that Cohen and some other lawyers filed a class-action lawsuit against SmithKline on behalf of Duboff and all the other denture-adhesive users out there who, because of a tragic lack of legal representation, had not yet noticed that they were victims.

And of course SmithKline, to avoid the hassle and publicity and legal expense of a trial, settled out of court. Three groups got money in the settlement:

1. *Mr. Duboff.* He got $25,000. Fair enough. It was his idea in the first place.

2. *The other denture-adhesive victims.* They were notified of their victimhood via newspaper advertisements and direct mailings, paid for by SmithKline. About 650 people sent in proof that they had purchased Orafix Special or Brace; each of these people received $7. Another 2,800 people— who did not have proof of purchase—filled out forms certifying that they

had purchased at least one tube of either product; each of these people received a package of discount coupons for SmithKline products.

3. *The lawyers for the plaintiff.* If you are a fan of Justice, American Style, you will be very excited when I tell you what the lawyers got, in expenses and legal fees.

They got $954,934.57.

"It's a lot of money," said Cohen. "But there's also a lot of money that goes into these cases."

I am sure there is! A lot of money! Also a lot of work! It cannot be easy, taking a case wherein it appears, to the naked untrained layperson eye, that nobody has suffered any observable harm, and, using legal skills, turning it into a financial transaction that involves thousands of people and a million dollars! Plus coupons!

So the lawyers certainly deserved this money, although I'm certain that, for them, the really important thing was simply the satisfaction of knowing that all those victims are now finally able, at long last, to put this horrible denture-adhesive nightmare behind them and begin leading happier lives, possibly by applying their $7 settlements toward world cruises, vacation homes, etc.

Yes, we owe a tremendous debt of gratitude to these lawyers and the estimated 14.2 billion other members of the American legal community, many of whom, I am sure, will write to me on their official letterhead stationery to respond to this column. I look forward to reading these letters; I just hope that, in handling them, I do not suffer paper cuts, which could cause me, as a writer, to become incapacitated, not to mention pain and suffering.

And I'm not settling for any stinking coupons.

Addendum

In response to claims by "anti Big Food" crusaders that certain high calorie snacks containing cheese are addictive, Barry writes:

Dave Barry, "The Tide is High,"

Funny Times, November, 2007, at 3.

The question is, what do I do now? One option would be to give up cheese, join the vegans and eat nothing but water and free-range soybean curd. But that seems extreme. So I'll just summon up my will power and accept personal responsibility for filing a huge lawsuit against Big Food. Big Food, if you're reading this column: Please understand that I am not doing this for money. I'm willing to settle today for a sincere apology on your part, plus a huge cash payment. Also, please send me some more Cheez–Its, OK? This box is almost gone.

Derek C. Bok, "A Flawed System of Law Practice and Training"

33 Journal of Legal Education 570, 571–74, 577–80 (1983).

One-half of our difficulty lies in the burdens and costs of our tangle of laws and legal procedures. Contrary to popular belief, it is not clear that we are a madly litigious society. It is true that we have experienced a rapid growth in the number of complaints filed in our courts. But filings are often only a prelude to some kind of voluntary settlement. The number of disputes *actually litigated* in the United States does not appear to be rising much faster than the population as a whole. Our courts may *seem* crowded, since we have relatively few judges compared with many industrial nations. Nevertheless, our volume of litigated cases is not demonstrably larger in relation to our total population than that of other western nations.

At the same time, the complexity of litigation seems to be increasing. Even if a case is settled without trial, preliminary motions and discovery procedures may occupy much time of judges and attorneys. Moreover, the country has experienced a marked growth in statutes and administrative regulations. . . . [L]egal costs are primarily people costs, and if we mark the growth in the total number of lawyers and the average compensation of attorneys, it is clear that legal expenditures have been climbing more rapidly than the gross national product for many years.

Is it wrong to spend so much on legal services? After all, people pay a lot for underarm deodorants, television soap operas, liquor, and drugs. If rules are passed by elected representatives and legal expenses are voluntarily incurred, is it clear that the nation is spending "too much" on law?

The catch in this argument, of course, is the quiet assumption that rules and regulations are all freely chosen through something akin to a market process. In fact, that is far from being the case. All lawsuits are heavily subsidized by the government and are usually desired by only one party to the dispute. Many rules are the work of judges or bureaucrats over whom the general public has little control. Although the public may support the general outlines of a statute, its details and complexities are rarely understood, let alone endorsed, by the average voter. Most of our laws and administrative regulations have been complicated by the efforts of pressure groups and lobbyists. Even legislation widely approved when enacted often proves unexpectedly cumbersome and ineffective, yet efforts at reform quickly die from inertia or from the opposition of vested interests. . . .

If these observations are even half true, our legal system leads to much waste of money that could be put to better purposes. But even greater costs result from the heavy use of human talent. Not only does the law absorb many more young people in America than in any other industrialized nation: it attracts an unusually large proportion of the exceptionally gifted. . . .

A nation's values and problems are mirrored in the ways in which it uses its ablest people. In Japan, a country only half our size, 30 percent more engineers graduate each year than in all the United States. But Japan boasts a total of less than 15,000 lawyers, while American universities graduate 35,000 *every year*. It would be hard to claim that these differences have no practical consequences. As the Japanese put it, "Engineers make the pie grow larger; lawyers only decide how to carve it up."

The elaborateness of our laws and the complexity of our procedures absorb the energies of this giant bar, raise the cost of legal services, and help produce the other great problem of our legal system—the lack of access for the poor and middle class. The results are embarrassing to behold. Criminal defendants are herded through the courts at a speed that precludes individual attention, leaving countless accused to the mercy of inexperienced counsel who determine their fate in hasty plea bargaining with the prosecution. On the civil side, the cost of hiring a lawyer and the mysteries of the legal process discourage most people of modest means from trying to enforce their rights. Every study of common forms of litigation, such as medical malpractice, tenant evictions, or debt collections, reveals that for each successful suit there are several others that could be won if the victims had the money and the will to secure a lawyer.

Congress has tried to address this problem by creating the Legal Services Corporation. But even in its palmiest days, the corporation was only empowered to help the poor and had money enough to address but a small fraction of the claims of this limited constituency. Since then, its budget has been cut severely. Middle-income plaintiffs often find that legal expenses eat up most of the amounts that they recover. In personal injury claims, contingent fees may help surmount the cost barrier, but legal expenses consume a third or more of the average settlement in most proceedings and can often rise to 50 percent in cases going to trial. As many observers have testified, the costs and delays of our system force countless victims to accept inadequate settlements or to give up any attempt to vindicate their legal rights.

This state of affairs has become so familiar that it evokes little concern from most of those who spend their lives in the profession. As I visit in different cities, however, and talk to laymen in other walks of life, these problems loom so large as virtually to blot out every other feature of the legal system. The blunt, inexcusable fact is that this nation, which prides itself on efficiency and justice, has developed a legal system that is the most expensive in the world, yet cannot manage to protect the rights of most of its citizens. . . .

An effective program will require not only multiple efforts but a mixture that involves attempts to simplify rules and procedures as well as measures that give greater access to the poor and middle class. Access without simplification will be wasteful and expensive; simplification without access will be unjust.

A program embodying these principles will include initiatives along a number of lines already described. Lawmakers will need to adopt no-fault car insurance everywhere and extend the no-fault concept to new fields of liability. Legislatures will have to take a hard look at provisions for treble damages and other artificial incentives that stimulate litigation. Agency officials will want to mount a broad review of existing laws to simplify rules and eliminate regulations that do not serve a demonstrable public purpose. These efforts at simplification must be accompanied by larger appropriations to make legal counsel available to the poor. But money alone will not suffice. In cases involving debtors and creditors, landlords and tenants, and other disputes that touch the lives of ordinary folk, judges will have to develop less costly ways of resolving disputes, since expensive adversary trials ultimately deny access, and therefore justice, to countless deserving people. Likewise, lawyers will need to devise new institutions to supply legal services more cheaply. Such changes, in turn, will undoubtedly force the organized bar to reexamine traditional attitudes toward fee-for-service and the unauthorized practice of law. . . .

In addition, judges, lawmakers, scholars will all have to recognize that our conception of the role of law has fallen into disrepair. In its place, they will need to search for a new understanding that is no less sensitive to injustice but more realistic in accounting for the limits and costs of legal rules in ordering human affairs. In such a world, the law may seem enlightened and humane, but its constant stream of rules will leave a wake strewn with the disappointed hopes of those who find the legal system too complicated to understand, too quixotic to command respect, and too expensive to be of much practical use.

NOTES

"Western society has chosen for itself the organization best suited to its purposes and one I might call legalistic. The limits of human rights and rightness are determined by a system of laws; such limits are very broad. . . . If one is right from a legal point of view, nothing more is required, nobody may mention that one could still not be entirely right, and urge self-restraint or a renunciation of these rights, call for sacrifice and selfless risk; this would simply sound absurd. Voluntary self-restraint is almost unheard of; everybody strives toward further expansion to the extremes of the legal frames. . . .

But a society with no other scale but the legal one is also less worthy of man. A society based on the letter of the law and never reaching any higher fails to take advantage of the full range of human possibilities. The letter of the law is too cold and formal to have a beneficial influence on society. Whenever the tissue of life is woven of legalistic relationships, this creates an atmosphere of spiritual mediocrity that paralyzes man's noblest impulses."

Aleksandr Solzhenitsyn[1]

1.   Aleksandr Solzhenitsyn, "A World Split Apart" in *Solzhenitsyn at Harvard* 7–8 (Ronald Berman ed. 1980).

> "We're a litigious society; everybody is suing, it seems like. There are too many lawsuits in America.... People who have got a claim, a legitimate claim, must have a hearing in our courts.... And they deserve a court that is uncluttered by junk and frivolous lawsuits."

George W. Bush[2]

Concerns about litigiousness and the legalization of American society are by no means a recent development. The last three centuries have witnessed countless variations on the themes raised by George W. Bush and Aleksandr Solzhenitsyn, elaborated by Derek Bok, satirized by Dave Barry, and fictionalized by Charles Dickens. It has been often asserted and widely assumed that America has had "too much law and too little justice," and that lawyers have contributed as much to the problem as the solution.[3] However, as the continuity of such critiques suggests, they have done little to discourage the nation's investment in legal process. Indeed, the history of Solzhenitsyn's denunciation of legalism provides an ironic illustration of our cultural ambivalence toward legalization. When some of his admirers sought to republish the address in a volume of commentary placing it in broader perspective, Solzhenitsyn initially withheld permission and threatened legal action. In the abstract, the "letter of the law" may have seemed too "cold and formal to have a beneficial influence on society" but in his own case, Solzhenitsyn (as well as his adversaries) apparently found it of some use.[4] It also bears note that President George W. Bush, who has long complained about "too many lawsuits," owes his own election to one.

Concerns about litigiousness generally presuppose but rarely defend some objective standard of evaluation. Consider, for example, Bok's indictment. By what criteria does he determine that America is too legalistic? What would be an appropriate level of reliance on law, and how would we know when we reached it?

Most complaints about American "hyperlexis" involve four related claims. Critics assert that we have too many lawyers, too much litigation, too much law, and too much legal expense. Each of these claims is worth exploring in some detail.

---

2. George W. Bush, Remarks on Medical Liability Reform, University of Scranton, Scranton, Penn. Jan. 16, 2003, available at http://www.whitehouse.gov/newsreleases/2003/01/print20030116–.html. See also Terry Carter, "New Name, New Strategies," *ABA J.*, Feb. 2007, 39, 43 (quoting George Bush's claim that the "plethora" of frivolous lawsuits was driving up health care costs).

3. For representative versions of such critiques, see Walter K. Olson, *The Rule of Lawyers: How the New Litigation Elite Threatens America's Rule of Law* (2002); Catherine Crier, *The Case Against Lawyers* (2002) and sources discussed in Myron Levin,

"Legal Urban Legends Hold Sway," *L.A. Times*, Aug 14, 2005, at C1; Deborah L. Rhode, "Frivolous Litigation and Civil Justice Reform: Miscasting the Problem, Recasting the Solution," 54 *Duke L. J.* 447 (2004). For discussion, *see* Thomas Burke, *Lawyers, Lawsuits, and Legal Rights* (2000); Deborah L. Rhode, *Access to Justice* 24–46 (2004).

4. After Solzhenitsyn and his publisher threatened to sue for copyright violations, the commentators filed a complaint alleging fair use. The case was settled when the publisher granted requests to reprint the address. *See* Ernest Lefever, "Foreword," in *Solzhenitsyn at Harvard, supra* note 1.

Too Many Lawyers

Since the Colonial era, Americans have complained about the number of lawyers, and have often blamed them for the nation's proliferation of laws and lawsuits. Yet such criticisms typically rely on misleading assumptions.

First, the facts are often wrong. For example, one widely repeated assertion that America has seventy percent of the world's lawyers is widely off the mark. Informed estimates put the figure somewhere between a quarter and a third, which is roughly the United States' share of the world's combined Gross National Products.[5] Cross-cultural comparisons can be misleading since they fail to reveal the number of practitioners in other countries who are not licensed members of the bar but who receive legal training or perform tasks that in this country are largely reserved for lawyers. In Germany, for example, in-house corporate counsel do not belong to the bar, and are not counted as members of the legal profession. The favorable references that Derek Bok and other critics often make to Japan are particularly in need of qualifications. There, a large number of individuals receive legal training in universities, and perform legal functions, but are not permitted to act as advocates in court because bar passage rates are set at extremely low levels, traditionally around two to three percent.[6]

Similarly, the frequent criticism that lawyers never "make the pie grow larger [but] only decide how to carve it up," works more effectively on the rhetorical than the empirical level. As a description of American attorneys' role in corporate planning, regulatory compliance, civil liberties litigation, or criminal defense, the pie metaphor seems somewhat lacking— "pie in the sky," as Luban has put it.[7] An engineer's product has value only if it can be developed, protected, and marketed within a complex network of legal relations. Contracts, collective bargaining agreements, property interests, securities sales, health and safety regulations, may all be implicated. Lawyers who sue to protect an engineer's patent rights aren't just "dividing the pie;" they are also enforcing a system of incentives that reward innovation and thereby make the pie larger.

Too Many Lawsuits

Claims about America's hair-trigger litigiousness are equally problematic. Although four-fifths of Americans believe that America has too much litigation, experts generally agree that current litigation rates in the United States are not exceptionally high, either in comparison with prior historical eras or with many other Western industrial nations not known for contentiousness. Higher per capita rates of litigation occurred in some communi-

5. Marc Galanter, "News from Nowhere: The Debased Debate on Civil Justice," 71 *Denver U. L. Rev.*1, 79–80 (1993).

6. Mariko Sanchanta, "Japan Set to Create Bonanza in Legal Jobs," *Financial Times.Com*, July 17, 2003, available at ft.com/nonFtArticle?id + 030717003834.   By

2010, the country is aiming to have increased substantially the number of lawyers who pass the bar. *Id.*

7. *See* Deborah L. Rhode, *In the Interests of Justice* 93 (2003).

ties in colonial and in nineteenth and early twentieth century America. Contemporary rates of United States court filings are in the same range as Canada, Australia, New Zealand, England, Denmark, and Israel.[8] The number of civil trials in U.S federal courts have dropped by half over the last four decades, and the number in state courts has also declined.[9]

Nor is it clear that rates of filings are an accurate measure of cultural combativeness or legal hypochondria. Over ninety-five percent of American litigation occurs in the state courts, where uncontested divorces account for much of the recent caseload increases. Yet the higher rates of marital dissolution may be attributable less to legal vindictiveness or "spiritual mediocrity" than to individuals' longer lives and higher expectations for intimate relationships. Such cases hardly constitute a major drain on judicial resources; the average hearing in many family courts is under five minutes. While business leaders raise the most complaints about litigiousness, disputes between businesses are the fastest growing category of civil cases. Almost three-quarters of businesses file at least one claim as a plaintiff and nearly half file up to five in a given year; tort cases that trigger the greatest criticism, such as personal injury and product liability claims, are declining.[10]

The other most frequently cited evidence for America's undue litigiousness relies on unrepresentative examples—disputes that are too big for courts, disputes that are too small, and disputes that shouldn't be disputes at all. The first category includes Jarndyce-like litigation that leaves endless paper trails and makes lawyers the major beneficiaries of the disputes they orchestrate. At the other end of the spectrum are the "trivial pursuits": football fans suing referees, beauty contestants suing each other, Cracker Jack purchasers denied a prize; students suing dates who stood them up, and prison inmates seeking to get chunky rather than smooth peanut butter.[11] In the third category are grievances that critics would prefer not to validate as disputes, much less legal disputes, such as the $350,000 damages claim by a 24–year–old man against his mother and father for improper parenting; the $67 million claim against a dry cleaner for a lost pair of pants; or the multimillion dollar award against McDonald's for injuries from hot coffee that a customer spilled.[12] Since litigants do not bear the expenses of the judicial system, the social costs of litigating even meritorious but minor claims may exceed their private

8. Burke, *supra* note 3, at 3; Rhode, "Frivolous Litigation," *supra* note 3, at 456–57; Herbert Kritzer, "Lawyer Fees and Lawyer Behavior in Litigation: What Does the Empirical Literature Really Say?," 80 *Tex. L Rev.* 1943, 1981 (2002).

9. Michael Grey, "The Vanishing Trial," *Business Week*, April 30, 2007, at 38. In the 21 states for which data is available, civil jury trials dropped by 40% between 1976 and 2004. *Id.*

10. Stephen C. Dillard, "Litigation Nation," *Wall St. J.*, Nov 25–26, 2006, at A9; Paul Davies, "Plaintiffs' Lawsuits Against

Companies Sharply Decline," *Wall St. J.*, Aug. 26–27, 2006, at A1; "Fighting with Footnotes," ABA J., Feb., 2007, at 42 (noting survey findings of 79 percent decline in federal tort filings and 31 percent decline in state filings).

11. *See* sources cited in Rhode, "Frivolous Litigation," *supra* note 3, at 447–48; and *Interests of Justice*, *supra* note 7, at 120–24.

12. Hansen v. Hansen, 608 P.2d 364 (Colo.App.1979); Andrea Stone, "Pants Suit: Ruling Goes to the Cleaners," *U.S.A. Today*, June 26, 2007, at 3A; note 13 *infra*.

benefits and create what economists view as an excessive incentive to litigate.

Such claims again demand closer scrutiny. Isolated anecdotes do not establish that America has exceptional numbers of frivolous suits or that they occupy a substantial amount of judicial time. Exceptional compared with what? Historical and cross-cultural research reveals comparable claims: a nineteenth century peasant suit for return of sunflower seeds to feed a pet crow, a 1965 Belgrade court coping with 9,000 slander suits.[13] What constitutes frivolity is often in the eye of the beholder, and media portraits can often be misleading.

A textbook illustration involves the multimillion dollar McDonald's case, which to most journalists served as an all-purpose indictment of the legal profession and legal process: an avaricious lawyer paraded a petty incident before an out-of-control jury and extracted an absurd recovery. Newspaper editorials, radio talk shows, and magazine commentaries replayed endless variations on the theme summarized by the national Chamber of Commerce: "Is it fair to get a couple of million dollars from a restaurant just because you spilled hot coffee on yourself?" On closer examination, the question no longer looks rhetorical. The plaintiff, a 79–year–old woman, suffered acutely painful third-degree burns from 180 degree coffee. She spent eight days in the hospital and returned again for skin grafts. Only after McDonald's refused to reimburse her medical expenses did she bring suit. At trial, jurors learned of 700 other burn cases involving McDonald's coffee during the preceding decade. Although medical experts had warned that such high temperatures were causing serious injuries, the corporation's safety consultant had viewed the number of complaints as "trivial." McDonald's' coffee is served hotter than that at comparable restaurants, and physicians testified that at the lower temperature of other restaurants' coffee the victim's burns would not have been nearly as severe. The jury's verdict of $2.3 million was not an arbitrary choice. Its punitive damages award represented two days of coffee sales revenues, and the judge reduced the judgment to $640,000. To avoid an appeal, the plaintiff then settled the case for a smaller undisclosed amount. McDonald's put up warning signs and other fast-food chains adopted similar measures. While evaluations of this final result may vary, it was not the patently "ridiculous" travesty that media critics described.[14]

That is not to discount the problem of meritless or vastly exaggerated damage claims and the personal and financial costs they impose. In the dry cleaners case, for example, the defendant owners, Korean immigrants, had to spend over $100,000 in legal costs after their proposed settlement offer $12,000 was rejected. Although they won in court, they may have lost in life; they had to shut down their cleaners in the aftermath of the suit.[15] Yet

13. Deborah L. Rhode, "The Rhetoric of Professional Reform," 45 *Md. L. Rev.* 274, 278 (1986).

14. Rhode, *In the Interests of Justice, supra* note 7, at 121–22. For other examples of exaggerated or false media claims, see Levin, *supra* note 3, at C1, C5.

15. Stone, supra note 12, at 3A. For discussion of the psychological costs of litigation, see Luther T. Munford, "The Peace-as is clear from the discussion of frivolous cases in Chapter IV, the boundary between vindictiveness and vindication is often difficult to draw, and disproportionate media coverage of large recoveries distorts public perceptions.[16] For every legal dispute that critics believe shouldn't have been a dispute, there may be countless other grievances that they would acknowledge as legitimate claims, but that remain unremedied due to the financial and other personal costs of formal proceedings. Claims about Americans' over-reliance on law must be evaluated against the evidence of unmet legal need discussed below.

A more productive debate over litigiousness will require a reformulation of its framework. Before leaping to categorical conclusions that Americans rely too heavily on law, litigation, or lawyers, we need to rethink certain factual and normative questions. How much are we prepared to pay for due process? How does law compare with other demands on our social resources? What are the alternatives to legal solutions? Are law and lawyers handling public needs in the most cost-effective manner? Which individuals and what interests aren't being adequately served? What institutional changes would be necessary to provide efficient and "just" resolutions of disputes or to prevent them from arising in the first instance?

Too Much Law/Too Much Expense

A related concern is that American society in general and business in particular suffer from too much law, which is too complicated, too costly, and too often ineffective. Over the last quarter century, regulation has rapidly increased in areas such as employment, environmental hazards, health and safety, financial institutions, education, intellectual property, and family life. Not only do we have more law, the law we have is more pervasive. Law intrudes into more areas of personal and commercial life and is not always a welcome guest. In the aftermath of disasters like Hurricane Katrina, courts are often inundated with lawsuits, and the spectacle of well-off lawyers profiting from others' miseries adds to public distrust.[17] The concerns are captured in cartoons such as the *New Yorker* portrait of a well-dressed lawyer with a cat on his shoulder confronting a dog. As he hands the dog some documents, he announces: "We're slapping you with a stress suit, pal."[18]

Concerns about the price of legal processes are widely shared. Over four-fifths of surveyed Americans believe that litigation is too slow and too costly, and about two-thirds think that lawsuits are damaging the country's economy.[19] In assessing such concerns, it is important to separate two

maker Test: Designing Legal Rights to Reduce Legal Warfare," 12 *Harvard Negotiation L. Rev.* 377, 384–389 (2007).

16. Myron Levin, "Coverage of Big Awards for Plaintiffs Helps Distort View of Legal System," *Los Angeles Times*, Aug. 15, 2005, at C1.

17. Laura Parker, "After Katrina, Courts Are Flooded By Lawsuits," *USA Today*, Jan. 16, 2006, at 1.

18. *See* Philip K. Howard, *The Death of Common Sense: How Law Is Suffocating America* (1995). *See also* Howard, *The Lost Art of Drawing the Line* (2001).

19. Robert A. Kagan, *Adversarial Legalism: The American Way of Law* 142–43

related but distinct questions. First, are the total costs of legal liability excessive in comparison with their benefits and are they a threat to American economic health? Second, are the transaction costs of resolving particular types of legal claims excessive, given the value they provide and the alternatives that could be devised?

Although we lack reliable assessments of the total costs of civil liability, some informed calculations are available for the tort system. Most figures are far lower than most popular debate assumes, and do not reveal a substantial effect on economic productivity. For example, Brookings Institution research estimates that tort liability could represent no more than two percent of the total costs of United States goods and services, an amount "highly unlikely" to have a substantial affect on American competitiveness.[20] Moreover, many critics of the costs of legalization fail to acknowledge the benefits. For example, commentators often complain that products cost too much or unnecessary medical tests are performed because of liability expenses. John Stossell in the *Wall Street Journal* asserts that "every football helmet costs $100 more because of lawsuits," and, that some "financially strapped schools no longer have football programs. The kids play in the streets. Is that safer?" Stossell wonders.[21] But what he doesn't wonder is how many students play other sports that are safer, or how many serious head injuries have been avoided due to helmet redesign. In commenting on the frequency of business litigation noted earlier, another *Wall Street Journal* op-ed put the question: "Are these statistics a confirmation of America's vicious, tail-chasing lawsuit crisis? Or are they a vote of high confidence in the judicial system as a means of enforcing contracts, safeguarding intellectual property, and stopping fraud?"[22] It is also important to ask whether eye-popping estimates of the "cost of the tort system" represents the transaction costs alone or, as is more common, includes the damages paid. Counting the damages as a "cost" of the tort system assumes that compensating victims for their injuries is the mark of an inefficient legal system rather than an efficient one.

A related concern about the expense of litigation is that undue risks of liability and excessive insurance premiums cause businesses not to distribute valuable products and force doctors to shift their practice location, change their specialty, or order unnecessary medical tests. Yet while some concern is clearly warranted, many commentators believe that the extent of the problem is often overstated. The exodus of doctors appears confined to a few geographic areas and a few fields like obstetrics. On the average, only about three percent of doctors' revenue goes to cover malpractice premiums, an amount not self-evidently excessive or likely to cause major career changes.[23] Most research has not found a systematic relationship between

---

(2001); Levin, *supra* note 16, at C5.

20. Robert E. Litan, "The Liability Explosion and American Trade Performance: Myths and Realities," *Tort Law and the Public.*

21. John Stossell, "Protect Us From Legal Vultures," *Wall Street Journal*, Jan. 2, 1996, at A8.

22. Dillard, *supra* note 10, at A9.

23. Peter Ostler, Julie Appleby, & Martin Kasindorf, "Hype Outraces Facts in Mal-

insurance premium increases and withdrawals from practice. The most recent comprehensive study by the Harvard School of Public Health concluded that the malpractice system "performs reasonably well in its function of separating claims without merit from those with merit and compensating the latter." Meritorious claims outnumber non-meritorious claims by two to one. Only three percent of the surveyed claims involved no adverse outcomes from medical care, and of those that experts judged to have no compensable injuries, only a handful received recoveries.[24] Studies of "defensive medicine" suggest that liability risks have led to both desirable *and* excessive precautions, and most find that unnecessary procedures are relatively infrequent, partly due to cost constraints imposed by managed care.[25] While product withdrawals have sometimes been a major problem, as in the case of vaccines for childhood illnesses, in other instances, litigation has resulted in the removal of major safety risks. Obvious examples include the tragedies prevented from toxic shock syndrome, flammable pajamas, and Dalkon shields.[26]

In short, whether the costs of additional litigation is worth the expenses involves complex value judgments. As Lawrence Friedman points out: "the benefits [of legal claims], to be sure, are often quite intangible and immeasurable: social justice, expanded opportunities for women and minorities, expansion of civil liberties, fair procedures within institutions, limits on government. Who would deny that these are significant gains? Whether they are worth the costs is a question that models and equations cannot answer."[27]

Recent increases in the reach and volume of law also reflect broader cultural needs, many of which are by no means unique to America. As societies become more technologically sophisticated and as patterns of life become more interdependent, the necessity of legal regulation becomes correspondingly greater. In many Western industrialized countries, improvements in the standard of living have led to increased expectations about the role of legal and governmental institutions in maintaining that standard. So, for example, industrial accidents, discriminatory conduct, and inadequacies in social services that were once accepted as a matter of course now prompt demands for remedial action. Throughout the last century, many societies have increased their expectations for what Fried-

---

practice Debate," *USA Today,* March 5, 2003, at A1.

24. David M. Studdert, et al., "Claims, Errors and Compensation Payments on Medical Malpractice Litigation, New England J. Medicine, May 11, 2006, at 2024, discussed in Jeffrey B. Bloom, Disproving Frivolous Myth," *Nat'l L. J.,* July 3, 2006, at 26.

25. Kagan, *supra* note 19, at 274 n. 28; Michelle M. Mello & Troyen A. Brennan, "Deterrence of Medical Errors: Theory and Evidence for Malpractice Reform," 80 *Tex. L. Rev.* 1595, 1606–09 (2002).

26. For unsafe products, *see* Peter A. Bell & Jeffrey O'Connell, *Accidental Justice: The Dilemmas of Tort Law* 189 (1997); Andrew D. Dyer, Todd E. Hymstead, & N. Craig Smith, "Dow Corning Corporation: Product Stewardship, Cases on Leadership, Ethics, and Organizational Integrity: A Strategic Perspective," 298 (Lynn Sharp Paine, ed., 1996).

27. Lawrence Friedman, "Litigation and Society," 15 *Annual Rev. Soc.* 17, 26–27 (1989).

man calls "Total Justice."[28] The sense is that individuals should be protected from an increasing array of harms and should be compensated for injuries and injustices that have not been prevented.

Moreover, as commentators since Alexis de Tocqueville have noted, the United States has always placed more reliance on law and courts to solve social problems than most other societies. Americans traditionally have distrusted centralized power, and have checked its exercise through a system of privately initiated lawsuits and judicial review. This culture's individualist ideology places a high priority on civil rights and liberties. Litigation offers protection for fundamental values such as freedom of speech, due process, and equal opportunity that are central to our cultural heritage and constitutional traditions. Privately-financed lawsuits are also a financially attractive way of enforcing public mandates and providing social safety nets without spending taxpayer dollars on legal costs. Much of this nation's environmental, antitrust, securities, consumer, and antidiscrimination regulation occurs through efforts of public interest and plaintiffs' lawyers. The same can be said of important conservative victories in recent years, such as rollbacks of affirmative action and the establishment of constitutional gun rights. As political scientist Robert Kagan notes, in the United States "demands for total justice and regulatory protections have been filtered through a political culture that mistrusts 'big' government and resists high taxes . . . [and a] political system that lacks strong national law enforcement, regulatory, medical care and welfare bureaucracies."[29] Americans turn to courts for needs that other countries meet through administrative measures, such as guaranteed health and no-fault wage replacement insurance systems. Without broader changes in cultural values and political structures, curtailing the role of law may be difficult to achieve.

Alternative Frameworks

Would the United States be better off if it relied less on law and lawyers to address social needs? As the preceding discussion made clear, that is a complex question, requiring complicated and contested tradeoffs. However, critics from all points on the political spectrum tend to agree on one point: American litigation is not a cost-effective way of achieving certain remedial objectives.

The most commonly cited problems include under-compensation of victims, over-compensation of intermediaries (including lawyers), inadequate checks on fraudulent or other non-meritorious claims, and inconsistency and unpredictability in outcomes.[30] In the cases that go to trial, results are too often idiosyncratic and not well related to the extent of the plaintiff's injury and the defendant's culpability. Which side has the most

---

28. Lawrence Friedman, *Total Justice* (1994).

29. Robert A. Kagan, "Do Lawyers Cause Adversarial Legalism?: A Preliminary Inquiry," 19 *Law Soc. Inquiry* 1, 8 (1994).

30. Kagan, *Adversarial Legalism, supra* note 19, at 146; Charles Silver, "Does Civil Justice Cost Too Much?," 80 *Tex. L. Rev.* 2073, 2076 (2002).

effective lawyers, whether the case is filed in a "plaintiff-friendly" region, and whether the defendant appears to have a "deep pocket" all play a critical role. These idiosyncrasies mute the deterrent value of litigation. A further problem involves the amount in recoveries that goes to compensate lawyers rather than victims. In cases of automobile accidents, almost fifty percent of the payments by insurance companies end up in the hands of attorneys for both sides. In other tort cases, the transaction costs are even higher, averaging over sixty percent.[31] Such problems have sparked a wide variety of reform proposals, some of which are considered in the materials on non-lawyer services in Chapter XII, Regulation of the Market, and in Part B below.

QUESTIONS

1. Do you believe America has "too much law, too little justice?" Both? Neither? What, if any, problems would you identify in the current system?

2. If you were a bar association leader, how would you respond to the claims about America's oversupply of law and lawyers? Would your response be different if you were a leader of a consumer organization?

B. PROBLEMS OF ACCESS: THE UNDERLAWYERED SOCIETY

Legal Services Corporation: Documenting the Justice Gap in America.

1, 4, 9, 11, 15, 18 (2005).

This report uses a variety of approaches to document the civil legal needs of low-income individuals and families and to quantify *necessary access to civil legal assistance*—that is, the level of assistance that would be required across the nation to respond appropriately to those needs. The civil legal needs of low-income people involve essential human needs, such as protection from abusive relationships, safe and habitable housing, access to necessary health care, disability payments to help lead independent lives, family law issues including child support and custody actions, and relief from financial exploitation. The difference between the current level of legal assistance and the level which is necessary to meet the needs of low-income Americans is the "Justice Gap."

HISTORICAL BACKGROUND

... A major step (in assessing the "Justice Gap") was the Comprehensive Legal Needs Study funded by the American Bar Association and released in 1994. Conducted by the Institute for Survey Research at Temple University

---

31. In the Rand Institute for Civil Justice Studies, plaintiffs in asbestos cases received only 42 percent of total spending on litigation and payouts. Stephen J. Carroll et. al., *Asbestos Litigation* (2005). That rate is consistent with earlier studies.

and based on well-established, rigorous social science methodology, the study was based upon more than 3,000 interviews with a randomly selected sample of low-and moderate-income Americans.

The ABA study documented the existence of a major gap between the civil legal needs of low income people and the legal help they received. Among its findings were the following:

> • Nationally, on the average, low-income households experienced approximately one civil legal need per year.

> • Only a small portion of these legal needs resulted in legal help of any type. Help was received from a legal aid provider or the private bar for roughly one in five of all problems identified.

The ABA study remains the most recent *national* study of the legal needs of low-income Americans and the extent to which they are or are not met. . . .

Principal Findings on Current Legal Needs and the Justice Gap

Taken together, these different methodologies confirm the existence of a major gap between the legal needs of low-income people and the legal help that they receive.

> • For every client served by an LSC-funded program, at least one person who sought help was turned down because of insufficient resources. [One million cases a year must be rejected for this reason].

> • Only a very small percentage of the legal problems experienced by low-income people (one in five or less) are addressed with the assistance of either a private attorney (pro bono or paid) or a legal aid lawyer.

> • Despite the changes in legal aid delivery over the last decade, a majority of legal aid lawyers still work in LSC-funded programs. The per capita ratio of legal aid attorneys funded by all sources to the low-income population is a tiny fraction of the ratio of private attorneys providing personal civil legal services to the general population. . . .

Continuing Documentation of Legal Needs

Analysis and Comparison of Recent State Legal Needs Studies

[Between 2000 and 2005, nine states had examined legal problems of low-income residents.] Key points of comparison are as follows.

> • The nine state studies found that low-income households experience a per-household average of legal needs ranging up to more than three legal needs per year

> • All nine recent state studies found that only a very small percentage of the legal problems experienced by low-income people (fewer than one in five) is addressed with the assistance of a private or legal aid lawyer.

- Taken together, the recent state studies indicate that a large percentage of low-income people experiencing a problem with a legal dimension do not understand that there may be a legal solution.

- The recent state studies show that a majority of low-income people either do not know about the availability of free legal services or do not understand that they are financially eligible for them.

- Finally, analysis of these studies shows that even if the problems considered are limited to those considered to be "very important" by the household experiencing them and understood by the household to call for legal help, a large majority of the problems are not addressed with the help of a lawyer.

Comparison of the recent state study findings to those in the 1994 ABA study confirms the continuing validity of the ABA study and indicates that, if anything, the ABA study actually *under-represents* the current level of need.

TABLE 3: Legal Needs

STATE	Average number of legal needs in preceding year per low-income household
Oregon	3.2
Vermont	1.1
Connecticut	2.7
Washington	2.9
Massachusetts	2.4
Tennessee	3.3
Illinois	1.7
Montana	3.5
State	**Average number of new legal needs in preceding year per low-income individual**
New Jersey	1.8

TABLE 4: Legal Help[32]

STATE	
Oregon	18.1% help received
Vermont	9% help received
Connecticut	10% help sought
Washington	12% help received
Massachusetts	15.4% help sought
Tennessee	29% Help sought
Illinois	16% help received

32. Editors' note: this table reflects a simplified version of Table 4; the figures for Tennessee refer to the largest problem encountered.

Montana	16.4% help received
New Jersey	16% help received

Findings: Importance of Problems

Several of the recent state studies also collected data about the respondents' assessment of the seriousness of the problem involved and/or the respondents' understanding of whether a lawyer was necessary to resolve it, yielding data about percentages of the most immediate serious problems.

Montana: Respondents characterized 53 percent of the problems identified as "currently important" and 91 percent as "important."

New Jersey: 84 percent of people with a legal problem thought the problem was highly serious and important. 52 percent thought that they needed a lawyer to help with the problem.

Washington: Respondents characterized 56 percent of their legal problems as "extremely important" and 93 percent as "important." ...

Findings: Why People Did Not Seek Help

Seven of the state studies explored the reasons why so many people with a legal need did not seek legal help, but instead either did nothing or sought to resolve the problem on their own. Key reasons emerging from these studies are as follows:

- *Lack of understanding that the problem has a legal dimension and potential solution.* The predominant reasons given by respondents were a sense that getting a lawyer would not help and that it would cost too much. Many responded that "there was nothing to be done" or that "it was not a legal problem, just the way things are."

- *Low awareness of legal aid for civil matters.* Many respondents gave as their reason for not seeking legal help that they were unable to afford a lawyer, even though most respondent households were financially eligible for free legal assistance under LSC guidelines. Most of the studies specifically asked the respondent whether they knew of a place that provides free legal services and whether they would be eligible for free services. All of these states found low awareness on the part of the respondents that they might be eligible for free legal assistance. The lowest percentages of people knowing about free legal aid were in Tennessee (21 percent), Illinois (23 percent), and New Jersey (26 percent).

Attorneys Per Capita

Legal Aid Lawyers Compared to Private Lawyers

The count shows that despite the expansion of non-LSC funded programs in the past decade, a substantial majority of attorneys serving the poor still work in LSC-funded programs: there were 3,845 lawyers in LSC-funded programs (this figure includes all lawyers in the program, including those funded with state, private and other funds) and an estimated 2,736 in programs that do not receive LSC funding. The LSC-funded network thus remains the primary source of civil legal aid for low-income Americans.

The number of legal aid attorneys available to serve the poor provides a simple demonstration of the justice gap when compared to the number of attorneys serving the general public. The number of attorneys in private practice can be presumed to reflect a market response to the legal needs of the U.S. population. Nationally, there are *more than ten times* the number of private attorneys providing personal civil legal services to the general public as there are legal aid attorneys serving the poor. While there is only one legal aid lawyer (including all sources of funding) per 6,861 low income people in the country, there is one lawyer providing personal civil legal services for every 525 people in the general population.

Conclusion: Providing Necessary Access to Civil Legal Assistance

While the available attorney comparison suggests there may be a much deeper problem, the more conservative "one-in-five-receive-help" data from the scientific legal needs studies appears to be the best benchmark to gauge the current size of the justice gap, and suggests what necessary access will require. Assuming that the other partners at least maintain their proportionate levels of efforts as the nation moves toward "necessary access," the one-in-five measure suggests that the *federal baseline share* must be at least five times greater than it is now, or $1.6 billion. It is essential that LSC move toward the necessary access level in firm, measured strides, designed to reach it (adjusted for inflation) and close the justice gap as quickly as possible. As an initial critical step, there must at least be enough funding to serve all of those *currently* requesting help from LSC grantees.

NOTES

In theory, access to justice is difficult to oppose. In practice, however, there is considerable fuzziness to the concept. How much "naming, blaming, and claiming" do we want to encourage and how much are we prepared to invest in that enterprise? There is broad agreement that quality of justice should not depend on ability to pay, but little consensus on an alternative. Although some commentators argue for "equal access," such claims raise the question R. H. Tawney once posed about equal opportunity generally:

> it is unclear what would terrify supporters most, "the denial of the principle or the attempt to apply it." Given the broad range of problems that could be considered legal, and the wide disparity of skills among lawyers, any serious attempt to equalize access would require massive public subsidies. More modest demands to expand, if not fully

equalize, access usually skirt the sticky points. How much are we prepared to pay for process? How do legal services compare with other demands on our collective resources?[33]

How to measure legal needs is also problematic. Even the most carefully designed studies, although useful for many purposes, have inherent limitations. First, they measure only subjective perceptions, and many individuals may be unaware of rights and remedies. For example, parties may not know that they are entitled to certain benefits, that their consumer loans fail to meet legal requirements, or that their apartment fails to meet housing code requirements. Most legal needs surveys also leave out collective problems with which public interest groups are concerned (e.g., environmental risks, consumer safety protections, school financing, or voting rights). A focus only on individual grievances can deflect attention from the structural forces that may prevent their recognition and redress.

Moreover, counting problems does not of itself provide an adequate profile of unmet needs because no distinctions are made between urgent concerns and minor grievances, between concerns that require extensive assistance and those that demand only minimal help, or between matters that call for attorney expertise and matters that could be addressed through less expensive means, such as aid from court ombudsmen and lay specialists. Legal needs research has also been criticized for assuming that the solution is more of the same—more access to law, lawyers, and judicial proceedings. Yet as Marc Galanter has questioned, "is the utopia of access to justice a condition in which all disputes are fully adjudicated?"[34] Moreover, access to the justice system will not necessarily bring disadvantaged parties closer to justice in a substantive sense. "Poor peoples' courts" that handle family, landlord/tenant, small claims, and minor criminal proceedings are often overburdened and understaffed. And in many contexts, the "haves" are often still likely to come out ahead, given other advantages apart from lawyers, such as the resources to take risks, tolerate delay, structure transactions in light of potential disputes, and lobby for the reversal of unfavorable legal decisions[35]

Law, of course, is not the only context in which "haves" enjoy an advantage. Yet as the following discussion of the right to legal counsel suggests, the ideal of equal access to justice occupies a special place in our governance structure. The gap between the aspirations and the operation of our legal system has prompted efforts along three basic lines: strategies that reduce the need for legal intervention and assistance; initiatives that minimize the cost of legal procedures and services; and attempts to expand the provision of subsidized aid.

The first strategy involves simplification or modification of legal rules or processes. Plain–English statutes, no-fault insurance schemes, standardized forms for simple wills and uncontested divorces, and automatic wage

33. Rhode, *Interests of Justice, supra* note 7, at 131.

34. Marc Galanter, "Justice in Many Rooms," in *Access to Justice and the Welfare State* 145, 150–151 (Mauro Cappelletti ed. 1981).

35. Marc Galanter, "Why the Haves Come Out Ahead: Speculations on the Limits of Legal Change," 9 *Law & Soc. Rev.* 95 (1974).

withholding for obligations such as child support payments are examples of efforts to minimize individuals' need for legal assistance. A second approach is to reduce the cost of such assistance through greater reliance on hotlines, computer programs, on-line assistance, qualified nonlawyers, courthouse facilitators, unbundled legal services, and alternative dispute resolution procedures that do not require lawyers. A third approach is to expand access to lawyers through public subsidies and private pro bono contributions. The materials that follow explore such strategies in greater depth.

C. THE RIGHT TO LEGAL SERVICES

NOTES

In this country, demands for access to legal assistance have drawn on a number of constitutional provisions: the Sixth Amendment guarantee of assistance of counsel for criminal defendants, the Fifth and Fourteenth Amendment due process clauses, and the Fourteenth Amendment equal protection clause.

Under early English common law, defendants in felony prosecutions except for treason were not allowed to have legal representation at trial. The Sixth Amendment was intended to eliminate that prohibition in federal cases; 12 of the original 13 states also eliminated it in their courts. It was not, however, until the mid-twentieth century that courts began interpreting constitutional guarantees to require counsel for criminal defendants who could not afford it. Prior to that point, some federal and state statutes authorized appointment of counsel in capital trials and courts sometimes asserted inherent authority to appoint counsel with or without compensation in other felony cases. But such appointments often occurred only after arraignment, when 70 to 80 percent of defendants had already pleaded guilty and others had made incriminating statements to the police.[36]

In the l930s, the inadequacies of this system began to attract greater judicial concern. In the notorious Scottsboro case, the Court reversed the conviction of two indigent blacks who were accused of raping white women and afforded only pro forma legal representation. In so holding, the Supreme Court reasoned that a state's failure to provide adequate legal assistance could violate the due process clause under certain circumstances. Writing for the majority, Justice Sutherland noted that the "right to be heard would in many cases be of little avail if it did not comprehend the right to be heard by counsel." *Powell v. Alabama,* 287 U.S. 45, 68–69 (1932). Several years later, the Court interpreted the Sixth Amendment to

---

36.   Rhode, *Access to Justice, supra* note 3; Emory Brownell, *Legal Aid in the United States* 35, 84 (1951).

mandate counsel for indigent defendants in federal criminal cases. *Johnson v. Zerbst,* 304 U.S. 458 (1938).

Over the next several decades, the Court overturned a number of state court convictions on due process grounds where defense attorneys were not provided and where the proceedings were complicated, the penalties were severe, or the defendants were particularly ill-equipped to represent themselves due to youth, illiteracy, or unfamiliarity with the English language. Under *Betts v. Brady,* 316 U.S. 455, 462 (1942), the test was whether "fundamental fairness" demanded counsel's assistance. Finally, in 1963, in response to a prisoner's handwritten *in forma pauperis* petition, the Supreme Court held that any indigent defendant in a state felony proceeding was entitled to an attorney. *Gideon v. Wainwright,* 372 U.S. 335, 344 (1963). It seemed an "obvious truth" that the ideal of insuring that "every defendant stands equal before the law ... cannot be realized if the poor man charged with a crime has to face his accusers without a lawyer to assist him." *Id.* The Court subsequently extended the guarantee of court-appointed counsel to juveniles, *In re Gault,* 387 U.S. 1 (1967), and to defendants charged with misdemeanors or given suspended sentences if the ultimate disposition could result in incarceration. *Argersinger v. Hamlin,* 407 U.S. 25 (1972); *Alabama v. Shelton,* 535 U.S. 654 (2002). In other proceedings involving the possibility of imprisonment, such as probation revocation hearings, the Court left decisions about appointment of counsel to be made on a case by case basis. *Gagnon v. Scarpelli,* 411 U.S. 778 (1973).

The Court was not, however, prepared to recognize a similar right in civil matters involving fundamental rights.[37] In *Lassiter v. Department of Social Services,* 452 U.S. 18 (1981), a woman imprisoned for second degree murder lost parental rights to her 3–year–old son after a hearing at which she lacked assistance of counsel. Applying the due process standards of *Mathews v. Eldridge,* 424 U.S. 319, 335 (1976) and *Gagnon v. Scarpelli,* 411 U.S. 778 (1973), the Court held that decisions about whether to provide counsel in the absence of a "potential deprivation of physical liberty" should depend on evaluation of three factors: the private interest at stake, the government's interest, and the risk that lack of counsel at the civil hearing would result in an erroneous decision. 452 U.S. at 26–27, 31. Under those standards, a majority of Justices found no reversible error in *Lassiter,* because the assistance of counsel would not have made a "determinable difference." Given the state's strong factual case and the absence of

---

37. One potentially fruitful line of analysis began when the Court struck down filing fees in divorce cases on the ground that such fees restricted access to the courts. Boddie v. Connecticut, 401 U.S. 371 (1971). But in subsequent decisions involving filing fees for bankruptcy and welfare claims, the Court distinguished *Boddie* as applicable only to circumstances where fundamental interests were at issue and where judicial procedures offered the only means of resolving disputes over those interests. United States v. Kras, 409 U.S. 434 (1973); Ortwein v. Schwab, 410 U.S. 656 (1973). For critiques of these decisions *see, e.g.,* David Luban, *Lawyers and Justice: An Ethical Study* 243–266 (1988). For a more recent Supreme Court decision requiring waiver of costs in cases involving an appeal of a decree terminating parental rights, see M.L.B. v. S.L.J., 519 U.S. 102 (1996).

"troublesome" issues of law, the failure to provide a lawyer did not make the procedure "fundamentally unfair." 452 U.S. at 32, 33.

A related series of equal protection decisions evolved in similar fashion. In decisions before *Gideon*, the Court required states to provide a free trial transcript to indigent appellate defendants, and to provide counsel to indigents appealing by right from a criminal conviction. *Griffin v. Illinois,* 351 U.S. 12 (1956); *Douglas v. California*, 372 U.S. 353 (1963). These cases raised the prospect of an equal protection argument for the right to legal assistance in civil cases. However, in *Ross v. Moffitt,* 417 U.S. 600 (1974), the Court found no constitutionally protected right to counsel's assistance in optional criminal appeals in federal court, and in *Pennsylvania v. Finley,* 481 U.S. 551 (1987), it extended that reasoning to post-conviction proceedings in state court. What is true for optional criminal appeals is *a fortiori* true for optional civil claims.

The unwillingness to recognize a right to counsel in civil matters has attracted criticism on several grounds. One line of critique challenges the results in cases such as *Lassiter* under the Court's own analytical framework. From this perspective, some civil proceedings implicate interests as significant as those at issue in many misdemeanor proceedings where counsel is required. The rationale for subsidized legal assistance seems particularly strong in cases like *Lassiter,* where crucial interests are at issue, legal standards are imprecise and subjective, proceedings are formal and adversarial, and resources between the parties are grossly imbalanced. 452 U.S. 18, 35 (1981) (Blackmun, J., dissenting); *id.* at 59 (Stevens, J., dissenting).

Some commentators have made broader claims, and have argued for recognition of a right to counsel in civil cases affecting fundamental rights. Under this line of analysis, access to legal assistance is necessary for access to the legal system; access to the legal system is necessary to realize equality before the law, and equality before the law is necessary to the legitimacy of our form of government.[38] As the Supreme Court has itself recognized, the right to "sue and defend" is a right "conservative of all other rights, and lies at the foundation of orderly government." *Chambers v. Baltimore & Ohio R.R.,* 207 U.S. 142, 148 (1907). More specifically, legal assistance fosters certain values central to our concept of a just society. Not only does it serve the instrumental function noted in *Lassiter* of preventing erroneous decisions, but it also promotes "self respect and a sense of having [one's] will counted in societal decisions."[39] Many European countries have recognized as much, and the ABA has endorsed a resolution

---

38. Luban, *supra* note 37, at 263–64. *See also* Rhode, *Access to Justice, supra* note 3; David S. Udell & Rebekah Diller, "Access to the Courts: An Essay for the Georgetown University Law Center Conference on Independence of the Courts," 95 *Geo L. J.* 1127, 1153 (2007). A National Coalition for a Civil Right to Counsel has organized around the need for a "Civil *Gideon*."

39. Frank Michelman, "The Supreme Court and Litigation Access Fees: The Right to Protect One's Rights—Part I," 1973 *Duke L.J.* 1153, 1172–1173.

calling for governmental authorities to provide counsel to low-income individuals in civil cases where crucial interests are at stake.[40]

Such arguments for assistance raise a number of a concerns. Could such rights be kept within economically manageable limits? In a country that has declined to insure adequate housing or health care for all its residents, should law be a higher priority? Suppose parties had a right to counsel but, as is true in indigent criminal defense, legal assistance programs had nowhere close to adequate funding? Under such circumstances, if clients were unwilling to accept quick settlements, the programs would be unable to provide meaningful representation. As the history of legal services here and abroad makes clear, rights to legal counsel coupled with inadequate resources for implementation produce the illusion rather than the reality of effective assistance of counsel.

In response to such concerns, some commentators have noted that many European nations have recognized rights to legal services that are limited through eligibility criteria, sliding fee scales, and restrictions on the fees recoverable by subsidized counsel.[41] As discussion in Part E notes, legal aid programs in this country also screen cases to stay within their limited budgets. Similar standards could be established for a broadened right to civil legal assistance, or at least a right in certain categories of civil cases where crucial interests are at issue and the claimant has a reasonable chance of prevailing.

Such a right to civil legal assistance raises broader distributional concerns about the appropriate allocation of resources in a good society. Consider Richard Abel's arguments for equalizing the distribution of legal services, and David Luban's analysis of equal justice under law. Is that ideal a realistic societal aspiration? What would be its policy implications?

Richard L. Abel, "Legal Services"

Handbook of Applied Sociology 417–421 (M. Micklin & M. Olsen, eds., 1981).

Equality in the distribution of legal services has a value beyond that of enhancing the welfare of the unrepresented or underrepresented. The very integrity of the U.S. legal system as an adversary system depends upon equal representation of all parties. The legitimacy of contemporary law rests on the assumption that optimally efficient allocations of scarce resources are produced by parties who freely negotiate with each other on the basis of equal information about the law and equal competence to use it. The adversarial model of litigation—whether in a civil action or a

40. Martha F. Davis, "We Need a Civil 'Gideon,'" *Nat'l. L. J.*, Aug. 7, 2006, at 26; Airey v. Ireland, 2 European Court Human Rights 305, 306–07 (1979) (requiring counsel where important interests are at stake and the complexity of the procedure or case made representation indispensable for effective access to the court); ABA Report to the House of Delegates No. 112A (2006).

41. Rhode, *Access to Justice, supra* note 3, at 117; Deborah L. Rhode, "In the Interests of Justice: A Comparative Perspective on Access to Legal Services and Accountability of the Legal Profession," 56 *Current Legal Problems* 93 (2003).

criminal prosecution—is grounded upon the belief that factual truth and fidelity to substantive and procedural rules are best achieved by partisan struggle between equal opponents, which at a minimum means opponents who are equally represented. Moreover, the theory of democratic pluralism assumes that all citizens are equally able to influence the making and application of laws. Given the influence of lawyers in U.S. politics, that assumption requires equal representation by lawyers before both the legislature and the executive at all levels of government.

David Luban, "Taking Out the Adversary: The Assault on Progressive Public–Interest Lawyers"
91 Calif. L. Rev. 209, 212 n. 9 (2003).

Critics will argue that access to justice is a concept with no real meaning because the level of access to lawyers that justice requires is impossible to specify. Does access mean every nonfrivolous litigable case should have a lawyer funded by the government? Such a notion raises two problems. First, it implies a higher level of access than even the wealthiest purchasers of legal services enjoy. Even wealthy clients have limited budgets and must pick and choose which cases to litigate. Second, the concept of a "litigable case" is inherently indeterminate. The point at which a dispute breaks through from the informal to the formal legal system depends in part on the cost of legal services; no dispute is intrinsically litigable or not. If lawyers were cost-free, then perhaps even extremely trivial disputes would migrate into the formal system. This hardly seems like a desirable state of affairs. Increasing the supply of free lawyers would undoubtedly drive up demand, so "access to justice" becomes a receding target.

Perhaps "access" ideally entails that every cost beneficial case should have a lawyer. Here, too, the concept is indeterminate: whether a case is cost beneficial depends on how expensive a lawyer is. Maybe a better approach is that every case that would be cost beneficial for a litigant to bring if the lawyer were charging normal market rates should have a lawyer. But this neglects the possibility that although the litigation is cost beneficial to the plaintiff, the total social costs of providing formal justice outweigh the benefit. Alternatively, access to justice could be defined in terms of access for any matter that concerns a significant interest of the litigant. This, however, seems too restrictive: surely, poor people should be able to use the formal system to redress grievances even if they do not involve major rights violations.

The definitional questions become even more vexing once we realize that lawyers can be useful for many law-related problems that do not involve litigation. A great many poor person's problems can be solved by a legally knowledgeable, articulate person making a few phone calls. But if the criterion of access means that everyone can obtain legal services whenever the services would be useful, we confront the fact that a good lawyer is an extremely useful person: a good lawyer is shrewd, adept at navigating the waters of institutional life, and prudent. Most of us could use one almost all the time, and this ideal of full access raises the nightmarish vision of everyone with their own personal general counsel accompanying them through daily life.

The conclusion of these arguments is that the ideal of access to justice—embodied most famously in the motto "Equal Justice Under Law" emblazoned on the Supreme Court building—threatens to land us on unacceptable slippery slopes under even the most plausible interpretations. But it is possible to cut those Gordian knots. Even if precise specification of equal justice under law eludes us, we know what equal justice is not. Creating legal institutions that can be navigated only by people with lawyers violates any meaningful interpretation of "equal justice under law" if large segments of the population cannot obtain a lawyer. Because lawyers are expensive, market-based distribution of legal services would exclude at least forty million people from access to legal institutions, and it follows that market-based distribution of legal services violates the equal-access ideal.... Our current system of subsidized legal services for the poor, however, is nearly indistinguishable from market-based distribution: it leaves 95 percent of poor people's legal needs unaddressed.... Whatever the definition of access to justice turns out to be, we are nowhere near it. And so any cutback or restriction in legal services from the little we do now represents a step in the wrong direction.

QUESTIONS

1. What is your view on the distribution of legal services? What if any reforms would you propose? How would you respond to critics? Does the adversary system presuppose that all parties have access to effective assistance of counsel?

2. Does the ideal of access to justice have determinate meaning? Would the standard endorsed by Luban or Abel be satisfied by the recommendations of the Legal Services Corporation or the American Bar Association as noted earlier? If not, what would be required and could it be made politically feasible?

D.   PUBLIC INTEREST LAW
PROBLEM 1

a) Two of the trustees of your environmental organization have asked you to challenge their city's plans to construct a baseball stadium on the only site that planners believe is economically feasible. The proposed stadium is necessary to attract a major league team, but its construction on that site would threaten crucial wetlands and an endangered wildlife habitat. If you file suit, you may be able to cause sufficient expense and delay to convince the team's owners to relocate in another city. Although you share the trustees' objections to the proposed development, you worry about the effects of opposition on the city's racial minorities and on your group's reputation as elitist and insensitive to such concerns. Various civil rights coalitions support the stadium as a way to increase inner-city jobs, expand tax revenues, build morale, and assist minority-owned businesses. Under the proposed plans, minority contractors, vending services, and professional firms (including lawyers, engineers, and architects) would receive a substantial share of the work connected with the stadium.

When you raise your concerns with your organization's board, the two trustees respond that your organization's mission is to protect environmental interests; it is up to the civil rights coalitions to address minority needs. As one individual puts it, "[W]ildlife has fewer and fewer places to go and paving over wetlands is an unacceptable way of providing cheap development sites."[42] The legal staff of your organization, however, feels that this is the wrong development plan to resist, and that they should spend scarce resources fighting toxic plant sites where their mission would be aligned with minority communities and other environmental justice organizations. How do you proceed?

b) You are the lawyer described in Shauna Marshall's article excerpted below. How do you proceed?

Shauna Marshall, "Mission Impossible?: Ethical Community Lawyering"

7 Clinical L. Rev. 147, 151–52 (2000).

[Susan was a legal aid housing lawyer for East Palo Alto, a low-income community.] ... At a macro level, Susan's goal was to help ensure that the community had a decent stock of affordable housing, particularly rental units. Some of her clients lived in large, dilapidated apartment buildings. One such building was located in one of the areas designated for redevelopment. Over the years Susan worked with and represented the tenants who lived in that building regarding issues of habitability. In fact, many of the tenants' habitability claims were still not completely settled and Susan was still actively representing them. Now, as part of the redevelopment plan, the city was going to acquire the building and have it torn down. In its place was going to be a shopping center with large warehouse retail outlets. Members of the City Council hoped the redevelopment project would bring employment opportunities to its residents along with badly needed tax revenues.

The tenants living in the building scheduled for demolition were entitled to relocation benefits. In fact, Susan as well as Jamie had conducted educational sessions about a tenant's right to relocation benefits when his property is demolished as part of a redevelopment plan. Susan had even

---

42. This hypothetical is based on a controversy over San Jose's proposed site for a stadium. The local chapters of the Sierra Club and the Audubon Society opposed the location. The quoted phrase is from Wetlands Committee Chairperson Tom Esperson in a Sierra Club Press Release (May 27, 1992).

helped other tenants in other locations obtain relocation benefits. When, however, it was time for this large complex to be torn down, the city was strapped for cash. Fearing a fiscal crisis which might threaten the entire redevelopment project, the city wanted to pay the tenants their benefits in installments. Many of the tenants objected to payment over time and wanted the lump sum to which they were entitled. Moreover, they wanted "their" lawyer Susan to represent them in their attempts to obtain full payment.

Susan, however, was concerned that the city did not have sufficient funds to pay these relocation benefits all at once. As she looked at the problem in the context of the larger community, she was not certain that she supported the tenants' objectives. But, these tenants had been her clients when she pursued habitability claims against their former, private landlord. In fact, some still were. Moreover, she had been a part of a public education program that informed them of their entitlement to full relocation payments. Could she now refuse to represent them because of her concerns for the city's financial health? After all, she was the only housing lawyer in town. . . .

Susan called a meeting of the tenants. She looked around the room. Almost all of the persons gathered were her clients, the tenants whom she had been representing in the habitability case. She explained to them what the city proposed. She tried to point out the pros and cons of the city's proposal. She did not express her opinion. The reaction of the tenants caught her off guard. They were not sympathetic toward the city's plight. Unlike tenants living in other areas designated for redevelopment, this group of tenants did not expect to relocate in East Palo Alto. Perhaps that fact led them not to have strong attachments to the community or to care too deeply about a successful redevelopment project. What Susan learned was that the tenants wanted full payment right away and they wanted her to represent them in their efforts to obtain those benefits.

Susan felt conflicted. She wanted to urge her clients, for the community's sake, to take the deal. Moreover, she feared that a challenge would just cause delays and put the city in a more precarious financial condition, making it even more difficult for her clients to collect any money.

What was her obligation to these tenants, her clients? To whom did Susan owe her loyalty? Who or what entities constitute the "community"? Should she urge the tenants to accept benefits over time? Was it not in the tenants' best interest for their advocate to zealously pursue full benefits?

NOTES

Although the term "public interest law" is relatively recent, the concept has its roots in earlier social movements including legal services for the poor, civil liberties, and civil rights.[43] The growth of an organized civil

43. Oliver A. Houck, "With Charity for All," 93 *Yale L.J.* 1415 (1984); Earl Johnson, *Justice and Reform: The Formative Years of the American Legal Services Program* (1978).

liberties movement began during World War I, when a small group of pacifists founded the American Union Against Militarism. It eventually spun off an organization that became the American Civil Liberties Union. Activities quickly broadened to include free speech and eventually to reproductive rights and anti-discrimination strategies. So too, America's first major civil rights organization, the National Association for the Advancement of Colored People, was founded in the early twentieth century by a small number of liberal activists. A brutal 1908 race riot in Springfield, Illinois prompted a group of predominantly white reformers to form an association that would focus on racial discrimination.[44] In 1939, the association spun off the NAACP Legal Defense Fund as a separate organization. Over the next several decades, the Fund orchestrated a systematic legal campaign against racial segregation and subordination. In the process, the Fund broadened its agenda to include related issues such as death penalty litigation. Other organizations, including the Lawyers' Committee for Civil Rights Under Law and the National Lawyers Guild, joined in the effort. These civil rights and civil liberties organizations served as models for other legal reform associations.[45]

During the late 1960s and early 1970s, a rise in political activism, together with a large increase in foundation founding, gave birth to new "public interest" legal groups. Judicial and legislative initiatives further encouraged this development. Test-case litigation became a more effective strategy as courts began liberalizing doctrines regarding ripeness, standing, and sovereign immunity, and as Congress began authorizing fee awards to "prevailing parties" in certain civil rights, consumer, environmental and analogous cases.[46]

Under the definition put forth by the Council for Public Interest Law (now the Alliance for Justice), such organizations qualified as "public interest" if they were tax-exempt non-profit groups that employed at least one attorney and devoted at least 30% of their total resources to the legal representation of previously unrepresented interests on matters of public policy.[47] By that definition, in the 1960s, there were approximately 23 public interest organizations with less than 50 full time attorneys in the

---

44. Charles Kellogg, *NAACP: A History of the National Association for the Advancement of Colored People* (1967).

45. *See* Richard Kluger, *Simple Justice* (1976); Mark Tushnet, *The NAACP's Legal Strategy Against Segregated Education, 1925–1950* (1987).

46. By the close of the 1980s, some 150 statutes authorized fee awards, and the California Supreme Court permitted recovery under a private attorney general theory. Nan Aron, *Liberty and Justice for All: Public Interest Law in the 1980's and Beyond* 55–56 (1989); Serrano v. Priest, 131 Cal.App.3d 188, 182 Cal.Rptr. 387 (1982).

47. Aron, *supra* note 46. In order to qualify for tax-exempt status, the organiza-

tion must: provide representation of a broad public interest rather than a private interest; structure its decision making through a board or committee representative of the public interest; receive financial support primarily from grants and contributions; accept only cases where the individuals or groups involved cannot afford, or do not have sufficient financial stakes to justify, the retention of private counsel. They may, however, accept fees from their clients under some circumstances. In private-party litigation between parties able to retain private counsel, tax-exempt public interest law firms are restricted to serving as amici curiae. *See* Rev. Proc. 92–59, 1992–2 C.B. 411.

entire nation. By the 1990s, there were over 200 organizations with more than 1,000 lawyers, and by 2006, under a more inclusive definition that encompassed government-funded legal services, there were over a thousand organizations with annual budgets ranging from a few hundred thousand to over a hundred million dollars.[48] In addition, a substantial number of private firms that did not qualify for tax-exempt status devoted a major portion of their work to public interest representation.

Conservative legal organizations also formed to broaden the groups represented. Groups such as the Washington Legal Foundation, the Rocky Mountain Legal Foundation, the Center for Equal Opportunity, and the Southwestern Legal Foundation have waged often successful campaigns against affirmative action, gun control, restrictions on property rights, small-business regulation, and—perhaps ironically—subsidized legal services for the poor.[49] Although these organizations operate with tax-exempt status, they often fall outside the definition of the Alliance for Justice (a coalition of liberal public interest organizations) because they take positions that are already well-represented by their corporate funders.[50] However, they qualify under definitions that are more inclusive, and encompass any group that seeks to use law in the service of social causes.[51]

The appropriate role and meaning of "public interest organizations" are matters of longstanding dispute. The conventional justification for public interest law rests on the failure of current political and market structures to take adequate account of the concerns of unorganized, diffuse, or subordinate groups. Where transaction costs in organizing are high, and parties have inadequate resources or small individual stakes in representation, the rationale for public interest advocacy is greatest. Yet this rationale raises as many issues as it resolves. Surely underrepresentation does not of itself qualify a legal position as being "in the public interest." For example, few individuals would apply that label to an organization of pedophiles who sought to eliminate prohibitions on child sexual abuse. If the concept of

---

48. Laura Beth Nielsen & Catherine R. Albiston, "The Organization of Public Interest Practice: 1975–2004," 84 *N.C. L. Rev.* 1591 (2006). It estimated that about 1000 organizations fit its definition: non profit organizations that "employ at least one lawyer at least part time and whose activities (1) seek to produce significant benefits for those who are external to the organization's participants and (2) involve at least one adjudicatory strategy." *Id.*, at 1601. For budgets and characteristics of leading public interest organizations, see Deborah L. Rhode, "Public Interest Law: The Movement at Midlife," 60 *Stan. L. Rev.* 2027 (2008).

49. The Legal Foundation of Washington challenged the use of IOLTA funding (Interest on Lawyers' Trust Accounts) to subsidize legal services. Had the lawsuit been successful, it would have cut off the largest source of nonfederal funds for civil legal aid

programs. *See* Brown v. Legal Foundation of Washington, 538 U.S. 216 (2003).

50. Aron, *supra* note 46, at 78; Houck, *supra* note 43.

51. For broader definitions, see *Cause Lawyers and Social Movements* (Austin Sarat & Stuart Scheingold, eds. 2006); *Cause Lawyering: Political Commitments and Professional Responsibilities* (Austin Sarat & Stuart Scheingold, eds. 1998); Rhode, *supra* note 48. For conservative organizations, see Steven M. Teles, *The Rise of the Conservative Legal Movement* (2008); *Bringing Justice to the People* (Lee Edwards, 2004); Ann Southworth, "Conservative Lawyers and the Contest over the Meaning of Public Interest Law," 52 *UCLA L. Rev.* 1223 (2005); John P. Heinz, Anthony Paik, & Ann Southwork, "Lawyers for Conservative Causes: Clients, Ideology, and Social Distance," 37 *Law & Soc'y Rev.* 5 (2003).

public interest presupposes some reference to widely shared values or socially defensible criteria, how should these be determined? In the absence of adequate funding for full representation, who should decide which interests should be heard and how loudly? On what basis should such decisions be made? Consider those issues in light of the criticisms that follow.

Public interest litigation raises concerns from all points on the political spectrum. Critics from the right complain that it vests too much power in non-majoritarian institutions, while critics from the left complain that is too limited to produce lasting social change. Conservative objections build on a long tradition of challenges to judicial activism, but they also direct particular opposition to public interest lawyers and lawsuits. Legal strategies that avowedly aim at restructuring institutions or redistributing resources have drawn fire on the ground that courts lack the competence or accountability for such a role. According to this line of criticism, such efforts invite rule by self-appointed representatives of the "public interest" who do not in fact reflect its concerns, and an "imperial judiciary" that does not have the necessary training, institutional familiarity, and enforcement mechanisms.[52]

Such arguments have prompted responses on several levels. As defenders of public interest advocacy note, it is not inconsistent with democratic principles for the public to delegate certain functions to non-majoritarian processes. Such a delegation is particularly appropriate to protect the needs of "discrete and insular minorities," or diffuse majorities that lack resources to organize in a political system increasingly captive to well-financed interests.[53] Courts can play a critical role in enforcing constitutional principles that other branches of government fail to vindicate.

Moreover, judicial oversight is not necessarily inconsistent with democratic authority. Public interest work often focuses on lobbying or on legal strategies designed to enforce the legislative intent underlying statutory guarantees. In many contexts, public interest organizations increase accountability in governmental policy making by providing review that is otherwise absent. For example, such groups provide a crucial check against the capture of agencies by the groups to be regulated. Elected representatives often lack the time, information, and technical expertise to supervise implementation of statutory mandates. Where courts face similar limitations in public interest litigation, they can rely on special masters or broker settlements that take account of all the interests at issue, and involve participants in the monitoring effort.[54]

While some critics worry that public interest law involves too much exercise of power, others worry that it involves too little. From their perspective, activist attorneys have placed too much emphasis on litigation

52. Ross Sandler & David Schoenbrod, *Democracy by Decree: What Happens When Courts Run Government* (2003); Jeffrey Rosen, *The Most Democratic Branch: How the Courts Serve America* (2006); Gerald N. Rosenberg, *The Hollow Hope* (1992).

53. United States v. Carolene Products Co., 304 U.S. 144, 152 (1938); Luban, *supra* note 37, at 358–70.

54. Charles Sabel & William Simon, "Debstabilization Rights: How Public Law Succeeds," 117 *Harv. L. Rev.* 1015 (2004).

and formal rights and have diverted efforts from the political organizing necessary to make such rights meaningful. In a landmark discussion of this issue, Harvard professor and longtime legal services activist Gary Bellow argued that

> the problem of unjust law is almost invariably a problem of distribution of political and economic power; the rules merely reflect a series of choices made in response to these distributions. If a major goal ... is to redistribute power, it is debatable whether the judicial process is a very effective means toward that end.... There is generally not much doctrinal judicial basis for adequately dealing with such problems, and lawyers find themselves developing cases whose outcomes are peripheral to the basic issues that these problems raise. Secondly, "rule" change, without a political base to support it, just doesn't produce any substantial results because rules are not self-executing; they require an enforcement mechanism.[55]

Too often, public interest lawyers lack resources to monitor compliance with test-case decrees and some defendants, particularly governmental institutions (such as prisons, schools, or mental hospitals), lack funds for adequately implementing judicial remedies. Decisions that lack public support are also vulnerable to statutory reversal or judicial retrenchment. According to this line of argument, the achievement of formal rights and procedural justice may leave intact a system that is substantively unjust. Public interest lawyers, it is claimed, continue to place undue reliance on doctrinal "victories" because their funding, credibility, and professional reputations depend on such visible achievements and because neither their professional nor personal backgrounds adequately equip them for grass roots organizing. In too many cases, attorneys do not empower clients to create the political and organizational structures necessary to challenge their subordination but instead only minister to its symptoms.[56]

In responding to such concerns, defenders of public interest lawyers have emphasized that litigation is not their sole focus. Much law reform activity serves multiple purposes and often helps raise public awareness, increase political leverage, mobilize communities, or broker internal reform efforts.[57] In recent decades, the increasing conservatism of the courts and stricter notice and standing requirements have prompted most public interest groups to rely less on litigation and more on lobbying, education,

---

55. Gary Bellow, *quoted in* Comment, "The New Public Interest Lawyers," 79 *Yale L.J.* 1069, 1077 (1970).

56. *See* Gerald Lopez, *Rebellious Lawyering* (1992); Lynn Jones, "The Haves Come Out Ahead: How Cause Lawyers Frame the Legal System for Social Movements," in *Cause Lawyers and Social Movements, supra* note 51, at 182–83; Michael Diamond, "Community Lawyering: Revisiting the Old Neighborhood," 32 *Colum. Human Rights L. Rev.* 67 (2000).

57. Rhode, "Public Interest Law," *supra* note 51, at 20–46–48; Susan Carle, "Pro-gressive Lawyering in Politically Depressing Times: Can New Models For Institutional Self–Reform Achieve More Effective Structural Change?," 30 *Harv. J. Law & Gender* 323, 326 (2007); Sandra R. Levitsky, "To Lead With Law: Reassessing the Influence of Legal Advocacy Organizations in Social Movements," in *Cause Lawyers and Social Movements, supra* note 51, at 145, 147–52; Ann Southworth, "Lawyers and the 'Myth of Rights' in Civil Rights and Poverty Practice," 8 *B.U. Pub. Int. L. J.* 469 (1998).

organizing, counseling, economic development, and related community-lawyering strategies. For many underrepresented groups, litigation has functioned most often as a threat that confers bargaining leverage in out-of-court settings, or as a catalyst for political action and organizing efforts. Bellow himself often acknowledged the strategic potential of litigation, and commentators such as Anthony Alfieri and Scott Cummings have documented its importance as a background threat and organizing tool in community development struggles.[58] In short, effective public interest advocates have learned to rely on multiple strategies that focus on long term change and that enlist and empower clients in the struggle to achieve it.

A final set of concerns raised by public interest law involves issues of accountability and conflict of interest such as those arising in Section G of Chapter X. The more unorganized the class, the fewer the constraints on counsel. In critics' view, lawyers who lack accountability become indistinguishable from the government official whose policy they often challenge: "[h]ow are [these attorneys] to succeed where government has failed? Bigger experts? Bigger hearts?"[59] In what sense can these lawyers claim to be more representative of the public than elected officials?

Responses to these concerns take a number of forms. Some commentators have acknowledged that public interest lawyers' choice of causes and reconciliation of competing client interests inevitably involve contested value judgments. Yet these commentators have also stressed that such judgments are, or at least can be, subject to some standards of accountability. The vast majority of contemporary public interest organizations work extensively in coalitions with community groups, government agencies, and other public interest groups, which help build responsiveness to the concerns and judgments of those most informed about the problems at issue.[60] In the long run, the influence of cause lawyers depends on credibility with funders, clients, peers, commentators, and policy makers. The effectiveness of public interest legal organizations turns on their ability to express widely shared values, vindicate critical principles, and justify a need for subsidized advocacy.

E.   Subsidized Legal Services

INTRODUCTION

The United States' first legal aid society formed in 1876 as part of an organization to assist German immigrants. By the turn of the century, legal

---

58. Bellow, *quoted in* Comment, *supra* note 55, at 1072 (tenants' lawsuit that lost in the courts but convinced clients that they could force change through collective action). See Anthony Alfieri, "Faith in Community: Representing Colored Town," 95 *Calif. L. Rev.* 1829 (2007); Scott Cummings, "Law in the Labor Movement's Challenge to Wal–Mart: A Case Study of the Inglewood Site Fight," 95 *Calif. L. Rev.* 1927 (2007).

59. Kenny Hegland, "Beyond Enthusiasm and Commitment," 13 *Ariz.L.Rev.* 805, 813 (1971).

60. Rhode, "Public Interest Law," *supra* note 51; Southworth, *supra* note 57; Alfieri, *supra* note 58; Cummings, *supra* note 58; Anthony V. Alfieri, "Practicing Community," 107 *Harv. L. Rev.* 1747 (1994).

assistance programs were operating in about a half a dozen cities, with funding from private charity and municipal subsidies. Program leaders generally viewed their mission as promoting social stability rather than social change. By demonstrating that justice was accessible through established means, many legal aid supporters hoped to undercut support for socialism, anarchism and other left political movements. Efforts to attract funding, however, met with limited success. In 1919, Reginald Heber Smith's *Justice and the Poor* reported a total of some 40 organizations throughout the country, with only 62 full-time attorneys and a combined budget of less than $200,000. Many programs also had highly restrictive policies. Only the "deserving poor" were eligible for assistance and only for what lawyers considered "deserving" cases. Subsequent surveys have found that among the cases typically excluded from coverage were those involving divorce or purchases of "luxury goods" like cars or televisions.[61]

The American Bar Association subsequently appointed Smith to head its Standing Committee on Legal Aid, which began providing modest assistance to local offices. Bar leaders supported assistance on the grounds that it reassured the public of the fairness of legal institutions and increased respect for lawyers. However, many leaders also opposed substantial government funding because of concerns about the "socialization" of legal practice. By 1963, some 250 offices were providing civil legal services with a combined annual budget of approximately $4 million, about 12% of which came from bar association contributions. That budget amounted to less than two-tenths of one percent of the nation's total annual expenditures for legal services and funded only 400 lawyers, about one for every 120,000 poor Americans.[62]

With the Johnson Administration's War on Poverty came a major influx of governmental aid and a new reformist vision. In 1965, the Office of Economic Opportunity (OEO) began allocating the first federal funds for civil legal assistance programs, and a cadre of progressive lawyers joined their staffs. In addition to traditional services, OEO programs encouraged a focus on law reform and political organizing. The consequences were quickly apparent, as legal aid offices achieved significant victories on consumer, welfare, housing, health, and related issues.

These victories resulted in political backlash. The Nixon Administration was unsuccessful in attempts to dismantle the federal program, but did manage to restrict its activities. To provide greater political insulation for poverty law offices, Congress in 1974 established the Legal Services Corporation, with board members appointed by the President and confirmed by the Senate. To gain support from conservative critics, the authorizing legislation prohibited Corporation-funded attorneys from engaging in lob-

61. Rhode, *Access to Justice, supra* note 3; Bryant Garth, *Neighborhood Law Firms for the Poor* 19–20 (1980); Jerold Auerbach, *Unequal Justice: Lawyers and Social Change in Modern America* 53–62 (1976); Lee Silverstein, "Eligibility for Free Legal Services in Civil Cases," 44 *J.Urb.L.* 549 (1967). To some

legal aid attorneys, divorces also seemed to be a "luxury;" for the poor, desertion appeared "just as good." *Id.* at 579–583.

62. *See* Johnson, *supra* note 43, at 6–9. The ratio of lawyers to non-poor clients was approximately 1 to 560. Caseloads were as high as 2500 per legal services attorney.

bying, political organization, and representation in certain controversial areas such as school desegregation, abortion, and military service. Under the new Corporation charter, earlier OEO rhetoric of "law reform" and "social change" was also absent; emphasis had shifted to the more neutral goal of enhancing "access to justice."

Further restrictions followed. The Reagan administration failed in its initial efforts to dissolve the Legal Services Corporation, but subsequently succeeded in reducing its budget and restricting its permissible activities. Recipients of government funds could not, for example, represent aliens, pursue cases involving gay rights, or initiate class actions except under limited circumstances.

In 1996, Congress again restricted the Corporation's activities and reduced its budget by about a third to under $300 million. Among the most controversial of the 1996 restrictions Congress imposed on Legal Services Corporation funding recipients are set out below. One important but subtle point about the restrictions is this: the legislation does not simply forbid legal services providers from using LSC funds for prohibited activities. By its terms, it prevents organizations engaging in these activities from receiving LSC funds, and thus in effect prohibits recipients of LSC grants from engaging in prohibited activities using their own funds or funds from private sources.

Omnibus Consolidated Rescissions and Appropriations Act of 1996: Legal Services Corporation

PL 104–134.

Section 504(a) None of the funds appropriated in this Act to the Legal Services Corporation for the provision of legal assistance may be used to provide financial assistance to any person or entity (which may be referred to in this section as a "recipient")—...

(2) that attempts to influence the issuance, amendment, or revocation of any executive order, regulation, or other statement of general applicability and future effect by any Federal, State or local agency;

(3) that attempts to influence any part of any adjudicatory proceeding of any Federal, State, or local agency if such part of the proceeding is designed for the formulation or modification of any agency policy of general applicability and future effect; ...

(7) that initiates or participates in a class action suit; ...

(11) that provides legal assistance for or on behalf of any alien, unless the alien is [lawfully present in the United States, or has applied to become a permanent resident, or is the spouse or parent of a U.S. citizen].

(13) that claims (or whose employee claims), or collects and retains, attorneys' fees; ...

(15) that participates in any litigation on behalf of a person incarcerated in a Federal, State, or local prison;

(16) that initiates legal representation or participates in any other way, in litigation, lobbying, or rulemaking, involving an effort to reform a Federal or State welfare system, except that this paragraph shall not be construed to preclude a recipient from representing an individual eligible client who is seeking specific relief from a welfare agency if such relief does not involve an effort to amend or otherwise challenge existing law in effect on the date of the initiation of the representation;

(17) that defends a person in a proceeding to evict the person from a public housing project if—

(A) the person has been charged with the illegal sale or distribution of a controlled substance; . . .

Section 50. None of the funds appropriated in this Act to the Legal Services Corporation may be used by any person or entity receiving financial assistance from the Corporation to file or pursue a lawsuit against the Corporation.

Legal Services Corp. v. Velazquez

Supreme Court of the United States, 2001.
531 U.S. 533.

■ Kennedy, J.

[The case involved a challenge to the LSC restrictions, brought by lawyers working for New York City LSC grant recipients, their clients, and contributors to their organizations. The plaintiffs challenged various of the restrictions on due process or First Amendment grounds. They argued that the restrictions unduly burden the client-lawyer relationship, and that they impose unconstitutional conditions on the receipt of LSC grants. Finally, they challenged some of the restrictions by arguing that they discriminate against certain lawyer speech based on viewpoint. The court of appeals rejected all the challenges except the last one. The court upheld the restriction on welfare-reform activities, because it bans lobbying and re-form litigation on any side of the issue. But it struck down one provision of subsection (a)(16) that was "inescapably viewpoint-biased." That provision permitted representation of welfare claims in suits for benefits only if they did not challenge a rule that led to the denial of benefits.

The plaintiffs did not appeal, but the LSC challenged the court of appeals' determination that the "suits for benefits" clause of subsection (a)(16) is unconstitutional. The Supreme Court affirmed in a 5–4 decision.]

By providing subsidies to LSC, the Government seeks to facilitate suits for benefits by using the State and Federal courts and the independent bar on which those courts depend for the proper performance of their duties and responsibilities. Restricting LSC attorneys in advising their clients and in presenting arguments and analyses to the courts distorts the legal system by altering the traditional role of the attorneys. . . .

[U]pon determining [that] a question of statutory validity is present in any anticipated or pending case or controversy, the LSC-funded attorney must cease the representation at once. This is true whether the validity issue becomes apparent during initial attorney-client consultations or in the midst of litigation proceedings. A disturbing example of the restriction was discussed during oral argument before the Court. . . . [A]s the LSC advised the Court, if, during litigation, a judge were to ask an LSC attorney whether there was a constitutional concern, the LSC attorney simply could not answer.

The restriction imposed by the statute here threatens severe impairment of the judicial function. Section 504(a)(16) sifts out cases presenting constitutional challenges in order to insulate the Government's laws from judicial inquiry. If the restriction on speech and legal advice were to stand, the result would be two tiers of cases. In cases where LSC counsel were attorneys of record, there would be lingering doubts whether the truncated representation had resulted in complete analysis of the case, full advice to the client, and proper presentation to the court. The courts and the public would come to question the adequacy and fairness of professional representations when the attorney, either consciously to comply with this statute or unconsciously to continue the representation despite the statute, avoided all reference to questions of statutory validity and constitutional authority. A scheme so inconsistent with accepted separation-of-powers principles is an insufficient basis to sustain or uphold the restriction on speech.

It is no answer to say the restriction on speech is harmless because, under LSC's interpretation of the Act, its attorneys can withdraw. This misses the point. The statute is an attempt to draw lines around the LSC program to exclude from litigation those arguments and theories Congress finds unacceptable but which by their nature are within the province of the courts to consider.

The restriction on speech is even more problematic because in cases where the attorney withdraws from a representation, the client is unlikely to find other counsel. . . . Congress was not required to fund an LSC attorney to represent indigent clients; and when it did so, it was not required to fund the whole range of legal representations or relationships. The LSC and the United States, however, in effect ask us to permit Congress to define the scope of the litigation it funds to exclude certain vital theories and ideas. The attempted restriction is designed to insulate the Government's interpretation of the Constitution from judicial challenge. The Constitution does not permit the Government to confine litigants and their attorneys in this manner. We must be vigilant when Congress imposes rules and conditions which in effect insulate its own laws from legitimate judicial challenge. Where private speech is involved, even Congress' antecedent funding decision cannot be aimed at the suppression of ideas thought inimical to the government's own interest. . . . For the reasons we have set forth, the funding condition is invalid.

NOTES AND QUESTIONS

1.   Although the court of appeals struck down one provision of the funding restrictions on welfare reforms, it upheld the other restrictions and legal aid grantees did not appeal that ruling. A similar constitutional challenge to the LSC restrictions was rejected by the Ninth Circuit Court of Appeals in *Legal Aid Society of Hawaii v. Legal Services Corporation*, 145 F.3d 1017 (9th Cir.1998). These rulings were based on *Rust v. Sullivan*, 500 U.S. 173 (1991). *Rust* involved a challenge to federal regulations forbidding medical providers who receive federal funds from counseling patients about abortion. The Court held that these regulations did not impose unconstitutional conditions on receipt of the funds, because Congress may legitimately refuse to use federal funds to advocate or promote abortion. In so ruling, the Court reasoned that the government is not discriminating among viewpoints because failing to fund constitutionally-protected speech is not the same as restricting or forbidding it. *Id.* at 193.

Do the Congressional restrictions upheld by these court of appeals' decisions impair representation by LSC recipients? Do any of these restrictions raise constitutional concerns analogous to those underlying the Supreme Court's ruling in *Velazquez*? Consider the following issues.

a) Section 504(a)(7) forbids LSC recipients from filing class actions, even if they believe that a class action will best serve the interests of their clients. Does this place recipients in violation of any ethical rules, such as:

> • Rule 1.8(f) "A lawyer shall not accept compensation for representing a client from one other than the client unless . . . (1) the client gives informed consent [and] there is no interference with the lawyer's independence of professional judgment or with the client-lawyer relationship. . . .";

> • Rule 5.4(c) "A lawyer shall not permit a person who . . . employs, or pays the lawyer to render legal services for another to direct or regulate the lawyer's professional judgment in rendering such legal services"?

Alternatively, does Rule 1.2 permit limited representation? It provides that "A lawyer may limit the scope of the representation if the limitation is reasonable under the circumstances and the client gives informed consent." If low-income clients have no alternative source of legal assistance, how meaningful is their consent?

> Critics of the decisions sustaining these restrictions raise several concerns.

> It is, of course, true that legal aid clients are no worse off as a result of the restrictions than they would have been if the government had never provided funding. But that is often true in cases where the Supreme Court has found unconstitutional conditions; the point of the doctrine is to require the government to respect constitutional rights if it chooses to provide assistance. Once Congress decides to subsidize certain attorney-client relationships, it should not be permitted to

undermine their effectiveness. Foreclosing strategies like class actions, requests for attorneys' fees, or legislative advocacy often has that effect. In many jurisdictions, no non-federally funded organizations are available to pursue restricted activities.

Moreover, contrary to courts' implication, the attorney-client relationship has long been recognized to serve crucial First Amendment values of expression and association. Current LSC restrictions undercut those values and compromise lawyers' ethical obligations to serve their clients' best interests. For example, it is generally advantageous for plaintiffs with similar claims to pursue them as class actions, since such collective efforts offer broader relief, higher stakes and visibility, and greater bargaining leverage. By foreclosing such strategies, LSC restrictions impair lawyers' ethical obligations to provide effective representation and to exercise independent professional judgment about what that representation requires.[63]

Do you agree? How might defenders of the restrictions respond?

b) An additional restriction in the 1996 Act, Section 504(a)(8), prohibits LSC recipients from filing a complaint or negotiating a settlement unless "each plaintiff has been specifically identified, by name ..." and all the facts known to the plaintiff are recorded and kept on file "and are made available to any Federal department or agency that is auditing or monitoring the activities of the Corporation or of the recipient...." The plaintiff may, however, be granted an injunction preventing his or her name from being disclosed "to prevent probable, serious harm to such potential plaintiff."

Consider a legal services client who is a residential patient in a psychiatric hospital suing hospital staff over alleged abusive treatment. Must the lawyer caution the client that the client may have to seek an injunction to avoid having her identity revealed to the hospital staff (and that the client may lose on the issue)? Must a legal services lawyer warn every litigation client that the client's identity and the facts of the client's case could be turned over to politicians searching for sound-bite stories in order to embarrass the LSC? Must a legal services lawyer require clients to consent to waive confidentiality before undertaking litigation on their behalf?

2.   LSC recipients report that among the most onerous of the restrictions are the "program integrity" regulations stipulating that recipients of federal funds may not spend their non-federal money on restricted activities. This led some recipients to split their organizations; one half continues to receive LSC funds while the other half declines the funds in order to engage in restricted activities. The result has been that these offices had to purchase duplicate equipment and hire duplicate staff, with less money available to serve clients. In programs that could afford only one office,

---

63.   Rhode, *Access to Justice, supra* note 3, at 113–14.

clients with legal problems requiring federally-prohibited legal representation often had to travel long distances to find legal assistance.[64]

3. Other burdensome restrictions include the prohibition on class actions, which requires offices to undertake expensive case-by-case relitigation of essentially identical matters, and the prohibition on collecting statutory attorneys' fees. Not only have these fees made up an important part of legal aid budgets in the past, but also the threat of statutory attorneys' fees has provided negotiating leverage that is essential to effective representation. Defenders of this prohibition generally claim that it is needed to prevent recipients from giving undue priority to fee-generating cases, and to prevent defendants who are already subsidizing legal services through their tax contributions from "double paying" their opponents' expenses. But that same objection could be made whenever any organization that receives government funding sues to recover fees. Does denying awards in such cases undermine any of the purposes of authorizing fees in the first instance, or is the restriction a legitimate way of prioritizing aid?

While the legislation imposing the 1996 restrictions was pending, the American Bar Association issued a Formal Opinion discussing the ethical issues they raise. See ABA Formal Opinion 96–399 (1996). The Opinion concluded that legal services lawyers must significantly limit their representation, withdrawing from some cases, declining others, or warning potential clients, in order to maintain their federal funding, but that none of these limitations violate the Model Rules. Do you agree with this assessment?[65]

4. Beginning in the mid–1990s, the Legal Services Corporation also mandated that legal services programs engage in a process of state-wide planning to develop a comprehensive, integrated delivery system. Long-standing programs were no longer presumptively entitled to renewal of their funding. Rather, the Corporation invited competitive bids, and evaluated candidates based on their capacity to maximize access of eligible clients to timely, effective, and appropriate legal services.[66]

Such changes responded to several criticisms of legal services programs. One recurrent complaint has been that legal aid programs have been insufficiently responsive to poor peoples' routine but pressing needs in order to pursue law reform objectives of greater interest to poverty lawyers. Progressive critics have viewed the resource allocation process as autocratic, while free-market defenders have found it inefficient. According to commentators such as Richard Posner, providing legal services in kind rather than through income transfers encourages clients to overuse free

64. *See* David S. Udell, "The Legal Services Restrictions: Lawyers in Florida, New York, Virginia, and Oregon Describe the Costs," 17 *Yale L. & Pol'y. Rev.* 337 (1998).

65. *See* Alan W. Houseman, "Restrictions by Funders and the Ethical Practice of Law," 67 *Fordham L. Rev.* 2187 (1999). *See also* David Luban, "Taking Out the Adversary: The Assault on Progressive Public–Interest Lawyers," 91 *Cal. L. Rev.* 209, 225–26 (2003).

66. *See* Alan W. Houseman, "Civil Legal Assistance for the 21st Century," 17 *Yale L. & Pol. Rev.* 369 (1998).

services and forces lawyers to make often inaccurate judgments about which needs are most acute.[67]

Another criticism is that lawyers' legal activism has in fact worked against the long-term interests of poverty communities. For example, conservative commentators claim that legal aid offices encourage welfare dependency and broken homes through their divorce and government benefits work. A related claim is that when these offices increase landlords' difficulties in evicting deadbeat or dangerous tenants, the price is paid by other non-litigious tenants in the form of increased rents and safety risks.[68] And when litigation costs prevent schools from expelling abusive students or enforcing sanitary ordinances against the homeless, the costs will be born by poor communities, not the attorneys who claim to protect them. According to critics, these lawyer "liberators" seldom confront the daily consequences of their advocacy; "abstract compassion" is the luxury of litigators who can "live in neighborhoods with more . . . coffee houses than drug dealers" and who can shield their own children from the educational disruption they perpetuate for others.[69]

So too, some commentators from the left who strongly support legal aid have questioned its quality of representation and its strategies for client involvement and empowerment. In their view, the landmark litigation victories that many lawyers seek may have little concrete effect, given the post-judgment power relations of the parties, the difficulties of enforcement, and the possibility of legislative reversal. The federal restrictions on LSC-funded organizing, lobbying, and class action activities have encouraged legal aid offices to focus on remedying individual problems rather than pursuing broader changes; the remedies sometimes achieve concessions in individual cases, but do not challenge basic power relations. Research on poverty lawyering over the last two decades has also identified problems of professional dominance and structures of legal representation that disempower clients, particularly when advocates are of different class, race, and ethnic backgrounds. As Anthony Alfieri puts it, "What do progressive lawyers give to subordinated people? The conventional answer is rights . . . What do progressive lawyers take from subordinated people? The answer is dignity: the values of independent action and respect."[70]

In response to such criticisms, defenders of legal services generally invoke the arguments supporting access to justice set forth in the preceding section. In addition, they point out that some criticisms of poverty law programs are attributable to limitations on resources and restrictions on program activities such as class actions and lobbying that conservative

---

67. Richard A. Posner, *Economic Analysis of the Law* 511–515 (5th ed. 1998).

68. Kenneth F. Boehm, "The Legal Services Program: Unaccountable, Political, Anti–Poor, Beyond Reform and Unnecessary," 17 *St. Louis U. Pub. L. Rev.* 321 (1998). For similar criticisms *see* sources cited in Rhode, *Access to Justice, supra* note 3, at 108–10.

69. George Will, "One for Santa Ana," *Washington Post*, May 7, 1995, at E5.

70. See Alfieri, *supra* note 60; Lopez, *supra* note 56; Troy E. Elder, Poor Clients, Informed Consent, and the Ethics of Rejection, 20 *Geo. J. Legal Ethics* 989 (2007); Lynn Jones, "The Haves Come Out Ahead," *supra* note 56, at 182, 183.

critics have themselves demanded. Other criticisms are really objections not to legal assistance per se, but to the rights it makes possible to assert. Opponents would have the same concerns about advocacy in welfare, homelessness, and school disciplinary proceedings no matter who was paying the legal bills. It is, moreover, by no means clear that all of the cases critics cite reflect counterproductive advocacy. Opponents generally assume that the costs of defending such lawsuits will all be passed on to other poor people. But whether the landlord will in fact raise honest tenants' rent because legal aid lawyers successfully fight evictions or force landlords to undertake expensive improvements is a complicated empirical question that depends heavily on context and local market conditions.[71]

Whether such consequences would be offset by other benefits is equally complicated, particularly if, as the research available suggests, cases taken to trial for low-income clients typically have valid claims.[72] Understaffed legal services offices have no reason to spend substantial scarce resources litigating the "marginal" or meritless cases that critics's arguments invoke. Similar points could be made about other litigation that assertedly hurts the poor more than it helps. For example, contesting expulsions does not necessarily result in more classroom disruptions; it can instead force school districts to respect appropriate procedural norms and to find more constructive solutions to disciplinary issues. This is not to suggest that society in general or the poor in particular would benefit if every potential claim were fully litigated. But neither is ability to pay for legal counsel an effective way of screening out meritless claims

While acknowledging certain limitations of legal aid as a redistributive device, defenders emphasize its role in monitoring the fairness of existing redistributive programs and in enforcing recognized entitlements. For many impoverished clients, legal services are the only way to meet fundamental needs in areas such as medical care, housing, education, protection from domestic violence, and hazardous working conditions. Also, since courts, unlike legislatures, are open as of right, they are often the most accessible if not always the most effective forum in which to seek expansion of existing rights.[73]

Proponents find conventional critiques of subsidized legal assistance problematic on other grounds as well. To argue that it is unfair to force taxpayers to subsidize legal services for indigent clients overlooks the

---

71. *See, e.g.,* Werner Z. Hirsch et al., "Regression Analysis of the Effects of Habitability Laws Upon Rent: An Empirical Observation on the Ackerman–Komesar Debate," 63 *Calif. L. Rev.* 1098 (1975) (finding little or no correlation between enforcing habitability laws and increased rent).

72. *See* Rhode, *Access to Justice, supra* note 3, at 109; Carol Seron et al., "The Impact of Legal Counsel on Outcomes for Poor Tenants in New York City's Housing Courts: Results of a Randomized Experiment," 35 *Law & Soc. Rev.* 419 (2001).

73. For analysis and criticism of arguments against subsidized legal services, *see* Luban, *Lawyers and Justice, supra* note 35, at 293–391. For an argument that courts, legislatures, and the organized bar have obligations to support adequate legal assistance of some form to those who cannot realistically afford it, *see* Rhode, *Access to Justice, supra* note 3, at 5–11, 20–23, and Rhode, *In the Interests of Justice, supra* note 7, at 129–41.

multibillion dollar subsidy already provided for non-indigent clients through tax deductions for legal services as business expenses. To assume that cash transfers to the poor would be more effective than direct provision of services ignores problems such as lack of information and collective needs that legal aid programs are meant to address. Moreover, at current governmental funding levels, which provide legal aid programs with less than $10 annually for every person below the poverty line, converting the LSC budget to income transfers scarcely seems promising. Similarly, proponents challenge critics' complaint that poverty lawyers pursue politically driven lawsuits and hollow courtroom victories instead of individual client needs. About 90 percent of legal services cases involve matters that are handled short of litigation; most of these cases involve relatively uncomplicated family, landlord/tenant, income maintenance, and consumer matters. Moreover, law reform cases are often the best means of addressing individual grievances because they provide broad relief, mobilize and educate potential claimants and deter subsequent legal violators.

Although sympathetic to certain concerns about the undue dominance of lawyers and the limitations of litigation, proponents generally believe that legal assistance has the potential of empowering some clients and meeting the fundamental needs of others. To that end, poverty lawyers should target their resources and give priority to widely shared problems and collaborative, community-based responses. Clients should also have a meaningful voice in decisions about the allocation of resources, and programs should engage in systematic evaluation of their cost-effectiveness.[74] By focusing on educational projects, self-help assistance, and aid to local organizations, legal services offices also can aid low-income groups not only in resolving individual problems but also in developing skills to address the structural causes of poverty.

QUESTIONS

1. What position would you take in these debates over legal services? Should the United States recognize a right to civil legal assistance in cases where important interests are at stake and the complexity of the proceeding makes adequate self-representation infeasible?

2. How should government decision makers and legal services administrators respond to the vast unmet need for civil legal assistance and how should they establish priorities for allocating limited resources?

PROBLEM 2

a) You are staff counsel to the Senate Committee that controls appropriations for the Legal Services Corporation (LSC). Your committee is reconsidering funding levels and restrictions on activities of poverty lawyers. The chair asks for your recommendations on several questions. In an

---

74. Lopez, *supra* note 56; Rhode, Access to Justice, *supra* note 3, at 120–23; Alan Houseman, "Civil Legal Assistance for Low Income Persons: Looking Back and Looking Forward," 29 *Ford. Urban L. J.* 1213, 1230 (2002); Elder, *supra* note 70.

era of restricted funding for all domestic programs, how much priority should be given to legal services? Should least partial subsidies be available to the near poor, who are over current eligibility cut-offs but who cannot realistically afford assistance? Which, if any, of the current restrictions on cases, clients, and staff activities should the committee attempt to repeal? How would you summarize the arguments favoring and opposing such restrictions?

The committee is also evaluating the strategies by which local programs establish their priorities. Current federal regulations require programs to:

> Include an effective appraisal of the needs of eligible clients in the geographic areas served by the recipient, and their relative importance, based on information received from potential or current eligible clients solicited in a manner reasonably calculated to obtain the attitude of all significant segments of the client population. The appraisal shall also include input from the recipient's employees, governing body members, the private bar, and other interested persons, and to the extent feasible should include outreach to eligible clients which may include the use of such techniques as questionnaires and surveys.[75]

Critics charge that many legal service offices are insufficiently responsive to client preferences in decisions about resource allocation. Defenders of the current approach respond that most poverty lawyers are highly knowledgeable and deeply concerned about community needs and that their assessments are more reliable than uninformed or unrepresentative responses on client surveys. According to many program directors, potential clients are often unaware of the full range of needs in the community and tend to focus on easily identifiable routine matters rather than fundamental causes and collective concerns. Given the difficulties that most offices already experience in attracting and retaining qualified staff at current salary levels, program directors are also wary of measures that would unduly limit staff discretion and channel resources to the least challenging and rewarding forms of assistance. What are your recommendations?

b) You are chair of a commission established in response to a report on unmet legal needs in Illinois. As in other jurisdictions, the report estimated that unmet needs totaled about ten times the cases handled by legal services attorneys; the state had only one attorney for every 4750 problems experienced by low income individuals.[76] Only a quarter of the eligible population was aware of how to obtain free legal services, and only a sixth of those who sought services obtained them. Legal advice and referral hotlines could handle only about 15% to 33% of the calls received, and certain groups were particularly underserved, such as disabled, elderly,

---

75.   45 C.F.R. § 1620.3(b).

76.   Mark Marquardt, *The Legal Aid Safety Net: A Report on the Legal Needs of Low Income Illinoisans* 157–58, 165 (2005). See also District of Columbia Bar Founda-

tion, *Civil Legal Services Delivery in the District of Columbia* (finding that 90% of the needs of low and moderate income residents were not being met).

institutionalized, and immigrant populations.[77] Among the report's recommendations were: simplification of legal forms and proceedings; self-help support services in every courthouse; trained non-lawyer facilitators in libraries and social service offices; additional web-based and telephone assistance; further outreach to vulnerable populations; changes in bar ethical rules to encourage more "unbundled" limited scope representation by lawyers in private practice, and increased funding through mandatory minimum contributions from attorneys and unclaimed damages in class actions. Other possibilities include a tax on legal revenues, and a sliding fee scale for clients who can afford to pay something but not the full cost of assistance.[78]

How would you evaluate these recommendations? Would a mandatory financial or hourly contribution from attorneys make sense in light of the material on pro bono in Section G? What other strategies might you consider?

Stephen Wexler, "Practicing Law for Poor People"

79 Yale Law Journal 1049, 1049–1059 (1970).

Poor people are not just like rich people without money. Poor people do not have legal problems like those of the private plaintiffs and defendants in law school casebooks. In so far as the law is concerned, [financially secure individuals] lead harmonious and settled private lives; except for their business involvements, their lives usually do not demand the skills of a lawyer. Occasionally, one of them gets hit by a car, or decides to buy a house, or lets his dog bite someone. The settled and harmonious pattern of life is then either broken or there is a threat that without care it may be broken. . . .

Poor people get hit by cars too; they get evicted; they have their furniture repossessed; they can't pay their utility bills. But they do not have personal legal problems in the law school way. Nothing that happens to them breaks up or threatens to break up a settled and harmonious life. Poor people do not lead settled lives into which the law seldom intrudes; they are constantly involved with the law in its most intrusive forms. For instance, poor people must go to government officials for many of the things which not-poor people get privately. Life would be very difficult for the not-poor person if he had to fill out an income tax return once or twice a week. Poverty creates an abrasive interface with society; poor people are

---

77. Marquardt, *supra* note 76, at 163–65. *See also* Robert A. Katzmann, "The Legal Profession and the Unmet Needs of the Immigrant Poor," 21 *Geo. J. Legal Ethics* 3 (2008).

78. The report proposed a $250 contribution. *Id.* at 170. A 2007 Illinois statute mandates that up to half of unclaimed class action damages be used to support legal services. Adam Liptak, "Doling Out Other Peo-

ple's Money," *N.Y. Times,* Nov. 26, 2007, at A12. For other proposals see Rhode, *Access to Justice*, *supra* note 3, at 112–13. For limited scope representation see Model Rule 1.2(c); Alicia M. Farley, "An Important Piece of the Bundle: How Limited Appearances can Provide an Ethically Sound Way to Increase Access to Justice for Pro Se Litigants," 20 *Geo. J. Legal Ethics* 563 (2007).

always bumping into sharp legal things. The law school model of personal legal problems, of solving them and returning the client to the smooth and orderly world in television advertisements, doesn't apply to poor people.

Additions to the law school curriculum like "Law and the Poor" serve a useful function by making it crystal clear that the remainder of the curriculum deals with law and the rich; they do little, however, to change the law schools' treatment of legal problems, or their perception of the proper roles and concerns of a lawyer. Law schools have rarely asked questions about how the law came to be as it is. They have never concerned themselves or their students with what led a client to become involved with the law, or with what happened to him after he won or lost in court. . . .

Similarly, and with similar consequences, lawyers have not seen that what causes a client to become involved in a civil action, or what happens to him after it is over, are lawyers' concerns. No law school course, including "Law and the Poor," concerns itself with what happened to Mrs. Smith after the Supreme Court decided that Georgia could not withhold her welfare payments because she was having sexual intercourse with a man who was not her husband. Few lawyers ask themselves whether Mrs. James has a decent place to live since a three-judge Federal court held that it was a violation of the Fourth Amendment for New York State to cut off her welfare grant when she refused to let a caseworker into her home without a warrant. The traditional practitioner is usually safe in forgetting about his client after the case is over and the bill is paid; but Mrs. Smith, Mrs. James, other welfare recipients, poor people who need but cannot get welfare, underpaid laborers, old or disabled people on fixed incomes, and other poor people will still be bumped and chafed and jostled by the law after the lawyers have completed their last appeal, shaken hands with those who opposed their clients, and snapped their brief cases closed.

Poverty will not be stopped by people who are not poor. If poverty is stopped, it will be stopped by poor people. And poor people can stop poverty only if they work at it together. The lawyer who wants to serve poor people must put his skills to the task of helping poor people organize themselves. This is not the traditional use of a lawyer's skills; in many ways it violates some of the basic tenets of the profession. Nevertheless, a realistic analysis of the structure of poverty, and a fair assessment of the legal needs of the poor and the legal talent available to meet them, lead a lawyer to this role.

If all the lawyers in the country worked full time, they could not deal with even the articulated legal problems of the poor. And even if somehow lawyers could deal with those articulated problems, they would not change very much the tangle of unarticulated legal troubles in which poor people live. In fact, only a very few lawyers will concern themselves with poor people, and those who do so will probably be at it for only a while. In this setting the object of practicing poverty law must be to organize poor people, rather than to solve their legal problems. The proper job for a poor people's lawyer is helping poor people to organize themselves to change things so that either no one is poor or (less radically) so that poverty does not entail misery.

Two major touchstones of traditional legal practice—the solving of legal problems and the one-to-one relationship between attorney and client—are either not relevant to poor people or harmful to them. Traditional practice hurts poor people by isolating them from each other, and fails to meet their need for a lawyer by completely misunderstanding that need. Poor people have few individual legal problems in the traditional sense; their problems are the product of poverty, and are common to all poor people. The lawyer for poor individuals is likely, whether he wins cases or not, to leave his clients precisely where he found them, except that they will have developed a dependency on his skills to smooth out the roughest spots in their lives. The lawyer will eventually go or be taken away; he does not have to stay, and the government which gave him can take him back just as it does welfare. He can be another hook on which poor people depend, or he can help the poor build something which rests upon themselves—something which cannot be taken away and which will not leave until all of them can leave. Specifically, the lawyer must seek to strengthen existing organizations of poor people, and to help poor people start organizations where none exist. There are several techniques for doing this, but all of them run counter to very deeply rooted notions in law school training, professionalism and middle-class humanism....

The starkest picture of the "proper" mentality for a poor people's lawyer is painted in a story told by a very successful welfare rights organizer:

> I once found a recipient who worked hard at organizing, and was particularly good in the initial stages of getting to talk to new people. I picked her up at her apartment one morning to go out knocking on doors. While I was there, I saw her child, and I noticed that he seemed to be retarded. Because the boy was too young for school and the family never saw a doctor, the mother had never found out that something was seriously wrong with her son. I didn't tell her. If I had, she would have stopped working at welfare organizing to rush around looking for help for her son. I had some personal problems about doing that, but I'm an organizer, not a social worker.

I have heard this story related several times; each time, the people who have not heard it before gasp, fidget in their seats, and shrink away from the organizer. It is natural for them to be repelled, for this story embodies the very hardest line about organizing. Not everyone can handle the "personal problems" which arise from a primary commitment to organizing. The very things which make a lawyer want to work for poor people make it difficult to help them in the most effective way. Few can accept the organizer's model fully; but the more one is able to accept it, the more he can give poor people the wherewithal to change a world that hurts them.

If organizing is the object of a poverty practice, what are the methods for achieving that object? One method by which an existing organization can be strengthened is for a lawyer to refuse to handle matters for individuals not in the organization.... [The alternative] seemingly neutral policy of "first-come, first-served" cuts against the least informed, the least mobile, and the most oppressed. . . .

Selection of clients is only the first step; the cornerstone of a practice is the kind of service a lawyer provides for his clients. The hallmark of an effective poor people's practice is that the lawyer does not do anything for his clients that they can do or be taught to do for themselves. The standards of success for a poor people's lawyer are how well he can recognize all the things his clients can do with a little of his help, and how well he can teach them to do more. . . . [The difficulty is that] lawyers are taught to believe, and have a three-year investment in believing, that what they have learned in law school was hard to learn, and that they are somehow special for having learned it. It is difficult for a lawyer to commit himself to believing that poor people can learn the law and be effective advocates; but until he believes that, a lawyer will create dependency instead of strength for his clients, and add to rather than reduce their plight.

Four ways in which a lawyer can help his clients use his knowledge are (1) informing individuals and groups of their rights, (2) writing manuals and other materials, (3) training lay advocates, and (4) educating groups for confrontation. None is particularly glamorous, but all are extremely important.

PROBLEM 3

a) If you had been a lawyer who worked with the welfare rights organizer described by Stephen Wexler in the excerpt above, how would you have responded? Do such examples suggest the need for more "holistic" approaches in which lawyers work on teams with other professionals such as social workers and medical specialists, to address clients' multiple needs?

b) Your federally-funded legal aid office, after its appraisal of client needs, has determined to target most of its available resources to housing reform, which it believes to be the most pressing issue facing the poor in its city. The office hopes to launch lawsuits attacking both the deteriorating condition of public housing stock and the semi-official tolerance of racial discrimination in public housing admissions. Lawyers also hope to work with a neighborhood organization seeking innovative ways to finance new housing projects, and to block developments that will reduce affordable residential units or increase environmental hazards.

For this reason, the office now turns away almost all prospective clients with non-emergency legal needs unrelated to housing. In addition, clients are now chosen partly on tactical grounds. For example, the office does not accept clients seeking admission to public housing if a family member has a history of violence. Once a client is accepted for representation, however, your office will handle non-housing-related legal problems as well, because you and the other attorneys believe that only in this way can you achieve an acceptable attorney-client relationship.

The Hispanic mother of a mentally disturbed teenage boy has asked your program to represent her in efforts to place her son in a special educational program. The boy has been suspended or expelled from public school twice as a result of assaults on classmates. The mother insists that the incidents were provoked by racist comments. After learning the reason that your office cannot handle her case, she returns and indicates that she has now applied for admission to public housing. Other attorneys report similar experiences, and express discomfort about the possibility that the office's targeting policy is too manipulative toward would-be clients.

Related concerns have surfaced about caseload restrictions. Some potential clients have questioned the meaning and appropriateness of the ban on representing families with a history of violence, since it penalizes innocent as well as guilty members. A local women's group has also complained about the office's refusal to handle divorce and domestic violence cases. In its view, the lawyers' interest in cutting edge litigation and community development work has come at the expense of poor women who remain ineligible for benefits and trapped in abusive relationships because of the absence of legal assistance. Another community group proposes broadening the kinds of cases the office will accept, but conditioning assistance on clients' willingness to provide a specified amount of community service, such as helping with neighborhood cleanup, and renovation or providing services to disabled elderly residents.

The staff and board of the office are meeting to reconsider caseload priorities. What is your recommendation?[79]

NOTES AND QUESTIONS

1.   Critics of targeting resources to limited kinds of cases are troubled that legal services offices will address an eligible client's problem only if enough other potential clients share the same problem. To critics, targeting raises the concern commonly voiced against utilitarianism: that privileging the welfare of the group denies equal respect and concern to the individual. Defenders of targeting reply that only by focusing on widely-shared problems can legal aid offices address the causes of poverty as well as its individual symptoms. Whose view is more persuasive?

Model Rule 1.2 provides that a lawyer may "limit the scope of the representation if the limitation is reasonable under the circumstances and the client gives informed consent." Does this adequately respond to the problem? How meaningful is a client's consent to limited representation if no alternative is available?

---

79.   Aspects of this problem are drawn from Edgar S. Cahn, "Co–Producing Justice: The New Imperative," 5 *U.D.C. L. Rev.* 105 (2000) (discussing programs with community service requirements); Gary Bellow & Jean Kettleson, "From Ethics to Politics: Con-fronting Scarcity and Fairness in Public Interest Practice," 58 *B.U. L.Rev.* 337, 343–44 (1978); and "Ethical Problems in Legal Services Cases," (unpublished training materials, Western Center on Law and Poverty, April 7, 1994).

2.   Legal aid attorneys inevitably confront a dilemma both in the initial selection of cases and in the determination of how much time and expense should be spent on any particular matter. On one hand, to limit client assistance to only predefined "targeted" areas identified by the program is to ignore the immediate, personal aspects of the lawyer-client relationship that are basic to providing legal or any other social service. On the other hand, to provide full representation for each client would require either a staggering increase in available legal services or a system of triage in which most will go without service in order that a few may get what they need. How should this tradeoff be resolved?

3.   Unless and until legal assistance is more widely available, are changes needed in adversarial norms? For example, should ethical codes include provisions such as those appearing in an earlier draft of the Model Rules that would have prohibited lawyers appearing against pro se opponents from "unfairly exploiting . . . ignorance of the law or the practices of the tribunal," and "procur[ing] an unconscionable result"?[80] After vigorous bar opposition, that provision was replaced with requirements in Rule 4.3 that lawyers dealing with an unrepresented adversary simply avoid implications that they are disinterested and make reasonable efforts to correct misunderstandings concerning their role. Are such requirements sufficient?

4.   After the cutbacks in federal subsidies for legal services during the 1980s, many jurisdictions attempted to fill the gap through funds from Interest on Lawyers Trust Accounts (IOLTA). Lawyers are required to maintain separate "trust accounts" for any client money in their possession. For example, defendants who have lost a civil case will typically write the check for damages to the plaintiffs' lawyer rather than to the plaintiff; the plaintiffs' lawyer will then deposit the money in a trust account for the few days it takes to transfer the award to the plaintiff. Traditionally, lawyers placed client funds in non-interest-bearing accounts because lawyers have no right to the interest and the administrative costs of distributing it to individual clients exceeded the benefits. In 1980, however, Congress amended banking laws and made it possible for money in lawyers' trust accounts to earn interest, provided that the interest would go to charitable organizations. Under IOLTA plans, states require or permit lawyers to place client funds in such interest-bearing accounts. Banks then pay the interest to state bar IOLTA programs, which use the funds for legal aid and other projects related to the administration of justice. Such programs collect an estimated $160 million a year, making them the second-largest source of legal aid funds, after the federal Legal Services Corporation. The Supreme Court has upheld that system against claims that it constituted an uncompensated taking of property without just compensation. *Brown v. Legal Foundation of Washington*, 538 U.S. 216 (2003). However, recent declines in interest rates have reduced the amount of

80. Model Rules of Professional Conduct, Rule 3.6 (Discussion Draft 1980); *id.* comment at 75.

IOLTA funds available to subsidize crucial services. Would other sources of revenue be feasible, such as those proposed in Problem 2(b)?

F.   ALTERNATIVE DISPUTE RESOLUTION

1.   THE RATIONALE FOR ALTERNATIVE DISPUTE RESOLUTION

NOTES

Alternative dispute resolution [ADR] procedures are not a new phenomenon; what is new is the level of interest in expanding their forms, availability, and effectiveness. Beginning in the late 1960s, such procedures began to attract greater attention. A broad range of factors fueled interest in these alternatives: dissatisfaction with the expense, delays, and contentious nature of adjudication; concerns about undue litigiousness and unequal access to justice; desires for increased client control, community empowerment, and remedial flexibility; heightened interest in preserving relationships and exploring root causes as well as legal symptoms of problems; and perceived inadequacies in other family, religious, and community institutions for mediating grievances.[81] The number of mediations and arbitrations through the American Arbitration Association tripled during the 1990s, and the volume of providers and publications also grew dramatically.[82] In its current form, ADR seeks to encompass more than just alternatives to litigation; it also aims to encompass different kinds of disputes through different, more cost-effective processes.[83]

Advocates of ADR advocate "fitting the forum to the fuss."[84] Their premise is that different types of disputes and dispute resolution procedures have distinctive characteristics and should be matched accordingly. Lon Fuller, one of the principal architects of this framework, argued that adjudication was appropriate for cases involving fundamental rights or unsettled legal principles, but that other procedures might be more suitable for routine matters, for parties with ongoing relationships, or for grievances that affect multiple stakeholders and do not lend themselves to

---

81. *See generally,* Carrie Menkel–Meadow, "Roots and Inspirations: A Brief History of he Foundations of Dispute Resolution," in *The Handbook of Dispute Resolution* 13–31 (Michael L. Moffit & Robert C. Bordone eds. 2005).

82. Charles Silver & Lynn Baker, "Does Civil Justice Cost Too Much?," 80 *Tex. L. Rev.* 2073, 2105 (2002). A rough gauge of current interest is suggested by a search effort that revealed over 270 internet sites and some 4,000 books related to dispute resolution. Deborah R. Hensler, "Our Courts, Ourselves: How the Alternative Dispute Resolution Movement Is Reshaping Our Legal System," (2003); David D. Hechler,

"ADR Finds True Believers," *Nat'l. L. J.,* July 2, 2001, at A1. For an overview of processes, see Stephen Goldberg et al., *Dispute Resolution: Negotiation, Mediation, and Other Processes* (4th ed. 2003).

83. Jacqueline M. Nolan–Haley, "Introduction: Lawyers' Ethics in ADR," in Professional Responsibility of Lawyers, 28 *Fordham Urban L. J.* 891 (2001).

84. Frank E. A. Sander & Stephen B. Goldberg, "Fitting the Forum to the Fuss: A User–Friendly Guide to Selecting an ADR Procedure," 10 *Negotiation J.* 49, 60 (1994) (crediting the phrase to Maurice Rosenberg).

principled win-lose decisions.[85] Building on that approach, many proponents refer to ADR as "appropriate" rather than "alternative" dispute resolution.

At the most abstract level, supporters of alternative dispute resolution share certain common objectives. They join in what then Chief Justice Burger summarized as the true goals of the legal profession: "to gain an acceptable result in the shortest possible time with the least amount of stress and at the lowest possible cost to the client."[86] At the concrete level, however, what constitutes "acceptable" remains subject to dispute, and these goals do not always push in the same direction. Conflicts often arise between cost and quality, between parties' desire for private, mutually acceptable outcomes, and societal interests in publicly accountable decision making, and between enhancing access and reducing congestion and delay. Faced with such tradeoffs, advocates of alternative dispute resolution have had diverse priorities and have championed an equally diverse set of proposals.

2.   FORMS OF ALTERNATIVE DISPUTE RESOLUTION

NOTES

Dispute resolution structures vary across multiple dimensions, such as the parties' control over the process, the formality of procedures, the finality of judgment, the role of neutral mediators or decision makers, and the allocation of expenses. These structures also vary in priorities. Some approaches have been principally concerned with facilitating justice as the current system defines it: providing cheaper, quicker, and more convenient ways of achieving results comparable to what a court would mandate (so-called "shadow verdicts"). Other advocates of alternative dispute resolution have hoped to revise existing notions of justice by empowering those disadvantaged under current procedures and by encouraging cooperative problem solving rather than win/lose outcomes.

Some alternative dispute resolution procedures have developed under federal and state legislation or judicial decrees; others have evolved through private initiatives. Among the most important federal statutes is the Judicial Improvements Act (Civil Justice Reform Act) of 1990, 28 U.S.C.A. § 471. It requires every federal district court to study its caseload and to develop a plan to "facilitate ... adjudication of civil cases on the merits, and ensure just, speedy and inexpensive resolution of civil disputes." Among the strategies courts should consider in formulating their plan is authority for trial judges to refer appropriate cases to alternative dispute resolution.

---

85. Lon Fuller, "The Forms and Limits of Adjudication," 92 *Harv.L.Rev.* 353 (1978); Lon Fuller, "Mediation: Its Forms and Functions," 44 *S.Cal.L.Rev.* 305 (1971).

86. Commission on Professionalism, American Bar Association, *In the Spirit of Public Service: A Blueprint for the Rekindling of Lawyer Professionalism* 41 (1986) (quoting Chief Justice Warren Burger).

a.   *Procedural Variations*

Alternative dispute resolution procedures differ along several lines:[87]

The role of the decision maker or facilitator. Who selects that individual and by what criteria? What expertise is required?

The enforceability of the outcome. Is the outcome binding or is it subject to review?

Consent. Is the procedure voluntary or mandatory?

Relationship to the adjudicative system. Is the procedure independent or connected to state or federal courts?

Formality. Is the procedure formally structured by fixed rules or by agreement of the parties, or is it relatively informal and flexible?

What constitutes a good outcome may depend on the nature of the process. In mediation, for example, assessments might turn on whether the process reflected principles such as mediators' neutrality and confidentiality, and parties' informed consent, self-determination, and ultimate satisfaction with the process and result. In arbitration, the criteria might include not only satisfaction, but savings in time and money, and compliance with the judgment. In adjudication, the concerns might be whether justice was achieved, rights vindicated, and an equitable result achieved.[88]

b.   *The Range of Alternative Structures*

Arbitration. In arbitration, parties submit their dispute to a neutral decision-maker, often someone who has particular expertise in the matters at issue. The American Arbitration Association handles close to 10,000 commercial disputes each year, and large numbers of additional labor and contract controversies are arbitrated under private arrangements. Typically, the arbitrator is chosen by mutual agreement of the contending parties from a list of professionals. Some consumer agencies and industry groups such as the Better Business Bureau also have systems for arbitrating claims.

Most states have statutes modeled on the Uniform Arbitration Act, 7 U.L.A. 5 (1985), which govern enforcement of arbitration agreements. Enforcement may also be available under the Federal Arbitration Act, and the Labor Management Relations Act of 1947. Arbiters' judgments are usually final; review is available only in limited circumstances, generally involving procedural violations. A number of federal and state courts require submission of certain cases to court-annexed arbitration, although parties typically have a right to trial de novo.

Private Adjudication. Some statutes and rules of court permit referral of cases to privately selected and compensated adjudicators, often

---

87. For an overview of approaches see Federal Judicial Center, *Guide to Judicial Management of Cases in ADR* (2001). *See also* Carrie Menkel–Meadow, *Dispute Processing and Conflict Resolution: Theory, Practice, and Policy* (2003).

88. Robert C. Burdone, "Fitting the Ethics to the Forum: A Proposal for Process–Enabling Ethical Codes," 21 *Ohio State J. Dispute Resol.* 1, 6–7 (2005).

retired judges. Under such referral programs, sometimes labeled "rent-a-judge," the private adjudicator's decision is entered as the judgment of the court. Unlike an arbitrator's award, this judgment is normally appealable.

Summary Jury Trial. Under this procedure, lawyers give a summary of their trial presentation to a jury, usually without witnesses or exhibits. The jury then renders a verdict that is not binding, although the jurors are not informed of this fact before reaching their decision. This verdict can assist parties to evaluate their claims and to negotiate a reasonable settlement.

Mini-trials. Mini-trials, or "structured settlement" negotiations, offer opportunities for lawyers to present an abbreviated version of their case to a decision-making panel. In one common variation, the panel includes a neutral advisor and executives of the opposing parties. The aim is to enable the parties to hear a forceful presentation of their adversary's case. After the advisor predicts what would happen if the case were litigated, the principals attempt to negotiate a settlement. In some mini-trials, the neutral advisor will render an advisory opinion only if the parties initially fail to reach an agreement.

Mediation. Mediation is an informal process in which a neutral third party helps the parties resolve a dispute or structure a transaction. Ordinarily, this third party facilitates but does not impose a solution, and the parties voluntarily choose the mediator. However, some jurisdictions require mediation for certain types of cases, such as child custody disputes. Distinctions are often drawn between "evaluative mediation," in which the mediator suggests an appropriate settlement range in light of the legal and factual strength of parties' claims, and "facilitative mediation," in which the mediator helps parties find a solution that reflects their underlying interests and maximizes opportunities for joint gains. See Chapter VIII (Negotiation and Mediation).

Ombudsperson. Ombudspersons are officials appointed by organizations to prevent, investigate, and informally resolve disputes. In the private sector, ombudspersons function primarily in employer/employee relations. In the public sector, their role is broader. The Administrative Conference of the United States recommended that all federal agencies with a significant public function consider establishing ombudsperson offices. See 1 C.F.R. § 305.90–2.

Community–Based Dispute Resolution. Neighborhood justice centers, citizen complaint bureaus, and other community-based centers function as free-standing institutions or court-affiliated agencies. These organizations typically receive referrals from courts, prosecutors, police, or other community agencies, as well as walk-in clients. Professional mediators or volunteers with mediation training handle a variety of disputes, including landlord-tenant, family, and neighbor relations. Some jurisdictions have also established specialized "holistic," "therapeutic," or "community" courts to deal with problems like domestic violence, homelessness, and misdemeanors such as prostitution, drug possession, and juvenile offences. Judges in these proceedings receive special training and partner with other social service providers to offer treatment approaches that can address root causes not just legal symptoms. By employing mediation and other alternative dispute resolution techniques, these courts seek to engage parties in productive, collaborative problem solving.[89]

Early Neutral Evaluation or Expert Evaluation. This technique, which is used both in private dispute resolution and in court-annexed programs involves reliance on an experienced attorney or technical expert to evaluate a case. After summary presentations by counsel and the parties, the evaluator assesses the issues in dispute in an effort to facilitate settlement negotiations.

Online Dispute Resolution. Recent technological innovations are providing an increasing array of online dispute resolution processes. They include: (a) online e-mail or instant messaging negotiation or mediation, such as services to resolve controversies over online auction purchases; (2) interactive blind bids, in which lawyers for a plaintiff and a defendant who have already agreed on liability can negotiate monetary damage amounts until their bids converge close enough for the computer to create a settlement; and (3) ad-hoc jury panels that allow parties with small claims to post arguments and evidence online and to respond directly to the panel's questions.[90]

Some of these processes require online mediators to adhere to ethical standards of professional responsibility adapted from the Ethical Standards set forth by the Society of Professionals in Dispute Resolution [SPIDR]. These standards encompass duties "to the parties, to the profession, and to themselves. They should be honest and unbiased, act in good faith, be diligent, and not seek to advance their own interests at the expense of their parties'." To ensure compliance with such standards, services like Square-Trade.com, which addresses online auction disputes, require mediators to sign a legally binding confidentiality agreement and encourage parties to inform the site if they believe the mediator has deviated from his or her duties.

3. ALTERNATIVE DISPUTE RESOLUTION: CRITICS AND THEIR CRITICS

NOTES

These varied dispute resolution procedures have sparked an equally varied set of critiques. Paradoxically enough, many of the same criticisms leveled at litigation-based strategies also have been directed at more

---

89. Greg Berman & John Feinblatt, *Problem Solving Courts: A Brief Primer* (2001); Margot Lindsay & Mary K. Shilton, "The Public Is Willing," 29 *Fordham Urb. L. J.* 1267, 1270 (200–; Anthony C. Thompson, "Courting Disorder: Some Thoughts on Community Courts," 10 *Wash. U. J. L. and Pol.* 63 (2002).

90. Jason Krause, "On the Web," ABA J., Oct., 2007, at 43–45; Online Dispute Resolution (ODR): Technology as the "Fourth Party," Papers and Proceedings of the 2003 United Nations Forum on ODR (Ethan Katsh and Daewon Choi, eds., Geneva, June 30–July 1, 2003), *available at* http://www.odr.info/unece2003/pdf/Tyler.pdf.

informal alternatives. Critics have often claimed that ADR procedures do more to defuse than to resolve conflict. For example, by individualizing grievances shared by many community residents—such as complaints by tenants against a large landlord—such procedures deflect attention from common problems and the collective efforts necessary to address them. By expanding "access to justice" for these individual claims, dispute resolution reforms also may foster the illusion that "justice" has been done when underlying problems remain unsolved. So too, many ADR processes do not result in the substantial savings in time or cost that their proponents sought to achieve.[91]

A second cluster of criticisms has an equally paradoxical quality; alternative dispute resolution is criticized for being both too available and not available enough. Some commentators complain that options such as rent-a-judge or mini-trials are affordable only by the wealthy. Such a market-based structure institutionalizes "legal apartheid"—convenient, speedy justice for the haves and cumbersome, inefficient processes for the have-nots. By creating a two-track system, alternative dispute procedures also may reduce pressure to reform the judicial system that makes such alternatives necessary.

Conversely, another group of critics charges that ADR is too often imposed on middle-and low-income clients with "simple" cases and that it too often offers second-class justice. Mandatory mediation for which parties must pay imposes special hardships on those of limited means. Informal, streamlined structures also can deprive less powerful parties of crucial protections. Problems are especially likely to arise in systems that pit repeat players against parties who are not. For example, in one study involving such cases, the odds of employers winning in disputes with employees were five to one. Only repeat players had incentives to investigate the past records and predispositions of ostensibly neutral decisionmakers and some of those decisionmakers had incentives to please sources of future business. In another survey of results under arbitration clauses imposed by First USA, the nation's second largest issuer of credit cards, the bank won 99% of the cases.[92]

A related problem is that mediation between parties with unequal power may reinforce their inequality and encourage negotiation of rights that should be non-negotiable. For example, battered wives may agree to avoid "nagging" in exchange for their husbands' promises to refrain from physical assaults.[93] Although some mediators attempt to mitigate certain disparities in parties' bargaining capacities, or refuse to ratify settlements

91. See studies reviewed in Silver & Baker, *supra* note 82, 1206–07; Hensler, *supra* note 82.

92. Richard C. Reuban, "Lawyer Turns Peacemaker," *ABA J.*, Aug. 1996 at 61; Jeffrey Stempel, "Reflections on Judicial ADR and the Multidoor Courthouse at Twenty: Fait Accompli, Failed Overture or Fledgling Adulthood," 11 *Ohio State J. on Dispute Resolution* 297, 319, 339, 351 (1996); Caroline E. Mayer, "Win Some, Lose Rarely?; Arbitration Forum's Rulings Called One–Sided," *Washington Post*, March 1, 2000, at E1.

93. Leigh Goodmark, "Alternative Dispute Resolution and the Potential for Gender Bias," *Judges Journal*, Spring 2000, at 21–27; Hensler, *supra* note 82 (reviewing empirical surveys).

that seem clearly unfair, such non-neutral conduct raises its own set of ethical difficulties. Not only can it compromise mediators' credibility and capacity to achieve solutions, it subjects participants to manipulation by mediators with undisclosed standards and no formal mechanisms of accountability.

These examples also suggest some of the concerns that Owen Fiss summarizes in the excerpt below: that informal processes oriented toward private settlements undervalue society's interest in having publicly accountable officials interpret and implement publicly acceptable norms. A process geared toward compromise may also provide inadequate deterrence of unlawful conduct. Where arbiters need not adhere to formal rules or give reasons for their reasons, the process appears arbitrary in a sense that adjudication does not.[94]

Yet as ADR supporters note, these critiques often proceed by comparing alternative processes to an idealized image of adjudication. Before denouncing such initiatives as second-class justice, it is important to inquire whether first class is likely to be available and on what terms. Under current adjudicative processes, informal settlement is the norm; less than 10% of cases filed receive the full process that Owen Fiss endorses, and the vast majority of grievances never even reach the filing stage. Even in the small minority of cases that are adjudicated, the due process that is available often looks more impressive in theory than in practice. For reasons noted in prior discussion, it seems unlikely that the poor generally fare better in formal than informal tribunals. In many respects the current system already offers "apartheid justice"; extensive resources are available for commercial litigation that parties can afford to subsidize, while other matters, such as those involving family issues for nonwealthy parties, receive only the most cursory attention.[95] Moreover, what limited empirical evidence is available suggests that many litigants do not place the high value on formal process that some legal commentators assume. Parties care about procedural fairness, but they often prefer some kind of alternative dispute resolution to courtroom trials.[96] Although parties' satisfaction should not be the sole criterion for evaluation, it is surely relevant.

These competing perspectives on alternative dispute resolution suggest one common insight. The evaluation of alternatives should not proceed in the abstract. Much depends on the form of dispute resolution at issue, the context in which it is implemented, and the other options realistically available. Sensible policy choices will also require more systematic information comparing outcomes, costs, and satisfaction in different dispute resolution processes, as well as more evaluation of efforts to increase accountability and protect vulnerable parties.

94. Owen Fiss, "Against Settlement," 93 *Yale L.J.* 1073, 1085–87 (1984). *See also* Deborah Hensler, "Suppose It's Not True: Challenging Mediation Ideology," 2002 *Dispute Resolution* 81 (2002).

95. Rhode, *In the Interests of Justice*, *supra* note 7, at 132–34.

96. Lisa Brennan, "What Lawyers Like: Mediation," *National L. J.*, November 15, 1999, at A1; Hensler, *supra* note 94; Michael Zander, *The Quality of Justice*, 29–32 (2000).

4.   ETHICAL RULES

A final area of concern involves the ethical rules governing alternative dispute resolution. Practices vary on issues such as confidentiality, conflicts of interest, and responsibility to promote procedural and substantive fairness. Significant differences are also evident in ethical codes drafted by various professional organizations, such as the American Arbitration Association, the Society of Professionals in Dispute Resolution, and the Georgetown Commission on Ethics and Standards in ADR.[97] Should ADR professionals be held to some uniform ethical standards? Should such professionals be required to demonstrate certain minimum qualifications for practice? If so, how should these requirements be defined and enforced?

PROBLEM 4

a) A former client asks your advice on whether to hire a retired judge or to stage a mini-trial to resolve a million-dollar contract dispute. Your sister also seeks your opinion about whether she should agree to her husband's proposal that they hire a mediator rather than lawyers to handle their divorce. What questions would you ask, and which considerations would be most relevant to your advice?

b) You represent the plaintiff in a contingent-fee products liability claim. The defendant has proposed to resolve the issue through a confidential arbitration proceeding. You are reluctant to agree because you have already incurred most of the costs necessary to try the case, and you believe that it could generate a larger award from a jury than from an arbitrator. Moreover, the potential adverse publicity of such a verdict might prompt a generous settlement on the eve of trial. In either case, your success is likely to attract more visibility and more new clients than a confidential arbitration award. Your client, however, is extremely risk-averse and might be tempted to accept the alternative dispute resolution offer, since it is likely to result in a substantial financial recovery and could not be appealed. Are you obligated to discuss the ADR proposal with the client and to disclose your own interests? See Model Rules 1.2 and 1.7; EC 7–7 and 7–8, and DR 5–105.

c) You are counsel to the Congressional committee that is establishing a seven billion dollar fund to compensate the victims of the 9/11 attacks. Individuals who agree to waive rights to sue for injuries or deaths resulting from those attacks will be eligible to participate. A threshold question is how to fix the level of compensation. Should it reflect lost earning potential, establish standardized amounts for death and or serious injury, or leave the amounts to the discretion of the special master who will adminis-

---

97. See the discussion of mediation ethics in Chapter VIII, *supra,* Symposium: "The Collision of Two Ideals: Legal Ethics and the World of Alternative Dispute Resolution," 21 *Ohio St. J. Dispute Resol.* 1 (2005); Burdone, *supra* note 88; Carrie Menkel–Meadow, "Ethics Issues in Arbitration and Related Dispute Resolution Processes: What's Happening and What's Not," 56 *U. Miami L. Rev.* 949 (2002); Symposium: "ADR and the Professional Responsibility of Lawyers," 28 *Fordham Urb. L. J.* 891–991 (2001); Georgetown Commission on Ethics and Standards in ADR, *Proposed Model Rule of Professional Conduct for the Lawyer as Third Party Neutral* (1999), and sources cited.

ter the fund? Supporters of the earning potential standard point out that it is the normal measure for personal injury and wrongful death claims, and a different approach might discourage individuals from participating in the program. Opponents argue that it will be hard to explain to the widow of a firefighter who died in a heroic effort to save victims that she will be entitled to "a million dollars less than the widow of a bond trader for Enron on the hundred third floor of the World Trade Center."[98] Another issue involves the scope of the compensation hearings. Should they be limited to the remedies at issue, or should families have an opportunity to introduce any information they choose concerning the lives of victims, such as videos from their weddings or bar mitzvahs, and pictures from family photo albums?[99] What do you advise, and what considerations would inform your decision?

d) You are a lawyer for the United States Agency for International Development (USAID). The Agency has recently come under criticism by U.S. women's rights organizations for sponsoring a mediation program in Nicaragua that includes domestic violence cases. Although a local feminist cooperative has supported the program, some observers are concerned that the program's emphasis on harmony and individual solutions may perpetuate victimization, as well as undercut broader political efforts. Given the widespread opposition to mandatory mediation of domestic violence cases in the United States, women's rights groups argue that American tax dollars should not subsidize such initiatives abroad. By contrast, supporters of the Nicaraguan program, although sensitive to its disadvantages, believe that it is often preferable to litigation, given the geographic inaccessibility of courts for much of the country, and the costs for victims who bring formal complaints. From supporters' vantage, the United States should support local understandings of appropriate conflict resolution, not impose its own standards.[100] How would you advise the Agency to proceed? When the United States sponsors "rule of law" initiatives abroad, how should government decision makers assess the procedural alternatives?[101]

Owen Fiss, "Against Settlement"

93 Yale Law Journal 1073, 1075–78, 1085–86 (1984).

The advocates of ADR are led to . . . exalt the idea of settlement . . . because they view adjudication as a process to resolve disputes. They act as

98. Kenneth Feinberg, "What is Life Worth," University of Massachusetts, Sept. 11, 2007, available at http://www.massachusetts.edu/uncommonleadership/kennethfeinberg.html.

99. *Id.*

100. For a description of the Nicaraguan program and its relative strengths and limitations, see Jean R. Sternlight, "Is Alternative Dispute Resolution Consistent With the Rule of Law? Lessons From Abroad," 56 *Depaul L. Rev.* 560, 577–78 (2007).

101. Since the 1990s, the World Bank alone has sponsored over three hundred projects, which have spent almost three billion dollars. David M. Trubek, "The 'Rule of Law' in Development Assistance: Past, Present and Future," in *The New Law and Economic Development: A Critical Appraisal* 74 (David M. Trubek & Alvarao Santos, eds. 2006). For examples of ADR in such projects, see Center for Democracy and Governance, USAID, *Alternative Dispute Resoution Practitioners' Guide* (1998).

though courts arose to resolve quarrels between neighbors who had reached an impasse and turned to a stranger for help. Courts are seen as an institutionalization of the stranger and adjudication is viewed as the process by which the stranger exercises power. The very fact that the neighbors have turned to someone else to resolve their dispute signifies a breakdown in their social relations; the advocates of ADR acknowledge this, but nonetheless hope that the neighbors will be able to reach agreement before the stranger renders judgment. Settlement is that agreement. It is a truce more than a true reconciliation, but it seems preferable to judgment because it rests on the consent of both parties and avoids the cost of a lengthy trial.

In my view, however, this account of adjudication and the case for settlement rest on questionable premises. I do not believe that settlement as a generic practice is preferable to judgment or should be institutionalized on a wholesale and indiscriminate basis. It should be treated instead as a highly problematic technique for streamlining dockets. Settlement is for me the civil analogue of plea bargaining: Consent is often coerced; the bargain may be struck by someone without authority; the absence of a trial and judgment renders subsequent judicial involvement troublesome; and although dockets are trimmed, justice may not be done. Like plea bargaining, settlement is a capitulation to the conditions of mass society and should be neither encouraged nor praised.

The Imbalance of Power

By viewing the lawsuit as a quarrel between two neighbors, the dispute-resolution story that underlies ADR implicitly asks us to assume a rough equality between the contending parties. It treats settlement as the anticipation of the outcome of trial and assumes that the terms of settlement are simply a product of the parties' predictions of that outcome. In truth, however, settlement is also a function of the resources available to each party to finance the litigation, and those resources are frequently distributed unequally. Many lawsuits do not involve a property dispute between two neighbors, or between AT & T and the government (to update the story), but rather concern a struggle between a member of a racial minority and a municipal police department over alleged brutality, or a claim by a worker against a large corporation over work-related injuries. In these cases, the distribution of financial resources, or the ability of one party to pass along its costs, will invariably infect the bargaining process, and the settlement will be at odds with a conception of justice that seeks to make the wealth of the parties irrelevant.

The disparities in resources between the parties can influence the settlement in three ways. First, the poorer party may be less able to amass and analyze the information needed to predict the outcome of the litigation, and thus be disadvantaged in the bargaining process. Second, he may need the damages he seeks immediately and thus be induced to settle as a way of accelerating payment, even though he realizes he would get less now than he might if he awaited judgment. All plaintiffs want their damages immediately, but an indigent plaintiff may be exploited by a rich defendant because his need is so great that the defendant can force him to accept a sum that is less than the ordinary present value of the judgment. Third, the poorer party might be forced to settle because he does not have the resources to finance the litigation, to cover either his own projected expenses, such as his lawyer's time, or the expenses his opponent can impose through the manipulation of procedural mechanisms such as discovery. It might seem that settlement benefits the plaintiff by allowing him to avoid the costs of litigation, but this is not so. The defendant can anticipate the plaintiff's costs if the case were to be tried fully and decrease his offer by that amount. The indigent plaintiff is a victim of the costs of litigation even if he settles....

Of course, imbalances of power can distort judgment as well: Resources influence the quality of presentation, which in turn has an important bearing on who wins and the terms of victory. We count, however, on the guiding presence of the judge, who can employ a number of measures to lessen the impact of distributional inequalities. He can, for example, supplement the parties' presentations by asking questions, calling his own witnesses, and inviting other persons and institutions to participate as amici. These measures are likely to make only a small contribution toward moderating the influence of distributional inequalities, but should not be ignored for that reason. Not even these small steps are possible with settlement. There is, moreover, a critical difference between a process like settlement, which is based on bargaining and accepts inequalities of wealth as an integral and legitimate component of the process, and a process like judgment, which knowingly struggles against those inequalities. Judgment aspires to an autonomy from distributional inequalities, and it gathers much of its appeal from this aspiration.

Justice Rather Than Peace

The dispute-resolution story makes settlement appear as a perfect substitute for judgment, as we just saw, by trivializing the remedial dimensions of a lawsuit, and also by reducing the social function of the lawsuit to one of resolving private disputes: In that story, settlement appears to achieve exactly the same purpose as judgment—peace between the parties—but at considerably less expense to society....

In my view, however, the purpose of adjudication should be understood in broader terms. Adjudication uses public resources, and employs not strangers chosen by the parties but public officials chosen by a process in which the public participates. These officials, like members of the legislative and executive branches, possess a power that has been defined and conferred by public law, not by private agreement. Their job is not to maximize the ends of private parties, nor simply to secure the peace, but to explicate and give force to the values embodied in authoritative texts such as the Constitution and statutes: to interpret those values and to bring reality into accord with them. This duty is not discharged when the parties settle.

In our political system, courts are reactive institutions. They do not search out interpretive occasions, but instead wait for others to bring matters to their attention. They also rely for the most part on others to investigate and present the law and facts. A settlement will thereby deprive a court of the occasion, and perhaps even the ability, to render an interpretation. A court cannot proceed (or not proceed very far) in the face of a settlement. To be against settlement is not to urge that parties be "forced" to litigate, since that would interfere with their autonomy and distort the adjudicative process; the parties will be inclined to make the court believe that their bargain is justice. To be against settlement is only to suggest that when the parties settle, society gets less than what appears, and for a price it does not know it is paying. Parties might settle while leaving justice undone. The settlement of a school suit might secure the peace, but not racial equality. Although the parties are prepared to live under the terms they bargained for, and although such peaceful coexistence may be a necessary precondition of justice, and itself a state of affairs to be valued, it is not justice itself. To settle for something means to accept less than some ideal.

NOTES AND QUESTIONS

In a comprehensive overview of the ADR literature, Marc Galanter and Mia Cahill argue that the appropriate task for policy makers is not "promoting settlements or discouraging them but regulating them."[102] The goal should be to promote the values that we consider most desirable in a particular context, such as encouraging full disclosure of relevant facts, offering adequate remedies, providing principles and guidance for future cases, fostering compliance with relevant laws, and maintaining good relations between the parties. As Galanter and Cahill note, available research does not establish that either adjudication or pre-trial settlement is necessarily more effective in accomplishing any of these objectives. Nor does that research suggest consistent differences between ADR and adjudication in cost, speed, and party satisfaction.[103]

If neither ADR nor adjudication is clearly preferable for all, or even most contexts, what follows from that fact? According to some commentators, consumers should have a broad range of dispute resolution choices and the information necessary to make them. And society should have a way to insure that the parties' procedural choices are subject to reasonable constraints based on the public values at stake. So, for example, multidoor courthouses could allocate different types of cases to "appropriate dispute resolution" processes based on several key criteria: the nature of the controversy; the relationship between the parties; the priorities that the participants attach to various features of the dispute resolution process; and the societal interests at issue. Crucial features of the controversy

---

102. Marc Galanter & Mia Cahill, "Most Cases Settle: Judicial Promotion and Regulation of Settlements," 46 *Stan.L.Rev.* 1339, 1388 (1994).

103. *Id.*; Rhode, *In the Interests of Justice, supra* note 7, at 132–34; text at note 91 *supra*.

include the remedies being sought, the novelty or complexity of relevant law, and the public policies implicated. Cases involving relatively small monetary damages and the application of settled legal precedents may not justify the expense of full-scale adjudication. In other contexts, the relationship between the parties may argue for procedures that are best able to address power disparities or to foster long-term working relationships.

How would Fiss respond to such a proposal? How would you? What considerations do you think are most critical in evaluating ADR and how would they affect your decisions in Problem 4?[104]

G.   PRO BONO REPRESENTATION

1.   THE ETHICAL OBLIGATIONS OF LAWYERS

INTRODUCTION

One primary way that "learned professions," including law and medicine, distinguish themselves from business occupations is by emphasizing their commitment to public service. Thus, the American Bar Association Committee on Professionalism entitled its widely-publicized report "*. . . In the Spirit of Public Service.*"[105] The bar has a long-standing tradition of providing assistance *pro bono publico* ("for the public good")—or "pro bono" for short. This concept encompasses work provided free or for a reduced fee for a wide range of organizations and individuals, including poor people, nonprofit organizations, bar associations, civic groups, and friends, relatives, or personal employees of lawyers or their clients.

Although the bar has long supported pro bono in principle, its commitment in practice has been less consistent. As the readings below note, a wide gap remains between the rhetoric and reality of pro bono service. The ABA Code of Professional Responsibility maintains that "[t]he rendition of free legal services to those unable to pay reasonable fees continues to be an obligation of each lawyer." (EC 2–25). In fact, however, this reference to a pro bono "obligation" in the Ethical Considerations finds no counterpart in the Code's mandatory rules. Nor do the Model Rules impose any such obligations. Rule 6.1 provides that a lawyer "should aspire to render at least 50 hours of pro bono public legal services per year" and should provide a "substantial majority" of such services to "persons of limited means" or to organizations that assist such individuals. The Comment to this Rule makes clear that it "is not intended to be enforced through disciplinary process."

Efforts by some courts and bar leaders to require a minimum contribution of assistance have provoked broad resistance. The ABA Ethics 2000 Commission rejected proposals to make pro bono work mandatory, and

---

104. For further discussion of Fiss's argument, *see* David Luban, "Settlements and the Erosion of the Public Realm," 83 *Geo. L.J.* 2619 (1995).

105. ABA Commission on Professionalism, "*. . . In the Spirit of Public Service*": *A Blueprint for the Rekindling of Lawyer Professionalism* (1986), excerpted in Chapter I.

recommended simply that Rule 6.1 include a statement in the Comment that "[e]very lawyer has a professional responsibility to provide services to those unable to pay." Reform efforts at the state level have followed a similar pattern. According to ABA data, by 2007, 19 states had a version of Rule 6.1 suggesting 50 hours, 19 specified no amount, 5 specified between 20 and 30, and 1 required 80, and 1 required 2% of professional time. Eight suggested a specific financial contribution, ranging from $200 to $500. Five states, Florida, Illinois, Maryland, Mississippi, and Nevada, required lawyers to report their pro bono contributions, and twelve had voluntary reporting systems. Compliance rates range between 35 to 99 percent.[106] Since Florida first enacted a reporting requirement in 1994, the number of lawyers providing pro bono assistance to the poor has increased 35%, the number of hours has increased 160%, and the amount of financial contributions has increased 243%. In Maryland, about half of lawyers reported some pro bono participation, but only a fifth donate at least 50 hours.[107] A few jurisdictions require limited service in civil or criminal cases. For example, New Jersey requires lawyers to accept current appointments in cases involving indigents, but exempts practitioners in specified categories such as prosecutors, public defenders, legal aid attorneys, and lawyers who have contributed 25 hours a year of pro bono assistance to the poor through qualifying legal aid organizations. *Madden v. Township of Delran*, 601 A.2d 211 (N.J. 1992). Arizona authorizes county courts to require attorneys to serve as arbiters for small cases. *Scheehle v. Justices of the Arizona Supreme Court*, 120 P.3d 1092 (Ariz.2005).

Whether courts or bar associations should do more to foster charitable contributions remains a matter of ongoing debate. The following selection offers an argument for greater pro bono commitments.[108]

Deborah L. Rhode, Access to Justice

145–84 (2004).

The provision of assistance "pro bono publico" often expresses what is most admirable in the legal profession. But not often enough. Over the course of their careers, many lawyers contribute hundreds of unpaid hours to causes that would otherwise be priced out of the justice system. Some lawyers also give significant financial support to legal services programs. Yet the majority do not. Most lawyers make no contributions, and the average for the bar as a whole is less than half an hour a week and fifty

---

106. ABA State by State Pro Bono Service Rules, available at http://www.abanet.org/legalservices/probono/stateethicsrules.html. For compliance rates, see Leslie Boyle, "Meeting the Demands of the Indigent Population: The Choice Between Mandatory and Voluntary Pro Bono Requirements," 20 *Geo. J. Legal Ethics* 415, 425 (2007).

107. For Florida's increase, see Standing Committee on Pro Bono Legal Service,

Report to the Supreme Court of Florida, The Florida Bar, and the Florida Bar Foundation on the Voluntary Pro Bono Attorney Plan (2006). For Maryland, *see Current Status of Pro Bono Service Among Maryland Lawyers* (2005).

108. For extended arguments, *see* Rhode, *Pro Bono in Principle and in Practice* (2005); Scott Cummings, "The Politics of Pro Bono," 52 *UCLA L. Rev.* 1 (2004); Boyle, *supra* note 106.

cents a day. Moreover, much of what passes for "pro bono" is not aid to the indigent or public interest causes, but either favors for friends, family, or clients, or cases where fees turn out to be uncollectible. The bar's pro bono commitments are, in short, a reflection of both the profession's highest ideals and its most grating hypocrisies....

How best to reduce the gap between professional ideals and professional practice has been the subject of longstanding debate but little data. To help fill the void, the discussion that follows reviews findings from my own recent study: the first comprehensive national survey of the factors that influence lawyers' pro bono work. This study includes both an overview of the literature on altruism in general and bar contributions in particular, as well as questionnaires and interview responses from a sample of some three thousand attorneys. [These findings suggest] changes in workplace and law school cultures that can more effectively translate public service principles into professional practices.

The Rationale for Pro Bono Responsibilities

The rationale for pro bono work rests on two central claims. One involves the value to society of addressing unmet legal needs. A second justification involves the value to lawyers, individually and collectively, of such charitable contributions. The first argument begins from the premise that access to legal services is a fundamental interest. That claim ... is that inadequate legal assistance jeopardizes individual rights, compounds other social inequalities, and undermines America's commitment to procedural fairness and social justice.

A second rationale for pro bono service rests on the benefits to those who provide it. A wide array of research, both on charitable involvement in general and lawyers' public service in particular, finds that participants benefit personally and professionally. Regular volunteering is correlated with physical as well as mental health. Compared with the population generally, people who regularly assist others apart from family and friends have longer lives, less pain, stress, and depression, and greater self-esteem. Volunteers also report a sense of physical well-being, both immediately after helping and when the service is remembered, and are more likely to be happy with their lives. Although the correlation between volunteer activities and well-being does not establish a causal relationship, other evidence suggests that such a relationship exists, and that selfless action is good for the self. Such evidence includes the high frequency of individuals' subjective experience of benefits, the consistent association of volunteering with objective measures of health, and the biological indications of a "helper's high." ...

Studies of the legal profession, including findings from my own survey, similarly confirm the benefits of charitable involvement. Particularly for young attorneys, pro bono work can provide valuable training, contacts, trial experience, and leadership opportunities. Through volunteer projects, lawyers can develop new areas of expertise and demonstrate marketable skills. Involvement in community groups, charitable organizations, high visibility litigation, and other public interest activities is a way for attorneys to expand their perspectives, enhance their reputations, and attract paying clients. Pro bono work also enables individuals to express the commitments to social justice that often motivated them to choose legal careers in the first instance. ABA surveys consistently find that lawyers' greatest dissatisfaction with their practice is a lack of "contribution to the social good." Volunteer work can provide that contribution.

So too, pro bono activity serves the interests of legal employers and the legal profession generally. Strong public service programs can produce tangible, although hard to quantify, organizational benefits in terms of retention, recruitment, reputation, morale, and job performance. Pro bono contributions also can enhance the reputation of lawyers as a group. In one representative survey, which asked what could improve the image of lawyers, the response most often chosen was their provision of free legal services to the needy; two-thirds of those surveyed indicated that it would improve their opinion of the profession.

For all these reasons, the vast majority of surveyed lawyers believe that the bar *should* provide pro bono service. However, the vast majority also oppose *requiring* such service. The most common objection is that it is unfair to make the profession satisfy a public obligation. If access to law is a societal value, then society as a whole should bear its cost. The poor have fundamental needs for food and medical care, but we do not require grocers or physicians to donate their help in meeting those needs. Why should the responsibilities of lawyers or their employers be greater?

One answer is that the legal profession has a monopoly on the provision of essential services. Lawyers have special privileges that should entail special obligations. In the United States, attorneys have a much more extensive and exclusive right to provide legal assistance than attorneys in other countries. The American legal profession is responsible for creating and protecting that right, and its success in restricting lay competition has helped to price services beyond the reach of millions of consumers. Some pro bono contribution is not unreasonable to expect from lawyers in return for their privileged status. Nor would it be unfair to expect comparable contributions from other professionals who have similar monopolies over provision of critical services.

An alternative rationale for imposing special obligations on lawyers stems from their historic role as officers of the court and their special role in our governance structure. As a prominent New York bar report explained, much of what lawyers do "is about providing *justice*, [which is] . . . nearer to the heart of our way of life . . . than services provided by other professionals. The legal profession serves as indispensable guardians of our lives, liberties and governing principles. . . ." Because lawyers occupy such a central role in our justice system, there is also particular value in exposing them to how that system functions, or fails to function, for the have-nots. Giving broad segments of the bar some experience with poverty-related problems and public interest causes can lay crucial foundations for change.

A second cluster of objections to pro bono responsibilities rests on moral grounds. To many lawyers, requiring pro bono service seems an infringement of their own rights, and a form of "involuntary servitude" or latent fascism. Other commentators view "compulsory charity" as a contradiction in terms. From their perspective, requiring assistance undermines its moral significance and compromises altruistic commitments. Drawing on studies of helping behavior, some critics argue that individuals are more likely to provide sustained and quality service if they are doing so voluntarily than if they are fulfilling a requirement.

There are problems with each of these claims, beginning with the assumption that pro bono service is "charity." Rather, as the preceding discussion suggested, pro bono work is not simply a philanthropic exercise; it is also a professional responsibility. The effect that some minimum service requirement would have on overall pro bono participation is difficult to gauge. Critics have produced no evidence that voluntary assistance has declined in the small number of jurisdictions where courts now appoint lawyers to provide uncompensated representation. Nor is it self-evident that most lawyers who already make public service contributions would cease to do so simply because others were required to join them. As to the large numbers of lawyers who do not voluntarily contribute pro bono assistance but claim that required service would lack moral significance, law professor David Luban has it right: "One hesitates to state the obvious, but here it is: You can't appeal to the moral significance of a gift you have no intention of giving." Asking lawyers to make a modest contribution of service, along the lines that bar ethics codes suggest, generally between a half an hour to an hour a week, hardly constitutes "servitude." And those who find it unduly burdensome could substitute a financial contribution.

The stronger arguments against pro bono obligations involve pragmatic rather than moral concerns. Many opponents who support such obligations in principle worry that they would not prove efficient in practice. A threshold problem involves defining the services that would satisfy a pro bono requirement. If the definition is broad, and encompasses any unpaid legal work, then experience suggests that poor people will not be the major beneficiaries; most work will help friends, relatives, middle-class non-profit organizations, and deadbeat clients. By contrast, if a pro bono requirement is limited to the low-income individuals given preferred status in some bar association's aspirational standards, then that definition would exclude many crucial public interest contributions, such as work for civil rights, civil liberties, or environmental organizations. Any compromise effort to permit some but not all charitable groups to qualify for pro bono credit would bump up against charges of political bias.

A further objection to mandatory pro bono requirements is that lawyers who lack expertise or motivation to serve under-represented groups will not offer cost-effective assistance. In opponents' view, corporate lawyers who dabble in poverty cases will often provide unduly expensive or incompetent services. The performance of some attorneys required to accept uncompensated appointments in criminal cases does not inspire confidence that unwillingly conscripted practitioners would provide acceptable representation. Critics also worry that some lawyers' inexperience and insensitivity in dealing with low-income clients will compromise the objectives that pro bono requirements seek to advance. The basis for such concerns is often apparent in surveys of pro bono programs. Some attorneys object to spending time on "piddling matters" or representing clients who have "messed up their lives" and then, even after assistance, do something to botch it up even more. Opponents also worry about the "Burgeoning Bureaucratic Boondoggle" that they assume would be necessary to monitor compliance. Even with a substantial expenditure of resources, it would be extremely difficult to verify the amount of time that practitioners reported for pro bono work or the quality of assistance that they provided.

From critics' perspective, requiring attorneys to contribute minimal services of largely unverifiable quality cannot solve the problem of unequal access to justice. Worse still, such minimal mandates may divert attention from more productive ways of addressing unmet needs. Preferable strategies would include those proposed in earlier chapters, such as simplification of legal procedures, expanded subsidies for poverty law programs, greater assistance for pro se litigants, and fewer restrictions on provision of routine legal services by nonlawyers.

These are significant concerns, but they are not nearly as conclusive as critics suggest. It is certainly true that some practitioners lack many of the skills necessary to serve those most in need of assistance. But, as law professor Michael Millemann notes, the current alternative is scarcely preferable: "Assume that after four years in college, three years of law school, and varying periods of law practice some lawyers are 'incompetent' to help the poor. . . . All this despairing assumption tells us is that the poor are far less competent to represent themselves, and do not have the readily available access to attaining competency that lawyers have." To be sure, subsidizing additional poverty law specialists or enlisting more willing volunteers would be a more efficient way of expanding services than relying on reluctant dilettantes. But neither strategy seems likely to be sufficient in this political climate. Nor is it clear that pro bono programs are diverting significant attention from better ways to address current needs. Whose attention? Most policy makers who have opposed adequate legal aid funding do not appear much interested in expanding access to justice through any method.

In any event, multiple strategies are available to reduce the likelihood of incompetent assistance and undue enforcement burdens. One is to allow lawyers to buy out their required service by making an equivalent financial contribution to a legal aid program. Another option is to permit lawyers in organizations to satisfy their obligations collectively by designating certain individuals responsible for fulfilling the hourly responsibilities of all their colleagues. A further possibility is to give continuing legal education (CLE) credit for time spent in training for pro bono work, and to rely on the same kind of honor system used in enforcing CLE requirements for pro bono obligations as well. Many voluntary public interest projects have effectively equipped participants through relatively brief educational workshops, coupled with well-designed manuals and accessible backup assistance. Bar associations could also provide free malpractice insurance for pro bono cases, supported by membership dues, that would cover practitioners who satisfied certain quality-related conditions.

In the absence of experience with such strategies, the effectiveness of mandatory pro bono programs is difficult to predict. But even without such experience, a threshold question is worth considering. Suppose critics are correct that attempts to assure competent performance would be inadequate or prohibitively expensive. Would a mandatory program still make sense, despite the risks of some noncompliance? At the very least, such requirements would support lawyers who want to participate in public interest projects but work in organizations that have failed to provide adequate resources or credit for these efforts. Many of the nation's most profitable law firms and leading corporate employers fall into that category. They could readily afford a greater pro bono commitment and a formal requirement could nudge them in that direction. For lawyers who have no interest in public interest work, buyout provisions could reduce resistance and the risks of unacceptable performance. A fallback position would be to require attorneys to report their contributions. Some evidence suggests that such requirements can result in modest increases in participation. Only through experience with mandatory pro bono initiatives will it be possible to gauge their relative costs and benefits. Yet rather than encouraging such requirements, the organized bar has remained firmly wedded to an aspirational approach. And that approach has left a wide gap between the rhetoric and reality of bar pro bono commitments.

The Extent of Pro Bono Responsibilities: Rules and Realities

. . . For most of this nation's history, the bar's commitment to pro bono service was noticeable for its absence. The limited data available indicate that most lawyers never provided significant charitable assistance and that little of their unpaid work went to the poor or to underrepresented public interests. [Most went to relatives, friends, and civic organizations.] Over the last two decades, the inadequacy of voluntary pro bono programs has prompted a series of proposals [largely unsuccessful,] for bar ethics codes to require service or at least reports of contribution levels. . . .

How many lawyers meet [the bar's current] aspirational standards or are subject to court-appointed requirements is impossible to gauge with any precision. Full information on participation is lacking because only two states mandate reporting of contribution levels, because the definition of pro bono is often expansive and ambiguous, and because lawyers responding to surveys often stretch its scope to include work for which they expected to be paid but which turned out to be uncompensated or undercompensated. Many lawyers also count services for friends, family members, bar associations, and organizations that could afford to pay for assistance. . . . [T]he best available research finds that the American legal profession averages less than half an hour of work per week and under half a dollar per day in support of legal services for the poor. . . .

Yet a strong pro bono commitment is clearly not inconsistent with commercial success. Many of the nation's most profitable firms have high contribution levels. Indeed, surveys of large firms have found that pro bono participation is positively correlated with profitability. Such findings are consistent with the evidence noted earlier of the professional benefits of charitable service in terms of recruitment, training, client development, and so forth.

The failure of so many lawyers to participate in pro bono work has prompted a broad range of initiatives. . . . A growing number of organizations and websites match lawyers with organizations needing assistance, and the ABA's Pro Bono Center gives assistance to more than 1000 volunteer programs. Major lawyers' periodicals like the *American Lawyer* and the *National Law Journal* now provide rankings and profiles of outstanding employer contributors. Yet . . . [t]he limitations of current bar initiatives have prompted calls for more efforts. . . .

Influences on Pro Bono Work: An Empirical Analysis of Workplace Factors

The objective of the empirical study summarized here was to provide the first broad-scale data about the personal characteristics, educational experiences, and workplace policies that influence pro bono participation. To that end, some 3,000 detailed questionnaires went to three groups: lawyers who were graduates of six schools that had different approaches to student pro bono work; recent individual and law firm winners of the American Bar Association's annual Pro Bono Publico Award; and firms for which annual pro bono data are available [namely firms that the *American Lawyer* has consistently listed among the top one hundred in terms of gross revenues]. . . .

To gauge the relative importance of factors influencing pro bono participation, the questionnaire asked lawyers to rank commonly cited factors on a scale of 1 to 5, with 5 being "very significant," and 1 being "not significant." In general, the rankings that emerged were consistent with the other research on altruistic behavior. It finds that people are motivated both by intrinsic factors, such as personal values and characteristics, and by extrinsic factors such as rewards and reinforcement. For surveyed lawyers, the most commonly emphasized forces driving pro bono participation were intrinsic: the satisfaction that came from the work (4.2) and a sense of obligation to pursue it (3.7). Of secondary importance were extrinsic factors such as: employer policies (2.7) or encouragement (2.7); and professional benefits such as contacts, referrals, and training (2.7), trial experience (2.5), involvement with clients (2.4), and opportunities for control over the work (2.4). Of slightly less significance were personal characteristics such as political commitment (2.3) or religious commitment (2.1). Awards by employers or bar associations had least importance (1.7). A regression analysis was also performed to determine whether any of the demographic characteristics of respondents were significantly correlated with pro bono work. As is the case with altruistic behavior generally, no such correlations were identified. Race, ethnicity, gender, income, and the importance of religion did not predict involvement. The only factors that were strongly positively correlated were political commitment and employer encouragement.

Some lawyers also volunteered comments about these influences on their pro bono work, as did many of the ABA award winners. The most significant motivations were a commitment to public service and the personal satisfaction that it provided. Some attorneys had gone to law school or had taken a particular job partly out of a desire to be involved in public interest work. For these lawyers, family influences, early volunteer involvement or personal hardships often instilled a commitment to community service in general or to certain causes in particular. Other attorneys developed interest in law school, or through exposure to pro bono programs at their firms, and some believed that such work was a "professional obligation. . . ." For many of those attorneys, pro bono matters provided their most rewarding professional experiences. As one ABA winner put it, after lawyers leave law school, the "altruistic sense of what the profession is about . . . disappears pretty quickly. Pro bono is a way to get this passion back. This makes you feel alive and like you are doing something worthwhile. . . ." Lawyers often contrasted their public service with their largely commercial practices, and reported greater satisfaction from promoting social reform or from helping a disadvantaged client than wrangling over money. . . . Many lawyers also cited professional benefits from pro bono service. It was often a way to develop expertise in a particular area in which they wanted to practice. Others gained trial experience or community contacts, which sometimes had direct payoffs in obtaining paid work.

Lawyers were also asked about the relative importance of factors limiting pro bono work. Here again, the findings are consistent with more general research on the factors discouraging altruistic behavior. For surveyed lawyers, the most important constraints were workload demands (4.5), family obligations (3.4), and billable hour expectations (3.0). Other factors included employer attitude (2.6), lack of opportunities in their practice area (2.6), lack of expertise (2.4), lack of information about opportunities (2.4), employer bonus policies excluding pro bono work (2.2), lack of interest (2.2), lack of resources (e.g., support staff) (2.2), inconvenient or unpleasant aspects of work (2.1), and lack of malpractice insurance (1.9). Again, many attorneys' written comments and interview responses amplified these views. . . .

Some attorneys cited negative pro bono experiences as the major factor limiting their participation. The work was uninteresting, unimportant, or emotionally draining, or the clients were unethical, unreasonable, or unappreciative. Other lawyers identified their field of practice as the main problem in finding appropriate cases. . . . Some lawyers had represented individuals who seemed to be dishonest or to be "abusing the system," [or were unreasonable] in rejecting settlement offers. . . . Some [c]lients [receiving fee assistance] reportedly found "no downside to rolling the dice and going to trial."

Finally, some attorneys felt that they simply could not afford to do pro bono work. One partner in a two-person civil rights/criminal defense firm already represented many low-income clients on a contingent fee basis. The firm ended up with "a lot of 'de facto' pro bono work" and the partner found it impossible at this point in her career to build the practice, support its staff, and take on additional matters that she knew would be pro bono.... Many lawyers cited family obligations, coupled with heavy workload pressures, as a primary constraint. One attorney who found it impossible to find time for optional public service when combining 2400 billable hours a year with a family, added: "*I* need pro bono!" Or at least, as noted below, lawyers in this situation need a policy that counts pro bono work as part of their billable hour quota.

Lawyers with substantial family responsibilities not only had competing demands on their time, they also had greater financial obligations, which pushed them to focus on paying work and client development activities that would generate it.... [Other lawyers] cited significant educational debts and the high cost of living in cities like New York as major deterrents to public service. These lawyers described themselves as "not driven by money," but rather as "realists" about supporting a family, especially if they had multiple educational tuitions to pay or children with special needs. A few interviewees were candid about their own lifestyle desires. As one attorney acknowledged, there are "certain comforts ... [I don't] want to live without." Yet by the same token, some lawyers, particularly ABA award winners, saw pro bono work as a way to reconcile their economic needs with their service commitments. Although they would have preferred full-time public interest work, a well-paying private-sector job offering pro bono opportunities was the next best alternative.

Taken together, the data collected and reviewed for this study make clear that financial considerations are neither decisive nor unimportant in explaining pro bono contributions. As is true with altruistic behavior generally, economic ability does not determine charitable involvement. Rather, the most powerful influences are a sense of satisfaction and obligation, together with the professional benefits or costs associated with pro bono work. Yet some of these benefits and costs are influenced by external factors, particularly workplace policies. Even seemingly personal motivations, such as the satisfaction that lawyers experience from pro bono involvement, may be in part a function of the opportunities, training, and support that their employers provide or fail to provide. So too, the negative pro bono experiences that some lawyers reported may reflect a mismatch between their interests or expertise and the volunteer options readily available. Certain adverse reactions to clients also may indicate a lack of understanding or "cultural competence" in dealing with low-income individuals....

Not only could well-designed workplace programs affect satisfaction with pro bono work, they also could reduce the costs of pursuing it. Yet as the survey findings make clear, most programs leave much to be desired.... Only a quarter of the employers fully counted pro bono work toward billable hours. Fewer than a third counted a certain number of hours (20 percent) or a certain kind of work (10 percent). Such findings are consistent with other recent survey data, and signal a priority structure that undermines public service commitments.... In effect, pro bono work was permissible only if it occurred "outside the normal work hours." Given what passes for "normal" in many firms, the price of public service is often prohibitive.

Other limitations on pro bono participation arise from workplace practices concerning resources, rewards, and recognition. Only about half of the surveyed workplaces (57 percent) subsidized all the costs of pro bono matters.... Only 10 percent of surveyed lawyers indicated that their organizations valued such work as much as billable hours. About a fifth (18 percent) believed that pro bono contributions were not viewed as important, and almost half felt they were negatively viewed (44 percent).... Over a third of surveyed lawyers noted that their organizations' informal reward structures were at odds with formal policies supporting pro bono work. Some attorneys volunteered comments that were highly critical: firm leaders simply paid "lip service" to pro bono work for purposes of recruiting or self-image; others "encouraged pro bono on the surface but [provided] ... no incentive to do it." ... Moreover, the economic trends in private practice suggest that bottom-line priorities are having an increasing impact. Almost half of responding attorneys (46 percent) believed that recent escalation in salaries and hourly work expectations had caused practitioners to decline pro bono work.

These trends are taking a toll on workplace satisfaction. Fewer than a quarter of surveyed attorneys were very satisfied (22 percent) with the amount of time that they spent on pro bono work. About a fifth (19 percent) were somewhat satisfied and a quarter (25 percent) were neutral. A third of the sample were dissatisfied, slightly over a quarter, somewhat dissatisfied, and about 10 percent very dissatisfied (11 percent).... Close to half (43 percent) of respondents were dissatisfied with the types of cases permitted, and one cluster of problems involved matters that lawyers classified as "not truly" pro bono, such as favors for clients or their relatives, or personal legal needs of partners or their families. A related concern involved the use of pro bono resources to subsidize the "pet organizations" of certain partners, particularly when these matters were objectionable to other members of the firm....

For lawyers in most practice settings, the treatment of pro bono activities leaves much to be desired. Yet although a majority of lawyers identify inadequacies in workplace policies, their criticisms have not been sufficiently pervasive or intense to force the necessary changes. Policies on pro bono generally are not a critical factor in influencing lawyers to choose a particular employer, according to data collected for this study. Only a third of attorneys considered such factors very important (13 percent) or somewhat important (20 percent) in their choices of employment. Almost half (44 percent) indicated that pro bono policies and practices were not important to their decisions, and about a quarter (23 percent) had no information about these norms at the time of decision. . . .

The priorities of most attorneys are undoubtedly a major obstacle to improving pro bono programs. Yet the evidence summarized above suggests that many lawyers are underestimating the personal and professional rewards that well-designed programs can provide. If so, the question then becomes how best to educate attorneys about those benefits . . .

An Agenda for Reform: Connecting Principles to Practice

The findings set forth above suggest a number of best practices to which organizations should aspire. The include:

- adoption of a formal pro bono policy;
- visible commitment by the organization's leadership;
- credit for pro bono work toward billable hour requirements;
- consideration of pro bono service as a favorable factor in performance evaluations and in promotion and compensation decisions;
- recognition and showcasing of service;
- recruitment efforts that emphasize the personal and professional benefits of service;
- establishment of a pro bono coordinator to develop opportunities, to match participants with appropriate placements, and to insure adequate training, supervision, and performance;
- compliance with the Law Firm Pro Bono Challenge of 3 or 5 percent of billable hours or the ABA Model Rules standard of fifty hours per lawyer per year or the financial equivalent.

This is not a modest agenda. But it surely merits greater efforts. Pro bono service reflects all that is best in the legal profession. . . .

QUESTIONS

1. Would it be possible to ensure reasonable levels of competence and compliance under a mandatory pro bono system? Are there strategies for increasing voluntary contributions that might be preferable?

Esther F. Lardent, president of the Pro Bono Institute, warns that mandatory systems make a "very small dent in a very large problem." In her estimation, the costs of training participants, administering referrals, and monitoring performance are likely to exceed the benefits:

> Unfortunately, the end product of a successful campaign for a mandatory pro bono program probably will fail to meet the original goals of the program's proponents. Experience demonstrates that the political compromises involved in securing approval of such a program will result in a definition of pro bono service so broad that it encompasses activities already undertaken by virtually all lawyers. All lawyers will

be in compliance, yet no additional services to address unmet legal needs will be provided.... Mandatory pro bono will not increase services, enhance professionalism, or improve the performance of existing pro bono programs.[109]

Do you agree? How would Rhode respond? Do differences in the context of lawyers' practices call for different requirements? Should they be imposed by legal employers rather than the bar and should more efforts focus on evaluating their quality?[110] If Lardent is right, should the advocates of increased legal services for the poor focus on changing the political climate within the bar? Should they push for a pro bono reporting requirement? Or should they concentrate on ways to increase funding for existing legal assistance programs and to reduce the need for lawyers? Which is most likely to make a difference in the long run?

2.   As Rhode's article notes, critics of mandatory pro bono believe that minimum requirements, such as 50 hours a year, by counsel unfamiliar with problems of indigents, would be grossly inadequate responses to current levels of unmet legal needs. The failure of most programs to monitor quality compounds these concerns. Yet voluntary programs are open to similar objections, and raise a further problem. The wider the disparity between lawyers' rhetorical and actual commitment to public service, the more vulnerable the profession becomes to charges of hypocrisy. Unenforceable pro bono "aspirations" enhance the bar's self-importance and entitlement to special status without the inconvenience of significant sacrifice on the part of most practitioners. How would supporters of the current Model Rule respond to this objection? How would you?

3.   Should the American Bar Association require that law schools establish adequate pro bono programs as a condition of accreditation? How should adequacy be defined? Should programs be mandatory if a majority of law students fail to volunteer? Consider the objection shared by many students: "I advocate volunteerism and try to do my part, but I would resent being told how to manifest my charity. Most important, I would resent the law school judging the merit of my charity choices."[111]

4.   Should pro bono requirements be imposed upon law faculty in schools that impose such requirements on students? At Tulane, architects of the mandatory student pro bono program felt that the faculty, "for academic freedom reasons, would not buy into imposing [a pro bono requirement] on themselves." At the University of Pennsylvania, professors approved what is now a "highly regarded student program, but were split on mandating

---

109. Esther Lardent, "Pro Bono in the 1990s," *in* American Bar Association, *Civil Justice: An Agenda for the 1990s* (1990); Esther Lardent "Mandatory Pro Bono in Civil Cases: The Wrong Answer to the Right Question," 49 *Md. L. Rev.* 78, 100–101 (1990).

110. For variations in pro bono based on the context of practice, see Robert Granfield, "The Meaning of Pro Bono: Institution-

al Variations in Professional Obligations Among Lawyers," 41 *Law & Soc'y Rev.* 113 (2007). For the need for evaluation, see Deborah L. Rhode, "Where is the Public in Lawyers' Public Service?: Pro Bono and the Bottom Line," *Ford. L. Rev.* (forthcoming).

111. Letter to the Editor, Thomas J. Plofchan, *Washington Post*, Jan. 23, 1991, at A16.

pro bono for themselves. That part of the proposal died."[112] Is it hypocritical for faculty to require the student body to do as they say, not as they do?

How would you respond to this argument? Consider that issue in light of the rationale for pro bono in law schools in Chapter XVI, Legal Education.

5. As Rhode indicates, many lawyers find the concept of a pro bono duty objectionable out of a gut-level sense that requiring a person to donate time and personal service against their will is a basic violation of their rights, different in kind and spirit from a merely financial tax. Defenders of pro bono typically respond with arguments that pro bono is not fundamentally a compulsory donation, but rather (as Rhode suggests) a quid pro quo for the many benefits that lawyers gain through their exclusive license to practice law.[113] To this, some critics respond that the legal profession is bitterly competitive, and lawyers' so-called "monopoly" is unreal.[114] Some proponents of the pro bono duty argue that it is a moral obligation but should not be made legally mandatory, either on principle or because under current conditions mandatory pro bono is unnecessary or counterproductive.[115] In effect, there are four possible positions: (1) no pro bono obligation, either moral or legal, is justifiable; (2) lawyers have a moral obligation of pro bono, but on principle it should not be legally mandatory; (3) lawyers have a moral obligation of pro bono, and in principle it would not be wrong to make it legally mandatory—but under current conditions it should not be made legally mandatory; (4) mandatory pro bono is justifiable and a good idea. Which of these positions seems most plausible to you?

2. COURT-APPOINTED PRO BONO REPRESENTATION

NOTES

As the preceding materials note, courts have exercised power to appoint lawyers to represent indigents in both criminal and civil cases. EC 2–29 of the Code of Professional Responsibility provides that when a lawyer is "appointed by a court . . . to undertake representation of a person unable to obtain counsel . . . he should not seek to be excused from undertaking the representation except for compelling reason." Model Rule 6.2 similarly instructs a lawyer not to "seek to avoid appointment by a tribunal to

112. David Luban, "Faculty Pro Bono and the Question of Identity," 49 *J. Legal Educ.* 58, 66 (1999). ("[H]ow can law faculties teach professionalism successfully if our own approach to pro bono is that we wouldn't touch it with a ten-foot pole?").

113. For other examples of such arguments, *see* Luban, *supra* note 112, at 63–66 (arguing that lawyers are analogous to trustees of the legal system); Luban, *supra* note 35, at 282–88 (arguing that pro bono is a quid pro quo for lawyers' oligopoly); Steven Lubet & Cathryn Stewart, "A 'Public Assets' Theory of Lawyers' Pro Bono Obligations," 145 *U.*

Pa. L. Rev. 1245 (1997) (arguing that pro bono is a quid pro quo for lawyers' possession of publicly-created assets such as privilege to maintain client secrets).

114. Roger Cramton, "Mandatory Pro Bono," 19 *Hofstra L. Rev.* 1113, 1135–36 (1991).

115. *See, e.g.*, Luban, *supra* note 112, at 58–59; Lardent, Esther Lardent "Mandatory Pro Bono in Civil Cases: The Wrong Answer to the Right Question," *supra* note 109.

represent a person except for good cause," including the likelihood that the representation will result in violations of the Rules or other law, impose "an unreasonable financial burden", or lead to impaired assistance because of the lawyer's repugnance for the client or cause. Both the Code (DR 2–110(A)(1) and DR 2–110(C)) and the Model Rules (1.16(c)) also forbid a lawyer who has undertaken representation to withdraw from a case pending before a tribunal without permission of the tribunal.

The duty to represent indigents without a fee has been traced back to Roman and medieval ecclesiastical traditions, as well as to a pathbreaking English statute enacted in 1495, which provided for the appointment of "learned Councell and attorneys" to represent paupers in all courts of record. It is unclear, however, how often courts actually made such appointments, and equally unclear to what extent appointed attorneys had to serve without compensation.[116] Evidence concerning the appointment power in this country is similarly sketchy.[117] Most experts, however, see no constitutional bar to courts exercising of their inherent authority over the practice of law in order to require reasonable amounts of service.

Court Appointments in Criminal Cases

As Chapter VI noted, indigent defendants are entitled to court-appointed counsel in all felony cases and in misdemeanor cases that could result in incarceration. Lawyers have been drafted to provide such representation under several circumstances. Sometimes government funding runs out before the end of the appropriations period. Needless to say, representation of accused criminals is not a high budget priority for most voters and their elected representatives. In other cases, funding does not run out but reimbursement rates are set so low that too few private practitioners volunteer for indigent defense.

Lawyers often have challenged courts' power to make involuntary appointments. The most common claim is that compelling pro bono service constitutes a violation of the Fifth Amendment, which prohibits taking property without just compensation. Most courts have rejected this claim, although a few have interpreted takings clauses in state constitutions to prevent uncompensated court appointments. The United States Supreme Court has never spoken directly to the issue. But, in dicta and in one summary dismissal, it has implied that uncompensated court appointment is permissible for criminal cases. In *Ex Parte Sparks,* 368 So.2d 528 (Ala.1979), the Alabama Supreme Court upheld an assignment system for indigent criminal defense, and the United States Supreme Court summarily dismissed an appeal, 444 U.S. 803 (1979). The Court has also suggested that "[t]he Fifth Amendment does not require that the Government pay for the performance of a public duty it is already owed," *Hurtado v. United States,* 410 U.S. 578, 588–89 (1973). And in earlier cases, the Court has

---

116. David L. Shapiro, "The Enigma of the Lawyer's Duty to Serve," 55 *N.Y.U. L. Rev.* 735, 739–49 (1980).

117. *Id.* at 749–62; Rhode, *supra* note 108, at 3–6; Michael Millemann, "Mandatory

Pro Bono in Civil Cases: A Partial Answer to the Right question," 49 *Md. L. Rev.* 18, 33–35 (1990).

concluded that attorneys, as "officers of the court" are "bound to render service when required." *Powell v. Alabama,* 287 U.S. 45, 73 (1932).

QUESTIONS

1. According to an influential Ninth Circuit decision, *United States v. Dillon,* 346 F.2d 633, 635 (9th Cir.1965), cert. denied 382 U.S. 978 (1966):

> An applicant for admission to practice law may justly be deemed to be aware of the traditions of the profession which he is joining, and to know that one of these traditions is that a lawyer is an officer of the court obligated to represent indigents for little or no compensation upon court order. Thus, the lawyer has consented to, and assumed, this obligation.

Do you find this claim persuasive? Does it permit the state to increase its powers over lawyers at will simply by giving timely notice of conditions attaching to the license to practice law? Or, as Rhode's article argues, is the obligation to provide reasonable services an acceptable condition on lawyers' monopoly over the provision of essential services?

2. Lawyers who are required to provide services for grossly inadequate fees have little incentive to defend a case zealously. In some instances, statutory ceilings on compensation have resulted in rates as low as $2.00 an hour.[118] Yet as Chapter VI on criminal defense and Chapter XV on malpractice note, the constitutional standards for assessing attorneys' performance remain notoriously lenient. Under *Strickland v. Washington,* 466 U.S. 668, 688 (1984), defendants must demonstrate a reasonable probability that the lawyer's actual incompetence caused a difference in the outcome of the trial.

Is this constitutional requirement an adequate means of insuring competence where lawyers are required to provide pro bono representation? If not, how should problems of deficient performance be addressed? See the discussion in Chapters VI and XV.

Court Appointments in Civil Cases

Uncompensated court appointments have been more controversial in civil than criminal matters. As noted earlier, in *Lassiter v. Department of Social Services,* 452 U.S. 18 (1981), the Court found a presumption against a right to appointed counsel in civil cases. Although the presumption is rebuttable under a balancing test, that test has rarely been met. Moreover, in *Mallard v. United States District Court for Southern District of Iowa,* 490 U.S. 296 (1989), the Supreme Court concluded that a statute authorizing the federal judiciary to "request an attorney to represent" indigents does not grant judges the power to compel such representation. (28 U.S.C. § 1915(d)). The Court expressly reserved, however, the question of whether the judiciary has authority to compel indigent representation as part of its "inherent power" to regulate matters pertaining to the justice system.

---

118. See Rhode, *supra* note 3, at 104–105.

A number of lower courts have addressed that issue. In *Scheehle v. Justices of the Arizona Supreme Court*, 508 F.3d 887 (9th Cir. 2007), the Ninth Circuit Court of Appeals upheld an Arizona rule authorizing superior courts to appoint active members of the bar to serve as arbitrators for two days a year in the courts' mandatory arbitration system for cases involving no more than $65,000. In the appellate panel's view, the economic impact of the required service was negligible and there was no showing that it significantly interfered with the plaintiff's legal work. Accordingly, under prior Supreme Court decisions on Fifth Amendment takings, the deprivation was not significant enough to call for compensation. In *Pennsylvania Coal Company v. Mahon,* 260 U.S. 393 (1922), Justice Holmes held that once the diminution of property value reaches "a certain magnitude," the government must provide just compensation. In subsequent cases, the Court has suggested that this "certain magnitude" is reached when the exercise of state power will "frustrate distinct investment-backed expectations." *Penn Cent. Transp. Co. v. New York City*, 438 U.S. 104, 127 (1978). It is not reached if the owner is still capable of realizing a reasonable profit on the investment. The *Scheehle* decision is consistent with other leading lower court decisions on pro bono requirements such as *Family Division Trial Lawyers v. Moultrie,* 725 F.2d 695 (D.C.Cir.1984).

QUESTIONS

1. At what point would pro bono requirements become unconstitutionally burdensome?

2. Could a court obligate lawyers to meet the ABA's standard of 50 hours a year? Should a court do so?

CHAPTER XIV

ADMISSION TO THE BAR

A. INTRODUCTION

NOTES: HISTORICAL PERSPECTIVES

For much of its history, the American bar made relatively little effort to ensure adequate qualifications among its members. As Chapter III noted, the courts traditionally asserted inherent power to regulate the practice of law, including authority to determine who could appear before them. However, until the twentieth century, formal admission standards were lax. Courts required applicants to demonstrate "fitness to practice," but generally required only perfunctory oral exams and/or some limited period of preparation. The absence of any legal degree requirement reflected both the inaccessibility and inadequacy of professional training in colonial universities and the legacy of English traditions. England placed responsibility for legal instruction under independent Inns of Court rather than academic institutions. Although some eighteenth-century Americans traveled to one of the Inns, the training they received there during this period was not extensive. Moreover, most practitioners, who could afford neither study abroad nor enrollment in an American university, prepared through apprenticeships.[1]

This system left much to be desired. The conventional arrangement was for aspiring attorneys to offer their services plus a fee to established lawyers in exchange for instruction and the right to use their masters' legal forms later in practice. In an era before typewriting, preprinted forms, and duplicating services, students often spent most of their apprenticeships copying writs and documents. Not only were such training experiences extremely tedious, they offered little chance for broader inquiry. All too often, the only opportunities for less technical instruction came through independent reading of treatises and other materials not intended as textbooks. Although a few law schools emerged in the late eighteenth century to supplement such instruction, they remained highly limited in number and scope until after the Civil War.

In the excerpt that follows, J. Willard Hurst describes the evolution of more formal admission requirements.

---

1. *See generally* Charles R. McKirdy, "The Lawyer as Apprentice: Legal Education in Eighteenth Century Massachusetts," 28 *J.* *Legal Educ.* 124 (1976); William Holdsworth, *A History of English Law* 3–101 (1938).

J. Willard Hurst, The Growth of American Law

256, 277–284, 292–293 (1950).

Indeed, over most of our history there were no official standards of preparation for the bar, and such standards as existed in fact were largely the product of the schools' traditions.... [By] 1860 only 9 of 39 states and territories had even nominal requirements of professional preparation. By 1890 nearly one half, by 1920 about three fourths, and by 1940 all states required some professional study preparatory to admission. The spread of this requirement was gradually attended by a lengthening of the period of professional preparation, up to the three-year requirement which by 1940 was fixed in forty states.

Naturally, through the years in which most states did not even set minimum requirements of professional training, they set no requirements for prelegal study. In 1921 the American Bar Association first committed itself to a substantial declaration in favor of higher standards. As late as this, only fourteen states had any requirements of preliminary general education, and only ten required the equivalent of graduation from high school as a condition of eligibility for admission to the bar. But advance was fast after the Association's action. By 1940 over two thirds of the states had adopted the requirement of at least two years of college preparation or its equivalent, as a prerequisite for admission....

Legal biography showed that, before he entered practice, the average lawyer of 1800 had a basic education a year or so short of finishing what the twentieth century would call grammar school, plus 6 to 14 months' training in law. A random sampling from over the country in 1931 showed an average basic education that reached through about one year of college and two and a quarter years in a law school or in office training. Clearly, during the whole period of 131 years the well-trained men from good law schools had been "a tiny stream—emptied into an ocean of inadequate preparation." Clearly, too, when one allowed for the comparative educational facilities of the times, and for the increased complexity of the society, the 1931 average of education was no startling degree beyond that of 1800.

The examination was throughout the main official instrument for enforcing standards of preparation for the bar. Before 1870 it was typically oral. In any case, oral or written, it was administered with casual leniency; the approach was characteristic of times and communities that were close enough to the frontier so that they had no awe of formality or specialized knowledge, and small enough so that personal acquaintance and relationships were a substantial check on conduct....

The movement to lengthen the required period of professional study went on for a generation after the Civil War before it was accompanied by a substantial effort to improve the examining machinery. Before 1890 only four states had boards of bar examiners, and in no more than half a dozen had written examinations been used. However, when the leading law schools began to use the written examination, this encouraged adoption of the practice in the states, where it became the invariable method of examination after 1900.... [However, surveys] showed that about 90 per cent of all who applied from 1922 to 1925 eventually passed....

Education, admissions policy, and organization wove together to form main strands in the character of the bar in the United States. The history of admissions policy and bar organization created a challenge to legal education. [In the nineteenth century, the] decline in admissions standards, and the disappearance of dominant local bar associations, gave the law schools the opportunity to assert a leadership in regard to bar standards and law reform that was without parallel in the Anglo–American legal world.

B. COMPETENCE

INTRODUCTION: BAR EXAMS

Although bar examinations have an extended history, their early forms bear little resemblance to their modern versions. Before the Civil War, exams were typically oral, and were administered by state judges or attorneys appointed by the court on an ad hoc basis. The procedures governing these examinations were often quite informal, as the following description of an examination by Abraham Lincoln suggests. The candidate, Jonathan Birch, encountered his examiner in a hotel room, in the process of taking a bath, which continued during the interview. According to Birch,

> [Lincoln] asked in a desultory way the definition of a contract, and two or three other fundamental questions, all of which I answered readily, and I thought, correctly. Beyond these meager inquiries, as I now recall the incident, he asked nothing more. Meanwhile, sitting on the edge of the bed he began to entertain me with recollections—many of them characteristically vivid and racy—of his own practice and the various incidents and adventures that attended his start in the profession. The whole proceeding was interesting yet so unusual, if not grotesque, that I was at a loss to determine whether I was really being examined or not.[2]

Eventually Lincoln sent Birch off with a note to the other member of the Springfield examining committee, who admitted him without further inquiry. The note read: "The bearer of this is a young man who thinks he can be a lawyer. Examine him if you want to. I have done so and am satisfied. He's a good deal smarter than he looks to be. Yours, Lincoln."[3]

In the late nineteenth century, states attempted to upgrade standards by establishing boards of bar examiners and requiring written exams. However, most early examiners were part-time or short-term employees, with limited expertise. The tests they devised usually demanded only rote

2. Len Yang Smith, "Abraham Lincoln as a Bar Examiner," 51 *Bar Examiner* 37 (1982).

3. *Id.*

learning and basic literacy skills. What limited data are available leaves doubt that these examinations functioned as an effective test of competence. All but a small minority of candidates ultimately passed.[4] Moreover, in many jurisdictions, a major impetus for screening candidates was not competence *per se,* but public image. Elite members of the bar often saw examinations as a means of stemming the tide of lower-class applicants, particularly religious and ethnic minorities, whose inadequate command of the "King's English" threatened to debase the profession's status.[5]

In 1931, a National Conference of Bar Examiners was created to upgrade standards for exams and examiners, as well as to promote cooperation among the states. Partly as a result of Conference efforts, examinations over the next half century became more uniform and comprehensive. The development of a multi-state multiple choice test in core subjects reflected and accelerated this trend. Yet whether this trend is to be welcomed, and whether bar exams in their current form are an appropriate means of assessing competence, remain matters of considerable dispute. Consider that issue in light of the readings that follow.

Richardson v. McFadden

Fourth Circuit Court of Appeals, 1976.
540 F.2d 744.

■ CRAVEN, CIRCUIT JUDGE:

This action for declaratory and injunctive relief was brought by four black law school graduates who had satisfied all requirements for admission to the South Carolina Bar except that they received failing scores on the bar examination. They challenge the constitutionality of the South Carolina Bar Exam as applied generally to black applicants. Appellants Spain and Kelly also attack its validity as applied to them personally.... The district court, after trial, rejected appellants' arguments, except as to the claim that due process was denied unsuccessful applicants by the failure of the Bar Examiners to provide a system for review of failing papers.

We affirm the district court, except as to the individual claims of Spain and Kelly.

I.

Appellants' main challenge to the South Carolina Bar Examination is that it is not job related. They argue that the State Bar's past history of

---

4. *See e.g.,* Esther L. Brown, *Lawyers and the Promotion of Justice* 117 (1938) (80–90% of applicants ultimately passed); J. Willard Hurst, *The Growth of American Law* 292–93 (1950) (90% passed).

5. *See* Jerold S. Auerbach, *Unequal Justice* 49, 112–14 (1976); Randall Collins, *The Credential Society: An Historical Sociology of Education and Stratification* 149–56 (1979). For example, prominent legal ethicist Henry Drinker, like other leaders of the bar,

saw a need to protect the profession from "Russian Jew boys ... up out of the gutter ... following methods their fathers had been using in selling shoe-strings and other merchandise." Robert Gordon, "The American Legal Profession, 1870–2000," in *The Cambridge History of Law in America* (Chris Tomlins and Michael Grossberg, eds., 2008) (quoting Drinker).

racial discrimination in admitting blacks to the practice of law and the disproportionate impact of the examination on blacks places on the Examiners the burden of showing that the exam is job related, and that in this context the standards for judging job relatedness should be those of Title VII of the 1964 Civil Rights Act rather than traditional Fourteenth Amendment tests. Appellants contend that to be constitutional the test in general must be shown to measure skills relevant to the practice of law, and the passing score must be selected so as to draw the line at minimal professional competency. While the main thrust of their argument goes to establishing Title VII standards as applicable to the bar examination, they contend that, regardless of the standard employed, the Examiners have failed to demonstrate the requisite job relatedness.

The district court, examining the question solely under the criteria of the Fourteenth Amendment, held that "the South Carolina bar examination as presently administered has a rational connection with any applicant's fitness or capacity to competently practice law in this state." He made no explicit finding concerning the passing score, probably because the question was not presented to him in those terms, but we believe that, in ruling that the bar examination "as presently administered" was "job related," he meant to indicate approval of both the test in general and the selection of a passing score.

But if Title VII's standards for job relatedness are applied, the test used must be "shown, by professionally acceptable methods, to be 'predictive of or significantly correlated with important elements of work behavior which comprise or are relevant to the job or jobs for which the candidates are being evaluated.'" *Albemarle Paper Co. v. Moody,* 422 U.S. 405, 431 (1975). While the Bar Examiners do not concede that they would lose under this requirement, we believe the record is inadequate to demonstrate either "criterion" ("predictive"), "content," or "construct" validity under professionally acceptable methods. Thus, if we were to determine that Title VII standards were applicable, it would be necessary to reverse and declare the South Carolina Bar Examination constitutionally invalid. [But] appellants agree that Title VII does not apply to the bar exam [because the statute by its terms covers only employers, labor organizations, and employment agencies]. . . .

[I]n *Washington v. Davis,* 426 U.S. 229 (1976), decided after oral argument in this case, the Supreme Court . . . [held] that, where discriminatory purpose by the state is not proven, it is inappropriate to "adopt this more rigorous [Title VII] standard for the purposes of applying the Fifth and the Fourteenth Amendments. . . ." We agree with the Fifth Circuit . . . that under the Equal Protection Clause of the Fourteenth Amendment the issue is still whether the examination is job related, albeit a less demanding inquiry. "The hallmark of a rational classification is not merely that it differentiates, but that it does so on a basis having a fair and substantial relationship to the purpose of the classification." And here the purpose of the classification is to distinguish between persons demonstrating minimal competence to practice law and those lacking such knowledge and skill.

The testimony introduced at trial on the validity of the test questions consisted primarily of testimony by the individual Bar Examiners. Each testified to basically the same facts: (1) that he is a successful practicing lawyer in the State and, from observation and experience, understands the skills necessary to practice competently; (2) that he has examined sample questions prepared by the National Council of Bar Examiners and/or discussed question formulation with others; and (3) that he designed the questions he placed on the Bar so as best to determine whether the applicant possesses the minimal level of competence necessary to practice law in the State. In addition, the Examiners' experts, Statler and Bernreuter, testified that they had performed correlation studies between performance on the bar examination and performance in law school as measured by the law school grades. Both experts testified that, in their opinion, the results demonstrated the "content validity" of the bar examination, where "content" is defined as law school performance. Appellants did not challenge the existence of such correlation; they only attacked its significance and argued that it was irrelevant to any then established procedure for showing content validity. They contend that, absent a job analysis, which was not performed here, there can be no demonstration of content validity.

In *Washington v. Davis,* the Supreme Court held that, at least in validating admission to a police training program, a "positive relationship between the [admission] test and training course performance [is] sufficient to validate the former, wholly aside from its possible relationship to actual performance as a police officer." ... In fact, the Court found this relationship to be "the much more sensible construction of the job relatedness requirement."

While the Court's treatment of the job relatedness requirement in *Washington v. Davis* has no direct application to professional licensing examinations because of the differing state interests involved, we believe the Court's general reasoning gives substantial support to the Examiners' argument that under the Fourteenth Amendment the relationship between law school performance and the bar examination is significant in establishing job relatedness.[11]

We believe that this statistical evidence plus the other efforts of the Examiners to intelligently relate the examination questions to the skills involved in the practice of law are sufficient to satisfy the demands of the Fourteenth Amendment.

11. If it were carried to its logical extreme, seldom the path of the law, the Court's opinion on this point surprisingly might invalidate almost all state professional examinations. If the only demonstration of job relationship required is that it has a positive relationship to training course performance—e.g., law school—then why does not training school performance itself demonstrate that the applicant is fit to practice his profession? It is certainly clear that nothing correlates better with training school performance than training school performance itself. An applicant for the Bar who has graduated from an accredited law school arguably may be said to stand before the Examiners armed with law school grades demonstrating that he possesses sufficient job-related skills. Why, then, any bar examination at all?

Whether the passing score selected by the Bar Examiners bears "a fair and substantial relationship" to the determination of minimal competency presents a much more difficult question. In *United States v. North Carolina,* 400 F.Supp. 343 (E.D.N.C.1975) (three-judge court), the district court, in a similar context, held that to satisfy the demands of the Equal Protection Clause the cut-off score selected must be reasonably related to minimal competency, and it held invalid the minimal passing score selected by North Carolina for a National Teacher Examination because of a total absence of evidence showing it to be related to minimal teaching competency.

In this case, some evidence was introduced to validate the cut-off score of 70 used by the Examiners, but it was very subjective and general in nature and hardly acclaimed by the educational testing experts who testified. Perhaps the testimony most supportive of the validity of the cut-off score was provided by Examiner David Freeman, who described his grading procedures as follows:

> My own approach is that, preliminary to the grading process, to go back to the exam question and in studying through them very carefully, I make a mental assessment of the importance to be attached to each one. I do not go through, for my own purposes: I feel that it's a mechanical process of assigning a point value to each question. I then read the examinations. I treat them not as questions to which so many points were assigned to this or to that issue of this question, but as a totality and assign to that paper a grade which I think is reflective of the student's evidence of ability in answering the whole.

> Q.   What form would that grade take, a letter grade?

> A.   It would be a numerical grade. And I think, for my own testing purposes, the magic passing point is 70, and I range upward or downward through that. . . .

> Q.   All right sir, as I understand it, you read the entire paper and then assign a single numerical grade, with 70 as passing?

> A.   That is right. . . .

> Q.   As I understand it, you don't attempt to assign points to any particular portion of the test?

> A.   Not in a numerical fashion. It is a matter, in the preliminary process, of giving a mental assessment of importance to this question, or lesser importance to this question, or lesser importance to that question. When I have finished grading a paper, what I would have is one grade that I put on there.

Other Examiners employed a very mechanical system, assigning points to particular parts of questions, summing those points, and then in some cases obtaining the 70 cut-off line simply by raising the highest score to an "A" or perfect score. We tend to agree with appellants' expert that, if this second system is utilized in the precise manner described by the Bar

Examiners, it would be almost a matter of pure luck if the "70" thereby derived corresponded with anybody's judgment of minimal competency.

But absent professionally validated, administered, and evaluated examinations, it is not clear that to require grading along the lines discussed by Freeman rather than the more mechanical and arbitrary method used by McFadden is anything more or less than to demand greater subjectivity. It is not at all certain which of these two, both of whom are competent lawyers but laymen at question design and evaluation, generates numerical scores which more accurately reflect their "true" evaluation of competency.

In view of the fact that all Examiners both designed their exams and assigned scores so as to indicate their judgment as to minimal competency, we cannot find the results obtained so unrelated to the State's objectives as to violate the Equal Protection Clause.

NOTES

The bar examination has often been challenged on both legal and policy grounds. Courts have rejected constitutional claims based on racially disparate impact and on the arbitrariness of grading standards.[12] However, criticism persists on several levels.

The most fundamental objection is that the capabilities that exams measure do not assess most of the skills necessary for competent practice. Standardized testing procedures place a high premium on rote memorization and ability to function under extreme time pressure. Most exams assess only a few of the essential core competencies identified by the ABA's blue ribbon (MacCrate) Commission on Law Schools and the Profession: legal analysis and reasoning, legal research, factual investigation, communication, counseling, negotiation, litigation and dispute resolution procedures, organization and management of legal work, and recognizing and resolving ethical issues.[13] Although most states have made some effort to supplement standard multiple choice and essay questions with some performance/skills assessment, the exam still focuses on mastery of general principles in a small number of subjects. As the MacCrate Commission noted, "the traditional bar exam does nothing to encourage law schools to teach and law students to acquire many of the fundamental lawyering skills.... [If anything,] the examination influences law schools, in developing their curricula, to overemphasize courses in the substantive areas covered by the examination at the expense of courses in the area of lawyering skills."[14] Reports by the Conference of Chief Justices and the Society of American Law Teachers have come to similar conclusions.[15] The problem is com-

12. See Kristin Booth Glen, "When and Where We Enter: Rethinking Admission to the Legal Profession," 102 *Colum. L. Rev.* 1696, 1716–17 (2002).

13. ABA Section of Legal Education and Admissions to the Bar, *Report of the Task Force on Law Schools and the Profession, Narrowing the Gap: Legal Education and Professional Development—An Educational Continuum* 138–40 (1992).

14. MacCrate Report, *supra* note 13, at 278.

15. Conference of Chief Justices, *National Action Plan on Lawyer Conduct and Professionalism* 32 (1999); Society of Ameri-

pounded by pressure that law faculty often feel to teach to the test, rather than to focus on material that would ultimately prove more valuable.

The result, according to critics, is to encourage a superficial knowledge of a few fields of law, which creates a false sense of complacency among successful applicants and the general public. A little knowledge can be a dangerous thing, and that is what bar examinations demand.[16] This screening method is both over- and under-inclusive. And in an era of increasing specialization in legal practice, the deficiencies have grown more apparent. The current admission requirements exclude individuals with experience and practice skills who could provide assistance for routine needs, while providing no assurance that those who pass law school and bar exams are, or will remain, competent in their chosen fields.

A second problem, according to critics, involves the arbitrariness of grading procedures and their adverse impact on diversity in the profession:

> Although bar exams do measure some relevant skills, the current grading system does not capture relevant distinctions. No effort has been made to correlate performance on admission exams with performance in practice. The most that bar officials can establish is a correlation between examination scores and law school grades. That relationship is scarcely surprising, since both measure similar skills. How well either predicts success as a lawyer is something else again, and has yet to be demonstrated. Charles Evans Hughes failed the New York bar exam six times and later became Chief Justice of the United States Supreme Court, and the list of less celebrated failures is extensive.

> The inadequate link between exam and job performance is of special concern because minority applicants have disproportionately low passage rates. Part of the problem is that these applicants are least able to afford the time and expense of bar review courses and multiple attempts at passing. Although courts have rejected claims that the exam process is racially discriminatory and insufficiently predictive of competence in practice, their reasoning has relied on evidence that they have found deficient in other occupational contexts: unsupported testimony by administrators who believe that their questions are unbiased and relevant. But even assuming that exam performance demonstrates some necessary lawyering skills, the current grading process is arbitrary at best. One California study found that a third of bar examiners disagreed about whether a particular set of answers failed or passed, and that a quarter of examiners, when presented with the same paper a second time, reversed their earlier decision.

> The selection of passing scores raises further difficulties. States that use the same multiple choice tests vary considerably in their selection of passing scores and in their ratios of successful to unsuccessful applicants. The percentage of candidates who pass ranges from

can Law Teachers, "Statement on the Bar Exam," 52 *J. Legal Educ.* 446 (2002).

16. Deborah L. Rhode, *In the Interests of Justice: Reforming the Legal Profession* 150 (2000).

the 30s to the 90s. Unsurprisingly, success rates tend to be lowest in the states with the greatest concentrations of lawyers, where new competitors are particularly unwelcome. By contrast, other jurisdictions pass such a high proportion of candidates that they become known as the "Tijuana[s] of the law admission world." No evidence suggest that these states experience exceptional problems with lawyer performance. If states swapped cut-off scores, the majority of applicants passing the bar in permissive jurisdictions would fail, and the majority of those failing in stringent jurisdictions would pass. So too, as statisticians point out, higher grading standards do not guarantee higher competence in a system where about 95 percent of candidates who keep taking the exam eventually pass. In states with low success rates, students simply "study harder" and more applicants have to take the test multiple times.[17]

Although most states do not collect statistics on the race of successful and unsuccessful bar applicants, those that do have found substantial racial and ethnic differences, as did the only national study. That survey by the Law School Admission Council reported eventual bar exam pass rates of 78 percent for African Americans and 96 percent for white applicants; the rates for other minority racial and ethnic groups were 8 to 15 percent lower than for white test takers. So too, a higher proportion of African–Americans than whites who fail the first time do not take the test again: 11 percent vs. 2 percent.[18] More recent state data reflects similar disparities.[19] The reasons for these differential success rates are not entirely clear, but many experts believe that the extent of the variance does not reflect differences in socioeconomic background, educational preparation prior to law school, or competence in practice. Other explanations include racial disparities in the learning experiences of law students, and the stigma of lower exam success rates, which constitutes a stereotype threat adversely affecting performance.[20]

The problems of justifying state passing scores and ratios emerged clearly in an antitrust suit against the Arizona Board of Bar Examiners. In *Hoover v. Ronwin,* 466 U.S. 558 (1984), an unsuccessful bar applicant

---

17. Rhode, *supra* note 15, at 51–52 (2000). *See also* Andrea Curcio, "A Better Bar: Why and How the Existing Bar Should Change," 81 *Neb. L. Rev.* 363 (2002) (criticizing states' arbitrary decisions to raise passing scores); Michael J. Thomas, "The American Lawyer's Next Hurdle: The State–Based Bar Examination System," 24 *J. Legal Prof.* 235, 256 (2000) (criticizing some states' refusal to accept transferred multistate bar exam scores from another jurisdiction).

18. Linda F. Wightman, *Law School Admission Council National Longitudinal Bar Passage Study* 27 (1998). The first time failure rates were 8 percent for whites and 39 percent for African Americans.

19. William C. Kidder, "The Bar Examination and the Dream Deferred: A Critical

Analysis of the MBE, Social Closure, and Racial and Ethnic Stratification," 29 *Law & Soc. Inquiry* 547, 570–571 (2004) (reporting Florida pass rates of 79.7% for whites and 65.6% for non-whites) ABA http:www.abanet.org/minorities/publications/g9/v11n1/mountains.html (reporting California pass rates of 74.6% for whites, 48.2% for African Americans, 53.4% for Hispanics, and 65.5% for Asians).

20. *Id.,* at 575–78; Claude Steele, "A Threat in the Air: How Stereotypes Shape Intellectual Identity and Performance," 52 *Am. Psychologist* 613, 616–18 (1997); sources cited in Glen, *supra* note 12, at 1701, n. 12, 1715, n. 65.

claimed that the Board's practice of setting passing scores after exams were graded constituted an anticompetitive effort to limit the number of licensed attorneys and thus violated the Sherman Antitrust Act. The United States Supreme Court rejected that claim. Under the majority's analysis, the administration of bar admission procedures occurred under Arizona Supreme Court auspices and therefore fell within the state action exemption to the Sherman Act. However, the majority also acknowledged the subjectivity involved in the choice of passing grades: "By its very nature, therefore, grading examinations does not necessarily separate the competent from the incompetent or—except very roughly—identify those qualified to practice and those not qualified. At best, a bar examination can identify those applicants who are more qualified to practice law than those less qualified." 466 U.S. at 578 n. 31.[21]

A final criticism of the current testing system involves its other costs. These include the time and effort spent on bar review cram courses, the inhibition of interest in law school work that does not aid exam preparation, and the barriers to practitioners' mobility across state lines.[22] If the bar exam system is justifiable despite these costs because it measures basic competence, critics question why graduation from an accredited school is also required. Conversely, if the test does not adequately screen for competence, why require it in addition to law school?[23]

In response to such arguments, defenders of the bar examination make several claims. First, they defend the test as a relatively inexpensive way to make standardized anonymous evaluations of basic legal knowledge. It also so provides an incentive for students to synthesize information, to familiarize themselves with local law, to improve writing and analytic skills, and to recognize legal issues in areas outside their expected speciality.[24] To the extent that current bar exams do not provide a useful learning experience, defenders wish to improve, not eliminate, testing procedures. A further claim is that the likely alternative to bar exams would be worse. Assessments relying on personal demonstration of practice skills increase expense, inconsistency, and the potential for bias. Alternatively, a diploma privilege admitting all graduates of ABA approved law schools might lead to more interference with those schools' curricular offerings, or graduation and admission requirements. Given faculty members' disinclination to fail students, elimination of the bar exam might leave no significant screening device for minimal competence.[25] It may, in part, be these concerns,

---

21. For similar concerns about passing scores, see The Committee on Legal Education and Admission to the Bar, "In Opposition to the Board of Law Examiners' Proposal to Increase the Passing Score on the New York Bar Exam," 58 *The Record* 97 (2003).

22. *See* Glen, *supra* note 12, at 1703–18; Society of American Law Teachers, *supra* note 15.

23. Herb D. Vest, "Felling the Giant: Breaking the ABA's Stranglehold on Legal Education in America," 50 *J. Legal Educ.* 494, 502 (2000).

24. Suzanne Darrow–Kleinhaus, "A Response to the Society of American Law Teachers Statement on the Bar Exam," 54 *J. Legal Educ.* 442 (2004); Susan Case, "Licensure in the Ideal World," Bar Examiner, Nov. 2005, at 26–30; Randall T. Sheperd, "On Licensing Lawyers: Why Uniformity is Good and Nationalization is Bad," 60 *N.Y. Ann. Surv. Am. L.* 453, 459 (2004).

25. Erwin Griswold, "In Praise of Bar Examinations," 42 *Bar Examiner* 136 (1973).

together with a sense of hard-won entitlement among admitted practitioners, that have blocked impetus for significant change.

The lack of reform does not, however, reflect a lack of reform proposals. Some states have expanded their reciprocal admission procedures or considered programs that would expand their evaluation processes. One recommendation, by a Tri–State Task Force of Maine, New Hampshire, and Vermont bar leaders and educators, would replace the bar exam with a comprehensive educational program designed to improve lawyer competence through in-depth skills training and evaluation.[26] Another pilot program proposed for New York would allow a selected number of applicants to elect a Public Service Alternative Bar Exam. Those applicants would spend ten to twelve weeks working in the state court system while being evaluated on a range of practice skills. Those who passed would also be obligated to provide 150 hours of pro bono service in the court system in the three years following admission.[27] New Hampshire has approved a pilot program in which a small number of students would be designated in the state's only law school to complete a coordinated sequence of courses and submit to periodic skills based assessments by a committee of representatives from the state courts, the faculty, the practicing bar, the Board of Bar Examiners, and the student participants.[28] An alternative proposal, developed by Minnesota law school deans, would require passage of a multistage examination and skills training program. Law students would take portions of the exam as they completed the relevant course work, and after graduation, would take the multistate bar exam. Those who passed these exams would be admitted on the condition that they successfully complete a postgraduate skills training program under the supervision of a certified mentor.[29]

Some commentators have also proposed licensing systems modeled on those in other countries or other professions. The United States is almost alone among other advanced industrial nations in admitting practitioners on the basis of written exams without skills based assessments or an apprenticeship period.[30] In most countries, legal education occurs at the undergraduate level, supplemented by a skills courses and an apprenticeship. For example, in Great Britain, after an undergraduate law degree (or a one year intensive course in the foundations of legal knowledge), students must either complete a one-year legal practice course for solicitors or a bar vocational course for barristers, and then work under the supervision of a

---

26. Report of the Working Group on Lawyer Conduct and Professionalism to the Conference of Chief Justices, *A National Action Plan on Lawyer Conduct and Professionalism* (1998); Linda Stewart Dalianis & Hulette H. Askew, "Three States Add or Revise Motion Admission Rules: New Hampshire and Vermont Establish Reciprocity and Georgia Resurrects Comity Admission," *Bar Examiner*, February, 2003, at 16 (discussing abandonment of the Tri State proposal).

27. Glen, *supra* note 12, at 1722–24.

28. Hon. Linda S. Dalianis & Sophie M. Sparrow, "New Hampshire's Performance–Based Variant of the Bar Examination: The Daniel Webster Scholar Program," *Bar Examiner*, Nov. 2005, at 23–26.

29. Sam Hanson, "The Relationship between Bar Admissions and Law Schools," *Bar Examiner*, August 2003, at 7, 8–9.

30. Clark Cunningham, "The Professionalism Crisis: How Bar Examiners Can Make A Difference," *Bar Examiner*, Nov. 2005, at 6, 7.

barrister for a one year pupilage, or under a solicitor for a two-year training contract. Australian practitioners complete an extended undergraduate law degree and a two year apprenticeship. Scotland requires a 28–month vocational course and a two-year traineeship. In Germany, students complete two years of theoretical study and an eighteen-month internship with a court, prosecutor, agency or private practitioner.[31] Canadian provinces typically require graduation from a law school, followed by a skills course and a ten-to twelve-month articling period in which the student works under supervision. Other professions like medicine, which also require a combination of written proficiency exams and supervised practice, have served as models for bar admission structures.[32]

According to most commentators, apprenticeship programs in this country have generally not been successful in insuring quality instruction.[33] Many have encountered problems in monitoring and certifying supervisors. Students who already carry substantial debt burdens are understandably reluctant to encounter another hurdle to paid work unless the apprenticeship period could substitute for part of current legal training. Yet at the same time, many commentators recognize that recent graduates often lack the skills necessary for practice and that law firms are reportedly cutting back on the on-the-job mentoring that they provide due to clients' unwillingness to pay. How might these competing concerns be addressed? Are other alternatives, such as bar sponsored "bridging the gap" skills programs for new attorneys, worth considering? See Chapter XVI on Legal Education.

QUESTIONS

1. Would you support any of these proposals? Are there other reforms that would be desirable? Would a national system of admission, or uniform bar passage rates for all states, be preferable to the current structure?

2. If you were a member of a court considering challenges to the bar examination based on its racially disparate impact, how would you rule?

31. Nigel Duncan, "Gatekeepers Training Hurdlers: The Training and Accreditation of Lawyers in England and Wales," 20 *Ga. State L. Rev.* 911 (2004); Murray Hawkins, "Australian Legal Education and Bar Admissions," *Bar Examiner*, Feb., 2008; Paul Maharg, "Transactional Learning Environments and Professional Legal Education in Scotland," *Bar Examiner*, Nov. 2005, at 9; Richard Zitrin, Carol Langford, & Nina W. Tarr, *Legal Ethics in the Practice of Law* 842 (3rd ed. 2006); John M. Law, "Canadian Bar Admissions," *Bar Examiner*, Nov. 2005, at 14.

32. One proposal is for a five-stage process that would include a general knowledge exam at the end of the second year in law school; a third year of clinical skills instruc-

tion followed by test; a three year provisional practice period in which candidates received mentoring and completed continuing legal education courses; and a final exam in an area of specialty. Successful completion of these requirements, together with a character and fitness assessment, would result in a permanent license to practice in any state. Jayne W. Barnard & Mark Greenspan, "Incremental Bar Admission: Lessons from the Medical Profession," 53 *J. Legal Educ.* 340 (2003).

33. For historical discussion, *see* Hurst, *supra* note 4, at 277–93. For a critical evaluation of the two existing state apprenticeship programs, *see* MacCrate Report, *supra* note 13, at 287–89.

3.   In 2006, the California Committee of Bar Examiners considered whether to increase the minimum multistate professional responsibility exam passage score from 79 to 86. The increase would require a score of 31 correct answers out of 50 questions and would bring California closer to the national average. A majority of the Committee believed that the increase would "ultimately increase the protection of consumers of legal services in California." Opponents claimed that a higher passing score could disadvantage students of color, encourage legal ethics courses to focus on the minutiae of rules, and do nothing to ensure more ethical lawyers. According to one Committee member, the change would be "window dressing."[34] Which way would you vote?

3.   Is significant reform in existing exam procedures politically practical or socially desirable? If nonlawyers controlled the admission process, what changes might they propose? Should their interests play a greater role in establishing licensing structures? How could that be accomplished?

C.   CHARACTER AND FITNESS

George Sharswood, An Essay on Professional Ethics
(4th ed. 1876).

There is no profession in which moral character is so soon fixed as in that of the law; there is none in which it is subjected to severer scrutiny by the public. It is well that it is so. The things we hold dearest on earth,—our fortunes, reputations, domestic peace, the future of those dearest to us, nay, our liberty and life itself, we confide to the integrity of our legal counselors and advocates. Their character must be not only without a stain, but without suspicion.

Schware v. Board of Bar Examiners of the State of New Mexico
Supreme Court of the United States, 1957.
353 U.S. 232.

[At issue was the denial of an applicant by the Board of Bar Examiners based on his prior membership in the Communist Party and related activities. These activities included participation in violent shipyard strikes, arrests for political activities, and use of aliases. However, the applicant quit the Communist Party in 1940 and served honorably in the Army before graduating from law school in 1953. In support of his application, he offered testimony of his rabbi, and the faculty, fellow students, and staff at the law school. No witnesses contradicted the testimony of current good

---

34. "Bar Gets Tougher on Ethics Exam," *California Bar J.*, Jan. 2006, at 1 (quoting Committee and Dorothy Tucker, a public board member).

character. The Supreme Court reversed the denial of admission, and Justice Frankfurter wrote a separate concurrence.]

■ MR. JUSTICE FRANKFURTER, whom MR. JUSTICE CLARK and MR. JUSTICE HARLAN join, concurring.

One does not have to inhale the self-adulatory bombast of after-dinner speeches to affirm that all the interests of man that are comprised under the constitutional guarantees given to "life, liberty and property" are in the professional keeping of lawyers. It is a fair characterization of the lawyer's responsibility in our society that he stands "as a shield," to quote Devlin, J., in defense of right and to ward off wrong. From a profession charged with such responsibilities there must be exacted those qualities of truth-speaking, of a high sense of honor, of granite discretion, of the strictest observance of fiduciary responsibility, that have, throughout the centuries, been compendiously described as "moral character." . . .

It is beyond this Court's function to act as overseer of a particular result of the procedure established by a particular State for admission to its bar. No doubt satisfaction of the requirement of moral character involves an exercise of delicate judgment on the part of those who reach a conclusion, having heard and seen the applicant for admission, a judgment of which it may be said as it was of "many honest and sensible judgments" in a different context that it expresses "an intuition of experience which outruns analysis and sums up many unnamed and tangled impressions,— impressions which may lie beneath consciousness without losing their worth." . . . .

But judicial action, even in an individual case, may have been based on avowed considerations that are inadmissible in that they violate the requirements of due process. Refusal to allow a man to qualify himself for the profession on a wholly arbitrary standard or on a consideration that offends the dictates of reason offends the Due Process Clause. Such is the case here . . . .

To hold, as the [lower] court did, that Communist affiliation for six to seven years up to 1940, fifteen years prior to the court's assessment of it, in and of itself made the petitioner "a person of questionable character" is so dogmatic an inference as to be wholly unwarranted. History overwhelmingly establishes that many youths like the petitioner were drawn by the mirage of communism during the depression era, only to have their eyes later opened to reality. Such experiences no doubt may disclose a woolly mind or naive notions regarding the problems of society. But facts of history that we would be arbitrary in rejecting bar the presumption, let alone an irrebuttable presumption, that response to foolish, baseless hopes regarding the betterment of society made those who had entertained them but who later undoubtedly came to their senses and their sense of responsibility "questionable characters." Since the Supreme Court of New Mexico as a matter of law took a contrary view of such a situation in denying petitioner's application, it denied him due process of law.

NOTES

Moral character as a professional credential has an extended history. For lawyers, the requirement dates to the Roman Theodesian Code, and its Anglo–American roots reach to thirteenth century England. In this country, every state bar currently makes certification of character a prerequisite for practice, and most other nations and licensed professions impose a similar mandate. In principle, the rationale for the requirement is straightforward: it serves both to protect the public from unethical practitioners, and to preserve confidence in the integrity of the system. In practice, however, the application of the standard has proven problematic. Historically, it has served to exclude a diverse and changing constituency, variously defined to include not only former felons, but religious, racial, and ethnic minorities, adulterers, political radicals, and bankrupts. In perhaps the high water of exclusivity, one Pennsylvania board rejected candidates deemed "dull," "colorless," "subnormal", "unprepossessing," "shifty," "smooth," "keen," "shrewd," "arrogant," "conceited," "surly," and "slovenly". Also rejected were those who lacked "well defined ideas on religion," or had family members with "unsavory" backgrounds or a "poor business reputation."[35] Although the number of applicants formally denied admission has always been small, in one study fewer than 1%, the number deterred or delayed has been more substantial.[36]

The Code of Recommended Standards for Bar Examiners, adopted by the American Bar Association, the National Conference of Bar Examiners, and the Association of American Law Schools, lists the following factors as relevant to determining an applicant's admission to the bar:

- unlawful conduct
- academic misconduct
- making of false statements, including omissions, in the application for admission
- misconduct in employment
- acts involving dishonesty, fraud, deceit, or misrepresentation
- abuse of legal process
- neglect of financial responsibilities
- neglect of professional obligations
- violation of an order of the court
- mental or emotional instability
- evidence of drug or alcohol dependency
- denial of admission to the bar in another jurisdiction on character and fitness grounds

35. For a comprehensive history and empirical study, see Deborah L. Rhode, "Moral Character as a Professional Credential," 94 *Yale L. J.* 491 (1985). For the Pennsylvania cases, see *id.*, at 501.

36. *Id.* at 516.

- disciplinary action by a lawyer disciplinary agency or other professional disciplinary agency of any jurisdiction.[37]

The Code further specifies that the "weight and significance" of prior conduct should be evaluated by considering factors such as the recency and seriousness of the conduct, evidence of rehabilitation and positive social contributions since the conduct, and candor during the admission process.[38]

The expansiveness of this list and the subjectivity of standards raise several concerns. One is the possibility for overly intrusive inquiries and inconsistent decisions. Historically, character committees have excluded individuals for a wide range of conduct that had little obvious relation to protection of the public, including everything from civil disobedience to cohabitation. Bar examiners and judges have often disagreed about the relative weight to be accorded to factors such as the severity or recency of offense, and the evidence of rehabilitation and remorse. In one study, conduct such as bankruptcies, and minor drug and alcohol offenses provoked widely differing responses, as did other criminal convictions. Violation of a fishing license statute ten years earlier was sufficient to cause one local Michigan committee to decline certification. But, in the same state, at about the same time, other examiners sitting on the central board admitted individuals convicted of child molesting and conspiring to bomb a public building. While Michigan's repentant bomber gained admission despite years in a maximum security facility, an unconfessed Peeping Tom in Georgia was viewed as too great a threat to warrant admission.[39] Some evidence also suggests that race and class bias may affect the evaluation process.[40]

A related problem involves the timing of character inquiries and the double standard operating in admission and disciplinary proceedings. In essence, the current screening process comes both too early and too late. It occurs before most applicants have faced situational pressures comparable to those in practice, but after candidates have made such a significant investment in legal training that denying admission imposes enormous costs. Yet the price of exclusion is even greater for practitioners, and courts and bar authorities are more willing to deny than to revoke a license based on evidence of misconduct. Both substantive and procedural requirements are more solicitous of practitioners than applicants, and as Chapter 15 indicates, disbarment occurs in only the most egregious cases. However, from the standpoint of protecting the public, misconduct is most probative of threats to clients when it is committed by individuals who are already officers of the court. If matters such as financial irresponsibility, disregard of legal obligations, or mental health disabilities can justify exclusion from

---

37. *Comprehensive Guide to Bar Admission Requirements* (Margaret Fuller Corneille & Erica Moeser eds., 2007).

38. *Id.*

39. Rhode, *supra* note 35, at 538, 545.

40. Keith Swisher, "The Troubling Rise of the Legal Profession's Good Moral Character," 82 *St. John's L. Rev.* 1037

(2008); M.A. Cunningham, "The Professional Image Standard: An Untold Standard of Admission to the Bar," 66 *Tulane L. Rev.* 1037–39 (1992) (describing survey finding that Ivy League applicants have received less searching scrutiny than other applicants and that candidates of color have received more stringent review than their white counterparts).

practice, why do they trigger inquiry only by admission and not disciplinary bodies?

A further difficulty with character screening involves problems of predicting future misconduct from prior acts that occur under quite different circumstances. Psychological research makes clear that moral behavior is highly situational, and that contextual norms, incentives, and pressures have a substantial impact on ethical conduct.[41] Past conduct is, of course, relevant in assessing how people will react to such contextual influences. One small scale survey of disciplined lawyers found that their admission applications had been more likely to disclose problems such as arrests, academic probation, financial problems and substance abuse than the general pool of applications.[42] Yet it is often necessary to know a good deal about why individuals responded to earlier situations in order to predict how they will react in different future circumstances.[43] Bar examiners frequently lack that level of knowledge.

What follows from that fact? How confident would you be in your predictive judgments about the applicants in Problem 1? Would you support a system of conditional admission for candidates with a history of difficulties such as substance abuse, mental health disabilities, or unpaid financial obligations? About a fifth of states have such systems, which place certain applicants on probation for a specified period, typically around two to five years. During that time, they must comply with terms set by bar examiners, such as participation in alcohol treatment programs, or timely payment of debts. In 2008, the ABA approved a Model Rule on Conditional Admission for applicants who demonstrate "recent rehabilitation from dependency or successful treatment for mental or other illness, or from any other condition that the court deems appropriate that has resulted in conduct or behavior that would otherwise have rendered the applicant currently unfit to practice law ..."[44] The commentary to the rule makes clear that it designed to avoid discouraging applicants from seeking treatment. Whether the conditional status should remain confidential is left to states to determine. Would such a system make sense for cases like *In re Stewart*?

In re Application of Stewart

Supreme Court of Ohio, 2006.
860 N.E.2d 729.

Per Curiam.

Applicant, William Howard Stewart III of Dayton, Ohio, graduated from Salmon P. Chase College of Law in May 2004. He applied to register

---

41. See studies summarized in Deborah L. Rhode, "Where Is the Leadership in Moral Leadership?," in *Moral Leadership* 23–33 (Deborah L. Rhode, ed., 2006); Walter Mischel and Yuichi Shoda, "A Cognitive Affective System Theory of Personality: Reconceptualizing Situations, Dispositions, Dynamics, and Invariance in Personality Structure," 102 *Psychol. Rev.* 246 (1995).

42. Carl Baer & Peg Corneille, "Character and Fitness Inquiry: From Bar Admission to Professional Discipline," *Bar Examiner* 5 (Nov. 1992) (finding that roughly half of 54 disciplined attorneys had problematic histories, compared with 20 percent of all applicants).

43. Mischel & Shoda, *supra* note 41.

44. James Podgers, "Endorsing Early Treatment," ABA J., March 2008, at 65.

as a candidate for admission to the Ohio bar on December 10, 2003.... In early July 2004, two members of the Dayton Bar Association's Admissions Committee, after interviewing the applicant, expressed concern over the applicant's indebtedness, history of litigiousness, and overly combative nature.... After much debate, the full committee approved the applicant's character and fitness ... but they [decided] against the applicant's immediate approval, recommending instead that he be permitted to reapply to take the bar examination when he was better able to demonstrate his character and fitness to practice law.

The Applicant's Considerable Indebtedness

The applicant, who was 47 years old at the time of the panel hearing, had a history of financial irresponsibility. The board was deeply troubled by this and his lack of candor about the extent of his indebtedness. The applicant confirmed during the hearing that he had outstanding debts ranging from $160,000 to $170,000, with all but $30,000 of the indebtedness being attributable to student loans. The applicant testified that he had applied for another six-month deferment for repaying the student loans but had not yet received notice of that determination.

The remaining $30,000 of debt, the applicant explained, was attributable to four credit cards. The applicant reported that he had recently tried to arrange payment plans with two of these creditors and had done so successfully with one, but had not gotten around to making similar arrangements with the two other credit card companies. When the panel inquired as to whether any of his credit card bills were 90 days past due when he filed his bar exam application in March 2004, the applicant replied, ''No,'' just as he had in response to this question on his application. What he meant by this statement and his answer, however, was that he had never allowed three months to pass without making some payment on each card, not that he had consistently kept up his payments even in the minimum amounts. In a marked understatement, the applicant acknowledged that he was a ''slow pay'' on his revolving credit accounts.

The applicant, who is now a self-employed painter, explained that he simply does not have the money to pay his obligations. He withdrew his contributions from the Public Employee Retirement System and used the money during law school and while studying for the bar exam, but that money ran out in August 2004. He promised the panel, however, to do better in paying his credit card debts with the $600 per week he was earning as a painter.

The panel asked the applicant to produce the credit card statements that he had received after he had filed his bar-candidacy application in December 2003. The applicant agreed to present the 13 months' worth of statements for all four cards promptly in order to accommodate review before the board meeting to be held on February 3, 2005. The applicant later contacted the panel chairperson and confessed that some of his credit card payments were, in fact, more than 90 days overdue. At that time, the panel chairperson again asked the applicant to forward the requested records, and the chairperson reminded the applicant immediately before the board meeting to send these reports. The applicant supplemented his application materials on February 13 and March 12, 2005, too late for the board's consideration.

In addition to his credit card and other debt, the applicant was delinquent during the years 1970 to 1990 in paying his federal, state, and local taxes. The applicant explained his tax liability as being in part the result of his ex-wife's failure to withhold payroll taxes for her family's accounting business. Tax consequences also resulted when the applicant failed to withhold payroll taxes for his own business as a contractor. The applicant eventually negotiated a settlement of his federal and state tax liability. He claimed that he had resolved all his tax problems except for a deficiency of $1,500 in state taxes and $350 in federal taxes for 2004.

The Applicant's History of Litigiousness

The applicant's bar application materials further confirmed that since 1976, he has been involved in 62 court cases concerning all manner of disputes. In at least three cases, the applicant claimed unfair labor practices. In at least nine cases, authorities attempted to collect the applicant's delinquent federal, state, or local taxes. Still other actions included 13 traffic citations and several disorderly conduct convictions, as well as a 2003 conviction for menacing, which was later reversed.

Despite this startling amount of legal activity, the board found that the applicant had never pursued a vexatious claim. Moreover, because at least 11 of the 62 cases were juvenile court proceedings in which the applicant had participated only as a parent, the board did not question the applicant's involvement in those proceedings. The 50 or so other cases were of considerable concern to the board, however, as was the applicant's cavalier attitude toward his litigious record.

As of the panel hearing date, all but three of the approximately 50 court cases had been resolved. Still pending was a mandamus action to contest the dismissal of the applicant's claims against his former employer, the city of Dayton, after the city allegedly denied him a day of vacation. A related dispute in which the applicant had sued Dayton for abuse of process was also pending. In the third case, the applicant was defending himself against a mortgage foreclosure action.

Despite this record, particularly the misdemeanor charges, the applicant disputed that he had shown any pattern of disregarding the law, a factor that weighs against an applicant's approval under Gov. Bar R. I(11)(D)(3)(f). The applicant insisted that "all kinds of people" had a record of minor misdemeanors similar to his and that he did not "see it as a serious problem." . . .

The Applicant's Combativeness

Also of concern was the applicant's inability to conduct himself without regularly resorting to behavior that the board referred to as pugnacious.

Members of the bar admissions committee described the applicant as an "arrogant, pompous * * * know it all." The applicant admitted his characteristic hot temper, but defended it as a mere verbal manifestation that never resulted in a physical altercation:

"I think I can handle myself, conduct myself according to a code, a code of honor, and a code of doing right to other people, and if they don't do me right, I'm like John Wayne, you're going to hear about it, and I'm going to get up in your face but, like I said, I don't beat anybody up."

Acknowledging that a pleasant personality is not a prerequisite to the practice of law in Ohio, the board nevertheless noted that an applicant must have the ability to conduct himself professionally and in a manner that engenders respect for the law and the profession. See Essential Eligibility Requirements, Requirement No. 10. Throughout his testimony, however, the applicant was confrontational without provocation and saw nothing unprofessional about his remarks. He also rejected the suggestion that he might benefit from anger-management therapy, tossing off the board's concern as "paternalistic." The applicant confessed that he had almost seen a psychiatrist in 2004 but had canceled the appointment because he considered it an empty gesture. The applicant was confident that he would be able to practice law in accordance with professional and ethical standards because he intended to secure a transactional legal job that did not require him to interact with clients.

In conclusion, the board agreed with the panel and bar admission committee that the applicant's poor temperament and litigious history were not by themselves sufficient to disapprove of his character and fitness. Based on the combination of these factors, the applicant's indebtedness, and his failure to candidly discuss or document his financial irresponsibility, however, the board found that he had not proved his character and fitness to practice law by clear and convincing evidence. Because the applicant had failed to sustain his burden of proof, the board recommended disapproval of his application to take the Ohio bar exam and, consistent with the panel's report, that he be permitted to reapply to take the bar examination at a later time. The applicant has not objected to this recommendation.

On review, we adopt the findings and recommendation of the board. Under Gov.Bar R. I(11)(D)(1), the applicant has the burden to prove by clear and convincing evidence that he possesses the requisite character, fitness, and moral qualifications for admission to the practice of law in Ohio. The applicant did not meet that burden.

An applicant's tendency toward financial irresponsibility makes him a poor risk to entrust with the duties owed clients, the courts, adversaries, and others in the practice of law. . . .

Financial irresponsibility alone is enough to disapprove a bar candidacy or bar exam application, as is an applicant's failure to provide requested information. See Gov.Bar R. I(12)(C)(6). The reservations expressed by the board about the applicant's financial condition are justified. The application to take the Ohio bar examination is therefore disapproved at this time. The applicant may reapply when he is able to demonstrate that he possesses the requisite character, fitness, and moral qualifications for admission to the practice of law in Ohio.

Judgment accordingly.

PROBLEM 1

a) Criminal Conduct and Rehabilitation

You are a member of your state supreme court. How would you vote in the following cases? What standard should the applicant meet in demonstrating rehabilitation, and what importance would you attach to evidence of remorse?

Application of King, 136 P.3d 878 (Ariz. 2006).

In 1977, Lee King was employed as a deputy constable in Texas. While depressed and drunk, he shot two unarmed men after a fight in a bar. He pled guilty to attempted murder, and served four months before a court suspended his sentence. He then graduated from college and law school, and was admitted to the Texas bar. He married, completed alcohol counseling, practiced in Texas, and after ten years moved to Arizona to work in his firm's Phoenix office. Although the Arizona character committee recommended his admission, the Supreme Court disagreed. In the majority's view, King had not made the " 'virtually impossible' showing needed to erase the stain of his serious misconduct." 136 P.3d, at 886. What most disturbed the court was King's suggestion that he might have had a defense to the charges of attempted murder, but that he had accepted the plea because of "anti-police" public attitudes, which might have compromised his ability to get a fair trial. Because King did not adequately show why he committed the murders or how he had overcome his weakness, he had not met his high burden of proof.

One justice dissented on the ground that King had been a "model citizen" for thirty years, and had never been subject to any disciplinary action. He also noted that King had attributed his assault to job-related stress and alcohol abuse, and had undergone counseling during and after his probation. He had never been diagnosed as having a mental health disability warranting further treatment, and in the dissent's view, he should not have been penalized for failing to obtain a mental health expert to diagnose his earlier character flaw trait and his "triumph over it." *Id.,* at 890 (Hurwitz, J., dissenting). The dissenting judge also questioned whether applicants would be better served by a bright line rule barring admission of those with serious offenses, because "if Mr. King's application cannot meet our 'non per se' standards, I doubt that any ever will." *Id.* at 891.

Application of T.J.S., 692 A.2d 498 (N.H. 1997).

In 1986, T.J.S. was convicted of six counts of felonious assault of two female students while he was employed as a junior high and high school teacher. He also admitted inappropriate sexual conduct with nine other students between the ages of 13 and 17, including kissing and sexual intercourse. While serving four years in prison, he completed sexual offender counseling and was, "by all accounts, a model prisoner," 692 A.2d, at 500. He subsequently married, graduated from law school, and found employment working as a nonlawyer in a law firm. In recommending against admission, the state character committee described his demeanor as "too articulate, glib, and adept at explaining away his past behavior." The court accepted that recommendation, noting that attorneys enjoy great trust and confidence from clients and the applicant "failed to convince us that, given the opportunity, he would not breach such trust and confidence." *Id.*, at 503.

In the Matter of Hamm, 123 P.3d 652 (Ariz. 2005) (en banc).

James Hamm, who mortally shot a man during a drug deal in 1974, spent the next 18 years in prison as a model inmate. While serving his sentence, he obtained a college degree summa cum laude and married a woman with whom he formed a prison reform organization. After his sentence was commuted, he performed thousands of hours of community service and graduated from the University of Arizona law school. Some state legislators were outraged by his admission. By threatening budget cuts, they forced the law school to review its policy concerning convicted felons. According to the president of the state senate, "Hamm's precious seat should go to one of the thousands of applicants who didn't shoot somebody in the head." Defenders of Hamm's admission argued that he should have the right, once he had served his sentence, to put the crime behind him. Hamm himself maintained that "I don't want to put it behind me. I want to bring it with me."[45] In his law school application, he argued that the time he spent behind bars tutoring other prisoners and working as an inmate legal assistant would enrich his career.

After passing the bar exam and working for several years as Director of Advocacy Services at the prison reform organization, he sought admission to practice. In denying his application, the Arizona Supreme Court cited several factors. One was his failure to make any child support payments to the son he had fathered in 1969 until after he applied to the bar in 2004. Although Hamm attempted to excuse his failure by claiming that he had learned in 1988 that his son had been adopted by his former wife's husband, that did not, in the court's view, explain his lack of concern prior to 1988. Nor was Hamm's account consistent with his son's testimony that he had never told his father that he had been adopted. 123 P.3d, at 660. The Committee was also disturbed by Hamm's failure to disclose an altercation with his wife that had caused a call to the police (but no arrest) in 1996, and his use of language in his petition for review from a prior supreme court decision without quotes or attribution.

b) Academic Misconduct

Four different students at four different law schools were found to have plagiarized papers off the internet during their final year. One school

---

45. Jane Gross, "A Killer in Law School: Admirable or Abominable?," *N.Y.* *Times* Sept. 13, 1993, at A14 (quoting John Greene).

simply gave the student an F in the course; a second suspended the student for a year; a third agreed not to report the conduct to the bar if the student performed 100 hours of community service; and the fourth learned of the plagiarism only after the student graduated, when a journal to which the paper was submitted discovered the earlier publication. What are the obligations of the law school and the applicant to report these incidents? Should bar examiners' response be affected by the severity of the school's response? Is one act of plagiarism sufficient grounds for exclusion? If, as some studies suggest, law schools experience a high incidence of unreported academic misconduct, what follows from that fact? How should bar examiners respond to conduct such as providing false information on a law school application or falsifying a resume and transcript? Should applicants be given clear guidance about how such acts will be treated?[46]

c) First Amendment Concerns

How should courts and character committees deal with conduct raising issues of freedom of speech such as the following cases?

In re Converse, 602 N.W.2d 500 (Neb. 1999)

The Bar Commission of Nebraska denied Paul Converse the right to sit for the state bar exam based on his history of repeated conflicts with administrators at the University of South Dakota Law School. The conflicts included a series of complaints about grades, internship procedures, parking violations, removal of a photograph of a female nude posted in his law school carrel, and marketing of a "Deanie on a Weanie" shirt depicting a nude caricature of the dean astride a large hot dog with a caption reading "astride the Peter Principle." Converse drew attention to many of these conflicts by circulating letters rather than relying on prescribed complaint channels. He sent correspondence to the judges of the South Dakota Supreme Court in the grade dispute, to the ACLU in the library carrel incident, and to the school newspaper in other matters. He also threatened litigation and contacted the university president to demand that the dean be fired for incompetence. Prior to law school, Converse sued a tenant for nonpayment of rent and referred to her as a "fucking welfare bitch." 602 N.W.2d, at 504. In affirming the Commission's decision, the Nebraska Supreme Court determined that behavior reflecting on character could be considered "even if it was protected by the First Amendment." Converse's record displayed "hostile, intemperate, threatening and turbulent conduct" incompatible with a profession committed to peaceful resolution of disputes through appropriate channels. *Id.*, at 501.

Hale v. Committee of Character and Fitness of the Illinois Bar, 530 U.S. 1261 (2000).

---

46. These hypotheticals are drawn from the ABA Section of Legal Education and Admission to the Bar, *Model for Dialogue: Bar Examiners and Law Schools* (1998) (hypotheticals I and K). For the incidence of cheating and a proposal that only aggravated misconduct be considered disqualifying, see Caroline P. Jacobson, "Academic Misconduct and Bar Admissions: A Proposal for a Revised Standard," 20 *Geo. J. Legal Ethics* 739, 740 (citing studies, including one survey finding that 45% of law students admitted some form of cheating); Terri Le Clercq, "Failure to Teach: Due Process and Law School Plagiarism," 49 *J. Legal Educ.* 236 (1999).

Matthew Hale was the leader of World Church of the Creator, a white supremacist organization that advocates racial separatism. In that capacity, Hale made racially derogatory statements, and engaged in various acts of civil disobedience. Members of his organization had been indicted or convicted of violent hate crimes.[47] Hale also ran his Church's web site, which demonizes Jews and "other mud races," and claims that Hitler had the right idea.[48] In public statements, Hale acknowledged that he would prefer not to represent black clients, but he also claimed that he did not advocate violence and that he would uphold state and federal constitutional prohibitions on discrimination, as well as bar rules against racially discriminatory treatment of litigants, jurors, witnesses, and lawyers.[49]

According to the Illinois committee panel, Hale is free to "incite as much racial hatred as he desires and to attempt to carry out his life's mission of depriving those he dislikes of their legal rights, but in our view, he cannot do this as an officer of the court. Under any civilized standards of decency, the incitement of racial hatred for the ultimate purpose of depriving selected groups of their legal rights shows a gross deficiency in moral character, particularly for lawyers who have a special responsibility to uphold the rule of law for all persons." Hale's requests for hearings before the Illinois and the United States Supreme Courts were summarily denied. The Montana Bar Association also subsequently denied Hale's admission.

Leaders of the Anti–Defamation League of B'nai B'rith opposed Hale's denial on the ground that individuals should not be excluded from the bar on the basis of their beliefs. According to League spokesman, the Illinois decision could set a precedent that would justify exclusion of others with unpopular opinions. Another critic of the *Hale* decision was George Anastaplo, who had been denied admission to the Illinois bar in 1961 because of his refusal to discuss possible Communist Party membership. Anastaplo observed:

> Mr. Hale is condemned by his character committee for espousing an unacceptable position on race relations in this country. Does this mean that any character committee members who had been *against* racial integration (in the 1950s and 1960s) would have been entitled to exclude from the practice of law in their States those applicants who threatened the prevailing system of segregation?[50]

47. Hale's offenses included: a $50 fine for distributing handbills; a conviction (later overturned) of obstructing justice (based on false statements to a police officer); an arrest for assault and battery in a confrontation with a mall security officer; and an arrest for burning an Israeli flag as part of a political protest. Hale also was the subject of a temporary restraining order based on verbal abuse of an ex-girl friend and a college disciplinary hearing based on calling someone "Jew-boy." Hale failed to disclose the disciplinary hearing and handbill fine. Bob Van Voris, "Mud-dying the Waters," *Nat. L. J.*, February 21, 2000 at A1, A6.

48. Pam Bellick, "Avowed Racist Barred From Practicing Law," *N.Y. Times*, February 10, 1999, at A12.

49. Bellick, *supra* note 48, at A12.

50. In re Anastaplo, 366 U.S. 82 (1961); George Anastaplo, "Lawyers, First Principles, and Contemporary Challenges: Explorations," 19 *N. Ill. L. Rev.* 353 (1999).

By contrast, supporters of the Illinois decision have noted that the police and military have been allowed to ban members of hate groups, in part because of concerns about the public credibility of law enforcement agents. These commentators argue that the same considerations argue for the bar's exclusion of an avowed racist: "If a white supremacist is admitted to the bar and thereby given the title of 'officer of the court,' the image of the profession would be tarnished. No longer would officers of the court be perceived by the public as fair-minded, respectable ministers of justice. Public confidence in the profession would be diminished."[51] If that is true, what role should public image play in admission and discipline decisions?

Reference: Model Rule 8.1.

NOTES AND QUESTIONS

1. If bar examiners are reasonably satisfied that an applicant's prior conduct will not recur, should that end the inquiry? Or does the profession have a substantial interest in protecting its public reputation and preserving respect for officers of the law that justifies excluding individuals guilty of heinous acts, regardless of their rehabilitation? If so, what acts should qualify? Does it matter how likely the acts would be to recur in a lawyer-client relationship?[52] Consider the opening of one newspaper article.

> Ex Cons Ply Other Side of Law by Practicing It
>
> A Convicted killer, a prostitute, drug dealers and common thieves. Sound like a cell block on Rikers Island?
>
> Try a meeting of the New York State bar.
>
> Dozens of felons are working as lawyers through out New York, gaining redemption in a a field that once judged them unfit for society. . . .[53]

By contrast, consider also the opinion of a federal district judge in a case involving a convicted drug dealer, who demonstrated substantial rehabilitation in the 24 years since his offense.

> Mr. Wiesner has apparently rehabilitated himself into a contributing member of society, and I must add he has done this without much help from our state courts despite the philosophy that applauds rehabilitation of ex-offenders. Without passing judgment on the crimes that Mr. Wiesner committed, most if not all agree that we should provide those convicted of crimes with a genuine chance to rehabilitate themselves

---

51. Carla D. Pratt, "Should Klansmen Be Lawyers? Racism as an Ethical Barrier to the Legal Profession," 30 *Fla. St. U. L. Rev.* 857, 881 (2003).

52. *See* cases discussed in Martha K. Treese, "Rehabilitation—An Update," *Bar Examiner*, February 2003, 6, 7–11; *In re* Hinson–Lyles, 864 So.2d 108 (La. 2003) (denying admission to former high school teacher con-

victed of felonies relating to sexual relationship with fourteen year old student).

53. Thomas Zambito, "Ex Cons Ply Other Side of Law by Practicing It; No Longer in Prison, New Attorneys Yearn for a Second Chance," *New York Daily News*, Aug. 20, 2006, at 30.

and thus, a genuine reevaluation of their circumstances as the time passes.[54]

Five states prohibit felons from practicing law; a sixth admits them only if they have a full pardon, and two other state supreme courts have ruled that particular applicants should be permanently excluded.[55] Would you support such a rule? Should any of the candidates described in Problem 1 be permanently barred from practice?

2. As a member of your state's Board of Bar Examiners, would you impose any limits on bar character inquiries? Do all criminal convictions demonstrate the kind of disrespect for law that ought not to characterize officers of the court? Should more states adopt bright line rules and make certain felony convictions a basis for disqualification, either permanently or for a prescribed period? Should more emphasis focus on disciplinary responses to misconduct rather than efforts to predict it?[56]

3. How should courts and bar examiners treat constitutionally protected speech that raises issues of character? Some law students report that they have been deterred from engaging in political protests that might involve civil disobedience out of concern that it might delay or jeopardize their admission to the bar.[57] Should states be required to publish specific standards or bar examiner decisions denying admission so that applicants would have greater notice of disqualifying conduct?[58] Did the courts in *Hale* and *Stewart* reach the right results? Did they arrive there by the right reasons or should they have placed more weight on conduct other than litigiousness or racist views? Did the *Converse* court appropriately consider the applicant's racial slur? Should political opinions, or non-vexatious "litigiousness" ever be the basis for denying admission to the bar? If lawyers could not be subject to discipline for bringing trivial cases or expressing racist views in nonlegal settings, should such conduct be grounds for denying admission?[59] Is your view in *Hale* affected by learning that he was subsequently convicted of obstruction of justice and soliciting the murder of a federal judge who had ruled against his organization in a dispute over its trade name? He is currently serving a 40 year sentence in a Colorado supermax prison.

---

54. Wiesner v. Nardelli, 2007 WL 211083 (S.D.N.Y. 2007) (expressing reservations about the decision but finding no basis for a federal court to intervene). For a fuller description of the facts, see Paul Davies, "The High Bar For Redemption," *Wall St. J.*, March 8, 2007, at A1.

55. See Davies, *supra* note 54 (describing ban by Indiana, Mississippi, Missouri, Oregon, and Texas, and pardon rule by Alabama); Thomas Arthur Pobjecky, "Beyond Rehabilitation: Permanent Exclusion from the Practice of Law," *Bar Examiner*, Feb. 2007, at 6, 10.

56. Rhode, *supra* note 35; Deborah L. Rhode, *In the Interests of Justice* 155 (2000).

57. Theresa Keeley, "Good Moral Character: Already an Unconstitutionally Vague Concept and Now Putting Bar Applicants in a Post–9/11 World on an Elevated Threat Level," 6 *U. Pa. J. Const. L.* 844 (2004).

58. Matthew A. Ritter, "The Ethics of Moral Character Determination: An Indeterminate Ethical Reflection Upon Bar Admission," 39 *Cal. Western L. Rev.* 1 (2002).

59. *See* W. Bradley Wendel, "Free Speech for Lawyers," 28 *Hastings Const. L. Q.* 305, 320 (2001).

4.   What kinds of character information should law schools provide to bar authorities? The National Conference of Bar Examiners has a form letter used by about half of the states in seeking law school deans' certification of the character and fitness of their graduates. That letter asks three questions:

> (1) Does the applicant's record raise question regarding the applicant's character or indicate a lack of integrity or trustworthiness?

> (2) Has the applicant engaged in any behavior, whether or not it was made part of the applicant's record, that reflects unfavorably on his or her character or fitness to practice law?

> (3) Is there any additional information of which you are aware that might impact the Board's determination of this person's character and fitness?

Other jurisdictions ask variations on these questions, sometimes broadly framed to cover any matters reflecting adversely on the applicant's reputation or character.

What information beyond what is part of the applicant's record do you think law schools have an obligation to provide and how much corroboration should they require?

5.   How much significance should the bar place on applicants' personal financial irresponsibility in general and student loan repayments in particular? Judges and bar examiners have long differed over the importance of these issues and over whether the discharge of educational debts in bankruptcy should be a grounds for exclusion.[60] Consider, for example, *In re C.R.W.*, 481 S.E.2d 511 (Ga. 1997), in which the Georgia Supreme Court denied admission to an applicant who, in the majority's view, had not made a "good faith effort" to establish a repayment schedule concerning credit obligations, including some of her student loans discharged in bankruptcy. By contrast, the two dissenting judges felt that "incurring debt for a legitimate purpose, using legitimate means to relieve oneself of the burden of that debt, and keeping current on repayment plans . . . [for claims that] survived the bankruptcy proceeding" did not constitute fiscal irresponsibility. Id., at 516 (Benham, J., dissenting). What is your view? Do you agree with how the majority handled the debt issues in the *C.R.W.* and *Stewart* cases?

6.   Consider the arguments supporting virtue-based ethical frameworks discussed in the Introduction. Is the moral character requirement an appropriate application of those frameworks? Could it be?

PROBLEM 2

Title II of the Americans with Disabilities Act provides that: "No qualified individual with a disability shall, by reason of such disability, be

---

60. The issue has come up with less frequency since amendments to the Bankruptcy Code prevented discharge of such loans absent "undue hardship" on the debtor and his or her dependents. 11 U.S.C. § 523. However what constitutes undue hardship has also been controversial, and recently proposed legislation would permit discharge of educational loans. *See, e.g.*, Student Borrowers Bill, S.511 (2007).

excluded from participating in ... or be subjected to discrimination by any ... [public] entity." 42 U.S.C. § 12132. Under Title II, disabled individuals are deemed "qualified" for purposes of occupational licensing if they can meet the "essential eligibility requirements for receiving the license or certification."[61] The Act provides an exception for exclusions "necessary" to providing the licensed services.

a) You are a lawyer with a disability rights organization. Several law school administrators and students have contacted you with concerns about the scope of questions on bar admission applications. The broadest question at issue asks: "From the age of 16 to the present, have you been treated for any mental, emotional, or nervous disorder?" A second, narrower question asks: "Have you ever had, been treated or counseled for, or refused treatment or counseling for, a mental, emotional, or nervous condition which permanently, presently or chronically impairs or distorts your judgment, behavior, capacity to recognize reality or ability to cope with ordinary demands of life?" A third question asks: "whether you have any mental or emotional condition ... that could adversely affect your capacity to practice law?"[62] Applicants also are required to waive confidentiality of records relating to the treatment disclosed.

Administrators report that some students have decided not to seek mental health counseling during law school partly out of concern that it might lead to delays or intrusive inquiries by bar examiners. Several students also express concern that they might be penalized for lack of candor if they fail to disclose conditions that have interfered with their academic performance or personal relationships, but which they do not believe will impair their ability to practice law. These students have asked whether they can justifiably refuse to answer such questions and whether you will represent them in proceedings against the state bar examining board if their applications are delayed or denied. How do you respond? Does it matter what psychological problems the students are unwilling to disclose?

b) Assume that you decide to represent at least some of the students and that you are engaged in negotiations with various state bar examining authorities about revising their questions. They appear open to reform but are not prepared to drop all questions. They note that a high proportion of lawyer misconduct and malpractice is related to substance abuse and mental health difficulties.[63] In the only study on point, prepared during a challenge to the Texas bar exam, most information concerning severe

---

61. Department of Justice (DOJ) Analysis, 28 C.F.R. § 35.104 (1991).

62. These questions are taken from the 2007 Indiana, Michigan, and New York bar applications. A number of states have a variation of the last question. California asks: "Have you been diagnosed or treated for a medically recognized mental illness, disease or disorder that would currently interfere with your ability to practice law?"

63. Erica Moeser, "Personal Matters: Should Bar Applicants Be Asked About Treatment for Mental Health? Yes: The Public Has the Right to Know About Instability," *A.B.A.J.*, October 1994, at 36. For the linkage between disciplinary problems and mental health difficulties, including substance abuse, *see* Chapter XV.

mental health concerns would not have come to light in the absence of mental health inquiries on bar admission forms.[64] Given the costs of detecting and remedying misconduct after the fact, examiners believe that the public has a legitimate interest in preventing admission of applicants who could pose a substantial risk to clients.

Attorneys in your office want to challenge any inquiry into mental health treatment. They point to evidence suggesting that law students would be significantly more likely to seek counseling and to encourage others to do so if they could be sure that bar examiners would not have access to information about that treatment.[65] Students' confidentiality concerns are not without basis. A comprehensive empirical study found substantial costs for many applicants who disclosed mental health treatment: invasion of privacy; financial and emotional consequences related to delay in their admission; fees for lawyers and expert witnesses; and reputational concerns in small communities where applicants might come in contact with lawyers on their character committee later in practice.[66]

Your staff attorneys also note that in states where litigants have challenged bar inquiries under the American with Disabilities Act, examiners have been unable to show that past mental health assistance predicts future problems in practice.[67] About half of those who seek such assistance do not have a diagnosable illness. Those who do may pose fewer risks than candidates with undisclosed and untreated problems. Even in the Texas study on which bar examiners rely, only thirteen individuals over a seven year period were identified as having serious mental health concerns that would not have otherwise emerged, and only five did not eventually receive unconditional admission.[68]

Litigation challenging mental health questions under the ADA has reached mixed results. In a minority of cases, courts have demanded empirical evidence that the questions have been necessary and effective in identifying applicants who pose a heightened risk to the public.[69] A majority of courts have applied a less rigorous test and reasoned that questions concerning serious mental illnesses are necessary to ensure that applicants "are capable of practicing law in a competent and ethical manner."[70]

64. Applicants v. Texas State Board of Law Examiners, 1994 WL 923404 (W.D.Tex. 1994) (citing a Board study finding that over a seven year period, thirteen of nineteen serious cases would have gone undetected).

65. *See* Phyllis Coleman and Ronald A. Shellaw, "Ask About Conduct, Not Mental Illness: A Proposal for Bar Examiners and Medical Boards to Comply with the ADA and Constitution," 20 *Legis.* 147, 162 (1994) (citing AALS Survey finding that the proportion of students who seek help for substance abuse increased from 10 percent to 41 percent, and the number who would encourage a classmate increased from 19 percent to 47 percent).

66. Jon Bauer, "The Character of the Questions, and the Fitness of the Process:

Mental Health, Bar Admissions and the Americans With Disabilities Act," 49 *UCLA L. Rev.* 93, 208–09 (2001).

67. Clark v. Virginia Board of Bar Examiners, 880 F.Supp. 430, 436 (E.D.Va.1995); In re Petition and Questionnaire for Admission to the Rhode Island Bar, 683 A.2d 1333, 1336 (R.I. 1996).

68. Bauer, *supra* note 66, at 146.

69. *See* cases cited in note 67 *supra*.

70. Applicants v. Texas State Board of Bar Examiners, 1994 WL 923404 (W.D. Tex. 1994).

NOTES AND QUESTIONS

According to the American Bar Association Commission on Mental and Physical Disability Law:

> research in the field, clinical experience and common sense all demonstrate that neither diagnosis nor the fact of having undergone treatment support any inferences about a person's ability to carry out professional responsibilities or to act with integrity, competence or honor. Nor does the evidence in the field indicate that bar examiners or mental health professionals can predict inappropriate or irresponsible behavior on the basis of the person's mental health history.[71]

Other extensive reviews of the relevant research have come to a similar conclusion.[72]

Should such evidence be sufficient to prevent the bar from asking any questions about treatment? Are there other sufficient ways to assess candidates' fitness to practice? Consider Jon Bauer's proposal that bar examiners establish a separate screening procedure, administered by trained mental health professionals, to review responses to narrowly focused mental health questions. Such questions might involve recent drug abuse or treatment for serious specified disorders such as schizophrenia and bi-polar disorders. This medical screening process would identify applicants whose records raise significant concern about fitness to practice. Bar examiners would receive mental health information only for these applicants, and only after examiners had conducted their own review of the application, uncontaminated by prejudices that may attach to mental health treatment.[73] Would you support such a system? How well would it address the concerns of applicants and the public?

D. INTERSTATE REGULATION

NOTES

The increasing mobility of the population and the interstate character of many transactions present substantial problems in a decentralized system of admission. These problems arise in a variety of contexts: attorneys relocating for family or professional reasons; attorneys representing local clients who need out-of-state services; attorneys with special expertise that offers them a national or global practice; and attorneys representing clients who have difficulty finding appropriate local counsel.

---

71. American Bar Association, Commission on Mental and Physical Disability Law, *Report to the House of Delegates* 17 (1994).

72. Bauer, *supra* note 66. The American Psychiatric Association recommends that psychiatric history not be the subject of admissions inquiries because it is not an accurate predictor of fitness. *See* Clark v. Virginia Board of Bar Examiners, 880 F.Supp. 430, 435 (E.D. Va. 1995).

73. *Id.*, at 213–17.

One way of responding to these difficulties has been to allow *pro hac vice* appearances by out-of-state lawyers. In *Leis v. Flynt,* 439 U.S. 438 (1979), the Supreme Court addressed the constitutional underpinnings of that practice. Defendants Larry Flynt and *Hustler Magazine* were charged with unlawful dissemination of harmful material to minors. The trial court declined to permit out-of-state lawyers Fahringer and Cambria to appear *pro hac vice* as counsel for defendants in association with local counsel. The United States District Court held, and the Sixth Circuit Court of Appeals affirmed, that these lawyers could not be denied the privilege of appearing *pro hac vice* without a meaningful hearing, application of reasonably clear standards, and a rational basis for exclusion. On petition for a writ of *certiorari*, the Supreme Court summarily reversed.

Leis v. Flynt

Supreme Court of the United States, 1979.
439 U.S. 438.

■ PER CURIAM.

. . . As this Court has observed on numerous occasions, the Constitution does not create property interests. Rather it extends various procedural safeguards to certain interests "that stem from an independent source such as state law."

The Court of Appeals evidently believed that an out-of-state lawyer's interest in appearing *pro hac vice* in an Ohio court stems from some such independent source. It cited no state law authority for this proposition, however, and indeed noted that "Ohio has no specific standards regarding *pro hac vice* admissions. . . ." Rather, the court referred to the prevalence of *pro hac vice* practice in American courts and instances in our history where counsel appearing *pro hac vice* have rendered distinguished service. We do not question that the practice of courts in most States is to allow an out-of-state lawyer the privilege of appearing upon motion, especially when he is associated with a member of the local bar. In view of the high mobility of the bar, and also the trend toward specialization, perhaps this is a practice to be encouraged. But it is not a right granted either by statute or the Constitution. . . .

Nor is there a basis for the argument that the interest in appearing *pro hac vice* has its source in federal law. See *Paul v. Davis, supra,* 424 U.S., at 699–701. The speculative claim that Fahringer's and Cambria's reputations might suffer as the result of the denial of their asserted right cannot by itself make out an injury to a constitutionally protected interest. There simply was no deprivation here of some right previously held under state law. Further, there is no right of federal origin that permits such lawyers to appear in state courts without meeting that State's bar admission requirements. This Court, on several occasions, has sustained state bar rules that excluded out-of-state counsel from practice altogether or on a case-by-case basis. Accordingly, because Fahringer and Cambria did not possess a cognizable property interest within the terms of the Fourteenth Amendment, the Constitution does not obligate the Ohio courts to accord them procedural due process in passing on their application for permission to appear *pro hac vice* before the Court of Common Pleas of Hamilton County.[5]

■ MR. JUSTICE STEVENS, with whom MR. JUSTICE BRENNAN and MR. JUSTICE MARSHALL join, dissenting.

A lawyer's interest in pursuing his calling is protected by the Due Process Clause of the Fourteenth Amendment. The question presented by this case is whether a lawyer abandons that protection when he crosses the border of the State which issued his license to practice.

The Court holds that a lawyer has no constitutionally protected interest in his out-of-state practice. In its view, the interest of the lawyer is so trivial that a judge has no obligation to give any consideration whatsoever to the merits of a *pro hac vice* request, or to give the lawyer any opportunity to advance reasons in support of his application. The Court's square holding is that the Due Process Clause of the Fourteenth Amendment simply does not apply to this kind of ruling by a state trial judge.[2]

. . .

The notion that a state trial judge has arbitrary and unlimited power to refuse a nonresident lawyer permission to appear in his courtroom is nothing but a remnant of a bygone era. . . . Interstate law practice and multistate law firms are now commonplace. Federal questions regularly arise in state criminal trials and permeate the typical lawyer's practice. Because the assertion of federal claims or defenses is often unpopular, "advice and assistance by an out-of-state lawyer may be the only means available for vindication." The "increased specialization and high mobility" of today's Bar is a consequence of the dramatic change in the demand for legal services that has occurred during the past century. . . .

History attests to the importance of *pro hac vice* appearances. As Judge Merritt, writing for the Court of Appeals [below] explained: . . .

"There are a number of reasons for this tradition. 'The demands of business and the mobility of our society' are the reasons given by the

---

5. The dissenting opinion of Mr. Justice Stevens argues that a lawyer's right to "pursu[e] his calling is protected by the Due Process Clause . . . when he crosses the border" of the State that licensed him. Mr. Justice Stevens identifies two "protected" interests that "reinforce" each other. These are said to be "the 'nature' of the interest in *pro hac vice* admissions or the 'implicit promise' inhering in Ohio custom." The first of these lawyer's "interests" is described as that of "discharging [his] responsibility for the fair administration of justice in our adversary system." As important as this interest is, the suggestion that the Constitution assures the right of a lawyer to practice in the court of every State is a novel one, not supported by any authority brought to our attention.

2. Although the Court does not address it, this case also presents the question whether a defendant's interest in representation by nonresident counsel is entitled to any constitutional protection. The clients, as well as the lawyers, are parties to this litigation. Moreover, the Ohio trial judge made it perfectly clear that his ruling was directed at the defendants, and not merely their counsel. . . . A defendant's interest in adequate representation is "perhaps his most important privilege" protected by the Constitution. . . . Whatever the scope of a lawyer's interest in practicing in other States may be . . . the client's interest in representation by out-of-state counsel is entitled to some measure of constitutional protection. . . .

American Bar Association in Canon 3 of the Code of Professional Responsibility. That Canon discourages 'territorial limitations' on the practice of law, including trial practice. There are other reasons in addition to business reasons. A client may want a particular lawyer for a particular kind of case, and a lawyer may want to take the case because of the skill required. Often, as in the case of Andrew Hamilton, Darrow, Bryan and Thurgood Marshall, a lawyer participates in a case out of a sense of justice. He may feel a sense of duty to defend an unpopular defendant and in this way to give expression to his own moral sense. These are important values, both for lawyers and clients, and should not be denied arbitrarily.''

The interest these lawyers seek to vindicate is not merely the pecuniary goal that motivates every individual's attempt to pursue his calling. It is the profession's interest in discharging its responsibility for the fair administration of justice in our adversary system. The nature of that interest is surely worthy of the protection afforded by the Due Process Clause of the Fourteenth Amendment. . . .

NOTES

Leis is an atypical case. Courts generally admit lawyers *pro hac vice,* although about half of all jurisdictions require association of local counsel. The stated justifications for restricting such special appearances usually involve concerns about out-of-state attorneys' familiarity with local practice and procedures, their availability for hearings and service of papers, and their accountability to local disciplinary authorities. Unstated concerns involve economic protectionism and political hostility.

The latter motivation emerged clearly in efforts by certain southern courts to prevent out-of-state appearances by civil rights attorneys during the 1950s and 1960s. The constitutionality of such practices remains open to question, particularly since the *Leis* majority did not reach the issue of whether defendants might in some circumstances be entitled to representation by out-of-state counsel of their choice. How should that issue be resolved?

A more general question involves the appropriateness of easing restrictions on out-of-state lawyers. Absent court approval, attorneys may provide representation only in jurisdictions where they are admitted to the bar. As Chapter XII's discussion of multijurisdictional practice noted, some decisions hold that attorneys may not even offer advice by phone or computer concerning a transaction or dispute arising in a state in which they are not licensed.[54] Such prohibitions cannot serve client needs that routinely cross state boundaries. Nor are these prohibitions possible to enforce in a technological age that makes such boundaries increasingly irrelevant.

54. Birbrower, Montalbano, Condon & Frank v. Superior Court, 70 Cal.Rptr.2d 304 (Cal. 1998).

Attorneys who attempt to avoid unauthorized practice by obtaining admission in multiple jurisdictions bump up against substantial obstacles. Many states require passage of their own bar exam, some require residency, including a local office, and others will waive exam requirements only for lawyers from jurisdictions that extend the same privileges to the states' own lawyers. Such reciprocity rules are difficult to justify from any consumer protection perspective. If experienced out-of-state attorneys are competent to practice, why should it matter how their local bars treat competitors? The situation is tolerable only because bar agencies rarely have sufficient information or resources to enforce prohibitions on out-of-state practice. However, the threat of sanctions can deter attorneys from providing cost-effective representation on multistate matters. Alternatively, clients may have to subsidize an affiliation with local counsel who provide no significant function other than compliance with protectionist admission requirements.

Critics of the current admission system argue that it cannot be justified on rational policy grounds, and that restrictions on out-of-state attorneys persist largely due to professional self-interest and public inertia. Once admitted to the bar, many lawyers have no incentive to eliminate arbitrary or overbroad restrictions if they lack a substantial interstate practice, particularly where the effect of reform would be to increase the number of potential competitors.

How would you address the needs of interstate law practice? In a series of cases in the late 1980s, the Supreme Court held that residency requirements for bar applicants or admitted lawyers were violations of the Privileges and Immunities Clause.[55] Although the Court did not challenge states' rights to impose exam requirements on out-of-state attorneys, its reasoning suggested decreasing tolerance for protectionist regulation. Similar concerns encouraged the ABA to appoint a Commission on Multijurisdictional Practice, and to adopt its recommended revision of Model Rule 5.5. As indicated in Chapter XII, that revised rule now provides "safe havens" for temporary practice by out-of-state lawyers under limited circumstances.

The Commission considered, but rejected proposals for a national admission system with uniform entrance requirements. Under such a system, states could still discipline attorneys for local misconduct and impose additional obligations to ensure familiarity with local rules. Another proposal, also rejected by the Commission, would be to follow the approach of the fifteen member European Community. Provisions in the Treaty of Rome provide that a lawyer licensed in one member country may provide legal services in another country, except for activities specially reserved to members of that country's bar, such as in-court representation. Under European Council Directives, an attorney licensed in one member country may be admitted to the bar of another after practicing the law of that

---

55. Supreme Court of New Hampshire v. Piper, 470 U.S. 274 (1985 as amended); Frazier v. Heebe, 482 U.S. 641 (1987); Supreme Court of Virginia v. Friedman, 487 U.S. 59 (1988).

country and the European Union for over three years. A lawyer admitted in only one country may also provide temporary legal services in another, subject to certain limited restrictions.[56] In Australia, lawyers are admitted by a state or territory, but under uniform standards so that their admission is recognized nationally.[57] Would you favor such an approach for interstate reciprocity in this country?

56.   *See* James M. Moliterno & George C. Harris, *Global Issues in Legal Ethics* 7–22 (2007); Roger J. Goebal, "The Liberalization of Interstate Legal Practice in the European Union: Lessons for the United States?" 34 *Int'l. L.* 307 (2000).

57.   Hawkins, *supra* note 31, at 18.

CHAPTER XV

DISCIPLINE AND MALPRACTICE

A. INTRODUCTION

American courts have traditionally asserted inherent power to regulate the practice of law. The tradition has its roots in thirteenth century English practices, when Edward I vested authority in the Lord Chief Justice of the Court of Common Pleas to determine those fit to appear before the bench. In disbarment proceedings before these early English courts, attorneys guilty of misconduct were literally cast over the "bar," a wooden barrier separating judges and clerks from lawyers, litigants, and witnesses.

In this country, eighteenth and nineteenth century courts seldom exercised their disciplinary power. Community disapproval and lack of referrals were the primary sanction for professional misconduct, and the inadequacy of this approach was a major impetus for the formation of bar associations. By the early twentieth century, all forty-eight states and several hundred localities had voluntary organizations of lawyers. Most of these associations established grievance committees to handle reports of attorney misconduct. Such committees were demonstrably inadequate for the task. As part of a voluntary governance system, the committees lacked power to compel attendance of witnesses or to impose discipline. Although the bar could report committee findings to the court, together with a request for sanctions, association members were reluctant to exercise that power. Given the low incidence of sanctions, few attorneys or clients made efforts to file complaints.[1]

The rise of integrated (*i.e.*, compulsory) bar associations in the early twentieth century brought an expansion in regulatory power. Under legislative or judicial mandate, both voluntary and integrated bars gradually acquired authority to investigate misconduct and to impose sanctions, subject to court oversight. The procedures governing lawyer discipline have varied from state to state, although they all must meet constitutional requirements. Because current disciplinary proceedings are "quasi-criminal" in nature, courts have extended basic due process safeguards such as (1) the opportunity to confront evidence and cross-examine witnesses, *Willner v. Committee on Character and Fitness*, 373 U.S. 96 (1963); (2) the right to present witnesses and argument, *In re Ginger*, 372 F.2d 620 (6th Cir.), *cert. denied*, 387 U.S. 935 (1967) and (3) the right to fair notice, *In re*

---

1. *See generally,* James Willard Hurst, *The Growth of American Law: The Law Makers* 286–93 (1950); George Martin, *Causes* *and Conflicts: The Centennial History of the Association of the Bar of the City of New York 1870–1970* (1970).

Ruffalo, 390 U.S. 544 (1968). Lawyers may not be disciplined for invoking the privilege against self-incrimination, but the privilege does not extend to testimony about non-criminal conduct even if it might lead to professional discipline. *Spevack v. Klein,* 385 U.S. 511 (1967). Lawyers granted immunity from criminal proceedings may be obligated to answer questions and supply information; failure to do so may give rise to adverse inferences. So too, incriminating testimony given by an attorney under a grant of immunity is admissible in disciplinary proceedings. Other procedural safeguards and the general rules governing lawyer discipline are set forth in state statutes, rules of court, and rules of professional conduct. A majority of jurisdictions require that disciplinary charges be proven by clear and convincing evidence. A minority demand only a fair preponderance of the evidence.

According to the ABA Standards for Lawyer Discipline and Disability Proceedings, Standard 1.1:

> The purpose of lawyer discipline and disability proceedings is to maintain appropriate standards of professional conduct in order to protect the public and the administration of justice from lawyers who have demonstrated by their conduct that they are unable or are likely to be unable to properly discharge their professional duties.

Similarly, the objective of civil malpractice proceedings is to enforce appropriate standards of professional conduct and to provide remedies for breaches of such standards.

The effectiveness of both disciplinary and civil liability structures is a matter of continuing concern. Only about a quarter of surveyed Americans believe that the profession does a good job of disciplining its members.[2] The readings that follow describe the capacities and limitations of bar disciplinary structures, as well as proposals for reform. Underlying this discussion are the broader questions about self-regulation raised in Chapter III. Are there inherent problems in a regulatory system controlled by the group to be regulated? If so, what follows from that fact?

B.   REGULATORY STRUCTURES AND STANDARDS

The Duty to Report Misconduct

PROBLEM 1

a) You are a junior partner in a prominent firm in a small city. Over the last several years, you have defended an insurance company in two separate personal injury suits handled by the same plaintiff's attorney. One of those cases settled for what you considered grossly inadequate sums because the attorney failed to do sufficient factual investigation or legal research. The lawyer did, however, recover a substantial contingency fee

---

2. American Bar Association, *Perceptions of the U.S. Justice System 77 (1999).*

for minimal work. In a second case, the lawyer bungled matters at trial through inept witness preparation, cross-examination, and argument before the jury. As a result, his seriously injured client recovered only a fraction of what the case was worth.

The attorney has now joined a small firm that does insurance defense work. You are currently defending a claim in which one of the co-defendants is represented by that attorney. The attorney, who is charging by the hour, has insisted on attending depositions and meetings at which he is unnecessary and unprepared. He has been persistently contemptuous of Hispanic witnesses and lawyers: for example, in off-the-record statements, he has referred to one of his opposing counsel, a young Hispanic woman, as "Taco Belle." In two instances, once to opponents and once to the court, the lawyer has misrepresented the reasons for seeking continuances. Although he claimed that he needed the schedule change to accommodate another trial, you know that he had planned a fishing trip for the time in question. The deception has not come to light because the attorney subsequently reported that the other case unexpectedly settled, which left him with an opportunity for a brief vacation.

Which, if any, of his practices violate Model Rules of Professional Conduct? What, if any action do you take? Would you act differently if the lawyer was representing your adversary or if you suspected that his inadequate preparation was related to substance abuse? Is any of your knowledge of the attorney's practices confidential? Would any of your client's interests be jeopardized by disclosure? If so, how do you reconcile the duty of confidentiality with the duty to report lawyer misconduct?

b) If you were chair of the state bar's disciplinary review board, what strategies would you propose for responding to such misconduct? What standards and enforcement policies would you advocate regarding lawyers who possess unprivileged knowledge of professional misconduct by other attorneys?

c) You are a former prosecutor having drinks with a close friend, law school classmate, and former colleague who tells you that he is that he is dying of colon cancer. In that same conversation, he reveals that he once suppressed exculpatory blood evidence in a criminal case. You urge him to "remedy the situation." He dies three months later without having done so. What do you do? Your state has a version of Model Rule 8.3 that requires reports to disciplinary agencies of unprivileged information that "raises a substantial question as to that lawyer's honesty, trustworthiness, or fitness as a lawyer in other respects. . . ."

d) Suppose that five years after the attorney dies you learn that one of the defendants involved in the case is scheduled to be executed, and that his lawyer had discovered an exculpatory blood test that had not been revealed. You provide the lawyer with an affidavit recounting the conversation and then report the misconduct to the Office of Disciplinary Counsel disclosing the conversation. You also testify for the defendant in a motion for a new trial and acknowledge that "I should have reported [the misconduct] sooner, I guess." Could, or should, the Office file disciplinary charges for your failure to make a prompt report? If so, what sanction would be appropriate?[3]

References:

Model Rules 1.1, 1.5, 3.1, 8.3.

In re Himmel

Supreme Court of Illinois, 1988.
533 N.E.2d 790.

[The case arose after Tammy Forsberg retained attorney John R. Casey to represent her in a personal injury action. Having settled the claim for $35,000, Casey (who was entitled to a one-third contingency fee) declined to provide Forsberg with her two-thirds share of the recovery. After several unsuccessful efforts to collect, Forsberg hired James Himmel to represent her. Casey subsequently agreed to pay $75,000 in settlement of the claim, and Forsberg agreed not to initiate criminal, civil, or disciplinary charges. When Casey failed to honor that agreement, Himmel sued and won a judgment of $100,000. However, he received no fee because despite the judgment, Forsberg ultimately collected only $15,400 and Himmel's retainer agreement gave him one-third of the recovery in excess of the amount owed on the original claim.

Prior to retaining Himmel, Forsberg had contacted the Illinois Attorney Registration and Disciplinary Committee (ARDC). When investigation revealed other complaints against Casey, ARDC initiated an action and subsequently disbarred Casey by consent. The ARDC then pursued charges against Himmel for failing to report Casey's misconduct. On appeal, the Illinois Supreme Court sustained those charges.]

■ JUSTICE STAMOS delivered the opinion of the Court.

We begin our analysis by examining whether a client's complaint of attorney misconduct to the Commission can be a defense to an attorney's failure to report the same misconduct. Respondent offers no authority for such a defense and our research has disclosed none. Common sense would dictate that if a lawyer has a duty under the Code, the actions of a client would not relieve the attorney of his own duty. Accordingly, while the parties dispute whether or not respondent's client informed the Commission, that question is irrelevant to our inquiry in this case. We have held that the canons of ethics in the Code constitute a safe guide for professional conduct, and attorneys may be disciplined for not observing them.... A lawyer, as an officer of the court, is duty-bound to uphold the rules in the Code....

Respondent contends that the information was privileged information received from his client, Forsberg, and therefore he was under no obligation to disclose the matter to the Commission. Respondent argues that his failure to report Casey's misconduct was motivated by his respect for

---

3. These facts are modeled on In re Riehlmann, 891 So.2d 1239, 1242 (La. 2005).

his client's wishes, not by his desire for financial gain. To support this assertion, respondent notes that his fee agreement with Forsberg was contingent upon her first receiving all the money Casey originally owed her. Further, respondent states that he has received no fee for this representation of Forsberg.

Our analysis of this issue begins with a reading of the applicable disciplinary rules. Rule 1–103(a) of the Code states:

> (a) A lawyer possessing unprivileged knowledge of a violation of Rule 1–102(a)(3) or (4) shall report such knowledge to a tribunal or other authority empowered to investigate or act upon such violation.

107 Ill.2d R. 1–103(a).

Rule 1–102 of the Code states:

> (a) A lawyer shall not
>
> (1) violate a disciplinary rule;
>
> (2) circumvent a disciplinary rule through actions of another;
>
> (3) engage in illegal conduct involving moral turpitude;
>
> (4) engage in conduct involving dishonesty, fraud, deceit, or misrepresentation; or
>
> (5) engage in conduct that is prejudicial to the administration of justice.

107 Ill.2d R. 1–102.

. . . . We agree with the Administrator's argument that the communication regarding Casey's conduct does not [fall under the attorney-client privilege.] The record does not suggest that this information was communicated by Forsberg to the respondent in confidence. We have held that information voluntarily disclosed by a client to an attorney, in the presence of third parties who are not agents of the client or attorney, is not privileged information. . . . In this case, Forsberg discussed the matter with respondent at various times while her mother and her fiance were present. . . . The record [also] shows that respondent, with Forsberg's consent, discussed Casey's conversion of her funds with the insurance company involved, the insurance company's lawyer, and with Casey himself. Thus, under [prior precedent] the information was not privileged.

Though respondent repeatedly asserts that his failure to report was motivated not by financial gain but by the request of his client, we do not deem such an argument relevant in this case. This court has stated that discipline may be appropriate even if no dishonest motive [exists]. . . . In addition, we have held that client approval of an attorney's action does not immunize an attorney from disciplinary action. . . .

The third issue concerns the appropriate quantum of discipline to be imposed in this case. . . . [Respondent's] failure to report resulted in interference with the Commission's investigation of Casey, and thus with the administration of justice. Perhaps some members of the public would have been spared from Casey's misconduct had respondent reported the information as soon as he knew of Casey's conversions of client funds. We are particularly disturbed by the fact that respondent chose to draft a settlement agreement with Casey rather than report his misconduct. As the Administrator has stated, by this conduct, both respondent and his client ran afoul of the Criminal Code's prohibition against compounding a crime, which states in section 32–1:

> A person compounds a crime when he receives or offers to another any consideration for a promise not to prosecute or aid in the prosecution of an offender. . . . Compounding a crime is a petty offense.

Both respondent and his client stood to gain financially by agreeing not to prosecute or report Casey for conversion. According to the settlement agreement, respondent would have received $17,000 or more as his fee. If Casey had satisfied the judgment entered against him for failure to honor the settlement agreement, respondent would have collected approximately $25,588.

We have held that fairness dictates consideration of mitigating factors in disciplinary cases. . . . Therefore, we do consider the fact that Forsberg recovered $10,400 through respondent's services, that respondent has practiced law for 11 years with no record of complaints, and that he requested no fee for minimum collection of Forsberg's funds. However, these considerations do not outweigh the serious nature of respondent's failure to report Casey, the resulting interference with the Commission's investigation of Casey, and respondent's ill-advised choice to settle with Casey rather than report his misconduct. . . .

Accordingly, it is ordered that respondent be suspended from the practice of law for one year.

Wieder v. Skala

New York Court of Appeals, 1992.
80 N.Y.2d 628.

■ Opinion by HANCOCK, JR., J:

Plaintiff, a member of the Bar, has sued his former employer, a law firm. He claims he was wrongfully discharged as an associate because of his insistence that the firm comply with the governing disciplinary rules by reporting professional misconduct allegedly committed by another associate. The question presented is whether plaintiff has stated a claim for relief either for breach of contract or for the tort of wrongful discharge in violation of this State's public policy. The lower courts have dismissed both causes of action on motion as legally insufficient . . . on the strength of New York's employment-at-will doctrine. For reasons which follow, we modify the order and reinstate plaintiff's cause of action for breach of contract. . . .

[Wieder, an associate at the defendant law firm, asked the firm to represent him in his purchase of a condominium. The firm assigned another associate, L.L., to represent Wieder. L.L. neglected Wieder's real estate transaction, and covered up his neglect by lying to him. When Wieder complained to partners at the firm, they admitted that L.L. was "a pathological liar." Wieder insisted that the firm report L.L. to the bar's disciplinary authorities. Eventually, and reluctantly, the firm did so, but fired Wieder.]

II.

We discuss first whether, notwithstanding our firmly established employment-at-will doctrine, plaintiff has stated a legal claim for breach of contract in the fourth cause of action.... The employment-at-will doctrine is a judicially created common-law rule "that where an employment is for an indefinite term it is presumed to be a hiring at will which may be freely terminated by either party at any time for any reason or even for no reason." [The Court notes that in preceding cases of retaliatory discharge of whistleblowers, the at-will employment doctrine prevented the employees from suing.]

As plaintiff points out, his employment as a lawyer to render professional services as an associate with a law firm differs in several respects from the employments in [previous cases]. The plaintiffs in those cases were in the financial departments of their employers, both large companies.... Associates are, to be sure, employees of the [law] firm but they remain independent officers of the court responsible in a broader public sense for their professional obligations.... It is in this distinctive relationship between a law firm and a lawyer hired as an associate that plaintiff finds the implied-in-law obligation on which he founds his claim.

We agree with plaintiff that in any hiring of an attorney as an associate to practice law with a firm there is implied an understanding so fundamental to the relationship and essential to its purpose as to require no expression: that both the associate and the firm in conducting the practice will do so in accordance with the ethical standards of the profession. Erecting or countenancing disincentives to compliance with the applicable rules of professional conduct, plaintiff contends, would subvert the central professional purpose of his relationship with the firm—the lawful and ethical practice of law.

The particular rule of professional conduct implicated here (DR 1–103 [A]), it must be noted, is critical to the unique function of self-regulation belonging to the legal profession.... To assure that the legal profession fulfills its responsibility of self-regulation, DR 1–103 (A) places upon each lawyer and Judge the duty to report to the Disciplinary Committee of the Appellate Division any potential violations of the Disciplinary Rules that raise a "substantial question as to another lawyer's honesty, trustworthiness or fitness in other respects." Indeed, one commentator has noted that, "[t]he reporting requirement is nothing less than essential to the survival of the profession."

Moreover, as plaintiff points out, failure to comply with the reporting requirement may result in suspension or disbarment....

Defendants, a firm of lawyers, hired plaintiff to practice law and this objective was the only basis for the employment relationship. Intrinsic to this relationship, of course, was the unstated but essential compact that in conducting the firm's legal practice both plaintiff and the firm would do so in compliance with the prevailing rules of conduct and ethical standards of the profession. Insisting that as an associate in their employ plaintiff must act unethically and in violation of one of the primary professional rules amounted to nothing less than a frustration of the only legitimate purpose of the employment relationship.... We conclude, therefore, that plaintiff has stated a valid claim for breach of contract based on an implied-in-law obligation in his relationship with defendants.

Bohatch v. Butler & Binion, et al.

Supreme Court of Texas, 1998.
977 S.W.2d 543.

■ Opinion by Enoch, J:

Partnerships exist by the agreement of the partners; partners have no duty to remain partners. The issue in this case is whether we should create an exception to this rule by holding that a partnership has a duty not to expel a partner for reporting suspected overbilling by another partner....

[In 1990, Collette Bohatch became a partner in the Texas law firm of Butler & Binion. She worked in the firm's three-person Washington, D.C. office, which did virtually all of its legal work for Pennzoil. Bohatch came to believe that Powers, the managing partner in the office, was substantially overbilling Pennzoil. She raised the issue with the office's other partner; then with the firm's managing partner; and finally with two other members of the firm's management committee. The firm's management committee investigated her charges and concluded that they were unfounded (a conclusion that Bohatch subsequently argued was a coverup). Bohatch was then informed that she should seek other employment. Subsequently, her partnership draw was reduced, and then her partnership was terminated. Bohatch sued the firm for breach of fiduciary obligation. A Texas jury awarded her $307,000 in compensatory damages and $4 million in punitive damages. On appeal, the Texas Court of Appeals held that Butler & Binion had not breached its fiduciary obligation to Bohatch, because the firm did not terminate her partnership for self-gain. It held that the firm had improperly withheld her partnership draw, however, and awarded her $35,000 plus attorneys' fees. Bohatch appealed.]

... The issue presented, one of first impression, is whether the fiduciary relationship between and among partners creates an exception to the at-will nature of partnerships; that is, in this case, whether it gives rise to a duty not to expel a partner who reports suspected overbilling by another partner....

The fiduciary duty that partners owe one another does not encompass a duty to remain partners or else answer in tort damages. Nonetheless,

Bohatch and several distinguished legal scholars urge this Court to recognize that public policy requires a limited duty to remain partners—*i.e.*, a partnership must retain a whistleblower partner. They argue that such an extension of a partner's fiduciary duty is necessary because permitting a law firm to retaliate against a partner who in good faith reports suspected overbilling would discourage compliance with rules of professional conduct and thereby hurt clients.

While this argument is not without some force, we must reject it. A partnership exists solely because the partners choose to place personal confidence and trust in one another. Just as a partner can be expelled, without a breach of any common law duty, over disagreements about firm policy or to resolve some other "fundamental schism," a partner can be expelled for accusing another partner, which may have a profound effect on the personal confidence and trust essential to the partner relationship. Once such charges are made, partners may find it impossible to continue to work together to their mutual benefit and the benefit of their clients. . . . The threat of tort liability for expulsion would tend to force partners to remain in untenable circumstance—suspicious of and angry with each other—to their own detriment and that of their clients whose matters are neglected by lawyers distracted with intra-firm frictions. . . .

We emphasize that our refusal to create an exception to the at-will nature of partnerships in no way obviates the ethical duties of lawyers. Such duties sometimes necessitate difficult decisions, as when a lawyer suspects overbilling by a colleague. The fact that the ethical duty to report may create an irreparable schism between partners neither excuses failure to report nor transforms expulsion as a means of resolving that schism into a tort.

We hold that the firm did not owe Bohatch a duty not to expel her for reporting suspected overbilling by another partner. . . . We affirm the court of appeals' judgment.

■ JUSTICE SPECTOR, joined by CHIEF JUSTICE PHILLIPS, dissenting:

> What's the use you learning to do right when it's troublesome to do right and ain't no trouble to do wrong, and the wages is just the same?
>
> —*The Adventures of Huckleberry Finn*

The issue in this appeal is whether law partners violate a fiduciary duty by retaliating against one partner for questioning the billing practices of another partner. I would hold that partners violate their fiduciary duty to one another by punishing compliance with the Disciplinary Rules of Professional Conduct. Accordingly, I dissent. . . .

[A]ttorneys organizing together to practice law are subject to a higher duty toward their clients and the public interest than those in other occupations. As a natural consequence, this duty affects the special relationship among lawyers who practice law together. . . . I believe that the fiduciary relationship among law partners should incorporate the rules of the profession promulgated by this Court. . . . In light of this Court's role in setting standards to govern attorneys' conduct, it is particularly inappropriate for the Court to deny recourse to attorneys wronged for adhering to the Disciplinary Rules. I would hold that in this case the law partners violated their fiduciary duty by retaliating against a fellow partner who made a good-faith effort to alert her partners to the possible overbilling of a client. . . . The duty to prevent overbilling and other misconduct exists for the protection of the client. Even if a report turns out to be mistaken or a client ultimately consents to the behavior in question, as in this case, retaliation against a partner who tries in good faith to correct or report perceived misconduct virtually assures that others will not take these appropriate steps in the future. Although I agree with the majority that partners have a right not to continue a partnership with someone against their will, they may still be liable for damages directly resulting from terminating that relationship. . . .

NOTES AND QUESTIONS: REPORTING MISCONDUCT

1. *In re Himmel* was the first reported decision imposing discipline solely for an attorney's failure to report collegial misconduct. The decision has provoked substantial controversy. Some commentators have noted with approval that Illinois lawyers' reports of misconduct have increased after the court's judgment in *Himmel* although subsequent prosecutions for failure to report misconduct are rare in that state, and almost nonexistent in others. Lawyers' reports are also more likely than clients' to result in disciplinary charges and often expose conduct that would not otherwise reach disciplinary agencies because clients benefit or have been compensated.[4]

Other commentators believe that the *Himmel* decision leaves troubling issues unresolved. For example, how prompt must the report be and how much knowledge is necessary to trigger attorneys' obligations? Should it be a "substantial basis," "a firm opinion that the conduct in question had more likely than not occurred," or some other standard? If the misconduct may be attributable to a substance abuse problem, would it be enough to contact a lawyer assistance program?[5] To what extent is the reporting requirement applicable to lawyers who represent other attorneys accused of misconduct? Should lawyers for malpractice insurance companies also have obligations to inform disciplinary authorities of misconduct that comes to light in investigations related to policy coverage?

2. Can *Wieder* be distinguished from *Bohatch*? How?

---

4. In the roughly two decades following the decision, there have been only four other prosecutions for failure to report misconduct. See Lance J. Rogers, "Conference Panelists Call for Clarification of Obligation to Report Peer Misconduct," 23 *ABA/BNA Lawyers' Man. Prof. Conduct* 297 (2007). For the value of complaints, see Mary T. Robinson, "A Lawyer's Duty to Report Another Lawyer's Misconduct: The Illinois Experience," 2007 *Professional Lawyer* 47.

5. *See* Rogers, supra note 4, at 298; In re Riehlmann, 891 So.2d 1239, 1248 (La. 2005) (a "reasonable" lawyer would "form a firm belief that the conduct in question had more likely than not occurred"). See also Attorney U v. Mississippi Bar, 678 So.2d 963, 972 (Miss.1996).

3. Who has the better argument, the *Bohatch* majority or the *Wieder* court and *Bohatch* dissent?[6]

4. How lawyers individually and collectively should respond to collegial misconduct, including the clear incompetence of adversaries, remains a matter of dispute. According to some commentators, the infrequency with which attorneys report fellow professionals is inevitable and in some measure justifiable. Law professor (now federal judge) Gerard Lynch, for example, has argued that the same values underpinning society's unwillingness to impose reporting requirements on citizens generally also apply in lawyer disciplinary contexts. In his view, the "impulse to protect one's friends and associates from harm, even from deserved punishment, is a moral and socially useful impulse precisely because it reaches beyond individual self-interest; it assimilates another's well being to that of oneself."[7] Professional relationships founded on trust serve an essential personal and societal function; they satisfy deep-seated interpersonal needs and provide essential buffers between the individual and the state. For lawyers, no less than other individuals, such considerations

> counsel *against* the imposition of a generalized duty to inform. Although it would sometimes be morally correct to report wrongdoing that comes to one's attention, such action would be morally incorrect in a great number of situations. The considerations relevant to sorting out these cases are highly complex. The preference for laws that are narrowly drawn and easy to apply would thus counsel that the law leave individuals free to follow their consciences in deciding whether or not to inform, except in a few carefully defined situations. Moreover, given the likelihood that people would disregard an unfocused and unpopular obligation to report the misconduct of others, little social benefit can be expected from a general rule even in those instances in which the moral obligation to inform is clearest. Whatever the reasons, the law has generally declined—correctly I believe—to impose a duty to provide unsolicited information, except in situations in which the information is especially vital and a definable category of persons is particularly likely to obtain it. The possibility of harm is too great, and the rewards too slim, to justify a general duty to inform.... The ethical codes applicable to lawyers ought to reflect the same approach that has proven acceptable to society as a whole.[8]

To Lynch, the bar's power of self-regulation imposes no special reporting responsibilities. A democratic society, he notes, is also self-regulating, but it delegates the police function to specialists:

> The legal profession also has its own disciplinary apparatus responsible for investigating and punishing violations of the rules of professional conduct. If these organs of discipline inadequately control lawyers, the bar should certainly act to strengthen them. But the disappointing

---

6. For a case history of *Bohatch,* see Leslie C. Griffin, "Bohatch v. Butler & Binion," in *Law Stories: Legal Ethics* (Deborah L. Rhode & David Luban eds. 2006).

7. Gerard Lynch, "The Lawyer as Informer," 1986 *Duke L.J.* 491, 531.

8. *Id.* at 535.

experience of mandatory informing hardly suggests that such a rule has been or can be the answer to inadequate self-policing.[9]

By contrast, most bar leaders and disciplinary authorities believe that reports of serious collegial misconduct are essential to protect clients and the public from abuses that would otherwise be impossible to detect or deter.[10] Rules imposing a duty to disclose misconduct and malpractice can provide essential support for those who would like to come forward but fear collegial hostility or retaliation. In effect, reporting requirements can make lawyers "feel less like a snitch."[11] Even lawyers who ultimately decline to report misconduct can find that a disclosure rule increases their leverage in seeking constructive responses to misconduct from errant attorneys or their firms. Under this line of analysis, reporting duties should be enforceable through professional disciplinary actions and civil liability. Such enforcement, it is claimed, would provide additional pressure for compliance with professional norms, as well as increase the remedies available to injured parties.

Supporters of the *Himmel* decision also note that the resulting increase in reports of misconduct cuts against claims that such an unpopular obligation would be disregarded in practice. However, these commentators also support greater protection of lawyer whistleblowers from retaliation through legislative or judicial protection for wrongful discharge.[12]

Do you agree? How would you respond to the issues presented in Problem 1 in light of the preceding arguments?

5. Should lawyers be subject to discipline for conduct reflecting bias on the basis of race, gender, religion, national origin, disability, age, sexual orientation, or socioeconomic status? Consider Canons 3(B)(5) and (6) of the Code of Judicial Conduct and the materials on bias in Chapter II. Canon 3(B)(5) states that "[a] judge shall perform judicial duties without bias or prejudice. A judge shall not, in the performance of judicial duties, by words or conduct manifest bias or prejudice, including but not limited to bias or prejudice based upon race, sex, religion, national origin, disability, age, sexual orientation or socioeconomic status, and shall not permit staff, court officials and others subject to the judge's direction and control to do so." Canon 3(B)(6) instructs judges to require lawyers in proceedings before the judge not to manifest any of the biases enumerated in clause (5). To that end, judges have imposed sanctions for litigation-related bias. Should they, or opposing counsel, also report such misconduct to bar disciplinary authorities? Under what, if any circumstances, would you impose sanctions for bigoted speech?

9. *Id.* at 537–38.

10. Rogers, *supra* note 4; American Bar Association Commission on Evaluation of Disciplinary Enforcement, *Report to the House of Delegates: Lawyer Regulation for a New Century* (1992).

11. Arthur F. Greenbaum, "The Attorney's Duty to Report Professional Misconduct: A Roadmap for Reform," 16 *Geo. J. Legal Ethics* 259, 271 (2003).

12. Lynn Bernabei & Jasen Zuckerman, "Protect the Whistleblower," *Nat'l L.J.* June 19, 2006, at 26.

Competence
The Florida Bar v. Neale

Supreme Court of Florida, 1980.
384 So.2d 1264.

William J. Neale, a member of The Florida Bar, petitions this Court for review of a referee's recommendation in a bar grievance procedure. . . .

This complaint against Neale arose from his representation of a Mrs. Mitchell for a claim of injuries she suffered as a result of being bitten by a dog in 1970. After attempts to negotiate a settlement failed, Neale filed suit on Mitchell's behalf in 1973. A few days before trial, Neale learned that the dog had a history of biting and that punitive damages might be available. His motion to amend the original complaint in order to allege punitive damages was denied, and Neale, believing that a four-year statute of limitations controlled, took a voluntary nonsuit with his client's concurrence. At that time, however, the statute of limitations on strict liability arising from dog bites was three years, and the defendants successfully raised this defense in the subsequent suit. On appeal, the district court affirmed the trial court's judgment against Mrs. Mitchell.

The referee found that Neale's late discovery of the dog's propensity to bite reflected inadequate preparation under the circumstances because Neale did not properly interrogate his client or make an independent investigation that would have resulted in his learning of the dog's history of biting.

Neale learned a fact that he deemed important late in the game. He then overlooked or misconstrued the statute of limitations on his statutory remedy. This neglect, however, is not of sufficient magnitude to warrant conviction of an ethical violation under Canon 6.

The power to disbar or suspend a member of the legal profession is not an arbitrary one to be exercised lightly, or with either passion or prejudice. Such power should be exercised only in a clear case for weighty reasons and on clear proof. . . . There is a fine line between simple negligence by an attorney and violation of Canon 6 that should lead to discipline. The rights of clients should be zealously guarded by the bar, but care should be taken to avoid the use of disciplinary action under Canon 6 as a substitute for what is essentially a malpractice action.

Neale had prepared to go to trial on his original complaint. Late in the proceeding he discovered a theory upon which he might have obtained a larger recovery for his client but then made the mistake of dismissing the action. His conduct might well be the basis of a negligence action against him, but, in our minds, it is insufficient to warrant a disciplinary action.

We therefore reject the recommendations of both the referee and the bar and dismiss the charges against the respondent.

It is so ordered.

Deborah L. Rhode, In the Interests of Justice: Reforming the Legal Profession

158–160 (2000).

In justifying [the profession's regulatory independence,] bar leaders have emphasized the importance of insuring that "those individuals . . . who pass judgment on attorney conduct be knowledgeable regarding the practice of law." But in fact, disciplinary complaint processes proceed on precisely the opposite basis. They rely almost exclusively on clients as a source of information about ethical violations. Those with the most knowledge concerning many violations—lawyers and judges—rarely report misconduct. And bar rules requiring reports are almost never enforced.

This failure to disclose ethical violations reflects a combination of social, psychological, and economic factors. Part of the problem is that many professional standards are formulated in highly general terms. What constitutes an "incompetent" performance or "unreasonable" fee is difficult to assess except at the extremes, and lawyers usually have no incentive to gather the relevant information. Disciplinary structures reflect classic free rider/common action problems. Reporting misconduct by another lawyer benefits society and the profession as a whole, but it seldom benefits complainants or their clients. Although implicit threats to file a grievance sometimes can provide useful bargaining leverage, more often they impose time-consuming burdens or start feuds that yield no personal advantage. For many practitioners, a reluctance to appear "holier than thou" or to expose the profession's "dirty linen" to public scrutiny also discourages disciplinary reports.

As a consequence, bar agencies depend almost entirely on complaints from clients, along with felony convictions, as a basis for disciplinary investigations. These sources are highly inadequate. Clients frequently lack sufficient information or incentives to file grievances. Many individuals have little understanding of their rights and remedies in disputes with lawyers and only two states provide a centralized source of consumer advice. Some forms of attorney misconduct, such as discovery abuse, benefit a client; others will not yield effective remedies. Bar disciplinary agencies generally dismiss about 90 percent of complaints without investigation or explanation to the claimant because they lack probable cause or fall outside agency jurisdiction. Grievances involving neglect, "mere" negligence, or fee disputes generally are excluded on the grounds that disciplinary agencies lack adequate resources, and other remedies are available through malpractice suits or alternative bar sponsored arbitration processes. However, as subsequent discussion suggests, malpractice litigation is too expensive for most of these matters and only a minority of states have alternative dispute resolution systems for client grievances. The procedures that are available usually are voluntary. Clients most in need of assistance seldom find their attorneys willing to cooperate. Many bar agencies also are reluctant to pursue powerful bar leaders or public officials. One survey of some 380 cases of serious prosecutorial misconduct found that none resulted in disciplinary actions.

QUESTIONS

1. At what point should incompetence, negligence and misrepresentation become grounds for disciplinary sanctions? Is the court's reasoning in *Florida Bar v. Neale* persuasive? Are current regulatory structures adequate to deal with minor misconduct?

2. In his study of insurance lawyers, Douglas Rosenthal reports the view of one defense attorney concerning the unpleasant aspects of his work:

> This is big business; it's dirty business. We're not a charity out to protect the plaintiff's welfare. Take the case I was trying today. The other lawyer [for the plaintiff] earns twice what I do and drives around in a Cadillac. But he doesn't know what he's doing. His client's got a good claim for a fractured skull. I want this bastard to win ... and he'll blow it. Today I laid the foundation for contributory negligence, which is very doubtful, and the other lawyer made no attempt to knock it down. The plaintiff is a sweet, gentle guy—a Puerto Rican. I met him in the john at recess and I told him that there was nothing personal in my working against him, that I was just doing my job. I think he understood this.

Rosenthal notes that the lawyer is "bothered by the cruelty and selfishness" in his work and needs to rationalize it:

> It's not my fault. I want him to win. It's his lawyer's fault and his own fault for not getting a better lawyer like me. If the client gets nothing ... it won't be my doing; it will be the jury's responsibility and that stupid contributory negligence rule.[13]

Is this an adequate response? Did the plaintiff's lawyer violate Model Rule 1.1, which requires competent representation, defined as reflecting the "legal knowledge, skill, thoroughness and preparation reasonable necessary for the representation?" If the lawyer fell below that standard, did it raise a "substantial question" as to his "fitness as a lawyer," which should be reported to the bar under Model Rule 8.3?

3. Consider the so-called "torture memo" discussed and excerpted in Chapter 9, Section E. This memo, written by DOJ Office of Legal Counsel lawyer John Yoo, offered highly controversial interpretations of U.S. laws against torture—controversial enough that the Justice Department eventually disowned them, withdrew the memo, and warned the Defense Department that it could no longer rely on other memos on the same subject written by Mr. Yoo. The fundamental criticisms of the memo were (1) that it stretched and distorted the law in a way that permitted harsh interrogation tactics that many regard as torture; (2) that it stated controversial views of presidential power that are Mr. Yoo's personal theories but are not broadly accepted in the legal community; and (3) that it did not indicate that its interpretations are controversial and in many respects out of the mainstream. Jack Goldsmith, the head of the Office of Legal Counsel who disowned the Yoo memos, has described them as "get-out-of-jail-free cards"

---

13. Douglas Rosenthal, *Lawyer and Client: Who's in Charge? 82–83 (1974).*

for torturers, and stated that the torture memo's "conclusion has no foundation in prior OLC opinions, or in judicial decisions, or in any other source of law."[14] Mr. Yoo, however, stands behind the legal reasoning in his opinions, and charges that they were withdrawn for political, not legal reasons.[15] As of summer 2008, Mr. Yoo is under investigation by the Justice Department's Office of Professional Responsibility. Reportedly one of the grounds for the investigation is incompetence, based on the theory that his memorandum badly misstated the law. Is this investigation an abuse of the competence standard? Should it matter that Mr. Yoo's theories have been published in distinguished law reviews? Given his assessment of the torture memo, should Goldsmith have reported Yoo?

NOTES: DISCIPLINARY STRUCTURES

Critics of the disciplinary process generally focus on two central problems: the low percentage of consumer grievances that ever reach regulatory agencies, and the low percentage of reported complaints that result in significant sanctions or other effective remedial responses. Some experts believe that such problems are rooted in a regulatory structure controlled by the profession. Although about half the states have disciplinary agencies that are nominally independent of the organized bar, they generally are staffed by lawyers and are dependent on good working relations with the profession and financial support from its members. Attorneys generally constitute at least two thirds of disciplinary panels. And state judges, who have final authority over the regulatory process often do not have adequate time or resources monitor its performance. Nor do they have incentive to institute reforms that might antagonize the bar, whose support is crucial to their reelection and advancement.[16] The result, according to critics, is a system more protective of the profession than the public. One limitation is the low likelihood that ethical violations will result in any disciplinary response As the preceding materials indicate, lawyers and judges seldom report misconduct and most clients who experience misconduct lack sufficient incentives or information to initiate disciplinary proceedings. Even more uncommon are complaints about ethical violations that benefit clients, such as lawyers' complicity in fraud or delay. And when cases are reported, the bar is unwilling to impose serious sanctions except in relatively egregious cases; fewer than 4 percent of cases end in public sanctions.[17]

---

14. Jack Goldsmith, *The Terror Presidency: Law and Judgment Inside the Bush Administration* 97, 149 (2007).

15. John Yoo, *War by Other Means: An Insider's Account of the War on Terror* 182–83 (2006).

16. For disciplinary panels, see HALT, Americans for Legal Reform, *HALT 2002 Lawyer Discipline Report Card*, available at www. HALT.org. For the limitations of judicial control, *see* Benjamin H. Barton, "An Institutional Analysis of Lawyer Regulation: Who Should Control Lawyer Regulation—Courts, Legislatures, or the Market?" 37 *Georgia L. Rev.* 1167 (2003).

17. The ABA's 2006 survey reported 123, 927 complaints with disciplinary agencies, of which 1903 resulted in private sanctions and 4309 in public sanctions; 893 were disbarred involuntarily or by consent and 1361 were suspended. ABA Center for Professional Responsibility, *Survey on Lawyer Discipline Systems*, Charts 1 and 2 (2007). For a

Several factors account for this attrition. Many complaints result in no formal action because they are inherently implausible or reflect dissatisfaction with outcomes rather than deficiencies in attorney performance. So too, disciplinary agencies are generally underfunded and understaffed. As a result, they cannot adequately investigate or prosecute complaints and must sometimes rely on volunteer counsel, who lack adequate time, experience, or skills.[18] The absence of resources also prevents agencies from undertaking independent investigations and limits the assistance that they can provide to individuals who wish to file grievances.

A related problem is that except in egregious circumstances, many disciplinary agencies decline jurisdiction over the kinds of conduct generating most consumer grievances: neglect, negligence, and fee disputes. Bar oversight is limited because of resource constraints and an assumption that other remedial alternatives are available through malpractice actions. However, as subsequent discussion suggests, malpractice litigation is too expensive for most of these matters. Although a growing number of states have alternative dispute resolution systems for minor client grievances and fee disputes, not all of these programs are mandatory and not all are perceived as effective by many clients.[19] Many states also lack effective diversion systems or remedial approaches that respond to the causes of ethical violations. Attorneys receive reprimands or mediated solutions for individual grievances rather than the training and oversight that will assist them in averting future problems. The twenty states that have diversion programs generally fail to track or publish statistics on the effectiveness of these programs in preventing future misconduct.[20] These limitations on bar disciplinary agencies lead to a mismatch between the focus of professional concern, which is controlling "deviance," and the needs of consumers for assurance of some basic level of quality, promptness, and cost-effectiveness.

Finally, procedural delays and protections, including the requirement of clear and convincing proof, result in dismissals of a significant number of complaints. Many jurisdictions have no time limits for resolving cases, and will "abate" disciplinary proceedings during the pendency of civil actions. Yet individuals are often reluctant to pursue bar complaints after the

general discussion, *see* Deborah L. Rhode, *In the Interests of Justice* 158–65 (2000); Fred Zacharias, "The Future Structure and Regulation of Law Practice: Confronting Lies, Fictions, and False Paradigms in Legal Ethics Regulation," 44 *Arizona L. Rev.* 829, 869 (2002).

18. Michael S. Frisch, "No Stone Left Unturned: The Failure of Attorney Self-Regulation in the District of Columbia," 18 *Geo. J. Legal Ethics* 325 (2005).

19. For disciplinary systems' lack of attention to performance issues and the rates of client dissatisfaction, *see* Rhode, *supra* note 17, at 159, 181. In Oregon's system, a majority of clients were not satisfied, al-

though it is unclear how much of that dissatisfaction was related to unrealistic expectations. Oregon State Bar, Annual Report of the Oregon State Bar Client Assistance Office (2006). Deborah Rosenthal, "Every Lawyer's Nightmare," *California Lawyer*, Sep. 2002, at 23, 24.

20. For failure to address underlying causes, *see* Vivian Berger, "Mediation: An Alternative Means of Processing Attorney Disciplinary Complaints," 16 *Prof. Lawyer* 21, 24 (2005). For the absence of data on diversion programs *see* Leslie C. Levin, "The Case for Less Secrecy in Lawyer Discipline," 20 *Geo. J. Legal Ethics* (2007).

termination of another lengthy civil suit. Extended delays also can prevent successful prosecution and expose more clients to misconduct.[21]

Most ethical violations by lawyers or inadequacies in bar responses are not visible to the public. Except in four states, bar disciplinary agencies will not disclose the existence of a complaint unless they have found a disciplinary violation or probable cause to believe that a violation has occurred. Nine states impose gag orders prohibiting complainants from discussing matters in which probable cause findings or sanctions have not resulted. Lawyers with as many as 20 complaints under investigation have received a clean bill of health when a consumer asked for information about their records, and it has sometimes taken as many as 44 complaints and three reprimands over eleven years to get a practitioner disbarred.[22] Even where sanctions are imposed, the public lacks a ready way of discovering them. Not all states publish information concerning disciplinary sanctions, and many do not so on line or in forms that are accessible to consumers.[23] Since the vast majority of complaints never result in public sanctions, and the vast majority of malpractice actions never result in published opinions, consumers lack crucial knowledge about lawyers' practice histories. The profession and the public also lack information that would enable them to assess the fairness of disciplinary processes. Many practitioners believe that the system is biased against small firms and solo practitioners, and racial and ethnic minorities, and the studies to date have been inadequate to evaluate those concerns.[24]

In responding to these inadequacies in bar disciplinary processes, the most significant, and some commentators believe most effective, strategy would be to create a regulatory body independent of the bar to replace or supplement current disciplinary structures. Some states have considered establishing such an oversight system and other Anglo–American nations have found to be an improvement over professional self-regulation. For example, England's Legal Services Act of 2007 creates an independent Legal Services Board, chaired by a lay person, with oversight over an Office for Legal Complaints, also headed by a lay Chair. The Office has broad power to ensure effective responses to individual complaints, including compensation for injuries resulting from professional misconduct.[25]

Some Australian states have also created more consumer-oriented disciplinary process. The New South Wales, Australia, Independent Legal

---

21. *See* Frisch, *supra* note 18, at 342–60.

22. Rhode, *supra* note 17, at 159–60; Levin, *supra* note 20, at 2, n. 9, 19. For a successful challenge to New Jersey's gag order, *see* R.M. v. Supreme Court of New Jersey, 883 A.2d 369 (N.J.2005).

23. Vesna Jaksic, "Attorney Discipline Web Data Uneven," *Nat'l L. J.*, Sept. 10, 2007, at 1, 7; Levin, *supra* note 20, at 20–21.

24. For example, almost half of Oregon lawyers believe that the disciplinary system is biased, largely based on the size of the lawyers firm, and a majority of African–American lawyers in Illinois, But only a small minority of white lawyers believed that race played a role in the disciplinary process. Levin, *supra* note 20, at 6–7. For the inadequacies of the studies, *see id.*

25. See Judith L. Maute, "Revolutionary Changes to the English Legal Profession or Much Ado about Nothing?," 17 *Prof. Lawyer* 1, 8–9 (2006); Richard Parnham, "The Clementi Reforms in a European Context: Are the Proposals Really That Radical," 8 *Legal Ethics* 194, 199 (2005).

Services Commissioner receives all complaints about a lawyer and refers them either to consumer-oriented mediation or to the bar's own regulatory bodies. Complainants who are unsatisfied with the results may seek review by the Commissioner, who has the power to substitute a new decision. The Commissioner also oversees the process for handling complaints and may take over a particular investigation or recommend more general changes.[26] Queensland, Australia has an independent Legal Services Commission headed by a non-lawyer. Its disciplinary system includes a Client Relations Center, which resolves minor disputes, and a Legal Practice Tribunal, composed of a Supreme Court Justice, one non-lawyer, and one practitioner as advisors. Problems of competence and diligence can be subjects for discipline and the standard is what the public is entitled to expect of a reasonably competent practitioner. All disciplinary actions are published on the Legal Service Commission website.[27]

Whether such structures would be effective in this country is subject to dispute. In defending self-regulation, many bar leaders note that government-controlled oversight agencies often suffer from the same problems of understaffing, underfunding, and delays as bar systems. Shifting jurisdiction is not of itself a greater guarantee of effectiveness. And unless the oversight agency is insulated from pressure from the legislative and executive branches, it could pose a threat to lawyers who represent unpopular positions, clients, or causes.

In any event, even without changes in regulatory structures, there is ample room for constructive reform. One cluster of strategies should focus on making the disciplinary process more visible, proactive, and effective. The jurisdiction of disciplinary agencies should be broadened to include concerns of neglect, negligence, and fees, and resources should be increased to insure adequate investigation and remedial responses. The standard of proof should be the same as for other civil matters, a preponderance of evidence, instead of clear and compelling evidence. Rather than relying almost exclusively on felony prosecutions and complaints brought to their attention, regulatory officials should initiate investigations based on malpractice filings, judicial sanctions, and random audits of trust funds. More steps should be taken to publicize the complaint process, to assist individuals in filing complaints, and to develop effective alternative dispute proceedings. Support services and diversion programs for lawyers with mental health, substance abuse, and office management difficulties should help these practitioners establish an appropriate remedial plan and supervise their compliance.[28] More efforts should also be made to track the effectiveness of these programs and identify cases of recidivism.

26. Christine Parker & Adrian Evans, *Inside Lawyers' Ethics* 54–55 (2007); David Nicolson & Julian Webb, *Professional Legal Ethics* 86 (1999); Deborah L. Rhode, "In the Interests of Justice: A Comparative Perspective on Access to Legal Services and Accountability of the Legal Profession," 56 *Current Legal Problems* 93 (2003).

27. Legal Profession Act of 2007; Leslie C. Levin, "Building a Better Lawyer Discipline System: The Queensland Experience," 9 *Legal Ethics* 187, 193–94 (2006); Parker & Evans, *supra* note 26, at 56.

28. *See* Rhode, *supra* note 17, at 163–64; Richard Abel, Lawyers in the Dock: Learning From New York's Disciplinary Cases (2008); HALT, *supra* note 16; Diane

A second set of reforms could focus on increasing the public's knowledge about the ethical records of attorneys. Lawyers could be required to provide information concerning their performance records and malpractice coverage, as well as information about client rights and remedies. Another promising alternative would be centralized data banks and toll-free hotlines that would provide information about judicial sanctions, disciplinary actions, and malpractice judgments. A useful model is the on-line clearinghouses for physicians required in about half the states. These clearinghouses include information such as education, practice area, professional affiliations, criminal convictions, disciplinary sanctions, malpractice actions, and liability insurance. More states are expected to adopt such clearinghouses and a national consumer organization, Public Citizen, also maintains a publicly available directory of disciplined doctors. No comparable, readily accessible databases exist for lawyers, although one commercial provider, Avvo, rates about 400,000 lawyers in ten jurisdictions based on information including disciplinary sanctions. According to the most systematic research available, four-fifths of surveyed Americans express a desire for a resource that they could consult concerning the records of particular lawyers.[29]

Attorneys often object to providing such a clearinghouse on the grounds that potential clients may attach undue importance to partial information or to minor transgressions, and that the reputations of practitioners would be unjustly impaired. However, no evidence for that claim has been forthcoming, and minor indiscretions rarely trigger public disciplinary action or malpractice judgements. As advocates of disclosure initiatives note, our nation's preferred response to incomplete information has been more rather than less. Databases can include background materials such as national malpractice and disciplinary statistics that would help consumers put profiles of particular lawyers in appropriate context. Moreover, by identifying practitioners with good records and adequate malpractice insurance, such clearinghouses would create additional incentives for appropriate conduct. In the long run, an informed public is the best guarantee of an accountable profession.

Another strategy for increasing accountability is to make disciplinary processes public from the time that complaints are dismissed, diverted or referred for investigation based on a finding of probable cause. Complainants should also be free to discuss their grievances. Although many lawyers oppose such an open process on the ground that disclosure of unfounded complaints would unjustly prejudice their reputations, no evidence has demonstrated those harms in states with open processes. If civil complaints and police arrests are matters of public record, it is not clear why griev-

M. Ellis, "A Decade of Diversion: Empirical Evidence that Alternative Discipline Is Working for Arizona Lawyers," 52 *Emory L. J.* 1221 (2002). For challenges in creating lawyer assistance programs that balance confidentiality and client protection, *see* Fred C. Zacharias, "A Word of Caution for Lawyer Assistance Programming," 18 *Geo. J. Legal Ethics* 237 (2004).

29.   Steven K. Berenson, "Is It Time for Lawyer Profiles?," 70 *Fordham L. Rev.* 645, 651–57, 680 (2001). For these and other reforms, *see* Rhode, *supra* note 17, at 163–64, and HALT, *supra* note 16.

ances against lawyers should be subject to special protection.[30] Because consumer surveys find deep suspicion about closed door proceedings, the ABA's disciplinary commission recommended public disclosure of complaints.[31]

Would you support any of these reforms? If so, how might they be achieved? If not, what, if any alternative strategies would you recommend?

C. DISCIPLINARY SANCTIONS

INTRODUCTION

In principle, the sanctioning process is designed to serve three main functions: protection of the public, protection of the administration of justice, and preservation of confidence in the profession. In fact, much lawyer discipline seems to fit within the classic justifications of punishment: incapacitation, rehabilitation, and deterrence.

Jurisdictions now vary in the range and characterization of disciplinary remedies. Disbarment is the most uniform but also the most infrequent response; it refers to a permanent or indefinite withdrawal of the license to practice law. Five states require all disbarments to be permanent. Another eight allow permanent disbarment in some situations, two almost never grant readmittance and the remainder permit attorneys to reapply at any time or after a prescribed period, typically five or seven years.[32] Suspension refers to a temporary prohibition on practice either for a specified period (usually ranging from several months to several years) or until compliance with certain specified conditions and an order of the court. Less stringent sanctions include public and private censures, reprimands, admonitions, warnings, and cautions. These responses define misconduct, promote specific deterrence, and create a record that can be relevant in cases of repeat offenders. Rehabilitative sanctions such as probation and mandatory education, are designed to correct specific conduct. Some jurisdictions permit lawyers under investigation to resign, although that act is generally treated as an admission of guilt. Attorneys who later seek reinstatement following resignation must make the same showing of rehabilitation as disbarred attorneys who seek reinstatement.

As noted earlier, few complaints result in public discipline and only a tiny minority end in disbarment. Does this suggest the need for reforms in the sanctioning process? If so, what would you propose?

PROBLEM 2

Consider the following conduct. If you were chair of your state bar's disciplinary committee, what sanctions would you recommend?

---

30. Levin, *supra* note 20, at 22–23.

31. ABA Commission on Evaluation of Disciplinary Enforcement, *supra* note 9; Levin, *supra* note 20.

32. Brian Finkelstein, "Should Disbarment be Permanent?," 20 *Geo. J. Legal Ethics* 587, 590–91 (2007).

Kevin A. Holloway

The petitioner was held subject to discipline because he "deceived clients, failed to promptly deliver unearned fees and other funds rightfully belonging to a client, neglected his clients' cases and abused his clients' trust."[33]

Robert E. Moore

The petitioner was found subject to discipline because he "knew [that] marijuana was growing on his premises and he failed to destroy the plants."[34]

Mahlon Perkins, Jr. and Joseph Fortenberry

Mahlon Perkins, Jr. was a partner at the Wall Street firm of Donovan, Leisure, Newton & Irvine. In order to avoid turning over certain documents during the discovery process in a contentious antitrust case, he falsely stated at a deposition that he had inadvertently destroyed them. He later repeated that statement under oath. He subsequently disclosed the perjury, was convicted of a misdemeanor, and served a one-month prison sentence. Joseph Fortenberry was a Donovan Leisure associate who was present at the deposition. He allegedly reminded Perkins that the documents were not destroyed, but remained silent after the partner did not correct the misstatement.[35]

Daniel Cooper

Daniel Cooper was a thirty-eight year old law firm partner who pled guilty to charges of overbilling a client $550,000 over two years. He avoided jail by cooperating with authorities and received a sentence of six months home confinement and 200 hours of community service. His defense was that he was under pressure to increase hours by a name partner who was a "father figure" to him in the firm.[36]

Laura Beth Lamb

Laura Beth Lamb, a 35–year–old lawyer, faced disciplinary charges for taking the 1985 California bar exam for her husband. At the time of the exam, she was seven months pregnant and suffering complications from chronic diabetes. Her husband, who had previously failed exams in both Texas and California, had bouts of rage and depression during which he threw heavy objects, and threatened to kill Lamb and her unborn child if she did not take the test in his place. She agreed, disguised herself as her husband, and scored ninth out of some 7,000 applicants. After an anonymous tip revealed the matter to the state bar, she pleaded guilty to felony impersonation and deception. She received a $2,500 fine, probation, and a

33. *In re* Holloway, 452 N.E.2d 934, 935 (Ind.1983) (per curiam).

34. *In re* Moore, 453 N.E.2d 971, 974 (Ind.1983) (per curiam).

35. James B. Stewart, Jr., "Kodak and Donovan Leisure" in *The Partners* (1983). The case is discussed in Chapter VII.

36. *In re* Cooper, 613 N.Y.S.2d 396 (App. Div.1994).

sentence of 200 hours of community service. When she was fired from her job at the SEC, she took a position as a legal secretary. She also divorced her husband and received psychological treatment.

In a letter to the court considering bar disciplinary charges, Lamb's therapist concluded that she "was unlikely to do anything remotely like this again. [Her] prognosis for the future is good provided that she remains in therapy long enough to develop the psychic structures that have not yet matured.... This will require a long-term commitment."[37]

Margita Dornay

Margita Dorney, a law firm partner and part-time prosecutor, had an extramarital affair with deputy sheriff David Hick while he was divorcing his wife. Hick's lawyer, who did not know about the affair, called Dorney as a witness during his divorce hearing to testify about exchanges of child visitation that she had witnessed between Hick and his wife. In her testimony, she stated that she had never witnessed him "rant and rave," "berate," or become "rageful at any time." In fact, Dorney had seen him become enraged after an argument and slam his head on a nightstand. He had also put a revolver in her hand and instructed her to shoot him, because if she did not love him he wanted to die. Dornay subsequently ended the affair and, several months after the divorce hearing, petitioned for a protective order against Hick on grounds that he was abusive and constituted a threat to herself and her family. She testified that Hick had screamed at her and ranted and raved during the course of their relationship, and signed a sworn declaration that she had perjured herself at the divorce hearing. Counsel for Hick's wife relied on the declaration to suspend Hick's visitation rights with his son.

In response to the bar's disciplinary complaint, Dorney claimed that she had acted under duress. However, she provided no evidence that she had been threatened at the time of the divorce hearing and the record indicated that she had sent Hick a dozen roses and romantic cards on the day following the hearing.[38]

Gerard Mullins

Gerard Mullins was a Queensland barrister who represented a quadriplegic client injured in an automobile accident. In mediation with an insurance company to settle the claim, Mullins failed to reveal that he had recently learned that his client was seriously ill with cancer. Rather, Mullins left uncorrected a medical report that estimated the lost earnings and cost of care for his 48–year–old client based on a 27 year life expectancy. After consulting his client and senior counsel, Mullins concluded that he was not obligated to disclose the change in his client's medical situation as long as he did not make any affirmative misstatements.[39]

---

37. *In re* Laura Beth Lamb, 776 P.2d 765, 767 (Cal.1989).

38. *In re* Dornay, 161 P.3d 333 (Wash. 2007).

39. Legal Services Commissioner v. Mullins [2006] LPT 012.

William Jefferson Clinton

Federal District Court Judge Susan Webster Wright referred an order sanctioning then-President William Clinton to the Arkansas Supreme Court Committee on Professional Conduct. Wright based her order on a finding that Clinton had made false statements in a sex harassment lawsuit brought by Paula Jones. The statements at issue concerned Clinton's relationships with other women who may have been targets of inappropriate sexual advances. At a pretrial deposition, Jones's lawyers asked Clinton whether he and Monica Lewinsky had ever been alone together, and whether they had ever engaged in sexual relations. The district court found:

> the record demonstrates by clear and convincing evidence that the President responded by giving false, misleading and evasive answers that were designed to obstruct the judicial process. . . . [40]

Arkansas rules governing sanctions permit disbarment for "serious misconduct for which a lesser sanction would be inappropriate." "Serious misconduct" is defined to include dishonesty, deceit, or misrepresentation. A disciplinary panel found that Clinton's conduct violated Arkansas Rules 8.4(c) and (d), which are identical to Model Rules 8.4(c) and (d).

In no other Arkansas case over the last decade had disciplinary sanctions been based on conduct as a party in a civil suit. In other cases involving false statements, attorneys were disbarred or suspended only if the misrepresentations were made in connection with some other offense, such as defrauding a client. If the only offense was misrepresentation, lawyers were subject to more lenient forms of discipline.

In his response to the complaint, Clinton maintained that his actions were "motivated in part by a desire to protect himself and others from embarrassment"; that the conduct occurred in a suit dismissed for lack of merit; that the testimony was not essential to Jones's lawsuit; that Jones was made whole by a settlement in excess of her original damages claim; and that the alleged misconduct did not involve official duties or actions as a lawyer.

Ethics experts were divided about what disciplinary action would be appropriate. Some emphasized Clinton's special responsibilities as President and as a role model for the nation, as well as his continued refusal to admit that he had lied. Southeastern Legal Foundation, which had also filed a disciplinary complaint against Clinton, pointed out that commentaries to the Arkansas ethical code hold public servants to a special standard. These commentaries provide that lawyers in public office "assume responsibilities beyond those of other citizens. A lawyer's abuse of public office can suggest the inability to fulfill the professional role of attorney." By contrast, other experts stressed that Clinton's conduct had occurred as a litigant not as a public official. These commentators also emphasized mitigating factors such as the political motivations underlying questions regarding Lewinsky; the peripheral relevance of those questions to Jones's

40. Jones v. Clinton, 36 F.Supp.2d 1118 (E.D.Ark.1999).

claims; and the President's understandable desires to preserve the privacy of all concerned.[41]

NOTES

The following sanctions were imposed in each case.

Holloway. The Indiana Supreme Court imposed a 45–day suspension because Holloway's "numerous acts of professional misconduct have served to tarnish the integrity of the legal profession [and] exemplify [his] repeated inability to grasp the importance of adhering to professional ethics."[42]

Moore. The Indiana Supreme Court ordered disbarment. Moore "acted in contravention of the laws of . . . Indiana at the time he was serving a public trust to enforce such laws. . . . A lawyer who betrays his public trust and ignores his responsibility for the impartial administration of justice, not only suggests to the public an absence of integrity, but also demonstrates an unfitness to continue in practice."[43] *Holloway* and *Moore* were decided within a few days of each other.

Perkins and Fortenberry. Perkins was not disbarred and Fortenberry was not charged with any disciplinary violations. See the discussion in Chapter VII, Supervisory and Subordinate Lawyers, *supra*.

Cooper. A discipline panel of one nonlawyer and three lawyers (including two former leaders of New York bar associations) recommended a one-year retroactive suspension, equivalent to the period of Cooper's interim suspension. The Court of Appeals affirmed, crediting the panel's finding of firm pressure and Cooper's cooperation with the government. Cooper's current Martindale–Hubble listing mentions his background, federal clerkship, and distinguished clients, but omits all mention of his criminal conviction or suspension.[44]

Mullins. According to a Queensland Legal Tribunal, no barrister could have reasonably approached the mediation as an "honesty free zone" in light of bar association rules. Those rules provided that barristers could not "knowingly make a misleading statement" and must "take all necessary steps to correct any false statement" to an opponent "as soon as possible after the barrister becomes aware that the statement was false." Rules 21 and 52. In mitigation, the Tribunal noted that Mullins had supplied many character references from senior practitioners and that his conduct was intended not to secure any "personal advantage." Still, the Tribunal imposed a public reprimand and substantial fine of $20,000 fine in order to

---

41. "Clinton Denies Lying, Violating Ethics Rules; Calls Disbarment Sanctions Excessively Harsh," 16 *ABA/BNA Manual of Professional Conduct* 496 (2000); David E. Rovella, "Clinton Has New Nemesis," *National L. J.*, July 17, 2000, at A1, A8.

42. *In re* Holloway, 452 N.E.2d 934, 935 (Ind.1983) (per curiam).

43. *In re* Moore, 453 N.E.2d 971, 974–975 (Ind.1983) (per curiam).

44. *In re Cooper,* 586 N.Y.S.2d 250 (App.Div.1992); Levin, *supra* note 20, at 83, n. 57.

"signify disapproval and deter future misconduct."[45] According to American law professor Leslie Levin, the case reflected the significance of an independent Legal Service Commission headed by a lay chair. As she noted, it was unlikely that a member of the legal profession, "or at least one who had practiced in Queensland—would have had the courage to prosecute the complaint."[46]

Lamb. By a 6–1 vote, the California Supreme Court revoked Lamb's license. In its view:

> [Lamb's] deceitful acts were of exceptional gravity. Her conduct threatened innumerable clients with significant injury through unknowing exposure to an unqualified practitioner. It undermined the integrity of the State Bar's admission system, on which public confidence in the competence of attorneys is founded.... Though replete with testimonials to her talent and general character, the record contains ... no "clear and convincing" indication of [her] *sustained and complete* rehabilitation from chronic personal problems which led to her catastrophic misjudgment.... The legal, ethical, and moral pressures of daily practice come in many forms. Besides raw avarice and self-aggrandizement, they may include the sincere but misguided desire to please a persuasive or overbearing client....
>
> Despite our sympathetic feelings, ... we believe that reinstatement proceedings are the means by which petitioner should demonstrate her clear rehabilitation after "the passage of considerable time."

In re Laura Beth Lamb, 776 P.2d 765, 768–770 (Cal.1989).

Justice Kaufman dissented:

> ... Contrary to the majority's premise, there is no danger to the public or anyone else from petitioner's one-time, aberrational conduct stemming from circumstances that no longer exist and as to which there is not the slightest possibility of recurrence.... [Disbarment] serves only to punish an apparently talented lawyer whose misconduct resulted from the most desperate, life-threatening circumstances. Indeed, such drastic discipline serves the public interest *less* well than would a long period of probation on appropriate conditions ... including proof of fitness before returning to the practice of law.

Id. at 771.

In responding to the court's decision in *Lamb,* one California columnist concluded:

> Over the years, I've written about lawyers who bilked senile clients of their last dollars, lawyers who deceived old people into making them beneficiaries of large estates, lawyers who grabbed fees so large that their clients received almost nothing. And they're still practicing.... Laura Beth Lamb, who behaved honorably after her deception came to light, is now working as a legal secretary in Los Angeles while she

45. Legal Services Commissioner v. Mullins, [2006] LPT 012.

46. *See* Levin, *supra* note 20, at 198.

performs what amounts to more than 62 40–hour weeks of community service. . . . I hope she gets back in [the bar]. California could use more lawyers like Laura Lamb.[47]

Ten years after her disbarment, Laura Beth Salant (formerly Lamb) was reinstated by the California Supreme Court over the objection of state bar disciplinary prosecutors. During the intervening decade, Salant worked as a paralegal for the IRS, and according to the State Bar court review department, compiled "a most impressive record of employment, outstanding character and psychological rehabilitation." After the bar court recommended reinstatement, prosecutors asked the California Supreme Court for review. They claimed that Salant had falsely represented that she had obtained a restraining order against her ex-husband and that she had failed to file a required affidavit informing clients of her disbarment. Salant maintained that her former attorney had agreed to file the affidavit and that, after eight years of psychotherapy, she had turned her life around. The California Supreme Court ordered reinstatement.[48]

Dornay. In adopting the state bar disciplinary board's recommendation of a three-year suspension, the Washington Supreme Court accepted findings that Dornay's dishonesty had been motivated by selfish motives and that her testimony might have affected the parenting plan for Hick's vulnerable three-year-old child. In mitigation, the court also noted the findings that Hick and Dornay's turbulent relationship exhibited a pattern common in cases of domestic violence.[49]

Clinton. The Arkansas panel unanimously recommended disbarment. While the matter was pending, Clinton reached a joint agreement with the Independent Counsel and the Arkansas Bar. Under that agreement, Clinton admitted that he had "knowingly made false statements" that were "prejudicial to the administration of justice." Clinton also accepted a $25,000 fine and a five year suspension of his law license.

QUESTIONS

1. Do you agree with the sanctions in these cases? Why or why not?

2. How would you deal with lawyers' criminal conduct that occurs outside a lawyer-client relationship? Consider the following cases

   a. A lawyer who willfully violated a court order to pay child support;

   b. A Northern California state judge who resigned from the bench after conviction for growing marijuana on his property, and a Utah judge removed from office for violating bigamy statutes for 35 years.

   c. An attorney convicted of indecent exposure in a public restroom;

47. Bill Mandel, "State Bar Persecutes a Victim," *San Francisco Examiner*, Aug. 14, 1989, at A4.

48. "Woman Who Impersonated Husband Ordered Reinstated," *California Bar Journal*, 1999, at 27, 28.

49. *In re* Dornay, 161 P.3d 333 (Wash. 2007).

d.   A law professor convicted of income tax violations;

e.   A lawyer who stole $1800 from her daughter's Girl Scout cookie account.

f.   A lawyer who, in a "one-time aberrational" act, hired three men to throw lye in the face of a woman who had threatened to break off their affair. The woman was blinded, and Pugach spent fourteen years in prison. After his release, he obtained work as a paralegal and married the woman.

g.   A lawyer who pled guilty to leaving the scene of an accident in which he struck and killed a bicyclist. At his sentencing to a year in prison, he acknowledged knowing that he had hit a person and explained that he had panicked and fled the scene.

h.   A lawyer who served 21 months in prison for bringing back sexually explicit child pornography magazines from Europe. The magazines were legal where purchased, and the models were of legal age where the magazines were published.

i.   A former New York Attorney General who patronized prostitutes while his office was targeting prostitution.[50]

Compare your decisions in these cases with your judgments about the admission of lawyer with criminal records discussed in Chapter XV. Should the standards be the same or different in disciplinary contexts? How should concerns about public confidence and the image of the legal profession weigh against concerns about rehabilitation, redemption, and threats of future misconduct?

3.   DuPont corporation and its law firm, Alston & Bird, settled a criminal investigation charging concealment of documents suggesting that a DuPont fungicide had been contaminated. As part of the settlement, the client and firm each agreed to pay $2.5 million to four Georgia schools to endow a chair in professional ethics, $1 million to endow an annual symposium on legal ethics, and $250,000 to support work by the state bar's professionalism commission.[51] Is this an appropriate response to lawyer misconduct? Would requirements of pro bono service ever be appropriate as a disciplinary sanction or plea agreement?[52]

---

50.   "California Bar Targets Deadbeat Dads," *National Law Journal*, July 12, 1995; Richard Marosi & Anne Gorman, "L.A. Gets Tough on Corrupt Lawyers," *L.A. Times*, Nov. 10, 2003, at B1; *In re* Steed, 131 P.3d 231 (2006); Mandel, *supra* note 47, at A4; Norimitsu Onishi, "A Tangle of Affairs of the Heart," *N.Y. Times*, April 21, 1997, at B8; *In re* Tidwell, D.C. No. 99–B6–1569 (Sep. 11, 2003); *In re* Boudreau, 815 So.2d 76 (La. 2002); Dean Slater, "If Spitzer Loses Law License, a Safety Net Will be Removed," *Wall St. J.*, March 13, 2008. For an historical overview of the bar's treatment of such cases, see Deborah L. Rhode, "Moral Character As a Professional Credential," 94 *Yale L. J.* 491, 552–54 (1985).

51.   Milo Geylin, "DuPont and Atlanta Firm Agree to Pay Nearly 13 Million in Benlate Matter," *Wall Street J.*, Jan. 4, 1999, at A18.

52.   Brian K. Pinaire, Milton J. Heumann, & Jennifer Lerman, "Barred From the Bar: The Process, Politics, and Policy Implications of Discipline for Attorney Felony Offenders," 13 *Virg. J. Soc. Pl'y & Law* 290, 326 (2006) (discussing New Jersey bar officials' reaction that such sanctions were "patronizing," and raised questions about why

4. Suppose that you are a member of a bar task force that is seeking to promote greater consistency in the sanctioning process. In drafting guidelines, task force members are divided on several questions:

a) Whether disbarment should ever or always be permanent or whether attorneys should be able to apply for reinstatement after a specified period;

b) Whether to allow discipline against law firms as well as individuals;

c) Whether to treat substance abuse or mental health difficulties as a mitigating factor;

d) Whether to adopt presumptive guidelines concerning specific offenses;[53]

e) Whether disbarment should be automatic following a felony conviction or whether mitigating factors should be considered;

References:

Model Rules 1.1, 1.3, 1.5, 3.1.

American Bar Association, ABA Standards for Imposing Lawyer Sanctions

(Revised edition, 2005, adopted 1992)

5. Violations of Duties Owed to the Public

5.1 Failure to Maintain Personal Integrity

Absent aggravating or mitigating circumstances, upon application of the factors set out in Standard 3.0, the following sanctions are generally appropriate in cases involving commission of a criminal act that reflects adversely on the lawyer's honesty, trustworthiness, or fitness as a lawyer in other respects, or in cases with conduct involving dishonesty, fraud, deceit, or misrepresentation:

5.11 Disbarment is generally appropriate when:

(a) a lawyer engages in serious criminal conduct, a necessary element of which includes intentional interference with the administration of justice, false swearing, misrepresentation, fraud, extortion, misappropriation, or theft; or the sale, distribution or importation of controlled substances; or the intentional killing of another; or an attempt or conspiracy or solicitation of another to commit any of these offenses; or

(b) a lawyer engages in any other intentional conduct involving dishonesty, fraud, deceit, or misrepresentation that seriously adversely reflects on the lawyer's fitness to practice. . . .

---

the poor should be served by those who had violated professional norms).

53. Pinaire, Heumann, & Lerman, *supra* note 52, at 327 (noting New Jersey's "going rate" of three-month suspensions for drug possession).

9.0   Aggravation and Mitigation

9.1   Generally

After misconduct has been established, aggravating and mitigating circumstances may be considered in deciding what sanction to impose.

9.2   Aggravation

9.22 *Factors which may be considered in aggravation.* Aggravating factors include:

(a) prior disciplinary offenses;

(b) dishonest or selfish motive;

(c) a pattern of misconduct;

(d) multiple offenses;

(e) bad faith obstruction of the disciplinary proceeding by intentionally failing to comply with rules or orders of the disciplinary agency;

(f) submission of false evidence, false statements, or other deceptive practices during the disciplinary process;

(g) refusal to acknowledge the wrongful nature of conduct;

(h) vulnerability of victim;

(i) substantial experience in the practice of law;

(j) indifference to making restitution;

(k) illegal conduct, including that involving the use of controlled substances.

9.3   Mitigation

Definition: Mitigation or mitigating circumstances are any considerations or factors that may justify a reduction in the degree of discipline to be imposed.

9.32 *Factors which may be considered in mitigation.* Mitigating factors include:

(a) absence of a prior disciplinary record;

(b) absence of a dishonest or selfish motive;

(c) personal or emotional problems;

(d) timely good faith effort to make restitution or to rectify consequences of misconduct;

(e) full and free disclosure to disciplinary board or cooperative attitude toward proceedings;

(f) inexperience in the practice of law;

(g) character or reputation;

(h) physical disability;

(i) mental disability or chemical dependency including alcoholism or drug abuse when:

(1) there is medical evidence that the respondent is affected by a chemical dependency or mental disability,

(2) the chemical dependency or mental disability caused the misconduct;

(3) the respondent's recovery from the chemical dependency or mental disability is demonstrated by a meaningful and sustained period of successful rehabilitation, and

(4) the recovery arrested the misconduct and the recurrence of that misconduct is unlikely.

(j) delay in disciplinary proceedings;

(k) imposition of other penalties or sanctions;

(l) remorse;

(m) remoteness of prior offenses.

NOTES AND QUESTIONS

The ABA Standards are the most common source of guidance in the sanctioning process. Some supreme courts rely heavily on those standards in imposing discipline, while others have modeled their own standards on the ABA's framework. The remaining jurisdictions generally have bright line rules or presumptive sanctions for specific offenses, or employ a case-by-case approach to all disciplinary decisions. This regulatory patchwork creates substantial inconsistencies in responses to similar conduct within and across jurisdictions.

According to the limited data available, disciplined attorneys are disproportionately likely to be in solo or small firm practice.[54] A number of factors may account for that overrepresentation. Solo and small firm lawyers have less collegial oversight and backup to deal with overwork. They also have less economic cushion, and fewer staff and technological resources to monitor deadlines, client funds, and so forth. The areas in which they practice, such as family law, criminal defense, and personal injury litigation, are disproportionately likely to attract complaints. That is, in part, because clients in these matters often lack the experience, knowledge, and economic leverage that helps protect commercial clients of large firms. Seldom do corporate clients experience the kinds of clear ethical violations that are the focus of disciplinary agencies.[55] The most common grounds for sanctions are misappropriation of funds; criminal convictions; and neglect, such as failure to perform services or communicate with

---

54. Levin, *supra* note 20, at 6; Report by the State Bar of California, *Investigations and Prosecutions of Disciplinary Complaints Against Attorneys in Solo Practice, Small Size Law Firms, and Large Law Firms* (2001) (finding that lawyers in solo practice or in firms of under 10 lawyers accounted for an estimated 56 percent of the state bar, 95 percent of disciplinary investigations, and 98 percent of sanctions); Mark Hansen, "Picking on the Little Guy," *ABA J.* March 2003, at 33.

55. *See* Hansen, *supra* note 54, at 33; Geoffrey C. Hazard, Jr., & Ted Schneyer, "Regulatory Controls on Large Law Firms: A Comparative Perspective," 44 *Ariz. L. Rev.* 593, 601–02 (2002).

clients. Underfunded disciplinary agencies generally find it cost-effective to target their limited resources to pursuit of these violations. By contrast, the kinds of violations that are more common in large firms, such as overbilling, discovery abuse, or complicity in fraud, are harder to prove, and individual responsibility is more difficult to locate. Consider these factors as you assess the sanction-related issues that follow.

At an abstract level, there is general agreement about most of the factors relevant in imposing disciplinary sanctions: for example, 1) the extent to which the lawyer's conduct injured others; 2) the "blameworthiness" of that conduct; 3) the lawyer's general character, demeanor, and prior disciplinary history; 4) the need for incapacitation or supervision; and 5) general or specific deterrence.[56] With respect to more concrete questions, however, such as what constitutes blameworthiness in a particular case, and what will provide sufficient public protection, there remains considerable disagreement.

Severity in Sanctions

One perennial dispute has involved the stringency of sanctions. While courts and disciplinary agencies have generally been reluctant to withdraw the means of earning a living, commentators have repeatedly criticized the leniency of discipline, particularly in cases involving repeated instances of neglect, misrepresentation, or incompetence.[57]

1.   What is your view? If non-lawyer consumer advocates were deciding the cases discussed in Problem 2, would their decisions have been different than the bar's? Would more than 4 percent of complaints result in public discipline and more than 2 percent of complaints result in disbarment?[58]

Permanent Disbarment

A related issue involves permanent disbarment. As noted earlier, most states allow disbarred attorneys to apply for reinstatement after a prescribed period, generally between three to six years, and the Rule 25 of the ABA Model Disciplinary Rules recommend the possibility of readmission after at least five years. The frequency of reinstatement varies. For example, over one ten year period, Pennsylvania granted three quarters of the applications from 44 lawyers who sought to resume practice. Its neighbor Delaware granted none. California grants only three percent.[59] Lawyers who are permanently disbarred in one jurisdiction can be readmitted in another and even those who have been disbarred more than once can apply for reinstatement.

56. Charles Wolfram, *Modern Legal Ethics* 110–11 (1986).

57. *See* Frisch, *supra* note 18; Rhode, *supra* note 17, at 160; Julie O'Sullivan, "Professional Discipline for Law Firms? A Response to Professor Schneyer," 16 *Geo. J. Legal Ethics* 3, 55 (2003).

58. See note 17 *supra*.

59. Chris Osher & Brad Burnsted, "Disbarment Not End for Lawyers," *Pittsburgh Tribune Review*, Feb. 17, 2003, at A1; Finkelstein, *supra* note 32, at 595.

According to David E. Johnson, Director of the Office of the Attorney of Ethics of the Supreme Court of New Jersey:

> Disbarment in America today is in truth a myth. It is what I call the great white lie of disciplinary sanctions. Very simply, disbarment in 20th century America does not mean permanent disbarment in the majority of states. As a result, we see repeated instances of thieves, liars, perjurers, rapists and other serious criminal offenders applying for, and sometimes securing, reinstatement to the practice of law. The specter of ever reinstating an attorney who has bribed a judge to fix a case, for example, or has committed other heinous criminal acts, is repulsive to most honest, ethical lawyers. To the public the prospect is inconceivable. Why? Because the public thinks in terms that are straightforward and honest, plain and simple, especially when it comes to core values like the administrat[ion] of justice.[60]

In Johnson's view, permanent discipline would provide a powerful deterrent lacking in the current system. In one study he conducted of New Jersey lawyers who were disciplined but not disbarred for financial violations, over a quarter were found guilty of further financial misconduct.[61] In other states, some attorneys have been disbarred multiple times for serious misconduct and one study found a 44 percent recidivism rate for disbarred attorneys.[62] Many commentators share Johnson's belief that such repeat offenders undermine public confidence and drains disciplinary system resources.

Legal ethics expert Ronald Rotunda disagrees. Given the absence of consensus on what misconduct is sufficiently abusive to preclude reinstatement, a system permitting permanent disbarment is likely to produce inconsistent and inequitable results. Rotunda argues:

> We must be careful not to let our hearts rule when our heads should be in charge . . . Because the purpose of discipline is to protect the public, if the court finds that the reason to impose the discipline has changed, and no longer exists, or that the risk to the public of future harm no longer exists, then the court should also reevaluate the need for continued discipline. Wisdom never comes to some people; we should not reject it in others merely because it comes a little late. . . . The possibility of reinstatement is a good policy because it serves the laudable purpose of giving the lawyer an incentive to mend his or her old ways. To take away this possibility is to take away an incentive to reform. . . .
>
> Proponents of permanent disbarment often claim that we should agree with their proposal because it will improve the public image of lawyers. We should resist that temptation: the organized bar should

---

60. David E. Johnson, "Permanent Disbarment: The Case For . . .," *The Professional Lawyer,* Feb. 1994, at 22. In two states, Ohio and New Jersey, all disbarments are permanent. In four others, permanent disbar-ment has been imposed in cases where the circumstances warrant it. *Id.*

61. *Id.* at 26.

62. *Id.* at 27; Finkelstein, *supra* note 32, at 595.

propose legal reforms because they are right, not because they might improve our public image. Lawyers engage in a lot of activities that are bad for their public image, from representing alleged Communists to representing alleged Nazis to using the Fourth Amendment in an effort to exclude probative evidence. If we do things that are proper but bad for the public image, we should respond by trying to educate the public. It is our job to lead, not to follow.[63]

2. Which position do you find most persuasive? If permanent disbarment were an option in your state, would you impose it in any of the cases described in Problem 2. Should lawyers who have been disbarred be required to disclose that fact to prospective clients?

Mitigating Circumstances

A related controversy has centered on the role of mitigating circumstances. As discussion below notes, some courts and commentators have been sympathetic toward offenses that appear attributable to factors such as substance abuse or mental health problems. Other courts and commentators, primarily concerned with client protection, have been reluctant to view such difficulties as adequate mitigation. The significance of lawyers' feelings of remorse and willingness to provide client compensation has provoked related disputes. According to HALT (Americans for Legal Reform), it is the job of disciplinary agencies to make sure that the risk of clients is "eliminated or minimized, not excused. The kind of leniency [granted for lawyers] is not accorded elsewhere—one can hardly imagine a bank forgiving a teller's theft of thousands of dollars and keeping them on the job based on excuses such as alcoholism, mental disability, or willingness to pay it back."[64]

3. Is that an appropriate analogy? What is your view?

Similar controversies involve questions about whether the attorney has "suffered enough." It is often asserted that disbarment is gratuitous for a prominent lawyer who has undergone the humiliation of public disciplinary proceedings, particularly those accompanied by criminal charges or involuntary resignation from employment. Such considerations influenced the decisions in several of the cases noted in Problem 2. Other courts and commentators are disturbed by the possible class bias underlying such assertions. In their view, those who have attained positions of wealth and status should be held to a higher, not lower, standard of conduct, particularly since their cases are likely to attract more attention than the usual proceedings and they have fewer extenuating financial circumstances. To the extent that the profession is concerned with general deterrence and the appearance of even-handedness, making special allowances for the "mighty who are fallen" carries obvious costs.

---

63. Ronald D. Rotunda, "Permanent Disbarment: The Case Against," *The Professional Lawyer*, Feb. 1994, at 22–24.

64. HALT (Americans for Legal Reform), *Attorney Discipline* 16 (1988).

4.   Which position seems more persuasive? Should courts have imposed disbarment in the cases involving Clinton, Cooper, and Perkins described in Problem 2?

Fines

Unlike the disciplinary systems in other countries, most American jurisdictions do not allow the imposition of monetary fines, although they do sometimes require compensation to injured clients as a condition of return to practice. The stated rationale is that such sanctions constitute punishment, while the purpose of disciplinary procedures is protection. A related concern has been that fines would make disciplinary procedures resemble those of the criminal justice system and would accordingly require comparable due process safeguards, such as proof beyond a reasonable doubt. Some legal ethics experts also argue that fines carry less stigma than disbarment or suspension, and therefore constitute a less effective deterrent.[65] Moreover, permitting fines in a system ostensibly based on the need for public protection may create the unseemly suggestion that lawyers can buy their way out of remedies designed to safeguard the public.

By contrast, some commentators have argued that fines are appropriate mechanisms of deterrence. Underlying such arguments is the presumption that individuals generally respond to enforcement in proportion to the level of sanction and the probability of its imposition. A lawyer, it is assumed, is even more likely than the average person to engage in cost-benefit calculations and to have information about the costs and risks of misconduct. In addition, courts may be less reluctant to impose fines than sanctions involving the loss of an individual's livelihood. And if the penalties were used to compensate injured parties, more of those individuals might be willing to report misconduct and to feel fairly treated by the disciplinary process.

5.   What is your view? Under what if any circumstances should fines be imposed for ethical violations?

Discipline of Law Firms

A related issue is whether disciplinary sanctions should be directed at law firms as well as individual lawyers. The bar has led the movement for organizational liability in other contexts, such as those involving securities, antitrust, and environmental regulation; and corporate criminal liability has been an accepted part of American law for over a century. *New York Central & Hudson River Railroad v. United States*, 212 U.S. 481 (1909). Many commentators believe that the reasons for seeking institutional accountability are just as relevant for legal workplaces. In some cases, it is impossible or inequitable to single out particular individuals for sanctions. Collective liability may encourage development of appropriate mechanisms

65. Linda Haller, "Disciplinary Fines: Deterrence or Retribution," 5 *Legal Ethics* 152 (2002) (discussing Australian experience with fines).

for preventing or responding to misconduct and may avoid the need for scapegoating any single lawyer in circumstances of diffuse or shared responsibility.[66]

Two states, New York and New Jersey, have pioneered rules permitting discipline of law firms. However, those rules have rarely been invoked, and when they are, the targets are typically small firms.[67] According to some New York bar disciplinary counsel, disciplining firms may be counterproductive because it enables regulators to take the "easy way out" and avoid identifying which lawyers are responsible for misconduct.[68] And because organizations cannot be disbarred or suspended, sanctions like admonitions or modest fines may be inadequate to insure compliance. Given the infrequency of imposition, the size of the penalty that would be necessary to discourage otherwise profitable misconduct is likely to be so high as to be impractical for bar disciplinary purposes.[69] Such considerations led the ABA's Ethics 2000 Commission to drop recommendations of law firm discipline.

Supporters of institutional liability respond that bar regulators can follow the model of other administrative agencies and place firms on probation. Firms could also be required to establish internal review procedures and to allocate responsibility to specialists to oversee compliance. The threat of collective liability could also encourage more firms to take such steps voluntarily. As Elizabeth Chambliss and David Wilkins argue, firm policies create economic incentives and social pressures that shape individual conduct: "To ignore that role is to abdicate a central duty of professional regulation."[70]

6. Do you agree? Under what, if any, circumstances should disciplinary agencies sanction law firms? Consider Model Rule 5.1(a), which requires "reasonable efforts to ensure that the firm has in effect measures giving reasonable assurance that all lawyers in the firm conform to the rules of professional conduct?" Should firms be subject to sanctions for violating this rule? Should the rule be amended to require appointment of internal compliance monitors?[71] Would institutional sanctions be appropriate for cases such as discovery abuse, overbilling, conflicts of interest, or complicity in client fraud?

---

66. Elizabeth Chambliss & David B. Wilkins, "A New Framework for Law Firm Discipline," 16 *Geo. J. Legal Ethics* 335 (2003).

67. O'Sullivan, *supra* note 57, at 84; (citing only five instances of reprimands of law firms); Chambliss & Wilkins, *supra* note 64, at 340 (citing only five instances).

68. "Law Firm Discipline: Easy Way Out or Getting More Bang for the Buck," 15 *ABA/BNA Lawyer Manual on Professional Conduct* 401 (1999) (quoting Robert J. Saltzman and Diane McShea).

69. *See generally* O'Sullivan, *supra* note 57, at 63, 88–90; "How Should We Regulate Large Law Firms? Is a Law Firm Disciplinary Rule the Answer?," 16 *Geo. J. Legal Ethics* 203, 205–06 (2002) (comments of William P. Smith).

70. Chambliss & Wilkins, *supra* note 66, at 338.

71. "How Should We Regulate Large Law Firms?," *supra* note 69, at 203 (comments of Elizabeth Chambliss).

D. Mental Health and Substance Abuse

INTRODUCTION

A related regulatory issue involves health-related difficulties. An estimated one-third of lawyers suffer from depression or from alcohol or drug addiction. Attorneys reportedly have almost three times the rate of depression and almost twice the rate of substance abuse as other Americans.[72] Such problems figure in a large percentage of disciplinary and malpractice cases.[73] Given the importance of the issue, it is striking to find little consensus among courts concerning the effect that addiction and other psychological difficulties should have in disciplinary cases.

This issue has provoked controversy on several levels. One area of disagreement involves the nature of the disciplinary process and the nature of substance abuse. Should discipline be seen purely as a protective system, concerned with an attorney's fitness to practice? Alternatively, should it incorporate elements of punishment and deterrence, which involve considerations of culpability? Under either framework, what implication does drug or alcohol addiction carry? To what extent should it figure as a mitigating factor rather than as an indication of unfitness? Should compulsive gambling also be considered in mitigation?[74]

Ironically enough, the "humanitarian" view that substance abuse and mental health difficulties are a disease and that the disciplinary system should be non-punitive does not provide the outcome that many addicted attorneys prefer. Under this view, careers can be subject to prolonged suspension based on the necessarily somewhat speculative assessments of medical experts as to an attorney's future abilities to avoid relapse.

A second set of problems involves causation. Some courts and disciplinary bodies have appeared to assume a relationship between addiction and misconduct; others have demanded a showing that but for the addictive

---

72. Zacharias, *supra* note 28, at 237, n. 1, 241, n. 15; Sue Shellenbarger, "Even Lawyers Get the Blues: Opening Up About Depression," *Wall St. J.*, Dec. 13, 2007, at D1; Jean Guiccione, "Attorneys Find Defense Against Dependence," *L.A. Times*, August 30, 2002, at B2.

73. Zacharias, *supra* note 28, at 241, n.15.

74. For conflicting views, see J. Nick Badgerow, "Apocalypse at Law: The Four Horsemen of the Modern Bar–Drugs, Alcohol, Gambling, and Depression," 18 *Professional Lawyer* 1, 14 (2007). *Compare* Disciplinary Proceeding Against Schwimmer, 108 P.3d 761, 765 (Wash. 2005) (addiction did not mitigate misappropriation; disbarment appropriate); Florida Bar v. Heptner, 887 So.2d 1036 (Fla. 2004) (cocaine did not mitigate multiple acts of misconduct; disbarment appropriate);

In re Brown, 912 A.2d 568 (D.C. 2006) (disbarment stayed; three year probation appropriate for attorney whose alcohol addiction was a substantial cause of misconduct); *In re* Mendelson, 780 N.Y.S.2d 801 (App.Div.2004) (gambling treated as mitigation; one year suspension stayed); State ex rel. Counsel for Discipline of Nebraska Supreme Court v. Reilly, 712 N.W.2d 278 (Neb. 2006) (ordering disbarment because compulsive gambling, "although regrettable and cause for sympathy, does not obviate the seriousness of the improper attorney conduct"); Iowa Supreme Court Board of Professional Ethics and Conduct v. Grotewold, 642 N.W.2d 288 (Iowa 2002) (sixty day suspension appropriate for attorney being successfully treated for depression).

behavior, the misconduct would not have occurred.[75] How strong a showing of causation should be required? If, as some courts require, addicted attorneys must enter counseling programs and submit to monitoring as a condition of practice, how long should such requirements remain in force? Consider those issues in light of *In re Kersey,* set forth below:

In re Kersey

District of Columbia Court of Appeals, 1987.
520 A.2d 321.

[After extended hearings, the District of Columbia Board on Professional Responsibility found that Franklin Kersey had committed 24 violations of the Code of Professional Responsibility, including extreme neglect and commingling of funds. The Board also accepted a committee finding that Kersey's misconduct would not have occurred but for his alcoholism and that he was unlikely to commit further abuses as long as he remained in structured rehabilitation programs. However, the Board rejected the committee's recommendation that Kersey should be placed on probation during a five-year suspension. In the Board's view, some period of actual suspension was necessary to deter similar misconduct by other lawyers and motivate them to seek treatment. The District of Columbia Court of Appeals rejected that conclusion. It disbarred Kersey but stayed execution and placed Kersey on probation for five years under the condition that he remain abstinent and submit to financial and sobriety monitoring].

■ Newman, J.

Today we hold that alcoholism is a mitigating factor to be considered in determining discipline. We agree with the Committee and the board that a sufficient nexus between Kersey's alcoholism and his misconduct has been established. But for Kersey's alcoholism, his misconduct would not have occurred. We hold that this "but for" test is the standard that must be met in order to prove causation in disciplinary cases involving alcoholism. We decline the opportunity in this opinion to write rules encompassing all future disciplinary cases involving alcoholism. These cases are necessarily decided on an individual basis. Factors that are generally considered in all disciplinary cases include the protection of the public, the vindication of public and private rights, and the deterrence to the bar. Our purpose in imposing discipline is not to visit punishment upon an attorney.... Ordinarily, the rehabilitation of the attorney's professional conduct does not play a major role in our choice of discipline. However, when alcoholism has been a causal factor leading to professional misconduct, rehabilitation from that condition will be considered a significant factor in imposing discipline. Deterrence, however, should not be considered a significant factor. Other alcoholic attorneys likely will fail to make the connection between the

---

75.   *See* American Bar Association Standards for Imposing Lawyer Sanctions (1989), Standard 9.3(h) (allowing "physical or mental disability or impairment" as a mitigating factor in the degree of discipline imposed, but noting in the commentary that this factor has been treated inconsistently by state courts and does not excuse the misconduct).

sanctioned attorney's alcoholic condition and their own drinking problem, and between their own drinking and their professional behavior. The record here is a testament to a pre-treatment alcoholic's persistent and virtually unshakable denial of his alcoholism.

We have given careful consideration to the Board's view that a period of actual suspension should be imposed on Kersey. While we acknowledge its legitimate concerns about the appropriate message to be given to other alcoholic attorneys, we give recognition to the element of choice inherent in alcoholism by creating an incentive rather than imposing a penalty. We conclude that where there is significant evidence of rehabilitation, a period of actual suspension is not always mandated. Hence, in those cases where the Board contemplates a suspension period, it should examine evidence concerning the impact of the suspension of the respondent, with particular attention to its effect on the respondent's continued rehabilitation. After consideration of these factors, there may be situations where a period of suspension is justified. In this case, however, we are convinced that the minimal deterrence value of suspension upon other alcoholic attorneys is substantially outweighed by the likely salutary effect upon Kersey's continued rehabilitation that continuation of his professional career will have.

NOTES AND QUESTIONS

1.   Which position do you find most persuasive, the Board's or the Court of Appeals'? In subsequent cases, courts have divided over whether lawyers should be placed on probation, or suspended indefinitely or for a prescribed period, with reinstatement conditional on their successful treatment and continued monitoring, and sometimes periodic reports from psychiatrist.[76] Which approach strikes you as most appropriate, or does it depend on a case-by-case assessment?

2.   Consider David Luban's observation:

> *In re Kersey* offers a powerful argument against regarding the disciplinary process as a system of punishment in cases concerning alcoholic lawyers, namely that one of the traditional justifications for punishment—deterrence—is inapplicable. . . .

> Though alcoholism is a disease, it is unlike most diseases in that it does not just happen to the victim. He brings it on himself by drinking alcohol, behavior which initially is voluntary. Thus, even though alcoholism is not a vice . . . it necessarily shares one characteristic of vices: if the recovered lawyer relapses, "goes off the wagon," it will not be through an accidental reinfection, but through willful behavior, namely taking the first drink. Even a purely medical judgment of whether the lawyer is recovered to the point of being fit to practice is therefore partly a judgment of will power, and thus of character. In this way it is

---

76. *In re* Brown, 912 A.2d 568 (D.C. 2006) (three year probation); State ex rel. Oklahoma Bar Ass'n v. Beasley, 142 P.3d 410 (Okla. 2006) (two year suspension); Disciplin-ary Counsel v. Hiltbrand, 852 N.E.2d 733 (Ohio 2006) (suspended indefinitely until completion of sustained period of recovery).

not after all so very unlike a moral judgment, at least where this is a judgment of a person's character rather than his conduct. Medical [experts] try as best they can to base their prognoses on external factors—the quality of the lawyer's support group (such as Alcoholics Anonymous), his responses to counseling, the changes he has made in his environment to protect himself from stresses to which he has in the past responded by drinking, the stability and happiness of his life, etc. But in the end ... although alcoholism is a disease, not a defect of character, recovery from it will be a perpetual test of character. Character, and not medical ingenuity, will make the difference, and this is a moral dimension that the medical conception of alcoholism as a disease should never be permitted to obscure.... To say that the recovery from alcoholism is a sign of moral strength is not to say that the disease itself is morally blameworthy, and is thus not an argument against mitigation of sanctions. Just the opposite, recovery displays a mettle in the attorney that should raise our estimation of him.[77]

Do you agree? Does it follow that lawyers whose substance abuse is a but-for cause of misconduct should always have the opportunity for probation if they are in a structured rehabilitation program? Or are there contexts in which disbarment (with or without the option of reinstatement) is appropriate?

3.　Do mental health difficulties stand on different footing?

Consider the case of Joel Greenberg, disbarred in New Jersey in July 1998, and admitted in Pennsylvania in July 1999. Greenberg lost his New Jersey license after stealing almost $35,000 from his law firm in 1993. Neither the state's disciplinary review board nor its supreme court accepted Greenberg's claim that his misconduct was a self-destructive act fueled by depression, not greed, and that his subsequent psychiatric treatment left him fit for legal practice. According to the New Jersey Supreme Court, Greenberg's complicated system of misappropriation did not suggest such a "loss of competency" as to prevent compliance with ethical rules. To permit his continued practice would impair public confidence and exonerate other attorneys who misappropriated funds in response to personal hardship. In the court's view, attorneys suffering from mental health or substance abuse should seek help before they engage in activities that would irreparably damage their own reputation and seriously compromise the profession's public standing. By contrast, Pennsylvania bar examiners obviously accepted Greenberg's claims of rehabilitation, but refused to make any public comment about their decision due to confidentiality concerns.[78] Which state had it right?

How would you respond to a lawyer who provided testimony by his physician attributing misconduct to "professional burnout?" At issue were several instances of serious neglect,/ refusal to return unearned fees, and

---

77. David Luban, "Commentary: A Professional Tragedy," *Nat. Rep. Legal Ethics and Prof. Resp.* (1988).

78. *In re* Greenberg, 714 A.2d 243 (N.J. 1998); Wendy Davis, "Advice for the Disbarred, Go West," *N.J. Law J.* July 19, 1999, at 1.

failure to cooperate with disciplinary officials. The lawyer subsequently obtained counseling, temporarily closed his practice, cooperated with bar officials, and according to the physician, had brought his problem under control. Was the court's 30–day suspension appropriate?[79]

Increasing recognition of health related difficulties among attorneys has led to increasing innovations in treatment programs. According to most experts, alcohol and drug addiction require early intervention before social stigma, physiological problems, and professional impairment become pronounced. Recovery rates among professionals who obtain adequate treatment are encouragingly high. Some type of program is available in every state, and many jurisdictions have implemented diversion systems for cases not involving serious misconduct. Under these programs, disciplinary action will be stayed, pending successful completion of a rehabilitation program. Encouraging greater participation in these programs, and more evaluation of their long-term effectiveness, should be a key priority for the profession.[80]

E.   COMPETENCE AND MALPRACTICE

1.   COMPETENCE

INTRODUCTION

Competence in lawyers' services is something "everyone wants more of, but no one has a very clear sense of what exactly 'it' is, how best to promote it, or which efforts will be worth the cost."[81] Since their beginnings, bar associations have been concerned with professional performance and its effect on public status, and bar ethical codes have included provisions on competence. The Code of Professional Responsibility mandates "preparation adequate in the circumstances," (DR 6–101(A)(2)) while the Model Rules of Professional Conduct require "the legal knowledge, skill, thoroughness, and preparation reasonably necessary for the representation." (Rule 1.1) By whose standards and at what cost are matters left unaddressed.

Almost no systematic research is available on the extent of incompetence among practicing attorneys, or the strategies most effective in addressing it. As chapters XIV and XVI note, although we have some evidence that performance in law school correlates with performance in bar examinations, we have no idea how well either correlates with competence in practice. However, the fragmentary research available reveals that most qualities rated most relevant by practitioners and employing organizations are not learned in law school or tested on bar examinations: e.g., fact-

---

79. State ex rel. Oklahoma Bar Association v. Schraeder, 51 P.3d 570 (Okl. 2002).

80. For a description of representative programs *see* Zacharias, *supra* note 28; Badgerow, *supra* note 74, at 17–18.

81. Deborah L. Rhode, "The Rhetoric of Professional Reform," 45 *Maryland L. Rev.* 274, 288–293 (1986).

gathering, instilling confidence, effective oral expression, maintaining client and collegial relations, document drafting, diligence, judgment, supervisory capability.

To address these problems, bar leaders generally propose continuing legal education; skills-oriented bar exams and law school courses; "bridging the gap" training and mentoring programs for new attorneys; support structures for solo and small firm practitioners; and improved in-house education by employers. Yet again, almost no systematic effort has been made to assess the effectiveness of such initiatives. Moreover, most clearly identifiable incompetence is a function less of cognitive deficiencies than attitudinal problems and economic pressure. To the extent that inadequate representation results from greed, indifference or mental health-related difficulties, or from inadequate stakes and limited client resources, these educational responses are clearly inadequate.

Given the increasingly complex and changing nature of many areas of legal practice, the profession's traditional reliance on entry-level screening also seems somewhat anachronistic. According to the ABA's Task Force on Law Schools and the Profession, lawyers are not adequately prepared for their first jobs in practice and their deficiencies are increasing as law becomes more complex and the range of necessary skills becomes more diverse.[82] To what extent can the strategies discussed below address these concerns? What reforms are likely to be most effective?

Continuing Legal Education

Continuing legal education [CLE] for practicing lawyers began a quarter century ago in the aftermath of Watergate, largely in response to public criticism of lawyers' ethics. About four-fifths of all states now require practicing lawyers to participate in CLE programs, generally ranging from ten to twelve hours. In most jurisdictions, some of the coursework must focus on ethics. A minority demand coverage of other topics such as bias in the profession and substance abuse.

Such requirements have been relatively uncontroversial. Who could object to having lawyers make minimal efforts to stay current in their fields and to familiarize themselves with significant ethical issues? The problem, however, is that few CLE programs make any significant effort at quality control or have demonstrated evidence of effectiveness. In order to gain acceptance from the bar, most educational requirements are minimal and user-friendly approaches are endless. Some courses on substance abuse and emotional distress have focused on stress reduction, and Tibetan relaxation methods; courses on sports law have occurred at sporting events, complete with hot dogs and peanuts.[83] The problem is not simply that some classes stretch the concept of "legal education"; the more fundamental difficulty, as a District of Columbia task force noted, "is that there have been no

---

82. American Bar Association, Section on Legal Education and Admission to the Bar, *Legal Education and Professional Devel-* *opment—An Educational Continuum* (1992) (MacCrate Report).

83. Rhode, *supra* note 17, at 156.

reliable, scientific demonstrations of the efficacy of continuing legal education." Research in other professions such as medicine and engineering has found no relationship between performance and participation in continuing education.[84] Neither is it self evident that passive attendance at ungraded courses will significantly increase competence in practice.

That is not to suggest that all CLE is unproductive. Rather as one expert notes, these program's "major benefit appears to be skill enhancement of already motivated and relatively competent practitioners."[85]

QUESTIONS

1. Consider the following reform options. Do any seem preferable to existing programs?

> One possibility might be to require both less and more in continuing legal education. States could demand fewer hours but impose greater quality controls. Bar officials should require passage of an exam and deny credit for courses that bear little demonstrated relationship to performance in practice. More programs should target the deficiencies in practice management that cause the greatest disciplinary problems, such as client neglect and financial improprieties. Providers could themselves be subject to educational requirements that insured some basic level of effectiveness....

> Alternatively, states could combine required and voluntary approaches. CLE could be mandatory for new lawyers and for other practitioners who have violated ethical rules. For example, attorneys who are subject to disciplinary, judicial, or malpractice sanctions could be required to take appropriate courses. Other attorneys who voluntarily complete CLE classes and pass a basic test could receive certification of their coursework. That credential could prove useful in attracting clients and in seeking lower malpractice insurance premiums. An increasing number of lawyers are now willing to complete demanding educational requirements in order to become certified as specialists in particular fields of practice. States could encourage this trend by expanding specialization programs, publicizing their value to consumers, and improving their educational quality.[86]

Disciplinary Diversion Programs

A further competence-related strategy involves educational programs in lieu of lawyer discipline. The ABA Commission on Disciplinary Enforcement recommended that all jurisdictions adopt such programs for matters in which a lawyer's action constitutes minor misconduct, incompetence, or

---

84. Task Force on Mandatory Continuing Legal Education, *Report to the Board of Governors of the District of Columbia Bar* 26–28 (1995).

85. Susan Martyn, "Lawyer Competence and Lawyer Discipline: Beyond the Bar," 69 *Geo.L.J.* 705, 725–32 (1981).

86. Rhode, *supra* note 17, at 157.

neglect. These programs could include arbitration, mediation, practice management, and substance abuse or psychological counseling.

Implementation of this recommendation has been uneven. Most states have some form of substance abuse diversion, and many have "ethics schools" or well-developed practice oversight systems. Under these approaches, lawyers accused of minor violations who might otherwise receive a reprimand have the option of participating in alternative programs. Participants then agree to comply with remedial requirements such as counseling, peer review, and office management courses. Evaluation of these programs has been highly limited. One in-house study of Arizona's diversion system found that those who adhered to the terms of their term had a lower likelihood of recidivism than those who did not.[87] However, it is not clear to what extent that difference was attributable to the characteristics of the program, as opposed to characteristics of those who choose to participate and who completed their term. Even less effort has focused on evaluating the long term impact of ethics schools.

In the absence of data indicating effectiveness, should such schools constitute a substitute for discipline? Should they be evaluated or run by a consumer protection commission independent of the organized bar? What initiatives are likely to be most effective in preventing and remedying the malpractice problems discussed below?

2.   Malpractice

PROBLEM 3

You are a senior associate in a large corporate firm. An old friend of your family asks for an interview. She believes that she may have a malpractice claim against a local hospital and one of its doctors. You arrange a meeting with your firm's leading trial attorney. After discussing the matter for about 45 minutes, he tells her that nothing in the facts she has related suggests that the claim is one that the firm would be "interested in handling." According to the woman, the lawyer told her that he would raise the matter with a colleague and let her know if that conversation changed his view of the case. He never called. Nor did he bill her for the interview.

After the two-year statute of limitations on the matter has run, the woman discovers that her claim would have been quite likely to succeed. She sues your firm. The partner maintains that he told her that because of the serious nature of the injuries, she might want to consult another lawyer, and that she "should do so promptly." He also recalls telling her that the firm had no expertise in medical malpractice and that he would call a specialist in another firm if she wanted a second opinion. He claims that he did raise the issue with that attorney but acknowledges that he did not review medical records or contact the woman. He also argues that there was no attorney-client relationship.

87.   Ellis, *supra* note 21.

How should your firm respond? Are there further facts that would affect your decision? What, if anything, should the partner have done differently?

NOTES

Three decades ago, malpractice claims against attorneys were so rare and practitioners were so unconcerned about liability that insurance coverage was generally not available on the domestic market. That situation has dramatically changed. Definitive data is impossible to come by because insurance companies do not disclose payouts and many settlements remain confidential. However, it has been estimated that 10 to 20 percent of attorneys face malpractice exposure in a given year, that annual insurance payouts total four to six billion dollars, and that claims, particularly large claims, are on the rise.[88]

What accounts for the increase is subject to dispute. Some commentators believe that incompetent representation is growing. As the profession becomes more competitive, as profit margins decrease, and as billable hour expectations escalate, lawyers are under more pressure to handle matters beyond their expertise. Other commentators believe that the increase in malpractice claims is attributable primarily to rising consumer expectations and greater willingness among lawyers to bring such claims. As these observers note, the bar's experience is by no means unique. Other professionals have also been subject to escalating malpractice complaints; even the clergy has felt the effects.[89]

Finally, the growth in claims against lawyers may reflect some factors linked to changes in the legal profession and its practice climate. Greater competition and stratification within the legal community have made colleagues less hesitant to testify against each other in malpractice suits. Risky financial speculation and corporate scandals have also generated more civil liability claims. Victims in search of deep pockets to sue have increasingly lighted on prosperous law firms. Attorneys who draft opinion letters and securities documents face a growing risk of malpractice actions.[90]

Yet despite the escalation of liability claims, the barriers to successful actions have remained considerable. Most individuals with grievances against a lawyer are unable or unwilling to incur the costs in time, money, and acrimony involved in filing charges. Unless liability looks clear, dam-

88. Rhode, *supra* note 17, at 165; "Law Firms Face Sharp Rise in Malpractice Suits," *Legal Times*, May 10, 2005; Joan C. Rogers, "Speakers Spot Trends, Assess Changes in Malpractice Claims and Insurance Market," 22 ABA/BNA *Law. Man. Prof. Conduct* 115 (2006).

89. Richard Pérez–Peña, "When Lawyers Go After Their Peers: The Boom in Malpractice Cases," *N.Y. Times*, Aug. 5, 1994, at B13; Jonathan Gaw, "Lawyers Shed Reluctance to Sue Their Own," *L.A. Times*, Dec. 14, 1992, at B1; Ramos, *supra* note 78.

90. Rosenthal, *supra* note 19, at 23; American Bar Association Standing Committee on Lawyers Professional Liability, *Legal Malpractice Claims in the 1990s* (American Bar Association, Chicago, 1996), 12, 16; John Gibeaut, "Good News, Bad News in Malpractice," *ABA Journal*, March 1997, 101.

ages are substantial, and the errant lawyer has sufficient insurance or legally accessible assets to make a judgment collectible, plaintiffs' attorneys will generally decline the case.

The burden of proof necessary to establish liability is also difficult to meet. Although the data on malpractice success rates are incomplete and conflicting, the best available evidence suggests that half of all claims result in no recovery, and three quarters are resolved for less than $10,000 in total expenses and indemnity settlement costs.[91] Most successful claims involve fairly obvious errors, such as missing deadlines, neglecting to file documents, fraudulent representations, or failing to consult clients and follow their instructions.[92] In cases presenting less objective proof of error, clients will often have difficulty establishing that what the attorney did or did not do fell below average performance standards, and that the incompetence was a but/for cause of substantial losses.

Current debates over malpractice liability center on several main issues: how to set performance standards; what proof of causation should be necessary; what should be the role of professional conduct codes; what remedies should be available; who should be entitled to sue; and how to encourage more effective preventive strategies.

NOTES AND QUESTIONS

1. *Performance Standards*

Courts and commentators have divided over whether average community standards are the appropriate benchmark of liability and, if so, how the legal community should be defined. Should the relevant community be the locality, the state, or the legal profession more generally? According to an influential Vermont Supreme Court decision, the "minimum knowledge required should not vary with geography. . . . The fact that a lower degree of care or less able practice may be prevalent in a particular local community should not dictate the standard of care." *Russo v. Griffin*, 510 A.2d 436, 438 (Vt.1986) (holding that the state was the relevant community). Some commentators have raised more fundamental objections to making liability depend on prevailing practices in the community. In their view, such an approach adopts a "perpetrator" rather than "victim" perspective; it grants the profession the power to dictate its own standard of conduct, a prerogative not generally granted to other occupations even in areas involving technical expertise. To these critics, a preferable approach is to determine what constitutes reasonable performance under the totality of the circumstances, including clients' legitimate expectations. That is the standard prevailing in other nations' disciplinary as well as malpractice systems.

91. ABA Standing Committee on Lawyer's Professional Liability, *Profile of Legal Malpractice Claims* 13 (2005). Of cases that go to trial, plaintiffs are successful in slightly over half. Rosenthal, *supra* note 19, at 26. For the difficulties of proof, *see id.*

92. Ramos, *supra* note 78; ABA Committee, *supra* note 81.

1.   What is your view? Consider the issue in light of a leading California Supreme Court decision, *Aloy v. Mash,* 212 Cal.Rptr. 162 (Cal.1985). There, a majority of justices voted to send a malpractice claim to trial where an attorney had done inadequate research in an unsettled area of marital pension rights, even though his advice turned out to be consistent with a later United States Supreme Court holding. In the majority's view, the defendant was not entitled to summary judgment because a subsequent legal decision had validated his earlier advice. Since it was unlikely that the subsequent decision would be retroactively applied, the California Court saw no reason to bar the plaintiff's claim. Three justices dissented on the theory that an attorney should not be held liable for advice that later turned out to be correct.

2.   Which side in *Aloy* had the better argument? The majority focused on the standard of care owed to the client, while the dissent focused on whether the client got the result that was ultimately held to be correct. Which emphasis makes more sense?

3.   Similar issues have risen in cases involving lawyer-client sexual relationships. (See the prior discussion of attorney-client sexual relationships in Chapter X, section I, *supra.*) In *Kling v. Landry,* 686 N.E.2d 33 (Ill. App. Ct. 1997) and *Suppressed v. Suppressed,* 565 N.E.2d 101 (Ill. App. Ct. 1990), Illinois appellate courts held that coercive sexual relationships between divorce lawyers and their clients did not establish malpractice unless it so adversely affected the lawyer's legal performance as to cause significant damages. In so ruling, the courts noted that attorneys were not exempt from "human frailties" and should not be subject to a cause of action in which the only damages would be intangible emotional distress and the potential for blackmail would be significant. By contrast, the Georgia Supreme Court held that a lawyer could be liable for breach of fiduciary duties based on an adulterous affair with a woman he successfully represented in a disability claims procedure. The couple who retained him alleged that he misused confidential information concerning the wife's emotional and mental condition to convince her to have an affair, resulting in significant damages to their relationship and well-being. *Tante v. Herring,* 453 S.E.2d 686 (Ga.1994). Which ruling would you support?

2. *Causation*

A further burden for malpractice plaintiffs involves causation. In effect, they must demonstrate not only that the lawyer was negligent, but that such negligence resulted in quantifiable damages. For claims involving litigation (which comprise about half of all malpractice complaints), that burden requires a trial within a trial; plaintiffs must establish that but for the lawyer's negligence, they would have prevailed in the original proceeding. That requirement has been severely criticized. Would a fairer standard be the test applicable in England and France, and in American medical malpractice cases? Under that test, plaintiffs who demonstrate that the defendant's substandard performance deprived them of a substantial possibility of recovery would be entitled to damages adjusted to reflect the likelihood of success.[93]

Defenders of the current legal malpractice standard argue that this alternative is only suitable for medical contexts in which an objective basis for predicting outcomes is available. It is, for example, possible to give reliable estimates of the survival chances of patients who receive appropriate treatment. By contrast, legal malpractice contexts lack "controlled studies ..., meaningful statistical information ..., [and a] well-defined body of expertise" that can ground predictions of success.[94]

QUESTIONS

1.   Are you persuaded? Is predicting the chance of success of a legal claim a significantly more speculative endeavor than other tasks of juries and expert witnesses in tort cases (e.g., assigning a value to pain and suffering or loss of consortium)? Consider consumer advocates' claim that an attorney who is guilty of incompetence should not be absolved of liability simply because objective proof of the value of the plaintiff's claim is unavailable.

2.   Should the same but-for standard be applicable to transactional representation? Consider *Viner v. Sweet*, 30 Cal.4th 1232 (2003). There, plaintiffs were the California founders of an audio book company who sold out their interest to a media conglomerate with the help of Charles Sweet, a transactional attorney from the Washington D.C. law firm, Williams & Connelly.

A jury awarded the Viners $13 million based on findings that Sweet was negligent on seven counts, including misrepresentation of a key non-solicitation clause and attorneys' fee provision, ignorance of important California law, and failure to negotiate an indemnity provision or exclude certain stock dividends from a general release. Sweet appealed, claiming that the plaintiffs needed to prove that but-for the negligence they would have obtained a more favorable agreement. An appellate court affirmed the verdict on the ground that such a standard would be inappropriate for transactions that did not have a clear winner and loser. The California Supreme Court reversed, and held that the Viners could recover only on two counts (worth $515,760) on which the parties had stipulated that the Viners would have obtained a more favorable result. In so ruling, the court noted:

> When a business transaction goes awry, a natural target of the disappointed principals is the attorney who arranged or advised the deal. Clients predictably attempt to shift some part of the loss and disap-

---

93.   John Leubsdorf, "Legal Malpractice and Professional Responsibility," 48 *Rutgers Law Review* 111–119 (1995); Lawrence W. Kessler, "Alternative Liability in Litigation Malpractice Actions: Eradicating the Last Resort of Scoundrels," 37 *San Diego L. Rev.* 401 (2000). For the traditional standard, see Charles Wolfram, "A Cautionary Tail: Fiduciary Breach as Legal Malpractice," 34 *Hofstra L. Rev.* 689, 718–19 (2006).

94.   John C. P. Goldberg, "What Clients Are Owed: Cautionary Observations on Lawyers and Loss of a Chance," 52 *Emory L. J.* 1202, 1212 (2003).

pointment of a deal that goes sour on to the shoulders of persons who were responsible for the underlying legal work ... Courts are properly cautious about making attorneys guarantors of their clients' faulty business judgment. 30 Cal.4th, at 1241.

Do you agree?

3.   What should the standard be in criminal cases? The dominant view is that complainants must establish that they were innocent and that their attorneys' substandard performance was responsible for their convictions.[95] Is that requirement appropriate? Consider *Ang v. Martin*, 114 P.3d 637 (Wash. 2005), in which the Washington Supreme Court held that defendants who withdrew a guilty plea and were subsequently acquitted could not recover against their attorney without showing that they were actually innocent. In so ruling, the court reasoned that the rule: prohibited criminals from benefitting from their own bad acts; maintained respect for the justice system; avoided harmful chilling effects on the defense bar; blocked suits by guilty criminals who believed that they could have gotten a better deal; and prevented a flood of nuisance litigation. 114 P.3d, at 642. Three justices dissented. Two believed that the standard should be the same as in civil cases. The third supported the standard applicable in a minority of jurisdictions, which puts the burden on a negligent attorney to prove that the complainants were guilty. According to that third justice, "[t]he Court should protect the public from lawyers misdeeds not the other way around." 114 P.3d 645 (Chambers, J., dissenting). Which approach do you find most convincing?

3.   *The Role of Ethical Codes*

A related issue involves the significance of bar ethical rules in establishing attorney malpractice. The Preliminary Statement of the ABA Code disclaims any effort to define standards for civil liability of lawyers. The Scope Note to the Model Rules similarly states that:

> [v]iolation of a rule should not give rise to a cause of action nor should it create any presumption that a legal duty has been breached. The Rules are designed to provide guidance to lawyers and to provide a structure for regulating conduct through disciplinary agencies. They are not designed to be a basis for civil liability. Furthermore, the purpose of the Rules can be subverted when they are invoked by opposing parties as procedural weapons.

QUESTIONS

1.   Is this reasoning persuasive? In some jurisdictions, violations of ethical rules can serve as evidence of negligence *per se*, or as evidence of failure to meet the proper standard of care. By contrast, other courts disallow any use of the rules, or only permit indirect use (as when an expert refers to

---

95. Wiley v. San Diego County, 966 P.2d 983 (Cal.1998); Wolfram, *supra* note 56, at 218–27.

them in testifying about the standard of care).[96] Which of these positions would you support?

2.   Does it make sense to require that ethical violations be proven by expert testimony rather than by reference to bar codes? Under what circumstances would violation of an ethics rule not be malpractice? Could judges or juries make that decision themselves? In other litigation contexts, judges and juries apply law—some of it very complicated law—to facts without the need of an expert. Should rules of professional responsibility be different? Do the disclaimers in bar codes serve a public interest?

4.   *Malpractice Remedies and Insurance*

A related question involves the adequacy of remedies for acknowledged malpractice. Courts are divided about whether damages should be available for non-economic losses. State bars also vary in their efforts to compensate victims where recovery against the attorney is impossible. Recent estimates suggest that about 20 to 50 percent of lawyers are uninsured, and malpractice judgments against these practitioners are seldom collectible.[97] Some compensation is generally available for fraud or dishonesty through bar-administered client security funds (which are subsidized by mandatory lawyer contributions). However, as noted earlier, most of these funds are too limited to cover more than a small fraction of client grievances, and payouts are capped at inadequate levels.

To insure more effective remedies, several strategies are possible. One response is to expand client security funds and make them available for additional forms of malpractice, such as neglect and incompetence. Another proposal involves establishing more low-cost alternative dispute resolution procedures for fee disputes and malpractice claims. A third strategy involves requiring forfeiture of fees not yet collected, or disgorgement of fees already obtained. Since such remedies are triggered by a breach of fiduciary obligation, they are typically available on a showing of misconduct; the client need not also prove damages. These claims often arise in countersuits where the attorney attempts to collect a bill, or in cases involving conflicts of interest. See *Restatement (Third) of the Law Governing Lawyers*, § 37.

A further strategy, pioneered in Oregon and debated in a growing number of jurisdictions, is to require all attorneys to carry adequate malpractice insurance and to establish some state-administered fund to provide coverage. Such proposals have attracted considerable controversy, particularly among members of the bar who do not practice full-time or who could not readily afford liability premiums. Critics also worry that mandatory coverage would encourage frivolous claims and would fail to distinguish between attorneys with widely varying needs. Supporters of mandatory insurance respond that no increase in claims has occurred in

---

96.   Gary A. Munneke and Anthony E. Davis, "The Standard of Care in Legal Malpractice: Do the Model Rules of Professional Conduct Define It?" 22 *Journal of the Legal Profession* 33, 69 (1998).

97.   Mark Hansen, "Undercovered," *ABA J.*, Nov. 2001, at 47.

Oregon and premiums there are below those of comparable jurisdictions. Part of the reason for Oregon's success is that it operates a mandatory nonprofit Professional Liability Fund that insures all the states' attorneys, eliminates expensive marketing and brokers' fees, and incorporates effective prevention initiatives. Over four-fifths of the state's attorneys support the state's program.[98]

It is, however, unclear whether such a plan would be practical for larger state bars with greater diversity in types of practice and risk levels. Some experts worry that a mandatory plan in a state like California would require premium levels that would be prohibitively expensive for those with limited incomes from their legal practice. A preferable strategy, in these experts' view, is to require attorneys who do not have malpractice insurance to disclose that fact. In South Dakota, which requires such disclosures on attorneys' letterhead, only two percent of practitioners are uninsured.[99] The ABA has adopted a Model Court Rule which, where adopted, requires lawyers to report malpractice insurance information to the state supreme court or other specified authority, and indicates that the information will be made available to the public in a manner designated by the court. About two fifths of states require lawyers to provide information on insurance coverage either to clients or to the bar.[100] Opponents of mandatory disclosure argue that the requirement would be unfair to lawyers and misleading to the public because the fact of coverage is not indicative of competence, or even necessarily of the chances for insurance coverage, given the exclusions written into most policies.[101]

QUESTIONS

1. Which of these strategies seem most productive? Should states require either that attorneys carry some minimum level of malpractice insurance or that they disclose their lack of insurance to prospective clients? Why or why not?

2. Would your answer differ if you were: a client; a solo or small firm practitioner; a state legislator; a bar president, or the director of your state's discipline system? If so, who should make the decision?

5. *Third Party Obligations*

A final area of controversy involves the extent to which non-clients should be able to sue for an attorney's violations of professional rules. Although the doctrine of privity traditionally blocked such actions, courts gradually began recognizing exceptions to that rule. Some jurisdictions now

98. ABA Commission, *supra* note 9, at 81–82; Rhode, *supra* note 17, at 168; Harry H. Scheider, "At Issue: Mandatory Insurance," *ABA Journal*, November, 1993, 45.

99. James E. Towery, "The Case in Favor of Mandatory Disclosure of Lack of Malpractice Insurance," *Professional Lawyer*, Winter 2003, at 22; "South Dakota Reform Works," HALT, *Legal Reformer*, Fall 2002, at 5.

100. *See* www.abanet.org/cpr/clientpr/malprac_disischart.pdf.

101. Lance J. Rogers, "Two States Pass Insurance Status Rules; California Bar Eschews Required Disclosure," 23 *ABA/BNA Law. Man Prof. Conduct* 531 (2007).

hold that lawyers who undertake responsibilities that foreseeably affect a third party owe a duty of care to that individual. For example, attorneys may be liable to intended beneficiaries of an estate if errors in drafting the will prevents them from receiving the bequest. Such holdings rely on fiduciary/agency principles, third party beneficiary theories, or a balancing test that considers the predictability and certainty of harm, the defendant's moral culpability, and the extent of the third party's justifiable reliance on the defendant's conduct.[102] Underlying this line of cases is a desire to place responsibility on the individual best able to prevent losses or to maintain adequate insurance.

By contrast, other courts have concluded that making a lawyer liable to persons other than clients would "inject undesirable self-protective reservations into the attorney's counseling role," would prevent him from devoting his "entire energies to his client's interests," and would be an undue burden on the profession.[103] A prominent case denying recovery is *Schatz v. Weinberg & Green,* 943 F.2d 485 (4th Cir.1991), *cert. denied,* 502 U.S. 62 (1991). In 1986, the plaintiffs, Ivan and Joanne Schatz, arranged to sell an 80 percent interest in two companies to Mark Rosenberg. The purchase price was $1.2 million in promissory notes that a holding company issued and that Rosenberg personally guaranteed. Prior to the closing, the plaintiffs relied on a financial statement and update letter describing Rosenberg's net worth. The documents, prepared by his law firm, Weinberg & Green, included material misstatements. Over the next several years, the Schatzes loaned an additional $150,000 to the companies while Rosenberg siphoned off all available corporate assets. When he declared bankruptcy, the Schatzes were left with worthless notes. They then sued the law firm, arguing that attorneys should be accountable for a representation that they know is false and that is incorporated into a document on which third parties will reasonably rely.

In affirming the dismissal of plaintiffs' complaint, the Fourth Circuit reasoned that attorneys owed common law duties only to clients and to direct beneficiaries of the lawyer-client relationship, not to other third parties such as the Schatzes. According to the court, only if lawyers had the specific intent to aid fraud should they be liable.

> Any other result may prevent a client from reposing complete trust in his lawyer for fear that he might reveal a fact which would trigger the lawyer's duty to the third party. Similarly, if attorneys had a duty to disclose information to third parties, attorneys would have an incentive not to press clients for information. The net result would not be less securities fraud. Instead, attorneys would more often be unwitting accomplices to the fraud as a result of being kept in the dark by their clients or by their own reluctance to obtain information. 943 F.2d at 493.

---

102. Leubsdorf, *supra* note 83, at 111, 130–135; Geoffrey Hazard, Jr., "The Privity Requirement Reconsidered," 27 *South Texas Law Review* 967 (1996); Forest Bowman, "Lawyer Liability to Non–Clients," 97 *Dickinson Law Review* 267, 276 (1993).

103. Goodman v. Kennedy, 556 P.2d 737 (Cal.1976).

In criticizing the *Schatz* holding, John Freeman and Nathan Crystal note that recent decisions have generally held professionals other than lawyers to a higher standard than intentional fraud. "Conscious avoidance" of facts indicating fraud will establish federal criminal liability for professionals such as underwriters. Many commentators argue that attorneys in civil cases should have no greater protection.[104] As these commentators note, in some respects the *Schatz* holding ill-serves the bar as well as the public. From an economic perspective, the decision undermines the value of having attorneys prepare financial documents. Paying a law firm to complete a net worth statement is valuable largely because the firm's reputation serves to corroborate the client's assertions. On this reasoning, the outcome in *Schatz* is inefficient because it permits negligent or willfully ignorant attorneys to devalue other lawyers' reputations.

QUESTIONS

1. Which way would you have ruled in *Schatz*? Some observers believe that the Court's ruling was based in part on a desire to deter a perceived epidemic of securities-fraud cases—the Schatzes sued for securities fraud as well as legal malpractice.

2. The trend in the case law is toward increased third-party liability, and to use a balancing test that considers: the extent to which the transaction was intended to benefit the plaintiff; the foreseeability of harm to the plaintiff; the degree of certainty that the plaintiff suffered injury; the closeness of the connection between the defendant's conduct and the injury; the public policy of preventing harm; and the burden on the profession.[105] For example, in litigation involving failures of savings and loan institutions, lawyers have been held accountable for failure to make a reasonable investigation. The Seventh Circuit reached the opposite conclusion from *Schatz* in a leading case *Greycas v. Proud*, 826 F.2d 1560, 1565 (7th Cir.1987). There, a lawyer was held liable for a letter to a third party that included negligent misrepresentations that induced detrimental reliance. By contrast, in *Talton v. Arnall Golden Gregory* LLP, 622 S.E.2d 589 (Ga.App.2006), a patient who received infected cadaver tissue during a knee operation could not recover from attorneys who provided confidential advice to the tissue supplier regarding appropriate warnings.

Under what circumstances should third parties be entitled to sue for malpractice? Should opposing parties have a claim against attorneys who violate ethical rules in contexts like discovery abuse?

6. *Prevention*

However these issues concerning the standard and scope of liability are resolved, attorneys are facing increased pressure to prevent disputes that

---

104. John M. Freeman & Nathan M. Crystal, "Scienter in Professional Liability Cases," 42 *S.C.L.Rev.* 783 (1991).

105. Marc A. Johnson & Sims Weymuller, "Irreconcilable Differences: The Duty of Undivided Loyalty Versus the Non–Client Duty of Care," *Prof. Lawyer* 79, 80–81 (2007). For an overview of the costs and benefits of third-party liability, see Fred Zacharias, "Coercing Clients: Can Lawyer Gatekeeper Rules Work?," 47 *Boston College L. Rev.* 455, 472–73, 494–95 (2006).

might trigger malpractice claims. Unsurprisingly, insurers have been at the forefront of this effort by auditing their policyholders for risky practices. To maintain insurance coverage, policyholders must establish risk management systems and follow ethical protocals.[106] Critical preventive techniques include systems for identifying conflicts of interest and for reminding lawyers of important deadlines. The latter systems are more effective if they allocate responsibility for monitoring compliance to someone other than the person responsible for performance. Peer review is also important in contexts where individual lawyers may have personal or financial interests in retaining matters that pose undue risks to the firm. An equally important strategy involves communication with clients. Attorneys should provide realistic assessments concerning chances of success as well as probable delays, costs, and fees. Disputes can also be preempted by detailed written retainer agreements and by ongoing reports concerning the status of the case (such as copies of major filings, notices of significant developments, and so forth). Increasing numbers of firms have also found it useful to designate a specialized general counsel position with responsibilities for compliance with ethical standards and malpractice prevention.[107] It is also critical to ensure that institutionalized risk management techniques do not displace lawyers' individual responsibility to consider factors other than client interests and malpractice prevention.[108]

Contrary to popular assumption, it is not young, inexperienced attorneys who experience most malpractice claims. Lawyers practicing over eight years account for a disproportionate share of suits. The same financial and psychological factors that help lead to disciplinary charges also contribute to malpractice: unrealistic caseloads, substance abuse, and personal stresses such as debts, divorce, and depression. The best protection for both lawyers and their clients is professional help when such problems arise, together with comprehensive malpractice coverage.

QUESTIONS: PREVENTION

1. Should all lawyers be exposed to prevention strategies through law school, bar examination, or CLE initiatives?

2. Of all the strategies reviewed above, which strike you as most critical in addressing malpractice issues?

106. Anthony E. Davis, "Legal Ethics and Risk Management: Complementary Visions of Lawyer Regulation," 21 *Geo. J. Legal Ethics* 93 (2007) (arguing for institutionalized risk management systems and cultures that promote compliance).

107. For a range of proposals including in-house counsel positions, *see* Milton C. Regan, Jr., *Eat What You Kill: The Fall of a Wall Street Lawyer* 358–59 (2004); Anthony

V. Alfieri, "The Fall of Legal Ethics and the Rise of Risk Management," 96 *Geo. L. J.* 1909, 1947 (2007); Elizabeth Chambliss, "The Professionalization of Law Firm In-House Counsel Positions," 84 *N. Car. L. Rev.* 1515 (2006).

108. Alfieri, *supra* note 107, at 1947–48 (2007) (expressing concerns about the way that risk management may displace individual responsibility).

CHAPTER XVI

LEGAL EDUCATION

A. THE STRUCTURE OF LEGAL EDUCATION

INTRODUCTION

As Chapter XIV on admissions indicated, apprenticeship was the dominant system for legal education during the American legal profession's formative years. In the late eighteenth century, a few universities began establishing chairs in law along the lines of some British universities. However, most of the legal education that occurred outside the apprenticeship system centered in small proprietary law schools. At the height of their popularity during the early nineteenth century, there were about nineteen or twenty of these institutions. The most famous was the Litchfield Law School in Connecticut. Formally established in 1784, it focused on adapting Blackstone's *Commentaries* to American contexts and was influential in the development of the nation's early legal culture.[1]

These independent schools, and a small number of university counterparts, fared poorly during the Jacksonian era. As the bar's formal educational requirements eroded in response to populist demands, enrollments correspondingly declined. In 1840, the nation had only nine university-affiliated law schools with a total of 345 students.[2]

The characteristic features of modern legal education originated at Harvard Law School after the Civil War era. The development had much to do with the appointment of Charles Eliot to the university's presidency and Christopher Columbus Langdell to the newly created post of dean of the law school in 1870. Both had great faith in scientific methodology and its application to legal education. Langdell's case method attempted to derive general principles of law from appellate decisions in the same way that scientists sought to extract rules of nature from biological specimens. Langdell's goals were to institutionalize the case method and the Socratic style of teaching, and to establish law school as a three-year post-graduate requirement. Although students initially resisted the method and could "see nothing in the system but mental confusion and social humiliation," it quickly became the dominant model.[3]

---

1. For a comprehensive history, *see* Robert Stevens, *Law School: Legal Education in America from the 1850s to the 1980s* (1983).

2. Stevens, *supra* note 1, at 8. In 1860 only 9 of 39 states required any specific period of legal study. *Id.*

3. Charles Warren, 2 *History of Harvard Law School* 372–73 (quoting a student at the time, Samuel F. Batchelder). *See generally* Robert W. Gordon, "The Geologic Strata of the Law School Curriculum," 60 *Vand. L. Rev.* 339 (2007).

These initiatives coincided with a period of increased concern about educational standards within the profession and the culture generally. The American Bar Association, formed in 1870, established a Committee on Legal Education that soon recommended tighter admission standards. One of its first proposals was that states require attorneys to complete three years of law school. Similar recommendations also began emerging from the Association of American Law Schools. The formation of that Association in 1900 reflected broader social trends supporting higher education. By the turn of the century there were over a hundred university-affiliated law schools, and the number continued to increase over the next several decades.[4]

This formalization of professional education was not unique to law. And the trend was not without its critics. One of the most prominent was sociologist Thorstein Veblen, who maintained that "vocational" schools like law "belong[ed] in the modern university no more than a school of fencing or dancing."[5] Other commentators, although more sympathetic towards efforts to make professional education more rigorous, were unpersuaded that all forms of legal practice required the same academic preparation. That view was reflected in a celebrated 1921 Report for the Carnegie Foundation, *Training for the Public Profession of Law.* At the time of the Report's release, the American bar varied considerably in its education. The author, Alfred Reed, was a non-lawyer who advocated maintaining that diversity. According to Reed, the profession should recognize the dual nature of legal education and legal practice—i.e., the need for an elite corps of highly qualified lawyers to serve corporate and governmental clients, and the need for general practitioners, trained in night and part-time programs accessible to the working classes, to fill more routine legal needs. By institutionalizing this division, through two separate exams for two divisions of lawyers, the profession could accommodate concerns of quality and accessibility.

Both the ABA and the Association of American Law Schools (AALS) flatly rejected that recommendation. Most leaders of the bar appeared disappointed that the Reed Report had not followed the model of Abraham Flexner's 1910 review of medical education for the Carnegie Foundation. Unlike Reed, Flexner had proposed that all medical students complete a rigorous four-year program of university training. That recommendation found sufficient support within the medical profession and state legislatures to upgrade licensing requirements.[6] By contrast, the organized bar during the early twentieth century lacked sufficient unity or leverage to impose a comparable model of legal education. At the time of the Reed report, the ABA represented less than 10% of the nation's lawyers. Over a third of all law students were enrolled in night programs, and many

---

4. Lawrence Friedman, *A History of American Law* 607 (2d ed. 1985).

5. Thorstein Veblen, *The Higher Learning in America* 211 (1918).

6. *See generally* Michael Schudson, "The Flexner Report and the Reed Report: Notes on the History of Professional Education in the United States," 55 *Soc. Sci. Q.* 347 (1974).

constituencies within and outside the profession were reluctant to impose stringent educational requirements.[7]

Over the next several decades, however, the ABA and AALS leadership had increasing success in the battle to upgrade standards. A growing number of jurisdictions began accepting law school attendance as a substitute for apprenticeship, and eventually such attendance became the dominant method of professional training.

Controversies over appropriate requirements for entry to the profession have been only one aspect of a broader debate over the structure of legal education. Who should teach what, to whom, for how long, and by what method, have all been matters of longstanding dispute. The following discussion focuses on the most important and most contested issues.

1. Educational Structure

Law schools are subject to multiple regulatory systems. The United States Department of Education recognizes the American Bar Association as the nation's accrediting authority for professional training in law. Under that authority, the ABA's Council of the Section of Legal Education and Admission to the Bar has developed detailed accreditation standards governing matters such as classroom hours, student-faculty ratios, use of adjunct professors, library resources, and so forth. Once a school has established its compliance with these standards, it is subject to a site visit every seven years to insure its continued adherence to accreditation requirements. About four-fifths of the states require applicants to the bar to graduate from an ABA–accredited law school as well as pass a bar exam. The other states have developed their own accreditation systems, and California permits practice by graduates of unaccredited schools who have passed the bar exam. The Association of American Law Schools also has a membership review system with standards that are similar to the ABA's but in some respects less specific or more demanding. These oversight processes have been subject to frequent criticism but little sustained challenge. Periodically some educators have sought to make the system less rigid and expensive, and more open to shorter degree programs. By contrast, other constituencies have sought to impose more rigorous requirements that would ensure greater competency in practice.[8]

One controversy has involved accrediting authority. In the late 1990s, the Massachusetts School of Law, responded to its failure to obtain accreditation by unsuccessfully suing the ABA and the AALS on antitrust grounds. According to the Massachusetts School of Law complaint, the current accreditation system functions as a cartel by setting standards that unjustifiably raise the cost of legal education.[9] The MSL claims were rejected on both procedural and substantive grounds, and prompted the ABA and AALS to undertake only modest reforms. *Massachusetts School of Law v.*

---

7. *Id.* at 353–54.

8. *See* Roy Stucky et al., *Best Practices for Legal Education* 2 (2006).

9. Margaret Slade, "A Little Law School Does Battle With the ABA," *N.Y. Times*, Feb. 4, 1994, at A19.

ABA, 107 F.3d 1026 (3d Cir.), *cert. den.* 522 U.S. 907 (1997); 142 F.3d 26 (1st Cir.1998). However, similar concerns have emerged from other educators. The American Law Deans Association has challenged the accreditation process as enforcing "a one-size-fits-all" model of legal education that is overly intrusive, inflexible, concerned with details not relevant to school quality and terribly costly in administrative time as well as actual dollar costs to schools.[10] In particular, the Association has asked the Department of Education to remove the ABA's authority to require tenure or long term contracts for clinicians, library directors and writing instructors; in the deans' view, these requirements lead to fewer appointments and limits program development.[11] So too, the Association and other educators have challenged the ABA's minimum LSAT scores and bar passage requirements, which restrict access to the profession by students of color, and other resource-related requirements, which prevent more affordable tuition.[12]

Despite significant dissatisfaction with the current accreditation structure, there is little consensus about how to fix it. Some educators and bar leaders would like to eliminate or substantially curtail accreditation requirements. From their vantage point, a free market of reasonably well-informed students and legal employers would promote more experimentation, competition, and ultimately cost-effective education than the current regulatory system.

By contrast, other lawyers and legal academics question how many students and legal employers would have sufficient knowledge to create a well-functioning free market. Some bar leaders would like to tighten, not loosen, accreditation standards in certain areas such as skills training. An influential report by an ABA Task Force on Law Schools and the Profession, *Narrowing the Gap* (the MacCrate Report), identified ten core skills and four central values necessary for any "well-trained generalist to practice law competently and professionally." The "Fundamental Lawyering Skills" describes functions common to nearly all areas of practice: (1) problem solving, (2) legal analysis and reasoning, (3) legal research, (4) factual investigation, (5) communication, (6) counseling, (7) negotiation, (8) litigation and alternative dispute-resolution procedures, (9) organization and management of legal work, and (10) recognition and resolution of ethical dilemmas.[13] Providing training in all of these areas requires enriching, not shortening, current degree programs.

10. Courtney Leatherman, "Rebellion Brews in Tight–knit World of Law Accreditation," *Chronicle of Higher Education*, June 1, 1994, at A14, A16.

11. Leigh Jones, "ABA's Tenure Power Is Disputed," *Nat'l L. J.*, April 3, 2006, at A1, A12.

12. Leigh Jones, "ABA Moves to Tighten Bar Passage Standards," *Nat'l L. J.*, July 9, 2007, 4; Michael Coyle, "End the ABA's Tyranny," *Nat'l L. J.*, Aug. 21, 2006, at A22;

George B. Shepherd, "Law School: Make it Optional," *Legal Times*, available at *Law. com, Legal News Online*, Oct. 5, 2005.

13. American Bar Association Section of Legal Education and Admissions to the Bar, *Legal Education and Professional Development—An Educational Continuum, Report of the Task Force on Law Schools and the Profession: Narrowing the Gap* (1992) [MacCrate Report].

Other constituencies also support stiffer standards for different, more self-interested reasons. Many lawyers advocate heightened qualifications as a way to reduce the number of new entrants to a bar that already seems overcrowded. So too, some law school administrators support stringent accreditation standards as leverage in resource negotiations with central university decision-makers. The need to comply with accreditation requirements governing libraries, faculty size, and so forth has enabled law schools to hold onto resources that might otherwise support poorer departments.

Part of what makes consensus in this area so difficult is that legal education has multiple constituencies with competing agendas. Law schools are expected to produce both "Pericles and plumbers"—lawyer–statesmen and routine service providers.[14] Faculty and students have differing interests, and ones that are not necessarily identical with those of the ultimate consumers—clients and the public. Education is one of the rare contexts where some buyers want less for their money. Many students find the current system too expensive and too removed from practice; they would like to earn a degree with the minimal effort required to pass a bar examination and land a job. In the absence of strict accreditation standards, law schools might need to reduce costs and quality standards in order to compete for applicants who viewed "less as more," regardless of the impact on the public.[15] Consider these issues in light of Richard Posner's argument for "letting the market decide." If you were the federal official charged with overseeing law school accreditation structures, would you agree with his proposal?

Richard A. Posner, "Let Employers Insist If Three Years of Law School is Necessary"

San Francisco Daily Journal, December 15, 1999, A4.

We have no theory of education, and so the only way an educational policy or program can be evaluated is by subjecting it to competition. When government prescribes educational policy, not just for public schools but for all schools, it thwarts the competitive process. That is the situation with regard to legal education.

Government has decreed that anyone who wants to be a lawyer must go to law school for three years. As a result, we have no experimental or otherwise empirical basis (and no compelling theoretical reason, simply because as I have said there is no good theory of education, including legal education) for believing that law school has to take so long, at enormous cost; not just the tuition, . . . but the foregone income that the student would have had, had he been working instead of going to school.

---

14. William Twining, "Pericles and the Plumber," 83 *L. Q. Rev.* 396 (1967). *See also* Herbert M. Kritzer, "The Future Role of 'Law Workers': Rethinking the Forms of Legal Practice and the Scope of Legal Education," 44 *Ariz. L. Rev.* 917 (2002).

15. Deborah L. Rhode, *In the Interests of Justice: Reforming the Legal Profession* 188 (2000).

Graduate schools of business grant an M.B.A. after only two years, and the business world seems not to be suffering as a result of the "abbreviated" education that their students receive. Business education, not incidentally, is an unregulated branch of education. The two-year M.B.A. is the upshot of a competitive process among business schools.

It will be argued that law students can't make a judgment whether they need a third year of law school; they are too immature and too ignorant about law. Maybe so. But employers know whether a third year of law school is necessary. If they think it is, they will not hire students who have not completed a third year of law school, or they will pay students who leave earlier much less. . . . There is no need for government to do the insisting.

I am willing to concede the case for some paternalism. Some newly graduated lawyers hang out their own shingle rather than going to work for a law firm or other knowledgeable employer, and perhaps consumers need protection from the under-educated lawyer, if that is how a person who has not completed the third year of law school should be described. If consumer protection is needed in this area, it can be provided by stiffening the bar exam, or perhaps by giving a special bar exam to students who don't complete the third year, or perhaps by confining the title "lawyer" to the three-year graduate and assigning another title, such as "legal advocate" or "legal counselor" to practitioners who have not had three years of law school.

Courts, too, need protection from lawyers who lack the skills or experience to handle a trial. But the necessary protection can be obtained by court rules requiring demonstrated skills and experience, not completion of an artificially determined period of schooling.

I don't think the deregulation of legal education would lead to the disappearance of the third year. Many employers and many students may decide that the educational benefits of a third year exceed the costs. What I think is certain, however, is that removing an artificial barrier to competition will result in a better third year. The law faculties will no longer have a captive audience. They will have to demonstrate to students and employers that the third year provides real value added to the students and to the profession. . . .

We might see the third year deferred rather than extinguished. It is typical now for students to enter graduate business schools after several years of working. Some lawyers may want after years of practice to return for a third year of law school to hone their skills or retool for a different practice.

NOTES AND QUESTIONS

1. If you were a member of the ABA or AALS committees charged with reassessing the accreditation process, what would you recommend? How much uniform national regulation is appropriate? Should all applicants to

the bar graduate from accredited law schools? Should accreditation be voluntary?[16] Who should decide?

2. Should accrediting authorities encourage greater diversity among law schools? For example, should institutions be able to offer two-year programs or adopt cost-cutting measures? The price of legal education grew dramatically during the 1990s, well beyond the rate of inflation or the increase in cost of undergraduate education.[17] By far the largest law school expenditure accounting for tuition hikes was financial aid. Other rising costs resulted from lower faculty-student ratios, expanded skills and writing instruction, improved technology, and additional bar preparation and student services.[18] The decline of mentoring in private practice has pushed more schools to focus on teaching students not just to *"think"* like a lawyer," but also to *"be"* a lawyer," which requires more expensive clinical course work.[19]

Could certain areas of law school budgets be cut without a significant loss in educational quality? Or should more financial assistance and loan forgiveness programs be available, as some commentary in Part II suggests? How should accrediting agencies assess educational quality? Should they focus less on inputs, such as faculty/student ratios, and library resources, and more on outputs, such as the effectiveness of instruction and the competence of graduates? How could such outputs be assessed? Are current measures of bar exam passage rates and placement statistics adequate?

3. Is there a sense in which law school accreditation is a "combination . . . or conspiracy in restraint of trade" even if not in the sense prohibited by the Sherman Antitrust Act? If so, what follows from that fact?

4. In 2008, Northwestern University's law school announced that it was introducing a two-year option; previously, the University of Dayton had done the same. Both are five-semester programs, and include the same number of courses and credits as the three-year option; the two-year alternative is designed for students willing to take more courses and credits each semester. At the time of the announcement, Northwestern had not decided whether students would continue to pay the full three-year tuition, but its dean pointed out that under the two-year option students would benefit financially by entering the work world a year sooner.[20] Do the Northwestern and Dayton plans fulfill the goals Judge Posner outlines in his proposal?

---

16. Shepherd, *supra* note 12.

17. John A. Sebert, "The Cost and Financing of Legal Education," 52 *J. Legal Educ.* 516 (2002) (noting that the Consumer Price Index grew 32%, the average private law school tuition grew 86%, and the average public non-resident tuition grew 113%); Coyle, *supra* note 12 (noting that undergraduate education increased 58% and law schools grew 88%).

18. Sebert, *supra* note 17, at 524.

19. Richard Matasar, "The Rise and Fall of American Legal Education," 49 *New York L. S. L. Rev.* 465, 472–73 (2004).

20. "An Elite Law Degree–In Two Years," *Inside Higher Ed*, June 20, 2008, available at http://www.insidehighered.com/news/2008/06/20/northwestern.

2. THE ROLE OF RANKINGS

Another factor that many observers believe has adversely affected law school diversity and priorities is rankings, particularly those of *U.S. News and World Report*. Students, faculty, alumni, donors, and funders are all concerned with how well their institutions measure up in comparison with rivals, and rankings have become a crucial index of status. These educational scorecards have had some benefits. Some relevant characteristics can be objectively assessed, and schools should be held accountable for their performance. Ratings can supply a counterweight to complacency and a check on puffing. In their absence, applicants would undoubtedly encounter an educational "Lake Woebegon," where all institutions were above average.[21] But the problem with rankings like those in *U.S. News and World Report* is that they assign a single score based on arbitrary weightings of a partial list of characteristics, many of which bear little relation to the quality of education. This pecking order then implies a false precision that assumes undue influence, and skews decision making by applicants and the institutions themselves.

U.S. News rankings typically place heavy reliance on reputation, measured by the subjective perceptions of top administrators. As these individuals freely acknowledge, they rarely possess enough systematic knowledge about other institutions to make accurate comparative judgments.[22] Those surveyed often depend on word-of-mouth reputations and prior rankings, which create a self-perpetuating dynamic. Past recognition provides a halo effect, which perpetuates high scores even when the evaluator knows nothing about current performance. This explains why Princeton's and MIT's law schools do so well, even though they do not exist.[23] Rankings also affect the size of applicant pools and resources from alumni giving, which are part of what the rankings measure, and which add to their self-reinforcing effects.

The more objective factors that influence ratings are problematic for other reasons. Almost all of these factors measure inputs, such as the test scores of the entering class, alumni contributions, and library books per student, which receive arbitrary weights and bear no necessary relationship to the quality of the learning experience. The main measure of output is placement rates, which are often subject to manipulation. Moreover, even minor changes in the way that data are collected or assessed can cause significant fluctuations in rankings, which affect admissions, morale, and alumni relations out of all proportion to what the changes signify about the

21. Deborah L. Rhode, *In Pursuit of Knowledge: Scholars, Status, and Academic Culture* 7 (2006); William Henderson with Andrew Morriss, "Rank Economics: Law Schools Have No One to Blame but Themselves for the Power of U.S. News Rankings," *The American Lawyer*, June 2007, at 81–82.

22. Wendy Nelson Espeland & Michael Saunder, "Rankings and Reactivity: How Public Measures Recreate Social Worlds," 113 *Am. J. Sociology* 1, 13–14 (2007); Colin Diver, "Is There Life After Ranking?," *Atlantic Monthly*, November, 2005, at 136–137; Leigh Jones, "Ranking Time Brings Rain of Glossy Promos: Law Schools Send 'Law Porn' to Gain Edge in Rankings," 28 *Nat'l L. J.*, October 31, 2005 (quoting Paul Caron), at 6.

23. Espeland & Saunder, *supra* note 22, at 11–14; Rhode, *supra* note 21, at 7; Matasar, *supra* note 19, at 478.

institutional environment. Worse still, the undue importance of these rankings among students, faculty, employers, and alumni donors has led to various unwelcome practices. Some institutions have fudged the facts or engaged in strategic behaviors, such as giving unjustly low evaluations to close competitors in reputational surveys; denying admission to qualified minorities with low test scores or placing them in night or part-time programs that do not count in ratings; manipulating academic leaves and titles to improve student/ faculty ratios, or hiring their own graduates on a short term basis to improve job placement records.[24] Moreover, the ranking system discourages investment in many areas that enhance educational quality but are not rated, such as access to clinical courses, well-designed public service programs, and a diverse faculty and student body. Instead, the premium placed on reputation encourages overinvestment in scholarship at the expense of teaching, and expensive public relations campaigns that do nothing to improve the learning environment.[25]

QUESTIONS

1. Is there anything that law schools or professional associations could do to counteract the unwanted affects of rankings?

2. Should law schools attempt a collective boycott of rankings, as have a number of liberal arts colleges? Although much of the data used in rankings is publicly available from the ABA, administrators and faculty could refuse to provide reputational information.[26] Another that some commentators advocate is for the ABA to collect and publish easily accessible standardized information on matters of particular student concern, such as bar passage rates, the proportion of graduates taking jobs in particular practice areas, the availability of skills courses, and so forth.[27] To what extent would this reduce the importance of *U.S. News* rankings? Should the ABA audit the information schools provide?

3. How would you weigh the benefits of rankings against their drawbacks? Are there better ways to provide public information about law schools and to hold them accountable?

3. Educational Content and Methodology

Other controversial issues in legal education involve curricular priorities and teaching approaches. Some of the disputes stem from the slightly

---

24. Diver, *supra* note 22, at 137; Linda Edwards, "The Rankings Czar," *ABA J.*, April 2008, at 38, 41 (quoting Brian Leiter's characterization of placement data as a "work of the imagination"); Alex Wellen, "The $8.78 Million Makeover," *N.Y. Times*, July 31, 2005, at 4A, 18–19; Espeland and Saunder, *supra* note 22, at 28–30; Henderson & Morriss, *supra* note 21, at 81.

25. Rhode, *supra* note 20, at 8; Espeland & Saunder, *supra* note 21, at 26. Nearly every dean interviewed in a recent study reported being inundated by materials they never looked at. As one put it, "I can't imagine how bored I'd have to be to read one of those things. But we send them out because.... we need to get our name out there." *Id.*

26. Leigh Jones, "Law Schools Unlikely to Boycott Magazine Rankings: Fallout From Liberal Arts Boycott Minimal—So Far" 29 *Nat'l L. J.*, June 25, 2007, at 22.

27. Henderson & Morriss, *supra* note 21, at 81.

schizophrenic role that modern legal education has attempted to play. In seeking to advance legal knowledge as well as convey practical skills, law schools have run the risk of doing neither very well. According to many critics, contemporary legal education offers too little theory and too little practice. It provides inadequate training in basic skills and too little grounding in disciplines that should inform legal analysis and legal practice, such as philosophy, psychology, history, finance, and management. Those criticisms, explored more fully in the excerpts below, raise several related issues: law schools' traditional reliance on the case method and the Socratic discussion format; their failure to support students' public interest commitments; their inadequate attention to practical and interpersonal skills; and their creation of highly stressful, competitive environments that may fail to provide adequate evaluation, mentoring, and support services.

Duncan Kennedy, Legal Education and the Reproduction of Hierarchy

i, ii, 3, 5–7, 16–17, 20–22, 58, 65, 68, 70, 101–03, 214–15 (Revised edition 2004).

This is an essay about the role of legal education in American social life. It is a description of the ways in which legal education contributes to the reproduction of illegitimate hierarchy in the bar and in society. . . .

The general thesis is that law schools are intensely *political* places, in spite of the fact that they seem intellectually unpretentious, barren of theoretical ambition or practical vision of what social life might be. The trade school mentality, the endless attention to trees at the expense of forests, the alternating grimness and chumminess of focus on the limited task at hand, all these are only a part of what is going on. The other part is ideological training for willing service in the hierarchies of the corporate welfare state . . .

The First Year Experience

The initial classroom experience sustains rather than dissipates ambivalence. The teachers are overwhelmingly white, male, and deadeningly straight and middle class in manner. The classroom is hierarchical with a vengeance, the teacher receiving a degree of deference and arousing fears that remind one of high school rather than college. The sense of autonomy one has in a lecture, with the rule that you must let teacher drone on without interruption balanced by the rule that teacher can't *do* anything to you, is gone. In its place is a demand for a pseudo-participation in which you struggle desperately, in front of a large audience, to read a mind determined to elude you. . . .

The actual intellectual content of the law seems to consist of learning rules, what they are and why they have to be the way they are, while rooting for the occasional judge who seems willing to make them marginally more humane. The basic experience is of double surrender: to a passivizing classroom experience and to a passive attitude toward the content of the legal system.

The first step toward this sense of the irrelevance of liberal or left thinking is the opposition in the first year curriculum between the technical, boring, difficult, obscure legal case, and the occasional case with outrageous facts and a piggish judicial opinion endorsing or tolerating the outrage. The first kind of case—call it a cold case—is a challenge to interest, understanding, even to wakefulness. It can be on any subject, so long as it is of no political or moral or emotional significance. Just to understand what happened and what's being said about it, you have to learn a lot of new terms, a little potted legal history, and lots of rules, none of which is carefully explained by the casebook or the teacher. It is difficult to figure out why the case is there in the first place, difficult to figure out whether one has grasped it, and difficult to anticipate what the teacher will ask and what one should respond.

The other kind of case usually involves a sympathetic plaintiff, say an Appalachian farm family, and an unsympathetic defendant, say a coal company. On first reading, it appears that the coal company has screwed the farm family, say by renting their land for strip mining, with a promise to restore it to its original condition once the coal has been extracted, and then reneging on the promise. And the case should include a judicial opinion that does something like awarding a meaningless couple of hundred dollars to the farm family, rather than making the coal company do the restoration work.

The point of the class discussion will be that your initial reaction of outrage is naive, non-legal, irrelevant to what you're supposed to be learning, and may be substantively wrong in the bargain. There are good reasons for the awful result, when you take a legal and logical view, as opposed to a knee-jerk passionate view, and if you can't muster those reasons, maybe you aren't cut out to be a lawyer . . . .

The Ideological Content of Legal Education

. . . Law schools teach . . . rather rudimentary, essentially instrumental skills in a way that almost completely mystifies them for almost all law students. The mystification has three parts. First, the schools teach skills through class discussions of cases in which it is asserted that law emerges from a rigorous analytical procedure called "legal reasoning," which is unintelligible to the layman, but somehow both explains and validates the great majority of the rules in force in our system. At the same time, the class context and the materials present every legal issue as distinct from every other, as a tub on its own bottom, so to speak, with no hope or even any reason to hope that from law study one might derive an integrating vision of what law is, how it works, or how it might be changed (other than in an incremental, case by case, reformist way).

Second, the teaching of skills in the mystified context of legal reasoning about utterly unconnected legal problems means that skills are taught badly, unselfconsciously, to be absorbed by osmosis as one picks up the knack of "thinking like a lawyer." Bad or only randomly good teaching generates and then accentuates real differences and imagined differences in student capabilities. But it does so in such a way that students don't know when they are learning and when they aren't, and have no way of improving or even understanding their own learning processes. They experience skills training as the gradual emergence of differences among themselves, as a process of ranking that reflects something that is just "there" inside them.

Third, the schools teach skills in isolation from actual lawyering experience. "Legal reasoning" is sharply distinguished from law practice, and one learns nothing about practice. This procedure disables students from any future role but that of apprentice in a law firm organized in the same manner as a law school, with older lawyers controlling the content and pace of depoliticized craft training in a setting of intense competition and no feedback. . . .

This whole body of implicit messages is nonsense. Legal reasoning is not distinct, *as a method for reaching correct results*, from ethical and political discourse in general (i.e., from policy analysis). It is true that there is a distinctive lawyers' body of knowledge of the rules in force. It is true that there are distinctive lawyers' argumentative techniques for spotting gaps, conflicts and ambiguities in the rules, for arguing broad and narrow holdings of cases, and for generating pro and con policy arguments. But these are *only* argumentative techniques. There is never a "correct legal solution" that is other than the correct ethical and political solution to that legal problem. . . .

[Conservative political] bias arises because law school teaching makes the choice of hierarchy and domination, which is implicit in the adoption of the rules of property, contract and tort, look as though it flows from legal reasoning, rather than from politics and economics. . . . The message is that the system is basically OK, since we have patched up the few areas open to abuse, and that it has a limited but important place for value-oriented debate about further change and improvement. If there is to be more fundamental questioning, it is relegated to the periphery of history or philosophy. The real world is kept at bay by treating clinical legal education, which might bring in a lot of information threatening to the cozy liberal consensus, as free legal drudge work for the local bar or as mere skills training. . . .

The Modeling of Hierarchical Relationships

Yet another way in which legal education contributes causally to the hierarchies of the bar is through . . . law teachers that model for students how they are supposed to think, feel and act in their future professional roles. Some of this is a matter of teaching by example, some of it a matter of more active learning from interactions that are a kind of clinical education for lawyerlike behavior. . . .

Often, it boils down to law review. At first, everyone claims they aren't interested, wouldn't want to put in the time, don't work hard enough to make it, can't stand the elitism of the whole thing. But most students give about equal time to fantasies of flunking out and fantasies of grabbing the brass ring. And even though the class has been together for a semester or a year, everything is still different after the lightning of grades. An instant converts jerks into statesmen; honored spokespeople retire to the margins, shamed. Try proposing that law review should be open to anyone who will do the work. Within a week or two, the new members have a dozen arguments for competitive selection. Likewise at the hour of partnership. . . .

The culmination of law school as training for professional hierarchy is the placement process, with the form of the culmination depending on where your school fits in the pecking order. . . . By dangling the bait, making clear the rules of the game, and then subjecting almost everyone to intense anxiety about their acceptability, firms structure entry into the profession so as to maximize acceptance of hierarchy. If you feel you've succeeded, you're forever grateful, and you have a vested interest. If you feel you've failed, you blame yourself, when you aren't busy feeling envy. When you get to be the hiring partner, you'll have a visceral understanding of what's at stake, but it will be hard even to imagine why someone might want to change it. . . .

What this means is that lawyers can have and should have workplace struggles, no matter where they are situated in the hierarchy of the bar, and whether or not they are actively engaged in political law practice. For law students, it means that it is important to have a law school struggle, even if they are spending most of their time on extra-curricular activities that support oppressed people.

Afterword

(From the 2004 edition of the original 1983 publication)

The system described in LERH [Legal Education and the Reproduction of Hierarchy] has gotten tighter in the ensuing twenty years. . . . The bar is even more highly stratified than it used to be, with greater differences in incomes but also in the organization of firms and in the class origins and current prestige of practitioners. The system rigidly determines a place for everyone and everyone in his or her place. . . .

Behind the hierarchy of law firms, there is the feeder system of the hierarchy of law schools. As one researcher recently put it, "the identity of the institution from which a graduate received the J.D. degree may be the single most important factor in the graduate's career path." Average student indebtedness has increased . . . for the maybe 80 percent of law students who borrow. Job security for associates has gone out the window as their first-year compensation has increased, so the chances that you will be let go or that your firm will go under or merge into an entity that no longer needs you are way up, and the chances that you will end up a partner in your first employer are way down.

Radicalism does *not* mean believing that by forming law student study groups you can abolish this system. It does mean finding some way to rebel in law school. . . . It means recognizing the system for what it is when, all around you, your fellow lawyers are denying that it exists or glorying in what they happen to be getting out of it at the moment. It means rejecting it as both unjust and socially unnecessary. It means trying to locate other people who feel the same way, without getting yourself fired. It means looking for small enactments of rejection and resistance that affirm that one is a person of moral substance. And it means looking for the targets of opportunity that might allow building a minoritarian alliance over time that could sustain itself. After graduation, it seems to me to mean first of all trying to find a morally tolerable law firm to work for, or to move to from whatever firm one is forced into working for by the status degradation ritual of the law school placement process.

QUESTIONS

1.   Compare Duncan Kennedy's critique to those offered by the Carnegie Foundation and by feminists and critical race theorists in Part B below. To what extent do these accounts match your own experience?

2.   Do Kennedy or the Carnegie Foundation offer an adequate explanation of the forces that sustain existing institutional practices and the forces that would encourage change? If not, what explanations would you offer?

3.   In commenting on Kennedy's article, Wisconsin law professor Stewart Macaulay predicts that few law professors would agree with his critique:

> Most would dilute his position greatly before they accepted it or, more likely, they would ignore it.... [My own view is that] Kennedy certainly is right that the first year of law school will be hard on students who question capitalism, liberal pluralism, or the existing distributions of wealth, privilege, and status in the society ..... A slightly idealistic first-year student often makes a statement in class which the professor can push into the form of "it is just to equalize wealth; X is the poorer of the parties and Y is a large corporation with a deep pocket; therefore X ought to win." When a master teacher is through, the student or one of his susceptible classmates will have asserted the virtues of rewards to the efficient who create wealth for all of us, the virtues of holding individuals responsible for their actions, and the evils of paternalism which robs the weaker of their choice and substitutes that of a purported expert. In a well-run class, all will see visions of grass growing in the streets if courts were to yield to softhearted sentiment. Other skilled teachers will drive home the message that the redistribution of wealth may be an appropriate function of legislatures in a pluralistic society but falls out of bounds for courts; however, they seldom examine seriously the likely consequences of this position. While such conclusions may flow from our political outlook, it would be hard to call them neutral or scientific with a straight face.

> Even when the message of a first-year classroom is not so openly political, there is another message which is part of the process of transforming entering students into apprentice lawyers. A strong les-

son is that there is always an argument the other way, and the Devil usually has a very good case. . . . The successful student learns that there are no answers but just arguments.[28]

This process, asserts Macaulay, tends to undermine ethical conviction and progressive political commitments. Kennedy has argued that the first year of law school undermines strongly-felt conservative commitments as well.

Do you agree with this description? Consider such claims in the light of the materials that follow. If Kennedy and Macaulay are right, what implications follow from their critique?

NOTES

Concerns about contemporary legal education cluster around four main themes: the dominant instructional methods of casebooks and Socratic dialogue; the erosion of public interest commitments; the inadequacy of skills instruction; and the nature of law school culture.

The Case Method and Socratic Style of Instruction

Modern legal education has largely rejected Langdell's premises about law as a science, based on deductive principles independent of political influence. Yet his approach is often said to "rule us from the grave." A diluted case method and quasi-Socratic style still characterize many law school classrooms. The reasons have much to do with the adaptability of this method for large classes; its corresponding low costs; and its perceived ability to sharpen analytic and verbal advocacy skills; as well as to accommodate different intellectual approaches.

However, the case approach is highly limited and somewhat of a misnomer. It does not require study of actual cases, although that, as legal realists noted, would be "little enough." It directs attention only to the text of judicial opinions, a censored account that leaves out much of the "living process" of the law.[29] What it often ignores is the translation of a dispute into a legal grievance; the investigation, negotiation, and presentation of parties' claims; the unstated factors influencing judicial decision making; the consequences of that decision on the individuals involved; alternative methods of resolving disputes; and the social, political, and economic backdrop of the process. The focus on American legal doctrine also marginalizes the importance of other legal institutions such as legislatures and administrative agencies, and the global context in which lawyers increasingly practice. These limitations in dominant teaching techniques have helped to produce corresponding limitations in legal scholarship.

The Socratic style of presenting cases has also provoked criticism. At its best, the Socratic method develops verbal and analytic skills, and

28. Stewart Macaulay, "Law Schools and the World Outside the Doors: Some Notes on Two Recent Studies of the Chicago Bar," 32 *J. Legal Educ.* 506, 521–25 (1982).

29. Jerome Frank, "Why Not a Clinical Lawyer–School?," 81 *U.Pa.L.Rev.* 907 (1933).

promotes self-critical understanding of varied viewpoints.[30] At its worst, in Ralph Nader's phrase, this controlled dialogue offers students only freedom to "roam in an intellectual cage."[31] Too often, faculty first invite the student to "guess what I'm thinking," and then find the response inevitably lacking; professors are "fishing for the 'right' answers and students [are] trying to catch the hook."[32] The result is a "culture of competition and conformity," in which "never is heard an encouraging word," and "thoughts remain cloudy all day."[33] Alternatively, professors who seek to be more humane, and to avoid interrupting or "putting down" students, may leave the rest of the class bored or confused.[34]

In either case, this classroom method rewards an ability to give quick, often superficial answers. And, as Martha Nussbaum notes, to acknowledge doubt, "a key Socratic virtue—will not get the student very far."[35] Critics argue that such an atmosphere can diminish students' self-confidence and encourage corrosive skepticism. By depersonalizing and decontextualizing inquiry, it also marginalizes issues of justice and can foster an impoverished understanding of the lawyer's role.[36] In response to such criticisms, increasing numbers of professors are seeking more egalitarian and reflective classroom approaches.

In contrast to these criticisms, Anthony Kronman (a philosopher as well as former dean of the Yale Law School) has defended the case method as an instrument for broadening the moral imaginations of law students, enhancing their ability to understand a variety of conflicting values that are not necessarily better or worse than each other (Kronman uses the term "incommensurable"), making lawyers more public-spirited, and cultivating a generally, and benignly, conservative outlook.

Anthony T. Kronman, The Lost Lawyer: Failing Ideals of The Legal Profession

113–19, 154–61 (1993).

The case method of law teaching presents students with a series of concrete disputes and compels them to reenact these disputes by playing the roles of the original contestants or their lawyers. It thus forces them to see things from a range of different points of view and to entertain the

30. Philip Areeda, "The Socratic Method," 109 *Harv. L. Rev.* 917 (1996).

31. Ralph Nader, "Law Schools and Law Firms," *New Republic*, Oct. 11, 1969, at 20–21, 23.

32. Susan Sturm & Lani Guinier, "The Law School Matrix: Reforming Legal Education in a Culture of Competition and Conformity," 60 *Vand. L. Rev.* 515, 532 (2007).

33. *Id.*; Grant Gilmore, "What Is a Law School?," 15 *Conn.L.Rev.* 1 (1983).

34. *See* Phillip E. Areeda, "The Socratic Method," 109 *Harv. L. Rev.* 911 (1996).

35. Martha C. Nussbaum, "Cultivating Humanity in Legal Education," 70 *Chi. L. Rev.* 265, 272 (2003).

36. William M. Sullivan et al., *Educating Lawyers: Preparation for the Profession of Law* (Carnegie Foundation Report, 2007); Rhode, *supra* note 15, at 197; Philip C. Kissam, *The Discipline of Law Schools: The Making of Modern Lawyers* 41–43 (2003). For a key early development of this criticism, *see* Roger Cramton, "The Ordinary Religion of the Law School Classroom," 29 *J.Legal Ed.* 247 (1978).

claims associated with each, broadening their capacity for sympathy by taxing it in unexpected ways. But it also works in the opposite direction. For the student who has been assigned a partisan position and required to defend it is likely to be asked a moment later for his views regarding the wisdom of the judge's decision in the case. To answer, he must disengage himself from the sympathetic attachments he may have formed as a committed, if imaginary, participant and reexamine the case from a disinterested judicial point of view. The case method thus works simultaneously to strengthen both the student's powers of sympathetic understanding and his ability to suppress all sympathies in favor of a judge's scrupulous neutrality. Most important, it increases his tolerance for the disorientation that movement back and forth between these different attitudes occasions. In this way the case method serves as a forcing ground for the moral imagination by cultivating that peculiar bifocality that [is] its most essential property.

One aim of this complex exercise in advocacy and detachment is the cultivation of those perceptual habits that lawyers need in practice. Forcing students to defend positions they do not believe in or that they consider morally offensive may seem arbitrary and insensitive, but it serves an important goal. The student who is put in this position must strain to see the claim he has been given to defend in its most attractive light. He must work to discover its strengths and to articulate them, and this he cannot do unless he temporarily puts his earlier convictions to one side. In this way students get used to looking with a friendly eye even at those positions they personally reject, and before long they acquire some skill at identifying the strengths and weaknesses of whatever claim is presented to them, those that are unfamiliar or morally distasteful as well as those they recognize and endorse. Gradually, much of this becomes habitual.... [I]n time it increases a person's powers of empathic understanding and relaxes the boundaries that initially restrict his sympathies to what he knows and likes.

Some students find this experience disturbing and complain that the case method, which makes every position respectable, undermines their sense of integrity and personal self-worth. It is easy to understand why. For the discovery in oneself of a developing capacity to see the point of positions that previously seemed thoughtless or unfair is often accompanied by a corresponding sense of more critical detachment from one's earlier commitments, and this can lead to the feeling of being unmoored with no secure convictions and hence no identity at all.

This experience, which law student sometimes describe, not inappropriately, as the experience of losing one's soul, strongly suggests that the process of legal education does more than impart knowledge and promote new perceptual habits. In addition it works—is meant to work—upon the students' dispositions by strengthening their capacity for sympathetic understanding. The strengthening of this capacity often brings with it the dulling or displacement of earlier convictions and a growing appreciation of the incommensurability of values, changes of attitude that many experience as personally transforming. It is this unsettling experience that underlies the law student's concern that his professional education threatens to rob him of his soul—an anxiety no mere increment in knowledge or refinement of perception can explain. . . .

The case method is largely an exercise in forced role-playing. But it is important to remember that among the roles students are invited to play is that of a judge, and to recognize that the priority of this role over others is embedded in the method itself.

If the effort to entertain the claims of the parties to a lawsuit demands enlarged powers of sympathy and leads to a loss of ideological conviction, to a blurring of the distinction between right and wrong, and to a diminished faith in the commensurability of values generally, the case method's emphasis on the priority of the judicial point of view underscores the need to conclude the dispute despite these uncertainties and to do so not by fiat but in a reasoned and publicly justifiable manner instead. In this way the case method provides its own counterweight to the student's growing acceptance of complexity and pluralism in the realm of values, and blocks the slide to what might otherwise become the cynical celebration of arbitrariness. It does this by habituating students to the need for reasoned judgment under conditions of maximum moral ambiguity, and by giving them practice at rendering such judgments themselves. The result is a combination of attitudes in tension with one another: an expanded capacity for sympathetic understanding coupled with the ability to see every claim with the coldest and most distant, most judicial, eye; a broad familiarity with diverse and irreconcilable human goods coupled with an indefatigable willingness to enter the fray, hear the arguments, render judgment, and articulate the reasons that support it, even when all hope of moral certainty is gone. At war with itself, this complex set of attitudes nonetheless describes a recognizable moral ideal, . . . distinguishable from the indifferent cynicism that some believe the case method of instruction tends inevitably to produce. . . .

The privileged position that the case method assigns the judicial point of view has another important consequence. Judges are expected to decide cases in a disinterested manner, meaning without concern for their own personal advantage. . . . By a process of transference that the case method deliberately exploits, the judicial attitude that a student begins by mimicking becomes to some degree his own, and the student himself takes on a measure of the public-spiritedness that distinguishes the judge's view of legal conflict. The student to whom this has happened tends instinctively to look at the law and to argue about its meaning in the same way that a judge would, and even more important, to care with new intensity about the good of the legal system and the community it represents. . . .

[T]he case method encourages . . . the tendency to take a conservative view of law and politics, in a sense I shall explain. . . . [T]his method tends inevitably to promote a certain skepticism regarding the power of abstract ideas and to encourage a kind of pragmatic gradualism that constitutes the core of one familiar species of legal and political conservatism. . . . Because it systematically selects for [close cases with plausible arguments on both sides], the case method tends to encourage a preference for narrow justifications over broad ones, and to discourage the belief that hard cases—the cases of greatest professional interest to lawyers—can be decided on the basis of abstract principles that sweep too broadly and omit too much of the peculiarities that distinguish the specific case at hand.

The case method thus undermines students' faith in the power of abstract ideas as instruments of analysis and control and focuses their attention on the details of specific cases instead, encouraging them to search in these details for some small distinguishing mark, some marginal qualification, that will permit them to decide a particular case one way or another without compromising too greatly the losing principle the case involves....

By encouraging a certain skepticism toward the usefulness of abstract ideas as instruments of legal judgment, the case method thus promotes a preference for gradualism in politics generally. This is one way in which it works to inculcate a conservative outlook among lawyers ... This ideal is an essentially conservative one.... Recognizing the moral imperative for change, the lawyer who embraces this ideal will nevertheless prefer to move slowly and by small degrees. He or she will be repelled by all programs of utopian ambition ..., and in the quirks and absurdities of the status quo will be likely to see what no utopian can: a whole series of unthought-out local compromises and adjustments that reflect the plurality of human goods and soften the consequences of their inevitable conflict.

The lawyer-statesman whose portrait I have sketched is not a mindless defender of the status quo, but is temperamentally inclined to see a value in the irregularities of the existing order and to proceed with caution in leveling them out.

QUESTIONS

1. Does Kronman accurately describe the intellectual and personal changes that the case method encourages?

2. Both Kennedy and Kronman believe that legal education makes law students more conservative in their outlook. It is important to realize that Kronman does not mean that law school promotes right-wing views. "Conservative" in his sense means "resistant to sweeping social change," in a right-wing as well as left-wing direction. Kennedy criticizes this conservatizing tendency of legal education, whereas Kronman praises it. How would each of them respond to the other's arguments? How would you?

The Erosion of Public Interest Commitments and the Rise of Student Debt
NOTES

The influence of the law school socialization process has been much studied and much debated. Most commentators, including those in a recent

Carnegie Foundation Report, *Educating Lawyers*, assume that legal education has a substantial effect in shaping student values, perceptions, and professional careers.[37] A frequent observation is that students enter law school talking of justice and leave talking of jobs.

Critics believe that several aspects of the educational experience contribute to this shift in perspective. First, the high tuition and limited financial aid and loan forgiveness programs at most law schools discourage some students from taking poorly-paid public sector and public interest jobs. Close to 90 percent of law students borrow to finance their legal education, and the amounts they

> borrowed grew over 400 percent between 1987 and 2006; the average debt burden at the end of that period was about $54,500 for graduates of public schools and $83,200 for graduates of private schools.[38] However, most systematic studies suggest that other factors other than debt are more important influences on job placement, primarily the lack of public interest/public sector positions and their low pay scales compared with private-sector salaries.[39] In 2006, the median starting salary for public interest jobs was $40,000 compared to $105,000 for law firm associate positions.[40]

Loan Repayment Assistance Programs [LRAPs] and public interest scholarships can significantly expand graduates' job opportunities. In one large scale study, half of the responding attorneys with public interest jobs reported that the availability of loan forgiveness was very important in their choice.[41] Other research suggests that scholarships and fellowships are even more effective in encouraging public interest placements.[42] Although most accredited schools offer some loan forgiveness, the amounts awarded and the numbers of graduates reached are quite modest.[43] However, recent federal legislation offers much more comprehensive coverage. It provides debt relief to graduates of any law school who take qualifying jobs

---

37. *See* Sullivan et al., *supra* note 36, at 145, 187; Robert Granfield, *Making Elite Lawyers* 38–39 (1992); Sturm & Guinier, *supra* note 32.

38. Henderson & Morriss, *supra* note 21, at 81; Vesna Jaksic, "Fine Tuning Eyed for Student Debt Program," *Nat'l L. J.*, Nov. 19, 2007, at A1, A18.

39. Christa McGill, "Educational Debt and Law Student Failure to Enter Public Service Careers: Bringing Empirical Data to Bear", 31 *Law & Soc' Inquiry* 677 (2006). The main study finding that debt had a significant impact on entry to public interest jobs had serious methodological limitations. *See id.*, at 679–80 discussing 4 percent response rate of Equal Justice Works, NALP, & The Partnership for Public Service, *From Paper Chase to Money Chase: Law School Debt Diverts Road to Public Service* (2002).

40. NALP, *2006 Public Sector and Public Interest Salary Report* 16–20 (2006); Sandhya Bathija, "Loans Not Filling Public Service Gap," *Nat'l L. J.*, Nov. 13, 2006, at A1, A26.

41. Ronit Dinovitzer, *After the JD: First Results of a National Study of Legal Careers* 72 (2004).

42. Erica Field, Educational Debt Burden and Career Choice: Evidence from a Financial Aid Experiment at NYU Law School, Working Paper #469, Princeton University Industrial Relations Section (October 2002).

43. Equal Justice Works, *Financing the Future: Responses to the Rising Debt of Law Students* 6 (2006) (reporting that programs at 100 schools benefitted an estimated 1778 students; the median annual award was $3400 and about half of schools cap salaries of eligible positions at below $45,000).

and total forgiveness to those who commit at least 10 years to public interest legal work.[44]

Whether law school could or should play a greater role in encouraging public interest commitments through full time or pro bono work is a matter of some dispute. Most research finds that issues of social justice receive relatively little attention in the core curricula.[45] However other studies suggest that law school does not have a large or negative effect on attitudes toward public interest law, and that the larger influence on career commitments comes from market forces, such as the comparatively low salary and prestige associated with most of the public interest work available.[46] To counteract these forces, some commentators believe that law schools could and should do more to support public interest commitments through pro bono programs, placement priorities, summer fellowships, curricular coverage, and related initiatives.[47]

Of course, these studies do not fully assess the qualitative, often unconscious, shifts in perspective that Duncan Kennedy describes. Nor do they undercut critics' claim that law schools could and should take more affirmative steps to sustain the public service concerns that motivate many students to attend law school but that decline in the face of market realities.

QUESTIONS

1. How much effect do you believe that law school and law school debt have on students' career choices?

2. Should alleviating the debt burdens of a group of relatively well-off professionals be a high government priority? Why or why not?

3. Should law schools do more to support public service? If so, what strategies seem most promising?

44. College Cost Reduction and Access Act (CCRAA) (2007), Pub. L. No. 110–84, 121 Stat. 784 (2007) (codified in scattered sections of 20 U.S.C.). The impact of this act on high indebtedness/low income law students–with guidance about how to take advantage of it–is discussed in Philip G. Schrag, "Federal Student Loan Repayment Assistance for Public Interest Lawyers and Other Employees of Governments and Nonprofit Organizations," 36 *Hofstra L. Rev.* 27 (2007). Professor Schrag was among the chief architects and lobbyists for CCRAA.

45. Sullivan, et al., *supra* note 36, at 187 (noting that such issues are treated as addenda if at all); Deborah L. Rhode, *Pro Bono in Principle and in Practice* 161 (2005) (finding in national survey that only about one percent of surveyed graduates reported coverage of pro bono issues in professional responsibility and orientation programs).

46. *See* Granfield, *supra* note 37, at 38–48, 88–90. *See also* McGill, *supra* note 39.

47. Granfield, *supra* note 36, at 8; Deborah L. Rhode, "Pro Bono in Principle and in Practice," 53 *J. Legal Educ.* 413 (2003) and Rhode, *supra* note 45, excerpted in Chapter XIII.

The Substance and Structure of Learning
William M. Sullivan et al., Educating Lawyers: Preparation for the Profession of Law

186–94 (Carnegie Foundation for the Advancement of Teaching 2007).

Law schools are impressive educational institutions. In a relatively short period of time, they are able to impart a distinctive habit of thinking that forms the basis for their students' development as legal professionals. In our visits to over a dozen schools of different types and geographical locations, our research team found unmistakable evidence of the pedagogical power of the first phase of legal education. Within months of their arrival in law school, students demonstrate new capacities for understanding legal processes, for seeing both sides of legal arguments, for sifting through facts and precedents in search of the more plausible account, for using precise language, and for understanding the applications and conflicts of legal rules. Despite a wide variety of social backgrounds and undergraduate experiences, they were learning, in the parlance of legal education, to "think like a lawyer." This is an accomplishment of the first order that deserves serious consideration from educators of aspirants to other professional fields. . . .

By questioning and having argumentative exchanges with faculty students are led to analyze situations by looking for points of dispute or conflict and considering as "facts" only those details that contribute to someone's staking a legal claim on the basis of precedent. Again, much like the signature pedagogies of other professions, the case-dialogue method drills students, over and over, in first abstracting from natural contexts, then operating on the facts so abstracted, according to specified rules and procedures; they then draw conclusions based on that reasoning. Students discover that thinking like a lawyer means redefining messy situations of actual or potential conflict as opportunities for advancing a client's cause through legal argument before a judge or through negotiation.

By contrast, the task of connecting these conclusions with the rich complexity of actual situations that involve full-dimensional people, let alone the job of thinking through the social consequences or ethical aspects of the conclusions, remains outside the method. Issues such as the social needs or matters of justice involved in cases do get attention in some case-dialogue classrooms, but these issues are almost always treated as addenda. Being told repeatedly that such matters fall, as they do, outside the precise and orderly "legal landscape," students often conclude that they are secondary to what really counts for success in law school—and in legal practice. In their all-consuming first year, students are told to set aside their desire for justice. They are warned not to let their moral concerns or compassion for the people in the cases they discuss cloud their legal analyses. . . .

Another unforeseen consequence results from the near-exclusive focus on systematic abstraction from actual social contexts, which suggests two major limitations of legal education. One limitation is the casual attention that most law schools give to teaching students how to use legal thinking in the complexity of actual law practice. Unlike other professional education, most notably medical school, legal education typically pays relatively little attention to direct training in professional practice. The result is to prolong and reinforce the habits of thinking like a student rather than an apprentice practitioner, thus conveying the impression that lawyers are more like competitive scholars than attorneys engaged with the problems of clients. Neither understanding of the law is exhaustive, of course, but law school's typically unbalanced emphasis on the one perspective can create problems gratuitously for what [the American Bar Foundation's study] *After the JD* calls "the transition to practice."

The second limitation is law schools' failure to complement the focus on skill in legal analysis with effective support for developing the ethical and social dimensions of the profession. Students need opportunities to learn about, reflect on, and practice the responsibilities of legal professionals. Despite progress in making legal ethics a part of the curriculum, law schools rarely pay consistent attention to the social and cultural contexts of legal institutions and the varied forms of legal practice. To engage the moral imagination of students as they move toward professional practice, seminaries and medical, business, and engineering schools employ well-elaborated case studies of professional work. Law schools, which pioneered the use of case teaching, only occasionally do so.

Both these drawbacks—lack of attention to practice and the weakness of concern with professional responsibility—are the unintended consequences of reliance on a single, heavily academic pedagogy to provide the crucial initiation into legal education....

Assessment is important in all forms of professional education. In law schools, too, assessing students' competence performs several important educational functions. In its familiar summative form, assessment devices such as both standardized and essay tests sort and select students....

Law schools give less attention and emphasis in their formal procedures to the second type of assessment, called formative assessment. Here feedback is provided primarily to support students' learning and self-understanding rather than to rank or sort. Contemporary learning theory suggests that efficient application of educational effort is significantly enhanced by the use of formative assessment. For educational purposes, summative devices have their place primarily as devices to protect the public by ensuring basic levels of competence. Formative practices directed toward improved learning ought to be primary forms of assessment....

We endorse a different strategy, which we call *integrative* rather than *additive*. Something like an integrative strategy has, in fact, begun to emerge recently in discussions of legal education. The core insight behind the integrative strategy is that effective educational efforts must be understood in holistic rather than atomistic terms. For law schools, this means that, far from remaining uncontaminated by each other, each aspect of the legal apprenticeship—the cognitive, the practical, and the ethical-social—takes on part of its character from the kind of relationship it has with the others. In the standard model, in which the cognitive apprenticeship as expressed in the Socratic classroom dominates, the other practical and ethical-social apprenticeships are each tacitly thought of and judged as merely adjuncts to the first. That is why adherents of the additive strategy resist the idea that all experiences are critical, that they are inseparable, and that all three will be strengthened through their integration .....

When thinking of the law school curriculum as a three-part model, whose parts interact with and influence each other, those elements are

1. The teaching of legal doctrine and analysis, which provides the basis for professional growth.

2. Introduction to the several facets of practice included under the rubric of lawyering, leading to acting with responsibility for clients.

3. A theoretical and practical emphasis on inculcation of the identity, values, and dispositions consonant with the fundamental purposes of the legal profession.

NOTES

> "We are uncertain what we think our students should learn, how best to teach it to them, and how to be sure when they have learned it."

> William Bennett[48]

One of the longstanding criticisms of legal education is that it offers too little theory and too little practice. The standard casebook approach offers no sense of how problems unfolded for the lawyers or ultimately affected the parties. Nor does it adequately situate formal doctrine in social, historical, and political contexts. According to critics:

> Much classroom discussion is both too theoretical and not theoretical enough; it neither probes the social context of legal doctrine or offers practical skills for using that doctrine in particular cases. Students get what Stanford professor Lawrence Friedman aptly characterizes as the legal equivalent of "geology without the rocks ... dry arid logic, divorced from society." Missing from this picture is the background needed to understand how law interacts with life.

> Also absent is any sustained effort to address the emotional and interpersonal dimensions of legal practice. Law schools claim, above all else, that they teach students to "think like a lawyer." In fact, they often teach how to "think like a law professor ..." The psychological dimensions of lawyering are largely relegated to clinical courses, ... [which] are still treated as a poor relation in most law schools. Without adequate resources, status, or class hours, clinical courses cannot compensate for the neglect of practical and interpersonal skills in the rest of the curricula. It is thinking about thinking—Grand Theory and

---

48. Stucky et al., *supra* note 8, at 2 (quoting Bennett, former Secretary of Education).

doctrinal analysis—that earns greatest academic respect. As [NYU] professor Gerald Lopez notes, law school is "still almost entirely about law and ... only incidentally and superficially about lawyering."

It is, moreover, about law from too insular a perspective. Despite growing recognition of the importance of cross-cultural and cross-disciplinary perspectives, the core curriculum stubbornly resists intruders. With the exception of law and economics, which has managed a fair amount of infiltration, these perspectives generally remain on the margins.... At most schools, a bit of borrowed intellectual finery dresses up the standard legal wardrobe, but the fashion remains the same. The consequence is to deprive students of approaches that could prove highly useful in their future practice. An obvious example involves problem solving, which most lawyers find central to their daily work and which only a small number of schools have begun to address directly. Adequate preparation for this role could offer background in risk analysis, cognitive psychology, game theory, and organizational behavior. Similar interdisciplinary approaches could enrich understanding of other equally critical roles. Students planning to specialize in corporate law should have more exposure to economics and finance. Future matrimonial lawyers would benefit from a better background in psychology....

Similar benefits would emerge from expanding clinical offerings and integrating more skills training in the core curriculum. Simulation exercises and supervised practice offer opportunities to develop a more diverse range of skills than is possible in conventional Socratic or lecture formats. Clinics serving low-income clients offer especially valuable opportunities for students to learn how the law functions, or fails to function, for the have-nots.[49]

In response to such criticisms, law schools have implemented a variety of curricular reforms. Many have added more skills training, and included more collaborative and experiential forms of learning in the core curricula. Some have refocused the first year to cover legislation, regulation, problem solving, and comparative materials. Other schools have encouraged interdisciplinary approaches and sequenced learning in the second and third years.[50] Relatively few institutions, however, have fully integrated analytic, practical and ethical approaches, or restructured student assessment along the lines that many education experts have suggested.[51]

QUESTIONS

1. How central a role do you believe that skills instruction should play in law school? Should accreditation standards require all law schools to insure

49. Rhode, *supra* note 15, at 197–98.

50. Jonathan D. Glater, "Training Law Students for Real–Life Careers," *N.Y. Times,* Oct. 31, 2007, at A22; Jill Schachner Chanen, "Re-engineering the J.D.,"*ABA J.* July, 2007, at 42–44.

51. Stucky et al., *supra* note 8; Sullivan et al., *supra* note 36; Sturm & Guinier, *supra* note 32.

some threshold level of competence of their graduates in core legal tasks? If so, how should additional skills training be financed? Would it make sense to require law school faculty to build practice and professionalism components into their standard curricular offerings? How would you respond to: (a) commentators who claim that if clinical training was so valuable, employers would demand it for those they hire, and one reason they don't is the "leftist" tilt of most offerings; (b) the dean of a dentistry school who, when asked by a law school colleague about clinical instruction, replied "Oh, we don't let [our students] work on patients. We just teach them to think like dentists"?[52]

2.   Would it be equally or more cost-effective to shorten law school and to offer skills training through post-graduate courses or apprenticeship, along the lines of legal education in other nations?[53]

3.   Are there other curricular areas apart from practice skills that you believe deserve more attention? Given the increasing globalization of much legal practice, should international issues be a higher priority? How should American law schools respond to the trend among European nations toward harmonization of curricula and quality assurance standards, and toward mutual recognition of educational degrees? Should American law schools join these efforts in order to remain attractive for foreign students, and to insure opportunities for international study and entrance to a foreign bar for their own graduates?[54]

4.   Are there ways to reduce the stress of legal education, which some research finds is greater than in other professional schools?[55] Some analysts believe the stress may contribute to substance abuse, which may in turn set the stage for future professional difficulties.[56]

5.   How serious are the problems in legal education? In a national law school survey of student engagement, about four-fifths of students (82%) rated their overall law school experience as "good" or "excellent," and about the same number (79%) would "probably" or "definitely" choose the same school again.[57] Are such satisfaction rates a sufficient measure of success? If you could make one change in legal education, apart from its expense, what would it be?

52.   Heather McDonald, "Clinical, Cynical," *OnlineWallSt.J.com* Jan. 11, 2006; Neil Hamilton, "Professionalism Clearly Defined," 18 *Prof. Lawyer* 4, 23 n. 20 (2008).

53.   Andras Jakob, "Dilemmas of Legal Education: A Comparative Overview," 57 *J. Legal Ed.* 253, 260–64 (2007). See the discussion of apprenticeship in Chapter XV.

54.   For example, 47 European nations are participating in the standardization and recognition initiatives for higher education launched by the Bologna Process. Some of these initiatives are beginning to involve law schools. *See* Laurel Terry, "The Bologna Process and its Implications for U.S. Legal Education," 57 *J. Legal Ed.* 237 (2007).

55.   *See* research summarized in Kennon M. Sheldon & Lawrence S. Krieger, "Understanding the Negative Effects of Legal Education on Law Students: A Longitudinal Test of Self–Determination Theory," 33 *Personality & Soc. Psych.* 883 (2007).

56.   Thomas Adcock, "Despite '93 Report, Substance Abuse Persists at Law Schools," *N.Y. Law J.*, June 30, 2003, at Law.com. *See* "Report of the AALS Special Committee on Problems of Substance Abuse in Law Schools," 44 *J. Legal Educ.* 35, 36 (1994).

57.   I Law School Survey of Student Engagement (LSSSE), *Student Engagement in Law Schools* (2004).

B.   Diversity

American Bar Association Task Force on Minorities in the Legal Profession, Report with Recommendations
(Jan. 1986).

Throughout most of the history of the legal profession in America, race discrimination made it virtually impossible for minority group members to obtain legal training. In this regard legal education, the gateway to practice, mirrored its profession.

The early history of legal education and minorities is portrayed principally and most vividly through the experiences of Blacks. Because of their unique relationship to the majority community following centuries of enslavement, Blacks endured particularly explicit and invidious discrimination. During the nineteenth century, when "reading the law" was an acceptable portal to the profession, few Blacks were able to find white lawyers with whom they could "read" or gain admission to practice in an openly hostile profession. Many states excluded Blacks from their law schools.

Formal legal education for Blacks began in 1868 when George Lewis Ruffin was admitted to Harvard. The decades which followed the turn of the twentieth century, formative years for American legal education, saw Blacks systematically denied opportunities to study law. The Howard University Law School opened in 1869. Notwithstanding many difficult years when its very existence was often in jeopardy, Howard trained the majority of Black lawyers in the United States between 1869 and 1967.

By 1900, four years after the United States Supreme Court's landmark "separate but equal" opinion in *Plessy v. Ferguson*, there were only 728 Black lawyers in the entire United States. *Plessy*, along with the Supreme Court opinion in *Dred Scott v. Sandford* and the *Civil Rights Cases* among others, made it clear that Blacks had been abandoned by the law. The already thin opportunities in legal education for Blacks were also decimated by racial discrimination during the post-Reconstruction period and the "Jim Crow" era that followed *Plessy*.

During most of the first half of the twentieth century, southern law schools were completely closed to Blacks. Northern schools, though ostensibly open to Black students, enrolled very few. The major responsibility for educating Black lawyers remained with Howard and the other Black law schools. Most of these schools had "Jim Crow" origins, and were maintained solely to segregate the races or to meet the barest requirements of *Plessy's* "separate but equal" mandate. The inadequate resources devoted to the Black schools and their resulting poor status eventually became critical issues in the legal efforts to overturn segregation in public institutions of higher learning. This movement, which began in the 1930s, was spearheaded by Black lawyers, and eventually resulted in a series of Supreme Court decisions generally known as the "graduate school desegregation cases." These cases culminated in the 1954 landmark Supreme Court decision, *Brown v. Board of Education*. In *Brown*, the Court addressed legal segregation directly, and concluded that separate public educational facilities are inherently unequal. In addition to culminating a century long struggle by Blacks for equal educational opportunity, *Brown* was an impetus for the new struggles of the 1960s and the 1970s in which legal education was a prominent subject.

It was not until 1964, ten years after *Brown* was decided, that the Association of American Law Schools (AALS) Committee on Racial Discrimination was able to report for the first time that no member school reported denying admission on the basis of race or color. Moreover, it was not until the late 1960s that virtually all the vestiges of overt discrimination in law school admissions were removed, and many law schools began programs to seek out and attract minority group students. These efforts were in part the result of a recognition that where a real desire to increase minority student enrollments existed, merely removing restrictions was not enough.

The civil rights movement and the urban rebellions during the 1960s led to national commitments to alleviate the poor status of Blacks and other minorities. Included were concerns over the lack of minority lawyers, and during the late 1960s law schools began to focus attention on minorities. This interest was accompanied by a recognition that special efforts were needed to attract and assist these students to gain admission to law school.

While substantial progress was made [during the late 1960s and 1970s], much remained to be done. In 1980, in response to the prospect of a decline in minority enrollments, and in recognition of the importance to legal education of a diverse student body, the House of Delegates, upon recommendation of the Section of Legal Education and Admissions to the Bar, adopted accreditation Standard 212. This standard reaffirms the ABA's commitment to minority law school admissions and requires the law schools to demonstrate by concrete actions, that full opportunities to study law, and to enter the profession were provided to racial and ethnic minorities.

Kimberlé Williams Crenshaw, "Foreword: Toward a Race–Conscious Pedagogy in Legal Education"

National Black Law Journal, Winter 1989, at 1.

Race in the Law School Classroom

Minority students across the country have waged a series of protests to draw attention to problems of diversity in the nation's law schools. Although the students' bottom line demand is often for the recruitment of more minority faculty and students, the anger and frustration apparent in these protests indicate that the disappointment is not simply over the lack of "color" in the hallways. The dissatisfaction goes much deeper—to the substantive dynamics of the classroom and their particular impact on minority students. In many instances, minority students' values, beliefs, and experiences clash not only with those of their classmates but also with those of their professors. Yet because of the dominant view in academe that legal analysis can be taught without directly addressing conflicts of individual values, experiences, and world views, these conflicts seldom, if ever, reach the surface of the classroom discussion. Dominant beliefs in the objectivity of legal discourse serve to suppress the conflict by discounting the relevance of any particular perspective in legal analysis and by positing an analytical stance that has no specific cultural, political, or class characteristics. I call this dominant mode "perspectivelessness."

This norm of perspectivelessness is problematic in general, and particularly burdensome on minority students. While it seems relatively straightforward that objects, issues, and other phenomena are interpreted from the vantage point of the observer, many law classes are conducted as though it is possible to create, weigh, and evaluate rules and arguments in ways that neither reflect nor privilege any particular perspective or world view. Thus, law school discourse proceeds with the expectation that students will learn to perform the standard mode of legal reasoning and embrace its presumption of perspectivelessness. When this expectation is combined with the fact that what is understood as objective or neutral is often the embodiment of a white middle-class world view, minority students are placed in a difficult situation. To assume the air of perspectivelessness that is expected in the classroom, minority students must participate in the discussion as though they were not African–American or Latino, but colorless legal analysts. The consequence of adopting this colorless mode is that when the discussion involves racial minorities, minority students are expected to stand apart from their history, their identity, and sometimes their own immediate circumstances and discuss issues without making reference to the reality that the "they" or "them" being discussed is from their perspective "we" or "us." Conversely, on the few occasions when minority students are invited to incorporate their racial identity and experiences into their comments, they often feel as though they have been put on the spot. Moreover, their comments are frequently disregarded by other students who believe that since race figures prominently in such comments, the minority students—unlike themselves—are expressing biased, self-interested, or subjective opinions. The result is that minority students can seldom ground their analysis in their own racial experiences without risking some kind of formal or informal sanction. Minority students escape the twin problems of objectification and subjectification in discussions when minority experiences are deemed to be completely irrelevant, or are obscured by the centering of the discussion elsewhere. The price of this sometimes welcomed invisibility, however, can be intense alienation. I will elaborate on these dilemmas below.

The Problem of Objectification

Instructors create the conditions that lead to the objectification of minority students by narrowly framing classroom discussions as simple exercises in rule application and by not giving students permission to step outside the doctrinal boundaries to comment on or critique the rules.

In each of these cases minority students confront difficult choices. To play the game right, they have to assume a stance that denies their own identity and requires them to adopt an apparently objective stance as the given starting point of analysis. Should they step outside the doctrinal constraints, not only have they failed in their efforts to "think like a lawyer," they have committed an even more stigmatizing *faux pas*: they have taken the discussion far afield by revealing their emotional preoccupation with their racial identity.

Given the infrequency with which most law teachers create the space for and legitimize responses that acknowledge the significance of a racially-informed perspective, it is not surprising that minority students often choose the role of "good student" rather than run the risk of appearing to be incapable of exercising the proper decorum and engagement in legal analysis. Such experiences teach minority students that in law school discourse, their cultural and experiential knowledge is not important or relevant. Indeed, they learn that any failure to observe the constructed dichotomy between the rational—read non-racial and non-personal—and the emotional—read racial and experiential—may elicit derision or disregard. . . .

Many of these problems could be averted if professors framed discussions so that the boundaries of acceptable responses were not so narrowly constructed. This would give students permission to drop the air of perspectivelessness, to stand within their own identity, and to critique the doctrine or rule directly. Yet instructors often fail to broaden the parameters of the discussion, perhaps believing that to do so would legitimize the inclusion of racial perspectives where none had existed before. Some may assert that since white students do not feel the need to fall back on personal, racialized views of the world, neither should minorities. This belief, however, is predicated on an erroneous view that white students—and indeed the instructors themselves—are not also reflecting racialized views when they frame and discuss issues. They accept the absence of an explicitly racial referent as evidence that the doctrinal or substantive framework being discussed is objective and race-neutral. However, majority as well as minority students view the world through a consciousness constructed in part through race. The appearance of perspectivelessness is simply the illusion by which the dominant perspective is made to appear neutral, ordinary, and beyond question. As a result, while the perspectives of minority students are often identified as racial, the perspectives of their majority classmates are not. . . .

An equally stressful, but conceptually more obscure experience is what I call subjectification. This is experienced by minority students when, after learning to leave their race at the door, their racial identities are unexpectedly dragged into the classroom by their instructor to illustrate a point or to provide the basis for a command performance of "show and tell." The eyes of the class are suddenly fixed upon the minority student who is then expected to offer some sort of minority "testimony".... Usually, the effort to elicit the minority perspective is a cue that the discussion is a policy—as opposed to a doctrinal—discussion. The racial conflict, if any, is seen as occurring outside of the classroom while the objective of the discussion is apparently to determine how best to address the problem. To the extent that the minority student can participate in this debate, she is viewed as a biased or specially interested party and thus, her perspectives are probably regarded as being too subjective to have a significant bearing on the ultimate solution.

[T]o raise race in this way imposes multiple burdens upon minority students. First, it reinforces the view that racial differences and minority students' distinct racial experiences are essentially peripheral to the main course of law. Such efforts to compartmentalize racial experiences present racism as a series of individualized anomalous occurrences rather than systematically connected to larger institutional practices and values which are reflected in and reinforced by law. Presenting minority viewpoints in such narrowly-framed and marginalized discussions ignores the possibility that these insights might have some bearing on larger issues involving the role of law in constructing societal relationships and on the appropriateness of discussing those relationships in law school classrooms....

Some of these dilemmas can be addressed by altering the way racial issues are framed, by presenting racism as a serious societal problem, and by explicitly deprivileging dominant perspectives. Instructors wishing to explore racial issues without contributing to the anxiety of minority students should resist framing minority experiences in ways that make such experiences appear to be disconnected to broader issues and that can be easily forgotten as soon as the policy discussion is over. Instead, the frame should be shifted so as to illuminate the connection between racial subordination and the values and interests that appear to be race-neutral or that are simply taken for granted. This would provide space for minority students to contribute to discussions in ways that value their perspectives and do not put them on the spot.

NOTES: PERSPECTIVES ON RACE, ETHNICITY, AND GENDER

Historical Background

As Chapter II and the preceding ABA Report have indicated, most law schools long discriminated on the basis of sex, race, ethnicity, and religion. Part of the impetus for tighter admission standards during the late nineteenth and early twentieth centuries reflected racial, ethnic and religious biases among many educational administrators. For example, Columbia Law School was urged to require that applicants have a college diploma or pass an examination including Latin as a way to "keep out the little scrubs whom the school now promotes from grocery counters...."[58] Discrimina-

---

58. D. Kelly Weisberg, "Barred From the Bar: Women and Legal Education in the United States 1870–1890," in 2 *Women and the Law* 231, 252 (D. Kelly Weisberg ed.,

tion against immigrants and Jewish students continued throughout the early twentieth century. Racial barriers were more enduring. Although the first black graduated from law school in 1869 and some black institutions formed graduate programs in law around the same period, few of these programs survived after the Reconstruction era. As the preceding ABA Task Force Report notes, a series of lawsuits beginning in the 1930s forced the establishment of separate black state law schools, and eventually the integration of existing institutions.

The history of the *Sweatt v. Painter* litigation illustrates the extent of the barriers confronting racial minorities. In 1940, the Texas legal profession included approximately 7570 white attorneys and 22 blacks. When a qualified black applicant sought admission at the University of Texas Law School, the state responded first by adding law classes at Prairie View University, an impoverished black institution that offered college credit for mattress and broom-making. Two of the three law classrooms lacked chairs and desks. Yet, in the *Sweatt* litigation, the state court concluded that the Prairie View facility was "substantially equal" to the University of Texas Law School.[59]

After the *Sweatt* decision, 339 U.S. 629 (1950), which held Texas's racially segregated law schools unconstitutional, the Association of American Law Schools passed a resolution designed to encourage, but not to require, member schools to abolish racially discriminatory practices. Not until 1964 did all schools do so. Even after law schools removed formal prohibitions against non-white applicants, the absence of financial aid, affirmative action, active recruiting strategies, and supportive academic environments worked against admission of minorities.[60] Until the 1960s, they represented less than two percent of the profession. For women of color, the barriers were especially great; only a tiny number of minority women managed to obtain legal training before the 1960s.[61]

For white women, the situation was better, but even the most intellectually qualified and economically privileged applicants faced significant discrimination. For most of this nation's history, "both normal policies and informal norms assumed that law was unfit for women and women unfit for law."[62] "No woman," declared one nineteenth-century Columbia trustee, "shall degrade herself by practicing law especially if I can save her."[63]

1982); Robert Stevens, *Law School: Legal Education in America from the 1850s to the 1980s* 100–101 (1983).

59. Douglas L. Jones, "The Sweatt Case and the Development of Legal Education for Negroes in Texas," 47 *Tex.L.Rev.* 677, 678–85 (1969); Richard Kluger, *Simple Justice* 261 (1975); Edward J. Littlejohn & Leonard S. Rubinowitz, "Black Enrollment in Law Schools: Forward to the Past?," 12 *T. Marshall L.J.* 415, 431 n. 81 (1987).

60. William C. Kidder, "The Struggle for Access From *Sweatt* to *Grutter*: A History of African–American, Latino, and American

Indian Law School Admissions, 1950–2000," 19 *Harvard Blackletter J.* 1 (2003).

61. *See* Geraldine Segal, *Blacks in the Law* 212–13 (1983); Karen Morrello, *The Invisible Bar: The Woman Lawyer in America, 1638 to the Present* 143–7 (1986).

62. Deborah L. Rhode, "Midcourse Corrections: Women in Legal Education," 53 *J. Legal Educ.* 475 (2003).

63. Janette Barnes, "Women and Entrance to the Legal Profession," 23 *J. Legal Educ.* 276, 283 (1970).

Such attitudes built on broader cultural assumptions about gender roles. A recurrent anxiety was that women's exposure to masculine education and pursuits would result in infertility, frigidity and "race suicide." Theories about the deadly "brain-womb" conflict warned that women who diverted their scarce energies to cognitive rather than reproductive pursuits risked permanent physical and psychological damage. The lower birth rate among female professionals appeared as both a cause and consequence of deep neuroses. Career women who remained single were viewed as morbid, sex-starved spinsters, while those who married were accused of neglecting their children's needs and irreparably injuring their husbands' self-respect and social status.[64]

Other rationales for women's exclusion from law school were more pragmatic. Some professors and administrators worried about distractions for male students in the classroom, and opportunities for unchaperoned interchanges in the library. Many faculties did not want to squander scarce places on female students who would presumably not have the same opportunities as male competitors to make full use of their legal training. Societal discrimination against women thus became a rationale for perpetuating it.[65]

Such attitudes discouraged women from applying to law schools and legitimated discrimination against their admission. Throughout the first half of the twentieth century, female students never constituted more than 3% of law school classes except during World War II. Not until 1972 did all ABA-accredited schools remove bans on women students. Moreover, even where formal admission policies were gender-neutral, educational experiences were not. Until women began entering law schools in substantial numbers during the 1970s, a common practice was to ignore their classroom presence as much as possible except for special issues or ceremonial occasions. For example, some professors observed Ladies Days, on which they called only on women students for selected cases or hypotheticals involving "women's concerns." Rape and needlework were favored topics.[66] Sol Linowitz, a prominent Washington practitioner, recalls that

> [t]here were only two women in my class at Cornell Law School, and to tell the truth we felt somewhat uncomfortable when they were around. It never occurred to us to wonder whether *they* felt uncomfortable.
>
> Nobody in those days thought of bigoted exclusion from the higher levels of legal practice as an ethical problem. For those who were excluded, it would have been pretentious; for others, with few exceptions, it was the way of the world—unfair, perhaps, but manageable. After all, you couldn't ask lawyers to be partners with people with whom they did not feel "comfortable."[67]

---

64. Rhode, *supra* note 62, at 477; Stevens, *supra* note 40, at 2, 82–84; Weisberg, *supra* note 58, at 252.

65. Rhode, *supra* note 62, at 478; Judith Richards Hope, *Pinstripes & Pearls: The Women of the Harvard Law School Class* of '64 Who Forged an Old–Girl Network and Paved the Way for Future Generations (2003).

66. Rhode, *supra* note 62, at 478; Cynthia Epstein, *Women in Law* 66–67 (1981).

67. Sol M. Linowitz with Martin Mayer, *The Betrayed Profession* 6 (1994).

Contemporary Challenges: Racial and Ethnic Diversity

As Chapter II indicates, overt discrimination declined over the next several decades. In the 1960s, the demographics of the profession began to change more rapidly, partly in response to the civil rights movements. During the late 1960s, a series of meetings under the auspices of the Office of Economic Opportunity led to the formation of a national Council on Legal Education Opportunity (CLEO) for minorities, with representatives from the ABA, AALS, and LSAC (Law School Admission Council). This group's efforts, coupled with other social and governmental pressures, led to increased financial aid, recruitment, and prelaw training. Support and protest activities by Black, Asian, and Hispanic law student organizations, also resulted in modest progress. During the early 21st century, when racial and ethnic minorities accounted for about 30 percent of the nation's population, they constituted about 22 percent of law schools' student population, 11 percent of law school deans, and 12 percent of full professors.[68]

Commentators have identified three major barriers to increasing diversity in law school. The first involves minorities' underrepresentation in the eligible applicant pool of college graduates, in part because of limited financial assistance and inequalities in educational preparation. A second major hurdle involves law school admission criteria and their disproportionate impact on minorities. On average, Blacks, Hispanics and Native Americans have lower LSAT scores and GPAs. A final barrier involves minorities' higher dissatisfaction, disengagement, and attrition rates.

How law schools should respond to these problems has been a matter of continuing controversy and concern. ABA accreditation standards as recently strengthened require law schools to demonstrate "by concrete action" a commitment to having a "law school body that is diverse with respect to gender, race, and ethnicity."[69] The most common and widely accepted strategies involve proactive recruitment and retention programs, adequate financial aid, and educational support services. A more controversial issue involves affirmative action programs that result in acceptance of targeted minorities with lower average LSATs and grade point averages than white applicants. In *Regents of the University of California v. Bakke*, 438 U.S. 265 (1978), the Supreme Court held that educational institutions may consider the ethnicity and race of an applicant in order to achieve diversity as long as they do not employ rigid quotas. Subsequent challenges to law school admission processes have involved the exclusion of white applicants with GPAs and test scores higher than those of racial and ethnic minorities. Plaintiffs in these cases argued that such admission systems function with de facto quotas. In *Hopwood v. Texas* and *Grutter v. Bollinger* lower federal courts agreed.[70]

68. ABA Section on Legal Education and Admission to the Bar (2007), available at http://www.abanet.org/legaled/statistis tics/stats.html; AALS Statistical Report on Law Faculty 24 (2006–07).

69. ABA Accreditation Standard 211 and Interpretation 211–3 (2006).

70. Hopwood v. State of Texas, 78 F.3d 932 (5th Cir.), cert. den. 518 U.S. 1033 (1996) (finding a constitutional violation in the University of Texas Law School diversity pro-

In *Grutter*, the United States Supreme Court reversed. There, five Justices joined a majority opinion holding that the University of Michigan Law School's admission process did not violate the Equal Protection Clause by considering the racial and ethnic diversity of applicants. *Grutter v. Bollinger*, 539 U.S. 306 (2003). Six Justices also joined the majority in a companion cases that struck down the undergraduate admissions program at the University of Michigan because it awarded a substantial and fixed number of points toward admission to members of targeted racial and ethnic minority groups. *Gratz v. Bollinger*, 539 U.S. 244 (2003).

These cases attracted a record number of amicus briefs. Support for the law school's program came from virtually all higher education associations, including the AALS, and a wide range of business organizations, as well as a group of highly distinguished retired military leaders. These defenders of affirmative action made several claims. The first is that institutions of higher education, including professional schools, have a compelling state interest in taking racial and ethnic diversity into account in the admission process. In supporters' view, it is essential to educate lawyers who will adequately reflect the diverse make-up of the population they will serve. Writing for the majority in *Grutter*, Justice O'Connor agreed: "In order to cultivate a set of leaders with legitimacy in the eyes of the citizenry, it is necessary that the path to leadership be visibly open to talented and qualified individuals of every race and ethnicity. All members of our heterogeneous society must have confidence in the openness and integrity of the educational institutions that provide this training." 539 U.S., at 326.

In addition, the *Grutter* majority stressed the wide range of research introduced in the court below and in amicus briefs indicating that a student body with varied backgrounds and perspectives enriches the learning environment for all participants. This research finds that students who experience racial diversity in education show less prejudice, more ability to deal with conflict, better cognitive skills, clearer understanding of multiple perspectives, and greater satisfaction with their academic experience.[71]

---

gram that had created separate applicant pools and admission committees for white and non-white applicants, and used different cut off scores); Grutter v. Bollinger, 16 F.Supp.2d 797 (E.D. Mich.1998), rev'd, 288 F.3d 732 (6th Cir. 2002) (en banc), aff'd, 539 U.S. 306 (2003), (finding a constitutional violation in the University of Michigan Law School diversity program that gave preference to racial and ethnic minorities with lower GPAs and test scores than white applicants).

71. American Council on Education and American Association of University Professors, *Does Diversity Make a Difference?* (2000); Richard O. Lempert, David L. Chambers & Terry K. Adams, "Michigan's Minority Graduates in Practice: The River Runs Through Law School," 25 *Law & Soc. Inq.*

395 (2000); Gary Orfield & Dean Whitla, *Diversity and Legal Education: Student Experiences in Leading Law Schools*, 14–16 (1999) (of some 1800 students at two leading law schools, over two-thirds reported positive effects of diversity on their educational experience). *But see* Stanley Rothman, Seymour Martin Lipset, & Neil Nevitte, "Does Enrollment Diversity Improve University Education?," 15 *Internat'l J. Public Op. Res.* 8 (2002) (describing a survey of 140 universities finding that students and faculty with higher black enrollment reported less satisfaction with the quality of education and work ethic of students and more experiences of discrimination). For an overview, see Justin Pidot, "Intuition or Proof: The Social Science Justification for the Diversity Ratio-

Proponents of affirmative action also argued, and the *Grutter* majority agreed, that the law school's admission system was narrowly tailored to achieve these compelling interests. That program neither established a fixed quota for minority admissions, nor restricted diversity considerations to those of race and ethnicity. Rather, the school considered candidates' whole file, and sought to achieve a "critical mass" of students of color. The number of African–American, Latino, and Native American students in each class varied between 14 and 20 percent during a previous seven year period, "a range inconsistent with a quota." 539 U.S at 330.

Proponents also argued, and the Court found, that law schools were justified in taking into account factors other than quantitative measurements such as test and grade point averages. Although formulas based on these quantitative measures help predict first-year law school performance, many experts believe that such screening devices have assumed too much importance in the admission process. As they note, such formulas account for only 16–36% of the variance in law school grades, and grades measure only some of the skills necessary for effective legal practice.[72] The most systematic attempt to follow students after graduation has not found a significant correlation between law school grades and later achievements. In a longitudinal survey by Michigan Law School, LSATs, and GPAs did not correlate with graduates' earned income, career satisfaction, or contributions to the community. Minorities admitted under affirmative action criteria did as well on these measures as other graduates.[73] Supporters of affirmative action for law students generally include similar diversity concerns to justify affirmative action in faculty hiring. In addition, supporters emphasize the importance of providing mentors and role models for students of color.

Opponents of preferential treatment, while not necessarily disagreeing about the value of diversity, worry that differential hiring and promotion criteria for minorities will reinforce the stereotypes of inferiority that the legal profession should be seeking to challenge. In his recent memoir, Justice Clarence Thomas attributed his inability to get the law firm jobs he wanted as evidence of what a "law degree from Yale was worth when it bore the taint of racial preference."[74] Many opponents also believe that affirmative action violates a moral principle of color-blindness. As Justice Thomas put it in his dissent in *Grutter*,

nale in *Grutter v. Bollinger* and *Gratz v. Bollinger*," 59 *Stan. L. Rev.* 761 (2006).

72. The correlation between law school grades and undergraduate test scores and GPAs is a strong one in terms of what social scientists consider statistically significant. However, its predictive power is still quite limited, which points up the risks in admission systems that give almost conclusive importance to such formulas in admitting or excluding some group of applicants. Rhode, *In the Interests of Justice, supra* note 12, at 196; Law School Admission Council, *New Models to Assure Diversity Fairness and Ap-*

propriate Test Use in Law School Admissions (1999); Jess Bravin, "Law School Admission Counsel Aims to Quash Overreliance on LSAT," *Wall St. J.* March 29, 2001, at B1.

73. Lani Guinier, "Confirmative Action," 25 *Law & Soc. Inq.* 565, 568 (2000); Richard O. Lempert & Terry K. Adams, "Doing Well and Doing Good, The Careers of Minority and White Graduates of the University of Michigan Law School, 1970–1996," 42 *Law Quadrangle Notes* 60 (1999).

74. Clarence Thomas, *My Grandfather's Son* 87 (2007).

The Constitution abhors classifications based on race, not only because those classifications can harm favored races or are based on illegitimate motives, but also because every time the government places citizens on racial registers and makes race relevant to the provision of burdens or benefits, it demeans us all.... Having decided to use the LSAT, the Law School must accept the constitutional burdens that come with this decision. The Law School may freely continue to employ the LSAT and other allegedly merit-based standards in whatever fashion it likes. What the Equal Protection Clause forbids, but the Court today allows, is the use of these standards hand-in-hand with racial discrimination. 539 U.S. at 346, 363 (Thomas, J., dissenting).

Critics of preferential treatment further argue that it masks rather than addresses the core problem, which is inadequate educational preparation for law school. According to Clint Bolick, director of litigation at the Institute of Justice, "So long as we have a regime of racial preferences that problem is not going to be addressed head-on.... When affirmative action is practiced that way it does not have any impact in expanding the pool of qualified applicants, which is what the goal should be. The way affirmative action is practiced today is cosmetic and superficial. It does not offer a systemic cure for serious social problems. It simply reshuffles the deck [among applicants]." In his view, current policies simply enable the most privileged nonwhite candidates to obtain better positions, and to attend better law schools than their credentials justify.[75]

In a widely publicized article, UCLA Law Professor Richard Sander raised similar concerns. He claimed that affirmative action was counterproductive for blacks because it enabled them to attend law school beyond what their credentials justified. This "academic mismatch" led them to have lower grades, graduation rates, and bar exam pass rates than if they had attended lower-ranked schools. By Sander's calculation, elimination of affirmative action would actually increase the number of black practitioners.[76] The article attracted extensive criticism. Looking at a wider data set than Sander, experts generally agreed that eliminating affirmative action would decrease the number of black lawyers, particularly those in leadership position who often graduated from top-ranked schools. Many commentators also questioned his assumption that if diversity initiatives were eliminated, black students would go to lesser-ranked schools, as opposed to pursuing other educational or employment opportunities.[77]

These controversies are likely to persist. Sander and colleagues have filed freedom of information requests seeking broader data from law

75. Tim Wells, "Affirmative Action in Law Schools: Is it Necessary?," *Washington Lawyer*, Jan/Feb 2000, at 48, 46 (quoting Clint Bolick). *See also* Charles W. Collier, "Affirmative Action and the Decline of Intellectual Culture," 55 *J. Legal Educ.* 3 (2005).

76. Richard H. Sander, "A Systematic Analysis of Affirmative Action in American Law Schools," 57 *Stan. L. Rev.* 367 (2004).

77. *See* the symposium devoted to Sander's article in 57 *Stan. L. Rev.* 1807 et. Seq. (2005) and Cheryl Harris & William Kidder, "The Black Student Mismatch Myth in Legal Education: The Systematic Flaws in Richard Sander's Affirmative Action Study," *J. Blacks in Higher Educ.* Winter, 2004–2005, at 102.

schools regarding the impact of affirmative action.[78] Voter initiatives banning race-based preferences for public institutions are pending or have passed in several states, and lawsuits have been filed against race-based policies that are allegedly inconsistent with *Grutter*, such as minority scholarships and supplemental educational programs. Critics have also objected to the ABA's use of its accreditation authority to press for more preferential treatment by schools with relatively poor diversity records.[79]

QUESTIONS

1. How would defenders of preferential treatment respond to these challenges? What is your view?

2. What strategies would be most effective in increasing law school diversity?

3. LSAT scores are significantly correlated with first year grades in law school, and combining the scores with college GPAs yields a slightly better predictor of those law school grades. In your view, how important are first year grades in relation to the goals of legal education? Should criteria apart from GPAs and test scores assume more weight in law school admissions? Do *U.S. News & World Report* rankings foster over-reliance on these latter criteria?[80] How much relevance should schools attach to factors such as socioeconomic background and leadership ability, community service, employment experiences, and perseverance in the face of disadvantages? Would greater reliance on such factors leave too much room for idiosyncratic or biased judgments? Is there any truly "neutral" basis on which to weigh relevant characteristics?

4. Public opinion polls consistently find that most Americans oppose preferential treatment, and most disagreed with the Court's holding in *Grutter*.[81] How relevant should this opposition be to courts or law schools?

5. Is the distinction that the *Grutter* drew between the permissible law school approach and the impermissible undergraduate formula convincing? In their *Grutter* dissents, both Justice Kennedy and Justice Rehnquist emphasized the small deviation from year to year among the percentages of

78. Peter Schmidt, "Scholars Mount Large–Scale Effort to Study Affirmative Action's Effects, Good and Bad," *Chron. Higher Ed.*, Jan. 8, 2008, available at http://chronicle.com/daily/2008/01/1130n.htm.

79. Rachel Moran, "Of Doubt and Diversity: The Future of Affirmative Action in Higher Education," 67 *Ohio St. L. J.* 201, 228–238 (2006); Gail Heriot, "The ABA's 'Diversity' Diktat," *Wall St. J.*, April 28, 2008, at A19.

80. *See* John Nussbaumer, "Misuse of the Law School Admission Test: Racial Discrimination and the De Facto Quota System for Restricting African–American Access to the Legal Profession," 80 *St. John's Law Rev.* 167–70 (2006) (claiming that schools

place undue importance on scores because it is convenient and improves their *US News* rankings, and noting that blacks make up less than 7% of law school classes, but 13% of the American population and that the number of black graduates of law school has fallen since 1998).

81. *See e.g.*, Harris Poll, "Public Sharply Divided on Recent Supreme Court Decisions," July 30, 2003 (finding 76% of Americans opposed the Court's decision that a university may use race as one factor in deciding whom to admit; 12% of whites, 20% of Hispanics, and 60% of blacks supported the decision).

admitted minority students during most of the period under review, and the fact that administrators actively monitored the number of minorities throughout the admission process. When does a preference for a critical mass of minority students become a quota?

6. Is "diversity" the best rationale for racial and ethnic preferences? Consider the views of one self-described "tepid" supporter of affirmative action, a black *Time* editor, Perry Bacon, who objects to placing a burden on students or workers to contribute a "uniquely black viewpoint."

> But the fact is, a Michigan Law School student would learn a lot more about the "unique experience" of blacks in America if he spent a day at an inner-city school in Detroit than he would in a torts class with me. In fact, a white person who grew up poor has an equally or perhaps more diverse perspective, and yet my blackness counts so much more in affirmative action.... Let's stop using this notion of diversity to sidestep the real issue. Colleges don't want more minority student so we can all hold hands and sing *It's a Small World*. Why can't we just say what the real goal is: the creation of a multiethnic élite? I think young minorities can help form that élite. But I want to join that élite and be expected to deliver the "unique experience" of my whole life rather than an assumed experience based solely on the color of my skin.[82]

7. Justice O'Connor's *Grutter* opinion indicated that race-conscious programs "must have a logical end point," and Justice Ginsburg adds that this view is consistent with other nation's approach. 539 U.S. at 339 (2003); *id.*, at (Ginsburg, J., concurring). The majority's decision goes on to note that "[i]t has been 25 years since Justice Powell first approved the use of race to further an interest in student body diversity in the context of public higher education. Since that time, the number of minority applicants with high grades and test scores has indeed increased.... We expect that 25 years from now, the use of racial preferences will no longer be necessary to further the interest approved today." Justice Ginsburg, joined by Justice Breyer, wrote separately to suggest that "[f]rom today's vantage point, one may hope but not formally forecast, that over the next generation's span, progress toward nondiscrimination and genuinely equal opportunity will make it safe to sunset affirmative action." 539 U.S., at 341. What is your view? By what criteria should law schools decide when to end preferential treatment?

8. In a major 2007 decision, the Supreme Court struck down a voluntary desegregation plan for Seattle and Louisville public schools. *Parents Involved in Community Schools v. Seattle School District No. 1*, 127 S.Ct. 2738 (2007). Noteworthy in the Court's decision was a strong assertion that race-consciousness in public schools, even for purposes of preventing de facto segregation, is unconstitutional. 127 S.Ct. at 2757–59. "The principle that racial balancing is not permitted is one of substance, not semantics.

---

82. Perry Bacon, Jr. "How Much Diversity Do You Want From Me?" *Time*, July 7, 2003, at 108.

Racial balancing is not transformed from 'patently unconstitutional' to a compelling state interest simply by relabeling it 'racial diversity.' While the school districts use various verbal formulations to describe the interest they seek to promote—racial diversity, avoidance of racial isolation, racial integration—they offer no definition of the interest that suggests it differs from racial balance." *Id.* at 2758–59. While Justice Stevens's dissent found "a cruel irony" in the majority's reliance on *Brown v. Board of Education* to overturn a voluntary plan designed to maintain racially integrated schools, *id.* at 2797 (Stevens, J. dissenting), the majority argued that the "fundamental principle" of *Brown* is that rights are individual and personal, not group-based. *Id.* at 2765. Justice Thomas, concurring, explicitly analogized the school systems using racial criteria to achieve integration with segregationist school systems that used racial criteria to the opposite end. "Disfavoring a color-blind interpretation of the Constitution . . . would give school boards a free hand to make decisions on the basis of race—an approach reminiscent of that advocated by the segregationists in *Brown v. Board.*" *Id.* at 2768 (Thomas, J. concurring). How should the principles of *Parents Concerned* affect programs of affirmative action in law schools?

9. What other steps could law schools take to improve the climate and graduation rates for students of color? Recent studies indicate that minority students generally participate less in class and have lower comfort and satisfaction rates than their white classmates, except when the class is taught by a professor of color or the students are enrolled in one of the historically black law schools.[83] What are the implications of such findings for educational reform efforts?

Gender

Progress on issues of gender has been more dramatic than on issues of race and ethnicity. In response to the socioeconomic, demographic, and ideological forces described in Chapter II, the percentage of female law students grew from 3 percent in 1960 to almost half by the turn of the 21st century. Women accounted for about 19 percent of deans and 29 percent of full professors.[84] However, despite that rapid numerical growth and the

---

83. See studies cited in Elizabeth Mertz, *The Language of Law School: Learning to "Think" Like a Lawyer* (2007), Elizabeth Mertz, "Inside the Law School Classroom: Toward a New Legal Realist Pedagogy," 60 *Vand. L. Rev.* 483, 510 (2007) (finding racial differences as high as 283% in some classes); Kevin R. Johnson & Angela Onwuachi-Willig, "Cry Me a River: The Limits of 'A Systematic Analysis of Affirmative Action in American Law Schools,'" 7 *Afr.–Am. L. & Pol'y Rep.* 1 (2005). As an Asian American woman in one study explained, she would not feel comfortable bringing up an issue of race that she though deserved class attention because she did not "want to look like the minority bitch by complaining." Wendy Leo Moore, *Reproducing Racism: White Space, Elite Law Schools, and Racial Inequality* 127 (2008).

84. AALS, *supra* note 68, at 20. For an overview of the barriers, *see* Sari Bashi & Maryana Iskander, "Why Legal Education is Failing Women," 18 *Yale J. Law & Feminism* 389 (2006); Adam Neufield, "Costs of an Outdated Pedagogy? Study on Gender at Harvard Law School," 13 *J. Gender, Social Pol'y & the Law* 511 (2005); and the symposium "Taking Stock: Women of All Colors in Legal Education," 53 *J. Legal Educ.* 467 et seq. (2003), including Deborah L. Rhode, "Midcourse Corrections: Women in Legal Education," 53 *J.Legal Educ.* 475 (2003).

demise of overtly discriminatory practices, many women feel that subtle barriers to equality remain.

American Bar Association Commission on Women in the Profession, The Unfinished Agenda: Women in the Legal Profession

(Prepared for the Commission by Deborah L. Rhode) (2001).

The experience of women in legal education again reflects a history of dramatic, but still only partial progress. Until the 1970s, women in law schools were noticeable largely for their absence. Only three schools had ever had women deans, and few had more than one or two women faculty. Female students constituted no more than 3 percent of entering classes and the atmosphere for those present was less than fully welcoming.... Justice Ruth Bader Ginsburg recalls that when she attended law school, there were associations for wives of law students but not for women students themselves.

By the turn of the 21st century, the academic landscape had been transformed.... But women, particularly women of color, remain overrepresented at the bottom and underrepresented in the upper ranks of legal education. And at many schools, the curriculum and climate for women still leaves much to be desired.

1. Underrepresentation

Despite substantial progress, women in legal education still have not achieved wholly equal opportunities, particularly for leadership positions.... Women faculty are still clustered in the least prestigious academic specialties and positions, such as librarians, research and writing instructors, and non-tenured clinicians. Gender inequalities persist within as well as across these specialties. For example, women account for two-thirds of legal writing instructors, but are only half as likely as their male counterparts to hold tenured positions or to direct writing programs. At many schools, women students are also underrepresented in the most prestigious positions such as law review editors, class officers, and members of academic honor societies. The limited research available finds that these gender and racial disparities cannot be entirely explained by objective factors such as academic credentials or experience. Some evidence also suggests that women of color are underrepresented in student bodies relative to their undergraduate performance and academic potential.

Such findings should come as no surprise. Racial, ethnic, and gender biases persist within the legal profession generally, and there is no reason to expect legal education to be different. Female students and faculty are subject to the same double standards and double binds that women encounter in other legal settings. Their competence is subject to heightened scrutiny and they risk criticism for being too assertive or not assertive enough. Women's disproportionate family responsibilities also carry a cost when pitted against substantial research, teaching, and committee obligations. Although work schedules in law schools generally permit more flexibility than those in legal practice, performance pressures and time demands can be even more unbounded. The problem is exacerbated by the overlap between women's biological and tenure clocks. About two-thirds of surveyed women law professors cite work/family conflicts as a significant problem.

Although there is no reason to expect law schools to be exempt from broader patterns of gender bias, there *is* reason to expect them to address the issue more effectively. Without a critical mass of similar faculty colleagues, women bear disproportionate burdens of counseling and committee assignments, and lack adequate mentoring and support networks. Institutions also lose valuable guidance and students lose valuable role models. And without adequate racial and ethnic diversity among faculty and students, prospective lawyers lack the informed classroom interchanges, and understanding of multiple perspectives that is critical to practice within an increasingly multicultural world....

2. Educational Climate and Curricula

A true commitment to equal opportunity will also require broader changes in the educational culture. Research over the last decade consistently finds that women, particularly women of color, are more likely than men to be silenced in the classroom. Female students volunteer less frequently and make fewer follow-up comments. The gender differentials are most pronounced in courses that are taught by men and that have high male-female ratios. Part of the reason appears to be the largely unconscious biases that continue to affect classroom experiences. When women speak in mixed groups, they are often heard differently than men. Female students' comments are more likely to be overlooked, devalued, or misattributed. The highly competitive atmosphere of many law school classrooms also tends to silence students with lower self-confidence, who are disproportionately women, especially women of color.

The marginalization of women's classroom participation is compounded by the marginalization of issues concerning race, gender, and sexual orientation in core curricula, as well as the disparaging treatment of students and faculty who introduce such concerns. Reviews of gender bias in casebooks disclose that issues generally receive insignificant coverage. And in class discussions, such topics are often tacked on as curricular afterthoughts—as brief digressions from the "real" subject. Some teachers exclude issues of obvious importance, such as domestic violence, same-sex marriage, or pornography, because the discussion may become too volatile. When such issues do arise, students or faculty who express strong views frequently are dismissed or demeaned. Most institutions have experienced racist, sexist, and homophobic backlash in e-mails, graffiti, or anonymous flyers, and many have experienced other egregious forms of sexual harassment. In Law School Admission Council surveys, discrimination is reported by about two-thirds of gay and lesbian students, a majority of African–American students, and a third of women, Asian American, and Hispanic students. Harassment is also common for conservative students who express unpopular views on gender and diversity issues.

What is especially disturbing about such patterns is the tendency among many faculty to dismiss their significance. A common response is simply to ignore inappropriate comments or to rely on other students to respond. Yet tolerance of intolerance falls short of ensuring the equal opportunity and mutual respect that professionally responsible educators should demand. Many schools have also failed to respond adequately to other forms of demeaning or biased treatment. Women faculty often experience classroom challenges to their competence and authority. Women of color, women who are open about their same-sex orientation, and women who take strong feminist positions have been especially likely targets of offensive comments, adverse student evaluations, and marginalization by their colleagues. The devaluation of teaching and scholarship that focuses on gender, race, ethnicity, and sexual orientation also discourages junior faculty from pursuing such interests and disadvantages those who persist.

In short, too many women, particularly women of color and lesbians, still feel uncomfortable in the educational environment and too few have advanced to positions where they can significantly affect it. And too few schools have committees or other administrative structures charged with addressing gender-related concerns. Given these patterns, it is scarcely surprising that women report higher levels of dissatisfaction and disengagement with the law school experience, and that women of color have the greatest likelihood of alienation. If our goal is to create an educational community, and ultimately a profession, of equal opportunity and mutual respect, we have a significant distance yet to travel.

NOTES

Other critiques of legal education have involved more fundamental challenges. Building on theoretical work popularized by Carol Gilligan, some feminists have argued that women bring a distinctive perspective to legal issues. These perspectives, which are especially attentive to care, cooperation, and context, are devalued in traditional legal educational approaches.[85]

However, other women's rights advocates worry that such critiques oversimplify and over-claim. They overlook the ways that sexual difference is experienced differently across race, class, ethnicity, age, and sexual orientation. And they make sweeping generalizations based on small statistical differences. Psychological research finds few characteristics on which men and women consistently differ along gender lines, and even on these characteristics, gender typically accounts for only about five percent of the variance.[86] Many feminists argue for a more contextual approach to gender

85. Carol Gilligan, *In a Different Voice* (1982); Rand Jack & Dana Crowley Jack, *Moral Vision and Professional Decisions: The* Changing Values of Men and Women Lawyers *(1989).*

86. Deborah L. Rhode, *Speaking of Sex* 37–38 (1999).

analysis that avoids sweeping claims about women's essential nature, but that also acknowledges the gender-based experiences and expectations that individuals bring to their professional lives.

The limited empirical research available on legal education underscores both the relevance of gender and the role of such contextual factors. For example, recent surveys suggest that the motivations and experiences of women currently in law school differ in substantial ways from men's. Women law students demonstrate greater commitment to public interest, are substantially less likely to speak in class, and report higher levels of dissatisfaction, disengagement, and self-doubt than men.[87] In some schools, women are underrepresented on the law review and among graduates receiving clerkships, and report fewer opportunities for mentoring and recommendations by faculty.[88] Technological innovations have created new opportunities for sexist conduct and widened its audience. One well publicized example was the posting of lewd and derisive statements about identified female students on AutoAdmit, a law school message board; another was a contest site to select the "hottest" woman attending a "Top 14" law school.[89] Photos and comments about the women were posted on multiple chat room threads accessible through Google searches. In a world in which over four fifths of surveyed legal employers report using search engines and social network sites to search for information about candidates, there are significant harms from what site owners claim is "fun" about anonymous postings.[90] Women students observed that malicious posters on AutoAdmit also "Google-bombed" their postings so that they would show up first when the victims' names were searched by prospective employers. At least one of the victims withdrew from law school.

The role of gender in law school is, of course, mediated by other factors. In most research where race is a variable, women of color have the highest levels of alienation. Women of color differ most significantly from white men, but also from men of color and white women. Some research also indicates that ideological factors may be more important than gender in explaining women's overall experience of legal education. In one study, women who entered law school primarily for reasons such as status, income, and job security were generally satisfied with their training, while women who entered with predominantly social justice motivations found the institution sexist and dehumanizing.[91]

87. See studies summarized in Mertz, "Inside the Law School Classroom," *supra* note 83, at 509 and Neufield, *supra* note 84, at 516–17, 530–39, and findings of Bashi & Iskander, *supra* note 84, at 404–13.

88. Neufield, *supra* note 84, at 554–559; Bashi & Iskander, *supra* note 84, at 423–37.

89. Ellen Nakashima, "Harsh Words Die Hard on the Web: Law Students Feel Lasting Effects of Anonymous Attacks," *Wash. Post*, March 7, 2007, at A1.

90. W. Erin Binns, "What Does the Web Say About You?," 35 *Stud. Law* 6, 16 (2007); Nakashima, *supra* note 89, quoting Jarret Cohen's explanation of why he did not keep identifying information about posters or require them to use their real names: "People would not have as much fun, frankly, if they had to worry about employers pulling up names on them."

91. For a review of the research, *see* ABA Commission on Women in the Profession, *Unfinished Agenda: Women in the Legal*

Taken together, these different accounts of gender difference highlight a longstanding paradox. By definition, the women's movement claims to speak from the experience of women. Yet that experience counsels attention to its own diversity, and to the role of contextual variations and multiple identities in mediating gender differences. Recognition of these factors argue for grounding critiques of legal education in normative principles not sweeping, sex-based premises.

Such principles argue for many of the reforms noted earlier: less reliance on large lectures or quasi-Socratic discussion and greater emphasis of clinics, simulations, and other opportunities for interactive experiential learning, collaborative projects, and ongoing feedback and mentoring. Less focus would center on doctrinal analysis, and more on the social context of legal decisionmaking. In addition, dimensions such as gender, race, class, ethnicity, and sexual orientation would become more central categories in analyzing legal institutions and lawyer-client relationships. Such analysis would move beyond the kind of "add woman and stir" approach that often passes for curricular diversity: an occasional case or reference to gender, race, or similar issues. Rather, as Catharine MacKinnon puts it, quoting Aldous Huxley, "Nothing short of everything will do."[92] Promising reform strategies include adding diversity-related issues to faculty workshops, lecture series, and curricular integration initiatives. Supplemental reading, case studies, and exercises can be developed to address issues of gender, race, ethnicity, class, and sexual orientation. Schools should also have a structure for addressing concerns and monitoring progress on gender and diversity-related issues.

QUESTIONS

1. Is there a "woman problem" at your institution. If so, what might be the most promising ways of addressing it?

2. How should sites like AutoAdmit be handled when their anonymous postings include false claims about sexual activity, as well as racist and anti-Semitic comments? Administrators at the University of Pennsylvania Law School unsuccessfully requested one of their students who founded AutoAdmit to remove offensive threads. He and his cofounder responded that they were "very strong believers in the freedom of expression and marketplace of ideas," and that "a much deeper and much more mature level of insight" is possible "in a community where the ugliest depths of human opinion are confronted rather than ignored."[93] One commentator on the site similarly maintained that a woman had no right to ask for removal of threads demeaning her. "If we want to objectify, criticize, and [expletive deleted] like her, we should be able to." Another commentator

---

Profession 30–32, (2001). For the Harvard study, *see* Granfield, *supra* note 25.

92. Catharine A. MacKinnon, "Mainstreaming Feminism in Legal Education," 53 *J. Legal Ed.* 199 (2003). Accord, Rhode,

"Midcourse Corrections," *supra* note 84, at 485–86, 488 (critiquing "add-woman-and-stir" approaches).

93. Nakashima, *supra* note 89, at A1 (quoting Cohen and Ciolli).

maintained, "If these girls can't handle a little humor, how can they handle life?"[94]

How might the "girls" respond? Was it appropriate for the law firm that had hired one of the site's founders before the controversy to withdraw its offer, and for students identified on the site to sue its founders as well as anonymous posters for defamation?[95] Alternatively, as a lawyer at the Electronic Freedom Frontier maintained, is the "cure to bad speech . . . more speech"?[96]

Sexual Orientation

Progress on sexual orientation issues is more difficult to assess because many gay and lesbian law students are still reluctant to be open about their sexual identity. However, as noted by the ABA Commission, gay and lesbian students report the highest incidence of discrimination by any group. One effort to raise awareness and build support on these issues involved a challenge to the Solomon Amendment by FAIR, a Forum for Academic and Institutional Rights. This forum includes law schools and faculties with policies prohibiting discrimination on the basis of factors including sexual orientation.

The Amendment is a statute that denies federal funding to colleges and universities that exclude military recruiters from their campuses. Law schools that belong to the Association of American Law Schools must have policies that bar use of their placement facilities to employers who discriminate on the basis of specified characteristics, including sexual orientation. Because the military engages in such discrimination, it would normally be denied recruitment privileges. However, to avoid funding cutoffs under the Solomon Amendment, AALS member schools have been allowed to permit the military's access to placement facilities provided that the schools engage in "ameliorative activities" expressing their opposition to discrimination. Some schools conveyed their opposition by requiring the military to use campus placement facilities outside the law school, by refusing to schedule interviews, or by declining to post military literature. Several of these schools were threatened with denial of federal funds.

The lawsuit, *Rumsfeld v. Forum for Academic and Institutional Rights, Inc. and Society of American Law Teachers*, claimed that the Solomon Amendment as applied to law schools infringes their First Amendment rights to freedom of speech and association. In a unanimous decision, the United States Supreme Court disagreed. 547 U.S. 47 (2006). Writing for the Court, Chief Justice Roberts found that the Solomon Amendment regulated conduct not speech. Nothing about granting access to recruiters suggested that the schools agreed with recruiters' speech and nothing in the Amendment restricted what schools could say about military policy; they "remain

---

94. *Id.*, "Comment by Inquiring Mind," June 12, 2007.

95. Peter Lattman, "Student Gets Costly Lesson in Defending Vicious Speech," *Wall St. J.*, May 9, 2007, at B3; Amir Efrati, "Students File Suit Against Ex–AutoAdmit Director, Others," *Wall St. J. Blog,* June 12, 2007.

96. Nakashima, *supra* note 89, at A1 (quoting Kurt Opsahl).

free under the statute to express whatever views they may have on the military's congressionally mandated employment policy, all the while retaining eligibility for federal funds." 547 U.S. 47, 60 (2006). Nor did the Amendment infringe associational interests. The schools were not forced to associate with the recruiters in any expressive sense and "students and faculty are free to associate to voice their disapproval of the military's message." *Id.*, at 69.

QUESTIONS

1. Do you agree with the Court's decision? What about the Solomon Amendment?

2. What are your school's policies regarding military recruitment and amelioration? A study conducted by the National Association of Law Placement after the FAIR decision found that 88% of schools had a GLBT student association; 86% posted policies on military recruiting; and 60% offered a course on sexual orientation and the law. Most schools also reported support for panels, events, and outreach to GLBT students, but only about a third reported student protests of the military presence on campus or discussion of the Solomon Amendment or the military's "Don't Ask, Don't Tell" policy in law school courses.[97] Do schools need to do more to address these issues? Should they ask students to request off-campus interviews with military recruiters?

3. How would you respond to a controversy that emerged at George Washington Law School, a member of FAIR, following the supreme court's decision? A GW student group, the National Security Law Association, held a career fair on employment opportunities in the national security law area and invited several military employers that adhered to the "Don't Ask, Don't Tell" policy. George Washington's Lambda Law association asked the school to rescind the invitation. Its members claimed that the Solomon Amendment requires equal access to military recruiters but not affirmative invitations to those who violate the school's non-discrimination policy, that a career fair is not a forum for expression of ideas, and information about employment opportunities was available from other sources. The National Security Law Association members responded that they have a first amendment interest in receiving information from military employers.[98] What is your view?

4. How is the climate for gay and lesbian students and faculty at your school?[99] What, if any reforms would you suggest?

---

97. James G. Leipold, "Law School Strategies for Amelioration and Protest: What Law Schools Can Do," 57 *J. Legal Edu.*72, 182–83 (2007).

98. Joan Schaffner, "Should Law Schools Bar Student Organizations from Inviting the Military to Campus for Recruitment Purposes?," 57 *J. Legal Ed.* 162 (2007).

99. For general discussion of sexual orientation bias in legal education, see Michael R. Siebecker, "To Be or Not To BE ... Out in the Academy," 22 *Law & Ineq.* 143 (2004).

C. PROFESSIONAL RESPONSIBILITY

NOTES

One significant change in legal education over the last two decades has involved professional responsibility. Although the first American courses in this field date back to the turn of the century, early instruction was quite limited. The typical offering was a brief ungraded sequence of lectures by a judge or local practitioner. "General piffle" was the description of these efforts by one of the first serious scholars in the field.[100]

Around the turn of the century, however, some law schools began offering more formal coverage, and others claimed that instruction occurred through the "pervasive method"—through "incidental" instruction throughout the curricula. So "incidental" was this form of instruction that most surveyed students were unaware that it had occurred. Nor did bar exams attempt to refocus their attention. Ethics questions were infrequent and typically invited undemanding reflection on topics such as "what the Code of Ethics means to me." Required courses were not necessarily better. Most were highly rule bound; some demanded simply that students memorize the ABA code and pass a true-false exam on its contents.[101]

This lack of interest in professional responsibility instruction was in part attributable to assumptions that it offered too little too late. A common view was that legal ethics like "politeness on subways [and] fidelity in marriage" could not be acquired through course assignments in professional schools.[102] However, by the 1970s, a new interest in the area began to emerge in response to several trends, including increased student activism, legal challenges to the bar's regulatory standards, and the Watergate scandal, which involved a high proportion of lawyers. Public confidence in the profession fell to new lows, which helped prompt the ABA to require accredited schools to provide some instruction in professional responsibility. A growing number of states also began to demand such instruction as a condition of admission to practice, and bar examinations increased their coverage of ethical issues, typically through a separate multistate exam.

These initiatives have had mixed results. Certainly the field of legal ethics has achieved greater academic credibility over the last several decades; three quarters of those responding to the Law School Survey on Student Engagement reported that their school placed "very much" or "quite a bit" of emphasis on the ethical practice of the law. Yet only a

---

100. George Costigan, "The Teaching of Legal Ethics," 4 *Am.L.Sch.Rev.* 290 (1917).

101. Michael J. Kelly, *Legal Ethics and Legal Education* 3–12 (1980); Deborah L. Rhode, "Ethics by the Pervasive Method," 42 *J.Legal Educ.* 31 (1992); Richard H. Underwood, "What I Think That I Have Learned About Legal Ethics," 39 *Idaho L. Rev.* 245, 252 (2003).

102. Eric Schnapper, "The Myth of Legal Ethics," *A.B.A. J.*, Feb. 1978, at 64.

minority of students felt that theses efforts had significantly helped them develop a "personal code of values and ethics," national surveys find little coverage of professional responsibility issues outside the required courses, and international studies reveal an absence of required courses except in practical training programs.[103] Moreover, many teachers of those courses believe that their efforts are undermined by a mandatory format and the perceived need to prepare students for a rule-oriented multistate bar ethics exam. This focus on the law of lawyering too often results in legal ethics without the ethics.[104] Other faculty and students are resistant to integrating ethical coverage in the core curriculum because they doubt that ethics instruction will significantly affect ethical reasoning or that improving moral reasoning will improve conduct.

Legal Education and Ethical Values

One common assumption is that professional responsibility is largely a matter of moral character, and that it is not possible to alter in a few classroom hours what students have acquired over long periods from family, friends, schools, churches, and popular culture. According to federal judge and law professor Richard Posner, "as for the task of instilling ethics in law students.... I can think of few things more futile than teaching people to be good."[105] Another variation of this argument is that law schools have no business making that effort; apart from rules-based issues, the ethical questions worth discussing have no "right" answers and faculty should not turn their podiums into pulpits. Alternatively, other commentators worry that if professors remain studiously neutral on value-laden issues, an ethics course can lapse into a form of "values clarification" that erodes commitment. If everyone's view is as good as everyone else's, what is the point of classroom debate?

This critique, however, ignores the possibility of a middle ground. As the Introduction to this book suggests, professional responsibility courses can encourage toleration without endorsing skepticism. Although many ethical questions have no objectively valid answers, not all answers are equally valid; some are more logical, consistent, coherent, respectful of evidence, and so forth. Nor do all issues of professional responsibility present unsolvable dilemmas, or the task of "teaching people to be good." Many regulatory questions call for the same skills of legal and policy

---

103. Law School Survey of Student Engagement, *supra* note 57, at 8, 12; Sullivan et al., *supra* note 36, at 145, 187; Ann Colby & William Sullivan, "Legal Education Gives Ethics Training Short Shrift," *S.F. Daily J.*, Jan. 18, 2007, at 6; Janine Griffiths–Baker, "Reviewing Legal Ethics and Legal Education in England and Wales–An Unenviable Task?," 10 *Legal Ethics* 121, 121–22 (2008).

104. Deborah L. Rhode, "Teaching Legal Ethics," 51 *Saint Louis U. L. J.* 1043. 1047–48 (2007); Steven Gillers, "Eat Your Spinach," 51 *Saint Louis U. L. J* 1215, 1219 (2007).

105. Richard Posner, "The Deprofessionalization of Legal Teaching and Scholarship," 91 *Mich. L. Rev.* 1921, 1924 (1993). *See also* David Barnhizer, "Profession Deleted: Using Market and Liability Forces to Regulate the Very Ordinary Business of Law Practice For Profit," 17 *Georgetown J. Legal Ethics* 246 (2004) (noting that "law schools have been educating for ethics for over 20 years ... I know no one who is claiming that lawyers are more ethical as a consequence").

analysis that are standard fare in law school classrooms. The most effective way to secure substantial changes in professional conduct is often through reforming regulatory standards and economic incentives, and legal education can contribute to that effort. So too, a substantial body of evidence suggests that ethical values are by no means as fixed as critics contend. Recent psychological research indicates that significant changes occur during early adulthood in people's basic strategies for dealing with moral issues. Through interactive education, such as mentoring, problem-solving and role-playing, individuals can enhance skills in moral analysis and build awareness of the situational factors that skew judgment.[106]

Ethical Reasoning and Ethical Conduct

The extent to which capacities for ethical analysis affect ethical conduct is more difficult to assess. Most research suggests that moral behavior is a function of four basic factors.

- moral awareness; the recognition that a situation raises ethical issues, which often involves empathy for those involved;

- moral reasoning; the capacity to overcome self-interest and cognitive biases and determine what course of action is ethically justifiable;

- moral intent; the motivation to act on moral convictions and subordinate other concerns such as status and financial interests;

- moral behavior; the ability to act on ethical decisions in the face of situational influences such as peer pressures, organizational reward structures, and diffusion of responsibility for action.[107]

Both historical experience and psychological research make clear that moral conduct is highly intuitive and situation-specific. Intuitions are non-conscious processes that respond to prototypes for stock ethical situations. Emotions often drive these responses; reasoning comes later to support intuitive judgments, and individuals often selectively seek out evidence and arguments that will be consistent with their self interest.[108] So too, although individuals may differ in their responses to pressures and temptation, contextual pressures have a substantial effect on moral conduct

---

106. Rhode, "If Integrity Is the Answer, What Is the Question?" 72 *Fordham L. Rev.* 333 (2003); Sullivan, *supra* note 36, at 135; M. Neil Browne, Carrie L. Williamson, & Linda L. Barkacs, "The Purported Rigidity of an Attorney's Personality: Can Legal Ethics be Acquired?," 30 *J. Legal Prof.* 55 (2006); Steven Hartwell, "Promoting Moral Development Through Experiential Teaching," 1 *Clinical L. Rev.* 505 (1995); Neil Hamilton & Lisa M. Brabbit, "Fostering Professionalism Through Mentoring," 37 *J. Legal Educ.* 102 (2007); National Research Council, "Learning and Transfer", in *How People Learn* 51–78 (2000).

107. Deborah L. Rhode, "Where Is the Leadership in Moral Leadership?," in *Moral Leadership: The Theory and Practice of Power, Judgment, and Policy* 22–33 (Deborah L. Rhode, ed. 2006); Milton C. Regan, Jr., "Moral Intuitions and Organizational Culture," 51 *Saint Louis U. L. J.* 941, 955 (2007).

108. Alan M. Lerner, "Using Our Brains: What Cognitive Science and Social Psychology Teach Us About Teaching Law Students to Make Ethical, Professionally Responsible, Choices," 23 *QRL* 643, 671–79 (2004–2005); Jonathan Haidt, "The Emotional Dog and its Rational Tail: A Social Intuitionist Approach to Moral Judgment," 108 *Psychological Rev.* 814 (2001).

independent of any generalized "integrity" or stated principles.[109] One sobering survey found no significant differences in the moral beliefs characteristic of Chicago ministers and inmates of the state penitentiary.[110] And as Chapter VII noted, in Stanley Milgram's well-known experiment, two-thirds of the subjects complied with directions to administer apparently dangerous electric shocks to co-participants despite their cries of pain.[111]

These patterns suggest reasons to avoid overstating the potential contributions of ethical instruction, but not reasons to avoid including it in professional school curricula. Despite the importance of situational pressures, most psychological research finds some modest relationship between moral judgment and moral behavior.[112] How individuals evaluate the consequences of their actions can be critical in shaping conduct, and education can affect those evaluative processes. It can also make individuals aware of ways that economic and peer pressures, structures of authority, and diffusion of responsibility skew judgment. For example, analysis of Milgram's obedience studies reveals that subjects were far less likely to impose shocks if other subjects refused to do so. That analysis highlights the importance of building support networks to help individuals withstand ethical pressures that arise in practice.

Such pressures do frequently arise, so a well-constructed ethics curriculum can address issues of far greater personal relevance than much of what is covered in law school. Many practitioners will never encounter the rule of perpetuities after a bar exam; all will confront questions of candor, confidentiality, and conflicts of interest. Practitioners who have taken legal ethics courses, even in early, ill-developed forms, have credited them with helping to resolve ethical issues, and most lawyers want to see more, rather than less ethics coverage.[113] What law schools model in their formal curriculum and social practices matter to the kind of "lives ... students will live, the profession they will constitute, and the public they will serve."[114]

The failure of law schools to institutionalize ethical discussion throughout the law school or to deal effectively with unprofessional student conduct itself raises ethical issues.[115] For faculty to treat professional

109. Research surveyed in John M. Doris, *Lack of Character: Personality and Moral Behavior*, 24–28, 123 (2002). *See* David Luban, "Integrity: Its Causes and Cures," 72 *Fordham L. Rev.* 279 (2003); Rhode, *supra* note 107, at 26–33, 45; David L. Rosenhan, Bert S. Moore & Bill Underwood, "The Social Psychology of Moral Behavior," *in Moral Development: Advances in Research and Theory* 241 (James R. Rest, et al., eds. 1986).

110. Peter Caws, "On the Teaching of Ethics in a Pluralistic Society," 8 *Hastings Center Report* 32 (Oct. 1978).

111. Stanley Milgram, *Obedience to Authority: An Experimental View* 35 (1974).

112. See sources cited in Rhode, *supra* note 107, at 22–24; Lerner, *supra* note 108,

at 680 (noting individuals' ability to override the effects of intuitive reactions through ethical reasoning).

113. *Id. See also* Robert Granfield & Thomas Koenig, " 'It's Hard to Be a Human Being and a Lawyer': Young Attorneys and the Confrontation With Ethical Ambiguity in Legal Practice," 105 *W. Va. L. R.* 495 (2003).

114. Rhode, "Teaching Legal Ethics," *supra* note 104, at 1043.

115. For law school responses to misconduct, see American Bar Association Standing Committee on Professionalism, Report on Survey of Law School Professionalism Programs 11–18 (2006).

responsibility as someone else's responsibility encourages future practitioners to do the same. One primary cause of unethical conduct, particularly in organizational settings, is the assumption that moral responsibility lies elsewhere. Legal educators cannot afford to mirror this approach in their own priorities. Evidence from the medical profession indicates that students who exhibit unprofessional conduct during medical school are three times as likely to be disciplined in practice.[116] A minimalist approach to legal ethics marginalizes its significance. Educational priorities are apparent in subtexts as well as texts. What the curriculum leaves unsaid, and what unprofessional practices by students and faculty go unchallenged, send a powerful message.[117] Although law school experiences cannot fully simulate, or insulate individuals from, the pressures of practice; it can provide a setting to explore their causes, and it can model appropriate conduct in personal interactions and collective priorities. The ethics we profess should be the ones we practice in all aspects of legal education.

D.   PROFESSIONAL VALUES AND PRO BONO OPPORTUNITIES

In 1996, the American Bar Association amended its accreditation standards to call on schools to "encourage students to participate in pro bono activities and to provide opportunities for them to do so." Standard 302(b)(2). Interpretation 302–10 of those standards, as revised in 2007, provides that "pro bono opportunities should at a minimum involve the rendering of meaningful law-related services to persons of limited means or to organizations that serve such persons; however, volunteer programs that involve meaningful services that are not law-related may be included within the law school's overall program." Schools can also include credit-bearing activities "so long as law-related non-credit bearing initiatives are part of the program." The revised ABA standards also encourage schools to address the obligations of faculty to the public, including participation in pro bono activities.

Although a growing number of schools have made efforts to increase pro bono involvement, substantial challenges remain. Only about 10 percent of schools require service by students, and fewer still impose specific requirements on faculty. Even at these schools, the amounts demanded are sometimes quite minimal: half of those responding to an ABA survey required only 10 to 20 hours of students.[118] Although most institutions offer voluntary public service programs, only a minority of students are involved. In short, most law students graduate without pro bono legal work

---

116. Maxine A. Papadakis et al., "Unprofessional Behavior in Medical School Is Associated with Subsequent Disciplinary Action by a State Medical Board," 79 *Ac. Medicine* 244 (2004). Examples of such behavior included irresponsibility in maintaining commitments and inability to respond constructively to criticism.

117. Rhode, *In The Interests of Justice*, *supra* note 15, at 203; Sullivan et al., *supra* note 36, at 14, 178.

118. ABA Standing Committee on Professionalism, *supra* note 115, at 46–47. Only two schools reported specific faculty requirements in the Committee on Professionalism's survey; one required only 10 hours and the other 21–30. *Id.*, at 47.

as part of their educational experience.[119] Moreover, the quality of some programs is open to question. Many students lack on-site supervision or a classroom opportunity to discuss their work or pro bono issues generally. In Rhode's survey, *Pro Bono in Principle and in Practice*, only 1 percent of law school graduates reported that pro bono service received coverage in their orientation programs or professional responsibility courses; only three percent observed visible faculty support for pro bono work.[120] In the American Bar Foundation's survey of recent law graduates, pro bono ranked last on a list of experiences that practitioners felt had significantly assisted them in practice.[121] In the nation's first comprehensive report on pro bono programs in legal education, an AALS Commission offered a diagnosis that remains apt: "law schools should do more."[122]

The inadequacy of support for public service is a missed opportunity for both the profession and the public. As the materials on pro bono in Chapter XIII notes, such work offers participants a wide range of practical benefits, such as training, trial experience, problem solving skills, and professional contacts. For many participants, this experience also provides their most direct exposure to what passes for justice among the poor and to the need for legal reforms. In addition to these educational and practical benefits, a positive public service experience in law school may help inspire future involvement.[123]

For these reasons, the AALS Commission recommended that schools seek to make available for every law student at least one well-supervised law-related pro bono opportunity and either require student participation or find ways to attract the great majority of students to volunteer.[124] Some commentators have also recommended that law schools impose pro bono requirements on faculty. If an important goal of legal education is to inspire a commitment to public service among future practitioners, then having faculty serve as role models makes obvious sense. As research on altruism makes clear, individuals learn more by example than exhortation.[125]

---

119. Law School Survey on Student Engagement, *supra* note 57, at 8.

120. Deborah L. Rhode, *Pro Bono In Principle and In Practice* 161–62 (2004). Only 60 percent of those responding to the ABA Professionalism Committee reported the availability of on-site supervision. ABA Standing Committee on Professionalism, *supra* note 115.

121. Ronit Dinovitzer, *After the JD.: First Results of a National Study of Legal Careers* 81 (2004).

122. Commission on Pro Bono and Public Service Opportunities in Law Schools, Association of American Law Schools, *Learning to Serve: A Summary of the Findings and Recommendations of the AALS Commission on Pro Bono and Public Service Opportunities* 2 (1999).

123. The experience need not come in a pro bono program as opposed to a clinic, and mandatory programs do not always insure a positive experience. Research to date does not find that participants in mandatory programs are more likely to engage in pro bono work after graduation or to meet the ABA's aspirational levels of service for practitioners. *See* Rhode, *Pro Bono*, *supra* note 120; Robert Granfield, *The Pedagogy of Public Service: Assessing the Impact of Mandatory Pro Bono on Young Lawyers* 2, 90 (Law School Admission Council, 2005).

124. AALS Commission, *supra* note 122, at 7.

125. *See* Rhode, *supra* note 120; David Luban, "Faculty Pro Bono and the Question of Identity," 49 *J. Leg. Ed.* 58 (1999). See the discussion of pro bono responsibility in Chapter XIII, Section G.

QUESTIONS

1) How would you assess your law school's professional responsibility curriculum and pro bono opportunities? What, if any, changes would you recommend?

2) What accounts for the inadequacies in many law schools' approach to legal ethics and public service? Would it help if *U.S. News and World Report* or some other organization ranked pro bono and public service programs by the number of placements provided or hours contributed per student?[126] What other strategies might be most effective in producing reform?

EPILOGUE

Whatever their other differences, legal ethics experts generally share one central conviction: that progress is possible on issues of professional responsibility, and that it matters. Though talk about ethics is cheap, silence about ethics is far too expensive. Legal institutions and practices will never change unless we—as students, teachers, and lawyers—are prepared to deliberate together about professional ideals and identity. That, after all, is the aim of this book.

126. Equal Justice Works provides an electronic guide to law school public service programs that does not include a ranking. See E–Guide, http://ejw.newsweek.com. Only 3% percent of students report being greatly influenced by pro bono opportunities in law schools; 84% reported not being influenced. Granfield, *supra* note 123.

INDEX

References are to pages.

ABORTION
American Bar Association resolutions, 111 et seq.
Access to Justice, 866–877, 884–902, 914–930

ADMISSION TO THE BAR
Bar Admission, this index

ADVERSARY SYSTEM
Abuses, Judicial controls on adversarial abuses, below
Advocate's role
  Generally, 137 et seq.
  Neutral Partisanship, this index
Civility and civility codes, 228 et seq.
Comparative perspectives, 166–175
Criminal Law, this index
Discovery abuses, judicial controls, 213–235
Frivolous litigation, 206–213
Historical background, 157, 158
Judicial controls on adversarial abuses
      Generally, 206–235
  Civility and civility codes, 228 et seq.
  Discovery abuses, 213–235
  Frivolous litigation, 206–213
Neutral Partisanship, this index
Protection of rights and "search for truth,"
  158–166
"Search for truth" and protection of rights,
  158–166

ADVERTISING
Market Regulation, this index

ADVOCACY
Adversary System, this index
Criminal Law, this index

ADVOCATE–WITNESS RULE
Conflicts of interest, 689, 690

AGE DISCRIMINATION
Generally, 103–105

ALTERNATIVE DISPUTE RESOLUTION
Distribution of Legal Services, this index

AMERICAN ACADEMY OF MATRIMONIAL ATTORNEYS
Counseling role of attorneys, 517 et seq.

AMERICAN BAR ASSOCIATION
ABA Standards for Imposing Lawyer Sanctions, 995 et seq.
Abortion resolutions, 111 et seq.
Canon of Ethics, 116 et seq.
Code of Professional Responsibility, 117 et seq.
Commission on Professionalism, 39–42
Commission on Women in the Profession, 82–90, 1061 et seq.
Committee on Ethics and Professional Responsibility, 445, 527 et seq.
Comprehensive Legal Needs Study, 866 et seq.
Constitution of the American Bar Association, 106
Market Regulation, this index
Model Rules of Professional Conduct, 118 et seq.
Report of the Committee on Code of Professional Ethics, 114 et seq.
Sexual orientation resolution, 101
Standards Relating to the Administration of Criminal Justice, The Prosecution Function, 361 et seq.
Task Force on Minorities in the Legal Profession, Report with Recommendations, 1047

ARBITRATION
Distribution of legal services, 903

ATTORNEY–CLIENT DECISION–MAKING
  Generally, 696–755
Authority versus tactical choices, 704 et seq.
Disabled clients, 743 et seq.
Informed consent, partially competent client and
  Generally, 736 et seq.
  Defining competence, 740 et seq.
  Disabled clients, 743 et seq.
  Juvenile clients, 745 et seq.
  Sophisticated clients, 753 et seq.
Juvenile clients, 745 et seq.
Paternalism
  Generally, 696 et seq.
  Ad hoc paternalism, 732–734
  Hypothetical consent, 731, 732
  Justification of paternalism, 727 et seq.

ATTORNEY–CLIENT DECISION–MAK-ING—Cont'd

Paternalism—Cont'd
  Moral Problem of Paternalism, 730 et seq.
  Objective conditions, 731
  Unabomber, 689 et seq.
Sophisticated clients, 725 et seq.
Unabomber, 716 et seq.

ATTORNEY–CLIENT PRIVILEGE

Generally, 236 et seq.
Background of privilege
  Generally, 239–244
  Confidentiality, distinction between duty of confidentiality and attorney-client privilege, 242, 243
  Elements, 240, 241
  Fees, information about attorney fees, 243
  Identity of client, 243
  Waiver, 240, 241
Burden of proof, crime-fraud exception, 252 et seq.
Code of Professional Responsibility, 277 et seq.
Confidentiality
  Client fraud, confidentiality and, 288–299
  Distinction between duty of confidentiality and attorney-client privilege, 242, 243
  Ethical duty of confidentiality, below, 243
Court orders, compliance with, 285 et seq.
Crime-fraud exception
  Generally, 250–267
  Burden of proof, 252 et seq.
  Furtherance crime or fraud, conversations in, 251 et seq.
  Intent of client to crime or fraud, 250 et seq.
  Temporal distinction, "past," "ongoing," and "future" events, 252 et seq.
  Tobacco litigation, 257 et seq.
  "War on terror," 265 et seq.
Elements, 240, 241
Ethical duty of confidentiality
  Generally, 277 et seq.
  Code of Professional Responsibility, 277 et seq.
  Court orders, compliance with, 285 et seq.
  Lawyer-client disputes, exception for, 287, 288
  Model Rules of Professional Conduct, 277 et seq.
Fees, information about attorney fees, 243
Fraud
  Client fraud, confidentiality and, 288–299
  Crime-fraud exception, above
Identity of client, 243
Justification of privilege
  Generally, 244–250
  Organizational clients, 274, 275
Lawyer-client disputes, exception for, 287, 288
Model Rules of Professional Conduct, 277 et seq.

ATTORNEY–CLIENT PRIVILEGE —Cont'd

Organizational clients
  Generally, 267–277
  Control group and subject matter tests, 268 et seq.
  Justification, 274, 275
  Scope of privilege, 267 et seq,
Terrorism, crime-fraud exception and "war on terror," 265 et seq.
Tobacco litigation, crime-fraud exception, 257 et seq.
Waiver, 240, 241

ATTORNEYS

Attorney–Client Decision Making, this index
Conflicts of Interest, this index
Counseling Role of Attorneys, this index
Criminal Law, this index
Mediators, lawyers as, 489 et seq.
Profession of Law, this index
Roles of Attorneys, this index

ATTORNEYS' FEES

Attorney-client privilege, information about attorney fees, 243
Conflicts of Interest, this index
Market Regulation, this index

BANKRUPTCY

Bar admission, 958 et seq.

BAR ADMISSION

Generally, 931–966
Apprenticeship requirement, 931
Bankruptcy, 958 et seq.
Bar exams, 933 et seq.
Character and fitness
  Generally, 944 et seq.
  Bankruptcy, 958 et seq.
  Communist Party membership, 944 et seq.
  Criminal convictions, 952 et seq.
  Mental, emotional, or nervous disorders, 959 et seq.
  Racist views, 955 et seq.
  Student loan defaults, 958 et seq.
Communist Party membership, 944 et seq.
Competence
  Generally, 933 et seq.
  Apprenticeship requirement, 931
  Bar exams, 933 et seq.
  Racial discrimination, 933 et seq.
  Title VII, 935 et seq.
Criminal convictions, 952 et seq.
Historical perspectives, 931 et seq.
Interstate regulation, 961 et seq.
Mental, emotional, or nervous disorders, 959 et seq.
Racial discrimination, 933 et seq.
Racist views, 955 et seq.
Student loan defaults, 958 et seq.
Title VII, competence, 935 et seq.

BAR ASSOCIATIONS
Generally, 107 et seq.
American Bar Association, this index
Integrated bars, 112 et seq.
Lobbying, 101 et seq.
Self-regulation, 113 et seq.

BURDEN OF PROOF
Attorney-client privilege, crime-fraud exception, 252 et seq.

BYBEE/YOO MEMO
548–51

CALI CARTEL LAWYERS
Generally, 196 et seq.

CANONS OF ETHICS
Generally, 116 et seq.

CATEGORICAL IMPERATIVE
Morality, 4

CHARACTER AND FITNESS
Bar Admission, this index

CHOICE OF LAW
Federal government lawyers, 134 et seq.
Federal-state choice of law, 134 et seq.
Jurisdiction, 132 et seq.
Professional regulation, 129 et seq.

CIVILITY AND CIVILITY CODES
Adversary system, 228 et seq.

CLASS ACTIONS
Conflicts of Interest, this index

**CODE OF PROFESSIONAL RESPONSI
BILITY**
Generally, 117 et seq.
Attorney-client privilege, 277 et seq.
Neutral partisanship, 141

CODES
Civility and civility codes, 228 et seq.
Code of Professional Responsibility, above
Code of Ethics, this index
Professional Independence and Professional
Codes, this index

CODES OF ETHICS
American Bar Association, this index
Civility and civility codes, 228 et seq.
"Law of lawyering," 1
Malpractice, 1015, 1016
Value, 122 et seq.

COERCION
Negotiation and mediation, 465 et seq.

COMPETENCE
Bar Admission, this index
Discipline and Malpractice, this index
"Torture memos" and, 981–982

CONFIDENTIALITY
Attorney–Client Privilege, this index
Conflicts of interest, confidentiality and
"substantial relation" standard, 615 et
seq.
Inadvertent receipt of confidential material,
141 et seq.
Mediation, 492 et seq.
Sarbanes–Oxley requirements, 416–423

CONFLICTS OF INTEREST
Generally, 563–695
Advocate-witness rule, 689, 690
Attorney fees, Fee-related conflicts of interest, below
Business transactions between attorneys and
clients, 686 et seq.
Civil matters
Class actions, below
Concurrent conflicts, 589 et seq.
Confidentiality and "substantial relation"
standard, 615 et seq.
Corporate practice, concurrent representation, 598, 599
Disqualification
Former client conflicts, disqualification
rationale, 615, 616
Imputed disqualification, 625 et seq.
Divorce, concurrent representation, 599
Former client conflicts
Generally, 613 et seq.
Confidentiality and "substantial relation" standard, 615 et seq.
Disqualification rationale, 615, 616
Former government lawyers, below
Imputed disqualification, 625 et seq.
Insurance defense, concurrent representation, 600 et seq.
Lawyer for the situation, 596 et seq.
Positional conflicts of interest, 609 et seq.
Real estate transactions, concurrent representation, 600
Class actions
Generally, 647 et seq.
Classes, conflicts between, 658 et seq.
Mass torts, 663 et seq.
Public interest class actions, 649 et seq.
Concurrent and former client conflicts, 565 et
seq.
Concurrent conflicts
Civil matters, 589 et seq.
Criminal law, defense, 583 et seq.
Confidentiality and "substantial relation"
standard, 615 et seq.
Constitutional standards, criminal defense,
570 et seq.
Corporate practice, concurrent representation, 598, 599
Criminal law, defense
Concurrent conflicts, 583 et seq.
Constitutional standards, 570 et seq.
Former client conflicts, 578 et seq.
Multiple representations of criminal defendants, 586 et seq.
Disqualification. Civil matters, above

CONFLICTS OF INTEREST—Cont'd
Divorce, concurrent representation, 599
Family relationships, conflicts based on, 690
   et seq.
Fee-related conflicts of interest
      Generally, 671 et seq.
   Attorney buyouts and secret settlements,
      680 et seq.
   In-kind settlements of consumer class ac-
      tions, 684
   Public interest representation, 671 et seq.
Former client conflicts
   Civil matters, above
   Criminal law, defense, 583 et seq.
Former government lawyers
      Generally, 632 et seq.
   Revolving door, 635et seq.
Government lawyers. Former government
   lawyers, above
Imputed disqualification, 625 et seq.
Insurance defense, concurrent representa-
   tion, 600 et seq.
Lawyer for the situation, 596 et seq.
Mass torts, class actions, 663 et seq.
Media contracts, 688, 689
Personal relationships, conflicts based on,
   690 et seq.
Positional conflicts of interest, 609 et seq.
Prospective clients, 690
Public interest class actions, 649 et seq.
Real estate transactions, concurrent repre-
   sentation, 600
Sexual relations between attorneys and
   clients, 693

CONSEQUENTIALISM
Morality, 9

CONSTITUTIONAL STANDARDS
Conflicts of interest, criminal defense, 570 et
   seq.

CONTINUING LEGAL EDUCATION
   Generally, 1008 et seq.

CORPORATE PRACTICE
Conflicts of interest, concurrent representa-
   tion, 589
Counseling Role of Attorneys, this index
Organizational Clients, this index

COUNSELING ROLE OF ATTORNEYS
   Generally, 498–562
American Academy of Matrimonial Attor-
   neys, 517 et seq.
Client-centered, collaborative, and contextual
   approaches, 499 et seq.
Corporate practice,
      Generally, 505 et seq.
   Whistleblowers. Organizational Clients,
      this index
Family practice, 516 et seq.

COUNSELING ROLE OF ATTORNEYS
—Cont'd
Frameworks
      Generally, 498 et seq.
   Client-centered, collaborative, and contex-
      tual approaches, 499 et seq.
Government practice, 542–562
Tax practice
      Generally, 522 et seq.
   Committee on Ethics and Professional Re-
      sponsibility, 527 et seq.
   Model Rules of Professional Conduct, 540,
      541
Tax shelters, 534–538

CRIME–FRAUD EXCEPTION
Attorney–Client Privilege, this index

CRIMINAL LAW
American Bar Association Standards Relating
   to the Administration of Criminal Jus-
   tice, The Prosecution Function, 361 et
   seq.
Bar admission, criminal convictions, 952 et
   seq.
Conflicts of Interest, this index
Defense attorneys
   Conflicts of Interest, this index
   Evidence, below
   Guilty clients, defending, below
   Truthful witnesses and lying clients, be-
      low
Disclosure obligations, prosecutorial ethics,
   380 et seq.
Discretion, prosecutorial ethics, 357 et seq.
Documents retention and destruction, 344 et
   seq.
Evidence
   Document retention and destruction, 344
      et seq.
   Possession of evidence, 340 et seq.
   Prosecutorial ethics, 380 et seq.
   Witness preparation, 351 et seq.
Guilty clients, defending
      Generally, 303–323
   Conviction, ravages of, 305 et seq.
   Ineffective assistance of counsel, 320 et
      seq.
   Partisanship, challenges to, 317 et seq.
   Plea bargaining, 305 et seq.
   Rights, 316
   Structural constraints and lawyer-client
      relationships, 318 et seq.
   Truth, 309 et seq.
Impeachment, truthful witnesses and lying
   clients, 332 et seq.
Ineffective assistance of counsel, 320 et seq.
Investigative function, prosecutorial ethics,
   362
Peremptory challenges, prosecutorial ethics,
   390, 391
Perjury, truthful witnesses and lying clients,
   323 et seq.

CRIMINAL LAW—Cont'd
Plea bargaining
    Defense attorneys, 304 et seq.
    Prosecutorial ethics, 363, 364, 377 et seq.
Possession of evidence, 340 et seq.
Preparation of witnesses, 351 et seq.
Press statements, prosecutorial ethics, 361, 362, 385 et seq.
Pro bono representation, court-appointments, 927 et seq.
Prosecutorial ethics
    Generally 355–391
    American Bar Association Standards Relating to the Administration of Criminal Justice, The Prosecution Function, 361 et seq.
    Disclosure obligations, 380 et seq.
    Discretion, prosecutorial, 357 et seq.
    Evidentiary practices, 380 et seq.
    Investigative function, 362
    Peremptory challenges, 390, 391
    Plea bargaining, 363, 364, 377 et seq.
    Press statements, 361, 362, 385 et seq.
    Trial conduct, 388 et seq.
Rape victims, impeachment of, 336 et seq.
Rights, defending guilty clients, 316
Trial conduct, prosecutorial ethics, 388 et seq.,
Truth
    Guilty clients, defending, 309 et seq.
    Witnesses. Truthful witnesses and lying clients, below
Truthful witnesses and lying clients
    Generally, 323 et seq.
    Impeachment, 332 et seq.
    Perjury, 323 et seq.
    Rape victims, impeachment of, 336 et seq.
White-collar crime, 344 et seq.
Witnesses
    Preparation of witnesses, 351 et seq.
    Truthful witnesses and lying clients, above

DECISION MAKING
Attorney–Client Decision Making, this index

DEFENSE ATTORNEYS
Criminal Law, this index

DEONTOLOGICAL THEORIES
Morality, 10, 11

DISABLED CLIENTS
Attorney-client decision making, 743 et seq.

DISCIPLINE AND MALPRACTICE
Generally, 967–1020
American Bar Association, ABA Standards for Imposing Lawyer Sanctions, 995 et seq.
Competence
    Generally, 1007 et seq.
    Continuing legal education, 1008 et seq.
    Disciplinary diversion programs, 1009
    Malpractice, below
    Regulatory structures and standards, 968 et seq.

DISCIPLINE AND MALPRACTICE—Cont'd
Continuing legal education, 1008 et seq.
Diversion programs, 1009
Malpractice
    Generally, 1010 et seq.
    Causation, 1013
    Ethical codes, role of, 1015, 1016
    Performance standards, 1012 et seq.
    Remedies and insurance, 1016 et seq.
    Third party obligations, 1017, 1018, 1019
Mental health, 1003 et seq.
Regulatory structures and standards
    Generally, 968 et seq.
    Competence, 979 et seq.
    Disciplinary structures, 982 et seq.
    Duty to report misconduct, 968 et seq.
    Reporting overbilling, partnership termination, 974 et seq.
Sanctions, disciplinary
    Generally, 968 et seq.
    Aggravation, 996, 997
    American Bar Association Standards for Imposing Lawyer Sanctions, 995 et seq.
    Fines, 1001, 1002
    Law firm discipline, 1001, 1002
    Mitigation, 996, 997, 998, 999
    Outside of professional relationships, 971 et seq.
    Permanent disbarment, 998, 999,1000
Substance abuse, 1003 et seq.

DISCLOSURE OBLIGATIONS
Negotiation and mediation, 480 et seq.
Prosecutorial ethics, 380 et seq.

DISCOVERY
Abuses, judicial controls, 213–234

DISCRIMINATION
Generally, 60–64
Age discrimination, 103 et seq.
Ethnic discrimination, 90 et seq.
Sex discrimination, 81 et seq.
Sexual orientation, 100 et seq.

DISQUALIFICATION
Conflicts of Interest, this index

DISTRIBUTION OF LEGAL SERVICES
Generally, 850–930
Access to Justice
    Generally, 866 et seq.
    American Bar Association, Comprehensive Legal Needs Study, 866 et seq.
    Minimizing need for legal intervention and assistance, 872
Alternative dispute resolution
    Generally, 902–914
    Arbitration, 904
    Criticisms, 906 et seq.

DISTRIBUTION OF LEGAL SERVICES
—Cont'd
Alternative dispute resolution—Cont'd
Forms of alternative dispute resolution, 903 et seq.
Mediation, 905
Mini-trials, 905
Ombudspersons, 905
Private adjudication, 904, 905
Summary jury trial, 905
American Bar Association, Comprehensive Legal Needs Study, 866 et seq.
Arbitration, 904
Civil cases, court appointments, 929 et seq.
Community-based dispute resolution, 905, 906
Court appointed pro bono representation, 927 et seq.
Criminal cases, court appointments, 928, 929 et seq.
Early neutral evaluation, 806
Expert evaluation, 806
Interest on Lawyers Trust Accounts (IOLTA), 901, 902
Legal Services Corporation, 885 et seq.
Litigiousness
Alternative frameworks, 865 et seq.
Too many lawsuits, 859 et seq.
Too much law at too much expense, 862 et seq.
Mediation, 905
Minimizing need for legal intervention and assistance, 871–72
Mini-trials, 905
Ombudspersons, 905
Online dispute resolution, 906
Poor people, legal needs of, 896 et seq,
Private adjudication, 904–905
Pro bono representation
Generally, 914–930
Civil cases, court appointments, 929–930 et seq.
Court appointed pro bono representation, 927–930
Criminal cases, court appointments, 928–929
Ethical obligations of lawyers, 914 et seq.
Public interest law, 877–884
Right to legal services, 872–877
Subsidized legal services
Generally, 884–902
Interest on Lawyers Trust Accounts (IOLTA), 901–902
Legal Services Corporation, 885 et seq.
Poor people, legal needs of, 896 et seq.
Summary jury trial, 905

DIVORCE
Conflicts of interest, concurrent representation, 599

DOCUMENT RETENTION AND DE-STRUCTION
Criminal law, 344 et seq.

EDUCATION
Continuing legal education, 1108 et seq.
Legal Education, this index

ETHICS
Codes of Ethics, this index
Custom-based ethics, 4
Definition, 3
Law and ethics, 7, 8
Morality, this index

ETHNIC MINORITIES
Racial and Ethnic Minorities, this index

EVIDENCE
Criminal Law, this index

FAMILY PRACTICE
Counseling role of attorneys, 516 et seq.

FEDERAL GOVERNMENT LAWYERS
Choice of law, 134 et seq.

FIRST AMENDMENT
Market regulation, this index

FRAUD
Attorney–Client Privilege, this index

FRIVILOUS LITIGATION
Judicial controls, 206–235

FUNCTIONALISM
Sociological theory, 35 et seq.

GAYS
Sexual Orientation, this index

GOVERNMENT LAWYERS
Conflicts of Interest, this index
Prosecutorial ethics. Criminal Law, this index
Counseling role of, 542–562

GROUP LEGAL SERVICES PLANS
Market Regulation, this index

GUANTANAMO BAY
Terrorism, this index

HOMOSEXUALITY
Sexual Orientation, this index

IDENTITY OF CLIENT
Attorney-client privilege 243–244

IMPEACHMENT
Criminal law, truthful witnesses and lying clients, 332 et seq.

INDEPENDENCE
Professional Independence and Professional Codes, this index

INEFFECTIVE ASSISTANCE OF COUN-SEL
Criminal law, 320 et seq.

INFORMED CONSENT
Attorney–Client Decision Making, this index

IN–HOUSE COUNSEL
Organizational clients, 424–438

INSURANCE DEFENSE
Conflicts of interest, concurrent representation, 600 et seq.

INTEREST ON LAWYERS TRUST ACCOUNTS (IOLTA)
Generally, 901–902

INTIMIDATION
Neutral partisanship, defense by intimidation, 148 et seq.

INTUITION
"Moral institutions," 12

JURISDICTION
Choice of law, 132 et seq.

JUVENILE CLIENTS
Attorney–Client Decision Making, this index

"LAW OF LAWYERING"
Codes of ethics, 1

LAWYER–CLIENT DECISION MAKING
Attorney–Client Decision Making, this index

LAWYER–CLIENT DISPUTES
Attorney-client privilege, exception for lawyer-client disputes, 287

LAWYER FOR THE SITUATION
Conflicts of interest, 596 et seq.

LEGAL EDUCATION
Generally, 1021–1074
Diversity
    Generally, 1047 et seq.
    American Bar Association
        Commission on Women in the Profession, the Unfinished Agenda: Women in the Legal Profession, 1061 et seq.
        Task Force on Minorities in the Legal Profession, Report with Recommendations, 1047 et seq.
    Racial and ethnic minorities, 1047 et seq.
    Sexual orientation, 1066–1067
    Women, 1051 et seq.
Pro bono opportunities, 1072
Professional responsibility, 1068 et seq.
Structure of legal education
    Generally, 1021 et seq.
    Case method and Socratic style of instruction, 1035 et seq.
    Curricular concerns, 1044 et seq.
    Educational content and methodology, 1029 et seq.
    Educational structure, 1023 et seq.
    Public interest commitments, erosion of, 1039 et seq.

LEGAL SERVICES CORPORATION
Generally, 885 et seq.

LESBIANS
Sexual Orientation, this index

LITIGIOUSNESS
Distribution of Legal Services, this index

LOBBYING
Bar associations, 110 et seq.

MALPRACTICE
Discipline and Malpractice, this index

MARKET REGULATION
Generally, 756–849
[Financing Litigation] Acquiring interest in litigation, 843 et seq.
Adverse selection, 756
Advertising
    Generally, 757 et seq.
    Cost and quality, 764
    Deception, 759
    First Amendment, 765 et seq.
    Professionalism and administration of justice, 819
American Bar Association
    Multidisciplinary practice, ABA Commission on Multidisciplinary Practice, 818
    Specialization, ABA-approved private programs, 794 et seq.
    Unauthorized practice of law, ABA Task Force on the Model Definition of the Practice of Law, 803
Attorneys' Fees
    Generally, 821 et seq.
    Contingent fees, 837 et seq.
    Excessive fees, 824 et seq.
    Price-fixing, 822 et seq.
    Referral fees, 836
    Types of fee arrangements, 822
    Underbidding, 822 et seq.
Externalities, 757
First Amendment
    Advertising, 759 et seq.
    Solicitation, 775 et seq.
Free riders, 757
Group legal services plans. Specialization and group legal services plans, below
Information barriers, 756
Mailings, solicitation by, 779 et seq.
Multidisciplinary practice
    Generally, 816 et seq.
    ABA Commission on Multidisciplinary Practice, 818
    State regulation, 819 et seq.
Multijurisdictional practice, 810 et seq.
Paralegals, 807 et seq.
Referrals
    Attorneys' fees, 836
    Systems, 797 et seq.
Solicitation
    Generally, 770 et seq.
    First Amendment, 775 et seq.
    In-person solicitations, 774 et seq.
    Mailings, solicitations by, 779 et seq.

MARKET REGULATION—Cont'd
Specialization and group legal services plans
    Generally, 794 et seq.
    Referral systems, 797 et seq.
    State certification plans, 795 et seq.
State certification plans, specialization, 795
    et seq.
Unauthorized practice of law
    Generally, 800 et seq.
    ABA Task Force on the Model Definition
        of the Practice of Law, 803
    Document preparation, 801 et seq.
    Multijurisdictional practice, 810 et seq.
    Paralegals, 807 et seq.

MEDIA CONTRACTS
Conflicts of interest, 688

MEDIATION
Negotiation and Mediation, this index

MENTAL HEALTH
Bar admission, 960 et seq.
Discipline and malpractice, 1003 et seq.

MINI–TRIALS
    Generally, 905

MINORITIES
Racial and Ethnic Minorities, this index

MODEL RULES OF PROFESSIONAL CONDUCT
Adoption, 117 et seq.
Attorney-client privilege, 277 et seq.
Neutral partisanship, 141
Roles of attorneys, 31–32
Tax practice, 539–540

MORALITY
Categorical imperative, 4
Consequentialism, 9
Deontological theories, 10–11
Ethics, relationship to, 3
"Moral institutions," 12
Pluralism, morality theories, 12
"Positive morality" and "critical morality"
    distinguished, 4
Relativism, 4–7
Theories
    Generally, 8–13
    Consequentialism, 9
    Deontological theories, 10–11
    "Moral intuitions," 12
    Pluralism, 12
    Relativism, 4–7
    Virtue ethics, 12
Theory-based morality, 4
Virtue ethics, 11–12

MULTIDISCIPLINARY PRACTICE
Market Regulation, this index

MULTIJURISDICTIONAL PRACTICE
Market Regulation, this index

NATIONAL LESBIAN AND GAY LAW ASSOCIATION
Sexual orientation, 100 et seq.

NEGOTIATION AND MEDIATION
    Generally, 457–497
Coercion, 465 et seq.
Confidentiality in mediation, 492 et seq.
Cooperative and competitive bargaining, 484
    et seq.
Disclosure, duty of, 480 et seq.
Fairness and impartiality in mediation, 493
    et seq.
Functions of mediation, 489 et seq.
Inappropriate cases for mediation, 495 et seq.
Mediation
    Generally, 488 et seq., 905
    Confidentiality in mediation, 492 et seq.
    Fairness and impartiality, 493 et seq.
    Functions of mediation, 489 et seq.
    Inappropriate cases, 495 et seq.
    Lawyers as mediators, 489 et seq.
Mediators, lawyers as, 489 et seq.
Truthfulness in bargaining, 467 et seq.

NEUTRAL PARTISANSHIP
Alternatives to neutral partisanship
    Neutrality, alternatives to, 181–186
    Partisanship, limits of, 187–202
    Role morality and group identity, 202–206
Code of Professional Responsibility, 140
Conception of lawyer's role, 137–148
Confidential material, inadvertent receipt of,
    141 et seq.
Group identity and role morality, 202–206
Intimidation, defense by, 148 et seq.
Justification, 154–157
Model Rules of Professional Conduct, 141
Neutrality, alternatives to, 181–186
Partisanship, limits of, 187–202
Role morality, 148–154, 202–206
SLAPP suits, 149 et seq.

OMBUDSPERSONS
    Generally, 905

ORGANIZATIONAL CLIENTS
    Generally, 392 et seq.
ABA Committee on Ethics and Professional
    Responsibility, 445
Attorney–Client Privilege, this index
Bureaucratic structure, 453
Corporate counseling and whistleblowing
    Generally, 392–411
    Cost/benefit frameworks, 397 et seq.
    Whistleblowing, 404 et seq.
In-house counsel, 424–438
Legal controls in organizational settings, 454
    et seq.
Perjury, supervisory and subordinate law-
    yers, 439 et seq.
Sarbanes–Oxley, 411–423
Securities, Sarbanes–Oxley, 411–423
Subordinate lawyers. Supervisory and subor-
    dinate lawyers, below

ORGANIZATIONAL CLIENTS—Cont'd
Supervisory and subordinate lawyers
    Generally, 438–456
      ABA Committee on Ethics and Profession-
      al Responsibility, 445
    Perjury, 439 et seq.
Whistleblowing. Corporate counseling and
    whistleblowing, above

PATERNALISM
Attorney–Client Decision Making, this index

PEREMPTORY CHALLENGES
Prosecutorial ethics, 390

PERJURY
Criminal law, truthful witnesses and lying
    clients, 323 et seq.
Supervisory and subordinate lawyers, 439 et
    seq.

PLEA BARGAINING
Criminal Law, this index

PLURALISM
Morality theories, 12

PRO BONO REPRESENTATION
Distribution of Legal Services, this index
Legal education, 1072–1074

PROFESSION OF LAW
Age discrimination, 103–105
American Bar Association, this index
American legal profession
    Age discrimination, 103–105
    Conditions of practice
      Generally, 68–81
      Discontent, 71 et seq.
      Profit, priority of, 74 et seq.
    Demographic profiles, 64–68
    Discontent, 71 et seq.
    Discrimination, 60–64
    Distrust of lawyers, 52 et seq.
    Employment distributions, 64
    English legal profession, 52
    Ethnic minorities. Racial and Ethnic Mi-
      norities, this index
    Exclusion, patterns of, 60–64
    Gender
      Employment in relation to sex, 64
      Sex discrimination, 60–62
      Women, this index
    Historical frameworks, 51–64
    Professional opportunities
      Age, 103–105
      Racial and Ethnic Minorities, this in-
        dex
      Women, this index
    Profit, priority of, 74 et seq.
    Racial and Ethnic Minorities, this index
    Religious discrimination, 62–64
    Sexual Orientation, this index
    Stratification, 52
    Women, this index.

PROFESSION OF LAW—Cont'd
Codes. Professional Independence and Pro-
    fessional Codes, this index.
Commercialism, concept of profession, 38 et
    seq.
Concept of profession
    Generally, 35–50
    American Bar Association, Commission on
      Professionalism, 38 et seq.
    Commercialism, 38 et seq.
    Contemporary controversies, 38–50
    Definition, profession, 35
    Functionalism, sociological theory, 35 et
      seq.
    Historical frameworks, 37–38
    Professionalism, 38 et seq.
    Sociology, 35 et seq.
Conditions of practice. American legal profes-
    sion, above
Contemporary controversies, concept of pro-
    fession, 38–50
Definition, profession, 35
Demographic profiles, 64–66
Discontent, 71 et seq.
Discrimination, 60 et seq., 90 et seq.
Distrust of lawyers, 52 et seq.
Employment distributions, 64–65
English legal profession, 52
Ethnic minorities. Racial and Ethnic Minori-
    ties, this index
Exclusion, patterns of, 60–64
Functionalism, sociological theory, 35 et seq.
Gender. American legal profession, above
Historical frameworks
    American legal profession, 51–64
    Concept of profession, 37
Independence. Professional Independence
    and Professional Codes, this index
Model Rules of Professional Conduct, this
    index
Professional opportunities. American legal
    profession, above
Professionalism, 38 et seq.
Profit, priority of, 74 et seq.
Racial and Ethnic Minorities, this index
Religious discrimination, 62–64
Sexual Orientation, this index
Sociology, concept of profession, 35 et seq.
Stratification, 52
Women, this index

**PROFESSIONAL INDEPENDENCE
AND PROFESSIONAL CODES**
Choice of Law, this index
Historical backdrop, 106 et seq.
Self-regulation, 113 et seq.

PROSECUTORIAL ETHICS
Criminal Law, this index

PUBLIC INTEREST LAW
Distribution of legal services, 877–884

RACIAL AND ETHNIC MINORITIES
Generally, 90–100
Bar admission, 934 et seq.
Ethnic discrimination, 62–64, 106 et seq.
Legal Education, diversity, 1047 et seq.
Race discrimination, 62–64, 106 et seq.
Unconscious racism, 91 et seq.

REAL ESTATE TRANSACTIONS
Conflicts of interest, concurrent representation, 600

REFERRALS
Market Regulation, this index

RELATIVISM
Moral relativism, 4–7

ROLES OF ATTORNEYS
Confidentiality, advocacy, and contextual de-
cision making, 32–34
Ethical principals, 31, 32
Model Rules of Professional Conduct, 31

SANCTIONS
Discipline and Malpractice, this index

SARBANES–OXLEY ACT
Securities, 411–423

SEX
Conflicts of interest, sexual relations between
attorneys and clients, 693

SEXUAL ORIENTATION
Generally, 100–103
American Bar Association resolution, 101
Discrimination, 100 et seq.
Legal Education, diversity, 1066–1067
National Lesbian and Gay Law Association,
101

SLAPP SUITS
Neutral partisanship, 149 et seq.

SOCIOLOGY
Profession, concept of, 34 et seq.

SOLICITATION
Market Regulation, this index

SOPHISTICATED CLIENTS
Attorney-client decision making, 753 et seq.

SPECIAIZATION
Market Regulation, this index

STRATIFICATION
Profession of law, 52

SUBORDINATE LAWYERS
Organizational Clients, this index

SUBSIDIZED LEGAL SERVICES
Distribution of Legal Services, this index

SUBSTANCE ABUSE
Discipline and malpractice, 1003 et seq.

SUMMARY JURY TRIAL
Generally, 905

**SUPERVISORY AND SUBORDINATE
LAWYERS**
Organizational Clients, this index

TAX PRACTICE
Counseling Role of Attorneys, this index

TERRORISM
Attorney-client privilege, crime-fraud excep-
tion and "war on terror," 265 et seq.
Guantanamo detainees, legal representation
of, 712–713, 729–730
Zeal on behalf of terror suspects, 197–202

TOBACCO LITIGATION
Attorney-client privilege, crime-fraud exception, 257 et seq.

**TORTURE, LAWYER INVOLVEMENT
IN**
542–562, 981–982
Bybee/Yoo memo, 548–550, 981–982

TRIAL CONDUCT
Criminal law, prosecutorial ethics, 388

UNABOMBER
Paternalism and attorney-client decision
making, 715 et seq.

UNAUTHORIZED PRACTICE OF LAW
See Market Regulation, this index

VIRTUE ETHICS
Moral theory, 11–12

WAIVER
Attorney-client privilege, 241

WHISTLEBLOWING
Organizational Clients, this index

WHITE–COLLAR CRIME
Criminal Law, 344 et seq.

WITNESSES
Criminal Law, this index

WOMEN
ABA Commission on Women in the Profes-
sion
Generally, 82–89
Context of gender issues, 86
Difference made by gender, 86
Agenda for change, 87–89
Barriers
Generally, 82–86
Sexual harassment, 85–86
Stereotypes, 82–83
Support networks, 83
Workplace structures, 83–84
Context of gender issues, 86
Legal education, 1052 et seq.
Professional opportunities, 81–90
Sex discrimination, 60–62

WOMEN—Cont'd
Sexual harassment 85–86
Stereotypes, 82–83

WOMEN—Cont'd
Support networks, 83
Workplace structures, 83–84

†